Guide to Financial Services Regulation

Guide to Financial Services Regulation

THIRD EDITION

Professor Barry A K Rider LLB (Hons); MA (Cantab); PhD (Lond); PhD (Cantab); Hon LLD (Dickinson); Barrister
Director of the Institute of Advanced Legal Studies, University of London and Fellow of Jesus College, Cambridge

Charles Abrams ACIArb
Partner, Head of the Securities Group, S J Berwin & Co

Michael Ashe QC
Member of the Bars of England and Wales, Ireland and Northern Ireland

CCH EDITIONS LIMITED

Disclaimer

This publication is intended to provide accurate information in regard to the subject matter covered. Readers entering into transactions on the basis of such information should seek the services of a competent professional adviser as this publication is sold on the understanding that the publisher is not engaged in rendering legal or accounting advice or other professional services. The publisher, its editors and any authors, consultants or general editors expressly disclaim all and any liability and responsibility to any person, whether a purchaser or reader of this publication or not, in respect of anything and of the consequences of anything done or omitted to be done by any such person in reliance, whether wholly or partially, upon the whole or any part of the contents of this publication.

Legislative and other material

While copyright in all statutory and other materials resides in the Crown or other relevant body, copyright in the remaining material in this publication is vested in the publisher.

The publisher advises that any statutory or other materials issued by the Crown or other relevant bodies are reproduced in this publication are not the authorised official versions of those statutory or other materials. In their preparation, however, the greatest care has been taken to ensure exact conformity with the law as enacted or other materials as issued.

Crown copyright material is reproduced with the permission of the Controller of HMSO.

Ownership of Trade Mark

The trade mark is the property of

Commerce Clearing House Incorporated, Riverwoods, Illinois, USA
(**CCH** INCORPORATED)

ISBN 0 86325 401 2

CCH EDITIONS LIMITED
(a business unit of Croner Publications Limited, part of the Wolters Kluwer Group)
Telford Road, Bicester, Oxfordshire OX6 0XD
Telephone (01869) 253300, Facsimile (01869) 874700
DX: 83750 Bicester 2

First published 1987 under the title *Guide to the Financial Services Act 1986*
Second Edition 1989

Typeset in the UK by Mendip Communications Ltd, Frome, Somerset.
Printed and bound in the UK by Clays Limited, Bungay, Suffolk.

About the Publisher

CCH Editions Limited is a business unit of Croner Publications Limited, part of the Wolters Kluwer Group. Wolters Kluwer is the leading international professional publisher specialising in tax, business and law publishing throughout Europe, the US and the Asia Pacific. The group produces a wide range of books and reporting services in different media for the accounting and legal professions and for businesses. The Oxfordshire premises are the centre for all CCH UK and European operations.

All CCH publications are designed to provide practical, authoritative reference works and useful guides, and are written by CCH's highly qualified and experienced editorial team and specialist outside authors.

CCH Editions Limited publishes information packages including bound books, loose-leaf reporting services, newsletters and electronic products on UK and European topics for distribution world-wide. The UK company also acts as distributor of the publications of the overseas affiliate companies.

CCH Editions Limited
Telford Road
Bicester
Oxfordshire
OX6 0XD
Telephone: (01869) 253300

A Business Unit of Croner Publications Limited,
Croner House, London Road, Kingston-upon-Thames,
Surrey, KT2 6SR, (0181) 547 3333
Part of the Wolters Kluwer Group

About the Authors

Barry Rider is a Professor of Law at the University of London and Director of the Institute of Advanced Legal Studies. He is also a Fellow of Jesus College, University of Cambridge, and President of the British Institute of Securities Laws. In this guide he was primarily responsible for Chapters 1, 2, 6, 7 and 13 and jointly with Mr Michael Ashe for Chapter 12.

Charles Abrams is a member of the CBI's City Regulatory Panel and of the editorial advisory board of European Financial Services Law. He was formerly an arbitrator for the SFA's Consumer Arbitration Scheme and IMRO's specialist adviser on venture capital and in this guide was primarily responsible for Chapters 3, 8 and 9.

Michael Ashe is a practising member of the Bars of England and Wales, Ireland and Northern Ireland. In this guide he was primarily responsible for Chapters 4, 5, 10, 11 and jointly with Professor Rider for Chapter 12.

Preface to the Third Edition

The authors in the prefaces to the first two editions of this book bemoaned the dynamic nature of financial services regulation in Britain and thus the inevitable difficulty that they encountered in attempting to give the subject the considered and pensive analysis that it clearly deserves. When we started on the third edition, we were optimistic that the structure of regulation had settled as far into the sand as it could! It has endured a series of overhauls and now while rather different from that envisaged, at least by the government and City in 1986, arguably illustrates but a process of maturing and refinement. Today the system of regulation is still a mixture of substantive legal regulation and various types of self-regulation. Still the day-to-day regulation of those doing business in the financial sector is based on the law of contract. Indeed, after the de-designation of most of its Core Rules and its decision to become a stand-back regulator of the regulators, the SIB has given even greater emphasis to the contractual form of regulation. While we may have reservations as to the efficacy and efficiency of the regulatory structure we had expected it to remain in its present form. This proved to be unfounded.

Shortly after assuming office, the government, through the Chancellor, Gordon Brown, announced a simplification and reform of the regulatory structure to the House of Commons on 20 May 1997. He said that the division of responsibility between the SIB and the self-regulatory organisations was inefficient and confusing to investors and lacked accountability and clear allocation of responsibilities. The object was to have a new regulator which the Economic Secretary, Mrs Helen Liddell, told the Institute of Economic Affairs on 4 June 1997 had to be a world leader. In a speech to the Westminster and City Programmes Conference on 25 June 1997 the Chief Secretary, Alastair Darling, made the point that self regulation did not work, that it was a cumbersome and expensive fiction and that it had had its day as it did not deliver the standard of supervision and investor protection that the public had come to expect.

The reform of financial services regulation followed an announcement by the Chancellor on 6 May 1997, in accordance with the Labour Party's manifesto promise to reform the Bank of England, that the Bank would have operational responsibility for setting interest rates. In the statement to the Commons on 20 May 1997, Mr Brown also said that the responsibility for banking regulation would be moved to the new regulator, thereby combining financial services and banking regulation.

At the time of writing it is difficult to say how quickly the reforms will be implemented. Moreover, it is difficult to ascertain details of what thought and consideration went into the Chancellor's announcement. At this time the regulatory bodies are finalising their submissions to the Chancellor. It is apparent that the initial thrust of the reform will be to move banking regulation to a revitalised SIB and legislation is expected in the autumn. We hope that some measures can be taken at the same time to implement or at least spell out the government's proposals on the Financial Services Act.

In addition to changes in the structure and character of regulation, we hope that particular attention will be given to the issue of enforcement. It is one thing to have well fashioned rules and regulations, yet quite another to ensure that they achieve the requisite degree of credibility through enforcement. Since the second edition of this book there have been significant developments in the attitude of government and the regulators to enforcement, or rather the means of enforcement. While we have long contended that in the financial sector the traditional criminal justice system is at best a rather blunt and often too expensive weapon, there has been resistance and downright opposition to the notion of utilising alternative weapons and devices. Today there would appear to be widespread agreement throughout the regulators and even in such bodies as the Serious Fraud Office, that the use of civil enforcement actions and the imposition of civil penalties might well prove to be more efficacious than resort to the criminal law in many areas of abuse. The government has shown sympathy with this view and legislation is likely in the not too distant future providing for the imposition of civil fines and other penalties in the case of insider dealing and certain other 'City' abuses. It has also been made clear that the ability of the regulators to proceed to enforcement through the civil law should be broadened. It remains to be seen whether these important matters will be addressed in the legislation that is currently being prepared to transfer supervisory functions from the Bank of England to the SIB.

The decision of the authors and publishers to expand the scope of this book to encompass matters that are not directly or for that matter indirectly addressed in the *Financial Services Act* 1986, but which are undoubtedly pertinent to the control and regulation of the financial services industry, has turned out to be even more justified than we thought, given Mr Gordon Brown's statement on 20 May. Indeed, even in the first edition of this work, we took the decision to include matters such as the regulation of insider dealing, which although not addressed in the *Financial Services Act* 1986, are obviously relevant to those who operate in the financial services sector. In the present edition, we have gone even further and examined such topics as the control of money laundering. Indeed, it is arguable that the impact of the anti money-laundering laws, and in particular the various compliance obligations that they have spawned, is greater on the way business is actually carried out by many financial intermediaries than that of the 1986 Act. Consequently, it has proved to be increasingly inappropriate for this work to be seen as merely a 'Guide' to the Financial Services Act 1986. Our third edition, therefore, seeks to address more or less every issue which pertains to the regulation of the financial services industry. There are, of course, marked differences in the depth of analysis of particular issues and given the interrelationship of what might be described as securities regulation with so many other areas of law and in particular company law, we have had to draw lines – some of which might well appear arbitrary. Consequently, the regulation of takeovers and mergers is only discussed en passant, save where other specific issues arise, such as the misuse of price sensitive information.

We would like to express our appreciation to the many individuals and organisations who have co-operated in the preparation, re-writing and updating of this work. It would not be practicable to select any single person for particular mention; suffice it for us here to record our sincere appreciation for the assistance and advice we have received from a number of quarters, some official, some unofficial and some in transit! Charles Abrams has asked that we express his particular gratitude to the other members of S J Berwin's Securities Group for their helpful suggestions and clarifications and also to the senior members of the legal, policy and technical divisions of the SIB, SFA and IMRO for the ready help and guidance which they have always given to him. Naturally, we are particularly grateful for the constant advice and support of our publishers CCH Editions Limited.

For our second edition, Dr Eilis Ferran of St Catherine's College, Cambridge, stepped into the breach, when Dr David Chaikin returned to Australia to take up a senior appointment in government. This has proved to be something of a hot seat, as Dr Ferran has herself stepped down for the third edition, to be replaced by Mr Michael Ashe QC. As is now customary in a work of this nature, we wish to record that the views expressed in this book are those of the authors themselves and should not necessarily be assumed to be those of S J Berwin & Co or for that matter any other organisation with which the authors are, or have been associated with.

The views expressed are stated as of July 1997 and we have attempted to indicate and even predict likely developments. However, given the inexorable pace of internationalism, if not globalisation of the markets and their regulation, the implications of technology and the apparent appetite of the present government for change – be warned!

Professor Barry A K Rider
Charles Abrams
Michael Ashe QC
July 1997

Useful Addresses

Centre for Corporate Law and Practice
Institute of Advanced Legal Studies
17 Russell Square
London WC1B 5DR
Tel: (0171) 637 1731

Securities and Investments Board (SIB)

Securities and Investments Board
Gavrelle House
2–14 Bunhill Row
London EC1Y 8RA
Tel: (0171) 638 1240

Self-Regulating Organisations (SROs)

Investment Management Regulatory
Organisation (IMRO)
Lloyds Chambers
1 Portsoken Street
London E1 8BT
Tel: (0171) 390 5000

Personal Investment Authority (PIA)
7th Floor, 1 Canada Square
Canary Wharf
London E14 5AZ
Tel: (0171) 538 8860

The Securities and Futures Authority (SFA)
1st Floor, Cottons Centre
Cottons Lane
London SE1 2QB
Tel: (0171) 378 9000

Recognised Professional Bodies (RPBs)

Association of Chartered Certified Accountants (ACCA)
29 Lincoln's Inn Fields
London WC2 3EE
Tel: (0171) 242 6855

Institute of Actuaries
Staple Inn Hall
High Holborn
London WC1V 7QJ
Tel: (0171) 242 0106

Institute of Chartered Accountants in England and Wales (IRAEW)
Chartered Accountants' Hall
Moorgate Place
London EC2P 2BJ
Tel: (0171) 920 8100

Institute of Chartered Accountants in Ireland
Chartered Accountant's House
87–89 Pembroke Road
Dublin 4
Tel: (00 353) 1 668 0400

Institute of Chartered Accountants of Scotland
27 Queen Street
Edinburgh EH2 1LA
Tel: (0131) 225 5673

Insurance Brokers Registration Council
63 St Mary's Axe
London EC3A 8NB
Tel: (0171) 621 1061

Law Society
Law Society's Hall
113 Chancery Lane
London WC2A 1PL
Tel: (0171) 242 1222

Law Society of Northern Ireland
Law Society House
98 Victoria Street
Belfast BT1 3JZ
Tel: (01232) 231614

Law Society of Scotland
The Law Society's Hall
26 Drumsheugh Gardens
Edinburgh EH3 7YR
Tel: (0131) 226 7411

Recognised Investment Exchanges (RIEs)

International Petroleum Exchange of London Ltd (IPE)
International House
1 St Katharine's Way
London E1 9UN
Tel: (0171) 481 0643

London Stock Exchange
Old Broad Street
London EC2N 1HP
Tel: (0171) 588 2355

London International Financial Futures and Options Exchange (LIFFE)
Cannon Bridge
London EC4R 3XX
Tel: (0171) 623 0444

London Metal Exchange Ltd (LME)
56 Leadenhall Street
London EC3A 2BJ
Tel: (0171) 264 5555

London Securities and Derivatives Exchange Ltd (OMLX)
107 Cannon Street
London EC4N 5AD
Tel: (0171) 283 0678

Tradepoint Financial Networks plc
35 King Street
Covent Garden
London WC2E 8JD
Tel: (0171) 240 8000

Recognised Clearing Houses (RCHs)

London Clearing House Ltd
Aldgate House
33 Aldgate High Street
London EC3N 1EA
Tel: (0171) 426 7000

Friendly Societies Commission

Friendly Societies Commission
15 Great Marlborough Street
London W1V 2LL
Tel: (0171) 437 9992

Building Societies Commission

Building Societies Commission
15 Great Marlborough Street
London W1V 2LL
Tel: (0171) 437 9992

Panel on Takeovers and Mergers

The Secretary
Panel on Takeovers and Mergers
P.O. Box No. 226
The Stock Exchange Building
London EC2P 2JX
Tel: (0171) 382 9026

Monopolies and Mergers Commission

Monopolies and Mergers Commission
New Court
48 Carey Street
London WC2A 2JE
Tel: (0171) 324 1467

Office of Fair Trading

Office of Fair Trading
Field House
Breams Buildings
London EC4A 1PR
Tel: (0171) 242 2858

Ombudsmen

Banking Ombudsman
70 Gray's Inn Road
London WC1X 8NB
Tel: (0171) 404 9944

Building Societies Ombudsman
35–37 Grosvenor Gardens
London SW1X 7AW
Tel: (1071) 931 0044

Friendly Societies Ombudsman
35–37 Grosvenor Gardens
London SW1X 7AW
Tel: (0171) 931 0044

Insurance Ombudsman
City Gate One
135 Park Street
London SE1 9EA
Tel: (0171) 928 7600

Investment Ombudsman
6 Frederick Place
London EC2R 8BT
Tel: (0171) 976 3065

Occupational Pensions Advisory Service
11 Belgrave Road
London SW1V 1RB
Tel: (0171) 233 8080

Pensions Ombudsman
11 Belgrave Road
London SW1V 1RB
Tel: (0171) 834 9144

PIA Ombudsman
Hertsmere House
Hertsmere Road
London E14 4AB
Tel: (0171) 216 0016

HM Treasury

For the purposes of financial services regulation, the address of HM Treasury is:
Securities and Investment Group
HM Treasury
3rd Floor
Parliament Street
London SW1P 3AG
Tel: (0171) 270 5000

Department of Trade and Industry

Department of Trade and Industry
Ashdown House
123 Victoria Street
London SW1E 6RB
Tel: (0171) 215 5000

Serious Fraud Office

Serious Fraud Office
Elm House
10–16 Elm Street
London WC1X 0BJ
Tel: (0171) 239 7272

European Communities Commission

The address for the sales office for Official Publications of the European
Communities is:
2 rue Mercier
L–2985 Luxembourg
Tel: (00 352) 49 92 81

The addresses of the European Communities Commission Information Offices are:
Bâtiment Jean Monnet
Rue Alcide de Gasperi
L–2920 Luxembourg
Tel: (00 352) 43011

Jean Monnet House
8 Storey's Gate
London SW1P 3AT
Tel: (0171) 973 1992

Windsor House
9/15 Bedford Street
Belfast BT2 7EG
Tel: (01232) 240708

4 Cathedral Road
Cardiff CF1 9SG
Tel: (01222) 371631

9 Alva Street
Edinburgh EH2 4PH
Tel: (0131) 225 2058

Bank of England

Bank of England
Head Office
Threadneedle Street
London EC2R 8AH
Tel: (0171) 601 4444

London Stock Exchange

The London Stock Exchange
Old Broad Street
London EC2N 1HP
Tel: (0171) 588 2355

HMSO

Her Majesty's Stationery Office bookshops are located at:
49 High Holborn
London WC1V 6HB
Enquiries
Tel: (0171) 873 0011
Postal address: P.O. Box 276, London SW8 5DT
Orders
Tel: (0171) 873 9090

71 Lothian Road
Edinburgh EH3 9AZ
Tel: (0171) 228 4888

9–21 Princess Street
Manchester M60 8AS
Tel: (0161) 834 4188

Southey House
33 Wine Street
Bristol BS1 2BQ
Tel: (0117) 929 4515

258 Broad Street
Birmingham B1 2HE
Tel: (0121) 643 3740

16 Arthur Street
Belfast BT1 4GD
Tel: (01232) 238451

Abbreviations

AFBD	Association of Futures Brokers and Dealers
AIBD	Association of International Bond Dealers
Amex	American Stock Exchange
CBRs	Financial Services (Conduct of Business) Rules 1987
CCU	Commercial Crime Unit, Commonwealth Secretariat
CFTC	Commodities and Futures Trading Commission (US Body)
Ch.	Chapter (of the Financial Services Act)
Cl.	Clause
CSI	Council for the Securities Industry
DIE	Designated Investment Exchange
DTI	Department of Trade and Industry
EEC	European Economic Community
EU	European Union
IMRO	Investment Management Regulatory Organisation
ISE	The International Stock Exchange of the United Kingdom and the Republic of Ireland Limited
LCE	London Commodity Exchange
LIFFE	London International Financial Futures Exchange
LME	London Metal Exchange
MIBOC	Marketing of Investments Board Organising Committee
MOU	Memorandum of Understanding
NASD	National Association of Securities Dealers (US Body)
NYSE	New York Stock Exchange (US Body)
OEIC	Open-ended investment company
OFT	Office of Fair Trading
OTC market	Over the counter market
para.	paragraph
PIA	Personal Investment Authority
Pt.	Part
r.	rule (of the Securities and Investments Board)
RCH	Recognised Clearing House
reg.	regulation (of the Securities and Investments Board or statutory instrument)
RIE	Recognised Investment Exchange
RPB	Recognised Professional Body
s.	section(s) (of the Financial Services Act unless otherwise indicated)
Sch.	Schedule (to the Financial Services Act)
Secretary of State	The Secretary of State for Trade and Industry
SEC	Securities and Exchange Commission (US Body)
SFA	Securities and Futures Authority
SFO	Serious Fraud Office
SIB	Securities and Investments Board
SRO	Recognised Self-Regulating Organisation
TSA	The Securities Association
The Tribunal	The Financial Services Tribunal
UCITS Directive	EEC Directive on the co-ordination of laws relating to undertakings for collective investment in transferable securities

Contents

3   Investment Business and the Need for Authorisation

10   Collective Investment Schemes

11   Insurance Businesses and Friendly Societies

1 Financial Services Legislation – the Historical Perspective

INTRODUCTION

¶101   Confidence in the market

Integral to the efficient operation of any market is the maintenance of confidence in the integrity of its functions. History records the concern of those charged with ensuring the proper operation of even the earliest and most embryonic markets with the maintenance of certain standards. For example, the English common law at a very early stage in its development outlawed any practice or device to falsely enhance the price of 'victuals' and other merchandise in the markets as being prejudicial to trade and commerce and therefore injurious to the public good. The ancient common law offences of forestalling, regrating and ingrossing were for a considerable period specifically prohibited by statute as being detrimental to the national economy and tending to undermine confidence in the public markets.

The desire to ensure honesty, if not fairness, in the markets was naturally reflected in regard to the market, such as it was, in shares and bonds. In fact, during the first part of the eighteenth century the degree of statutory regulation and control within the City of London at least was, in some respects, commensurate with our new regime of regulation. Contrary to what many think, securities regulation is not a new science. Indeed, many of the problems that face us today had to be resolved or contained, at least in some measure, in the past. Whilst in the context of dynamic activities such as trading in securities it is necessary to be forward looking, it would be rash for us to ignore the often expensive experience of our forefathers. In some measure dealings on the financial markets of today are motivated by the same human emotions and desires that were manifest in the early physical markets. Perhaps the boundary between acceptable and unacceptable greed and exploitation has changed, particularly in regard to things like insider dealing, but the raw material remains constant. Therefore, there is value in setting out present system and structure of regulation in its historical context.

THE SECURITIES MARKETS

¶102   The market

We cannot know precisely at what stage the informal and *ad hoc* meetings of buyers and sellers of various commercial and financial instruments, including shares and bonds, actually became sufficiently regular and predictable to properly be described as a market. In fact, it is difficult enough to determine as a matter of definition at what stage it is reasonable to describe these instruments as securities in the modern sense of that word. It seems, however, that in the early days of the London securities market the main product traded was paper issued, at first, by the new joint stock companies and then a little later by the permanent national debt.

Given recent concern over the internationalisation of securities markets it is not without interest that some of the earliest joint stock companies were concerned with 'foreign trade' and overseas ventures. For example, in 1553 Sebastian Cabot formed a company with 240 shareholders to trade with Russia. A year or so earlier a company was formed with the rather romantic object of 'discovery of regions, dominions, islands and places unknown'. Obviously a very sound investment! Dealing in the market in these essentially partnership shares was sporadic and exceedingly limited. It was not until the end of the seventeenth century, after a costly war with France and considerable government borrowing, that dealings in shares and bonds developed and the profession of stockbroking was born. It would appear that a regular and reasonably sophisticated market with option and time dealings had developed in the City of London by 1694. In this market there was no separation between brokers and jobbers and the description often applied to both functions was 'stock-jobbing'.

¶103   A pernicious practice

The term 'jobber' carried a certain amount of opprobrium. Daniel Defoe in a paper entitled '*The Anatomy of Change Alley: A System of Stock-jobbing Proving that Scandalous Trade as it is now carried on to be knavish in its Private Practice and Treason in its Publick*', stated 'there is not a man but will own 'tis a complete System of Knavery; that 'tis a Trade in Fraud, born of Deceit and nourished by Trick, Cheat, Wheedle, Forgeries, Falsehoods and all sorts of Delusions'. From other writings in the late seventeenth and early eighteenth centuries it is clear that Defoe's view of the financial services industry was not exceptional.

Parliament appointed commissioners to 'look after the Trade of England', and in a report submitted to Parliament in November 1696 the commissioners stated 'the pernicious Art of Stock-Jobbing hath ... so wholly perverted the

End and Design of Companies' (*House of Commons Journals*, 25 Nov 1696). The commissioners chronicled examples of promotional frauds, asset stripping operations, insider dealing and market manipulation.

SECURITIES REGULATION

¶104 Regulating the market

Under a number of statutes dating back to the time of Edward I, brokers who acted as agents were required to be licensed by the Lord Mayor and Aldermen of the City of London. As a condition of this licence they were required among other things to make an oath to be of good behaviour. Once a licence had been issued it appears that there was no restriction on the commodity in which these agents could trade. Stockbrokers were thus simply brokers who traded in a wide variety of vendible commodities on behalf of their principals. This limited degree of regulation was scant protection and, with the development of an embryo financial services industry, scandals and abuses became commonplace.

¶105 The Act of 1697

After two unsuccessful attempts in 1693 and 1696 an 'Act to restrain the number and ill practice of Brokers and Stock-jobbers' was enacted in 1697. The preamble to this statute recorded that 'divers Brokers and Stock-jobbers, or pretended Brokers' had been guilty of 'most unjust practices and designs' and had 'unlawfully combined and confederated themselves together to raise or fall from time to time the value of securities'. The Act simply outlawed stockbroking in regard to virtually all financial instruments and shares of corporations, but not unincorporated companies, unless a licence were obtained from the Lord Mayor and Court of Aldermen. On admission the stockbroker was bound to swear that he would execute his duties 'without fraud or collusion, to the best of my skill and knowledge' according to the word and spirit of the law. Furthermore, a broker was required to enter into a bond of £500 which could be forfeited in case of misconduct. For acting as a broker without a licence there was a fine of £500 for each offence and anyone knowingly employing an unlicensed broker was liable to a fine of £50 for each offence. Brokers were prohibited from acting as principals on pain of perpetual disqualification. Further, they were bound to maintain a register recording all the details of their transactions.

The Act limited the number of licences to one hundred. Consequently there was considerable pressure from unlicensed brokers to repeal the statute or prevent its continuance. For a variety of reasons, more associated with apathy than design, the Act was allowed to lapse in 1704. It is most interesting, however, to observe how developed this legislation was in attempting to resolve many of the problems that have only just been tackled again in the *Financial Services Act* 1986.

¶106   Curbing speculation

The scandal and fiasco associated with the so-called 'South Sea Bubble', although testifying to the greed and gullibility of investors, did surprisingly little long-term harm to the embryonic securities market. Because of the perceived extent of abuse and speculative dealing, an 'Act for the better establishing of public credit by preventing for the future the infamous practice of stockjobbing' was passed by the House of Commons, but was thrown out by the Lords in 1721. In 1734, however, an 'Act to Prevent the Infamous Practice of Stock-Jobbing' was passed. Generally referred to as Barnard's Act, after its sponsor, The Act outlawed and rendered void all option dealings. Short-selling was also made illegal and a broker who knowingly executed such a bargain was liable to a fine of £100. Another interesting aspect of this Act was that brokers had to record all transactions in the name of the principal. Criminal penalties under the Act were rarely applied, however, and its main impact was in impugning transactions. Given the extent of speculative and technically illegal business the market developed a strict code of honour between members of The Stock Exchange which did not depend upon written or recorded undertakings. A member's word was his bond. Furthermore while brokers were agents *vis-à-vis* their clients, they were treated as principals when transacting business with other members of The Stock Exchange. All this tended to strengthen brokers' dislike for lawyers and the courts!

¶107   The City's authority

The ancient authority of the Lord Mayor and Court of Aldermen to license and supervise brokers in the City of London was reaffirmed several times during the seventeenth and eighteenth centuries. Perhaps the most important aspects of this somewhat loose regulation were the oath to avoid all deceit, to make known the identity of a principal, to maintain a dealing book, not to deal on one's own account and to report any dealings by unlicensed brokers to the Court. While it seems that prosecutions under these provisions were not rare, convictions were most infrequent. Perhaps one of the most significant implications of these regulations was that they contributed to the separation of broking and jobbing as businesses. A jobber, dealing as a principal, was not bound by the laws relating to agents.

THE STOCK EXCHANGE

¶108 Introduction

Given the degree of centralisation within the British economy and the overwhelming supremacy of the City of London in providing finance and services, it is surprising that The Stock Exchange did not really take shape, in a form that we would recognise today, until the nineteenth century. For example, the notion that the market should be confined to 'elected' members faced considerable opposition, and for a time even the Bank of England advocated a public market. The Stock Exchange had to use its wits and influence in 1810 to avoid legislation which would have rendered it a public market. After accepting that its administration had been 'loose and careless' in 1812 The Stock Exchange published its first Rule Book. During the nineteenth century the market had to face an onslaught of fraud and abuse invariably associated with the promotion of companies, particularly under the *Joint Stock Companies Act* 1844. It is a fine testament to the honour, and possibly enlightened self-interest, of those responsible for the development of this great market that procedures were developed and generally applied to mitigate the worst and most damaging abuses.

¶109 A precursor to Professor Gower!

The Report of the Royal Commission, appointed in March 1877 under Lord Penzance, to look into the administration and operation of The Stock Exchange, 'recognised a great public advantage in the fact that those who bought and sold for the public in a market of such enormous magnitude ... should be bound in their dealings by rules for the enforcement of fair dealing and the repression of fraud, capable of affording relief and exercising restraint far more prompt and often more satisfactorily than any within reach of the Courts of law'. Although the Commission's report was on the whole a vindication of The Stock Exchange and in particular endorsed the jobbing system which had developed on the London market but not in the provinces, it considered that there were serious deficiencies in investor protection. The commissioners recommended that inquiries into fraud and suspicious dealings should be undertaken promptly by 'some public functionary and enforced by law'. Furthermore, a majority of the Commission considered that The Stock Exchange should be constituted under a statute. Its rules and regulation could then be amended only by 'the President of the Board of Trade or some other public authority'. It was argued that this element of 'external control' would boost public confidence and resolve complaints about The Stock Exchange's monopolistic privileges. The Commission was also of the opinion that dealings on the market should be far more visible so that investors would see justice done! It is also not without interest that the Commission did not consider it desirable to 'fix commissions'. It also recommended the marking and recording of all bargains. All very radical, isn't it?

INTO THE MODERN ERA

¶110   Share pushing

While the general law, and in particular the criminal law, showed that it had teeth in dealing with some of the more excessive promotional frauds during the last century, there were few provisions that could be effectively deployed against some of the more sophisticated and abusive operations both on and off the market, especially in regard to marketing and share pushing. Given the prevalence of such undesirable practices, in 1936 the Government set up a committee under Sir Archibald Bodkin 'to consider operations commonly known as share-pushing and share-hawking and similar activities'. At about the same time another committee was appointed under Sir Alan Anderson to inquire into 'fixed trusts' and to report what action was desirable in the public interest. This report in fact addressed itself to 'unit trusts'. The recommendations (see Cmnd 5259 and Cmnd 5539) of both committees were largely accepted by the Government and this led to the enactment of the *Prevention of Fraud (Investments) Act* 1939. In 1958 this Act was replaced by another of the same title, which was virtually a re-enactment.

¶111   Prevention of Fraud (Investments) Act 1958

The *Prevention of Fraud (Investments) Act* 1958 prohibited dealing in securities except by persons who obtained a licence from the Department of Trade and Industry (DTI) or who were within certain exceptions. For example, a member of a recognised stock exchange or recognised association of dealers in securities was not required to obtain a licence. The Bank of England, statutory and municipal corporations and those declared by the DTI were exempted from this prohibition. Under the Act the DTI was empowered to exempt certain dealers. The DTI exercised its discretion in regard to banks, discount houses and similar institutions of standing which dealt in securities only to a degree incidental to their main activities or who dealt essentially as 'wholesalers' rather than directly with members of the public. Until comparatively recently the DTI was for a variety of reasons – some more justified than others – unwilling to exercise adequate supervision over the grant and renewal of licences.

Under s. 7 of the Prevention of Fraud (Investments) Act, the DTI was empowered to make rules governing the conduct of licensed dealers and to varying degrees these were regarded as minimum standards by the various organisations and institutions not required to have a licence. The *Licensed Dealers (Conduct of Business) Rules* 1983 (SI 1983/585) introduced into the system of securities regulation a number of new and radical concepts. 'Chinese Walls' (see ¶615) were recognised as providing some defence to the non-disclosure of material interests. An obligation to 'know your client' was implicit in the obligation to ensure investment advice was 'suitable' to the circumstances of a client. 'Cold calling' was significantly restricted and dealers were held to 'generally accepted standards' as to what constitutes 'good market practice'. While no less than a breakthrough, at least in conceptual terms, the rules lacked any real sanction other than an unlikely disciplinary jurisdiction vested unenthusiastically in the DTI.

In addition to licensing dealers, the Prevention of Fraud (Investments) Act provided for authorisation by the Department of unit trusts and the setting down of conditions as to the status of managers and trustees. Furthermore, the Schedule 1 to the Act also set out matters to be covered by the trust deed. Although this provided some degree of regulation, the law relating to the management of unit funds, and for that matter investment funds generally, was left almost entirely to the few and outdated principles of equity and common law.

The 1958 Act was essentially by its name and terms an anti-fraud statute in the traditions of the so-called North American 'Blue Sky' laws. Section 13 of the Act emphasised this by making it a crime for any person to induce or attempt to induce another to enter into an investment transaction by a misleading, false or deceptive statement, promise or forecast or by any dishonest concealment of a material fact. Although by its wording an apparently wide provision, it was rarely used and was to some extent emasculated by restrictive interpretation. Section 14 of the Act imposed a general prohibition on the distribution of investment circulars inviting investment, although the prohibition was subject to certain important exceptions. These extended on a general and continuing basis to exempted or licensed dealers and to persons dealing with dealers in securities. Others could apply to the DTI for permission to distribute a particular circular.

¶112   Investor protection

To some extent British securities regulation bears a resemblance to the British Constitution. Although there is no enactment or document which can be described as the British Constitution it would be misguided to think that we do not have one. It is derived from a number of sources and is the umbrella concept under which a host of rules, laws and practices operate more or less effectively and are referrable to each other. The same is and was perhaps, before the recent legislation, even more true of securities regulation. In addition to the *Prevention of Fraud (Investments) Act* 1958, there were a number of other statutory provisions. Indeed, many still remain outside the main corpus of securities regulation. Thus the provisions in the *Companies Act* 1985 relating to the creation, issue and maintenance of capital may be considered as within securities regulation. The provisions in the *Companies Act* 1985 relating to substantial interests in shares and disclosure of aggregated interests or 'concert parties' can also be regarded as falling within securities regulation. Provisions empowering the DTI to inquire into the affairs of companies and the beneficial ownership of securities and in some instances freeze such interests can properly be considered within our remit. The provisions in Pt. V of the *Criminal Justice Act* 1993 outlawing insider dealing as part of securities regulation. There are, of course, many other provisions in fiscal, banking and insurance law which might equally be regarded as falling within the broad area of securities regulation.

Although the courts are willing to interfere when they perceive fraud and abuse, as they did during the nineteenth century in regard to various forms of promotional fraud and more recently in relation to what might be described as 'criminal breach of trust' and knowing assistance in the laundering of the proceeds of fraud, they are very concerned not to become involved in matters where there is a sensitive balance of regulation. Thus, in *R v International Stock Exchange of the United Kingdom* (1993) 1 All ER 420, Bingham MR observed 'in a highly sensitive and potentially fluid financial market ... the courts will not second guess the informed judgment of responsible regulators steeped in knowledge of their particular market'. Therefore, the courts have shown themselves reluctant to be drawn into contested takeover bids and the like. As Lord Templeman emphasised in *Prudential Assurance Co Ltd v Newman Industries & Ors* (No 2) (1982) Ch 204 at 224, speaking for the Court of Appeal, 'in our view the voluntary regulation of companies is a matter for the City. The compulsory regulation of companies is a matter for Parliament.'

¶113   The balance of regulation

The debate on whether and how to regulate the financial services industry in Britain, as in many other countries, has tended to be dominated by the dark shadow of scandals and abuses. For example, the efficacy of self-regulation during the 1970s tended to be judged almost wholly in terms of its ability to combat such abuses as insider dealing. While it is not surprising that the media, and thus political and public opinion, tend to be shocked by sensational frauds and abuses, there is nonetheless a grave danger of the 'tail being allowed to wag the dog'. By concentrating excessively on the role of regulation in the financial services sector to promote and assure integrity and thereby protection from abuse, there is a real danger that the positive aspects of regulation may be ignored.

In Canada, the influential Kimber Committee (Report of the Attorney-General's Committee on Securities Legislation in Ontario (1966) 1.09) recognised that:

> 'While the underlying purpose of legislation governing the practices and operation of the securities market must be the protection of the investigating public, it is equally true that the character of securities legislation will affect the development of financial institutions and their efficiency in performing certain economic functions. The principal economic functions of a capital market are to assure the optimum allocation of financial resources in the economy, to permit maximum mobility and transferability of those resources, and to provide facilities for a continuing valuation of financial assets.'

Even the controversial report published in Australia under the chairmanship of Senator Rea (Report of the Senate Select Committee on Securities and Exchange (1974) Australian Government) observed that the purpose of securities regulation was firstly to 'maintain, facilitate and improve the performance of the capital market in the interests of economic development, efficiency and stability'.

As in the case of the US it was concerned about the justification of apparently restrictive practices which precipitated fundamental changes in the regulatory structure. Although there has long been debate – mostly outside the City – about the adequacy or otherwise of self-regulation the debate until 1980 tended to concentrate almost exclusively on the competence of regulation to control or at least inhibit fraud and abuse. Of course, this ignores the positive side of regulation.

THE CITY AND SELF-REGULATION

¶114   Self-regulation

By far the most important area of corporate securities regulation before and for that matter after the enactment of the Financial Services Act is that of self-regulation. Self-regulation in the financial services industry has worked reasonably effectively in the past, and in a significantly modified form may be expected to do so in the future, largely because of the nature and character of the City of London. The 'village atmosphere' in the City of London, reinforced by its traditions, institutions, self-interest and, until comparatively recently, by the essentially homogeneous character of its inhabitants, proved a fertile ground for self-regulation to develop and attain a degree of respect unrivalled in any other system of corporate securities control. It is impossible to understand the workings of the present system of control and supervision without fully appreciating this factor.

The institutions of self-regulation in the City of London have been diverse and have operated with differing standards of success. At one end of the spectrum the Panel on Takeovers and Mergers acquired an international reputation for efficiency, integrity and professionalism that even the US Securities and Exchange Commission (hereafter referred to as the SEC) envied (see Rider, 'Self-regulation: the British approach to policing conduct in the securities business, with particular reference to the role of the City Panel on Take-overs and Mergers' [1978] *Journal of Comparative Corporate Law and Securities Regulation* 319). At the other end was the ill-fated Council for the Securities Industry (CSI) which Professor LC Gower, perhaps with some charity, mentioned *en passant* in his Discussion Document as having been considered by some a 'fifth wheel on the carriage' (*Review of Interior Protection – A Discussion Document* (HMSO, 1982) para. 8.22). The degree of actual regulation administered by The Stock Exchange and bodies such as the Panel should not be underestimated. Of course there were and still are weaknesses in any system of self-regulation, but on the whole it cannot be doubted that before the City became a different place from the one it had been for the last 600 years, it all worked surprisingly well.

¶115   The City

It is appropriate to look, albeit briefly, at the financial services industry in Britain, and, thus, at the City of London. The story of the City of London is in many ways a 'tale of two cities'. The international city and the domestic city. Both cities were distinct in all respects before the 'suspension' of exchange control in Britain in 1979. The international city, in more recent years, centred upon the Euromarkets and in particular on providing services and facilitation for the vast amounts of money essentially in non-sterling denomination that sloshed around the world economy. The City provided a 'wholesale' market, with countries such as Switzerland providing the 'retail' service. The oil crisis in 1973 created a new demand for international finance on the one side and produced fantastic sums on the other. Intermediating these needs and essentially recycling 'petrodollars' confirmed the international role of the City. Relatively lax banking regulation, a reputation for discretion and confidentiality and an essentially stable political system all played their role.

On the other side of the formal dividing line, the relatively strict exchange control regulation, lay the domestic city. This centred on The Stock Exchange and the domestic operations of the banks and insurance companies. Not only was there a striking difference in the nature of the two cities, but also in the 'players' on their respective markets. The offshore city was virtually dominated by foreign houses, yet the domestic market was able through various devices, including exchange control and restrictive practices, to shield itself from foreign penetration. It was largely the domestic market that attracted concern so far as regulation was concerned. The scandals and abuses which were identified were far closer to home. (See generally Hadden, 'Fraud in the City, The Role of the Criminal Law [1983] Crim. LR 500). Consequently the international city was allowed to operate in the shadow, well out of reach and largely beyond the interest of the media and public.

With the lifting of exchange control in 1979, the formal barrier between the two cities was destroyed. Very quickly it became apparent that there were large parts of the City which were internationally uncompetitive. The protection that had so long been afforded to British houses was gone probably for ever. Compounding this was the fact that other centres were beginning to emulate the City. With the developments in technology and in particular telecommunications this was a real threat. Shares in traditional British companies could be and are traded in New York just as easily as on The Stock Exchange. 'Follow-the-sun' trading had become a practical reality. It was obvious that if London was to retain its pre-eminence in the European time-trading zone, something fundamental had to be done and quickly. The third world debt crisis also played its part as it throttled the role of the banks in borrowing and lending across international boundaries. This business had made the City probably the foremost international banking centre in the world. Instead, borrowers were seeking to raise capital through the issue of securities. Thus, if the City was to retain this business there was considerable pressure upon it to develop as an international securities centre. All these pressures, as in primeval chaos, finally contributed to the so-called 'Big Bang'. It would be difficult to isolate a single significant factor behind this phenomenon. However, there is little doubt that pressure on the City from overseas, the failure for a variety of reasons of stockbroking firms and merchant banks to move adequately into the international securities business, as well as the developments that were taking place in the field of regulation, all had their role.

THE PRELUDE TO THE FSA

¶116 A weakening system

Self-regulation has proved to be an effective and reasonably efficient system for the British securities industry until very recently. The British financial services industry, given its virtual dependence on the City of London, developed within a very small and intimate environment. Until comparatively recently there was

¶116

a village atmosphere in the City. In the senior levels of the various institutions and professional firms there was a degree of homogeneity which ensured common values and reinforced the informal 'codes' within which this society operated. The class system, with its institutions of social control invariably subtle and exclusionary in their orientation, functioned with a predictability and efficiency which probably surpassed any practical system of legal regulation. However, things have changed not only domestically but, perhaps more importantly, internationally. Today the City lacks the homogeneity it once had. The fear of exclusion – whether from business or the right clubs – no longer carries the stigma and social consequences that it once did.

On a political level, it has become increasingly clear that government cannot remain aloof from manifest abuses and breakdowns in control. The 'unacceptable face of capitalism' may appear to some as the only one that capitalism wears, thereby bringing directly into question the public's confidence in the integrity and, thus, the efficiency of the markets. This has been recognised in regard to insider dealing. It is true that there is precious little evidence of the extent of this form of activity and the arguments as to whether it causes serious harm are equivocal. However, if enough people consider that insiders and their associates are 'unfairly' taking advantage of the markets, this will inevitably undermine investor confidence. Thus the state has not only the right but also, as ultimate custodian of the integrity of the national economy, the obligation to intervene.

¶117   A Securities and Exchange Commission

In 1974 the DTI sent out questionnaires inquiring as to the adequacy of supervision and regulation of the securities market. Although the replies were not published the predominant view of those who did not bother to reply was that the self-regulatory system was likely to be as effective as any other. The City has always harboured an almost paranoid fear that it would have a governmental body similar to the United States' SEC imposed upon it. Indeed, it would not be merely cynical to observe that it was usually the case that the City only reacted with any real enthusiasm to getting its house in order when such talk was heard in Westminster or Whitehall. The establishment of the Panel on Takeovers and Mergers, and its refinement into probably one of the most effective self-regulatory organisations anywhere, was largely a response to such fears. It is probable that the City, and for that matter those who spoke so glibly about the United States' SEC, failed to comprehend that that body is just as unique, and just as much a creature of its own peculiar history and environment, as anything one is likely to find in the City. The DTI's review did show, however, that legislation was required in certain areas to prevent abuses such as insider dealing. A Joint Review Body consisting of officials from the

Bank of England and the DTI was also set up. The City, not to be outdone, set up the ill-fated Council for the Securities Industry.

During the 1970s a number of organisations and interest groups considered the question of supervision and published their views and recommendations. It is perhaps surprising that so many called for the setting up of a statutory authority with legal powers. This view was not confined to those of a left wing or radical standpoint. For example, Justice, the British Section of the International Commission of Jurists, in 1974, recommended a body that bears an uncanny resemblance to the 'designated agency' in the *Financial Services Act* 1986. The Senate of the Inns of Court and Law Society also advocated a similar body.

¶118   The Wilson Committee

The Committee, appointed to review the functioning of financial institutions, under Sir Harold Wilson, in delivering its report in 1980 (1980 Cmnd 7939; see also Report of the Committee under Lord Radcliffe, on the Working of the Monetary System (1959 Cmnd 827)), to the surprise of many, was prepared to give the system of self-regulation a clean bill of health. Although it did recognise the need to improve certain aspects of the system, on the whole it thought that it worked tolerably well, and was probably better than any other system that could reasonably be devised. Unfortunately, however, the scandals continued and some assumed proportions that were impossible to ignore (see generally, Clarke, *Regulating the City, Competition, Scandal and Reform* (1986, Open University). The CSI never proved itself a competent or even efficient body. It lacked virtually every characteristic that would have enabled it to resolve the many problems and tensions that were fast developing within the City. Its mandate was unclear, it lacked leadership, its composition was inappropriate and it could never find the resources and support it needed to enable it to operate effectively.

THE GOWER REVIEW

¶119   Terms of reference

The unique quality of British securities regulation is nowhere better illustrated than in the manner in which the onus of developing a comprehensive scheme for supervision and regulation was placed on the strong but aged shoulders of a single, although an eminent and uniquely qualified academic. In July 1981 the government appointed Professor LCB Gower, the former Vice-Chancellor of Southampton University, to undertake a review with the following terms of reference:

(1) to consider the statutory protection now required by (a) private and (b) business investors in securities and other property, including investors through unit trusts and open-ended investment companies operating in the UK;

(2) to consider the need for statutory control of dealers in securities, investment consultants and investment managers; and

(3) to advise on the need for new legislation.

In addition, if this was not enough, Professor Gower was asked to take into account any relevant developments in the European Economic Community (EEC). What in most countries would have been no modest task for a team of experts with competent and adequate support, Professor Gower was required to do alone. Given the desire of everyone to see that the discussion advanced as quickly as possible, Professor Gower published a discussion document (*Review of Investor Protection – A Discussion Document* (1982), HMSO) in January 1982 and then invited comments.

¶120   Gower's provisional views

Professor Gower recognised that one of the most serious problems was simply to determine the scope of his review and, thus, the reach of his proposals. He decided that it should cover all forms of investment other than those in any form of property over which the investor has exclusive control after its acquisition. Although property such as an antique may be bought as an investment, the circumstances concerning acquisition and retention are very different from the case of, for example, a share, where its 'value' will depend largely upon what the investor is told and on the stewardship of those in whom the investment property is vested. Professor Gower considered that there were four main ways of protecting investors:

(1) by regulating the *modus operandi* of the body in which the investor invests;

(2) by regulating the terms of investment;

(3) by providing for full disclosure about what those terms are; and

(4) by regulating those who act as intermediaries.

Professor Gower considered that it was not practical for him to look at (2), which was really a matter of company law. He considered that self-regulation and government regulation 'should not be regarded as antithetical but as complementary'. He was convinced that 'the Government should be the decider of major questions involving public policy – a role which it cannot abdicate though it may, within limits, delegate subject to its general supervision'. He thought that 'the ideal would be to weld self-regulation and governmental regulation into a coherent statutory framework which would cover the whole field that needs to be regulated and in which each would perform the role which it does best, working harmoniously together'. The Wilson Committee had thought that balance between government and self-regulation and statutory and non-statutory regulation was acceptable. Professor Gower disagreed with this. He thought that the Wilson Committee had erred in considering that the balance between statutory and non-statutory control was sufficiently effective in protecting investors.

In developing his proposals, Professor Gower was circumscribed by a number of practical and 'political' considerations. Firstly, he was aware of the Government's desire to see a substantial reduction in the number of 'Quasi-Autonomous Non-Governmental Organisations' or QUANGOS. Gower recognised that while *caveat emptor* was a discredited policy there were serious differences in the nature and character of both investors and securities. He thought that it was desirable to 'adjust' regulation to reflect this and the differing expectations associated with each. He acknowledged the 'cost benefit' balance in regulation. It would be 'self-defeating' to introduce regulation which could only be complied with at considerable expense. 'The likely effect would be to drive out the scrupulous who would be unwilling to continue in practice in breach of the regulations and leave matters in the hands of the unscrupulous.' Prevention was both in principle and practice better than cure. However, breaches were to some extent inevitable and 'the only effective ultimate safety net for investors is some form of compensation fund'. Gower was also mindful of the need to ensure that in the international arena London was regarded as sufficiently well regulated to promote confidence in its integrity, but not excessively onerous in its conditions.

Considering various approaches to regulation, Professor Gower stated that 'if I were writing on a *tabula rasa* I suspect that I should provisionally recommend the setting up of a securities commission'. However, due to the 'political' constraints he recognised emphatically 'but I am not. And I don't'.

In the practical world, Gower considered that the most likely and profitable approach was to adjust the balance between governmental and self-regulation. In this process Gower recognised that the collaboration in the City was imperative. Indeed, it was largely because he recognised the City's extreme dislike of securities commissions that he accepted the inevitability of the political reaction to a recommendation to establish such.

Gower considered that the statutory framework should be provided by a

¶120

Securities Act, which at a later stage he renamed Investor Protection Act, which would require firms engaged in business within the financial services industry to register. This process of registration would occur through appropriate and recognised self-regulatory bodies. Recognition of such bodies would be by the DTI which would be charged with general oversight and would have the power to add to their rules. The DTI's powers would, however, be confined to circumstances where such action was necessary for the protection of investors or the orderly functions of the market. An independent tribunal would be required to hear appeals from the determinations of self-regulatory authorities.

Gower considered that effective self-regulatory authorities would be required in the following areas:

(1) issues and distributions of securities, acquisitions and takeovers;

(2) operation of the securities markets;

(3) broking and jobbing, on or off the market in securities;

(4) investment management and advice; and

(5) operation of unit trusts and pools.

He recognised that none were then effectively covered by a single organisation. He consequently, and somewhat controversially, proposed that the Takeover Panel's terms of reference should be expanded so as to include public issues. It would be charged with prescribing the contents of, and scrutinising for accuracy and fairness, all prospectuses and not only those circulated in takeover merger operations. In regard to broking, jobbing, investment management and advice, Professor Gower contemplated that there was a need for at least two organisations; one for The Stock Exchange and another for the over-the-counter market (OTC). It would also be necessary to establish an organisation to assume responsibility for unit trusts and mutual funds.

These organisations would need to be co-ordinated and Professor Gower considered that this role might usefully be undertaken by a revamped and more realistically resourced Council for the Securities Industry. The cost of this new scheme of self-regulation would be borne by investors who are the beneficiaries. Professor Gower also advocated that laws and rules seeking to ensure honesty in the markets were probably not sufficient and that regulations should be devised to ensure the competence of those entering the industry.

¶121   Gower's considered opinion

Professor Gower's proposals met with a mixed reception which was divided along the expected lines of tradition and self-interest. Most in the City thought that his ideas were 'interesting' but many dismissed them as 'academic'. In his report, *Review of Investor Protection*, which was published in two parts, the first in January 1984 (1984 Cmnd 9125) and the second in March 1985 (1985 HMSO), Professor Gower had obviously taken account of many of the points raised. His later recommendations also manifested a greater maturity both of thought and experience. In essence they are the same, although refined, and in some respects there is a change of emphasis. Of course, during his review there were a number of developments. The DTI itself published new Licensed Dealers (Conduct of Business) Rules in 1983 which introduced into British securities regulation a number of novel and potentially far-ranging provisions. The DTI also significantly tightened up its procedures for licensing and monitoring dealers under the *Prevention of Fraud (Investments) Act* 1958 (see ¶112). Legislation was passed which implemented the three EEC Directives on listed securities, and the issue of restrictive practices and The Stock Exchange was resolved (see ¶801). Not only did all these mean that Professor Gower had to attempt to maintain the focus on a number of fast-moving targets, but also that he was largely bereft of administrative support.

Professor Gower felt it necessary to restate his philosophy in his report. He stated that 'logic and tidiness ... are of importance only in so far as they contribute to a legal regime which can be understood, which will be regarded as fair by those it affects and which, as a result, will be generally observed and can be effectively enforced'. Professor Gower emphasised that unintelligibility and the failure to treat alike undermines enforcement and credibility. Nor did he 'favour regulating for the sake of regulation'. He recognised fully the dangers of over-regulation. In assessing the optimum degree of regulation Professor Gower did not consider that it was practical or that he was sufficiently well qualified to attempt any cost-benefit analysis. He accepted that 'there is a tension between market efficiency and investor protection which often pulls in different directions'. In the end, it has to be a value judgment as to how much weight is given to a free market and how much to investor protection. His judgement was simply that regulation should 'be no greater than is necessary to protect reasonable people from being made fools of. Recognising the national interest in properly regulated markets, Professor Gower modified his view as to who should bear the cost. While the market should pay for the day-to-day regulation, the ultimate regulatory authority should be funded from the public purse.

Professor Gower was obliged to revise his proposals in regard to the structure of regulation. His idea of super 'activity' based on self-regulators was considered to be unworkable. He had hoped that there would be a need for only four or five such agencies. It was clear, however, that this would not be feasible. Professor Gower persisted in his view that the basic principle of a comprehensive system of regulation within a statutory framework based so far as possible on self-regulation subject to government surveillance (which was intended to be enshrined in the original *Prevention of Fraud (Investments) Act* 1939), was desirable. While accepting that self-regulation could be undermined by too much oversight, he stated that 'if self-regulation is to survive, the surveillance to which it is subject must be sufficient to provide a genuine curb on undesirable restrictive practices and sufficient spur to ensure that rules are kept under review and their observance efficiently monitored'.

Reluctantly Professor Gower had to accept that self-regulation based upon a functional division of investment business was unworkable and that instead it had to be built on professional and commercial groupings. Professor Gower's attachment to this approach was not simply because he found it neat in academic terms, but also because it is difficult for professional bodies orientated to the protection and advancement of their members' interests to adapt themselves into an organisation able to take full account of the wider public interests. Devices such as lay members on governing bodies may, in the words of Professor Gower, be nothing more than 'window dressing'.

He considered, in some detail, whether the DTI or some other body should be entrusted with overall responsibility within this framework. Although he found the argument in logic for a securities commission inescapable, he accepted that this was not practical politics. Furthermore, he found the notion that the CSI should be converted into a commission charged with administering the new structure 'even more impracticable'. While accepting that his revised proposals had inevitably resulted in a blurring of the borderline between governmental and self-regulation he felt that general oversight must be the responsibility of the DTI.

¶122   Overtaken by events

The pace of developments both in the City and in Whitehall continued, and Professor Gower and his parliamentary counsel who were attempting to prepare a draft bill were overtaken by events. In the circumstances it was considered inappropriate to publish those parts of his draft bill that had been prepared and thus the second and final part of Professor Gower's report was confined to a commentary on the government's own White Paper which had been published a couple of months earlier in January 1985. (*Financial Services in the United Kingdom: A New Framework for Investor Protection* (1985 Cmnd 9432)).

In his second report, Professor Gower acknowledged that there had been a change of heart in the City and that there was an increasing feeling that a proliferation of small self-regulatory organisations might not be beneficial. He also noted that while there was still little real support for a security commission, most took the view that the DTI even if it assumed the 'expertise' of the CSI, would not be capable of effectively discharging its oversight role.

Consequently, and somewhat tentatively, many were coming round to the notion that a new super self-regulatory agency should be established: a 'son of CSI'.

REACTION TO GOWER

¶123 The City

The feeling in certain quarters that the 'tail was begging to wag the dog' led in May 1984 to the surprise appointment by the Governor of the Bank of England of a high-powered practitioner-based advisory group under Mr Martin (later Sir Martin) Jacomb. This group was mandated to advise him urgently on the structure and operation of self-regulatory agencies, and whether a practitioner-based system could be fashioned in the near future. Under a little pressure from the DTI another such group was formed, under Mr Marshall Field, to advise on the prospects for practitioner-based regulation of the marketing of life assurance and unit trusts.

These committees concentrated essentially on the issue of whether a new institutional structure was required. They decided it was, and considered it would be preferable to have the government delegate powers to a private body resembling a more powerful version of the CSI. The Bank of England and The Stock Exchange must have preferred this solution to the 'dangerous logic' of Professor Gower. This was pressed on a tolerably receptive DTI, and a White Paper was rushed to the printers. This neat and typically British solution allayed the increasing embarrassment felt in Whitehall. Professor Gower had put ministers in a difficult position by so blatantly arguing in terms of a securities commission, but resiling from logic and efficiency, on the grounds of overt political expediency. He had presented the arguments with a disturbing polarity – a commission or, alternatively and equally unpalatable, an enlarged role for the DTI. There was no middle road, the sort that ministers, civil servants and the City cherish. Professor Gower, always the academic, saw only black and white; it is the practitioner, whether in the City or in Whitehall, that envisages grey! It was from this 'grey region' that the Securities and Investments Board (SIB) was born.

¶124 The Government

The White Paper (see ¶208), while adopting most of Professor Gower's detailed recommendations, departed in several important respects from his views. It underlined the clear national interest in a healthy and well run financial services industry. While accepting the need to improve laws relating to investor protection which are 'outdated and incomplete', the White Paper emphasised that the government was well aware of the dangers of excessive regulation. Regulation should 'be no more than the minimum necessary to protect the investor'. The government also made it clear that 'regulation cannot eliminate risk' and that an element of risk is inherent in investment as distinct from savings.

In developing its new framework, which builds upon the best aspects of self-regulation, the government stated its objectives as: the promotion of efficiency in the financial services industry, promoting competitiveness both domestically and internationally, inspiring confidence in issuers and investors that the financial services industry is a 'clean' place to do business, and finally ensuring that the regulatory framework is flexible and clear enough to guide but not to cramp structural and other changes so that it has the resilience not to be overrun by events.

To achieve these laudable objectives, the government prefered to espouse the following principles. The primary assurance that the industry will meet the needs and expectations of customers is simply market force. The government sought to facilitate this by ensuring that better and more information is disclosed, and the forces of competition are brought to bear upon the industry. The law should be clear and should lay down a set of principles which facilitate the proper conduct of business. As a general rule prevention is better than cure, but vigorous enforcement of a simplified and clear investment law is necessary to deter fraud and abuse. Self-regulation should be promoted to ensure that those practising in the industry voluntarily adhere to the highest principles of integrity. Furthermore, the law should ensure equivalence of treatment between products and services competing in the same market.

It is not without interest that the then Economic Secretary to the Treasury, during a debate in 1964, stated that 'the first duty of the Government is to ensure that so far as possible investors are protected against the cheat' but not the foolish, reckless and greedy investor. The White Paper states 'no regulatory system can, or should, relieve the investor of responsibility for exercising judgment and care in deciding how to invest his money'. While the White Paper is prepared to acknowledge that 'proper prominence "should be given to" the time honoured principle of *caveat emptor*', this principle alone is not enough. In the interests of confidence the likelihood of fraud must be reduced and high standards must be encouraged.

As some have pointed out, it remains to be seen to what extent the promotion of competition can be seen to be an effective or efficient means of eradicating or reducing the scope for fraud. Surely the more pressure there is on financial intermediaries to cut corners and operate at the margins, whether of credit or

¶124

accepted practice, the more risk there is of fraud and abuse. The Wilson Committee acknowledged the essential paradox by recommending that 'regulation and competition should be complementary, the one providing the framework within which the other can be allowed to operate safely'. To expect competition itself to evoke and ensure compliance with regulatory norms is misconceived. The government's approach was that of the two City advisory groups, in proposing the creation of a super self-regulatory agency to which virtually all the powers of regulation and supervision under the new Act could be delegated. The White Paper refers to two such agencies, one to cover securities and investment, and another the marketing of packaged investments. Professor Gower, in the second part of his report, criticised this 'two headed scheme' as a 'fundamental error'. He considered that it would be wasteful, duplicative and confusing. He thought that a single authority was far more sensible. That an amalgamation of the functions of these two bodies was foreseen even by the government is clear in the White Paper. It specifically states that with the benefit of experience it may be beneficial to have a single body.

The White Paper described how these bodies would be given, through delegation, statutory authority to authorise persons conducting investment business and impose on such. They would also be given the power to recognise various practitioner-based self-regulating authorities whose rules and procedures are no less onerous than theirs. These other bodies would be responsible for the admission and conduct of their own members under supervision of the recognising authority. Thus, authorisation required for conducting investment business could be secured from either the super self-regulatory agencies directly or through a self-regulatory organisation recognised by such. An independent tribunal as a final determinant of any dispute about authorisation or penalties for breaches of the rules was proposed.

The White Paper acknowledged that 'to provide for a statutory power of authorisation and regulation to be given to a private sector body is unprecedented' and consequently certain safeguards are provided for (see Page *'Self-regulation: Constitutional Dimension* (1986) 49 MLR 141). For example, the Chairman of the Securities and Investments Board (SIB) is appointed by the Secretary of State with the agreement of the Governor of the Bank of England, while the members of the Board are appointed by the Governor, subject to the agreement of the Secretary of State. Rather than a manifestation of constitutionality this was, of course, a compromise!

It is debatable whether entrusting such powers to a private body is 'unprecedented'. However, what is clear is that given the public functions and statutory powers that the Boards possess, they are subject to, and amenable to, the public law and, in particular to judicial review.

¶124

THE BIG BANG

¶125   Introduction

Having regard to the lack-lustre circumstances surrounding the introduction of The Stock Exchange's then novel computer-assisted dealing system in 1986, which showed a remarkable propensity to 'go-down' at key moments, the description 'Big Bang' was singularly inappropriate. This unfortunate phrase was coined to describe 27 October 1986 as it was on this day that The Stock Exchange abolished its system of minimum commissions in the domestic securities market and introduced its new dealing system. As a consequence, it also abolished its time-honoured practice of insisting on the strict segregation of broker and dealer function on its markets.

Although the financial services legislation was going through Parliament at the same time as the 'Big Bang' occurred, and the media naturally linked the two events, the reasons behind each were very different, although to some degree related. As in the case of the US, it was concerned with the justification of apparently monopolistic and restrictive practices which to some extent precipitated fundamental changes in the regulatory structure of the markets. However, the need to revitalise and restructure the economic and financial institutions of the City was dictated more by political and economic considerations than an admitted deficiency in regulation and supervision. The social economic, political and technological pressures which contributed to the substantial weakening of traditional self-regulation and compelled the government and the City to adapt its procedures and institutions to meet foreign competition and domestic needs have already been discussed. It is not necessary to recount them here. It is important, however, to appreciate that the debate on regulation and supervision tended to be dominated by the desire to prevent and minimise frauds and scandals in the City. Although abuses are an inevitable risk in the markets, there was, and sadly is, a real danger of the City's reputation being significantly undermined.

Thus, while the fundamental changes that have occurred and are still after nearly fifteen years occurring in the form and structure of regulation and supervision are related to the so-called Big Bang, the pressures that brought each about are not necessarily the same. The need for a radical restructuring of regulation, while emphasised by the 'Big Bang', existed independently from it. By the same token, the need to revitalise and restructure the business of the securities industry is largely unrelated to the issues of regulation and de-regulation. However, both have to be seen in the context of the other. The Act and the structure it ordains is the framework within which the industry must work – at least for the time being!

¶126   The new players

Members of The Stock Exchange discovered in the early 1980s that in order to compete with overseas dealers and because of the demands of institutional investors and companies seeking to raise long-term funds, they needed substantially more capital than they possessed; this was particularly true in the case of jobbers. The Stock Exchange, in an effort to ensure that the owners or member firms were subject to its rules, had insisted that no more than 29.9 per cent of a member firm could be owned by any single non-member. However, the need for outside capital proved irresistible and in March 1986 this limit was removed so that member firms could be owned entirely by a non-member. As a result, most of the leading member firms were acquired by English merchant and clearing banks and overseas commercial and investment banks and securities dealers. In addition, non-members set up their own new member firms, and some of the world's largest securities brokers have joined The Stock Exchange. As a result, we have seen the growth in the UK of financial conglomerates on the American pattern. They can act like merchant banks by advising companies how to raise funds by issuing securities; they can act like brokers by distributing those newly-issued securities through their own network of clients; and after the offering they can act like jobbers and operate as market-makers in the securities.

It is perhaps surprising that so little thought was given to the inevitable conflicts of interest which must exist within these new financial conglomerates. Of course, to a considerable extent the City and its institutions have never eschewed conflicts of interest – wearing two hats has become almost a way of life! Nonetheless, obvious dangers exist and have been exacerbated by the structure and operations of these new institutions.

¶127   Prelude to a 'Bang'

In 1976 the then Labour Government issued the Restrictive Trade Practices (Services) Order extending the scope of the restrictive practices legislation to financial services. Despite fervent pleas by The Stock Exchange it was not exempted from this Order, unlike banks, building societies and unit trusts. The Stock Exchange's worst fears were realised in February 1979 when the Office of Fair Trading (OFT) formally referred The Stock Exchange's rule book and certain practices to the Restrictive Trade Practices Court. The OFT based its case on 173 alleged restrictive practices, of which The Stock Exchange had already registered 139 under the provisions of the Act.

The Stock Exchange was disappointed, although perhaps not too surprised, when the Conservative Government refused to interfere, despite urging from the Bank of England. The Bank took the view that this action was inappropriate and did not take proper account of the special role and responsibilities of The Stock Exchange. Baroness Thatcher has never been a supporter of the 'club mentality' which characterised the City during her premiership and still does to some degree. She particularly resented the association of fraud and abuse with capitalism – albeit recognised as 'its unacceptable face'. She and her colleagues were also concerned about the efficiency of the market in digesting large chunks of the public commercial sector when it came to privatisation. Furthermore, there is a deep-seated antagonism within the Tory Party towards 'restrictive practices' which to many the City establishment and its institutions appeared to perpetuate.

Whilst the grounds upon which the OFT based its reference to the Restrictive Trade Practices Court were wide and encompassed a sizeable proportion of the Stock Exchange's Rule Book, in essence there were only three broad issues which were under direct challenge. These were minimum commissions, separation of capacity and access to membership. The Stock Exchange, in its expensively prepared and on the whole well deliberated response, did not seek to justify the structure of minimum commissions for their own sake nor for the wellbeing of its members. Rather, it attempted to establish that a system of minimum commissions was vital for the maintenance of a structure of separate capacity. This argument, which came to be known as the 'link' argument, emphasised the inter-dependence of the rules on minimum commissions and those relating to strict segregation of broker and jobber function. The Stock Exchange maintained that the purpose of minimum commissions was to ensure observance of single capacity. The Stock Exchange also argued that abolition of minimum commissions would affect the nature of the securities market. In particular, it would result in a reduction of advice and research by member firms. Furthermore, it would result in greater fragmentation of the market and an increase in foreign ownership and control.

The government was less convinced than the OFT that single capacity was unjustified. The Stock Exchange and the Bank of England have long maintained that the segregation of function between brokers dealing as agents and jobbers dealing as principals is beneficial. Apart from providing a counter to self-interest, to some extent it assures liquidity and stability. However, the Bank of England and increasingly The Stock Exchange recognised that because of a whole series of factors, this system required modification. There had long been concern over the reduction in the numbers of jobbing firms and the implications that this had for competition within the market. Technological changes also placed increasing pressure on the defenders of the traditional system to justify it. Institutionalisation, with its attendant implications on liquidity, and the degree of capitalisation required to perform the obligations of a jobber also raised serious issues.

By its constitution and private status, The Stock Exchange has complete discretion over its membership, subject to the various statutory provisions

¶127

outlawing discrimination and the application of the principles of natural justice. The Stock Exchange traditionally resisted outside membership of its various constitutional committees, and although always keen to exhibit the appropriate degree of 'public spirit', had in practice, functioned much in the same manner as a tolerably select West End club. The Stock Exchange considered, with some justification, that many of its rules relating to membership, both of itself and its various committees, prevented or reduced the risk of conflict of interest and that it had a 'public responsibility' to ensure that it is satisfied as to the integrity and competence of those it endorses by election to membership. The OFT was far from convinced that the restrictive nature of its rules and practices were justified.

Under a certain amount of pressure from the Bank of England and with a more sympathetic attitude within the DTI, an accord was arrived at between The Stock Exchange and the Government in 1983. In an exceptional piece of legislation – the *Restrictive Trade Practices (Stock Exchange) Act* 1984 – the litigation between the OFT and The Stock Exchange was discontinued on the basis that The Stock Exchange agreed voluntarily to introduce a package of changes.

Notwithstanding The Stock Exchange's arguments concerning the need for and advantages of minimum commissions, the government felt that they must go. On the other hand, it was accepted that to simply abolish them would seriously disrupt and even de-stabilise the market. Consequently, it was agreed that they should be phased out. In fact The Stock Exchange abolished minimum commissions on dealings in overseas shares almost immediately and from 27 October 1986 all commissions became negotiable between brokers and their clients.

From the first attack on its minimum commissions structure, The Stock Exchange pointed out the implications for its compensation fund. Such a scheme is of considerable importance to investors and is a key factor in securing investor protection. The Stock Exchange emphasised that, quite reasonably, its members would resent 'underwriting' the possibly incautious activities of those few members who might be prepared to 'sail too close to the wind' once minimum commissions were abolished. To a very significant extent this debate became academic with other developments in the industry. In particular, the merger of The Stock Exchange with The International Securities Regulatory Organisation (ISRO) and the creation of The International Stock Exchange added considerably to the complexities of administering the fund. In the result, The Stock Exchange's Compensation Fund was discontinued, with the coming into operation of the Securities and Investment Board's own compensation scheme.

As has been pointed out, the DTI was not as sure as the OFT that single capacity was an unjustified restrictive practice and would not have been against

¶127

a continuation of this system – with suitable modifications. However, The Stock Exchange considered that the logic of the 'link arrangement' was inescapable and consequently developed a new trading system which in effect provides for dual capacity trading much in line with the practice in North America and most other developed markets. Members of The Stock Exchange rejected the notion of a gradual move towards abolition of minimum commissions and consequently the 'Big Bang' necessitated the introduction of an entirely new dealing system.

Under the new system, member firms are able to choose whether to become broker-dealers, thus being able to conduct traditional broking business as well as dealing directly with 'clients' as principals. A firm of broker-dealers also has the option of becoming a committed market maker in specific securities. Broker-dealers are required to deal with the market maker offering the best price unless they can transact the deal themselves on more advantageous terms as principals. Naturally all deals are recorded so that it is possible to ensure that the best execution rule has been observed. Central to the new system of dealing is SEAQ – Stock Exchange Automated Quotations. This service displays prices on a continuously updated basis. Transactions are executed by telephone, on the floor of the Exchange, or through the London Stock Exchange's new electronic dealing system, CREST.

¶127

2   The Regulatory Structure

INTRODUCTION

¶201   General outline of structure

In the White Paper which preceded the *Financial Services Act* 1986 (FSA), the government was at pains to describe the proposed system as 'self-regulation within a statutory framework'. The continued emphasis upon self-regulation was clearly intended to alleviate City fears to the effect that a system similar to that in existence in the US was about to be introduced. The enactment of a statute which, for the first time, subjects investment business in the UK to comprehensive statutory regulation has inevitably increased the significance of legal controls, and, with some justification, Professor Gower has commented that a more accurate description of the new regulatory structure would be 'statutory regulation monitored by self-regulatory organisations recognised by, and under the surveillance of a self-standing Commission' (*Big Bang and City Regulation* (1988) 51 MLR 1, at p. 11).

In general terms, the FSA vests statutory and regulatory powers in the Secretary of State. Until 1992, this was the Secretary of State for Trade and Industry, but by the *Transfer of Functions (Financial Services) Order* 1992 (SI 1992/1315), most of these responsibilities and powers have been assigned to the Treasury. Therefore, references in the Act to the Secretary of State now refer in most cases to the Economic Secretary. The government, under the terms of the FSA is empowered to delegate most, but not all, of its statutory and regulatory powers to the 'designated agency' (s. 114). The SIB, a private company rather than a government agency, is identified as the first designated agency (s. 114(2)). The Act allows powers to be delegated to the SIB only once the Secretary of State is satisfied that a number of specified statutory conditions have been met. Furthermore, the activities of the SIB are subject to the continued scrutiny of the Treasury which possesses the ultimate weapon in the form of a statutory power (s. 115) to take back those powers which have been transferred. Thus, although the SIB is a private company, its position as the body vested with primary responsibility for the regulation of investment business in the UK depends upon satisfaction of statutory criteria and is subject to continued statutory regulation and control. The SIB, as the designated agency, is in turn empowered to recognise other self-regulating bodies, each of which is responsible for particular aspects of investment business. The principal self-regulating bodies are the self-regulating organisations (SROs), of which there are, at present three. Other important self-regulating bodies within the framework are the Recognised Professional Bodies (RPBs), Recognised Investment Exchanges (RIEs) and Recognised Clearing Houses (RCHs). The criteria which must be satisfied before recognition may be granted to such bodies by the SIB are specified by the Act; thus, again, statutory conditions rather than private regulations determine whether or not a body may regulate investment business in the UK.

A Financial Services Tribunal (FST) has been set up. The function of the FST is to review certain decisions of the SIB. The availability of a right of appeal to a statutorily constituted body is a further clear illustration of the encroachment of public law upon the principles of self-regulation (Page *Self-regulation: The Constitutional Dimension* (1986) 49 MLR 141).

An important aspect of the new regulatory structure is the relationship between the bodies operating under the Financial Services Act and other regulatory bodies, both governmental and self-regulating in origin. Apart from the Treasury and the DTI, the new regulatory bodies interact with the Bank of England, the Office of Fair Trading (OFT) and the Panel on Takeovers and Mergers.

¶202   Transfer of powers to the SIB

On 18 May 1987, the *Financial Services Act 1986 (Delegation) Order* 1987 (SI 1987/942), having been approved by both Houses of Parliament (in accordance with s. 114(11)) was made, and came into force the following day. This Order delegates most, but not all, of the powers specified in s. 114(4) to the SIB. Subsequent orders have, however, delegated additional powers.

The recitals to the Order indicate that the Secretary of State was satisfied that the SIB had met the detailed statutory criteria and was able and willing to discharge the functions to be transferred to it (s. 114(1)). The detailed criteria which the SIB had to satisfy are set out in Sch. 7 to the Act. They include: the implementation of requirements relating to the constitution and decision making powers of the Board; the establishment of a satisfactory monitoring and enforcement system, of effective arrangements for the investigation of complaints and of satisfactory record-keeping systems; and the acceptance of an obligation to promote and maintain high standards. The recitals also record that the Secretary of State was satisfied that the SIB's proposed rules and regulations (at that stage no continuing guidance releases were in existence under s. 114(10)) afforded investors with an adequate level of protection (as required by s. 114(9) and Sch. 8), were not anti-competitive (after due consultation with the OFT in accordance with s. 121–122) and took proper account of Pt. II of the *Insurance Companies Act* 1982 (as required by Sch. 10, para. 4(6)).

¶203　Delegated powers

As anticipated, the majority of the delegable powers vested by the FSA in the Secretary of State have been delegated to the SIB in accordance with s. 114. Functions which have not been transferred are set out in Sch. 1 to the *Financial Services Act 1986 (Delegation) Order* 1987 (SI 1987/942). Functions which have been transferred to the SIB, subject to the reservation that they are to be exercisable concurrently by the Treasury and in some instances the DTI, are set out in the main body of the Order (art. 4–5 and 7) and in Sch. 2.

The powers which have been delegated include:

(1) power to recognise and revoke the recognition of SROs (s. 10–11);

(2) power to recognise and withdraw recognition from RPBs (s. 18–19);

(3) power to authorise investment businesses directly and to withdraw and/or suspend such authorisation (s. 25–30); however, in the circumstances detailed in Sch. 1, para. 1 to the Order, power is reserved to the Treasury and is not delegated;

(4) power to terminate or suspend the authorisation of Euro-persons (s. 33–34); again this delegation is subject to reservations (Sch. 1, para. 1–2 to the Order);

(5) power to recognise and to revoke the recognition of investment exchanges and clearing houses (s. 36–39 and s. 41); this power does not extend to overseas investment exchanges and clearing houses (s. 114(6) and Sch. 1, para. 3–4 to the Order);

(6) power to make conduct of business rules (s. 48), financial resources rules (s. 49), cancellation rules (s. 51), notification regulations (s. 52), compensation fund rules (s. 54), client money rules (s. 55) and unsolicited calls rules (s. 56);

(7) power to make disqualification orders (s. 59), subject to a reservation (Sch. 1, para. 6 to the Order);

(8) powers under s. 60–61 have been transferred subject to the reservation that they are, in general, concurrently exercisable by the Treasury (Sch. 2, para. 2 to the Order. Functions also subject to this reservation are specified in Sch. 2 and in art 5 and 7 of the Order); furthermore, in a number of specific circumstances, powers under s. 60–61 have not been delegated and remain in the sole control of the Treasury (Sch. 1, para. 1, 7–10 to the Order); and

(9) power to institute proceedings in respect of the offences specified in Sch. 3 to the Order; concurrent powers are reserved to the Treasury (art. 7 of the Order).

The most significant function which was not delegated to the SIB in May 1987 was that of regulator in respect of collective investment schemes (Ch. VIII, Pt. I of the Act). A second Delegation Order transferring this function (and a number of other less important powers) was made on 5 April 1988 and came into force the following day (the *Financial Services Act 1986 (Delegation) (No. 2) Order* 1988 (SI 1988/738)). A number of detailed reservations have been made (art. 3(3)–3(4) of the Order); in particular, concurrent powers of investigation under s. 94 have been reserved to the Treasury. The trend for more and more powers to be delegated to the SIB has continued, as the SIB's competence and self-confidence have increased. The DTI was perhaps less willing to see its powers handed over to the SIB than the Treasury has been. Indeed, in a review of its responsibilities under the FSA, conducted towards the end of 1994, the Treasury expressed the view that important additional duties should be assigned to the SIB, including the day-to-day responsibility for supervising the Listing Department of the London Stock Exchange, assessing overseas stock exchanges wishing to carry on business in the UK, to see whether their rules provide adequate protection for investors and also to assess other jurisdictions to ascertain whether their laws and rules are capable of providing the requisite degree of investor protection, (see *Fundamental Review of HM Treasury's Running Costs; A Report to The Chancellor of The Exchequer*, by Sir Colin Southgate (Oct 1994)).

¶204   Continuing position

Under s. 115 of the FSA, all or any of the powers which have been transferred to the SIB may be resumed by the government. Such resumption of responsibility may result from a request from the SIB itself or may be imposed upon it by the Treasury if it ceases to satisfy the statutory criteria or becomes unwilling or unable to discharge the functions which have been transferred. Rule making powers may also be resumed if the rules and regulations produced by the SIB no longer provide investors with adequate protection (s. 115(A)). A resumption order may also be made if the rules, regulations, guidance notes or practices of the SIB, or any person subject to its rules, appear to the Secretary of State to be anti-competitive (s. 121(2), (3)). Alternatively and less drastically, the Treasury may direct the SIB to remove the anti competitive effect of such provisions (s. 121(3)(b)). The Treasury may only exercise its powers under s. 121(3) on the advice of the OFT (s. 122(7)). Resumption orders are subject to the affirmative resolution procedure (s. 115(6)).

The resumption of powers by the Government is an extreme option which is unlikely to be lightly chosen. A less radical control weapon is contained in Sch. 7, para. 1(2) to the Act, which provides that the chairman and other members of the governing body of the SIB are to be appointed and removed by the Secretary of State and the Governor of the Bank of England: unlike other private companies, the composition of the governing body is not controlled by the members of the company. The replacement of the first chairman of the SIB, Sir Kenneth Berrill, by Sir David Walker, who was thought to be rather more of the same mind as the Bank of England in regard to the way in which the SIB should guide regulation, has been referred to as an example of the use of these powers. Whether this is true or for that matter fair, the point remains that government does have significant control over the regulatory structure through the machinery of appointment. As an additional safeguard, the SIB is required to submit an annual report on its activities to the Secretary of State, who is required to put it before Parliament (s. 117). Furthermore, the Trade and Industry Select Committee of the House of Commons has made it clear that it intends to review the work of the SIB on an annual basis, despite the fact that it is, at least constitutionally, a private sector body. The Secretary of State is empowered to give directions to the SIB with regard to its accounts and audit (s. 117).

¶205   Constitutional position of the SIB

The SIB (which by virtue of Sch. 9 para. 2 is exempt from the obligation to attach the word 'limited' at the end of its name) is a private company limited by guarantee. As such, it is financed by the payment of fees by SROs and other recognised bodies and authorised persons (s. 112–113), thereby retaining a flexibility which, it is argued would not be available to a body dependent upon government funding.

The exercise of the SIB's statutory powers is of course subject to judicial review. Despite the SIB's somewhat anomalous legal status, there is no doubt that it has a public regulatory function. So far there have been few instances when decisions of the SIB have been specifically challenged in review proceedings before the courts, although the risk of such proceedings is never very far away. In *R v The Securities Investment Board, ex parte the Independent Financial Advisers Association and London Insurance Brokers Mutual,* ((1995) 2 BCLC 76) the Divisional Court held that the SIB had not exceeded its powers in issuing guidance to self-regulatory bodies on how they should insist on the investigation of pensions mis-selling and the compensation of those who were adversely affected. Staughton LJ noted that the industry was facing 'a problem of exceptional magnitude and a proper solution was urgently required'. The SIB was entitled to intervene in the public interest to discharge its statutory mandate to protect investors. However, it is not without interest that the court recognised that there were distinct limits to the SIB's jurisdiction and that while it was appropriate for it to give advice to self-regulatory authorities it had no legal right to enforce compliance by individuals, this being the responsibility of the relevant SRO. The Court of Appeal in *R v International Stock Exchange of the United Kingdom and the Republic of Ireland Ltd, ex parte Else* [1993] 1 All ER 420, emphasised that when legislation left regulators with discretion to act in the public interest in the context of the financial markets, 'the courts will not second-guess the informed judgment of responsible regulators steeped in knowledge of their particular market'. The more so, when the issue is related to the public interest in protecting the markets and investors.

Whilst the SIB may therefore be the object of review proceedings, the members of the Board and its staff are given legal immunity from civil claims for damages (s. 187(3)), unless bad faith can be established. In *Melton Medes Ltd v The Securities and Investments Board* [1995] 2 WLR 247, a claim was brought against the SIB under s. 187(3) in respect of two alleged contraventions of s. 179, which controls the use of 'restricted' information, which it was claimed had been committed in bad faith. The complaints related to information that the SIB had obtained in the course of its duties and which it had disclosed to investors and their advisors. The plaintiffs, who administered certain pension funds, claimed that but for the relevant disclosures there would have been a satisfactory settlement of a dispute between them and various beneficiaries of the funds. Lightman J had no difficulty in dismissing the actions on the basis that the SIB had quite properly disclosed the information in question to the beneficiaries given its responsibility to promote and facilitate the protection of investors. Furthermore, the court doubted whether the information was 'restricted' within the terms of s. 179. Furthermore, Lightman J held that even if s. 179 had been violated this did not give rise to a cause of action on the part of those whose consent to disclosure would have been required. The court also explored the concept of bad faith in the context of s. 187 and held that it involved proof of lack of probity. Lack of good faith connotes either malice in the sense of personal spite or a desire to injure for improper reasons, or knowledge of absence of power to make the decision in question. Lightman J rejected the argument that it was sufficient to show merely that a power had been used for a purpose other than that for which it had been granted, such as in the field of administrative law. Of course, despite the existence of statutory immunity, it is obviously necessary for there to be a viable cause of action in the first place and the courts have shown reluctance in finding a duty of care on the part of regulators to those served by those who are regulated. Thus, banking regulators have been held not to owe a duty of care in supervising and licensing deposit takers, to customers and depositors. Although justified by virtue of lack of proximity, in reality such decisions have rather more justification in considerations of public interest, see generally

¶205

Davis v Radcliffe [1990] 1 WLR 821, *Johnson Matthey Plc v Arthur Young and The Bank of England* [1988] FLR 345 and *Yuen Kun Yeu v The Attorney-General of Hong Kong* [1988] AC 175.

¶206 The SIB and SROs

The relationship of the SIB and various self-regulatory organisations (SROs) has changed and developed since the 'new' structure of regulation was established just prior to the enactment of the FSA. Having regard to the significance of self-regulation in the financial services sector, and the unwillingness of government to assume a greater political or financial role in supervision, the creation and maintenance of a viable structure of self-regulatory agencies is vital to the success of the regime. Professor Gower recognised that the then existing structure of regulation was inadequate, because there were important areas of activity for which there was no effective self-regulatory authority in place and in others a real danger of overlap and regulatory competition. Professor Gower advocated activity based self-regulation, rather than a structure which reflected the traditional interests of defined groups and the professions. The present structure now resembles rather more what Professor Gower had in mind, than took form around the time that the FSA became law. Over the last decade a number of new SROs, have been created *de novo* or through mergers. This tier of regulation has proved to be rather more dynamic than many thought possible given the vested interests which militated against Professor Gower's proposals.

Largely because of pressure to improve the perceived effectiveness of enforcement and to facilitate the setting of standards for those engaged in investment business, the SIB has recognised the need for recasting and re-emphasising certain aspects of the self-regulatory tier which it is primarily responsible for overseeing. In 1990 the SIB published *The SIB and the New Regulatory Structure Over the Next Few Years; A Forward Look*, in which an attempt was made to identify issues which would have a significant impact on the regulatory and supervisory responsibilities of the SIB. Rather more important was the report by the then chairman of the SIB, Andrew Large, commissioned by the Chancellor of the Exchequer in 1993 entitled *Financial Services Regulation – Making the Two Tier System Work*. Like so much in British securities regulation this report was commissioned in the wake of a scandal: the Maxwell affair. The review undertaken by Mr Large (since knighted) and the discussions which surrounded it, both inside and outside the City, had a significant impact on the self-regulators. Widespread concern that the system was not working effectively in preventing and controlling abuses was recognised by Mr Large and in the result the SIB has re-positioned itself. The SIB has 'stepped back' leaving the self-regulators with a clear responsibility over their members. The SIB remains responsible for those whom it directly authorises, (through the Securities and Investments Board Regulatory Organisation – SIBRO) but as has already been pointed out, it is the declared policy of the SIB to discourage this form of authorisation and eventually to transfer responsibility to a self-regulator. The SIB now sees itself as the regulator of the regulators – coordinating and setting industry-wide standards. To this end the SIB has persuaded the main SROs to draw up regulatory aims and objectives and to publish on a regular basis statements as to how these are being achieved and observed, as the SIB now does itself.

Mention has already been made of the practice that has developed in recent years of the House of Commons' Select Committee on Trade and Industry reviewing the SIB on an annual basis. Of course, traditionally select committees have confined their monitoring role to government departments and public agencies. There would appear to be an increasing willingness to also review the work of self-regulatory agencies performing a significant public, albeit non-statutory, function. Several SROs, and in particular IMRO, have been called to give evidence on their operations to a number of House of Commons' Committees in recent years, reflecting the degree of public and political concern as to how effective the second tier of regulation is.

The SIB has also been rather more mindful in recent years of the changing nature of capital markets. In 1994 the SIB published a far ranging discussion paper on the regulation of United Kingdom equity markets and established the Market Conduct Regulators Group to examine and monitor certain market practices which had attracted criticism. In June 1995 the SIB published *Regulation of the United Kingdom Equity Markets* which sets out not only the SIB's conclusions following its review but also looks ahead taking account of developments in the nature and operation of the markets and in particular the international dimension. The SIB sets out the overall objective for equity market regulation – namely, to enable investors to use the markets with confidence. This is achieved, according to the SIB, by providing investors with 'fair and clean markets and with an appropriate level of protection, without being so burdensome as to reduce the overall volume of trading'. Harking back to the government's original White Paper on the regulation of financial services (see ¶124) the SIB identifies three guiding principles for the development of regulation 'market freedom, cost effectiveness, and regard for the interests of issuers'. In regard to 'market integrity' the SIB focuses upon 'fairness, a clean market and efficient price formation'. The SIB, conscious of the development of new financial products, trading methods and even markets, stresses the importance of maintaining a centralised market in an economic sense, albeit the market has more or less ceased to be centralised organisationally. In achieving this the SIB's report emphasises the importance of consistent standards of transparency, monitoring and enforcement throughout the marketplace and underlines the role of the various self-regulatory organisations in achieving this.

THE SIB AND THE RECOGNISED SELF-REGULATING ORGANISATIONS

¶207 Role of SROs

As we have seen self-regulating organisations occupy a central position in the new regulatory structure. Although the SIB is able to authorise investment businesses directly (s. 25), it was intended that the vast majority of businesses will obtain authorisation by virtue of their membership of one or more SROs (s. 7). An investment business which is authorised by an SRO is, in general, subject to the rules and regulations of that SRO rather than the SIB (in particular, the Conduct of Business Rules made under s. 48(1)) and the SIB's enforcement powers will not normally apply, e.g. injunctions and restitution orders (s. 61(2)), intervention powers (s. 64(4)), winding-up powers (s. 72(5)) and investigation powers (s. 105(2)). Yet, despite the lack of general direct regulation of investment business by the SIB, it does retain ultimate control by virtue of its supervisory powers over SROs.

A self-regulating organisation is described by the Act as a body (whether or not incorporated) which regulates the carrying on of investment business of any kind by enforcing rules which are binding on persons carrying on business of that kind because they are members of that body or because they are otherwise subject to its control (s. 8(1)). 'Membership' of an SRO is extended by statute to cover persons who have not joined the organisation but who are subject to its rules in carrying on the investment business in question (s. 8(2)).

¶208 The recognised SROs

Professor Gower recognised that the self-regulatory tier would take a number of years to settle down. The Securities Association (TSA) and the Association of Futures Brokers and Dealers (AFBD) merged in April 1991 to become the Securities and Futures Authority (SFA). In October 1991 the SIB appointed Sir Kenneth Clucas to conduct an enquiry into the scope of regulatory oversight by the then existing authorities and the boundaries of their responsibilities. He was asked to consider in particular the regulation of pooled retail investment products. Sir Kenneth recommended that a new SRO should be created to regulate investment business done with or directly for the private investor, (see *Retail Regulation Review Report of a study by Sir Kenneth Clucas on a new SRO for the Retail Sector* (1992)). This reflected widespread concern in the industry and to some extent in Parliament, that the regulatory structure established under the *Financial Services Act* 1986 was unable, given the spectrum of interests, to properly attain its objectives in seeking to regulate the professional markets and promote investor protection at a retail level, at one and the same time, using essentially the same or very similar vehicles. Sir Kenneth argued that the new authority should be given responsibility over investment business regulated by FIMBRA and LAUTRO, and to a lesser degree IMRO and the SFA. The SIB also seized the opportunity to advocate a transfer of those firms directly regulated by SIBRO, to the proposed SRO.

A formation committee was established to consider how best to implement these recommendations and a detailed consultative document was published by the SIB on 24 September 1992. It was proposed that the new SRO, to be named the Personal Investment Authority (PIA) would be constituted by the end of the summer 1993. The establishment of the PIA proved to be a rather more difficult and controversial process than was first anticipated. A number of major intermediaries and banks opposed the initiative and the implications that this had for the development of the PIA as a competent and adequately funded SRO were, and to some degree remain, significant. However, the SIB recognised the PIA with effect from July 1994 and its regulatory scope includes activities formerly regulated by FIMBRA and LAUTRO, together with some activities previously overseen by IMRO and the SFA who have redefined their jurisdiction. The SIB has been an influential promoter of the PIA, although not always an entirely uncritical supporter, primarily to reduce regulatory overlap and thus, regulatory arbitrage within the self-regulatory structure.

On 18 February 1994 the SIB acting under powers delegated to it by the Secretary of State pursuant to s. 114(1) of the Act gave notice pursuant to s. 11(3) of its intention to revoke the recognition of FIMBRA and the LAUTRO as SROs. The statutory process for revocation is lengthy and requires that the SIB give those affected by its decision an opportunity to make representations.

The Securities and Futures Authority (SFA)

This is a body which resulted from an agreed merger, in April 1991, between The Securities Association (TSA) and the Association of Futures Brokers and Dealers (AFBD). TSA was itself created out of a merger in late 1986 between The Stock Exchange and the International Securities Regulatory Organisation (ISRO). ISRO had been set up to regulate major dealers in Eurobonds, international securities and money market instruments. By mid-1986 many of its members either owned or had substantial interests in a good number of The Stock Exchange's member firms. The SIB recognised TSA on 19 February 1988. The AFBD was concerned with regulating dealers in commodity and financial futures and options. The SIB granted recognition to the AFBD on 13 January 1988. Consequently, SFA member firms will be involved in carrying on business in connection with dealing or arranging deals in shares, debentures, government and other public securities: rights and interests in securities, foreign currency, commodities or other property to which they relate to their derivatives; and in connection with advising corporate finance customers and arranging deals and managing portfolios for them. Furthermore, member firms may also be concerned, but not as their main activities, with advising on deals in all of these investments, with managing such investments, or with arranging and advising on transactions in life assurance and collective investment schemes.

Investment Management Regulatory Organisation (IMRO)
Member firms of IMRO are primarily engaged in managing investments, the management of Occupational Pension Scheme (OPS) assets, acting as managers or trustees of authorised unit trust schemes, managing or operating unregulated collective investment schemes and the provision of investment advice to non-private investors. Thus, its members are drawn from merchant banks; investment trusts; pension fund managers; unit trust managers and insurance companies. Although recognition was given on 27 January 1988, special conditions were imposed as a result of the Maxwell affair and perceived deficiencies in the regulation of pension related investment business. After a period of intensive liaison between officers of IMRO and the SIB and the drawing up of a new monitoring plan, the SIB removed the special conditions on IMRO's recognition in late 1994.

The Personal Investment Authority (PIA)
As has already been indicated the PIA was recognised on 18 July 1994 and took over the responsibilities of FIMBRA and LAUTRO which will cease to exist as SROs. The Financial Intermediaries Managers and Brokers Regulatory Association (FIMBRA), arose from a merger in 1986 of the National Association of Security Dealers and Investment Managers (NASDIM) and the Life and Unit Trust Intermediaries Regulatory Organisation (LUTIRO). FIMBRA first received recognition on 14 December 1987. The Life Assurance and Unit Trust Regulatory Organisation (LAUTRO) was recognised on 28 April 1988. The PIA's member firms are, for the most part, insurance companies; friendly societies, financial advisers and bancassurers whose main activities are marketing, advising on and arranging deals, primarily for private clients, in life assurance products; friendly society products; unit trusts; investment trust saving schemes; shares, warrants and debt instruments which are readily realisable (this usually means that they are traded on a recognised or designated investment exchange). PIA members also provide private client portfolio management including the use of derivatives for the purpose of

¶208

efficient portfolio management of securities, or where the derivative is a traded option. The PIA's regulatory authority also extends to regulating investment management for private clients.

¶209   The lead regulator

One of the most serious criticisms that was made of the pre-FSA system of supervision was that it was incomplete and lacked proper interface. While certain areas were well served by a self-regulatory authority others were not. There were instances of regulatory overlap and even competition, compounded by regulatory lacunæ. On the other hand, as is clear from the above discussion the new structure does not provide a seamless and uniform web of self-regulation. The SIB has always recognised that the appropriate SRO for an applicant will not always be readily apparent and has indicated that SROs should be prepared to discuss the particular circumstances of each case and to refer the applicant to a more appropriate SRO if necessary. Where there is an overlap of jurisdiction it is for the applicant to choose which SRO to join (*SIB Guidance Release 1/87* July 1987). Of course, recent developments in the second tier and the reduction in the number of SROs have reduced the risk of overlap. Furthermore, in so far as the SROs now publish clear statements of their regulatory objectives and aims and the SIB plays a rather more obvious coordinating role the potential for 'regulatory arbitrage' is reduced.

Given the possible need for an investment business to obtain membership of more than one SRO because its activities are sufficiently wide to fall within the jurisdiction of two or more SROs, the notion of a lead regulator has been developed. Of course, there is always the possibility of seeking direct authorisation from the SIB. However, as has already been pointed out, the SIB has never been enthusiastic about taking on the responsibility of monitoring investment businesses. In its Annual Report for 1993/94, the SIB states whilst 'the option of direct regulation by the SIB remains legally available; ... as we have repeatedly made clear, it is our view in the long-term interests of customers and the industry that all retail firms should join the PIA. To the extent that they do not, it is our intention to delegate to the PIA, as far as possible under the FSA, monitoring of retail directly authorised businesses, in order to permit the SIB to concentrate on its main priorities of standard setting, supervision and enforcement'.

The SIB proposed and endorsed the notion of a lead regulator in *The Regulation of Investment Business; The New Framework* (Dec. 1985 p. 9) even before enactment of the FSA. The SIB was particularly concerned about the efficient monitoring of capital adequacy and liquidity standards in financial conglomerates which were members of more than one SRO or were within the regulatory purview of several authorities. The SIB took the view that there must be a lead regulator with sole resposibility for the financial affairs of multi-authorised investment businesses. The lead regulator would normally be the SRO which is responsible for the largest part of the firm's business. Indeed, in some instances it is conceivable that this could be the SIB itself. If the firm is also a bank, the lead regulator would normally be the Bank of England.

The SROs have adopted the lead regulator concept (e.g. SFA's rules provide 'These financial regulations shall apply to all firms except where and to the extent the Association determines otherwise. This will be in order to avoid the duplication of the assessment of a firm's financial soundness and of its monitoring in cases where the firm is adhering in whole or in part to the financial regulations of another regulator'. In so far as the lead regulator concept involves the delegation of an SRO's monitoring and enforcement functions to another regulator, that delegation is expressly authorised by the Act (Sch. 2, para. 4(2)). Similar power to delegate monitoring and enforcement responsibility is given to the SIB (Sch. 7, para. 3).

The lead monitor will monitor the financial resources of all investment firms. It will receive and assess all information relevant to the capital adequacy of the firm and set requirements for the firm as a whole. It will keep other regulators, including other SROs, informed and will co-ordinate remedial action should this be necessary.

In regard to overseas institutions wishing to conduct investment business in the UK through branches, both the SIB and SROs are prepared to enter into lead regulation arrangements with home state supervisors to disapply the UK's financial resources requirements, where the home state supervisory system is judged sufficient for the protection of UK investors. The purpose of such arrangement is to facilitate international business and relieve such firms from what might be an intolerable compliance burden. There are over 60 such arrangements in place. Of course, within the European Union it is unnecessary for the regulators, whether of the financial or banking sectors, to negotiate specific agreements as the notion of lead regulator is central to the passport scheme of regulation.

¶210   Criteria for recognition

If a prospective SRO meets the statutory conditions and standards, it must be recognised (s. 10(2)). If not, the application can be refused. The SIB must give reasons for the refusal but there is no right of appeal to the Financial Services Tribunal. Section 10 of, and Sch. 2 to, the Act, establish criteria that a prospective SRO needs to meet in order to qualify for recognition by the SIB. The most important requirement is that it must have rules which afford investors an 'adequate level' of protection (Sch. 2, para. 3 as amended by s. 203(1) of the *Companies Act* 1989). Under the original wording of Sch. 2 the applicant had to show that its rules would give investors protection 'at least equivalent' to that provided by the rules issued by the SIB for directly authorised persons. The requirement of 'equivalence' caused many problems and the so-called 'new settlement' substituted a rather more flexible if not relaxed criteria. It is, of course, for the SIB to determine what is an adequate level of protection. This certainly does not mean that the SRO must have identical rules to those of the SIB and the SRO may adapt the rules for particular markets and businesses.

In addition, the SRO must have arrangements and resources for the monitoring and enforcement of its rules (Sch. 2, para. 4). Although the SRO is able to delegate such monitoring to other 'regulators' (see below), it cannot delegate its enforcement function. The SRO is expected to have the capacity, resources and willingness effectively to enforce its rules.

The rules and practices of the SRO must secure that its members are 'fit and proper persons' to carry on 'investment business' of the kinds which it regulates (Sch. 2, para. 1); this mirrors the SIB's own obligation for directly authorised businesses. The SRO must have fair and reasonable procedures for admission and expulsion and this includes suitable appeal arrangements (Sch. 2, para. 2).

There is a risk that an SRO will regulate in the interests of its members at the expense of the interests of the public. In order to deal with this potential problem, the membership of the governing body of the SRO must include a sufficient number of persons independent of its members and its organisation to secure a proper balance (Sch. 2, para. 5). The SRO must also make effective arrangements for the investigation of complaints, whether against the SRO or against its members, and this may include an independent ombudsman (Sch. 2, para. 6). In addition, it must be prepared to cooperate with other regulators and to share information about its members with them (Sch. 2, para. 7).

Other conditions for recognition are that the SRO's rules are no more anti-competitive than is necessary for the protection of investors. Further, the rules of the SRO must provide that if any investment business is not regulated by that SRO its members cannot carry on that business except by virtue of authorisation by some other means or unless it is exempted in relation to that business (s. 10(3)) which will apply mainly to money market activities. Finally, if the SRO includes among its members insurance companies authorised under the *Insurance Companies Act* 1982, the SIB will not be able to recognise it unless the Secretary of State certifies that its rules take proper account of the provisions of the Insurance Companies Act concerning the protection of policy holders (Sch. 10, para. 3(2)).

¶211   Complete or partial revocation of recognition

Recognised SROs are subject to the general supervisory control of the SIB. The SIB possesses a number of powers derived from the Financial Services Act which may be used against an SRO where necessary. The most drastic of these powers is the power to revoke recognition (s. 11(1)). This power may be exercised if the SRO ceases to satisfy the criteria set out in Sch. 2 and s. 10(3), if it has failed to comply with obligations imposed upon it by the Act, or if its continued existence becomes unnecessary or undesirable as a consequence of duplication of jurisdiction with another organisation (s. 11(1)). Hence the revocation of recognition of both FIMBRA and LAUTRO. The Treasury may direct the SIB to revoke recognition where an SRO had introduced rules which are anti-competitive and notwithstanding delegation to the SIB, the Treasury may always exercise the power of revocation itself in these particular circumstances (s. 120(4)); in so acting or directing, the Treasury must act on the advice of the OFT (s. 122(7)). An SRO whose recognition is to be revoked has no right of appeal to the FST, but before a revocation order is made, the reasons for it must be published. The SRO and its members may then make representations which must be taken into account before the decision is finalised (s. 11(3)–(5) and s. 128). (See for example *Reports to The SIB by Lord Oliver of Aylmerton and Dame Margaret Booth in regard to the Revocation of Recognition of FIMBRA and LAUTRO as SROs,* June 1994). An order revoking recognition generally does not take effect until three months after it is made (s. 11(2)); however, this and the other procedural safeguards may be overridden if it is essential to do so in the interests of investors (s. 11(6)).

An SRO may be partially de-recognised uder s. 13(2). If it is found that the rules of an SRO fall below the statutory standard of adequacy for the protection of investors in regard to one (or more) of the classes of investment business for which it acts as a recognised SRO, recognition in respect of that class (or classes) may be withdrawn with the consequence that members engaging in the investment business placed outside the scope of the SRO must obtain alternative authorisation.

¶212 Compliance orders and alteration of rules

Revocation of recognition has been described as a 'nuclear deterrent'. It is a threat hanging over the heads of recognised SROs but it is unlikely to be used except in very extreme circumstances. As has already been pointed out, whilst there had been some criticism of the way in which in particular FIMBRA discharged its regulatory and enforcement functions as an SRO, revocation on this basis was never seriously considered. The revocation of FIMBRA and LAUTRO's recognition was part and parcel of establishing the PIA. At least in the initial stages of dissatisfaction with the activities of an SRO, the SIB is much more likely to use one of its less draconian powers. For example, in July 1992 the SIB issued a statement on IMRO's regulation of two Maxwell fund management companies. In it the SIB stated that, although the Maxwell affair had exposed serious weaknesses in IMRO, its failings were not so fundamental that the SIB should withdraw its recognition. Instead the SIB imposed a number of 'conditions' for continued recognition. These resulted in a thorough overhaul of IMRO's procedures for admissions, monitoring and emergency case handling, the introduction of a tighter regime governing the conduct of 'in house' managers of pension scheme assets, greater attention to the development of regulatory expertise and new rules on board members' interests. Indeed, it was largely as a result of the perceived failure of IMRO's monitoring of the Maxwell companies, that Andrew Large, the then chairman of the SIB was commissioned by the Chancellor of The Exchequer in July 1992 to review the efficacy of self-regulation (see *Financial Services Regulation – Making the Two Tier System Work*, May 1993). In November 1994 the SIB announced that it was in a position to lift the special conditions or caveats that it had imposed on IMRO, although it also emphasised that like all other SROs, IMRO will be subject to a more systematic supervisory regime by the SIB, (see *The SIB, Annual Report for 1993/94*). Under s. 12 the SIB may apply to court for an order requiring an SRO to comply with its statutory obligations or with the requirements of s. 10(3) and Sch. 2. Under s. 13 the SIB may direct the alteration, or itself alter the rules of an SRO where these do not provide adequate protection for investors. The SIB must consult with the SRO before obliging it to change its rules and its decision may be challenged in the courts (s. 13(4)–(5)). The rules of an SRO may also be altered if they become anti-competitive (s. 120(4)) or if they are incompatible with international obligations (s. 192).

¶213 Disclosure

In accordance with s. 14 of the Act, the SIB has imposed disclosure and notification requirements upon SROs (the *Financial Services (Notification by Recognised Bodies) Regulations* 1995 contained in the SIB rule book). Amongst other things, SROs are required to send copies of their annual reports account and budget to the SIB (reg. 2.07) to keep it informed of the principal details of members (reg. 3.01) and to notify the SIB of any refusal of membership or suspension or expulsion (reg. 3.02).

¶214 Constitutional position

The Financial Services Act does not vest enforcement powers in the SROs. It is the contract of membership which enable SROs to enforce their rules and regulations against members. Some doubts were raised as to whether this meant that the decisions of SROs were to be regarded as purely private exercises of powers, challengeable only in the event of breach of contract, or whether they were amenable to judicial review. These doubts were effectively quelled by the decision of the Court of Appeal in *R v Panel on Takeovers and Mergers, ex parte Datafin plc & Anor* [1987] 1 All E.R. 564; [1987] 2 WLR 699; (1987) 3 BCC 10 (see also *R v Panel on Takeovers and Mergers, ex parte*

Guinness plc [1989] 2 WLR 863; (1988) 4 BCC 325) where it was held that the supervisory jurisdiction of the High Court was not limited to bodies which derived power fom the prerogative or from statutory provisions but was applicable to other bodies operating in the public domain.

In *The Governor and Company of the Bank of Scotland, Petitioners* [1989] BCLC 700, the Court of Session held that IMRO was subject to the supervisory jurisdiction of the Court as the objects and activities of IMRO were for the purpose of implementing and fulfilling the system of self-regulation established pursuant to the Financial Services Act. The court considered that in reviewing decisions by such public bodies there was no reason why an administrative action should not also be a failure to perform a contractual obligation. Thus, whilst it is the law that judicial review is not available in regard to the exercise of purely contractual powers, the authority, albeit of a contractual nature, that the various SROs have over their members is to enable the performance of their public function. (See also *R v FIMBRA, ex parte Cochrane* [1991] BCLC 106; *SIB & Anor v FIMBRA & Anor* [1992] Ch 268; *R v LAUTRO, ex parte Ross* [1992] 1 All ER 422 and *R v SIB & ors, ex parte Sun Life Assurance Society plc* (1996) 2 BCLC 150.)

While the courts have been prepared to recognise the public interest in regulatory authorities taking proactive action to protect investors, see for example, *Melton Medes Ltd v The Securities and Investments Board* [1995] 2 WLR 247, the Court of Appeal has arguably placed a significant obstacle in the way of effective and timely regulatory action, where there is a risk that this might prejudice the position of the parties in other legal proceedings. In *R v The Institute of Chartered Accountants in England and Wales, ex parte Brindle* (1994) BCC 297, the Court of Appeal disagreed with the Divisional Court's rejection of an application by the sometime auditor of BCCI, Price Waterhouse, for judicial review of decisions affecting the conduct of a disciplinary inquiry by the relevant professional bodies. The applicants contended that given the numerous civil, administrative and criminal proceedings relating to the BCCI affair, in some of which they were involved as a party or as a probable witness, the conduct of a disciplinary inquiry possibly leading to action within the Joint Disciplinary Scheme for the accounting profession, was both inappropriate and unfair. The complaint was not directed at the decision to initiate inquiries, but the decision of the panel appointed to make the investigation not to postpone their inquiries until after the completion of the other proceedings. Thus, the issue before the court was whether allowing the investigation to proceed would produce a real risk of prejudice or injustice.

In *R v Panel on Takeovers and Mergers, ex parte Fayed* [1992] BCC 524 it was recognised that 'the court has power to intervene to prevent injustice where the continuation of one set of proceedings may prejudice the fairness of the trial of

¶214

other proceedings ... but it is a power which has to be exercised with great care and only where there is a real risk of serious prejudice which may lead to injustice', per Neill LJ. In the present case Price Waterhouse contended there was such a risk because of a number of factors. These included: the fear that they would not be able to defend their actions before the investigation committee without breaking confidences; that documents might be produced which would be thereby obtainable by other parties; that they may be prejudiced in the eyes of a juror, albeit in a foreign jurisdiction; that there would be a danger of co-incidence of issues and that for the committee to proceed would place an intolerable burden on the resources of applicants. Whilst Nolan LJ observed that 'the court should be slow to interfere with the assessment of risk carried out by a body such as the Committee ... in the context of litigation on such a scale that, if only partly successful, it might well destroy the appellant's business, the risk of prejudice, even if this amounts to no more than forensic disadvantage, clearly demands careful appraisal'. Whilst the Court of Appeal was not impressed with all the applicants' fears, and it recognised that 'it is unsatisfactory from the point of view of the applicants, as well as that of the public, that a question mark should be left hanging over their observance of professional standards ... for so long,' the interests of justice are paramount and therefore the investigation should be adjourned.

The effect of this decision on the ability of regulatory authorities to act effectively against those within their jurisdiction remains to be seen. It has already been noted that the circumstances in this case are exceptional and as the Court of Appeal specifically noted there was no realistic prospect that the Committee would be able to complete its inquiries with alacrity given the complexity and nature of the issues. On the other hand, delaying the Committtee's work is hardly likely to facilitate the accountancy bodies being able to come to an appropriate decision on the position of Price Waterhouse.

In a subsequent case before the Divisional Court, *R v Chance, ex parte Smith* (1995) BCC 1095, the court refused to review a decision by the Executive Council of the Joint Disciplinary Scheme to continue an enquiry into the activities of Coopers & Lybrand as auditors of the Maxwell Group of companies. Coopers & Lybrand contended that the firm was already involved in several other investigations and proceedings and that it was unfair to place the additional burden of such an enquiry upon it at this point in time. Despite, as Henry LJ acknowledged the 'superficial similarities' between the present case and *ex parte Brindle*, the Divisional Court thought it would be wrong for the courts to interfere. Referring to the test set out in *R v Panel on Takeovers and Mergers, ex parte Fayed*, and the need to balance possibly competing public interests, Henry LJ emphasised that *ex parte Brindle* was not authority for the proposition that it was unfair to allow a firm or individual to be subject to proceedings before different tribunals at the same time. It was also not the case

¶214

that disciplinary or regulatory proceedings were in any sense inferior to judicial proceedings. They served different purposes. The Divisional Court, although appearing to have no great sympathy with the decision in *ex parte Brindle,* distinguished it on the facts. In the present case the circumstances and implications of the various proceedings were of a different order. This approach was followed by Dyson J in *R v Executive Counsel, Joint Disciplinary Scheme, ex parte Hipps*, 12 June 1996 (QBD). (See also *Report of the Financial Services Tribunal, In The Matter of Peter James West and In The Matter of Paul Bingham*, 18 November 1994.) Thus, it is possible that the approach in *ex parte Brindle* may be justified only in the exceptional circumstances of the BCCI affair. Nonetheless, the decision remains as a constraint on the effectiveness of self-regulation in an area of activity where prompt action by the relevant professional bodies may be highly desirable.

Multiple proceedings also give rise to serious problems in regard to the admissibility and useability of evidence. For example, may documents seized pursuant to statutory or self-regulatory powers be handed over to another agency or a prosecutor to facilitate other proceedings? Of course, in some cases, such as under s. 2 of the *Criminal Justice Act* 1987 where the Director of the Serious Fraud Office wishes to inquire into a serious or complex fraud, the person served with a notice requiring testimony or production of documents had no privilege or right to refuse cooperation. We have already seen in the *Melton Medes* case, Lightman J considered that it was quite proper for the SIB to pass information that it had arguably obtained as a regulator, to private litigants seeking compensation. In the recent case of *Kaufmann v Credit Lyonnais Bank* (1995) CLC 300, Arden J granted an application for the production of documents which a bank had disclosed to the SFA and the Bank of England. Whilst the case concerns a claim by a former client against a regulated firm, it has implications for the relationship between the regulator and those within its jurisdiction. The litigant seeking to bring a s. 62 action against the bank sought discovery of certain documents which the bank had passed voluntarily to the Bank of England and the SFA. The bank contended that these documents were protected from discovery on the basis that they had been disclosed in confidence to assist the regulators and there was therefore a public interest in respecting this confidence. Both the SFA and Bank of England supported this argument and emphasised that if disclosure was ordered lawyers would advise their clients to be cautious in making voluntary disclosures to their regulators with the result that this would undermine the effectiveness of self-regulation. Arden J having regard to the purpose of the Financial Services Act 1986 in promoting investor protection was reluctant to recognise such a broad class-based public interest immunity. Indeed, to accept it might allow misleading documents to be protected. Arden J also noted that the claim for privilege related to disclosures which had been voluntary and not

¶214

pursuant to specific obligations in the SFA's rules. The Bank of England which was not the prime or lead regulator had no independent right to assert privilege. In ordering disclosure Arden J departed from the decision in *MGM Pensions Trustees v Invesco Asset Management Ltd* 14 October 1993, where the High Court granted public interest immunity to correspondence addressed to IMRO on the basis that the House of Lords in *R v Chief Constable of West Midlands, ex parte Wiley* [1994] 3 WLR 433 had reiterated and reinforced the heavy onus on anyone seeking to establish a new class claim to public interest immunity.

Mention has already been made (see ¶205) on the statutory immunity that the Financial Services Act affords to the SIB and its officials from the threat of civil liability. Section 187(1) also affords SROs, members of their governing bodies and their staff immunity from liability in damages, unless they have acted in bad faith. It would seem that the test for bad faith requires proof of dishonesty or at least a lack of probity.

RECOGNISED PROFESSIONAL BODIES

¶215   Recognition and immunity

Members of professions such as law and accountancy may be required to engage in investment business in the course of their professional work. Instead of requiring such professionals to join an SRO, the Financial Services Act enables authorisation to be obtained by certification from an RPB (s. 15). A 'professional body' is a body which regulates the practice of a profession other than a business consisting wholly and mainly of investment business (s. 16(1)). Such a body may apply to the SIB for recognition (s. 17(1)). The nine professional bodies which have obtained recognition to date are the Institute of Chartered Accountants in England and Wales, the Institute of Chartered Accountants of Scotland, the Institute of Chartered Accountants in Ireland, the Chartered Association of Certified Accountants, the Law Society, the Law Society of Scotland, the Law Society of Northern Ireland, the Institute of Actuaries and the Insurance Brokers Registration Council.

An RPB may confer authorisation on corporate practices as well as on partnerships and individuals practising on their own account. In this Guide references to members of RPBs are references to persons certified by RPBs whether or not they are members, but not to members who are not certified.

Thus, solicitors and accountants who engage in incidental investment business may obtain authorisation through certification from the relevant RPB. However, it is a condition of recognition that the rules of the professional body must impose acceptable limits upon the carrying on of investment business

(s. 18(3)). An RPB can only grant authorisation to a person who engages in investment business incidentally to his profession. If the investment business is a distinct and separate business, authorisation must be obtained by the normal method of joining an SRO.

The other statutory criteria which must be satisfied by a prospective RPB are specified in Sch. 3. These include a requirement that the rules of an RPB must satisfy the adequacy test (Sch. 3, para. 3). The rules of an RPB need not be subjected to the scrutiny of the OFT before recognition is granted. Notably, in contrast to an SRO, an RPB which satisfies all of the statutory criteria is not entitled to recognition and the SIB retains a discretion in this respect.

Recognition of an RPB may be revoked (s. 19) and the SIB may apply to court for compliance orders (s. 20); however, the SIB has no power to alter, or to direct the alteration of the rules of an RPB. There is no right of appeal to the FST. In accordance with s. 21, the SIB has imposed disclosure obligations upon RPBs (the *Financial Services (Notification by Recognised Bodies) Regulations* contained in the SIB rulebook); the most notable difference between these regulations and those applicable to SROs is that RPBs are not required to send annual financial reports to the SIB. The SIB has issued a number of Guidance Releases which are specifically directed at RPBs. These include guidance on compliance, monitoring and client confidentiality.

The RPBs enjoy no civil immunity by virtue of the Act. It was considered that the dual function of RPBs made an extension of the s. 187 immunity impractical: it might be impossible to determine in particular circumstances whether the RPB was acting in its primary role as regulator of professional business (in which case, the Financial Services Act would not be relevant) or as a regulator of investment business. Exceptionally, an RPB may make it a condition of certification that the RPB, and its governing body, officers and servants are not to be liable in damages to the member in the absence of bad faith (s. 187(6)). This is a limited immunity and will not affect other persons, including members who have not agreed to the condition.

RECOGNISED INVESTMENT EXCHANGES AND CLEARING HOUSES

¶216 Recognised investment exchanges and designated investment exchanges

The characteristics of markets for trading securities will to some extent depend upon history, geography and the political and social environment within which the market operates. However, markets – whatever their particular nature will be concerned with ensuring that a product, which is capable of objective and perhaps standard evaluation, may be efficiently valued and its ownership transferred. A primary means of attaining marketability, liquidity and effective settlement will be the regulatory structure pertaining to the admission of the product on to the market, the circumstances in which it may be traded and the terms upon which ownership may be transferred and settlement achieved. As we have already seen those responsible for operating markets soon recognised the importance of creating a system of rules and customs determining these and related issues. Legislation in Britain has long accorded certain privileges and responsibilities to 'recognised stock exchanges'. For example, under the old *Prevention of Fraud (Investments) Act* 1958 and its predecessor, a member of a recognised stock exchange was not required to obtain a licence for dealing in securities. As the structure and operation of the traditional stock market became more sophisticated and in particular given developments in technology, the term recognised stock exchange was broadened to that of recognised 'investment exchange'. This term is broad enough to encompass not only those markets which have a central and physical location, but also markets which operate through electronic systems of communication.

The Financial Services Act enables any body corporate or unincorporated association to apply to the SIB (to whom this function has been delegated (*Financial Services Act 1986 (Delegation) Order* 1987 (SI 1987/942)) for recognition as an 'investment exchange' (s. 37). The importance of recognition is that an RIE is an exempted person as regards anything done in its capacity as such which constitutes investment business and does not require authorisation (s. 36).

The Act does not define what is meant by an 'investment exchange' but it is clear that this category is intended to cover organised markets for the trading of investments. An RIE may provide its own clearing services or may arrange for them to be provided by an RCH (Sch. 4, para. 2(4)).

Under s. 36 of the *Financial Services Act* 1986, the SIB may recognise an investment exchange if it satisfies the requirements set out in Sch. 4 and in Sch. 21 to the *Companies Act* 1989. Its rules and practices must ensure that business is conducted in an orderly manner and so as to afford proper protection to investors (Sch. 4, para. 2(1)). It must also limit dealings on the exchange to investments in which there is a proper market and, where relevant, impose information requirements so that persons dealing in the investments have proper information for determining their current value. To that end it must provide arrangements for the recording of bargains (Sch. 1, para. 2(5)).

The rules of a prospective RIE must not be unduly anti-competitive (s. 119–123). Recognition does not follow automatically upon satisfaction of the statutory conditions but remains in the SIB's discretion.

¶216

An RIE may have its recognition revoked (s. 37(7) and s. 120(4)), compliance orders may be obtained against it (s. 37(8)) and it may be required to change its rules (s. 120(4) – this power may only be exercised where the rules are unduly anti-competitive). Under the SIB rules made in accordance with s. 41, RIEs are subject to disclosure obligations (the *Financial Services (Notification by Recognised Bodies) Regulations* 1995).

The roles of an RIE and an SRO were often fulfilled in one organisation, as in the case of the London Stock Exchange. The separation of these functions in the Act had created some confusion and resulted in fairly arbitrary decisions as to what is the responsibility of an SRO and what is the responsibility of an RIE. For example, financial resources of investment firms are determined by the rules of SROs even though the RIEs have a fundamental interest in the financial ability of firms to perform their contracts.

The following recognised investment exchanges (RIEs) are recognised by the SIB:

the International Petroleum Exchange (IPE);
the London Stock Exchange (LSE);
the London International Financial Futures and Options Exchange (LIFFE);
the London Metal Exchange (LME);
the London Securities and Derivatives Exchange (OMLX);
Tradepoint Financial Networks plc (Tradepoint)

Electronic information and dealing systems, such as Crest have changed to a very significant extent the character and operation of the securities markets. The pace and extent of technological developments are perhaps most dramatically illustrated, however, by the creation of entirely electronic markets, some interfaced with the internet. While there are few such systems in operation at this point in time, there are a number in the pipeline. By the time it comes to publish a fourth edition of this work it is certain that there will already be examples of such markets in operation in the United Kingdom. They will offer to investors and companies seeking to obtain a market for their shares, direct access to a sophisticated computer-based dealing and information system. The service and market can be accessed, without any form of intermediation, from any terminal, once access clearance has been achieved. The regulatory implications of such markets, which by nature do not recognise the physical and jurisdictional constraints of more traditional markets, are profound. However, the Government has indicated a desire to see such markets develop, as they will ensure competition both in the provision of services to investors, and in providing issuers with access to a market on considerably cheaper terms. Of course, in addition to such initiatives, The London Stock Exchange is in the course of taking steps to ensure that it remains relatively attractive and competitive as a market for smaller issuers' securities. This involves not only the development of its existing services for information dissemination and settlement, but also the creation of an Alternative Investment Market (see generally *Consultative Document on The Alternative Investment Market – For smaller and growing companies* (1994) and also *Regulation of the United Kingdom Equity Markets Report by the SIB*, June 1995).

¶217   Recognised clearing houses

A clearing house has the function of providing clearing services in respect of transactions effected on an investment exchange (s. 38(2)). Traditionally, clearing houses match contracts to facilitate the settlement process and guarantee the performance of contracts on the investment exchange. Under s. 39 the SIB may recognise a clearing house if it has financial resources sufficient for the proper performance of its functions and if it provides the clearing services required for the recognition of an investment exchange. In addition the anti-competition obligations specified in s. 119–123 must be satisfied.

The supervisory powers and controls available to the SIB in respect of RCHs are similar to those which are available in respect of RIEs (s. 39(7)–(8)). The power to change or direct the changing, or anti-competitive rules under s. 120(4) is also available. Notification obligations have been imposed under s. 41 (the Financial Services (Notification by Recognised Bodies) Regulations 1995 contained in the SIB rule book).

The SIB has recognised the London Clearing House and CrestCo Ltd as an RCH.

¶218   Overseas investment exchanges and clearing houses

Overseas investment exchanges and clearing houses may be recognised by the Treasury under the Act (s. 40). This function cannot be delegated to the SIB (s. 114(6)). An overseas investment exchange or clearing house which is so recognised is an exempted person in respect of investment business which is carried on in the UK. The investment business must be effected in its capacity as investment exchange or clearing house as the case may be.

The investment exchanges which have been recognised by the SIB to date include:

Belgian Futures and Options Exchange (Belfox);
Chicago Board of Trade ((BOT);
Chicago Mercantile Exchange (Globex);
Delta Government Options Corporation (Delta);
(France): MATIF, MONEP;

(Spain): MEFF Renta Fija, MEFF Renta Variable;
National Association of Securities Dealers Inc (NASDAQ);
New York Mercantile Exchange (NYMEX);
Paris Bourse;
Stockholm Stock Exchange;
Sydney Futures Exchange.

¶219 Designated investment exchanges

The SIB has prepared a list of so called 'designated' overseas exchanges, which while not requiring authorisation, are considered by the SIB to provide protection for investors of an equivalent standard to that afforded by recognised investment exchanges. For the purpose of the SIB's conduct of business rules, transactions taking place on these exchanges will be regarded as though they had occurred on a recognised exchange. The current list of several dozen exchanges is maintained in a schedule to the SIB's Glossary and Interpretation Rules and Regulations 1990, and is subject to change.

FINANCIAL SERVICES TRIBUNAL

¶220 Composition and function

An interesting innovation introduced by the Financial Services Act was the establishment of the Financial Services Tribunal (FST) (s. 96–101). This Tribunal is an independent administrative body, vested with power to review the exercise of specified statutory powers. Subject to a few minor exceptions (*Financial Services Act 1986 (Delegation) Order* SI 1987/942, Sch. 1), the relevant powers in terms of review are those which have been delegated to the SIB. In exercising these powers, the SIB thus, bears little similarity to an entirely private, self-regulating body. The FST has no authority to review the decisions of SROs or other regulatory bodies.

The circumstances in which a complaint may be referred to the FST are specified in s. 97. A decision by the SIB to refuse direct authorisation or to withdraw or suspend authorisation previously granted (s. 25–29 and s. 33–34) is open to challenge, as are decisions to make disqualification orders (s. 59), to issue public statements as to misconduct (s. 60) or to use (or vary or rescind the use of) a power of intervention (s. 64–71). The person against whom the relevant decision is to be made is entitled to bring a claim before the Tribunal (s. 97(1)(a)). This right must be exercised within 28 days of receipt of the notice served in accordance with the relevant section (s. 97(1)). Any third party named in the relevant notice may also have the matter referred to the FST within the same time period (s. 97(1)(b)).

Three persons nominated by the Secretary of State must sit in the case (s. 96(3)). They must be chosen from a panel of not less than ten persons, including persons with legal experience appointed by the Lord Chancellor and persons with other relevant qualifications or experience appointed by the Secretary of State (s. 96(2)). The Secretary of State's functions under s. 96 are not delegable (s. 114(5)(f)). The chairman of the Tribunal must be legally qualified and, so far as practicable, at least one of the other two members should be a person with recent practical experience in business relevant to the case (s. 96). Rules regulating the conduct of proceedings before the FST are to be drawn up in accordance with Sch. 6.

If a case is referred to the FST at the instigation of a person against whom the relevant decision is directly aimed, it must be investigated and the FST must then make a report to the SIB outlining what it considers to be the appropriate course of action; the SIB is under a statutory duty to decide the matter in accordance with that report (s. 98). If the reference to the FST is made by a third party (s. 97(1)(b)), the Tribunal must report to the SIB whether the reasons relating to that party in the relevant notice are substantiated. A copy of the Tribunal's report must be sent to the person who is the subject of the notice and to the third party.

FINANCIAL SERVICES AND BANKING

¶221   Interrelationship of Banking and Financial Supervision

Traditional banking business, that is, the taking of deposits and the on-lending of those deposits to borrowers has been regulated by the Bank of England under the *Banking Act* 1987. Under this Act, the acceptance of deposits in the course of a deposit taking business by any person in the UK is prohibited unless that person is authorised or exempted under the Act or unless the transaction is itself exempted (s. 3–4 of the *Banking Act* 1987). Given the importance of prudential regulation and supervision of banks and the way in which control over the financial markets has developed, successive governments have sought to maintain clear regulatory boundaries between the regulation of banking and investment business. However, the historical distinctions between these businesses are breaking down. In particular the emergence of financial conglomerates offering a wide range of banking and investment services inevitably has given rise to problems of overlapping regulation and responsibility.

The SIB first issued a Guidance Release relating to the membership of SROs by banks in July 1987. This makes it clear that a bank may be required to join one or more SROs in order to lawfully engage in its full range of business activities but that in such circumstances, the Bank of England would act as lead regulator of the bank's financial position.

Under the Financial Services Act, institutions approved by the Bank of England are exempted from the need for authorisation in respect of certain money market activities (s. 43). As originally enacted, s. 193 of the *Financial Services Act* 1986 provided that authorised and exempted persons who accepted deposits in the course, or for the purpose of their investment business, were not subject to the *Banking Act* 1979. That section was repealed by the *Banking Act* 1987, and has been replaced by a similar exemption under reg. 14 of the *Banking Act 1987 (Exempt Transactions) Regulations* 1988 (SI 1988/646) which came into force on 29 April 1988.

The policing of serious fraud has tended in recent years to span a number of regulatory systems and, indeed, jurisdictions. Whilst the creation of the Serious Fraud Office by the *Criminal Justice Act* 1987 has centralised both the responsibility for prosecution and also investigation in the case of what the Director considers to be a 'serious or complex' fraud, it is common ground that all those agencies involved in monitoring conduct in the financial sector have a role to play. This has blurred responsibilities and led to a realisation that inter-agency cooperation must be fostered. Thus, the Bank of England has, with the SIB, taken responsibility for developing the Financial Fraud Information Network and developing the Shared Intelligence Service. A series of major banking and banking-related scandals, such as the collapse of Barings, have dramatically underlined the need for those concerned with ensuring the observance of high standards and probity in the investment services industry to work closely with banking supervisors in Britain and for that matter elsewhere. The development of comprehensive anti-money laundering legislation has further underlined the significance of cross-sector cooperation and monitoring. Indeed, the impact of anti-money laundering laws, particularly those introduced in the *Criminal Justice Act* 1993 and *Drug Trafficking Act* 1994, on those engaged in handling other people's money has been profound. The requirements of the *Money Laundering Regulations* (SI 1993/1933) in terms of compliance and customer identification place upon financial intermediaries obligations which have serious implications for the conduct of their business.

While it was widely appreciated that the Labour Party when in opposition had profound concerns about the efficacy of the system of supervision for banks and in particular its interface with those authorities concerned with the financial services industry, it came as a shock to all, and not least the Governor of the Bank of England, that within days of assuming office, the new Labour Chancellor of the Exchequer announced on 20 May 1997, that legislation would be introduced by the end of the year to transfer responsibility for supervision of banking to a strengthened and expanded SIB. Whether this will involve more than the Banking Supervision Department simply decamping to the SIB's new premises, or something rather more meaningful, remains to be seen.

At the same time, Mr Gordon Brown announced that Sir Andrew Large would step down as chairman of the SIB and Mr Howard Davies, the Deputy Governor of the Bank of England, would be the first chairman of the enhanced SIB responsible for integrating the supervision of banking and financial services. Given the limited amount of consultation that appears to have been conducted prior to these significant announcements, reaction from the City and the relevant regulators has so far been rather non-committal. Although a small working group, chaired by Dr Mads Andenas of Kings College, University of London, did prepare a report for the Labour Party in the Autumn of 1996, it remains to be seen whether the more thorough-going consideration of the issues involved in bringing supervision over such a broad spectrum of activity, that should have been undertaken, has been carried out. It is difficult to find those who are prepared to admit that they were consulted, let alone involved in the decision! Of course, subsequent to Mr Brown's announcement a joint committee consisting of officers from the Bank of England and the SIB, with additional expert members, has been convened. While the determination of the government to reinforce investor and depositor confidence must be applauded, the manner in which this process is being carried out must be disruptive, even if in the final analysis beneficial.

¶222   Non-Financial Services Act regulators

Whilst it was the intention, or perhaps rather hope, of those responsible for the new regulatory structure to ensure a much greater degree of cohesion than the former essentially self-regulatory regime of supervision was able to offer, there are inevitably a number of agencies and authorities which properly remain outside the new structure, but whose jurisdiction might well on occasion be relevant in regulating or controlling the activities of those engaged in investment business.

Outside the Act the DTI remains solely responsible for the prudential regulation and authorisation of insurance companies and continues to supervise standards of corporate behaviour under the Companies Acts. The DTI also has the exclusive power to investigate the beneficial ownership of shares and appoint inspectors to inquire into suspected cases of insider dealing.

The Treasury regulates reciprocal facilities for overseas businesses and can approve overseas RIEs so as to allow them to play an important role in public offers of unlisted securities dealt in on them. It may also direct the SIB or any SRO to refrain from taking any proposed action if such action would be incompatible with the UK's EEC or other international obligations or to take any action which is required by them (s. 192). The negotiation of international information exchange agreements relating to securities and futures is also under the direction of the Treasury.

Although the SIB is given power to prosecute, for certain regulatory offences under the *Financial Services Act* 1986, until recently there has not been a great deal of enthusiasm for the SIB to assume a significant prosecutorial role. The SIB is, of course, armed with civil enforcement powers under s. 6 and 61 of the 1986 Act. The prosecution of more serious offences is left with the DTI (this has not been transferred to the Treasury), Serious Fraud Office (SFO) and Crown Prosecution Service (CPS). Furthermore, under the *Criminal Justice Act* 1993 it is possible for the Secretary of State to appoint other authorities to prosecute cases of insider dealing and this power has been exercised to enable the London Stock Exchange to bring several such cases, albeit rather minor ones.

PREVENTION OF RESTRICTIVE PRACTICES

¶223   Scrutiny of competition

The relationship of those laws which seek to prevent and control restrictive and monopolistic practices and the investor protection is not always clear or for that matter happy. Mention has already been made of widespread concern at various stages in the development of the capital markets about procedures which appeared to be tantamount to restrictive practices. Indeed, it was the referral of The Stock Exchange's Rule Book, by the Director General of Fair Trading, to the Restrictive Trade Practice's Court in February 1979 which was one of the more significant factors in the so called 'Big Bang' (see ¶213). To a large extent issues of competition regulation in regard to trading practices and procedures, admission to membership of exchanges and in particular minimum dealing commissions have proved to be an impetus for reform and change in securities regulation in a number of other countries, including the USA, Canada and Australia. Of course, those involved as regulators or professional intermediaries in the markets tend to maintain that certain restrictions are necessary to advance investor protection – either through a process of exclusion – or by rendering it financially possible to fund effective investor protection service. Governments have tended to be rather cynical of such arguments particularly in an era of deregulation. The British Government has always maintained the importance of ensuring that anti-competitive devices are only permitted where such can be manifestly seen to advance the public interest, such as in the protection of investors. In fact, it has been a significant element in the Government's strategy of supervision to contend that the promotion of free competition in the financial sector will of its nature promote better standards, (see ¶208 and *Financial Services in the United Kingdom; A New Framework for Investor Protection* (1985) Cmnd 9432). The SIB has also adopted a similar view, albeit with perhaps not the same degree of enthusiasm (*Regulation of the United Kingdom Equity Markets*, Report by the SIB, June 1995).

The Financial Services Act seeks to create a modified anti-competitive regime for the financial services sector where proper weight can be given to the special interest of investors and in particular their protection.

Under the *Financial Services Act* 1986, the rules, regulations, guidance, notices, clearing procedures and practices of SROs, RIEs, RCHs and the SIB are subject to a special regime. Sections 119–128 of the Act apply in a different system of competition scrutiny from that in the general law. The most important point is that the Act replaces the judgment of the Restrictive Practices Court by the decision of the Secretary of State. The justification for this is that the Secretary of State is thought to be in a better position to balance the requirements of investor protection against the anti-competitive effects of regulation.

The transfer of functions to the SIB under the Act was conditional upon the Secretary of State being satisfied that the SIB's rules did not have, nor were intended nor likely to have, a significant anti-competitive effect which was greater than was necessary for the protection of investors (s. 121(1)). Before reaching his decision, the Secretary of State was required to consult with the Director-General of Fair Trading (s. 122(1)). Similarly, it is a prerequisite of recognition of SROs, RIEs and RCHs that their rules do not restrict, distort or prevent competition to a greater extent than is necessary to protect investors (s. 119(1), 122(2)).

The rules, regulations, guidances and practices of the regulatory bodies remain subject to the scrutiny of the OFT (s. 122(4)). If, at any time, the OFT considers that the rules are, or are intended or likely to be, significantly anti-competitive, it must investigate and report to the Treasury (s. 122(4)–(6)).

The OFT's responsibility to monitor the rules and practices of, in particular, RIEs is one that is taken seriously. The Director General prepared a substantial report to the Secretary of State in April 1988 which was part of the process leading to the recognition of the then International Stock Exchange as an RIE. The Director General also submitted a report to the Secretary of State on Trade Publication and Price Transparency in April 1990 and a report to the Chancellor of the Exchequer on Trade Publication Rules of The London Stock Exchange relating to market makers in March 1995. The SIB in all cases responded and attempted to balance the public interest in preventing anti-competitive devices with that of protecting investors, (see generally on this *Regulation of the United Kingdom Equity Markets,* report by the SIB, June 1995.)

¶223

The OFT may also scrutinise the practices of the SIB or the other regulatory bodies but is under no obligation to do so. In order to facilitate the conduct of its investigations, the OFT is given the power to obtain documents and information (s. 124). The Secretary of State is required to consider the OFT's reports but the Act does not oblige him to follow them (s. 122(2) and (7)).

There are considerable exemptions from competition and other related laws for regulatory agencies under the Act. While they are recognised, SROs, RIEs and RCHs and their rules and practices will be exempted from the *Fair Trading Act* 1973, the *Restrictive Trade Practices Act* 1986 and the *Competition Act* 1980 (s. 124–126 of the *Financial Services Act* 1986). Similar exemptions apply to the SIB.

THE PANEL ON TAKEOVERS AND MERGERS AND THE CITY CODE

¶224   The regulation of takeovers and mergers

It has long been the view of government and the City that there are overwhelming advantages in retaining a significant degree of flexibility in the administration of rules relating to the conduct of takeovers and mergers. Consequently, the Panel on Takeovers and Mergers and the City Code remain formally outside the regulatory structure established by the Financial Services Act. Whether the provisions of the City Code and for that matter the Substantial Acquisition Rules, will remain non-statutory, remains to be seen. The proposal for a 13th European Parliament and Council Directive on Company Law Concerning Takeover Bids (95/0341 (COD) provides in its preamble '... the Directive does not exclude the possibility of control being exercised by a self-regulatory body which will have the power to decide on complaints with regard to a takeover bid. The extent to which courts may intervene will be a matter for each member State provided that there is at least a right to bring proceedings to claim compensation'. It is hard to see that the present status of the code could endure in such circumstances, albeit the preamble does state 'There is no requirement to suspend or interrupt the takeover process if a party takes the matter to court'.

However, it should be noted that whilst not law in the strict sense, the Takeover Code has been looked at by judges as setting appropriate standards and practices, see *Gething v Kilner* (1972) 1 WLR 337 and *Dunford & Elliot Ltd v Johnson & Firth Brown* (1977) 1 Lloyd's Rep 505. It has also been held in the case of a criminal prosecution where the interpretation of the Code had some

¶224

relevance to the issues, that the interpretation of the Code was a matter of law for the judge, see *R v Spens* (1991) 4 All ER 421. Breaches of the Code have also provided justification for other proceedings including the appointment of inspectors under the *Companies Act* 1985 and have been taken into consideration in winding up and disqualification proceedings. Whilst the courts have been keen to avoid the danger of participants in contested takeovers seeking to use legal proceedings to frustrate the proper aspirations of others, it has been accepted in a number of cases that decisions of the Panel are subject to judicial review, albeit on an historic basis, (see for example *R v Panel on Takeovers and Mergers, ex parte Datafin plc* (1987) 1 QB 815, *R v Panel on Takeovers and Mergers, ex parte Guinness* (1989) BCLC 255 and *R v Panel on Takeovers and Mergers, ex parte Fayed* (1992) BCLC 938). The Code has also been endorsed by the SIB for the purposes of Principle 3, which requires firms to observe high standards of market conduct and in particular comply with any code or standard approved by the SIB. (The SIB's *Financial Services (Statements of Principle) (Endorsement of Codes and Standards) Instrument* 1995, para. 4.) A breach of the principles, or any code endorsed by the SIB, does not of itself give rise to a right of civil action (see s. 47A(3), but it may well justify disciplinary action by the relevant SRO or RPB, and the SIB has authority to initiate proceedings for disqualification (see s. 59) or for an injunction under s. 61. However, in endorsing the Takeover Code, the SIB has made it clear that responsibility for enforcement and, of course, interpretation will remain with the Panel and its Executive. Under the terms of the SIB endorsement disciplinary action and intervention by the SIB for breaches of the Code or ruling made under it, can only occur at the specific request of the Panel. Furthermore, the possibility of seeking an order under s. 61 is also expressly excluded.

The Takeover Panel is a designated authority for the purpose of disclosure of information under s. 180 (the *Financial Services (Disclosure of Information) (Designated Authorities No. 2) Order* 1987 (SI 1987/859)).

DATA PROTECTION ACT 1984

¶225   Exemption from access

Section 190 of the *Financial Services Act* 1986 makes it clear that data held by SROs and RPBs for the purpose of their regulatory functions may be exempted by order under s. 30 of the *Data Protection Act* 1984 from its subject access provisions. The SIB has made such an order: the *Data Protection (Regulation of Financial Services etc.) (Subject Access Exemption) Order* 1987 (SI 1987/1905).

If this order had not been made an individual could have invoked his rights of access under the 1984 Act to find out what information was held about him by the regulatory authorities, which it was argued would impede the efficacy of vetting and monitoring procedures.

PUBLIC REGISTER OF AUTHORISED PERSONS AND RECOGNISED ORGANISATIONS

¶226   Access to information

In accordance with s. 102 of the Financial Services Act, the SIB has established a register of authorised persons. The register also contains the names of all SROs, RPBs, RIEs and RCHs and of authorised unit trust schemes and recognised collective investment schemes. Persons subject to a disqualification direction are listed.

There are sufficient powers in the Act to ensure that the information required to maintain the register is supplied to the SIB on a timely basis. All directly authorised persons must provide information in accordance with the regulations made under s. 52 (*the Financial Services (Notification) Regulations* 1988). Similarly, SROs, RPBs, RIEs and RCHs are also subject to notification requirements (the Financial Services (Notification by Recognised Bodies) Regulations 1995 (s. 14), s. 21 and s. 41).

The SIB publishes lists of the above information and the register is available in computer-readable form. Most of this information is open to public inspection (s. 103(1). Inspection is limited in relation to that part of the register concerning individuals subject to a disqualification direction. Section 103(2) enables an applicant to check whether a particular person specified by him is currently disqualified. Anyone who has good reason for seeking information about disqualified persons may inspect entries about disqualification more generally (s. 103(3)).

PUBLICATION OF INFORMATION AND ADVICE

¶227   SIB's powers

Section 206 of the *Financial Services Act* 1986 enables the SIB, to whom this function has been delegated (*Financial Services Act 1986 (Deregulation) Order*

1987 (SI 1987/942)), to publish information or give advice with regard to the operation of the Act and the rules and regulations made thereunder. The SIB may charge for the services which it provides under this section (s. 206).

The provision of essentially informal advice by the Executive of the Panel on Takeovers and Mergers has always been perceived as one of its strengths. On the other hand there are obvious dangers in regulatory bodies, such as the SIB, expressing views as to the interpretation of the law or for that matter in regard to issues which have not been entirely thought out. Hence, whilst officers of the SIB do try to be helpful the advice that they proffer is given on the clear understanding that it cannot, even if followed, be necessarily relied upon as correct. Of course, to what extent such disclaimers protect the SIB remains to be seen.

¶228   Appraisal of the new structure

It was the intention of the government and the City that the new structure of regulation and supervision should retain as much flexibility and sensitivity as possible.

There was a fear that the SIB could easily become a formalistic bureaucracy dominated by lawyers. Others feared that too much emphasis on enforcement would not only project the wrong image but be destructive of the co-operation and goodwill that is vital if the system is to operate smoothly. In the result the SIB has not degenerated into a lawyer dominated bureaucracy, like so many of its foreign equivalents, and it has not, until recently, underlined its enforcement role. While it is still a relatively small organisation, it has proved to be expensive, or rather more expensive than the City had hoped. It has also found it difficult to recruit persons with relevant experience, or to retain some of its key personnel. The SIB has also been criticised for making its rules and regulations far too legalistic and technical. Indeed, it has been reported that both the cost of maintaining the SIB and in complying with these new regulations contributed significantly to the unpopularity of the SIB's first chairman Sir Kenneth Berrill.

Sir Kenneth's successor, Sir David Walker, who remained a non-executive director of the Bank of England, was no doubt a little more political and circumspect. During his period of office, from May 1988 until June 1992, he strove to project the SIB as being sensitive to the legitimate concerns if not aspirations of the City. He tended to play down enforcement, whilst under this chairmanship significant steps forward did occur in the development of both a framework and network for international cooperation. Sir David's main achievement was undoubtedly the so-called 'new settlement', This was achieved largely by agreement, although given legislative blessing in the *Companies Act* 1989 which introduced several important amendments to the Financial Services Act. The conduct of business rules, drawn up by the SIB and

applicable directly to only those authorised by the S~~I~~
an inflexible standard against which the rules of the
measured and tested so as to give investors 'equiv
excessive technicality and specificity of the SIB ~~1~~
inadequate and insensitive drafting constituted a majo~~i~~
City practitioners were especially worried given the pr~~(~~
under s. 62 of the 1986 Act should a violation of one of th
an investor.

After a certain amount of discussion and the publication of a first attempt,
known as the 'new approach', the SIB resolved upon a three-tier structure of
rules. Ten very general, if not banal, commandments which are to be applied to
everyone, then a second-tier of Core Rules which subject to limited and agreed
exceptions are applicable to all authorised firms, either directly or through
'adoption' by the SROs in their own rulebooks, and then a third-tier which
allows the requirements of particular sectors of the industry to be catered for.
Furthermore, the absolute standard of 'equivalence' was watered down to a
determination by the SIB that the relevant SRO rules provide an adequate
level of investor protection. In addition, s. 62 was emasculated so as to provide
a civil statutory tort action for harm caused by a violation of the Core Rules, at
the behest of only private investors. In other words, investors who in many
instances are unlikely to be able to afford the costs of litigation. Of course, there
were other important aspects to the 'new settlement' but the restructuring of
the rules adequately sets the tone.

The third chairman of the SIB, Sir Andrew Large, came into office in June
1992 after a series of major scandals in the City, most of which although highly
damaging to confidence in the integrity of the system of supervision and
regulation, had relatively little to do with the SIB. In July 1992 the Chancellor
of the Exchequer asked Sir Andrew to undertake a review of the regulatory
system and to give particular attention to the way in which both the SIB and
IMRO had discharged their respective duties in relation to the so-called
Maxwell affair. The Large report (*Financial Services Regulation – Making the
Two Tier System Work*) was published in May 1993. Perhaps one of the most
significant issues raised by him was that of enforcement. Sir Andrew recognised
that there was a widespread perception that fraudsters were escaping and sharp
practices were not being controlled. He accepted that the SIB had a role in the
coordination and support of enforcement action by other agencies and in
particular the self-regulators. He clearly anticipated a role for the SIB as a
'central policeman' for the financial sector, although he also accepted that this
might be well into the future. Of course, Sir Andrew had already observed,
before publication of his report that he would like to see more effective
enforcement not just of the Financial Services Act but also related matters such
as insider dealing and fraud. As we have seen, the Serious Fraud Office was

¶228

...lished in 1987 to investigate and prosecute cases of serious or complex ...aud. Although the SFO has never shown a great willingness to get involved in the prosecution of cases involving merely breaches of the Financial Services Act or anti-insider dealing law, it has brought a number of cases before the courts in regard to what might be described as City fraud. Its conviction rate has not been less than other prosecutorial agencies in the UK or for that matter elsewhere. However, it has had an unfortunate number of very high profile and extremely expensive failures. Of course, given the SFO's arguably wider responsibilities in discouraging serious fraud, it is debatable whether the number of convictions that it is able to secure is the only or the most appropriate measure of its success (see ¶1,201). However, there can be little doubt that the media and thus, the public, have not been reassured by the SFO's record in regard to these well publicised cases, that the criminal justice system is capable or willing to bring the perpetrators of major frauds effectively to book.

The former Director, Mr George Staple, publicly expressed his view, on a number of occasions, that notwithstanding the special investigatory powers that his office enjoys under s. 2 of the *Criminal Justice Act* 1987, it would often be better and more efficacious to deal with cases through the disciplinary jurisdiction of the SROs and RPBs. This view would appear to be shared by Sir Andrew and George Staples's successor Mrs Rosalind Wright, who before her appointment had served as General Counsel of the SFA and the London Stock Exchange. The Select Committee of the House of Commons on Trade and Industry, in its *Report on Company Inspections*, published in June 1990 (Third Report. HC 36), was less than complimentary about the record of the DTI and other 'enforcement' agencies in policing the City and advocated the use of civil enforcement procedures along the line of those employed by the Securities and Exchange Commission in the US. Of course, the SIB is given statutory power under s. 61 of the 1986 Act to bring injunctive and restitutionary suits for violations of the Act and Core Rules, but has exhibited little enthusiasm in so doing other than in cases of unauthorised investment business. The SIB has expressed support on a number of occasions for consideration to be given to the efficacy of civil enforcement actions and the imposition of civil penalties. Sir Andrew expressed the view that civil penalties would be a useful sanction against insider abuse. In September 1996 the Treasury commissioned a study from a US consultancy company and Dr Mads Andenas of King's College, University of London, into the efficacy of such devices in the USA. It would also seem that despite its traditional opposition to dealing with serious public wrongs, such as insider abuse, other than through the criminal law, the DTI has also come round to the view that alternative enforcement procedures might prove rather less expensive and more efficient. It is thought that the new Labour Government will introduce legislation in the not too distant future reinforcing the SIB's enforcement powers and enabling civil penalties to be assessed and imposed for breaches of the 1986 Act and for such matters as insider dealing. Of course, it is one thing for the SIB to become more aggressive even armed with additional powers, and yet quite another ensuring that it has the resources necessary to do more than bark.

While there is no doubt a popular perception that the regulatory regime has failed adequately to prevent and punish wrongdoing it would also appear that significant personalities in the industry itself have profound reservations as to the efficacy of the system. The then chief executive of Britain's biggest investor, the Prudential Corporation, in a public speech to the Institute of Actuaries (London, 3 November 1992) described the system as a complete failure and called for the creation of a statutory authority along the lines of a securities and exchange commission. The 300-strong audience comprised of practitioners in the financial services industry indicated complete agreement with Mr Mick Newmarch's indictment of the 'failed experiment' of practitioner-based regulation. Others have voiced similar disillusionment including individuals, such as Mr S M Yassukovich, a former chairman of the London Stock Exchange (see letter to the *Financial Times*, 10 November 1992).

No doubt as a result of many factors and pressures, but not least Andrew Large's own initiative, the SIB has since 1994 given rather more attention to enforcement and the protection of ordinary investors. The degree of inter-agency coordination and cooperation, both at a national and international level, has increased significantly. The creation of the Financial Fraud Information Network (FFIN) and the Shared Intelligence Service (see ¶222) in regard to which the SIB has been a prime mover, has contributed greatly to both prevention and the better handling of cases. The establishment of a 'civil enforcement' arm within the SIB had underlined the Board's willingness to use all its powers under the *Financial Services Act* 1986 and this together with an increase in resources for monitoring and enforcement may be expected to achieve better results. The SIB has also used its statutory powers of disqualification (see ¶59) to ban individuals from being involved in investment business within the UK for life.

The desire to improve the actual and perceived efficiency of the regulatory system in terms of the prevention and control of abuse is not new. Indeed, as we have seen this was one of the driving forces behind the creation of the present system. Sir Andrew, during his chairmanship of the SIB, has given considerable emphasis to the role of the SIB in enforcement and the promotion of good standards of conduct. Whether his strategy of the SIB becoming a 'stand-back' super-regulator and leaving so much responsibility on the second-tier regulators, was wise or not has to be questioned. The de-designation of the SIB Core Rules created the impression in many people's minds that the structure was being weakened rather than tailored to the regulatory needs of specific activities in the industry. Stand-back regulation inevitably appears as aloof

¶228

regulation, and given the number of scandals that have occurred, albeit often properly outside the SIB's remit, such an approach can justly earn the rebuke of the former Economic Secretary that the SIB had become 'toothless'. On the other hand, given the many achievements that were made during Sir Andrew's reign, it is perhaps sad that on the occasion of the new Chancellor of the Exchequer's announcement that he was stepping down and being replaced by Mr Howard Davies, the Deputy Governor of the Bank of England, Mr Gordon Brown also took the opportunity to brand the system as a failure. The Chancellor stated 'it has long been apparent that the regulatory structure introduced by the *Financial Services Act* 1986 is not delivering the standard of supervision and investor protection that the industry and the public have the right to expect'. He added that the current two-tier system 'splits responsibility between the SIB and SROs, together with the RPBs – this division is inefficient, confusing for investors and lacks accountability and a clear allocation of responsibilities'. The Chancellor emphasised that the 'reform is long overdue' and that legislation would be introduced by the end of the year to bring the second self-regulatory tier into a new and strengthened SIB (statement to the House of Commons and Press Release, 20 May 1997). The government's decision also to transfer responsibility for the supervision of banks under the *Banking Act* 1987 to the SIB has already been referred to.

While it was known that there was considerable sympathy in the Labour Party for the establishment of a statutory commission to regulate and oversee the whole of the financial sector, armed with the weapons necessary to deal with abuses, it came as a shock to many that the new government was prepared to move so far so quickly. The degree of deliberation let alone consultation that preceded these announcements appears to have been minimal. Although the reaction of regulators, the industry and investors is on the whole favourable there is widespread concern as to how the creation of a new system will be achieved in the relatively short time scale intimated by the Chancellor. Draft legislation transferring responsibility from the Bank of England to the SIB is now in preparation and should be public by the autumn of 1997. Whether the other matters to which the Chancellor referred, will also be included in this measure remains unclear. A working group has been convened to ensure as far as possible that the transfer of responsibility under the Banking Act is as smooth and as efficient as possible. Absorbing the second regulatory tier is a much more difficult and larger task. There is a profound uncertainty as to whether the SIB will merely be strengthened by the addition of SRO staff, or whether it will be recast. There is a view in the Labour Party and for that matter elsewhere that merely transferring offices and giving people new designations will not alter much. There is a need for a real change of philosophy and the manner in which the responsibility for ensuring investor confidence is carried

¶228

out. This may well mean a change of personnel and a radical restructuring within the SIB.

In a letter from Mr Gordon Brown to Sir Andrew Large, he states –

'legislation will deliver the government's manifesto commitment to give the SIB direct responsibility for the regulatory regime covered by the 1986 Act. It will do this principally by transferring to it all the functions of the SROs, so establishing the SIB as the single financial services regulator, with full responsibility and accountability. The legislation will also give to the SIB the full range of powers and discipline, established in statute, which are currently available to the SROs under contract law'.

Obviously, when this legislation comes into effect it will have a very wide ranging and significant effect on the regulatory structure and the character of regulation itself.

¶228

3 Investment Business and the Need for Authorisation

THE FSA'S AUTHORISATION REQUIREMENT

¶301 Introduction

The *Financial Services Act* 1986 provides in s. 3 that no-one may carry on FSA-regulated investment business in the United Kingdom unless he is an 'authorised person' or an 'exempted person' (see ¶347–¶355). As a result of the regulations implementing into UK law the 'single European passport' provisions of, respectively, the EU investment services directive (ISD)(as from 1 January 1996) and the EU second banking coordination directive (2BCD) (as from 1 January 1993), a non-UK EEA investment firm or bank or other credit institution may also carry on FSA-regulated investment business in the UK under its passport even if it is neither an authorised person nor an exempted person (see ¶356). In addition, the UK has unilaterally granted qualifying non-UK EEA credit institutions a passport equivalent to the ISD passport for ISD services which are not covered by their 2BCD passport (see ¶356).

To contravene the s. 3 prohibition is a criminal offence punishable by imprisonment or an unlimited fine (s. 4). Contraventions of s. 3 may also lead to civil actions (s. 5(1)(a)), as indeed may the involvement, in contravention of s. 3, of a firm which is not FSA-authorised in concluding investment agreements subject to the FSA which are entered into by an FSA-authorised or exempted firm or a passporting firm (s. 5(1)(b)). It is the threat of civil sanctions which is in practice the most effective deterrent to contravention; these include, in particular, unenforceability at the option of the investor and the possibility of restitution orders, which in effect give the investor an indemnity against loss.

Importantly, the FSA applies to both banks and non-banks without distinction. In contrast to the EU's financial institutions 'single market' directives, in particular the ISD and the 2BCD, regulation applies on a functional, rather than an institutional, basis; firms which carry on FSA-regulated investment activities are subject to the FSA even if they are banks or insurance companies. It is this which has made implementation of those directives into UK law exceedingly complicated. Indeed, UK banks and building societies could only qualify for the 2BCD passport in relation to the

FSA-regulated investment business covered by it by providing in the regulations implementing the 2BCD passport into UK law that, in effect, their authorisation as credit institutions authorised them to carry on the FSA-regulated investment business covered by the passport if they were FSA-authorised for it (see ¶356).

Assuming that the investments concerned are FSA-regulated investments (see ¶323–¶328), that carrying on the activity is treated as carrying on a business in the UK (see ¶304, ¶310 and ¶311) and that no exemption applies, the FSA in general terms applies to not only broker-dealers, market-makers and investment managers, but also investment advisers and intermediaries, investment exchanges, underwriters, anyone who manages unit trusts or other unincorporated collective investment schemes, or who acts as the depositary or sole director of a UK open-ended investment company, anyone who engages in interest rate swaps, anyone who acts as a CREST sponsor or, as from 1 June 1997, as a custodian or nominee and even anyone who buys or sells investments for his own account outside an investment exchange (unless, in particular, his counterparty is an FSA-authorised firm). Importantly, if a firm carries on FSA-regulated investment activities from a UK office or with UK clients or counterparties by way of business as a 'normal' activity (and, as explained in ¶302, that normally includes even merely offering or agreeing to carry on the substantive activity) and no exemption applies, it will usually be regarded as carrying on FSA-regulated investment business in the UK and, accordingly, will normally need to be FSA-authorised.

¶302   Definitions of terms used

The terminology adopted by the Financial Services Act in relation to FSA-authorisation is unfortunately difficult to use in an explanation of when FSA-authorisation is required. For example, if it is treated as carried on in the UK, the FSA regulates 'investment business', which is defined in s. 1(2) as the activities listed in Pt. II of Sch. 1 which are not excluded by Pt. III and are carried on as a business, yet it heads Pt. II as 'activities constituting investment business'. Accordingly, it is legitimate in trying to explain when a firm needs to be authorised (or, licensed) under the FSA to use a slightly different terminology, although the expressions so used cannot be found in the FSA. In this chapter, the following expressions have the respective meanings set out below:

(1) 'FSA-regulated investment activities' means those activities which would require FSA-authorisation if carried on as a business in the UK in relation to FSA-regulated investments and if the FSA contained no exemptions; advertisements and cold-calls relating to them are FSA-regulated even if the activity itself is exempted from the FSA's

authorisation requirement (see Ch. 9). These activities are listed in Pt. II of Sch. 1 (see ¶312–¶322) under the heading 'activities constituting investment business' and, in general terms, consist of the following activities, and (except in the case of (e) and (f) below) even merely offering or agreeing to carry them on:

(a) 'dealing in investments', whether as principal or as agent (except, in particular, effecting transactions on an investment exchange or off-exchange with an FSA-authorised firm as counterparty);

(b) 'arranging deals in investments', or making arrangements to market investments or which would result in the purchase or sale of investments;

(c) 'managing investments', whether on a discretionary or a non-discretionary (or, advisory) basis;

(d) 'advising [an investor] on investments', on an ad hoc basis or, seemingly, after reviewing a portfolio without responsibility for implementing the recommended transaction (reviewing the portfolio with that responsibility is in (c) above);

(e) 'establishing, operating or winding up collective investment schemes [including open-ended investment companies]';

(f) acting as a depositary or sole director of a UK open-ended investment company;

(g) providing, or arranging for the provision of, safe custody services (except, in particular, where an FSA-authorised 'primary custodian' acting from a UK office has responsibility); and

(h) acting as a sponsor in CREST for shareholders on the register whose holdings are dematerialised (and so within the CREST computerised book-entry settlement system) but who do not want to be system-participants themselves.

Although the FSA refers to the conduct it regulates as 'activities', most FSA-regulated conduct is in fact the provision of a service. Entering into own account transactions as a market-maker is the provision of a service as, indeed, is doing so as a broker-dealer if this involves the firm's holding itself out as ready to buy or sell investments for or from its own book if asked to do so or buying or selling investments for or from its own book to meet a client's agency order. It is noteworthy in this context that the investment services directive refers to the kinds of activity regulated by it as 'services' and that, of course, the FSA and the ISD both include the word 'services' rather than 'activities' in their title. In reviewing whether an activity falls within the FSA (or the ISD) it is therefore often helpful first to see whether any service is in fact being provided to third parties. Among the few FSA-regulated investment activities which are subject to the FSA's authorisation requirement but do not in fact constitute a service to third parties is own account transactions with non-professionals entered into on the firm's own initiative; they need FSA-authorisation in order to protect the non-professional counterparty. Many of these transactions do not fall within the FSA's limited 'own account' exemptions, for example, there is no exemption for the purchase from a 'member of the public' (as defined and, importantly, normally including investment trusts) of a holding in a company carrying less than 20 per cent of the company's voting rights, (see ¶331 and ¶332). These 'own initiative' own account transactions are not within the ISD's passport (or its authorisation requirement) as they are not 'services'; however, they are within the 2BCD's passport, as it applies to 'activities' rather than 'services';

(2) 'FSA-regulated investment business' means those FSA-regulated investment activities which fall outside the exemptions contained in Pt. III of Sch. 1 (see ¶329–¶333 and ¶335–¶346) and are carried on as a business (see ¶304); importantly, several of these exemptions have been restricted as a result of the UK's implementation of the ISD (see ¶330). This is the same as 'investment business' as used in the FSA (s. 1(2)) and a firm must normally be FSA-authorised to carry it on in the UK; the firm will not carry it on in the UK for this purpose, even if the client or counterparty is in the UK, if the 'overseas persons' exemptions apply (see ¶334);

(3) 'firm' means a securities firm, bank or other credit institution or insurance company carrying on FSA-regulated investment activities, and indeed anyone else doing so, (whether as a corporation, partnership, individual or otherwise and whether or not as a business);

(4) 'exempted firm' means a firm which is exempted from the FSA's authorisation requirement by one of the FSA's 'status' exemptions (in particular, a listed institution approved for the purpose by the Bank of England and carrying on restricted kinds of FSA-regulated investment business in qualifying short-term debt securities or other qualifying assets within the 'money market' exemption in s. 43 and an appointed representative within s. 44); this is the same as the FSA's 'exempted person'. Passporting firms are not 'exempted firms' in relation to their passported business even if they are listed institutions (see ¶357);

(5) 'overseas firm' means a UK or non-UK firm which does not carry on FSA-regulated investment business from its own UK office (unless, perhaps, it is doing so only within a 'status' exemption from FSA-authorisation, in particular the 'money market' exemption, see ¶347)

¶302

and accordingly is entitled to the FSA's 'overseas persons' exemptions (see ¶334);

(6) 'overseas securities firm' means a UK or non-UK firm whose head office is outside the UK and whose ordinary business involves it in carrying on FSA-regulated investment activities but which is not an FSA-professional;

(7) 'qualifying overseas securities firm' means an overseas securities firm which, in relation to the 'own account' exemption for securities transactions, is solicited for the relevant transaction at an office outside the UK and, in relation to the 'own account' exemption for derivatives transactions, is party to the relevant transaction, or arranges it, except that the firm is not a qualifying overseas securities firm in relation to the 'own account' exemption for derivatives transactions unless the transaction is entered into through a non-UK office of a party to the transaction;

(8) 'EEA firm' means a firm incorporated in (or, if not a body corporate, formed under the law of or with its head office in) any part of the European Economic Area, namely the European Union, Iceland, Liechtenstein and Norway (and so, importantly, not including Switzerland) and, in relation to the single European passport and unless the context indicates differently, means an EEA firm entitled to the passport granted by either the ISD or the 2BCD;

(9) 'EEA investment firm' means an EEA firm whose regular occupation or business is the provision of one or more of the 'core investment services' specified in the ISD, all of which qualify as FSA-regulated investment activities, (see ¶358) to third parties on a professional basis, other than insurance companies and other firms excluded from the ISD by art. 2(2) (see ¶330). EEA banks and other credit institutions which provide one or more core investment services as their regular occupation or business also qualify as EEA investment firms but if as is normal they are authorised to do so under their banking licence or authorisation, and so as banks rather than as investment firms, they are not subject to the ISD's authorisation requirement and they do not have a passport under the ISD;

(10) 'passporting firm' means a non-UK EEA firm when it is using its ISD or 2BCD passport to carry on FSA-regulated investment business in the UK outside the 'overseas persons' exemptions (see ¶303) and without being FSA-authorised for it (see ¶356), except that ISD credit institutions may perhaps not be passporting firms in relation to their ISD passport, but only in relation to their 2BCD passport, (see ¶357). Non-UK EEA firms only providing FSA-regulated investment

¶302

services, or carrying on other FSA-regulated investment activities, falling within the exemptions in Pt. III of Sch. 1 are not carrying on FSA-regulated investment business, and are therefore not subject to the FSA's authorisation requirement anyway; they are accordingly not using their passport, and therefore are not passporting firms, when doing so;

(11) 'ISD credit institution' means a non-UK EEA bank or other credit institution which is an EEA investment firm but is excluded from the ISD passport because it is authorised to provide core investment services under its banking licence. ISD credit institutions have been granted by the Treasury, in addition to their 2BCD passport, a passport equivalent to the ISD passport which, as from 1 January 1996 and without any need to notify UK regulators, enables them to carry on in the UK FSA-regulated investment business which is covered by the ISD passport, but not by the 2BCD passport, and for which they are authorised by their domestic regulator under the First and Second Banking Directives, without being FSA-authorised for it, and references to their ISD passport are references to that equivalent passport;

(12) 'passported' means covered by the ISD or the 2BCD single European passport or, in relation to ISD credit institutions, their ISD passport;

(13) the 'ISD' means the EU investment services directive of 10 May 1993, which grants a 'single European passport' to EEA investment firms for the services covered by it (most of which are FSA-regulated investment activities) and, as from 1 January 1996 and subject to their making the appropriate notifications to UK regulators, accordingly allows non-UK EEA investment firms from EEA member states which have implemented it to carry on FSA-regulated investment business in the UK which is covered by their ISD passport, and for which they are authorised by their domestic regulator under the ISD, without being FSA-authorised for it (see ¶356). EEA investment firms otherwise entitled to the ISD passport are excluded from it if they are credit institutions authorised to provide one or more ISD core investment services under their authorisation as a credit institution; however, if they are non-UK firms, they qualify as ISD credit institutions and the Treasury have granted them a passport equivalent to the ISD passport in relation to FSA-regulated investment business carried on by them in the UK, in addition to their 2BCD passport;

(14) the '2BCD' means the EU second banking coordination directive of 15 December 1989, which grants a 'single European passport' to EEA firms which are banks or other credit institutions for the activities

covered by it (including several FSA-regulated investment activities) and, as from 1 January 1993 and subject to their making the appropriate notifications to UK regulators, accordingly allows non-UK EEA credit institutions from EEA member states which have implemented it to carry on FSA-regulated investment business in the UK which is covered by their 2BCD passport, and for which they are authorised by their domestic regulator under the first and second banking directives, without being FSA-authorised for it (see ¶356). UK credit institutions are, in effect, authorised by the Bank of England for this purpose to carry on the FSA-regulated investment business covered by the 2BCD passport as credit institutions under the first and second banking directives if they are authorised to carry on that FSA-regulated investment business under the FSA;

(15) 'FSA-professional' means an FSA-authorised firm, an exempted firm (see ¶347), a passporting firm or a 'permitted person' (see ¶335), except that in relation to the 'overseas persons' exemptions (see ¶334), an exempted firm is an FSA-professional only in the case of transactions within its exemption and 'permitted persons' are not FSA-professionals; and

(16) 'non-professional' means a firm which is neither an FSA-professional nor, in relation to the own account exemptions (see ¶331 and ¶332 below), a qualifying overseas securities firm; the typical non-professional is a private individual or, importantly, in particular, a firm with a UK head office which carries on FSA-regulated investment activities only within the 'own account' exemptions from the FSA's authorisation requirement, such as an investment trust.

¶303   Over-view

It is fair to say that most of the businesses which one would colloquially call 'investment businesses' need to be authorised (or, licensed) under the Financial Services Act if their function is, in general terms, to provide investment services to clients (including dealing on their behalf or with them as counterparty) and that, conversely, private individuals will not need to be FSA-authorised if they merely dabble from time to time on the London Stock Exchange for their own account. The problems come with what lies between these two extremes. All transactions on an investment exchange are normally within the FSA's 'own account' exemptions, (see ¶331 and ¶332). It should, however, be emphasised that other own account transactions may need FSA-authorisation if they are with non-professionals; the counterparty needs to be protected, even though he is not a client and the firm is dealing on its own initiative and not as a service responding to investment enquiries (as in the case of market-makers or broker-dealers). This is because, despite the 'own account' exemptions, the FSA normally requires the firm to be authorised in these circumstances for dealings in securities as principal if it 'regularly solicits' non-professionals; it should be allowed to solicit non-professionals regularly only if it is FSA-authorised. It is significant that the FSA refers in this context to the solicitation of 'members of the public' and important that it defines them not as 'private investors' but, instead, as everyone except FSA-professionals and qualifying overseas securities firms (or, in an attempt to be helpful, where qualifying large holdings are involved). Indeed, in the case of derivatives, all own account transactions may need FSA-authorisation, even if they are not solicited by the firm, if the firm is FSA-authorised for other activities or the counterparty is a non-professional, unless, in this latter case, an FSA-professional or a qualifying overseas securities firm arranges the transaction.

Accordingly, off-exchange own account dealings in securities may need FSA-authorisation unless the counterparty is an FSA-professional or is an overseas securities firm solicited at an office outside the UK. Passporting firms are FSA-professionals for this purpose; the exemptions can therefore apply even if they are solicited at their UK offices for passported transactions. The only safe practice for City institutions which wish to avoid having to be FSA-authorised for their own account off-exchange dealings in securities is therefore to confine their transactions to FSA-authorised firms (and other FSA-professionals). Whether FSA-authorisation is necessary for particular investment transactions or other activities is probably the most difficult question in the whole FSA system of investor protection and requires a detailed review of all the investment activities which it is intended to engage in. This detailed review is now even more important because the scope of many of the FSA exemptions has been narrowed in order to comply with the investment services directive (see ¶330). This review will need to be repeated before any new kind of activity is entered into because, as will be seen, the FSA-authorisation obtained for some investment activities may not be sufficient for others.

This Chapter seeks to explain the very complicated questions and analyses that are relevant to determining whether a particular activity needs FSA-authorisation; this in essence depends on whether:

(1) the activity concerned is FSA-regulated (see ¶302);

(2) the activity relates to investments to which the FSA applies (see ¶306);

(3) any exemption is available (see ¶307); and

(4) whether carrying on the FSA-regulated activities relating to FSA-regulated investments outside the exemptions provided by the FSA

constitutes the carrying on of a business in the UK (see ¶304, ¶310 and ¶311).

Investment activities accordingly need to be authorised under the Financial Services Act if, in short, they constitute FSA-regulated investment activities falling outside all the exemptions provided by the FSA and (when taken together) they are carried on as a business in the UK. In general terms, exactly the same test applies to determine whether the investment activity is regulated by the rules of the SIB or an SRO, which normally apply only to FSA-regulated investment business needing FSA-authorisation. However, r. 1.02(1) of the *Financial Services (Conduct of Business) Rules* 1990 provides that the SIB conduct of business rules apply also to own account transactions by a firm regulated by it which are exempted by the 'own account' exemptions in para. 17 of Sch. 1 to the FSA (see ¶331 and ¶332). Importantly, this approach has been followed by SFA (see r. 5-1(1)(d) of the SFA Rules), although not by IMRO. Accordingly, firms which are members of SROs, or directly regulated by the SIB, also need to review their activities in light of Sch. 1 to see if they are subject to regulation and whether particular activities have to be included in their permitted business or business profile; passporting firms are directly regulated by the SIB for their passported investment business unless they join an SRO or become listed money market institutions for it (see ¶357). In addition, the SIB and SROs now regulate ISD 'non-core services' even if they do not themselves require FSA-authorisation (see ¶330 and ¶358). It is hoped that this chapter will therefore be of help to FSA-authorised firms and to passporting firms as well as to firms trying to decide whether they need to be authorised under the Financial Services Act for particular investment activities.

Section 3 of the Financial Services Act requires a firm to be FSA-authorised only if it carries on FSA-regulated investment business 'in the United Kingdom' (see ¶310–¶311) and only if it is not exempted from the FSA's authorisation requirement. FSA-regulated investment business will be carried on in the UK for the purposes of s. 3 if either of two different conditions is fulfilled. The first relates to firms which carry on FSA-regulated investment business from a permanent place of business maintained by them in the UK (s. 1(3)(a)) and the second to firms which do not, at least if they are not 'exempted persons' in respect of it, for example under the 'money market' exemption (s. 1(3)(b)). Section 1(3)(a) provides that a firm carries on FSA-regulated investment business in the UK if it does so from its own office (or, branch) in the UK. Section 1(3)(b) is a 'disguised' exemption for overseas firms, which the FSA terms 'overseas persons', (Sch. 1, para. 26 and 27); it provides that they require FSA-authorisation only for certain kinds of FSA-regulated investment business they carry on in the UK. An FSA-regulated investment activity carried on (or, engaged in) in the UK which falls

¶303

outside both the tests in s. 1(3) is therefore treated in this Chapter as entitled to the FSA's (additional) exemptions for overseas firms; these exemptions are contained in Pt. IV of Sch. 1 and apply only to overseas firms, whether UK or non-UK, (see ¶334).

Even a firm carrying on FSA-regulated investment business in the UK may, however, not need FSA-authorisation. First, it may fall within one of the FSA's special exemptions for 'exempted persons', which exempt firms in very tightly-defined circumstances (see ¶347). The key exemption is that for listed money market institutions which apply to and are approved by the Bank of England for the purpose (see ¶349); the exemption applies only to a very narrow range of transactions (essentially, qualifying transactions entered into outside an RIE and relating to short-term debt securities or currencies or to derivatives linked to them). The exemption is not available to passporting firms even if they are listed money market institutions (as they do not need to be FSA-authorised for transactions within their passport), although they will be exempted persons for FSA-regulated investment business outside their passport which falls within the 'money market', or any other, exemption. Practically all listed institutions are in fact FSA-authorised for activities outside this very narrow exemption; accordingly, the only real benefit in practice of being a listed institution is normally that the Bank of England is substituted for the SIB or SRO as the primary conduct of business regulator. Secondly, non-UK EEA firms are exempted for business carried on under their single European passport, even from a UK office, or, in the case of non-UK EEA insurance companies, are automatically FSA-authorised for it (see ¶357). It should, however, be emphasised that many FSA-regulated investment activities fall outside the passport and non-UK EEA firms may therefore need 'top-up' FSA-authorisation for those activities.

Importantly, the 'overseas persons' exemptions can still be used by non-UK EEA firms even if the FSA-regulated investment activities concerned would have been covered by the passport (see below). Accordingly, the ISD and 2BCD passports are only needed for activities carried on in the UK if they fall outside not only the 'normal' exemptions in Pt. III of Sch. 1 but also the 'overseas persons' exemptions; if all the FSA-regulated investment activities of the non-UK EEA firm carried on in the UK fall within those exemptions, it is treated as not carrying on FSA-regulated investment business 'in the UK' and therefore does not need to be FSA-authorised, and is not FSA-regulated, for those activities anyway. Accordingly, the regulations implementing the two passports both provide that, although in effect the passports exclude the FSA's authorisation requirement whether or not it applies, the non-UK EEA firm is only FSA-regulated for FSA-regulated investment business carried on by it in the UK as a passporting firm, and so under the passport but outside the 'overseas persons' exemptions (see ¶356); similarly, the non-UK EEA firm is not treated as an 'exempted person' for business carried on by it as a passporting firm.

¶304   Carrying on a business

The requirement that an FSA-regulated investment activity falling outside the exemptions in Pt. III and Pt. IV of Sch. 1 must be carried on in the UK as a business in order for the investment activity to require FSA-authorisation is misleading. It does not confine regulation only to investment businesses in colloquial parlance (and was clearly not intended to). Instead, it is looking at the other end of the spectrum, and seeking merely to exclude from the need for FSA-authorisation firms which enter into FSA-regulated investment transactions or engage in other FSA-regulated investment activities only on isolated occasions or where they are not doing so by way of business.

A firm may carry on a business in legal terms on the basis of far less activity than in colloquial terms and much seems to depend on the purpose of the legislation concerned. Essentially, however, a firm will carry on a business if it engages in the relevant activities with repetition and continuity rather than only on one or several isolated occasions (*Edgelow v MacElwee* [1918] 1 KB 205). Indeed, the draftsman of the *Consumer Credit Act* 1974 even thought it necessary to provide expressly in s. 189(2) of that Act that a firm is not to be treated as carrying on a business 'merely because occasionally [it] enters into transactions belonging to a business ...'; similarly, the insider dealing provisions of the *Criminal Justice Act* 1993 define a 'professional intermediary' as a firm which carries on the specified activities as a business and, again, s. 59(3)(b) of that Act provides that a firm does not carry on a business consisting of a specified activity merely because it 'occasionally conducts one of those activities'. It is arguable, however, that, even if an activity is engaged in only once (for example, marketing a particular share issue), it may still be carried on as a business if it is carried on over a lengthy period.

The FSA's authorisation requirement does not apply unless the firm carries on 'investment business' in the UK (s. 3). The FSA defines 'investment business' as the business of engaging in FSA-regulated investment activities outside the exemptions in Pt. III of Sch. 1 and these include, for example, the business of merely offering to buy or sell investments or to give investment advice (s. 1(2) and Pt. II of Sch. 1). This makes it clear that activities can constitute a business for this purpose even though they are merely preparatory to the substantive activities. If the FSA did not have such a wide definition of 'investment business' it would be likely that, if a firm merely solicits business for itself in the UK (with the substantive business carried on only outside the UK), that soliciting would not in itself constitute carrying on a business in the UK (see, for example, *Vogel v R & A. Kohnstamm Limited* [1973] QB 133).

However, as the FSA does define 'investment business' as including the business of offering or agreeing to carry on the substantive activity, that must over-rule this line of cases. When the Financial Services Act was first introduced as a bill, it required authorisation if the specified activities were carried on 'by way of business'; while the bill was going through parliament, the test was changed to that of carrying on the business of engaging in the specified activities, but it would seem that this was to exclude occasional business activities rather than to change the required quality of the activities themselves. It is therefore suggested that, if a firm carries on FSA-regulated investment activities outside the Pt. III exemptions on several occasions as a 'regular' or 'normal' activity (so that it is not 'unusual' for the firm to carry them on), it will usually be regarded as carrying on the business of engaging in them (and so carrying on FSA-regulated investment business) unless it can be shown that they are carried on privately and not for reward, whether direct or indirect, or for other commercial reasons. Moreover, when considering whether FSA-regulated investment activities are entered into only on isolated occasions or as a business, it is necessary to look at all of them taken together rather than at each different type of FSA-regulated investment activity separately; the Financial Services Act refers to the business of engaging in 'one or more' of such activities (s. 1(2)).

The traditional common law approach is to review all the facts and determine whether the indicia of a business are more important than the factors which indicate that no business is being carried on. For the reasons outlined above, this balancing act will in practice be needed in only the marginal cases and normally only in order to establish that no business is being carried on. Because of the 'own account' exemptions (see ¶331), securities transactions entered into as principal are normally excluded from the FSA's authorisation requirement even if they are carried on as a business, for example, by an investment trust. If, however, the firm enters into transactions in securities with 'members of the public' as a result of regularly soliciting them (so that the 'own account' exemptions do not apply), the question of whether the firm is carrying on a business may be vital.

A very important factor to be taken into account in relation to investment services, such as advice, is whether they are provided on a commercial basis or only 'between friends'. The absence of any monetary reward is not in itself determinative if there are other commercial or 'public' reasons for providing the service (*Rolls v Miller* (1884) 27 Ch. 71 CA); however, it is, of course, normally an important indication that no business is being carried on, at least if no other benefit is being obtained. Conversely, the fact that the activity is engaged in by a company is prima facie evidence that it is carried on as a business; it has even been held in one Privy Council tax case (per Lord Diplock) that 'in the case of a company incorporated for the purpose of making profits

¶304

for its shareholders any gainful use to which it puts any of its assets prima facie amounts to the carrying on of a business' (*American Leaf Blending Co Sdn Bhd v Director-General of Inland Revenue* [1979] AC 676 PC at p. 684). It should also be noted that, in relation to the test of whether a particular transaction was entered into 'by way of business' for the purposes of s. 63 of the FSA (validation of gaming contracts), it has been held that the appropriate distinction is between a business transaction and something personal or casual, so that a local authority could enter into debt management transactions, or transactions seeking to obtain a profit for the local authority, 'by way of business' (*Morgan Grenfell v Welwyn Hatfield District Council* [1995] All ER1). Finally, the Investment Services Directive imposes its authorisation requirement on firms which provide the services covered by it either as their business or even merely as their 'regular occupation'; it is significant that the Treasury saw no need to expand the FSA's authorisation requirement similarly, presumably on the basis that the FSA's formulation was already wide enough to include this. It is therefore likely that an activity carried on by one member of a group of companies without remuneration but for the benefit of other members of the group or their clients may be regarded as carried on as a business for the purposes of the FSA's authorisation requirement if it is carried on regularly as a 'normal' activity, for example, in the case of a group nominee company used by a stockbroker.

A firm may therefore be regarded as carrying on the business of engaging in FSA-regulated investment activities even though it is not an 'investment business' in colloquial terms and even though that is not its main business. Indeed, this is implicit in the terms of the 'own account' exemptions (see ¶331) and is expressly stated in the 'permitted persons' exemption (see ¶335). It may perhaps help with an understanding of the expressions 'carrying on the business of engaging in FSA-regulated investment activities' or 'carrying on FSA-regulated investment business' to paraphrase them for the reasons explained above as 'carrying on FSA-regulated investment activities as a "normal" activity (that is, one which is not "unusual") and in a commercial or business context'.

The position can therefore be summarised as follows. If a firm does not engage in FSA-regulated investment activities in the UK as a business, it does not need FSA-authorisation. Conversely, if it does, it may need to be FSA-authorised unless it confines its UK FSA-regulated investment activities to those falling in the exemptions in Pt. III (and, in the case of overseas firms, Pt. IV) of Sch. 1 or, alternatively, carrying on the FSA-regulated investment activities falling outside these exemptions does not constitute the carrying on of a business. This is why it is so crucial to review whether an FSA-regulated investment activity falls within an exemption or, exceptionally, the investments concerned are outside the Financial Services Act altogether.

¶304

¶305 The different kinds of exemption

The FSA is in itself a very complicated statute but it is founded on a relatively simple concept: if a firm carries on FSA-regulated investment business in the UK, it normally needs FSA-authorisation (s. 3). For this purpose, 'FSA-regulated investment business carried on in the United Kingdom' is, in general terms, one or more of the investment activities specified in Pt. II of Sch. 1 which fall outside the exemptions contained in Pt. III or Pt. IV of Sch. 1 and which, taken together, are carried on as a business in the UK from the firm's UK office or with clients or counterparties who are in the UK. Pt. III contains the normal exemptions for all firms. Pt. IV provides detailed additional exemptions for overseas firms (see ¶334). There are, in addition, special exemptions for 'exempted persons', such as listed money market institutions (see ¶349) and appointed representatives (see ¶350).

It is important to be aware of the reasons for these three layers of exemptions. If an FSA-regulated investment activity falls within the exemptions contained in Pt. III, it does not constitute 'investment business' even if it is carried on as a business and, accordingly, no FSA-authorisation is needed for it. The exemptions in Pt. IV acknowledge that the investment activity can constitute 'investment business', but provide that the activity is treated as not carried on 'in the United Kingdom' and therefore does not need FSA-authorisation even if it does. Finally, the special exemptions for 'exempted persons' acknowledge that, again, the investment activities can constitute FSA-regulated investment business, but nonetheless provide that, in relation to those firms, no FSA-authorisation is required in the specified circumstances even if the business is treated as carried on in the United Kingdom.

There is in fact an even more sophisticated layer of exemptions. Several exemptions are contained not in Pt. III but in Pt. II, in the very definition of the FSA-regulated investment activity. The difference is important. An activity exempted in Pt. II, such as introductions to an FSA-authorised investment manager (note 6 to para. 13), is outside the regulatory scope of the FSA altogether. Conversely, activities exempted by Pt. III (or, *a fortiori,* Pt. IV) are nonetheless FSA-regulated investment activities. Accordingly, even though they do not require FSA-authorisation, they are subject to the FSA's investment advertisements and cold-calling rules (see Ch. 9), which the activities exempted in Pt. II are not. An important new consequence of this distinction is that the restrictions on FSA exemptions imposed as a result of the UK's implementation of the ISD (see ¶330) apply only to specified Pt. III exemptions and do not apply to the exemptions contained in Pt. II itself.

Superimposed on the FSA's own architecture are the 'exemptions' constituted by the single European passports granted under art. 52 and 59 of the Treaty of Rome to all non-UK EEA firms, under the ISD to non-UK EEA investment firms and under the 2BCD to non-UK EEA banks and other credit institutions (see ¶356). The passport granted to non-UK EEA insurance companies under the third insurance directives has been implemented differently, by giving them automatic FSA-authorisation for their passported investment business under s. 22 of the FSA (see ¶357).

¶306   FSA-regulated investments

The authorisation regime established by the FSA applies not only to securities but also to the other investments listed in Pt. I of Sch. 1, for example, financial and commodity futures and options on them (even if cash-settled), currency and precious metals options, 'speculative' forward foreign exchange contracts, life policies taken out as investments, personal pension policies and units in unit trusts (and participations in limited partnerships, shares in mutual funds or other open-ended investment companies and interests in other collective investment schemes) even if they invest in land or in other assets which are not themselves FSA-regulated investments, and rights to or interests in any of these investments (except in the case of interests under occupational pension schemes). The FSA also makes it clear that certificates of deposit are to be treated as debt securities (technically, 'debentures'), thus overriding the arguments of those who argued that they are not debt securities but merely banking documents. As required by the ISD, bankers acceptances (or, bills of exchange accepted by bankers) are treated as if they were debt securities for the purposes of the FSA, although they are not treated as such for the purposes of the *Public Offers of Securities Regulations* 1995 (para. 22 of Sch. 10 to the *Investment Services Regulations* 1995, SI 1995/3275), which normally apply to all the corporate securities covered by the FSA.

¶307   Exemptions

The FSA brought many sectors of the financial services industry under statutory regulation for the first time. However, the FSA clearly cannot seek to regulate everyone merely because they buy or sell investments; a private investor on the London Stock Exchange needs to be protected, not regulated. The FSA accordingly provides a key 'own account' exemption for transactions as principal with FSA-professionals, at least where it is only FSA-professionals who are solicited, (see ¶331 and ¶332) and also a multitude of other exemptions to cover those situations where (for commercial or other reasons) the counterparty, or the person on whose behalf the firm is acting, does not need protection (see ¶329–¶346). The FSA provides exemptions from the FSA's authorisation requirement either by qualifying the description of the investment which is FSA-regulated or by providing that no FSA-authorisation is required for particular FSA-regulated investment activities carried on in particular circumstances or by particular kinds of firm; these exemptions are precisely defined and therefore need to be reviewed in detail when deciding whether or not FSA-authorisation is necessary or, in the case of FSA-authorised firms or passporting firms, the service or activity is regulated under the FSA.

It is vital to realise that the FSA treats as investors needing protection not only the Aunt Agathas of this world but also, normally, City institutions and major trading and manufacturing companies, unless they are FSA-professionals. There is no specific exemption in the Financial Services Act for transactions with UK professional securities investors or large corporations (except in the case of own account dealings by overseas firms), and that has major implications when it comes to considering whether or not FSA-authorisation is required.

¶308   Employees and agents

Under the Financial Services Act, employees do not need their own FSA-authorisation. FSA-authorisation is not required unless the firm carries on the business of engaging in FSA-regulated investment activities, and an employee does not carry on a business; it is his employer who does. Instead, the rules of SROs in effect make FSA-authorised firms responsible for the selection and monitoring of suitable employees.

The position of consultants and seconded employees is more controversial. Although the FSA does not refer to consultants expressly, a consultant who carries on an FSA-regulated investment activity as part of the services he provides to a firm will normally not need his own FSA-authorisation. In the normal case, and subject to what the consultancy agreement provides, his business is the provision of his services to the firm and, when he carries on the FSA-regulated investment activity, he is doing so as part of the firm's business rather than his own. The consultant will normally be engaged to represent the firm in its business with third parties or the marketing of investments. As such, the consultant should be treated as an employee of the firm for regulatory (although not tax) purposes; this is preferable to seeking to make him an appointed representative of the firm, which is rather more restrictive (see ¶350) and, in any event, is not appropriate in these circumstances as the consultant is not carrying on his own business but is merely acting in the firm's name as part of the firm. This applies equally in the case of seconded employees, and is indeed more clearly the case; the seconding employer is not carrying on an FSA-regulated investment activity by seconding the employee (but is merely providing the services of the employee to the firm to which the employee is seconded) and, accordingly, does not require FSA-authorisation for the secondment. Investors are nonetheless protected because in these circumstances the SIB and SROs treat the consultant or seconded employee as an employee of the firm for which he carries on the FSA-regulated investment activity for the purposes of their conduct of business rules.

In contrast, there is no general 'status' exemption for firms which carry on business on behalf of another firm. Under the Financial Services Act, anyone who carries on an FSA-regulated investment activity as a business in the UK normally requires his own FSA-authorisation, unless one of the FSA's exemptions applies to the transaction concerned (see ¶329–¶346). This is also the case even though he may carry on that business on behalf of someone else. Accordingly, if one firm delegates its function as a stockbroker or investment manager to another to act on its behalf, that other firm also normally needs to be FSA-authorised for carrying on that business. The one exception to this general rule is in the case of appointed representatives, and this exception does not apply to transactions but applies only to advisory and 'arranging' services (see ¶350); however, this is an exception in only some cases because the appointed representative does not normally carry on business belonging to his principal, on behalf of his principal, but instead carries on his own business of providing the relevant services, albeit for the benefit of his principal. It is, perhaps, noteworthy that the ISD takes the same approach as the FSA, with the same exception for where, as in the case of an appointed representative, one firm carries on the business of 'receiving and transmitting orders' for the account (or, benefit) of another in qualifying circumstances (see ¶350).

This scenario also gives rise to FSA-authorisation problems the other way round. The firm which owns the business ('the principal') may in law be carrying on business through the agent (*Bedford Insurance Co Ltd v Instituto de Resseguros do Brasil* [1984] 3 All ER 766, *Stewart v Oriental Fire and Marine Insurance Co Ltd* [1984] 3 All ER 777 and *DR Insurance Co v Seguros America Banamex* [1993] 1 Lloyd's Reps. 120) In some cases, the courts express this by saying that it is carrying on business 'by' the agent (*The Lalandia* [1933] p. 56). Whether one firm is in fact to be treated as carrying on business on behalf of another (rather than merely entering into particular transactions or carrying on particular activities on its behalf), so that its transactions and activities are to be attributed to that other, is always a question of fact (see *The Lalandia*, above); this would seem to apply also in relation to whether the agent's UK office should also be treated as the office of his principal. Accordingly, not only the agent but also the principal may need FSA-authorisation for the same activities. This may be of great significance where the principal is carrying on FSA-regulated investment activities through the agent from the agent's UK office and hopes to qualify as an overseas firm. If the facts are sufficient, the principal would seemingly be regarded as carrying on FSA-regulated investment activities in the UK through the agent from what is, indirectly, the principal's UK office and accordingly would not be entitled to the 'overseas persons' exemptions (see ¶334); this is the case even if the agent is an

FSA-authorised firm. It is, though, unclear whether the SIB accepts this analysis or is willing to take enforcement action against the principal.

It is likely that the fundamental test for attribution (although it is not actually spelt out in the cases) is whether the agent carries on substantially the whole of his business on behalf of the principal (rather than carrying on his own business in which he acts as an agent, as a stockbroker does for his clients), or, at least, whether the agent's activities on behalf of the principal are so extensive and important as to constitute the carrying on of business on his behalf (*DR Insurance*). A key consequence of this relationship is that the commissions and profits earned by the agent in the business which he carries on on behalf of his principal 'belong' to the principal and the agent's only remuneration is his agency fee (however it is described). It is important (and difficult) to identify the business that the agent is actually carrying on. If he does not enter into transactions on behalf of the principal but, like an introducing broker, merely solicits business on his behalf (so that he is strictly not an agent at all), it is by no means clear that the agent's activities should necessarily be attributed to the principal even if that is all that the agent does; however, the prudent view unless the facts are very clear is that they should be. In some circumstances, the agent's activities are attributed by the FSA to the principal even if this 'attribution' test is not met (see s. 44(7) in the case of soliciting by appointed representatives). Even if they are not attributed, the principal may in effect be liable for the defaults of the agent in any event; if the principal relied on the agent to discharge the principal's regulatory or contractual obligations, the failure by the agent to do so means that the principal is accordingly also in default. The question of whether the agent's soliciting should be attributed to the principal is important, in particular, in determining whether the principal is to be treated as offering in the UK to enter into the investment transactions or to carry on other FSA-regulated investment activities which his agent solicits or markets in the UK; if he is, he may require FSA-authorisation even if all his substantive transactions or other activities are outside the UK.

¶309   Alteration of conditions for FSA-authorisation

The government is given the power to alter the conditions for FSA-authorisation and, indeed, the applicability of the Financial Services Act generally by secondary legislation without the need for a new statute (s. 2). This power is important as a means of keeping up with developments in the financial markets and for targeting more precisely the activities sought to be FSA-regulated and has already been used several times (see ¶312). The government's powers in this area cannot be delegated to a designated agency such as the SIB. Similarly, the government has been able to make the changes required by the EU financial institutions 'single market' directives by secondary legislation under the *European Communities Act* 1972, as extended to non-EU EEA firms by the *European Economic Area Act* 1993 (see ¶357).

TERRITORIAL LIMITATIONS

¶310   Carrying on FSA-regulated investment business in the UK

The Financial Services Act requires a firm to be authorised (or exempted) if it carries on FSA-regulated investment business 'in the United Kingdom' but not otherwise (s. 3). It will be treated as carrying on FSA-regulated investment business in the UK if it meets either of two separate tests, depending on whether or not it has a UK office (or, branch) for FSA-regulated investment business. First, if the firm carries on FSA-regulated investment business from a permanent place of business maintained by it (rather than, for example, by its independent stockbroker) in the UK (s. 1(3)(a)), even if all its clients or other customers are outside the UK. This wording would seem to include any sort of office, whether freehold, leasehold or merely rented, and whether it is 'permanent' will depend on the facts. It would seem that an office can be 'maintained' by a firm if it is regarded in practice as the firm's office, even if the firm does not directly pay any rent or expenses itself. Thus a company has 'an established place of business in England' for the purposes of the 'registration of charges' provisions of the *Companies Act* 1985 if it has 'some more or less permanent location [in England]', not necessarily owned or even leased by the company, but at least associated with the company and from which habitually or with some degree of regularity business is conducted (*Re Oriel* [1985] 3 A11 ER 216 CA per Oliver LJ at p. 220). Secondly, and even if it does not carry on FSA-regulated investment business from a UK office maintained by it, if the firm engages in FSA-regulated investment activities in the UK which fall outside both the exemptions in Pt. III of Sch. 1 and a series of special 'overseas persons' exemptions for overseas firms, which are contained in Pt. IV of Sch. 1, and by engaging in those non-exempted activities it is carrying on a business in the UK in the sense described in ¶304 (s. 1(3)(b)). If the firm does not fall in either s. 1(3)(a) or s. 1(3)(b), it does not need FSA-authorisation even if it carries on investment business with UK customers and, indeed, even if it does so on occasional visits to the UK. These special exemptions for overseas firms have been brought in to avoid frightening away overseas firms and will be reviewed later (see ¶334).

The 'overseas persons' exemptions apply, and accordingly an overseas firm is not treated as carrying on in the UK the FSA-regulated investment activities covered by them, in certain circumstances even if the firm does in fact have a

UK office. This is the case if the overseas firm uses the UK office to carry on only activities falling outside the FSA (for example, taking deposits), activities which are exempted from the FSA's authorisation requirement (for example, in the normal case and assuming that the firm does not hold itself out as a market-maker or dealer in the kind of securities concerned (see ¶331), effecting transactions in securities only if they are entered into as principal with FSA-authorised firms) or, probably, activities in relation to which the firm is an 'exempted person' and accordingly is exempted from the need to be authorised under the FSA (for example, activities within the 'money market' exemption if the firm is approved by the Bank of England as a listed institution), although this is not clear (see below).

It would seem that FSA-regulated investment business carried on by a listed institution under the 'money market' exemption is disregarded for the purposes of the 'overseas persons' exemptions, although this is not spelled out expressly, (para. 32 of Sch. 1); the 'overseas persons' exemptions can therefore probably apply even if the 'money market' exempted activities are carried on from a UK office. However, although it is, again, not clear, FSA-regulated investment business carried on under the single European passport is seemingly not disregarded for this purpose; carrying it on from a UK office (rather than on a cross-border basis) may therefore exclude the 'overseas persons' exemptions in relation to other FSA-regulated investment activities carried on from non-UK offices. This problem is aggravated by the fact that, in effect, the 'money market' exemption does not apply to passported investment business by passporting firms (see ¶357). If a passporting firm carries on FSA-regulated investment business from a UK office under its passport, it therefore seems to exclude the 'overseas persons' exemptions in relation to FSA-regulated investment business the firm carries on from non-UK offices, even if the business carried on from the UK office would have fallen within the 'money market' exemption if it had not been covered by the passport; if the firm did not have a passport for these activities, the activities would not have excluded the 'overseas persons' exemptions because, as the firm would therefore have been an 'exempted person' in respect of them, they would have been disregarded (see above). This analysis applies to all the FSA's 'status' exemptions from the FSA's authorisation requirement (see ¶347) but in practice it is most likely to be a problem with the 'money market' exemption.

As explained above, a firm which carries on any FSA-regulated investment business from its own UK office will normally not be entitled to the 'overseas persons' exemptions for other FSA-regulated investment activities carried on by it in the United Kingdom, even if those other activities are not carried on from its UK office; it will not qualify as an 'overseas person' (see para. 26(1) of Sch.1). This is of great importance to firms which establish a UK office for some only of their FSA-regulated investment activities and are as a result FSA-

¶310

authorised; they may accordingly need to be FSA-authorised for other FSA-regulated investment activities carried on in the UK only from non-UK offices. However, the position is mitigated in practice to a substantial extent because the SIB and SROs have limited the territorial scope of their conduct of business rules so far as those other activities are concerned. For example, the SFA and IMRO conduct of business rules normally do not apply to activities from a non-UK office within the 'foreign business carve-out'; these are activities which would have been within the 'overseas persons' exemptions if the firm had not maintained an office in the UK for FSA-regulated investment business. However, the SRO's marketing rules would normally apply, in particular the requirement to give private customers the 'prescribed disclosure' that FSA protections do not apply to business from non-UK offices. In consequence, the firm can carry on this FSA-regulated investment business in the UK from a non-UK office only if it is permitted to do so by the SRO but the SRO will nonetheless normally not regulate the business. This 'exemption' from SRO rules applies to all non-UK offices wherever the firm is incorporated and is nothing to do with the single European passport for non-UK EEA firms; it is accordingly available to both EEA and non-EEA firms.

¶311   Where is investment business carried on?

It is often not at all clear where investment business is carried on for the purposes of securities regulation. The question is relevant to:

(1) the territorial scope of the FSA;

(2) the 'overseas persons' exemptions (see ¶334);

(3) the use of and need for the single European passport (see ¶356); and

(4) the requirement for non-UK EEA firms to notify UK regulators that they intend to provide or carry on ISD or 2BCD services or activities in the UK (see ¶356).

With regard to the scope of the FSA, the normal canons of statutory construction provide that UK statutes regulate only conduct in the UK unless something express is said (as it is, for example, in relation to the offence of misleading statements and practices in s. 47 of the FSA); in principle, therefore, investment activities are normally regulated by the FSA only if they are carried on (or, engaged in) in the UK. The 'overseas persons' exemptions provide exemptions from the FSA's authorisation requirement for specified investment activities carried on in the UK from non-UK offices by providing, in effect, that they are nonetheless to be treated as not carried on in the UK; in doing so, the 'overseas persons' exemptions may, indeed, perhaps extend the territorial reach of the FSA in relation to investment activities from non-UK offices outside the exemptions. Similarly, both the ISD and the 2BCD provide that the single European passport granted by it can be used, in relation to the UK, only if the non-UK EEA firm's service or activity is provided or carried on 'within' the UK; in addition, the ISD provides that the principal regulator of ISD services is the member state 'in which the service is provided' (which it refers to as the 'host member state'). Finally, the SIB (or the Bank of England) must normally be notified before any service or activity within the ISD or 2BCD passport is provided or carried on 'in' the UK by a non-UK EEA firm entitled to it, even if not under its passport, (see ¶356); the one exception is that ISD credit institutions do not need to notify services to be provided under their ISD passport (but outside their 2BCD passport).

The FSA does not spell out where activities are to be treated as carried on or services as provided; the ISD and the 2BCD also do not do so. It may therefore be helpful to provide a very general summary of what the position currently seems to be, although it is likely to be changed by agreement between the EU regulators in the near future (see below); in any event, the UK and appropriate non-UK regulators should be consulted where relevant. The position is clear where both the client or counterparty and the relevant executive of the firm are in the same country when the activity is carried on or service is provided by the firm (even if one is visiting the other from another country at the time); it is carried on or provided within the country where both are present. Much more difficult is the situation where they are in different countries and the firm carries on the activity or provides the service by a means of remote communication (for example, post, telephone, fax or screen), in EU language 'on a cross-border basis'. The traditional UK approach to the FSA-regulated investment activities is that:

(1) Where communication is instantaneous, transactions are normally to be treated as entered into where (and when) the acceptance of the offer to enter into the transaction is received by the offeror (in other words, where the offeror is), which assumes that the facts can identify which party is making the offer, rather than merely an invitation to treat (*Brinkibon Ltd v Stahag Stahl* [1982] 1 All ER 293, HL). This contrasts with the position where communication is not instantaneous, for example acceptances by post, which take effect when the acceptance is posted (and so before it is received) (*Adams v Lindsell* (1818), 1B & Ald. 681); the transaction is presumably entered into where the offeree is. A business is normally treated as carried on by a firm where its contracts, and in particular sales contracts, are entered into and not merely where independent commission agents receive and pass on orders (*Grainger v Gough* [1896] AC 325). However, this is not always determinative and much depends on the precise facts (*FL Smidth v Greenwood* [1922] 8 TC 193 HL), where the House of Lords held that, even where a firm used its

¶311

own UK branch to receive and pass on to the main office in Denmark orders for machinery, the firm did not carry on a trade 'in the UK' because the UK branch had no authority to enter into the contract for the order. It, must, however, be remembered that the FSA's authorisation requirement can apply even before the substantive business is actually begun (see ¶304).

(2) Advice is treated as given where it is received, in the same way as documents are treated as issued where they are received; it surely makes no difference whether the advice is ad hoc or results from reviewing a portfolio, even though different conduct of business rules may apply. However, it is unclear whether this necessarily leads to the conclusion that an investment advisory business is treated as carried on everywhere the clients are, although the 'overseas persons' exemption for investment advice would be otiose unless the draftsman thought that it is. The prudent view, at present, is that it is; this does indeed seem also to be the better view once it is understood that all that this expression means is that the firm carries on the FSA-regulated investment activity of giving advice on a frequent and regular basis as a 'normal' part of its activities and in a commercial or business context to investors who are in the UK or other country concerned (see ¶304).

(3) It seems clear that a discretionary investment management activity or service is carried on or provided where the firm is, as the client is not contacted except for marketing or reporting; there is therefore no 'overseas persons' exemption within para. 27 for the actual decision-taking but only for offering or agreeing to act as investment manager.

(4) It is, however, unclear where non-discretionary (or, advisory) investment management for UK clients is treated as carried on. As it is in a sense more akin to advice than discretionary management, the prudent view is that it is treated as carried on in the UK (see (2) above). However, it would seem reasonable to regard the business as carried on where the investment manager is, as in the case of discretionary management, because the advice is only part of the process and the fundamental service being provided is actually reviewing the portfolio and then implementing the reconstruction once accepted; this is especially the case where, as is normal, the investment manager actually enters into the recommended transaction himself and, in effect, is merely asking the client's permission to do so. If the business is treated as carried on in the UK because the client is in the UK, even though the investment manager is not, this is the worst of both worlds; it falls in para. 14 rather than para. 15 and, in contrast to advice within para. 15, there is no 'overseas persons' exemption for the substantive activity itself (see ¶334).

¶311

(5) The SIB is understood to have taken the helpful position that arranging activities are carried on where the 'arranger' is; this is likely to apply also in relation to the FSA-regulated investment activities relating to collective investment schemes and, arguably, custodial services.

All of this has now been thrown into the melting pot by the need to determine where services are provided or activities are carried on for the purpose of regulation under, and the passports granted by, the ISD and the 2BCD. As explained more fully in ¶360, the better view seems to be that services provided and activities carried on by a means of remote communication (even if not instantaneous) are to be treated for these purposes as provided or carried on where the relevant branch of the firm is located, rather than where the client is. This indeed is the view which currently is being advanced by the Treasury and the SIB, except for advisory services, and seems to have been regarded as persuasive by the EU Commission; the exception for advisory services, which has not been expressly referred to by the Commission, may well be dropped in due course. It is likely that whatever position is finally taken for the purposes of the EU directives throughout the EEA will be adopted by the UK for domestic purposes even in the case of non-EEA firms.

It must not, however, be forgotten that the FSA, importantly, usually requires a firm to be FSA-authorised if it is carrying on in the UK the business of offering or agreeing to carry on the substantive FSA-regulated investment activity, even if the substantive activity (for example, selling securities) is on the above tests carried on only outside the UK and even if offering to do so does not itself generate any income directly (see ¶304); decisions in cases such as *Grainger* and *Smidth* (see (1) above) must therefore be applied with great caution. It is also important to remember that the FSA in effect regards FSA-regulated investment business as carried on 'in the UK' wherever the client is if it is carried on 'from' a UK office (s. 1(3)(a)); it is therefore subject to the FSA's authorisation requirement even if, on the above tests, it is actually carried on outside the UK.

FSA-REGULATED INVESTMENT ACTIVITIES

¶312   Introduction

The Financial Services Act regulates eight different types of investment activity, assuming of course that they relate to FSA-regulated investments. These are listed in Pt. II of Sch. 1 and subsequent 'Extension of Scope of Act' Orders as follows:

(1) dealing in investments (see ¶313);

(2) arranging deals in investments (see ¶314);

(3) managing investments (see ¶315);

(4) advising on investments (see ¶316);

(5) establishing, operating or winding-up collective investment schemes (see ¶317);

(6) acting as depositary or sole director of a UK open-ended investment company (see ¶318);

(7) acting as a custodian or nominee (see ¶319); and

(8) acting as a sponsor in CREST (see ¶320).

Importantly, it is not only the substantive investment activity (for example, dealing) which is an FSA-regulated investment activity, but, normally, also even merely offering or agreeing to carry on that activity; the only exceptions are in the case of the FSA-regulated investment activities relating to collective investment schemes and UK open-ended investment companies (see (¶317 and ¶318). This means that FSA-authorisation may be needed even before a firm actually does any business. Merely offering to deal 'once FSA-authorised' may therefore be a criminal offence; this is exactly where the FSA's authorisation requirement and the FSA's investment advertisements regime (see Ch. 9) overlap. It may be strange to regard a firm as carrying on a business of offering or agreeing to enter into its own transactions, but it should be remembered that an activity carried on by a firm in a business or commercial context and on more than isolated occasions can itself constitute a business for this purpose, even if it does not earn any fee itself (see ¶304). The better (and certainly the prudent) view is that, for the purposes of the FSA's authorisation requirement, a firm can indeed be treated as carrying on the business of offering or agreeing to enter into its own transactions (or provide its own services) and accordingly may need FSA-authorisation in order to do so.

One consequence of this approach is that, as indicated above, FSA-authorisation may be needed earlier than might have been expected. More importantly, however, this approach brings within the FSA's reach firms which carry on business only outside the UK (for example, discretionary investment managers or agency stockbrokers without a UK office) but actively solicit customers in the UK; they will indeed be offering in the UK to manage investments or deal in investments as agent (albeit outside the UK). Accordingly, unless the 'overseas persons' exemptions apply (see ¶334), they may require FSA-authorisation even if all their transactions, and indeed the investment management or agency brokerage agreements, are entered into outside the UK. Indeed, the terms of the 'overseas persons' exemptions in para. 27 of Sch. 1 confirm this analysis, as they provide an exemption for qualifying FSA offers or agreements (for example, to manage investments) but,

¶312

except in the case of transactions and advice, not for the substantive activity itself; offers or agreements which do not fall within the 'overseas persons' exemptions (see ¶334) accordingly may need FSA-authorisation. If, as is normal, the substantive activity takes place outside the UK (see ¶311), it falls outside the FSA's jurisdiction without any need for an exemption.

Schedule 1 has been amended several times by the Government under powers granted by the FSA (see ¶322) in order to provide further exemptions from the need for FSA-authorisation. The initial amendments were contained in the *Financial Services Act 1986 (Restriction of Scope of Act) Order 1988* (SI 1988/318) and the *Financial Services Act 1986 (Restriction of Scope of Act and Meaning of Collective Investment Scheme) Order 1988* (SI 1988/803). In certain cases, the new exemptions were inserted into Pt. II, so qualifying the definition of the particular FSA-regulated investment activity, rather than put into Pt. III, where most of the exemptions appear. This is because the activities concerned are intended to fall outside regulation altogether and, if the exemptions are merely put into Pt. III, they continue to constitute FSA-regulated investment activities, even though they do not need FSA-authorisation itself; for example, the FSA's investment advertisements regime would apply to them if the exemptions were in Pt. III but it does not apply to them once they are excluded from Pt. II altogether (s. 57 read together with s. 44(9)).

Conversely, the scope of the FSA has been extended by two amendments made by the *Financial Services Act 1986 (Extension of Scope of Act and Meaning of Collective Investment Scheme) Order 1988* (SI 1988/496), which added two additional precious metals (palladium and platinum) to the metals options over which constitute investments (see ¶323) and also restricted the 'supply of goods or services' exemption (see ¶341). The FSA has also been extended to cover, as from 15 July 1996, acting as a sponsor in CREST, the UK's new computerised book-entry settlement system for transactions on the London Stock Exchange, (the *Financial Services Act 1986 (Uncertificated Securities) (Extension of Scope of Act) Order 1996*, SI 1996/1322). The FSA also now covers, as from 6 January 1997, acting as a depositary or sole director of a UK open-ended investment company (an OEIC), a new addition to the UK's stable of collective investment scheme vehicles, and, as from 1 June 1997, acting as a custodian or nominee (the *Financial Services Act 1986 (Extension of Scope of Act) Order 1996*, SI 1996/2958).

Finally, several of the FSA exemptions in Pt. III of Sch. 1 have been restricted so as to comply with the authorisation requirements of the investment services directive (see ¶330). The order which restricted the exemptions, and so extended the scope of the FSA, (the *Financial Services Act 1986 (Investment Services) (Extension of Scope of Act) Order 1995*, SI 1995/3271) actually went further than was necessary and, accordingly, was itself restricted before it came into force, so far as the FSA's authorisation requirement was concerned, on

¶312

1 January 1997 (the *Financial Services Act 1986 (Restriction of Scope of Act and Meaning of Collective Investment Scheme) Order* 1996, SI 1996/2996). The restrictions on the FSA exemptions apply to all firms which provide 'core investment services' within the ISD outside the exemptions contained in art. 2(2) of the ISD, which are all listed in the 1995 order; importantly, this is the case whether or not those firms are EEA-incorporated, and even if they are banks or other credit institutions, but the restrictions do not apply to insurance companies (see further ¶330).

A firm does not need to be FSA-authorised merely because it engages in FSA-regulated investment activities; it has to be FSA-authorised only if it does so outside the exemptions provided by Pt. III and (in the case of overseas firms) Pt. IV of Sch. 1 to the FSA (see ¶329–¶346) and its doing so outside those exemptions constitutes the carrying on of FSA-regulated investment business in the UK (see ¶304 and ¶310). These FSA-regulated investment activities are also relevant for the FSA's on-going provisions, in particular those relating to the conduct of FSA-regulated investment business and marketing. This is why some of the definitions in Sch. 1 may seem strange if looked at only in the context of FSA-authorisation.

In addition to these eight investment activities, the FSA in certain circumstances also exceptionally treats the management of an occupational pension scheme by its trustees as FSA-regulated investment business (s. 191); an exemption may, however, apply (see ¶344).

¶313   Dealing in investments (Sch. 1, para. 12)

The first class of FSA-regulated investment activity is the buying and selling, and underwriting, of investments (para. 12). It is essential to realise that, although the FSA refers to this as 'dealing in investments', it does not cover only dealers or firms whose dealing constitutes trading for tax purposes; it also covers investors. In the sense in which it is used in para. 12, 'dealing' means buying, selling, subscribing for or underwriting investments, whether as principal (that is to say, for one's own account or as trustee) or as agent (for example, in the case of a stockbroker). Thus, if an investor merely bought or sold shares for his own account on the London Stock Exchange, he would still in principle be carrying on an FSA-regulated investment activity (although an exemption would apply).

A firm is treated as buying or selling investments if it acquires or disposes of them for valuable consideration (Sch. 1, para. 28(1)(d)). Accordingly, acquisitions or disposals otherwise than for cash are included. It is also treated as selling an investment if it enters into the obligation which gives rise to the investment, for example writing an option or a futures contract, or if it issues or creates the investment concerned, for example units in a unit trust (para. 28(2)). However, the issue of shares or debentures (or warrants or other instruments giving the right to subscribe them) does not in itself constitute the sale of an investment by the issuer except in the case of the issue of shares (or rights to subscribe shares) by an open-ended investment company (para. 28(3), as limited by para. 28(4)); a company therefore normally does not need to be FSA-authorised in order to issue its own shares or debt securities, although its marketing of them is nonetheless subject to the FSA's investment advertisements regime and ban on cold-calling (see Ch. 9).

In addition, the acceptance of loan notes, such as promissory notes, by the lender or his agent is also expressly excluded (note 1 to para. 12); the exemption also covers promissory notes or other debt securities relating to a guarantee or other financial accommodation. The making of the underlying loan is banking rather than investment business and accordingly the acceptance by the lender of a loan note or other debt security creating or acknowledging the loan (which is used in order to make it easier to sue on the loan) is also outside the FSA's authorisation requirement; similarly, issuing the loan note is also exempted as this constitutes the issue of a debenture, which is not an FSA-regulated investment activity (see above). A loan agreement is itself also not a 'debenture' for the purposes of the FSA; this is the case even though a secured loan agreement is often called a 'debenture'. The exemption for accepting loan notes also makes this clear; if a loan agreement were a debenture for FSA purposes, this exemption would be otiose as the lender would accordingly usually have needed FSA-authorisation in any event for the underlying loan agreement. However, the subsequent sale and purchase of the loan note are FSA-regulated investment activities, as in the case of other debt securities; the syndication of the loan may therefore constitute an FSA-regulated investment activity if it involves the assignment of the loan note (although the 'own account' exemptions would usually apply, see ¶331).

A firm will also fall within para. 12 if it merely offers to buy or sell investments or invites applications to do so. The FSA makes it clear that a firm may fall within para. 12 even though it establishes a clever legal structure in which only the proposed counter-party actually makes the technical offer (even if that can in fact always be achieved in the real world in cases where no application form is used); the FSA provides that 'offer' includes an invitation to treat, in other words an invitation to the prospective counter-party to make the actual offer (Sch. 1, para. 28(1)(c)). However, the exclusion of the issue of shares or debentures (and subscription rights relating to them) from the definition of 'selling' equally applies to such offers or invitations by the issuer. Conversely, the offer of its shares (or of instruments giving a right to subscribe them) by an open-ended investment company does constitute an FSA-regulated investment activity. The new UK class of open-ended investment company needs FSA-authorisation for this reason in a similar way to unit trusts, but, in contrast to unit trusts, must be FSA-authorised as a firm (in addition to

¶313

being authorised, as in the case of unit trusts, as a product) even if there is no offer to the general public within s. 76(1) (see Ch. 9); it is, accordingly, FSA-authorised automatically under a new s. 23A (see ¶318).

However, if a firm enters into an investment transaction in the name of its client, or offers or agrees to do so, or markets investments to be sold directly by a client (such as the issuer) to the investor, it is not itself buying or selling, or offering or agreeing itself to buy or sell the investment, but only offering or agreeing that its client will do so; this offer accordingly falls outside para. 12. However, it is exactly in this case that para. 13 may apply (see ¶314). Where the firm deals in the name of its client, it will, however, probably be regarded as effecting the transaction for the purposes of the SIB's or its SRO's conduct of business rules, even though this technically falls outside para. 12.

¶314   Arranging deals in investments (Sch. 1, para. 13)

The second FSA-regulated investment activity is described as 'arranging deals in investments' (para. 13); it covers making arrangements with a view to the effecting of investment transactions and seems directed at firms which match buyers and sellers, such as name-passing brokers, but is actually rather wider. To avoid overlap with para. 12 (dealing), it is specifically provided that no one will be regarded as making arrangements with a view to the effecting of investment transactions to which he himself will be a party as principal or which he will enter into as agent (note 1); although the position is not clear, this would seem to cover not only the firm which actually executes an agreement or transaction but also all firms in the contractual chain, even if it is executed on their behalf by someone else, such as their stockbroker.

If a firm enters into investment transactions in the name of its client (rather than in its own name), it is unclear whether it falls within para. 12 or para. 13. If it enters into transactions in its own name, albeit as an agent, it will fall in para. 12; however, it would seem that doing so in the name of the client falls in para. 13. Paragraph 13 would clearly apply unless note 1 excludes it; however, although the firm is executing the agreement on behalf of the client as his agent, and in his name, it is very difficult to say that the firm is actually entering into the transaction, albeit as agent, (as required if it is to fall into note 1). Technically, all that the firm is doing is binding the client to the contract because the firm is, in effect, representing the client in entering into the transaction; note 1 surely applies only if the firm is itself in the contractual chain and in these circumstances it is not. The firm would therefore seem to fall in para. 13 despite note 1. In any event, the firm would not fall in para. 12 as it is not buying or selling as agent; it is not even offering or agreeing that it will do so, but only that the client will (see ¶313).

Paragraph 13 includes both making arrangements intended to bring about (or, for) a particular transaction (para. 13(a)) and making *a priori*

¶314

arrangements with a view to the effecting of investment transactions generally (para. 13(b)); however, in the former case, arrangements are covered only if they themselves bring about the transaction, or would do so if something else had not happened, such as transmitting to an issuer the application form signed by an investor, (note 2). Presumably, company marriage brokers are intended to fall within para. 13; however, they will not necessarily do so as merely effecting introductions without more does not seem enough to constitute 'making arrangements'. In addition, the introduction may not be something which 'would' in itself bring about the contemplated transaction, which is required for para. 13(a) arrangements (see note 2). However, if the introducer is also involved in the negotiations for the ultimate transaction, he would seem to be making arrangements for it within para. 13(a). If, moreover, the marriage broker or other intermediary makes arrangements with 'clients' to find or refer to them potential investee companies or counterparties (normally, in return for a fee), the making of those arrangements would in itself fall within para. 13(b).

This contrasts with the ISD and the 2BCD, which cover making para. 13(a) arrangements for particular transactions in existing securities (although, in the case of the 2BCD, only in limited circumstances) but does not expressly cover the making of these para. 13(b) *a priori* arrangements; however, if there is a passport for making arrangements for a particular transaction, it is perhaps unlikely that it would not also cover an *a priori* agreement with one of the parties to the transaction to make those arrangements, in the same way as the passport is treated by the UK regulators as covering not only the substantive FSA-regulated investment activity but also offering or agreeing to carry it on (see ¶356). Accordingly, arrangements can fall within para. 13 whichever side of the transaction they relate to, although arrangements with the seller are perhaps more likely to fall within para. 13(b) and those with the buyer within para. 13(a). This is important as arrangements made (or offered or agreed) with the seller by an intermediary acting from an office outside the UK to sell or offer investments on the seller's behalf to a buyer in the UK are likely to fall outside the FSA's territorial scope where the seller is outside the UK, but the consequent arrangements made by the intermediary with the buyer may be within the FSA's territorial reach because the buyer is in the UK. However, merely making an offer to the investor without more (for example, also sending in his application form for him) is unlikely to fall within para. 13(a) in itself.

It would seem that entering into brokerage agreements or indeed investment management agreements under which the investment manager deals himself does not constitute 'arranging deals' within para. 13. This is because (as part of the avoidance of overlap with para. 12 (dealing)) para. 13 does not cover arrangements with a view to transactions which the arranger will enter into himself, even as agent; the broker or investment manager will enter into the contemplated transactions as agent for the other party to the arrangement

¶314

(namely, his client) and the client will also enter into them, through the broker or investment manager.

This exemption from para. 13, which is provided to avoid overlap with para. 12, may, in fact, have wider implications than appears at first sight. This is because the exemption applies generally and not just where para. 12 applies. This is for good reason; if it was so limited, the exemption would not apply if the 'own account' exemptions from para. 12 (see ¶331 and ¶332) applied and, accordingly, an 'own account' investor would need FSA-authorisation to arrange his own exempted transactions. However, the result is that the exemptions from para. 13 also apply in the case of arrangements for transactions to be entered into by the arranger outside the UK, even though those transactions may be outside the scope of the FSA and, accordingly, not require FSA-authorisation. This prima facie provides a loophole for overseas brokers or investment managers who arrange in the UK (even from their own UK office) for transactions to be executed by them from their 'home' office, for example on their local stock exchange; as a result of note 1, the arranging in the UK will accordingly not fall in para. 13. However, in these circumstances, para. 12 itself would seem to apply, so that FSA-authorisation is nonetheless needed; the broker is offering in the UK within para. 12 to buy or sell investments as agent (through an office outside the UK), albeit that the person to whom the UK offer is made is the client for whom he will buy or sell rather than the counter-party with whom he will enter into the purchase or sale transaction (see ¶313). The passing of the order from an office in the UK to an office of the same firm outside the UK has no legal impact itself but accordingly changes the characterisation of the activity for FSA purposes from a para. 13 activity to a para. 12 activity.

Paragraph 13 does not apply to certain arrangements linked to life assurance or pension policies (note 3). This is to avoid bringing within the FSA the specified providers of finance who use life assurance or personal pension policies as security; the list includes building societies and money-lending companies. The problem arises if they arrange, in advance of the life or pension policy being issued, for the life office to introduce prospective borrowers to them for loans on the security of the policy or for it to 'guarantee' the amount payable on surrender or maturity of the policy; para. 13 would seem to apply because of the *a priori* arrangements between the lender and the life office involving investments, even if it is the life office which introduces the prospective borrower to the lender (rather than vice versa) and the lender's primary intention and business activity is to advance a secured loan (which, as referred to in ¶313 above, is in itself outside the FSA). Note 3 is intended to avoid lenders having to be FSA-authorised in these circumstances. It should, however, be emphasised that the exemption is only one-way. It applies only where the arrangements are for the referral of borrowers by the life office to a

¶314

prospective lender. Importantly, it does not apply where the arrangements are for the referral of borrowers by the lender to the life office, even if the policy is to be used as security for the loan; arrangements for this referral are FSA-regulated investment activities in the same way as other arrangements for referrals to product providers.

It is also made clear that lenders do not make 'arrangements' within para. 13 merely because their loans will finance an investment transaction, even if that purpose is known to the lender (note 5). Further, in the same way as the acceptance of loan notes, or other debentures relating to a loan, guarantee or other financial accommodation, is excluded from para. 12 (see ¶313), arrangements for loans involving the acceptance of loan notes, or such other debentures, also fall outside para. 13 (note 4). Both the issue and arranging for the issue of loan notes, and other debentures, are also exempted from the FSA's authorisation requirement (para. 28(3)). Accordingly, neither side of the loan arrangement needs FSA-authorisation even though a loan note or other debenture is issued. This confirms that this sort of 'pure' banking business is outside the FSA.

Finally, there is an important exemption for introductions to certain categories of FSA-authorised or exempted firms which are intended to lead to the introducer's client, or the firm on its behalf, entering into investment transactions (note 6). The exemption also covers introductions to the same categories of other firms if they are not carrying on FSA-regulated investment business in the UK unlawfully; this may, for example, be because their business is exempted from the FSA's authorisation requirement (for example, because of the ISD or 2BCD passport, see ¶356), or because it is not treated as carried on in the UK at all, either by reason of the 'overseas persons' exemptions (see ¶334) or because it is outside the territorial scope of the FSA altogether (see ¶311). This exemption is seemingly intended to avoid the double regulation inherent in regulating introductions to firms which are themselves FSA-authorised and is of great help to solicitors, accountants and bank managers. However, it is both wider and narrower than that. As indicated above, the exemption applies to introductions not only to FSA-authorised and exempted firms but also to other firms which engage in the relevant FSA-regulated investment activities; importantly, these include overseas firms which are not FSA-authorised. Conversely, however, the exemption applies only if the introduction is made with a view to the provision of independent advice to the introducer's client or the independent exercise of discretion on his behalf, the independence being presumably from the introducer and being required for reasons of anti-avoidance. The exemption therefore applies to introductions to advisory or discretionary stockbrokers and investment managers but it does not apply to introductions to 'own account' dealers as such or, importantly, to execution-only brokers. This is perhaps surprising but it may perhaps be

¶314

because in their case the person introduced would be placing more reliance on the introducer. It should however be remembered that mere introductions (at least without an on-going or *a priori* relationship) may not actually fall within para. 13 at all (see above).

¶315   Managing investments (Sch. 1, para. 14)

Investment management, or offering or agreeing to act as an investment manager, is also an FSA-regulated investment activity (para. 14). If, therefore, a firm enters into investment management agreements, or offers to do so, in the UK, it may need to be authorised under the FSA regardless of where it actually conducts its investment management activities. Obviously, the investment activity falls within para. 14 if the portfolio includes FSA-regulated investments. However, it will also fall within para. 14 if the investment manager is authorised by the investment management agreement or arrangements to include FSA-regulated investments in the portfolio, even if it does not in fact do so. As a practical matter, it may be advisable in these perhaps unusual investment management agreements or arrangements specifically to exclude all FSA-regulated investments. Moreover, it would appear that, if the portfolio has in the past (but on or after 29 April 1988, the date s. 3 came into force) included FSA-regulated investments, the agreement is forever 'tainted'; in these circumstances, it is necessary to enter into a new agreement which is confined to assets which are not FSA-regulated investments in order to avoid the FSA's authorisation requirement in relation to it.

The FSA-regulated investment activity of 'managing investments' covers both discretionary and non-discretionary (or, advisory) portfolio management; although para. 14(b) refers to the investment manager's discretion, this is only in relation to the possible inclusion in the portfolio of FSA-regulated investments and does not relate to the investment manager's authority in relation to a portfolio which does include them. This contrasts with the ISD which does not expressly refer to non-discretionary investment management at all; the ISD requires authorisation only for qualifying discretionary investment management and its passport covers in addition only investment advice, albeit that the UK regulators seem to accept that this covers advisory management within para. 14 as well as investment advice within para. 15 (see ¶316). It should be noted that, where the portfolio includes, or can include, both FSA-regulated investments and assets falling outside the FSA, even the management of the non-FSA assets is FSA-regulated.

The term 'managing investments' is arguably confined to where a firm both makes or recommends investment decisions (depending upon whether or not it has discretionary authority) and carries them out. This is, indeed what investment managers normally do; more importantly, the key function to which para. 14 applies is 'managing' the investments rather than merely reviewing a portfolio and management surely involves doing something with the assets, the difference between discretionary and non-discretionary investment management being exactly that the investment manager must obtain the client's consent before carrying out his 'decisions'. If the firm does not carry out the decision, it would normally be an investment adviser within para. 15 (see ¶316). In many cases, the investment manager deals in the name of the client rather than his own name (for example, so as to avoid liability to the counterparty) or, indeed, merely directs an external custodian (or even the client) to buy or sell the investment concerned; this technically seems to fall in para. 13 rather than para. 12 (see ¶314) but the investment manager is nonetheless carrying out the investment decision (through the custodian or the client) and therefore still falls in para. 14.

The term 'investment manager' is defined in the rules of both IMRO and SFA as including a firm which merely reviews a portfolio, without requiring that it must actually deal. However, the SROs can attach whatever label they like to members performing particular functions without that affecting the legal analysis; firms may, for example, need FSA-authorisation as investment advisers within para. 15 but can have special rules applied to them as 'investment managers'. Similarly, some statutory provisions distinguish between the 'management' and the 'acquisition or disposal' of property or securities, for example, s. 75(1) (collective investment schemes), and, indeed, reg. 7(2)(a) of the Prospectus Regulations (exempted offers to qualifying securities professionals) (see Ch. 8); however, this is likely to be an attempt to 'catch' investment managers who are 'arrangers' within para. 13 (or, indeed, fall outside both para. 12 and para. 13) as well as those who fall in para. 12.

Much will depend on both the contractual position and the facts on the ground. Many offshore funds have an investment manager who is advised by an 'investment adviser'. If the investment manager has no real experience and is, in practice, just introduced into the arrangement to obtain some beneficial tax or regulatory treatment, accepting the advice without question, the investment adviser may well fall within para. 14. Accordingly, if one person has authority to sanction or veto investment 'decisions' relating to another's investments which are made by a third party, and depending on the arrangements and the particular facts concerned, that person may be regarded as managing those investments himself if he can direct the third party what to do, even if the third party is contractually described as the 'investment manager'. This could be the case, for example, if a management committee has the final say on investment 'decisions' made for a unit trust or limited partnership by the investment manager and, on the facts, the 'investment manager' is really the adviser of the management committee; if the management committee decides on the investment and directs the 'investment manager' to effect the transaction, the management committee is likely to fall in para. 14. Conversely, if the

¶315

management committee only has a right of veto for defined 'external' reasons, not related to the merits of the particular investment or its price (but related, for example, to the size of the investment or compliance with the investment parameters), this problem should not arise (see ¶317). Moreover, it is understood that IMRO and SFA regard 'investment management' as not being limited to where an actual portfolio (or cash) is transferred to the investment manager. It is therefore likely to include the case where one firm (for example, a stockbroker) is given discretionary authority to acquire or dispose of investments on behalf of another (normally, up to an agreed maximum), for example in the context of Stock Exchange investment.

In certain circumstances, investment management may include the management of a broker bond (where a life policy can be linked to various unit trusts and the 'linkage', that is the unit trust to which it is linked, can be switched at the direction of the intermediary). This analysis does indeed seem to be correct in relation to the management of the switching facility itself; the effect of the switch is the same as if a policy linked to the replacement unit trust was substituted for the policy linked to the unit trust which is replaced, and it is surely irrelevant that no replacement policy was in fact issued but, instead, the existing policy was continued. Similarly, the management of the right to convert, surrender or extend a policy should also be regarded as investment management within para. 14 as this affects the description or quality of the investment itself. However, it is unlikely that the mere administration of the policy (such as providing for the payment of premiums or notifying claims) should be regarded as investment management. The argument that it is 'investment management' is very difficult to refute as a matter of English, because that is, indeed, managing the investment in a wide sense. However, it is on balance thought that the courts would not regard this as 'managing investments' within para. 14, in the same way as having discretion to vote someone else's shares in a particular way is not treated as 'managing investments'; even though these services are normally part of the services provided by an investment manager, the provision of the services is administrative only and does not in itself require the provider to be regarded as an investment manager requiring FSA-authorisation under para. 14. Similarly, investment management may include managing investee companies for the investor, typically in the case of venture capital investments; however, the better view seems to be that managing the business of the investee company is not as such investment management unless, exceptionally, that business includes investments.

¶316   Advising on investments (Sch. 1, para. 15)

Giving investment advice, or offering or agreeing to do so, is also an FSA-regulated investment activity (para. 15). However, investment advice will require FSA-authorisation only if it is given to persons in their capacity as 'investors or potential investors' and relates to the merits of buying, selling, subscribing for or underwriting investments, or exercising any right conferred by an investment to acquire, dispose of, underwrite or convert an investment (para. 15). This means that, for example, giving advice as to the exercise of other rights, such as voting rights, does not fall within para. 15. Similarly, if a firm merely gives advice as to the taxation consequences of an investment, it will accordingly not have to be FSA-authorised for it (and, in any event, the exemption for necessary incidental advice may apply, see ¶343). However, giving advice to an investment manager would seem to be within para. 15 if the investment manager himself enters into the resulting transaction (personally or through an agent); he must surely be an 'investor' even if he is acting merely as an agent, especially where he is acting 'account client'. There is no exemption merely because the investor being advised is FSA-authorised; he presumably needed specialist external advice (for example, for the venture capital portion of the portfolio) and therefore needs FSA protection even though he is himself FSA-authorised. If, however, the investment manager being advised does not himself enter into transactions but, for example, only gives instructions to brokers to acquire or sell the investment for a client, and so acts as an 'arranger', it would perhaps be difficult to regard him as an 'investor'; nevertheless, the prudent view is that he does indeed qualify as an 'investor', as he causes the investment to be made, so that the investment adviser falls in para. 15. This problem arises where the adviser is advising the investment manager for his own benefit; however, if on the facts the advice is really being given to the investment manager's client, or the investment manager is a mere cypher, then the adviser would in any event fall in para. 15 or para. 14 as appropriate.

More generally, para. 15 talks about advice on 'an investment' which indicates that a particular investment must be in contemplation. Accordingly, a firm does not need FSA-authorisation in order to give generic advice about the comparative merits of different types of investment, for example, to advise that investing in shares is safer than investing in financial futures, and this may be of help to bank managers. Conversely, even if the adviser actually keeps the portfolio under review for an investment manager which makes his own decisions, albeit taking the advice into account, the investment adviser would still fall in para. 15; the advice does indeed result from reviewing the portfolio but each item of advice relates to a particular investment (within para. 15) and para. 15 does not exclude investment advice given in such circumstances.

Uncertainties still remain, however. In particular, it is arguable that directors of a company may need FSA-authorisation if they advise shareholders on whether or not to accept a takeover offer. It is likely that that does not constitute an FSA-regulated investment activity because the advice is being given to them as shareholders rather than as investors, although the line is a difficult one to draw. In addition, it is also normally arguable that the directors are not carrying on a business of giving investment advice (see ¶304).

Whether the provision of corporate finance advice falls within para. 15 depends on the matters to which it relates. Advice given to a potential offeror as to the merits of a bid would seem to fall within para. 15 even if the advice is only as to the price; an investment will nearly always be good if the price is low enough! Conversely, however, advice given to a prospective issuer as to the price at which to issue its securities does not fall within para. 15; the subscribers will be investors but they are not being advised, and the issuer is hardly an investor!

¶317   Acting in relation to collective investment schemes (Sch. 1, para. 16)

Establishing, operating or winding up a collective investment scheme also constitutes an FSA-regulated investment activity (para. 16); in contrast to the normal position, however, merely offering or agreeing to do so does not. Unit trusts, limited partnerships and open-ended investment companies are typical examples of collective investment schemes, although it is not necessary that there is a 'formal' fund so long as there are arrangements for 'collective' investment. It is expressly provided that acting as trustee of an authorised unit trust scheme also falls within para. 16.

The FSA defines an operator of a collective investment scheme only obliquely (s. 75(8)). If the manager of a unit trust is separate from the trustee, as it must be in the case of authorised unit trusts (s. 78(2)), it is the manager who is the operator, and for this purpose a custodian or depositary of a non-UK collective investment scheme is treated as a trustee even if he does not hold under trust. Conversely, in the case of a scheme constituted as an open-ended investment company, the operator is the company itself notwithstanding that (as is usual in the case of common law jurisdictions) there is a separate management company.

It may in practice be very difficult to determine who is the operator (or, manager) of an unincorporated collective investment scheme. It is clearly the case that 'operator' or 'manager' is not the same as 'investment manager'. The operator is more the firm which (in colloquial parlance) 'runs' the scheme than the firm which merely selects its investments; indeed, if one firm manages the scheme on behalf of another, as may be the case for internal reasons, for example, where they are both members of the same group, it may be the agent who is the 'operator'. It would also seem possible to conceive of the same scheme having more than one manager, and so operator, where the relevant functions are shared. From a regulatory point of view, the operator is normally the firm which deals with investors and accordingly is to be treated as 'responsible' for the operation and activities of the scheme. The two different functions of an operator and an investment manager are, however, often combined in the same firm; this makes the analysis difficult and would mean that the investment manager is, in fact, often the operator, although it is strictly better to rephrase this to say that the firm which (coincidentally) is the investment manager is also the operator. In the case of a limited partnership, the general partner may therefore be the operator depending on the facts, even if there is a separate investment manager. Conversely, if, as is often the case in practice, the general partner does not take part in the management of the limited partnership, the investment manager would normally be the operator; this would be the case where it is the investment manager which actually establishes and manages the limited partnership, rather than merely its investments, and the partnership has a general partner (usually 'supplied' by the investment manager) merely because the *Limited Partnerships Act* 1907 requires every English limited partnership to have at least one general partner to be liable for its debts. This analysis would seem to apply even where the general partner, at the direction of the investment manager, executes agreements, for example subscription agreements, on behalf of the limited partnership, which is the actual party to the agreement. The execution of the agreement would in fact be by the limited partnership through the general partner (as the only partner allowed by the Limited Partnerships Act to act for the limited partnership), and not by the general partner as part of a business of managing the limited partnership or of dealing or arranging deals in investments.

Both managers and trustees of authorised unit trusts are required to seek FSA-authorisation under para. 16. UK managers of unauthorised unit trusts also need FSA-authorisation (as operators). Although the position is by no means clear, it would seem that being a trustee of unauthorised unit trusts or a trustee or depositary of other kinds of collective investment scheme is not as such an FSA-regulated investment activity, provided that the scheme is not an authorised unit trust or a UK open-ended investment company (see ¶318) and, where relevant, that there is a separate manager who 'runs' the scheme, at least if he is appointed by the trust deed or other constitutional document; that manager will be the operator and indeed, in the normal case, he will also have established the scheme. The reason that trustees of authorised unit trust schemes are specifically referred to in para. 16 is that, although no one can be a trustee of an authorised unit trust scheme unless he is himself FSA-authorised (s. 78(4)), requiring the trustee to be FSA-authorised does not in itself help protect investors unless the FSA provides that by so acting he is carrying on FSA-regulated investment business, so that his business is subject to regulation under the FSA. The depositary or sole director of a UK open-ended investment company is specifically referred to in para. 16 for similar reasons (see ¶318).

¶317

This analysis is also relevant in the case of limited partnerships and authorised unit trusts (and indeed other collective investment schemes) where the 'manager' is subject to the supervision and control of a separate committee, usually composed of selected investors, or their representatives, or 'the great and the good'; this committee may well be constituted as the board of directors of a general partner or of an open-ended investment company. The rules of the collective investment scheme would normally provide that the consent of this committee is needed in 'conflict of interest' situations or other situations where investors need specific protection however competent the manager is, particularly if the manager of the scheme is also its investment manager. In the normal case, and although it all depends on the actual facts and the terms of the relevant documentation, the better view is that it is the manager which is the operator rather than the committee, even though ultimate control or responsibility lies with the committee; operating a collective investment scheme is a 'conduct' rather than a 'control' function, although it would help not to call the committee a 'management committee'. Indeed, the same would seem to apply to the ISD exemption for managers of collective investment undertakings (see ¶330). This is the case whether the committee is a stand-alone committee or a board of directors; indeed, the same analysis applies also to any separate corporate entity which monitors and supervises the manager, such as the general partner of a limited partnership with a separate manager.

It is also important to ensure that the 'controller' does not have the final decision on investments because, if it is an entity separate from the collective investment scheme or is a stand-alone committee, this runs the risk of its constituting an investment manager within para. 14 (as distinct from an operator within para. 16), at least if it reviews the portfolio (see ¶315); a veto right would in any event seem not to constitute the 'controller' an investment manager if it is exercisable only for specific 'external' reasons, such as size or falling outside the approved investment parameters, rather than because the controller does not think that the proposed investment is a good one.

¶318   Acting in relation to UK open-ended investment companies (Sch. 1, para. 16)

In early 1997, a new form of collective investment scheme became available under UK law for the first time, a UK open-ended investment company (the *Open-Ended Investment Companies (Investment Companies with Variable Capital) Regulations* 1996, SI 1996/2827, (the 'ECA regulations')). These corporate unit trusts are one of the three kinds of undertaking entitled to the single European passport for 'public' investment funds provided for by the EU directive of 1985 relating to undertakings for collective investment in transferable securities, No. 85/611/EEC, (the 'UCITS directive'); the UCITS directive provides that a qualifying investment fund which is authorised by its 'home' EEA member state to be marketed to the public in that member state can also be marketed to the public in all other member states without needing local authorisation and was implemented into UK law by Ch. VIII of the FSA (collective investment schemes). This is the first time that UK law permits the incorporation of open-ended companies (companies whose shares are redeemable at any time at the option of the investor); it is hoped by the Government that these open-ended 'investment companies with variable capital' (as they are referred to in the ECA regulations) will be products which can be sold successfully to the general public in Europe, who are not familiar with UK unit trust vehicles.

UK OEICs (their rather ungainly acronym) are collective investment schemes even though they are bodies corporate; the exclusion of bodies corporate from the definition of collective investment scheme (in s. 75(7)) does not apply to them as they are 'open-ended investment companies' within s. 75(8). Accordingly, para. 16 requires their operators (and anyone whose business it is to establish or wind them up) to be FSA-authorised (see ¶317); the 'operator' of an OEIC is in fact the OEIC itself (s. 75(8)), and the OEIC therefore needs to be FSA-authorised under para. 16. In addition, OEICs also need to be FSA-authorised, under para. 12, in order to offer and issue their shares to investors, even if only by private placements (see ¶313). A new s. 24A has therefore been inserted into the FSA giving OEICs automatic FSA-authorisation (para. 11 of Sch. 8 to the ECA regulations). OEICs are only incorporated when the SIB makes an 'authorisation order' under reg. 9 of the ECA regulations (reg. 3 of the ECA regulations); this is not FSA-authorisation but 'product' authorisation (as in the case of 'authorised' unit trusts) which allows OEICs to be marketed to the general public in the UK (see Ch. 9).

The UCITS directive also requires member states to vet the directors and depositaries of OEICs incorporated in them as the price of the single European passport granted for marketing to the public throughout the EEA. Accordingly, the *Financial Services Act 1986 (Extension of Scope of Act) Order 1996* (SI 1996/2958) amends para. 16 so that the depositary or sole director of an OEIC must also be FSA-authorised; in addition, all its directors must be 'fit and proper' (reg. 10(5) of the ECA regulations). This means that the conduct of business rules and financial resources requirements of the SIB or, if as is likely they join IMRO, IMRO can apply to them in the same way as they can apply to trustees of authorised unit trusts (see ¶317); depositaries are equivalent to trustees but, depending on the circumstances, may hold the assets under a contract rather than in trust (see the definition of 'depositary' inserted into s. 207(1) of the FSA by the ECA regulations, namely, a person to whom the property of the OEIC is 'entrusted for safe keeping'). Accordingly,

¶318

depositaries of OEICs are subject to FSA-regulation even though custodians generally were not until June 1997 (see ¶319).

¶319   Acting as a custodian or nominee (Sch. 1, para. 13A)

Although many FSA-authorised firms also act as custodian of the investments included in the portfolios they manage or deal for, and are accordingly regulated by conduct of business rules when acting as custodian in relation to them, the FSA for many years did not require 'mere' custodians to be authorised. There was an argument that firms which, as was normal in the case of banks, held assets in safe custody and bought or sold (or delivered) them when instructed by the customer might need to be authorised for their custodial activities under the FSA if they were also, quite separately, brokers or investment managers in relation to other assets; this was, however, a technical argument (based on the view that, as a result of the exclusion in para. 22(1)(c) for firms holding themselves out as providing a service of buying or selling investments, the FSA-exemption in para. 22(1) for nominees accordingly did not apply) and seems to have been ignored historically.

Whatever the previous position, a new para. 13A expressly made acting as a custodian or nominee authorisable under the FSA as from 1 June 1997 (the *Financial Services Act 1986 (Extension of Scope of Act) Order* 1996, SI 1996/2958). As a result, a customer's money held by a custodian or nominee together with his securities will constitute 'client money' subject to the *Financial Services (Client Money) Regulations* 1991, except when it is held by an 'approved bank' in an account in the name of the customer. Paragraph 13A provides that, unless an exemption applies, not only acting as a custodian or nominee for someone else's investments (or, 'safeguarding and administering them') requires FSA-authorisation but also merely arranging for someone else to do so, or (as is normal in Pt. II) offering or agreeing to do so. Although it is unclear, it would seem that a firm can be an 'arranger' within para. 13A both where it is a primary custodian using a nominee or sub-custodian actually to safeguard and administer the assets on its behalf and where it incurs no custodial liability at all but merely acts as an introducer to a custodian. However, it is not necessary to be FSA-authorised merely to keep someone else's share certificates in safe custody; this is safeguarding them but is not administering them. Conversely, and subject to the important exemption referred to below, a mere nominee would seem to be within para. 13A as it does administer the shares it holds (for example, by exercising the rights attached to them, or transferring them); it only does so on the instructions of the beneficial owner, but this applies to all custodians. Although the nominee has legal title to the shares, they are assets 'belonging to another' within para. 16A as they 'belong' to the beneficial owner for whom the nominee is acting. In particular, banks acting as custodians and corporate trustees now clearly need to be FSA-authorised, unless an exemption applies.

There are two important exemptions in para. 13A itself from the FSA's authorisation requirement, although it should be noted that these are not comprehensive. First, para. 13A does not apply if the safe custody arrangements involve a qualifying 'primary custodian' who undertakes to the owner of the assets that he will be as responsible for any problem as if he was safeguarding and administering them himself (note 1). This seems to be directed at exempting nominees or sub-custodians used by the primary custodian; however, it means that the primary custodian seemingly cannot in practice avoid liability for the negligence or default of a nominee or sub-custodian in the UK which he wants to use (and which is not FSA-authorised under para. 13A) even if it is not connected with the primary custodian. This exemption applies only in relation to the firm actually looking after the assets under the first limb of the FSA-regulated activity and not to a firm which merely arranges for someone else to do so under the second limb. Secondly, the FSA's authorisation requirement does not apply if all that the 'arranger' does by arranging the provision of custodial services is to introduce the customer directly to a qualifying custodian (whether the custodian merely arranges for someone else to safeguard and administer them under a contract with the customer or himself contracts directly with the customer) and the qualifying custodian is not in the same 'group' as, or remunerated by, the arranger (note 4); 'group' has the normal enlarged meaning used in Sch. 1 (see ¶333). The SIB indicated in its consultation document on 'Custody' (Consultative Paper 107 of March 1997) that it regards 'arranging' as a continuing activity if the 'arranger' has continuing obligations to supervise the custodian; this would seemingly be its view also if the arranger (rather than the customer) was responsible for giving the custodian settlement instructions. The exemption for introductions seemingly only applies if the 'arranger' drops out of the picture completely after the introduction and a continuing involvement would therefore seem to mean that the 'arranger' must become FSA-authorised as a 'custodian' because he arranges custody by someone else; this is a reasonable result as the customer still relies on the 'arranger', albeit to a limited extent.

In relation to both exemptions, a custodian will be a qualifying custodian only if the custodian's safe custody or 'arranging' service is provided in the UK (which seemingly means from a UK office) and the custodian is FSA-authorised for the service or is an exempted firm in relation to the service or, finally, because acting as a custodian in relation to securities is within both the ISD and the 2BCD passports, the custodian is a non-UK EEA firm and provides the service under its passport (note 5). The 'primary custodian' does not need actually to be a custodian in the colloquial sense; the expression covers

¶319

FSA-authorised firms which merely arrange for the use of a custodian, for example, an in-house nominee, provided that the firm is authorised under para. 13A for arranging custody or, indeed, seemingly to hold customer assets itself. At time of writing, the 'money market' exemption (in s. 43) has not been amended to cover custodial services in relation to qualifying investments, although the Treasury are considering whether it might be; if the investments are held by a listed institution for the purpose of a particular transaction within the 'money market' exemption (rather than as a 'custodian' properly so-called), the exemption is, however, likely to apply even in its present form (s. 43). It seems that a custodian operating from a non-UK office will not be a 'qualifying' custodian for this purpose; the secondary custodian, or the arranger introducing the 'offshore' primary custodian, may therefore have to be FSA-authorised even if the primary custodian is himself FSA-authorised.

Importantly, para. 13A expressly provides that it applies even if the assets are held by book-entry (note 3(a)). Accordingly, apart from the 'primary custodian' exemption, nominees and other custodians are in principle subject to para. 13A if they hold securities in book-entry depositary or settlement systems such as CREST or, for example, Euro-clear, CEDEL or Intersettle (the depositary system used by EASDAQ). Paragraph 13A also provides that it applies even if the assets may be transferred to a third party subject to a commitment by the custodian that they will be replaced by equivalent assets (note 3(b)). This seems to refer both to 'undesignated' nominees (where the assets of all customers are held in a single 'omnibus', or pooled, account) and also to nominees or custodians, or, indeed, depositaries of OEICs (see ¶318), who do not hold the assets in trust but are subject only to a contractual obligation to return assets of the same quantity and description. In both cases, the nominee or custodian is therefore still to be treated as safeguarding or administering assets within para. 13A even though the actual assets delivered to the nominee or custodian do not need to be returned (as the safe custody arrangements accordingly allow the nominee or custodian to use them for his own purposes).

Paragraph 13A applies only if the assets subject to the custodial arrangements consist of or include FSA-regulated investments or the arrangements are held out as potentially applying to them; if this is the case, however, para. 13A applies to all the assets, even if they are not FSA-regulated investments, and, accordingly, assets which are not FSA-regulated investments should be held under a separate custodial agreement. Helpfully, it is expressly stated that para. 13A does not apply to a person who merely receives documents of title for onward transmission in the course of or as a result of settlement (note 2(c)); indeed, the Treasury and the SIB have indicated that, as would be expected, para. 13A also does not normally apply to lenders holding investments as collateral or security. Stock loans as such are also not within

¶319

para. 13A. The 'borrower' actually acquires the securities and has to replace them with others; accordingly, he does not actually hold them while they belong to another. Finally, many of the Pt. III exemptions are extended to cover safe custody services, for example, the 'group exemptions' in para. 18 and the 'overseas persons' exemptions in para. 27 (but, strangely, not those in para. 26). Similarly, there is a new exemption for trustees, even professional trustees, who do not hold themselves out as providing safe custody services and do not receive additional remuneration for acting as a custodian, rather than merely as a trustee or legal representative (para. 22(2A). There is also a special exemption for insurance companies which are authorised under the *Insurance Companies Act* 1982 but are not automatically FSA-authorised under s. 22 in relation to their holding of investments belonging to their qualifying group pension fund(s) (para. 24A).

¶320   Acting as a CREST sponsor

Acting as a CREST 'sponsor' is also now an FSA-regulated investment activity (para. 16A). This was introduced in order to protect investors using 'sponsorship' services in CREST, the new settlement system launched in July 1996 for transactions on the London Stock Exchange. CREST is a computerised book-entry settlement system established under the aegis of the Bank of England and can be extended to gilts and other markets. Book-entry systems only work efficiently if share certificates and their accompanying stock transfer forms are done away with (the securities then being referred to as 'dematerialised'), although dematerialisation in CREST is optional for investors, as indeed is joining CREST for quoted companies. Even if CREST shares are dematerialised, legal title is still constituted by entry in the company's share register, as in the case of certificated securities. However, and crucially, the beneficial interest in dematerialised securities is transferred by book-entry in the computers of CRESTCo, the private company which operates CREST, by debiting the seller's account with CRESTCo and crediting the buyer's account; it is the transmission of computer instructions to CRESTCo which replaces the delivery to the buyer of a share certificate and stock transfer form and authorises CRESTCo to request the company to register the buyer in place of the seller.

Many investors, especially sophisticated private investors, would like the benefits of being in CREST but still want to be on the register themselves rather than use a professional nominee (for example, so as to be clearly entitled to attend company meetings and receive 'shareholder' perks), even if they accept that they can no longer have share certificates. Every shareholder on a company's register for his dematerialised securities must have his own account with CRESTCo and accordingly must have his own computer access. Because many shareholders are unlikely to want to incur the costs and time involved in running their own computer access, shareholders are allowed by CRESTCo to authorise a third party, typically their stockbroker, to run their computer accounts in CREST for them; the third party is referred to as a 'CREST sponsor'. CREST can only work efficiently if CRESTCo is allowed to act on computer instructions from the CREST sponsor without query and this means that the CREST sponsor is enabled to operate the shareholder's account as if it was his own.

The Government has therefore decided that CREST sponsors have to be vetted and regulated under the FSA and a new para. 16A has been inserted into Pt. II of Sch. 1 to require all CREST sponsors to be FSA-authorised. This is important because, although stockbrokers would of course have to be FSA-authorised anyway, their conduct as CREST sponsors can be regulated under the FSA only if acting as a CREST sponsor is FSA-regulated investment business; in addition, other CREST sponsors, such as registrars and software houses, would not necessarily have been FSA-authorised otherwise, as they are usually involved only in settlement not in execution and do not carry on any other FSA-regulated investment activity. Accordingly, acting as a sponsor in CREST (or offering or agreeing to do so) is an FSA-regulated investment activity under para. 16A (the *Financial Services Act 1986 (Uncertificated Securities) (Extension of Scope of Act) Order* 1996, SI 1996/1322).

Paragraph 16A refers in terms only to the activity of sending (or causing someone else to send) dematerialised instructions relating to an investment on behalf of another person where the instructions are sent by means of a relevant system to its operator approved under the *Uncertificated Securities Regulations* 1995 (SI 1995/3272) and does not mention CREST; however, at present the Regulations relate only to CREST, the operator is CRESTCo, dematerialised instructions are the computer messages (in particular, to transfer or accept delivery of securities) sent through CREST and, under the CREST rules, the only person who can send instructions relating to another person's account is a person appointed as a sponsor of that other person in relation to that account. Paragraph 16A makes it clear that an offeror making a takeover offer is not a sponsor merely because he can require accepted securities in the target company to be transferred to him when the offer has gone unconditional, as he can by means of the CREST 'escrow account' to which acceptances are credited while the offer is still conditional, (note 1(b)). In addition, the 'trustee' and 'group' exemptions in para. 22 and 18 are extended to cover, respectively, trustees and personal representatives acting as such and companies sponsoring group companies, as they will often do, especially in the case of group nominee companies (art. 2(3) and 2(4)); unusually , the group exemption accordingly applies where the group company is (or will be) merely the registered holder rather than having to own the assets. The 'overseas persons' exemptions in para. 27 are also extended to cover CREST sponsorship (art. 2(4)).

¶320

¶321 Marketing

It is remarkably unclear whether or not marketing is an FSA-regulated investment activity. The problem arises because the FSA does not refer to marketing expressly but it would be strange if it is not an FSA-regulated investment activity. It would in fact often fall within para. 13 as 'arranging deals' (see ¶314). In practice, it is perhaps unlikely that soliciting a prospective investor is in itself making arrangements with him for the resulting transaction within para. 13(a) unless something else is done, for example the salesman transmits an application form to the manager of an authorised unit trust, or at least the salesman offers to do so. Conversely, however, where one firm agrees to solicit investment transactions on behalf of another firm, it would seem that it is indeed thereby making relevant arrangements within para. 13(b), albeit with the other firm (its principal) rather than with the investor. This is because it is intended that, as a result of those arrangements, the principal will enter into investment transactions with or (if it is his agency brokerage services which are being marketed) on behalf of the investor; the solicitation will not be excluded by note 1 from para. 13(b) because the note 1 exclusion will not apply to the firm doing the soliciting if (as would be normal) it is the principal who enters into the consequent transactions and not the firm itself (see ¶314). If the principal does enter into the consequent transactions personally (rather than through the firm as his agent), it is para. 13(b) which applies to the firm soliciting rather than para. 12, even if the firm offers the investments for sale on behalf of the principal (as it would, for example, in a placing); although the firm is 'offering. . . as an agent', so that para. 12 seems to apply, it is merely offering that the principal will sell rather than that the firm will sell as agent for the principal and para. 12 applies only if the firm is 'offering to do so [that is, actually to sell]' albeit as an agent (see ¶313).

If, however, the marketing does not fall within para. 13, it will normally not be an FSA-regulated investment activity. This may be the case, for example, because (as where a firm markets its principal's corporate finance advisory services to a prospective client) neither the firm nor the principal is to enter into investment transactions, but only the client. The client is not party to the arrangements (so that para. 13 (b) does not apply) and the appointment of the corporate finance house in relation to the acquisition or disposal of a particular holding would not in itself bring about the desired transaction (so that para. 13(a) does not apply).

Certain provisions of the FSA make it clear that marketing is normally FSA-regulated. Thus, for example, the FSA stresses that (apart from giving advice) the only FSA-regulated investment business which appointed representatives can carry on within their exemption (see ¶350) is exactly to procure, or endeavour to procure, prospective customers to enter into an investment agreement with their principal or others (s. 44(3)). Similarly, the

FSA provides that amongst the few kinds of FSA-regulated investment business that an operator of a collective investment scheme recognised under s. 86 (EEA recognised schemes) carries on which the SIB can regulate is procuring persons to become participants (s. 86(7)).

Many subsidiaries of overseas dealers act as 'introducing brokers' for their parent companies, for example UK subsidiaries of some American brokers; they seek to induce the investor either to enter into an on-going brokerage or investment management agreement with the overseas dealer or to place orders with him through the introducing broker. As indicated above, there seems to be enough in the FSA for the courts to consider that to be an FSA-regulated investment activity even though marketing is not referred to expressly. However, where the marketing is by a self-standing subsidiary, the 'group' exemption in Sch. 1, para. 18(3) may, perhaps, apply in relation to the para. 13 marketing arrangements, although it possibly does not do so where the overseas parent company deals as agent (see ¶333). The very act of marketing is itself regulated by the FSA's restrictions on investment advertisements and cold-calling (see Ch. 9) and accordingly the investor is not totally unprotected even where marketing is not an FSA-regulated investment activity. However, the position is clearly not very satisfactory. The FSA allows the Government to extend the definition of FSA-regulated investment activity (see ¶322) and, on the basis that the courts will look at what the FSA says rather than what everybody intended or indeed assumed that it says, marketing is an obvious candidate for such extension.

¶322   Alteration of FSA-regulated investment activities

The FSA empowers the Government to extend or restrict the activities that constitute FSA-regulated investment business or the circumstances in which it is regarded as carried on in the UK (s. 2(1)(b)). This allows the Treasury to vary not only the exemptions (see ¶329–¶346) but also the activities which constitute FSA-regulated investment activities and the terms of the 'overseas persons' exemptions (see ¶334); it can also use this power to bring into UK law (even in relation to non-EEA firms) whatever is agreed for the purposes of the ISD and the 2BCD as to where services or activities are to be treated as provided or carried on. As explained above, the Government has already made some important alterations (see ¶312). This power cannot be delegated to the SIB or any other designated agency.

FSA-REGULATED INVESTMENTS

¶323   Introduction

In general terms, the Financial Services Act applies to all investments other than physical assets (such as antiques or land) over which the investor has control. However, an investment will be FSA-regulated only if it falls within one of the different paragraphs of Pt. I of Sch. 1 and is not excluded from that paragraph by means of the notes which have been introduced to provide exemptions or to define more closely what is included or not included. Certain of these paragraphs are analysed below. The FSA does not expressly state what the legal effect is of the notes in Pt. I (or indeed Pt. II) of Sch. 1. However, it is inconceivable that the courts would do anything other than treat them as qualifying or limiting the paragraphs to which they apply, as they are clearly intended to do.

The investments to which the FSA applies are, in general terms, the following:

(1) shares in UK or non-UK companies or other bodies corporate or in overseas unincorporated bodies (but not shares in open-ended investment companies, which are in 5 below, or in building societies) (para. 1);

(2) Eurobonds, gilts and other government bonds, loan stock, certificates of deposit, commercial paper, bills of exchange accepted by a banker and other debt securities or debentures (but not letters of credit, other bills of exchange, mortgages or trade finance instruments) (para. 2 and 3);

(3) warrants and other instruments entitling the holder to subscribe for shares or debentures (para. 4);

(4) depositary receipts or other certificates representing securities (para. 5);

(5) shares in or securities of open-ended investment companies, units in unit trusts and other participations in 'collective investment schemes' (including limited partnerships and schemes for common management of physical assets) even if they invest not in FSA-regulated investments but, for example, in land, pigs or, famously, ostriches and even if the scheme does not constitute a formal fund (para. 6);

(6) traded options or other put or call options over existing securities (but not subscription rights relating to unissued securities, which fall in 3 above), currency options, gold, palladium, platinum or silver options, options over futures contracts or other FSA-regulated investments and options over such options (para. 7);

(7) financial and commodity futures and other deferred delivery contracts, if the contract is for investment rather than commercial purposes, as to which the FSA contains certain presumptions or indications (para. 8);

(8) interest rate swaps, stock market 'bets' and contracts for differences or other contracts whose value is 'linked' to an underlying asset, index or factor, including interest rate futures, cash-settled options and spread-betting (para. 9);

(9) life assurance contracts with an investment element and personal pension policies, but not pure protection policies falling within very restricted criteria (para. 10); and

(10) rights to and interests in the investments listed above, but not interests under the trusts of an occupational pension scheme (or rights or interests which in themselves qualify as FSA-regulated investments, such as subscription rights, which fall in 3 above) (para. 11).

¶324   Debentures (Sch. 1, para. 2 and 3)

Debentures (or, debt securities) are normally FSA-regulated investments; they are defined as instruments creating or acknowledging indebtedness and expressly include certificates of deposit and bills of exchange accepted by bankers. It is irrelevant for this purpose whether or not they are secured. However, many exemptions are available for dealings in them, including the 'own account' exemption in para. 17(1)(c) and, in the case of qualifying short-term debentures, the very important exemption for wholesale (or 'deemed' wholesale) money market transactions (see ¶349). Further, the notes to para. 2 and para. 3 provide that, for the purpose of both paragraphs, a cheque or other bill of exchange not accepted by a banker, a banker's draft and a letter of credit are not 'debentures', nor are statements showing a balance in a current or deposit account. Paragraphs 2 and 3 of Sch. 1 also provide an exemption for trade finance, and in particular export credit activities; a loan note for money borrowed to pay for goods or services does not constitute an FSA-regulated investment nor, indeed, does any document acknowledging or creating the obligation to pay for those goods or services. However, the excluded instrument must relate to the contract which it is financing and should probably refer to it expressly. Note (c) to para. 2 provides that a mortgage (or other disposition of property) does not constitute a 'debenture' merely because it contains an obligation to repay. It is perhaps arguable that a loan agreement is a 'debenture' but the better view is that it is not (see ¶313).

Debentures are split into two paragraphs, one for those issued by governments or local authorities or international organisations which have an EEA member state as a member (para. 3) and the other for those issued by anyone else, in particular companies (para. 2). Although securities fall within para. 3 if they are actually issued by or on behalf of a government, they fall within para. 2 if they are merely guaranteed by one. It may in practice be difficult to determine whether bonds issued by a government agency are to be treated as issued by a government.

It is unclear how convertible loan stock should be categorised for the purposes of Pt. I of Sch. 1. Loan stock is clearly a debenture within para. 2 because it is primarily a document creating or acknowledging indebtedness. However, it is arguable that the right to convert is an instrument within para. 4. It is thought on balance that this argument is not correct as the conversion right is not a 'stand-alone' instrument, as in the case of warrants attached to bonds, and only 'instruments' fall within para. 2 and 3, albeit that 'instrument' has an extended meaning (para. 28(1)(b)).

¶325   Futures (Sch. 1, para. 8)

The Financial Services Act includes both financial futures and commodity futures as FSA-regulated investments; this contrasts with the passports granted by the ISD and the 2BCD which do not apply to commodity futures. Paragraph 8 of Sch. 1 to the FSA applies whatever the underlying property, but only if the commodity or other property is actually to be sold and delivered; in practice, futures contracts are normally not held to maturity but are 'closed out' by an opposite and matching contract, so realising a profit or loss, but there is no actual delivery (although, importantly, that is required if they are not closed out). If no property is to be sold or delivered, as in the case of interest rate futures, then the contract will not fall in para. 8, although it will often be a 'contract for differences' falling in para. 9 (see ¶326). Paragraph 8 also covers forward foreign exchange contracts in certain circumstances (see below).

The FSA finds it very difficult to define futures, in the sense of differentiating futures contracts from ordinary commercial contracts to buy or sell commodities for forward delivery. Because the FSA does not seek to regulate physical assets under the control of the investor, it equally does not want to treat a contract to buy a commodity or other physical property as an investment merely because, as in the normal case, such contracts provide for deferred delivery. However, the FSA does want to treat as an investment the type of contract which the producer or manufacturer would enter into to hedge his exposure under that forward contract. This is because it is exactly those hedging contracts which prove so attractive to speculators who are prepared to take on the very risks that the producer or manufacturer wishes to hedge against. These hedging contracts are normally futures contracts. In order to distinguish between forward and futures contracts, para. 8 provides that it does not cover contracts for forward delivery if the contracts are entered into for commercial rather than investment purposes (note 1); the difficulty lies in drawing the line.

The FSA fights shy of using the term 'futures contracts' and therefore sets out detailed criteria which are determinative or, in some cases, merely indicative of whether a contract is or is not made for investment purposes and so is or is not an FSA-regulated investment. However, para. 8 makes it clear that, if forward contracts are made or traded on recognised investment exchanges, such as LIFFE, they are FSA-regulated investments; contracts made off an exchange are also FSA-regulated investments if they are expressed to be as traded on, or on the same terms as equivalent contracts made on, a particular RIE, for example, an over-the-counter contract between a securities house and its client (note 2). 'Cash' contracts on RIEs will therefore be para. 8 futures whatever the stipulated delivery period. Conversely, if a contract is not made or traded on an RIE (or equivalent to such a contract), it will not fall in para. 8 if it is a 'spot contract' with an original delivery period of less than seven days after the contract date (note 3). This 'safe harbour' conclusive presumption applies if the seven days contract is a 'customised' contract made over-the-counter and not 'linked' to or 'matching' a contract traded on an RIE or, seemingly, if the contract is made on a non-UK investment exchange, even if it is a futures exchange treated by the SIB as a 'designated investment exchange' or is a 'regulated market' for the purposes of the ISD. It should be noted that the seven days delivery period is seven calendar days, not seven business days. This is important as the timing must be watched carefully. For example, the Bank of England informally advised in October 1994 that, when dealers are trading for 'seven days forward', the market convention is that the maturity date is seven calendar days from the spot settlement date which is itself two working days from the day on which the deal is done; a 'seven days forward' transaction is therefore outside the 'seven days' safe harbour.

The SIB issued guidance in 1996 ('Foreign Exchange and the Financial Services Act 1986', Guidance Release 1/96) in relation to the somewhat provocative practice of some foreign exchange dealers regularly to 'roll-over' contracts which required delivery of the currency bought or sold within seven days, so that delivery took place only after a much longer period; the SIB took the position that note 3 did not apply in these cases if the whole arrangement was based on this rolling-over.

Similarly, it is an indication of a commercial purpose that either of the parties intends to make or to take delivery and an indication of an investment purpose that neither do (note 4(b)); although it is unclear, the better view is that this test is met if, literally, either party (and not necessarily both parties) intends to make or take delivery and even if delivery is not in fact made, for example because the intention changes. It may be difficult in practice to prove this intention and, also, to indicate the intention (or lack of it) to the other party to the transaction where that is relevant; it may accordingly become the practice to declare this intention expressly in contracts. Even if neither party intends to make delivery, the contract may still be an FSA-regulated investment as a

¶325

contract for differences within para. 9 (see ¶326). Many of the detailed and complicated 'indications' are directed at specific factual circumstances. For example, it is an indication of a commercial purpose that either party is a manufacturer or producer of the property to which the contract relates or uses it in his business, and an indication of an investment purpose that this is not the case (note 4(a)). Again, it is an indication that a contract is made for commercial purposes if it is not made by reference to standard terms (note 5); however, it is not an indication that it is made for investment purposes if it is, as some 'physicals' trade associations publish standard terms for their members.

Note 6(a) provides that it is only an indication that the contract is made for investment purposes if it is expressed to be as traded on an exchange; this seems to conflict with note 2 which makes it a conclusive presumption in the case of an RIE and note 6(a) should therefore perhaps be read as referring to an exchange which is not an RIE. It is, however, unclear why there is no conclusive presumption that contracts traded on a non-UK exchange, or at least a designated investment exchange or (now) an ISD regulated market, are to be regarded as made for investment purposes, and so qualify as para. 8 futures, in the same way as contracts traded on an RIE (note 2). However, it is an indication of an investment purpose if margin is required (whether the contract is on or off exchange), and futures exchanges normally require it. It is an indication that the contract is made for investment purposes if performance of the contract is ensured by an investment exchange or clearing house (note 6(b)), although, as this is required for all RIEs (para. 2(4) of Sch. 4), this probably means merely that facilities for settlement are provided, rather than that settlement is guaranteed.

Prima facie, forward foreign exchange contracts fall within para. 8 unless they happen to be excluded by one of the notes to para. 8 (for example, if their original maturity is less than seven days). This is because para. 8 applies to contracts for the sale of any property and property is defined to include currency (Sch. 1, para. 28(1)(a)). This may originally have been an unexpected result but it follows from the wide scope of para. 8; this is the case even though there is a clear distinction between contracts which are tradeable in themselves and accordingly should fall within para. 8 (one buys and sells futures contracts) and mere contracts for deferred delivery, where only the underlying asset is tradeable, which should not fall within para. 8. That said, many forward foreign exchange contracts are for commercial purposes, for example, where the foreign currency acquired is actually to be used (for example, to pay holiday expenses). Again, they would seem to be for commercial purposes if they are intended to fund a liability payable in foreign currency or to sell anticipated future foreign currency proceeds, because they are transactions not for an investment purpose but for the very opposite, the avoidance of a currency risk. This would seem to be the case even if the liability or proceeds arise from an

¶325

investment transaction. Conversely, however, the contract would clearly be for an investment purpose where the currency concerned is bought or sold short for speculative purposes, at least where both the bank and the customer intend that to be the case. Any doubt that forward foreign exchange contracts fall within para. 8 if they are for investment purposes (and even 'hedging' is usually an investment purpose) was laid to rest by the SIB's 1996 guidance note on foreign currency dealers (see above). All forward foreign exchange contracts fall within the FSA's money market exemption if they are between listed institutions or qualify as 'wholesale' (see ¶349). In addition, both spot and forward foreign exchange transactions are regulated by the Bank of England's London Code of Conduct whether or not they relate to assets which qualify as FSA-regulated investments; the London Code of Conduct has been adopted by SFA as relevant to compliance with its 'fit and proper' standard.

¶326   Contracts for differences etc. (Sch. 1, para. 9)

Many futures or options contracts are cash-settled, requiring a payment or net payment to be made rather than actual delivery of the underlying asset to which the contract relates. If the contract makes this clear, or the intention of both parties to this effect is established, then the contract is outside para. 8, as indeed it may be if even one of the parties does not intend that there should be delivery (see ¶325). However, the FSA normally treats these cash-settled contracts as FSA-regulated investments, nonetheless, on the basis that they are within para. 9, rather than para. 8. Conversely, if both parties intend that there should be delivery of the underlying asset, the contract falls outside para. 9 (note to para. 9).

Paragraph 9 expressly covers 'contracts for differences', contracts under which a payment can be made either way depending on the movement from the defined reference price or other factor. However, although it may be loosely referred to as covering contracts for differences, para. 9 is much wider than this; it covers even payments which can only be made one-way, if the purpose of the contract is to secure a profit or avoid a loss, without delivery of the asset concerned, by reference to movements in the price or value of any asset (not merely securities) or in an index or other measure; the Court of Appeal has held that 'secure' means 'obtain' and that para. 9 investments are accordingly not confined to the protection of commercial interests by hedging (*City Index Ltd v Leslie* [1991] 3 WLR 207, CA). This is why index futures fall in para. 9 rather than para. 8 and why para. 9 covers also cash-settled options, under which the option will in practice only be exercised if a payment reflecting the movement in the price of the underlying asset is to be made by the writer of the option to the person exercising it. Again, bonds which link the principal payable on redemption to returns on a specified investment exchange fall within para. 9.

It is unclear whether para. 9 applies to income profits or losses as well as capital ones. Many banks and building societies tie the interest payable on deposits made with them to returns on a specified investment exchange. It would seem that, in principle, the contracts governing these deposits should be treated as falling within para. 9, as well as para. 2 (debentures) if applicable. This is because 'profits' and 'losses' include revenue profits and losses as well as capital profits and losses; for example, it was held in the *Spanish Prospecting Co Ltd* [1911] 1 Ch 92 CA that 'the fundamental meaning [of profits] is the amount of gain made...', without distinguishing between capital and income (per Fletcher Moulton LJ at p. 98). Indeed, if it were otherwise, para. 9 could easily be avoided by providing the investor's 'return' as interest, with a fixed repayment of principal, rather than by increasing the amount of principal. However, in May 1992, the SIB issued guidance in relation to building societies stating that, although the position was not free from doubt, it would not treat an interest element tied to para. 9 factors as falling within para. 9. Conversely, para. 9 is regarded as applying to spread-betting, even on non-financial bets such as horse-racing, and sports book-makers offering spread bets have therefore had to become FSA-authorised (by joining SFA) in the same way as 'financial book-makers'; one by-product of this analysis is that, under s. 63(2), these bets have become enforceable despite the Gaming Acts (*City Index v Leslie* (above).

It is important to review carefully whether a particular investment falls within para. 9 or within para. 7 (options) when applying to an SRO for authorisation for particular activities. This is because options over contracts for differences seem to fall in para. 7 if the result is that the right to the contract is transferred on exercise (para. 7(a)). However, there must actually be an underlying contract which can be transferred: if, for example, what is called an index option actually provides for cash settlement based on the movement in the index (as in the case of the LIFFE index option) then this would seem to fall in para. 9. If the FSA-authorised firm intends to exercise a para. 7 call option over a futures contract or a contract for differences, it must in any event ensure that both para. 8 and para. 9 are within its business profile.

¶327   Long term insurance contracts (Sch. 1, para. 10)

The FSA treats as FSA-regulated investments rights under what it terms 'long term insurance contracts', namely insurance contracts which constitute long term business within the meaning of the *Insurance Companies Act* 1982, whether or not the contract itself is 'long term'. They may, however, not be FSA-regulated investments if they are taken out for pure protection. Long term business includes the making and performance of 'investment' life assurance contracts, the managing of pension funds, contracts to pay annuities on human life (for example, personal pension policies) and certain permanent health insurance contracts (Sch. 1 to the Insurance Companies Act).

Life assurance contracts with an investment element (and, seemingly, also these permanent health insurance contracts) are therefore FSA-regulated investments, even if they are not unit-linked. Endowment policies under which benefits are payable even if the insured person survives, and pension policies, will always be treated as investments. However, the policy exceptionally will not be treated as an FSA-regulated investment if it is intended purely for protection and falls (or, if it constitutes both long term and general business, the benefits related to the long term business element fall) within the cumulative restrictive criteria specified in note 1; these are that benefits are payable only on death, by accident or within ten years or before a specified age not exceeding 70, or on incapacity, that the policy has no surrender value or that it is a single premium policy and the surrender value does not exceed the premium and that, finally, the policy does not provide that it can be converted or extended so as to fall outside these restrictions. It is not necessary that the specific value of the benefits is stated in the policy for it to fall within this exemption, and benefits can therefore be index-linked. It is, however, expressly provided that rights under reinsurance contracts do not constitute FSA-regulated investments (note 3).

Although para. 12 does not expressly classify the writing of regulated insurance policies as an FSA-regulated investment activity, this falls within para. 12 by virtue of the 'deeming' provision in para. 28(2) that references to the disposal of an investment (for example, in para. 12) include references to issuing it. However, insurance companies authorised under the Insurance Companies Act are normally automatically authorised under the FSA (s. 22), as indeed are non-UK EEA insurance companies using their single European passport, (see ¶415).

¶328   Alteration of FSA-regulated investments

The types of investment which are covered by the FSA may be altered by the Government (s. 2(1)(a)); this power cannot be delegated to the SIB or any other designated agency.

EXEMPTED ACTIVITIES

¶329   Introduction

The Financial Services Act provides detailed 'transactional' exemptions for various classes of FSA-regulated investment activity. These exemptions are contained in different paragraphs of Pt. III of Sch. 1, and, in the case of overseas firms, also in Pt. IV. The government is empowered to alter the Sch. 1 exemptions (s. 2(1)(b)); this power cannot be delegated to the SIB or any other designated agency. The Pt. III exemptions work by excluding the exempted activity from the relevant paragraph in Pt. II; accordingly, the activities do not constitute FSA-regulated investment business, and therefore do not require FSA-authorisation even if engaging in them constitutes carrying on business in the UK. The Pt. IV exemptions work by treating the exempted activity as not carried on in the UK; accordingly, the activities do not require FSA-authorisation even though engaging in them constitutes carrying on FSA-regulated investment business with customers in the UK. Agreements to do the exempted activity will however constitute 'investment agreements' (s. 44(9)) and, accordingly, exempted activities will be subject to the FSA's restrictions on marketing (see Ch. 9).

It should, however, not be forgotten that, even if carrying on an activity constitutes carrying on FSA-regulated investment business in the UK, a firm which is an 'exempted person' in relation to it does not need FSA-authorisation for it (see ¶347–¶355). In particular, the exemption for certain money market activities of listed institutions (see ¶349) is very important both for these institutions and for corporate treasurers who seek to deal with them as a counterparty (see ¶331 and ¶332). There is also an exemption in specified circumstances for non-professional trustees of occupational pension schemes (s. 191). This is a very different type of exemption but it is more like the 'transactional' exemptions than the 'exempted persons' exemptions and accordingly it is convenient to deal with it in this section (see ¶344).

In addition, non-UK EEA investment firms and banks and other credit institutions do not need FSA-authorisation for FSA-regulated investment business carried on by them in the UK under the single European passports granted by the ISD and the 2BCD respectively or, in the case of ISD credit institutions, by the Treasury (see ¶301). The single European passport has been implemented into UK law by disapplying the FSA's authorisation requirement in s. 3 of the FSA rather than by excluding the passported service or activity from Pt. II. The exemptions therefore work more like the 'exempted persons' exemptions than the 'overseas persons' exemptions. However, the expression 'exempted person' is an FSA term of art and that term of art does not include passporting firms; indeed, passporting firms are often treated as if they were in fact FSA-authorised firms (Sch. 7 of the ISD regulations and Sch. 9 of the 2BCD regulations). The exemptions for non-UK EEA firms using their ISD or 2BCD passport (or, indeed, using the general Treaty of Rome freedom) to establish UK branches or to provide cross-border services to, or carry on cross-border activities with, clients or counterparties in the UK are reviewed at the end of this chapter (see ¶356).

Four 'transactional' exemptions which are particularly important are analysed in detail below. These are the exemptions for 'own account' transactions (see ¶331 and ¶332), for certain 'group' activities (see ¶333), for

¶329

qualifying overseas firms (see ¶334) and for 'permitted persons', namely, holders of a para. 23 permission, (see ¶335). In addition, the most important elements of the other exemptions are also highlighted below.

As will be apparent, the most important practical consideration arising from the fact that the exemptions are so detailed is that each type of transaction must be analysed in detail. This applies in many contexts, for example:

(1) in considering whether FSA-authorisation is required at all and (if, as is now normally required in practice, FSA-authorisation is to be sought by membership of an SRO rather than directly from the SIB) which SROs need to be joined;

(2) what activities need to be specified or included in the business plan or business profile to be filed on application to the SIB or an SRO;

(3) whether it is necessary to file a revised business plan or business profile to cover a new investment activity and whether it is necessary to join another SRO to give FSA-authorisation for it; and

(4) generally, whether the transaction is subject to the SIB's or an SRO's conduct of business rules.

As a result of the implementation of the ISD, the UK has restricted many of the FSA's exemptions in order to make the FSA's authorisation requirement apply to all 'core investment services' which require authorisation under the ISD (see ¶330). As from 1 January 1997, the FSA's 'own account', 'group' and 'permitted persons' exemptions (see ¶331, ¶332, ¶333 and ¶335) have all been restricted, as have the 'sale of body corporate' exemption relating to qualifying sales of companies (see ¶338) and the 'supply of goods or services' exemption (see ¶341). Importantly, these restrictions apply to both EEA firms and non-EEA firms alike but only if those firms are EEA investment firms for the purposes of the ISD (see ¶358) and are not exempted from the ISD by art. 2(2), or would have been EEA investment firms for the purposes of the ISD, and would not have been exempted from it by art. 2(2), if they had been UK firms (see ¶330).

¶330   ISD restrictions on exemptions

As explained in more detail in ¶356, the investment services directive, the second banking coordination directive and the two third insurance directives grant 'single European passports' to, respectively, qualifying EEA investment firms, EEA banks and other credit institutions and EEA insurance companies authorised under them for specified investment services or activities; this means that their domestic licences or authorisations for those services or activities cover the whole of the European Economic Area (the EU and Iceland, Liechtenstein and Norway). EEA firms authorised in their own member state can accordingly provide passported services or carry on passported activities to or with clients in any other EEA member State on a cross-border basis (either from a branch in their own, or a third party, member state, or on visits into the client's state from the branch), or establish a branch in another member state to provide passported services or carry on passported activities, without the need for a local licence or authorisation. The passports are granted on the basis of mutual recognition of the minimum authorisation standards imposed under these four 'single market' financial institutions directives by all EEA member States. The 2BCD harmonises the minimum standards for the authorisation of EEA credit institutions and works on the 'universal bank' model seen on the continent; it grants EEA authorised banks and other credit institutions the passport for specified investment (and banking) activities. The third insurance directives similarly harmonise the minimum standards for authorisation of EEA insurance companies and grants them the passport for investment activities carried on as part of their insurance business. Neither the 2BCD nor the third insurance directives impose minimum standards for the conduct of the 'investment business' activities covered by the passport. However, the ISD does exactly this.

An EEA investment firm can obtain a passport under the ISD only if it is authorised under the ISD (as implemented by its home member state) to provide one or more of the 'core investment services' set out in Pt. A of the Annex to the ISD; these services include dealing for own account or as agent, order-passing and arranging secondary market transactions, underwriting primary issues and discretionary investment management in ISD investments (see ¶358). EEA investment firms which are banks or other credit institutions do not qualify for the ISD passport (in addition to the 2BCD passport) if (as is normal in many member States) they are authorised to provide one or more core investment services by their banking licence under the first and second banking directives. UK credit institutions are treated as authorised for core investment services on this basis if (as is required by UK law) they are authorised to provide core investment services under the FSA. An EEA investment firm can only become authorised under the ISD if it complies with minimum conditions, which closely follow the FSA's 'fit and proper' standard. A firm subject to the ISD must have minimum levels of financial resources (or, regulatory capital) in approved form (as elaborated in the Capital Adequacy Directive of 15 March 1993, No. 93/6/EEC) and must be of good repute. Once authorised, the firm must comply with conduct of business rules covering specified investor protection matters.

Importantly, the ISD requires EEA member states normally to impose authorisation (or, licence) requirements on any firm incorporated in them (other than an ISD credit institution or an EEA insurance company) which provides as a regular occupation or business one or more of the 'core

¶330

investment services' listed in it to third parties on a professional basis. The ISD does not require authorisation for the non-core services listed in the ISD; non-core services are additional services covered by the ISD passport for firms authorised under the ISD, and include investment advice, safe custody services and services relating to mergers and the purchase or sale of undertakings (see ¶358). However, EEA member States are allowed to impose their own domestic authorisation requirements on non-core services (and indeed on investment services exempted from or completely outside the ISD) if they want to; the passport covers non-core services in case a member State does choose to require authorisation for them. As in the case of the FSA, various exemptions from the ISD's authorisation requirement are provided by art. 2(2) for qualifying EEA firms (which are therefore not 'EEA investment firms' for the purposes of this chapter). As a result, these firms also do not have the ISD's single European passport, which, indeed, was often the reason for the exemption; however, they are entitled to the passport to provide cross-border services, or establish branches, throughout the EEA granted by the Treaty of Rome itself (see ¶360). The art. 2(2) exemptions are listed in the *Financial Services Act 1986 (Investment Services) (Extension of Scope of Act) Order* 1995 (see below). The exemptions apply, for example, to firms which are acting as managers of 'collective investment undertakings', qualifying firms authorised only to pass orders to 'authorised investment firms' and firms which provide core investment services only to group companies; the 'group' exemption may apply in limited circumstances even to firms which provide services to companies with which they are affiliated but which are technically not group companies (see ¶333). The ISD similarly does not apply to EEA insurance companies (which are also exempted by art. 2(2)). Finally, if a firm arranges deals in existing securities or transmits orders (both referred to in the ISD as the 'reception and transmission of orders') solely for the account of and under the full and unconditional responsibility of an EEA investment firm, that activity is regarded as the activity of the EEA investment firm and not of the firm itself; appointed representatives under s. 44 of the FSA therefore do not need ISD authorisation for these activities.

The ISD accordingly requires an EEA member State to impose an authorisation requirement for the core investment services listed in the ISD only in the case of EEA investment firms incorporated in it (and only if they are not ISD credit institutions authorised to provide core investment services under the first and second banking directives; however, it forbids member states to grant more favourable treatment to branches of non-EEA firms in relation to those services (art. 5). Because of these two requirements, and perhaps in order to avoid providing the consequent competitive advantages to non-EEA firms, the UK has extended the scope of the FSA in relation to both EEA investment firms and, importantly, non-EEA firms which would be EEA

¶330

investment firms if they were UK firms, in order to cover all services within the ISD's authorisation requirement (namely, core investment services outside the exemptions in art. 2(2) of the ISD). The ISD is not in fact much wider than the FSA, on which much of it seems based, but the resulting extensions of the FSA are important at the margin; as all ISD core investment services would be within the FSA apart from the exemptions in Pt. III of Sch. 1, the extensions were accordingly effected by restricting some of those exemptions.

The restrictions to the FSA exemptions are contained in the *Financial Services Act 1986 (Investment Services) (Extension of Scope of Act) Order* 1995, SI 1995/3271, as, in effect, amended by the *Financial Services Act 1986 (Restriction of Scope of Act and Meaning of Collective Investment Scheme) Order* 1996, SI 1996/2996, (together 'the FSA Extension Order'). The FSA Extension Order also applied the conduct of business rules of the SIB (or, where the firm is authorised for them by an SRO, of the SRO) to non-core services, as required by the ISD. Although the FSA extension order came into force on 1 January 1996 in relation to conduct of business rules, the fundamental prohibition in s. 3 of the FSA on carrying on FSA-regulated investment business in the UK without FSA-authorisation did not apply to the extensions made by it until 1 January 1997.

In essence, the FSA extension order removes the FSA exemptions specified in it (namely, the exemptions in para. 17–19, 21 and 23 of Sch. 1 to the FSA) to the extent that they are, in effect, incompatible with the authorisation requirement of the ISD for EEA investment firms. The restrictions accordingly apply only in the case of firms providing ISD core investment services, as listed in Sch. 1 to the order, to third parties on a professional basis as a regular occupation or business and only if they are not within the exemptions specified in art. 2(2) (which are also listed in the order). Non-core services are irrelevant in this context as the ISD does not require authorisation for them, but only gives them the passport in the case of EEA investment firms. The restrictions on the specified FSA exemptions apply even to EEA banks and other credit institutions if they are EEA investment firms, even though they are exempted from the ISD's authorisation requirement if (as is normal) they are authorised to provide one or more core investment services by their authorisation under the first and second banking directives as a credit institution; this is because their exemption from the ISD's authorisation requirement is in art. 2(1), not art. 2(2), (see above). However, ISD credit institutions (in other words, all non-UK EEA credit institutions which are exempted from the ISD's authorisation requirement on this basis) have been granted an ISD passport by the Treasury for core investment services, and ISD non-core services, falling outside their 2BCD passport; they therefore do not need FSA-authorisation for these services and are in effect accordingly exempted from the restrictions so far as the FSA's authorisation requirement is concerned. In addition, the

¶330

restrictions do not apply to insurance companies because their exemption from the ISD is contained in art. 2(2). The restrictions also apply to non-EEA firms if they would have been subject to the ISD's authorisation requirement if they had been UK firms; they therefore do not apply if on this basis the firm would have been exempted by art. 2(2), for example, because it is an insurance company.

The FSA extension order does not amend the terms of the affected exemptions themselves; it only provides that they are restricted and it is accordingly necessary to determine in each case the extent of the restriction. The order lists the ISD 'core investment services' and the art. 2(2) exemptions as they appear in the ISD without explaining them. It provides that, in general terms, the FSA Sch. 1, Pt. III exemptions specified in the order apply in relation to core investment services only to the extent that the ISD allows them for EEA investment firms as a result of the art. 2(2) exemptions (such as those for managers of collective investment undertakings, for firms providing ISD core investment services exclusively to group companies and for insurance companies). As explained above, the restrictions on the exemptions apply whether or not the firm is an EEA firm (because all firms are treated for this purpose as if they were UK firms). Accordingly, some services formerly covered by the specified Pt. III exemptions now need FSA-authorisation unless another exemption applies, such as the 'overseas persons' exemptions (see ¶334), which are not affected by the FSA extension order, or, indeed, the ISD or 2BCD passport itself. The Treasury have decided that the 'money market' exemption (see ¶349) can continue despite the ISD, although that had been in doubt; this is on the basis that the 'approval' process which allows eligible banks and other firms to qualify as listed money market institutions for the exemption is in effect an authorisation regime so far as the ISD is concerned, with the Bank of England as the SRO. Indeed, in the regulations implementing the ISD passport, the Treasury define listed institutions as 'authorised' for the purposes of the outgoing passport (reg. 18 of the *Investment Services Regulations 1995*, SI 1995/3275) and UK listed institutions can therefore use the ISD passport for their exempted money market transactions as if they were FSA-authorised for them. Conversely, the 'permitted persons' exemption for dealings (see ¶335) is subject to the FSA Extension Order and 'permitted persons' may therefore need FSA-authorisation; if, however, the 'permitted person' only deals for its own account (for its own purposes and not as a service) or on behalf of 'group companies' within the ISD 'group' exemption, as is normal for corporate treasurers, or, indeed, in investments outside the ISD (such as commodity futures), it can normally still use the exemption.

The FSA Extension Order provides that the FSA's exemptions for 'own account' dealings (see ¶331 and ¶332), for FSA-regulated investment activities in connection with the sale of goods or supply of services (see ¶341) and for para. 23 'permitted persons' (see ¶335), and the 'group' and the 'sale of body corporate' exemptions (see ¶333 and ¶338), apply in relation to the core investment services covered by them only to the extent that the services are exempted from the ISD in the case of UK firms. It must be emphasised that these FSA exemptions still apply in full where they can stand with the ISD; this will be the case if the FSA-regulated investments concerned fall outside the ISD (such as commodity futures), if the firm or service is exempted from the ISD under art. 2(2) (or would have been if it was a UK firm), if the services provided by the firm which fall outside art. 2(2) are not core investment services or, indeed, if the relevant activity (typically, dealing for own account) is not a 'service' for the purposes of the ISD. Accordingly, the 'own account' acquisition of holdings carrying at least 20 per cent of a company's voting rights is still seemingly exempted (by para. 17(1)(c)) provided that, as would be normal, they are acquired for the investor's own purposes and at his own initiative, as this is not a 'service' for third parties (see ¶331). Again, the 'group' exemption still applies to core investment services at least if the firm provides them only to ISD group companies (see ¶333), even if it also advises other companies outside the ISD group exemption (as investment advice is not a core investment service but only a non-core service).

Finally, the 'sale of body corporate' exemption in para. 21 still applies in particular circumstances. In the view of the UK regulators, the exemption is not restricted at all by the ISD if the firm's only FSA-regulated investment activities all fall within the exemption. SFA wrote in February 1997 to member firms to whom this applied informing them that, after consultation with the Treasury, the SIB had reached the view that such firms accordingly did not need FSA-authorisation as had originally been thought. It is understood that this revised view was reached on the basis that the transactions to which the 'sale of body corporate' exemption applies are really the acquisition or disposal of a business, albeit one which is incorporated, rather than of securities as such, and should therefore be regarded as falling outside the ISD altogether; the transaction is between 'proprietors' and prospective 'proprietors' rather than investors and prospective investors. This conclusion is very helpful where the firm's FSA-regulated investment activities do indeed all fall within the 'sale of body corporate' exemption. However, it is unclear why the SIB's view is not equally applicable where the firm provides no core investment service falling outside the 'sale of body corporate' exemption, or the exemptions in art. 2(2), (so that on this view it is not an EEA investment firm or treated as one), even if it carries on other FSA-regulated investment activities not qualifying as core investment services, in particular giving advice on transactions falling outside the 'sale of body corporate' exemption. Indeed, it is arguable that, where the transaction is the sale of the whole company (or substantially the whole company, perhaps down to the crucial 75 per cent level referred to in the 'sale of

¶330

body corporate' exemption), not only advisory but also arranging services provided in relation to it are in any event only non-core services (see ¶358), and it is also arguable that this is the case whether or not the firm provides core investment services outside the 'sale of body corporate' exemption or, indeed, whether or not that exemption applies at all; the relevant non-core service is 'services relating to ... the purchase of undertakings'. If, however, the firm is outside the art. 2(2) exemptions and does provide core investment services falling outside the 'sale of body corporate' exemption, its activities within the 'sale of body corporate' exemption are within the ISD passport, and are subject to the SIB's conduct of business rules (or those of its SRO), whether those activities are technically core investment services or non-core services; this is because the firm will be an EEA investment firm and accordingly, even if they are non-core services, they will be FSA-regulated as well as within the passport (see above). It should, however, be noted that, whichever is the correct analysis, the 'sale of body corporate' exemption does not apply to public takeovers. It applies only to the qualifying transactions between limited classes of counterparty to which the 'sale of body corporate' exemption historically applied (typically, the sale of a wholly-owned subsidiary to a corporate purchaser); although this is accordingly stricter than the ISD's authorisation requirement, it complies with the ISD because the ISD only lays down minimum standards and member states can impose stricter requirements if they want to, subject, of course, to the single European passport 'exemptions' (see ¶356). Advisory services are only non-core services for the purposes of the ISD and, as indicated above, the FSA's 'group' exemption and 'sale of body corporate' exemption accordingly continue to apply to them without restriction.

¶331   Own account dealings in securities (Sch. 1, para. 17(1)(c))

The 'own account' exemption in para. 17(1)(c) for dealings in securities as principal is the most important of all the exemptions from the FSA's authorisation requirement as it is this exemption which exempts ordinary investors from the need to be FSA-authorised for dealings with FSA-authorised firms, other FSA-professionals and qualifying overseas securities firms. The exemption primarily applies only in relation to investments which constitute 'securities' in colloquial language (other than traded options), namely investments falling in para. 1–6 of Pt. II of Sch. 1. However, it also applies to the assignment of life assurance and pension policies.

As a result of the implementation of the ISD, the 'own account' exemption in para. 17(1)(c) does not apply if the ISD would have required the activity to be authorised under the ISD in the case of a UK firm (see ¶330). The ISD only applies to 'services' and accordingly would seem to restrict the exemption only if the own account transaction constitutes a service; the key examples are where the firm is a market-maker in the kind of securities concerned or is a broker-dealer or an agency broker which sells an investment to a client from its own book, or buys an investment from a client for its own book, in order to fill an order from the client. In these cases, the 'own account' exemption accordingly does not apply even if the client who is the counterparty is in fact an FSA-authorised firm; if relevant, the agency side of a 'dual capacity' transaction (where for example, the broker sells from its own book) would normally be subject to FSA-authorisation in any event. However, the 'own account' exemption will not be restricted if no service is provided at all, typically where the firm wants to rely on the exemption for dealings in relation to 20 per cent holdings of voting rights in a company which it wants to buy or sell on its own initiative or the counterparty is an FSA-authorised firm; it will also not be restricted if, exceptionally, the investment is outside the ISD (typically, where it is a life policy). Finally, although it is unclear, it would seem that, except in the case of market-makers, agreeing to act as a counterparty when solicited for a particular transaction is also not a service, even in the case of dealers, at least where there is no fiduciary relationship, as the firm agrees to the transaction on its own initiative and for its own purposes. It is unclear how wide the ISD's investment service of 'dealing for own account' is (see ¶329). It is arguably restricted to 'dealing' in general parlance, in other words 'trading', and not to be synonymous with 'dealing in [ISD] investments' within para. 12. Crucially, it would therefore normally cover only acting as a dealer (or, of course, a market-maker) and not investing as such; however, even this means that professional dealers might need FSA-authorisation even if they do not hold themselves out as such within para. 17(1)(b) if they are in practice providing a service. If, however, 'dealing' in the ISD is synonymous with para. 12 (apart from the exemptions), then none of the exemptions in Pt. III would seem to apply unless they are covered by one of the limited ISD exemptions. Even in these circumstances, however, it would seem arguable that no service is being provided to third parties in the normal case; even a holding out or other solicitation (for example, a press advertisement by a venture capital firm indicating that it can provide funds for a growing business) does not really result in its providing a service, as the better analysis would seem to be that it is merely encouraging prospective counterparties to approach it. The FSA's authorisation requirement seemingly applies to securities dealers, under para. 17(1)(b), in the same way as it does to investors under para. 17(1)(c), namely in order to protect counterparties where a dealer in effect invites approaches, not because it is a service. If this argument is correct, the 'own account' exemption in para. 17(1)(c) for transactions not solicited by the firm is therefore not restricted by the ISD in normal circumstances, perhaps even in the case of dealers who do not hold themselves out as dealers within para. 17(1)(b).

¶331

The 'own account' exemption in para 17(1)(c) only applies in relation to securities in the cash market, including subscription warrants (even if they are, misleadingly, called 'options'), and to the assignment of FSA-regulated insurance and pension policies, for example 'second-hand' endowment policies, (see ¶327); the 'own account' exemption for derivatives transactions, and other transactions in FSA-regulated insurance and pension policies, is contained in para. 17(4) (see ¶332).

Paragraph 17(1)(c) provides that, except in the case of firms holding themselves out as market-makers or dealers in the kind of securities concerned, securities transactions as principal (which otherwise fall within para. 12) normally do not require FSA-authorisation unless 'members of the public' have been regularly solicited and the transaction results from that soliciting; importantly, FSA-authorised firms are not 'members of the public' for this purpose, nor are other FSA-professionals or qualifying overseas securities firms (see ¶302). Indeed, para. 17(1)(c) is drafted on the basis not that it provides an exemption but that, conversely, transactions as principal will be subject to the FSA's authorisation requirement only in the relevant, exceptional, circumstances. Nonetheless, it is easiest to approach para. 17(1)(c) as providing a back-to-front exemption for own account securities transactions not covered by it, in that (except in the case of firms holding themselves out as market-makers or dealers in the kind of securities concerned) FSA-authorisation is not required except where para. 17(1)(c) applies.

The 'own account' exemption will normally apply to dealings by investors on the London Stock Exchange or other investment exchanges and in the Eurobond market. It would seem that in principle it is available to trustees (whether of private settlements or of unit trusts or pension funds) because, when they deal, it would seem that they deal as principal for the purpose of the exemption; they are not as such agents for their beneficiaries (see *Bowstead & Reynolds on Agency*, 16th Edition p. 22), and, accordingly, if they are not to be treated as principals, para. 12 (which applies only to transactions as principal or as agent) will not apply at all. The term used in the FSA is 'as principal' rather than 'for his own account' and this seems wide enough to include trustees even though they are, indeed, not acting for their own account (although 'own account' is an acceptable short-hand title for the exemption). Conversely, the exemption may in practice not be available to venture capital companies, or other firms which subscribe new securities rather than buy existing securities (which may well think that the 'own account' exemption would necessarily apply), unless they limit their investments so that the exemption relating to 'substantial holdings' applies (para. 17(1)(c) taken together with para. 17(2) (d)); this important problem is dealt with below.

The exemption applies to all own account securities transactions except in the three cases listed in para. 17(1):

¶331

(1) in the case of firms holding themselves out as market-makers in the kind of securities concerned (para. 17(1)(a)); this exclusion of the exemption relates at most only to securities in the same paragraph in Sch. 1 as those in which the market-maker actually makes a market, and arguably is even more restricted;

(2) in the case of transactions by firms holding themselves out as dealers in securities in the kind of securities concerned (para. 17(1)(b)); again, this exclusion of the exemption relates at most only to securities in the same paragraph in Sch. 1 as those in which the firm holds itself out as a dealer, and arguably is even more restricted; and

(3) in the case of a firm which regularly solicits what are referred to in para. 17(1)(c) as 'members of the public' if the transaction results from that soliciting (para. 17(1)(c)). This means that own account transactions with counterparties who are not 'members of the public' (in particular, with FSA-professionals and qualifying overseas securities firms) will not need FSA-authorisation unless they result from the soliciting of members of the public, for example as a result of advertisements in a newspaper, which will be unusual. Similarly, transactions with 'members of the public' also will normally not need FSA-authorisation under para. 17(1)(c) if they are entered into by the members of the public on their own initiative and were not in any way solicited or, indeed, they result from the soliciting only of FSA-professionals or qualifying overseas securities firms. Conversely, however, both types of transaction may need FSA-authorisation (under para. 17(1)(b) or, indeed, para. 17(1) (a)) even if para. 17(1)(c) accordingly does not apply; this potential trap is discussed below.

The persons who are not 'members of the public' for the purpose of para. 17(1)(c) (and who accordingly can be solicited for securities transactions within the 'own account' exemption) are listed in para. 17(2); in summary, they are FSA-professionals, qualifying overseas securities firms and shareholders or other persons solicited in relation to 'substantial holdings' transactions. 'Members of the public' accordingly do not include FSA-authorised firms, exempted firms (see ¶347–¶355) and 'permitted persons', in other words holders of a para. 23 permission, (see ¶335). Importantly, non-UK EEA firms carrying on FSA-regulated investment business in the UK under their ISD or 2BCD passport are treated as FSA-authorised firms for this purpose, although the treatment of ISD credit institutions doing so under their ISD passport is not totally clear, (para. 42 of Sch. 7 to the Investment Services Regulations and para. 44 of Sch. 9 to the 2BCD regulations, see ¶357); non-UK EEA firms will

¶331

be carrying on FSA-regulated investment business in the UK under their passport if they carry it on from a UK office or otherwise with clients or counterparties in the UK outside the 'overseas persons' exemptions (see ¶334), in which case the business is referred to as 'home-regulated investment business [carried on] in the UK' (see ¶359). Overseas broker-dealers, investment managers, fund managers and investment advisers and other overseas securities firms are also not 'members of the public', even if they are not FSA-professionals if their head office is outside the UK and they are solicited at an office outside the UK. Accordingly, transactions on the London Stock Exchange, in the Eurobond market or on non-UK exchanges will normally not need FSA-authorisation even if the firm solicits members of the market or exchange direct rather than through brokers. A firm will be an overseas securities firm within para. 17(2) whether it acts as a principal or as an agent (such as a broker or an investment manager). However, it will be important, and perhaps difficult, to check whether, as required for it to qualify as an overseas securities firm, its ordinary business (or, normal activity) does involve it in carrying on FSA-regulated investment activities; it does not need to be actually carrying on FSA-regulated investment business, even outside the UK. Importantly, the person solicited does not need to be the actual counterparty, and he will not be in the case of an investment adviser. Investment trusts and some other City institutions are, however, normally treated as 'members of the public' (see below).

If para. 17(1)(a) or 17(1)(b) applies to a transaction, FSA-authorisation may be required for that transaction, even if it does not fall within para. 17(1)(c) so that the 'own account' exemption otherwise applies. As indicated above, they apply to a transaction if the firm entering into that transaction as principal holds itself out as a market-maker in securities of the relevant kind or as carrying on the business of buying securities of the relevant kind with a view to selling them; this must surely refer to 'dealers' rather than 'investors'. This presents a nasty trap because it is accordingly not sufficient merely to review whether para. 17(1)(c) applies to the transaction concerned on the basis that it results from the regular solicitation of 'members of the public'. It is also necessary to review all other FSA-regulated investment activities carried on by the firm concerned to see whether it holds itself out as a market-maker or dealer in any securities and whether, if that is the case, those securities (or some of those securities) fall in the same paragraph in Pt. I of Sch. 1 as the securities to which the transaction concerned relates; if they do, the prudent view is that the firm will need to be FSA-authorised for that transaction. Accordingly, if a firm holds itself out as a market-maker or dealer in corporate Eurobonds, it may need to be FSA-authorised even for long-term own account investments in loan stock, although it will not need to be FSA-authorised by virtue of that holding out for own account investments in shares; conversely, if the firm's business develops and it

¶331

holds itself out as a market-maker or dealer not only in Eurobonds but also in Euro-equities, then it may have to be FSA-authorised even for venture capital investment in shares.

The position is not, however, as bad as it might at first appear because the tests in paras. 17(1)(a) and 17(1)(b) are quite stringent. They do not apply to a firm merely because it is a market-maker or a dealer in securities. They apply only if it actually holds itself out as a market-maker or dealer (they do not refer merely to a firm carrying on the business of market-making or dealing but to a firm which actually holds itself out as doing so) and accordingly they do not necessarily apply even if the firm concerned is a market-maker or (which is more relevant in practice) a dealer. For a firm to hold itself out there must be a positive representation (whether by word or by conduct) and, if it deals only on its own initiative, or receives invitations to deal by virtue of its reputation or previous dealings and does not positively represent that it is a market-maker or dealer, para. 17(1)(a) and 17(1)(b) do not apply. Although the position is not totally clear, it would seem that a statement in the firm's accounts or (if the firm is a company) a provision in its memorandum of association that it is a market-maker or dealer is not a holding out for this purpose; indeed, this would accord with the philosophy behind para. 17(1)(a) and 17(1)(b), that it is necessary to regulate firms which invite investors to approach them. Similarly, mere regular dealing without more is normally not in itself a holding out (as evidenced by the 'group own account' exemption in para. 18(2)(a), which refers to a holding out 'directed' only at group companies); the SIB has, stated that this is, indeed, its view as well (see s. 5 of Guidance Release 1/88 on para. 17(1)(b), issued in March 1988), although it may since have changed its view somewhat (see s. 5(i) of the 1994 Permitted Persons Explanatory Memorandum (see ¶335)).

It is in fact arguable that the exclusion in para. 17(1)(a) and 17(1)(b) does not necessarily apply to all securities falling in the same paragraph in Sch. 1 as the securities in relation to which the firm holds itself out. Much may depend on what is actually held out. If, for example, the firm represents that it deals in 'shares', the exclusion will clearly apply to all shares. However, if it represents that it deals in 'Swiss equities' or in 'Eurobonds' or that it is an ISMA market-maker, it should be possible to persuade the UK regulators (and a court) that it is not representing that it deals in UK equities or domestic loan stock. However, although this is perhaps the better view on a mischief basis, the only safe view until there is an actual court decision on this matter is that, however restricted the holding out, the exemption will normally not apply to any securities in the same paragraph of Sch. 1 as those to which the representation relates (or should be regarded as relating). The one exception is where the firm is registered on an investment exchange as a market-maker for identified securities and is not a market-maker in any other case. In addition,

¶331

there are excluded from the 'holding out' test for dealers any transactions which fall outside para. 12; this may mean that only transactions resulting from the solicitation of 'members of the public' are included (para. 17(2)), but this is unclear. If para. 17(1)(a) and 17(1)(b) do not apply and the firm restricts its securities transactions so that it does not solicit 'members of the public' within para. 17(1)(c), it will not need FSA-authorisation for its own account dealings in securities.

The firm can also solicit other companies in its own 'group' (see ¶333). In addition, para. 17(2)(d) helpfully also allows a firm which is acting as principal to use the exemption in para. 17(1)(c) to acquire shares carrying 20 per cent of the voting rights in companies, or to increase or decrease such holdings of the firm or its group, or to sell shares to groups which already have such a holding. This applies in relation to any company, whether UK or overseas and whether listed or unlisted, and 'group' has the wide Sch. 1 meaning (see ¶333); however, shares are not included unless their voting rights are or have become exercisable generally, so that, for example, preference shares are typically not included until the issuer is in default, (para. 17(2)(d)(i)). This 'substantial holdings' exemption will, however, not be of help to investment companies if, as is normal, they seek to acquire or increase non-notifiable stakes, although it would seem to allow the acquisition of investments even by way of subscription.

It must always be remembered that City institutions and other UK professional securities investors are treated as 'members of the public' unless they (coincidentally) are FSA-professionals or the 'substantial holdings' exemption applies; as most insurance companies and investment managers of pension funds are FSA-authorised firms, the City institutions which can normally qualify as 'members of the public' are primarily investment trusts, venture capital trusts and other investment companies. There is no exemption within para. 17(1)(c) for transactions with them merely because they are professional investors or qualify as 'non-private customers' for the purposes of SRO conduct of business rules; this contrasts strongly with the position of overseas securities firms, which are not 'members of the public' if they are solicited at an overseas office, even though they are not FSA-professionals and, indeed, with the safe harbour given to overseas firms by the 'overseas persons' exemptions (see ¶334) for own account dealings with large companies even if they are not FSA-professionals.

The 'money market' exemption for listed institutions (see ¶349) may, however, be of help to their counterparties; as listed institutions are exempted firms, they are not 'members of the public' for the purposes of the 'own account' exemption in relation to the soliciting of securities transactions by ordinary trading and manufacturing companies. Such companies can therefore solicit listed institutions for 'exempted' wholesale transactions without needing FSA-authorisation. Indeed, it is arguable that this particular class of 'FSA-professional' permitted counterparty is even wider. In contrast to the para. 26 exemption for 'overseas firms' (see ¶334), para. 17(2) does not qualify the exemption by limiting it to exempted firms acting in the course of the FSA-regulated investment business in respect of which they are exempt. Accordingly, a listed institution can seemingly be solicited within the 'own account' exemption for any transaction, even if outside the 'money market' exemption, in the same way as FSA-authorised firms can be solicited for any transaction, even if their FSA-authorisation does not cover it; the position is very unclear but this result would be reasonable as firms which are not themselves listed institutions cannot be expected to know the applicability of this very complicated exemption. In addition, exempted firms are defined as firms 'exempted under Ch. IV of Pt. 1 of [the FSA]' (s. 207(1)); listed institutions are indeed so exempted, although not perhaps for the transaction in question. Similarly, because, *ex hypothesi*, the listed institution did not solicit the transaction, it may itself be able to rely on the 'own account' exemption for the transaction even if it is outside its exemption. However, this depends on the facts and may be a dangerous route for listed institutions to take as a matter of practice (rather than ad hoc) if they are not also FSA-authorised firms; in particular circumstances, the courts may, perhaps, hold that the transaction did indirectly result from regular solicitation of 'members of the public' by the listed institution, even though its solicitation of exempted money market transactions is ignored (para. 32). Indeed, this all applies equally where the counterparty FSA-professional is a 'permitted person' (see ¶335) and in this case the firm hoping to rely on the 'own account' exemption cannot know the extent of the permission, which is additional support for this analysis in relation to listed institutions.

It is unclear whether the 'own account' exemption applies if the firm seeking to use the exemption does not solicit 'members of the public' itself but appoints an agent to do so. This is not a big problem in the case of Stock Exchange transactions as the firm's counterparty will normally be an FSA-authorised firm; this probably also applies in the case of other UK domestic markets, and a firm's counterparties in the Eurobond market are likely to be FSA-authorised firms or other FSA-professionals or qualifying overseas securities firms. In other circumstances, however, this will be a very important question, but unfortunately it is also a very difficult one. If the exemption does not apply in these other circumstances, it means that the firm will need to be FSA-authorised if it regularly solicits, for example, private companies even though it uses an FSA-authorised firm to solicit on its behalf, such as a stockbroker or merchant bank (as the FSA clearly wants it to do). Conversely, if the exemption does apply, this would seem to allow a firm to use the 'own account' exemption if it appoints any third party to solicit 'members of the public' on its behalf even if the appointee is not an FSA-authorised firm. This is particularly significant

¶331

because it is not clear that the actual act of marketing itself always requires FSA-authorisation, although the agreement by the appointee to market on the firm's behalf is likely to fall within para. 13 and so require FSA-authorisation itself (see ¶321) unless the 'overseas person' exemption (see ¶334) or the 'group' exemption (see ¶333) applies.

The law is very unclear as to whether, if one firm solicits on behalf of another, that other will be regarded as doing the soliciting. On balance, the better view is that if the firm soliciting is doing so as part of its own independent business (as, for example in the case of a stockbroker) that soliciting will normally not be attributed to its principal, although the principal may have legal responsibility for torts committed during the solicitation. If the firm seeking to use the 'own account' exemption employs an independent stockbroker or merchant bank which is an FSA-authorised firm, that would seem to be doing exactly what the FSA wants it to do, and (even if the firm is properly regarded as doing the soliciting done by the stockbroker or merchant bank) it is surely very unlikely that the courts would regard the 'own account' exemption as excluded in those circumstances. Indeed, the FSA expressly makes certain exemptions available if an FSA-authorised or exempted firm arranges the transaction (see, for example, the 'own account' exemption for derivatives transactions, the 'overseas persons' exemptions and the 'money market' exemption discussed in, respectively, ¶332, ¶334 and ¶349). These exemptions would normally involve the FSA-authorised or exempted firm soliciting prospective counterparties on behalf of the firm seeking to rely on the exemption; the availability of these exemptions in these circumstances testifies to the FSA's approval of such soliciting and indicates that the much broader 'own account' exemption in para. 17(1)(c) should not be excluded in relation to the firm in the same circumstances. It is, however, unfortunate that the wording of the FSA allows room for doubt on this most fundamental point. Conversely, if one firm ('the principal') employs another firm ('the agent') to solicit on its behalf and the agent can properly be regarded as carrying on business on behalf of the principal, rather than his own independent business, (see ¶308), the courts will probably attribute the soliciting by the agent to the principal; although, it will depend on the facts, this may well be the case if the agent solicits exclusively on behalf of the principal and, *a fortiori*, if the agent is in the same group as the principal (in which case, indeed, the courts may also feel able to pierce the corporate veil). In addition, the agent's soliciting may also be attributed to the principal if he acts without discretion in a purely ministerial role and solicits prospective counter-parties nominated by the principal.

Venture capital companies which invest for their own account in small unquoted companies ('investee companies'), which will hopefully go public in due course, may need to become FSA-authorised firms under para. 17(1)(c) for this activity. This applies equally in the case of development capital companies

¶331

and other firms which in a sense provide finance by means of investment in share or loan capital rather than bank loans. This is because they normally solicit prospective investee companies, or their shareholders, for example by advertising the availability of private equity finance. Not only the shareholders but also the investee companies themselves are 'members of the public' in the normal case; this is because para. 17(2) defines 'members of the public' as 'any ... person' other than the permitted categories listed in para. 17(2)(a)–(e), and issuers as such are not on the list. Accordingly, investment as a result of such advertising falls outside the 'own account' exemption unless the exemption in relation to 'substantial holdings' applies (para. 17(2)(d)); if the firm wants to rely on this, it would be helpful if the soliciting made it clear that only holdings carrying at least 20 per cent of the voting rights are to be acquired. If the investment falls outside the 'own account' exemption, the acquisition of the venture capital stake will require FSA-authorisation even though it is acquired for the account of the venture capital company itself and not for a managed fund. This would not, however, be the case if the solicitation is in fact by a third party and is not attributed to the venture capital company itself. Accordingly, members of limited partnerships or other investment funds, or of syndicates of 'parallel' investors, managed by an FSA-authorised firm (or with an FSA-authorised investment manager) which alone solicits investee companies, and their shareholders, do not require FSA-authorisation, provided that the solicitation is not attributed to the fund or syndicate (which it normally will not be).

¶332 Own account dealings in derivatives (Sch. 1, para. 17(4))

The 'own account' exemption for transactions in derivatives, such as traded options or futures, is much easier. The exemption also applies to transactions relating to life assurance and pension policies, except that assignments of such policies fall within the tighter 'own account' exemption for securities transactions (see ¶331). It provides an exemption for own account derivatives transactions with FSA-professionals and qualifying overseas securities firms, as in the case of securities transactions (see ¶331), although the qualification for overseas securities firms is different, but it extends the exemption to cover also derivatives transactions arranged by them or entered into by them as agent for the firm seeking to rely on the exemption (para. 29).

There is, however, a potential trap here. In contra-distinction to the securities 'own account' exemption (see ¶331), the derivatives 'own account' exemption is available to a firm only if it is not already an FSA-authorised firm, or a passporting firm, which is treated as one (see ¶331). On many exchanges, futures brokers in fact deal as principal with their clients and with the market under matching transactions (in order, for example, to facilitate the settlement and margining of transactions with the clearing house). The restriction of the exemption to firms which are not FSA-authorised firms is intended to ensure that the broker's transactions with clearing (or other clearing) members of the exchange constitute FSA-regulated investment business and will accordingly be subject to the conduct of business rules of its SRO (or the SIB). This problem would not arise in the case of securities transactions because para. 17(1)(a) and 17(1)(b) require members of the exchange in a similar position to be FSA-authorised firms (see ¶331). However, the exclusion of the exemption applies to all FSA-authorised firms and not just those which might enter into matching transactions with 'members of the public'. Accordingly, a bank or securities dealer which is an FSA-authorised firm for securities transactions and which enters into derivatives transactions for its own account merely with FSA-professionals or qualifying overseas securities firms, (for example, and typically, on a futures or options exchange) will not be entitled to rely on the 'own account' exemption in para. 17(4), even though it is in this context an investor needing protection rather than a provider of financial services. Accordingly, the bank or securities dealer will need to ensure that its business profile or business plan includes derivatives transactions and will be subject to conduct of business rules in relation to them. Alternatively, the futures or options business could be transferred to a separate subsidiary which is not an FSA-authorised firm and therefore would be entitled to the exemption.

The application of the derivatives 'own account' exemption in relation to counterparties outside the UK, in particular in the case of transactions on overseas futures or options exchanges, is complicated. This is because transactions with or through overseas securities firms are covered by the exemption only if the transaction is actually entered into through a non-UK office of a party to the transaction, whether the counterparty or, indeed, the firm seeking to rely on the exemption or its broker (para. 17(4)(b)); this contrasts with the securities 'own account' exemption where what is important is not that the transaction is entered into through a non-UK office but that the overseas securities firm is solicited at a non-UK office. Transactions executed on an overseas exchange will therefore normally be within the exemption if the firm uses its own broker; the potential problem is that transactions executed on an 'open outcry' exchange are entered into in the exchange and not in the office of either party. They will be, however, within the exemption where the order is routed directly or indirectly through a non-UK office of the firm's broker, at least where the broker is acting as the firm's agent (and so enters into the transaction itself); they will also be within the exemption where the broker actually deals a transaction with the firm from its non-UK office which matches the one the broker deals with the market. Finally, it may be that only the broker's UK office is involved, for example it executes the order with the market itself; the broker must, however, be an FSA-professional in order to do this and, accordingly, the exemption will apply even if no non-UK office is

¶332

involved, because a non-UK office does not need to be involved if the transaction is with or through an FSA-professional (para. 17(4)(a), see above).

The derivatives 'own account' exemption is restricted by the ISD where the transaction forms part of an ISD core investment service (see ¶330). This is likely to be the case only where the firm seeking to rely on the exemption holds itself out as an options or futures market-maker or dealer (see ¶331). However, in exactly this case, it is likely to be an FSA-authorised or exempted firm or a passporting firm, and so treated as an FSA-authorised firm (see ¶331), at least if it is acting from a UK office, and the exemption would therefore not apply anyway. If the firm is acting from a non-UK office, and is not an FSA-authorised firm, the 'overseas persons' exemptions are likely to be available and to apply to the transaction. Accordingly, the ISD restriction of the exemption is unlikely to be significant in practice; the restriction will in any event not apply if the transaction relates to an investment outside the ISD, typically a commodity futures contract.

¶333   Group activities (Sch. 1, para. 18)

Paragraph 18 provides a series of exemptions for FSA-regulated investment activities which one company in a 'group', or one member of a joint enterprise, carries on with or on behalf of another. The exemptions are substantially restricted as a result of the ISD (see below) and this must be borne in mind when reviewing the exemptions as written, which are what is described below. The exemptions acknowledge that corporate groups, or members of joint enterprises, first, do not need to be protected from each other, and, secondly, are a single economic entity so far as third parties are concerned. Transactions with, and advice given to, other members of a 'group' or joint enterprise are therefore excluded from para. 12 (dealings) and para. 15 (advice) respectively (but see below if the advice is given as part of managing a portfolio). Transactions by one member of a 'group' or joint enterprise (the 'agent') on behalf of another member are also excluded from para. 12 if, in general terms, they would have fallen within the 'own account' exemption if the transaction had been entered into by the agent as principal (para. 18(2)); in the case of a transaction in securities (see ¶331), the agent must accordingly not regularly solicit 'members of the public' within para. 17(2) (para. 18(2)) and for this purpose the 'permitted connections' within para. 17(2) are the agent's, rather than the principal's, (para. 18(6)), although it is expressly stated for the avoidance of doubt that the 'substantial holdings' in relation to which the agent can solicit (para. 17(2)(d)) are those to be acquired or disposed of by the principal rather than the agent. There are, however, two differences from the 'own account' exemption in para. 17 which may be important in practice. First, the 'group own account' exemption for derivatives may apply even if the group company principal or agent is itself an FSA-authorised firm (contrast ¶332).

¶333

Secondly, the assignment of life assurance and pension policies falls within the derivatives exemption rather than the securities exemption (contrast ¶331). The 'group' exemption also applies to the arranging of transactions, or investment management, by one member of a 'group' or joint enterprise for, or on behalf of, another (para. 18(3) and 18(4) respectively), to the provision of safe custody services for group companies or in connection with a joint enterprise (para. 18(3A)), and to acting as a CREST sponsor in relation to securities where a group company is the registered shareholder, in particular where, as is often the case, it is a nominee for the CREST sponsor's clients (para. 18(5A)).

For the purposes of the 'group' exemptions (and, indeed, throughout Sch. 1), a 'group' includes every company in which (in general terms) a member of the Companies Act group holds a long-term voting equity shareholding in order to give it control or influence over the company (a 'qualifying capital interest') and there is a rebuttable presumption that a 20 per cent holding qualifies for this purpose (para. 30); there must, however, already be a Companies Act group before these companies can be included. A 'joint enterprise' is a joint venture between two or more firms entered into for commercial purposes relating to a business carried on by them which is not FSA-regulated investment business (para. 31). All companies in the same 'group' (seemingly with the extended definition) as a participator in the enterprise are regarded as being participators themselves, and accordingly the exemption also applies to transactions with or on behalf of them (for example, transactions between a holding company of one member of a joint enterprise and a finance company subsidiary of another).

There are three important points to note. First, the exemption in para. 18(4) for investment management by one member of a 'group' on behalf of another applies only to the investment management function (reviewing a portfolio and making investment decisions or recommendations) and does not apply to the dealings effected by the investment manager for the 'group' client when implementing them; his dealings will be exempted only if the 'group own account' exemption in para. 18(2) applies. These two exemptions are, in effect, intended to avoid one member of a 'group' having to be regulated merely in order to protect another member, which imposes too much regulation; nonetheless, any counterparty non-professionals or other 'members of the public' still need to be protected, whether the firm dealing with them is treated as a single company or as part of the single 'group' economic entity. Secondly, the exemption in para. 18(3) for arrangements made by one member of a 'group' or joint enterprise for a transaction to be entered into by another seemingly applies whether the relevant arrangements are made with that other member or with the third party concerned (or, indeed, both). Thirdly, if the company seeking to rely on the 'group' exemption advises a company in the

¶333

same group which is the 'investment manager' for an external client (a structure often adopted in the case of offshore funds), it is important to review the facts carefully to determine whether the 'investment adviser' seeking to rely on the 'group' exemption is on the facts an investment adviser within para. 15 or an investment manager within para. 14 (see ¶315 and ¶316 above); this is especially important as the 'group' exemption can apply to para. 15 even if the investments being advised on belong to an external client but cannot apply to para. 14 in these circumstances. Similarly, if the investment manager is discretionary (and falls, as normal, in para. 14) and he delegates his function to a group company, which then takes the investment decisions in its own discretion, the group company would itself be a para. 14 investment manager and the 'group' exemption does not apply.

It is unclear whether the exemption in para. 18(2) from para. 12 (dealing) applies even if the group company 'principal' itself acts as an agent, for example if it is a broker or investment manager and the firm relying on the exemption is therefore a sub-agent. On balance, the better view is that it does not. First, one of the main reasons for the 'group' exemptions is to avoid regulating one member of a group or joint enterprise in order to protect another; it is not looking beyond the group or joint enterprise and seeking to avoid protecting its clients or counterparties merely because there are, in effect, two companies carrying on the FSA-regulated activity rather than one. The exemption is clearly supposed to parallel the 'own account' exemption and in effect to allow it to apply even if the firm acting as principal, and soliciting the counterparty, is 'divided' into two group companies; where the 'principal' is in fact acting as agent, there is no reason for the 'group own account' exemption to apply. Secondly, several of the group exemptions are written in terms which make it clear that no-one outside the group or joint enterprise is involved, for example the 'custody' and 'investment management' exemptions apply only if the assets belong to a member of the group or joint enterprise (para. 18(3A) and 18(4) respectively). Thirdly, as a technical matter, the 'group' agent would in the putative 'group own account' transaction commit not just the 'group' client to the transaction but also the client of that 'group' client; that indirect client is not a 'group' company and, accordingly the exemption cannot apply. It might, conversely, be argued that the 'group own account' exemption is intended to avoid double regulation; a typical case for example, is where one member of a group is a US broker-dealer and the other is a UK stockbroker and the UK stockbroker executes deals only on behalf of the US broker-dealer's clients. However, the stronger argument seems to be that it is better to have double regulation in this case, rather than no regulation at all if the broker-dealer is for some reason not itself regulated (and the exemption does not differentiate between these situations); in any event, the 'group' exemption would clearly not apply if a UK investment manager was sub-investment manager for a US

¶333

investment manager, and there is no reason to suppose that the 'group own account' exemption for dealings should work differently.

Finally, assuming that the 'group' exemption is indeed only for 'internal' group activities, the logical consequence is that the 'arranging' exemption in para. 18(3) should also apply only where the member of the group or joint enterprise which enters into the resulting transaction, and accordingly brings the exemption into play, does so as principal and not as agent. A restriction of the exemption to arrangements for transactions by the member of the group or joint enterprise as principal would also avoid the potential loop-hole relating to the marketing of non-UK agency brokerage and most investment management services (see ¶315). Conversely, however, the wording of the exemption is wide enough to cover a transaction entered into by the member of the group or joint enterprise as agent. Indeed, it is in a sense irrelevant in relation to the exemption that the company entering into the transaction does so as an agent; its clients can still rely on it to protect them by not entering into the transaction even when it has been arranged by the 'arranger' (which is a choice not open when the member of the group or joint enterprise itself enters into the transaction in the case of the 'group own account' exemption). This applies also in relation to the 'group counterparty' exemption in para. 18(1), which is clearly not restricted to where the group company counterparty is acting as principal; again it is up to that group company counterparty whether or not to enter into the transaction. Finally, it would seem that the 'group arranger' exemption in para. 18(3) is intended to parallel for a group or joint enterprise the exemption from para. 13 (arranging deals) where the firm which arranges the transaction also enters into it (note 1); that exemption applies whether the firm enters into the transaction as principal or as agent. It is thought on balance that the exemption is therefore available even where the group company enters into the transaction as agent, but, as the scope of the exemption is not clear, it would be prudent to check what view the UK regulators would take in any particular situation.

It is also important to remember that the 'group' exemptions for agency transactions and arranging activities apply only in relation to the group company acting as agent or arranging the transaction (the 'group company agent') and not in relation to the group company for which it acts (the 'group company principal'). The group company principal will itself need to be FSA-authorised under para. 12 unless it qualifies for the 'own account' or another exemption from the FSA's authorisation requirement; where the group company agent relies on the exemption in para. 18(3), it would be prudent to regard the group company principal as itself soliciting the counterparty for the purposes of the 'own account' exemptions if the group company agent does so.

As indicated above, the 'group' exemptions are substantially restricted as a

¶333

result of the UK's implementation of the ISD (see ¶330). The exemptions cannot apply if they relate to activities which are core investment services for the purposes of the ISD (see ¶358) and are not excluded from the ISD by art. 2(2); the only relevant exclusions are normally if the firm is an insurance company or where the only core investment services provided by the firm are to group companies. Accordingly, the para. 18 exemptions relating to members of the same joint enterprise do not apply in relation to 'group own account' transactions where the firm acts as agent for another member of the joint enterprise, to discretionary investment management for it or to the arranging of secondary market transactions for it within para. 13 or if the firm is acting as counterparty to it as a service; these are all core investment services for clients outside the group. Importantly, the ISD 'group' exemptions do not apply if the firm also provides any core investment service to clients outside the group, seemingly even if the service is itself excluded from the ISD by art. 2(2); this would be the case for example, where the 'non-group' service consists of acting as discretionary investment manager for an open-ended investment company which the firm manages. IMRO seems willing not to regulate 'group' services in this situation which is very helpful, but IMRO is only concerned with firms which are FSA-authorised firms already and therefore is able to take a more relaxed view. It should be emphasised that it is very unclear whether the ISD would treat as within the 'group' any company which is not in the Companies Act group even though the FSA does in the case of qualifying affiliates (para. 30); subsidiary undertakings may perhaps be included, at least if they are consolidated in group accounts, but confirmation of this treatment must be sought from the SIB or the Treasury.

¶334 Exemptions for overseas firms (Sch. 1, Pt. IV)

'Overseas firms' are UK or, much more importantly, non-UK firms which do not carry on any FSA-regulated investment business from their own UK office, at least if they are not exempted persons in respect of that business (see ¶310); they are referred to in the FSA as 'overseas persons'. They are entitled to all the 'normal' exemptions in Pt. III of Sch. 1 to the FSA, which allow firms to carry on FSA-regulated investment activities without carrying on FSA-regulated investment business (for example, the 'own account' exemptions, see ¶331 and ¶332); they can also become 'exempted persons' for qualifying activities (for example, as listed institutions under the 'money market' exemption, see ¶349). In addition, however, they are also entitled to a special series of 'exemptions' as a result of which qualifying business with UK clients or counterparties is treated as not carried on 'in the UK' so that, again, they do not need to be FSA-authorised for it, even if it constitutes FSA-regulated investment business (see ¶310); these 'overseas persons' exemptions are contained in Pt. IV of Sch. 1. The exemptions apply whether the firm carries on the relevant activity from a non-UK office (for example, by telephone or fax) or on visits to the UK. Importantly, they also apply even if the overseas firm has an ISD or 2BCD passport which covers business within the exemptions; this means that the firm is not FSA-regulated for it, as it would normally be if the passported business did not fall within the 'overseas persons' exemptions (see ¶356).

The exemptions fall into two classes. First, there are 'FSA-professionals' exemptions (in para. 26) from para. 12 (dealing) and para. 13 (arranging) where the transaction involves an FSA-professional; however, in contrast to the 'own account' exemptions (see ¶331 and ¶332), if the FSA-professional is an exempted firm, it must be acting within its exemption from FSA-authorisation (in particular, a listed institution must be acting within the 'money market' exemption, see ¶349). These exemptions cover transactions involving passporting firms because they are treated for the purposes of para. 26 as FSA-authorised firms (para. 42(1) of Sch. 7 to the ISD regulations and para. 44(1) of Sch. 9 to the 2BCD regulations); however, it must be emphasised that, in contrast to the 'own account' exemptions, permitted persons holding para. 23 permissions, and overseas securities firms which are not FSA-professionals, are not within the 'FSA-professionals' exemption as they are treated as 'non-professionals' for this purpose. Secondly, there are the more general exemptions (in para. 27) which apply to all FSA-regulated investment activities and whether or not FSA-professionals are involved; in relation to para. 12 and 13, these are more restricted than the equivalent exemptions in para. 26. The 'overseas persons' exemptions have not been restricted on the implementation of the ISD (see ¶330). Indeed, a non-UK EEA firm which carries on FSA-regulated investment activities within both the 'overseas persons' exemptions and its passport is in effect treated as doing so under the exemptions and not by virtue of its passport (see ¶356); accordingly, it is not a passporting firm, and is not subject to the conduct of business rules of the SIB (or its SRO), in relation to them (see ¶359).

The 'FSA-professionals' exemption from para. 12 (dealing) applies where the transaction is entered into with or through an FSA-authorised or relevantly exempted firm or a passporting firm, or is arranged by one, (para. 26(1)); it applies whether the overseas firm acts as principal or as agent, and accordingly applies even to overseas brokers or investment managers. The 'FSA-professionals' exemption from para. 13 (arranging deals) applies where the arrangements are made with an FSA-authorised or relevantly exempted firm or a passporting firm (para. 26(2)(a)). There is a similar 'FSA-professionals' exemption whoever the arrangements are made with if all transactions entered into in the UK under those arrangements are confined to FSA-authorised or relevantly exempted firms and passporting firms (para. 26(2)(b)).

The overseas firm may also avoid the need for FSA-authorisation under para. 12 even if it engages in transactions with firms outside these 'FSA-professionals' categories, provided that either it did not solicit anyone or, if it did, it did not solicit their business in a way which contravenes the FSA's restrictions on investment advertisements and cold-calling (see Ch. 9). This applies whether the firm acts as principal with a UK counterparty or, in restricted circumstances, as agent for a client in the UK; the exemption applies where the overseas firm is acting as agent for a client in the UK only if the counterparty is outside the UK or the overseas firm, again, either did not solicit anyone or, if it did, it did not solicit the transaction in a way which contravenes the FSA's restrictions on investment advertisements and cold calling (para. 27(2)). However, the 'overseas persons' exemptions in para. 27 strangely do not apply to transactions with non-professional UK counterparties where the overseas firm is acting as agent for a non-UK client, as in the case of an agency broker or an investment manager. In addition, and subject to the same requirement of non-contravention of the FSA's marketing restrictions, the exemption also applies to offers or agreements made to or with a person in the UK to arrange transactions (para. 13), provide or arrange for safe custody services (para. 13A), provide investment management services (para. 14), give investment advice (para. 15) or act as a CREST sponsor (para. 16A) (para. 27(1) and para. 27(3)), and to investment advice given to a client in the UK (para. 27(1)). However, except in the case of investment advice, the exemption does not apply where the overseas firm actually carries on in the UK any of the substantive FSA-regulated investment activities resulting from these offers or agreements. As the firm *ex hypothesi* would not do so from a UK office and is unlikely to do more than marketing whilst on visits to the UK, it is unlikely that it would in fact carry on the substantive activities in the UK, except where it makes arrangements for investment transactions (for example, it negotiates with a prospective investor) or gives investment advice (see ¶311). Giving investment advice is within the exemption (para. 27(1)), but there is no 'overseas persons' exemption for the making of arrangements for investment transactions or for establishing or winding-up collective investment schemes, or acting as depositary or sole director of a UK OEIC, (see ¶317 and ¶318). However, if the arrangements are made from a non-UK office (rather than on a visit to the UK) the making of the arrangements is treated as outside the territorial reach of the FSA, and this may perhaps apply also in the case of these other activities (see ¶311).

¶335   Paragraph 23 permitted persons (Sch. 1, para. 23)

Paragraph 23 of Sch. 1 creates an important exemption from para. 12 (dealings) for businesses which are not investment businesses in colloquial parlance and, in particular, the treasury operations of trading and manufacturing companies. It has, however, been substantially restricted as a result of the ISD (see below).

If a firm engages in relatively few FSA-regulated investment activities which require FSA-authorisation, it can apply to the SIB for permission to carry on those activities as principal (or as agent for another company in the 'group' or another participator in a joint enterprise) without FSA-authorisation. This exemption is intended to help corporate treasurers with the management of the company's debt or currency exposures, as it allows dealings in short-term debt securities and interest rate and currency futures and options. An application fee will be payable. The Financial Services Act specifies that in considering the application it is necessary to take into account the persons with whom and the purposes for which the applicant wishes to engage in those activities (para. 23(3)(c)). Permission will therefore probably not be granted in relation to dealings with ordinary private investors.

The exemption is clearly intended for trading and manufacturing companies; finance company subsidiaries are also eligible because the test for eligibility relates to the main business of the 'group' (rather than just that of the applicant). It is unclear whether a company which is a member of a 'group' and is otherwise eligible taken by itself is excluded from eligibility because of the activities of its 'group' taken as a whole. However, given that the FSA applies on a 'single company' basis and the 'group' eligibility test was intended as a concession, it is arguable that the company will nonetheless remain eligible for the para. 23 permission even though the main business of the 'group' may in fact be FSA-regulated investment business.

A permission is not needed if other exemptions apply, in particular, of course, the 'own account' exemptions (see ¶331 and ¶332) which would normally apply as the firm's counterparty is usually an FSA-authorised firm or a listed money market institution. A firm may still be able to rely on the 'own account' exemption in para. 17(1)(c) even if it regularly engages in investment transactions, for example, buying and selling gilts or commercial paper, (see ¶331).

As indicated above, the exemption has been restricted as a result of the ISD (see ¶330). In contrast to being listed by the Bank of England for the purposes of the 'money market' exemption, a para. 23 permission is not regarded as a form of ISD authorisation; although a detailed application pack must be completed and a 'permitted person' is subject to notification requirements imposed by the SIB, a 'permitted person' is not subject to regulation in relation to the permitted transactions. In particular, the exemption can therefore no longer apply to transactions by a firm as agent for other participators in a joint enterprise with it which are ISD core investment services outside the art. 2(2) exemptions (see ¶358), so that the exemption in para. 23(1)(c) no longer applies in many cases. However, if the firm applying for the permission deals only for its own account or for group companies, and only on its or their own initiative, or only in non-ISD investments (for example, commodity options or futures), it should be able to use the exemption; out of caution, it would be best to deal as

¶335

agent in ISD investments only for Companies Act group companies and not other companies in its extended 'FSA' group (see ¶333).

The para. 23 permission may also be available to City institutions as their 'licence' to deal for their own account (but not, for example, as a fund manager) with other City institutions, even if dealings with them fall outside the 'own account' exemptions because they are non-professionals (see ¶331 and ¶332). This is because the fundamental criterion is that the main business of the applicant (or its 'group') does not consist of activities for which FSA-authorisation is actually required (rather than that it does not consist of FSA-regulated investment activities as such). If most of the applicant's FSA-regulated investment activities fall within the 'own account' exemptions (because, for example, they consist of transactions with FSA-authorised or exempted firms or other FSA-professionals), then he will meet that test and the para. 23 permission will effectively be available for 'own account' transactions with one or more categories of 'members of the public' or non-professionals, which would be outside the exemptions. The requirement in para. 23(3)(c) to take into account the purposes for which the permission is wanted may be a little ominous in this context, but it would seem that City institutions should in principle be able to qualify for the permission in relation to 'own account' dealings with other City institutions or other UK professional securities investors which, like investment trusts, are technically non-professionals. Conversely, the 'own account' exemption will also allow City institutions (and anyone else) without the permission to deal for their own account with any City institution which holds it. If City institutions are granted a para. 23 permission, they will therefore be able to deal with each other without FSA-authorisation. However, it must be stressed that, at time of writing, the SIB seems to have adopted the policy that it will not grant a para. 23 permission to a firm, such as a City institution, whose main business does in fact consist of FSA-regulated investment activities even though most of its dealings are exempted from the need for FSA-authorisation because they are for its own account and fall within the 'own account' exemptions (see section 6 of the SIB's Explanatory Memorandum on 'Permitted Persons', issued in March 1994). The restrictions imposed on the exemption by the ISD should not in themselves prevent a City institution, and in particular an investment company, using a permission in this way, provided that all its transactions are on its own initiative or for its own reasons and not as a 'service' on a professional basis (see above). However, given the status accorded to an FSA-authorised firm and its easier access to transactions, and the SIB's position on the use of the exemption, it is far more likely that City institutions will seek FSA-authorisation or use an FSA-authorised investment manager.

If a para. 23 permission is granted and is subject to a condition, the SIB can take action under s. 61 for contravention of the condition and (as in the case of a

¶335

breach of its rules) can recover any profits, or require the holder of the permission to reimburse any losses, made as a result of the contravention (para. 23(6)).

¶336   Issues of shares or debentures (Sch. 1, para. 28(3))

The issue of shares or debentures, or warrants to subscribe shares or debentures, constitutes the sale of securities for the purposes of the FSA unless an exemption applies (see ¶313). However, their issue is normally excluded from para. 12 (dealing) and para. 13 (arranging deals) so far as the issuer is concerned (para. 28(3)) and the issuer therefore does not need FSA-authorisation to issue them or to arrange for them to be marketed or underwritten. Offers to issue shares or debentures (or warrants) within the exemption, and agreements to issue them, are also exempted. The exemptions apply only to the issuer and not to his agent, for example an issuing house. The exemptions do not apply to the issue of shares (or share warrants) by open-ended investment companies (para. 28(4) and para. 1), and UK OEICs are accordingly automatically FSA-authorised to issue their shares and arrange for their marketing (see ¶318); however, the exemption does apply to the issue of debentures (or debenture warrants) by open-ended investment companies. The marketing of shares or debentures (or warrants to subscribe them) by the issuer is, however, subject to the FSA's investment advertisements and cold-calling regimes (see Ch. 9) and, in the case of corporate issuers or listed securities, to the public issues regimes (see Ch. 8).

¶337   Employee share schemes (Sch. 1, para. 20)

Certain transactions relating to the administration of employee share schemes or share option schemes, or to 'share shops' linked to them, are exempted from the FSA's authorisation requirement. The exemption excludes from para. 12 (dealing) and para. 13 (arranging deals) transactions, or the arranging of transactions, in shares or debentures of a company or in subscription rights or depositary receipts relating to them provided that the transactions are between or (more importantly) for the benefit of present or former group employees or specified classes of their 'close relatives'. The exemptions apply in favour of the company which issued or is to issue the shares or debentures (or the subscription rights) and every connected company, and also of the trustee (if any) who is to hold the investments under the arrangements. The exemption also exempts them from para. 13A (safe custody services) in respect of these arrangements. A 'connected company' is a 'group' company or a company which (by itself or with other companies in its 'group') controls the majority of the voting rights in the issuer or its holding company; 'group' has the extended Sch. 1 meaning in both cases (para. 30 and see ¶333). The exemption does not apply to the provision of advice in connection with such schemes or, seemingly, although this is not clear, in relation to shares in open-ended investment companies.

¶338   Sales of companies (Sch. 1, para. 21, as amended)

This exemption excludes from para. 12 (dealing), para. 13 (arranging) and para. 15 (investment advice) certain transactions to acquire or sell shares in a company or other body corporate which carry at least 75 per cent of the voting rights, or bring an existing holding up to at least 75 per cent, and arranging or advisory services in connection with them. The exemption has been significantly restricted by the ISD (see below).

The exemption applies in relation to shares in any body corporate (even public non-UK companies) other than an open-ended investment company. The sale must normally be from and to a single party to qualify for the exemption, typically the sale of a wholly-owned subsidiary to a corporate purchaser, (para. 21(1)(c)); the exemption therefore does not apply to public takeovers. However, a partnership is treated as a single party for this purpose, as also is a 'group of connected individuals', namely the directors or managers, or proposed directors or managers, of the company and their 'close relatives' (as defined). Holdings of 'group' companies are not aggregated. There are problems with family shareholders as they also are not aggregated unless they are, or are to be, directors or managers or are 'close relatives' (as defined) of them; trustees are not 'close relatives' and therefore if there is a family trust or settlement the exemption will not apply unless the trustees are themselves directors or managers. Although it is not totally clear, it seems that, as would be commercially logical, the exemption can apply to preference shares even if they do not (yet) carry voting rights if their sale forms part of the exempt transaction; the sale must 'include' shares carrying the qualifying voting rights but, if it does, it can also include other shares. Strangely, even in this case the exemption does not apply to the sale of debentures. The exemption also applies to the arranging of, or the giving of advice in connection with, transactions to which the exemption applies, typically by a corporate finance advisory firm. The exemption may in practice be of help mainly where wholly-owned subsidiaries are being sold by their parent company, for example, in the case of management buy-outs or to a trade purchaser.

The para. 21 exemption has been restricted by the FSA Extension Order so as to comply with the ISD where the activities concerned constitute ISD core investment services (see ¶330 and ¶358). In the view of the UK regulators, the exemption still applies in full if the firm's only FSA-regulated investment activities all fall in para. 21 but, if any fall outside para. 21, the para. 21 exemption does not apply at all in relation to para. 13 (arranging) activities or, seemingly, para. 12 (dealing) activities, which are ISD core investment services. It would, however, seem arguable that the para. 13 (and para. 15) services covered by the para. 21 exemption are not restricted by the ISD at all, as they constitute (or, in the case of these para. 13 services, seem to constitute) only non-core services (see ¶330). The exemption from para. 12 (dealing) is not normally affected by the ISD unless the firm seeking to rely on the exemption buys or sells the holding as agent; a purchase or sale as principal is normally not a service to third parties, and therefore is unlikely to be a 'core investment service' for the purpose of the ISD.

¶339   Nominees (Sch. 1, para. 22(1))

Non-discretionary transactions by bare trustees or nominees are excluded from para. 12 (dealing) if they act on instructions from the beneficial owner whose nominee they are unless they hold themselves out as providing a service of buying and selling investments. Where a firm acts as bare trustee or nominee and only on instructions, it is this exemption which applies and not the 'own account' exemptions in para. 17(1)(c) and para. 17(4) (see ¶331 and ¶332), which are expressly excluded (para. 22(5)); if the firm holds itself out as providing a service of buying and selling investments, it therefore cannot rely on either the para. 22(1) exemption or, even if they would otherwise apply, the 'own account' exemptions.

It is arguable that, if the bare trustee or nominee does not actually enter into a para. 12 transaction, it does not need to rely on the exemption. If it is party to the contract (as some nominees are), then it will be buying or selling (as principal or as agent for the beneficial owner) and needs the exemption. However, if it merely transfers or receives the securities on settlement, and does not enter into the transaction itself, it would be difficult to argue that it is buying or selling, as only the beneficial owner can do so. However, 'buying' and 'selling' include any acquisition or disposal for valuable consideration (para. 28(1)(d)) and the bare trustee or nominee does indeed acquire or dispose of the legal title for a valuable consideration, albeit one payable to the beneficial owner. It is therefore prudent to fall within the para. 22(1) exemption and to ensure that (as is in any event the normal practice) the bare trustee or nominee does not hold itself out as providing a service of buying or selling investments within para. 22(1)(c). However, depending on the facts, the beneficial owner may itself need to rely on the 'own account' exemptions (see ¶331 and ¶332).

¶340   Trustees and personal representatives
(Sch. 1, para. 22(2)–22(4))

Trustees and personal representatives often engage in FSA-regulated investment activities by virtue of discharging the functions of their office. They are, however, already subject to regulation (under, for example, the *Trustee Act* 1925 and the *Trustee Investments Act* 1961) and are therefore normally exempted from the FSA's authorisation requirement in relation to normal 'trustee' activities (even if they are professional trustees). If, however, they are paid special fees for services which constitute FSA-regulated investment activities, in addition to fees for their normal 'trustee' activities, or hold themselves out as providing them they normally need to be FSA-authorised for them.

Subject to these exclusions, trustees and personal representatives are accordingly exempted by para. 22(2) to (4) in relation to their function as trustee or personal representative from para. 13 (arranging), para. 13A (safe custody services), para. 14 (investment management), except in the case of pension fund trustees (see below), para. 15 (investment advice), in relation to advice given to fellow trustees or personal representatives, or the beneficiaries, about the investments included in the trust or estate, and para. 16A (CREST sponsors), in relation to investments held by them as trustee or personal representative. Trustees of pension funds cannot use the para. 22 exemption in relation to para. 14 (investment management) because they are subject to a special FSA authorisation requirement under s. 191 which excludes that para. 22 exemption (see ¶344).

Trustees and personal representatives can also use the normal 'transaction' exemptions, namely the 'own account' exemptions in para. 17(1)(c) and 17(4) or, in the case of bare trustees or nominees the 'nominees' exemption in para. 22(1) (see ¶331, ¶332 and ¶339).

¶341   Supply of goods or services (Sch. 1, para. 19)

Many FSA-regulated investment activities in connection with the supply of goods or services are exempted in restricted circumstances, and so also are arranging, advisory and investment management services in connection with them; the exemption has been further restricted as a result of the ISD (see below).

The exemption is intended primarily to allow the supplier to arrange finance, or currency or interest rate hedging, for his customer. However, promissory notes and other debentures relating to payment for goods or services are normally not themselves FSA-regulated investments (see ¶324) and therefore their issue, purchase or sale (or the arranging of transactions in them) do not need FSA-authorisation even if the exemption does not apply; similarly, the issue of loan notes and their acceptance by the lender, and arranging for their issue or acceptance, are outside para. 12 (dealing) and para. 13 (arranging deals) in any event (see ¶313 and ¶314). The exemption applies only if the supplier's main business is to supply goods or services and not to engage in 'activities falling within Sch. 1, Pt. II'. It is unclear whether activities which are excluded from Pt. II by Pt. III or Pt. IV are or are not to be taken into account as activities falling within Pt. II for this purpose. As para. 19 is presently drafted, it would seem that they are not (contrast s. 44(9)) and therefore they do not exclude the exemption; although s. 1(2) and s. 1(3) (investment business) refer to activities which fall in Pt. II and are not excluded by Pt. III (or Pt. III or IV), this surely accepts that the excluded activities do not fall in Pt. II and merely draws attention to the Part which excludes them. If the supplier's main business is to engage in activities falling in Pt. II (despite the exclusions in Pt. III and Pt. IV), the para. 19 exemption therefore does not apply, even if the supplier does not need to be FSA-authorised for the Pt. II activities, for example, because it engages in those activities only outside the UK quite apart from the 'overseas persons' exemptions (see ¶311). In addition, it is unclear whether 'services' include financial services falling outside the FSA, for example the provision of mortgages. However, the exclusion of individuals and of life or pension policies from the exemption (see below) makes this question less important.

The exemption excludes investment transactions by a supplier with a customer in connection with a supply of goods or services from para. 12 (dealing). It also excludes investment transactions entered into on behalf of a customer in connection with the supply of goods or services, if, in general terms, the transaction would have fallen within the 'own account' exemptions (see ¶331 and ¶332) if it had been entered into by the supplier as principal and, accordingly, the supplier can solicit his own 'connections', as would be the commercial intention; the 'substantial holdings' exemption in para. 17(2)(d) applies but, in contrast to the 'group own account' exemption, the 'relevant person' acquiring or disposing of the holding is, seemingly, the supplier rather than the customer (contrast para. 18(6)). The exemption also applies to the arranging of transactions (para. 13), and investment management (para. 14) by a supplier for a customer in connection with a supply of goods or services, and to the giving of advice (para. 15) by a supplier to a customer or a lender or other third party in connection with a supply (for example, as to how to finance a purchase); it also applies to the provision or arranging of safe custody services (para. 13A) by the supplier in relation to assets held in connection with a supply of goods or services.

The exemption does not apply where the customer is an individual (para. 19(9)(a)) nor where the investments concerned are units in collective investment schemes (whether or not authorised unit trusts) or life assurance or pension policies (para. 19(9)(b)–(d)).

For the purposes of the exemption, companies in the same 'group' as the supplier or customer are treated as if they were actually the supplier or customer so that, for example, a finance company subsidiary of the supplier can accordingly arrange the financing of the supply for a holding company of the customer without FSA-authorisation (para. 19(7)); 'group' has the wide Sch. 1

¶341

meaning (para. 30 and see ¶333). The exemption also extends to FSA-regulated investment activities relating to supplies by third parties if they are made for the same purposes as the supplies by the supplier concerned.

The exemption has now been restricted by the FSA Extension Order on the implementation of the ISD (see ¶330). Even 'own account' transactions by the supplier with the customer are likely to be excluded from the exemption, as they would seem normally to be services provided on a professional basis within the ISD's authorisation requirement; so also are agency transactions for the customer and the arranging of transactions or discretionary investment management services for the customer. However, the exemption will still apply in full to the other FSA-regulated investment activities covered by the exemption or if an art. 2(2) exemption from the ISD applies (for example, the restricted exemption in art. 2(2)(i) for core investment services provided by commodity traders to producers and professional users of the commodity); indeed, it is this exemption for commodity traders which indicates that suppliers may be regarded as providing core investment services 'on a professional basis' even if they are provided only as part of the firm's ordinary business and without a separate fee.

¶342 Advice in newspapers and other media (Sch. 1, para. 25 and 25A)

Investment advice given in 'bona fide' newspapers, journals, magazines or other periodicals is excluded from para. 15 (advice) but advice given in, for example, tip-sheets is not. The SIB can certify that a publication falls within the exemption if an application is made by the proprietor (para. 25(2)), which is an invitation that should be taken up. The exemption can apply even if the publication does not have a certificate, but only if the principal purpose of the publication (including, importantly, any advertisements in it) is not to lead to investment; the precise wording is 'to lead persons to invest in any particular investment' and it is unclear how widely this expression is to be interpreted if there are advertisements relating to, for example, three or four different FSA-regulated investments.

A similar exemption is provided for advice given in television or radio programmes or a teletext service; this is more general than in the case of newspapers and, indeed, 'programme' is specifically defined to include advertisements as such (para. 25A). The Internet is perhaps unlikely to fall within this exemption. Importantly, the exemption does not apply to the FSA's rules on investment advertisements, and even having a certificate therefore does not protect a publication from infringing s. 57 (see Ch. 9).

¶343 Necessary advice and arrangements (Sch. 1, para. 24)

Investment advice is exempted if it is a necessary part of other advice or services given in the course of a profession or business which is not FSA-regulated investment business and it is not separately remunerated. In addition, the making of arrangements, and the provision or arranging of safe custody services, is also exempted in the same circumstances. This will help solicitors and accountants who on one view are making arrangements within para. 13 if they, for example, circulate draft share purchase agreements. The exemption is supposed to help solicitors, accountants and tax advisers acting as such (rather than as investment advisers or dealers) and it does not apply to advice given or arrangements made in the course of a profession or business which constitutes FSA-regulated investment business in any event. The exemption only applies if it is in fact necessary to give the advice or make the arrangements (which requires a difficult standard of proof) and the fact that it is only incidental is not in itself sufficient. If it is correct that 'investment advice' does not include 'generic' advice (see ¶316), it is difficult to see that this exemption will in fact be very useful in practice in the case of advice, except, perhaps, in permitting discussion of investments proposed by the client in response to non-investment advice.

¶344   Occupational pension schemes (s. 191)

The investment management of the assets of occupational pension schemes by trustees, such as directors or employees, is normally deemed to be FSA-regulated investment business if the assets include FSA-regulated investments (s. 191). The provisions of para. 22, which otherwise would normally exclude the services of even a professional trustee from the definition of investment management in para. 14 (see ¶340), are expressly disapplied (s. 191(5)). However, the deeming provision does not apply (and, accordingly, such investment management is exempted from the need for FSA-authorisation) if all day-to-day investment decisions relating to FSA-regulated investments (and so not necessarily, for example, to land or paintings) are taken by 'approved managers', and the exemption still applies in these circumstances even if the trustees determine investment policy and, in addition, decide whether or not to place money awaiting investment on deposit; 'approved managers' are FSA-authorised firms, FSA-exempted firms acting within their exemption, passporting firms carrying on business within their ISD or 2BCD passport (see ¶356) and overseas firms falling within the 'overseas persons' exemptions (see ¶334) or, seemingly, outside the territorial reach of the FSA altogether (s. 191(2), para. 39 of Sch. 7 to the ISD Regulations and para. 42 of Sch. 9 to the 2BCD regulations, see ¶357). Alternatively, even if day-to-day investment decisions relating to FSA-regulated investments are not all taken by 'approved managers', s. 191 does not apply if the scheme falls within an exemption provided by the Government for small schemes which are, in effect, controlled by their members.

The government has, indeed, issued an exemption for 'small' schemes which are controlled by their members (the *Financial Services Act 1986 (Occupational Pension Schemes) (No. 2) Order* 1988 (SI 1988/724), which replaced an earlier 1988 Order). Two categories of scheme qualify for this exemption. The first category is schemes constituted under an irrevocable trust which have 12 or fewer 'relevant members' all of whom are trustees (except for members who are unfit or incapable) and whose rules provide that all day-to-day investment decisions relating to FSA-regulated investments have to be taken by all the relevant members who are trustees, or a majority of them, or by 'approved managers' (see above) acting either alone or jointly with all or a majority of member-trustees; 'relevant members' are employees or former employees who are beneficiaries or potential beneficiaries under the scheme. The second category is schemes where there are no more than 50 members, the only assets are life policies or annuities on their lives (or cash to be used to buy them) and each member can select the policy or annuity on his own life. Where the 'small schemes' exemptions apply, trustees do not need FSA-authorisation under s. 191 if they are beneficiaries or potential beneficiaries or if they take no day-to-day decisions relating to the management of scheme assets which are FSA-regulated investments. However, they will need to be FSA-authorised if they do take part in day-to-day investment management decisions relating to FSA-regulated investments but are not themselves beneficiaries or potential beneficiaries (although trustees are often employees or directors); trustees who are trade union representatives but not group employees are normally not beneficiaries. This is all very complicated, but it must not be forgotten that, if all day-to-day investment decisions relating to FSA-regulated investments are taken by 'approved managers' (see above), there is no need to rely on the 'small schemes' exemptions because the 'deeming' provision in s. 191 will not apply anyway (see above).

¶345   International SROs (Sch. 1, para. 25B)

The government has power to exempt from para. 13 (arranging deals) organisations which provide dealing facilities for and regulate international securities business in what are professionals-only markets. The exemption applies if the organisation cannot become a recognised investment exchange for certain specified structural reasons, for example that it does not provide protection to UK investors at least equivalent to that provided by RIEs, which it does not need to do if it is not used by private investors, (para. 25B). This power was inserted to allow for the exemption of the International Securities Market Association (ISMA) from the FSA's authorisation requirement and ISMA has indeed been exempted; the exemption is, however, of more general application, although it applies only to organisations with head offices outside the UK.

¶346 Aggregation of exemptions

The 'own account' exemption for transactions in securities with, for example, FSA-authorised firms (see ¶331) does not apply if (exceptionally) they result from the regular solicitation of 'members of the public'. However, it would seem that it will still apply if that solicitation is directed only at transactions within other exemptions in Sch. 1, for example the exemption which allows a supplier to enter into investment transactions with a customer (see ¶341) or the 'sale of body corporate' exemption (see ¶338). The exemptions are therefore cumulative. Regular solicitation excludes the 'own account' exemption for securities transactions only if the solicitation is to induce 'members of the public' to enter into transactions to which para. 12 applies (para. 17(1)(c)); the other 'transactional' exemptions work on the basis that para. 12 does not apply to the transactions exempted by them and therefore those transactions do not fall in para. 17(1)(c). If other residual transactions are solicited which do fall in para. 12, the 'own account' exemption may accordingly nonetheless apply to them. This is on the basis that the solicitation is only occasional and not 'regular', as required by para. 17(1)(c) in order to exclude the 'own account' exemption; in addition it may also be arguable that on the facts these residual transactions are in any event too unusual to constitute carrying on FSA-regulated investment business (see ¶304).

Doubt is, perhaps, cast on this analysis by para. 32 which expressly provides that, effectively, the exempted activities of an FSA-exempted firm are to be disregarded when determining whether any exemption applies to its other activities. For example, the solicitation of City institutions and corporate treasury departments, which may constitute 'members of the public' (see ¶331), for the purpose of transactions within the 'money market' exemption (see ¶349) can be disregarded when ascertaining whether the 'own account' exemption applies to other transactions. Accordingly, such solicitation does not prejudice that exemption. As there is no similar provision for the 'transactional' exemptions in Sch. 1, this seems at first sight to imply that they are not disregarded, and may exclude the 'own account' exemption. However, in the case of an FSA-exempted firm, the exemption works by dispensing with the need for FSA-authorisation for the transaction but the 'exempted' transaction nonetheless falls in para. 12. In contrast to the Sch. 1 'transactional' exemptions, the exempted 'own account' transactions of an FSA-exempted firm therefore are transactions to which para. 12 applies and, if nothing else was said, might indeed exclude the 'own account' exemption for the FSA-exempted firm's other FSA-regulated investment activities. That is why para. 32 is needed for FSA-exempted firms but not for the transactions exempted by Pt. III and IV of Sch. 1.

Although it is not totally clear, para. 32 seems to provide that FSA-regulated investment activities carried on from a UK office entirely within an FSA exemption, typically the 'money market' exemption, can also be disregarded in determining whether the 'overseas persons' exemptions can apply to FSA-regulated investment activities carried on from the firm's non-UK offices. The firm is accordingly deemed by para. 32 not to be carrying on FSA-regulated investment business from a UK office; it accordingly qualifies for the 'overseas persons' exemptions (see ¶334). Even if this is correct, there seems unfortunately to be no similar exemption if the FSA-regulated investment activities carried on from the UK office of a non-UK EEA firm all fall within the firm's ISD or 2BCD passport, even if they would have fallen within the 'money market' exemption if the firm had not had the passport, (see ¶310).

EXEMPTED FIRMS

¶347   Introduction

An exempted firm is in general terms exempted from the need for FSA-authorisation not on the basis of what it does but on the basis of what it is. In its attempt to be comprehensive, the Financial Services Act has limited the classes of firm which are exempted by virtue of their status to the minimum, and accordingly there are only seven, of which three would not have been expected to require FSA-authorisation anyway.

The FSA confers its 'status' exemptions on:

(1) Lloyd's and Lloyd's underwriters (see ¶348);

(2) listed institutions (see ¶349);

(3) appointed representatives (see ¶350);

(4) the Bank of England (see ¶351);

(5) recognised investment exchanges and clearing houses (see ¶352);

(6) non-UK EEA 'regulated markets' (see ¶353); and

(7) certain public officials (see ¶354).

These exemptions are restricted to the particular activities associated with the status concerned. An exempted firm may accordingly need FSA-authorisation if it engages in other FSA-regulated investment activities. In addition, the government has declared certain other categories of firm to be exempted firms, either generally or to a specified extent, by FSA exemption orders. These categories of exempted firm include certain supra-national banks, the Official Solicitor and the Public Trustee.

¶348   Lloyd's insurance business (s. 42)

The Society of Lloyd's and Lloyd's underwriting agents are exempted for activities in connection with insurance business at Lloyd's. This exemption applies to two sorts of activities. The first relates to the investment business carried on by underwriting agents for the 'passive' underwriters, the Lloyd's 'Names', whose agents they are, and includes, for example, the investment of premiums received by the agents on behalf of the underwriters. For the moment the Government prefers to rely on the protection provided to 'Names' by the *Lloyd's Act* 1982. The writing of long-term business is also exempted. However, Lloyd's is in practice concerned predominantly with general business (for example, marine insurance) rather than long-term business, and policy holders are in any event protected by other legislation.

¶349   Listed money market institutions (s. 43)

Listed institutions are firms on a list maintained by the Bank of England for the purpose of the 'money market' exemption. The exemption relates to dealings in the money markets and was brought in in order to leave the regulation of the money markets to the Bank of England, which regulates them on a non-statutory basis (but subject to the ISD, where applicable). However, being on the list does not solve all problems, because the exemption is very restricted as to both the description and the maximum maturity of the instruments within the exemption. In addition, the exemption applies in the case of transactions involving unlisted firms only if the transaction is of a specified minimum value, which varies according to the kind of instrument concerned; if the transaction is of the requisite value so that the exemption applies, the unlisted firm is generally referred to as a 'wholesale counterparty' and the transaction as a 'wholesale transaction'.

The 'money market' exemption continues fully despite the implementation of the ISD, as the Bank of England is treated as an ISD regulator. Passporting firms (see ¶302) still qualify as 'listed institutions' if they are admitted to the list, but they are not 'exempted persons' despite being listed. Being listed is, however, useful for them because it substitutes the Bank of England as their regulator for exempted money market activities instead of the SIB; in addition, if the counterparty is itself a listed institution, it means that there is no need for the counterparty to qualify the passporting firm as a 'wholesale counterparty' in order to fall within the exemption. Conversely, UK listed institutions can use the outgoing ISD passport for their exempted money market activities, even if they are not FSA-authorised firms, (see ¶330). However, exactly because the Bank of England has regulatory functions under the ISD, it has to regulate UK listed institutions, and deal with applications from UK firms applying to be listed, if they qualify as EEA investment firms (see ¶302), but are neither FSA-authorised firms nor authorised institutions under the Banking Act 1987, in accordance with statutory rules under the ISD Regulations (see ¶357). For example, the Bank of England must restrict the ISD core investment services they can provide as a listed institution; indeed, the firm must comply with detailed requirements under the ISD before the Bank of England can admit it to the list (reg. 26).

Firms which enter into non-wholesale transactions with their customers (including corporate treasurers) will normally need to be FSA-authorised for those transactions even if they are listed institutions. However, even in their case being on the list will at least substitute the Bank of England's non-statutory regulation for the 'statutory' regulation of SROs or (in the case of passporting firms in particular) the SIB in the case of wholesale transactions; this is because the conduct of business rules of the SROs and the SIB are expressed not to apply to exempted transactions or (in the case of passporting firms which are listed institutions) transactions which would have been exempted transactions if they were not passporting firms.

Corporate treasurers had asked for a 'money market' exemption in order to avoid the need to be FSA-authorised merely because they deal in the wholesale money markets. However, it is not the total exemption they were looking for. This is because, unusually, the FSA does not grant exemption on the basis adopted in Pt. III of Sch. 1 (namely, exempting the permitted transactions themselves from the need for FSA-authorisation, which would mean that anybody could enter into them) but instead grants FSA-exempted status only to particular participants in the market in relation to those permitted transactions. The permitted transactions are listed in Sch. 5. Because the exemption applies only to listed institutions, it does not help corporate treasurers to deal with each other unless the transaction is arranged by a listed institution, which is permitted in defined circumstances by Pt. III of Sch. 5; this may restrict the benefits of the exemption so far as unlisted firms are concerned. The Bank of England has stated in its 'grey paper' issued in December 1995 and entitled 'The regulation of the wholesale cash and OTC derivatives markets (in sterling, foreign currency and bullion)' that it will allow onto the list only firms which trade in the interbank wholesale markets as professionals; these include in particular brokers, which arrange deals (within para. 13) by bringing together two counterparties to a transaction and passing their names over, and principals (dealing for their own account or, perhaps, as agent for a group company within para. 12), which are referred to as 'core principals' if they are banks, building societies or other financial institutions acting as principal and authorised under the Financial Services Act or using their ISD or 2BCD passport. The Bank of England has stated that it will not list customers or end-users of the interbank wholesale markets, for example industrial or commercial companies and local authorities. The Bank of England issues its list of listed institutions, or changes to the list, on a regular basis and firms must ensure that the list they use is up to date. Listed institutions must comply with

¶349

the Bank of England's London Code of Conduct (the latest edition of which at time of writing is July 1995) and the Association of Corporate Treasurers and SFA also expect their members to comply with it.

The Bank of England is the regulator of the wholesale markets; it is like an investment exchange regulator rather than an SRO. In principle, it accordingly regulates transactions in the wholesale money markets by regulating the duties and responsibilities of the counterparties to each other, rather than the relationship between a listed institution and its clients (the firms it deals for or for which it arranges deals). Accordingly, the 'money market' exemption does not apply to all FSA-regulated investment activities; it refers expressly only to transactions (if they fall in Sch. 5) and 'anything done for the purposes of' a Sch. 5 transaction and accordingly probably applies only to para. 12 (dealing) and para. 13 (arranging deals), and, even in their case, only in relation to short-term money market products. The Bank of England issued a Notice on 20 May 1991 in which it made it clear that the 'money market' exemption does not apply to discretionary management; the notice implicitly stated that it also does not apply to non-discretionary management and, importantly, the SIB has given informal guidance that this is indeed the case. Although the position is not clear, the prudent (and probably the better) view is that the exemption also does not apply to investment advice, even in relation to money market products; this view is, however, seemingly not universally accepted. At time of writing, the Treasury and the Bank of England are considering whether the exemption should apply to para. 13A (safe custody services); it would seem to apply to debt securities held for a client's exempted transactions even now.

The 'money market' exemption is very restricted and complicated and its application must be checked each time there is any doubt. If it applies, it has three separate but linked uses. First, of course, it provides an exemption for listed institutions from the FSA's authorisation requirement; secondly, it provides an exemption from the conduct of business rules of SROs and the SIB in the case of listed institutions which are FSA-authorised firms or passporting firms; thirdly, it provides an 'own account' exemption for unlisted firms (such as the corporate treasury departments of industrial or commercial companies) in relation to transactions with listed institutions or, in the case of derivatives transactions and securities transactions where the firm solicits the listed institution itself, transactions arranged by them (see ¶331 and ¶332). The exemption does not need to be used by listed institutions (or their counterparties) for transactions which are within their 'own account' exemptions anyway, although the London Code of Conduct nonetheless applies; on balance, it is likely that the counterparty can use the 'own account' exemption for dealings with listed institutions even if the transaction is outside the 'money market' exemption (see ¶331).

Listed institutions are allowed to deal freely with each other and with the

Bank of England without being FSA-authorised, although most listed institutions are in practice also FSA-authorised firms, both because of activities outside the 'money market' exemption and to avoid committing a criminal offence, as a result of falling outside what is a very complicated exemption. The exemption extends to where the listed institution deals as agent for another listed institution. It also normally applies where its counterparty is a listed institution, whether the counterparty deals as principal or agent and, indeed, even if it is an agent for an unlisted firm; this is because it is difficult for the listed institution seeking to rely on the exemption to know the capacity in which its counterparty deals and the value of the exemption would accordingly be reduced in practice if it was not so extended. However, listed institutions cannot normally deal with or on behalf of anyone outside the list (other than the Bank of England), unless the transaction is 'wholesale' rather than retail; this is determined by a 'size' test and the transactions are accordingly referred to in Sch. 5 as transactions subject to a monetary limit (or, threshold). If the transaction does qualify as 'wholesale', a listed institution can act as the unlisted firm's counterparty or as its agent. Unlisted firms can deal as principal or as agent (typically, for other companies in the group) and corporate treasurers can accordingly deal on a group basis.

The 'money market' exemption also normally allows a listed institution to arrange transactions for other listed institutions and even for unlisted firms if they are its 'wholesale counterparties' (Sch. 5, para. 9). It may, however, perhaps not allow a listed institution to arrange a transaction between two other listed institutions if each is acting as agent for an unlisted firm, because this is not referred to expressly in the list of permitted transactions in Sch. 5; however, it is arguable that it does. The exemption expressly applies if a listed institution arranges a transaction to be entered into between two unlisted firms (if they are both its wholesale counterparties) and the transaction in question will indeed be entered into by them, albeit through their 'listed institution' agents; in addition, it would be as inappropriate to require a listed institution to ask both listed institutions which are party to a transaction it arranges whether they are acting as agent and, if so, who for as it is to ask the same question of a listed institution it deals with as counterparty (which is not required); finally, there is no reason to allow a transaction between two unlisted firms if they enter into it personally (without being protected by a listed institution) but not allow the transaction if they use listed institutions as their agents which can accordingly protect them. The 'money market' exemption also applies in different circumstances to repurchase agreements, sale and buy back transactions and stocklending (all referred to below as 'repos') and the arranging of them (Sch. 5, para. 3 and 11).

The FSA specifies in great detail in para. 2 of Sch. 5 those money market instruments which fall within the exemption. Exempted instruments are, as might be expected, restricted to 'short term' debentures (for example, commercial paper), derivatives (such as warrants, options and financial futures) related to them, and derivatives related to interest rates, currencies, gold or silver (Sch. 5, para. 2(2)). The Treasury added 'medium term notes' to this list in 1990 (the *Financial Services Act 1986 (Listed Money Market Institutions and Miscellaneous Exemptions) Order* 1990); 'medium term notes' are debt securities issued by qualifying companies which have an original maturity of less than five years but which cannot be redeemed until after one year from issue. The qualifying original maturities of each kind of instrument are set out in para. 2(2), and it is necessary to check in each case whether a particular instrument falls within the exemption. As just one example, a certificate of deposit which is issued by an authorised institution under the *Banking Act* 1987 will be within the exemption if it has an original maturity of no more than five years (Sch. 5, para. 2(2)(a)); however, if it is issued by an overseas bank which is not a Banking Act authorised institution, it will qualify for the exemption only if its original maturity is no more than one year (Sch. 5, para. 2(2)(b)). Similarly, government bonds must have a maximum original maturity of one year, whereas bonds issued by UK local authorities qualify if their original maturity is no more than five years. There is no maximum maturity required in the case of repos, but they qualify only if the second part of the transaction is entered into within twelve months. It should also be noted that (except seemingly in the case of repos) the exemption does not apply at all to transactions in securities or warrants which are regulated by the rules of a recognised investment exchange or, in the case of qualifying derivatives such as financial futures, are made on an RIE or expressed to be as so made (para. 2(1)); however, there is no such exclusion in the case of other investment exchanges even if they are designated investment exchanges or, indeed, EEA 'regulated markets'.

To complicate the exemption even more, different minimum sizes of permitted transactions apply to different money market instruments for the purpose of seeing whether the transaction is wholesale or retail (that is, whether an unlisted firm involved in it qualifies as a 'wholesale counterparty' where that is relevant). For example, the acquisition or disposal of a certificate of deposit or a Eurobond is wholesale only if the consideration payable is not less than £100,000 (Sch. 5, para. 5(2)), whereas the acquisition or disposal of a warrant which entitles the holder to subscribe for that certificate of deposit or Eurobond is wholesale only if the consideration payable on subscription is not less than £500,000 (Sch. 5, para. 5(3)). The measure which is used to determine whether or not the transaction is wholesale also varies from instrument to instrument, and it is therefore vital always to check. For example, in the case of bonds, it is the consideration payable (Sch. 5, para. 5(2)), and not the principal amount, which may have negative implications for deep discount bonds. Again,

¶349

in the case of futures contracts, it is the price payable 'under' each futures contract (Sch. 5, para. 5(5)), not the consideration for the futures contract or the aggregate price payable under the several contracts acquired if more than one is acquired in a single transaction. Due to a deficiency in the drafting of the 1990 'medium term notes' order (see above), it is not clear whether any transaction in them qualifies as 'wholesale', and can accordingly fall within the exemption in the case of unlisted firms.

The FSA provides that once a listed institution has entered into a wholesale transaction with or on behalf of an unlisted firm, or has arranged one for it, the 'money market' exemption applies to non-wholesale money market transactions entered into by the listed institution with or for it, and to the arranging by the listed institution of non-wholesale transactions for it, for the next 18 months thereafter, as they are deemed to be wholesale transactions so far as that listed institution is concerned, except in relation to renewals of the safe harbour, (Sch. 5, para. 6, 10). This is a useful liberalisation but the 18-month 'safe harbour' must be watched very carefully and a 'diary' kept for each qualifying unlisted firm showing the actual wholesale transactions entered into with or for it, or arranged for it, by the listed institution. The liberalisation does not, however, apply to repos, which must always have a minimum consideration of £100,000 to qualify as wholesale transactions (Sch. 5, para. 7).

¶350   Appointed representatives (s. 44)

The typical appointed representative sells insurance products or units in unit trusts but the exemption is not limited to this. It applies not to employees, who do not need FSA-authorisation in any event (see ¶308), but only to company representatives or tied agents (who are, typically, companies). If they market investments or investment services for the benefit of an FSA-authorised firm (the 'principal') and the principal undertakes in writing to be responsible for them, they are allowed effectively to shelter under its FSA-authorisation for that marketing. It is unclear exactly who the recipient of the written undertaking is to be but, at the least, it should be included in the contract of appointment (which must contain certain specified provisions). Importantly, the appointed representative does not necesarily actually carry on its business 'on behalf of' (that is, as agent for) its principal. If it did, it would be entitled to an agency fee rather than commission; more importantly, if it is not acting as agent but for its own account, its main function is 'arranging deals' within para. 13 for its principal, rather than actually dealing within para. 12 on behalf of the principal. Although s. 44 allows the appointed representative to act for other firms if its principal consents, the rules of the SIB and SROs impose further restrictions under the principle of polarisation to ensure that the appointed representative cannot be mistaken for an independent intermediary. The appointed representative can be 'tied' on a group basis, and sell units in unit trusts for one company in the group and insurance products for another.

The 'appointed representative' status should be used only by firms which themselves carry on FSA-regulated investment business, normally in their own name, albeit for the benefit of an FSA-authorised firm, and therefore need an exemption to avoid the FSA's authorisation requirement. This normally means that it is not appropriate to appoint as appointed representatives individuals who represent the firm as 'consultants'; they should instead be treated as 'employees' of the firm for regulatory (although not taxation) purposes. Appointed representatives are therefore normally companies and the firm normally has on-going regulatory responsibilities and duties in respect of them.

The exemption has been affected by the ISD in two separate respects. First, although s. 44 refers in terms only to firms whose principal is an FSA-authorised firm, passporting firms are now treated as FSA-authorised firms for this purpose (para. 7 of Sch. 7 to the ISD regulations and of Sch. 9 to the 2BCD regulations, see ¶357); the appointed representative's principal must therefore be an FSA-authorised firm or a passporting firm if its business is to qualify for the exemption. Secondly, a UK appointed representative which is an EEA investment firm (see ¶302), because it passes on orders, or arranges deals in the secondary market, is not an 'exempted person' under s. 44 unless it does so solely for the account of a firm which is an EEA investment firm (see ¶302) or, seemingly, a firm which would be an EEA investment firm if it was a UK firm (reg. 27 of the ISD regulations, see ¶357); the appointed representative will of course, normally do so for the benefit of the FSA-authorised firm or passporting firm which is its principal and it will therefore surely be regarded as passing on orders or arranging deals for the account of its principal. If it does, and if the principal has full and unconditional responsibility for that activity, the ISD treats the business as being carried on by the principal rather than the appointed representative (art. 1(2)); given that the principal must accept responsibility for the appointed representative for the 'appointed representative' exemption to apply at all, this allows the exemption to continue. The problem does not arise in relation to the appointed representative's advisory services, as investment advice is not an ISD core investment service and accordingly is outside the ISD's authorisation requirement (see ¶330).

The 'appointed representative' exemption applies only to FSA-regulated investment business which consists of endeavouring to procure persons to enter into investment agreements, advising persons about whether or not to enter into investment agreements and giving advice as to the sale of investments issued by the principal or as to the exercise of rights conferred by an investment (s. 44(3)). The exemption therefore does not cover para. 12 dealings; however, as indicated above, an appointed representative does not normally act as agent

¶350

for the principal or enter into transactions within para. 12 on his behalf. Although the position is not clear, it would seem that the exemption allows the appointed representative to carry on business as an investment adviser in relation to any FSA-regulated investment (even if the resulting transaction is not with its principal) and even to act as a corporate finance advisory firm (arranging or advising on transactions to which its principal is not a party), provided only that it carries on that business for the benefit of an FSA-authorised firm or a passporting firm. However, this may not have been the intention of the legislation and an FSA-authorised firm or passporting firm which wants to use the 'appointed representative' exemption for these purposes should discuss them in detail with its SRO or the SIB as appropriate.

The 'appointed representative' exemption applies only to marketing or advisory activities (see above). Accordingly, the appointed representative would need FSA-authorisation if, rather than passing the investor's application for units or life policies on to its principal, it applies or accepts them itself as agent. It is understood that it has been suggested in certain quarters that half-commission men (dealers or salesmen who are not employees or consultants of the securities house but are employed under a contract for services as dealers or salesmen in return for a share of the commission earned from 'their' clients) can use the appointed representative status to deal on behalf of their principal; however, it is difficult to see how that can be correct if they actually deal in investments themselves on behalf of their principal (rather than merely arrange for others to deal). Conversely, however, it is arguable that in certain circumstances they may not in fact need FSA-authorisation at all, at least if they deal only as part of their principal's staff (see ¶308); indeed, if this is the case, they should normally not be engaged as appointed representatives at all, but merely treated as the principal's employees for regulatory purposes in the same way as consultants (see above).

¶351 The Bank of England (s. 35)

The Bank of England is exempted for everything it does.

¶352 Investment exchanges and clearing houses (s. 36, 38 and 40)

UK investment exchanges (such as stock, options or futures exchanges) and clearing houses are exempt for activities as such if they are recognised (or, approved) by the SIB; they regulate a market place and transactions on it (for example, imposing certain terms on bargains and specifying settlement periods) rather than the relationship of member firms with clients. RIEs and RCHs can be recognised in the discretion of the SIB but only if they fulfil certain minimum criteria, in particular that they have sufficient financial resources and adequate arrangements for supervision and enforcement. They must also 'ensure' settlement although, in the case of RIEs, it will be sufficient if they employ an RCH to do so (Sch. 4). It is unclear whether this involves some sort of guarantee rather than merely the provision of facilities, which is a vital question, but it is understood that it requires only the provision of facilities. If they are not exempted as RIEs or RCHs (and are not non-UK EEA 'regulated markets', see ¶353), investment exchanges and clearing houses which otherwise need to be FSA-authorised must join an SRO as a para. 13 'arranger' or be registered as a 'service company'.

Overseas exchanges and clearing houses can also be recognised if they satisfy different criteria, in particular that there is equivalent investor protection to that afforded by UK RIEs and RCHs and, importantly, that they are willing to co-operate with UK regulators, for example by sharing information, and there must be mutual assistance arrangements between the relevant regulating authorities and the UK (s. 40). In this case recognition must be by the Treasury, not the SIB, (s. 114(6)) and the Treasury can take into account whether there is reciprocity of access to the home financial markets of the applicant. Amongst recognised overseas investment exchanges is NASDAQ, which provides dealing facilities in the UK.

Recognition confers on an investment exchange or clearing house only an exemption from the FSA's requirement for FSA-authorisation. Accordingly, it is normally not an appropriate status for overseas exchanges or clearing houses unless they have a branch or otherwise do business in the UK. Nonetheless, the SIB has accepted that it is useful to direct investors to use 'approved' overseas exchanges by conferring privileges on them and it has therefore established a special category of investment exchange, the 'designated investment exchange'. DIEs include, for example, the New York Stock Exchange and many futures and options exchanges. In particular, the SRO's reporting requirements for firms regulated by them are substantially relaxed in the case of DIEs as well as RIEs. In addition, securities quoted on DIEs are normally treated as readily realisable, which avoids detailed disclosure requirements, and have lower financial resources requirements than securities not quoted on either an RIE or a DIE (or, if the relaxation has been extended to them by the firm's regulator, an EEA regulated market, see ¶353. However, it must be emphasised that DIEs have no formal status so far as the Financial Services Act itself is concerned; for example, dealings on DIEs may still be within the 'money market' exemption and deferred delivery contracts on them are not 'automatically' 'futures', in each case in contradistinction to the position of RIEs (see ¶349 and ¶325 respectively).

Recognition is likely to confer commercial advantages and qualifies an investment exchange for 'approval' by the Government which will allow it to play an important role in the new regime for offerings of unlisted securities. (see Ch. 8).

¶352

¶353   EEA regulated markets

The ISD in effect grants a 'single European passport' to screen-based markets which are established in the EEA (art. 15(4)). The ISD allows EEA member states to grant a special status to markets based in them which trade ISD investments, if they comply with certain requirements, in particular the ISD's transaction reporting and transparency rules. These markets must be listed as such by their home member state under ISD rules before they can qualify as 'regulated markets'; the 'home member state' is the state in which the body which provides the trading facilities has its registered office or, if it does not have a registered office, has its head office, seemingly even if the trading facilities are provided from a different member state. The ISD normally allows EEA investment firms (importantly, including EEA credit institutions) which deal for their own account or as agent to become members of, or have access to, ISD regulated markets, and their clearing systems, without the need for a local licence under the equivalent of an ISD or 2BCD passport, although they may have to establish a local branch in order to do so, (art. 15(1)). It also allows regulated markets which do not require a physical presence to provide trading screens or other appropriate facilities in all EEA member states, also without the need for a local licence, (art. 15(4)) so that the 'passport' can be used by securities firms without establishing a local branch. This is a great help to markets such as EASDAQ, the new pan-European market for enterprise companies.

The Treasury has accordingly granted non-UK EEA regulated markets an exemption from the FSA's authorisation requirement under the power granted to it by s. 46 (see ¶355). The exemption applies to all investment exchanges which, like EASDAQ, provide the trading facilities constituting an EEA regulated market which has a home member state (see above) other than the UK, if the market does not require that firms dealing on it must have a physical presence in the EEA member state from which the trading facilities are provided or on any trading floor the market may have (the *Financial Services Act 1986 (EEA Regulated Markets) (Exemptions) Order* 1995, SI 1995/3273). The exemption is essentially from para. 13 and applies to anything done in connection with or for the purposes of the provision of those trading facilities (art. 2). Like an RIE, EEA regulated markets are accordingly 'exempted persons' for the purposes of the FSA, and this allows them to market themselves in the UK without being subject to the FSA's restrictions on investment advertisements (s. 58(1)(b), see Ch. 9).

Because non-UK EEA regulated markets have this special exemption for screen-based trading facilities (or other trading facilities not requiring a physical presence) they are not treated as 'exempted persons' under s. 36 in relation to those trading facilities even if they become RIEs (reg. 25 of the ISD regulations, see ¶357).

¶353

¶354   Public officials (s. 45)

The FSA exempts certain specified public officials, such as official receivers, when acting in the relevant official capacity. Administrators under the *Insolvency Act* 1986 do not seem to be included, nor are receivers and liquidators; they may accordingly require FSA-authorisation if they engage in FSA-regulated investment activities.

¶355   Alteration of exempted firms (s. 46)

The government may alter these exemptions by secondary legislation. The government's powers under s. 46 cannot be delegated to a designated agency such as the SIB.

PASSPORTING FIRMS

¶356   Introduction

The scope and effect of the exemptions for non-UK EEA firms using their passport to carry on FSA-regulated investment business in the UK are very complicated, and an over-view may therefore be helpful.

The EU Treaty of Rome and the four 'single market' financial institutions directives issued under it, for EU investment firms, for EU banks or other credit institutions and for EU life and non-life insurance companies, respectively, have tried to create a single European market for FSA-regulated investment business (and banking and insurance business). The single market was extended to the whole European Economic Area (the European Union, Iceland, Liechtenstein and Norway) by the European Economic Area Treaty of May 1992.

The four 'single market' financial institutions directives issued under the Treaty of Rome are, respectively, the *Investment Services Directive* of 10 May 1993, No. 93/22/EEC, (the ISD) in the case of EEA investment firms, the *Second Banking Coordination Directive* of 15 December 1989, No. 89/646/EEC, (the 2BCD) in the case of EEA banks and other credit institutions, the *Third Insurance Directive* of 10 November 1992, No. 92/96/EEC, in the case of EEA life assurance companies and the *Third Insurance Directive* of 18 June 1992, No. 92/49/EEC, in the case of EEA non-life companies. Each of these directives requires member states to impose authorisation requirements on, and grant a single European passport to, the financial institutions subject to it. The 2BCD passport covers many FSA-regulated investment activities; however, it does not cover all the FSA-regulated investment activities covered by the ISD passport. In particular, it does not normally cover the arranging of transactions in existing securities, or the receipt and transmission of orders within para. 13 of Sch. 1 to the FSA, even though they are usually covered by the ISD passport. The Treasury has allowed UK credit institutions to use the 2BCD passport by providing in the regulations implementing the 2BCD that they are authorised for the purposes of the passport by their authorisation as banks or building societies under the first and second banking directives to carry on any activity within the 2BCD passport which is an FSA-regulated investment activity (and indeed any other activity covered by it) if it is lawful for them to carry it on in the UK (reg. 21 of the 2BCD regulations, see ¶357); it is lawful for them to do so in relation to FSA-regulated investment business if they are FSA-authorised for it or, in the case of credit institutions which are listed money market institutions, FSA-exempted for it and their FSA-authorisation or FSA-exemption is accordingly treated as merely a condition of their banking licence.

As a result, and provided that the relevant provisions of the directives have all been fully implemented into domestic law, as they all should have been by the end of 1995, every EEA investment firm, bank or other credit institution and insurance company can carry on the activities or provide the services covered by the relevant directive in all EEA member States on the basis of the authorisation (or licence) granted to it by its domestic regulator under the directive without any need for a local licence for that business, provided only that they comply with the notification procedures required by the directive. UK listed money market institutions, which are exempted from the FSA under s. 43 (see ¶349), are helpfully treated as being authorised under the FSA for this purpose and they can accordingly use the outgoing 2BCD or ISD passport for their money market activities if they qualify as passported services (reg. 18(2) of the ISD regulations, see ¶357). Accordingly, all non-UK EEA investment firms, credit institutions and insurance companies have a 'single European passport' enabling them to carry on FSA-regulated investment business in the UK without FSA-authorisation if they comply with the required notification procedures, provided that the investment business is within their passport and that they are authorised for it by their domestic regulator. In the case of non-UK EEA investment firms and credit institutions, the passport is granted as a disapplication of the requirement in s. 3 of the FSA to be authorised under the FSA. The passport for non-UK EEA insurance companies is granted as an automatic authorisation under s. 22 of the FSA, as in the case of UK insurance companies, and it can accordingly be ignored for present purposes. The passports granted to non-UK EEA investment firms and credit institutions cover most FSA-regulated investment business but, importantly, not all of it. However, the FSA's 'overseas persons' exemptions (see ¶334) continue to apply to all firms despite the implementation of the ISD and 2BCD directives and they are therefore still available to non-UK EEA firms when they are carrying on FSA-regulated investment business falling within them; accordingly, the passport does not need to be used where they apply. Similarly, the passport does not need to be used if the firm carries on FSA-regulated investment activities only within the FSA's 'normal' exemptions in Pt. III; as it is not carrying on FSA-regulated investment business when doing so, it does not need to be FSA-authorised anyway. In both these cases the firm is therefore not a passporting firm in relation to these FSA-regulated investment activities. Importantly, the Treasury have granted ISD credit institutions, which are authorised to provide one or more ISD core investment services by their authorisation as a credit institution under the first and second banking directives and accordingly are not entitled to the ISD passport (art. 2(1)), a passport equivalent to the ISD passport for FSA-regulated investment business carried on by them in the UK in relation to ISD services falling outside the 2BCD passport (see below).

It is unclear whether or not the passport is in fact used where the 'overseas persons' exemptions apply; the same notification procedures are required (see below) if the non-UK EEA firm wants to provide or carry on passported services or activities in the UK whether or not the 'overseas persons' exemptions apply (or, indeed, any of the 'normal' exemptions in Pt. III applies) so that no choice actually needs to be made. However, the Treasury have provided in relation to both the ISD passport and the 2BCD passport that for FSA purposes the regulatory approach to the non-UK EEA firm should depend on whether or not the firm is carrying on FSA-regulated investment business and, if so, whether the 'overseas persons' exemptions apply to the passported FSA-regulated investment business concerned (or, at least, would have applied if there had been no passport) the firm is treated as using its passport only if (in the absence of any 'exempted person' exemption) (see ¶347–¶355) it can only carry on the FSA-regulated investment activity concerned in the UK by using it. The firm is therefore treated as not using it when an exemption in Pt. III or Pt. IV applies; in that sense, it is easiest to regard the exemptions as having priority to the passport and so excluding it where they apply, and the relevant parts of this Section are written on that basis. The expression which is used in the regulations implementing into UK law the ISD passport and the 2BCD passport respectively to refer to FSA-regulated investment business carried on with clients or counterparties in the UK, or from a UK office, under the passport but outside the 'overseas persons' exemptions is 'home-regulated investment business [carried on] in the UK' (see ¶359). However, ISD credit institutions carrying on business in the UK under their ISD passport (and not under their 2BCD passport) may in fact not be regarded as carrying on 'home-regulated' investment business for this purpose; this is because business carried on under the ISD passport is treated as 'home-regulated' only if the non-UK EEA investment firm or credit institution is authorised for it as an 'investment firm' and ISD credit institutions are, seemingly, authorised for FSA-regulated investment business carried on under

¶356

their ISD passport under the first and second banking directives, and therefore seemingly only as credit institutions.

The difference between carrying on business under the passport and carrying it on under the 'overseas persons' exemptions is important in practice because a non-UK EEA firm is treated for many purposes as if it was an FSA-authorised firm when it carries on home-regulated investment business in the UK (in other words, when it carries on FSA-regulated investment business in the UK under its passport but outside the 'overseas persons' exemptions); a key example is that non-UK EEA firms are normally subject to the SIB's conduct of business rules when they use the passport (or the rules of an SRO if they join the SRO for their passported services) but not when they use the 'overseas persons' exemptions (para. 10(1) of Sch. 7 of the ISD regulations and of the 2BCD regulations, see ¶357). This treatment may, however, not apply to ISD credit institutions (see above and ¶357).

However, it is necessary for non-UK EEA firms to notify the relevant UK regulator through their domestic regulator if they want to provide any passported service or carry on any passported activity in the UK on a cross-border basis (even if they do so under the 'overseas persons' exemptions rather than by using the passport or, indeed, even if it falls within a Pt. III exemption) or if they want to establish a branch in the UK to provide passported services or carry on passported activities. The notification requirement accordingly applies even if the passported firm is not carrying on FSA-regulated investment business at all. Although the Pt. III exemptions do not apply to the ISD's core investment services subject to the ISD's authorisation requirement, they can apply to non-core services (see ¶330) even though non-core services are within the notification requirement; similarly, the Pt. III exemptions can apply to 2BCD passported activities if they do not constitute ISD core investment services subject to the ISD's authorisation requirement. The relevant UK regulator for the notification requirement is normally the SIB in the case of non-banks and the Bank of England in the case of banks and other credit institutions; however, it is the Bank of England in the case of non-banks which are listed institutions and which confine the FSA-regulated investment business they carry on or propose to carry on in the UK under their ISD passport to activities falling within the FSA's 'money market' exemption (see ¶349) (Sch. 3 of the ISD regulations, see ¶357). ISD credit institutions are not subject to this notification procedure for ISD services outside their 2BCD passport, perhaps because their ISD passport is not granted by either the ISD or the 2BCD (which would have required notification) but is, instead, granted by the Treasury. It should be noted that, under the provisions of the ISD and the 2BCD, UK investment firms and credit institutions must also notify the local regulators if they want to use their ISD or 2BCD passports to do business in another EEA member state; the notification is made through their

¶356

UK regulator and, indeed, it is normally an offence for UK firms to do business in another EEA member state which falls within their ISD or 2BCD passport without going through this notification procedure, and so in effect using the passport, (reg. 20 of the ISD regulations, see ¶357).

The ISD and the 2BCD (and indeed the third insurance directives) are intended to make it clear that the Treaty of Rome freedoms to establish branches and provide cross-border services throughout the European Economic Area (essentially, continental Europe other than Switzerland) do in fact apply in the postulated circumstances, so avoiding the definitional questions raised by the Treaty of Rome itself and arguments that a local licence can nonetheless be required under the EU concept of the 'general good' (see below). However, the Treaty of Rome is still relevant where the directives do not apply. As explained in ¶360, it is likely that the Treaty of Rome will in practice be relevant even in relation to the investment services covered by the ISD and, perhaps, the investment activities covered by the 2BCD, although this depends on whether member States agree with the UK's view on where services are provided (see ¶360); as the FSA and the 2BCD refer to investment activities rather than investment services, the expressions 'activities' or 'carrying on activities' will be used for convenience in this Section to include services or providing services, but it must be remembered that activities are outside the ISD if they are not actually services provided to third parties by an EEA investment firm (but are, for example, 'own initiative' own account dealings). The Treaty of Rome has been amended by the EEA Treaty of May 1992 in light of the EU's arrangements with members of the European Free Trade Association (EFTA) which are not themselves members of the European Union and therefore applies to all members of the EEA; it should be emphasised that Switzerland is not a member of the EEA even though it is a member of EFTA.

Article 52 of the Treaty of Rome gives EEA investment firms, credit institutions and insurance companies (and other EEA nationals) the right to establish a branch in all other member States of the EEA; art. 59 of the Treaty of Rome allows them to carry on cross-border activities from a branch in one EEA member State with or for customers in any other EEA member State. EU jurisprudence has established that these freedoms are subject to licensing and other regulatory requirements justifiable as being in the interest of the 'general good' (see ¶360). The directives were issued (under powers granted by the Treaty of Rome) in order to coordinate the provisions relating to these two freedoms which are a matter for regulation or administrative action; importantly, they accordingly prevent EEA member States raising a 'general good' justification for imposing a local licensing requirement for the activities covered by them on firms from other member States which are authorised under them.

¶356

¶357   Implementation of the passport

The 'single market' directives require EEA member States to grant access, in the relevant circumstances, to EEA firms authorised under them in other EEA member States, whether they want to establish a local branch or merely carry on cross-border activities from a branch in another member state. The directives accordingly prohibit 'host member States' from imposing their own licensing requirements for activities within the directives for which they are authorised by their 'home member State'. The ISD passport is granted to EEA investment firms. The 2BCD passport is granted to EEA credit institutions and their qualifying 90 per cent subsidiaries; although the position is not totally clear, these subsidiaries would seem to be entitled to both the 2BCD and the ISD passports and, indeed, the ISD Regulations are written on that basis. The 2BCD passport does not seem to be used very much in the case of qualifying subsidiaries; this is because not only must the subsidiary be authorised, and carry on the relevant business, in the same member state as the credit institution but, in addition, the credit institution must guarantee the liabilities of the subsidiary and consolidate it in its regulatory supervision. The third insurance directives passport is granted to EEA life assurance companies and other EEA insurance companies for their 'insurance business' activities; the passport is relevant in the present context because these activities (typically, the issue of qualifying endowment or unit-linked policies) may constitute 'investment business' for the purposes of the FSA.

In general terms, the single European passports granted by the ISD and the 2BCD allow qualifying non-UK EEA firms to carry on FSA-regulated investment business in the UK without needing FSA-authorisation if the relevant business falls within the passport and they are authorised for it by their domestic regulator. The Treasury might have implemented the passport requirements of the ISD and the 2BCD by giving passporting non-UK EEA firms automatic FSA-authorisation, as the UK did in the case of EEA insurance companies (see below). However, the Treasury have instead followed the style of the ISD and 2BCD directives themselves to provide that non-UK EEA firms do not need FSA-authorisation for passported activities which they are authorised, or permitted, to carry on by their home member State.

The ISD passport provisions were implemented into UK law as from 1 January 1996 by the *Investment Services Regulations* 1995, SI 1995/3275, (the ISD regulations) and the 2BCD passport provisions as from 1 January 1993 by the *Banking Coordination (Second Council Directive) Regulations* 1992, SI 1992/3218, (the 2BCD regulations). The ISD regulations and the 2BCD regulations follow the same structure and are very long and complicated. Their detail is beyond the scope of this guide but, in essence, qualifying non-UK EEA firms do not need FSA-authorisation for the FSA-regulated investment business covered by their passports once they have duly notified the relevant

UK regulators through their own domestic regulators; the prohibition in s. 3 of the FSA on carrying on FSA-regulated investment business in the UK without FSA-authorisation does not apply to those notified activities (reg. 5(1)(a) of the ISD regulations and reg. 5(1)(b) of the 2BCD regulations). The ISD passport covers a core investment service only if the firm is authorised to provide it by its domestic regulator, and also covers all non-core services for which it is authorised by its domestic regulator if it is authorised by it for at least one core investment service. The 2BCD passport covers all listed activities which the firm is authorised or (in the case of qualifying subsidiaries) permitted by its domestic regulator to carry on (see ¶358). The notification is required if the firm wants to carry on investment (or, indeed, banking) activities covered by the passport 'in the UK' even if its doing so does not constitute carrying on FSA-regulated investment business in the UK, for example because the 'overseas persons' exemptions apply (reg. 6(1) of the ISD Regulations and of the 2BCD Regulations). After notification, non-UK EEA firms can accordingly carry on passported activities in the UK, either from UK branches or on a cross-border basis from branches in other EEA member States, without FSA-authorisation; it is unclear whether they can also carry on passported activities from non-EEA branches and, as this is on balance unlikely, this should be discussed with UK regulators if relevant. A separate notification is needed for each new activity or UK branch. The regulations provide, as required by the directives, that cross-border services can begin as soon as the notification is made by the home member State regulator (which must be within one month) but that a branch can be established only after not only the notification is made (which must be within three months) but also the host member State has notified the firm of the conduct of business and other rules under which it will operate or two months have passed since the notification was made. The firm's domestic regulator cannot prohibit the firm from carrying on cross-border activities, and it can prohibit it from establishing a branch in another member State only on very limited prudential grounds.

Importantly, EEA credit institutions which are authorised under the first and second banking directives to provide one or more ISD core investment services are allowed by the Treasury to provide all ISD services falling outside the 2BCD passport as if they are entitled to the ISD passport, even though they are excluded from it under art. 2(1), (reg. 5(1) of the ISD regulations); however, they do not need to notify the UK regulators of these ISD passported services but only about their 2BCD activities (reg. 6 of the ISD regulations and of the 2BCD regulations). This 'additional' passport is important because the ISD passport is different from the 2BCD passport; in particular, the ISD passport normally covers the arranging of secondary market transactions and the receipt and transmission of orders but the 2BCD passport usually does not (see ¶358). The Treasury may perhaps have given these ISD credit institutions an ISD passport because it is a neat way of complying with two ISD requirements. First, EEA member states must regulate all EEA investment firms (including credit institutions authorised to provide one or more core investment services) which provide ISD services in them; secondly, credit institutions authorised to provide one or more core investment services under the first and second banking directives are outside the ISD's authorisation requirement (because they are authorised for them as banks). If, unlike firms excluded from the ISD under art. 2(2) (see ¶330), they have to be regulated for ISD services even though they are not subject to an authorisation requirement under the ISD, the easiest model to use is the passport. However, it is unclear why the Treasury passport was not restricted to only the FSA-regulated investment activities covered by the FSA extension order, as that was all that was strictly necessary to ensure that ISD credit institutions were not prejudiced by the implementation of the ISD (see ¶330).

A non-UK EEA firm's passported FSA-regulated investment business will normally be regulated by the conduct of business rules of the SIB (or its SRO) if it is carried on in the UK (para. 10 (1) of Sch. 7 to the ISD regulations and of Sch. 9 to the 2BCD regulations); however, it will not be FSA-regulated if it falls within the FSA's 'overseas persons' exemptions and so does not constitute 'home-regulated investment business [carried on] in the United Kingdom' (see ¶359) or, indeed, it falls within one of the FSA's 'normal' exemptions in Pt. III of Sch. 1 and therefore does not qualify as FSA-regulated investment business at all. ISD credit institutions are, however, seemingly not FSA-regulated for ISD services falling outside the 2BCD passport even if they fall outside the 'overseas persons' exemptions; this is the case even though the ISD requires all ISD services provided by EEA investment firms outside the art. 2(2) exemptions to be regulated by the member State in which they are provided, and the requirement applies even if they are provided by an ISD credit institution (even though it is not subject to the ISD's authorisation requirement). Passporting firms can still join SROs and, indeed, become listed money market institutions (see ¶349) for their passported activities. They will not thereby become FSA-authorised or exempted firms in relation to those services (reg. 21 and 26 of the ISD regulations and reg. 48 and 52 of the 2BCD regulations); however, they will, as a result, be subject to the relevant SRO and Bank of England rules, rather than those of the SIB.

It is important to remember that non-UK EEA firms still need FSA-authorisation if they want to carry on FSA-regulated investment business in the UK which falls outside their passport, unless an exemption applies, such as one of the 'overseas persons' exemptions; membership of an SRO for this non-passported business will give them FSA-authorisation for it (but not for passported business, as none is needed). In this context, it should be noted that, under reg. 24 of the ISD regulations and reg. 51 of the 2BCD regulations, the traditional FSA exemption for 'Euro-persons', which grants non-UK EEA firms without a place of business in the UK automatic authorisation for their domestically authorised FSA-regulated investment business (s. 31), is still available for business which is not 'home-regulated investment business carried on in the UK' or is not covered by the passport (for example, dealings in. commodity futures); this exemption, which was extended from the EU to the whole EEA by the *European Economic Area Act* 1993, is very little used but it may be of help in particular circumstances (see ¶414).

The passport granted to insurance companies has been implemented in a different way from the ISD and the 2BCD passports; the passport confers automatic authorisation rather than an exemption from the need for authorisation. Section 22 of the FSA grants UK insurance companies whose insurance business includes investment business automatic authorisation for that investment business (see ¶415); this is the case whether or not they are life assurance companies. Automatic authorisation under s. 22 has accordingly been extended to cover non-UK EEA insurance companies (reg. 57 of the *Insurance Companies (Third Insurance Directives) Regulations* 1994, SI 1994/1696, taken together with the *Insurance Companies (Amendment) Regulations* 1994, SI 1994/3132, and the *Insurance Companies (Amendment No. 2) Regulations* 1996, SI 1996/944). In general terms, the automatic authorisation applies where the carrying on of the insurance business constitutes the carrying on of FSA-regulated investment business 'in the United Kingdom' for the purposes of the FSA (see s. 1(3) of the FSA); automatic authorisation is also granted for any other FSA-regulated investment business the insurance company is entitled to carry on under its domestic law (for example, buying or selling investments outside the 'own account' exemptions). Any cross-border business falling within the 'overseas persons' exemptions is, however, not automatically FSA-authorised (see above); this is because that business is exempted by the 'overseas persons' exemptions from the FSA's authorisation requirement and accordingly does not need authorisation under the passport, even if the relevant service is provided in the UK. Because the passport for insurance companies works so differently from the ISD passport and the 2BCD passport, this section will not refer to it again but it must always be remembered that references in this Section to 'EEA firms' (or 'EEA investment firms') do not include EEA insurance companies.

¶358   Passported activities

The FSA-regulated investment activities covered by the ISD passport for EEA investment firms, or which would be covered apart from the exemptions in art. 2(2) of the ISD, are listed in the 1995 FSA Extension Order (see ¶330).

They consist in general terms of the following activities, if they are carried on as a service for third parties and (taken together) they are provided to third parties on a professional basis as a regular occupation or business:

(a) dealing in ISD investments (for own account or as agent); in the case of own account transactions, this seems to be more limited than para. 12 and to cover in the normal case only trading (rather than investing) activities, typically, 'dual capacity' transactions (for example, a broker dealing off its own book with a client) and acting as a market maker (see ¶329 and ¶331);

(b) receiving and transmitting orders in ISD investments, including arranging deals in existing ISD investments but, probably, not arranging the purchase or sale of an entire company (which is either outside the ISD altogether in particular circumstances or, arguably, falls in (f) below, see ¶330);

(c) managing ISD investments on a discretionary client-by-client basis;

(d) underwriting issues of ISD investments and placing ISD investments on their issue by taking them on to the firm's book and then selling them on; although the ISD refers to 'placing', the UK regulators have taken the position that this refers only to offers for sale, or US-style underwriting, and that UK-style placings (namely, offers by the firm as agent for the issuer where the resulting contract is entered into directly by the issuer) are covered only if the application or acceptance forms are sent back to the placing agent for transmission to the issuer (see (b) above);

(e) advising on ISD investments, or non-discretionary portfolio management of portfolios including ISD investments;

(f) advice and other services relating to mergers and the purchase or sale of undertakings;

(g) safe custody services relating to ISD investments (but not, for example, life policies); and

(h) foreign exchange services in connection with transactions in ISD investments (for example, selling pounds sterling for US dollars in order to buy US securities).

The services in (a) to (d) above are the 'core investment services' specified in the ISD (and the 1995 FSA extension order). A firm does not qualify for the ISD passport unless it provides one or more of these core investment services as a regular occupation or business to third parties on a professional basis outside the ISD's art. 2(2) exemptions. If, however, the firm does do so, it is defined in the ISD as an 'investment firm' and, if it qualifies for the ISD passport, it is commonly referred to as an 'ISD firm'. An EEA investment firm must be authorised for core investment services under its domestic legislation implementing the ISD (unless it falls within an art. 2(2) exemption or is an ISD

¶358

credit institution) and will accordingly obtain the ISD passport for them. Its passport will also cover the 'non-core services' specified in the ISD (and the 1995 FSA extension order), including those in (e), (f) and (h), if, as allowed, but not required, by the ISD, the firm is authorised for it under its domestic laws. A firm which only provides non-core services, and no core investment services, is not entitled to the ISD passport for those non-core services but, conversely, is not subject to the FSA Extension Order restricting various FSA exemptions in Pt. III of Sch. 1 (see ¶330). As explained in ¶357, the UK has granted an ISD passport to non-UK EEA credit institutions which provide one or more core investment services even though this is not in fact required by the ISD (see ¶357).

ISD 'investments' are shares, debentures (or, debt securities), units or shares in collective investment undertakings, money market instruments, financial options and futures (even if cash-settled, and so constituting contracts for differences), currency, interest rate and equity options and swaps and forward rate agreements. Collective investment undertakings are, in general terms, both formal funds and, probably, arrangements for parallel investment, at least if they are co-investing with a formal fund; closed-ended investment companies (such as investment trusts) are also collective investment undertakings. It is unclear whether other FSA collective investment schemes also qualify; however, given that the UCITS directive of 20 December 1985 (No. 85/611/EEC), the only EU directive on the harmonisation of laws relating to collective investment undertakings, refers to 'undertakings constituted [by contract, trust or statute]', this is perhaps unlikely. Commodities and derivatives linked to commodities are not covered. Similarly, stand-alone transactions in forward foreign exchange are also not covered even though they often constitute FSA-regulated investment transactions (see ¶325).

The FSA-regulated investment activities covered by the 2BCD passport for EEA credit institutions and their qualifying subsidiaries consist in general terms of the following activities (even if they are not provided as 'services', as required by the ISD passport):

(a) trading (for own account or the account of customers) in money market instruments, financial futures and options (even if cash-settled) and transferable securities; 'transferable securities' was deliberately not defined but the Treasury regard it as meaning all FSA-regulated securities in para. 1–6 of Sch. 1 which are freely transferable;

(b) portfolio management (whether discretionary or non-discretionary) and advice;

(c) advice and other services relating to securities issues;

¶358

(d) advice and other services relating to mergers and the purchase or sale of undertakings;

(e) money broking, which the Treasury regard as meaning acting as name-passing intermediary in the money markets;

(f) safe custody services relating to securities; and

(g) dealings in spot or forward foreign exchange.

In contrast to the ISD, the 2BCD passport does not as such cover the arranging of transactions in existing securities or the receipt and transmission of orders; however, it will do so if the activity falls within one of the specified heads of passported activity (for example, arranging takeovers, money broking or portfolio management). It also does not cover safe custody services relating to FSA-regulated investments which do not qualify as 'securities' within para. 1–6 of Sch. 1 to the FSA; non-UK EEA credit institutions may therefore need FSA-authorisation for safe custody services relating to other investments (para. 13A). Non-UK EEA credit institutions which are investment firms authorised to provide one or more ISD core investment services by their authorisation as credit institutions (and are accordingly excluded from the ISD passport) have, however, been granted a passport equivalent to the ISD passport by the Treasury (see ¶356) and their extended passport does cover the arranging of transactions in existing securities, and the receipt and transmission of orders generally (see ¶357) and safe custody services relating to all ISD investments. Conversely, dealings in forward foreign exchange are covered by the 2BCD passport but, seemingly, not by the ISD passport (see above).

The ISD and 2BCD passports only cover expressly the listed substantive activities; they do not cover expressly offering or agreeing to carry them on, in the same way as the FSA does. However, it would clearly be contrary to the concept of the single European passport to require local authorisation for offers and agreements to carry on passported activities and accordingly the UK accepts that the passport covers them as well; it therefore excludes the FSA's authorisation requirement in relation to them by the general requirement that nothing in the FSA prevents non-UK EEA firms carrying on passported activities in the UK (reg. 5(1) of the ISD regulations and of the 2BCD regulations).

¶359 FSA status of passporting firms

As non-UK EEA firms using their ISD or 2BCD passport do not obtain FSA-authorisation for passported activities, they are not 'authorised persons' for the purposes of the FSA in relation to the FSA-regulated investment business covered by their ISD or 2BCD passport. As they do not in fact need FSA-authorisation for passported activities, and indeed cannot be made subject to an 'exemption' process for them, they are also not 'exempted persons' in respect of that business. This is the case even if they are approved by the Bank of England as listed money market institutions but the SIB gave informal guidance in 1996 that they do nonetheless qualify as 'listed institutions' for the purposes of that exemption; other listed institutions are therefore within the exemption when they deal with them (see ¶349). However, many of the FSA provisions relating to FSA-authorised firms nonetheless apply in relation to passporting firms if, in using the ISD or 2BCD passport, they are carrying on 'home-regulated investment business in the UK'; this is presumably intended to apply to ISD credit institutions using their ISD passport for activities outside their 2BCD passport, although this is not totally clear from the wording. As a result, passporting firms are subject to UK conduct of business rules (of the SIB, their SRO or, if they are listed institutions carrying on business within the 'money market' exemption, the Bank of England); in addition, they do not need to have investment advertisements which are to be issued by them approved by an FSA-authorised firm (and, indeed, they can 'approve' them for others) and the 'own account', 'group' and 'overseas persons' exemptions apply in relation to business with or through them as if they were FSA-authorised firms. Similarly, they are subject to the restrictions in s. 76 of the FSA on the marketing by FSA-authorised firms of collective investment schemes which are not approved by the SIB (see Ch. 9). This is because the ISD regulations and the 2BCD regulations provide that many specified references in the FSA to FSA-authorised firms include references to passporting firms.

The expression 'home-regulated investment business [carried on] in the United Kingdom', which is used to determine when non-UK EEA firms are passporting firms, was specially coined for the purposes of the ISD regulations and the 2BCD regulations. It essentially means FSA-regulated investment business within the passport which would be treated as carried on in the UK for the purposes of s. 1(3) of the FSA, and so despite the 'overseas persons' exemptions (see ¶310); in the case of the 2BCD passport, the investment business must be regulated by a domestic supervisor, but this would normally be the case. In general terms, 'home-regulated investment business carried on in the UK' covers all business carried on from a UK branch; it also covers business carried on from a non-UK branch (even by a firm which has no UK branch) if it comes within the territorial reach of the FSA and falls outside the 'overseas persons' exemptions (which would have treated it as not carried on in the UK). As *ex hypothesi* the 'overseas persons' exemptions do not apply, the non-UK EEA firm must be using the passport in order to carry on this FSA-regulated investment business; accordingly, the passporting firm is 'relying on' the disapplication of the FSA's authorisation requirement as a result of the passport, which is required in order to qualify as 'home-regulated investment business [carried on] in the UK'. Conversely, business which falls within the 'overseas persons' exemptions (see ¶310) is not treated as carried on

¶359

'in the United Kingdom' for the purposes of the FSA, and these deeming provisions do not apply to it.

Importantly, the ISD regulations and the 2BCD regulations provide that non-UK EEA investment firms and banks or other credit institutions are normally not allowed to carry on activities 'in' the UK which are covered by their ISD or 2BCD passport unless they have notified the SIB or the Bank of England through their domestic regulator (reg. 6(1) and 7(1) of the ISD regulations and the 2BCD regulations). The notification requirement applies even if the firm does not have or establish a UK office and uses the 'overseas persons' exemptions for all its FSA-regulated investment business; activities can be treated as carried on in the UK for the purposes of the notification requirement even though they form part of FSA-regulated investment business which is treated as not carried on in the UK for the purposes of the FSA's authorisation requirement (see further ¶357). Indeed, passported activities have to be notified even if they are within the FSA's Sch. 1, Pt. III exemptions. Conversely, the notification requirement does not apply to FSA-regulated investment activities within the 'overseas persons' exemptions which fall outside the passport, although the better practice is, perhaps, to notify those services as well, at least if passported services are being notified. As indicated in ¶357, ISD credit institutions also do not have to notify activities within their ISD passport which are not within their 2BCD passport.

¶360 Applicability of the passport

Strangely, it is very unclear when the ISD and 2BCD passports actually apply or, indeed, have to. If the non-UK EEA firm wants to establish a branch in the UK for passported FSA-regulated investment business outside any exemption, it clearly must use the passport. Similarly, if executives of the non-UK EEA firm actually carry on passported FSA-regulated investment activities (including offering to carry on the substantive activity) whilst on temporary visits to the UK, which would be unusual, these activities would surely be treated for the purposes of the ISD and the 2BCD as carried on where the client is, namely in the UK; indeed, this is indicated by art. 60 of the Treaty of Rome which provides that in such cases the rules of the 'client's state' (namely, the state where the client is) apply. Accordingly, the prohibitions in the ISD regulations and the 2BCD regulations on carrying on activities covered by the ISD or 2BCD passport 'in the UK' except after using the notification procedures would apply; notification would therefore be required, even if the 'overseas persons' exemptions apply. Conversely, if the firm carries on the activity with the client when the client visits the firm at an office outside the client's state, the activity is treated as carried on where the firm is located. However, the analysis of where activities are to be treated as carried on for ISD or 2BCD purposes if they are carried on by a branch in another member state by telephone, fax or another means of remote communication is not yet settled. It is therefore prudent to notify the SIB (or the Bank of England) through the domestic regulator even if the activity is arguably not carried on in the UK (see below). This is certainly the prudent course in relation to advisory services provided to clients in the UK, which the Treasury regard as being provided in the United Kingdom even if they are provided to the UK client from a non-UK branch without physical entry into the UK.

Nonetheless, if (as would be normal) the passported activities fall within the 'overseas persons' exemptions, those activities are not regulated in the UK under SIB rules (or indeed the rules of SROs) even though they are subject to the notification requirement. This is because the provisions which apply SIB conduct of business rules (and so, indirectly, SRO rules) to passported activities only apply if the activities are 'home-regulated investment business carried on in the UK' (see para. 10 of Sch. 7 to the ISD regulations and of Sch. 9 to the 2BCD regulations); if the 'overseas persons' exemptions apply to them they are treated as not 'carried on in the UK' for this purpose. This rather complicated structure has been adopted in order to allow the 'overseas persons' exemptions to continue for non-EEA firms; the ISD forbids member States to grant more favourable treatment to branches of non-EEA firms (art. 5) and therefore the exemptions have to continue for EEA firms, despite the requirements of the Treasury that the ISD passport or at least its notification procedure must be used if it is available.

A firm may in fact not need the passport at all if it carries on its activities on a cross-border basis by a means of remote communication (such as telephone or fax) from a branch outside the client's state. The better view seems to be that those activities are not carried on in the client's State at all. Indeed, at time of writing, this is the view which is being advanced by the SIB and the Treasury, except in relation to advisory services, and seems to have been found acceptable by the EU Commission (see also ¶311).

If this view is accepted by the other EEA regulators, the ISD and 2BCD passports are not directly needed (and cannot be used) for cross-border activities unless the firm carries on the activities on a visit to the client's state (or, perhaps, is providing investment advice); the passports can be used only for investment activities carried on 'within' the host member State. Instead, the firm can normally rely on the passport provided by art. 59 of the Treaty of Rome to provide cross-border services when carrying on activities in a member State by a means of remote communication from a branch in another member state, at least if they are ISD core investment services. The art. 59 freedoms must surely apply to core investment services, and perhaps other activities within the ISD or 2BCD passport, by EEA firms entitled to them, as they comply with the (minimum) requirements regarded as acceptable for mutual recognition purposes by all EEA member States; the ISD is therefore useful not only for its own passport but also because it supports the view that there is normally no justifiable 'general good' objection to EEA firms using the art. 59 passport without a local licence. At time of writing, the position is unresolved, but the EU Commission seems to be sympathetic to this approach, at least in relation to the 2BCD, which is at present all that it has given guidance on, and it does indeed seem to be justified by EU jurisprudence. The UK's exception for advisory services seems to be pragmatic (and based on traditional UK law) rather than to arise from any difference in analysis.

Subject to what may be called the 'ISD defence', it should, however, be emphasised that EU jurisprudence allows the client's state to restrict the scope of all three passports (and the third insurance directive's passport), and indeed to impose its own conduct of business rules, if doing so can be justified as being in the interest of 'the general good' under EU jurisprudence. The client's State can therefore restrict the carrying on of investment activities with its residents under art. 59 (for example, by imposing a local licensing requirement or by banning cold-calling) if the restriction is justified by the general good. In particular, the restriction must be proportionate, must not be discriminatory and must not duplicate equivalent rules to which the provider is subject in its state of establishment. The ISD requires member States to impose most of the important investor protection rules on ISD activities carried on 'in' them (so giving primacy to the host member State, which, on the UK view, is normally the state where the firm's branch carrying on the activities is located), and, accordingly, the client's State may find it difficult to argue in many cases that the firm is not already subject to equivalent rules. Indeed, as indicated above, it would seem that no 'general good' objection can be raised against an EEA firm using the Treaty of Rome passport in respect of ISD core investment services (or perhaps other ISD or 2BCD activities) for which it is authorised under the ISD (or the 2BCD); accordingly, no local authorisation requirement can be imposed. The 'general good' test applies whether the rules are imposed by the firm's State or the client's State and whether or not the ISD or 2BCD passport is available; indeed, in relation to the art. 59 freedom to carry on cross-border activities, it is irrelevant where the activity is actually treated as carried on. EU case-law has indicated that it may, however, be more difficult to justify restrictions on art. 59 activities if there is no physical movement into the client's State or the client is a professional. As the ISD itself acknowledges that business with professionals needs less regulation than business with non-professionals, this may allow EEA investment firms and credit institutions doing passported business in other member states only with banks and other financial institutions to operate without substantial regulation.

4 How to be Authorised

INTRODUCTION

¶401 Routes to authorisation

The *Financial Services Act* 1986 provides seven different routes to authorisation, which are described in Ch. III of Pt. I:

- by membership of an SRO (see ¶403–¶404);
- by direct authorisation by the SIB (see ¶405–¶407);
- by certification by an RPB (see ¶408–¶410);
- by 'automatic' authorisation as a 'Euro-person' (see ¶411–¶413);
- by 'automatic' authorisation as operator or trustee of an 'EEC-wide' recognised collective investment scheme (see ¶414);
- ¶by 'automatic' authorisation as an authorised insurer (see ¶415);
- ¶by 'automatic' authorisation as a registered friendly society (see ¶415).

A system of interim authorisation operated for those who had applied for authorisation before 27 February 1988 but whose applications had not been determined by 29 April 1988, the day when s. 3 came into force. The applicant would normally be treated as if he were authorised during the period until the application was determined (Sch. 15, para. 1). The position of such persons was governed by the *Financial Services (Interim) Rules and Regulations* 1988 and 1990 (now revoked)

¶402 Reciprocity bar to authorisation

The 1986 Act contains an important power to prohibit or cancel the authorisation, or restrict the regulated investment activities, of 'foreign businesses' (s. 183); it cannot be delegated to the SIB. This sanction can be exercised if the home jurisdiction of the foreign business does not allow reciprocal facilities for investment business. This power applies not only to branches of foreign companies but also to UK subsidiaries and also, perhaps, to other UK companies where a person connected with the foreign country concerned has, together with associates, a holding carrying 15 per cent of voting rights. Similar powers in respect of banking business, and insurance business. They are exercised by the Treasury save in respect of insurance businesses which are not also investment businesses when the powers are exercised by the Secretary of State for Trade and Industry. Because of unhappy drafting, it is unclear whether authorisation can be refused or investment business due to lack of reciprocity in the field of banking or insurance. It is also unclear whether, if a commercial bank in the overseas country is forbidden by its local laws to deal in or underwrite securities (as for example in the US or Japan), it will be regarded as a lack of reciprocity if UK banks are accordingly refused securities licences on that ground. The power can only be exercised if it is in the national interest to do so. Restrictions on notices under s. 183 are provided in relation to UK investment firms by reg. 29 of the *Investment Services Regulations* 1995 (SI 1995/3275) to insurance companies established in the UK by reg. 8 of the *Insurance Companies (Amendment) Regulations* 1993 (SI 1993/174) and to credit institutions established in the UK by reg. 53 of the *Banking Coordination (Second Council Directive) Regulations* 1992 (SI 1992/3218). Effectively these regulations prevent a notice being given to such businesses if a subsidiary undertaking of a person connected with a non-UK country if the sole ground for the notice is that the business cannot be conducted in that country on terms as favourable as the UK.

MEMBERSHIP OF SROs

¶403 Right to membership

No one can be admitted to an SRO unless he is 'fit and proper' to carry on the investment business or businesses regulated by the SRO which he wishes to carry on (Sch. 2, para. 1). There is no definition of 'fit and proper' in the 1986 Act but the Financial Services Tribunal in *Re Noble Warren Investments Ltd* (1988) has treated the term as extending to the conduct of an applicant both in its dealings with the public and the ordering of its internal affairs. In practice, SROs take into account matters such as financial integrity, absence of convictions or civil liabilities, competence, good reputation and character and efficency and honesty. The 'fit and proper' test must include the matters relevant in the case of directly authorised persons, including in particular the applicant's financial resources (see ¶405) (Sch. 2, para. 1(3)). This requirement will not, however, apply to a person who is not an authorised person by virtue of his membership, which (under s. 7(2)) seemingly means members who are authorised insurers, registered friendly societies and Euro-person insurance companies (see ¶411 and ¶415) (Sch. 2, para. 1(4)). Conversely, no one has the right to insist that an SRO admits him as a member. However, if an applicant is 'fit and proper' to carry on the investment business he wishes to carry on, clearly it would be unfair, and would mitigate against the effectiveness of the proposed new system, if he could be unfairly refused admission or unfairly expelled. It is accordingly a condition of the recognition of an SRO that its rules and practices relating to admission and expulsion are fair and reasonable (Sch. 2, para. 2). In addition, those rules must include adequate provision for appeals. This is particularly important for branches or UK subsidiaries of overseas firms who may be anticipating discrimination, although the 'reciprocity' provisions of s. 183 may be relevant (see ¶402).

There is no right of appeal to the SIB or the Financial Services Tribunal although an applicant or member who is refused admission or expelled can apply for direct authorisation (or to join another SRO regulating the same kind of investment business if there is one), but it may be much harder to prove he is 'fit and proper'. A member of an SRO is not allowed to resign in order to avoid investigation or punishment; indeed, it is a condition of authorisation that the rules of the SRO must forbid that (Sch. 2, para. 3(4)).

¶404   Restrictions on investment business

An SRO must ensure that its members are fit and proper to carry on the kinds of investment business within its jurisdiction which they carry on (Sch. 2, para. 1(2)). 'Investment business' is, in general terms, the regulated investment activities which fall outside the exemptions in Pt. III of Sch. 1 and so require authorisation if carried on as a business, except perhaps in the case of overseas persons (see Ch. 3).

The SRO can therefore restrict the kinds of investment business regulated by it which can be carried on by particular members. In addition, and more fundamentally, an SRO can itself only regulate particular kinds of investment business and the SIB can refuse to recognise a prospective SRO if it seeks to regulate investment business of a kind carried on by another existing or prospective SRO. In line with this restriction, SROs are required to introduce 'scope' rules which prohibit members from carrying on investment business of a kind which the SRO does not itself regulate unless that member is an authorised person by some other means or is an exempted person in respect of that business (s. 10(3)). A bank or investment firm which is regulated in another EEA state where the business is home-regulated are excepted from s. 10(3) (reg. 55 *Banking Co-ordination (Second Council Directive) Regulations* 1992 (SI 1992/3218) and reg. 32 of the *Investment Services Regulations* 1995 (SI 1995/3275) (see Ch. 3). Where an authorised person obtains his primary authorisation by membership of an SRO, it is probable that he will seek to obtain authorisation for the kinds of investment business which that SRO does not regulate by joining another SRO rather than by being directly authorised, but there is no legal compulsion to do so. Each applicant has to describe his proposed business in a business plan or business profile and he cannot carry on any kind of investment business by virtue of his membership other than the kinds of investment business described in that business plan or profile and agreed to by the SRO. The member can at any time expand his business plan or profile subsequently and the additional kinds of investment business will thereafter also form part of his 'permitted business' if they fall within the SRO's scope and are acceptable in his case to the SRO.

A member of an SRO is an authorised person for all purposes. Accordingly, if he contravenes the 'scope' prohibition he will not be in breach of the general prohibition in s. 3 against carrying on investment business in the UK without authorisation (see ¶304 and ¶305 or commit any other criminal offence, and 'investments agreements' will be fully enforceable. He will, however, be in breach of the rules of the SRO and (as described in Ch. 12) may accordingly be subject to civil claims by investors for loss (s. 62), or ultimately the SIB for reimbursement of losses or a disgorgement of profits, arising from investment business in breach of the prohibition (s. 61). In an extreme case, he may be thrown out of the SRO.

The Act unfortunately does not contain any criteria to determine whether investment business is of one kind or another. It is probable that different types of investment business will be regarded as being of different 'kinds' if they constitute different regulated investment activities as described in Ch. 3 (that is, if they fall within different paragraphs of Pt. II of Sch. 1). However, within each class of activity they may also be of different kinds if they relate to different classes of investments (that is, if the investments fall within different paragraphs of Pt. I of Sch. 1, although paras. 2 and 3 would probably be treated as a single paragraph).

For some reason, the s. 10(3) prohibition is not limited territorially and applies in principle even to branches outside the UK and even if they would not themselves need to be authorised as a result of the general prohibition in s. 3 because they do not carry on investment business in the UK (see ¶304 and ¶305). Indeed, for this reason it can cause particular problems in the case of overseas investment firms (which term normally in this Guide includes banks doing investment business) which are members of an SRO because they need to be authorised for one or more regulated investment activities carried on by them in the UK (for example, because they have a branch here). In practice, IMRO expressly limits the relevant prohibition to investment business carried on in the UK (see ¶313ff.), leaving firms free to carry on business not regulated by them provided that it is not carried on in the UK. However, if the SRO does not so limit the prohibition it is very important for overseas investment firms to obtain a dispensation from the SRO rule reflecting the s. 10(3) prohibition in relation to their investment business which is not carried on in the UK.

In principle, all investment business carried on in the UK will be regulated by the conduct of business rules of the SRO, even if it is carried on from a non-UK branch. Indeed, if their conduct of business rules are similarly not restricted to

¶404

business carried on in the UK those rules also apply to all investment business of the kind authorised by it which is carried on from a non-UK branch even if not in the UK. However, the SROs in practice disapply their conduct of business rules to the business of overseas investment firms (and, indeed, UK firms) which is done from non-UK branches if that business meets certain conditions. Thus they will not apply if the client or counter-party is not in the UK, so that the business is not actually carried on in the UK. Moreover, they also will not apply, even if the business is carried on in the UK, if in effect the UK branches of the overseas investment firm are not involved in a relevant way. The details of the exemption vary from SRO to SRO (and must be reviewed carefully in each case) but the important point is that normally the business of the non-UK branch is not regulated by the SRO even if it does business with UK clients or counter-parties if they are authorised persons or they were not solicited in breach of the Act's or the SRO's marketing rules. The result in these cases is 'UK authorisation without UK regulation' (which is a precedent that the EEC Investment Services Directive will follow if it adopts 'host member state' regulation for conduct of business rules) but, conversely, the need for authorisation even if the SRO's 'foreign business' exemption applies must not be overlooked.

DIRECT AUTHORISATION

¶405   Eligibility for authorisation

In order to become 'directly authorised' by the SIB, it is necessary for applicants to apply to the SIB for authorisation and to prove that they are 'fit and proper persons' to carry on the 'investment business' they propose to carry on (s. 27(2)). Once authorised, they are subject to the conduct of business rules made by the SIB and the matters referred to in ¶404 apply in a similar way. The SIB has stressed that the 'fit and proper' test must involve consideration of the applicant's financial resources and it has accordingly proposed minimum liquidity margin requirements and other financial resources rules. Direct authorisation will be available not only to individuals and companies or other bodies corporate but also to partnerships and unincorporated associations (s. 26(1)). Authorisation will be granted to partnerships in the partnership name and will continue to apply notwithstanding changes in the partnership (s. 27(6)), which is a significant improvement to the previous practice.

As the SIB had hoped, direct authorisation is extremely rare. In practice, the SIB rulebook is important not as rules of direct application (although they apply to automatically authorised persons to differing degrees) but as the benchmark standard with SRO rules must reach.

¶406 Application for authorisation

An applicant must apply for direct authorisation in the prescribed manner, must make the prescribed disclosures and must pay the appropriate fee. He will also need to file a 'business plan' giving specified details of the 'investment business' he wants to carry on (s. 26(2)(b)). The authorisation will cover all kinds of investment business, even if it is not included in the business plan, although the 'fit and proper' test applies only to the business plan activities. However, the authorisation as a practical matter is confined to the 'business plan' activities by 'scope' rules made by the SIB under s. 48(2)(a)(ii) (the *Financial Services (Conduct of Business) Rules* 1990, r. 2.01). Breach of these rules has its own sanctions (for example, investors can sue for loss (see Ch. 12)) but (as in the case of members of SROs) it will not be illegal to carry on kinds of investment business other than those specified in the 'business plan' and contracts made in the course of such other kinds of business will be fully enforceable. This, is perhaps, not the best way of dealing with 'unauthorised' investment business.

To become authorised, the applicant will have to make the disclosures prescribed by the SIB (s. 26(2)). As permitted by the Act, the prescribed disclosures include information about directors and controllers of the applicant and about group companies. A person (including a company) will be a 'controller' of a company if he controls 15 per cent of the voting power of the company or a holding company (s. 207(5)). For this purpose, there will be aggregated with that person's own holding the holding of any company of which he is a director even if he owns no shares in that company and (in the case of companies) the holding of any subsidiary and, significantly, of any employee of the company or a subsidiary. Similarly, disclosures must also be made about the partners in a partnership or the governing body of an unincorporated association, as appropriate.

The Act expressly allows the SIB to take 'controllers' and partners (and also, crucially, employees and proposed appointed representatives) into account when deciding whether or not to authorise an investment business (s. 27(3)). The SIB must also take into account any authorisation the applicant has to carry on investment business in a member State of the EU other than the UK. This will be of help to persons outside the 'Europerson' automatic authorisation, for example if they carry on investment business from a permanent place of business in the UK (see ¶411–¶413) (s. 27(5)). It may also take into account any other business the applicant will carry on in connection with his investment business (s. 27(4)).

¶406

¶407   Refusal and revocation of authorisation

The SIB will be required to authorise the applicant if he is a 'fit and proper' person to carry on the investment business described in the application and will have no discretion to refuse authorisation (s. 27(2)). However, it seems that the applicant cannot be authorised unless all the prescribed information is actually provided (s. 27(1)).

Unlike the former position with licences, the Act does not require authorisation to be renewed each year; this will be a great saving of management time and expense, although a periodical fee will be payable (and the SIB may impose its own additional requirements). However, authorisation may be withdrawn or suspended for 'misconduct' reasons, such as contravention of the SIB's conduct of business rules (or, if he is also a member of an SRO or RPB, their conduct of business rules) or of any of the provisions of the Act (s. 28). The refusal, withdrawal or suspension of authorisation will be subject to a right of appeal to the Financial Services Tribunal (s. 29(4)). It would seem that an authorised person cannot of his own volition cease to be authorised but that he, effectively, needs the consent of the SIB (s. 30(1)). This parallels the position of members of SROs and, as indicated by s. 30, seems to be provided so that he cannot avoid the sanctions which apply to authorised persons.

CERTIFICATION BY RPBS

¶408   Right to certification

No one can be certified by an RPB unless he is either an individual who is a member of the RPB (and not carrying on business in partnership) or a partnership or company which is managed and controlled by individuals all of whom are members of RPBs and of whom at least one is a member of the certifying RPB (Sch. 3, para. 2(2)). 'Members' include persons who although not actually members of the RPB practise the profession regulated by it and in doing so are subject to its rules (s. 16(2)). As para. 2(2) indicates, the Act has looked a little into the future and has provided that partnerships need not be limited to one profession (but, for example, can include both solicitors and accountants) and that professional corporations can also be certified. In the case of a partnership, the certificate is issued to the partnership and survives changes in partners (s. 15(3)) and the authorisation is therefore similar to that given to partnerships who are directly authorised see ¶405). No UK investment firm can be certified by an RPB unless it provides core investment services incidentally to its professional activity (reg. 31 the *Investment Services Regulations)* 1995 (SI 1995/3275)). The Act contemplates that overseas persons may be certified (Sch. 3, para. 2(4)).

¶409 Effect of certification

Once a member of an RPB has been certified he is an authorised person; this usually is for all investment business (s. 15(1)), but (as in the case of members of SROs) his authorisation is in fact qualified. First, the RPB must impose 'acceptable limits' on the investment business which persons certified by it can carry on (s. 18(3)) and must prohibit them from carrying on investment business outside those limits unless they are authorised to do so by another means (for example, membership of an SRO) or are exempted persons in relation to it. The Act does not define what are 'acceptable limits' but it is likely that they must be acceptable to the SIB rather than merely the RPB; as just one example, the Law Society has imposed a limit by reference to the fee income derived from investment business. The unexpected extent of this 'scope' rule and the sanctions if it is contravened are the same as in the case of members of SROs, who are subject to their own 'scope' rule (see ¶404). Secondly, and more fundamentally, the main business of the certified person must be the practice of the profession which the RPB regulates (Sch. 3, para. 2(3)) and it is expressly provided that 'profession' does not include a business consisting wholly or mainly of investment business (s. 16(1)).

¶410 Attractiveness of certification and recognition

A solicitor or accountant will not be able to buy or sell investments on behalf of a client or give investment advice outside the exemption for 'necessary' advice unless he is authorised, and certification seems easier than joining an SRO because he will at least be regulated by his own (or another) profession. However, like SROs, the RPB must have rules in relation to the investment business regulated by it which provide investor protection at least equivalent to that provided by the SIB's rules (including those relating to financial resources, indemnity and compensation funds) (Sch. 3, para. 3). In addition, the RPB must monitor and enforce compliance and investigate complaints and the persons responsible for enforcement must include lay representatives, although both monitoring and enforcement can be delegated, as can the investigation of complaints, for example to an ombudsman (Sch. 3, para. 4 and 5). At present most relevant professional bodies have sought recognition. However, it may well be that over the course of time not many professional bodies will find recognition (and the need to act as quasi-SROs) attractive or want to risk public criticism if they fail to regulate their members for what are really activities outside their normal jurisdiction. This may be especially the case as there is no immunity from damages as exists in the case of SROs and such bodies also will have to monitor capital adequacy. As indicated above, investment advice, or indeed the arranging of deals, in the course of business is exempted if it is necessary and professional bodies may properly take the view that they should be concerned with the regulation only of their profession and not of investment business.

EURO-PERSONS

¶411   Eligibility for authorisation

Certain persons 'established in a member State (of the EU) other than the United Kingdom' who are authorised to carry on investment business in that member State are authorised as of right to carry on investment business in the UK provided that the law of that State recognises them as nationals of that or another member State (s. 31). The SIB somewhat inelegantly refers to persons automatically authorised under s. 31 as 'Euro-persons'.

A person will be 'established in a member State other than the United Kingdom' for this purpose if his head office is in that member State and he does not transact investment business from a permanent place of business maintained by him in the UK (s. 31(2)). Indeed, the use of the word 'transact' rather than 'carry on' may imply that he cannot engage in any regulated investment activities from a UK place of business, even if not amounting to the carrying on of a business. The authorisation is thus granted (only) to EU 'overseas persons' who fall outside the special exemptions in Pt. IV of Sch. 1. They will accordingly be able to send salesmen and investment advertisements into the UK and effect transactions even with UK private investors.

A member State investment business will not be authorised under s. 31, however, unless he carries on in his 'home' member State at least one kind of qualifying investment business. Investment business will 'qualify' for this purpose if the provisions of the law authorising that business afford to investors in the UK (and not just investors in the 'home' State) protection which is 'at least equivalent' to that afforded to investors by the SIB's rules or those of the SROs (s. 31(3)). The Treasury can certify compliance with this requirement but the absence of a certificate will not be fatal (s. 31(4)). Alternatively, investment business will 'qualify' if the authorising law complies with EU harmonising directive or other instrument (s. 31(3)(b)) and the authority granting such authorisation certifies that it does in fact comply (s. 31(5)). Section 31 does not apply to banks and investment firms which are authorised in other EEA States and came within the *Banking Co-ordination (Second Council Directive) Regulations* 1992 SI 1992/3218 or the *Investment Services Regulations* 1995

SI 1995/3275 (see Ch. 3). These firms are not authorised persons but gain the single market passport by reference to the EU directives giving rise to these regulations. Special provisions apply to a Euro-person who is an insurance company (Sch. 10 para. 2(3)(3A)). As the Channel Islands are not member States of the EU, Channel Island investment businesses are not automatically authorised under s. 31. Conversely, Gibraltar can be deemed to be a 'member State' for the purposes of s. 31 (s. 208(1)) and accordingly investment businesses established in Gibraltar can qualify as 'Euro-persons', although this section is still not in force, except in relation to certain contracts of insurance: see the *Financial Services Act 1986 (Commencement) (No. 8) Order* 1988 (SI 1988/740 (C. 22)).

Although authorised as of right, a Euro-person will not be able to carry on investment business in the UK until he has given the SIB not less than seven days' notice that he intends to do so and has provided certain prescribed information (s. 32(1)). Contravention of this prohibition is a criminal offence (s. 32(4)). The prescribed information will include details of the investment business he proposes to carry on in the UK.

¶412   Limitations of authorisation

Although the drafting of s. 31 is not clear, it would seem that, if he carries on any 'qualifiying' investment business, a Euro-person will be an authorised person for all investment business (not just the 'qualifying' business). The 'home' regulator has to be consulted in certain circumstances (see ¶413 and s. 33(6) which relates to this requirement refers to the regulator who is responsible 'for the kind of investment business' which the Euro-person is (or was) carrying on, seemingly in his home member State. This is a standard EU requirement and does not indicate whether or not he will be authorised under s. 31 only for investment business he is authorised for by his home member State. However, a Euro-person must disclose information as to his authorisation in the member State in which he is established and the SIB would seem to be able to restrict his regulated investment business to that for which he is authorised in his home member State (s. 48(2)(a)(i)). Moreover, as in the case of the business plan of a directly authorised person (see ¶406) the rules of the SIB can prohibit a Euro-person from carrying on any regulated investment business not specified in his notice (s. 48(2)(a)(ii)). Following the normal pattern, it is not a criminal offence to contravene these restrictions and investment agreements are enforceable, but investors who suffer loss from the contravention may be able to sue for damages (see Ch. 12).

A Euro-person can join an SRO for authorisation in respect of investment business outside his 'automatic' authorisation (see s. 32(2)) and, presumably, can also become directly authorised.

¶412

¶413   Suspension or withdrawal of authorisation

'Automatic' authorisation cannot be refused. However, as in the case of directly authorised persons, the SIB will be able to suspend or withdraw authorisation for 'misconduct' reasons (for example, breach of conduct of business rules or providing false or misleading information or, in particular, contravention of the Act's cold-calling or investment advertisement rules) (s. 33), subject to a right of appeal to the Financial Services Tribunal (s. 34) and normally only after consulting the 'home' regulatory authority (s. 33(4)).

'EEC-WIDE' COLLECTIVE INVESTMENT SCHEMES

¶414   'Automatic' authorisation

In addition to authorisation under s. 31, if they are eligible (see ¶411), operators and trustees of recognised 'EU-wide' under s. 86 open-ended investment companies or other collective investment schemes are authorised as of right to operate (or act as trustee of) or to market those schemes in the UK, or, it would seem, to deal in UK markets but for no other purposes (s. 24). This complies with the Government's obligations under the UCITS directive and at present would apply only to schemes authorised under that directive. Section 24 also applies to any other collective investment schemes which may obtain 'Community-wide' authorisation in the future, not just the schemes investing in transferable securities 'authorised' by the UCITS directive. The SIB takes the view that authorised person status is not conferred upon an EU operator who chooses not to carry on investment business in the UK (para. 23, SIB Guidance Release No 3/89 'Marketing in the United Kingdom: Guidance for Operators of Recognised Collective Investment Schemes').

The custodian of the scheme's assets is treated as a trustee for this purpose, whether or not it actually holds them under a trust (s. 75(8)). The 'operator' is normally the manager of the scheme, but in the case of an open-ended investment company with a separate management company it is the investment company itself (s. 75(8)). Accordingly, the management company will not be automatically authorised and must seek its own authorisation if it carries on any investment business in the UK, for example, dealing in the UK on behalf of the operator outside the Act's exemptions from authorisation (see Ch. 3).

Contrary to the position before the Act, the managers of authorised unit trust schemes are not automatically authorised as it will be a condition of the scheme's authorisation that the manager and the trustee are already authorised persons. The managers and trustees (if any) of collective investment schemes recognised on a 'designated country' or 'individual' basis (see Ch. 10) are also not automatically authorised.

INSURANCE COMPANIES AND FRIENDLY SOCIETIES

¶415 'Automatic' authorisation

An insurance company authorised under the *Insurance Companies Act* 1982 to carry on insurance business which constitutes investment business is automatically authorised under the Act for that business (s. 22). This includes, for example, issuing regulated insurance contracts. It is also authorised in respect of any other investment business it can carry on without contravening the restrictions in that Act against engaging in activities which are not connected with its insurance business. Authorisation is also granted as of right to certain registered friendly societies in relation to business carried on for certain purposes under the *Friendly Societies Act* 1992 (s. 23).

Such authorised insurance companies and registered friendly societies are automatically authorised in order to avoid the need to satisfy competing requirements for authorisation. They will be able to join an SRO but, whether they do or not, an insurance company which is an authorised person by virtue of s. 22 cannot be authorised by virtue of any other provision and special regimes apply to both such insurance companies and friendly societies authorised under s. 23 (see Ch. 11).

5   Conduct of Investment Business

AN OVERVIEW OF THE SIB'S RULES

¶501   Standards for all investment businesses

In accordance with s. 114 of the *Financial Services Act* 1986, extensive rule-making powers have been vested in the SIB (*Financial Services Act 1986 (Delegation) Order* 1987 (SI 1987/942), *Financial Services Act 1986 (Delegation) (No. 2) Order* 1988 (SI 1988/738), *Financial Services 1986 (Delegation) Order* 1991 (SI 1991/200) and the *Financial Services 1986 (Delegation) (No. 2) Order* 1991 (SI 1991/1256)). The SIB has power, which it has exercised, to make detailed rules in respect of the following aspects of investment business:

   (1)   statements of principle (s. 47A);
   (2)   conduct of business (s. 48);
   (3)   financial resources (s. 49) and administrative arrangements regarding the keeping of financial records (s. 48), the drawing up of financial statements (s. 48, 52 and 55), the notification to the SIB of relevant financial information (s. 52) and the appointment of auditors (s. 48 and 107) (since these rules do not impinge directly on the day-to-day organisation of investment business, they are not considered in any detail in this chapter);
   (4)   cancellation of investment agreements (s. 51);
   (5)   compensation fund scheme (s. 54);
   (6)   clients' money (s. 55);
   (7)   unsolicited calls (s. 56);
   (8)   collective investment schemes (s. 75–95, considered in Ch. 10);
   (9)   administrative matters such as the payment of fees (s. 113) (these rules are not considered in any detail in this chapter);
   (10)   to designate provisions of rules regarding conduct of business, financial resources, clients' money and unsolicited calls to a member of a recognised SRO (s. 63A); and
   (11)   to issue codes of practice (s. 63C).

Since most investment businesses are authorised by SROs and RPBs, the SIB's rules have little direct day-to-day effect. Their importance lies in the fact that they establish the benchmark of protection, the Secretary of State not being able to make a delegation order unless he is satisfied that the rules will afford investors an adequate level of protection (s. 114(9) as substituted by s. 206 *Companies Act* 1989) and that they will provide high standards of integrity and fair dealing in the conduct of investment business (Sch. 8 para. 1A as substituted by s. 206 *Companies Act* 1989). The rules of an SRO or an RPB must afford an adequate level of protection to investors in order for the SRO or RPB to be recognised by the SIB. In recognition of the fact that they are the 'bench-mark' of investor protection, this chapter focuses mainly upon the SIB's rules.

¶502 The SIB's Conduct of Business Provisions

(1) Overview

The conduct of business provisions are the rules made under s. 48 of the Act, the statements of principle and codes of practice. The SIB has issued both conduct of business rules and statements of principle but has not issued any codes of practice. In exercise of its powers to designate provisions of the conduct of business rules to a member of an SRO the SIB issued the Core Conduct of Business Rules under its powers in s. 63A. Apart from the rule in Chinese Walls (r. 36) the substantive rules have now been 'dedesignated' so that they no longer apply directly to SRO members, though the fact that (with certain exceptions) these core rules have been incorporated into SRO rule books still makes them useful as a picture of the basic standard to be followed.

(2) Statements of Principle

Section 47A of the *Financial Services Act* 1986 provides for the issue of statements of principle with respect to the conduct and financial standing expected of those who are authorised to conduct investment services. They then apply to all authorised persons whatever the source of their authorisation and to European credit institutions carrying on home-regulated investment business in the UK. Failure to comply with a statement of principle may result in disciplinary action (see Ch. 12) or the exercise of powers of intervention. However such failure neither gives a right of action nor affects the validity of any transaction. There is statutory provision (s. 47B) for modification or waiver of any statement of principle in order to provide flexibility in certain situations but this provision has yet to be brought with force.

Ten principles have been issued by the SIB and are expressed to provide a universal statement of the standards expected without being exhaustive.

(1)   *Integrity*
A firm should observe high standards of integrity and fair dealing.

(2)   *Skill, Care and Diligence*
A firm should act with due skill, care and diligence.

(3)   *Market Practice*
A firm should observe high standards of market conduct. It should also, to the extent endorsed for the purpose of this principle, comply with any code or standard as in force from time to time and as it applies to the firm either according to its terms or by rulings made under it.

(4)   *Information about Customers*
A firm should seek from customers it advises or for whom it exercises discretion any information about their circumstances and investment objectives which might reasonably be expected to be relevant in enabling it to fulfil its responsibilities to them.

(5)   *Information for Customers*
A firm should take reasonable steps to give a customer it advises, in a comprehensible and timely way, any information needed to enable him to make a balanced and informed decision. A firm should similarly be ready to provide a customer with a full and fair account of the fulfilment of its responsibilities to him.

(6)   *Conflicts of Interest*
A firm should either avoid any conflict of interest arising or, where conflicts arise, should ensure fair treatment to all its customers by disclosure, internal rules of confidentiality, declining to act, or otherwise. A firm should not unfairly place its interests above those of its customers and, where a properly informed customer would reasonably expect that the firm would place his interests above its own, the firm should live up to that expectation.

(7)   *Customer Assets*
Where a firm has control of or is otherwise responsible for assets belonging to a customer which it is required to safeguard, it should arrange proper protection for them, by way of segregation and identification of those assets or otherwise, in accordance with the responsibility it has accepted.

(8)   *Financial Resources*
A firm should ensure that it maintains adequate financial resources to meet its investment business commitments and to withstand the risks to which its business is subject.

¶502

(9) *Internal Organisation*

A firm should organise and control its internal affairs in a responsible manner, keeping proper records, and where the firm employs staff or is responsible for the conduct of investment business by others, should have adequate arrangements to ensure that they are suitable, adequately trained and properly supervised and that it has well-defined compliance procedures.

(10) *Relations with regulators*

A firm should deal with its regulator in an open and cooperative manner and keep the regulator promptly informed of anything concerning the firm which might reasonably be expected to be disclosed to it.

Under the third statement of principle (market practice) the SIB has endorsed the City Code on Takeovers and Mergers and the Rules Governing Substantial Acquisitions of Shares published by the Panel on Takeovers and Mergers (the *Financial Services (Statements of Principle) (Endorsements of Codes and Standards) Instrument* 1995). At the request of the Panel the SIB could use disciplinary action or exercise its powers of intervention in respect of a breach of the Takeover Code.

The statements of principle are, as previously indicated, applicable to European credit institutions carrying on home-regulated investment business in the UK. However the principles are not taken to include for that purpose either provisions as to the fitness of such an institution to carry on any such business or as to any matter reserved by the Second Banking Co-ordination Directive (No. 89/646/EEC) for the home state regulator. (The *Financial Services (European Institutions) Instrument* 1993, reg. 2.01.) The second disapplication in favour of the home regulator also applies to insurance companies with a head office in another EU State (see Ch. 13) (reg. 58(1), *Insurance Companies (Third Insurance Directive) Regulations* 1994 (SI 1994/ 1696).

(3) Application of the SIB's Conduct of Business Rules (CBRs)

The SIB's existing CBRs apply to persons directly authorised by the SIB under s. 25 of the Financial Services Act 1986 and to persons authorised in other EU member States under s. 31 of the Financial Services Act 1986. Subject to certain limitations, they also apply to insurance companies and registered friendly societies authorised under s. 22–23 of the Act and to operators or trustees of recognised (under s. 86) EU collective investment schemes authorised under s. 24 of the Act. Special provision is currently made for persons who engage in corporate finance and capital markets activities, and for service companies, journalists, broadcasters, authors and publishers. In individual cases not covered by special provision in the rules, the SIB also has a statutory power under s. 50 of the Financial Services Act to modify its CBRs, but before doing so it must be satisfied that compliance with the CBRs would be unduly burdensome for the investment business concerned and that the modification will not result in any undue risk to investors.

It is emphasised that the SIB's CBRs do not apply directly to persons who are authorised by virtue of membership of an SRO or certification from an RPB, but SROs and RPBs must impose their own CBRs upon the persons whom they authorise.

However, as indicated previously, s. 63A permits the application of dedicated rules and regulations to members of self regulating organisations. Contravention of these are treated as a contravention of SRO rules (s. 63A(2)). Core conduct of business rules were designated for IMRO (the *Core Conduct of Business Rules Commencement (IMRO) Order* 1991) and for SFA (the *Core Conduct of Business Rules Commencement (SFA) Order* 1992). However the core conduct of business rules (apart from the Chinese Wall rule) were subsequently dedesignated (the *Financial Services (Dedesignation) Rules and Regulations* 1994) though they remain incorporated into the SRO rulebooks.

(4)   Statutory scope of the rule-making power
Under s. 48 of the Financial Services Act 1986, the SIB has the power to make whatever rules it considers appropriate in respect of the conduct of investment business. In particular, the CBRs may make provision as follows:

(1) prohibit a person from carrying on an investment business of a particular kind or on a particular scale (s. 48(2)(a);

(2) restrict a person to dealing with persons of a specified class or description (s. 48(2)(b));

(3) regulate the manner in which a person may hold himself out as carrying on investment business (s. 48(2)(c));

(4) regulate market making (s. 48(2)(d));

(5) regulate the form and contents of advertisements (s. 48(2)(e));

(6) require principals to impose restrictions on the investment business carried on by their appointed representatives (s. 48(2)(f));

(7) require the disclosure of, but not impose limits on, the amount or value of commissions (s. 48(2)(g) and (3));

(8) permit or require the erection of a Chinese Wall (see ¶509) (s. 48(2)(h));

(9) regulate the procedures used in stabilising the price of investments of any specified description (s. 48(2)(i));

(10) make arrangements for the settlement of disputes (s. 48(2)(j));

(11) require the keeping of and the inspection of records (s. 48(2)(k)); and

(12) require a person to make provision for the protection of investors in the event of the cessation of his investment business in consequence of his death, incapacity or otherwise (s. 48(2)(l)).

The CBRs apply to the conduct of home-regulated investment business carried on in the UK by European investment firms but cannot prohibit such a firm carrying on, or holding itself out as carrying on any home-regulated investment business or deal with any matter which the investment services directive reserves to the home-state regulator (Sch. 7, para. 10 of the *Investment Services Regulations* 1995 (SI 1995/3275)).

(5) Territorial scope of the rules

Both the existing CBRs and the new approach are consistent with the Financial Services Act with regard to the question of territorial application: investment business which has no connection with the UK is not regulated. This means that any business which does not involve a firm in having a permanent place of business in the UK or in engaging in any activity in the UK is not subject to regulation by the SIB, nor is a foreign branch of a firm regulated with regard to its dealings outside the UK. A firm which engages in investment business which is not regulated by the CBRs must make that fact clear to customers (SIB Rules, Ch. III, Pt. 2, r. 2.17). Similarly, a firm must not direct its customers to conduct their investment business through an unregulated foreign branch of the firm without making it clear to the customer that the protection of the CBRs will no longer apply (SIB Rules, Ch. III, Pt. 2, r. 2.18(2)).

(6) Customers and investors

In determining the standards required of firms, the SIB has recognised that flexibility is required. Firms may engage in a vast range of transactions and activities which fall within the phrase 'investment business' and a system of regulation which is sufficient but not excessive demands that different circumstances must be taken into account in determining the level of protection to be afforded to investors.

A customer of an investment business includes a potential customer, an identified principal of an agent customer and a customer of a firm's appointed representative but does not include a market counterparty or a trust beneficiary (the *Financial Services Core Glossary* 1991).

A customer is a private customer when he is an individual who is not acting in the course of carrying on investment business or, unless he is believed to be an ordinary business investor, a customer who is a small business investor. Accordingly a distinction is drawn between a private customer and an ordinary business investor, the latter being afforded less protection than private customers.

An 'ordinary business investor' is a government or local or public authority, a

¶502

company or partnership which satisfies certain criteria relating to the size of its shareholding or the value of its share capital or net assets, or a trustee of a trust the assets of which exceed a certain value. The membership criterion is a minimum of twenty members and the size criterion is a called up share capital or net assets of £50,000 or more. A small business investor falls below one or other of these criteria.

EXAMPLES OF SPECIFIC RULES

¶503   General outline

By way of example this section examines the broad areas of scope of the CBRs using the headings of the now dedesignated core rules to do so as these rules have been incorporated into SRO rulebooks and reflect the benchmarks of the SIB rules.

¶504   Independence

If a firm holds itself out as offering independent advice it should not compromise that position through its association or arrangements with others. The CBRs cover four main areas: inducements, material interests, soft commission and polarisation.

The making or receiving of inducements such as gifts and other benefits which are intended to attract investment business is restricted and reciprocal arrangements, whereby a firm agrees to introduce investment business to another firm in return for that firm introducing investment business to it, are generally prohibited. It is important to note that the payment of introduction commissions is not entirely outlawed; it is only where they are so great or are paid so often that they can reasonably be expected to distort the advice or service provided to investors, that there is infringement.

The point is that firms should avoid conflicts of interest (cf Statement of Principle 6) and accordingly where a firm has a material interest in a transaction to be entered into with or for a customer it must not knowingly advise or deal in exercise of discretion in relation to that transaction unless it takes reasonable steps to ensure fair treatment for that customer. A similar approach relates to soft commissions where goods and services are provided to, for example, a fund manager in exchange for placing insurers with a broker. Soft commissions for order flow are prohibited but broadly permitted where it assists in the provision of investment services for the customer. An example of soft commission to a fund manager benefiting the customer might be information technology. Finally polarisation, often a controversial subject, is also designed to ensure independence. Accordingly only an independent intermediary may advise a private customer on packaged investment products from a range of services. A product company must only advise a private company on its own products.

¶505   Advertising and marketing

The CBRs are concerned to set out rules on the advertising and marketing of investment products and thus make provision for the structure, issue and approval of advertisements as well as for communications with the customer and the provision of information (see Ch. 9).

¶506   Customer relations

The CBRs provide for customer agreements, customer rights, the suitability of recommendations and discretionary deals, standards of advice on packaged products, charges and information on transactions. Although there is nothing generally to prevent oral investment agreements, where there is a written customer agreement it must set out in adequate detail the basis on which the investment services are provided. However, what are termed 'two-way customer agreements' (which are in writing and to which the customer has signified his assent in writing in circumstances where the firm is satisfied that the customer has had a proper opportunity to consider its terms) are required in two circumstances. First in a derivative transaction under which a private customer has a contingent liability to make further payments. Secondly where there is discretionary management of a private customer's assets. So far as customer rights are concerned a firm should not seek to exclude its statutory or regulatory duty under the Financial Services Act and in relation to private customers, unless it is reasonable to do so, restrict any other duty to act with skill, care and diligence.

A general requirement is imposed on a firm to ensure that certain products are suitable to the customer. The suitability principle along with the know your customer principle are central to the regulatory system and mark an advance on the obligations imposed on financial intermediaries by the general law. Accordingly a firm must take reasonable steps to ensure that it does not in the course of business make any personal recommendation to a private customer of an investment or an investment agreement or effect or arrange a discretionary transaction with or for a private customer when the recommendation or transaction is suitable for him, having regard to the facts disclosed by that customer and other relevant facts about the customer of which the firm is, or reasonably should be, aware.

An extension of the suitability principle may be seen in standards of advice set for packaged products. For example, if a firm acts as an independent intermediary it must not advise a private customer to buy a packaged product or buy a packaged product for him if it is aware of a packaged product which is generally available which would better meet his needs. Such a firm must take reasonable steps to inform itself and relevant agents about packaged products which are generally available on the market and on which it can advise.

On charging, the rules provide that these must not be unreasonable in the circumstances. The aim is to prevent unfair or unreasonable charges for the services provided. The broad rule is, subject to exception, that there must be disclosure to a private customer of the basis or amount of its charges. The object of this would appear to be openness and also to give some guide, by way of comparison, to reasonableness of charge. This is all part of a policy of openness to customers which is also seen in a rule which requires information sent to customers setting out the essential details of the transaction.

¶507   Dealing for customers

A group of rules deal with what are essentially principles of fairness in acting for customers. These concern customer order priority, timely execution, best execution, allocation of transactions, dealing ahead of publication, churning and switching.

These rules are intended to ensure that a firm does not treat some customers more favourably than others or are otherwise disadvantaged. Thus, for example, if customers' orders are 'lumped', the basis of allocation must be fair as between the relevant customers and must be decided upon before dealing. This rule augments the existing case law on the practice of aggregating and allocating customer orders (e.g. *Scott & Horton v Godfrey* [1901] 2 KB 726). Similarly, a firm must not discriminate between customers in the use of its research information and must not act to its customers detriment to its own benefit.

Accordingly a firm should deal with customers' and own account orders fairly and in due turn and, unless on reasonable grounds a firm believes that postponement of an order is in the best interests of the customer, it must effect or arrange the execution of an order as soon as reasonably practicable in the circumstances. As well as timely execution, a firm must provide best execution. This best execution rule requires a firm to take all reasonable steps to ensure that transactions for customers are effected upon the best terms available at the time. Whilst price is an important factor, other considerations such as the other terms of the transaction and the reliability of the counterparty are also relevant (cf. *Maxted v Paine* (1871) LR 6 Exch. 132, at p. 149). A firm may contract out of the best execution requirement with regard to its business and experienced investors and it does not apply to certain types of investment, notably, life policies and units in regulated collective investment schemes (but a duty of 'best advice' attaches to those investments). Closely connected with these rules is the requirement for timely allocation and fair allocation which are relevant where a firm has aggregated orders. The object is to ensure allocation without preference.

In general a firm is not permitted to deal for its own account ahead of publication to customers of a recommendation or a piece of research or analysis. The principle is that the firm should only deal for an account after the customers for whom the publication was intended are likely to have had a reasonable opportunity to react to the publication. A similar fair dealing principle is to be found in the prohibition of churning and switching. Churning will occur where the dealing would be reasonably regarded as too frequent. Accordingly a firm must not make a personal recommendation to a private customer or exercise a discretion for any customer in these circumstances. Switching will occur where a change of investment is not reasonably justified. Accordingly a firm must not make a personal recommendation to a private customer to switch within a packaged product or between packaged products or effect such a switch in the exercise of discretion for a private customer unless it believes on reasonable grounds that the switch is justified from the customer's viewpoint.

¶508   Market integrity

Under the heading 'Market Integrity' the Core Rules deal with four matters: insider dealing, stabilisation, off exchange market makers and reportable transactions. The criminal law prohibits insider dealing by virtue of Pt. V of the *Criminal Justice Act* 1993 and what the core rules seek to do is to place certain prohibitions and obligations on a firm, the 1993 Act dealing only with individuals. Accordingly a firm must not effect (either in the UK or elsewhere) an own account transaction when it knows of circumstances which mean that it or its associate, or an employee of either, is prohibited from effecting that transaction by the statutory restrictions on insider dealing. Furthermore, a firm must use its best endeavours to ensure that it does not knowingly effect a transaction for a customer who it knows is prohibited from doing so by the statute. As regards this obligation, there are three exceptions, first where the statutory prohibition applies only because of knowledge of the firm's own intentions, secondly where the firm is a recognised market maker with obligations to deal in the investment, and thirdly where the firm is a trustee or personal representative who acts on the advice of a third party appearing to be an appropriate adviser who is not so prohibited.

Stabilisation of price of securities must comply with the stabilisation rules. The aim of price stabilisation is to facilitate an orderly distribution of securities being issued by pegging their price in order to prevent a decline (see House of Commons, Parliamentary Debates *Hansard* 30 Oct. 1986, cols. 538–547). It is a technique which is widely used in the international securities markets. The SIB now recognises that effective stabilisation will often require an international stabilising operation and accordingly, provision is made for the modification of the relevant rules in such circumstances.

The distinction between legitimate price stabilisation and market manipulation is fine. Under s. 48(7) and the recently inserted s. 47(7A) of the *Financial Services Act* 1986, price stabilisation is permitted in certain circumstances. In order to fall within this permission, one of the conditions which must be satisfied is that the stabilisation must conform to the SIB's rules. These rules are now contained in the existing SIB rulebook at Pt. 10 of Ch. III.

Under the rules, stabilisation is only permitted in relation to cash issues of shares, debentures, or government securities, and of instruments entitling the holder to subscribe for such securities and certificates representing such securities. They must be securities which may be dealt in on an exchange which is specified in the rules (at the time of writing, the specified exchanges are: Amex, AIBD, ISE, NASD, NYSE, Paris Stock Exchange and Toronto Stock Exchange). The fact that the issue may be stabilised must be disclosed to the relevant exchanges and generally, potential purchasers must be warned that stabilisation is possible. The statements which are required to be included in various sorts of announcements and documents are set out in a helpful table.

'Permitted stabilisation' under the rules means purchases of the newly issued securities and of certain associated securities and call options by the stabilising manager (which is usually the manager of the original issue). These purchases must be made on one or more of the specified exchanges. The maximum price at which purchases may be made is specified and time limits within which the purchases must be effected are imposed: broadly, the maximum price at which the new securities may be purchased is the price at which they were first issued and the latest permitted expiry date of a stabilising period is the thirtieth day after the issuer of the securities receives the proceeds of the issue.

Securities that may be affected by stabilisation should not usually be recommended to or acquired for private investors.

Further important requirements imposed under the 'market integrity' heading relate to off-exchange market makers who must give notice to the customer that they are required to ensure that a reasonable price for repurchase of the investment is available for at least three months and to a reporting requirement about transactions in securities effected other than on a recognised investment exchange.

¶509   Administration

Six core rules are concerned with administration. Accordingly there is an obligation to safeguard customer investments, to maintain a business profile describing the kind of investment business which the firm carries on in the UK, to establish compliance procedures and complaints procedures. Finally a firm must establish, where necessary a 'Chinese Wall'. This rule, r. 36, is the only one of the core rules which has not been dedesignated (see ¶216).

Liability for breach of various principles and rules of conduct turns upon what the firm knows or ought to have known. Under the general law, the knowledge of each department within a firm is usually attributed to the firm and its liability is judged accordingly, but where the different services offered by a financial supermarket have been hived off into separate companies, these rules are modified. In the first place, each of the companies is regarded as a separate entity and its knowledge is not attributed to its parent, subsidiary or sister companies, but if the division of the businesses is simply a technical device, and the companies operate as one business in practice, the courts are able to ignore the technicality and attribute the knowledge of one company to the other companies in its group.

The concept of 'firm' or 'group' knowledge raises problems when taken in conjunction with the operation of Chinese Walls. Chinese Walls are procedures which are designed to stop the unnecessary flow of information between different departments or companies within a group and are an essential weapon in the task of minimising conflicts of interest in investment business (s. 48(2)(h) of the Financial Services Act 1986). However, if a Chinese Wall works effectively, it may incidentally cause a breach of a CBR which imposes liability in respect of what a firm knows or ought to have known. For example, the broking arm of a firm may recommend a transaction to a customer in circumstances where another department within the firm is aware of information which makes that investment unsuitable for the customer. In order to avoid a breach of the suitability rule in these circumstances, it is necessary to provide that if information is unknown to the brokerage department because of the operation of the Chinese Wall, the firm is deemed not to know (and to be under no obligation to know) the information. Chinese Wall exemptions are provided in relation to all of the CBRs which impose liability in respect of knowledge (see further on the benefits and problems associated with Chinese Walls: Poser, 'Chinese Walls or Emperor's New Clothes?' (1988) 9 Co. Law 119 *Part XVI Fiduciary Duties and Regulatory Duties* (Law Com No. 236); Lipton and Mazor, *The Chinese Wall Solution to the Conflicts of Securities Firms* 50 NYUL L Rev 549; *Lee (David) & Co. v Coward Chance* [1991] Ch. 259; *Kelly v Cooper* [1993] AC 205; Clark *Boyce v Mouat* [1994] 1 AC 428).

Core Rule 36.1 provides that where a firm maintains an established arrangement which requires information obtained by the firm in the cause of carrying on one part of its business of any kind to be withheld in certain circumstances from persons with whom it deals in the course of carrying on another part of its business then the information may be withheld. Accordingly, for the purpose of the rules, knowledge will not be attributed to the firm if none of the relevant individuals had that knowledge, even though across the Chinese

Wall other individuals in the firm clearly had that knowledge. Further, nothing done in conformity with r. 36.1 is regarded as a contravention of s. 47 of the Act (see s. 48(6)).

CONDUCT OF BUSINESS RULES OF SROs

¶510   General outline of the rules

Since the SIB has only a limited role with regard to the direct authorisation of investment businesses, in practice, it is the SROs' CBRs which are relevant on a day-to-day basis to the majority of firms. Each of the SROs have produced their own CBRs and each set of rules is different both in detail and, in some respects, in general approach. However, it is important to reiterate that they are all linked and must continue to reflect the standards of investor protection inherent in the SIB's rules. Since for an SRO to be recognised by the SIB its rules must afford an adequate level of protection to investors.

OTHER RULES MADE BY THE SIB

¶511   Contents of the rulebook

As already outlined, the SIB's rule-making power is extensive. The full rulebook contains not only the Conduct of Business Rules but also:

(1) rules on financial supervision;

(2) other special subjects such as unsolicited calls, cancellation and client money;

(3) rules to create and administer the compensation scheme;

(4) rules about product regulation (collective investment schemes, etc.);

(5) rules about regulation itself (notification, fees, etc.);

   (source: New Approach, Introduction).

¶512   Cold calling

Section 56 of the Financial Services Act 1986 prohibits any person from doing any investment business during or in consequence of an unsolicited call made on a person in the UK or from the UK on a person elsewhere. Essentially there are two restrictions, a dealing restriction on the entering into an investment agreement and a marketing restriction on the procuring or endeavouring to procure a person to enter into an investment agreement. This amounts to a ban on cold calling and applies to all persons, including firms. The ban is subject to regulations made by the SIB, the SROs and the RPBs under which cold calling is permitted in certain specified circumstances. The prohibition on cold calling relates only to personal visits, telephone calls or other oral communications made without invitation (s. 56(8)). It does not apply to letters or mail shots to potential customers, which are normally regulated by s. 57.

A person who contravenes s. 56 is not guilty of a criminal offence but is subject to the following civil sanctions:

(1) any resulting investment agreement is unenforceable against the person called; and

(2) the person called is able to recover any money or other property transferred, as well as interest or other compensation (s. 56(2)).

However, the court has a discretion to enforce investment agreements which have been generated by cold calls and to allow money or property to be retained in the following circumstances:

(a) if the person on whom the call was made was not materially influenced by anything done in the course of or in consequence of the call;

(b) if the agreement was entered into pursuant to discussions other than those made during the unsolicited call, provided that the investor was aware of the nature of the risks involved in the agreement; or

(c) if the call was not made by or on behalf of the person seeking to enforce the agreement or by a person (e.g. an insurance intermediary) to whom he pays a commission or other inducement (s. 56(4)).

The burden of proof would appear to be on the person seeking the order of enforcement or retention.

The circumstances in which cold calling is allowed by the SIB are outlined in the Common Unsolicited Calls Regulations which came into effect on 1 January 1992. They do not apply to persons certified by an RPB.

The circumstances in which cold calling is permissible are outlined in the principles of conduct. These are as follows.

(1) Anyone may cold call persons within the investment community or persons whose corporate finance experience makes them well able to look after themselves (reg. 1). This enables cold calls to be made on (amongst others) authorised persons, exempted persons and business investors.

(2) Authorised persons may cold call their existing customers if the customer agreement permits it, and overseas persons may cold call overseas customers (reg. 4).

¶512

(3) Cold calling is permitted between persons within the same family, company, group, partnership, or enterprise (reg. 8).

(4) It is permitted to use cold calls for the sale of non-geared packaged products such as units in unit trusts or for life policies (where cancellation rules frequently apply); (reg. 2) or where the investment agreement is a contract to manage the assets of an occupational pension scheme (reg. 10).

(5) Cold calling is permitted for the supply of 'callable investment services' under a cancellable agreement for these services with an authorised or exempted person. Included under this head are agreements for generally marketable non-geared packaged products and readily realisable securities other than warrants (reg. 3).

(6) Cold calling is allowed to permit the purchaser of an investment business to invite the customers of that investor to establish a customer relationship with him (reg. 5).

(7) The restrictions are lifted in connection with public takeovers (reg. 6) certain corporate acquisitions (reg. 7) and in relation to employee share schemes (reg. 9).

(8) The cold calling restrictions are also lifted where a person was not acting by way of business and who has been provided with no incentive to make the call (reg. 11), where the call was made in the course of a non-investment business and the investment advice or service was a necessary part of that business and was not separately remunerated (reg. 12) and where the cold call was made by an exempted person in the course of investment business covered by that exemption (reg. 13).

It should be noted that the marketing restriction and the dealing restriction are lifted only to the extent that the caller or dealer can demonstrate that he believes on reasonable grounds in the existence of circumstances which would mean that the restriction is lifted from him (reg. 17). A regulator may issue formal guidance on cold calling and a person will be taken to have acted in conformity with the Common Unsolicited Calls Regulations to the effect that he believes on reasonable grounds that he is acting in conformity with such guidance (reg. 18). Finally as regards an overseas person call where the regulations do not specifically refer to such a call the regulations lift the marketing and dealing restrictions only to the extent that the marketing or dealing is due through an authorised or exempted person (reg. 14).

¶513   Client money regulations

Section 55 of the Financial Services Act 1986 enables the SIB to make client money regulations. These are contained in the *Financial Services (Client*

¶513

Money) Regulations 1991 and *The Financial Services (Client Money) (Supplementary) Regulations* 1991.

In general terms, the primary purpose of the client money regulations is to protect investors in the event of a firm's insolvency. It is an established principle of insolvency law that property which, although in the possession of an insolvent firm, is not beneficially owned by it, must be returned to its true owner in priority to the claims of both the secured and unsecured creditors of the firm (*Barclays Bank Ltd v Quistclose Investments Ltd* [1968] 3 All ER 651). A subsidiary aim is to prevent the doctrine of set-off operating to the detriment of customers. The doctrine of set-off enables the creditors of a firm to obtain repayment of their debts by deducting amounts which they owe to the firm from amounts due from the firm (see Wood, *English and International Set-off*, p. 5). A simple example of set-off arises where a firm operates two bank accounts, one of which is in credit and the other of which is in debt: by setting off the two accounts, the bank may be able to clear the overdraft. However, the availability of set-off is qualified by the proviso that, normally, only mutual debts may be set off (see Wood, *ibid.*, p. 766). With regard to the example of the two bank accounts, this means that the account which is in credit cannot be set off against the overdrawn account if persons other than the firm have beneficial interests in the credit balance.

In order to achieve these objectives, the SIB's rules require client money to be held on trust (s. 55(2)(a) of the *Financial Services Act* 1986. Detailed rules of conduct define 'client money' for these purposes (r. 2.01) and money received from a private customer will normally be subject to the regulations unless any such customer is reasonably believed by the firm to have sufficient experience to be able to waive customer protections, that the customer is warned that his money will not be subject to client money protections and that person has given his written consent (r. 2.02(2)). If the client is a business or experienced investor who is not an authorised person, he may notify the firm that he wants the regulations to apply to his money (r. 2.02(4)). If the firm is unwilling to treat this money as client money they must return it.

The trust obligation is to be fulfilled by the opening of a client account (or accounts) at an 'approved bank'. This client account must be held in the EU unless there is written agreement to the contrary between the firm and client (r. 2.14(1)). All client money must be paid into the client account as soon as possible (r. 2.08(1)) and this account must be segregated from any account holding money belonging to the firm (r. 2.12). Generally, money which is not client money should not be paid into the client account.

It is a principle of conduct that firms account properly and promptly for client money. In order to fulfil this, firms must be sure at all times how much client money stands to the credit of each client and must ensure that money belonging to one client is not used on behalf of another. There is a general obligation to

¶513

pay interest on client money but this may be excluded by agreement to the contrary (s. 55(2)(f) and (r. 4.02).

Section 55(2)(e) enables the SIB to require a firms' accounts to be examined by an accountant for the purposes of establishing whether the client money regulations have been complied with. These requirements are embodied in r. 4.11 which requires auditors of firms to report to the relevant regulatory authorities on the existence of adequate accounting systems and on compliance with the regulations.

One point about the client money regulations which requires specific mention is their application in respect of firms. Although the general position is that the SIB's rulebook applies directly only to firms authorised by the SIB, the client money regulations are unusual in that they apply, to some extent, to all persons who have obtained authorisation by virtue of membership of an SRO or by virtue of certification from the Chartered Association of Certified Accountants or the Institute of Actuaries. This extended application is necessary because only regulations made under statutory authority can first, create a binding trust and secondly, enable payments of interest gross (commentary to *Client Money Regulations 1989, New Approach 2*, pp. 11–12).

¶514   Risk disclosure statements

Various CBRs require specific warnings, in the form of risk disclosure statements, to be given to investors about the risks involved in particular investment transactions, e.g. transactions in futures, options, contracts for differences and in securities which have been stabilised.

¶515   Cancellation rules

Under s. 51 of the Act rules may be made to enable a person who has entered or offered to enter into an investment agreement with an authorised person to rescind that agreement or withdraw that offer as the case may be. In accordance with s. 51, the SIB has made cancellation rules which came into force on 1 April 1989 (the *Financial Services (Cancellation) Rules* 1989). These rules were amended by the *Financial Services (Cancellation) (Amendment) Rules* 1989 and in respect of life policies the *Financial Services (Cancellation) Rules* 1994 apply from 1 January 1995 thereby implementing Article 15 of the Second Life Directive (90/619/EEC) and Article 30 of the Third Life Directive (92/96/EEC). These rules apply to persons who are authorised by SROs and RPBs as well as to directly authorised persons. The broad scope of the cancellation rules is as follows.

The purpose of cancellation rules is to provide investors with a 'cooling-off' period, or, in the words of the SIB: 'to give investors the opportunity to make considered and well informed investment decisions' (r. 2.01, Explanation). Since it would be excessive to afford the luxury of a re-think to investors who are, or who should be, capable of protecting themselves, business investors are not given cancellation rights. That these rules are intended to protect smaller and relatively inexperienced investors is also reflected in the products to which cancellation rights attach: investors are given the right to cancel life assurance contracts and contracts relating to the sale of units in regulated collective investment schemes, such as unit trusts. Execution-only investors are excluded from the protection of the rules: there is no danger that such investors will have been subjected to a 'hard sell' from the relevant life office or unit trust manager.

Notice of the right to cancel must be sent to the investor by post at the very latest within the period of 14 days after the investment agreement is entered into. The rules do not limit the period by which the cancellation notice may precede the investment agreement. The usual cancellation period under the rules is 14 days after receipt of the notice of the right to cancel. If a cancellation notice is served by the investor within this period, it operates to rescind the investment agreement to which it relates or, if that agreement has not been concluded, to withdraw any offer to enter into an agreement. If an investor is not informed of his cancellation rights, then, in addition to any other claims arising out of this breach, he retains the right to cancel the agreement. However, a 'prescriptive period' of two years from the making of the investment agreement has been introduced and a notice of cancellation may not be given after that period has expired (r. 2.02 and r. 2.03).

¶516   The SIB's compensation scheme

Under s. 54 of the Act rules may be made to establish a compensation scheme for investors where authorised persons are unable or likely to be unable to satisfy claims in respect of any description of civil liability incurred by them in connection with their investment businesses.

In accordance with s. 54, the SIB has established a compensation scheme. (See the *Financial Services (Compensation of Investors) Rules* 1994 as amended by the *Financial Services (European Institutions) Investment Rules* 1993 and the *Financial Services (Investment Firms) Rules* 1995.)

The compensation scheme applies in situations where authorised persons whose business includes scheme business ('participant firms') are unable, or are likely to be unable, to satisfy civil liability claims made against them in respect of their investment business. Scheme business is investment business carried on by any person in respect of which he is an authorised person including a European investment firm carrying on home-regulated investment business in the UK. Excluded are RPB regulated business, management of investments for an occupational pension fund, registered friendly societies, certain participants in the oil market and overseas schemes providing comparable protection.

The scheme is managed by Investors Compensation Scheme Limited. It operates only where a participant firm is 'in default', as defined by the rules. In general terms, mere failure to pay a debt does not constitute default. The management company may determine a participant firm to be in default where it appears that the firm is unable, or likely to be unable, to satisfy claims in respect of any description of civil liability incurred in connection with its investment business and that as a result compensation is likely to be payable (r. 2.01(1)).

If an investor wishes to make a claim on the investment fund, he must normally apply within six months of becoming aware of the default, or within six months of the time when he ought to have become aware of it. Claims in respect of defaults which occurred before 27 August 1988, when the scheme came into force, are permitted (see *SIB v FIMBRA* [1992] Ch 268). The circumstances in which claims may be made on the fund by business or experienced investors are limited. Claims made by any person implicated in the firm's financial difficulties will be rejected (r. 2.02(4b)). Claims may only be made in respect of eligible liabilities, which, broadly, are civil liabilities owed to the investor by the firm in respect of its investment business (r. 2.03 and 2.04).

Subject to the requirements that payments must not exceed either the amount of the liability which the firm is unable to meet or the financial limits imposed by the rules, the appropriate amount of compensation payable to an investor is to be determined by the management company (r. 2.06 and 2.07).

The financial limits are as follows:

(1) claims in respect of liabilities of up to £30,000 may be met in full;

(2) claims in respect of liabilities of between £30,000 and £50,000 may be met in full up to £30,000 and up to 90 per cent in respect of the excess;

(3) a maximum of £48,000 is imposed on claims in respect of liabilities which exceed £50,000.

Furthermore, the maximum amount which may be paid out of the fund in any one year is limited to £100 million. In order to ensure that this total limit is not exceeded, the management company is entitled to reduce the amounts payable to investors but, in so far as is reasonably possible, should ensure that such reductions are suffered rateably by all claimants (r. 2.07).

The funding of the compensation fund is crucial. The management company may raise funds from a number of sources and has already entered into loan agreements for this purpose. Contributions levied on participant firms will go towards repayment of these loans. Participant firms are required to make contributions in respect of both the management costs and compensation costs of the management company. Essentially, the levy required of each participant firm depends upon the management costs and compensation costs incurred in the previous year; these costs are to be divided up amongst participant firms by reference to their declared incomes.

¶516

Aspects of the compensation scheme have already been the subject of considerable criticism. Particular complaints include:

(1) the maximum annual compensation ceilings are regarded as inadequate; even losses caused by a single default, such as Barlow Clowes, may exceed the overall maximum; comparable schemes, such as under the Policyholders Protection Act 1975, do not have any ceilings;

(2) the discretion of the management company to scale down claims where the overall limit is likely to be exceeded, may result in an appearance of unfairness where the claims of other investors have been satisfied earlier in the year;

(3) claims cannot be carried forward to the following year;

(4) compensation which draws no distinction between the quality of the firms in default may be a spur to inefficiency, causing investors to place funds in risky ventures of dubious merit, in the knowledge that they are insulated from loss; the discretion to reduce payments where the investor would receive benefits disproportionate to those which might reasonably have been expected, does not address the point: even if the discretion can be used so as to reduce a claim by losses which might reasonably have been expected in risky ventures, inefficiency will be deterred only by imposing penalties on investors who consciously assume extraordinary risks;

(5) there is no appeal mechanism against the decisions of the management company; investor confidence might have been better served in this respect by extending the powers of the Financial Services Tribunal.

Despite these criticisms, the scheme does overcome the burdens imposed on working capital by funded schemes. It was recognised early on that no cost-effective insurance was obtainable.

Legal decisions relevant to the scheme may be found in *SIB v FIMBRA* [1992] Ch 268 (scheme covers liabilities incurred on and after 18 December 1986), *R v Investors Compensation Scheme Ltd ex parte Weyell* [1994] 1 All ER 601, *R v Investors Compensation Scheme ex parte Bowden* [1994] 1 WLR 17 (personal representatives may claim).

6 Insider Dealing

¶601 Insider dealing in perspective

The abuse of a privileged position to take advantage for oneself or another is nothing new – it is simply human nature. The taking advantage, however, of information which is available because of one's special position, by dealing on the basis of it in securities the price of which are materially affected by this inside information is a practice which has attracted rather more attention over the last 30 years. Nonetheless, it is not novel and it is possible to find references to concern about insider dealing as early as the seventeenth century (see for example, *House of Commons Journal*, 25 November 1696). As with most sharp practices, attitudes to its undesirability have not been uniform over the years.

There are today those who contend that there are economic and other advantages to the market in permitting those in privileged positions to avail themselves of the opportunity to trade on the basis of inside information. Whether such arguments are justifiable or not, and the present author admits to scepticism of most, it has generally been assumed that investors consider insider dealing unfair. It matters little that this perception may not be entirely the product of logic and may, indeed, be rather more a manifestation of human jealousy than moral outrage if it appears that confidence in the integrity and thus, arguably, the efficiency of the markets is harmed.

Investors who consider that unfair practices occur in a particular market may according to this view lose confidence in that market and put their money elsewhere. Therefore, those who are custodians of the market have a responsibility to be seen to be acting against such practices. In Britain we have accepted this justification for intervening against insider abuse as the primary basis for regulation. Given the perceived threat to public confidence in the operation of the public securities market, it has generally been assumed that it is the criminal law which is the appropriate weapon to deploy. The criminal law is cast in the role of protecting the public good in the markets, even though it is clear that the traditional criminal justice system is not particularly well suited to dealing with complex economic activity. While the results in prosecuting insiders in Britain since 1980 are better than every other jurisdiction, with the exception of the USA, which generally uses alternative enforcement procedures rather than the criminal law, it cannot realistically be argued that the record would give members of the public confidence that insiders would dare not trespass on the integrity of the market.

¶602 The regulation of insider dealing

Insider dealing was not specifically rendered a criminal offence until 1980, but it was recognised as an abuse necessitating legislative action long before this. One of the justifications for imposing a statutory obligation (see s. 324–328 of and Sch. 13 to the *Companies Act* 1985) on directors to report to their companies all dealings by them, their spouses and infant children, in the securities of their company and related companies, was to discourage the taking advantage of inside information. Indeed, the requirement that companies receiving such information should then be obliged to pass it on to the market, was specifically justified on this basis. See s. 329 of the *Companies Act* 1985. Whilst non-compliance with these provisions constitutes a criminal offence there have been precious few prosecutions. It is, of course, unlikely that a person who is willing to deliberately abuse his position by taking advantage of such information is going to be significantly inhibited by the prospect of evading or ignoring these reporting obligations. In addition to these statutory provisions there are a host of other legal and extra-legal requirements relating to the disclosure of directors' and various other insiders' interests. Many of these are not aimed directly at insider dealing. This is particularly so in regard to the statutory obligation on substantial shareholders to report their holdings and changes in regard to such to the company – see s. 198–220 of the *Companies Act* 1985. This obligation was justified on the basis that those dealing with companies should be in a position to know who has significant influence over the company. Indeed until 1993, shareholders, whether their holding is considered substantial or not, were not considered to be candidates for insider status. The traditional view of the English law is that a shareholder as a shareholder has no privileged access to information and even a substantial shareholder has no special rights or responsibilities.

The first substantive provision aimed at least in part against insider dealing was introduced in the *Companies Act* 1967 which prohibits directors, their spouses and infant children, purchasing options in the securities of their company or a related company. See s. 323 and 327 of the *Companies Act* 1985. It is important to note that this prohibition applies irrespective of whether there is any allegation that the director has inside information. The provision is aimed at insider speculation rather than insider dealing, although it was recognised that the acquisition of options did enable insiders to take advantage of inside information in a particularly cost effective manner. As in the case of the reporting provisions there have been precious few prosecutions.

It has been argued that in certain circumstances where an insider, or for that matter anyone else, induces an investment transaction by virtue of a dishonest

¶602

concealment of a material fact, a crime is committed contrary to what is now s. 47(1) of the *Financial Services Act* 1986. Whether it is possible to argue that a concealment has occurred when there was no prior and independent duty to disclose the information in the first place is open to question. Furthermore, it has been doubted whether it is possible dishonestly to refrain from disclosing information which one may well be under a duty to another person to keep confidential. Nonetheless, where a person does conceal material facts which he is under an obligation to disclose either because there is an independent duty of disclosure or an obligation to correct a false or misleading impression, then if what has transpired can be described as dishonest, there is a prospect of a charge under s. 47(1).

Perhaps the most significant area of regulation prior to 1980 and arguably even today is the area of self-regulation or perhaps more accurately non-statutory regulation. In addition to the various reporting obligations to which reference has already been made, the *City Code on Takeovers and Mergers* and the *Listing Rules* of the London Stock Exchange have long contained provisions designed to discourage insider abuse. Both the Code and the Rules promote timely disclosure as a means of ensuring fair, well-informed and orderly markets. Obviously the more effective disclosure is, and in particular timely disclosure of information, the less opportunity there will be for insiders to take advantage of informational imbalances in the markets. Furthermore, the Code and Rules contain provisions for the handling of sensitive information and require such information to be kept confidential until it is appropriate to disseminate it. The Code and the Stock Exchange's Model Code (set out in an appendix to Ch. 16 of the *Listing Rules*) also condemn insider dealing and provide thereby a basis for disciplinary action. See B Rider and T M Ashe, *Insider Crime* (1993) Jordans, at p. 79ff. The Model Code which the Stock Exchange requires listed companies to apply to its directors and certain other insiders provides a minimum standard, which it has been accepted by the court places directors under an obligation to their companies to comply with: *Chase Manhattan Equities Ltd v Goodman & Ors* [1991] BCC 308. Of course, many companies and institutions incorporate provisions for controlling and monitoring dealings within their terms of employment. The SIB's Statements of Principle underline the importance of those in the investment business having and operating effective compliance procedures for their staff – see Principle 9.

The SIB's Core Conduct of Business Rules address insider abuse at many levels, but in r. 28 it is provided that subject to the operation of an acceptable Chinese Wall, authorised persons should not engage in transactions when one of their staff is prohibited by the general law on insider dealing from acting, and that a firm should use its best endeavours to ensure that it does not transact business for a client when that client would commit such an offence. The

¶602

various self-regulatory organisations have adopted similar provisions. Of course, in the case of all such rules the possibility exists for a civil enforcement action to be brought by the Treasury or SIB under s. 61 of the *Financial Services Act* 1986, or by an investor who can prove loss as a result of a breach of the rules, under s. 62 of the 1986 Act.

¶603   The civil law

The position of those who engage in insider dealing, or who benefit from insider abuse under the civil law has received attention from academics although not from the courts, at least in Britain. See B Hannigan, *Insider Dealing* (1988) Kluwer, Ch. 5; J Suter, *The Regulation of Insider Dealing in Britain* (1989) Butterworths, Ch. 4; and B Rider and H L Ffrench, *The Regulation of Insider Trading* (1979) Macmillan. It has long been the position in English law that a person is under no duty to disclose even highly material information that may even be peculiarly within his possession or cognisance, to the other party during the negotiation of a contract: *Bell & Anor v Lever Bros Ltd & Ors* (1932) AC 161. There are certain exceptions, but none are particularly relevant in the context of the vast majority of securities transactions on anonymous markets. In most transactions the buyer and seller will be willing traders at the relevant market price and their marriage will be simply random, the notion of privity being little more than an ex post factor fiction. Traditional notions of reliance and causation in the context of an abusive transaction are practically and legally meaningless. Of course, where the relevant transaction is not indirect and wholly impersonal, it may be more practicable to construct an expectation of fair dealing so as to give rise to some form of obligation of disclosure. Furthermore, in face to face transactions and the like, the general law of misrepresentation may provide remedies where it is possible to locate half truths, continuing representations and representations by conduct. See generally B Rider and T M Ashe, *Insider Crime* (1993) Jordans at p. 63. Nonetheless, in the vast majority of market transactions it is extremely unlikely that a duty will arise between the insider and his casual counterpart so as to afford that person any realistic opportunity for compensation or rescision.

Where directors deal with shareholders, and possibly although far less likely persons who by virtue of that transaction become shareholders, the courts, at least in Australasia, have been more willing to assist. See in particular *Coleman v Myers* (1977) 2 NZLR 298 and (1977) 2 NZLR 225 (discussed in (1977) 40 MLR 471 and (1978) 41 MLR 585 and *Glandon Pty Ltd v Strata Consolidated Pty Ltd* (1993) 11 ACLC 895 (New South Wales (Court of Appeal)). The traditional attitude of the English law is that directors can only be regarded as owing their duties as directors to the company which is, of course, a separate legal person totally distinct from its shareholders. See *Percival v Wright* [1902] 2 Ch 421. Thus, directors in their position and office as directors therefore owe no fiduciary or other obligation to shareholders collectively or individually. Whilst this as a general principle must remain so, the courts have been prepared to hold individuals, who happen to be directors or other insiders of a company, to duties of fair dealing and candour, when because of special facts they have stepped into an exceptional relationship with shareholders. See *Allen v Hyatt* (1914) 30 TLR 444, *Briess v Woolley* (1954) AC 333 and *Walsham v Stainton* (1863) 1 De G J and S 678. Indeed, in a recent Australian decision the Court of Appeal of New South Wales appeared to be willing to find such a relationship on relatively unexceptional facts. See *Glandon Pty Ltd v Strata Consolidated Pty Ltd*. The judges remarked that attitudes as to the commercial morality of insider dealing had changed since the decision in *Percival v Wright* (and see B Rider 'Insider Beware', 14 Co Law (1993) 202) which is taken as establishing the traditional rule. It is certain that where a fiduciary or confidential relationship can be found, then there will be a duty of good faith, which will involve an obligation of full disclosure and avoidance of profiting by virtue of undisclosed conflicts of interest.

It follows that as directors are in a fiduciary relationship, by virtue of their office, with their company then they are not allowed to profit by virtue of any conflict of interest that arises. See *Regal (Hastings) Ltd v Gulliver & Anor* [1942] 1 All ER 378. Thus, if a director takes advantage of information and opportunity which comes to him by virtue of his position as a director to make a profit for himself, without obtaining the fully informed consent of the company, he will be accountable to the company for the benefit he has received. It is less clear whether such an insider would be accountable for the benefit that he has facilitated another receiving or whether he would be liable to the company for the value of any loss that he has avoided, by virtue of using the information in question. To follow the illicit profit into the hands of others and possibly also establish liability for so called 'negative profits' it has been thought necessary for there to be a proprietary element in the breach of duty upon which a constructive trust relationship can be based. It has generally been assumed that a mere duty to account for a 'secret profit' much in the same way as where there is liability to account for a bribe, cannot of itself give rise to a constructive trust relationship.

This restrictive view of the law must now be doubted and it is probable that where a fiduciary uses his position to obtain a 'secret profit' then the courts may well regard the profit in question as being subject to a constructive trust. See *Attorney General for Hong Kong v Reid & Ors* [1994] 1 All ER 1. This would mean that anyone who received this profit otherwise than bona fide and for value might be called upon to yield it up, and where the third party knows of the circumstances they themselves might be liable as a constructive trustee, or as if they were a constructive trustee when they facilitate the laundering of the proceeds without actually taking the profit into their own hands. See *Nanus*

Asia Co Inc v Standard Chartered Bank [1990] 1 HKLR 396; *Agip (Africa) Ltd v Jackson and Ors* [1992] 4 All ER 385 and 451, and P Millett, 'Tracing the proceeds of fraud', (1991) 107 LQR 71. The possibility of invoking a constructive trust also has possible implications under the so called rule in *Foss v Harbottle* (1843) 2 Hare 461 and the availability of a minority shareholder's action (see B Rider, 'A company lawyer's lot...!' 15 Co Law (1994) 34). The traditional and perhaps somewhat academic view has been that a breach of trust cannot be ratified by the appropriate organs of the company so as to place it beyond the reach of a derivative action. Whilst this may well be a rather too simplistic analysis of the law, it is probable that a judge will be concerned to examine the good faith of those seeking to prevent or disrupt such a suit when there is an allegation of knowing assistance or receipt of trust property.

What is tolerably certain is that no matter what courses of action may exist for breach of fiduciary and other relationships, the commission of an offence under Pt. V of the *Criminal Justice Act* 1993 does not of itself have implications in the civil law. Section 63(2) of the Act provides 'no contract shall be void or unenforceable by reason only' that it amounts to an offence under s. 52. This reflects the dislike which has been evident in the debates throughout the history of insider dealing regulation in Britain of having to unravel market transactions for what are generally assumed to be undeserving litigants. It should be noted that this provision does not, however, effect the viability of any action based on a course of action other than that of statutory illegality. For example, it might be argued, probably without much chance of success, that insider dealing is so undesirable that transactions involving insider abuse should be struck down on the grounds of public policy at common law. See *Innovisions Ltd v Charles Chan Sing-chuk & Ors* [1992] 1 HKLR 71 and 254, where such an argument was rejected, but see in particular *Chase Manhattan Equities v Goodman & Ors* [1991] BCC 308. It has been decided, on the basis of the slightly differently worded provision in the *Company Securities (Insider Dealing) Act* 1985 that a court is entitled to deny its powers to a litigant who seeks to enforce a partially completed transaction which he has entered into on the basis of inside information. In other words the court will not allow an insider to enforce such a transaction against an innocent party. See *Chase Manhattan Equities v Goodman*.

¶604   The legislative background

It became increasingly recognised during the 1970s that the substantive regulation of insider dealing could not be left to essentially self-regulatory authorities bereft of legal powers of investigation. See generally B Rider and H L Ffrench, *The Regulation of Insider Trading* (1979) Macmillan. After various attempts to enact legislation aimed at insider dealing, it was made a specific criminal offence by Pt. V of the *Companies Act* 1980. (See B Rider, *Insider*

Trading (1983) Jordans). The law, with one or two amendments, was re-enacted as the *Company Securities (Insider Dealing) Act* 1985. These provisions whilst being politically and to some degree philosophically justified on the basis that insider dealing undermined public confidence in the markets, were nonetheless orientated to traditional corporate relationships. Thus, primary insiders were essentially those in an essentially confidential relationship with the relevant issuer. Insider status was based on being connected to a particular company and it was through or by virtue of this relationship that the information had to flow to imbue it with privileged status. The information in question had to be such that would not have been disclosed otherwise than in the interests of or for the purposes of the issuer in question. In short it had to be more or less confidential information.

Of course, the net of liability was thrown wide enough to catch those who received the information in question from those whom they knew were connected. But in practice secondary insiders only risked prosecution if they had acquired the information in full knowledge of all the circumstances and therefore appreciated they themselves were in a confidential relationship of sorts to the company. Thus, to some extent the former law in the UK resembled the prevailing principle of liability for insider abuse in the USA. That liability should depend primarily on the misappropriation of information which 'belongs' at least in terms of disposal and utilisation to another. The determination of what is and what is not a misappropriation inevitably involves analysis of relationships and expectations. Liability is much wider than notions of stewardship except in a very attenuated form, and involves issues of relational unfairness, but not abstract unfairness.

The various agencies of the European Union concerned with the development of a single financial market have long identified insider abuse as a specific problem. Attempts were made during the harmonisation period to fashion provisions which would satisfy member countries and be considered sufficiently credible by the USA, but without success. The initiative to achieve co-ordination, if not actual equivalence, was rather more successful. In the result, after well over 20 years of discussion and debate, the European directive co-ordinating regulations on insider dealing was promulgated on 13 November 1989 (Directive 89/592). The directive has a rather different philosophical basis than the former English law had. Its preamble makes it clear that the purpose of regulating insider abuse is to assure investors that they are on an 'equal footing'. Investors will not have confidence in the markets unless they are convinced that there is equality of access to information. See B Bergmans, *Inside Information and Securities Trading* (1992) Graham and Trotman and B Rider and T M Ashe, 'The Insider Dealing Directive?' in *EC Financial Market Regulation and Company Law*, M Andenas and S Kenyon-Slade (eds.) (1993) Sweet & Maxwell.

¶604

Ironically the courts and regulators in the US after many years of experience jettisoned this notion as a basis for effective regulation of insider abuse over a decade ago. Thus, the new law on insider dealing in Britain, introduced in the *Criminal Justice Act* 1993 which implements the directive, moves significantly away from the company law stance to a market-orientated approach. Now liability is based on knowledge that you have information which is inside information almost regardless of how or where you acquired it. Of course, as might be expected Britain has not gone the whole way, and as with so many other instruments, the law that we now have does not entirely espouse market egalitarianism and a ghost of the old principles of stewardship can be perceived – albeit faintly.

¶605 The crime of insider dealing

Instead of the 12 separate offences under the 1985 Act, there is only one offence of insider dealing in Pt. V of the 1993 Act, although it can be committed in three ways; by dealing in securities the price of which will be affected by the inside information which is in that person's possession (s. 52(1)); encouraging another person to so deal (s. 52(2)(a)); and disclosing the inside information to another person (s. 52(2)(b)). For an offence to be committed in the case of dealing or encouraging another to deal, the transactions must occur on a regulated market or the person dealing in the price-affected securities must rely on a professional intermediary or himself be acting as such. It should also be noted that as in the previous legislation criminal liability, as a principal offender, is confined to individuals and, thus, corporations and other artificial legal persons cannot be charged with the substantive offence of insider dealing. However, there is no objection to an artificial legal person being charged with such offences as incitement, conspiracy, counselling and abetting.

The new legislation seeks to impose criminal liability on insider dealing committed within the UK, although by s. 63 a charge cannot be brought in regard to anything done by an individual acting on behalf of a public sector body in pursuit of monetary policies, policies with respect to exchange rates or the management of either public debt or foreign exchange reserves. There are, in addition to this limitation on the scope of the law, a number of defences which relate either to the reasons for the transaction in question or to particular market practices.

It has been the view of successive governments that prosecutions for insider dealing should only be brought in cases where there can be little doubt as to the individual's dishonesty. As in the previous law, prosecutions may only be instituted in England and Wales and Northern Ireland with the consent of the Secretary of State or Director of Public Prosecutions, and in Scotland all prosecutions are instituted by the Lord Advocate. Section 209 of the *Companies Act* 1989 permitted the Secretary of State to consent to prosecutions being brought, rather than to initiate proceedings himself, or leave the matter in the hands of the Director of Public Prosecutions. Section 61(2) of the 1993 Act leaves this power to consent to others bringing prosecutions with the Secretary of State and Director. Since 1989 the London Stock Exchange has been given permission to initiate prosecutions in several instances. Under s. 62(1) an individual convicted of insider dealing after summary trial is liable to the imposition of a fine not exceeding the statutory maximum and/or to a term of imprisonment not exceeding six months. However, on conviction on indictment there may be an unlimited fine and/or a term of imprisonment of up to seven years. Insider dealing is a serious offence and is, thus, an extradition crime and one to which the provisions for the seizure and forfeiture of profits in both the *Criminal Justice Act* 1987 and 1993 apply. It should also be noted that where a victim can be identified and his loss quantified it has been suggested that a compensation order might be made on the conviction of an offender. See *Powers of the Criminal Courts Act* 1985.

¶606   Securities covered by the offence of insider dealing

Under the former law there was a degree of divergence between the list of securities covered by the law on insider dealing and investments within the scope of the *Financial Services Act* 1986. Given the purpose of the anti-insider dealing law to promote and protect confidence in the integrity of the financial markets such a divergence was not logical. Thus the list of securities in regard to which insider dealing will now amount to a criminal offence, is much more in line with the scope and coverage of the Financial Services Act. This also conforms with the philosophy and wording of the European directive on insider dealing which seeks to extend regulation to gilts, local authority securities and instruments derived from them, in addition to corporate securities. Given the policy to protect public markets it is not all dealings in such securities, however, that are within the purview of the new Act. Only dealings in securities which are traded in the market or where there is a ready trade are included. This is achieved by a relatively complicated process of first defining the securities which are covered, then defining the circumstances and conditions which will bring those securities within the parameters of the law and then setting out the circumstances of dealing in those securities with which the provisions on insider dealing are concerned.

The securities which are included within the purview of the new law are set out in the Act, although the list can be added to by the Treasury by order (s. 54 and Sch. 2). The present list includes:

(1) shares and stock in the share capital of a company ('shares');

(2) any instrument creating or acknowledging indebtedness which is issued by a company or public sector body, including, in particular, debentures,

debenture stock, loan stock, bonds and certificates of deposit ('debt securities');

(3) any right (whether conferred by warrant or otherwise) to subscribe for shares or debt securities ('warrants');

(4) the rights under any depositary receipt; a 'depositary receipt' being a certificate or other record whether or not in the form of a document, which is issued by or on behalf of a person who holds any shares, debt securities or warrants of a particular issuer and which acknowledges that another person is entitled to rights in relation to those securities or securities of the same kind;

(5) any option to acquire or dispose of shares, debt securities, warrants, depositary receipts, futures or contracts for differences ('options');

(6) rights under a contract for the acquisition or disposal of shares, debt securities, warrants, depositary receipts, options or contracts for differences under which delivery is to be made at a date and price determined in accordance with the contract ('futures'); and

(7) rights under a contract which does not provide for the delivery of securities but whose purpose or pretended purpose is to secure a profit or avoid a loss by reference to fluctuations in a share index or similar factor connected with securities or the price of particular securities or the interest rate offered on money placed on deposit ('contracts for differences'; in *City Index v Leslie* [1992] 1 QB 98 the comparable albeit slightly different wording in Sch. 1, para. 9 of the Financial Services Act was considered to include not only hedging transactions, but also bets).

The circumstances in which a dealing in these securities, will be within the purview of the Act are that the transaction occurs on a regulated market or that the person either relies on, or is himself acting as, a professional intermediary. This confines the scope of the insider dealing offence to organised public markets and to where a professional intermediary is directly involved in the transaction. Regulated markets for the purpose of these provisions are set out by the Treasury in an order (the *Insider Dealing (Securities and Regulated Markets) Order* 1994, (SI 1994/187)) and include recognised investment exchanges, such as the International Stock Exchange of the United Kingdom and the Republic of Ireland, the National Association of Securities Dealers Automated Quotations System (NASDAQ) and now given the wider scope of the definition of securities, the London International Financial Futures Exchange (LIFFE).

In addition to these markets the order includes a number of major investment exchanges in the European Community. Even markets that are not specifically named in the order will be considered to be regulated markets for the purpose of the insider dealing offence if the head office of the relevant investment exchange under the rules of which the market is established, is situated in a member State of the European Community, and the market is subject in that member State to regulation as to the manner in which it operates, the means by which access may be had to its facilities, the conditions to be satisfied before a security may be dealt in by means of, or before its price may be quoted on, its facilities and the reporting and publication of dealing effected by means of its facilities. All such markets will be regulated markets for the purpose of the anti-insider dealing law. It must be remembered that the prospect of a criminal charge is limited by s. 62 which sets out the territorial scope of the offence. However, subject to this provision, insider dealing on any of these markets or in reliance on or by a professional intermediary in the defined securities may well fall within the scope of the offence, provided the following conditions are also satisfied, namely:

(1) in relation to any security, it must be dealt in or under the rules of, or have its price quoted on, a regulated market;

(2) in relation to a warrant, the rights to subscribe must be for any shares or debt security dealt in or under the rules of, or have their price quoted on, a regulated market;

(3) in relation to a depositary receipt, the rights under it must be in respect of any share or debt security dealt in or under the rules of, or have their price quoted on, a regulated market;

(4) in relation to an option or future, that the options or rights under it are in respect of any share, debt security or depositary receipt which is dealt in or under the rules of, or have their price quoted on, a regulated market or in respect of a depositary receipt the rights under which are in any share or debt security so dealt in or has its price so quoted; and

(5) in relation to a contract for differences, that the purpose or pretended purpose of a contract for differences is to secure a profit or avoid a loss by reference to fluctuation, either in the price of any shares or debt securities or depositary receipt which are dealt in on or under the rules of, or have their price quoted as a regulated market or any depositary receipt in respect of such share or debt security.

¶607 Relevant deals

The Act seeks to set out deals or transactions which are relevant for the offence of insider dealing. The determination of whether a deal is relevant or not, is not only necessary for the offence of dealing in securities but also in regard to the encouragement offence. It is only an offence to encourage another to enter into such relevant deals. If the transaction does not take place on a regulated market it will not be within the purview of the law, unless the person dealing relies on a professional intermediary or is himself in such a position. A person will rely on a professional intermediary for the purposes of the Act if the professional intermediary either acquires or disposes of securities, whether as a principal or as an agent, in relation to the dealing or acts as intermediary between persons taking part in the dealing. It is provided in s. 59(1) that for the purposes of the Act a professional intermediary is a person who carries on a business of acquiring or disposing of securities, again whether as an agent or principal, or a business of acting as an intermediary between persons taking part in any dealing in securities. Employees of such a person will also be considered to be a professional intermediary, although a person will not be so considered if the activities in question are merely incidental to other activities or if he only occasionally conducts one of those activities. The purpose of these provisions is to exclude from the scope of criminal liability a truly private deal executed off the market without the involvement of a market professional.

¶608   Inside information

It is in regard to the definition of what constitutes or may constitute inside information that the greatest amount of controversy has arisen. For information to be considered sufficient to justify criminal liability if it be used or disclosed under the former law it had to be unpublished, price sensitive, of a specific nature and confidential. Section 55(1) retains these characteristics, save the need of confidentiality. It is the intention of the government to impose liability on the abuse of information that can be expected to have a significant impact on the market. The Act prescribes (s. 56) four characteristics of information, knowledge of which is considered sufficient to ground liability. Firstly, it must relate to particular securities or to a particular issuer of securities or particular issuers of securities, and not to either securities or issuers in general. It must be specific or precise. It must not have been made public and finally, it must be such as if it were made public it would be likely to have a significant effect on the price of any securities.

It is clear that information which relates to a specific sector will give rise to liability as will information which relates to a specific security. Thus, information may still be inside information even though it is not specifically related to a particular issuer or for that matter its securities, but does relate to the industry within which the relevant issuer operates. It is also the case that the information may come from inside or outside the issuer. Therefore, a decision to make a take-over bid for the securities of a particular company will constitute inside information in regard to the target company and its securities. It may not always be easy to determine whether the relevant information does relate in a specific manner to a particular company. To address this problem,

s. 60(4) provides that 'information shall be treated as relating to an issuer of securities which is a company not only where it is about the company but also where it may affect the company's business prospects'. The government made it clear that the purpose of this 'gloss' on s. 55(1)(a) is to 'catch as inside information, information which, while not relating directly to a company, would nonetheless be likely to have a significant effect on the price of its shares'. (*Parliamentary Debates*, House of Lords, 3 December 1992, col. 1495.)

It should be noted that the information can be either specific or precise. The European directive only speaks in terms of precision not specified. It is therefore probable that in this regard our law is wider than the provisions of the directive. Of course, it may be that information is specific, albeit it has a vague quality to it. It is not necessary that every facet of the information in question has a degree of specificity which would leave no doubt as to its implication. It must, however, be more than rumour. The more detailed the information in question the more likely it would be considered material by an investor.

¶609   Undisclosed information

In addition to the information being referable, specific or precise, it must be undisclosed to the market. It is not necessary, as it is in some countries, that the information should have been discounted, that is digested by the market, before the prospect of liability is removed. The determination of when an item of information ceases to be privileged is not an easy one to make in the abstract. Section 58 of the 1993 Act sets out four circumstances in which such information will be considered to have been sufficiently disclosed. The Act makes it clear, however, that these four situations are not exclusive and there are other ways in which information may become public. The four specified situations are:

(1) when information is published in accordance with the rules of a regulated market for the purpose of informing investors and their advisers;

(2) when information is placed in records which by virtue of any enactment are open to inspection by members of the public;

(3) if the information can be readily acquired by those that are likely to deal in any of the securities to which the information relates or of an issuer to which the information relates; or

(4) if the information is derived from information which has been made public.

It is further provided in s. 58(3) that information may be treated as having been made public, even though it can be acquired only by persons exercising diligence or expertise, or where it is communicated to a section of the public and not to the public at large, or where it can be acquired only by observation, or it is communicated only on the payment of a fee, or it is published only outside the UK. It must be emphasised that these provisions state only that the information may be considered as made public, not that it must. Obviously, there must be some degree of flexibility as there is all the difference between information being published in a relatively obscure magazine as compared with publication in a major financial newspaper.

Section 58(2)(c) provides, as we have seen, that information will be made public if it can be readily acquired by those likely to deal in any securities to which the information relates or of an issuer to which the information relates. The determination of exactly who might be considered to be likely to deal is not always an easy one. The appropriate standard should be whether those generally in the market would have had ready access to the information in question. If such persons did have ready access then it might be assumed with some degree of confidence that the information has already been discounted in the price of the relevant securities and thus could not have had any significant impact. The door is therefore only open to those insiders who take advantage of such information which has been negligently ignored or distrusted by the market. Of course, it may be that an insider, being in a better position to evaluate the information which is admittedly readily available is less inclined to distrust it. He commits no offence, however, by utilising this advantage, unless his insight can be considered to constitute an item of inside information which is not publicly available.

By the same token, the fourth category of when information ceases to be non-public, makes it clear that information which is derived from publicly available information cannot be considered inside information. This provision was added to placate analysts, who considered that despite the assurances of government that this was already implicit in the notion of public information, there was still some degree of uncertainty. Thus, the superior insight of an insider will not be counted against him, if he uses it to derive insight from information which is generally available.

The situations set out in s. 58(3) where information may be regarded by a court as having been made public, albeit they are not fairly within the criteria of s. 58(2) are merely stated by way of example. A court is at liberty, on the facts, to determine the issue one way or the other.

¶610 Price impact

The 1993 Act focuses on price sensitivity. Section 56(1) provides that the information must, if it were made public, be likely to have a significant effect on the price of any securities. The decision whether the impact is significant or not is essentially a determination of materiality. It can be assumed that only significant movements of price would influence the decision of if and when to trade of an investor motivated primarily albeit, given the defence, not solely by the effect of the information on price. It is expressly provided in s. 56(3) that price includes value.

¶611   Who is an insider?

As has already been observed, perhaps the most significant change in the law is the abandonment of the traditional requirement that the insider should be in some clearly defined way 'connected' with the company in whose securities he makes his illicit profit. A person will have information as an insider, if and only if, it is – and he subjectively knows that it is – inside information, and he has it from an inside source. Thus, before a person can be convicted, it will be necessary for the prosecution to prove beyond all reasonable doubt that the individual concerned was fully aware that the information was within the terms of s. 56, and that he had it from an inside source. Section 57(2) provides that a person will have such information from an inside source, if and only if, he has it through being a director, employee or shareholder of an issuer of securities, or had access to the information by virtue of his employment, office or profession; or the direct or indirect source of his information was such a person. Therefore, a person can only be charged with an offence under Pt. V of the 1993 Act if he has information that he appreciates he has come into possession of through being a director, employee or shareholder of a relevant issuer, or through having access to the information by virtue of his employment, office or profession. Nor can he be charged with an offence as a 'secondary' insider or tippee, unless it can be proved that he was aware that the source of his information was one of these 'primary' or access insiders.

There are only two significant expansions in the category of insider and both have been dictated by the European directive. The first is the inclusion of shareholders. The second is to bring into the net those occupying similar insider relationships with public sector bodies. Thus, a minister or civil servant will be an insider in relation to UK gilts, as will for that matter local government officials in regard to municipal and council securities, as well as officers and employees of foreign public sector institutions in regard to their securities.

There will also be those who have been aptly described as 'temporary insiders' who whilst being essentially outsiders, gain access to information nonetheless by virtue of their position. These will include professional advisers such as lawyers, merchant bankers, accountants, public relations specialists and the like. While it is not unreasonable to expect such persons to assume the responsibilities of insider status on a temporary basis, the wording of the section is wide enough to bring in many others performing rather more peripheral services to an issuer. Thus, it may be argued that office cleaners, temporary secretarial staff, postmen and couriers have access to information by virtue of their employment. Whilst it is no doubt the case that an opportunity to acquire inside information may well have been presented through engaging in the activities of their employment it is not clear whether it is appropriate to cast the net so widely. The better view under the previous legislation was that the information had to be obtained in the proper course and performance of the employment in question. An office cleaner rummaging through a waste paper bin could not be considered to be acting in the course of his or her employment. The present legislation, unlike the earlier law, does not require a connection between the insider and the relevant issuer.

Therefore, given this and the philosophy of the directive to penalise the taking of informational advantages, more or less irrespective of the status of the individual concerned, it has been argued that the new Act imposes considerably wider potential liability than the 1986 legislation. It has been argued that a journalist or analyst who deals prior to the publication of his own recommendations, even though the price-sensitive information is essentially nothing more than his own recommendations, will be guilty of insider dealing. It is submitted that this is not the law. The Act requires that as a precondition for liability the relevant information must emanate from an inside source. An individual will have inside information from an inside source if, for example, he has it through being a director or he has access to it by virtue of his employment. Thus, it is reasonable to assume that information created by an employee would not be regarded as information to which that individual has access to, by virtue of that employment. The notion of having access would seem to require that the information in question is in existence independently of the person seeking to obtain it or access to it. Thus, a journalist's or analyst's own recommendations would not on this argument be inside information as far as that individual is concerned, because he is incapable of accessing his own information. However, whilst a journalist's or analyst's own recommendations may not be considered inside information in regard to his own dealings, any other person who acquires knowledge of the relevant information, in the course of their employment would presumably be within the scope of the offence.

¶612 Tippees

Secondary insiders or tippees are persons who have information directly or indirectly from an insider source. This source must be a person who falls within the terms of s. 57(2) namely directors, employees or shareholders of issuers, or those who have access to inside information by virtue of their employment, office or profession. As under the old law, the secondary insider must know that the information is inside information and he must know that it was ultimately from an inside source. While it is necessary to prove that the source was an insider, it is not necessary to prove any fault on the part of the informant. It is not necessary, for example, to prove that the informant was guilty of the offence of encouraging another to deal.

¶613   The dealing offence

The two essential elements in the dealing offence are that an individual has information as an insider and he must then deal in securities that are price-affected securities in regard to that information. As we have seen, price-affected securities in regard to an item of inside information are those securities the price of which would be significantly affected if the information in question was made public. The obligation on an insider in such a position is not to deal, either as a principal or as an agent for someone else. Dealing is comprehensively defined to encompass acquisitions and disposals, agreements to do such, the entering into a contract which creates a security or the bringing to an end of such a contract. It is important to note that as the offence is committed at the time of agreement, it matters not that the relevant contract is never executed.

While the 1993 Act, as did the previous law, confines the offences of insider dealing to individuals, the definitions of dealing in s. 55 refer to persons and thus, presumably encompass bodies corporate. Thus, by s. 55(4) a person will be considered as dealing if he procures an acquisition or disposal of a security, if that security is acquired or disposed of by a person who is his agent, nominee or is acting at his direction in regard to the transaction. It is expressly provided in s. 55(5) that notwithstanding the express extension of the concept of dealing in this manner, subs. (4) is not to be considered an exhaustive statement as to the circumstances in which a person may be regarded as procuring an acquisition or disposal of securities by another person.

¶614   Encouraging persons to deal

The Act creates a new and general offence of encouraging another person, including a body corporate, to deal knowing or having reasonable cause to believe that the person who is the object of this encouragement would in fact deal in securities, in the circumstances covered by the dealing offence. It is important to appreciate that the offence is proved even if the person who is encouraged to deal does not know that the securities in question would be affected by the information that the insider has, or for that matter he is unaware that the person is an insider or has possession of inside information. The offence fastens solely upon the conduct and state of mind of the insider. If he does encourage another to deal, knowing or having reasonable cause to believe, which is, of course, an objective test, on a recognised market or through or as a professional intermediary, the offence is committed regardless of whether that person does in fact deal.

¶615   The disclosure offence

It is an offence under s. 52(2)(b) for an individual who has information as an insider to disclose the information otherwise than in the proper performance of the functions of his employment, office or profession to another person. The offence is complete when the insider discloses the information whether he intends or suspects that the person to whom he has disclosed it will deal or not. It is simply an offence for an insider to disclose inside information otherwise than in the proper and lawful performance of his duties as an employee, officer or professional intermediary. Of course, if he is bound to disclose the information pursuant to a general or specific obligation arising by law, then it is probable that this would be subsumed with the proper execution of his duties.

¶616   Territorial scope of the offence

The purpose of the European directive was to create a community-wide system of insider dealing regulation. Given the ease of structuring transactions so as to involve another jurisdiction in a significant aspect of the relevant conduct and the traditional approach of the criminal law to confine itself to essentially territorial jurisdiction, compounded by the difficulties and cost involved in such investigations, there was considerable pressure on the government to address the problem of jurisdiction. Part I of the 1993 Act renders a number of fraud related offences both result and conduct crimes in relation to jurisdiction in accordance with the recommendations of the Law Commission. (*Jurisdiction over Fraud Offences with a Foreign Element – A Consultation Paper* (1987) Law Commission.) However, the Law Commission refrained from making recommendations in this regard in relation to insider dealing and, thus, the offences in Pt. V are dealt with specifically in s. 62.

As under the previous law a territorial link is required in that the prohibited conduct must either take place on the markets in the UK or with or through professional intermediaries who are based there. To commit the dealing offence an individual must be in the UK at the time of any act forming part of the dealing, the regulated market on which the dealing occurs must be one regulated in the UK, or the professional intermediary with or through whom the offence was committed, must be in the UK at that point in time. Thus, provided the dealing takes place on, for example, the London Stock Exchange it matters not that the issuer is out of jurisdiction. Moreover, provided a professional intermediary in the UK is utilised it matters not that the insider instructs him from outside the UK to execute a deal on, for example, the French stock exchange.

The disclosure and encouragement offences will be committed within the jurisdiction of the UK courts if the insider was within the UK at the time that he disclosed the information or encouraged the dealing, or the recipient of the information or encouragement was within the UK when he received the information or encouragement.

¶617   The defences

Section 53 sets out a number of defences to charges under s. 52. It is important to note at the outset that the accused has both the burden of raising a defence and then establishing it. Section 53(1) states that an individual is not guilty of insider dealing by virtue of dealing in securities 'if he shows' certain justifications. The better view is that this would impose upon the defendant the burden of establishing what is contended, to the civil standard of proof, namely to a balance of probabilities. In respect of both the dealing offence and the encouragement offence an individual is not guilty if he shows that he did not, at the relevant time, expect the dealing to result in a profit which was attributable to the fact that the information was price-sensitive information in relation to the securities. It is expressly provided in s. 53(6) that in the context of the defence, a profit will also include the avoidance of a loss.

Section 53(1)(b) provides that if an individual charged with dealing can show that at the time he agreed to deal in the relevant securities, he believed on reasonable grounds that the information had been disclosed widely enough to ensure that none of those taking part in the dealing would be prejudiced by not having the information he is entitled to a defence. Section 53(2)(b) provides, in slightly wider terms, a similar defence to a charge of encouraging another person to deal. This provision entitles the defendant to an acquittal if he shows that he believed, on reasonable grounds, that either the information had been disclosed at the time he sought to encourage the dealing, or that it would be sufficiently disclosed at the time the dealing in question took place.

Section 53(1)(c) and (2)(c) provide a defence for those charged with dealing and encouraging another to deal where the defendant can show that he would still have acted as he did even if he had not had the information. Thus, if he can show that he already intended to deal in the relevant securities or encourage another to so deal, at that point in time, then he is entitled to an acquittal, even though at the time he dealt or gave encouragement he was in possession of inside information.

It might well be that this provision would also be useful for trustees, who come into possession of inside information and find themselves impaled on the horns of dilemma. If they deal or instruct someone else to deal they commit an offence and if they do nothing, it is conceivable that they might well be considered to be in breach of trust or even negligent. The Act does not include specific provisions addressing such conflicts of interest. However, under the previous law if a trustee did in fact act upon the advice of an independent adviser, there was a presumption that the transaction was unobjectionable, even if the trustee himself was in possession of inside information relevant to the transaction. It would now, presumably, be open to a trustee in such circumstances to argue that the transaction would have taken place in any case on the basis of independent professional advice. In the final analysis this is a question of fact.

There are also specific defences in relation to the offence of disclosing information. Firstly, an individual is entitled to a defence if he shows that he did not, at the time he disclosed the information, expect any person, because of the disclosure, to deal in the securities on a regulated market, or through or with a professional intermediary (s. 53(3)(a)). Secondly, he is entitled to be acquitted if he proves that although he has such an expectation, at the time of the disclosure, he did not expect the dealing to result in a profit, or avoid a loss, attributable to the fact that the information was price-sensitive information in relation to the securities (s. 53(3)(b)). It is noteworthy that in both cases the defence need not establish that the expectation was reasonable. Furthermore, it must also be borne in mind that no offence is committed in the first place if the disclosure was in the proper performance of the insider's office, profession or employment.

In addition to these rather general defences a number of special defences are set out in Sch. 1 to the Act. The Treasury is empowered by s. 53(5) to amend Sch. 1 by statutory instrument. There are three special defences relating to the dealing and encouragement offences in Sch. 1, which are given effect to by virtue of s. 53(4). The three defences relate to market makers, stabilisation and to market information. It has long been recognised that there are quite proper and necessary operations and practices in the securities market which might be unnecessarily inhibited, or even outlawed by the strict application of anti-insider dealing laws. The special defence for market makers operates where a market maker can show that he acted in good faith, in the course of his business as a market maker, or in the course of his employment in the business of a market maker. A market maker is defined in para. 1(2) of Sch. 1 to the Act as a person who holds himself out, at all times, in compliance with the rules of a regulated market or an international securities self-regulating organisation approved by the Treasury under the *Financial Services Act* 1986, as willing to acquire or dispose of securities, and is recognised as doing so under the relevant rules.

The defence relating to stabilisation is available only if the rules promulgated by the Securities and Investments Board under s. 48 of the *Financial Services Act* 1986 are complied with. Basically, if a manager of an issue of securities complies with these rules in seeking to stabilise or maintain the market price of the securities he will be entitled to a defence to any charge under Pt. V of the 1993 Act. As with the other defences it is for the defendant to show due compliance.

The wider 'market' defence which does not depend upon the status of the defendant relates to what is described in the schedule as market information. An individual will have a defence to any charge of insider dealing if he shows that the information which he had was market information, and that it was reasonable for an individual in his position to have acted as he did, despite having the information as an insider at the material time. Market information is information relating to activities in the market which will themselves impact on the market, or knowledge that their impending occurrence will of itself have a measurable impact on price. Typically it is knowledge that a significant transaction is about to take place in securities or that a particular security is about to be 'written up' by a financial journalist. Market information is defined extensively albeit in broad terms in the 1993 Act. Paragraph 4 of Sch. 1 provides that market information is information consisting of one or more of the following facts:

(1) securities of a particular kind have been or are to be acquired or disposed of, or that their acquisition or disposal is under consideration or the subject of negotiation;

(2) securities of a particular kind have not been or are not to be acquired or disposed of;

(3) the number of securities acquired or disposed of or to be acquired or disposed of or whose acquisition or disposal is under consideration or the subject of negotiation;

(4) the price or range of prices at which securities have been or are to be acquired or disposed of or the price or range of prices at which securities whose acquisition or disposal is under consideration or the subject of negotiation may be acquired or disposed of; and

(5) the identity of the persons involved or likely to be involved in any capacity in an acquisition or disposal.

It is important to appreciate that this list is exhaustive as to the type of market information which will come within the terms of the special defence. The defence is limited to information that someone acquiring or disposing of securities may acquire as an inevitable consequence of the activities in question. The Act provides that in deciding whether it is reasonable for an individual to do any act, despite being in possession of market information at the material time, the content of the information, the circumstances in which he first had the information, and in what capacity, and the capacity in which he now acts, are to be taken into account.

An additional defence is provided in regard to the use of market information, where an individual shows that he acted in connection with an acquisition or disposal, which was under consideration or the subject of negotiation, with a

¶617

view to facilitating the accomplishment of the acquisition or disposal and the information arose directly out of his involvement (Sch. 1, para. 3). This would seem to provide a defence to, for example, an institutional shareholder who having decided to enter into a series of transactions which would affect the market commences its programme without making a public announcement. This particular defence is not conditional, as are the others in regard to the use of market information, on the individual acting reasonably. There has long been discussion as to whether an individual's own intentions should constitute inside information in certain circumstances, but the general view has been that it would be wrong and possibly against the interests of the market to invoke the criminal law in regard to such conduct.

¶618 Enforcement

Perhaps one of the most telling criticisms of the regime introduced by the *Financial Services Act* 1986 is that too little attention was given to the issue of enforcement. Of course, in this context enforcement means rather more than simply investigating and prosecuting those who offend the various rules. In the context of securities regulation, effective enforcement necessitates a proactive stance much in the same way as prudential supervision of the banking sector. In regard specifically to insider dealing it has long been recognised that the problem needs to be addressed at a number of levels and to place reliance simply on the traditional criminal law is unlikely to achieve impressive results. Thus, as has been seen, emphasis was placed on prompt reporting of insider transactions and the development of compliance and in-house procedures designed to control and monitor potentially objectionable transactions.

Most developed markets also operate sophisticated monitoring and stock watch programmes which attempt to identify unusual and suspicious movements and enable the regulators to initiate appropriate action. Of course, these programmes are interfaced with others designed to ensure proper disclosure of information by issuers. It is beyond the scope of this chapter to discuss disclosure, but reference should be made in particular to the *Traded Securities (Disclosure) Regulations* 1994 (SI 1994/188) and *Guidance on the Dissemination of Price-Sensitive Information* (1994) issued by the London Stock Exchange.

Whilst special investigatory provisions, akin to those relating to the inspection of companies' affairs under the general Companies Acts, were thought necessary to assist in policing the statutory reporting obligations on directors and their spouses, it was not thought necessary or for that matter desirable to introduce similar powers for policing the substantive offence of insider dealing created in 1980, until the *Financial Services Act* 1986. See s. 446 of the *Companies Act* 1985, and B Rider *Insider Trading* (1983) Jordans. Sections 177 and 178 of the Financial Services Act provide for the appointment

¶618

of inspectors armed with full inquisitorial powers akin to ordinary Companies Acts inspectors, to inquire into suspected cases of insider abuse. Of course, in so far as such inquiries are specifically designed to ascertain whether a prosecutable offence has been committed they are rather more like an exercise of powers by the director of the Serious Fraud Office under s. 2 of the *Criminal Justice Act* 1987 than an ordinary inspection.

Under s. 177(1) of the Financial Services Act, if it appears to the Secretary of State that there are circumstances suggesting that an offence has been committed under Pt. V of the *Criminal Justice Act* 1993, he may appoint one or more inspectors to carry out 'such investigations as are requisite to establish whether or not any such contravention has occurred' and to report the results to him. Traditionally, inspectors appointed under the provisions in the Companies Act have been Queen's Counsel and senior chartered accountants in private practice. In recent years, however, the government has been prepared to appoint – very occasionally – its own officials and even more rarely members of the Stock Exchange. It is probable that under these provisions the DTI will be far more willing to appoint its own officials and those of the various self-regulatory authorities. This would be both sensible and much more effective.

If the inspectors consider that any person is or may be able to give information concerning any such offence they may require that person to produce any documents in his possession or control relating to the issuer of the relevant securities or its securities, to attend before them and to give them all other assistance which 'he is reasonably able to give' in regard to the investigation. Inspectors may administer oaths and examine any such person under oath. A statement made by a person in compliance with a request made under this section can be used in evidence against him. Under s. 177(7) of the Financial Services Act it is expressly provided that information that is subject to legal professional privilege cannot be demanded by the inspectors. Furthermore, under s. 177(8) banks need not disclose confidential information unless required by the Secretary of State. It remains to be seen how often inspectors will seek to utilise this power, and how willing the Treasury will be to sanction it.

¶619   Penalties for non-cooperation

Section 178(2) of the Financial Services Act imposes penalties in case of failure to comply with a request for assistance or for information by an inspector. Where there is a refusal to cooperate, the inspectors are empowered to certify this to the court and the court is empowered to inquire into the matter. If after hearing evidence from both parties, the court is of the opinion that the refusal to cooperate is unreasonable, it may punish the person concerned as if he stood guilty of contempt (s. 178(2)(a)). The court may also direct that the Secretary of

State can exercise his powers under s. 178 (s. 178(2)(b)). Section 178(2) also provides, most importantly, that the court may so direct, notwithstanding that the offender is not within the jurisdiction, if the court is satisfied that he was notified of his right to appear before the court and the powers available under this section.

The courts, recognising the seriousness of insider dealing cases, have been prepared to interpret the test of reasonableness in refusing to co-operate with inspectors both robustly and in a practical manner. In *Re an Inquiry under the Company Securities (Insider Dealing) Act 1985*, Mr Jeremy Warner, a financial journalist, refused to identify his sources for two articles that he had written accurately predicting how two cases that had been referred to the Monopolies and Mergers Commission would be dealt with. These articles appeared prior to any public announcement by the DTI or Office of Fair Trading. The inspectors had been appointed to inquire into suspected instances of insider abuse, possibly involving public officials. At first instance, (1987) 3 BCC 195, Hoffmann J, whilst accepting the seriousness of the crimes under investigation by the inspectors, accepted Mr Warner's argument that the generally accepted public interest in protecting journalists' sources and now recognised in s. 10 of the *Contempt of Court Act* 1981, would be outweighed where disclosure was shown to be necessary for the prevention of a specific crime. It was not enough, in Hoffmann J's opinion, for the inspectors to show that disclosure would have been expedient, but rather they had to show that it was probable that in the absence of disclosure further crimes were likely to be committed. The court decided that the inspectors had not surmounted this hurdle. The House of Lords and the Court of Appeal ([1988] AC 660; (1988) 4 BCC 35 and (1987) 3 BCC 301) disagreed with Hoffmann J and considered that the appropriate standard was whether the information was 'really needed' for the prevention, detection and deterrence of crime. In the present case the inspectors had shown that it was, and accordingly Mr Warner was ordered to comply with their request. When he refused, he was fined £20,000 for contempt.

When the court does direct that the Secretary of State may exercise his powers under s. 178(3) in respect of an authorised person he is empowered by service of notice, to cancel any authorisation after the expiry of a specified period. He may also disqualify that person from becoming authorised to carry on investment business after the expiry of a specified period. Restrictions may also be imposed on any authorisation in respect of investment business during that specified period to the performance of contracts entered into before the notice comes into force. The Secretary of State may also prohibit a person from entering into transactions of a specified kind, or entering into them except in specified circumstances, or to a specified extent. Furthermore, that person may be prohibited from soliciting business from persons of a specified kind or otherwise than from such persons or from carrying on business of a specified kind or otherwise than in a specified manner. The period specified in the Secretary of State's notice must be such as appears to the Secretary of State reasonable to enable the person concerned to complete the performance of the contracts in question and to terminate such of them as are of a continuing nature before the notice comes into force.

When the court gives a direction under s. 178(2)(b) in regard to a person who is unauthorised, the Secretary of State is empowered under s. 178(5) to direct that any authorised person who knowingly transacts investment business of a specified kind or in specified circumstances, or to a specified extent, with or on behalf of that unauthorised person shall be treated as being in breach of the rules made under Pt. I, Ch. V of the Financial Services Act or, in the case of a person who is authorised by virtue of his membership of a recognised self-regulating organisation or recognised professional body, the rules of that authority.

The Secretary of State may revoke a notice at any time if it appears to him that the person concerned has agreed to comply with the request in question. Revocation of such a notice does not revive authorisation except where, apart from the effect of the notice, the person concerned would be authorised by virtue of his membership of an SRO or RPB. Of course, after revocation the person concerned can apply for re-authorisation. An obligation is placed on the Secretary of State to serve copies of his notices on the designated agency and other self-regulatory authorities where the person concerned falls under their jurisdiction, or did before service of his notice.

Section 178(6) of the Financial Services Act provides that a person who is asked to provide information or furnish a document shall not be taken to have a reasonable excuse for refusing to co-operate where the suspected offence relates to dealing by him on the instructions of, or for the account of, another person simply because at the time of his refusal he did not know the identity of that other person. In addition it is not a reasonable excuse that he was subject to the law of another jurisdiction prohibiting him from disclosing information relating to that transaction without the consent of that other person if he might have obtained that consent or obtained exemption from that law. Numerous investigations into suspected cases of insider dealing by official as well as self-regulatory authorities have been frustrated by agents simply asserting that they are unaware of the true identity of their principal.

Of course, the obligation to 'know your customer' has implications beyond that of assisting in enforcement (s. 178(2)(b)). It has proved to be a useful device in the US, however, as it places an obligation upon a person within jurisdiction who is amenable to not only the law but also a variety of disciplinary and professional pressures to co-operate in such an inquiry. It should be noted, of course, that the agent need not know the ultimate customer or beneficiary. In practice it is common to use foreign banks or other intermediaries and the implicit obligation in this section to 'know your client' is discharged by simply disclosing who instructed the transaction. Where this person is overseas it is going to be as difficult as it always has been for the investigator to determine whether the information with which he has been provided is accurate and exactly what is the status of that other person.

It has also been a convenient excuse for financial intermediaries simply to assert against a request for information concerning a party in another jurisdiction that the laws of that country or territory prohibit the disclosure of such information. Invariably the laws of that other jurisdiction are not as restrictive as they are assumed to be. The cost and practical difficulties involved in attempting to force the issue, however, often persuade the investigator to abandon that line of inquiry. Section 178(6)(b) is a most useful device. It would seem from the wording of this provision which is not entirely unambiguous, that such an agent will now have to show that he actually attempted to secure authority, according to the relevant foreign law, for the disclosure of the information or documents in question before he can be credited with a justified excuse for not cooperating with the inspectors. This may well encourage financial intermediaries to obtain from overseas clients advance authority to disclose relevant information to such an inquiry, as is now the practice in Switzerland and certain other jurisdictions.

It is provided in s. 178(10) that the functions of the Secretary of State under this section may be transferred to a self-regulatory authority under s. 114. It is also provided, however, that the Secretary of State is to retain a concurrent jurisdiction and that any exercise of these powers by the designated agency is subject to such conditions or restrictions as the Secretary of State may impose. It is important to note that this provision applies only to the various powers under s. 178 where there has been a failure on the part of a person to cooperate with an inspector appointed by the Secretary of State. The Secretary of State cannot designate the power to appoint inspectors.

Whilst a number of investigations have been ordered and on the whole the conviction rate for insider abuse is no less encouraging than in other areas of economic crime, it is the view of many that the blunderbuss of the criminal law is not always cost effective or appropriate. See generally *'Company investigations', Third Report of the Select Committee of the House of Commons on Trade and Industry* (1990) and J Naylor, 'The use of criminal sanctions by UK and US authorities for insider trading', (1990) *11 Co Law 53*. Thus, there is discussion about relying rather more on administrative action, disciplinary procedures and even the introduction of civil penalties.

¶620   Conclusion

There is little doubt that the efficacy of insider dealing regulation within a given system is often seen as an appropriate test of that system's ability to promote and protect investors. Thus, to a very large degree the 'tail has wagged the dog' and the debate on the suitability and efficiency of regulation has become side-tracked. This is perhaps understandable given the nature of insider abuse which has been described as one of the most unacceptable warts on the ugly face of capitalism and in so far as it illustrates by its very name and substance the taking advantage of inequalities in the market it is almost the capitalist crime, par excellence.

Whether, however, all the time and trouble that has been taken in recent years to fashion both preventive and responsible devices to control insider abuse are worth it remains to be seen. In the view of the present writer there are instances of insider abuse, particularly where concerted and deliberate attempts have been made to appropriate price-sensitive information and then deploy it to spectacular effect, which have to be controlled. Insider trading has become an attractive activity for organised and serious criminals, given the high rewards, and relatively small risk of effective action against them or their profits. See B Rider, 'The Financial World at Risk', 8 *Managerial Auditing Journal* (1993) 3 and B Rider, *Organised Crime* (1994) House of Commons Home Office Committee. However, it seems that most systems of regulation are ineffective against such operations and there remains the danger that it is only the hapless, the 'shopped' and the witless that stand any real chance of ending up in court. One answer, but obviously not the only one, is to devote even more attention to the issue and control of tentative information through timely disclosure policies. But a search for a panacea to the problem is a search in vain.

7 City Fraud

¶701 Investor protection

It has long been recognised in Britain that one of the most significant justifications for regulation in the financial services industry is the protection of investors. This was emphasised by Professor LCB Gower in his review of investor protection (¶119) and more recently by the SIB in its report on the *Regulation of the United Kingdom Equity Markets* (June 1995). However, whilst references to the importance of ensuring adequate levels of investor protection are frequently encountered, even Professor Gower in his reports did not seek to set out exactly what he thought the protection of investors actually encompasses.

Much will depend upon the underlying philosophy of those seeking to set definitional perimeters, and the character and expectations of those investors that it is sought to bring within the fold. For example, there has been discussion as to whether the same sort of protection should be afforded to those who are essentially speculators as that provided to small private investors with relatively long-term aspirations in regard to their investments. Indeed, much criticism has been directed at the present legal and regulatory regime on the basis that it does not seek to significantly differentiate between small private investors and professional investors. Of course, distinctions have been made between those investors with different expectations of the market, at the self-regulatory level and to some extent now in legislation, such as, for example s. 62A of the Financial Services Act. Generally speaking, however, the view is taken that all investors, no matter what their character and aspirations, should be entitled to protection against certain risks. These would certainly include the risk of being defrauded.

However, it is not always the case that all investors can reasonably expect or require the same degree of care and skill to be shown in the advancement of their interests. As a general proposition the larger and more well resourced the investor, the less reasonable it may be for him to rely upon the 'advice' of another including his professional advisers. For example, there have been cases in Britain and for that matter elsewhere, where the courts have refused to hold a stockbroker to be under a duty of care to his client, on the basis that given the relationship of the parties it was not reasonable for one to expect that the other was under such a duty. In cases where such a duty has arisen, the courts have been very willing to examine carefully how reasonable it was, on the particular facts, for the individual concerned to rely upon the person in question. In one unreported decision of Foster J (*Briggs v Gunner*, Chancery Division, 16 January 1979, discussed in Rider and Ffrench, *The Regulation of Insider Trading* (1979) Macmillan, p. 441), the learned judge thought that it was unreasonable for an investor who was a practising solicitor to rely upon the advice of his stockbroker, who claimed that he had access to inside information. Where a duty of care does arise, then it may well be that by virtue of the Core Rules (i.e. r. 16), or even the general law, that the advice must be suitable to the circumstances and aspirations of the person to whom the duty is owed. This is an example of the law seeking to 'accommodate' the subjective characteristics of the investor, although it must be remembered that the determination as to whether the advice in question was reasonable or not remains wholly objective.

¶702 The prevention of fraud

Traditionally, English securities law has been primarily if not exclusively concerned with protecting investors against fraud. But it would be wrong to think that the law sought to do this only through the imposition of liability under the criminal law. Some of the earliest laws, as we have seen in Ch. 1, sought to establish a regulated environment into which only those who were regarded as sound and honest could enter as professional intermediaries. These early laws may well have had rather more to do with raising revenue and promoting restrictive practices, than imposing a 'fit and proper' standard, but nonetheless they do indicate, at least an awareness of the need to throw the regulatory net somewhat wider than the control of criminal fraud.

However, even if the purpose of regulation is simply to prevent and control fraud, much will depend upon what is meant by the term. The courts and Parliament have resolutely refused to define fraud in English law, unlike in many other countries. This has been largely to prevent attempts at circumvention. On the other hand, it would be misguided to perceive the concept of fraud as merely a protean one which can be drawn down and modelled by the courts or regulators so as to bring within the legal net conduct which has hitherto been considered unobjectionable. Fraud will inevitably require the elements of subjective dishonesty, misrepresentation and legally recognised harm. The law is sufficiently flexible to include within the notion of harm not only deprivations of property, but also, for example, the exercise of an official discretion induced on the basis of a dishonest misrepresentation. In some jurisdictions even conduct such as insider dealing is considered to be fraud. However, it is hard to justify such a categorisation according to English law.

Thus, the protection of investors certainly involves preventing and controlling fraud against investors, whether they be speculators, institutional investors or small private investors. The dishonesty of the perpetrator's design renders the particular circumstances of his victim irrelevant in terms of law, albeit perhaps not in terms of response. However, what else is involved in protecting investors? It would seem that preventing and controlling insider dealing is today, also considered to be part and parcel of protecting investors. Indeed, the conventional justification for attempting to discourage insider dealing in Britain has been that it undermines public confidence in the integrity of the financial markets. Whether the inhibition and control of money laundering can be viewed in the same light is more debatable.

The dangers presented by the laundering of the proceeds of serious crime through the facilities of the exchange are both real and serious. The US Presidential Commission on Organised Crime reported in 1984 that there is no financial institution or intermediary that is safe from the risk of becoming involved in a money laundering operation at some stage or other in the laundering cycle. More recently evidence submitted to the Home Affairs Select Committee of the House of Commons during its hearings on organised crime in Britain in the Spring 1994 indicates that the problem has not gone away, but has rather become more significant particularly in the context of the UK. It is certainly the view of the National Criminal Intelligence Service (NCIS) that City institutions are at risk and it would be dangerous for any organisation that seeks to offer services to the financial community not to have regard to this threat. (*Organised Crime, Minutes of Evidence and Memoranda*, Home Affairs Committee, 16 November 1994 HMSO and *Organised Crime, Third Report*, Home Affairs Committee, 17 July 1995, HMSO).

The protection of investors in addition to requiring action against fraudsters, insider dealers and money launderers, also requires action against those involved in abusive trading and manipulation practices. As we have seen, some of the earliest laws were directed at conduct which sought to interfere with the proper operation of supply and demand on public markets (see ¶101). Abusive trading and manipulation of prices on the market whilst directly undermining fairness and, thus, confidence in the integrity of the markets may also impact adversely on those in the market or who have an interest in it. Abusive trading can take many forms, some of which, but certainly not all, may amount to manipulation. Of course, in so far as terminology is not always precise, and the stratagems of those who wish to profit at the market's expense often diverse, it is not uncommon to find conduct of a manipulative nature, which involves outright fraud as well as insider dealing. Indeed, on narrow markets and developing markets, it is rather more common to find primary insiders engaging in insider manipulation rather than traditional insider dealing on the basis of inside information. It is said, particularly in the USA, that one of the main justifications for anti-insider dealing regulation is that it discourages and penalises insiders manipulating corporate disclosure so that they can take advantage of the resulting informational imbalances.

Abusive trading may involve transactions which are, for example, in breach of the provisions of the City Code on Takeovers and Mergers or the Substantial Acquisitions Rules, (SARs). Such breaches may or may not involve breaches of the law as well. For example, in many instances where there is a breach of the concert party provisions in the Code, there will also be a breach of the aggregated reporting obligations on substantial shareholders under Pt. VI of the *Companies Act* 1985. However, there may well be situations where transactions take place which are objectionable under the Code or SARs, but which do not involve the commission of a specific criminal offence. For example, under the Code it is objectionable for transactions to take place in a company's shares or assets without the approval of the shareholders, which might frustrate a takeover bid. Such 'defensive tactics' may involve violations of the spirit or specific rules of the Code, but not amount to conduct which could be considered illegal or for that matter unlawful. Transactions which are in breach of, for example, the duties imposed on directors under the general law, might be considered unlawful, but might also be susceptible to ratification. Until such takes place it would be appropriate to categorise these as abusive. Hence, investor protection involves giving attention to matters which are not always illegal and unlawful in the black and white sense of the criminal law.

¶703   False markets

Recognition that certain forms of conduct can undermine and damage the proper and orderly function of markets has long been chronicled. In England there were common law offences of 'forestalling, regrating and cornering' as early as the eleventh century. These were for a time put into statutory form and today survive to some degree within the scope of conspiracy to defraud. However, these affairs were rarely employed and although there were many scandals during the eighteenth and nineteenth centuries the market, which was primarily centred on the London Stock Exchange, remained subject to only essentially self-regulatory procedures. A major exception was in the area of the promotion of new issues, an area of activity particularly susceptible to fraudulent schemes. By the end of the nineteenth century the law imposed on those promoting companies and floating off their shares to the public reasonably onerous disclosure obligations and regarded the deliberate non-disclosure of material facts as fraud.

Whilst the Royal Commission on The London Stock Exchange (see ¶109), sitting under Lord Penzance, reported in 1876 that more effective action was required against fraudulent practices on the stock market, very little happened until the 1930s when concern over abusive practices, in regard to collective investment schemes and share-hawking, led to the appointment of two government committees. Their reports led to the enactment of the *Prevention of Fraud (Investments) Act* 1939 which was slightly amended and re-enacted in 1958. This Act in large measure exemplified the anti-fraud stance of traditional 'Blue Sky' laws. Of particular importance in addressing abusive conduct, was s. 13(1) of the Act. This made it a serious criminal offence to induce an investment transaction by making a false statement either dishonestly or recklessly, or by dishonestly concealing a material fact. This provision, with slight amendments, is now s. 47(1) of the FSA 1986. Whilst a few prosecutions were brought under s. 13(1) for inducing investment transactions by making a fraudulent misrepresentation, there was little attempt to address the problem of creating a false impression by manipulative conduct in the markets. This was left, prior to the enactment of the *Financial Services Act* 1986, and in particular s. 47(2), to the general criminal law and to various self-regulatory procedures, such as the Rules and Regulations of The Stock Exchange and the City Code on Takeovers and Mergers – in so far as they addressed the creation and promotion of false markets. Thus, statutory control of manipulative practices as opposed to the inducement of transactions by fraudulent misrepresentations is in Britain a relatively new development. It follows that our jurisprudence in England on such matters is virtually nonexistent and our experience of enforcement and to some degree compliance limited.

¶704   The common law

The most significant area of law in England in regard to manipulation was, prior to the enactment of s. 47(2), the common law. The judiciary have rarely shown much sympathy for those involved in manipulating public markets. For example, in the case of *Rubery v Grant* (1872) XIII LR 443, Sir Robert Malins VC, considered that to allege that a person was a member of a share rigging syndicate amounted to an allegation that they were dishonest. He added, 'going into the market pretending to buy shares by a person whom you put forward to buy them, who is not really buying them, but only pretending to buy them, in order that they may be quoted in the public papers as bearing a premium, which premium is never paid – is one of the most dishonest practices to which men can possibly resort'. The learned judge added 'there is a class of people who think it is a legitimate mode of making money; but if they would only examine it for a moment they would see that a more abominable fraud, and one more difficult of detection, cannot be found'.

Perhaps the first English case to be decided by the English Courts, or at least reported, is that of *Rex v de Berenger*, 105 Eng Rep 536 (KB 1814). This case involved one of the most audacious frauds ever perpetrated on a stock market. Britain had been at war with France for over two years and the price of British Government stock was naturally depressed. The conspirators sort to raise the price of stock on the London Stock Exchange enabling them to dump securities that they had already acquired, by spreading rumours that the Emperor Napoleon had been killed and that peace was certain. The London Stock Exchange appointed a committee of inquiry which discovered the relevant facts. De Berenger and seven others were indicted of –

> 'unlawfully contriving by false reports, rumours, acts and contrivances, to induce the subjects of the King to believe that a peace would soon be made ... thereby to occasion without any just or true cause a great increase and rise of the public government funds and the Government securities of the Kingdom ... with a wicked intention thereby to injure and aggrieve all the subjects of the King who should, on the 21 February, purchase or buy any part or parts, share or shares of and in said public Government funds and other Government securities.'

The defendants contended that seeking to raise the price of securities in the market was not of itself a crime, and that there was no criminal conspiracy without some allegation that they had intended to cheat certain investors, or cause harm to the Government. Indeed, it was argued that it was in the Government's interest that the price of its securities should be kept high.

The court, however, had little sympathy for such arguments and held that it was not necessary for the Crown to allege, let alone prove, that any one had in fact been misled and injured. Both the means used, and the object of the enterprise were wrong. The public had a right to expect that the market had not been interfered with by wrongful means. Lord Ellenborough stated:

> 'A public mischief is stated as the object of this conspiracy; the conspiracy is by false rumours to raise the price of the public funds and securities; and the crime lies in the act of conspiracy and combination to effect that purpose, and would have been complete although it had not been pursued to its consequences, or the parties had not been able to carry it into effect. The purpose itself is mischievous, it strikes at the price of a vendible commodity in the market, and if it gives a fictitious price, by means of false rumours, it is a fraud levelled against all the public, for it is against all such as may possibly have any thing to do with the funds on that particular day. The excuse is, that it was impossible that they should have known, and if it were possible, the multitude would be an excuse in point of law. But the statement is wholly unnecessary, the conspiracy being complete independently of any persons being purchasers. I have no doubt it must be so considered in law according to the cases'.

The decision in *de Berenger* does not address directly, however, the issue as to whether it is an indictable conspiracy, to interfere with the proper operation of the markets, not through the circulation of false rumours and information, but by a course of dealing. Of course, under the ordinary law it is possible to make a statement by word or by conduct, so as a matter of principle manipulative conduct could be regarded as constituting a false and misleading representation. Nonetheless, in *de Berenger*, one of the learned judges said:

'... the raising or lowering the price of the public funds is not per se a crime. A man may have occasion to sell out a large sum, which may have the effect of depressing the price of stocks, or may buy in a large sum, and thereby raise the price on a particular day, and yet he will be guilty of no offence. But if a number of persons conspire by false rumours to raise the funds on a particular day, that is an offence; and the offence is, not in raising the funds simply, but in conspiring by false rumours to raise them on that particular day'.

In a subsequent civil case involving an action for rescission against a stockbroker, who had agreed to purchase shares on the Stock Exchange on behalf of the plaintiff, for the sole purpose of creating trading on the market at a premium in order to create the impression that there was a thriving market, and thereby induce other investors to purchase, in denying rescission the court expressed the view that the relevant agreement amounted to a criminal conspiracy to defraud the public. (*Scott v Brown, Doering, McNab & Co*, 1892 QB 724.) The view was expressed by Lopes LJ that there is 'no substantial distinction between false rumours and false and fictitious acts'.

¶705 The fair price

On the other hand it is also clear that not every concerted intervention into the market to hold a price will be considered manipulative. In *Sanderson & Levi v British Westralian Mine & Share Corporation*, 43 Solicitors Journal 45 (QB 1898) affirmed *London Times*, 19 July 1899, a contract was enforced pursuant to which a jobber on the Stock Exchange had made a market at a fair price, whilst the defendant distributed a substantial block of shares. In the rather less authoritative decision in *Landon v Beiorley* 10 LT 505 (Ex 1848), where a new trial was ordered (see 13 LT 122 (Ex 1849)), the court also denied rescission of an allotment, on the basis that the pegging of share prices during the launch of the company was to prevent 'undue depreciation below their actual worth'.

Thus, it is clear on the English authorities, that there is a distinction between manipulation and what we describe today as stabilisation. It is not without interest, however, that the courts of other jurisdictions have not always been prepared to accept such a distinction. For example, in *Harper v Crenshaw* 82 F.2d 845 (DC cir. 1936) the US Court of Appeals for the District of Columbia went further than the English Court of Appeal in *Scott v Brown* , and held that an agreement to stabilise the price of shares whilst a large block of shares was brought on to the market, was illegal and unenforceable. There was no evidence that the agreement sought to create a fictitious price for the securities in question, or to raise the price higher than the real value of the relevant securities. In *Bigelow v Oglesby* 303 Ill. App. 27, 36, 23 NE 2d 382 (1939) an appellate court in Illinois declined to enforce a syndicate agreement among underwriters because it contained what was then a standard clause for stabilisation. The court distinguished the English case of *Sanderson & Levi* (supra) on the basis that in the present case the agreement was to stabilise the price of the relevant shares at a level which had not already been determined by the market itself.

¶706   Conspiracy

It is important to remember when considering these authorities that the law might not necessarily be the same in the case of a criminal and a civil conspiracy, and different considerations apply as to whether the persons concerned are being prosecuted for a criminal offence, or are seeking to enforce an agreement inter-party, or are being sued before the civil courts by a innocent third party. Unfortunately, the judges in categorising certain conduct as illegal do not always observe these distinctions. It would seem that a conspiracy to influence the price of shares or other securities on a market by making false statements, or by engaging in purposeful conduct, such as a series of transactions with the intention of misleading the market, will be a conspiracy at criminal law. Conspiracy to create a public mischief no longer exists, but the facts in the relevant cases would today fall within the scope of conspiracy to defraud. Generally speaking, however, it would be appropriate for the prosecution to allege a statutory conspiracy to breach either s. 47(1) or s. 47(2) of the FSA 1986. (See *R v Cooke* (1986) AC 909 modifying the strict rule in *R v Ayres* (1984) AC 447 to the effect that a conspiracy to defraud could not be charged where a substantive offence could be alleged.)

Considerable discussion has taken place over the years as to the proper scope of conspiracy in the criminal law. The Law Commission's Working Party published a consultation document in 1973 (*Working Paper No 50, Inchoate Offences*) in which it concluded that the crime of conspiracy should be confined to an agreement to commit a specific offence. In other words, the mere agreement to engage in a course of conduct, no matter how malicious, should not of itself constitute a crime, unless the conduct in question was itself a specific offence. The Law Commission took the view, however, that there were situations covered by the crime of conspiracy to defraud which might not be susceptible to this approach, (see *Law Commission Working Paper 56, Conspiracy to Defraud*).

Section 1 of the *Criminal Law Act* 1977 enacted a statutory offence of conspiracy to replace the common law offence of conspiracy. This reflected the Law Commission's view that the crime of conspiracy should be limited to circumstances where the object of the agreement is to commit an act which would itself be a substantive offence known already to the criminal law. However, s. 5(2) of the Act excepted the common law offence of conspiracy to defraud which remains outside s. 1. Discussion has taken place as to whether conspiracy to defraud should remain an exception to the general rule. The Law Commission in its report *Criminal Law: Conspiracy to Defraud* (1994) HMSO takes the view that it still has a role to play. This is illustrated in the recent case of *The Queen v Adams* (1995) 1 WLR 52. The Privy Council was of the opinion that an agreement to conceal transactions in regard to which there was a fiduciary duty of disclosure, so that those responsible might avoid being called to account for their unauthorised profits, amounted to an indictable conspiracy to defraud.

¶707   Enforcing the bargain

The agreement between the parties to the conspiracy, would generally be unenforceable before the civil courts as being contrary to public policy. Indeed, Sir Frederick Pollack in an article published in the Law Quarterly Review in 1893 (9 LQR 105 (1893)), referring to the case of *Scott v Brown* in which an attempt was made to enforce such an agreement, described it as reminiscent of the 'well known legal legend ... of a highwayman coming into equity for an account against his partner'. Indeed, some American courts have taken this approach quite far and refused to enforce agreements involving the touting of shares, such as in *Ridgely v Keene* 134 AD 647, 119 NYS 451 (2d dept.1875). In England the courts have certainly declined to allow a wrongdoer to enforce such a transaction against the other party, when that party is innocent and where both parties are involved in the wrongdoing. The general rule is that the courts should remain aloof. Losses and profits remain where they fall.

In a case involving insider dealing Knox J, despite a statutory provision to the effect that breach of the then insider dealing law did not render the relevant contract void or voidable, declined to lend the court's support to the enforcement of a partially completed transaction. (*Chase Manhattan Equities Ltd v Goodman* (1991)BCLC 897). It has long been the English law that an innocent party can seek rescission or cancellation of a fraudulent transaction and the courts will not be keen to allow formalities or technical arguments to stand in the victim's path, see *Gillett v Peppercorne* (1840) 3 Beav 81. It is rather less likely that the courts would be prepared to see such an agreement enforced rather than rescinded by an innocent party. This is particularly so when the purpose of the agreement is to achieve something which is contrary to the public interest. An innocent party in such circumstances would generally have other remedies than those based on the relevant agreement. It is unclear to what extent third parties who have been damnified by manipulative practices can pursue those responsible in the civil courts. Where a market has been manipulated and a false price achieved, all those who come to the market or rely upon the market at the relevant time are harmed. In the leading US case of *US v Brown*, at first instance, Judge Woolsey, referring to the English cases, observed 'when an outsider, a member of the public, reads the price quotations of a stock listed on an exchange, he is justified in supposing that the quoted price is an appraisal of the value of the stock due to a series of actual sales between various persons dealing at arm's length in a free and open market on the exchange, and so represents a true chancering of the market value of that stock thereon under the process of attrition due to supply operating against demand' (5 F. Supp. 81 at 85 (SDNY 1933). In *Scott v Brown*, there is a statement to the effect that a third party who was induced to buy shares with inflated prices from the manipulators may be able to sue them for their loss.

Whilst in theory and principle there is some justification for according to all those who have suffered loss as a result of the fraudulent conduct a remedy, it remains to be seen whether those who cannot establish a contractual or special relationship with the manipulators can recover. Where such a relationship can be established, third parties have been allowed to sue for compensation, (see *Barry v Croskey* (1861) 2 J. & H. 1, 70 Eng rep 945). However, outside such relationships the courts have shown considerable reluctance to find sufficient reliance and causation, (see for example, *Salaman v Warner* 64 LTR (NS) 598 7 TLR 431 (QB 1891) affirmed 65 LTR (NS) 132). By the same token the courts have been very reluctant to permit market participants to recover for losses occasioned by their not unreasonably relying upon statements made by auditors of listed companies, which turn out to be negligent. (See *Caparo Industries plc v Dickman* (1990) 2 AC 605.) For similar reasons it is very difficult to see how even a counter party could recover compensation against a person engaging in insider dealing on the market (see generally Rider and Ashe, *Insider Crime* (1993) Jordans).

¶708   Misleading the regulators

Finally, before leaving these cases it is necessary to consider briefly the position where the form of the manipulation is such to persuade the Stock Exchange to take a certain course of action with the result that the relevant market price may be affected. In *R v Aspinall* 1 QBD 730 (1876) affirmed 2 QBD 48 (1876) it was held to be an indictable conspiracy at common law to obtain a listing of securities on the Stock Exchange by falsely representing that the requisite amount of shares had been allotted and amounts paid. It should be noted that it was decided that it was sufficient for the conspiracy to be established that the purpose of the defendants was to mislead the officials of the Stock Exchange into granting a listing and consequently to mislead investors, 'who should thereafter buy and sell the shares of the company, to believe that the company was duly formed and constituted, and had in all respects complied with the rules of the Stock Exchange, so as to have their shares quoted in the official list'. It should be noted that it was not necessary for the prosecution to allege or prove that the purpose was to injure public traders by inducing them to buy shares that were valueless or worth less than they appeared to be. It was sufficient that the defendants had agreed to mislead the officials of the Stock Exchange into granting the company a listing, by making false statements to them. Brett JA was prepared to take judicial notice of that fact that, 'a purchaser of ordinary intelligence' would rely upon the relevant market price as an indication of worth and that he would consider the fact that the relevant security was listed in accordance with the rules of the Stock Exchange gave it a certain value.

It may amount to the crime of conspiracy to defraud, to agree with others to induce by false statements made by word or conduct, a public official to do or not to do an act in the course of his duties. It has been argued that the same rule should apply to, for example, officials of the Panel on Takeovers and Mergers and other self-regulatory authorities. It should also be noted that under s. 200(1) of *Financial Services Act* 1986 it is a criminal offence for anyone who is required to furnish information under the Act or pursuant to some authority derived from it, to make a false or misleading statement. Therefore, misleading an official of the Securities and Investments Board could be a specific offence under this provision. It is less certain that misleading an official of a self-regulatory organisation would be covered, as it is not certain that the information would be required pursuant to an obligation imposed by or under the Financial Services Act.

¶709 Concert parties and nominees

Transparency in the sense of requiring disclosure of transactions and dealings which lend themselves to possible abuse, has long been a characteristic of commercial and corporate legislation in Britain. Thus, there are statutory provisions in the *Companies Act* 1985 requiring directors to disclose their dealings in the shares and other securities of their company and related companies on their own behalf or that of their spouses and infant children (s. 324–329). There are also provisions requiring substantial shareholders and those who acting together in concert, have a substantial interest in a particular company to disclose their holdings and report subsequent transactions. Under s. 199 of the *Companies Act* 1985 a person has a notifiable interest when he is interested in shares in the relevant share capital of a public company, whether listed or not, of an aggregate value equal to, or more than 3 per cent of, the nominal value of that share capital. Relevant share capital is defined in the Act as meaning the company's issued share capital of a class carrying rights to vote in all circumstances in general meetings of the company. Furthermore, a person will be deemed to be so interested in such shares held by a spouse, infant child and trusts and companies which he controls. To address the practice of 'warehousing,' there are 'concert party' provisions in s. 204 of the Act. Under

s. 204 persons will be regarded as acting in concert if there is an agreement or arrangement between them for the acquisition by any one or more of them of interests in shares of a particular public company. The agreement, to activate the section, must impose obligations or restrictions on any one or more of the parties concerning the use, retention or disposal of an interest in shares of the relevant company, acquired in pursuance of the agreement, and an interest being in fact acquired by any one or more of those persons. In such cases the holdings of each member of the concert party are aggregated and the obligation to report the total holding is placed on each individual member of the party.

Although the Act makes non-compliance with these reporting obligations a criminal offence and there are wide ranging investigatory powers, (s. 212–219 and 442–446), in practical terms an individual who is prepared to engage in manipulative conduct is unlikely to be overly concerned about the prospect of a derisory fine. In practice there have been virtually no prosecutions under these provisions (see *Meridian Global Funds Management Asia Ltd v New Zealand Securities Commmission* (1995) 2 BCLC 116 in regard to a prosecution under the differently worded New Zealand provisions, where the Privy Council emphasised the importance of effective timely disclosure of substantial acquisitions), and relatively few examples of action by issuers and the Department of Trade, under these statutory powers, to freeze interests in shares the beneficial ownership of which is uncertain. The obligation to disclose dealings and interests imposed under the companies Acts are mirrored and to some extent extended by various self-regulatory disclosure obligations such as those included in the Listing Rules and Takeover Code.

There are other provisions in the Companies Act relating to disclosure of directors and certain other insiders' interests (s. 317), controlling such persons' involvement with substantial property transactions with the company and related companies, (s. 320–322) and regulating the circumstances when they might receive loans and other financial facilities, (s. 330–344). There are also provisions regulating the circumstances in which companies can become involved directly and otherwise in providing financial assistance in the purchase of their own securities and in buying their own shares, and in reducing capital, (s. 151–169). All these provisions, together with the general law relating to directors' duties are more or less relevant to controlling abuses on the market.

¶710   False statements

Some practices have attracted legislative attention resulting in specific prohibition, rather than merely promoting transparency. Many of these relate to matters which tend to disrupt or undermine confidence in the operation of the markets, or which can facilitate abusive transactions. Perhaps the best example is the outlawing of insider trading which has been discussed in Ch. 6.

The main statutory provisions directed at the control of market abuse in

Britain are contained in s. 47 of the *Financial Services Act* 1986. Section 47(1) renders it a serious criminal offence for anyone to make a misleading statement, promise or forecast so as to induce someone to enter into an investment agreement or to exercise any rights conferred by an investment agreement, or to refrain from doing so. The making of a statement, promise or forecast may take either two forms. First, the making of a statement which the defendant knows to be misleading, false or deceptive, or dishonestly concealing a material fact. Secondly, the reckless making, dishonestly or otherwise, of a statement which is in fact misleading, false or deceptive. In the first situation the prosecution must prove that the person making the statement or concealing the relevant material fact did so dishonestly and was therefore essentially fraudulent. On the other hand, in the second situation dishonesty is not required. Recklessness will be sufficient for criminal liability. Recklessness in this context may mean 'a high degree of negligence without dishonesty' (*R v Bates & Anor* (1952) 2 All ER 842), or a rash statement without any real basis of facts, (*R v Grunwald & Ors* (1963) 1 QB 935). In *R v Caldwell* (1982) AC 341 it was said that if a person fails to address his mind to the possibility that there is an obvious risk that a statement might not be true, he may be considered reckless.

There has been some debate as to what 'dishonest concealment of a material fact' means. It would seem to be the better view that before the defendant can be said to have concealed a fact there must be an independent duty upon him to disclose it. Generally speaking the law of contract does not impose an obligation on one party to a transaction to disclose facts to the other, no matter how material those facts may be, even when it is clear that the other party does not have access to the information in question. There are certain exceptions to the general rule of *caveat emptor* such as where there is a pre-existing fiduciary relationship, but these are narrow and would not normally be present in the context of investment transactions. It has been argued that in cases of extreme self-interest where the circumstances indicate obvious dishonesty on the part of the defendant, a duty of disclosure should arise. There is no authority, however, for such a view. It has also been argued that it cannot be dishonest for a person to refrain from disclosing information which may be confidential to another person. This argument is misconceived as the issue of dishonesty is one of fact for the jury. Nonetheless, unless the defendant can be proved to have been under a duty to disclose the information in question, and few in the market will be under such a duty, then it cannot be said that mere non-disclosure amounts to concealment. It should be noted in this context that it will be rare for an insider to be under any duty to disclose the facts which constitute his inside information. The issuer may be under a duty of timely disclosure, but such duties would hardly ever apply to individuals. Where what is said by what is omitted creates a false impression, the law imposes a duty to correct the half truth. By the same token if later events falsify what has innocently been said before, the law expects the statement to be corrected. In such cases a dishonest failure to correct what has been said might well constitute concealment for the purposes of s. 47(1).

It should be noted that s. 47(1), as its statutory predecessor s. 13 of the *Prevention of Fraud (Investments) Act* 1958, applies whether the relevant investment agreement is to occur on or through the market or is a face to face transaction. The jurisdictional scope of s. 47(1) is wide and it is essentially both a conduct and results offence. Thus, if the statement is made, or the facts are concealed in or from the UK, or the person affected is in the UK, or the agreement is or would be entered into in the UK or the rights are or would be exercised in the UK there will be sufficient jurisdiction for the English courts.

In the context of false and misleading statements it is also helpful to refer to s. 19 of the *Theft Act* 1968. This makes it a serious criminal offence for a person who is or who purports to be an officer of a company to publish or cause to be published a written statement which he knows is misleading false or deceptive in a material particular with the intention of deceiving the shareholders or creditors of the company about its affairs.

¶711 Other crimes

There are a number of other offences that to a greater or lesser extent may be relevant in controlling abusive conduct in the financial sector. It may well be possible to establish that what has occurred amounts to theft, contrary to s. 1 of the *Theft Act* 1968, although there would appear to be a reluctance on the part of prosecutors and in particular regulators to label misconduct as simple theft! (But see *R v Clowes (No. 2)* (1994) 2 All ER 316. Apart from the more usual offences associated with forgery, uttering false documents and false accounting, it must be remembered that there are numerous offences of a more specific nature in the Companies Acts, insolvency legislation, banking laws and, of course, tax laws, (see generally, Smith A, *Property Offences* (1994) Sweet & Maxwell). Perhaps the most significant offences in practice are, however, those associated with obtaining property or services by deception. Mention has already been made of conspiracy to defraud (see also *Criminal Law, Conspiracy to Defraud*, Law Commission, Law Cons No. 228 (1994) HMSO) but it will generally be preferable to charge a conspiracy to commit a specific statutory offence, and the most usual one will be that of obtaining property by deception, contrary to s. 15 of the *Theft Act* 1968. The importance of this particular offence is illustrated in regard to the practice of 'stagging' – which has manifested itself in the UK, perhaps rather more than in other developed markets. This practice occurs when a person in the expectation that a particular issue is likely to be significantly over subscribed and therefore in anticipation that his application will be scaled down, applies for a greater number of shares than he could in fact purchase. On notice of allotment he will then sell in the market, in the firm expectation that he will receive a premium and be able to cover with the money he has obtained the cost of subscription.

Stagging has not been considered objectionable in itself, although in recent years some judges have expressed doubts as to its integrity. In a number of the major privatisation issues, given the declared policy of the government to favour small investors and spread the issues as widely as possible, the terms of issue made it clear that allocation would be restricted to stipulated amounts and that multiple applications would not be accepted. Indeed, in one or two instances this was provided for in the relevant legislation contemplating de-nationalisation. In such circumstances the courts had no difficulty in regarding those who deliberately and thus, dishonestly, made multiple applications as obtaining the relevant shares by deception, contrary to s. 15 of the *Theft Act* 1968, (see for example, *R v Best, The Times*, 6 October 1987). Furthermore, it has been held in cases where the person engaging in stagging is aware that a cheque sent with his application, which is normally required, cannot be honoured by his bank on the first presentation, also commits a deception (see *R v Goldstein and Green* (1976) 1 All ER 1). The fact that he expects to be in funds on the occasion of a subsequent representation is irrelevant. Nor did it make any difference that what had happened was not an uncommon practice and one in which bankers had seemingly connived in.

¶712 Manipulation

Section 47(2) of the *Financial Services Act* 1986 is an entirely new provision unlike s. 47(1) which as we have seen is, with one or two minor amendments, the old s. 13 of the *Prevention of Fraud (Investments) Act* 1958. The UK is probably one of the last common law jurisdictions with a developed financial market, to enact legislation directed specifically at market rigging. It had been considered for many years that the self-regulatory provisions on the avoidance and control of false markets in the Stock Exchange's Yellow Book and its Rules and Regulations, together with the Takeover Code and Substantial Acquisition Rules were adequate, reinforced by the common law offence of conspiracy to defraud. However, there were situations in the market in regard to which it was thought desirable there should be a provision on the statute book which more directly addressed manipulative practices rather than simply fraudulent inducements to deal.

By s. 47(2), of the FSA, it is a serious offence to deliberately undertake an act or course of conduct which gives a false or misleading impression as to the price or value of an investment if that is done for the purpose of creating that impression and thereby inducing other persons to deal in investments. It also applies to misleading investors as to the size or liquidity of a market for the investment in question.

The section applies to any person, whether they be a body corporate or a natural person. As in the case of s. 47(1) it applies whether the dealings take place on or off the market. The main thrust of the offence is to penalise an act or course of conduct which creates a false or misleading impression as to the market in or the price of an investment. It is not entirely clear as to whom the misleading impression must be directed. If the conduct in question is directed at a particular type of investor, such as professional investors or institutional investors, it is arguable that the issue is whether such persons and not the general market, would have been given the relevant impression. The use of the word impression is also worthy of note. It would seem to mean that the conduct in question must be directed towards creating a perception in the minds of those concerned. It is a rather different test than that, for example, in determining whether there has been a sufficient inducement to contract in the law of misrepresentation.

The impression that is conveyed, or that it is intended should be given, must be directed at either the state of the market or the value of the investment. Thus, acts or conduct which create a false impression as to the state of the market in terms of activity, depth, or, indeed, any other relevant characteristic would be within the scope of the offence. It should be noted that not only artificial transactions, in the sense of washed transactions may give rise to liability. Transactions which actually do involve independent consideration and result in proper execution, but which are inherently misleading, because they are, for example, matched or pool operations, would be also caught. Indeed, the scope of the offence would be wide enough to catch conduct which would not necessarily be considered to involve manipulative trading. Thus, if an underwriter who is left with a large inventory of shares that are not taken up in a new issue, made additional market purchases in the expectation of teasing the market into action, he might well be guilty of an offence under s. 47(2).

It is also an offence, as we have seen, where the misleading impression is as to the price or value of the investment in question. The problem with this and similarly worded offences in other jurisdictions, is that it presupposes the existence of a fair price or real value. In the case of securities that are listed on a stock exchange the correct value is the market price which is arrived at by the consensus of the *bona fide* purchasers and sellers. This principle has been regularly applied by the courts not only in relation to securities but to commodities and land. It follows that any attempt to interfere with this market equilibrium is potentially unlawful under s. 47(2). Thus, many forms of share support and market making may, at least in theory, be caught by this provision. Wherever there is an attempt to influence the price of a security to a level above or below that which the market has or would set if unimpeded by the conduct in question, there be at least *prima facie* evidence of the commission of a criminal offence. Both the courts and those charged with bringing prosecutions may be expected to have regard to commercial and market regularity and provided what is done comports with generally accepted practices then it remains unlikely that the sledgehammer of the criminal law will come crushing down.

Nonetheless, it cannot be assumed that the mere fact that what has been done is a reasonably widespread practice and something to which most people would not take exception, will discourage a prosecution being brought or a conviction being recorded. It must be remembered that in the Blue Arrow prosecutions the defendants maintained that what they had done in attempting to support the price of shares in the market at the time of a sensitive rights issue was common practice. This did not prevent their conduct being characterised by the Serious Fraud Office as manipulative and fraudulent. Of course, in the result the jury took a rather different view. As long ago as 1840 Lord Langdale MR, in the case of *Gillett v Peppercorne*, 3 Beav 81, observed 'it is said that this conduct is every day's practice in the City. I certainly should be very sorry to have it proved that such sort of dealing is usual; for nothing can be open to the commission of fraud than transactions of this nature'. Of course, in criminal prosecutions the tribunal of fact, usually the jury, will have to be satisfied beyond a reasonable doubt that the defendant has acted dishonestly in the case of fraud and with the appropriate degree of intent in relation to s. 47.

The intent or state of mind (*mens rea*) that must be proved in the case of s. 47(2)), is that the defendant had an intention to create an impression as to the market in or the price or value of a security, and that he intended to induce another person to deal in the relevant security. It is very important to note that the prosecution does not need to establish that he intended to create a false or misleading impression as such. It is enough that he intended to create an impression as to the value or price of the investments. The implication is then fairly raised that he intended to create a false and misleading impression. This much is clear from the relationship of the statutory defence in s. 47(3) to the offence. Section 47(3) provides a defence to a charge under s. 47(2) if the defendant reasonably believed that his conduct would not create an impression that was false or misleading. Thus, if s. 47(2) could not be breached unless the purpose of the conduct was to create a false or misleading impression, s. 47(3) would be unnecessary. It must also be proved that what has been done has been to induce others to deal in the relevant securities. Therefore, no offence would be committed if the defendant could establish that he shuffled his investments for tax or for that matter any other reason than to induce a transaction. As was pointed out by Mason J in the Australian case of *North v Marra Developments Ltd* (1982) 56 ALJR 106, 'purchases or sales are often made for indirect or collateral motives ... plainly enough, it is not the object of the section (i.e. the equivalent provision) to outlaw all such transactions.'

Of course, in a criminal prosecution it is for the prosecution to prove beyond a reasonable doubt all the elements of the offence. Where, however, a statute places an evidential burden on the defendant, it is generally speaking necessary for him to establish the relevant facts to the standard of the civil law, that is to a balance of probabilities. The prosecution will, however, be able to rely on proper inferences from evidence, circumstantial and otherwise. Thus, in the Canadian case of *The Queen v Lampard*, (1968) 2 OR 470, in a prosecution of a stockbroker for manipulative practices, McLennan JA observed, in regard to the defendant's intent, 'he had been in the brokerage business for many years and must be taken in the absence of evidence from which some other reasonable explanation may be inferred, not only to have foreseen that each wash trade would create a false appearance of active public trading, but to have intended that result.' In the leading Canadian case of *The Queen v Macmillan* (1968) 66 DLR (2d) 680, the Court in dismissing the defendant's appeal, stated 'in the absence of any explanation ... and in the absence of evidence of circumstances which might reasonably lead to another conclusion, the only logical inference to be drawn from her conduct is that her real and dominant intention was to create a false or misleading appearance of active public trading in the shares of Golden Arrow (i.e. the manipulated stock). The suggested intent to benefit friends could amount to no more than a mere subsidiary consideration ...'.

As has already been pointed out under the common law it is not necessary in a charge of conspiracy to defraud to establish that the defendant intended to defraud a specific individual. It is enough that his statements are directed at the market and those who happen to be on the market on the particular day. It is not entirely clear from the wording of s. 47(2) whether the same rule would apply in a prosecution under this provision. It does refer to the conduct in question 'thereby inducing another person'. Thus, need the prosecution prove that the manipulator had the intention to induce a transaction with a particular and ascertained person? To so require would be to unduly restrict the scope of s. 47(2) and it is probable that a court would not require such a narrow interpretation. It should be sufficient for an offence to have been committed under this provision that the defendant intended to affect investors generally or a class thereof.

¶713   Stabilisation and defences

Mention has already been made to the statutory defence available in regard to a prosecution under s. 47(2), but not under s. 47(1), where the defendant can show that he reasonably believed that his conduct would not create a false or misleading impression. This means that if the defendant can prove that he acted honestly, believing that what he was doing would not create a false impression, he is entitled to an acquittal. Of course, his belief must be reasonable, which will be determined on objective criteria. Thus, an unreasonable, albeit honest, belief would not entitle the defendant to an acquittal.

¶713

There are further defences provided for in s. 48. This section empowers the SIB to make rules on the conduct of business. It is provided in s. 48(6), that nothing done in conformity with rules promulgated under s. 48(2)(h) will amount to an offence under s. 47. It should be noted that this applies to both false statements and dishonest concealment of material facts under s. 47(1) and manipulative practices under s. 47(2). Basically, s. 48(2)(h) empowers the SIB to promulgate rules relating to withholding information from clients or employees in certain circumstances in the conduct of investment business – in short the creation and maintenance of 'Chinese Walls'. Thus, there would be no offence if a misleading impression was created because relevant information had not been passed, because an item of information in question had remained behind a Chinese Wall and was not therefore accessible to the person making the relevant representation or engaging in the particular conduct in question.

Section 48(7) is perhaps of greater significance. It provides a defence only in regard to manipulative conduct under s. 47(2). There will be no offence in regard to anything done for the purpose of stabilising the price of investments, if it is done in conformity with rules made under s. 48. However, the rules may only cover investments referred to in the first five paragraphs of Sch. 1 to the Act, which broadly encompasses shares, debentures, government and public securities, warrants and other instruments entitling the holder to subscribe for shares, debentures and gilts and certificates representing securities, furthermore the rules must specify the investments that they cover. Moreover, the rules must in the case of public issues set time limits and in the case of public offers cover only until thirty days after the closing date.

Furthermore, an offer for the purpose of this provision means an offer for cash where either the investments have been admitted to dealing on an RIE or any other exchange of repute outside the UK, or the offer is on the occasion of such admission and the total cost of the investments subject to the offer at the price stated in the first public announcement is at least £15 million or its equivalent in other currency, (see the *Financial Services Act 1986 (Stabilisation) Order* 1988, SI 1988/717). The SIB has promulgated comprehensive rules relating to stabilisation – see the SIB's *Financial Services (Conduct of Business) Rules* 1990, Pt. 10.

¶714 Civil consequences

It should be noted that neither s. 47 nor s. 48 affect the operation of the general criminal law or directly the civil law. Nonetheless, it is usually the case that where it is possible to frame a charge of conspiracy to commit a specific statutory offence, then the more general charge of conspiracy to defraud is inappropriate. Section 47 would seem to give rise to no direct civil consequences. Of course, a contract to further the commission of an offence under s. 47 would be illegal and unenforceable at common law on the grounds of public policy. Section 62 which gives private investors a right of action for compensation for losses caused by a breach of certain statutory provisions, and in particular the relevant conduct of business rules, does not apply to s. 47. Furthermore, in the circumstances it is highly unlikely that the courts would find a statutory tort. However, s. 61 which gives the SIB and Treasury power to bring essentially injunctive suits, to which orders for restitution and disgorgement of profits may be added, is broad enough in its scope to extend to offences committed under s. 47.

¶715   High pressure selling

There has long been concern to discourage the grosser aspects of high pressure selling of securities to unsophisticated investors. The Government set up a Committee under Sir Archibald Bodkin 'to consider operations commonly known as share-pushing and share-hawking and similar activities' in 1936 (see ¶110). The recommendations of this Committee found their way into the *Prevention of Fraud (Investments) Act* 1939. Nonetheless, in recent years there would appear to have been a considerable growth in high-pressure selling operations, often referred to as 'boiler rooms'. Section 56 of the Financial Services Act seeks to address this. It provides that except to the extent permitted by regulations made by the SIB, no person shall in the course of or in consequence of an unsolicited call, made on a person in the UK, or made from the UK on a person elsewhere, by way of business, enter into an investment agreement with the person on whom the call is made or procure or endeavour to procure that person to enter into such an agreement. It should be noted that this prohibition bites on those calling into and those calling out from the UK.

In *Alpine Investments BV v Minister van Financien* (Case C-384/93) (Opinion of Advocate General Jacobs, delivered 26 January 1995) the European Court of Justice accepted that whilst rules seeking to prohibit 'cold calling' was a restriction on a person's freedom to provide cross-border services they were justified on the basis that a member State had the right to ensure the protection of investors and the integrity of its financial markets.

Under s. 56(2), however, it is provided that a contravention of the prohibition does not constitute a criminal offence, but the agreement will not be enforceable against the person to whom the call was made, and that person will be able to recover any money or other property paid or transferred by him under the agreement, together with compensation for any loss sustained by him as a result of having parted with it. As in the case of s. 57, however, if the innocent party elects not to perform an agreement which is unenforceable against him, by virtue of this provision, he must repay and account for any money or property that he has received. Thus, a violation of s. 56 will give rise to civil consequences, but not criminal. The absence of a penal aspect permits the offence to reach overseas without impinging the sovereignty of other States.

It should be noted, however, that both the SIB and Treasury may initiate enforcement actions for an injunction and restitution order under s. 61 of the Act. Where an order is made by a court and it is then breached this could give rise to contempt proceedings.

The SIB has initiated enforcement action against several individuals involved in 'high pressure' selling operations. In *SIB v Pantell SA* (1989) BCLC 590 the defendant company sent advertisements from Switzerland offering investment advice to investors in the UK and stressing the impartiality of the advice it offered. The advertisements recommended securities in certain US issuers which were closely associated with the defendant. The defendant had sent cheques that it had received from investors to its solicitors in London for them to pay into the defendant's bank account. The SIB, alleging that the defendants were engaged in unauthorised investment business contrary to s. 3 of the Act and were engaged in making misleading statements and unsolicited calls to investors in the UK, commenced proceedings under both s. 6 and s. 61 of the *Financial Services Act* 1986. The SIB also sought a Mareva injunction in favour of the SIB restraining the defendant from dissipating its assets. The court held that notwithstanding that the SIB itself had no beneficial interest in the assets and no private cause of action against the defendant, it was in the public interest that the SIB's statutory right of action under s. 6 and s. 61 should be supported by the court and an injunction was issued (see also *SIB v Lloyd-Wright* (1993) 4 All ER 210). In *SIB v Pantell SA (No. 2)* (1992) BCLC 58 the SIB joined the defendant's solicitor in the enforcement action, claiming that he was knowingly concerned in a contravention of the Act, in that he was aware that the defendant was not authorised to conduct investment business. The courts have also been prepared to impose restitutory liability on those who knowingly assist in the handling of moneys which have been misapplied in breach of a fiduciary obligation in 'boiler room' operations (see *El Ajou v Dollar Land Holdings plc* (1993) 3 All ER 717 (see ¶603).

Under s. 56(4) a court may uphold an agreement which would otherwise be prohibited, where the person called was either not influenced or not influenced to a material extent, in entering into the agreement 'by anything said or done in the course of or in consequence of the call'. Furthermore, the agreement may be upheld where the person on whom the call was made, entered into the agreement following discussions between the parties of such a nature and over such a period, that his entering into the agreement can fairly be regarded as a consequence of those discussions rather than the call itself, and he was aware of the nature of the agreement and any risks involved in entering into it. The agreement may also be enforced if it can be shown that the call was not in fact made by the person seeking to enforce or take commission in regard to it, or by a person on his behalf. By s. 56(8) an unsolicited call is defined as meaning a 'personal visit or oral communication made without express invitation'. Thus, it would apply to solicitation through the use of the telephone, but not electronic mail. For further discussion of 'cold calling' see Ch. 9.

¶716   Insolvency offences

It is sadly the case that in a large number of cases it is only when an insolvency occurs that fraud will be discovered. This is dramatically illustrated by the Maxwell affair and the collapse of both the Barlow Clowes and Levitt groups of companies. There are a number of specific investigatory powers available under both the Companies Acts and *Insolvency Act* 1986. (See for example *Re British & Commonwealth Holdings plc (Nos. 1 & 2)* (1992) 2 All ER 801 and *British & Commonwealth plc (Joint Administrator) v Spicer & Oppenheim* (1992) 4 All ER 876.) Whilst such provisions almost inevitably involve shutting the stable door after the horse has bolted, they can be important in tracing misappropriated funds and facilitate the imposition of compensatory liability on directors and officers who have some degree of responsibility in the insolvency. There are provisions in the companies and insolvency legislation as well as the *Financial Services Act* 1986 (see s. 72 and 73) relating to winding up which may well be of relevance in cases of fraud and other misconduct. For example, under s. 440 of the *Companies Act* 1985 and s. 124 of the *Insolvency Act* 1986, and in the case of an authorised person, s. 72 of the *Financial Services Act* 1986 the Secretary of State may present a petition to the court to have a company wound up if he is of the opinion that it is just and equitable to do so. Thus, in *Re Walter L Jacob & Co Ltd* (1989) BCLC 345 a financial intermediary that was a member of FIMBRA was wound up on the order of the Court of Appeal on the basis that this was in the public interest. It had been established to the satisfaction of the court that the company's financial records were inadequate and the company had been involved in pushing shares of dubious value in related US issuers without proper disclosure of the company's material interests.

There are a number of specific offences relating to malpractice and abuses before and during liquidation. Section 206 of the *Insolvency Act* 1986 provides that a present or former officer of a company in liquidation, who within the previous year conceals, fraudulently removes, or pawns any of the company's property or conceals or falsifies any records relating to the company's property, will be deemed to have committed an offence. By the same token an officer, or former officer, who is privy to any of these actions will also be deemed to have committed an offence. It should be noted that the term officer includes shadow directors. Section 206 not only applies to things done prior and in anticipation of a liquidation, but also to things done during a winding up. The defendant is entitled to a defence if he can establish that he had no intent to defraud, or conceal information from the company or defeat the law.

Section 207 provides when a company is being wound up, a person is deemed to have committed an offence if he, being at the time an officer of the company, has made or caused to be made any gift or transfer of, or charge on, or has caused or connived at the levying of any execution against, the company's property, unless the transaction in question took place more than five years before the commencement of winding up or if he proves that, at the time of the conduct constituting the offence, he had no intent to defraud the company's creditors. There are further offences (s. 208–211) relating to the conduct of officers during the winding up, which place an obligation on such persons to cooperate fully with the liquidator in identifying the company's property and require accurate statements and records to be made. Perhaps the most important provision is, however, s. 213 which relates to fraudulent trading.

In addition to these offences, there are provisions facilitating contribution and restitution. Section 212 provides for summary proceedings in cases of misfeasance. Where, in a winding up, it appears that a person involved in the management or promotion of the company has misapplied or retained, or become accountable for, any money or other property of the company, or been guilty of any misfeasance or breach of any fiduciary or other duty in relation to the company, the court may, on the application of the liquidator or a creditor, examine the person concerned and make an order requiring restoration or contribution. Section 213 is concerned with fraudulent trading and empowers the court, again on application, to make orders in regard to a person who it appears has carried on a business with intent to defraud the company's creditors. Given the requirement of intent to defraud, as in the case of a prosecution brought under s. 206 of the Insolvency Act (see *Re Patrick and Lyon Ltd* (1933) 1 Ch 786) it is necessary to prove 'actual dishonesty, involving real moral blame'. Consequently, the provision is of limited use, and proceedings for wrongful trading under s. 214 are usually far more efficacious.

¶717   Disqualification proceedings

It is appropriate in discussing the control of fraud to refer to the *Company Directors Disqualification Act* 1986 which has an important role in preventing further frauds as well as constituting an additional sanction in regard to conduct that has already taken place. It should be noted that in certain circumstances an order may be made in regard to a foreign citizen in relation to conduct taking place outside Britain. Arden J construing s. 6 of the Act decided that the fact that modern communications enabled companies to be controlled across frontiers, given parliament's intention to create an effective and integrated response to misconduct, justified an interpretation of the provisions which could extend to foreigners who were out of the jurisdiction and to conduct which occurred out of the jurisdiction. (See *Re Seagull Manufacturing Co Ltd (No. 2)* (1994) 1 BCLC 273). An order made under the Act against a director or in many cases a shadow director, renders it unlawful for him to be a director, liquidator, administrator, receiver of a company, or be in any way, either directly or indirectly, concerned with the promotion, incorporation or management of a company in Britain, during the currency of the order.

There are a number of statutory grounds upon which an application can be made by the Secretary of State, or in some instances the liquidator or even a creditor, to the court under the Act. Conviction for an indictable offence in connection with the promotion, formation, management or liquidation of a company is a ground under s. 2 of the Act. It has been held that a conviction for insider dealing, when the conduct in question clearly had a relevant factual connection with the management of the company, was sufficient to justify a disqualification order. (See *R v Goodman* (1994) 1 BCLC 349). Under s. 3, a court may make a disqualification order where there has been persistent default in making returns or delivering accounts and other documents required under the Companies Acts. Section 5 empowers the court to make an order on summary conviction for failing to comply with the statutory provisions relating to the filing of returns where there has been three such convictions within a period of five years.

Section 4 empowers the courts to make an order where it appears to the court in the course of insolvency proceedings, which need not necessarily end in a determination of insolvency, that there has been fraudulent trading or a breach of duty to the company. It should be noted that a conviction is not a prerequisite to the court exercising its powers under this section. Section 5 gives the court power to disqualify a person.

Section 6 relates to the disqualification of directors who have been associated with an insolvent company and are found to be unfit to be a director. It has been accepted by the courts that deliberately concealing transactions from the company and its shareholders is sufficient for the court to determine that a person is unfit to be a director (see *Re Godwin Warren Control Systems plc* (1993) BCLC 80).

By s. 8 the Secretary of State is empowered to seek an order for disqualification when he has received a report from inspectors appointed under the Companies Acts or the *Financial Services Act* 1986, or information pursuant to his own powers of investigation, indicating that it is in the public interest that an individual should be so disqualified. Before the court can make an order it must be satisfied that the conduct in relation to the company makes the person concerned unfit to be involved in corporate management under s. 9. In determining the issue of unfitness it is further provided that the court have regard to the matters set out in Pt. 1 of Sch. 1 to the Act which relates to the question of unfitness in cases brought under s. 6. Thus a director who abuses his power in circumstances indicating a lack of commercial probity, was held to be unfit (see *Re Looe Fish Ltd* (1993) BCLC 1160). The House of Commons' Select Committee on Trade and Industry severely criticised the refusal of the

Secretary of State to initiate such proceedings against the Fayed brothers following a recommendation by inspectors appointed to inquire into the House of Fraser affair. Although there was evidence that the Fayeds and their advisers had misled the City Panel on Takeovers and Mergers, the Department of Trade and Industry took the view that their conduct was not related to the management of a company, albeit that it is arguable that their misconduct facilitated the acquisition of the House of Fraser (see company investigations, Third Report of The Trade and Industry Committee (1990) HMSO).

Finally in regard to the grounds for disqualification, s. 10 permits a court to disqualify a person against whom it decides to make an order under either s. 213 of the *Insolvency Act* 1986 for fraudulent trading or under s. 214 for wrongful trading.

Breach of a disqualification order constitutes a criminal offence under s. 13 of the Act as well as contempt of court. Under s. 15 a person who is involved in the management of a company in violation of an order made under the Act, or a person who acts or is willing to act as a 'frontman' for a person who he knows to be subject to disqualification will be personally liable for all debts of the company. It should be noted that the same rules apply in regard to undischarged bankrupts (see s. 11 and s. 15 of the *Company Directors Disqualification Act* 1986).

The Secretary of State and the SIB are empowered by s. 59 of the *Financial Services Act* 1986 where it appears to them that any individual is not a fit and proper person to be employed in connection with investment business or investment business of a particular kind, to direct that he shall not, without the consent of the Secretary of State or the SIB, be employed in connection with investment business or business of that particular kind, by an authorised or exempted person, or by any specified person, or persons of a specified description being persons involved in the conduct of investment business. It is an offence for a person who is subject to such a disqualification order to breach it and under s. 59(6) a duty is imposed on authorised persons and appointed representatives to take reasonable care not to employ or continue to employ a person in contravention of a disqualification order. This duty may be enforced by action pursuant to s. 61 of the Act. It should also be noted that once an order has been made, the Secretary of State and the SIB have a discretion to impose conditions on giving consent to any variation. Those subject to such an order or refusal to consent to a variation may have the matter referred to the Financial Services Tribunal. The SIB has been somewhat coy about using this power, although an order was made against Mr Roger Levitt (29 April 1994) who was also disqualified under the *Company Directors Disqualification Act* 1986.

¶718   Money laundering

Mention has already been made of the impact of anti-money laundering laws on the operation of those engaged in the financial services business. Whilst there has always been 'secret money' the increase in organised crime and in particular highly profitable criminal activity has generated vast amounts of money in the hands of criminals, the source of which they need to obscure. It must always be remembered that the processes involved in hiding the origin of wealth are neither risk free or inexpensive. Therefore, organisations, whether illicit or not, are unlikely to go to the trouble of laundering money unless there is a practical and compelling reason. Obviously possession of significant amounts of wealth, that cannot be readily explained, attracts attention and may well lead to suspicion and, therefore investigation. Furthermore, the development of laws enabling the authorities to confiscate the proceeds of serious crime inevitably gives criminals an incentive to try and place their ill-gotten gains beyond the reach of the courts. Thus, with the enactment of provisions in the Criminal Justice Act 1988 empowering the courts, on conviction, to deprive criminals of the proceeds of their crimes the need to launder the profits of crime was emphasised. Before 1988 where the criminal activity was not related to drug trafficking there was little risk of confiscature. Whilst the devices that launderers employ to hide the source of money and other forms of wealth are legion there is little doubt that the financial services industry is attractive both in terms of placement and layering operations. Financial intermediaries may be used to translate cash, which represents the proceeds of a crime into, for example, securities which can then be negotiated and exchanged for other valuable instruments at a subsequent stage in the layering process. Of course, the financial intermediary may or may not be a knowing participant in this operation. Obviously the further the transaction that the intermediary is involved with, is from the initial placement of the 'dirty money' in the financial system, the less likely he will have knowledge of the facts or be suspicious as to the true origin of the wealth in question.

The financial services industry is therefore not only at risk from being inveigled into money laundering operations and thereby facilitating criminal activity, but also being 'penetrated' by criminals and their organisations. Given the vast amounts of money that pass through the so called 'criminal pipeline' there have been a number of instances where organised crime has decided that it is cost effective to takeover the operation of a bank of financial intermediary, both to facilitate its own financial operations and as an investment in itself. Another danger is that with an increase in law enforcement activity and the tendency for law enforcement agencies to attack those who facilitate criminal activity, rather than those primarily responsible for the commission of the crimes which give rise to the profit in the first place, intermediaries are finding themselves the subject of enforcement operations. Governments have recognised the importance of the financial sector in ensuring that as far as possible criminal organisations should be discouraged, if not prevented, from using their banks and financial intermediaries to retain their ill-gotten gains and invest them in other anti-social activity. Therefore onerous compliance and record keeping obligations have increasingly been imposed on banks and other intermediaries in the financial system. Whilst significantly increasing the costs of doing business in certain cases, there are clear legal and other risks in failing to diligently comply with these requirements. Furthermore, given the significant contribution that imposing this level of compliance has made to the prevention and control of other criminal and abusive activity there is a tendency for law enforcement agencies and in particular the regulators to broaden these initiatives to throw up information in regard to other conduct. Therefore, devices which were constructed to inhibit money laundering are now being employed to furnish the authorities with information and investigatory assistance across a wider spectrum of activities. The criminal law in imposing various obligations on those handling other people's money has not always been satisfactorily interfaced with the obligations imposed by the civil law and regulatory regimes. Therefore, the burden placed on financial intermediaries in terms of compliance is made significantly more onerous and precarious.

¶719   The offences

The provisions relating to the laundering of the proceeds of drug trafficking have been consolidated and re-enacted in the *Drug Trafficking Act* 1994. Section 50 of the 1994 Act provides that it is an offence for anyone to assist a drug trafficker to launder money by assisting them to retain or control the benefits of their criminal activity, even if this merely amounts to providing advice. It is necessary for the prosecution to prove that the accused knew or suspected that the other person is, or was engaged in drug trafficking, or has benefited from the drug trafficking activities of another person. The accused is entitled to a defence if he can prove that he did not know or suspect that this was the case, or that he would have informed the authorities but for a factor which reasonably prevented him from so doing. If a person does make disclosure of his suspicions to the proper authorities, which include, in the case of employees of banks and financial intermediaries, the relevant compliance officer, do not commit an offence even if they subsequently at the request of the authorities provide assistance that would otherwise be within the scope of the offence. Section 52 in an attempt to further encourage reporting of suspicious transactions provides that it is an offence to fail to disclose knowledge or suspicion of money laundering activity to the authorities provided this is acquired in the course of certain professional duties or certain types of employment. It is a defence, however, to prove that the person concerned had a reasonable excuse for not passing on the information in question or that it was passed to a designated compliance officer within the relevant business or organisation. In regard to disclosure under both s. 50 and s. 52 there is immunity from the consequences of what might amount to a breach of contract or confidence. However, this does not extend to, for example, liability for defamation, although there is likely to be a defence of qualified privilege.

Section 53 of the 1994 Act renders it an offence to 'tip off' another person that an investigation into money laundering is in progress or is about to be commenced, which is likely to be prejudicial to the investigation. This is a widely drawn provision, although the accused is entitled to a defence if he can prove that he did not know or suspect that the disclosure was likely to prejudice any money laundering investigation. Legal advisers are given specific protection from this offence, but on condition that the information in question is not communicated in the furtherance of a criminal offence. Finally, in regard to the proceeds of drug trafficking it should be noted that the offences relate to the proceeds of such activity wherever it takes place. It is not necessary that the proceeds in question have to be a result of activity which is an offence under United Kingdom law, although it must be such as would have been an offence had it occurred within jurisdiction.

The provisions relating to the laundering of terrorist funds remain in the *Prevention of Terrorism (Temporary Provisions) Act* 1989 and are in some respects more draconian than those relating to the laundering of the proceeds of drug trafficking. Under s. 9 of the 1989 Act it is an offence for a person to engage in certain conduct with the intention that or having reasonable cause to suspect, that the funds in question will be used to commit or further acts of terrorism in Britain or elsewhere. The conduct in question includes, soliciting or inviting another person to give, lend or otherwise make available any money or other property, receiving or accepting from any other person any money or property or using or having possession of any money or other property whether for consideration or not. It is also an offence if a person, knowing or having reasonable cause to suspect that the money or other property will be used to commit or further acts of terrorism, gives, lends or otherwise makes available to any other person such property or is concerned in an arrangement whereby money or other property is to be made available to another person either immediately or at some time in the future. Section 10 provides that it is an offence for a person to solicit or invite any person to give, lend or otherwise make available any money or other property, whether for consideration or not, or himself lends or otherwise makes available such property, or receives or accepts or uses or has possession of any money or property, or is concerned in an arrangement whereby money or other property is to be made available, for the benefit of a proscribed terrorist organisation. Except where the offence involves solicitation, it is a defence for the accused to establish that he did not know or have reasonable cause to suspect, that the money or property in question was for the benefit of a proscribed organisation or related to such.

Section 11 of the 1989 Act is similar to s. 50 of the *Drug Trafficking Act* 1994 insofar as it renders it an offence for a person to enter into or be otherwise concerned in an arrangement which facilitates the retention or control of terrorist funds by or on behalf of another person. However, there is an important difference in terms of the statutory defence to such a charge. In the case of s. 11 the accused must establish that he did not know or have reasonable cause to suspect that the relevant arrangement related to terrorist funds. The test being objective rather than subjective. As in the case of the other provisions, s. 11, applies to acts done or intended outside the UK provided they constitute offences triable in the UK.

Section 12 provides immunity to those who might otherwise be in breach of contract or the law of confidence in reporting their suspicions to the authorities, and provides a defence for those who engage in activity which would otherwise constitute a crime, provided they have made proper disclosure to the authorities and have been permitted to proceed, or who can establish that he informed the authorities as soon as is reasonable after engaging in the relevant activity. It is also a defence, as in the case of the drug trafficking provisions, that the accused had a reasonable excuse for not informing the authorities, or that he informed an appropriate person according to the terms of a compliance procedure within the relevant organisation.

The *Criminal Justice Act* 1993 added to the 1989 Act a further provision to bring the law relating to terrorist funds in line with that relating to the laundering of drug related funds. Section 18A makes it an offence to fail to disclose knowledge or suspicion that financial assistance is being given to promote terrorism. The obligation to report knowledge or suspicion is imposed on those who in the course of their trade, profession, business or employment learn of the relevant facts. They will be guilty of an offence if they do not 'blow the whistle' to the authorities unless they prove that they have a reasonable excuse or that an appropriate person, such as a compliance officer, has been notified. As in the case of the other provisions relating to the reporting of suspicions a defence is provided in regard to allegations of breach of contract and confidentiality.

Section 17 of the *Prevention of Terrorism (Temporary Provisions) Act* 1989 as amended by the *Criminal Justice Act* 1993 broadens the offence of 'tipping off' along the same lines as s. 58 of the *Drug Trafficking Act* 1994. It is now an offence for anyone to disclose information relating to an investigation, actual or contemplated, in regard to the relevant offences with the intention of prejudicing the inquiry.

The *Northern Ireland (Emergency Provisions) Act* 1991 also contains provisions relevant to the funds of terrorist organisations. Section 53 renders it an offence to assist another person to retain the proceeds of terrorist related activities, knowing or suspecting that the person is or has been engaged in such activities or has benefited by virtue of such conduct. It is a defence for the accused to prove that what is done has been done with the prior consent of the authorities after proper disclosure to them, or that there has been disclosure as soon as is reasonable after the assistance in question has occurred. Furthermore, it is also open to the accused to establish that he is not guilty because he did not know or suspect that the arrangements related to the proceeds of terrorist related activity or that he intended to inform the authorities and had a reasonable excuse for delaying. As in the case of the provisions relating to drug trafficking there is immunity from the civil law for proper disclosures where the liability would be based on breach of contract or an obligation of confidentiality.

It is an offence under s. 54 of the 1991 Act to conceal, disguise, convert or transfer property which in whole or part, directly or indirectly, represents the proceeds of terrorist related activity, or to remove it from the jurisdiction of the courts. Section 54(1) is directed at the terrorist racketeer who seeks to avoid confiscature of the proceeds of his crimes, whereas s. 54(2) is aimed at those who assist such persons in 'laundering' the proceeds of terrorist related activity, knowing or having reasonable cause to suspect its source. It is also an offence for a person to acquire, use or possess property which they know or have reasonable cause to suspect represents, in whole or in part, directly or indirectly, another person's proceeds of terrorist related activity. However, to such a charge, since the 1993 Act, it is a defence if proper consideration, other than in services, was given, or that the person concerned intended to report his suspicions, but had a reasonable excuse for delaying. It is also a defence, as in the other provisions, that what has been done, was done after proper disclosure to the authorities with their consent. There are also the usual provisions protecting against liability for breach of contract and the law of confidence.

Section 54A of the 1991 Act, which was added by the *Criminal Justice Act* 1993, makes it an offence to fail to disclose knowledge or suspicion of an offence under both s. 53 and s. 54 of the 1991 Act. As in the case of the provisions relating to drug trafficking this obligation to 'blow the whistle' applies where the facts were learnt in the course of a trade, profession, business or employment. The usual protections are provided in regard to civil liability, or where the disclosure was to an appropriate person pursuant to a compliance procedure. Furthermore, legal advisers are given protection provided they are acting within the confines of accepted legal privilege.

The provisions in the *Drug Trafficking Offences Act* 1986 relating to money laundering were extended by the *Criminal Justice (International Cooperation) Act* 1990. These additional and important provisions have been codified in the *Drug Trafficking Act* 1994. Section 49(1) of the 1994 Act provides that it is an offence for a person to conceal or disguise any property which wholly or partly, directly or indirectly, represents his own proceeds of drug trafficking. It is also an offence if the trafficker converts or transfers the property or removes it from the jurisdiction of the courts. This provision is aimed at the drug trafficker himself attempting to launder the proceeds of his crime, whereas s. 49(2) renders it a crime for another person to engage in such acts for the purpose of assisting any person to avoid prosecution for a drug trafficking offence or the making of a confiscation order, knowing or having reasonable grounds to suspect that the property in question is derived from the proceeds of drug trafficking. Obviously there is some overlap with s. 50 which as we have seen, renders it an offence to assist another to retain the benefits of his illicit trafficking.

Section 51 is a particularly significant provision as it renders it an offence to acquire, possess or use property, knowing that it directly or indirectly represents another person's proceeds of drug trafficking. It is important to note that before the offence can be committed the person concerned must actually know that the property in question is derived from drug trafficking, mere suspicion is not sufficient. Whilst the section will not apply to property transferred under a legitimate contract, where the consideration is unreal, wholly inadequate or illegal, there may well be an offence under this provision provided there is the requisite degree of knowledge. Statutory protection is afforded to those who legitimately provide goods and services provided that this does not assist in the drug trafficking activities of the recipient, even if the provider of the relevant services is aware that payment is from the proceeds of a drug related offence. Thus, a lawyer receiving payment for defending a drug trafficker would not commit an offence under this provision. It is also a defence to a charge under this section that proper disclosure has been made to the authorities, or where appropriate to a compliance officer, or that the person concerned would have made due disclosure but delayed in so doing for a reasonable cause.

It has already been pointed out that prior to the *Criminal Justice Act* 1993 attempts to launder the proceeds of crimes other than those relating to drug trafficking and terrorism did not amount to a specific criminal offence. Where a freezing or confiscation order had been made under the *Criminal Justice Act* 1988 an attempt to evade it might constitute contempt of court. There are also a variety of disparate provisions such as those in the *Companies Act* 1985 relating to the freezing of rights attaching to shares in certain circumstances which in particular circumstances might have relevance in preventing activity which resembles laundering. Furthermore, the handling of the proceeds of a theft or deception is a specific offence under s. 22 of the *Theft Act* 1968. The *Criminal Justice Act* 1993 extends most of the provisions relating to money laundering to property derived from such criminal activity as is susceptible to the making of a confiscature order, after conviction, under the 1988 Act. Thus, the proceeds from all offences that are triable on indictment and certain summary offences, which have the smell of organised crime about them, such as those relating to sex establishments, supplying video recordings of unclassified work, possessing unclassified videos for the purposes of supply and the use of unlicensed premises for the exhibition of videos are within the reach of the new anti-money laundering provisions.

Section 93A, which has been added to the 1988 Act, makes it an offence for a person knowing or suspecting that another is, or has been engaged in, or has benefited from criminal conduct, to enter into an arrangement, or be otherwise concerned, in facilitating the retention or control by or on behalf of another's proceeds of criminal conduct, whether by concealment, removal from the jurisdiction of the courts or transfer to nominees or otherwise. It is also an offence to enter into an arrangement or be otherwise concerned, whereby the proceeds of a person's criminal conduct are used to secure that funds are placed at his disposal or are used to acquire property by way of investment for that person's benefit. As in the case of the drug related offences, an accused is entitled to a defence if he proves that what he did was done after proper disclosure to the authorities and with their approval, or that he reported what had happened as soon as reasonable. Protection is also provided for those who disclose in breach of contract or an obligation of confidentiality. An accused will also be entitled to a defence if he can prove that he neither knew nor suspected that any arrangement related to the proceeds of criminal conduct or that the arrangement involved facilitating the laundering of such proceeds. Section 93B mirrors s. 51 of the *Drug Trafficking Act* 1994 in that it makes it an offence to acquire, use or possess property, knowing that it is in whole or part directly or indirectly derived from the proceeds of criminal conduct. As in the case of s. 51, it is necessary that the prosecution establishes actual knowledge, mere suspicion not being sufficient for liability. The same defences are also available, namely the payment of adequate consideration, provision of goods and services in the ordinary course of business and 'whistle blowing'. By s. 93C(1) it is an offence to conceal, disguise, convert, transfer or remove from the jurisdiction of the courts, any property which is directly or indirectly, in whole or part the proceeds of criminal conduct. Section 93C(2) renders it a crime for anyone else to assist another to do this, provided they have knowledge or reasonable grounds to suspect that any of the property represents directly or indirectly the proceeds of criminal conduct. The objective element should be noted. Finally, s. 93D makes it an offence for a person knowing or suspecting that a money laundering investigation is in progress or is about to be initiated, discloses this knowledge or suspicion to another if such is likely to prejudice the inquiry. In addition to the substantive offences, regard must be had to the Money Laundering Regulations which came into force

¶719

1 April 1994. These are concerned with putting into place within financial and other institutions mechanisms to ensure due compliance with the substantive provisions, to deter money laundering and to facilitate effective and efficient detection and investigation. Financial institutions which come within the scope of the regulations are required to create, implement and operate internal procedures. Failure to do this is a criminal offence, although it is a defence for the institution to show that it took all reasonable steps and exercised proper due diligence in seeking to comply with the requirements of the regulations.

¶720 Civil fraud

The dividing line between the criminal and civil law in regard to fraudulent conduct has never been entirely clear in English law. Indeed, one of the earliest causes of action, that of deceit, involved considerations of almost a penal nature. Given the harm that allegations of dishonesty can cause to individuals, particularly if they are in business, the courts have always been concerned by way of procedure and proof to ensure as far as is practical that such allegations are not made and pursued wantonly. Therefore, as a matter of pleading in the civil law, averments of fraud must be specially plead with all the relevant facts establishing the specific averment set out. Whilst there is a difference between standard of proof in an ordinary criminal trial and one for fraud in the civil law, the judges have often emphasised that as the seriousness of the allegation increases in civil proceedings the standard of proof that is required to be met will be more exacting. Therefore, in practice there may not be a great deal of difference between the standards of proof required to establish fraud in the civil and criminal law, particularly when it is remembered that in most cases considerable reliance will need to be placed on documentary evidence. Where allegations of fraud or deliberate misconduct, involving moral turpitude, are made and persisted with in circumstances which the court considers unjustified, then there will be serious costs implications for the plaintiff and on occasion judges have expressed their disapproval of counsel.

The issue of fraud may arise in the civil law in a number of ways. However, since *Pasley v Freeman* (1789) 3 TR 51 it has been the rule that if a person knowingly or recklessly, that is to say not caring whether it is true or false, makes a false statement to another, with the intention that it shall be relied upon by that person, who in fact does rely on it and as a consequence suffers harm, then the action in deceit will be available. It is the need for the plaintiff to establish that the defendant acted with actual knowledge or could not care less whether what he said was true or not, which distinguishes liability in fraud from, for example, liability in the tort of negligence (see *Derry v Peek* (1889) 14 App Cas 337). In the case of negligent misstatement the defendant will be liable if an ordinary reasonable person would have known that what was said was untrue, in other words the standard is objective. Where a person has been induced to enter into a contract as a result of a fraudulent misrepresentation, the law provides remedies of rescission and damages. Whilst rescission may be a more attractive remedy in the case of investment transactions it will not always be available. There is a strict rule which requires full restoration of property transferred under the relevant contract. In other words the parties must be restored to their original position. It follows that if the victim of the fraud, rather than run the risk of a further, perhaps unrelated, diminution in the value of his securities disposes of them, he will have lost his right to rescind. In *Smith New Court v Scrimgeour Vickers* (1994) 4 All ER 225) Nourse LJ observed that, in the case of a fungible asset like quoted shares, the rule which requires restitution *in specie* is a hard one and in cases of fraud it was clear that the court had little sympathy with it, although in the circumstances it was not appropriate to depart from it. The rule works harshly, particularly in the case of an omission to disclose information which does not give rise to an independent cause of action for damages (see *Banque Keyser Ullman v Skandia* (1989) 2 All ER 952).

In an action for damages, the courts have been concerned to ensure that a fraudster takes no benefit from his fraud or the false circumstances that he has created. Lord Atkin in *Clark v Urquhart, Stracey v Urquhart* (1930) AC 28 at 68 emphasised that the measure of damages is 'the actual damage directly flowing from the fraudulent inducement' and this includes consequential loss (see *Doyle v Olby (Ironmongers) Ltd* (1969) 2 All ER 119). On the other hand, depreciation of the value of shares by market forces operating after the date of acquisition does not flow directly from the fraudulent inducement, but from the purchaser's decision to retain the shares and accept the hazards of the market rather than sell at once (see *Waddell v Blockey* (1879) 4 QBD 678). The measure of damages will therefore be the difference between the price that the plaintiff paid and the 'true value' of the securities at the time he was fraudulently induced to acquire them. Valuation is always a difficult task and determination of the price depends upon a number of assumptions. One of the most important being what assumption should be made about the information which was available to the market (see *Lynall v IRC* (1971) 3 All ER 914 and in regard to insider trading). The Court of Appeal in *Smith New Court v Scrimgeour Vickers* considered that there were only two plausible possibilities in determining what assumption should be made as to information in the case of fraud. First, to assume that the market knew everything it actually did know but was not influenced by the misrepresentation itself, or secondly, to assume that the market was omniscient. The Court of Appeal thought that the first approach was rational, but the second arbitrary and therefore disagreed with Chadwick J who at first instance appeared to have assumed that the market was omniscient. In the result the Court of Appeal held that the correct measure of damages in a case where a person is induced to acquire shares by deceit, is the difference between the price that was actually paid and the price which, absent the misrepresentation the parcel of shares would have fetched on the open market at that time.

The relationship between actions for deceit and in the tort of negligence have already been alluded to. As it is not necessary for a plaintiff in an action for damages to specify the particular tort which he is seeking to rely for a remedy, provided he asserts and establishes the facts required for liability under at least one accepted cause of action, there may in practice be little lost in not alleging or being able to prove dishonesty, given the court's attitude to allegations of fraud. Apart from the desire to brand a person as a fraudster, it remains possible to obtain exemplary damages in cases of proven fraud and the statute of limitation may be more favourable (see s. 32, *Limitation Act* 1980), but in the majority of cases plaintiffs are well advised to refrain from specific averments of fraud. In the case of misrepresentations inducing a contract between the parties the statutory remedies for negligent statements, provided by s. 2(1) of the *Misrepresentation Act* 1967 are in practical terms superior to an action in tort. Under s. 2(1) the person responsible for the misrepresentation has the burden of establishing that he had reasonable grounds for believing and did in fact believe what he said to be true.

The issue of fraud may also be relevant in other actions, as we have seen such as conspiracy and under specific statutory provisions giving rise to a civil remedy. Equity follows the law, and will not enforce a bargain that has been procured by fraud. Furthermore, the courts have developed a form of restitutionary liability for those who receive property transferred in breach of trust or who facilitate the laundering of such property with the requisite degree of dishonesty (see *AGIP (Africa) Ltd v Jackson* (1992) 4 All ER 385 and 451, *El Ajou v Dollar Land Holdings plc* (1993) 3 All ER 717 and *Royal Brunei Airlines Sdn Bhd v Tan* (1995). Indeed, such is the apparent efficacy of such proceedings that some have advocated a greater degree of reliance on civil 'enforcement' actions than on the traditional processes of the criminal law (see Rider B, Civilising the Law – The use of civil and administrative proceedings to enforce financial services law (1995) 3 *Journal of Financial Crime* 11). It must also be remembered that whilst there have been significant developments in the criminal law facilitating the taking and receipt of evidence from overseas, the civil law provides far greater weapons in obtaining evidence and discovery, in freezing funds and in enforcing orders of the court (see Ch. 12). Whilst the criminal courts possess statutory power, in certain circumstances, to order restoration and even compensation, as we have seen in the context of insider dealing, such orders are rarely appropriate in the case of securities related fraud.

8 Public Issues

INTRODUCTION

¶801 The need for prescribed disclosures

When securities are offered to the public in the UK for the first time, it is normally necessary for the issuer (or other offeror) to publish a prospectus containing prescribed disclosures about the issuer and the securities. The disclosures are normally those required by the London Stock Exchange if the securities are subject to an application for listing on the London Stock Exchange and those required by the *Public Offers of Securities Regulations* 1995, SI 1995/1537, (the prospectus regulations) if they are not. Prescribed disclosures are also normally needed when securities are admitted to listing on the London Stock Exchange, even if there is no public offer; the disclosures are those required by the London Stock Exchange. If the public offer is of securities which are already listed on the London Stock Exchange, no prescribed disclosures are normally required by either statute or the London Stock Exchange itself. However, in all cases, documents containing or constituting an offer, and indeed other marketing materials, must normally contain the risk warnings and other information about the securities being offered which are required by the SIB or the relevant SRO (or RPB) as a result of the FSA's Marketing Prohibition (see Ch. 9); this is the case whether the offer is to the public or is a private placement, although there is an exemption for the actual prospectus or listing particulars. Unfortunately, the public issues rules are not written on this straightforward basis but differentiate (in form although not really in substance) between most securities to be listed on the London Stock Exchange and all other securities. This is for historical reasons.

Originally, all public offers of shares and corporate debt securities were regulated by the Companies Acts, ultimately the *Companies Act* 1985. This was changed in 1984, where the securities were listed, or were subject to an application for listing, on the London Stock Exchange. Offers of securities to be listed on the London Stock Exchange were normally taken out of the Companies Act and made part of a separate regime applying only to securities to be listed in London; offers of securities which were already listed on the London Stock Exchange were also normally moved to the new regime. The London Stock Exchange became the 'competent authority' for listing, and had to ensure compliance with the three EU directives relating to 'official listing' (the listing directives): the *Admission Directive* of 1979 (Council Directive No.79/279/EEC), the *Listing Particulars Directive* of 1980 (Council Directive No. 80/390/EEC) and the *Interim Reports Directive* of 1982 (Council Directive No. 82/121/EEC). The governing factor was listing, rather than a public offer; whenever securities subject to the listing directives were to be admitted to listing on the London Stock Exchange, it was necessary to publish and file 'listing particulars' approved by the London Stock Exchange, unless an exemption applied; this was the case whether or not there was a public offer. Conversely, there was no need to publish a Companies Act prospectus even if the admission to listing was accompanied by a public offer. If securities which were already listed on the London Stock Exchange were offered to the public, there was no need to publish either a prospectus or, indeed, listing particulars.

This 'listing particulars' regime for the admission to listing on the London Stock Exchange of securities subject to the listing directives is now contained in Pt. IV of the FSA, which came into force in 1987. The 'prospectus' regime contained in the Companies Act, for securities which were neither listed, nor subject to an application for listing, on the London Stock Exchange under the listing directives, continued in force until 1995, although it was supposed to be replaced in due course by the new regime in Pt. V of the FSA.

This regulatory regime has also now been changed, as a result of the prospectus regulations, which came into force in June 1995 and implemented into UK law the EU's directive relating to public offers of transferable securities, the *Prospectus Directive* of 1989 (Council Directive No. 89/298/EEC). The prospectus directive normally applies whenever a public offer is made for the first time in an EEA member State of securities which are not already listed on an exchange in that member State, whether or not the securities are subject to an application for official listing there. It is therefore now again normally necessary to publish and file a 'prospectus' containing prescribed disclosures whenever securities are offered to the public in the UK for the first time, unless they are already listed on the London Stock Exchange under Pt. IV. In addition, the marketing of all securities is subject to the FSA's Marketing Prohibition (see Ch. 9); this is the case even if they are already listed on the London Stock Exchange and, indeed, even if the securities are not subject to the special 'public issue' regimes.

The prospectus regulations normally apply to 'first time' UK public offers even if the securities are subject to an application for listing on the London Stock Exchange. However, if they are securities subject to an application for listing on the London Stock Exchange under Pt. IV (LSE securities), the prospectus must be approved by the London Stock Exchange and, importantly, the prescribed disclosures are those required by the listing particulars directive, and so the London Stock Exchange under Pt. IV (as amended by the prospectus

¶801

regulations), rather than those required by the prospectus regulations themselves. If there is no 'first time' UK public offer (either because there is no UK public offer at all or because the securities have previously already been the subject of a UK public offer), or the securities are not subject to the prospectus directive (which applies to slightly different categories of securities from those to which the listing directives apply), it is still necessary to publish and file 'listing particulars' before securities subject to the listing directives can be admitted to listing on the London Stock Exchange, unless an exemption applies.

Public offers of securities which are not listed, or subject to an application for listing, on the London Stock Exchange under Pt. IV ('non-LSE securities') are also no longer subject to the 'public offer' provisions of the Companies Acts, although certain regulatory provisions in the *Companies Act* 1985 (or the Northern Ireland equivalents) still apply to them in the case of UK companies (see ¶825). Instead, they are regulated by Pt. II of the prospectus regulations (which, as mentioned above, implemented the EU's prospectus directive into UK law), unless they are exempted from Pt. II or (in limited circumstances) outside its scope.

Except in the case of securities already listed on the London Stock Exchange under Pt. IV of the FSA, the prospectus regulations apply whenever securities subject to them are offered to the public in the UK for the first time (in what may be called, in the American phrase, an 'IPO', an initial public offering). The prospectus regulations apply to most securities falling in para. 1–5 of Sch. 1 to the FSA; however, they therefore do not apply to shares in open-ended investment companies, which are in para. 6. The prospectus regulations apply to IPOs of securities to be listed on the London Stock Exchange under the listing directives by way of amendments to Pt. IV of the FSA, but apply in the case of IPOs of non-LSE securities subject to them in their own right. Accordingly, the term 'prospectus regulations' is for convenience used below to refer only to the new regime for IPOs of non-LSE securities, which is contained in Pt. II of the prospectus regulations. The proposed 'prospectus' regime in Pt. V of the FSA has never been brought into force and has been replaced by the prospectus regulations.

The prospectus regulations require all offerors, whether of new or existing non-LSE securities, to publish and file a prospectus containing the detailed disclosures set out in Sch. 1 to the prospectus regulations (and, importantly, all other material information) before they can make an IPO in the UK; in the case of a new issue, the offeror is often the issuer itself (see ¶823). As a result of helpful exemptions, many 'restricted' offers of non-LSE securities to UK offerees do not need a prospectus, although they will normally be subject to the FSA's Marketing Prohibition (see Ch. 9); this will help, in particular, private placements in or into the UK. Offers to offerees outside the UK are ignored

¶801

altogether for this purpose (although they will normally be subject to local prospectus requirements where the offeree is). As indicated above, this new regime applies even to securities listed, or subject to an application for listing, on the London Stock Exchange if, exceptionally, they are outside Pt. IV because the listing directives do not apply to them; they are for convenience therefore also referred to in this guide as 'non-LSE securities'. In the UK context, IPOs of non-LSE securities normally occur on the London Stock Exchange's Alternative Investment Market for young and growing companies (AIM); indeed, the new regime accordingly came into force on the day that dealings started on AIM. IPOs in the UK of securities quoted on overseas exchanges, and indeed of securities of unquoted non-UK companies, are also subject to the prospectus regulations as 'non-LSE securities', although, because of the private placement exemptions, they will in practice normally be exempted from them.

If a holding of securities already listed on the London Stock Exchange under Pt. IV is marketed by way of a public offer, however, no prospectus is needed even if, exceptionally, the offer is an IPO (because, for example, it is the holding of a controlling shareholder whose shares were listed by way of an introduction, for example, on a privatisation); nor it is necessary to publish listing particulars. This is because an offer of securities which are already listed on the London Stock Exchange under Pt. IV is excluded from Pt. II of the prospectus regulations as well as offers subject to an application for such listing (reg. 3(1)(a)) and an IPO requires a prospectus under Pt. IV only if the securities are offered to the public in the UK for the first time 'before admission' to listing (s. 144(2), as substituted by the prospectus regulations). In addition, no listing particulars are necessary because the securities have already been admitted to listing. This lack of disclosure requirements is probably because information about the issuer is already available under Stock Exchange rules, but it does mean that the primary remedy for misleading statements made by the offeror is at common law rather than under statute (see ¶812). Accordingly, it would seem that the only statutory regulation applicable to public offers of securities already listed on the London Stock Exchange under Pt. IV is the FSA's Marketing Prohibition (see Ch. 9); public offers of securities traded on AIM or, for example, EASDAQ are therefore better regulated than public offers of securities listed on the London Stock Exchange.

¶802 Over-view of the new public issues regimes

When securities not already listed on the London Stock Exchange under Pt. IV are offered to the public in the UK for the first time, a prospectus containing prescribed information must normally be published and filed by the offeror (see ¶818) and, in the case of non-LSE securities, the offeror must refer to the prospectus in all marketing materials (see ¶818); as indicated in ¶801, 'non-LSE securities' include securities listed on the London Stock Exchange which are outside Pt. IV. The prospectus regulations contain several important exemptions for UK private placements of non-LSE securities (see ¶821); similar exemptions apply also to the amended Pt. IV regime (see ¶804). As a result of these exemptions and of exemptions from the FSA's marketing restrictions, offers to FSA-authorised or passporting firms which are also 'qualifying securities professionals' and, in addition, to up to 50 'qualifying corporations in the UK', or to any number of 'qualifying corporations' where the minimum purchase price for every UK offeree is ECU40,000 (currently, approximately £33,000), are normally not regulated by UK law; for this purpose, 'qualifying corporations' are primarily companies which are FSA-authorised or passporting firms or fall within the art. 11(3) exemption from the FSA's Marketing Prohibition on the size test (see ¶821(b)). There are also provisions for the mutual recognition of prospectuses or listing particulars approved by the competent authorities of other member States (see ¶824). Finally, the revised Pt. IV now contains a voluntary regime for the approval of UK prospectuses by the London Stock Exchange in the case of public offers of non-LSE securities which want to use the 'passport' provided by the prospectus directive (see ¶824); the prescribed disclosures are in this case those required by the London Stock Exchange (under Pt. IV, as reduced by the London Stock Exchange in the light of the reduced requirement of the prospectus directive) rather than by the prospectus regulations.

In principle, every offer of securities (and, indeed, any marketing related to it) is subject to the FSA's normal Marketing Prohibition (see Ch. 9), whether or not the offer constitutes an IPO. There are, however, specific exemptions for the actual prospectus itself (whether under Pt. IV or the prospectus regulations), for listing particulars (which, as explained above, are used if there is no public offer or the public offer is not an IPO) and for any other admission document required by a 'relevant EEA market' (see ¶905(5)).

¶803   Differences in applicability of the new public issues regimes

Because of the complicated way in which the new regimes have evolved (see ¶801), there are exceptional cases where certain categories of securities are outside one or more of the three public issues regimes, that for IPOs of securities subject to an application for listing on the London Stock Exchange under Pt. IV ('the LSE IPO regime', where a prospectus approved by the London Stock Exchange may be required), that for non-IPOs of such LSE securities, whether they are merely to be admitted to listing on the London Stock Exchange without any offer at all (where, for example, the securities are transferred from another exchange, such as AIM, by way of an introduction), or their admission to listing is accompanied by an offer which does not constitute

¶803

an IPO, (the 'LSE non-IPO regime', where listing particulars are normally required) and, finally, that for IPOs of non-LSE securities (the 'non-LSE IPO regime', where a prospectus may be required under the prospectus regulations); as explained above (see ¶801), there is no public issues regime for the fourth alternative, an IPO of securities already listed on the London Stock Exchange under Pt. IV.

Securities are not subject to either the LSE IPO regime or the LSE non-IPO regime unless Pt. IV applies to them. The securities to which Pt. IV applies are listed in s. 142(3) by reference to the paragraphs in Sch. 1 to the FSA which list the investments to which the FSA applies. Part IV applies to debt securities issued by a government (which term includes a local authority) of a non-EEA country but not of an EEA member State. However, debt securities issued by any government are outside the prospectus directive. They are therefore also outside the LSE IPO regime, on the basis that offers of them are treated as not being 'offers to the public' (Sch. 11A to the FSA); accordingly, they do not need a prospectus even if there is a public offer, although listing particulars must normally be published before they can be admitted to listing if the government is outside the EEA. Debt securities issued by governments are similarly outside the prospectus regulations. Conversely, corporate debt securities are normally subject to all three regimes. However, where their original maturity is less than one year, they are only subject to the LSE non-IPO regime if they are to be listed on the London Stock Exchange under Pt. IV; they are excluded from the prospectus regulations if they are non-LSE securities and, similarly, offers of them are treated as not being 'offers to the public' if they are LSE securities (Sch. 11A to the FSA). Accordingly, a public offer of such short term securities, such as commercial paper, does not need a prospectus but, if they are to be admitted to listing on the London Stock Exchange and no exemption applies, only listing particulars. Conversely, warrants and options relating to corporate debt securities are not subject to Pt. IV; even if they are to be listed on the London Stock Exchange, they are therefore outside both the LSE non-IPO regime and, even if there is a public offer, the LSE IPO regime. Warrants and options relating to corporate debt securities are therefore treated as non-LSE securities even if the warrants or options, or indeed the underlying debt securities, are listed on the London Stock Exchange, exactly because Pt. IV does not apply to them; they are accordingly always subject to the non-LSE IPO regime (unless the securities have an original maturity of less than one year). Finally, shares issued by companies are normally subject to all three regimes, as are warrants and options relating to them. However, if the company is an open-ended investment company, public offers or listings on the London Stock Exchange are outside all three regimes; instead, their marketing is subject to the FSA's Marketing Prohibition and the special restrictions on the marketing of collective investment schemes (see Ch. 9), and their listing on the

¶803

London Stock Exchange is subject to the London Stock Exchange's own, domestic, rules.

SECURITIES LISTED ON THE LONDON STOCK EXCHANGE

¶804   Overview

The admission of securities to official listing on the London Stock Exchange is normally regulated by Pt. IV of the FSA, as amended by the *Public Offers of Securities Regulations* 1995. So also is an offer to the public in the UK for the first time of securities within Pt. IV which are subject to an application for listing on the London Stock Exchange (LSE securities). In each case, Pt. IV requires the publication and filing with the Registrar of Companies of a document approved by the London Stock Exchange and containing the disclosures required by the listing particulars directive, and so the listing rules; where there is an IPO of LSE securities, the document is called a 'prospectus' and, in other cases (where there is an introduction only or an offer not constituting an offer to the public in the UK for the first time or the securities are outside the IPO regime), it is called 'listing particulars'. Schedule 11A to the FSA, inserted by the prospectus regulations, explains when securities are treated as offered to the public in the UK, so that the offer is an IPO requiring a prospectus if this is the first time that the securities concerned (rather than merely other securities of the same class) are offered to the public in the UK. The circumstances are the same as in the case of non-LSE securities, where it is much more important to know if the offer is an IPO requiring a prospectus, as only then is it necessary to publish and file a document containing prescribed disclosures, and the position is therefore explained in the context of an offer of non-LSE securities (see ¶821).

Part IV also regulates the issue of advertisements or other information about LSE securities in certain circumstances; if so provided in 'listing rules' issued by the London Stock Exchange (see ¶806), they cannot be issued without the approval or the authorisation (without approval) of the London Stock Exchange (see ¶813). As indicated in ¶803, the FSA's Marketing Prohibition, which normally requires investment advertisements to be approved by an FSA-authorised firm unless they are actually issued by one, will also be relevant (see ¶902 to ¶907), although there are certain exemptions in the case of LSE securities, for example one for listing particulars (see ¶905(2)).

The Financial Services Act adopts a flexible approach to the incorporation of the listing directives. Instead of spelling out their requirements, it merely empowers the London Stock Exchange to introduce 'listing rules' (see ¶806), gives it the requisite powers to comply (or require issuers to comply) with the other requirements of the listing directives and leaves it at that, except that it expressly sets out the general duty to disclose adequate 'financial condition' information, as required specifically by art. 4.1 of the listing particulars directive (see ¶810). However, and this is what this approach is based on, the requirements of the listing directives must still be observed even though that is not specifically spelled out in the FSA. Indeed, the Treasury is empowered to ensure that the London Stock Exchange observes the requirements of the listing directives if it does not do so of its own accord (s. 192).

¶805   The securities to which Pt. IV applies

Part IV of the FSA applies to all applications for admission to listing of securities on the London Stock Exchange under the listing directives, whether the securities are yet to be issued (even for a consideration other than cash, for example on a takeover) or are existing securities which are offered by the present owner or are merely 'introduced' to listing without any offer. For convenience, the term 'listed securities' is used in this guide to mean both securities which are already listed under Pt. IV of the FSA and securities subject to an application for listing under Pt. IV. However, Pt. IV does not apply to securities which, rather than being listed, are dealt in on the Alternative Investment Market of the London Stock Exchange or on Tradepoint or to securities listed or quoted on an overseas stock exchange rather than in London. IPOs of these securities, and of securities not quoted on any exchange, are subject to the prospectus regulations, as also are IPOs of securities listed on the London Stock Exchange but falling outside Pt. IV, if they are securities within the prospectus regulations regime.

Part IV applies only to shares and debt securities (technically, 'debentures' within para. 2 or 3 of Sch. 1 to the FSA), to warrants or other rights to subscribe for shares and to depositary receipts for, or other certificates representing, shares (s. 142(2) and (3)(c)). However, Pt. IV does not apply to other investments, for example traded options and warrants or other rights to subscribe for or acquire debt securities; nor does it apply to shares in industrial and provident societies or bills of exchange accepted by a banker, even though, as a result of the ISD, they are now FSA-regulated investments, falling in para. 1 and 2 of Sch. 1 respectively (para. 35 of Sch. 7 to the *Investment Services Regulations* 1995 (SI 1995/3275)). Part IV also applies to listed shares in building societies (s. 142(3)(a)). As permitted by the admission directive, Pt. IV does not, however, apply to debt securities issued by the government of, or a local authority in, the UK or another member State of the European Economic Area. Conversely, Pt. IV does apply to debt securities issued by other governments or local authorities, or by international organisations of which the UK or another member State of the EEA is a member (s. 142(3)(b)). As permitted by the admission directive, Pt. IV does not apply to shares in open-ended investment companies (see Ch. 10). However, the Treasury may at a later stage apply the provisions of Pt. IV to such shares or to other units or interests in collective investment schemes (s . 142(4)); indeed, it has already applied Pt. IV to 'single property' schemes (the *Official Listing of Securities (Units in Single Property Schemes) Order* 1989 (SI 1989/29)). The investments to which Pt. IV applies are referred to in this part of this chapter as 'securities', which is the term used both in normal speech and in the FSA itself.

¶806   The London Stock Exchange as competent authority

The FSA delegates responsibility to regulate admission to stock exchange listing under the listing directives to the 'competent authority' which may make rules (referred to as 'listing rules') for the purposes of Pt. IV (s. 142(6)) and which is protected from legal liability in damages for anything done or omitted in good faith (s. 187(4)). The competent authority also vets prospectuses issued on IPOs of securities to be listed under Pt. IV. The competent authority is the London Stock Exchange but the FSA authorises the Treasury to transfer the functions of the competent authority to another body (s. 157(1)). The Treasury will be able to transfer those functions either at the request of the London Stock Exchange or if it appears to the Treasury that it is necessary to do so for the protection of investors or that the London Stock Exchange exercises its powers in a way which is unnecessary for the protection of investors (that is, abuses its powers) and fails to take into account the proper interests of issuers (s. 157(1)); this latter condition may be particularly relevant where the London Stock Exchange pre-vets IPO prospectuses in respect of non-LSE securities if the offeror wants to use the 'single European passport' granted by the prospectus directive (see ¶824). This 'threat' that an external body will have jurisdiction over admission to its own Official List will therefore always hang like a Damoclean sword over the London Stock Exchange, but in this guide the competent authority is referred to as 'the London Stock Exchange'.

¶807   Applications for listing

The FSA provides that no securities within Pt. IV can be admitted to the Official List of the London Stock Exchange except in accordance with the provisions of Pt. IV (s. 142(1)). An application for listing must be made as provided in the listing rules (s. 143(1)) ; unless the listing rules are complied with, the securities cannot be listed (s. 144(1)). This gives statutory authority to the London Stock Exchange's rules (which are set out in the Listing Rules, known colloquially as the 'Yellow Book'). The listing rules must be in writing and must be made available to the public, although the London Stock Exchange is allowed to charge for copies (s. 156(4)). The FSA imposes its own requirements in addition to those imposed by the London Stock Exchange.

Thus, it provides that no application can be made for listing except by or with the consent of the issuer of the securities (s. 143(2)); in the case of depositary receipts for, and other certificates representing, shares, the 'issuer' is the issuer of the underlying shares (s. 142(7)) and it is accordingly his consent which is needed. The FSA states expressly that Pt. IV does not prejudice the powers of the London Stock Exchange to make rules for investments which are not securities within Pt. IV (s. 142(9)). The London Stock Exchange is therefore still able to impose similar requirements on open-ended investment companies even though they have not been brought into the Pt. IV statutory regime (see ¶805); however, these requirements would remain matters of private contract.

The FSA specifies two circumstances where the London Stock Exchange is entitled to refuse a listing to securities within Pt. IV even if the applicable conditions are satisfied. These are if the London Stock Exchange considers that the admission of the securities would be detrimental to the interests of investors for a reason relating to the issuer, or if the issuer has failed to comply with obligations to which it is subject in relation to official listing in another member State of the EEA (but not, for example, in relation to listing on the New York Stock Exchange) (s. 144(3)). The statement of these two circumstances implies that the London Stock Exchange does not have a total discretion as to whether or not to admit securities to the Official List. Indeed, the admission directive requires that applicants should have a right of judicial review, although there is no statutory right to a listing. The London Stock Exchange has six months (or longer if it requires extra information) to notify the applicant whether the securities will be admitted to listing. If it has given no answer within this period, the application is deemed to have been refused (s. 144(5)) and the applicant can seek judicial review of the 'decision'. It is likely that judicial review can be sought only by the applicant itself, and not by shareholders, as in the case of a de-listing (the *Titaghur* case, see ¶816). Conversely, the FSA prohibits the London Stock Exchange from admitting securities to listing unless the application has been duly made and it is satisfied that all its listing rules relating to applications generally (including the requirement for listing particulars (see ¶809)) and any particular requirements relating to that application have been complied with, even if not required by the FSA (s. 144(1)). Effectively, however, admission will be conclusive evidence that all the listing requirements have in fact been fulfilled (s. 144(6)). This statutory exclusion of the London Stock Exchange's right to grant or refuse listing in its sole discretion does not apply to investments which are not subject to Pt. IV.

¶808   Prohibition on listing by private companies

The FSA provides that no application can be made by a private company for the listing of shares or debt securities to be issued by it (s. 143(3)). Strangely, this prohibition does not seem to apply to existing shares or debt securities and if this is correct it would allow a listing to be effected by means of an 'introduction', which does not require a new issue, if the London Stock Exchange accepts that there is a sufficient spread of investors (which may be unlikely in practice).

¶809   Publication of listing particulars

As allowed or, in the case of IPOs, required by the FSA, and unless an exemption applies, the London Stock Exchange requires as a condition of admission to listing that the applicant publishes a document containing specified disclosures; if the securities are to be offered to the public in the UK for the first time after the application for admission but before the admission actually takes place, the document is called a 'prospectus' and, if not, it is normally called 'listing particulars' (s. 144(2)). Both classes of document are referred to below in this chapter as 'listing particulars'. The listing particulars have to be approved by the London Stock Exchange and registered with the Registrar of Companies before publication (s. 144(2)(a) and s. 149(1)), and must state that a copy has been delivered to the Registrar (s. 149(1)).

Although the FSA does not impose an express obligation on the London Stock Exchange to require the publication of listing particulars if there is no IPO, such an obligation is normally imposed by the listing particulars directive. The Treasury can make the London Stock Exchange comply with the directive (s. 192). The London Stock Exchange therefore has to require the disclosures required by the listing particulars directive. However, the London Stock Exchange has provided certain exemptions, for example, if the issue is of shares and would increase the shares of a class already listed by less than ten per cent, it will normally not need listing particulars. Even if no listing particulars are in fact required by the London Stock Exchange in certain cases, the London Stock Exchange nonetheless normally requires certain prescribed disclosures to be published (for example as an 'exempt listing document', an 'equivalent offering document' or what may be called 'equivalent listing particulars').

¶810   Contents of listing particulars

Prospectuses and other listing particulars must contain such detailed information as the London Stock Exchange prescribes, and also the prescribed 'financial condition' information which the FSA (and, indeed, the London Stock Exchange) requires, in compliance with the listing particulars directive. As required by the prospectus directive, this information must also be given even where there is an IPO in connection with the application for listing; a prospectus therefore normally contains the disclosures required by the Yellow Book rather than the prospectus regulations, although the requirements are amended to cater for the fact that there is also a UK public offer. The listing particulars must normally contain not only all the prescribed detailed information but also all such other information as investors and their professional advisers would reasonably require to make an informed assessment of the assets and liabilities, financial position, profits and losses and prospects of the issuer of the securities and would reasonably expect to find in listing particulars (s. 146(1), reflecting art. 4.1 of the listing particulars directive). The FSA allows the nature and extent of this 'financial condition' information to be determined by the circumstances, for example the nature of the issuer and the prospective market and, in particular, existing public information (s. 146(3)). The FSA requires the persons 'responsible' for the preparation of the listing particulars (see ¶812) to make reasonable enquiries to ascertain any such information not within their personal knowledge, but the disclosure obligation is restricted to information which they actually know or ought to know (s. 1 46(2)). Strangely, there is no express requirement in s. 146 to publish such information about guarantors of debt securities, which would be a substantial improvement so far as investor protection was concerned because, *ex hypothesi*, investors would be investing in reliance on the financial strength of the guarantor rather than of the issuer. However, the inclusion of certain financial information about guarantors is required by the listing particulars directive and, accordingly, the London Stock Exchange does require certain information about guarantors. In addition, it will of course be necessary to give a full description of the rights attaching to the securities to be listed (s. 146(1)(b)).

The London Stock Exchange has a general right to grant derogations from the listing particulars requirements in particular cases if authorised by the listing rules (s. 156(2)) and to the extent permitted by the listing particulars directive. In addition, the London Stock Exchange may authorise the omission from listing particulars generally of particular 'financial condition' information otherwise required by s. 146 (s. 148). The London Stock Exchange may allow information to be omitted under s. 148 only on particular grounds: that its disclosure would be contrary to the public interest, as to which a certificate from the Treasury will be conclusive (s. 148(3)); that its disclosure would be seriously detrimental to the issuer, although the London Stock Exchange cannot allow anything to be omitted on this ground if its omission would mislead a prospective investor as to any essential facts; or, finally, in the case of debt securities of any class prescribed by the listing rules, because its disclosure would be unnecessary for persons of the kind who may be expected normally to buy or deal in the securities concerned, which is intended to help preserve the speed and informality so vital in the Eurobond market.

¶811 Supplementary listing particulars

It may be necessary for the issuer to publish a supplementary prospectus or other supplementary listing particulars (for example, during the course of an offer) in certain circumstances (s. 147). They will be required if, after the preparation of listing particulars for submission to the London Stock Exchange and before the commencement of dealings following admission, there is a significant change affecting any matter required to be contained in those particulars (for example, the financial condition of the issuer). They will also be required if a significant new matter arises which would have had to have been included in the original listing particulars if it had arisen before they were prepared. For this purpose, 'significant' does not necessarily mean 'price-sensitive'; it means significant for making an informed assessment of the issuer's 'financial condition' (see ¶810) (s. 147(2)). The supplementary listing particulars will have to be approved by the London Stock Exchange and registered before publication (s. 147(1) and 149(1)). If necessary, more than one set of supplementary listing particulars may have to be published (s. 147(4)). The FSA requires the persons 'responsible' for listing particulars (see ¶812) to notify the issuer if they become aware of any such circumstances (s. 147(3)). The issuer is not required to issue supplementary listing particulars if he did not know of the relevant change or new matter, and was not informed of it by a 'responsible' person, (s. 147(3)). The obligation to publish supplementary listing particulars is on the issuer of the securities rather than any different offeror, presumably because no application for listing can be made under Pt. IV except by or with the consent of the issuer.

¶812   Compensation payable by persons 'responsible'

The FSA enforces the requirement to publish listing particulars or supplementary listing particulars by imposing civil liabilities on the persons 'responsible' for them if they contain false or misleading statements or omit any matter required to be included by the FSA or the listing rules and the statement or omission results in loss (s. 150(1)). The FSA thus contains a civil sanction for mere non-disclosure of prescribed information. The issuer of the securities will be similarly liable if he fails to publish supplementary listing particulars when he is required to do so, as will anyone else who is responsible for listing particulars if he fails to notify the issuer of the significant change or new matter requiring supplementary listing particulars to be issued (s. 150(3)). If the facts are sufficient, the issuer or offeror may also be guilty of an offence under s. 47 of the FSA (misleading statements), which would enable the SIB to bring a civil action for compensation and disgorgement of profits under s. 61.

Subject to certain defences, compensation will be payable under s. 150 to any person who suffers loss because the securities are as a result worth less than (effectively) they were represented to be. Although s. 150 is not totally clear, the better view is that compensation is payable, unless a statutory defence is available, even if the investor did not invest in reliance on the listing particulars and, indeed, even if he did not see them or he bought the securities in the secondary market (see ¶822); however, no compensation will be payable to a person who bought with knowledge of the default (s. 151(5)).

The FSA provides the reasonable defences that would be expected, for example that the person 'responsible' published a correction (s. 151(3)), or reasonably believed that the statement was true and not misleading or that nothing that should have been disclosed was omitted (s. 151(1)). However, in this latter case, ignorance of the facts will not itself be an excuse unless he has made all reasonable enquiries to ascertain the true position. In addition, he must have continued in that belief not just until admission to listing but until the securities were acquired, or must have had no time to publish a correction or bring it to the attention of prospective investors, or (which may help limit liability to purchasers in the market) the securities must have been acquired after a material lapse of time, provided, in this last case, that he had continued in his belief at least until the commencement of dealings (s. 151(1)). There are similar defences for reasonable reliance on an expert's statements provided that the expert consented to their inclusion in (in the hallowed phraseology) the form and context in which they were included (s. 151(2)). In the case of a failure to publish supplementary listing particulars, there will be no liability if the issuer or other person 'responsible' reasonably believed that there was no need for them.

As required by the listing particulars directive, the FSA spells out (in s. 152) the persons who are deemed to be responsible for all or part of listing particulars or supplementary listing particulars. The persons 'responsible' are the issuer, every director or person who authorised himself to be named as a director of the issuer, every person who expressly accepts responsibility (for example, under the listing rules) and every other person who authorised their contents. Where the listing particulars are a prospectus relating to an IPO, references to the 'issuer' include references to the 'offeror' (s. 154(A)(b)), except that directors of the offeror are not 'responsible' as such. The question of who is an 'offeror' for this purpose is often a difficult one (see ¶823). The offeror is, however, not 'responsible' by virtue of his status where the offer is not an IPO, for example, where the offerees do not constitute the 'public' in the UK or the securities have already been offered to the public in the UK on an earlier occasion; the offeror would, however, be 'responsible' for the contents of the listing particulars that he has authorised himself, which is likely to be most of them. The issuer is a person 'responsible' even in the case of an IPO by a shareholder of existing securities; this is presumably because the application to listing cannot be made without the issuer's consent (s. 143(2)) and therefore it should ensure that it has verified the statements made about it. The fact that anyone who has allowed himself to be named as a director is 'responsible' may in practice cause problems in the case of a recommended takeover where a director of the target company is named as joining the offeror.

¶812

However, there are several helpful exemptions from responsibility. A director or ostensible director is not responsible for particulars published without his knowledge or consent if he publicised that fact when he became aware of their publication (s. 152(2)). There is an exemption for persons who merely give advice in a professional capacity (s. 152(8)); however, it is unlikely that that exemption applies to exclude, for example, a merchant banker who approves particular wording rather than merely giving advice and it is thought that, accordingly, the exemption will not exclude the responsibility of sponsors even if they are not themselves offerors in an IPO, which is an important question. There is a special exemption in the case of recommended take-overs; if the target company and its directors expressly accept responsibility for particulars about the target company, the offeror and its directors will not be regarded as 'responsible' for them (s. 152 (4)). In addition, directors of the issuer or an offeror are not 'responsible' for the listing particulars in the case of 'international securities' of a class prescribed by the London Stock Exchange for 'reduced disclosure' purposes (see ¶810), unless they accept responsibility or authorise the contents of the listing particulars; 'international securities' are debt securities likely to be dealt in by overseas residents, or denominated in a foreign currency or otherwise connected with an overseas country (s. 152(5)–(6)). Finally, there is an interesting exemption from responsibility as directors for directors with conflicts of interest or who are in other circumstances which the London Stock Exchange certifies make it 'inappropriate' for them to be so responsible (for example, in a takeover where they are directors of both companies) (s. 152(5)).

The FSA provides that its 'listing particulars' liability does not exclude other liabilities, for example in deceit or misrepresentation (s. 150(4)); accordingly, there are still many different varieties of potential prospectus liabilities. However, it does exclude liability for non-disclosure of matters which do not have to be disclosed in listing particulars by the person or persons responsible for them (s. 150(6)). A recent case has held that even purchasers in the market may be entitled to sue directors of an issuer for negligence on a prospectus if the facts showed that it had the additional, intended, purpose of informing and encouraging purchasers in the market and the purchaser established that he had reasonably relied on the negligent misrepresentation and reasonably believed that the representor had intended him to act on it (*Possfund Custodian Trustee v Diamond* [1996] 2 All ER 1774, Ch. D). This liability may be relevant even in the case of listing particulars if for some reason there is no statutory liability.

¶813   Advertisements in connection with listing applications

Section 154(1) provides that, where listing particulars are or are to be published in connection with an application for listing, no advertisement or other information of a kind specified by listing rules can be issued in the UK unless its contents have been approved by the London Stock Exchange or the London Stock Exchange has authorised its issue without such approval. Contravention will be treated as a breach of conduct of business rules in the case of FSA-authorised firms and passporting firms and as a criminal offence in the case of anyone else (s. 154 and para. 36 of Sch. 7 to the *Investment Services Regulations* 1995). Although the FSA does not refer to the point, art. 22 of the listing particulars directive requires this prohibition to apply to certain specified documents relating to the admission of the securities to listing and intended to be published by or on behalf of the issuer. The London Stock Exchange can however, require other documents relating to a listing to be also subject to this prohibition, and all these documents will also fall in s. 154. The Yellow Book lists the documents subject to these approval or authorisation requirements and they include offer notices and formal notices (which need LSE approval) and mini-prospectuses, summary particulars and announcements of a public offer or the admission to listing (which need only LSE authorisation and some prescribed disclosures). The FSA provides that the issuer of the document (and the persons responsible for the prospectus or other listing particulars) will be protected against liability for non-disclosure or misleading statements in relation to that information if the information is appropriate when read together with the listing particulars (s. 154(5)).

An advertisement or information will be treated as issued 'in the UK' even if it is issued outside the UK if it is directed or made available to persons in the UK, unless it is in a newspaper or other periodical published and circulated principally outside the UK or in a broadcast transmitted principally for reception outside the UK (s. 207(3)). The same test is therefore used as in the Marketing Prohibition (see ¶902). In addition, any documents actually sent to recipients in the UK will in any event be 'issued' in the UK (as a document is issued, and, indeed, an offer is made, where it is received) and accordingly will be subject to s. 154 quite apart from s. 207(3). There is a defence for 'innocent issuers' who are not themselves investment firms, such as newspapers (and, perhaps, advertising agencies) who reasonably believe that the advertisement or information was approved or authorised as required. Advertisements subject to s. 154 which constitute 'investment advertisements' are exempted from the Marketing Prohibition and so can be issued direct by the issuer without the approval of an FSA-authorised firm (see ¶905(1)).

¶814   Mutual recognition of EEA prospectus and listing particulars

As part of the single European market programme, the listing particulars directive (as amended by the prospectus directive) provides for mutual recognition by all EEA member States in which an application is made for official listing under the listing particulars directive of prospectuses (and listing particulars) which have been approved in another member State; mutual recognition is, however, required only where the application for listing is made contemporaneously with or within a short period after the approval and member States have the option to provide that mutual recognition applies only in the case of issuers incorporated within the EEA. The securities normally do not need to have been subject to an application for official listing in that other member State provided that the prospectus was published under the prospectus directive; if it was, it does not matter whether it contains listing particulars directive disclosures or prospectus directive disclosures (see ¶824). The prospectus regulations accordingly provide for mutual recognition for the purposes of Pt. IV of prospectuses and listing particulars (or supplementary prospectuses or listing particulars) approved in another member State of the EEA (reg. 20 and Pt. I of Sch. 4). These documents, which are referred to in Sch. 4 as 'recognised European documents', must contain the information required by the 'approving' member State and any additional information required by the London Stock Exchange's listing rules, although presumably only if permitted by the listing particulars directive, (para. 2, Sch. 4); however, they do not need to be 'approved' by the London Stock Exchange (para. 4(a) of Sch. 4). In the case of a European document which has been approved as a prospectus, the approving 'member State' must have given its approval to the prospectus within the period of three months before the application for listing on the London Stock Exchange is made (para. 1(c)(ii), Sch. 4 and art. 24b of the listing particulars directive, as amended, to which it refers). The 'approving member State' is the State where the issuer has its registered office if the relevant IPO or application for listing (or one of the relevant IPOs or applications for listing) is made in that State; if it is not, the issuer or offeror can select the approving member State from the member States concerned (art. 24 of the listing particulars directive, as amended). If the prospectus or listing particulars have been translated into English, it is normally the English translation which is the recognised European document (para. 1, Sch. 4).

¶815   On-going obligations and contravention of listing rules

As contemplated in s. 153(1), the Yellow Book imposes on-going obligations on issuers of listed securities, in particular to disclose information whenever that is necessary to avoid a false market; they apply also to the issuers of securities which were already listed when Pt. IV came into force (s. 153(2)). The FSA does not expressly declare breaches of the listing rules to be actionable, as it does, for example, contraventions of conduct of business rules which cause loss (FSA, s. 62). It is an interesting question whether civil claims can be brought by investors, for example on the ground of breach of statutory duty, and, indeed, whether the London Stock Exchange's interpretation or application of those rules is subject to judicial review, which would in fact seem to be likely, as in the case of the Takeover Panel (*R v Panel on Takeovers and Mergers, ex parte Datafin plc & Anor* [1987] 1 All ER 564; [1987] 2 WLR 699; (1987) 3 BCC 10; *R v Panel on Takeovers and Mergers, ex parte Guinness plc* [1989] 2 WLR 863; (1988) 4 BCC 325). The FSA allows the listing rules to provide for sanctions, which in the interests of self-regulation are left to the discretion of the London Stock Exchange. However, the FSA expressly allows the listing rules to authorise the London Stock Exchange not only to publish the fact that an issuer has contravened those rules but also itself to publish any required information which an issuer has failed to publish (s. 153(1)).

¶816   Termination or suspension of listing

As permitted by the FSA in circumstances precluding normal regular dealings (whether relating to the market or the issuer itself), the Yellow Book provides that the London Stock Exchange is able to discontinue the listing of any securities at any time and in any circumstances (s. 145(1)). This is the only ground on which the admission directive allows securities to be de-listed and it provides that delisting must be subject to judicial review; however, although the company itself can claim judicial review, shareholders in the company cannot do so (*The International Stock Exchange of the United Kingdom and the Republic of Ireland Limited, ex parte Else (1982) Ltd* [1993] BCC 11, CA (relating to the delisting of Titaghur plc)). The London Stock Exchange is also able to suspend listing in similar circumstances (s. 145(2)). These provisions apply even to securities which were already listed when Pt. IV came into force (s. 145(4)).

OFFERS OF UNLISTED SECURITIES

¶817   Overview

When corporate securities which are not listed, or subject to an application for listing, on the London Stock Exchange under Pt. IV of the FSA ('non-LSE securities') are offered to the public in the UK for the first time, it is normally necessary for the offeror to publish and file a prospectus containing prescribed disclosures (and a supplementary prospectus, if one is needed) and to refer to the prospectus in all marketing materials. Unless an exemption applies, the prospectus requirements apply to offers even of existing securities (by a shareholder) except where the particular securities themselves (and not merely other securities of the same class) have been offered to the public in the UK on an earlier occasion.

The prospectus regime which applies to these initial public offers (IPOs) is contained in Pt. II of the *Public Offers of Securities Regulations* 1995 (SI 1995/1537) (the prospectus regulations), which implement into UK law the requirements of the EU prospectus directive of 1989 and came into force on 19 June 1995. Importantly, similar compensation provisions for non-disclosure apply to prospectuses registered under the prospectus regulations as to listing particulars (including prospectuses) registered under Pt. IV (see ¶812 above). Because the prospectus regulations implement the prospectus directive, they also contain the directive's provisions for mutual recognition of non-UK EEA prospectuses (even if they relate to an issuer which is not an EEA company). The prospectus regulations also establish the reciprocal regime enabling mutual recognition of UK prospectuses (although individual member States may not recognise prospectuses relating to non-EEA issuers); this new, voluntary, regime allows offerors to seek pre-vetting by the London Stock Exchange in order to qualify for mutual recognition and is accordingly contained in the revised Pt. IV (see ¶824).

There are, however, many important exemptions from the prospectus requirements in the case of qualifying restricted offers. These work on the basis that the offer is not an offer to the public in the UK for the purposes of the prospectus regulations; importantly, only offerees in the UK are taken into account for this purpose. If there is no need for a prospectus (and, indeed, even if there is), the FSA's Marketing Prohibition and ban on cold calling (see Ch. 9) will normally apply. To avoid regulation of offers to offerees in the UK, it is therefore necessary to fall within exemptions from both regimes; this will typically be the case where the UK offerees are restricted to FSA-authorised firms and passporting firms or other 'business investors' (see ¶302) which are also 'qualifying securities professionals' for the purpose of the prospectus regulations; the offer can be made, in addition, to 'qualifying corporations' which are not 'qualifying securities professionals' (see ¶821(b) in the UK, although they must be limited to 50 unless the minimum purchase price for UK offerees (including qualifying securities professionals) is at least ECU40,000. The prospectus regulations do not apply to open-ended investment companies; however, the marketing of their securities is subject to both the FSA's Marketing Prohibition and, as they are regarded as 'collective investment schemes' (s. 75(8) of the FSA), the special regime applicable to 'collective investment schemes' (see Ch. 9).

¶818   The requirement for a prospectus

The prospectus regulations provide that, when 'unlisted securities' are offered to the public in the UK for the first time, it is normally necessary to publish a 'prospectus' containing prescribed disclosures and to register it with the Registrar of Companies. A 'prospectus' is the document containing the disclosures and is not necessarily the offer document itself; indeed, the offer does not actually need to be in writing. 'Unlisted securities' is not a glamorous term but it means all securities subject to the prospectus regulations which are not listed, or subject to an application for listing, on the London Stock Exchange under Pt. IV of the FSA; they are therefore referred to in this chapter as 'non-LSE securities'. They include practically all corporate securities (and warrants, options and depositary receipts relating to them) which are not listed, or subject to an application for listing, on the London Stock Exchange under Pt. IV of the FSA, including not only unquoted securities but also securities quoted on AIM and securities listed or quoted on non-UK exchanges, such as the New York Stock Exchange or EASDAQ. Indeed, certain classes of securities are subject to the prospectus regulations even if they are listed on the London Stock Exchange. This will be the case if, exceptionally, they are not subject to the rules relating to listing contained in Pt. IV of the FSA (for example, covered warrants, traded options and warrants to subscribe debt securities); they are in effect treated as not being listed and accordingly are also referred to in this chapter as 'non-LSE securities'.

The prospectus regulations provide that, whenever non-LSE securities are offered to the public in the UK for the first time (and even if other securities of the same class have previously been offered to the public in the UK), a prospectus containing specified information about the issuer and the securities must normally be filed in a public register in the UK, and copies must be made available at a UK address (reg. 4). There is no requirement actually to send the prospectus to the offerees; however, that would certainly be best practice and would normally need to be done for commercial reasons. Where the securities are convertible into, or otherwise give a right to acquire, securities issued by a different issuer or are guaranteed, the prescribed financial information must also be given in respect of the issuer of the underlying securities and the guarantor (para. 50 and 51 of Sch. 1). The information must be presented in as easily analysable and comprehensible a form as possible (reg. 8(3)). In addition, any marketing materials relating to the offer, for example a newspaper advertisement, must state that a prospectus is or will be published and give an address in the UK from which it can be obtained (reg. 12). If an FSA-authorised firm (or a passporting firm) fails to comply with these requirements (other than those relating to disclosures, see ¶822), the failure is treated as a contravention of SRO (or SIB) rules (reg. 16(1) and (6)); the firm can therefore be sued under s. 62 of the FSA by a qualifying investor (who must normally be an individual) for any loss suffered as a result or under s. 61 by the SIB. Non-compliance by anyone else is a criminal offence and any investor who suffers loss as a result can normally sue for compensation (reg. 16(2) and (4)).

The registered prospectus must normally contain the detailed disclosures about the issuer and the securities being offered which are set out in Sch. 1 of the prospectus regulations. In addition, as in the case of Pt. IV prospectuses and

¶818

listing particulars, there is a specific obligation (in reg. 9(1)) to provide all information which investors would need in order to make an 'informed assessment' of the issuer's assets and liabilities and its profits and losses, of the financial condition of the issuer and of its prospects, and of the rights attaching to the securities, with consequent civil liability for any failure to do so (see ¶822). Although reg. 9(1) does not specify what period should be covered by 'prospects', the detailed disclosure provisions of the prospectus regulations follow the prospectus directive by requiring details of prospects for at least the current financial year (para. 49 of Sch. 1); reg. 9(1) should therefore be read as referring to at least that period. A supplementary prospectus must be issued (and registered) if there is a significant change affecting the required disclosures or a significant new matter arises which would have had to be disclosed or a significant inaccuracy is discovered in any information contained in the prospectus (whether or not a required disclosure); in all these cases, 'significant' means important for the purpose of making that informed assessment (reg. 10). Strangely, there is no requirement to send the supplementary prospectus to the original offerees or advertise its publication.

If an offeror who is not the issuer or acting under an arrangement with the issuer is subject to the prospectus requirements, he is not required to provide information about the issuer which is not in the public domain and is not known by the offeror after making reasonable efforts to obtain it (reg. 11(2)).

¶819   Scope of the prospectus regulations

It must be emphasised that, unless the IPO falls within an exemption, the prospectus requirements apply whenever non-LSE securities are offered to the public in the UK for the first time, even if the offer is not for cash (but, for example, for shares) and even if the offer is not in writing (but, for example, by fax or screen, such as a stock exchange screen or the Internet).

The prospectus regulations normally apply to IPOs of non-LSE securities even if securities of the same class have previously been offered to the public in the UK or, indeed, are listed on the London Stock Exchange. As indicated in ¶818, the prospectus regulations apply even if the securities are being offered by a shareholder rather than by the issuer itself (or by a securities firm or underwriter by arrangement with the issuer) and even if the shareholder is not a 'controller'. However, the offeror's disclosure obligations in relation to the issuer are necessarily qualified (see ¶818). Finally, the prospectus regulations apply not only to offers of shares or corporate debt securities (other than shares in, or perhaps debt securities of, open-ended investment companies) but also to offers of debt securities, call options or warrants (including covered warrants), or depositary receipts, convertible into or relating to shares or corporate debt securities to which the prospectus regulations apply (reg. 3(1)(b)). All of these derivatives are referred to in the Prospectus Regulations as 'convertible securities' (reg. 2(1)) and special disclosure obligations apply in relation to the underlying securities if the issuer of the underlying securities is different from the issuer of the convertible securities (para. 50 of Sch.1).

However, the prospectus regulations do not apply to debt securities with an original maturity of less than one year, such as commercial paper (reg. 3(2)). They also do not apply to government securities or securities issued by a local or public authority. In addition, the prospectus regulations do not apply to an offer of securities which were originally issued at the same time as other securities of the same class if a UK prospectus was then published in relation to those other securities (see ¶821(6)).

The prospectus regulations make it clear that an offer is to be treated as an offer to the public if it is made to any section of the public, including shareholders or holders of debt securities of a particular company (such as the issuer) or clients of the offeror (reg. 6). However, there are some important exemptions from the need for a prospectus, although not necessarily from the FSA's Marketing Prohibition or ban on cold calling (see Ch. 9); these exemptions apply to most private placements in or into the UK (see ¶821).

¶820   Exemptions from prospectus requirements even where there is an offer to the public

The prospectus does not need to include the prescribed detailed information about the issuer's assets and liabilities, financial condition and profits and losses (or its principal activities and its directors) if the omission is authorised in specified circumstances by a person or body designated by the Treasury (reg. 8(4)). Those circumstances are that the securities being offered are shares, that the shares are to be dealt in on an 'approved exchange', that the shares are being offered on a pre-emptive basis (for example, by a rights issue) to some or all of the existing holders of shares (seemingly, not necessarily shares of the same class, although that is unclear) and that up-to-date information equivalent to the omitted prescribed information is already available under that exchange's rules. An 'approved exchange' is a recognised investment exchange under the FSA (an RIE) which has been specifically approved by the Treasury for this purpose; the RIE does not need to have a head office in the UK. The Treasury has in fact 'approved' AIM for this purpose and has designated the London Stock Exchange as the 'competent authority'.

In addition, the Treasury can designate a UK regulator who can authorise public offers of shares to be made without a registered prospectus at all if they are of the same class as shares which have already been admitted to dealings on an approved exchange (typically, AIM), the number or value of the offered shares is less than ten per cent of the number or value of the shares already quoted and up-to-date information equivalent to the detailed disclosures required by Sch. 1 to the prospectus regulations is already available under that exchange's rules (reg. 8(5)). The offered shares seemingly do not need to be quoted themselves. The Treasury has designated the London Stock Exchange as the competent authority.

The London Stock Exchange can also authorise the omission from the prospectus of information relating to the issuer in specified circumstances (reg. 11(3)). It can do so even though the securities are non-LSE securities and, as is normal, the London Stock Exchange does not have to approve the prospectus (but see ¶823). The specified circumstances are either that the publication of the information would be 'seriously detrimental' to the issuer and its omission would not be likely to mislead investors or that the information is of only minor importance.

There is also an important exemption under which a full prospectus is not needed even if the securities (whether or not shares) are being offered to the public in the UK for the first time and the 'approved exchange' exemptions do not apply (for example, because the issuer is not quoted on an RIE but, for example, only on a non-UK stock exchange without a UK office). The exemption applies only to offers for subscription (and not to secondary offers, namely, offers of existing securities). The exemption will apply if, within the 12 months preceding the date when the new securities are first offered to the public in the UK, the same issuer has published a full prospectus in relation to other securities issued by the issuer, whether or not of the same class, (reg. 8(6)); a prospectus published by the issuer in relation to a secondary offer of securities owned by the issuer will not qualify (because it will not have contained most of the prescribed information about the issuer) and neither will even a prospectus about shares which were issued by the same issuer where the IPO was by a shareholder (as the prospectus was not published by the issuer, as required by the prospectus directive for the exemption to apply, and in any event may not have included all the required information about the issuer). Instead of a full prospectus, the issuer must either publish that earlier full prospectus (and any supplementary prospectus) or merely refer to it (or them) in its offer document and, in either case, must publish disclosures about any changes to the information contained in that earlier prospectus (and supplementary prospectus) which are likely to influence the value of the securities. This 'bring down' prospectus is a very helpful development in UK prospectus law. It would seem best practice (and certainly more prudent) to publish a copy of the earlier full prospectus rather than just to state that there was one and indicate changes.

Finally, as the prospectus regulations implement the prospectus directive, which requires member States to accept prospectuses used in other member States, prospectuses approved by regulators in other EEA member States can normally be used in the UK without needing to set out the disclosures required by Sch. 1 of the prospectus regulations or, indeed, to be approved by UK regulators (see ¶823).

¶821 Exemptions from prospectus requirements where there is deemed to be no 'offer to the public'

The prospectus regulations contain important private placement exemptions; where they apply, the offer is not a 'public offer' and therefore no prospectus is required, although the FSA's Marketing Prohibition and ban on cold calling may still apply (see Ch. 9). The statutory exemptions will cover most private placements in or into the UK, even if they are part of a public offer made outside the UK (for example, in a non-UK issuer's home territory). This is because the prospectus regulations apply on a territorial basis only; the question of whether an offer is made to the public 'in the UK' is therefore determined by reference only to recipients of the offer who are in the UK (reg. 7(1)) and it is irrelevant that the offer is part of a private placement or public offer made in another country. The exemptions therefore need to be reviewed only in the context of offerees physically in the UK; in the case of offers to banks or companies, this means a UK office.

As a result of these prospectus exemptions and of the exemptions in, or introduced under, the FSA from the FSA's Marketing Prohibition and ban on cold calling (see Ch. 9), private placements in or into the UK will not be regulated by UK law, provided that the prospectus is sent to UK recipients only if they are:

(a) firms authorised under the FSA or passporting firms which are also qualifying securities professionals (see (1) below); or

(b) qualifying corporations. A corporation will qualify if it is an FSA-authorised or passporting firm or, alternatively, if it, or a holding company or subsidiary, has a called-up share capital or net assets of at least £5m (or, if it or a holding company is quoted or otherwise has more than 20 shareholders, £500,000). However, the number of qualifying corporations (including FSA-authorised and passporting firms) which are not qualifying securities professionals must be limited to 50 (see (2) below) unless there is a minimum purchase price for UK offerees (including qualifying securities professionals) of at least ECU40,000 or the equivalent (see (4) below).

These private placements are unregulated by UK securities law even if the offeror is a firm authorised under the FSA. If, conversely, the offer is made to individuals or small companies, or other prospective investors, who are neither qualifying corporations nor, indeed, other 'business investors', then it will normally be regulated under the FSA (see Ch. 9). In all cases, however, it will normally be a criminal offence (under s. 47 of the FSA) if the offering materials contain misleading or untrue statements, or any information is dishonestly concealed, and the SIB is able to bring an action on behalf of investors (under s. 61 of the FSA) for an indemnity for any loss suffered as a result.

The private placement exemptions are normally written in terms of particular classes of offeree. However, the better, and certainly the prudent, view is that the exemption applies only if the offer can be accepted only by the offerees themselves. The only exception to this is in the case of offers to qualifying employees (see (11) below) but, even in this case, the exemption would not apply if the offer can be renounced (or, assigned) outside the permitted offerees.

The main exemptions from the prospectus requirements (on the basis that the offer is not treated as an offer to the public in the UK) apply to the following types of offer, looking only at offerees in the UK:

(1) Offers to qualifying securities professionals (reg. 7(2)(a)). 'Qualifying securities professionals' are firms which buy or sell securities (as principal or agent), or hold securities or act as investment manager, as part of their ordinary activities (rather than merely advise on securities or arrange transactions). As a result, offers to stockbrokers, investment banks, investment managers, nominee companies and most commercial banks will be exempted on this basis; the offer can be accepted by them for the account of clients but seemingly cannot be passed on to a client to accept personally. Offers to investment trusts, including venture capital trusts, and life assurance companies will also be exempted.

(2) Offers to no more than 50 persons (reg. 7(2)(b)). This is the first time that UK prospectus law has provided a private placement exemption for a specified number of offerees (in the UK). The relevant number is the number of people in the UK who receive the offer and are not in another applicable exemption (see below); the number who actually accept the offer is irrelevant. The Prospectus Regulations contain aggregation provisions to prevent the splitting up of offers to get within the exemption. In order to see whether the 50 person limit is reached for a particular offer, it is accordingly necessary to include all offerees in the UK who have previously received any offer from the same offeror in respect of the same class of securities, if the previous offer was open (rather than merely first made) during the 12 months before the proposed offer is first made and was exempted from the prospectus regulations by this '50 persons' exemption (reg. 7(6)); qualifying securities professionals and other offerees within any other exemption which can be used in relation to the same offer (see below) do not need to be included (reg. 7(3) and (4)). Although it may not be intended, it is,

¶821

perhaps, arguable that if the issuer 'places' the securities with a small number of firms, who separately buy for their own account and sell on, each placee (for example, a member of a 'selling group' or US style 'underwriter') should be treated as an 'offeror' (see ¶823) and each can, accordingly, sell to his 'own' 50 offerees in the UK without needing to publish a prospectus. However, the better view is surely that this simplistic avoidance device will not work: the regulators and the courts would regard all the 'offers' as one offer (and so an 'offer to the public') for the purposes of the prospectus regulations and the splitting up of the offer as a mere mechanism.

Under UK law, English limited partnerships are not separate legal entities; accordingly, the prudent view is that an offer to them is treated as made to each partner and, as there can be up to 20, this may restrict the use of the '50 persons' exemption. All offers should therefore be made to their managers if, as is normal, they are also the investment managers. If they are, and even though they normally do not enter into transactions themselves, they will be qualifying securities professionals (see (1) above). If they are not, or if they do not want to be subject to the ISD as brokers (which would subject them to heavy financial resources requirements under the CAD), which might not otherwise apply, the most useful exemption will normally be the exemption for offers with a minimum purchase price of not less than ECU40,000 (see (4) below).

(3) Offers to a restricted circle of experienced investors (in the UK) whom the offeror reasonably believes to be sufficiently knowledgeable to understand the risks involved in accepting the offer (reg. 7(2)(d)); any information supplied by the offeror is to be disregarded for this purpose, apart from information about the issuer (reg. 7(7)). As there is no statutory test, it would be prudent not to rely on this exemption, unless the position is clear.

(4) Offers where the minimum purchase price which may be paid under the offer by each offeree is not less than ECU40,000 or an equivalent amount (reg. 7(2)(i)); importantly, this is to be calculated at the latest practicable date (but not more than three days) before the offer is first made in the UK (reg. 7(9)). Although it is unclear, it is prudent to use the rate of exchange applicable to a purchase of ECUs with the currency of the offer. The exemption applies even if it is only the UK offerees who are subject to this threshold, even though non-UK offerees under a simultaneous local offer are not; however, all UK offerees must be included, even if they are qualifying securities professionals. This is the first time that UK prospectus law has provided an exemption for what may be called 'non-retail' offerings.

¶821

(5) Offers of Euro-securities (reg. 7(2)(s)). Offers of Euro-securities are typically offers of Eurobonds and Euro-equities where the principal market is outside the country of incorporation of the issuer (see para. 3(2) of Sch. 11A to the FSA, applied by reg. 2(1)). The exemption applies only where the underwriting syndicate and selling group include members with registered offices in different countries; this test can seemingly be satisfied even if they all act through offices in one country. For this purpose, a separate State or other territory is treated as a separate country. In addition, there must be no marketing to the general public in the UK; accordingly, marketing materials must be either sent direct to securities professionals (including in this case all FSA-authorised firms) or contained in professional journals and there should be no advertising in newspapers. If that is the case, ordinary investors can seemingly apply for the securities, although they can do so only if they use a bank, building society or securities professional as intermediary, which should be made clear in the marketing materials. If this interpretation is correct, this exemption is actually wider than the general exemption for offers to qualifying securities professionals (see (1) above); however, it would seem easiest to use either that general exemption or the exemption for offers with a minimum purchase price of ECU40,000 (see (4) above).

(6) Offers which relate to securities which were originally issued at the same time as a public issue of other securities of the same class (reg. 7(2)(t)). The exemption applies only if those other securities have already been offered to the public in the UK, and a UK prospectus was accordingly registered, whether under the prospectus regulations, Pt. IV of the FSA or the *Companies Act* 1985; seemingly, it does not matter how long before the new offer the prospectus was published and therefore how out of date the information in it is, although the information should be updated for a variety of reasons. The exemption cannot, of course, apply to an offer by the issuer.

(7) Offers made in connection with a 'takeover offer' (reg. 7(2)(k) and 7(10)). For this purpose, a 'takeover offer' is a qualifying offer to acquire all the shares, or all the shares of a particular class, not owned by the offeror or a qualifying partial offer. Accordingly, no prospectus normally needs to be issued in relation to securities offered as consideration in a bid.

(8) Offers by a UK private company to members or employees of the company, and qualifying family members, or to holders of its debt securities (reg. 7(2)(f) and reg. 7(8)). The exemption covers offers to restricted classes of family members of the shareholders or employees

(but not of the holders of debt securities), including, helpfully, family trusts (reg. 7(8)(b)). However, it does not cover holders of debt securities with an original maturity of less than one year, as they are not 'securities' for the purpose of the prospectus regulations (reg. 2(1)). This exemption (which mirrors that in the *Companies Act* 1985) shows that even private companies can make public offers within the prospectus regulations, if the offer is not a 'public offer' within the old *Companies Act* 1985 definition (see ¶825).

(9) Offers where the securities being offered are not transferable (reg. 7(2)(u)).

(10) Offers where the total consideration payable is limited to ECU40,000 (reg. 7(2)(h)). This is a maximum limit on the whole offer (to UK offerees) rather than the minimum threshold for each application or acceptance as referred to in (4) above.

(11) Offers restricted to qualifying employees of the issuer or its group, or specified classes of their family members, not, however, including family trusts, (reg. 7(2)(o) and reg. 7(12)).

The prospectus regulations do not give any guidance as to when an offer is treated as first made, which is relevant to the '50 persons' and ECU40,000 exemptions (and indeed to when a prospectus must be registered and made available at a UK address in the case of a public offer). The better view is that an offer is made when, as well as where, it is received; however, that may not apply to currency conversions in the case of the ECU40,000 exemption, if only on practical grounds, provided that the latest practicable date is used for the conversion rate.

Importantly, the '50 persons' and 'experienced investors' exemptions (see (2) and (3) above) are cumulative and apply in addition to the exemption for offers to qualifying securities professionals (see (1) above), (reg. 7(3)); as a result, an offer will be exempted from the prospectus regulations provided that all the offerees in the UK fall within one or other of these exemptions. The offer will therefore be exempted from the prospectus regulations (but not necessarily the FSA's Marketing Prohibition (see Ch. 9), if, typically, it is made in the UK only to qualifying securities professionals and 50 other persons. The exemptions in 6 to 8 above can also be used cumulatively with these three exemptions (reg. 7(3)). Each of the other exemptions listed above (for example, the ECU40,000 minimum purchase price described in (4) above) can be used only if it applies to all offerees in the UK; none of them can be used together with any other exemption.

¶822   Compensation payable by person 'responsible'

The prospectus regulations introduce for public offers of non-LSE securities a compensation regime similar to that relating to securities listed on the London Stock Exchange under Pt. IV (see ¶812). They provide that, if a prospectus (or supplementary prospectus) for non-LSE securities does not comply with the applicable disclosure requirements or contains any untrue or misleading statement, the person or persons 'responsible' for the prospectus or supplementary prospectus must normally compensate investors who suffer loss as a result (reg. 14(1)). If the facts are sufficient, the offeror may also be guilty of an offence under s. 47 of the FSA (misleading statements), which would enable the SIB to bring a civil action for compensation and disgorgement of profits under s. 61.

Although it is not clear, the generally accepted view is that reg. 14 does not require that the investor has relied on the statement or the prospectus; it is enough that he acquired the securities (whether or not in the offer) and that he lost money because of the non-compliance or untrue or misleading statement (for example, because the securities were worth less than they would have been worth if the statement was true). The general view is supported by the fact that compensation is also normally payable if a supplementary prospectus should have been issued but was not (reg. 14(3)). The investor surely cannot be expected to have invested in reliance on the fact that, if any statement was or became untrue or a new matter arose, a supplementary prospectus would have been issued in accordance with reg. 10. This is especially the case as the offeror is not required to send the supplementary prospectus to the original offerees or publicise its issue, although it must be made available to the public (reg. 10(3)); even if it were published in a newspaper, as required in the case of AIM under London Stock Exchange rules, investors would not necessarily see it. In addition, there is no obligation to send even the original prospectus to the offerees but only to 'make it available' free of charge (reg. 4(1)); compensation cannot be predicated on the basis that the offeree should have gone to look at the prospectus if it was not sent to him; it must surely be payable on the basis that he would have been misled if he had looked at it.

The persons 'responsible' for the prospectus are listed in the 'prospectus regulations' (reg. 13). They include the issuer and its directors (unless the offer is a secondary offer, of existing securities, and the issuer has not authorised it), anyone who is named in the prospectus with his consent as a director or proposed director of the issuer and, if the offeror is not the issuer, the offeror and its directors. It is not always clear who is the 'offeror' for the purposes of the Prospectus Regulations (see ¶823). The persons 'responsible' also include everyone who has authorised the contents of the prospectus or supplementary prospectus (or, as the case may be, part of it) or who has accepted responsibility for it and is described in it as having done so; where a person has authorised the contents only of part of the prospectus or supplementary prospectus, he is 'responsible' only for that part. Even if a firm which sponsors an offer is technically not an offeror, which is unlikely, (see ¶823), it will normally be a person 'responsible' on the basis that it authorised the contents of the prospectus; its directors will, however, normally not be persons 'responsible' unless, perhaps, they personally authorised the contents of the prospectus. Professionals such as lawyers who advise on the contents of a prospectus or supplementary prospectus only in a professional capacity are expressly stated not to be 'responsible' for it (reg. 13(4)). The prospectus must state the names of the persons 'responsible' for it (para. 9 of Sch. 1 to the prospectus regulations).

The prospectus regulations contain detailed exemptions from the liability of persons 'responsible' to pay compensation, which mirror those under Pt. IV of the FSA (see ¶812) (reg. 15). As would be expected, they depend on the lack of knowledge of the person 'responsible', his taking of reasonable steps to issue a correction, his reasonable belief that no supplementary prospectus was necessary or the knowledge of the person suffering the loss as to the true position. The burden of proving that an exemption applies is on the person 'responsible'. In addition, a director of the issuer is not responsible for a prospectus or supplementary prospectus if it is published without his knowledge or consent and he makes this public as soon as he finds out (reg. 13(2)). Strangely, there is no similar exemption for directors of the offeror.

¶823 Who is the 'offeror'?

The prospectus regulations impose compensation liability on the 'offeror', and indeed make the 'offeror' the person who has to publish the prospectus (reg. 4(1)). It defines the 'offeror' of securities as the person who 'as principal' makes an offer which, if accepted, would give rise to a contract for the issue or sale of the securities or who invites such an offer (reg. 5); this definition applies also in the case of the 'offeror' of listed securities, where the term is similarly important in the case of compensation liability (see ¶812). It is irrelevant whether the securities subject to the offer are to be issued or sold by the offeror or by another person with whom he has made arrangements for their issue or sale (reg. 5(a)).

Where the offer is made by the issuer himself or by the owner of existing securities, it is quite clear that the 'offeror' is the issuer or owner. Where there is an 'offer for sale' by an issuing house or other 'sponsor' of securities to be issued by the issuer to the sponsor and then sold on to the investor, it is, again, clear that it is the sponsor which is the 'offeror'; the securities are technically to be 'sold' under an offer made by the sponsor and issued directly by the issuer under arrangements made with the sponsor (albeit at the request of the issuer).

It is, however, not totally clear who the 'offeror' is where the sponsor makes the offer to investors on behalf of the issuer or shareholder but does not himself buy the securities on the way; the typical case (applying to both new and existing securities) is where the securities are 'placed' by a sponsor acting as 'placing agent' (assuming that the placing is technically an offer to the public) or securities are floated on AIM by way of a public offer made by a sponsor. The 'obvious' view is that the offeror is the issuer or shareholder, since he issues or owns the securities and the sponsor is acting as his 'agent', not 'as principal'. As the shareholder is liable as an 'offeror', it is accordingly 'responsible' for the whole prospectus and not just the portion (perhaps about itself) which it has authorised; all the directors are therefore also responsible and there is no clear exemption for them as in the case of the directors of the issuer (see ¶822).

However, it is possible (albeit perhaps unlikely) that even in this case it is the sponsor who is the 'offeror'. For example, the definition of 'offeror' refers to the making of the offer rather than the ownership of the securities, and prospectus law is a law regulating documents, not the mere issue or sale of securities. In addition, it is arguable that the conduct of the sponsor as part of its own business should not be attributed to the issuer or owner of the securities and, accordingly, the offer does not need to be treated as made by the sponsor as 'agent' in the same way as the contract resulting from the offer would be treated as made by the sponsor as 'agent' if he had actually entered into the contract (and so created a contractual relationship) on behalf of the issuer or owner. Nonetheless, the only 'safe' view where existing shareholders are selling securities along with the issuer is that each selling shareholder is an offeror 'responsible' for the whole prospectus. In order to protect them, there should therefore be two separate prospectuses; the selling shareholders would incorporate the information from the issuer's prospectus in their own prospectus. This would seem to limit the shareholders' liability, and the costs of a separate prospectus would be an acceptable price to pay. Indeed, the existing shares can usually be sold by way of a private placement at the same time as the public offer of the new shares.

¶824   Mutual recognition of prospectuses

As the prospectus regulations implement into UK law the provisions of the EU prospectus directive, there are provisions for mutual recognition in the UK of prospectus disclosures made in relation to IPOs of securities not already officially listed in an EEA member State, whether or not the IPO is accompanied by an application for official listing, if the IPO was made in one or more other EEA member States and the prospectus was pre-vetted by the relevant local regulator (reg. 20 and Pt. II of Sch. 4).

The mutual recognition provisions apply only if the public offer was made in the member State concerned not more than three months earlier and are similar to the mutual recognition provisions applying to listing particulars and

Pt. IV prospectuses (see ¶814). The prospectus (and any supplementary prospectus already issued) must be translated into English. The mutual recognition provisions can apply even if the issuer (and, if different, the offeror) is incorporated outside the EEA; this is a member State option which the UK has exercised in relation to 'incoming' prospectuses.

As provided in the prospectus directive, the detailed disclosures to be contained in the 'recognised' prospectus are in principle those required by the prospectus directive. However, where the public offer relates to securities subject to an application for admission to official listing on a stock exchange in the same member State, the disclosures are instead those required by the listing particulars directive, with modifications appropriate for a public offer, (art. 7). In addition, and even if there is to be no official listing, member States can also allow the offeror to provide instead the listing particulars directive disclosures provided that there is prior scrutiny by a competent authority (art. 12); indeed, importantly, if there are such prior scrutiny requirements the member State in which the public offer is to be made is actually required to allow this if the securities are to be officially listed in another member State (art. 8). Although it is not totally clear, these two provisions seem to be designed to allow offerors to choose whichever of the two disclosure regimes they prefer. It is also necessary to include (perhaps by way of a 'wrap-around') information about taxation of UK investors, details of UK paying agents and a statement of how notices are to be given to UK investors (para. 8(1) of Sch. 4). Mutual recognition may not be available if the member State which approved the prospectus granted a partial exemption or derogation, and this needs to be reviewed in each case. The recognised prospectus (and any supplementary prospectus issued in the 'approving' member State) must be filed in the UK and made available at an address in the UK, in the same way as UK prospectuses, and the provisions relating to the subsequent need for a supplementary prospectus will also apply (see ¶818 above); this is because mutual recognition applies only to the disclosure requirements of reg. 8 and 9 (see para. 8(1) of Sch. 4) and the other provisions relating to prospectuses continue to apply.

Although it is not totally clear, it would seem that the compensation provisions (see ¶822) apply to recognised non-UK EEA prospectuses in a similar way to the way they do to UK prospectuses, except that, as would be expected, references to the detailed disclosures required by the Prospectus Regulations are to be read as references to the detailed disclosures required by the law of the 'approving' member State (reg. 9 of Sch. 4). It is not totally clear that the general duty of disclosure contained in reg. 9(1) (see ¶818) is similarly replaced by local law requirements; however, even if it is not, that general duty merely reflects the requirements of the prospectus and listing particulars directives and therefore is also imposed by every other EEA member State under its own law.

¶824

Mutual recognition of course applies both ways. In order that UK prospectuses can similarly be entitled to mutual recognition in other EEA member States (subject to the provision of similar additional information and to the possible non-recognition of derogations as in the case of UK recognition), the prospectus regulations allow offerors to apply to the London Stock Exchange (or any other competent authority designated by the Treasury) to vet the prospectus under Pt. IV even if the securities offered are not going to be listed on the London Stock Exchange but, for example, are only to be dealt in on AIM or EASDAQ (reg. 17 and new s. 156A inserted into the FSA). If the offeror is not the issuer, however, the application can be made only with the consent of the issuer (s. 156A(1)(c)). The disclosures are those required by the London Stock Exchange, rather than the prospectus regulations (s. 156A(2); accordingly, the London Stock Exchange sets out its disclosure requirements in a special section of the Yellow Book. In essence, there are the normal Yellow Book disclosures with the exclusion of disclosures found in the listing particulars directive and not also in the prospectus directive and therefore in effect are those required by the prospectus regulations. Any additional requirements imposed by the Yellow Book would need to be discussed with the London Stock Exchange if they cause a problem in practice; this is likely to occur in particular where the Yellow Book still requires trading information for periods longer than those for which the company has filed accounts, although most of these requirements have been reduced appropriately.

In addition, as the relevant regime is the Pt. IV regime rather than that relating to non-LSE securities, the provisions requiring compensation for untrue or misleading statements are those relating to listing, which are contained in Pt. IV of the FSA (see ¶812), rather than those in the prospectus regulations (reg. 4(3)). The prospectus directive allows member States to refuse mutual recognition to prospectuses for offers of securities issued by issuers from outside the EEA, which is an option the UK has not exercised itself; this will need to be reviewed in the case of each member State where the outgoing UK prospectus is to be used.

¶825 Continuing Companies Act restrictions on 'public offers'

Three key 'public offer' provisions in the *Companies Act* 1985 still continue to apply to public offers of non-LSE securities, despite the general repeal of the Companies Act's prospectus provisions on the coming into force of the prospectus regulations *(the Financial Services Act 1986 (Commencement) (No. 13) Order 1995, SI 1995/1538)*. They continue because the prospectus regulations are regulations made under the *European Communities Act 1972* only for the purpose of implementing the prospectus directive and so cannot affect statutory provisions not related to the 'public offers' matters covered by the directive.

The first key Companies Act provision which remains in force is the prohibition on allotments if the minimum amount which must be raised by the prospectus to fund certain prescribed matters is not achieved (s. 83 of the *Companies Act* 1985). Although Sch. 3 of the Companies Act has been repealed generally, para. 2 of Sch. 3, which lists the matters to which s. 83 refers, is still in force for the purposes of s. 83(1); indeed, these matters are in fact also required to be stated in the prospectus by the prospectus regulations (para. 21 of Sch. 1). Accordingly, if the stated minimum amount is not raised within the 40 day period specified in s. 83, the offer period cannot be extended and the offer must be aborted.

The second key Companies Act provision which remains in force is the prohibition on public offers by UK private companies (s. 81 of the *Companies Act* 1985). The prohibition applies to the offer of shares or debt securities to the public; it does not apply to the other securities covered by the prospectus regulations, unless they can be regarded as an indirect offer of the shares or debt securities. Because the prospectus regulations do not affect this prohibition, the definition of 'offer to the public' remains that in s. 59–60 of the *Companies Act* 1985, which are retained in force for this purpose. The Companies Act definition is much wider than that in the prospectus regulations; for example, it includes most offers which are treated as not being 'offers to the public in the UK' for the purposes of the prospectus regulations (see ¶821) and also includes offerees outside the UK. An offer by a UK private company may therefore be prohibited by the Companies Act even though it could have been made without a prospectus under the prospectus regulations.

The third key Companies Act provision which remains in force is the prohibition on allotments under a 'prospectus issued generally' (s. 82 of the *Companies Act* 1985). Although the FSA did indeed envisage the repeal óf the definition of 'prospectus issued generally', that definition has not in fact been repealed; it means a prospectus issued to persons who are not existing members of the company or holders óf its debt securities (s. 744 of the *Companies Act* 1985). However, and importantly, the Companies Act definition of 'offer to the public' used in the definition of 'prospectus' has been repealed in this context; it has been retained for the purposes of s. 81 and 83 (see above) but not s. 82 (the *Financial Services Act 1986 (Commencement (No. 13) Order* 1995). Accordingly, 'offer to the public' must surely be interpreted in accordance with the prospectus regulations, in other words, under the new public issues regime. Section 82 therefore applies to a 'prospectus' under the prospectus regulations for non-LSE securities; it does not apply in relation to a 'prospectus' under Pt. IV because (like s. 83) it has been repealed for that purpose (the *Financial*

Services Act 1986 Commencement No. 3 Order 1986). Accordingly, s. 82 does not apply in the case of offers which are not 'offers to the public' under the prospectus regulations (see ¶821) even if they would have been 'offers to the public' under the Companies Act.

9 The Marketing of Investments

¶901 Introduction

The *Financial Services Act* 1986 imposes tight controls on the marketing of investments because in a sense that is where prospective investors are most at risk. The FSA imposes three separate marketing restrictions:

(1) on the issue of marketing documents to recipients in the UK;

(2) on cold-calling investors in the UK or from the UK; and

(3) on the marketing by FSA-authorised firms or passporting firms to investors in the UK of 'unregulated' collective investment schemes and on advising investors in the UK on investment in them; 'passporting firms' are non-UK EEA firms carrying on FSA-regulated investment business in the UK outside the 'overseas persons' exemptions but under their 'single European passport' (see ¶302 and ¶355).

The FSA provides that (except where an exemption applies) no one may issue marketing documents (referred to in the FSA as 'investment advertisements') in the UK, or cause them to be issued in the UK, unless it is an FSA-authorised firm or a passporting firm, or they have been 'approved' by one, (s. 57); advertisements are issued 'in the UK' for this purpose if they are delivered or sent to recipients in the UK or, even if this is not the case, if they are treated by the FSA as issued in the UK (see ¶902), and issue or 'approval' involves the firm verifying the statements made and providing the risk warnings and other disclosures required by the firm's regulator (see ¶902–¶907). As a result of this prohibition on the issue of investment advertisements (the Marketing Prohibition), the FSA in effect delegates responsibility for investor protection in this context to FSA-authorised firms and passporting firms.

Further, the FSA also effectively bans cold calling (which it refers to as 'unsolicited calls') on investors in the UK, even from outside the UK, or from the UK to investors outside the UK, even by FSA-authorised firms, except where permitted by regulations made by the SIB (s. 56).

Finally, the FSA also contains (in Ch. VIII of Pt. I) a separate regime restricting the marketing of shares, units or other interests in 'collective investment schemes', such as open-ended investment companies and unit trusts, to investors in the UK; the restrictions also apply to recommending or advising, or procuring, investment in collective investment schemes and accordingly references in this chapter to the marketing of collective investment schemes include recommending or advising, or procuring, clients to invest in them. Unless an exemption applies, collective investment schemes cannot be marketed by FSA-authorised firms or passporting firms to investors in the UK if they are 'unregulated schemes', in other words collective investment schemes which are not approved and accordingly regulated (at least to a limited extent) by the SIB (s. 76(1)); the only collective investment schemes which are so approved and regulated by the SIB (and accordingly are not 'unregulated schemes') are authorised unit trusts, UK open-ended investment companies (OEICs, see ¶318) and (non-UK) schemes 'recognised' (or, approved) by the SIB. However, the FSA and regulations issued by the SIB permit the marketing of unregulated schemes to particular kinds of investor, typically non-private customers, (see ¶914).

As a result of the implementation of the ISD and the 2BCD, passporting firms are treated as if they were FSA-authorised firms for the purposes of all of these marketing restrictions and permissions (para. 17 and 23 of Sch. 7 and para. 10 of Sch. 11 to the *Investment Services Regulations* 1995 and para. 17 and 25 of Sch.9 and para. 16 of Sch. 11 to the *Banking Coordination (Second Council Directive) Regulations* 1992). References in this Chapter to FSA-authorised firms therefore include passporting firms, unless the context indicates otherwise. Terms and expressions defined in ¶302 bear the same meanings when used in this chapter.

Passporting firms can accordingly issue investment advertisements to recipients in the UK without their being 'approved' by an FSA-authorised firm and, indeed, can 'approve' them for others. Non-UK EEA firms acting outside the ISD or 2BCD passport are also exempted from the need for s. 57 'approval' of investment advertisements issued by them in particular circumstances, although they cannot 'approve' investment advertisements for others, (s. 58(1)(c)). The SIB can make rules regulating the form and content of advertisements relating to FSA-regulated investment business (s. 48(2)(e)), except in the case of certain advertisements relating to listed securities (s. 48(5)). The 'form and content' rules can be imposed by UK regulators on investment advertisements issued by non-UK EEA firms provided that they can be justified as being 'in the general good' (see ¶360) and, indeed, the investment services directive expressly allows this even in the case of EEA investment firms subject to it and even if they are acting as passporting firms (art. 13). The s. 58(1)(c) exemption granted to non-UK EEA firms which are not acting as passporting firms is conditional on their compliance with the SIB's form and content rules (s. 58(1)(c)); this applies whether or not the firm is actually subject to the ISD. The SIB can accordingly regulate the form and content of investment

¶901

advertisements, which allows it to restrict the investments to which an investment advertisement can relate; it has used this power to prohibit non-UK EEA firms which are not acting as passporting firms from issuing investment advertisements under s. 58(1)(c) which market unregulated collective investment schemes to investors in the UK in contravention of s. 76(1), or, rather, in what would have been in contravention of s. 76(1) if they had been FSA-authorised firms or acting as passporting firms (r. 7.27 of the *Financial Services (Conduct of Business) Rules* 1990). The SIB can also regulate the manner in which an FSA-authorised firm or a passporting firm may hold itself out as carrying on FSA-regulated investment business (s. 48(2)(c)).

The most important aspect of all these marketing restrictions is that the FSA and the SIB have built a ring-fence around private individuals and small companies, partnerships or trusts in the UK. In general terms, no-one can market FSA-regulated investments or investment services to private individuals in the UK, however rich or sophisticated they are, or to small companies, partnerships or trusts in the UK without involving an FSA-authorised firm or a passporting firm and, in addition, it is normally not possible to cold call then; small companies, partnerships or trusts are those which do not qualify as 'business investors' and 'partnerships' include limited partnerships, which are a common vehicle for institutional investment in private equity and are normally not themselves FSA-authorised firms. Even FSA-authorised firms and passporting firms normally cannot market unregulated collective investment schemes to them, or cold call them, unless they are qualifying clients; these clients qualify for the marketing of unregulated collective investment schemes only if investment in the scheme is suitable for them (and they did not become clients in contravention of s. 76(1)) and qualify for cold calling only if they have given the appropriate consent required by the SIB permissions.

Conversely, however, none of these marketing restrictions apply in relation to investors physically outside the UK (except that the cold calling restrictions apply to calls to them from the UK) or in relation to what may be termed 'business investors'. In this chapter, 'business investors' means: FSA-authorised firms and passporting firms; FSA-exempted firms (except, in relation to the marketing of collective investment schemes, appointed representatives and firms which would be acting outside their exemption if they invested in the scheme and, in relation to cold calling, where the resulting investment agreement is to be entered into by an appointed representative); governments, public or local authorities and international organisations the members of which include the UK or another member State of the EEA ('government bodies'); and qualifying companies and trusts and, probably in relation only to the restrictions on cold calling and on marketing unregulated collective investment schemes, qualifying partnerships if they are, as usual, not

¶901

bodies corporate. Companies, trusts and partnerships qualify on a size test which in general terms is as follows:

(1) in the case of companies, the company (or any holding company or subsidiary) has net assets or paid-up share capital of at least £5 million or (if the company or its holding company has over 20 shareholders) £500,000; this size test applies to all bodies corporate even if they are not companies;

(2) in the case of trusts (whether unit trusts, pension funds or family settlements), the trustee is himself a business investor or the aggregate value of the cash and FSA-regulated investments in the trust is at least £10 million or was at least £10 million at any time during the previous two years; and

(3) in the case of partnerships (which normally are probably not business investors in relation to the Marketing Prohibition), the partnership has net assets of at least £5 million, taking into account loans granted or loan capital subscribed by partners.

If it is intended to market FSA-regulated investments or investment services to unit trusts or pension funds in the UK, the best procedure (even if they are business investors) is to market to their manager or investment manager if, as is usual, they have one and if, as is again usual, it is FSA-authorised. It is unclear whether partnerships can qualify as business investors in relation to all three marketing restrictions and the prudent view is that they cannot qualify in relation to the Marketing Prohibition. The concept of a 'business investor' is not found in the FSA; it results from reviewing which investors fall within exemptions from all three marketing restrictions and, in the case of the Marketing Prohibition, the only 'general' exemption is in relation to art. 11(3) 'expert investors' (see ¶906(1)). However, the only category of 'expert investor' which might cover English partnerships which are not FSA-authorised or passporting firms is the category of 'unincorporated association'. This arguably includes 'partnerships' and, indeed, the FSA expressly treats the term 'unincorporated association' as including partnerships in relation to penalties for offences (s. 202(4)); however, the FSA distinguishes between unincorporated associations and partnerships in relation to FSA-authorisation (see s. 27(6) and s. 27 (7)) and the SROs also distinguish between them, and cover them both, in the definition of 'ordinary business investor', which is the key category used in the exemptions relating to cold calls and the marketing of unregulated schemes. Conversely, however, the SIB definition of 'ordinary business investor' relates only to partnerships and not to unincorporated associations. The safer view, therefore, is that there is no art. 11(3) exemption from the Marketing Prohibition in relation to partnerships, and that they are

¶901

accordingly not 'business investors' in relation to the Marketing Prohibition. However, if they are English limited partnerships, their manager or investment manager will normally be an FSA-authorised firm and, if this is the case, the Marketing Prohibition will accordingly not apply if the investment advertisement is sent to him, as would be preferable commercially anyway. In addition, some partnerships are seemingly bodies corporate, for example Scottish partnership and Delaware limited partnerships; they are likely to be treated as business investors if they meet the size test for companies.

INVESTMENT ADVERTISEMENTS

¶902 The marketing prohibition

Section 57(1) provides that, subject to certain exemptions, no person other than an FSA-authorised firm can issue (or cause to be issued) an investment advertisement in the UK unless its contents have been approved by an FSA-authorised firm. The Marketing Prohibition applies even if the advertisement is issued (or, delivered or sent) to the recipient at his request (*Hudson v Bishop Cavanagh* [1982] Crim LR 114) and even if, as in the case of an offer for subscription, the investments have not yet been issued. Passporting firms are treated as FSA-authorised firms for these two purposes (para. 17 of Sch. 7 to the *Investment Services Regulations* 1995 and of Sch. 9 to the *Banking Coordination (Second Council Directive) Regulations* 1992); they accordingly do not need to have investment advertisements issued by them 'approved' under s. 57. Non-UK EEA firms which are not acting as passporting firms (because, for example, they are carrying on FSA-regulated investment business in the UK not under their ISD or 2BCD passport, but under the 'overseas persons' exemptions (see ¶334)) can also issue investment advertisements which have not been 'approved' by an FSA-authorised firm, if they are doing so in the course of carrying on FSA-regulated investment business lawfully in their home state, provided that they comply with the SIB's form and content rules (s. 58(1)(c)); they can use s. 58(1)(c) if they are not acting as passporting firms even if they are entitled to the ISD or 2BCD passport. The FSA-authorised or passporting firm acts as a policeman and must comply with the risk warning and other disclosure requirements of its SRO (or the SIB); non-UK EEA firms using the s. 58(1)(c) exemption must similarly comply with the SIB's disclosure rules. Accordingly, there is a difference between the disclosure requirements for passporting firms and those for non-UK EEA firms using the s. 58(1)(c) exemption only if the passporting firm has joined an SRO.

¶902

The FSA contains several exemptions from the Marketing Prohibition by reference to the nature of the issuer of the advertisement or in the case of public issues (see ¶904 and ¶905). In addition, the FSA allows the Treasury to issue other exemptions in the case of 'restricted' advertisements and, because this structure was adopted only to provide flexibility, the exemptions the Treasury have provided are just as important in practice as those contained in the FSA (see ¶906).

The Marketing Prohibition applies to the marketing of all FSA-regulated investments to investors in the UK (see ¶323–¶328). Accordingly, it applies to the marketing of both listed and unlisted securities, and also to the marketing of collective investment schemes even though special, additional, restrictions also apply to them under s. 76(1) (see ¶911–¶920); indeed, it is the Marketing Prohibition that, in effect, often brings the s. 76(1) restrictions into play. The Marketing Prohibition also applies to the promotion of investment management and investment advisory services and, on the better view, brokerage services (see ¶903). It also applies to advertisements promoting the exercise of certain 'transactional' rights conferred by an investment, namely, the right to buy, underwrite, convert or sell FSA-regulated investments; it does not, however, apply to advertisements to refrain from exercising such rights, although s. 47 (offence to make misleading statements) does. In addition, although the FSA does not say expressly that it applies to application forms the better view is that it does (see ¶907).

As in the case of investment agreements entered into without FSA-authorisation where that is required, contravention of the Marketing Prohibition is a criminal offence; contravention is punishable by two years' imprisonment and an unlimited fine. In addition, and (probably more important in practice) investment agreements entered into as a result of investment advertisements issued in contravention of the Marketing Prohibition are normally not enforceable against the investor, but only by him; contravention also normally entitles the investor to an indemnity against loss (see ¶1201) and may lead to a civil action by the SIB under s. 61.

An investment advertisement is issued 'in the UK' (and accordingly is subject to the Marketing Prohibition) if it is delivered or sent to recipients in the UK even as part of another document, for example a newspaper. In addition, an advertisement is also treated as issued in the UK (even though it is not delivered or sent to recipients in the UK) if it is directed at or made available to persons in the UK (s. 207(3)). However, in the latter case, it will not be treated as issued in the UK (and accordingly the Marketing Prohibition will not apply to it) if it is in a newspaper or other periodical published and circulating principally outside the UK or is in a broadcast transmitted principally for reception outside the UK (like a French television channel received by satellite in the UK); properly, this exemption does not apply if the advertisement is

¶902

actually directed at investors in the UK. It is understood that the DTI (and accordingly now also the Treasury) regard a newspaper as published outside the UK even if it is physically printed here provided that editorial control is exercised only outside the UK; however, and, importantly, the DTI (and therefore now also the Treasury) also seem to regard advertisements in a newspaper or other publication as issued in the UK (without regard to s. 207(3)) if the publication is available for sale in the UK. Although it is not clear, it would seem that material circulated on the Internet would be treated as subject to the Marketing Prohibition because of s. 207(3) if it is available to people in the UK who want to access it; information on the Internet is seemingly not a 'sound or television broadcast' within s. 207(3) so that it is unlikely that the exemption from s. 207(3) is available in these circumstances.

Although the position is not totally clear, it would seem that a person 'issues' an investment advertisement by publishing it and 'causes the issue' of one by causing someone else to publish it physically as the advertisement of that person rather than of the 'publisher', the 'causing' relating to mechanical publication of the advertisement (for example, by a newspaper, or by distributing it) so that the advertisement is issued to the order of the person causing it to be issued (see the exemption in s. 57(4)). A client will therefore not 'cause' the issue of investment advertisements issued as its 'own' advertisement by an FSA-authorised firm or a passporting firm even if it does so for his benefit, which is presumably one reason why there is no express exemption for persons who 'cause' an FSA-authorised firm or passporting firm to issue an investment advertisement.

The possibility of mere approval by an FSA-authorised firm was introduced into the FSA at the very last moment in the House of Lords and may have significant implications in practice. Although the position is not yet totally clear, it is likely that the liabilities which apply to an 'approver' are as great as those which apply to an 'issuer' and, indeed, this view can be justified by the very structure of the FSA in this context. Under the rules of the SROs (and the SIB), investment advertisements 'approved' by an FSA-authorised or passporting firm regulated by them must normally state that fact and contain similar disclosures to those which would have been required had the investment advertisement actually been issued by it. If this practice is extended, as seems legally acceptable, to offer documents issued on take-overs and promotional documents relating to public issues, such documents will no longer need to be issued by an FSA-authorised firm, as is the current practice, at least if the FSA's authorisation requirement does not apply (see Ch. 3) and subject to the requirements of the Takeover Code, if applicable. In addition, the use of the 'approval' route has important implications for the effectiveness of the restrictions on the marketing of 'unregulated' collective investment schemes (see ¶919).

¶902

¶903 Investment advertisements

An 'investment advertisement' is any 'advertisement' which either invites persons to enter into an 'investment agreement' (or to exercise rights conferred by an FSA-regulated investment to buy, underwrite, convert or sell an FSA-regulated investment) or contains information calculated to lead directly or indirectly to persons doing so, even if not the recipient, (s. 57(2)). Both classes of advertisement are referred to in this chapter as 'marketing documents' but an advertisement which does not constitute an-offer but merely contains information is also sometimes referred to as a 'promotional document'. An 'advertisement' is defined (in s. 207(2)) to include 'every form of advertising' whether in a document (for example, mailshots or letters to clients) or a newspaper, on television, radio or otherwise, and accordingly the Marketing Prohibition will apply to newspaper advertisements and, for example, pages on Reuters, Bloomberg or Internet screens. However, it normally does not include oral marketing, for example the practice of effecting private or vendor consideration placings on the telephone or calling shareholders in a target company during a bid. Oral marketing will, however, be subject to the rules governing 'unsolicited calls' (see ¶908–¶909).

It has in fact been argued by some lawyers and regulators that mere oral marketing statements can constitute 'investment advertisements' notwithstanding that there is a clearly separate ban on cold calling contained in s. 56 (see ¶908). It is thought on balance that the Marketing Prohibition in s. 57 is a ban on proscribed kinds of marketing media and that a mere oral statement is not one of those proscribed media; it would be otiose to state expressly (as does s. 207(2)) that sound broadcasting is a proscribed medium if ordinary oral statements are also covered. Indeed, the very concept of advertising involves standard, normally repeated, marketing and a statement made only once to one recipient (even in a letter) seems not to be an 'advertisement' at all; a statement made orally to a group of people (for example, at a shareholders' meeting or a 'roadshow') would similarly seem normally not to be advertising either but this is more problematic. It is very difficult to regulate oral statements. The FSA should surely be regarded as accordingly not requiring their 'approval', together with appropriate disclosures, as in practice this would be to prohibit most oral statements about FSA-regulated investments altogether, which is an unlikely regulatory objective. The route chosen is, instead, to prohibit cold calling about FSA-regulated investments and, indeed, contravention of that ban is deliberately not made a criminal offence; to impose a criminal penalty of two years' imprisonment on failure to obtain regulatory 'approval' for a mere oral statement, without any untrue or misleading statement having to be involved, is a very unlikely approach. Conversely, however, written marketing by standard form documents or oral statements on TV or radio (which are likely to be 'permanent' or recorded and to which the cold calling 'ban' is unlikely to apply) are subject to the Marketing Prohibition and so also is reading out standard statements (which is otherwise an obvious avoidance route). The SIB has confirmed that this is indeed its view and that it is appropriate to draw the regulatory line in this way in a 1991 guidance release, in which it indicated that even scripted telephone messages were unlikely to constitute 'advertisements' despite being made to several people at different times as they were normally difficult to standardise ('Telephone selling by telephone marketing agencies', SIB Guidance Release 3/91).

An 'investment agreement' is an agreement the making or performance of which by either party constitutes an FSA-regulated investment activity (see ¶322) even if it falls within an exemption from the FSA's authorisation requirement, for example, the issue of shares by a closed-ended company, (s. 44(9)). Investment agreements therefore include agreements to acquire or dispose of securities or other FSA-regulated investments, and take-over offer documents are accordingly subject to the Marketing Prohibition; however, 'defence' documents are not, as they do not invite shareholders to sell their holdings but the opposite, although they are within the scope of the FSA's offence of misleading statements (s. 47). They also include investment management and investment advisory agreements. The better view is that brokerage agreements are also investment agreements, as they are agreements to buy or sell investments in the future as an agent, albeit for the other party to the brokerage agreement (the client) rather than from or to the counterparty to the subsequent transaction, and that the Marketing Prohibition therefore applies to them. As indicated above, an advertisement will also be an investment advertisement if it promotes the exercise of certain 'transactional' rights conferred by an investment; those are the rights to acquire, dispose of, underwrite or convert an investment (for example, by the exercise of a warrant or the conversion of loan stock). These rights do not include voting and accordingly, proxy circulars are not 'investment advertisements'.

¶904 Exemptions provided by the FSA

The Marketing Prohibition does not apply to certain types of investment advertisement listed in s. 58:

(1) advertisements issued or caused to be issued by any government, local authority or central bank (including the Bank of England), or any international organisation the members of which include the UK or another member State of the EEA, provided that the advertisement relates to investments issued by the 'advertiser' (s. 58(1)(a));

(2) advertisements issued or caused to be issued by exempted persons, other than the Bank of England (see ¶347–¶355), provided that the advertisement relates to matters in respect of which they are exempt

s. 58(1)(b)). Advertisements by appointed representatives or listed money market institutions in relation to the marketing of FSA-regulated investments or activities within their respective exemptions (see ¶350 and ¶349) can therefore be issued directly by them without 'FSA-authorised firm' approval; so also can advertisements issued by RIEs and, indeed, non-UK EEA regulated markets about their exempted trading facilities (see ¶352 and ¶353). Passporting firms are not exempted persons even if they are listed money market institutions (see ¶357) but they are not subject to the Marketing Prohibition Agency (see ¶902);

(3) except in the case of advertisements relating to depositary receipts for or other certificates representing securities (s. 58(6)), advertisements issued or caused to be issued by nationals of a member State of the EEA other than the UK in the course of investment business lawfully carried on by them in that State, provided that such advertisements conform with any 'form and content' rules made by the SIB under s. 48(2)(e), (s. 58(1)(c), as extended to non-EU member States of the EEA by the *European Economic Area Act* 1993). These advertising rules can restrict the investments which can be advertised (see ¶901). The non-UK EEA firm does not need actually to be licensed (or, authorised) by its home member State provided that it is carrying on the relevant FSA-regulated investment business without contravening its domestic law. In particular, it does not need to be authorised under the ISD or the 2BCD in order to use this exemption and indeed, if it is acting as a passporting firm, for example, marketing its passported ISD services, it does not need to rely on this exemption at all as it is treated as if it was an FSA-authorised firm; in both cases, however, it must comply with the SIB's (or its SRO's) 'form and content' rules (see ¶901); and

(4) certain advertisements relating to public issues of securities (see ¶905).

In addition, the FSA provides that persons who issue investment advertisements in the ordinary course of business (other than FSA-regulated investment business) to the order of another person will not be guilty of an offence if they reasonably believed that the issue complied with or was exempted from the Marketing Prohibition (s. 57(4)). This exemption is available to newspapers (for example, for advertisements issued in the name of the advertiser) but it imposes a heavy duty on them. It would seem that they must have actually considered whether the Marketing Prohibition applied, must have asked the right questions and (probably) must have checked in the public register of FSA-authorised firms maintained under s. 102. Indeed, it is the practice of some newspapers to insist that advertisers complete a 'compliance' questionnaire.

¶904

¶905 Exemptions provided by the FSA for public issues

The *Financial Services Act* 1986 contains several exemptions from the Marketing Prohibition in order to avoid double regulation under the investment advertisements regime and the public issues regimes for listed securities and unlisted securities contained in, respectively, Pt. IV of the FSA and (now) the *Public Offers of Securities Regulations* 1995 (the prospectus regulations) (see Ch. 8). There is, however, no comprehensive exemption from the Marketing Prohibition for marketing documents relating to offers subject to the public issues regimes and it is therefore necessary to analyse each investment advertisement to determine whether or not it falls within an exemption. The public issues regimes do not at present apply to collective investment schemes, although the listed securities regime may be applied to them in due course, and accordingly there is no exemption for public issues of shares, units or other interests in open-ended investment companies or other collective investment schemes even if they are listed on the London Stock Exchange (but see ¶906(6)). The 'public issues' exemptions also do not apply to securities which are outside the relevant regime in Pt. IV of the FSA or the prospectus regulations. Conversely, unless an exemption applies, the public issues regimes will apply even on a take-over if the consideration is the issue of new shares or debentures and therefore the 'public issues' exemptions from the Marketing Prohibition may also apply in these circumstances (see below).

The relaxation of the Marketing Prohibition to allow mere approval means that in practice the main problem for domestic public issues will not be s. 57 (as long as it is not overlooked) but ensuring compliance with the SRO's disclosure rules applicable to the issuer or 'approver'. Normally any important 'public issues' document of a UK company would in practice not be issued unless it was approved by the company's broker or merchant bank in any event. The exemptions will however be important in the context of overseas issuers who would normally not want to have to involve 'UK' FSA-authorised firms in the preparation of the offer document but would rely on their 'local' banks or brokers. If the local bank or broker is an FSA-authorised firm, even only by reference to a UK office, there is no problem in this respect; indeed, even if it is not, but it is a non-UK EEA firm, it may be able to issue (or alternatively, if it is a passporting firm, 'approve') the offer document in any event (see ¶901).

The FSA and the *Financial Services Act 1986 (Investment Advertisements) (Exemptions) (No. 2) Order* 1995 (the 1995 investment advertisements order) provide 'public issues' exemptions in the following circumstances:

(1) an advertisement which is approved or authorised for issue by the London Stock Exchange under s. 154 and which relates either to securities subject to an application for listing or to unlisted securities for which a UK registered prospectus is approved by the London Stock

Exchange for mutual recognition purposes under s. 156A (see ¶824) (s. 58(1)(d)(i) as expanded by s. 156A); these advertisements include mini-prospectuses and summary particulars but seemingly not placing letters;

(2) an advertisement which consists of (or of any part of) listing particulars or supplementary listing particulars or a prospectus or supplementary prospectus (either relating to a public offer of securities subject to an application for listing or which relates to unlisted securities and is approved by the London Stock Exchange as referred to in (1) above) or any other document required or permitted to be published by listing rules (s. 58(1)(d)(ii) as amended by para. 6(a) of Sch. 2 to the prospectus regulations); the similar exemption in s. 58(1)(d)(ii) relating to 'approved exchanges' has been replaced, now that Pt. V has been repealed without coming into force (see Ch. 8), by a wider exemption in relation to all 'relevant EEA markets', including AIM, (see (5) below);

(3) an advertisement which is a prospectus or supplementary prospectus for unlisted securities issued in accordance with Pt. II of the prospectus regulations (art. 14(a) of the 1995 investment advertisements order);

(4) a qualifying advertisement relating to a prospectus or supplementary prospectus referred to in (3) above (art. 14(b) of the 1995 investment advertisements order). An advertisement qualifies if the only invitation or marketing information which it contains is restricted to: the name and address of the offeror or his other contact details; the nature, nominal value, number and price of the securities being offered; a statement that a prospectus or supplementary prospectus is or will be available, and (if relevant) when; and instructions for obtaining a copy;

(5) a qualifying advertisement relating to unlisted securities which is an admission document required by a 'relevant EEA market' (as defined in art. 2 of the order) (art. 14(c) of the 1995 investment advertisements order). The advertisement qualifies if (in a similar way to listing particulars) it contains the information required by the prospectus regulations on a public offer, even if there is only a private placement or, indeed, no offer at all (but only an introduction), and if, apart from that, it does not contain any information which is not required or permitted to be published by the rules of that market; 'relevant EEA markets' include AIM and other EEA stock exchanges and some options or futures markets and (although it is not actually specified) EASDAQ, assuming, as seems to be the case, that it meets the relevant criteria set out in Pt. II of Sch. 1 to the order; and

(6) a qualifying advertisement relating to shares (other than shares in open-ended investment companies) or debentures, options or warrants

¶905

to subscribe them or depositary receipts relating to them which are traded or dealt in on a 'relevant EEA market' (see (5) above) or a market designated in the order for the purpose (art. 11 of the 1995 investment advertisements order). An advertisement qualifies if it consists of, or of any part of, a document which is required or permitted to be published by the rules of that market or its regulator or a body which regulates offers or issues of securities to be traded on that market; the designated markets include NASDAQ and other North American stock exchanges (and the Chicago Board Options Exchange) and the Tokyo and Osaka stock exchanges. Open-ended investment companies and other collective investment schemes, such as unit trusts, are excluded because public offers of their securities are not regulated by the prospectus regulations; indeed, it is exactly for this reason that they do not need expressly to be excluded in the exemptions referred to in (4) and (5) above.

The exemption referred to at (4) above is perhaps really aimed at providing an exemption for advertisements about a prospectus or supplementary prospectus which are intended to publicise the offer and invite applications for the prospectus, rather than applications for the securities concerned. However, it confirms the view that these advertisements are themselves investment advertisements. Accordingly, they must be issued or approved by an FSA-authorised firm if they fall outside the exemption, for example (and importantly) in the case of open-ended investment companies (see (6) above). This indirectly restricts the marketing of offshore funds because it brings into play the special restrictions on the marketing of unregulated collective investment schemes (see ¶911).

¶906   Additional exemptions for particular kinds of 'restricted' advertisements

Although the Marketing Prohibition applies whether or not the investment advertisement is issued to the public, the Treasury are able to exempt investment advertisements issued on a more limited basis in particular circumstances (s. 58(3)). This power of exemption cannot be delegated to a designated agency such as the SIB (s. 114(5)(d)).

The Treasury have in fact issued a large number of exemptions, which apply in restricted circumstances and are now consolidated in two exemption orders: the *Financial Services Act 1986 (Investment Advertisements) (Exemptions) (No. 2) Order* 1995 (SI 1995/1536) (the 1995 investment advertisements order), which contains most of the exemptions for public issues of unlisted securities referred to in ¶905, and the *Financial Services Act 1986 (Investment Advertisements) (Exemptions) Order* 1996 (SI 1996/1586) (the 1996 investment

¶906

advertisements order); the 1996 investment advertisements order has itself been amended, in relation to the exemptions relating to investment advertisements issued to 'expert investors' or issued by 'overseas persons' (see (1) and (7) below), by the *Financial Services Act 1986 (Investment Advertisements) (Exemptions) Order* 1997 (SI 1997/963) (the 1997 order). The two exemption orders must always be referred to if a person other than an FSA-authorised firm or a passporting firm (for example, a listed company or a non-EEA firm) proposes to issue an investment advertisement to recipients in the UK without seeking the 'approval' of the advertisement by an FSA-authorised firm or a passporting firm under s. 57 and the exemptions in s. 58(1) do not apply. The exemptions are very detailed and apply in many different circumstances (see below); the exemptions apply to both issuing advertisements and causing their issue but for convenience both are referred to in this section as issuing them.

In general terms, the exemptions apply to:

- advertisements issued by a company to its shareholders, creditors or (in connection with an employee share scheme, which term covers most employee offers) its employees about securities issued by the company or a member of its Companies Act group;

- advertisements issued to certain categories of expert investor, or investors deemed 'expert' because they are 'business investors' (see ¶901), but not private investors even if they are 'sophisticated' or 'high net worth';

- advertisements issued in many circumstances where the resulting investment agreement itself is exempted from the FSA's authorisation requirement, or would be apart from the ISD, (see Ch. 3), and accordingly an FSA-authorised firm does not need to be involved in investment advertisements relating to these 'exempted' FSA-regulated investment activities; and

- advertisements relating to investment in UK private companies.

Most of the exemptions are cumulative in that they allow the investment advertisement to be issued not only to recipients covered by the exemption but also to other recipients 'to whom [the investment advertisement] may otherwise be lawfully issued'; accordingly, an investment advertisement sent to shareholders within one exemption and also to qualifying expert investors within another (for example, in connection with a placing) will be exempted. Importantly, the Marketing Prohibition does not apply at all to investment advertisements which are not issued to recipients in the UK, and are not deemed to be issued in the UK under s. 207(3), (see ¶903); it is therefore not necessary to try to find a relevant exemption in their case and, indeed, the exemptions which apply in the case of investment advertisements issued to UK

¶906

recipients in the circumstances described below accordingly still apply even though they may also be issued to recipients outside the UK who fall outside any exemption.

The two exemption orders provide exemptions for investment advertisements issued (or caused to be issued) to UK recipients in the restricted circumstances set out below:

(1) Advertisements issued or made available only to certain categories of 'expert investor' (art. 11 of the 1996 investment advertisements order, as amended by the 1997 order); importantly, the exemption does not apply if the advertisements can be seen by other people in the UK, for example, in newspapers, even if they cannot themselves acquire the investment (but see (2) below)). The exemption applies to overseas issuers (for example, investment banks) as well as UK ones, provided in each case that they are not unlawfully carrying on investment business in the UK. Accordingly, it applies both to issuers not carrying on FSA-regulated investment activities at all (such as companies, other than open-ended investment companies, placing their own shares) and also to those who do carry on FSA-regulated investment activities if all their investment business in the UK falls within Pt. III or, if relevant, Pt. IV of Sch. 1 (see ¶329) or, as in the case of listed money market institutions, they are FSA-exempted for it (see ¶347). The categories of 'expert investor' are set out in art. 11(3), which is what is often referred to in the normal UK selling restriction in non-public marketing documents. They include FSA-authorised or exempted firms, passporting firms and persons holding a para. 23 'permitted person' permission (see ¶333); passporting firms were originally introduced into art. 11(3) by para. 11 of Sch.10 to the investment services regulations and para. 44 of Sch. 10 to the banking coordination (second council directive) regulations, and are now reflected in specific amendments to art. 11 made by the 1997 order. In addition, they include government bodies, qualifying companies and other business investors (see ¶901). Importantly, the list does not, however, include private individuals even if they are sophisticated or high net worth investors, in other words, the rich private investors who are a much desired target of investment advertisements; indeed, they are not included even if they qualify as 'experts' for the purposes of SRO 'non-private customer' rules or the SIB's permissions for cold calls (see ¶910) or the marketing of unregulated schemes (see ¶914(2)) and that is why they are not 'business investors'.

(2) Advertisements directed at informing or influencing only qualifying professionals or government bodies (see ¶901) (art. 8 of the 1995

investment advertisements order). This is a very helpful exemption similar to the exemption for expert investors (see (1) above); however, and importantly, it can apply where the advertisement is made available to persons even if they are outside the 'expert investors' exemption, because for example they are in ordinary newspapers or other publications or on screens. For this purpose, 'qualifying professionals' are firms whose ordinary activities involve them in acquiring, holding, managing or disposing of FSA-regulated investments for the purposes of a business carried on by them, and who are therefore 'qualifying securities professionals' for the purposes of the exemption from the prospectus requirements of the prospectus regulations (see ¶821). Qualifying professionals also include firms whose ordinary business involves them in giving investment advice or arranging transactions; these terms are more general than the FSA-regulated investment activities relating to them and, for example, include advising even investment advisers. The exemption applies even if the putative qualifying professionals carry on FSA-regulated investment business in the UK only under the 'overseas persons' exemptions (see ¶334) so that they are not FSA-authorised or exempted firms or passporting firms within the 'expert investors' exemption; if they are not in the UK, there is no need for an exemption anyway (see above). The exemption sets out certain factors which indicate that the target of the advertisement is or is not restricted to qualifying professionals and government bodies (for example, that it states that it is available only to professionals or, conversely, that the minimum investment is not likely to deter investors who are not qualifying professionals or government bodies).

(3) Advertisements issued by a company to the holders of shares, bonds, loan stock or other debentures (or options, warrants or other rights to subscribe them) issued by, or to the creditors of, the company or another body corporate in the same Companies Act group or persons entitled to become holders even only conditionally (for example, purchasers in the market) about securities of these kinds issued or to be issued by a group company (art. 3(1) of the 1996 investment advertisements order). The exemption does not apply if the advertisement relates also to other FSA-regulated investments; accordingly, it does not apply if, for example, the target company in a recommended offer tells its shareholders to accept a share for share offer, although it would seem to apply if the offer is only for cash. The exemption also does not apply to investment advertisements (or in relation to FSA-regulated investments) issued by an open-ended investment company, although there are similar exemptions for them

¶906

(see (6) below). The exemption applies *mutatis mutandis* in relation to a body corporate which is not a company.

(4) Advertisements relating to an offer of securities to present or former employees of the issuer of the securities or of another company in its group (for example in respect of employee share or share option schemes) in the circumstances in which the similar exemption from the FSA's authorisation requirement applies (see ¶337) (art. 6 of the 1996 investment advertisements order); 'group' includes companies in which a member of the Companies Act group holds a qualifying capital interest within para. 30 of Sch. 1. Advertisements are within the exemption whether they are issued by a group company or by a company 'connected' with it or by a 'relevant trustee' within that exemption.

(5) Any of the advertisements issued by one member of a group to other group companies and any advertisement relating to a joint enterprise issued by one member of the joint enterprise to other members (art. 7 and 8 of the 1996 investment advertisements order). 'Group' and 'joint enterprise' have the meanings used in the Sch. 1 exemptions (see ¶333) and 'group' therefore includes companies in which a member of the group holds a qualifying capital interest within para. 30 of Sch. 1. The exemption applies even if the similar exemption from the FSA's authorisation requirement is excluded by the ISD (see ¶333).

(6) Certain advertisements relating to collective investment schemes (art. 3(2) and 14 of the 1996 investment advertisements order). First, an open-ended investment company can issue advertisements about its own shares or debentures, or subscription rights over its debentures, to the holders of any of those securities (or persons entitled to become holders, such as purchasers) and its creditors (art. 3(2)). Secondly, the operator of any sort of collective investment scheme (for example, an open-ended investment company or a unit trust) which is 'recognised' (or, approved) by the SIB under s. 87 or s. 88 for marketing to the general public in the UK can issue advertisements to participants in that scheme (typically, holders of its shares or units) which relate to other recognised collective investment schemes managed by him (art. 14); although this is not clear, it would seem the better view as the alternative reading is that the operator can issue investment advertisements only about the scheme in which they are already investors and a large part of the art. 3(2) exemption would accordingly be otiose. Operators of schemes recognised under s. 86 (and of authorised unit trusts and UK OEICs) are always FSA-authorised firms (see ¶414) and therefore do not need an exemption.

¶906

(7) Any advertisements issued in very restricted circumstances by overseas firms which do not carry on FSA-regulated investment business from a UK office to recipients who, in effect, are or were their 'non-UK clients' (art. 10 of the 1996 investment advertisements order, as amended by the 1997 order). The recipient must be a person with or for whom the overseas firm effected or arranged a transaction, or to whom it gave investment advice, or to or for whom it provided or arranged custody services within para. 13A or for whom it acted as a CREST sponsor, in each case within Pt. II, and outside the exemptions in Pt. III, of Sch. 1, in the previous 12 months. In addition, the recipient (the overseas firm's client) must have been non-resident and have had no place of business in the UK at that time; alternatively, even if he was resident or had a place of business in the UK at that time, the exemption still applies if the client was non-resident and had no place of business in the UK at any earlier time that the overseas firm had effected or arranged a transaction with or for him, or given him investment advice, or provided or arranged the custody services to or for him or acted as his CREST sponsor within Pt. II and outside the Pt. III exemptions. Finally, in the case of para. 13A custody services, the overseas firm must have provided, or arranged, the custody services from a non-UK office, and, in the case of investment advice, the recipient must also have been outside the UK when he received the advice. If the advertisement qualifies for this exemption, the overseas firm can send it to the client and still qualify for the 'overseas persons' exemptions from the FSA's authorisation requirement for the resulting transaction (see ¶334).

(8) Qualifying advertisements issued by a company which is not an open-ended investment company (art. 4 of the 1996 investment advertisements order). An advertisement qualifies if the company (or, if the company is a wholly-owned subsidiary, its holding company) has its shares or debentures, or warrants or options issued by it to subscribe its shares or debentures or depositary receipts or other certificates issued by it for or representing its shares or debentures ('relevant securities') quoted on a 'relevant EEA market' or an 'approved securities market'; warrants or options, or depositary receipts or other certificates, are treated as issued by it (and so as 'relevant securities') for the purposes of the order if they are issued by it or by a Companies Act group company or (as in the case of sponsored ADRs) are issued by a third party under arrangements with it (art. 2(2)). Alternatively, if no relevant securities are quoted on such a market, the advertisement qualifies if it consists of or is accompanied by the directors' report or audited annual accounts (or summary financial statement) of the company, or any part of the accounts, and the directors' report has been

approved by the board of directors (or equivalent) under UK law or the corresponding law of any other EEA member State. 'Approved securities markets' are the non-EEA stock exchanges specified in the order and include North American exchanges such as the NYSE and NASDAQ, Japanese exchanges and the Australian Stock Exchange. As would be expected, the exemption does not apply if the advertisement contains an actual offer or invitation, or any recommendation, to buy or sell, or underwrite, any FSA-regulated investments; nor does it apply if the advertisement contains any information likely to lead to anyone buying or selling FSA-regulated investments, or exercising any right given by an FSA-regulated investment to buy, sell, underwrite or convert FSA-regulated investments, other than 'relevant securities' issued by the company or any other body corporate in the same Companies Act group (or, in the case of subscription options or warrants relating to, or depositary receipts for or other certificates representing, shares or debentures issued by it, any third party who issued the option, warrant or certificate under arrangements with it, see above). The exemption also does not apply if the advertisement contains an invitation or offer to effect a transaction with, or make use of any services provided by, the company or any person named in the advertisement in the course of FSA-regulated investment activities not excluded by Pt. III of Sch. 1. Nor does it apply if the advertisement contains information about prices or, normally, the yield of securities, unless there is a warning that past performance cannot be relied on, or if the company issuing the advertisement is an open-ended investment company. The exemption applies *mutatis mutandis* in relation to a body corporate even if it is not a company.

(9) Qualifying advertisements issued by a company and addressed to persons entitled to relevant bearer securities issued by the company or a holding company or subsidiary (or treated as issued by it, see (8) above), provided that none of these companies is an open-ended investment company (art. 5(1) and art. 5(2) of the 1996 investment advertisements order); for this purpose, relevant bearer securities are bearer securities which are 'relevant securities' (see (8) above). The two exemptions are needed because the holders of bearer securities normally cannot be contacted except by public notices. The first exemption applies to advertisements containing offers or invitations to buy or sell the relevant bearer securities, or FSA-regulated investments which the relevant bearer securities entitle the holders to buy or sell; it applies only if the offer or invitation can be accepted only by persons entitled to 'relevant securities' issued by the company or by its holding

company or subsidiary (other than a company which is an open-ended investment company) and only if there is no offer or marketing information relating to FSA-regulated investments which are not 'relevant securities' issued (or treated as issued) by the company or any such holding company or subsidiary. The second exemption applies to advertisements issued by the company or any such holding company or subsidiary if it has relevant bearer securities issued (or treated as issued) by it traded on a 'relevant EEA market' (see ¶905(5)) or an 'approved securities market' (see (8) above), if they are investment advertisements only because they contain information required or permitted by that market to be given to the holders of 'relevant securities' of the same class as the relevant bearer securities. The exemption applies *mutatis mutandis* in relation to any body corporate even if it is not a company.

(10) Advertisements issued by a 'relevant EEA market' (see ¶905(5)), by an 'approved securities market' (see (8) above), by ISMA or by options or futures markets established by a specified non-EEA investment exchange which is only an investment advertisement because it contains information about the facilities provided by the market or because it identifies an option, a futures contract or a contract for differences as one which may be traded or dealt in on the market (art. 16 of the 1996 investment advertisements order and art. 12 of the 1995 investment advertisements order). The specified non-EEA investment exchanges whose options or futures markets are within the exemption include the Chicago Board of Trade, SOFFEX and the Singapore International Monetary Exchange. This exemption is additional to the general exemption (in s. 58(1)(b)) for RIEs and non-UK EEA regulated markets, which applies because they are exempted persons (see ¶352 and ¶353).

(11) Certain advertisements to be placed in publications or in other media. First, there is an exemption for qualifying press releases (art. 11(3)(c) of the 1996 investment advertisements order); the exemption applies to advertisements issued to financial journalists and to other people whose business involves the dissemination of information about FSA-regulated investments or investment activities in periodical publications, television or radio (but seemingly not the Internet). Secondly, there is a technical exemption for actual advertisements in very limited circumstances (art. 7 of the 1995 investment advertisements order). The exemption applies to advertisements issued to an advertising agency for the purposes of its business, or which is in a publication sent to other advertisers in that publication for the purposes

of their advertising or because they have advertised themselves; the exemption is needed because, although the publication is read only by professionals within, for example, the art. 11 exemption (see (1) above), the advertisers in that publication may not fall within that exemption.

(12) Advertisements required or authorised by or under other enactments (which are seemingly restricted to UK enactments other than the FSA itself), for example the report and accounts required under the *Companies Act* 1985 (art. 15 of the 1995 investment advertisements order, and see also (8) above).

(13) Advertisements issued by the holder of a para. 23 'permitted person' permission (see ¶335) for the purposes of or in connection with the para. 12 (dealing) activities engaged in by him under the terms of the permission (art. 6 of the 1995 investment advertisements order).

(14) Advertisements issued by or on behalf of either party to a management buy-out, trade sale or other sale of a body corporate within the para. 21 exemption for such sales from the FSA's authorisation requirement (see ¶338) if the advertisement is issued in connection with that sale (art. 5 of the 1995 investment advertisements order); the exemption applies even if the para. 21 exemption is excluded by the ISD.

(15) Advertisements containing specified disclosures and issued in connection with recommended take-over offers for UK private companies provided that their shares had not been the subject of public marketing arrangements (as defined) in the previous ten years (art. 4 of the 1995 investment advertisements order). Because, exceptionally, no FSA-authorised firm will be involved in the offer, the investment advertisement must contain many detailed disclosures and specified financial information and, in addition, the offer itself must comply with certain standards, in particular that the offer must be recommended by all the independent directors of the target company and must normally be conditional on the offer resulting in the offeror holding the majority of voting rights. The terms of the exemption are so complicated and restrictive (in order to protect shareholders in the target company) that in practice most offerors will probably ignore the exemption and use an FSA-authorised firm (for example a stockbroker or perhaps a firm of solicitors or accountants) to make or, at least, approve the offer and thus comply with the Marketing Prohibition.

(16) Advertisements relating to offers of shares in or debentures of a UK private company if the advertisement states expressly that the offer is restricted to an identified group of persons who have a pre-existing common interest with each other and with the company in the affairs of the company and in what is to be done with the proceeds of the offer

¶906

(art. 12 of the 1996 investment advertisements order). Offerees will not have this pre-existing common interest merely because they have a business relationship with the company. The exemption is directed at special situations, for example, supporters of a football club incorporated as a private company, where the involvement of the holders of the relevant securities is more than merely financial. It applies only if the advertisement contains: a responsibility statement by the directors or promoters for the statements actually contained in it; either a statement that all material information is included or, alternatively, a warning that the subscription is to help the company and not as an investment; and a warning to take professional advice on the offer.

(17) Advertisements relating to offers of shares in or debentures of a UK private company issued by a qualifying body corporate unconnected with the company in connection with the promotion by that body corporate of UK industrial or commercial activities or enterprises if the body corporate does not have a pecuniary interest in the offer (art. 3 of the 1995 investment advertisements order). The advertisement must contain a 'health warning' in prescribed form.

(18) Advertisements issued by an industrial and provident society about its own loan stock or other debentures (art. 13 of the 1995 investment advertisements order). Advertisements relating (instead or in addition) to transferable shares issued by it are also now subject to the Marketing Prohibition as they were added to the list of FSA-regulated investments as from the end of 1995 (art. 3 of the *Financial Services Act 1986 (Investment Services) (Extension of Scope of Act) Order* 1995); there seems to be no exemption for advertisements relating to them, although there is an exemption under the prospectus regulations (para. 22 of sch. 10 to the investment services regulations 1995).

(19) Advertisements issued by trustees or personal representatives about the trust or estate to fellow trustees or personal representatives or to beneficiaries (art. 13 of the 1996 investment advertisements order).

(20) Advertisements issued by suppliers to customers in relation to the financing of goods or services supplied in circumstances where the relevant financing transaction is exempted from the FSA's authorisation requirement, or would have been exempted apart from the ISD, (see ¶341) (art. 9 of the 1996 investment advertisements order); neither exemption applies to unit trusts or other collective investment schemes or to life or pension policies or where the customer is an individual.

¶906

(21) Advertisements relating to property management companies (art. 17 of the 1996 investment advertisements order). This is a technical exemption relating to the purchase of shares in a private company which manages flats or offices if the buyer of one of the flats or offices is required to buy them when he buys the property.

(22) Advertisements which relate to qualifying publications or programmes containing investment advice (art. 15 of the 1996 investment advertisements order). This is a technical exemption for 'indirect' investment advertisements which allows the issue of advertisements about periodical publications or TV or radio programmes if those publications or programmes contain investment advice but are exempted from the FSA's authorisation requirement (see ¶342).

As indicated above, it may be necessary in any particular case to look at all of these exemptions (and those contained in the FSA itself) (see ¶904) because more than one may be relevant.

The DTI (the predecessor to the Treasury as a regulator of investment advertisements) has very helpfully clarified the position with regard to corporate information in a guidance note which was copied by TSA (the predecessor to SFA) to its members with Board Notice No. 27 of 12 August 1988 but unfortunately some doubts still remain. In particular, a listed company can issue its report and accounts without approval by an FSA-authorised firm, because that is required both by the London Stock Exchange (see ¶905(2)) and under the Companies Act (see (12) above), and it can include a chairman's statement in the report and accounts sent to its shareholders (see (3) above) and to the London Stock Exchange, which is an exempted person (see ¶352 and (1) above). However, it is unclear whether it can publish a chairman's statement or extracts from it in a newspaper without such approval unless the rules of the London Stock Exchange require the publication of a chairman's statement if one is in fact made. The DTI has, however, stated in the guidance note that the London Stock Exchange considers it to form part of the report and accounts if it is contained in them. Further, the continuing obligation in the listing rules to disclose all material information will also exempt many corporate advertisements. However, the DTI guidance note does not expressly refer to extracts from a chairman's statement (or indeed from the report and accounts) which appear in a newspaper with the implicit intention of seeking new investors; such extracts would seem to be investment advertisements and certainly the prudent course, especially in the case of the chairman's statement, or if the advertisement is anything more than a mere extract, is for the advertisement to be approved by the company's brokers (who should as a matter of good practice vet it in any event quite apart from s. 57).

In addition to these exemptions, the FSA also allows the Treasury to issue other exemptions. Thus, they can exempt advertisements issued to private individuals who are 'sophisticated investors' because they would seem to constitute 'expert' investors within s. 58(3)(c), as there is no requirement that they must carry on a business. It could perhaps be argued that it may be too difficult to determine whether a private individual, however rich or experienced he is, knows so much about the relevant investments that he does not need to be protected; the SIB and the SROs do, however, relax their rules in the case of what they refer to as 'expert' private investors and that is perhaps a good precedent to follow but, equally, where those rules apply, there is an FSA-authorised firm involved in any event. No exemption for such marketing has yet been issued (see (1) above).

¶907   The issue of application forms

It is unclear whether or not application forms constitute investment advertisements, which is a matter of some significance in practice. Application forms were regulated as circulars by the *Prevention of Fraud (Investments) Act* 1958 (the predecessor to the FSA) but nothing is said expressly in the Financial Services Act. However, the FSA seems to assume that they are investment advertisements and, indeed, the FSA's transitional provisions contained a temporary exemption from the Marketing Prohibition, during the period that the Companies Act 1985 prospectus provisions remained in force, for not only prospectuses but also 'forms of application' (para. 8(1)(b) of Sch. 15). Further, the *Banking Act* 1987 has effectively the same definition of 'advertisement' as the Financial Services Act and the advertising regulations made under it clearly assume that they apply to application forms and accordingly contain certain exemptions for them (the *Banking Act 1987 (Advertisements) Regulations* 1988, reg. 2(4)). The better view, therefore, is that application forms are investment advertisements. This, indeed, has been confirmed by the exemption for recommended offers for private companies referred to at ¶906(15): thus, the exemption expressly states that it applies to 'an investment advertisement . . . issued in connection with a relevant offer [which] is a form of application for shares or debentures' (art. 4(5) of the 1995 investment advertisements order).

The problems do not end there however. Because there is no express reference to application forms, there is also no express exemption for application forms from the Marketing Prohibition as there was in the *Prevention of Fraud (Investments) Act* 1958 (and is in the banking regulations) if the application form is issued together with complying or exempted documents. An exemption for particular documents, for example listing particulars or a prospectus, will extend to application forms issued with them only if they are regarded as part of the same document, which is by no means clear. It may therefore be necessary for listing rules or the rules of an RIE or relevant EEA market to require application forms to be required or permitted to be published, so that they fall in one of the 'public issues' exemptions in their own right (see ¶905(2) and (6)). Otherwise application forms may have to be issued or 'approved' by FSA-authorised firms. This may be so even if they are issued with a document which itself complies with or is exempted from the Marketing Prohibition unless it is clear that the two documents must be read together. If they do need to be issued or 'approved' even if issued with an exempted investment advertisement, it may be that in practice reputable banks, brokers and other FSA-authorised or passporting firms will not issue or 'approve' an application form unless they also have some say in the contents of the exempted document.

THE BAN ON COLD CALLING

¶908   The 'ban'

Cold calling is, in effect, banned, even for FSA-authorised or exempted firms, unless an exemption applies (s. 56). It is not a criminal offence, however, and is not forbidden as such. Instead, s. 56 provides that if an 'unsolicited call' is made on a person in the UK, or from the UK on a person outside the UK, and the call is not permitted by the SIB's regulations, no-one can enter into an investment agreement by way of business (see ¶304) with the person on whom the call is made or try to persuade that person to enter into the investment agreement with him; in other words, it is the investment agreement which is prohibited if it results from the cold call, not the cold call itself, and the prohibition applies to everyone, not just the person making the call. An investment agreement which is entered into in breach of the prohibition will normally be unenforceable against the investor, although it may be enforced by him (s. 56(2)). In addition, the SIB can bring a civil action on behalf of investors for an indemnity against loss, or to recover profits, resulting from the contravention (s. 61). The SIB has provided detailed exemptions from this prohibition (or, permissions) which apply to everyone other than members of RPBs and therefore apply, importantly, to members of SROs and passporting firms (the *Common Unsolicited Calls Regulations* 1991); RPBs can provide different exemptions for the firms regulated by them.

¶909   Unsolicited calls

An 'unsolicited call' is a personal visit or oral communication made without express invitation (s. 56(8)). Although it is not totally clear, the regulators seem to have taken the generally accepted view that this includes talking without express invitation about FSA-regulated investments during a meeting or telephone call arranged or made for other purposes.

¶909

The ban is likely to be of most practical effect in the case of financial intermediaries (whether independent or appointed representatives), offshore share dealers who market by telephone and high-pressure salesmen who canvass door-to-door. However, it applies in principle to all unsolicited marketing of FSA-regulated investments or FSA-regulated investment services or other FSA-regulated investment activities carried out on the telephone or by personal visit; the ban therefore applies even in relation to corporate finance transactions, for example vendor consideration or private placings, although the exemptions for calls on investors who are not 'private investors' and on 'non-private customers' and for qualifying calls in relation to take-overs (see ¶911) will be of help in this context.

The exemptions are often very detailed and it is necessary to review them in detail. However, there are some general points which should be made before the exemptions are described briefly below. First, the exemptions actually help to indicate the scope of the ban. There are special exemptions for cold calls in a non-business context, where the person making the call is not acting by way of business nor for any sort of reward (such as, for example, a commission or fee) and for calls on 'close relatives' (as defined); these exemptions indicate that even calls on friends or business acquaintances to sell shares in the caller's own private company are within the ban. Secondly, there are special additional restrictions on 'overseas person calls'. Overseas person calls are calls made to market the FSA-regulated investment services or other FSA-regulated investment activities falling outside the exemptions in Pt. III of Sch. 1 (see ¶329) of an overseas investment firm or bank which is not an FSA-authorised firm or a passporting firm, if the call is made by or on behalf of that firm or bank or by or on behalf of another overseas investment firm or bank; examples of these services or activities are the sale of investments outside the FSA's 'own account' exemptions (see ¶331 and ¶332) and investment management services. For this purpose, an 'overseas investment firm or bank' is a securities firm, insurance company or bank or other credit institution which carries on FSA-regulated investment business but not from a UK office so that, for example, it qualifies for the 'overseas persons' exemptions; indeed, it may in fact be an FSA-authorised firm or a passporting firm, except in the case of the firm whose services or activities are being marketed. Finally, as indicated above, passporting firms are treated as if they were FSA-authorised firms for the purposes of the cold-calling permissions (para. 10 of Sch. 11 to the *Investment Services Regulations* 1995 and para. 16 of Sch. 11 to the *Banking Coordination (Second Banking Directive) Regulations* 1992); accordingly, calls relating to FSA-regulated investment services or other FSA-regulated investment activities are not 'overseas person calls' if they are to be provided or carried on by passporting firms within their ISD or 2BCD passport but outside the 'overseas persons' exemptions (see ¶334).

¶909

¶910 The exemptions

There is no general exemption for cold calls on private individuals, and accordingly they cannot be cold-called even by an FSA-authorised firm or a passporting firm unless a specific exemption applies. Cold calls on 'non-private investors' are, however, permitted unless they are overseas person calls; non-private investors are everyone except private individuals and therefore, except in the case of overseas person calls, there is no restriction on calling even small companies, partnerships or trusts which are not 'business investors' (see ¶901). If the call is an overseas person call, however, it normally cannot be made on individuals, or on companies, partnerships or trusts not qualifying as 'business investors' on the size lists, unless they are acting in the course of carrying on FSA-regulated investment business (for example, as an FSA-authorised firm or a listed money market institution). In addition, FSA-authorised firms or passporting firms can make unsolicited overseas person calls on individuals, companies, partnerships or trusts even if they were originally private customers if the firm has properly re-categorised them as 'experts', after warning them in writing of the 'private customer' protections they will lose and receiving consent to the re-categorisation; the consent must be in writing except in the case of customers who are ordinarily resident outside the UK and who the firm reasonably believes do not want to consent in writing. The specific permissions for cold calls on private individuals are the following (although the permissions are restricted in the case of overseas person calls):

(1) calls relating to the sale to the investor of a 'generally marketable non-geared packaged product', (reg. 2); these are units or shares in a 'regulated collective investment scheme' (such as an authorised unit trust or a 'recognised' scheme, see ¶913), an investment trust savings scheme or a life policy which can be marketed in the UK without contravening s. 130 of the FSA if the scheme or policy is not 'geared' (as defined in the Financial Services Core Glossary); for example, an investment trust savings scheme is 'geared' if it invests in an investment trust whose borrowing exceeds 50 per cent in value of the shares owned by it, a securities fund or a futures and options fund is 'geared' if it qualifies as a 'geared securities fund' or a 'geared futures and options fund' and a life policy is 'geared' if it is a unit-linked policy and is linked to a 'warrant fund' or a geared securities or futures and options fund (all as respectively defined in the *Financial Services (Regulated Schemes) Regulations* 1991) (reg. 2). Although the SIB has amended the definition of 'packaged product' to include UK OEICs, they do not seem to fall within this exemption as the definition of 'generally marketable' has not been amended to include them, although it is understood that they were intended to do so. Overseas person calls

relating to these products are also permitted but only if the call is by an FSA-authorised firm, a passporting firm or an FSA-exempted firm, such as a listed money market institution or an appointed representative, acting within its exemption (see ¶347); appointed representatives normally cannot make cold calls by virtue of the exemption for 'exempted persons' (see (9) below);

(2) calls relating to the provision by an FSA-authorised or exempted firm or a passporting firm of 'callable investment services' (reg. 3); these are FSA-regulated investment services (for example, sales) where the only FSA-regulated investments involved are 'generally marketable non-geared packaged products' (see (1) above) or readily realisable securities (other than warrants) provided that the acquisition of those investments is subject to (or is exempted from) cancellation or delayed entry procedures;

(3) calls made on existing customers of the person calling or, if different, the firm entering into the consequent investment agreement, or 'associates' of either (such as 'group' companies, where 'group' has the extended, 20 per cent affiliate, meaning given by para. 30 of Sch. 1, see (7) below), provided that the customer relationship envisaged cold calls (for example, they are referred to in the customer agreement) (reg. 4). In the case of 'geared packaged products' (see (1) above) the call is allowed only if it is by the investor's investment manager; in the case of 'contingent liability transactions' or discretionary investment management services, there must normally be a written consent to cold-calls; and, in the case of overseas person calls, there must be a written consent, the customer relationship must have existed while the customer was resident outside the UK and the customer must have been given a 'prescribed disclosure' that the FSA protections and, if this is the case, the FSA's compensation scheme do not apply;

(4) calls made by or under the supervision of an FSA-authorised firm or a passporting firm in connection with a take-over or substantial acquisition regulated by the Takeover Code or equivalent regulations in a non-UK EEA member State (reg. 6); this exemption applies even if the call is an overseas person call;

(5) calls made on existing customers of an investment business (for example, a stockbroker's local office) which has been taken over, if the call is by or on behalf of the new owner of the business asking them to be his customer (reg. 5);

(6) calls made on employees of a company (or other business) for the purpose of arranging a management buy-out from their employer or a

¶910

management buy-in involving them or a para. 21 corporate acquisition or disposal (see ¶338) (reg. 7);

(7) calls relating to employee share or option schemes, if the call is made by or on behalf of a group company or the trustee (reg. 9); 'group' has the wide para. 30 meaning and so includes not only a member of the same Companies Act group but also any other company in which any member of the group has, in general terms, a long-term equity shareholding, normally of at least 20 per cent, (see ¶333);

(8) calls made by a firm seeking to be appointed as investment manager of an occupational pension scheme or by the company (or the trustee) seeking to appoint one (reg. 10);

(9) calls relating to business with FSA-exempted firms (for example, listed money market institutions) for business within their exemption (reg. 13); the call can seemingly be made not only by or on behalf of the FSA-exempted firm but also on the FSA-exempted firm by a person who is (or is seeking to become) a client or counterparty. The exemption does not apply, regardless of who makes the call or on whom he makes it, if the investment agreement to which the call relates is to be entered into by an appointed representative;

(10) calls made in the course of non-FSA business in order to give investment advice or make arrangements for transactions within the 'necessary advice or arrangements' exemption from the FSA's authorisation requirement (see ¶343) (reg. 12);

(11) calls made in a non-business context (reg. 11). Calls are made in a non-business context if the person calling is not acting 'by way of business' (see ¶909) and has been provided with no incentive to make the call, regardless of the 'non-business' status of the resulting agreement;

(12) calls made on 'close relatives' (reg. 8(1)); 'close relatives' are spouses, parents, children and brothers and sisters; and

(13) calls made in relation to a trust between the settlor, the trustee and the beneficiaries or in relation to the deceased's estate between the personal representative and the beneficiaries, or their respective agents (regs. 8(2) and (3)).

Finally, it should be noted that, if the call is an overseas person call and the relevant permission does not expressly allow it, the call can be made by an FSA-authorised firm or a passporting firm if the consequent investment agreement is entered into on behalf of the overseas person, or is arranged, by an FSA-authorised firm or passporting firm or an FSA-exempted firm (for

¶910

example, a listed money market institution or appointed representative) acting within its exemption.

THE MARKETING OF COLLECTIVE INVESTMENT SCHEMES

¶911   Introduction

Chapter VIII of Pt. I of the Financial Services Act contains detailed provisions regulating the marketing to investors in the UK of unit trusts, mutual funds, open-ended investment companies, limited partnerships and other 'collective investment schemes' whether relating to securities or other FSA-regulated investments or to other property such as land. Chapter VIII prohibits FSA-authorised firms and passporting firms from marketing any collective investment scheme to the general public in the UK unless it is 'authorised' or 'recognised' (or, approved) by the SIB or is a UK OEIC (see ¶318), and so subject to some regulatory supervision; a firm 'markets' a collective investment scheme for the purposes of this prohibition if it recommends or advises clients, or procures them, to invest in it or if it issues investment advertisements relating to investment in it (s. 76(1)). The s. 76(1) restrictions are additional to the general marketing rules, for example the ban on unsolicited calls and, in particular, the Marketing Prohibition (see ¶902), which will apply in the normal way. Accordingly, unless an exemption applies, the prospectus or other marketing document for the collective investment scheme must be issued or 'approved' by an FSA-authorised firm or a passporting firm (see ¶902); as explained below, both routes are blocked by the s. 76(1) prohibition in relation to collective investment schemes subject to it.

Indeed, the s. 76(1) prohibition is actually much wider than merely a prohibition on marketing to the public. There is a total prohibition on marketing any collective investment scheme which is not authorised or recognised or a UK OEIC (an 'unregulated scheme') to any investor in the UK (even if there is no public offer) unless the marketing is restricted to: FSA-authorised firms and passporting firms; people who buy or sell property of the kind to which the collective investment scheme relates, namely, the underlying property, (s. 76(2)); and people who fall within the exemptions granted by regulations made by the SIB (see ¶914). Conversely, as open-ended investment companies are treated as collective investment schemes (s. 75(7)), they are not subject to the FSA's public issues regimes, whether they are listed or unlisted (see Ch. 8). The marketing restrictions in Ch. VIII apply in terms only to FSA-authorised firms and passporting firms (which are included by para. 23 of Sch. 7 to the *Investment Services Regulations* 1995 and para. 25 of

Sch. 9 to the *Banking Coordination (Second Council Directive) Regulations* 1992); however, they have now in effect been extended significantly by the SIB (see ¶919). Importantly, there are no restrictions under the FSA on the marketing of collective investment schemes to investors at addresses or offices outside the UK, although there may well be restrictions under their local law.

¶912   Authorisation and recognition

The only authorised schemes are authorised unit trusts or UK OEICs; a unit trust can be 'authorised' only if its manager is incorporated in the UK or another member State of the EEA and has a place of business in the UK (s. 78(3)). Only overseas schemes can be recognised, and there are three categories of such schemes:

(1) 'EEA-wide' schemes;

(2) 'designated country' schemes; and

(3) schemes recognised on an 'individual' basis.

¶913   The prohibition on marketing unregulated schemes

The FSA provides that, subject to the exemptions referred to in ¶914 and ¶915, FSA-authorised firms and passporting firms cannot issue investment advertisements (see ¶903) in the UK (or cause them to be issued in the UK) if they invite people to become, or to offer to become, participants (or, investors) in an unregulated scheme, or if they contain information calculated to lead to anyone becoming or offering to become a participant in an unregulated scheme, for example by applying for units or, in the case of open-ended investment companies, for shares in the scheme (s. 76(1)(a)). An 'unregulated scheme' is a collective investment scheme which is neither an authorised unit trust nor a recognised scheme nor a UK OEIC. The FSA also provides that, subject to the same exemptions, FSA-authorised firms and passporting firms cannot advise or procure anyone to become or offer to become a participant in an unregulated scheme (s. 76(1)(b)). This prohibition would seem to apply also to discretionary investment managers who want to put clients into a particular scheme. Moreover, the SIB has informally indicated that in its view mere 'offers' may constitute 'procuring' within s. 76(1)(b) and, indeed, that even mentioning unregulated schemes as a class as an investment possibility, or even asking a prospective investor whether he qualifies for an exemption, may contravene s. 76(1).

The prohibition only applies expressly to the 'issue' of investment advertisements by FSA-authorised firms or passporting firms but, as a result of the Marketing Prohibition (see ¶902), it normally applies in relation to all investment advertisements issued to individuals and other investors in the UK who are not 'business investors'. This is because advertisements falling in s. 76(1) are all 'investment advertisements' falling in s. 57(1) and, if they are not issued by an FSA-authorised firm, they accordingly need to be 'approved' by one under s. 57 unless an exemption applies (see ¶902). The SIB has in effect extended the prohibition so that it applies also where an FSA-authorised firm directly authorised by it or a passporting firm regulated by it proposes to 'approve' an investment advertisement for an unregulated scheme (rather than issue it) (see ¶919). Indeed, SFA and IMRO have gone even further and prohibited firms regulated by them from 'approving' investment advertisements relating to an unregulated scheme whoever they are to be issued to; as a result, investment advertisements about unregulated schemes must be issued by those FSA-authorised firms and the prohibitions will apply.

Contravention of the s. 76(1) prohibition is not a criminal offence, but investors are able to recover any loss and the other sanctions applicable to breach of conduct of business rules will apply. The FSA does not contain any exemption from these prohibitions for 'unregulated' schemes listed on the London Stock Exchange. It therefore does not help open-ended investment companies in this context to be listed on the London Stock Exchange. Indeed, the London Stock Exchange was accordingly originally minded to delist all open-ended investment companies which were not 'recognised'; it did not refer to UK OEICs because they were not yet in existence. However, it accepted that this was not necessary in light of the exemptions provided by the SIB (see ¶914) and wrote to listed open-ended investment companies in August 1988 to notify them that they could keep their listing if they thought that their shares could continue to be 'adequately marketed to UK investors'.

An advertisement will be treated as issued in the UK (and so subject to the s. 76(1) prohibition) if it is delivered or sent to an investor in the UK; as in the case of the Marketing Prohibition, it will also be treated as issued in the UK if it is directed at persons in the UK or is made available to them, unless it is so made available only in a newspaper or journal published and circulating principally outside the UK or is broadcast principally for reception outside the UK (s. 207(3), see ¶903). Because the prohibition applies only to the issue of an advertisement in the UK, it seemingly does not prohibit the posting from the UK of prospectuses or information memoranda to overseas recipients; this view is based on the argument that a document is issued in the UK only if its recipient is in the UK. The investor's local law must, however, always be reviewed.

¶914 Exemptions for 'professionals only' and restricted schemes

The prohibition in s. 76(1) does not apply to advertisements issued or advice given by FSA-authorised firms or passporting firms to, or their procuring of, other FSA-authorised firms or passporting firms (s. 76(2)(a), as extended by para. 23 of Sch. 7 to the *Investment Services Regulations* 1995 and para. 25 of Sch. 9 to the *Banking Coordination (Second Council Directive) Regulations* 1992) or 'ordinary business investors', namely persons whose ordinary business involves the acquisition and disposal of property of the same kind as the (underlying) property to which the scheme relates, (s. 76(2)(b)). The 'ordinary business investors' exemption thus applies to investors in the kind of property involved (for example, land) rather than (only) professional investors in securities. If marketing is confined to these two classes of investor, the scheme can be totally unregulated. Further, quite apart from these statutory exemptions for 'professionals only' schemes, it is also possible to market other unregulated schemes on a restricted basis as a result of exemptions issued by the SIB (s. 76(3)). The SIB has issued several exemptions from the prohibition in s. 76(1); they are contained in the *Financial Services (Promotion of Unregulated Schemes) Regulations* 1991. Although s. 76(3) applies these exemptions, and the regulations refer, in terms only to FSA-authorised firms, they also both apply to passporting firms in the same way as the s. 76(1) prohibition itself (para. 23 of Sch. 7 to the *Investment Services Regulations* 1995 and r. 2.03 of the *Financial Services (Investment Firms) Rules* 1995, in the case of non-UK EEA firms entitled to the ISD passport, and para. 25 of Sch. 9 to the *Banking Coordination (Second Council Directive) Regulations* 1992 and art. 1.02(4)(b) of the *Financial Services (European Institutions) Instrument* 1993, in the case of non-UK EEA firms entitled to the 2BCD passport).

Under the regulations and the exemptions in s. 76(2), FSA-authorised firms and passporting firms can promote (that is, issue investment advertisements about, give advice on and procure investment in) unregulated schemes of particular kinds to investors who are reasonably believed by the firm to fall in the particular class specified in the exemption (see below) and to FSA-authorised firms, passporting firms and ordinary business investors (see above). However, and importantly, unregulated schemes cannot be marketed by FSA-authorised firms or passporting firms directly to private individuals (however rich or sophisticated they are) or to companies, partnerships or trusts not qualifying as 'business investors' (see ¶901) if they are not their qualifying customers, although they can be approached indirectly through the broker, investment manager or other FSA-authorised firm or passporting firm whose customer they are; like the unsolicited calls regime, the exemptions seem to restrict the protection offered by the FSA primarily to private or retail investors.

The promotion of unregulated schemes regulations provide for the following main exemptions for marketing by FSA-authorised firms and passporting firms (in addition to those provided by s. 76(2), see above):

¶914

(1) all unregulated schemes can be marketed to 'business investors' (see ¶901) (s. 76(2) and reg. 1.04(6));

(2) all unregulated schemes can be marketed to other 'non-private customers' (reg. 1.04(6)); this allows marketing in particular to individuals, companies and trusts not qualifying as 'business investors' if they are properly categorised as 'experts' after sending them a clear written warning of the private customer protections they will accordingly lose and receiving consent from them to this treatment. It is in practice very difficult to use this exemption as the investor must have sufficient experience and understanding to know what he is doing (at least in relation to the underlying assets) and to waive the private customer protections and the firm must have reasonable grounds to believe this, and that the 'experts' procedures have been properly complied with, before first contacting the investor. The SIB has indicated informally that the firm may contravene s. 76(1) if it merely asks the investor to confirm that it is qualified as an 'expert' investor;

(3) unregulated schemes can be marketed to their existing investors or investors in schemes with substantially similar investment and risk profiles, and to people who were investors in them in the previous 30 months (reg. 1.04(1)); the 'similar' unregulated schemes do not need to be of the same kind so far as structure is concerned (for example, one can be a unit trust and one an open-ended investment company);

(4) all unregulated schemes can be marketed to existing customers of the firm or any group company ('group' having the wide Sch. 1 meaning by virtue of para. 30) if investment in the scheme is suitable for them (reg. 1.04(3)); however, prospective investors cannot be made customers merely so as to market unregulated schemes to them on this basis, and, indeed, the regulations indicate that making them customers for this purpose might itself be a contravention of s. 76(1). It is this exemption which allows indirect marketing to high net worth investors through their broker or investment manager;

(5) tax-exempt unregulated schemes can be marketed to pension funds and other qualifying investors (reg. 1.04(9));

(6) qualifying unregulated schemes can be marketed to employees or former employees of the firm marketing the scheme or a group company ('group' having the wide Sch. 1 meaning by virtue of para. 30) or to employees or former employees of an employer who has accepted responsibility for the marketing (reg. 1.04(11)); 'employees' include non-executive directors. A scheme qualifies if it is constituted as a limited partnership with the employer as the general partner and the employees as limited partners; alternatively, the general partner can be

¶914

not the employer but a group company ('group' having the wide Sch. 1 meaning by virtue of para. 30) or another company connected with the employer by virtue of one holding the majority of the voting rights in the other, whether alone or together with other group companies. In addition, a scheme qualifies if it is constituted as a trust and the firm reasonably believes that the employees are not potentially liable to make further payments into the trust (for example, because the trust writes options). Finally, a scheme also qualifies however it is constituted if it invests only in shares in and debentures of the employer, or a company connected with it (see above), or warrants or options to subscribe them (or depositary receipts or other certificates representing them); and

(7) an unregulated scheme can be marketed to an investor who has asked an unauthorised person to include the investor's name in a list of persons willing to receive details of unregulated schemes with underlying property of the same description as that scheme (reg. 1.04(12)). The exemption applies only if the firm seeking to rely on it is not an 'associate' of the unauthorised person compiling the list and only if the firm had no reason to believe that the investor's name was included in the list as a result of a contravention of s. 76(1) or of conduct of business rules relating to any FSA-authorised or passporting firm (for example, the prohibition on 'approving' investment advertisements for unregulated schemes).

¶915   Single property schemes

The *Financial Services Act* 1986 gives the DTI (and now the Treasury) the power to exempt 'single property schemes' from the Ch. VIII regime if they meet certain specified criteria (s. 76(4) and 76(6)); this is intended to promote the financing of substantial office blocks and other property developments. This power has not been delegated to the SIB. The regulations under which the exemption is provided can include extra conditions, but the FSA requires certain conditions to be satisfied in any event. These are that the property consists of a single building (or a group of adjacent buildings) managed as a whole by or on behalf of the operator of the scheme, and that the shares, units or other interests issued to the participants in the scheme are dealt in on a recognised investment exchange (for example, the London Stock Exchange, even if only on AIM). The DTI has in fact issued regulations exempting qualifying single property schemes from the s. 76(1) restrictions, allowing them to be either based on a trust or to involve a corporate structure and containing very detailed extra conditions which must be satisfied if the exemption is to apply: the *Financial Services Act 1986 (Single Property Schemes) (Exemption) Regulations* 1989 (SI 1989/28). However, the SIB has seemingly restricted marketing nonetheless to marketing allowed by the exemptions for 'professionals only' and restricted schemes (reg. 8(1) of the *Financial Services (Single Property Schemes) (Supplementary) Regulations* 1989). In addition, the SIB's Regulations require the publication by the operator of 'scheme particulars' relating to the exempted scheme (see ¶917).

Under reg. 8 of the SIB's regulations, an FSA-authorised firm or a passporting firm cannot 'market' a single property scheme unless scheme particulars have been published in accordance with the rules of the exchange on which the scheme will be quoted; however, a short-form advertisement relating to the prospectus may be published similar to that referred to in the similar exemption from the Marketing Prohibition (see ¶905(4)). As explained above, 'passporting firms' are treated as FSA-authorised firms for this purpose (reg. 1.02(4)(b) of the *Financial Services (European Institutions) Instrument* 1993 and of the *Financial Services (Investment Firms) Rules* 1995).

¶916 UK collective investment schemes

UK collective investment schemes can be marketed to the public in the UK by FSA-authorised firms or passporting firms only if they are authorised unit trusts or UK OEICs; UK schemes cannot be 'recognised'. However, UK OEICs are only incorporated if the SIB authorises them for marketing to the public (reg. 3 of the *Open-ended Investment Companies (Investment Companies with Variable Capital) Regulations* 1996 (the ECA regulations). The prohibition therefore simply means that FSA-authorised firms and passporting firms cannot market to the public in the UK unincorporated UK collective investment schemes other than authorised unit trusts, for example unauthorised unit trusts and contract-based schemes (such as venture capital limited partnerships), even if they relate to FSA-regulated investments. Similar overseas schemes, however, may be marketed to the public by FSA-authorised firms or passporting firms if they are 'recognised' by the SIB; accordingly, for example, limited partnerships will have to go offshore if they are to be marketed to the public in the UK. However, UK limited partnerships (and other UK schemes) can be marketed by FSA-authorised firms and passporting firms to restricted groups of investors (see ¶914), which may be all that is normally commercially required.

¶917 Publication of 'scheme particulars' and other information

The SIB can require authorised unit trusts and UK OEICs (s. 85(1), as extended by reg. 6 of the ECA regulations) and both 'designated country' schemes (s. 87(5)) and collective investment schemes recognised on an 'individual' basis (s. 88(10)), whether open-ended investment companies or unincorporated, to publish scheme particulars containing prescribed information. 'Scheme particulars' are the equivalent of listing particulars and prospectuses and, indeed, they are actually referred to as a 'prospectus' in both the ECA regulations relating to UK OEICs and the UCITS directive itself. The FSA provides that scheme particulars have to contain such information and have to comply with such requirements as are specified in regulations issued by the SIB.

The SIB has indeed issued detailed regulations: the *Financial Services (Regulated Schemes) Regulations* 1991 and the *Financial Services (Open-ended Investment Companies) Regulations* 1997. These provide that scheme particulars must be published by the 'operator'; the operator is the manager or (in the case of open-ended investment companies) the company itself (s. 75(8)). Where relevant in this section, references to scheme particulars include prospectuses and references to a 'scheme' include a UK OEIC. Scheme particulars must be revised at least every 12 months and supplementary scheme particulars must be issued whenever the material facts change, as in the case of listing particulars, (reg. 3.07). Copies must be given to the SIB, to the trustee (if any) and, normally, to prospective investors. Scheme particulars must contain details of the manager and operator, any investment manager or adviser, any trustee and the custodian and of the constitution of the scheme; they must also set out the objectives of the scheme and its hedging, borrowing and investment powers. However, non-UK EEA schemes authorised for marketing under the UCITS directive, as implemented into UK law by s. 86 ('EEA-wide' schemes) do not have to publish UK scheme particulars (reg. 3.01, see below). In addition, the SIB has exempted 'designated country' schemes established in Jersey, Guernsey and the Isle of Man from the requirement to issue scheme particulars complying with its rules if they comply with the requirements of the designated country concerned as to scheme particulars and those requirements have broadly the same effect as those of the SIB (reg. 3.05).

Scheme particulars and other information must be permanently available for inspection in the UK. There are special requirements for 'authorised securities funds'; these are authorised schemes for investment in transferable securities (and so falling within the UCITS directive). These schemes must issue translations of their scheme particulars in the language of any member State in which they are to be marketed; this is why the SIB's 'scheme particulars' requirements do not apply to them (see further below). The regulations provide that the operator is to be responsible for the scheme particulars and he is accordingly liable to compensate investors for loss arising from false or misleading statements and non-disclosure; this is without prejudice to his liability apart from the regulations, for example under the *Misrepresentation Act* 1967 (s. 85(3)). Directors of a UK OEIC are similarly usually liable for the prospectus issued by it, as also are persons who are named in the prospectus with their agreement as having agreed to be a director or as having accepted responsibility. If the operator of a scheme recognised on an 'individual' basis is not himself an FSA-authorised firm, the scheme's UK representative appointed under s. 88(5) is also responsible for the scheme particulars (reg. 3.06); this attempt to ensure that there is someone in the UK who is responsible to indemnify investors is an important protection.

As indicated above, this regime does not apply to 'EEA-wide' schemes; however, non-UK UCITS schemes are required by the UCITS directive and the SIB regulations to issue a prospectus in English containing prescribed disclosures equivalent to scheme particulars (art. 47 and reg. 14.01); the same will presumably apply to any other kinds of 'EEA-wide' scheme. The requirement for scheme particulars also does not apply to unregulated schemes subject to restricted offers (see ¶914).

The SIB can also require the operator of any recognised scheme (including 'EEA-wide' schemes) to include in investment advertisements which it issues or causes to be issued in the UK such 'explanatory information' as the SIB directs (s. 90(2)). This, seemingly, allows the SIB to single out particular operators or schemes rather than issue 'general' requirements as in the case of scheme particulars.

¶918   Advance notice to be given by 'EEA-wide' schemes

An 'EEA-wide' scheme cannot be marketed until it is, in effect, 'confirmed' to be a recognised scheme. Accordingly, it will be necessary to give at least two months' advance notice to the SIB that the scheme is to be marketed, specifying the manner in which offers are to be made, and to supply the SIB with the required documents and information (s. 86(2) and reg. 14.01).

¶919   Scope of the new regime

The new regime in Ch. VIII applies directly only to marketing by FSA-authorised firms and passporting firms (s. 76(1)). It therefore does not itself apply to the operator or manager of the scheme (see ¶917) unless it is an FSA-authorised firm or a passporting firm. However, the SIB has in effect extended the regime to directly authorised firms (see below). The operator of a UK scheme has to be an FSA-authorised firm, and Ch. VIII therefore applies to it. Similarly, the operator of an 'EEA-wide' scheme or a UK OEIC is also an FSA-authorised firm in relation to the marketing of that scheme (s. 24), but, as it can be marketed to the public, nothing turns on that. However, operators of other overseas schemes are not necessarily FSA-authorised firms.

It seems to have been the intention that the new regime should be comprehensive. Indeed, it normally would have been as a result of the Marketing Prohibition if the Marketing Prohibition had remained in its original form and had not been relaxed so as to allow investment advertisements to be issued (merely) with the 'approval' of an FSA-authorised firm or (now) a passporting firm (see ¶902). Apart from the relaxation allowing mere 'approvals', the offer or other marketing document would have had to be issued by an FSA-authorised firm or a passporting firm unless it fell within an exemption from the Marketing Prohibition and the new regime would have applied; conversely, it would not have applied in relation to 'business investors' or to 'expert investors' within the art. 11(3) exemption from the Marketing Prohibition (see ¶906(1)). As a result of the relaxation, however, s. 76(1) is not as comprehensive as was intended.

The SIB has, however, restored the position so far as directly authorised firms are concerned by in effect reversing the effect of the relaxation of the Marketing Prohibition in relation to 'approvals' by them; this applies also in the case of passporting firms unless they have joined an SRO for their activities relating to the marketing of unregulated schemes. The SIB has extended the new regime by, in effect, applying s. 76(1) to the 'approval' of advertisements as well as their issue. The SIB's rules therefore prohibit firms authorised by it (and passporting firms) from 'approving' investment advertisements relating to collective investment schemes unless they are regulated schemes or they are to be issued only within the exemptions to the prohibition in s. 76(1) (see ¶914) (r. 7.04(3)(a)) of the *Financial Services (Conduct of Business) Rules* 1990). In addition, the firm cannot 'approve' an investment advertisement about a collective investment scheme to be issued by an 'overseas person' (that is, a firm which carries on FSA-regulated investment business but not from a UK office) unless that overseas person is the 'operator' and, importantly, the scheme is a regulated collective investment scheme (r. 7.04(3)(b)); accordingly, the firm cannot approve investment advertisements for many non-UK unregulated schemes. The r. 7.04(3)(a) prohibition has been followed by SFA, IMRO and the PIA who, indeed, have prohibited all 'approvals' relating to unregulated schemes whoever issues the investment advertisement and whoever it is issued to.

The SIB has also blocked another similar potential gap. Section 58(1)(c) allows nationals of other EEA member States to issue qualifying investment advertisements without 'approval' under s. 57 even if they are not FSA-authorised firms or passporting firms (see ¶904(3)). This would in effect allow them to market unregulated schemes freely because, as the offer documents are neither issued nor 'approved' by FSA-authorised firms or passporting firms, the prohibitions in s. 76(1), and in the SIB's rules, would not apply. However, the SIB has prohibited firms directly authorised by it from issuing advertisements relating to unregulated schemes unless, again, they fall within an exemption from the prohibitions in s. 76(1) (r. 7.27 of the *Financial Services (Conduct of Business) Rules* 1990). This rule is actually otiose for directly authorised firms

¶919

(because s. 76(1) applies to them in any event). However, it is important for non-UK EEA firms relying on the s. 58(1)(c) exemption from the Marketing Prohibition; s. 58(1)(c) provides that advertisements issued under it must comply with the SIB rules for directly authorised firms relating to investment advertisements, and r. 7.27 accordingly subjects advertisements exempted by s. 58(1)(c) from the Marketing Prohibition to the prohibition in s. 76(1).

These prohibitions apply not only to the prospectus itself but also to advertisements in newspapers or on the Internet marketing an unregulated scheme or, indeed, announcing the availability of the prospectus, because they are 'investment advertisements' (see ¶905); this is in practice the principal way that offshore funds without a UK connection can attract the UK public and clearly it is important that the regime should apply to them.

¶920   No need to register

Chapter VIII of the Financial Services Act does not require marketing documents to be registered even if they contain scheme particulars (see ¶917) and even in the case of public offers. This is the case even in relation to UK or non-UK open-ended investment companies; this is exactly because the FSA's marketing restrictions apply to them on the basis that they are collective investment schemes rather than ordinary companies subject to the public issues regimes (see Ch. 8).

10 Collective Investment Schemes

INTRODUCTION

¶1001 Overview

Chapter VIII of Pt. I of the *Financial Services Act* 1986 introduced a new regime for the regulation of collective investment schemes marketed to the public. As explained in the previous chapter, the only collective investment schemes which can be marketed to the public in the UK by authorised persons are authorised unit trusts and 'recognised' overseas schemes. UK collective investment schemes can accordingly be marketed to the public in the UK by authorised persons only if they are constituted as unit trusts and are authorised (see ¶1005–¶1008). Chapter VIII describes the arrangements which will constitute collective investment schemes, the criteria for authorisation and recognition, and the new regime which will apply to authorised or recognised schemes.

'Collective investment schemes' are, in general terms, arrangements under which the participants participate in or receive profits or income arising from the acquisition, holding, management, or disposal of property of any description (including money) or sums paid out of such profits or income (s. 75(1)). They are colloquially referred to as 'funds', and where they are constituted outside the UK as 'offshore funds', and include unit trusts, mutual funds, limited partnerships and open-ended investment companies such as many currency or venture or development capital funds (see ¶1003). However, other bodies corporate are excluded (s. 75(7)), and accordingly ordinary investment companies and investment trusts (which are actually companies) will not constitute 'collective investment schemes'.

The Act places regulatory responsibilities on the 'operator' of a collective investment scheme. In the case of a unit trust with a separate trustee, the 'operator' is the manager (s. 75(8)). In the case of an open-ended investment company, however, the 'operator' is the company itself, even if there is a separate manager; this follows the EEC's UCITS directive (see ¶1013), but outside the EEC, for example in the Channel Islands, open-ended investment companies are normally established with a separate manager on the basis that the manager takes investment decisions and markets the fund while the company merely holds the assets like a trustee, and accordingly it may have been more satisfactory in the case of such companies if the manager had been the 'operator'. There is no special definition of 'operator' in the case of other collective investment schemes, and the 'operator' will therefore be the person who actually operates the scheme rather than the depositary or custodian, if any. 'Trustee' has a special meaning in Ch. VIII in the case of overseas schemes (but not UK schemes); it means the custodian or depositary of the scheme's assets, even if they are not held under a trust (s. 75(8)). Finally, the Act refers to the shares, units or other interests of the participants in a collective investment scheme by the collective term 'units' (s. 75(8)) and the holders of units as 'participants' (s. 75(2)).

¶1002   What are collective investment schemes?

Arrangements may constitute a collective investment scheme even if they are only contractual and even if the underlying property would not itself be a regulated investment if held direct (for example, land). They will be only contractual if the assets are not held under a trust and the scheme is not constituted as an open-ended investment company, for example if the arrangements provide merely for common management of separately owned assets or the scheme is constituted as a limited partnership or the participants have only a contractual right to share in a common fund. Arrangements will constitute a collective investment scheme only if the participants do not have day-to-day control over the management of the property in question and only if, in addition, either the contributions of the participants, and the profits or the income out of which payments are made to them, are pooled or the property is managed as a whole by or on behalf of the operator of the scheme (s. 75(2) and (3)). Further, where the arrangements provide for pooling in relation to separate parts of the property, the arrangements will constitute a single scheme only if the participants can exchange rights in one part for rights in another (s. 75(4)). This may help with the selective marketing of particular parts of a property within a particular exemption from the marketing restrictions.

The Act – as amended by various orders (SI 1988/496, SI 1988/803, SI 1990/349, SI 1990/1493) – provides that certain arrangements otherwise within the definition will not, however, constitute collective investment schemes. Thus it excludes certain arrangements where the contributions made by participants are deposits for the purposes of the *Banking Act* 1987, arrangements confined to members of a group, joint ventures and other cooperative arrangements entered into for commercial rather than investment reasons, franchise arrangements, clearing house services operated by an authorised person or a recognised clearing house or investment exchange, contracts of insurance, certain employee share schemes and occupational pension schemes, arrangements operated otherwise than by way of business, and arrangements relating to a particular property if the predominant purpose of the arrangements is the use of the property (for example, a time-share or a house lived in by the participants in the arrangements) (s. 75(6)). In addition, arrangements under which the rights of the participants are represented by certificates representing securities will not constitute a collective investment scheme if they fall in para. 5 of Sch. 1 because they are in any event regulated investments (s. 75(6)(h)). This exemption is necessary because in certain circumstances such certificates, for example bearer depositary receipts, may constitute unauthorised unit trusts.

The Act provides expressly that 'parallel' investment management schemes under which the portfolios are managed 'in parallel' as if they were a single fund (which they are not) do not constitute collective investment schemes if three conditions are satisfied. These are that the portfolios consist only of securities (other than traded options), shares, units or other interests in collective investment schemes which are authorised or recognised and cash awaiting investment; that the portfolios are not pooled (but only held, for example by a nominee, directly and separately for each participant); and that each participant remains the owner of his own portfolio and can withdraw it at any time (s. 75(5)). If this express exclusion had not been provided (and it was not in the Financial Services Bill as originally published), it would have been strongly arguable that such 'parallel' schemes were not within s. 75(1) at all. However, it is now arguable that they will always be unless the terms of the exclusion are kept to exactly (which will require, for example, an immediate right of withdrawal and, probably, separate certificates); however, the better view is that transactions can still be dealt on an aggregate basis, which is where the cost savings come from.

¶1003   Open-ended investment companies

Open-ended investment companies have existed in other countries for many years and provide a simpler investment mechanism than the unit trust which developed in the UK.

A company will be 'open-ended' for the purposes of the Act if (following the UCITS directive) either its shareholders can require the company to redeem their shares or, alternatively, the company ensures that its shares can be sold on an investment exchange at a price related to the value of the property to which they relate (for example, at net asset value less notional realisation and other expenses). As a legal matter, it would seem that redemption does not need to be related to net asset value, although it does if the company is to be recognised on an 'individual' basis (see ¶1015). The rights of the participants can be represented by securities other than shares and so may include some of those more sophisticated financing vehicles which do not give all the equity interest in the underlying property to investors. References in this chapter to shares, shareholders and redemption should therefore be read (where the context permits) as including those other securities, security holders and re-purchase. A company will be an 'investment company' if its economic purpose is to manage its funds in order to spread investment risk for the (economic) benefit of its members (or, rather, participants) (s. 75(8)), although as a legal matter the managed property will belong beneficially to the company, its participants having instead shares or securities in the company. In practice many offshore open-ended investment companies are managed by a separate management company and such externally managed companies also constitute collective investment schemes if they fulfil these criteria although (as seen in ¶1001) the 'operator' to whom regulation applies is the company rather than the manager.

Section 75(8) makes it clear that the 'redemption-right' test is not satisfied merely by virtue of the statutory right given to English and Scottish companies to redeem their shares under the *Companies Act* 1985 subject to the statutory conditions. UK company law effectively precludes a UK company being 'open-ended' if it wants to offer its shares to the public and, even if it is, there are normally substantial tax disadvantages. The Government indicated in the White Paper (*Financial Services in the United Kingdom: A New Framework for Investor Protection* (1985 Cmnd 9432)) that it would remove the company law restrictions.

The *Open-Ended Investment Companies (Investment Companies with Variable Capital) Regulations* 1996, SI 1996/2827 came into force on 6 January 1997 and made provision for such companies. These investment companies will be collective investment schemes within s. 75, open-ended investment companies within s. 75(8) and will be an undertaking for collective investment under the UCITS directive. Such companies must be authorised by the SIB which for this purpose issued on 16 January 1997 the *Financial Services (Open-Ended Investment Companies) Regulations* 1997. OEICs are discussed further at ¶1009ff.

¶1004   Fees

The SIB charges the operators of collective investment schemes both a 'one-off' fee on application for authorisation or recognition (or on the requisite notification) and also periodic fees once they are authorised or recognised: the Financial Services (Collective Investment Scheme Fees) Regulations 1992 (as amended), issued under s. 112(5) and 113(8) (see SIB Rules, vol. 3).

AUTHORISED UNIT TRUSTS

¶1005 Introduction

Although collective investment schemes may be constituted as unit trusts, as open-ended investment companies, or as contractual arrangements, UK schemes can be authorised only if they are constituted under a trust and have a separate trustee (s. 77(1)) (but see ¶1003). The SIB has made the *Financial Services (Regulated Schemes) Regulations* 1991 which inter alia provide for the constitution and management of authorised unit trusts schemes including price arrangements and scheme particulars and powers of investment and borrowing. An authorised unit trust satisfies the requirements of the UCITS directive so that such schemes may be marketed elsewhere in the EU.

As required by the UCITS directive, the Act provides that the manager must restrict his activities to those of acting as manager of a unit trust (which need not itself be authorised), of an open-ended investment company, or any other investment trust or investment company, or of an unincorporated collective investment scheme, for example a mutual fund under which the contributions of the participants and the profits or income out of which payments are made to them are pooled (s. 83). It therefore cannot act as manager of 'parallel investment' schemes or, indeed, as an ordinary investment manager for institutional or private clients outside these categories.

¶1006 Applications for authorisation

The manager and trustee of the unit trust have to apply jointly to the SIB for authorisation (s. 77(1)). They have to make prescribed disclosures and also have to lodge a solicitor's certificate that the trust deed complies with the SIB's regulations (see ¶1007) (s. 77(5) and 78(1)(b)). Authorisation will be discretionary and a decision must be made and notified within six months (s. 78(7)).

A unit trust can be authorised only if certain conditions are fulfilled (s. 78). The manager and the trustee must be independent of each other (see SIB Guidance Release No. 1/90) and must not be prohibited by the 'scope' rules from acting as a manager or trustee as appropriate (see ¶404 and ¶406). They must each be a company or other body corporate incorporated in the UK or in another member State of the EU. Their affairs must be administered in the country in which they are incorporated and each must have a place of business in the UK. In addition, each must himself be an authorised person (s. 78(4)), which is in direct contrast with the previous position under the Prevention of Fraud (Investments) Act where the manager and trustee were exempted exactly because they were a manager and trustee of an authorised unit trust. No minimum capitalisation is specifically required of the manager or trustee even though it was previously required of trustees; they must comply with the financial resources rules, however, in order to be authorised at all (see ¶403 and ¶407) and that is presumably why it is not required as a condition of authorisation of the unit trust. Further, a unit trust will not be authorised unless its units are redeemable at a price related to net asset value or, alternatively (as in the case of open-ended investment companies (see ¶1003)), the scheme requires the manager to ensure that participants can sell their units on an investment exchange (not necessarily the London Stock Exchange) at a price not significantly different from one related to net asset value (s. 78(6)). A price will be 'related' to net asset value if it is determined by reference to the net asset value less notional realisation and other expenses, although other formulae should be possible. Finally, if the manager is incorporated in a member State outside the UK, the unit trust cannot be authorised if it satisfies the requirement for 'EEC-wide' schemes because it then falls under the new regime for such schemes and, for example, the manager and trustee do not need to be authorised persons as a condition of recognition (see ¶1013) (s. 78(3)). If the SIB proposes to refuse authorisation, it must notify the applicants; they have 21 days to make oral or written representations, which the SIB must take into account, but there is no right of appeal (s. 80).

Existing authorised unit trusts were 'automatically' regarded as authorised for the purposes of Ch. VIII (Sch. 15, para. 9(1)). In the normal case, however, both the manager and the trustee nonetheless had to become members of an SRO (normally IMRO) or obtain direct authorisation (see Ch. 4).

¶1007   Regulation of authorised unit trusts

The regulation of authorised unit trusts is the responsibility of the SIB, and the relevant rules for the constitution and management of a unit trust are contained in the *Financial Services (Regulated Schemes) Regulations* 1991. These regulations provide the secondary legislation for the constitution and management of unit trusts. Accordingly they deal with requirements for the trust deed, powers and duties of the manager and trustee, payment of the manager and trustee, the pricing of units on their issue purchase, sale, redemption and cancellation.

The Act requires managers of authorised unit trusts to give written notice to the SIB of any proposed alterations to the trust and it will be necessary to deliver a certificate by a solicitor that the alteration will not affect compliance with the regulations made under s. 81 (s. 82(1)). The manager or the trustee will also have to notify the SIB of any proposal to replace the trustee or manager, as appropriate (s. 82(1) and (2)). No such proposal to alter the trust or replace the trustee or manager will be effective unless the SIB approves the proposal or fails to notify the manager or trustee, as appropriate, within one month that the proposal is not approved (s. 82(3)). The SIB will therefore have a power of veto if it does not like the proposed alteration or the proposed new trustee or manager, who must in any event be an authorised person and must comply with the statutory criteria (see ¶1006). The Act also provides that any provision of the trust deed of an authorised unit trust which purports to exempt the manager or trustee from liability for failure to exercise due care will be void (s. 84).

The SIB, in the 1991 regulation, requires the manager of an authorised unit trust to publish scheme particulars (see ¶917) and makes him liable to investors for untrue or misleading statements and for omissions. In addition, if the SIB restricts the activities of the manager under its powers of intervention, it can also restrict the marketing of the authorised unit trust to overseas investors (s. 83(3)).

¶1008   Revocation of authorisation

The SIB may revoke the authorisation of an authorised unit trust on various grounds. These are that any of the requirements for authorisation are no longer satisfied; that it is undesirable in the interests of the participants that the trust should continue to be authorised; or that the manager or trustee has contravened any provision of the Financial Services Act or any rules made under it (by the SIB or an applicable SRO), for example the conduct of business rules or the regulations relating to the trust (see ¶1007), or has furnished the SIB with false or misleading information (s. 79). In determining whether authorisation is 'undesirable' the SIB may take into account not only matters relating to the manager or trustee but also any matter relating to any employee or to a director or controller of the manager or trustee or any person associated with him in connection with the scheme, for example an appointed representative (s. 79(2)). 'Controller' includes anyone who (together with associates) holds at least 15 per cent of the voting rights in the manager or trustee (as appropriate) or in any holding company (s. 207(5)). The SIB must give notice that it proposes to revoke the authorisation, and the manager and trustee have 21 days to make oral or written representations (which the SIB must take into account), but there is no right of appeal (s. 80).

Conversely, the manager or trustee may request the SIB to revoke authorisation but the SIB can refuse to do so on various grounds. These are that any matter should first be investigated; that revocation would not be in the interests of participants; or because to do so would be in breach of an EU obligation, for example under the UCITS directive which (if the authorised unit trust qualified as a UCITS scheme) would not allow it to transform itself into a collective investment scheme falling outside the directive (s. 79(4)).

OPEN ENDED INVESTMENT COMPANIES

¶1009   Introduction

If the SIB makes an authorisation order an investment company with variable capital is incorporated notwithstanding that at the time the body has neither shareholders nor property (reg. 3 *The Open Ended Investment Companies (Investment Companies with Variable Capital) Regulations* 1996 (SI 1996/2827, the OEICs regulation)). On receipt of such an authorisation order the registrar of companies is obliged to register the company (reg. 4(2)) and thereafter the company may carry on business (reg. 4(3)). Unless designated by SIB regulations the collective investment scheme property of an open ended investment company is to be entrusted for safekeeping with a depositary (reg. 5).

¶1010   Authorisation

Application for authorisation is made to the SIB which may make an authorisation order in respect of the company (reg. 9). The OEIC Regulations specify ten criteria for authorisation which, in summary, are as follows:

(1) the company and its instrument of incorporation must comply with the OEIC Regulations and SIB regulations;

(2) the head office must be in England and Wales, Wales or Scotland;

(3) there must be at least one director;

(4) the directors must be fit and proper;

(5) a single director must be a body corporate which is an authorised person;

(6) if there are two or more directors their experience and expertise must be appropriate;

(7) the depositary must be a company incorporated in the UK or another EEA State which has a place of business in the UK, is an authorised person, and have its affairs administered in its country of authorisation and must be independent of the directors;

(8) the company's name must be neither undesirable nor misleading;

(9) the aims of the company must be capable of being achieved; and

(10) the rights of participants are either that shareholders are entitled to have their shares redeemed or repurchased upon request at a price related to the net value of the scheme property and determined in accordance with the instrument of incorporation and SIB regulations or that the shareholders are able to sell their shares as an investment exchange not significantly different to net value as determined above (reg. 10).

In determining fitness and propriety of directors the OEIC regulations provide that the SIB may take into account any matter relating to any person who is or will be employed by or associated with the proposed director, where the director is a body corporate to all those in control of the company and other companies in the same group, where the director is a partnership, to any of the parties or where the proposed director is an unincorporated association, to any controller of that association (reg. 9(2)).

If the SIB proposes to refuse authorisation it must give notice of its intention so to do with reasons and representations may then be made within 21 days to which the SIB must have regard in determining whether to refuse authorisation (reg. 11). The SIB has power to revoke an authorisation order on various grounds (reg. 16(1)) and where it proposes to revoke then it must seek the winding up of the company before that revocation comes into effect (reg. 16(3)). There is provision for representation against revocation (reg. 17). In addition the SIB is given powers of intervention under which, for example, it may require the company to cease the issue or redemption of shares (reg. 18(2)(a) or may apply to the court for the removal of a director (reg. 20(1)(a)). Both the Secretary of State and the SIB may appoint one or more inspectors to investigate the affairs of an open-ended investment company (reg. 21–24).

¶1011   Framework of the company

In Part III of the OEIC Regulations, there is provided a Corporate Code setting out regulations as directors, shares, shareholders, operation of the company, reports and mergers and divisions. The SIB regulations make provision for a wide range of operational details including prospectus requirements, the pricing and dealing of securities, investment and borrowing powers and the powers and duties of the directors and depository.

Looked at together the OEIC regulations and the SIB regulations provide a comprehensive code blending principles applicable to unit trusts with those of company law. This blend is no more better demonstrated than in the capital structure of an OEIC. Just as the number of units of a unit trust may fluctuate so an OEIC is fundamentally an investment company with variable capital.

The statutory characteristics of an OEIC are set out in s. 75(8) of the *Financial Services Act* 1986. The SIB regulations require the company to be a securities company, a warrant company or an umbrella company (reg. 2.03). A securities company is a company dedicated to investment in transferable securities, though it may invest up to 5% of its property in warrants (reg. 5.16). A warrant company is permitted to invest entirely in warrants (see reg. 5.08). An umbrella company is one which provides for the contributions of the participants and the profits or income out of which payments are to be made to be pooled in relation to separate parts of the scheme property and whose shareholders are entitled to exchange rights in one part for rights in another (reg. 2(1) OEIC Regulations).

An OEIC will exist as a corporate body on the making by the SIB of an authorisation order (reg. 3(1) OEIC regulation). In terms of existing company law this is a departure from company legislation because at this stage there will be no shareholders.

In terms of administration two functionaries require special mention, the authorised corporate director (ACD) and the depositary. While the OEIC regulations require the company to be managed by the board this is subject to the allocation by the SIB of responsibilities between the individual directors (reg. 28(4)(b)). The SIB regulations require an ACD (reg. 6.01) unless there is only a sole director when the regulations allocating responsibilities do not apply.

The SIB regulations (reg. 6.02) required the ACD to be responsible for and have the duty to carry out such functions as are necessary to ensure compliance with the SIB regulation imposing obligations on the company or ACD. Five categories of functions of the ACD are identified.

(1) Making decisions as to scheme assets in accordance with the company's investment objectives and policy.

(2) Instructing the depositary regarding rights attaching to ownership of scheme property.

(3) Taking all reasonable steps and exercising due diligence to ensure the shares are priced in accordance with the regulations.

(4) To take action to rectify any breach of the pricing and dealing regulations.

(5) Ensuring compliance by the company of certain specified breaches of the OEIC regulations.

In addition the ACD is made responsible for the keeping of records (reg. 6.04).

The depositary is entrusted with the safeguarding of the scheme property (reg. 5(1) OEIC regulations) and is given six rights:

(1) to receive all notices and communications relating to general meetings;

(2) to attend any general meetings;

(3) to be heard at general meetings;

(4) to convene a general meeting;

(5) to require information and explanations; and

(6) to have access to reports, statements and papers for meetings (reg. 4(1)).

¶1011

The SIB Regulations make the depositary responsible for the safekeeping of the scheme property (reg. 6.06) and also to take reasonable care that the company is managed in accordance with certain parts of the SIB regulations (reg. 6.05). Annually the depositary is required to report to shareholders (Sch. 2, Pt. III).

The depositary is required to be independent of both the company and the persons appointed as its directors (reg. 10, OEIC regulations). In January 1997 the SIB issued Guidance Release 1/97 on this independence. The Release stresses that there should be no links between a depositary and a director including no link through employment of even an associate of a director, although it states that listed shares in a depositary carrying no more than 0.5 per cent of the votes will not be considered to give rise to a potential conflict of interest.

OVERSEAS COLLECTIVE INVESTMENT SCHEMES

¶1012   Introduction

Three types of recognised collective investment schemes from overseas may be marketed to the public in the UK.

(1) Schemes authorised in other EU member States which comply with the UCITS directive and are recognised under s. 86 of the Financial Services Act;

(2) schemes which obtain recognition under s. 87 of the Act which are authorised in designated countries and which are of a class specified by H.M. Treasury; and

(3) other overseas schemes which get recognition under s. 88.

The statutory powers of recognition have been transferred to the SIB which has a Collective Investment Schemes Authorisation and Recognition Committee. The regulations for recognition made by the SIB are contained in the *Financial Services (Regulated Schemes) Regulations* 1991.

¶1013   UCITS and other 'EU-wide' schemes

Section 86 of the Financial Services Act gives 'automatic' recognition to certain collective investment schemes constituted in a member State of the EU other than the UK. It gives effect to the UK's obligations under the UCITS directive but the door is opened to similar recognition for any other scheme enjoying 'rights conferred by a Community instrument' in anticipation of further similar 'harmonising' directives in the future. Indeed, the Act does not even refer expressly to the UCITS directive or to schemes for collective investment in transferable securities (which is all that the UCITS directive applies to).

The EU's Directive on the coordination of laws relating to undertakings for collective investment in transferable securities, Directive 85/611/EC (the 'UCITS directive') was adopted on 20 December 1985. Under the UCITS directive a collective investment scheme which complies with its conditions (which, for example, limit the securities which it can invest in which are not transferable and traded on a regulated market and prohibit over-concentration in a single company) and which is authorised in any member State of the EU can be marketed without further authorisation in any other member State subject only to the local marketing laws: art. 1(6). The UCITS directive sets minimum standards and any member State can impose higher standards for schemes established in it; however, it must still accept schemes established in other member States which comply with the directive's minimum standards, and accordingly its domestic schemes would be at a disadvantage. The UCITS directive applies not only to unit trusts and mutual funds but also to open-ended investment companies which are therefore treated differently from other companies. The same is true in the case of the three EEC listing directives (see ¶801) and the Financial Services Act itself.

Section 86 of the Act provides that a collective investment scheme which is constituted in a member State of the EU other than the UK and which falls within the terms of the relevant Community instrument will not need to seek authorisation. It will automatically be a recognised scheme if it satisfies the prescribed requirements. In addition, the authorities of the 'home' State must certify that the scheme complies with the applicable Community instrument. The scheme will be 'constituted' in a member State if it is constituted under the law of that State in contract or trust or takes the form of an open-ended investment company incorporated under that law. In addition, it must also be managed by a body corporate incorporated under that law; however, if it is constituted as an open-ended investment company the manager (if there is one) may seemingly be incorporated anywhere, perhaps because in this case it is the company rather than the manager which is the operator (s. 86(8)).

As permitted by the UCITS directive, the Act provides that if the proposed methods of marketing the scheme do not comply with the Act, the scheme will not be recognised as an 'EU-wide' scheme (s. 86(2)). In order for the SIB to be able to determine whether or not they do comply, the Act provides that the operator of the scheme must give at least two months' written notice to the SIB before it begins marketing the scheme and must specify in the notice the proposed methods of marketing (s. 86(2)). The notice must also give the address of a place in the UK for service of notices and other documents (including, presumably, process) on the operator and must also give such

¶1013

information as may be prescribed by the SIB (s. 86(3)). Unless the SIB notifies the operator and the authorities of the 'home' State within two months of receiving this written notice that the scheme fails to comply with the Act's requirements as to marketing, the scheme will be a recognised scheme *ipso facto* if it complies with the relevant Community instrument. If the SIB refuses recognition, it must state in its notification of refusal the reasons why the Act's marketing requirements will not be complied with and the operator (or, indeed, the 'home' authorities) has 21 days to make oral or written representations, although there is no right of appeal to the Financial Services Tribunal (s. 86(5)).

Although the operator and trustee of the 'EU-wide' scheme will be authorised persons in connection with the scheme, the SIB's own conduct of business rules will not apply to them in that capacity except in so far as they relate to marketing and advising persons on the scheme and the exercise of rights conferred by it (s. 86(7)). Conversely, the SIB may require the operator to maintain certain facilities in the UK (see ¶1016). The SIB cannot require the operator to issue scheme particulars but that will be required by the 'home' regulator (at least in the case of UCITS schemes); however, the SIB can require him to provide specified explanatory information (see ¶918).

UCITS schemes will accordingly be recognised, and can be freely marketed to the public, provided that the operator gives at least two months' advance notification in writing to the SIB, complies with the marketing rules contained in or made under the Act (see Ch. 9) and meets the prescribed requirements.

¶1014 'Designated country' schemes

Collective investment schemes which are both managed in and authorised under the laws of a country or territory outside the UK can be recognised if the country or territory (for example, a state in the US) is designated by an order made by the Treasury, and they are in a class specified by that order (s. 87(1)). The power to make a designation order cannot be delegated to a designated agency (s. 114(5)(*e*)). For this purpose, 'management' seems to mean 'administration' rather than investment management. Although the Act is not clear, it seems that the SIB will be able to refuse recognition even to a 'qualifying' scheme (s. 87(3)). Provided it meets the statutory criteria (see below) any country or territory outside the UK can be 'designated', even member States of the EU, and designation is therefore an alternative route to recognition for EU collective investment schemes not covered by an EU 'harmonising' directive or other instrument (see ¶1013). At time of writing, the Isle of Man, Jersey, Guernsey and Bermuda have been designated for certain categories of schemes.

A country or territory can be designated only if the applicable local law under which the scheme is authorised and supervised gives investors in the UK (and not just local investors) protection which is 'at least equivalent' to that provided for them in relation to authorised unit trusts (s. 87(2)). Crucially, this includes the establishment of a satisfactory compensation scheme. In practice this condition may cause overseas countries, such as the Channel Islands and the Cayman Islands, where offshore funds and other collective investment schemes are at present often established, to amend their own laws if they do not meet this standard so that they can be 'designated'. Indeed, this was the case with the Isle of Man and the Channel Islands; Bermuda adopted an interesting two-tier approach with the introduction of a special category of 'UK scheme' for funds which want to meet the stricter standards needed for recognition under s. 87. Once a country is designated, its collective investment schemes which fall within the 'approved' classes can accordingly be marketed to the public in the UK by authorised persons without needing to apply for recognition on an 'individual' basis, which will presumably be more difficult to obtain (see ¶1015).

The operator of the scheme must apply to the SIB for recognition, giving the address of a place in the UK for service of notices and other documents (including, presumably, process) on the operator and providing such information as may be prescribed by the SIB. The SIB may refuse recognition in its discretion but the scheme is seemingly deemed to be recognised unless the operator is notified within four months that it is not to be recognised: the *Financial Services (Schemes Authorised in Designated Countries or Territories) (Notification) Regulations* 1989 (SI 1989/1584), issued under s. 87(3). The SIB can withdraw recognition on specified grounds. The Act will not regulate the scheme as it will leave that to the law of the 'home' country, but it requires it to maintain facilities here (see ¶1016). If the operator actually carries on investment business himself in the UK (for example, selling units or shares in the scheme) he must obtain authorisation unless an exemption applies; in particular under Sch. 1, Pt. IV; authorisation is not conferred by virtue of his status as it is in the case of operators of 'EU-wide' schemes. In addition, the SIB requires him to. issue scheme particulars and provide other specified explanatory information (see ¶918).

¶1015   Recognition on an 'individual' basis

Collective investment schemes managed in a country or territory outside the UK may also be recognised by the SIB on an 'individual' basis on the application of the operator (s. 88(1)). Recognition will seemingly be possible even if the local law does not itself provide adequate investor protection, although that will surely be an important factor. Unless it is an 'EU-wide' scheme this route will be the only route to recognition available to the scheme if there is no relevant designation order (see ¶1014), for example because it is established in a country without adequate investor protection laws or if it is managed from outside the country where it is authorised. It is therefore recognition on an 'individual' basis which will be crucial to many open-ended investment companies unless they are established in designated countries and fall within the specified classes. It is important to note that this is a third alternative route to recognition; it does not in itself imply any lesser status than the other routes, although it is likely to be very difficult in the case of all but the best names to persuade the SIB to grant recognition on an 'individual' basis and the SIB charges such schemes significantly higher fees, which is an important disincentive.

The provisions for application for recognition are similar to those for authorised unit trusts (see ¶1006). Schemes can be recognised on an 'individual' basis, however, only if they afford adequate protection to participants (perhaps, in the case of open-ended investment companies, by having an independent custodian) and make adequate provision for the matters dealt with by the regulations relating to authorised unit trusts (see ¶1007) (s. 88(1)).

Moreover, a scheme cannot be recognised under s. 88 unless either the operator is a body corporate or the scheme is an open-ended investment company (s. 82(2)). The operator and (if there is one) the trustee (which term includes a mere custodian or depositary, see ¶1001) need not be an authorised person, but if either the operator or the trustee is not (or he is prohibited by 'scope' rules from acting as operator or trustee) he must be a 'fit and proper person'. For this purpose the SIB may take into account matters relating to his employees or to persons associated with him for the purposes of the scheme (which includes persons who market it), to other companies in the same group and to directors or controllers of the operator (or trustee) or such other companies. 'Controllers' are persons who together with 'associates' (as defined) hold at least 15 per cent of the voting rights of the operator (or trustee) or a holding company (see ¶406). In addition, a scheme can be recognised on an 'individual' basis only if the operator has a representative in the UK who is an authorised person (and so subject to the jurisdiction of the SIB) and is authorised to act generally and to receive service of notices and other documents (including, presumably, process) on his behalf (s. 88(5)). It is unfortunate that the operator is required to have a general agent in the UK (which is perhaps further than it was necessary to go for the protection of investors), because that may well have adverse UK tax consequences unless great care is taken.

Finally, a scheme normally cannot be recognised on an 'individual' basis unless, as in the case of an authorised unit trust (see ¶1006), its units are redeemable at a price related to net asset value, or the operator is required by its rules to ensure that participants can sell their units on an investment exchange (not necessarily the London Stock Exchange) at a price not significantly different from a price related to net asset value (s. 88(7)). However, in order not to prejudice schemes already marketed here, s. 88(7)

¶1015

does not apply to schemes in existence on 7 November 1986 (when the Act was passed) which are prohibited by the law of the country or territory in which they are established from actually providing for compliance with s. 88(7), provided that the units were listed on the London Stock Exchange throughout the five years ending on that date and s. 88(7) was in fact regularly complied with in practice (although not legally required) throughout that period (Sch. 15, para. 11).

If the collective investment scheme applies for recognition it will effectively submit to the jurisdiction of the SIB and the latter will be able to prohibit proposed alterations to the rules of the scheme in the same way as in the case of the rules of authorised unit trusts (see ¶1007), although no solicitor's certificate will be required (s. 88(9)). If alterations are made without approval, recognition may presumably be revoked (see ¶1017), and it is possible that participants may be able to claim compensation for loss arising from any prejudicial alteration, although that is not clear (see ¶1214). If the operator or trustee of the scheme is to be replaced he, or the person who is to replace him, must give at least one month's notice to the SIB, but it would seem that the SIB has no power to prevent such replacement (s. 88(9)). If the operator himself carries on investment business in the UK (for example, selling units or shares in the scheme) he must obtain authorisation unless an exemption applies, in particular under Sch. 1, Pt. IV; authorisation is not conferred by virtue of his status as in the case of operators of 'EU-wide' schemes. The SIB requires the operator to issue scheme particulars as in the case of authorised unit trusts and to include certain explanatory information in investment advertisements (see ¶917). Finally, it also requires the scheme to maintain facilities in the UK (see ¶1016).

¶1016   Provision of facilities

The SIB in the *Financial Services (Regulated Schemes) Regulations* 1991 requires the operators of recognised schemes (whether they are recognised on an 'EU-wide', a 'designated country' or an 'individual' basis) to keep copies of the scheme's constitutional documents and scheme particulars, and to maintain certain other facilities, in the UK (s. 90(1)).

¶1017   Withdrawal of recognition

The SIB may at any time withdraw the recognition of a 'designated country' scheme or of a scheme recognised on an 'individual' basis on any of three grounds. These are: that it is undesirable in the interests of UK participants that the scheme should continue to be recognised; that the operator or trustee has contravened the Act or any rules made under it or has supplied false or misleading information; or (in the case only of a scheme recognised on an 'individual' basis) that it no longer qualifies for recognition (s. 89(1)). In the case of the first mentioned ground, the SIB can take into account not only matters relating to the scheme itself but also matters relating to any director or controller of the operator or trustee or any person employed by or associated with the operator or trustee in connection with the scheme (see ¶1015) (s. 89(2)). The SIB must give the operator of the scheme notice of its intention to withdraw recognition. The operator has 21 days to make oral or written representations, which the SIB must take into account, but he has no right of appeal to the Financial Services Tribunal.

Conversely, the SIB can refuse withdrawal of recognition when requested by the operator or trustee to withdraw it and, seemingly, the scheme cannot cease to be recognised without its consent (s. 89(4)). The SIB can refuse to withdraw recognition if it considers that any matter should first be investigated or if withdrawal is not in the interests of the participants (s. 89(4)).

PROFESSIONALS ONLY AND RESTRICTED SCHEMES

¶1018 Freedom from regulation

'Professionals only' schemes can be marketed by authorised persons to other authorised persons or to 'professional investors' as of right under the Financial Services Act (see ¶915). It seems that these schemes will be completely unregulated (so that, for example, they can invest in anything and there will be no restriction on borrowing). Similarly, the Act does not provide for the regulation of 'restricted' schemes (see ¶915). However, the SIB has issued the Financial Services (Single Property Schemes) (Supplementary) Regulations 1989, which require the operators of 'single property' schemes exempted from the marketing restrictions (see ¶916) to issue scheme particulars and audited financial statements.

11 Insurance Businesses and Friendly Societies

INTRODUCTION

¶1101 Background

Professor Gower in his report (*Review of Investor Protection Report: Pt. I* (1984) Cmnd 9125)) considered that the general regulation of insurance companies was beyond the scope of his review of investor protection and in any case there had been major changes in insurance legislation to bring it into line with various EEC Directives. However, he did think that 'something clearly needs to be done to tackle the problems raised by the growing popularity of bonds linked to life policies'. According to his overriding policy that in any new regime of investor protection 'like should be treated as like', he considered that 'all forms of bonds, whether or not linked to life policies, should be treated as "securities" ... and so should all life policies, for investment is what they undoubtedly are'. He was concerned that, largely for historical reasons, the degree of regulation applicable to the marketing of bonds masquerading as life assurance policies was substantially less than that relating to unit trusts.

In recent years concern has centred not so much on fraud, although inevitably there have been instances of it, but rather on the marketing practices adopted by insurance companies and intermediaries and the competence of salesmen in particular. The regulatory problem presented by life assurance and unit trust marketing is immense. Substantial numbers of people are engaged in the full time selling of life assurance policies and unit trusts in the UK, together with tens of thousands of employees of banks, building societies and estate agents engaged to varying extents in selling life assurance. There are also tens of thousands of solicitors and accountants who, in the course of their professional functions, are involved in advising clients in regard to life assurance and unit trusts.

The government accepted Professor Gower's main recommendations concerning the regulation of investment business in the context of insurance, and while the prudential regulation and authorisation of insurance companies under the *Insurance Companies Act* 1982 remains firmly in the hands of the Insurance Division of the DTI, regulation and supervision of the marketing of such investments is the responsibility of the SIB. The SRO principally concerned with exercising authority in this area is the PIA which is the lead regulator for activities consisting of the marketing of packaged products together with other business done with or for private investors. The term 'packaged products' embraces life insurance contracts, units in regulated collective schemes and shares bought through investment trust savings schemes.

Life assurance intermediaries who describe themselves as insurance 'brokers' are required to register with the Insurance Brokers Registration Council and to comply with its rules on separate insurance broking accounts and solvency margins, under the terms of the *Insurance Brokers (Registration) Act* 1977.

In so far as both the investment business aspect of life assurance and unit trusts are essentially forms of 'collective investments' there is of course considerable overlap between the provisions in the *Financial Services Act* 1986 and in the various regulatory bodies. For the sake of clarity it has been thought preferable in this guide to discuss insurance and collective schemes separately as the Act itself does.

SCOPE OF THE ACT

¶1102   Investments

The insurance companies legislation distinguishes between long term business and general insurance business. The former embraces various categories of what might be described as life assurance. The latter is really concerned with indemnity insurance for such risks as fire and general accident. Indemnity insurance is concerned with protecting against loss and is not a means of investment, whereas in most cases of life assurance there is a clear and significant investment element. It is therefore with long term insurance that the Financial Services Act is concerned. Paragraph 10 of Sch. 1 to the Act provides that rights under a contract the effecting and carrying out of which constitutes long term business within the meaning of the *Insurance Companies Act* 1982 will for the purposes of the Financial Services Act be regarded as an investment. Under Sch. 1 to that Act the classes of long term business are as follows:

(1) Life and annuity	Effecting and carrying out contracts of insurance on human life or contracts to pay annuities on human life, but excluding (in each case) contracts within Class 3 below.

¶1102

(2) Marriage and birth	Effecting and carrying out contracts of insurance to provide a sum on marriage or on the birth of a child, being contracts expressed to be in effect for a period of more than one year.
(3) Linked long term	Effecting and carrying out contracts of insurance on human life or contracts to pay annuities on human life where the benefits are wholly or partly to be determined by reference to the value of, or the income from, property of any description (whether or not specified in the contracts) or by reference to fluctuations in, or in an index of, the value of property of any description (whether or not so specified).
(4) Permanent health	Effecting and carrying out contracts of insurance providing specified benefits against risks of persons becoming incapacitated in consequence of sustaining injury as a result of an accident or of an accident of a specified class or of sickness or infirmity, being contracts that –

    (a) are expressed to be in effect for a period of not less than five years, or until the normal retirement age for the persons concerned, or without limit of time, and

    (b) either are not expressed to be terminable by the insurer, or are expressed to be so terminable only in special circumstances mentioned in the contract.

(5) Tontines	Effecting and carrying out tontines.
(6) Capital redemption	Effecting and carrying out capital redemption contracts.
(7) Pension fund management	Effecting and carrying out –

    (a) contracts to manage the investments of pension funds, or

    (b) contracts of the kind mentioned in paragraph (a) above that are combined with contracts of insurance covering either conservation of capital or payment of a minimum interest.

(8) Collective insurance etc.	Effecting and carrying out contracts of a kind referred to in art. 1(2)(e) of the first long term insurance directive (79/267 EEC).
(9) Social insurance	Effecting and carrying out contracts of a kind referred to in art. 13 of the first long term insurance directive.

¶1102

However, certain long term insurance contracts are excluded from the definition of investment under the Financial Services Act. Rights under a contract of insurance will be outside this definition if the benefits are payable only on death or disability; if no benefits are payable under the contract on a death (other than one due to accident) unless it occurs within ten years of the date on which the life of the person in question was first insured under the contract or before that person attains a specified age not exceeding 70; if the contract has no surrender value, or the consideration is a single premium and the surrender value does not exceed this; and if there are no rights of conversion into a policy which would not fall within the above exceptions. Rights under a reinsurance contract are also beyond the scope of the definition of investment. The effect of this paragraph is to include within the definition of investment all long term insurance, other than reinsurance, except where the insurance is a whole life or similar policy with no lifetime savings element.

¶1103　Application of the Act

Insurance companies are subject to a considerable amount of specific statutory regulation and supervision by a variety of enactments which it is beyond the scope of this guide to discuss. It is important to note that the Financial Services Act does not detract from or replace these provisions. However, in attempting to place its new regime of regulation and supervision over investment business the Act inevitably impinges on these other provisions though it does not confer authorisation on a person to carry on insurance business where he could not lawfully do so otherwise (FSA, Sch. 10, para. 4).

The basic framework of regulation is provided in s. 22 of the Act through recognition of an authorisation under s. 3 or 4 of the *Insurance Companies Act* 1982 as authorisation under the Financial Services Act. Accordingly a company authorised to carry on insurance business in the UK is authorised also to conduct investment business by reference to its long term insurance contracts and any other investment business carried on or in connection with and for the purposes of its insurance business including the management of pension funds. The basic framework extends to Eurocompanies such as insurance companies from the European Economic Area carrying on business in the UK through a branch on the basis of the insurance single passport (reg. 57 *Insurance Companies (Third Insurance Directive) Regulations* 1994 SI 1994/1696) and insurance companies in the EU authorised by another member State to conduct investment business which do not transact investment business from a permanent place of business in the UK (s. 31, Financial Services Act).

By virtue of s. 129 of the Financial Services Act, Sch. 10 applies the provisions of the Act to such companies. It needs to be stressed that these companies cannot be authorised persons for the conduct of investment business except by virtue of the above provisions (para. 2 and 3). Further their authorisation does not extend beyond the scope of their respective limited authorisations. Schedule 10 also applies to UK companies which carry on business in a member State of the EU other than the UK. However such a company can only be authorised for investment business as respects the management of the investments of any pension fund which is established solely for the benefit of the officers and employees of the company and their dependants, or of any other body corporate in the same group as that company.

FORM OF REGULATION

¶1104   Recognition of SROs

The provisions in the Financial Services Act relating to recognition apply to those bodies whose members include regulated insurance companies. However, it is provided in Sch. 10 that the rules of such SROs must take account of the provisions of Pt. II of the Insurance Companies Act 1982. In delegating his powers to a designated agency, the Secretary of State is bound to retain authority to revoke recognition of an SRO if its rules fail to take proper cognizance of the provisions of the 1982 Act. Furthermore, the SIB cannot recognise an SRO unless the Secretary of State has certified that he is satisfied that proper account has been taken of these statutory obligations.

The original SROs which were relevant to the insurance industry were LAUTRO and FIMBRA. LAUTRO was concerned with authorising companies whereas FIMBRA was concerned with the authorisation of financial intermediaries. The PIA emerged as a result of a report by Sir Kenneth Clucas that there should be a single SRO to regulate investment business primarily done with and for the private customer. Accordingly among the range of investments covered by PIA's scope are those falling within Sch. 1, para. 10 Financial Services Act (long term insurance contracts). The recognition of FIMBRA and LAUTRO was revoked by the SIB in June 1994 subject to a transitional winding down period to ensure continuity of regulation.

¶1105   Conduct of business

As indicated above the authorisation of an insurance company to conduct investment business is dependent either on authorisation under s. 22 (authorised insurers) or under s. 31 (authorisation in the member States). It therefore cannot gain authorisation or further authorisation by becoming either a member of an SRO or by seeking direct authorisation from the SIB.

Accordingly if an insurance company does join an SRO it will not have to satisfy the 'fit and proper' test (Sch. 2, para. 1(4) Financial Services Act) in order to become a member. Modifications have been made by Sch. 10 to the Financial Services Act of the conduct of business provisions in that Act. The purpose of this is to confine the rule-making authority provided by the Act to matters relating to investment business rather than insurance. Rules made under s. 48 (in effect the SIB Conduct of Business Rules) do not apply to regulated insurance companies except in so far as they make provision in regard to procuring proposals for policies the rights under which constitute an investment for the purpose of the Act, and advising persons on such policies and the exercise of rights conferred thereby, managing the investments of pension funds, procuring persons to enter into contracts for the management of such investments and advising persons on such contracts and the exercise of rights conferred by them and all matters incidental to this. This also applies to statements of principle under s. 47A and to codes of practice under s. 63C so far as they relate to matters within the rule-making power of s. 48.

The rules made under s. 49 of the Act relating to required minimum financial resources for those authorised to carry on investment business are not applicable to insurance companies that are authorised persons under s. 31 of the Act. The provisions relating to indemnity under s. 53 and compensation under s. 54 of the Act do not apply to losses arising as a result of a regulated insurance company being unable to meet its liabilities under a contract of insurance. Protection against an insurance company being unable to discharge its liabilities under an insurance contract is dealt with of course by the solvency requirements in the Insurance Company Regulations administered by the DTI and by the provisions for identifying policy holders with failed insurance companies under the *Policy Holder Protection Act* 1975.

Schedule 10 to the Financial Services Act also modifies the application of s. 59 in regard to regulated insurance companies. A person prohibited by an order under this section from being employed in an investment business will not be prevented from working for a regulated insurance company except in regard to business to which the conduct of business rules are made applicable under s. 48; in other words, the investment business activities of insurance companies.

Schedule 10 makes it clear that the provisions in the *Insurance Companies Act* 1982 relating to advertisements do not apply to so much of an advertisement issued by an authorised person as relates to a contract of insurance the rights under which constitute an investment. Similarly, no requirement imposed under the 1982 Act relating to intermediaries in insurance transactions will apply in respect of an invitation issued by an authorised person or appointed representative in relation to a contract of insurance the rights under which constitute an investment. The provisions in the 1982 Act relating to withdrawal from long term policies will not apply in regard to investments except where the relevant statutory notice is served, or should have been served, before the Financial Services Act came into force.

¶1106   Powers of intervention

The Schedule also adapts the provisions in Ch. VI of Pt. I of the Act (relating to powers of intervention) to take account of the special provisions elsewhere relating to insurance companies. It is provided that the statutory powers of intervention afforded by these provisions will not be exercisable in relation to regulated insurance companies on the basis of s. 64(1)(a), namely that the exercise of the powers is desirable for the protection of investors, for reasons relating to the ability of the company to meet its liabilities to policy holders. By the same token, the powers conferred by s. 66 (restriction on dealing with assets) and s. 68 (maintenance of assets in the UK) and, so far as those powers are applicable by s. 67 of the Act (vesting of assets in a trustee) to the assets belonging to the authorised person, are not exercisable in regard to regulated insurance companies.

The SIB or, when appropriate, a recognised SRO may not impose any prohibition or requirement under s. 65 (restriction of business) or s. 67 in regard to a regulated insurance company, or vary such an order, unless it has first informed the Secretary of State of its intentions and explained upon which ground in s. 64(1) it seeks to justify its exercise of power. The Secretary of State is empowered to instruct the designated agency or SRO not to proceed where he considers that it would not be in the interests of policy holders.

Finally, in this context, the provisions in s. 72 and 73 relating to winding up and administration orders are not applicable to regulated insurance companies, given the special provisions that apply to such in other enactments.

¶1107   Withdrawal of authorisation

The *Insurance Companies Act* 1982 is amended by Sch. 10 to the Financial Services Act to provide that the Secretary of State may withdraw authorisation that has been given under s. 3 and s. 4 of the 1982 Act in regard to an insurance company or class of business where, among other things, it has failed to satisfy an obligation imposed upon it by the Financial Services Act or an SRO of which it is a member. The Schedule also modifies the provisions in s. 33(1)(a) and s. 34 of the Financial Services Act in regard to termination and suspension of authorisation and notice of proposed termination or suspension. Where the Secretary of State's functions under the latter Act are exercisable by a designated agency, he is bound to consult that agency before authorising a regulated insurance company under s. 3 of the 1982 Act. The Secretary of State is required to take into account the advice of the designated agency and may furnish it with any information obtained in connection with the application. The Schedule also provides that the designated agency is bound to notify the Secretary of State forthwith when it has reasonable grounds for believing that an authorised insurance company is in breach of its obligations, and would if it was subject to s. 28 of the Financial Services Act be in peril of losing its authorisation.

PROMOTION OF INSURANCE

¶1108   Advertisements

The Financial Services Act restricts advertisements for insurance contracts classified as investments. Broadly, s. 130 makes it a criminal offence to advertise, advise or procure unauthorised insurance investments. Section 130(1) provides that no person shall issue, or cause to be issued, an advertisement inviting any person to enter, or offer to enter, into a contract of insurance rights which constitute an investment for the purpose of the Financial Services Act, or an advertisement containing information calculated to lead, directly or indirectly, to any person doing so. In its scope therefore, s. 130(1) is, as regards insurance products, wider than s. 57, in that it applies to everyone including authorised persons. There are, however, important exceptions to this general prohibition thereby bringing the exempted advertisements only within the scope of s. 57. Under s. 130(2) advertisements are allowed in relation to contracts to be made with insurance companies, a registered friendly society, or an insurance company which has a head office or a branch or agency in another member State and which is entitled to carry on insurance business of the relevant class in that jurisdiction. The relevant class refers to the type of insurance business and this must fall within the first two Schedules of the 1982 Act. The advertisement must relate to the class of business that the company is authorised to undertake in that other jurisdiction. Furthermore, the Secretary of State is empowered to designate any other jurisdiction, so that an insurance company authorised in that country or territory to conduct such business may also advertise, in regard to that class of business, within the UK. Before the Secretary of State can designate such a jurisdiction, however, he must be satisfied that the other country or territory subjects its insurance companies to sufficient regulation and supervision so as to ensure proper protection for policy holders.

This general prohibition of s. 130(1) also extends to advising or procuring any person in the UK to enter into such a contract. Thus, as with similar but more general provisions under the Act, its reach is very wide.

¶1108

¶1109   Contraventions

Subject to s. 130(7) and (8) any person who contravenes the prohibition on promoting contracts of insurance is guilty of a criminal offence and is liable to a term of imprisonment of two years and/or fine for conviction on indictment, and six months and/or a fine not exceeding the statutory maximum on summary conviction (s. 130(6)). Section 130(7), however, provides that a person who, in the ordinary course of business other than investment business, issues such an advertisement shall not be guilty of an offence if he proves that the matters contained therein were not wholly or in part devised or selected by him, or any person for whom he is responsible, and that he had reasonable grounds for believing, and did in fact believe, after due enquiry, that the person ordering the advertisement was an authorised person. Similarly, s. 130(8) provides that a person other than the insurance company with which the contract of insurance is to be made will not be guilty of an offence, if he proves that, after due enquiry, he believed on reasonable grounds that the advertisement was ordered by a person with due authority under the section to issue it. Apart from the criminal penalties for violation of this general prohibition, there are the usual civil implications for violation of such a prohibition under the Act. Section 131 provides that where there is a contravention of the Act, the insurance company shall not be entitled to enforce any contract of insurance tainted by the unlawful advertisement, advice or procurement which was entered into after the contravention occurred. Furthermore, the other party is entitled to recover any money or other property paid or transferred under the contract, together with compensation for any consequential loss. This is subject to the provisions in s. 131(3) and (4), however. Under s. 131(3), where the contravention is by the insurance company with which the contract was made the court may allow it to be enforced and money and property transferred under it may be retained if the court is satisfied that the person against whom enforcement is sought, or who is seeking restoration of his property, was not influenced to any material extent by the advertisement or advice in making his decision to enter into the contract. Alternatively, the court may uphold the contract where it is of the opinion that the advertisement, or advice, was not misleading as to the nature of the company or terms of the contract and that it fairly stated any risks involved in entering into the contract. Where the contravention was by a person other than the insurance company, the court, by virtue of s. 131(4), may allow the contract to be enforced, and money and property transferred under it to be retained, if it is satisfied that at the time of contract the company had no reason to believe that any contravention of the Act had in fact occurred.

Where a person chooses not to perform on such an unenforceable contract, or recovers money or property transferred under such a contract, he must return to the other party any property or money that he has obtained under the contract. In other words he cannot 'have his cake and eat it too!'

Finally in regard to these provisions, it should be noted that s. 131(7) provides that a contravention of s. 130 by an authorised person shall be actionable at the suit of any person who suffers loss as a result of the contravention. It is not clear why those other than authorised persons to which the section applies are not also referred to. The provisions in s. 61 concerning injunction and restitution orders are also rendered applicable to s. 130 (see ¶1210).

¶1110   Misleading statements

Section 47 of the Act renders it a criminal offence to induce an investment agreement through misleading statements and deceptive and manipulative devices. Section 133, which replaces s. 73 of the 1982 Act, enacts legislation similar to the provision of s. 47(1) above relating to misleading statements and concealing material facts to insurance contracts. Section 133(2) adopts the same principles of jurisdiction as in s. 47(4), while s. 133(3) provides for the same criminal penalties as s. 47.

AMENDMENTS TO INSURANCE STATUTES

¶1111   Unauthorised insurance business

The Financial Services Act, s. 132 provides that any contract of insurance entered into by a person in the course of carrying on insurance business in violation of s. 2 of the *Insurance Companies Act* 1982 shall be unenforceable, and that money and property transferred under it may be recovered as in the case of a violation of s. 130. This applies only to contracts which are not agreements to which s. 5(1) of the Financial Services Act applies. This section renders unenforceable contracts entered into in violation of s. 3, in other words by or through unauthorised persons (see ¶1217). Thus the effect of s. 132 is to provide a mirror provision in regard to insurance contracts which are not within the scope of the Financial Services Act. Section 2 of the 1982 Act, as we have seen, requires insurance business to be authorised in similar terms to investment business under the Financial Services Act, a provision made only for criminal penalties prior to the 1986 Act.

Section 132(3) provides that a court may uphold a contract if it is satisfied that the person carrying on insurance business reasonably believed that he was not in violation of s. 2 of the Insurance Companies Act, and that it is just and equitable for the contract to be enforced or for the money or property to be retained. It is also provided that, as in the case of violations under s. 5(4) of the Financial Services Act, any benefits received under such a contract that is to be set aside must be accounted for. Finally, s. 132(6) states that a contravention of

s. 2 of the 1982 Act shall not make a contract of insurance illegal or invalid, to any greater extent than is provided in s. 132 and, in particular, it shall not affect the validity of any reinsurance contract.

¶1112   Communications by auditors

The controversial but necessary provisions in the Financial Services Act emphasising that auditors do not breach their duties to their clients in communicating, in good faith, to the Secretary of State, information which is relevant to enforcement and supervision of the Act, are extended by s. 135 to encompass insurance companies. Under a new s. 21A of the *Insurance Companies Act* 1982 a provision substantially the same as s. 109 of the Financial Services Act is added. The only significant difference is that if an auditor fails to comply with a duty of disclosure consequent upon the Secretary of State issuing regulations requiring communication of certain matters, the Secretary of State may disqualify that person either from acting as an auditor for a specific insurance company or in regard to any company to which Pt. II of the 1982 Act applies.

¶1113   Avoiding unfairness

Section 136 of the Financial Services Act amends the *Insurance Companies Act* 1982 by adding an additional s. 31A. This provision is designed to ensure fairness between the separate insurance funds that are required pursuant to s. 28 of the 1982 Act. Section 28 provides that if the company carries on ordinary long-term business and industrial assurance business it must have separate accounts for each. Section 31A of the 1982 Act now provides that in such cases the company must ensure that adequate arrangements are in force for securing that transactions affecting assets of the company, other than those beyond its control, do not operate unfairly between these funds and the other assets of the company. Given the rather vague standard, it remains to be seen how this provision will work in practice.

¶1114   Registration

Section 138 of the Financial Services Act provides that rules made pursuant to s. 8 of the *Insurance Brokers (Registration) Act* 1977 may require an applicant for registration or enrolment to state whether he is an authorised person or exempted under Pt. I of the Financial Services Act and, if so, to give particulars of the authorisation or exemption. Furthermore, such an applicant will be treated as satisfying s. 3(2)(a) of the 1977 Act which requires that the Insurance Brokers Registration Council must be satisfied of his character and suitability, if he is authorised or a member of a partnership or unincorporated association which is an authorised person. This provides the necessary interface between the Financial Services Act and the pre-existing scheme of regulation. By the same token, s. 138(2) provides that in exercising its various rule-making powers the Insurance Brokers Registration Council must take proper account of the relevant provisions of the Act and powers exercisable under it in regard to insurance brokers.

The 1977 Act provides in s. 15 that the Council's Disciplinary Committee may erase from the register the name of a registered insurance broker for certain crimes or unprofessional conduct. Section 138(4) of the Financial Services Act adds an additional subsection to this provision. Thus s. 2A now provides that the Disciplinary Committee may if it thinks fit direct that a name be erased if it appears to the Committee that any responsible person has concluded that the broker, or a related person, has contravened or failed to comply with any provision of the Financial Services Act or rule of any SRO or RPB to which that person was subject. A responsible person within the meaning of this provision is a person who under the 1986 Act or the rules of an SRO or RPB is responsible for determining whether a relevant rule has been contravened. A related person means a partnership or unincorporated association of which the broker in question is, or at the material time was, a member or a body corporate of which he is or was a director.

Section 138(5) brings the Council into the overall regulatory framework by stating that the Council shall cooperate by sharing information and otherwise with the Secretary of State, or any other body responsible for supervision of investment business or other financial services. This is a very wide provision.

¶1115 Industrial assurance

Section 139 of the Financial Services Act attempts to interface the new provisions in the Act with those relating to industrial assurance. Section 139(1) simply provides that a policy issued by a society or company in violation of s. 3 of the Act, or s. 2 of the Insurance Companies Act, in the course of carrying on investment or insurance business, will not be within the prohibition on illegal policies in s. 5 of the *Industrial Assurance Act* 1923. In the circumstances it would be confusing, and in practical terms unnecessary, for this section to apply.

Under s. 139(3), where it appears to the Industrial Assurance Commissioner (who is in practice the Chief Registrar of Friendly Societies) that the rules of an SRO made pursuant to s. 48(2)(j) of the Act make provisions for the settlement of a dispute which would otherwise have been referred to him under s. 32 of the 1923 Act, he may delegate his functions in resolving such to the SRO. The rules of an SRO may provide that the Industrial Assurance Commissioner may deal with any matter in dispute referred to him in pursuance of those rules. In such cases he may determine the matter or delegate his functions to another person under s. 139(4) of the Act.

MARKETING

¶1116   Introduction

As has already been pointed out, the Financial Services Act will not have a major impact on the regulation and supervision of regulated insurance companies. Its main impact, and that intended by both Professor Gower and the government, is in relation to the conduct of intermediaries and in particular in regard to their activities in marketing investments in the context of insurance-related business. Given the nature of many of the rules and regulations in this field it is only possible for this guide to allude to the more important devices and controls. Of course, much of what has already been said in regard to conduct of investment business generally applies with full force here, in particular the provisions requiring disclosure by life assurance intermediaries of their interests and the provisions for a statutory cooling-off period.

¶1117   Intermediaries

The effect of the Act on life assurance intermediaries depends very much on their status. Although there are many variations it is possible to distinguish two types of intermediary. Firstly, there is the 'tied agent' or company representative who is the agent of the insurance company. Secondly, there is the independent intermediary who will invariably be the agent of the client seeking insurance or investment. Professor Gower recognised in his report that while as a matter of theory it is possible to distinguish these roles so nicely, in practice the situation is far more confusing and complex. The SIB has taken a 'purist approach' which requires complete polarity. Intermediaries must either act as appointed representatives of the company or be completely and demonstrably independent. This very strict approach was criticised during the debates on the Bill in Parliament and is not particularly popular with the industry. However, the approach of the SIB is that the onus is on those who argue in favour of a deviation from polarisation to justify it convincingly. To date this has not been done, although some powerful arguments have been put by influential groups.

The Act provides that a company representative, an intermediary acting as an agent for an insurance company, does not need to be separately authorised as the insurance company is the agent's principal, and is accordingly held responsible for his actions. Such persons are covered in s. 44 of the Act. An appointed representative is an exempted person in regard to investment business carried on by him as such a representative. An appointed representative is a person who is employed by an authorised person under a contract for services which permits or requires him to carry on investment business and which either contains a prohibition in regard to procuring persons to enter into investment agreements with persons other than his principal or giving advice on such transactions, or which gives his principal the right to restrict the scope and circumstances of such. Furthermore, the principal must have accepted, in writing, responsibility for the carrying on of this investment business. It is also necessary that the relevant investment business is the business for which the principal has accepted responsibility. During the passage of the Bill through Parliament the SIB proposed that the control which regulated insurance companies could be expected to exert over their salesmen needed to be strengthened by a statutory provision requiring registration of company representatives. Under this proposal an authorised firm would not be able to permit a person to sell or advise on life assurance unless that person is on a register maintained by the SIB. Only salesmen who had met the minimum standards of competence, and whose employers were satisfied that they were fit and proper, would be capable of being entered on the register. The government rejected this proposal on the basis that it was too expensive to implement. The government considered that it is sufficient to place the onus on the companies to ensure the competence and probity of their representatives and that the provisions in s. 59 concerning prohibited persons would give rise to a 'blacklist' which would serve the same purpose.

Section 44 applies to investment business carried on by an appointed representative which consists of procuring persons with whom he deals to enter into investment agreements with his principal, giving advice to such persons concerning such agreements, or in both cases with any other person, to the extent that he is permitted by his contract. This provision also covers giving advice as to the sale of investments issued by his principal or as to the exercise of rights conferred by an investment whether issued by his principal or not. It should be noted that from the wording of s. 44 an appointed representative, under the terms of his contract of services, may be able to 'introduce' and even transact business for another principal. The SIB's purist approach would not tolerate this. Although there are arguments in favour of allowing the scope of the exemption to be extended to those who are permitted to place business outside their host office, such as where the client requires diversification or a product that is not suitably available, the SIB is not enthusiastic about permitting its fundamental principle of polarisation to be violated.

Under s. 44(6) the principal shall be responsible for anything done, or omitted to be done, by his appointed representative in carrying out investment business for which he has accepted responsibility, to the same extent as if he had expressly authorised it. In determining whether a contravention of the Act, or a rule of a recognised SRO or RPB has occurred, the conduct of the appointed representative will be imputed to his principal. However, this imputation will not necessarily extend to the appointed representative's state of mind. In the

¶1117

case of a criminal offence the guilty mind of the appointed representative will only be imputed to his principal where in all the circumstances it is reasonable to so attribute it.

In the case of a company representative the SIB considers that the conduct of business rules must make it clear that the appointed representative is under a duty to explain to the client that he is unable to offer impartial advice. This is achieved through a series of detailed rules setting out exactly how the agent is to be presented to the client. Thus the rules provide controls to ensure that the representative discloses his status and that the company sends the investor notice that he is not independent.

The second category of intermediary relates to those who operate essentially independently. A person or firm acting as an intermediary in the sale of long-term insurance, who is not tied to a single life office, is required to be authorised under s. 3 of the Act. This applies both to firms engaged full time and those who act as intermediaries in the course of some other activity, such as building societies, accountants and solicitors. These independent intermediaries need to secure authorisation either directly from the SIB or through membership of a recognised SRO or RPB. Independent intermediaries are therefore themselves subject to the conduct of business rules and, unlike appointed representatives, are directly answerable for their own compliances.

An independent intermediary is also an agent of the investing client, unlike an appointed representative who acts on behalf of his principal. Consequently an independent intermediary is subject in his dealings to far more stringent controls both under the Act and the general law. The SIB has identified two principal duties to the investor client: first, a duty to ensure that the client obtains a deal that is to the client's best advantage, which is described as 'the best execution rule', and secondly, a duty to ensure that there is no conflict between the intermediary's own interests and those of his client. Both rules stem from the fiduciary nature of the agent's relationship with his client, of course, and would be imposed to some degree under the general law regardless of the provisions in the Act and the rules of the various recognised SROs and the RPBs.

In discharging the first of these fundamental duties the intermediary must take sufficient action to ensure that he can genuinely and reasonably believe that the client is recommended the best product that is available at that time. The second duty requires that the intermediary maintain and demonstrate independence from the life assurance companies to whom client business is passed. It is of fundamental importance that there is no suggestion of subordination of the client's best interests to those of anyone else. In discharging this duty of viable independence the intermediary might reasonably be expected to disclose all commissions to be earned in relation to

¶1117

the business. However, the exact amount of disclosure that is required is determined by the SIB and the recognised SRO.

The subject of commissions is inevitably a controversial one. Not only is there the fear that excessive commissions will serve to undermine the value of the investment in question, but 'overrider' commissions and similar advantages offered to salesmen tend to encourage perhaps an undesirable determination on the part of the prospective recipient to market one investment product to the exclusion of others, thus, possibly harming the interests of clients. Of course in the case of independent brokers the chance for company bias is reduced by the willingness of companies competing with each other to offer the maximum scale of commissions. Under PIA rules commission may be accepted by an intermediary but he is required to make disclosure of the amount if required to do so by the client.

Another controversial area is cold calling. Professor Gower considered that it was this practice which probably resulted in the greatest risk to investors. However while in principle unsolicited calls are prohibited by s. 57 these restrictions have been lifted in many cases by the *Unsolicited Calls Regulations* (see Appendix) and cold calls in relation to life policies are allowed provided they are not linked to highly volatile investment products.

FRIENDLY SOCIETIES

¶1118   Background

Friendly Societies are either registered under the *Friendly Societies Act* 1974 or are from 1 February 1993, when it became no longer possible to register under that Act, registered and incorporated under the *Friendly Societies Act* 1992. The 1992 Act established a Friendly Societies Commission as the principal regulatory body for friendly societies and under Sch. 11 to the *Financial Services Act* 1986 the Commission is given powers in relation to their investment business activities. These powers the Friendly Societies Commission has delegated to the SIB (para. 28).

¶1119   Authorisation

Section 23 of the *Financial Services Act* 1986 provides that a friendly society which carries on investment business in the UK is an authorised person under the Financial Services Act. It is provided, however, that authorisation relates only to investment business which the society carries on for, or in connection with, any of the purposes referred to in Sch. 2 to the 1992 Act. These are the proper and accepted purposes for which such societies may provide. Accordingly if a friendly society were to carry on other investment business it would require authorisation from the SIB or through membership of an SRO.

The 1986 Act, in s. 140, simply provides that Sch. 11 to the Act shall have effect in respect of the regulation of friendly societies. Given the nature of this guide, and the complexity of detail in this Schedule, only those provisions of particular interest will be discussed here.

¶1120 Self-regulation

An SRO for friendly societies may apply to SIB for an order declaring that it is a recognised SRO for the purposes of the Act. This recognised SRO is the PIA. The procedures for application, consideration and granting of recognition are essentially the same as those for recognition by the designated agency under the general provisions of the Act. There are one or two minor differences, such as for example the requirement that the rules of this organisation should take proper account of the provisions of the 1992 Act. The most significant difference, however, is that the Secretary of State must be consulted and, indeed, must consent to recognition. The SIB is entrusted with the power to revoke recognition and as a designated agency has similar powers over the rules and operation of the recognised SRO. The Secretary of State is also empowered to intervene, either directly or through the Registrar, to ensure that action is taken to avoid the creation or perpetuation of restrictive practices.

¶1121 Conduct of business

While the provisions of s. 48 of the Act do not apply to regulated friendly societies, the SIB may, with the consent of the Secretary of State, make such rules as may be made under that provision in regard to the conduct of business of such societies provided they are not members of a recognised SRO for friendly societies. These rules may be made in regard to the procuring of persons to transact regulated business with it, and to advising persons as to the exercise of rights conferred by investments acquired from the society in the course of such business, managing the investments of pension funds, procuring persons to enter into contracts for the management of such investments, and advising persons on such contracts and the exercise of the rights conferred by them, and matters incidental to these. Regulated business is simply investment business which the friendly society is authorised to conduct by virtue of s. 23 of the Act. The provisions in the Act relating to amendment and modification of rules and regulations promulgated by the SIB or by a recognised SRO apply under Sch. 11 with suitable adaptations. The SIB is entrusted with the general powers of the Secretary of State to intervene, seek information and conduct investigations.

12 Enforcement

¶1201 Introduction

Professor L C B Gower, in his Review of Investor Protection (see ¶120 and ¶121), emphasised that rules that could not or were not enforced were a snare and delusion for investors. While as a matter of theory rules which cannot be enforced in practice might have value as normative or educational standards, in the real world and in particular in areas of human endeavour where greed may well be the primary motivating factor, rules that are not enforced are of no use. The failure of authorities in most jurisdictions to effectively enforce provisions in the criminal law against insider dealing has been seized upon by those who, for whatever reason, wish to criticise the efficacy of the regulatory system as a whole. In this way the effectiveness of the law outlawing insider abuse has become, in many cases, the acid test for the integrity and competence of the structure and system of supervision over the financial markets as a whole. Whilst allowing the tail to wag the dog in this manner is both misconceived and illogical, the experience of countries such as the UK, France, Australia, Canada and South Africa clearly attest to the reality.

By giving proper emphasis to the importance of enforcement of securities regulations, there is little doubt that the relevant authorities have been able to obtain legal powers, privileges and in some instances resources, which they might otherwise have not been able to justify. On the other hand, when it is perceived that they have failed to deliver, the media are quick to underline the critical significance of their failure to protect the public and hence promote investor confidence in the integrity and fairness of the system. Thus, giving enforcement a priority in the regulatory system has proved to be a 'two edged sword'. The traditional approach of putting reliance on the criminal law to protect what are public markets and to vindicate the public good, has proved disappointing in terms of achieving successful convictions. Despite major legislative and administrative initiatives the government has not been able to secure an acceptable level of convictions. This failure to exhibit that the system is capable of bringing those accused of serious fraud effectively and efficiently to book, is compounded by the vast expense that has been involved in trying to secure convictions. This has led some to question whether the 'blunderbuss' of the criminal law is an appropriate weapon in the fight against many forms of financial fraud. Even the Director of the Serious Fraud Squad has stated that it might be better for many cases to be dealt with by the self-regulators as essentially disciplinary matters (see ¶228). Thought is also being given to developing procedures, in the civil law, to deprive fraudsters of their illicit profits.

The then chairman of the SIB, Sir Andrew Large, in his report, *Financial Services Regulation – Making the Two Tier System Work* (May 1993), accepted that there was widespread concern that the system was not achieving sufficient results in preventing and controlling fraud and other forms of misconduct. Whilst observing 'investor protection cannot be directed at totally eliminating market risk' and 'short of imposing a straitjacket, no regulatory system will keep out all fraudsters' (para. 9), he recognised the responsibility that the SIB has to improve enforcement, particularly by its own leadership and central role. The SIB's *Report on the Regulation of the United Kingdom Equity Markets* (June 1995) also emphasised the vital importance of clean markets where investors could rely upon the integrity of those participating in them.

While it is now being recognised at all levels of the regulatory system that enforcement involves rather more than trundling into battle the clumsy institutions of the traditional criminal justice system, which by orientation and mandate are essentially re-active, the criminal law still plays a very important role in the policing of the financial markets. Furthermore, given the significance that many procedures for obtaining international legal assistance still place on at least the prospect of criminal proceedings, the criminal law will inevitably continue to play a role in ensuring integrity in the financial markets. It must also be remembered that given the seriousness of many cases and the ever present risk of organised crime involvement with or penetration of the industry, it is appropriate to have access to the most powerful weapon in the law's armoury – the criminal law. It must also be remembered that there is a social and political significance in the denoucery effect of a criminal charge and conviction. Thus, this chapter fastens on the use of the criminal justice system to enforce financial services law. (But see ¶228.)

INVESTIGATORY POWERS OF THE SIB

¶1202   General overview

The *Financial Services Act* 1986 contains a number of powers which enable the SIB to investigate the conduct of investment business in the UK. It should be noted, however, that in *R* v *Secretary of State for Trade and Industry and Others, ex parte R* [1989] 1 WLR 372 BCLC 377, it was held that these powers could be exercised only in regard to transactions which took place prior to the Act coming into force, that is 18 December 1986 and not in regard to 'investment business' before this. The powers given to the SIB complement those which are available to other law enforcement agencies under the general law and under specific statutes, such as the *Companies Acts* 1985 and 1989, the *Criminal Justice Acts* 1988, 1990 and 1993, the *Drug Trafficking Act* 1994 and the *Proceeds of Crime Act* 1995.

¶1203 Power to call for information

Under s. 104 of the Act, the SIB may request information by notice in writing. The persons on whom such a notice may be served are directly authorised persons (s. 25), authorised insurers (s. 22), operators and trustees of recognised collective investment schemes (s. 24), investment companies with variable capital (s. 24A) and authorised Europersons (s. 31, s. 104(1)). Requests for information may also be made upon SROs, RIEs and RCHs but the SIB has no power to request information directly from firms which are authorised by virtue of membership of an SRO or certification from an RPB (s. 104(2)).

The only qualification to the SIB's power to request information under this section is that it must be reasonably required for the exercise of its functions under the Act (s. 104(1) and (2)). Since there is no specific requirement that the SIB should have 'good reason' for its request, the SIB can act on tip-offs or rumours of misconduct. The power may be used to investigate complaints from the public or to follow up inadequate or questionable filings by authorised person or recognised bodies.

The SIB may impose reasonable time-limits upon responses to requests and verification of the information, perhaps by an auditor, may be required (s. 104(3)).

In keeping with the informal nature of this power, failure to comply with a s. 104 request does not give rise to criminal penalties, but the civil enforcement powers under s. 60–62 may be used (s. 104(4)). Non-compliance with a s. 104 request may also provide the SIB with 'good reason' to launch a formal investigation under s. 105.

¶1204 Investigation in the affairs of an investment business

More extensive investigatory powers are contained in s. 105. Under this section, the affairs of any person so far as relevant to any investment business actually or apparently engaged in, may be investigated. There is no requirement that the person under investigation be authorised. However, the affairs of exempted persons (other than appointed representatives) cannot be investigated unless the investigation relates to investment business which is not covered by the exemption (s. 105(2)). Members of SROs and persons certified by RPBs may not be investigated under s. 105 unless the relevant body has requested the SIB to exercise its powers, or it appears to the SIB that the relevant body is unable or unwilling to conduct a satisfactory investigation itself (s. 105(2)).

Before a s. 105 investigation may be launched, the SIB must be satisfied that there is 'good reason' to do so (s. 105(1)); what amounts to 'good reason' is left open but it would seem to include reasonable suspicion of fraud, misconduct, breach of statutory duty, breach of conduct of business rules and failure to comply with a s. 104 request. However, as we have seen, activities prior to the Act coming into force may not be the subject of a s. 105 investigation (*R v Secretary of State for Trade and Industry and Ors, ex parte R* [1989] 1 WLR 372; (1989) 5 BCC 202).

An investigation may be conducted in two ways. First, the SIB may require the person under investigation to attend before it in order to answer questions and provide information (s. 105(3)). 'Connected persons' may also be required to attend such interviews; 'connected persons' include the employees, agents, appointed representatives, bankers, auditors and solicitors of the person under investigation (s. 105(9)). Secondly, the SIB may require the production of specified documents which appear to be relevant to the investigation (s. 105 (4)). The requirements that the relevant documents must be specified precludes a general fishing expedition by the SIB. A request for the production of documents may be made against any person and there is no requirement that the requested documents should be in that person's ownership or possession. If the documents cannot be produced, the SIB may require that person to state, to the best of his knowledge and belief, where the documents are (s. 105(4)(b)). The SIB may take copies of any documents which are produced (s. 105(4)(a)) and may request that documents which are not in legible form, such as computer records, be produced in legible form (s. 105(9)). Explanations of the documents may be required (s. 105(4)(a)).

Failure to comply with a requirement imposed under the section without reasonable excuse is a criminal offence (s. 105(10)). Since it is specifically provided that statements made by any person in the context of a s. 105 investigation may be subsequently used in civil or criminal proceedings against him (s. 105(5)). Furthermore, reliance upon professional privilege as a means of resisting a request for information or production of documents is substantially curtailed. Legal professional privilege is respected: information or documents which fall within the proper limits of this privilege need not be disclosed and the only information which a solicitor can be required to disclose is the name and address of his client (s. 105(6)). Other professionals, in particular auditors, are not so protected and cannot refuse to cooperate with the SIB on the ground that it would violate the duty of confidentiality owed to clients or customers.

The investigatory powers under s. 105 are also available concurrently to the

¶1204

Treasury (s. 114(8) and Sch. 2, para. 4 to the *Financial Services Act 1986 (Delegation) Order* 1987 (SI 1987/942)).

Both the Treasury and the SIB may authorise any officer or other competent person to conduct a s. 105 investigation (s. 106). However, inspectors cannot be given the power to initiate investigations at their own discretion; in all cases, the person(s) to be investigated must be specified by the SIB or the Treasury. It is possible that 'competent persons', which is not defined, will include SRO inspectors, officers of foreign regulatory organisations and firms' compliance officers.

¶1205   Investigation of collective investment schemes

The SIB and Treasury have the power to appoint inspectors to investigate the affairs of collective investment schemes or the affairs of the managers, operators or trustees of such schemes (s. 94). Before appointing inspectors, the SIB or the Treasury must be satisfied that it appears to be in the interests of the participants in the scheme to do so or that the matter is of public concern.

In conducting investigations, inspectors appointed under s. 94 have equivalent powers to those given to DTI inspectors under s. 434–436 of the *Companies Act* 1985. This means that the inspectors may demand the production of books, examine persons on oath and require the production of bank records. A person who refuses to cooperate with the inspectors may be punished as if he were in contempt of court (s. 436 of the *Companies Act* 1985). The inspectors may be required to prepare and submit reports on their investigations to the SIB or the Treasury; these reports may be supplied to certain concerned and interested parties upon payment of a fee and may also be published.

¶1206   Search and seizure powers

Sanctions, or the threat of sanctions, may encourage persons to cooperate with inquiries and investigations under the Financial Services Act, but ultimately do not in themselves guarantee the production of information and documents. This can only be achieved through the use of powers which enable documents to be seized irrespective of the cooperation or consent of their owner or keeper. Such powers are contained in s. 199 of the Act as amended by the *Companies Act* 1989.

Under this section, justices of the peace are empowered to issue search warrants. An application for a warrant may be made in any of three circumstances. First, a warrant may be sought if there are reasonable grounds for suspecting that an offence has been committed under certain sections of the Financial Services Act or the anti-insider dealing provisions in the *Criminal Justice Act* 1993 and that documents relevant to the case are on the premises specified in the information (s. 199(1)(a)). In this case, there is no qualification as regards the ownership or occupation of the premises in respect of which the application is sought. An application for a warrant on this ground may be made by the Treasury or, in limited circumstances, by the SIB (s. 199(7) and art. 6 of the *Financial Services Act 1986 (Delegation) Order* 1987 (SI 1987/942)). Secondly, if the affairs of an authorised person or a person whose authorisation has been suspended are being investigated under s. 105 and that person refuses to cooperate with a request to produce documents, a warrant may be sought (s. 199(1)(b)). Such a warrant may only be made in respect of premises owned or occupied by that person. In this case, the SIB's powers are co-extensive with those of the Treasury. Finally, search warrants may also be sought by inspectors appointed under s. 94 (s. 199(2)).

A warrant issued under s. 199 enables a police constable and any other person named in it to enter and search the specified premises. Relevant documents may be seized or other steps taken to prevent destruction or interference with them and any such documents may be copied (s. 199(3)). Seized documents may be retained for three months or longer if certain criminal proceedings to which they are relevant have been commenced (s. 199(5)).

Any person who obstructs the execution of a warrant is guilty of an offence (s. 199(6)).

¶1207   Investigations into insider dealing

Reference should be made to the discussion of the provisions in the Financial Services Act empowering the DTI to appoint inspectors to inquire into suspected cases of insider dealing at ¶618. In June 1988, the Secretary of State for Trade and Industry announced that following a review of the DTI's various powers to appoint inspectors, his Department was happy with the way in which inspections were being conducted, but that, in future appointments under the provisions in the Financial Services Act relating to cases of suspected insider dealing would not normally be announced except where it was in the public interest to do so.

Controversy has arisen in regard to the refusal of the Secretary of State to publish reports prepared by inspectors appointed to inquire into allegations of insider dealing. It has been argued that once it is known that an investigation has taken place, albeit a prosecution is not commenced, a possible slur is placed against the character of those who have been investigated. The DTI has consistently emphasised that the purpose of an investigation under s. 177 of the Financial Services Act is different from an inspection or investigation under the relevant provisions in the Companies Acts. In the case of an inquiry under the 1986 Act the only purpose is to discover whether an offence has been committed and to obtain evidence for a prosecution. Therefore, the process is rather more akin to an inquiry by the Serious Fraud Office under its powers under the *Criminal Justice Act* 1987, than an ordinary company inspection.

In recent years there has been a growing concern about the efficacy and efficiency of inquiries and inspections under the Companies Acts and the *Financial Services Act* 1986. The Secretary of State has long enjoyed special statutory powers to appoint inspectors to inquire into the affairs of companies and in certain circumstances companies have the right to request or call for the conduct of an investigation, (see generally Pt. XIV of the *Companies Act* 1985, as amended). While the Secretary of State does have powers to conduct investigations such as under s. 446 into possible contraventions of the law relating to the reporting of directors' share dealings, the preponderance of these wide ranging statutory powers exist to enable the Secretary of State to discover what has in fact taken place as a matter of public interest. Thus, whilst an inquiry may expose a crime or abuse and the processes of the inquiry, and in particular the exercise of inquistorial powers, may facilitate a prosecution or other regulatory action, the primary purpose is not the investigation of crime.

¶1208 Inspection and investigation

Controversy has arisen due to actual or perceived confusion as to the purpose or, indeed, the results of inspections under the general provisions in the Companies Acts. In particular, as to whether it is lawful or appropriate for evidence which has been obtained through the exercise of inquisitorial powers to be used in a subsequent criminal prosecution. A person under examination by inspectors may not refuse to answer questions or produce documents on the basis that such would tend to incriminate him or expose him to civil or regulatory liability (see *Re Pergamon Press Ltd* [1970] 1 WLR 1075 affirmed (1971) Ch 388). However, if incriminating questions are put, the inspectors must as a matter of natural justice allow the person under examination to see adverse testimony by other persons and give him an opportunity to test that testimony by cross examination (see *Maxwell v Department of Trade and Industry* [1974] QB 523), or at least the inspectors must inform the person concerned of the charges made against him and allow him an opportunity to respond. It is not, however, necessary as a matter of law, for the inspectors to give a person who they intend to criticise an opportunity to see and comment on their draft paragraphs.

The House of Commons' Select Committee on Trade and Industry in its Report on Company Investigations (1990 HC 36) thought that this might be unfair and recommended that those who were to be publicly criticised should be given an opportunity to comment. In *Fayed v United Kingdom*, the European Court did not consider that failing to do this amounted to a breach of The European Convention on Human Rights ((1994) October). However, as we shall see, there are indications that the European Court may be more prepared to take a robust attitude to such procedures in the future.

Given the fact that most of the statutory provisions in the *Companies Act* 1985 are designed to assist in finding out what happened in a case where there is a public interest in ascertaining what went wrong and not for identifying and securing evidence which may then be used in a legal action, whether civil or criminal, there has inevitably been some controversy as to when it is appropriate to use evidence that has been obtained through the cumpulsory provisions in the 1985 Act in such a proceeding. Until recently it was thought that any answer given on oath by a person in the course of a statutory investigation may be used as evidence against him in subsequent civil or criminal proceedings. This was notwithstanding that the evidence had been obtained pursuant to statutory powers which required cooperation regardless of almost any privilege that might otherwise arise. It was also thought that this was the case even where the relevant evidence did not relate to the matter under investigation. It was held in *London and County Securities Ltd v Nicholson* (1980) 1 WLR 948 that unsworn statements and supplementary correspondence between the Secretary of State and the person concerned could be properly admitted into evidence against him. Of course, the judge at trial has a discretion to exclude such evidence if he considers that to admit it would be unfair or against the public interest. However, it was thought unobjectionable for evidence to be required under compulsion and then utilised in evidence against the person concerned, whether in a civil, criminal or for that matter some other proceeding. Such a view is no longer tenable after the decision of the European Court in *Saunders v United Kingdom* (case 43 1994 490 572 (see *The Times*, 18 December 1996). The European Court held that use by the prosecution of evidence obtained by inspectors pursuant under these statutory powers, in a case involving allegations of fraud and breaches of the Companies Act, amounted to 'a remarkable departure from one of the basic principles of fair procedure' contained in the Convention. It must be remembered that the relevant statutory powers were not those given to the Department of Trade and Industry to investigate suspected crimes, such as those under s. 177 of the FSA 1986. Furthermore, it is probable that the special investigatory powers enjoyed by the Serious Fraud Office under s. 2 of the *Criminal Justice Act* 1987 are outside the court's censure. Nevertheless, this decision sends out a clear warning to the DTI and the various regulatory authorities that have similar investigatory powers. As we have already seen, under the present structure of regulation the various self-regulatory authorities do not have access to statutory powers of inquiry, although they can request bodies such as the SIB or DTI to exercise their's on their behalf. The investigatory authority of many self-regulators is purely a matter of contract law. The Chancellor of the Exchequer in his statement to the House of

¶1208

Commons on 20 May 1997 that the self regulatory tier would be merged into the SIB specifically stated that these powers need to be placed on a statutory footing. Therefore the issue raised in the *Saunders* case will need to be addressed in this context.

It should also be remembered that in English law the fact that an item of evidence has been improperly obtained and is therefore rendered inadmissible does not preclude other evidence that is obtained or deduced as a result of that excluded evidence from being admitted. Of course, in such cases the judge will be expected to exercise a discretion and ensure fairness. Another problem that has arisen, particularly in the context of financial services regulation, is whether evidence that has been quite properly obtained in one legal proceeding might be adduced in other, albeit related proceedings (see generally T M Ashe and B Rider *International Tracing of Assets* (1997) FT Law & Tax, and at ¶1214 and ¶1221 in regard to parallel proceedings).

ENFORCEMENT OPTIONS

¶1209   Disqualification directions

Although the general approach of the Financial Services Act is to authorise firms rather than individuals, s. 59 enables the SIB to exclude individuals from employment in investment business. The SIB has used these powers sparingly, but to some effect. If the SIB considers that an individual is not a fit and proper person to be employed in investment business, it may serve a disqualification direction upon that person (in this section, 'person' and 'individual' are used interchangeably). However, before such a direction is given, the SIB must give notice of its intention and of its reasons. The individual must be informed of his rights to have the case referred to the Financial Services Tribunal.

A disqualification direction may be absolute, barring the person affected from being employed in any investment business by authorised or exempt persons or may be restricted, barring the individual from employment in particular kinds of investment business. Although the date upon which the direction is to take effect must be specified (s. 59(2)), the Act does not indicate whether the SIB can limit the duration of a disqualification order. However, an individual who is subject to such a direction may nonetheless be employed by an investment business with the written consent of the SIB. Such consent may be general or limited to employment of a particular kind, may be subject to conditions and restrictions and may be varied from time to time. Disqualification directions may also be revoked subsequently by the SIB. 'Employed' in this context is widely defined and covers persons working under contracts for services as well as those engaged under contracts of employment.

If a person accepts or continues in employment in contravention of a disqualification direction, he commits an offence. In addition, a statutory duty is imposed upon authorised persons and appointed representatives (but not exempt persons) to take reasonable care to ensure that they do not employ a person in contravention of a disqualification direction. Under s. 102(1)(e) the SIB is required to keep a register of disqualified persons; failure to check this register is likely to expose an authorised person which employs a disqualified person to a claim for breach of statutory duty. Breach of this statutory duty may also trigger a public reprimand (s. 60), a civil action by the SIB (s. 61) and a claim for damages by other persons who have suffered loss as a result of the contravention (s. 62). Disciplinary action may be taken against the authorised person by its relevant organisation.

In addition to exclusion from the financial services industry, in certain cases it may well be appropriate for disqualification orders to be sought under the *Company Directors Disqualification Act* 1986. Under this Act, the DTI, and in some instances the Official Receiver or a liquidator, may apply to the court for an order making it a criminal offence for a person named in the order to be involved in the management, promotion or winding up of a company based in the United Kingdom, for a period of up to fifteen years. In recent years the DTI has shown itself to be far more willing to seek such orders and there have been one or two instances in which individuals have been banned under s. 59 of the FSA and the Company Directors Disqualification Act. The circumstances in which an order can be sought under the latter Act are wider than under the FSA. In addition to insolvency related matters and persistent default in filing in accordance with obligations imposed under the Companies Acts, an order can be made where a person is convicted of an offence involving the management of a company. It has been held, in *R v Goodman* [1993] 2 All ER 789, that insider dealing is such an offence. A person might also be disqualified on application by the DTI where the Secretary of State considers that it is in the public interest following the report from an inspector appointed under the Companies Acts or under s. 105 of the FSA, or pursuant to an investigation by the Serious Fraud Office. The DTI has taken the view that the relevant observations and criticisms by inspectors must relate to matters of management and simply misleading the City Panel on Takeovers and Mergers would not justify such an order. This has been questioned and is almost certainly a too narrow construction of the provision (see *Company Investigations, Third Report of the Trade and Industry Committee* [1990] HMSO). The DTI may also make an application for disqualification on the basis that the conduct of a director, either taken alone or together with his conduct as a director of any other company or companies, makes him unfit to be concerned in the management of a company. Schedule 1 of the Act sets out the circumstances in which a court might consider a person to be unfit and these include, for

¶1209

example, conduct by a director giving rise to an obligation to account for property of the company. Therefore, it would seem that this provision is wide enough to catch directors who are under a fiduciary duty to yield up to their company profits that they have made by use of the company's property and in circumstances where they have taken a bribe, but possibly not where their breach of duty is essentially nothing more than taking a 'secret profit' which arises merely from their position, (see *Attorney-General for Hong Kong v Reid* [1994] 1 All ER 1, *Nelson v Rye* [1996] 2 All ER 186 and *Warman International Ltd v Dwyer* [1995] 69 ALJR 362).

¶1210 Public reprimand

Despite the disappearance of much of the traditionally perceived atmosphere of the City of London as an exclusive club ('The City is not a club which one can join or not at will', Lloyd LJ said in *R v Panel on Takeovers and Mergers, ex parte Datafin plc & Anor* [1987] 3 BCC 10, at p. 582; [1987] QB 815, at p. 846; [1987] 3 BCC 10, at p. 28) adverse publicity remains an important weapon in the armoury of the SIB. A public reprimand can damage the reputation of a firm thereby undermining its clients' confidence and resulting in loss of business. It can also serve as a warning to others in the investment community.

Under s. 60, the SIB may make public the fact that an authorised person, other than a person authorised by an SRO or RPB or a registered friendly society, has breached certain requirements imposed by the Act. The types of misconduct which may give rise to a public reprimand include a breach of the Conduct of Business Rules, a violation of the cold-calling ban under s. 56, a contravention of s. 59 of the Act by employing a disqualified person, or a breach of a condition imposed under s. 50 of the Act.

The SIB must give the authorised person prior written notice of its intention to issue a public statement. The notice must set out the SIB's reasons and must give particulars of the right to have the case referred to the Financial Services Tribunal. If the notice refers to any person other than the authorised person, where practicable, that person must also be sent a copy of the notice if the SIB considers that the reasons specified are prejudicial to that person in any office or employment. The third person also has the right to refer the case to the Financial Services Tribunal (s. 97(1)(b)).

Publication of criticism of an investment firm cannot give rise to a claim for damages against the SIB unless that publication is shown to have been in bad faith (s. 187(3)).

¶1211 Injunctions and restitution orders

Under the Financial Services Act, the SIB is able to bring civil actions against wrongdoers in certain circumstances. Sums recovered by the SIB are payable to the investors who entered into the transactions tainted by the wrongdoing. In effect, the SIB is the respresentative but not the agent of the investors. The representative status of the SIB has two important consequences. First, it is for the SIB to decide whether or not to bring actions and it cannot be obliged to do so by investors. On the other hand, it is the SIB rather than the investors which is required to carry the costs of any action. Since the SIB's resources are likely to be greater than those of many investors, this means that lack of cash will not operate as a bar to redress.

The first representative power is contained in s. 6 of the Act. The SIB may apply to court if it considers that there is a reasonable likelihood that an unauthorised person will engage in investment business in breach of s. 3 or that a breach has already occurred and there is a reasonable likelihood of continuance or repetition. If satisfied that these suspicions are reasonable, the court can grant a restraining injunction. If transactions have been entered into in breach of s. 3, the court can require the unauthorised person and any other person knowingly concerned in the contravention to take steps to restore the parties to their original position (see *SIB v Pantell SA* (No. 2) [1993] Ch 256). In addition, the court can require the wrongdoer to pay a sum which appears to be just having regard to the profits made as a consequence of contravening s. 3 (s. 6(3) and (4)). In this case, it is not necessary to show that any person has suffered loss as a consequence of the contravention. This claim enables the court to recover profits in circumstances where it is not practicable to order a reversal of transactions under s. 6(2) or to impose a just penalty over and above the amount of the profits which the wrongdoer is required to return under s. 6(2).

Furthermore, the court has power to require a person who has acted in contravention of s. 3 to make a payment in circumstances where he has not made a profit but investors have suffered a loss or been otherwise adversely affected (s. 6(3) and 4)). The exact meaning of adverse effect is presently unclear but it would seem to cover loss of opportunity to make a profit. The loss or adverse effect must stem from the issue of misleading statements or involvement in misleading practices in contravention of s. 47, or from a breach of the cold calling ban or, notwithstanding the fact that the unauthorised persons are not strictly subject to rules made under Pt. I, Ch. V of the Act, e.g. CBRs, from a failure to act substantially in accordance with those rules. In this case, the payment must be just having regard to the extent of the loss or other adverse effect. This payment may be combined with a payment based upon profits.

Payments ordered under s. 6(4) must generally be paid into court (s. 6(4)). If necessary, the court can appoint a receiver to collect the payments on its behalf. Amounts recovered are then to be paid out or distributed in accordance with the directions of the court. The intended recipients of the money are the

¶1211

persons who entered into the transactions with the unauthorised person which gave rise to the profits or to the loss or other adverse effect.

In order the determine the amount of any payment under s. 6 and the method of distribution, the court can order the wrongdoer to produce accounting and other information; if necessary, the court can require this information to be verified (s. 6(7)).

In *SIB v Pantell S.A. & Anor* [1990] Ch 426, the High Court granted an interlocutory order freezing the assets of Pantell SA, a Swiss company, and Swiss Atlantic Holdings Ltd, an associated English company. The substance of the SIB's claim is that Pantell breached s. 3 and that Swiss Atlantic Holdings was knowingly concerned in the contravention. Brown Wilkinson VC held that although the SIB had no private cause of action it was, by virtue of the statutory right of action conferred on it by s. 6 for the benefit of investors, entitled to Mareva relief in an appropriate case.

Section 61 is the other provision under which the SIB can bring actions in a representative capacity on behalf of investors. There is some overlap between s. 6 and s. 61: for example, an unauthorised person who issues misleading statements in breach of s. 47 may be pursued under both s. 6 and s. 61. However, s. 61 is much wider than s. 6 and enables the SIB to proceed against authorised, as well as unauthorised persons.

The SIB can act under s. 61 if it considers that there is a reasonable likelihood that any person will contravene specified provisions or, where a contravention has already taken place, if it considers that there is a reasonable likelihood that it will be continued or repeated or that there are steps which could be taken for remedying that contravention (see *SIB v Vandersteen Associates NV* [1991] BCLC 206).

The types of wrongdoing which give rise to a potential claim under s. 61 are:

(1) contravention of the rules made under Pt. I, Ch. V such as the Conduct of Business Rules;

(2) breach of s. 47 (misleading statements and practices), s. 56 (the cold-calling ban), s. 57 (restrictions upon investment advertisements), or s. 59 (employment of a disqualified person);

(3) contravention of any restrictions to an order made by the Secretary of State under s. 58(3) permitting the issue of investment advertisements otherwise than by or with the approval of an authorised person;

(4) breach of the rules of an SRO, RPB, RIE or RCH; or

(5) breach of any condition modifying the application of the conduct of business and financial resources rules in particular cases (s. 50).

The SIB may only proceed in respect of breaches of the rules of an SRO, etc.

¶1211

where the relevant regulatory itself is unwilling or unable to take appropriate steps itself (s. 61(2)).

The court's powers under s. 61 are very similar to those which it enjoys under s. 6. If satisfied that there is a reasonable likelihood of a breach or continuance of a breach, the court may grant a restraining injunction. Reflecting the wider scope of s. 61, the court's power to restore the status quo is broadly stated: the wrongdoer and any other person knowingly concerned in it can be required to take whatever steps are necessary to remedy the contravention. As in s. 6, the court can require a wrongdoer who has made profits or caused investors to suffer loss or other adverse effect to make payments into court. These payments must be just having regard to the extent of the profits, loss or adverse effect in question. The method of distribution of these payments to investors is to be determined by the court. For the purpose of fixing the amount of payments and the method of distribution, the court may require the wrongdoer to provide accounting or other information.

¶1212   Revocation of authorisation

In a perfect world, the system of regulation established under the Act would prevent wrongdoers and incompetents from entering the system. However, it is more reasonable to expect that some mistakes will be made which will require rectification. Accordingly, the Act enables the SIB to withdraw authorisation or recognition in certain circumstances. The threat of withdrawal of authorisation will also encourage persons who are fit and proper at the time of authorisation to maintain standards and to observe the obligations imposed by the Act.

Under s. 28 of the Act, the authorisation of a directly authorised person may be withdrawn or suspended if it appears that he is not a fit and proper person or that he has contravened any provision of the Act or any rules or regulations made under it. The SIB has no power to withdraw or suspend the authorisation of a person authorised only by virtue of membership of an SRO or certification from an RPB. However, if an SRO or RPB fails to discipline the firms which it has authorised, the recognition of the SRO or RPB (and hence the authorisation of all persons authorised by that body) will be put at risk (s. 11 and s. 19).

¶1213   Powers of intervention

The SIB also has wide powers to intervene in the conduct of business of authorised persons (s. 64–71). These powers are necessarily less drastic in effect than the power to revoke authorisation but may be a prelude to revocation if the authorised person fails to comply with imposed restrictions.

Intervention powers may be used against directly authorised persons, including persons whose authorisation has been suspended. They may also in certain circumstances be used against appointed representatives. Generally, they may not be used against persons authorised by virtue of membership of an SRO or certification from an RPB; however, an SRO or an RPB may request the SIB to use its power to order assets to be vested in a trustee against firms which it has authorised. Special powers of intervention in the affairs of authorised unit trust schemes and certain recognised collective investment schemes also exist (s. 91–93).

The SIB may intervene if it considers this to be desirable for protection of investors or if it determines that an authorised person is not fit to carry on investment business to the extent that he is presently doing so. Contravention of the Act or rules made under it by an authorised person may also trigger intervention (s. 64).

Under s. 65, the SIB can restrict an authorised person with regard to the transactions which it can enter into, or with regard to the persons it deals with, or, more generally, with regard to the manner in which it carries on business. The SIB can even restrict non-investment business under this section, provided that it is a business carried on in connection with or for the purposes of investment business.

An authorised person may be prohibited from disposing of or otherwise dealing with its assets (s. 66). This order may extend to assets outside the UK. If necessary, the SIB can even require assets (including overseas assets) which belong to the authorised person or which are held by that person on behalf of investors to be vested in an approved trustee (s. 67). Assets vested in a trustee can only be leased or otherwise dealt with in accordance with the SIB's directions. The SIB can also require an authorised person to maintain assets of a specified value in the UK (s. 68). The value of assets required to be maintained in any case is such amount as appears to the SIB to be desirable to ensure that the person is able to meet his liabilities in respect of investment business carried on in the UK.

The SIB can rescind or vary any prohibition or other requirement if it considers that it is no longer needed or that it requires modification (s. 69). In this case, the SIB may act of its own accord or may be requested to act by the person subject to the prohibition or requirement. The SIB exercises its powers of intervention by giving written notice of the imposition, rescission or variation of any requirement or prohibition. The notice takes effect on the date stated in it. The reasons for the notice must be stated. There is provision for the authorised person affected and certain third parties to refer the matter to the Financial Services Tribunal. Public notice of any prohibition or requirement (or of its rescission or variation) may also be given if the SIB thinks fit. Any public notice must state the reasons for the imposition, variation or rescission of the prohibition or requirements (s. 70).

If an authorised person breaches a restriction or prohibition, the SIB can issue a public reprimand under s. 60 or may use its powers under s. 61. Individual investors may bring claims under s. 62. Any applicable equitable claims for breach of trust may also be pursued.

¶1214 Winding-up and administration orders

The SIB is afforded standing to petition for the winding-up of authorised persons and persons whose authorisation has been suspended. No application may be made in respect of a person whose authorisation is derived solely from membership of an SRO or certification from an RPB unless the regulatory body consents. In certain circumstances, the SIB can petition for the winding-up of appointed representatives.

There are only two grounds upon which the SIB may seek a winding-up order. The first is that the person is unable to pay his debts: in addition to the circumstances specified in s. 123 and 221 of the *Insolvency Act* 1986, a person is deemed to be unable to pay his debts if he fails to pay any sum due under an investment agreement. Secondly, a winding-up order may be sought on the just and equitable ground.

The SIB may also seek administration orders against corporate authorised persons and appointed representatives under s. 9 of the *Insolvency Act* 1986 (s. 74). The condition in s. 8 of that Act must be satisfied before any order is granted. The SIB has no standing with regard to persons whose authorisation stems entirely from an SRO or RPB but the regulatory bodies may themselves seek administration orders against firms which they have authorised. The SIB's power to petition for winding-up under the Financial Services Act is in addition to the DTI's power to present a winding-up petition under s. 440 of the *Companies Act* 1985. This section is itself slightly extended by the Financial Services Act: the DTI may now present a petition for winding-up based upon information obtained as a result of an investigation under s. 94 or s. 105 of the Financial Services Act (s. 198). Section 440 was recently used by the DTI to obtain a winding-up order against *Walter L Jacob & Co Ltd, a firm of securities dealers* [1989] 5 BCC 244. The DTI may also seek orders against individual directors under s. 8 of the *Company Directors Disqualification Act* 1985 upon the basis of information obtained through an investigation under s. 94, 177 or 105 of the Financial Services Act (s. 198).

INVESTIGATION AND ENFORCEMENT BY SROs

¶1215 Relevant powers

The powers of the SROs over their members are essentially a matter of contract law. As a condition of recognition by the SIB, the rules of an SRO must provide adequate monitoring and enforcement arrangements. These are binding upon persons authorised by the relevant SRO by virtue of their contract of membership. Of course, as a condition of authorisation, members firms will also have to ensure that they have in place adequate compliance and monitoring systems over their staff and representatives – and again this will be a matter of contract law. The position of the RPBs is a little different, as their authority may well, as in the case for example of the Law Society, be partially statutory. The SROs, however, do not have the benefit of the statutory investigation and enforcement powers enjoyed by the SIB, except in so far as the SIB can delegate its powers under, for example, s. 105. Of course, the SIB in recent years had made it clear that it is ready and willing to make available its own powers in support of the SROs, and in appropriate circumstances the RPBs and RIEs, given its role as the 'central policeman'. The main statutory power which is vested in the SROs is the power to present a petition for an administration order against a member under s. 74. In practice, this is a significant power, although obviously one of limited application. The SROs also have what might be described as 'negative' enforcement powers, which can be used to block the SIB in the exercise of its powers, such as under s. 72(5). Of course, unreasonable obstruction of the SIB would inevitably jeopardise the standing of the SRO in question.

CIVIL ACTIONS BROUGHT BY INVESTORS

¶1216   Claims open to an investor

The SIB's powers to bring civil actions on behalf of investors are without prejudice to the rights of investors to sue on their own behalf. In addition to the causes of action which may be available to investors under the general law (e.g. claims for breach of contract, breach of fiduciary duty or in tort) the Financial Services Act creates a number of new statutory claims which may be brought against persons who engage in investment business to the detriment of investors. The exact details of the claims open to an investor depend upon whether the person with whom he deals is authorised or not and, if it is an authorised person, upon the route whereby that authorisation has been obtained. In this part, the respective positions of persons authorised by SIB or by an SRO or RPB are considered; whether a claim may be brought against a person who has obtained authorisation through another means will require close consideration of the relevant sections.

¶1217   Authorised persons

Under FSA 1986, s. 62 as restricted by s. 62A of the Act private investors who suffer loss as a result of a contravention of specified provisions may bring an action for breach of statutory duty. Section 62(1) provides that the contraventions which give rise to a potential claim against an authorised person are:

(1) breach of the rules and regulations made under Pt. I, Ch. V (excepting the capital adequacy rules);

(2) breach of any condition imposed under s. 50 (except conditions relating to capital adequacy);

(3) breach of the duty not to employ a disqualified person.

Whilst the duty not to employ a disqualified person is imposed equally upon persons authorised by the SIB and by SROs and RPBs, the rules and regulations made under Ch. V and conditions imposed under s. 50 only apply to persons authorised by the SIB. However, persons authorised by SROs and RPBs do not escape liability: under s. 62(2), contravention of the rules of an SRO and RPB is actionable provided that the rules contravened relate to matters in respect of which rules have been or could have been made by the SIB under the Act. While the heading of s. 62 states 'Actions for damages' there is nothing in the section which confines the remedy for an action brought under the section to damages.

The enactment of s. 62(2) met with the opposition of many in the financial services industry. Bowing to pressure, the government did postpone the operation of the provision for six months: it was accepted that firms should be allowed some time to become accustomed to the working of the new regulatory structure in practice and that mistakes made in the 'teething' period should not give rise to civil actions by investors. The section was brought into force on 1 December 1987 except for contraventions covered by subsection (2) and on 3 October 1988 in respect of such contraventions (see the *Financial Services Act 1986 (Commencement) (No. 6) Order* 1987 (SI 1987/1997 (C. 59)).

Because there was concern that litigation in the financial markets would increase if practitioners and professional users of the market could take action under s. 62, s. 62A enacted by s. 193 of the *Companies Act* 1989 removed that right. In consequence only 'private investors', with certain exceptions, may sue under s. 62. For this purpose a 'private investor' is an investor whose cause of action arises as a result of anything he had done or suffered in the case of an individual, otherwise than in the course of carrying on investment business and in the case of any other person, otherwise than in the course of carrying on business of any kind. A government, local authority or public authority cannot be a private investor (reg. 2(1) of the *Financial Services Act 1986 (Restriction of Right of Action) Regulations* 1991 SI 1991/489). There are four circumstances where an action may be brought under s. 62 by a person who is not a private investor:

(1) contraventions not mentioned in s. 62(1) or (2) i.e. contraventions under other sections which apply s. 62 viz s. 71(1), 91(4), 104(4) and 184(8);

(2) contravention of any rule, etc. prohibiting a person from excluding or restricting any duty or liability;

(3) contravention of any rule prohibiting insider dealing;

(4) action brought in a fiduciary capacity for a private investor whose recovery was exclusively for that person and could not be effected otherwise than through suit of the representative (reg. 3, SI 1991/489).

By express cross-reference to s. 62, breach of other sections of the Act also give rise to a claim for breach of statutory duty under that section. For example, breach of a prohibition or requirement imposed by the SIB under s. 64–69 also gives rise to a s. 62 claim (s. 71). The SIB has only limited powers to impose requirements or prohibitions on persons authorised by SROs/RPBs under these sections; however, breach of any similar requirement or prohibition imposed by an SRO/RPB is also actionable (s. 71(2)). Similarly, failure to comply with a request for information issued by the SIB under s. 104 is actionable under s. 62; however, the SIB has no power to require persons authorised by SROs/RPBs to provide information under this section. (See also s. 91(4) – breach of a direction by an authorised person who is the the manager or trustee of an authorised unit trust, s. 184(8) – breach of a partial restriction notice served upon investment business).

Other sections of the Act which impose duties upon authorised persons do not refer expressly to s. 62 but provide simply that contravention is to be treated as if the authorised person were in breach of the SIB's rules or the rules of an SRO/RPB if so authorised. Sections which are drafted in this way include s. 95 (contravention of rules relating to collective investment schemes), s. 178(5) (failure to comply with an insider dealing inquiry), s. 154(2) (issue of investment advertisements in connection with a listing application in contravention of s. 154) and s. 171 (issue of investment advertisements relating to unlisted securities or the securities of a private company in contravention of Pt. V of the Act).

As the s. 62 action is a claim for breach of statutory duty, the defences and other incidents applying to such an action apply. Thus, the plaintiff must establish a breach of duty occasioning foreseeable loss (*Grant v National Coal Board* [1956] AC 649) on a balance of probabilities. Breach of s. 62 is not, of itself, a criminal offence.

Additionally, various sections of the Act afford investors with claims against authorised persons which do not depend upon or cross refer to s. 62. In some cases, investors are given the right to sue for compensation for breach of duty (e.g. s. 150 – compensation for false or misleading listing particulars, s. 166 – compensation for false or misleading prospectus, s. 171(6) – contravention of Pt. V of the Act and s. 185(6) – contravention of a partial restriction notice relating to banking business), whilst in other cases, the investor is given the right to set aside offending transactions and to recover compensation for having parted with any money or property as a consequence of those transactions (e.g. s. 56 – unsolicited calls).

¶1218   Unauthorised persons

Although s. 62 is primarily of use against authorised persons, an unauthorised person may be sued under that section if he issues an investment advertisement which has not been approved by an authorised person unless its issue is sanctioned by an order of the Secretary of State under s. 58(3). Similarly, under s. 95, unauthorised persons who contravene obligations imposed upon them as operators of recognised collective investment schemes are to be treated as having contravened rules made under Ch. V and are liable accordingly.

Generally, any transaction entered into by an unauthorised person in contravention of s. 3 of the Act is unenforceable by that person (s. 5). The person with whom he deals is entitled to recover any money paid or property transferred by him under the agreement and may recover compensation for any loss sustained as a consequence of having parted with it. However, the investor has the option of holding the unauthorised person to his agreement and, in certain circumstances, the court may enforce the agreement even against the investor's wishes (s. 5). Similar rights and claims against unauthorised persons are afforded to investors who enter into agreements or undertake obligations as a result of cold calls made in breach of s. 56 or investment advertisements issued in breach of s. 57.

Other sections under which civil claims may be made against unauthorised persons include s. 150, 166, 171 and 185(6) (as above).

CRIMINAL SANCTIONS AND PROSECUTIONS

¶1219   The offences

The Financial Services Act redefines certain existing offences and creates numerous new offences. The criminal provisions of the Act range from technical or regulatory offences to serious crimes of commercial fraud. The application of an offence may differ according to whether or not the person concerned is an authorised person.

Under the Financial Services Act it is a criminal offence:

(1) to engage in investment business unless authorised (penalty – a maximum of two years' imprisonment and/or a fine for conviction on indictment, or a maximum of six months' imprisonment and/or a fine of up to the statutory maximum for summary convictions: s. 4(1);

(2) to induce another person to enter an investment agreement by knowingly making a false or misleading statement (penalty – a maximum of seven years' imprisonment and/or a fine of up to the statutory maximum for summary convictions: s. 47(1) and (6);

(3) to knowingly engage in any act or course of conduct which creates a false or misleading impression of the market (penalty – a maximum of seven years' imprisonment and/or a fine for conviction on indictment, or a maximum of six months' imprisonment and/or a fine of up to the statutory maximum for summary convictions s. 57(3);

(4) to issue an investment advertisement unless authorised (penalty – a maximum of two years' imprisonment and/or a fine for conviction on indictment, or a maximum of six months' imprisonment and/or a fine of up to the statutory maximum for summary conviction: s. 57(3);

(5) to accept or continue in any employment in breach of a disqualification direction (penalty – fine: s. 59(5));

(6) to fail to obey a summons issued by the Financial Services Tribunal (penalty – fine: s. 96(6) and Sch. 6, para. 5(3)(a) and 5(4));

(7) to alter, suppress, conceal or destroy, or refuse to produce a document for the purpose of a proceeding before the Financial Services Tribunal (penalty – a maximum of two years' imprisonment and/or a fine for conviction on indictment, or a fine of up to the statutory maximum for summary conviction: s. 96(6) and Sch. 6, para. 5(3)(b) and 5(4).

(8) to fail to comply with an investigatory requirement without reasonable excuse (penalty – a maximum of six months' imprisonment and/or a fine: s. 105(10));

(9) knowingly to furnish false or misleading information to an auditor (penalty – a maximum of two years' imprisonment and/or a fine for conviction on indictment, or a maximum of six months' imprisonment and/or a fine of up to the statutory maximum for summary conviction: s. 111(1);

(10) to promote a contract of investment-related insurance (penalty – a maximum of two years' imprisonment and/or a fine for conviction on indictment, or a maximum of six months' imprisonment and/or a fine of up to the statutory maximum for summary conviction: s. 130(6);

¶1219

(11) to induce another person to enter into an insurance contract by knowingly making false or misleading statements (penalty – a maximum of seven years' imprisonment and/or a fine for conviction on indictment, or a maximum of six months' imprisonment and/or a fine of up to the statutory maximum for summary conviction: s. 133(1) and (3);

(12) to issue an advertisement offering securities without a prospectus (penalty – a maximum of two years' imprisonment and/or a fine for conviction on indictment, or a maximum of six months' imprisonment and/or a fine of up to the statutory maximum for summary conviction: s. 159 and s. 171(3));

(13) to breach the rules regulating the terms and implementation of an offer of securities (penalty – a maximum of two years' imprisonment and/or a fine for conviction on indictment, or a maximum of six months' imprisonment and/or a fine of up to the statutory maximum for summary convictions: s. 169 and s. 171(3));

(14) to breach the restrictions on disclosure of information (penalty – a maximum of two years' imprisonment and/or a fine for conviction on indictment, or a maximum of three months' imprisonment and/or a fine of up to the statutory maximum for summary convictions: s. 179(6) and s. 181(7);

(15) to contravene a notice restricting the deposit-taking business operations in the UK of an authorised institution within the meaning of the *Banking Act* 1987 (penalty – fine for conviction on indictment, or a fine of up to the statutory maximum for summary conviction: s. 185(5);

(16) to obstruct the exercise of any rights conferred by a search warrant (penalty – fine for conviction on indictment, or a fine of up to the statutory maximum for summary conviction: s. 199(6);

(17) knowingly to furnish false or misleading information in connection with any application under the Financial Services Act or in purported compliance with any requirement under the Act (penalty – a maximum of two years' imprisonment and/or a fine for conviction on indictment, or a maximum of six months' imprisonment and/or a fine of up to the statutory maximum for summary convictions: s. 200(1) and (5));

(18) to describe or hold oneself out as an authorised person or an exempted person where one is not such a person ((penalty – a maximum of two years' imprisonment and/or a fine for conviction on indictment, or a maximum of six months' imprisonment and/or a fine of up to the statutory maximum for summary convictions: s. 200(2) and (5));

(19) for an unauthorised person to issue an investment advertisement in connection with a listing application in breach of s. 154 ((penalty – a maximum of two years' imprisonment and/or a fine for conviction on

¶1219

indictment, or a fine on indictment, or a fine not exceeding the statutory maximum for summary conviction: s. 154(3)); and

(20) for an authorised Euro-person to fail to give notice of the commencement of business in the UK (penalty – an indictment, a fine, or on summary trial, a fine not exceeding the statutory maximum: s. 32).

The offences included in the 1986 Act are, of course, in addition to those, some of which have already been discussed in Ch. 6 and 7 under the general law. It must always be remembered that most authorised persons will be incorporated and therefore the plethora of offences in the *Companies Act* 1985, as amended, will be relevant. In cases of insolvency and bankruptcy charges may well be appropriate under the *Insolvency Act* 1986 and, as has already been pointed out, it may well be desirable for proceedings to be initiated by the DTI, Official Receiver or liquidator under the *Company Directors' Disqualification Act* 1986. In cases of banks proceedings will often be more appropriately brought under the relevant provisions of the *Banking Act* 1987 as amended. It must be remembered that the Bank of England for the time being (see ¶221) is under a duty to ensure that those who hold licences and those associated with the management of an authorised banking or deposit taking institution are fit and proper. Similar powers and provisions exist in regard to building and friendly societies and, of course, insurance companies. Fraud and theft charges under the Thefts Act may also be appropriate and the offence of conspiracy to defraud, as we have seen, will often be appropriate and the offence of conspiracy to defraud, as we have seen, will often be appropriate in cases involving misconduct in the financial sector.

The SIB has been given the power to carry out criminal prosecutions in respect of the majority of the offences created by the Financial Services Act (s. 114 and 201(4) and the *Financial Services Act 1986 (Delegation) Order* 1987 (SI 1987/942). Concurrent enforcement powers are reserved, however, to the DTI. Powers to investigate prosecutions under s. 133 or 185 of the Act cannot be delegated to the SIB (s. 201(2) and (3)). Enforcement of the provisions relating to insider dealing under the *Criminal Justice Act* 1993 is also outside the SIB's remit, although it is possible for the Director of Public Prosecutions or the DTI to authorise someone else to bring charges. This has been done in relation to the Stock Exchange, but not the SIB or other self-regulatory authorities. The SIB, although initially reluctant to contemplate a wider prosecutorial role for itself than enforcement of the law relating to authorisation, has increasingly realised the political advantage in having the power to attack misconduct across a broader canvas. Indeed, there have been suggestions within the SIB and elsewhere that it would be sensible for the SIB, in furthering its role as 'central policeman' to have broader powers of prosecution (see ¶228). At present most cases of fraud or serious misconduct in the markets or industry would involve several agencies with prosecutorial authority. Of course, this is not to say that liaison and cooperation cannot resolve many of the consequential difficulties. Even very close cooperation, however, does not always resolve the problems of rivalry, disharmony of regulatory objectives and, most importantly, political accountability and public responsibility.

¶1220   The Serious Fraud Office

The Fraud Trials Committee under the chairmanship of Lord Roskill observed that 'the public no longer believes that the system in England and Wales is capable of bringing the perpetrators of serious fraud expeditiously and effectively to book. The overwhelming weight of the evidence laid before suggest that the public is right' (Report 1986 HMSO, para. 1). The Criminal Law Team of the Law Commission in a consultative paper on jurisdiction in fraud offences (published in 1987), warned that other countries might well regard the inability of the British authorities to adequately deal with individuals who set up operation in the City to defraud persons overseas as 'insular, indeed chauvinistic, indifference to their interests' and that this would inevitably work against the interests of the UK. The Government concerned about the apparent inability of the system to handle competently complex fraud cases established the Serious Fraud Office (SFO) which commenced operations in April 1988.

Before the establishment of the SFO responsibility for the prosecution of serious fraud cases was the responsibility of the Director of Public Prosecutions. Attempts had been made by the DPP to improve the level of expertise available to investigators and prosecutors by establishing multi-disciplinary Fraud Investigation Groups on an ad hoc basis since 1978. Of course, as has already been pointed out, the Royal Commission on the Stock Exchange, under Lord Penzance, had reported in 1878 that the prosecution of complex financial frauds in the financial sector should be the responsibility of a specially appointed expert functionary, rather than left to be dealt with as any other offence. Whilst the SFO does not exactly resemble the multi-disciplinary agency that Lord Roskill's Committee called for in 1986, it does represent a very dramatic development in the manner that serious or complex cases are handled from investigation through to prosecution. The SFO brings together, under the director, who is appointed by and under the superintendence of the Attorney-General, the prosecution and investigation functions. The SFO has its own lawyers and accountants, albeit some of the latter serve under secondment from private practices, and is supported by police officers attached to it, although remaining accountable to their own forces. Whilst prosecutions are handled by members of the bar, the SFO's own lawyers are involved at the investigatory stage and instruct independent counsel. The decision whether to prosecute or not is made by a lawyer within the SFO, who has not been involved in the conduct of the investigation.

The SFO is constituted as an independent prosecutory authority under the Attorney-General by s. 1 of the *Criminal Justice Act* 1987. The director of the SFO is empowered to investigate any 'suspected offence which appears to him on reasonable grounds to involve serious or complex fraud'. The director, may, as he thinks fit, conduct any such investigation in conjunction with the police or any other person, whom he considers to be appropriate. This would include officials from the DTI, SIB and various self-regulatory authorities and their professional advisers.

Perhaps the most controversial aspect of the SFO is its wide ranging powers to obtain evidence under s. 2 of the *Criminal Justice Act* 1987. Under s. 2(2) 'the Director may by notice in writing require the person whose affairs are to be investigated or any other person whom he has reason to believe has relevant information to attend before the Director at a specified time and place and answer questions or otherwise furnish information with respect to any matter relevant to the investigation'. By s. 2(13) a failure to comply with such a notice may result in a fine or imprisonment. It is also an offence to furnish false or misleading information or to interfere with evidence. In *Smith* v *Director of the Serious Fraud Office* (1992) 3 All ER 546 the House of Lords held that the director's statutory powers to demand evidence did not cease once the individuals in question had been charged for an offence (see also *R* v *Director of the Serious Fraud Office, ex parte Saunders* [1988] Crim LR 837). The courts have consistently recognised that it is Parliament's intention to furnish the SFO with inquisitorial powers to obtain evidence and information without regard to virtually any traditional privilege, other than that between a lawyer and a client.

Protection is to some extent provided in s. 2(8) for those who are required under compulsion to answer questions or provide evidence in circumstances which might incriminate them. This provision states that a statement made by a person in response to a s. 2 notice may only be used in evidence against him in a prosecution for knowingly or recklessly giving false information pursuant to the notice, or in any other case where he makes a statement inconsistent with the evidence that he has furnished. Thus, generally speaking, the SFO cannot use evidence obtained under its inquisitorial powers to base a prosecution upon. However, evidence obtained pursuant to information or evidence produced under a s. 2 notice may well be useable. Furthermore, in *Re Arrows Ltd (No. 4)* [1994] 3 All ER 814 the House of Lords decided that s. 2(8) did not apply where the director obtains documentary evidence under s. 2(3). This provision is worded in much the same way as s. 2(2) but relates to specified documents. In Re Arrows, the director issued a notice under s. 2(3) requiring a liquidator to produce transcripts of oral evidence taken under the statutory powers that liquidators possess under s. 236 of the *Insolvency Act* 1986 to

¶1220

demand answers even though they might be incriminating. The House of Lords held that as the relevant answers had not been given in response to a notice under s. 2 of the *Criminal Justice Act* 1987, they were not within the protection of s. 2(8). The House of Lords acknowledged that 'if the SFO had itself asked the same questions acting under the inquisitorial procedure laid down by s. 2(2) of the 1987 Act, the appellant's answers to such questions would not have been admissible against him in criminal proceedings' (per Lord Browne-Wilkinson). Their Lordships expressed concern about this anomaly and indicated that judges should consider exercising their discretion to exclude evidence taken unfairly under s. 78 of the *Police and Criminal Evidence Act* 1984, in appropriate cases.

Of course, under the investigatory provisions in the Companies Acts, *Insolvency Act* 1986 and the *Financial Services Act* 1986, where information is demanded there is no privilege against self-incrimination. In the Guinness trials the courts ruled that evidence that had been fairly taken pursuant to the DTI's inquisitorial powers in the Companies Acts was admissible at a subsequent trial even if that evidence amounted to a confession (see *R* v *Seelig and Spens* [1991] 4 All ER 429. However, subsequently the European Court of Human Rights has ruled that this is in breach of the Convention (see supra at ¶1207). It has been held that it is not a reasonable excuse for a person to refuse to cooperate with such an inquiry simply because he anticipates that there will be a subsequent inquiry by the SFO.

The Act sweeps away numerous restrictions on access by the SFO to official information including information from the tax authorities. In virtually all cases, with the notable exception of tax information, the SFO is empowered to pass this information to other appropriate authorities, including those exercising merely a disciplinary function, for proper action against those suspected of offences. The SFO is also authorised to pass information to foreign regulatory authorities and to enter into arrangements for the exchange of information. Therefore, it is important to note the role of the SFO in the various bilateral arrangements that are currently being developed with other jurisdictions for mutual assistance in criminal matters.

The establishment of the SFO and the strengthening of the Fraud Investigation Group, within the Crown Prosecution Service, have to be seen in the context of the very significant changes that have taken place in the law and procedure relating to criminal trials, the admissibility of evidence and in particular international cooperation. A series of enactments have improved the law and given prosecutors a much better chance of securing convictions. The Criminal Procedure and Investigations Bill, which is currently passing through Parliament will also contribute to making trials of complex issues rather more efficient, if it does become law. However, whilst the results of the SFO and for that matter the Crown Prosecution Service have not been significantly worse

¶1220

than those obtained in other jurisdictions, there remains a widespread perception that the criminal justice system has not been able to secure convictions to the extent that Lord Roskill and his Committee thought desirable if public confidence was to be restored and preserved. The reputation of the SFO has undoubtedly suffered badly as a result of a number of spectacular failures to secure convictions of high profile defendants in what the press has reported as major frauds and scandals. The vast costs of trials that have too often resulted in acquittals or derisory penalties has been another indictment of the prosecutors. Consequently, successive directors of the SFO have called for far more attention to be given to sanctioning 'City fraud' through non-criminal procedures, such as the civil law and disciplinary actions. Whether the 'scaling down' of the penal process in this manner is acceptable or practical remains to be seen.

¶1221　Parallel proceedings

A given set of facts may well justify proceedings and action at various levels within the legal and regulatory system (see ¶214). Mention has already been made of the view of the present Chairman of the SIB and Director of the SFO, that it might well be preferable to utilise civil and disciplinary proceedings to sanction misconduct, rather than embark on a costly and protracted criminal prosecution. Of course, the purpose of disciplinary and regulatory action may well be rather different than that of the traditional prosecution. In the case of regulatory intervention the primary objectives will be to minimise harm and ensure a better degree of prevention for the future. This may well involve an element of punishment by way of condemnation and deterrence, but it will also involve issues of compliance and possibly curtailing the ability of the person responsible for the problem to cause similar difficulties in the future. Hence the importance that is attached in regulatory systems to maintaining a standard of 'fit and proper' conduct either by exclusion or disqualification. As regulatory initiatives, by their very nature, are more likely to involve preventative action, they will invariably occur at an earlier stage in the relevant conduct and will be justified on different grounds and upon different standards of evidence than a criminal prosecution. Whilst only certain regulatory actions may be accurately described as pro-active or prudential, most will need to be initiated on a timely basis if further harm and exposure to risk are to be limited.

It follows that in a given case there may well be a number of actions which have differing objectives and operate upon different standards of proof. For example, there may be regulatory action of a disciplinary and essentially contractual nature by an SRO, possibly reinforced by the statutory powers of the SIB, or in certain cases an RPB, together with action by the DTI, perhaps under its investigatory powers in the Companies Acts, the police and possibly the SFO and even internal action within the firm concerned. We have already seen that there is an inconsistency in the approach of the law in regard to evidence obtained pursuant to statutory powers of investigation under the Companies Act in relation to self-incrimination, and similar powers under the *Criminal Justice Act* 1987. The SFO has been able to obtain and use in prosecutions, evidence that it has obtained from regulators and others, that has been obtained by use of their powers, whereas if the SFO had sought to utilise its own powers directly against the person concerned, incriminating evidence would not have been able to justify a charge.

In *R v Institute of Chartered Accountants of England and Wales, ex parte Brindle* [1993] BCC 736, civil actions were brought against partners of Price Waterhouse by or for the benefit of persons who had suffered as a result of the collapse of the Bank of Credit and Commerce International. The essence of these claims were that the auditors had been negligent. The Institute of Chartered Accountants of England and Wales also initiated under the Joint Disciplinary Scheme an inquiry into the conduct of the firm. There was also the prospect that the firm might be involved as a witness in criminal proceedings in the USA and conceivably in the UK. Whilst Price Waterhouse did not dispute the Institute's decision to initiate an inquiry, it sought to enjoin the Committee of Inquiry from proceeding until at least the trial stage of the various negligence actions. The Court of Appeal considered that it was appropriate to quash the decision of the Committee to proceed even if this meant delaying the regulatory authority with responsibility for ensuring the fitness of professional auditing firms, could not proceed to the end of the century. The Court of Appeal's decision in this case reflects the notion that where there is a coincidence of issues and more than one legal proceeding, it is desirable for the court to determine the primary cause and stay the rest. Whether the Court of Appeal intended to establish such a rule remains to be seen. The facts of the BCCI are exceptional, and the factors referred to by the court in justifying this approach relatively unusual. Indeed, Hirst LJ stated 'the power to intervene must be most sparingly exercised and it is only in exceptional cases that the disciplinary process ... should not be allowed to go ahead unhindered'. On the other hand, the Court of Appeal considered in balancing the various interests, the responsibility of the self-regulatory authority to ensure the fitness of its members was not an 'over-riding factor'. In *R v Chance, ex parte Smith* (1995) BCC 1095, the Divisional Court on somewhat similar facts distinguished *ex parte Brindle.* The Divisional Court was reluctant to stay the proceedings as the allegations were serious, the disciplinary action specific, the regulatory action was likely to be completed prior to the civil proceedings advancing to a burdensome stage and that the civil proceedings were not such as to bring into question the very survival of the firm. (See also *R v Regulatory Board of Lloyd's of London, ex parte Macmillan,* (unreported) 24 November 1994).

Where disciplinary and criminal proceedings are more or less concurrent, the attitude of the courts has traditionally been rather more robust. For example, in *ex parte Lavelle* (1983) 1 WLR 23, Woolf J permitted the regulatory action to proceed, although he pointed out the court must have jurisdiction to intervene if there was a real issue of injustice. The Court of Appeal in *Jefferson v Bhetcha* (1979) 1 WLR 898 held that a defendant who is subject to criminal proceedings has no automatic right to be excused from procedural steps in a civil suit, which may well have the result of disclosing the defence to a criminal charge. In *R v Panel on Take-overs and Mergers, ex parte Guinness* [1990] 1 QB 146, the Court of Appeal refused to interfere with a decision of the Panel to proceed, before it had had the opportunity of considering the results of a DTI inspection. The Court of Appeal, took the view that the Panel was entitled to proceed on what it considered to be satisfactory grounds, provided it did so within its jurisdiction. In *R v Panel on Take-overs and Mergers, ex parte Fayed* [1992] BCC 524, it was argued that the Panel's proceedings constituted a real risk to the conduct of concurrent civil litigation. The Court of Appeal, whilst accepting there was jurisdiction in the court to interfere if there was a real risk of unfairness – 'it is a power which has to be exercised with great care and only where there is a real risk of serious prejudice which may lead to injustice'. As the civil proceedings would be determined by an experienced judge, the court thought that there was no risk. (See also *R v Solicitors Disciplinary Tribunal, ex parte Gallagher* (unreported) 30 September 1991).

In *ex parte Fayed*, the Court of Appeal accepted that the fact that a regulatory authority and a court of law might reach inconsistent conclusions was not necessarily constitutive of prejudice. Steyn LJ observed 'the unexpressed, but implied contention ... was that compared to court proceedings the disciplinary proceedings will only afford a second class form of justice to the applicants. There is no warrant for such an assumption'. However, it must also be remembered that the court did refer to the highly developed procedures that the Panel operated to ensure justice and that the Panel's decision had been formulated by none other than Lord Roskill. It is open to question whether the courts would be rather more concerned if the disciplinary proceedings were less developed and not superintended by such a qualified 'judge'.

ROLE OF AUDITORS AND INTERNAL COMPLIANCE BY INVESTMENT FIRMS

¶1222   Auditors

Every company incorporated under the *Companies Act* 1985 must appoint an auditor (s. 384). The person chosen must be eligible for appointment as a company auditor (s. 25 of the *Companies Act* 1989). Section 107 of the

Financial Services Act 1986 enables the obligation to appoint auditors to be extended to authorised persons who carry on investment business otherwise than in corporate form. Part 10 of the SIB's Financial Supervision Rules 1990 require all firms, except from those conducting only low risk investment services, to have an auditor (reg. 10.02). The qualifications which must be satisfied by an auditor appointed under the SIB's rules are specified and broadly equate to the requirements imposed under Pt. II of the *Companies Act* 1989.

Section 107A of the 1986 Act permits the SIB to designate its audit rules as applicable to members of SROs. No designation order has been made as IMRO, SFA and PIA have comparable requirements.

The SIB can require a directly authorised person to submit to a second audit if there appears to be good reason to do so (s. 108). The person who carries out the second audit must be approved by the SIB and it is the duty of the firm's auditor to cooperate fully with the investigation (s. 108(2) and (3)). The expense of the second investigation must be borne by the authorised person. It is thought that one case where this power may be used is if it appears that the work of the first auditor is substandard.

The function of an auditor is to inspect and report on the accounts of his client and under both the *Companies Act* 1985 (s. 237 inserted by s. 9 of the *Companies Act* 1989) and the rules made under the *Financial Services Act* 1986, auditors of firms carrying on investment business are given extensive investigatory powers. Under the general law, auditors are required to keep information which they discover through their position confidential unless disclosure is necessary in order to fulfil the inspection and reporting obligation. Failure to observe this obligation is a breach of contract (*Weld-Blundell v Stephens* [1920] AC 957). However, in order to maximise the flow of information from auditors to the regulatory authorities, the Financial Services Act provides auditors with some protection against claims for breach of confidence: if an auditor becomes aware of information or forms an opinion in his capacity as auditor of an authorised person, he may communicate that information or opinion to the SIB or an SRO/RPB without threat of liability (s. 109). Communications requested by the regulatory authorities and communications made at the auditor's initiative are equally protected. Indeed, an auditor may be under an obligation to take the initiative; although, it is anticipated that such a duty will be imposed upon the majority of auditors by virtue of rules made by the professional bodies of the accountancy profession, the Treasury (a non-delegable function) has the power to impose disclosure obligations upon any auditors who are not otherwise subject to satisfactory rules in this respect (s. 109(2)).

¶1223   Internal compliance

As part of the compliance function, the SIB's rules require authorised persons to establish and maintain compliance rules and procedures. These rules and procedures must be reviewed at least once a year to ensure that they are effective (r. 15.01 SIB Conduct of Business Rules). Similar obligations are imposed by the SRO's rules. The SIB Rules do not impose an express obligation upon authorised persons to appoint a compliance officer or to establish a compliance team but do require an annual compliance review of a reasonable representative sample of a firm's investment services (r. 15.02) so that in practice many investment businesses have appointed compliance officers whose function it is to ensure that the firm does not infringe the Act or any applicable regulatory rules.

¶1224   The Agencies of enforcement

Mention has already been made of the insitutional aspects of regulation and enforcement. Indeed, a pertinent criticism of the way in which the present system of regulation was established was that relatively little thought was given to the institutional aspects of supervision. It is not without interest that in his statement announcing the government's intention to establish a new and strengthened SIB, with full statutory powers, the Chancellor of the Exchequer, recognised, 'simply reforming the Financial Services Act is not enough in itself. In today's world of integrated global markets, the financial services industry transcends geographical and political boundaries. The regulatory response must meet this challenge. The UK financial services industry needs a regulator which can deliver the most effective supervision in the world . . .' (Statement 20 May 1997). As we have already pointed out (see ¶227) it remains to be seen how this laudable goal will be realised and in what time frame. Looking at the experience of other jurisdictions may be informative, but it is important to take account of the particular characteristics of each legal system and the various markets. For example, a culture of regulation exists in the USA which has bred lawyers and other professionals who are prepared to serve the public good on terms far less than they could expect in the private sector. It must also be remembered that in the USA there is much greater mobility between sectors than there is in the UK. On the whole, experience of secondment in Britain has produced mixed results and it remains to be seen whether the new regulator will be able to attract candidates of the right calibre as recruits. The notion that agencies such as the SIB and even the SFO are able to recruit better people because they are 'outside' the ordinary public service scales, has not produced convincing results. Much will depend upon whether the new SIB is able to create, very soon in its existence, the sort of esprit de corps that encouraged so many able young professionals to join the US Securities and Exchange Commission in its formative years. Still today, time spent with the SEC is seen as a positive investment for the future in terms of employment. The same could hardly be said about the SIB or the SROs in Britain! The only body that has achieved such a reputation in the UK system is the Takeover Panel's Executive.

13 International Aspects

¶1301 The global imperative

It is not only for criminal and anti-social reasons that so much in the world of finance and commerce today stretches beyond national frontiers. Development in communications, technology, and the general mobility of capital and persons, have all irresistibly contributed to a highly interdependent world economy, with truly international markets. For a host of sound commercial reasons, a significant proportion of any nation's business transaction will involve a multiplicity of jurisdictions.

This is perhaps no more so apparent as in the corporate securities industry. The international 'character' of securities markets is nothing new. As we have already seen in Ch. 1 some of the earliest English joint stock companies were concerned with foreign trade and some of the earliest recorded trading in script and bonds within the City of London was in regard to such companies. The securities markets of today often constitute markets for paper issued by foreign issuers and may be operated by members who have direct or indirect foreign interests, trading for or on behalf of persons outside jurisdiction. While the degree of internationalisation obviously varies from one market to another, virtually every market is subject, to some extent, to the essentially international imperative of money. Surprisingly, little attention has been given to the implications of internationalisation of the securities markets on what are essentially domestic structures of securities regulation. While economists and even politicians have long recognised the significance of internationalisation, few lawyers have, and those that have, have perceived relevant issues solely in terms of national jurisdiction.

¶1302 The problem

When questioned as to how far his Writ ran, King Henry II responded: as far as his arrows reached! Given the developments that have since taken place in ballistics, such an approach to jurisdiction might have accommodated the extraterritorial zeal of the US Securities and Exchange Commission (see for example, *Leasco Data Processing Equipment Corp v Maxwell* 468 F2d 1326 (2nd Cir 197)). However, the law relating to jurisdiction has not kept pace with technology and in England, within those jurisdictions that follow English common law, the criminal law and most public law confines itself within the strait-jacket of the 'territorial principle'. In other words, the Queen's writ in criminal matters generally runs to the edge of territorial waters and no further. In a world where transactions can occur on an almost instantaneous basis in or through a number of sovereign jurisdictions, the limits of the criminal justice system become immediately apparent.

¶1303   The traditional response

Traditionally, the approach of the common law to the control and regulation of foreign financial transactions has been to simply assert domestic jurisdiction through whatever normative system was applicable. Thus, in England, a foreign issuer seeking a quotation for its securities on the Stock Exchange was required to comply with English law as scrupulously as was possible. This naturally varied a great deal in practice, given the general requirements available for domestic issuers. Indeed, in some instances, because specific statutory exemptions might not be available for a foreign company, the more demanding 'self-regulatory' requirements of the market would be applied. Until relatively recently, members of the various organised markets were required to be domestic and the strict requirements of exchange control regulation effectively separated the domestic and international financial worlds.

In Britain, the general criminal law was, and still is, equally simplistic and parochial. In the context of the securities markets, the most relevant area of the criminal law is that relating to fraud and cheating. A special working party of the English Law Commission in 1987 described the primary feature of the present common law rules on jurisdiction in fraud matters as that of 'insularity'. (*Jurisdiction over Fraud Offences with a Foreign Element – A Consultation Paper* (The Criminal Law Team of The Law Commission, 1987)). These rules generally provide that a triable crime will be committed where and only where its last element takes place within territorial jurisdiction.

The common law distinguishes between so called result crimes and conduct crimes. In the case of the first category, there will be jurisdiction if the proscribed result occurred within territorial jurisdiction. In the case of conduct-crimes, it does not generally matter that the consequences occurred beyond the shores, if the proscribed result occurred within the territorial jurisdiction. This seemingly clear application results in ludicrous decisions. The development of electronic and other modern methods of transferring money and dealing in securities across national boundaries has naturally produced further problems. The implications of the restrictive attitude of the English courts were manifest in *R v Tomsett* (1985) (Crim L Rev 369), where a telex operator employed by a Swiss bank in London wrongfully diverted a large sum of money in an account in New York to another account in Geneva. English common law rules exclude from jurisdiction conspiracies to commit frauds outside the country. Consequently, when the operator successfully argued that the theft did not take place in England, he was successful in avoiding the jurisdiction of the English courts.

The English Law Commission's working party recognised that the approach of the English courts 'may well be perceived by other countries as an insular, indeed chauvinistic, indifference to their interests, a perception that may be damaging to the interests of the United Kingdom'. Thus, the Law Commission's working party recommended that if any 'act or omission forming part of the offence, or any event necessary to the completion of any offence' occurs within England, English courts have jurisdiction to hear such matters. The Commission excluded from its proposals offences relating to investments, as such offences often involve other considerations. The Law Commission's proposals have now been enacted in Pt. 1 of the *Criminal Justice Act* 1993 in regard to the more general offences in English law, and those crimes relating specifically to the financial investments are now governed by their own special rules relating to jurisdiction.

¶1304 The FSA – a safe environment

In regard to financial services regulation, the US Securities and Exchange Commission's Division of Corporate Finance, in its report on internationalisation to the US Congress in July 1987, observed that 'the extent of extraterritorial jurisdiction claimed by the UK regulatory agencies has never been subject to much discussion'. (*US Securities and Exchange Commission*, Report to US Congress on Internationalisation of Securities Regulation (US Securities and Exchange Commission, Division of Corporate Finance, 1987)). Before the *Financial Services Act* 1986 and the new regime of regulation and supervision that it gave rise to, the structure of control was essentially self-regulatory, as has already been pointed out. The various authorities that sought to 'police' the City before 1986 were able to exercise their powers without excessive regard to the normal constraints of legal jurisdiction. For example, the City Panel on Takeovers and Mergers was prepared to 'apply' the strict letter of the Takeover Code to overseas companies and individuals who attempted to take control over a British public company. Indeed, one of the alleged advantages of self-regulation was its ability to reach beyond the strict limits of legal jurisdiction.

The philosophy of the *Financial Services Act* 1986 is simply to control the financial services industry within the traditional territorial jurisdiction. A senior civil servant in the Department of Trade and Industry observed that 'the fundamental purpose of the Financial Services Act is to create a safe environment in which those who consume investment services within the United Kingdom can do so with confidence'. (J Rickford, *Developments in the UK – Securities Regulation, an International Perspective* (1986)). Thus, where the relevant activity occurs outside the United Kingdom, the controls 'go no further than is justifiable in accordance with established rules of international law and the principles of international good manners'. Of course, the weakness with this somewhat gentlemanly approach is that crooks do not invariably observe 'good manners'! There is a convincing argument in favour of responsible states not permitting their jurisdictions to be abused by crooks as 'safe havens'. In the *SEC v Kasser* (548 F 2d 109 (3d (in 1977)) a US Court of Appeals was '... reluctant to conclude that Congress intended to allow the US to become a "Barbary Coast" ... harbouring international securities "pirates" '.

The Financial Services Act and the regime that it creates has been described as little more than a 'compromise package'. It makes a determined, albeit not entirely successful, effort to satisfy everyone's vested interests and preconceptions. It is no less a compromise in its attempt to accommodate the foreign aspects of securities regulation. To some extent the hands of the government were tied by the Treaty of Rome, and in other cases, such as in regard to the USA and Japan, economic and political considerations dictated a spirit of compromise. Under the new regime, an investment business that is based in, and regulated by, the laws and regulations of another member country of the European Union is allowed to operate freely in Britain. 'Harmonisation' of financial services regulation within the Union was the original goal, but today this has been watered down to the attainment of mere 'equivalence'. The primary structure of regulation for financial and banking institutions within the Union is 'Home State' authorisation, with mutual recognition of each other's authorisation procedures on the basis that they are broadly equivalent. In practice, this might well mean that some European countries operate systems of regulation that are far less demanding than others. It is certain that some systems of regulation will be far less exacting, both in terms of application and administration, than those set down under the Financial Services Act in Britain. The temptation for British and overseas firms to relocate in a more 'hospitable' and probably warmer jurisdiction are obvious. Consequently, it may well be that, in time, European integration of financial services will, instead of enhancing the effectiveness of regulation, militate in favour of a lowering of standards, at least in Britain.

¶1305   Equivalence

The concept of equivalence was, of course, a primary regulatory concept in the system of regulation prior to the amendments introduced by the *Companies Act* 1989 to the Financial Services Act. The rules and regulations of recognised self-regulatory bodies had to give equivalent protection to investors to those promulgated by the SIB. It was thought, however, as we have seen, that the standard of equivalence was too onerous and inflexible. Now the SIB needs to be satisfied that the relevant rules are only adequate in terms of protection.

Nonetheless, the concept of equivalence is still found in the international context. Where an investment business operates in more than one country and the regulatory system of the state in which it is primarily established provides an appropriate degree of control and protection, then the concept of 'home state' supervision comes into play. The SIB has negotiated a number of agreements with 'lead regulators' in various countries to facilitate the working of this scheme. The Financial Services Act recognises that in certain circumstances, such as in relation to Europersons, under s. 40, overseas investment exchanges and clearing houses, under s. 87 and 88, collective investment schemes, under s. 130, contracts of insurance under s. 161 and the prospectus requirements, that if satisfactory regulatory obligations are imposed by another jurisdiction, then there is no need to impose the same degree of control as is applied to investment businesses which carry on their activities primarily in the UK. However, in general, the provisions of the Financial Services Act may only be disapplied or modified where either it is clear that the relevant foreign law provides investors in the UK with protection which is at least equivalent to that provided by the Financial Services Act (see s. 31(3)(a) (note also s. 31(3)(b)), s. 40(2)(a), 87(2) and 161(4)) or it is established that UK investors are provided with 'adequate protection' (s. 88(1) and 130(4)). Whether or not the relevant foreign laws provide investors in the UK with sufficient protection usually only has to be established to the satisfaction of the Secretary of State (s. 40 (in conjunction with s. 37(4) and 39(4)) s. 87, 88, 130 and 161(4)) (this function may only be delegated to the SIB in relation to collective investment schemes falling within s. 88 (s. 114)), but in s. 31 it is expressly provided (s. 31(4)) that the Secretary of State's decision to the effect that the equivalence test is not satisfied is not conclusive; consequently, such cases may be referred to the courts for objective determination.

The Treasury has issued guidance notes on applications for recognition of overseas investment exchanges or clearing houses under s. 40. In these it is emphasised that the issue of equivalence will be treated flexibly in order to ensure that regulatory requirements are not duplicated.

¶1306   Reciprocity

The internationalisation of the markets has highlighted the problem of reciprocity – should a country open its markets to foreigners whose own domestic markets are not open to outsiders? For economic reasons, closed domestic markets are becoming less common; in order to compete effectively in the international markets, investment businesses require access to amounts of capital which may be far in excess of domestic resources and for which they are obliged to become part of a large financial conglomerate which may be owned by a foreign bank. Similarly, a market to which access is limited is itself unlikely to have the necessary capital base with which to feature significantly as an international market. However, in strong national markets, vestiges of protectionism do remain.

The attitude of the British Government to this issue is that authorisation or permission to carry on investment, insurance or banking business in the UK is a privilege which may be withdrawn from foreigners. Under s. 183, the Secretary of State or the Treasury may, if it is considered to be in the national interest to do so, serve a notice upon any person who is carrying on or who appears to be intending to carry on an investment, insurance or banking business in the UK if that person is connected with a country (s. 183(4)) which, by reasons of its laws or governmental action, does not allow persons connected with the UK to carry on such businesses there on terms which are equally favourable to the terms offered to participants in the UK markets. A notice relating to investment or insurance business (which may only be served by the Secretary of State) may be a disqualification notice, a restriction notice or a partial restriction notice (s. 184), whilst a notice relating to banking business (which may only be served by the Treasury) may be a disqualification notice or a partial restriction notice (s. 185, as amended by the *Banking Act* 1987). A s. 183 notice may be revoked and a partial restriction order may be varied (s. 186). Except for those authorised to engage in investment business by an SRO or RPB, revocation of a s. 183 disqualification order does not revive authorisation (s. 186(3)) but a person who has been subject to a disqualification notice is not prevented from again becoming authorised (s. 186(5), as amended by the *Banking Act* 1987).

Furthermore, in order to pre-empt the need for a s. 183 notice, it is expressly provided that before deciding to recognise an overseas investment exchange or clearing house, the Secretary of State should have regard to the extent to which persons in the UK and persons in the country where the applicant's head office is situate have access to each other's financial markets (s. 40(3)).

¶1307   Enforcement

Undoubtedly, the most difficult problems raised by the progressive internationalisation of financial markets lie in the area of enforcement. While computerisation and technological advances have facilitated international trading, they have also increased the opportunities for undetectable fraud and abuse.

The first difficulty facing those involved in the enforcement of securities laws is, as we have seen above, that of establishing jurisdiction. Notwithstanding the fact that financial business and financial fraud may operate easily on an international level, as is common in English law, the provisions of the Financial Services Act are subject to a territorial limit. Thus, only those carrying on investment business in the UK (s. 1(3)) need to be authorised or exempt (s. 3); and offences and other infringements of the Act generally depend upon a territorial link (e.g. s. 47(4), 47(5), 56(1), 57 (and s. 207), 76 (and s. 95), 130, 133, 154 and 171). In one case, however, jurisdiction may be asserted even if there is no territorial connection: if the Secretary of State makes an order under s. 181, any British citizen, British Dependent Territories citizen, British Overseas citizen or body corporate incorporated in the UK who knowingly contravenes it is guilty of an offence, irrespective of whether that contravention takes place in the UK or abroad (s. 181(8) (see Glanville Williams, *Venue and the Ambit of Criminal Law* (1965) 81 LQR 276, 395, 518).

It has already been pointed out that the recommendations of the Law Commission in regard to jurisdiction in fraud cases which have been implemented in Pt. 1 of the *Criminal Justice Act* 1993 do not extend to investment related offences such as those in s. 47 of the Financial Services Act and the insider dealing provisions in the 1993 Act itself. The view of the Law Commission and the government was that it was better to provide specific rules in relation to these offences. Whilst it is hard to justify this in logic or on the basis of experience, in the result there is not a substantial difference, as the specific rules relating to jurisdiction do not differ materially from those relating to general fraud offences.

In the context of international fraud, high pressure selling of securities, either through cold calling or from 'bucket shops', has become an increasing problem in Europe and, consequently, attracted some discussion. The 'boiler room merchants' who learned their trade in Canada and the United States moved their operations to Europe, and in particular Amsterdam, during the late 1970s. The practice of 'share hawking' is not new in Britain; the British Government set up a committee under Sir Archibald Bodkin in 1936 to inquire into such undesirable practices, and the recommendations of this committee led to the enactment of the *Prevention of Fraud (Investments) Act* 1939.

Section 56(1) of the Financial Services Act prohibits any person from doing any investment business in consequence of an unsolicited call made on a person in the UK or from the UK on a person elsewhere. This prohibition creates a 'civil offence', in so far as any resulting contract will not be enforceable against the investor approached, and the investor will be able to recover money or property transferred under the contract or compensation. It is important to note that this provision extends to 'cold calling' by individuals in the UK on persons overseas. One of the reasons that criminal liability was not imposed is that it was thought unjustifiable to extend the reach of the criminal law in this way. It is of interest to note that in the recent judgment of the European Court in *Alpine Investments BV v Minister van Financiën* (Case C–384/93, 10 May 1995), the court held that similar 'cold calling' regulations in the Netherlands, whilst inhibiting freedom of services within the Communities, were nonetheless justified on the basis of a member state's right to protect investors.

Even if jurisdiction is established, it will be very difficult to detect and investigate a suspected fraud which has been channelled through the financial systems of a number of countries, unless the regulatory authorities of the relevant countries are willing to cooperate and to disclose information to each other. The Financial Services Act contains a number of provisions which formally recognise the importance of international cooperation and seek to promote its growth. Reference should also be made to the powers of the Director of the Serious Fraud Office under the *Criminal Justice Act* 1987, which are discussed in Ch. 12 and the DTI under the *Companies Act* 1989. Section 180(qq) of the Financial Services Act provides the principal statutory authority for the disclosure of information that would otherwise be restricted to authorities of countries or territories outside the UK. Section 179 restricts the disclosure of certain information (s. 179(2)) by the bodies specified in s. 179(3) and by others who have obtained the restricted information directly or indirectly from such specified persons. Contravention of s. 179 is a criminal offence. The specified bodies include the SIB but not the SROs (which therefore are covered only if they receive information directly or indirectly from a specified person). However, under s. 180(qq), restricted information may be disclosed to foreign authorities without infringing s. 179. The purpose for which information may be disclosed is to enable or assist the foreign authorities in exercising its regulatory functions. Section 180, prior to the amendments introduced by the *Companies Act* 1989, provided that disclosure was only lawful if it was to assist the overseas regulator to discharge duties of a similar nature to those performed in the UK by the Secretary of State under the Financial Services Act and the *Insurance Companies Act* 1982, the Bank of England under the *Banking Act* 1987, the competent authority (see s. 142(6)) under the Financial Services Act, or to enable them to investigate insider dealing (see s. 180(6) now repealed). Under s. 180(qq), as we have seen, information can now be disclosed to enable the overseas regulator to discharge any of its regulatory functions. Section 180 has also been amended so as to permit the disclosure of information to enable or assist the Secretary of State or the Treasury to exercise powers of investigation, including those under the 1989 Act, on behalf of a foreign regulatory authority (s. 180(bb) and (c)).

The courts, in regard to similar provision in the *Banking Act* 1987, have recognised the clear public interest in facilitating effective international cooperation against fraud and, thus, the need to permit the disclosure of information. (See *A v B Bank (Bank of England Intervening)* (1993) QB 311 and also *R v Crown Court at Southwark, ex parte Customs and Excise Commissioners, ex parte Bank of Credit and Commerce International SA* (1989) 3 All ER 673.

The importance of international cooperation is also reflected in s. 40. Before deciding whether or not to grant recognition to an overseas investment exchange or clearing house, the Secretary of State must be satisfied that the

¶1307

applicant is able and willing to cooperate in regulating and supervising investment business and financial services with the relevant UK authorities and bodies (s. 40(6)). Furthermore, it must also be established to the satisfaction of the Secretary of State that there are adequate arrangements for cooperation between those responsible for supervising the applicant in the place where its head office is situate and the UK authorities. Before recognition will be granted to an investment exchange under the Financial Services Act, it must be established that the applicant must be willing to cooperate, by the sharing of information or otherwise, with other regulatory bodies (Sch. 4, para. 5).

An obligation to cooperate, by the disclosure of information or otherwise, with other regulatory authorities is also imposed upon SROs and RPBs (Sch. 2, para. 7 and Sch. 3, para. 6). Although the relevant schedules do not expressly mention international cooperation, it is clear from the rule-books that the SROs consider that they are required to cooperate with foreign governments and with other foreign authorities, bodies and persons engaged in regulating investment business and financial services.

¶1308   Bilateral cooperation

The unilateral assertion of jurisdiction over conduct or individuals outside territorial boundaries, no matter what theory of justification is invoked, inevitably raises the prospect of conflict between the sovereignty of two states. Governments, often out of a sense of frustration with the level or standard of cooperation that they have been able to obtain from the authorities in other countries, have on occasion resorted to actions of a character which can hardly be expected to promote mutual respect and cooperation. In recent years most states, and in particular the USA, have recognised that it is much better to achieve cooperation on a consensual basis, albeit in many situations the balance between those asking and those from whom help is requested, will be unequal. Nonetheless, today it is widely accepted that the preferable approach is one of cooperation through agreement and therefore of paramount importance is the existence of bilateral arrangements whereby assistance in legal matters may be requested and obtained. The nature and character of such bilateral arrangements range across a broad spectrum, from informal contacts at essentially an operational level to full blown mutual assistance treaties implemented by legislation. Of great importance in practice are Memoranda of Understanding (MoUs). Again these instruments range fom little more than an exchange of undertakings between regulatory agencies to use their best efforts to assist each other in discharging their regulatory and supervisory responsibilities, to formal vehicles for the exchange of intelligence and assurance of cooperation in enforcement matters. Much will depend upon the underlying political relationship between the two states. Not surprisingly, many of these arrangements have developed from informal contacts and in some cases there has been a progression from rather weak instruments to rather more exacting agreements. In many instances, an MoU is seen to be a step along the road to the implementation of a full Mutual Legal Assistance Treaty (MLAT).

It is important to appreciate that most MoUs cannot be considered treaties, in so far as they may not involve acts of government and will not seek to impose 'legal' obligations on the parties to the agreement. Therefore, they can be negotiated and settled with rather more flexibility and expedition than is usually the case in developing full treaty arrangements. Consequently, there now exists a network of such arrangements involving many different agencies, with very different mandates and authorities. These range from 'lead regulator' agreements to arrangements to facilitate the monitoring of capital adequacy obligations and to enforcement. Even when such do not import mutual 'obligations' to cooperate, insofar as they acknowledge the importance of cooperation, they facilitate the determination of reciprocity and thereby often enable mandatory procedures to be initiated under domestic law. The first MoU of any significance to the UK was signed by the DTI and the US Securities and Exchange Commission in September 1986. Since then the DTI, Treasury, the SIB, Bank of England and various self-regulatory authorities have signed MoUs with their respective opposite numbers in a great many countries.

Although there is a great deal of variation in the form and content of MoUs as instruments, they do not impose 'legal' obligations and, consequently, do not need to be implemented by domestic legislation. On the other hand, treaties that do seek to impose legal obligations have to be implemented through legislation. Perhaps the best illustration of mutual assistance in legal matters in this context is the extradition arrangements that exist with most countries. Extradition or, in the case of Commonwealth countries, rendition of fugitives is now governed by the *Extradition Act* 1989 as amended. Obviously, it serves little purpose for courts to take jurisdiction over a matter if the fugitive is out of jurisdiction and cannot be returned to face trial. Problems did arise in that many securities related crimes involving specific statutory provisions, such as insider dealing, were not included in the schedules of extradition crimes. Now that the test for what is an extradition crime fastens inter alia on the length of sentence that a court may impose on conviction, many of these difficulties are removed. In the context of the Financial Services Act, offences under s. 47 would be within the scope of extradition arrangements currently in force with most jurisdictions. It is not only necessary for the law to have subject matter and personal jurisdiction, but also for the judicial process to be able to take and admit evidence from overseas. In this regard, considerable advances have been made in recent years. The *Criminal Justice Act* 1988, the *Criminal Justice (International Cooperation) Act* 1990 and the *Criminal Justice Act* 1993 have significantly improved the ability of prosecutors to obtain and adduce before

¶1308

the English courts evidence from overseas. These developments in domestic law have also facilitated the negotiation of international arrangements, including MLATs, for the identification, securing and taking of evidence in criminal matters out of jurisdiction. Furthermore, it must be remembered that there have been very important developments in both the law and practice relating to international cooperation in regard to the tracking, freezing and confiscature of property associated with serious criminal activity. Indeed, it is the worldwide concern about fighting the illicit trade in drugs that has given the impetus to international cooperation, particularly in regard to combatting money laundering.

¶1309   Multilateral cooperation

As we have seen, until recently, those states that sought to take a firm stand against fraudsters and others engaged in abusive conduct affecting their domestic capital markets generally contemplated some form of extraterritorial jurisdiction as the only practical means of bringing such persons to book. Whilst the US Federal Courts and in particular the SEC have achieved some success, both in jurisprudential and enforcement terms, in asserting extraterritorial jurisdiction over operations conducted beyond US territory, but which harm investors and markets within the US, the impact of such actions on international cooperation is not always positive. Whilst it is true that, as a consequence of occasionally rather 'excessive enforcement action' by the US authorities, other countries have been persuaded to negotiate bilateral agreements for legal cooperation, merely having a treaty, let alone an MoU, does not ensure that its provisions are going to be respected or that adequate resources are going to be made available to service it.

Whilst informal arrangements for sharing information have long existed, and in fact the DTI has deliberately initiated a series of annual meetings of key regulatory authorities to promote this sort of informal cooperation, it has become increasingly apparent that it is necessary for a facility to be developed which is able to develop and maintain information on a truly international basis in regard to fraudsters and securities law violators. Indeed, proposals have been made for the establishment of regional and even international securities regulatory authorities to not only promote cooperation in regard to loss prevention and enforcement, but also the standardisation of regulations and requirements for international trading in securities. Whilst a Euro-SEC is many years away, it is perhaps an inevitability.

The ICPO-Interpol network is not a satisfactory facility for passing information relating to securities law violators. The General Secretariat of ICPO-Interpol is concerned to facilitate cooperation in fighting serious crime and securities offences are invariably regarded by traditional police agencies as at best merely technical or regulatory offences. Consequently, ICPO-Interpol has not given any priority to this area. Furthermore, the ICPO-Interpol Constitution limits the mandate of Interpol to 'ordinary criminal law offences' and this has been construed as ruling out many 'offences' in securities regulation. It is also important to appreciate that the Interpol network is not an intelligence or investigatory facility, it is simply a dedicated communications system between police forces. Non-police agencies, such as securities regulators, cannot be members of this network and generally cannot interface directly with it. Whilst there have been instances where police agencies have been able to use the Interpol communications network with considerable effect to assist in the investigation of transnational securities related frauds, especially those involving organised crime and money laundering operations, it cannot be supposed that Interpol will, in its present form, ever be able to provide the sort of facility for developing effective loss prevention that is so obviously needed at the international level.

It must also be recognised that there is a very important difference in the 'culture' of traditional police agencies and that normally encountered in regulatory authorities. Consequently, there has been a reluctance at both national and international levels on the part of police agencies, always under resourced, to become involved in what are often regarded as regulatory matters – not involving real crime. It must also be remembered that it is not always easy or, indeed, acceptable for traditional law enforcement agencies to move forward into a proactive or preventive posture, such as is required in prudential monitoring of the banking and financial communities. By orientation, training and in many instances authority, police officers are cast in a reactive role. On the other hand, as police agencies increasingly recognise the significance of intelligence and the importance of tracing the profits of crime through the financial system, they have become more aware of the useful contribution that financial regulators, and in particular central banks, who have greater expertise, resources and political clout, can make in the fight against serious organised crime. Thus, ICPO-Interpol has attempted in recent years to involve representatives from central banks and regulatory authorities in its deliberations and initiatives, particularly those involving the control of money laundering.

Regional police initiatives, such as the newly created Europol and the embryonic Asiapol, have also recognised the need for interface with those governmental and official agencies concerned with 'policing' the financial markets. Again this has been largely a result of concern to improve enforcement against the assets of organised crime and, to some extent, terrorist groups. In practice, however, there is little indication that regional police initiatives, let alone international programmes, are concerned with facilitating the enforcement of securities regulation as an end in itself. Such concern as exists is almost entirely a result of the desire of police agencies to facilitate the

¶1309

fight against what they perceive to be 'real criminals'. Of course, given the move of organised crime into the financial world, this parochial attitude is to be regretted (see B Rider, *Organised Crime*, Memoranda and Minutes of Home Affairs Committee, *Organised Crime*, 16 November 1994, HMSO).

Commonwealth Law Ministers meeting in Canada in 1977 and in Barbados in 1980 clearly recognised the dangers to economic stability presented by organised crime entering the financial sector and acknowledged that police force to police force cooperation was insufficient. The Commonwealth Secretariat initiated a number of programmes, at the request of Commonwealth governments, including the establishment of a Commercial Crime Unit to act as a focal point in facilitating cooperation against financial and, after the Law Ministers' Meeting in Harare in 1986, organised crime. Despite Commonwealth Finance Ministers recognising at their meeting in Kingston, Jamaica in 1995 that the economies of many states were more at risk than ever before, the Commonwealth Secretariat's initiatives have suffered due to lack of resources and political interference. In the result, whilst significant steps forward were taken with the development of the Commonwealth Scheme for Mutual Assistance in Criminal Matters and in particular the 'operational' work of the Commercial Crime Unit, the Commonwealth is unlikely to provide a vehicle for facilitating the effective control of abuses in the financial world.

Of far greater significance in this regard are the initiatives that have been taken on a regional basis, primarily in Europe. Nonetheless, it must also be remembered that there are developments, albeit nowhere near as impressive, in other regions. Regulators in the Far East and South East Asia have established a contact group along the lines of one that has long existed in South and North America, and which in large measure spawned the International Organisation of Securities Commissions (IOSCO). IOSCO has gone through a number of incarnations since it was first established. In the initial years, the organisation was primarily concerned to facilitate cooperation on enforcement related matters and many saw it in terms of an Interpol type network for agencies involved in policing the financial markets. As its membership and constituency developed, the organisation has become rather more concerned with promoting international standards in regulation. The organisation's annual meeting is a curious combination of an assembly of regulators and organisations which have a responsibility over the markets and a conference for anyone who wishes to attend. IOSCO does provide a forum for promoting international awareness of issues and some of its working parties have produced documents which carry the debate on certain issues further. IOSCO, as an organisation, has underlined the importance of bilateral arrangements for the exchange of information and has encouraged its members to enter into MoUs. It has not, however, been able to assume any responsibility itself, given its limited resources and somewhat ambiguous mandate.

¶1309

The work of organisations such as the International Federation of Stock Exchanges Fédération Internationale des Bourses de Valeurs (FIBV), the Organisation for Economic Cooperation and Development (OECD) and various banking institutions and groups, must not be forgotten or underestimated, particularly in regard to fostering a climate for cooperation on matters such as money laundering and in setting standards such as in relation to capital adequacy.

¶1310   Investigators on behalf of foreign regulators

Part III of the *Companies Act* 1989 contains a number of provisions designed to facilitate international cooperation and the passing of information. Mention has already been made of the amendments to s. 180 of the Financial Services Act which now permits the passing of restricted information to overseas regulatory agencies for the proper performance of their functions, regardless of whether they are exercising a responsibility which has a counterpart under certain specified provisions of English law. Of course, in exercising its discretion whether or not to cooperate, the relevant UK authority would be expected to exercise a degree of circumspection that was appropriate in the circumstances. The disclosure of information for an improper or malicious purpose would be an offence and could also result in civil liability.

Apart from introducing a number of important amendments to the statutory powers of the Secretary of State, which are now administered by the Treasury, to conduct or order investigations under the *Companies Act* 1985, Pt. III introduced radical new provisions enabling the Secretary of State to initiate investigations, along the lines of those provided for in s. 105 and 106 of the Financial Services Act (see Ch. 12) on behalf of an overseas regulatory authority. The Secretary of State may require the giving of evidence, under oath, or the provision of documents on behalf of an overseas regulatory authority (s. 83). The full 'inquisitorial' powers that the Secretary of State possesses under the *Companies Act* 1985 apply and a statement by a person in compliance with an order under these provisions may be used in evidence against him. The Secretary of State may initiate an investigation on behalf of a foreign agency where the agency in question is exercising functions corresponding to those of the Secretary of State, the SIB or competent authority under the Financial Services Act, the Secretary of State under the *Insurance Companies Act* 1985 or the *Insurance Companies Act* 1982 or the Bank of England under the *Banking Act* 1987, or the investigation of insider dealing, whether or not such conduct is rendered unlawful or not in that other jurisdiction, and any function prescribed for the purposes of these provisions by an order of the Secretary of State, being a function which in his opinion relates to companies or financial services (s. 82(2)). Therefore, the scope of regulatory responsibility covered by these powers is very wide. It is important to note that the Secretary of State can initiate inquiries on behalf of a foreign agency, even if its jurisdiction is merely of a self-regulatory character. The Secretary of State is, however, under a duty not to exercise his powers unless he is satisfied that the assistance requested by the overseas regulatory authority is for the purposes of its regulatory functions. Obviously, the ease with which the Secretary of State may be satisfied of this will depend upon the circumstances and the relationship that exists between the two countries.

In exercising his discretion, the Secretary of State may take account of whether corresponding assistance would be given in that country to an authority exercising regulatory functions in the UK. It is important to note that an inability, or even perhaps a perceived unwillingness, to cooperate in the future and extend reciprocal assistance, would not necessarily rule out the Secretary of State exercising his discretion in favour of a present request. Reciprocity is but a factor, although no doubt an important one to be considered. Of course, where there is an MoU already in place, the issue of reciprocity is easily resolved.

The Secretary of State may also take into account whether the inquiry relates to a possible breach of law or other rule which has no close parallel in the UK, or involves the assertion of jurisdiction in circumstances which the UK would not recognise. Thus, the Secretary of State might well decide to initiate inquiries using his mandatory powers to acquire evidence in regard to a matter which is neither unlawful nor, for that matter, regulated in the UK. Of course, it would still be necessary for the Secretary of State to be satisfied that the overseas regulator was exercising a function similar to that exercised by a corresponding authority in the UK. However, this still leaves a great deal of scope for the conduct of investigations into matters which might not be considered objectionable under English law. The Secretary of State may also have regard to the seriousness of the matter under investigation and as to whether assistance may be better obtained in some other manner. Finally, the Secretary of State may take into account whether it is otherwise appropriate in the public interest to give the assistance that has been requested and, in cases of requests from overseas banking regulators, he is required to consult the Bank of England.

It should be noted that under s. 85 it is an offence for a person to refuse to comply with a request for evidence made under s. 83 by the Secretary of State or one of his officers, and it is also an offence to knowingly or recklessly give false information. There are provisions in s. 86 and 87 imposing restrictions on the use to which information obtained either as part of the request for assistance, or in the course of the inquiries, may be put and to whom it may be properly disclosed. The *Company Directors Disqualification Act* 1986 was also amended by the 1989 Act in order to provide for the possibility of

¶1310

disqualification as a consequence of an investigation carried out for the purposes of assisting a foreign regulatory authority.

¶1311   Non-cooperation

In direct contrast to the arrangements and agreements designed to facilitate the international flow of information, the Financial Services Act also contains provisions whereby the communication of information to persons outside the UK may be blocked.

Under s. 181, the Secretary of State may prohibit the disclosure of information to which the section relates (s. 181(3)) to any person(s) in a country or territory outside the UK if it appears to be in the public interest to do so. Alternatively, conditions may be applied to its disclosure. The relevant information includes certain information obtained directly or indirectly by SROs (s. 183(3)(b)). This power may not, however, override any relevant community disclosure obligations (s. 181(6)). Knowing contravention of a s. 181 direction is a criminal offence (s. 181(7)).

This provision is similar in effect to s. 2 of the *Protection of Trading Interests Act* 1980, which enables the Secretary of State to block the disclosure of information required by overseas courts and authorities. However, that section only applies to information which is *required*; in a notable extension of principle, s. 181 enables the Secretary of State to prevent the disclosure of information which is being supplied on a voluntary basis. Nonetheless, it is apparent from the Parliamentary debate which preceded the enactment of s. 181 (HL Vol 479, col 749) that it is a power which is intended to be used sparingly and that it should not be regarded as a detraction from the Government's policy of promoting international cooperation between regulators.

¶1312   Civil aspects

As the public law has increasingly had to come to terms with the international character of business, so has the civil law. Obviously, this is not the place to enter into an analysis of the rules and procedures relating to the enforcement of orders obtained from civil courts outside the UK, or for that matter the enforcement of foreign orders in Britain. Nor is this the place to discuss the many significant developments that have taken place in obtaining evidence from overseas and, in particular, in freezing foreign assets. (See generally T M Ashe and B Rider (Eds) *International Tracing of Assets* (1997) FT Law and Tax.) Suffice it here to emphasise that the civil law has proved equally as flexible as the criminal law in reaching overseas. The courts have also been mindful of the need to ensure that the substantive law accommodates international business. For example, the observation of Vinelott J in *Re*

Maxwell Communications Corporation plc (No. 2) (1994) 1 All ER 737 at 754, that 'it would be a matter of grave concern if, at a time when insolvency increasingly has international ramifications, it were to be found that English law alone refused to give effect to a contractual subordination.' In a similar vein, albeit to a different purpose, Lord Templeman in *Attorney General of Hong Kong v Reid* (1994) 1 All ER 1 at 12, considered that it was important that the law did not permit the proceeds of corruption being 'whisked away to some Shangri-La which hides bribes and other corrupt monies in numbered bank accounts'.

¶1312

Appendices

Appendix 1
Financial Services Act 1986

Appendix 2
Criminal Justice Act 1993, Pt. V

Appendix 3
Selected statutory instruments

Appendix 4
Extracts from Securities and Investment Board rules

Appendix 5
Annex to the second banking coordination directive

FINANCIAL SERVICES ACT 1986

(1986 Chapter 60)

ARRANGEMENT OF SECTIONS

PART I — REGULATION OF INVESTMENT BUSINESS

CHAPTER I — PRELIMINARY

SECTION

CHAPTER IV — EXEMPTED PERSONS

CHAPTER V — CONDUCT OF BUSINESS

SECTION

PART VI — TAKEOVER OFFERS
172. Takeover offers.

PART VII — INSIDER DEALING
173–176.   (Repealed by Criminal Justice Act 1993, sec. 79(14) and Sch. 6, Pt. I.)
177. Investigations into insider dealing.
178. Penalties for failure to co-operate with sec. 177 investigations.

PART VIII — RESTRICTIONS ON DISCLOSURE OF INFORMATION
179. Restrictions on disclosure of information.
180. Exceptions from restrictions on disclosure.
181. Directions restricting disclosure of information overseas.
182. Disclosure of information under enactments relating to fair trading, banking, insurance and companies.

PART IX — RECIPROCITY
183. Reciprocal facilities for financial business.
184. Investment and insurance business.
185. Banking business.
186. Variation and revocation of notices.

PART X — MISCELLANEOUS AND SUPPLEMENTARY
187. Exemption from liability for damages.
188. Jurisdiction of High Court and Court of Session.
189. Restriction of Rehabilitation of Offenders Act 1974.
190. Data protection.
191. Occupational pension schemes.
192. International obligations.
193. (Repealed by Banking Act 1987, sec. 108(2) and Sch. 7, Pt. I.)
194. Transfers to or from recognised clearing houses.
195. Offers of short-dated debentures.
196. Financial assistance for employees' share schemes.
197. Disclosure of interests in shares: interest held by market maker.
198. Power to petition for winding up etc. on information obtained under Act.
199. Powers of entry.
200. False and misleading statements.
201. Prosecutions.
202. Offences by bodies corporate, partnerships and unincorporated associations.
203. Jurisdiction and procedure in respect of offences.
204. Service of notices.
205. General power to make regulations.
205A. Supplementary provisions with respect to subordinate legislation.
206. Publication of information and advice.
–207. Interpretation.
208. Gibraltar.
209. Northern Ireland.

SECTION
210.   Expenses and receipts.
211.   Commencement and transitional provisions.
212.   Short title, consequential amendments and repeals.

SCHEDULES

FINANCIAL SERVICES ACT 1986

(1986 Chapter 60)

An Act to regulate the carrying on of investment business; to make related provision with respect to insurance business and business carried on by friendly societies; to make new provision with respect to the official listing of securities, offers of unlisted securities, takeover offers and insider dealing; to make provision as to the disclosure of information obtained under enactments relating to fair trading, banking, companies and insurance; to make provision for securing reciprocity with other countries in respect of facilities for the provision of financial services; and for connected purposes.

[*7th November 1986*]

PART I — REGULATION OF INVESTMENT BUSINESS

Chapter I — Preliminary

SEC. 1   Investments and investment business

1(1)   ["Investment"] In this Act, unless the context otherwise requires, "investment" means any asset, right or interest falling within any paragraph in Part I of Schedule 1 to this Act.

1(2) **["Investment business"]** In this Act "investment business" means the business of engaging in one or more of the activities which fall within the paragraphs in Part II of that Schedule and are not excluded by Part III of that Schedule.

1(3) **[Carrying an investment business in the UK]** For the purposes of this Act a person carries on investment business in the United Kingdom if he—

(a) carries on investment business from a permanent place of business maintained by him in the United Kingdom; or

(b) engages in the United Kingdom in one or more of the activities which fall within the paragraphs in Part II of that Schedule and are not excluded by Part III or IV of that Schedule and his doing so constitutes the carrying on by him of a business in the United Kingdom.

1(4) **[Construction of Sch. 1]** Parts I to IV of that Schedule shall be construed in accordance with Part V.

SEC. 2   Power to extend or restrict scope of Act

2(1) **[Power of Secretary of State]** The Secretary of State may by order amend Schedule 1 to this Act so as—

(a) to extend or restrict the meaning of investment for the purposes of all or any provisions of this Act; or

(b) to extend or restrict for the purposes of all or any of those provisions the activities that are to constitute the carrying on of investment business or the carrying on of such business in the United Kingdom.

2(2) **[Amendments for sec. 2(1)(b)]** The amendments that may be made for the purposes of subsection (1)(b) above include amendments conferring powers on the Secretary of State, whether by extending or modifying any provision of that Schedule which confers such powers or by adding further such provisions.

2(3) **[Approval of order by Parliament]** An order under this section which extends the meaning of investment or extends the activities that are to constitute the carrying on of investment business or the carrying on of such business in the United Kingdom shall be laid before Parliament after being made and shall cease to have effect at the end of the period of twenty-eight days beginning with the day on which it is made (but without prejudice to anything done under the order or to the making of a new order) unless before the end of that period the order is approved by a resolution of each House of Parliament.

2(4) **[Period in sec. 2(3)]** In reckoning the period mentioned in subsection (3) above no account shall be taken of any time during which Parliament is dissolved or prorogued or during which both Houses are adjourned for more than four days.

2(5) **[Annulment of order by Parliament]** Any order under this section to which subsection (3) above does not apply shall be subject to annulment in pursuance of a resolution of either House of Parliament.

2(6) **[Transitional provisions]** An order under this section may contain such transitional provisions as the Secretary of State thinks necessary or expedient.

Note
For orders made under s. 2, see SI 1988/318, SI 1988/496, SI 1988/803, SI 1990/349, SI 1990/1493, SI 1991/1516, SI 1992/273, SI 1995/3271, SI 1996/1322 and SI 1996/2827.

s. 2(6)

Chapter II — Restriction on Carrying on Business

SEC. 3   Persons entitled to carry on investment business

3 No person shall carry on, or purport to carry on, investment business in the United Kingdom unless he is an authorised person under Chapter III or an exempted person under Chapter IV of this Part of this Act.

SEC. 4   Offences

4(1) [Offence penalty] Any person who carries on, or purports to carry on, investment business in contravention of section 3 above shall be guilty of an offence and liable—

(a)   on conviction on indictment, to imprisonment for a term not exceeding two years or to a fine or to both;

(b)   on summary conviction, to imprisonment for a term not exceeding six months or to a fine not exceeding the statutory maximum or to both.

4(2) [Defence] In proceedings brought against any person for an offence under this section it shall be a defence for him to prove that he took all reasonable precautions and exercised all due diligence to avoid the commission of the offence.

SEC. 5   Agreements made by or through unauthorised persons

5(1) [Unenforceable investment agreements] Subject to subsection (3) below, any agreement to which this subsection applies—

(a)   which is entered into by a person in the course of carrying on investment business in contravention of section 3 above; or

(b)   which is entered into—

    (i)   by a person who is an authorised person or an exempted person in respect of the investment business in the course of which he enters into the agreement; but

    (ii)   in consequence of anything said or done by a person in the course of carrying on investment business in contravention of that section,

shall be unenforceable against the other party; and that party shall be entitled to recover any money or other property paid or transferred by him under the agreement, together with compensation for any loss sustained by him as a result of having parted with it.

Note

Concerning European investment firms, see the Investment Services Regulations 1995 (SI 1995/3275), reg. 32 and Sch. 7, para. 2.
Concerning European institutions, see the Banking Coordination (Second Council Directive) Regulations 1992 (SI 1992/3218), reg. 55 and Sch. 9, para. 2.

5(2) [Compensation under sec. 5(1)] The compensation recoverable under subsection (1) above shall be such as the parties may agree or as the court may, on the application of either party, determine.

5(3) [Condition for court allowing agreement] A court may allow an agreement to which subsection (1) above applies to be enforced or money and property paid or transferred under it to be retained if it is satisfied—

(a)   in a case within paragraph (a) of that subsection, that the person mentioned in that paragraph reasonably believed that his entering into the agreement did not constitute a contravention of section 3 above;

(b)   in a case within paragraph (b) of that subsection, that the person mentioned in sub-paragraph (i) of that paragraph did not know that the agreement was entered into as mentioned in sub-paragraph (ii) of that paragraph; and

(c)   in either case, that it is just and equitable for the agreement to be enforced or, as the case may be, for the money or property paid or transferred under it to be retained.

5(4)   [Where agreement not performed] Where a person elects not to perform an agreement which by virtue of this section is unenforceable against him or by virtue of this section recovers money paid or other property transferred by him under an agreement he shall repay any money and return any other property received by him under the agreement.

5(5)   [Where property has passed to third party] Where any property transferred under an agreement to which this section applies has passed to a third party the references to that property in subsections (1), (3) and (4) above shall be construed as references to its value at the time of its transfer under the agreement.

5(6)   [Effect of contravention of sec. 3] A contravention of section 3 above shall not make an agreement illegal or invalid to any greater extent than is provided in this section.

5(7)   [Application of sec. 5(1)] Subsection (1) above applies to any agreement the making or performance of which by the person seeking to enforce it or from whom money or other property is recoverable under this section constitutes an activity which falls within any paragraph of Part II of Schedule 1 to this Act and is not excluded by Part III or IV of that Schedule.

SEC. 6   Injunctions and restitution orders

6(1)   [Power of court] If, on the application of the Secretary of State, the court is satisfied—

(a)   that there is a reasonable likelihood that a person will contravene section 3 above; or

(b)   that any person has contravened that section and that there is a reasonable likelihood that the contravention will continue or be repeated,

the court may grant an injunction restraining the contravention or, in Scotland, an interdict prohibiting the contravention.

6(2)   [Power of court where sec. 3 contravened] If, on the application of the Secretary of State, the court is satisfied that a person has entered into any transaction in contravention of section 3 above the court may order that person and any other person who appears to the court to have been knowingly concerned in the contravention to take such steps as the court may direct for restoring the parties to the position in which they were before the transaction was entered into.

6(3)   [Power of court to make sec. 6(4), (5) order] The court may, on the application of the Secretary of State, make an order under subsection (4) below or, in relation to Scotland, under subsection (5) below if satisfied that a person has been carrying on investment business in contravention of section 3 above and—

(a)   that profits have accrued to that person as a result of carrying on that business; or

(b)   that one or more investors have suffered loss or been otherwise adversely affected as a result of his contravention of section 47 or 56 below or failure to act

s. 6(3)

substantially in accordance with any of the rules or regulations made under Chapter V of this Part of this Act.

6(4)   [Order re payment into court, etc.] The court may under this subsection order the person concerned to pay into court, or appoint a receiver to recover from him, such sum as appears to the court to be just having regard—

(a)   in a case within paragraph (a) of subsection (3) above, to the profits appearing to the court to have accrued;

(b)   in a case within paragraph (b) of that subsection, to the extent of the loss or other adverse effect; or

(c)   in a case within both paragraphs (a) and (b) of that subsection, to the profits and to the extent of the loss or other adverse effect.

6(5)   [Order re payment to applicant] The court may under this subsection order the person concerned to pay to the applicant such sum as appears to the court to be just having regard to the considerations mentioned in paragraphs (a) to (c) of subsection (4) above.

6(6)   [Payment of sums in sec. 6(4), (5)] Any amount paid into court by or recovered from a person in pursuance of an order under subsection (4) or (5) above shall be paid out to such person or distributed among such persons as the court may direct, being a person or persons appearing to the court to have entered into transactions with that person as a result of which the profits mentioned in paragraph (a) of subsection (3) above have accrued to him or the loss or other adverse effect mentioned in paragraph (b) of that subsection has been suffered.

6(7)   [Information on sec. 6(3) application] On an application under subsection (3) above the court may require the person concerned to furnish it with such accounts or other information as it may require for establishing whether any and, if so, what profits have accrued to him as mentioned in paragraph (a) of that subsection and for determining how any amounts are to be paid or distributed under subsection (6) above; and the court may require any such accounts or other information to be verified in such manner as it may direct.

6(8)   [Exercise of jurisdiction] The jurisdiction conferred by this section shall be exercisable by the High Court and the Court of Session.

6(9)   [Other persons bringing proceedings] Nothing in this section affects the right of any person other than the Secretary of State to bring proceedings in respect of any of the matters to which this section applies.

\Chapter III — Authorised Persons

MEMBERS OF RECOGNISED SELF-REGULATING ORGANISATIONS

SEC. 7   Authorisation by membership of recognised self-regulating organisation

7(1)   [Authorised person if member] Subject to subsection (2) below, a member of a recognised self-regulating organisation is an authorised person by virtue of his membership of that organisation.

7(2)   [Exception] This section does not apply to a member who is an authorised person by virtue of section 22 or 23 below or an insurance company which is an authorised person by virtue of section 31 below.

s. 6(4)

Note
Concerning European investment firms, see the Investment Services Regulations 1995 (SI 1995/3275), reg. 1, 21(1).
Concerning European institutions, see the Banking Coordination (Second Council Directive) Regulations 1992 (SI 1992/3218), reg. 48(1).

SEC. 8   Self-regulating organisations

8(1) **["Self-regulating organisation"]** In this Act a "self-regulating organisation" means a body (whether a body corporate or an unincorporated association) which regulates the carrying on of investment business of any kind by enforcing rules which are binding on persons carrying on business of that kind either because they are members of that body or because they are otherwise subject to its control.

8(2) **[References to members]** In this Act references to the members of a self-regulating organisation are references to the persons who, whether or not members of the organisation, are subject to its rules in carrying on the business in question.

8(3) **[References to the rules]** In this Act references to the rules of a self-regulating organisation are references to the rules (whether or not laid down by the organisation itself) which the organisation has power to enforce in relation to the carrying on of the business in question or which relate to the admission and expulsion of members of the organisation or otherwise to its constitution.

8(4) **[References to guidance]** In this Act reference to guidance issued by a self-regulating organisation are references to guidance issued or any recommendation made by it to all or any class of its members or persons seeking to become members which would, if it were a rule, fall within subsection (3) above.

SEC. 9   Applications for recognition

9(1) **[Application to Secretary of State]** A self-regulating organisation may apply to the Secretary of State for an order declaring it to be a recognised self-regulating organisation for the purposes of this Act.

9(2) **[Requirements for application]** Any such application—

(a)   shall be made in such manner as the Secretary of State may direct; and
(b)   shall be accompanied by such information as the Secretary of State may reasonably require for the purpose of determining the application.

9(3) **[Further information to be furnished]** At any time after receiving an application and before determining it the Secretary of State may require the applicant to furnish additional information.

9(4) **[Directions, requirements under sec. 9(2), (3)]** The directions and requirements given or imposed under subsections (2) and (3) above may differ as between different applications.

9(5) **[Form, verification of information]** Any information to be furnished to the Secretary of State under this section shall, if he so requires, be in such form or verified in such manner as he may specify.

9(6) **[Material to accompany application]** Every application shall be accompanied by a copy of the applicant's rules and of any guidance issued by the applicant which is intended to have continuing effect and is issued in writing or other legible form.

SEC. 10   Grant and refusal of recognition

10(1) [Power of Secretary of State] The Secretary of State may, on an application duly made in accordance with section 9 above and after being furnished with all such information as he may require under that section, make or refuse to make an order ("a recognition order") declaring the applicant to be a recognised self-regulating organisation.

10(2) [Duty of Secretary of State if sec. 10(3), Sch. 2 requirements satisfied] Subject to subsection (4) below and to Chapter XIV of this Part of this Act, the Secretary of State shall make a recognition order if it appears to him from the information furnished by the organisation making the application and having regard to any other information in his possession that the requirements of subsection (3) below and of Schedule 2 to this Act are satisfied as respects that organisation.

10(3) [Where investment business with which sec. 20 not concerned] Where there is a kind of investment business with which the organisation is not concerned, its rules must preclude a member from carrying on investment business of that kind unless he is an authorised person otherwise than by virtue of his membership of the organisation or an exempted person in respect of that business.

Note
Concerning European investment firms, see the Investment Services Regulations 1995 (SI 1995/3275), reg. 32 and Sch. 7, para. 3.

10(4) [Where Secretary of State may refuse to make order] The Secretary of State may refuse to make a recognition order in respect of an organisation if he considers that its recognition is unnecessary having regard to the existence of one or more other organisations which are concerned with investment business of a kind with which the applicant is concerned and which have been or are likely to be recognised under this section.

10(5) [Notice re refusal] Where the Secretary of State refuses an application for a recognition order he shall give the applicant a written notice to that effect specifying a requirement which in the opinion of the Secretary of State is not satisfied, stating that the application is refused on the ground mentioned in subsection (4) above or stating that it is refused by virtue of Chapter XIV.

10(6) [Order to include date] A recognition order shall state the date on which it takes effect.

Note
Concerning European institutions, see the Banking Coordination (Second Council Directive) Regulations 1992 (SI 1992/3218), reg. 55 and Sch. 9, para. 3.

SEC. 11   Revocation of recognition

11(1) [Where recognition order may be revoked] A recognition order may be revoked by a further order made by the Secretary of State if at any time it appears to him—

(a)   that section 10(3) above or any requirement of Schedule 2 to this Act is not satisfied in the case of the organisation to which the recognition order relates ("the recognised organisation");

(b)   that the recognised organisation has failed to comply with any obligation to which it is subject by virtue of this Act; or

(c)   that the continued recognition of the organisation is undesirable having regard to the existence of one or more other organisations which have been or are to be recognised under section 10 above.

s. 10(1)

11(2) **[Revocation order to include date]** An order revoking a recognition order shall state the date on which it takes effect and that date shall not be earlier than three months after the day on which the revocation order is made.

11(3) **[Duties of Secretary of State before revocation]** Before revoking a recognition order the Secretary of State shall give written notice of his intention to do so to the recognised organisation, take such steps as he considers reasonably practicable for bringing the notice to the attention of members of the organisation and publish it in such manner as he thinks appropriate for bringing it to the attention of any other persons who are in his opinion likely to be affected.

11(4) **[Contents of sec. 11(3) notice]** A notice under subsection (3) above shall state the reasons for which the Secretary of State proposes to act and give particulars of the rights conferred by subsection (5) below.

11(5) **[Where sec. 11(3) notice written representations may be made]** An organisation on which a notice is served under subsection (3) above, any member of the organisation and any other person who appears to the Secretary of State to be affected may within three months after the date of service or publication, or within such longer time as the Secretary of State may allow, make written representations to the Secretary of State and, if desired, oral representations to a person appointed for that purpose by the Secretary of State; and the Secretary of State shall have regard to any representations made in accordance with this subsection in determining whether to revoke the recognition order.

11(6) **[Secretary of State may revoke recognition order in spite of sec. 11(2), (3)]** If in any case the Secretary of State considers it essential to do so in the interests of investors he may revoke a recognition order without regard to the restriction imposed by subsection (2) above and notwithstanding that no notice has been given or published under subsection (3) above or that the time for making representations in pursuance of such a notice has not expired.

11(7) **[Transitional provisions in order]** An order revoking a recognition order may contain such transitional provisions as the Secretary of State thinks necessary or expedient.

11(8) **[Revocation on request]** A recognition order may be revoked at the request or with the consent of the recognised organisation and any such revocation shall not be subject to the restrictions imposed by subsections (1) and (2) or the requirements of subsections (3) to (5) above.

11(9) **[Written notice etc. re revocation order]** On making an order revoking a recognition order the Secretary of State shall give the organisation written notice of the making of the order, take such steps as he considers reasonably practicable for bringing the making of the order to the attention of members of the organisation and publish a notice of the making of the order in such manner as he thinks appropriate for bringing it to the attention of any other persons who are in his opinion likely to be affected.

SEC. 12   Compliance orders

12(1) **[Application by Secretary of State]** If at any time it appears to the Secretary of State—

(a)   that subsection (3) of section 10 above or any requirement of Schedule 2 to this Act is not satisfied in the case of a recognised organisation; or

(b)   that a recognised organisation has failed to comply with any obligation to which it is subject by virtue of this Act,

he may, instead of revoking the recognition order under section 11 above, make an application to the court under this section.

12(2)   [Court may make compliance order] If on any such application the court decides that subsection (3) of section 10 or the requirement in question is not satisfied or, as the case may be, that the organisation has failed to comply with the obligation in question it may order the organisation to take such steps as the court directs for securing that that subsection or requirement is satisfied or that that obligation is complied with.

12(3)   [Exercise of jurisdiction] The jurisdiction conferred by this section shall be exercisable by the High Court and the Court of Session.

Note
For application of s. 12 to a listed person see the Financial Markets and Insolvency (Money Market) Regulations 1995 (SI 1995/2049), reg. 1, 6, 7.

SEC. 13   Alteration of rules for protection of investors

13(1)   (Omitted by Companies Act 1989, sec. 206(1) and Sch. 23, para. 1(1), (2) as from 15 March 1990.)

Note
For transitional provisions in relation to the omission of s. 13(1) see SI 1992/354 (C. 12), art. 6.

13(2)   [Direction to alter if Sch. 2, para. 3(1) not satisfied] If at any time it appears to the Secretary of State that—

(a)   a recognised self-regulating organisation is concerned with two or more kinds of investment business, and

(b)   the requirement in paragraph 3(1) of Schedule 2 to this Act is not satisfied in respect of investment business of one or more but not all of those kinds,

he may, instead of revoking the recognition order or making an application under section 12 above, direct the organisation to alter, or himself alter, its rules so that they preclude a member from carrying on investment business of a kind in respect of which that requirement is not satisfied, unless he is an authorised person otherwise than by virtue of membership of the organisation or is an exempted person in respect of that business.

Note
Concerning European investment firms, see the Investment Services Regulations 1995 (SI 1995/3275), reg. 32 and Sch. 7, para. 4.
Concerning European institutions, see the Banking Coordination (Second Council Directive) Regulations 1992 (SI 1992/3218), reg. 55 and Sch. 9, para. 4.
For transitional provisions in relation to the amendment to s. 13(2) see SI 1990/354 (C. 12), art. 6.

13(3)   [Enforcement of direction] A direction under this section is enforceable on the application of the Secretary of State by injunction or, in Scotland, by an order under section 45 of the Court of Session Act 1988.

Note
For transitional provisions in relation to the amendment to s. 13(3) see SI 1990/354 (C. 12), art. 6.

13(4)–(6)   (Omitted by Companies Act 1989, sec. 206(1) and Sch. 23, para. 1(1), (5) as from 15 March 1990.)

13(7)   [Application of sec. 11(2)–(7), (9)] Section 11(2) to (7) and (9) above shall, with the necessary modifications, have effect in relation to any direction given or alteration made by the Secretary of State under subsection (2) above as they have effect in relation to an order revoking a recognition order.

13(8) **[Subsequent alteration, revocation by organisation]** The fact that the rules of a recognised organisation have been altered by or pursuant to a direction given by the Secretary of State or pursuant to an order made by the court under this section shall not preclude their subsequent alteration or revocation by that organisation.

SEC. 14   Notification requirements

14(1) **[Regulations re notification of certain events]** The Secretary of State may make regulations requiring a recognised organisation to give him forthwith notice of the occurrence of such events relating to the organisation or its members as are specified in the regulations and such information in respect of those events as is so specified.

14(2) **[Regulations re furnishing information]** The Secretary of State may make regulations requiring a recognised organisation to furnish him at such times or in respect of such periods as are specified in the regulations with such information relating to the organisation or its members as is so specified.

14(3) **[Extent of notices and information]** The notices and information required to be given or furnished under the foregoing provisions of this section shall be such as the Secretary of State may reasonably require for the exercise of his functions under this Act.

14(4) **[Regulations may require specified form, verification]** Regulations under the foregoing provisions of this section may require information to be given in a specified form and to be verified in a specified manner.

14(5) **[Manner of giving notice, information]** Any notice or information required to be given or furnished under the foregoing provisions of this section shall be given in writing or in such other manner as the Secretary of State may approve.

14(6) **[Notice where organisation amends rules, etc.]** Where a recognised organisation amends, revokes or adds to its rules or guidance it shall within seven days give the Secretary of State written notice of the amendment, revocation or addition; but notice need not be given of the revocation of guidance other than such as is mentioned in section 9(6) above or of any amendment of or addition to guidance which does not result in or consist of such guidance as is there mentioned.

14(7) **[Offence]** Contravention of, or of regulations under, this section shall not be an offence.

PERSONS AUTHORISED BY RECOGNISED PROFESSIONAL
BODIES

SEC. 15   Authorisation by certification by recognised professional body

15(1) **[Authorised person]** A person holding a certificate issued for the purposes of this Part of this Act by a recognised professional body is an authorised person.

15(2) **[Issue of certificate]** Such a certificate may be issued by a recognised professional body to an individual, a body corporate, a partnership or an unincorporated association.

15(3) **[Certificate issued to partnership]** A certificate issued to a partnership—

(a)   shall be issued in the partnership name; and

s. 15(3)

(b)   shall authorise the carrying on of investment business in that name by the partnership to which the certificate is issued, by any partnership which succeeds to that business or by any person who succeeds to that business having previously carried it on in partnership;

and, in relation to a certificate issued to a partnership constituted under the law of England and Wales or Northern Ireland or the law of any other country or territory under which a partnership is not a legal person, references in this Act to the person who holds the certificate or is certified shall be construed as references to persons or person for the time being authorised by the certificate to carry on investment business as mentioned in paragraph (b) above.

SEC. 16   Professional bodies

16(1)   ["Professional body"] In this Act a "professional body" means a body which regulates the practice of a profession and references to the practice of a profession do not include references to carrying on a business consisting wholly or mainly of investment business.

16(2)   [References to members] In this Act references to the members of a professional body are references to individuals who, whether or not members of the body, are entitled to practice the profession in question and, in practising it, are subject to the rules of that body.

16(3)   [References to notes] In this Act references to the rules of a professional body are references to the rules (whether or not laid down by the body itself) which the body has power to enforce in relation to the practice of the profession in question and the carrying on of investment business by persons practising that profession or which relate to the grant, suspension or withdrawal of certificates under section 15 above, the admission and expulsion of members or otherwise to the constitution of the body.

16(4)   [Reference to guidance] In this Act references to guidance issued by a professional body are references to guidance issued or any recommendation made by it to all or any class of its members or persons seeking to become members, or to persons or any class of persons who are or are seeking to be certified by the body, and which would, if it were a rule, fall within subsection (3) above.

SEC. 17   Applications for recognition

17(1)   [Application to Secretary of State] A professional body may apply to the Secretary of State for an order declaring it to be a recognised professional body for the purposes of this Act.

17(2)   [Effect of sec. 9(2)–(6)] Subsections (2) to (6) of section 9 above shall have effect in relation to an application under subsection (1) above as they have effect in relation to an application under subsection (1) of that section.

SEC. 18   Grant and refusal of recognition

18(1)   [Power of Secretary of State] The Secretary of State may, on an application duly made in accordance with section 17 above and after being furnished with all such information as he may require under that section, make or refuse to make an order ("a recognition order") declaring the applicant to be a recognised professional body.

18(2) [Conditions for recognition order] The Secretary of State may make a recognition order if it appears to him from the information furnished by the body making the application and having regard to any other information in his possession that the requirements of subsection (3) below and of Schedule 3 to this Act are satisfied as respects that body.

18(3) [Requirements for body's rules] The body must have rules which impose acceptable limits on the kinds of investment business which may be carried on by persons certified by it and the circumstances in which they may carry on such business and which preclude a person certified by that body from carrying on any investment business outside those limits unless he is an authorised person otherwise than by virtue of the certification or an exempted person in respect of that business.

18(4) [Written notice re refusal] Where the Secretary of State refuses an application for a recognition order he shall give the applicant a written notice to that effect, stating the reasons for the refusal.

18(5) [Order to include date] A recognition order shall state the date on which it takes effect.

SEC. 19   Revocation of recognition

19(1) [Where sec. 18 order may be revoked] A recognition order under section 18 above may be revoked by a further order made by the Secretary of State if at any time it appears to him—

(a)   that section 18(3) above or any requirement of Schedule 3 to this Act is not satisfied in the case of the body to which the recognition order relates; or

(b)   that the body has failed to comply with any obligation to which it is subject by virtue of this Act.

19(2) [Effect of sec. 11(2)–(9)] Subsections (2) to (9) of section 11 above shall have effect in relation to the revocation of a recognition order under this section as they have effect in relation to the revocation of a recognition order under subsection (1) of that section.

SEC. 20   Compliance orders

20(1) [Power of Secretary of State] If at any time it appears to the Secretary of State—

(a)   that subsection (3) of section 18 above or any requirement of Schedule 3 to this Act is not satisfied in the case of a recognised professional body; or

(b)   that such a body has failed to comply with any obligation to which it is subject by virtue of this Act,

he may, instead of revoking the recognition order under section 19 above, make an application to the court under this section.

20(2) [Order re non-compliance] If on any such application the court decides that subsection (3) of section 18 above or the requirement in question is not satisfied or, as the case may be, that the body has failed to comply with the obligation in question it may order the body to take such steps as the court directs for securing that that subsection or requirement is satisfied or that that obligation is complied with.

20(3) [Exercise of jurisdiction] The jurisdiction conferred by this section shall be exercisable by the High Court and the Court of Session.

SEC. 21   Notification requirements

21(1) [**Regulations re notice**] The Secretary of State may make regulations requiring a recognised professional body to give him forthwith notice of the occurrence of such events relating to the body, its members or persons certified by it as are specified in the regulations and such information in respect of those events as is so specified.

21(2) [**Regulations re furnishing information**] The Secretary of State may make regulations requiring a recognised professional body to furnish him at such times or in respect of such periods as are specified in the regulations with such information relating to the body, its members and persons certified by it as is so specified.

21(3) [**Notices and information required**] The notices and information required to be given or furnished under the foregoing provisions of this section shall be such as the Secretary of State may reasonably require for the exercise of his functions under this Act.

21(4) [**Form and verification of information**] Regulations under the foregoing provisions of this section may require information to be given in a specified form and to be verified in a specified manner.

21(5) [**Manner of giving notices, information**] Any notice or information required to be given or furnished under the foregoing provisions of this section shall be given in writing or in such other manner as the Secretary of State may approve.

21(6) [**Notice re amendment etc. of rules or guidance**] Where a recognised professional body amends, revokes or adds to its rules or guidance it shall within seven days give the Secretary of State written notice of the amendment, revocation or addition; but—

(a)   notice need not be given of the revocation of guidance other than such as is mentioned in section 9(6) above or of any amendment of or addition to guidance which does not result in or consist of such guidance as is there mentioned; and

(b)   notice need not be given in respect of any rule or guidance, or rules or guidance of any description, in the case of which the Secretary of State has waived compliance with this subsection by notice in writing to the body concerned;

and any such waiver may be varied or revoked by a further notice in writing.

21(7) [**Offence**] Contravention of, or of regulations under, this section shall not be an offence.

INSURANCE COMPANIES

SEC. 22   Authorised insurers

22 A body which is authorised under section 3 or 4 of the Insurance Companies Act 1982 to carry on insurance business which is investment business and carries on such insurance business in the United Kingdom is an authorised person as respects—

(a)   any insurance business which is investment business; and

(b)   any other investment business which that body may carry on without contravening section 16 of that Act.

Note

Regarding application to EC companies, see the Insurance Companies (Third Insurance Directives) Regulations 1994 (SI 1994/1696), reg. 1, 57.

FRIENDLY SOCIETIES

SEC. 23   Friendly societies

23 A friendly society which carries on investment business in the United Kingdom is an authorised person as respects any investment business which it carries on for or in connection with any of the activities mentioned in Schedule 2 to the Friendly Societies Act 1992.

COLLECTIVE INVESTMENT SCHEMES

SEC. 24   Operators and trustees of recognised schemes

24 The operator or trustee of a scheme recognised under section 86 below is an authorised person as respects—

(a)   investment business which consists in operating or acting as trustee in relation to that scheme; and

(b)   any investment business which is carried on by him in connection with or for the purposes of that scheme.

INVESTMENT COMPANIES WITH VARIABLE CAPITAL

SEC. 24A   Investment companies with variable capital

24A An investment company with variable capital is an authorised person as respects—

(a)   investment business which consists in operating the collective investment scheme constituted by the company; and

(b)   any investment business which is carried on by the company in connection with or for the purposes of operating that scheme.

PERSONS AUTHORISED BY THE SECRETARY OF STATE

SEC. 25   Authorisation by Secretary of State

25 A person holding an authorisation granted by the Secretary of State under the following provisions of this Chapter is an authorised person.

SEC. 26   Applications for authorisation

26(1) **[Applicants]** An application for authorisation by the Secretary of State may be made by—

(a)   an individual;
(b)   a body corporate;
(c)   a partnership; or
(d)   an unincorporated association.

26(2) **[Manner and contents of application]** Any such application—

(a)   shall be made in such manner as the Secretary of State may direct;
(b)   shall contain or be accompanied by—

  (i)   information as to the investment business which the applicant proposes to carry on and the services which he will hold himself out as able to provide in the carrying on of that business; and

s. 26(2)

(ii)   such other information as the Secretary of State may reasonably require for the purpose of determining the application; and

(c)   shall contain the address of a place in the United Kingdom for the service on the applicant of any notice or other document required or authorised to be served on him under this Act.

Note
See note after s. 26(5).

26(3)   [Additional information] At any time after receiving an application and before determining it the Secretary of State may require the applicant to furnish additional information.

26(4)   [Differing requirements] The directions and requirements given or imposed under subsections (2) and (3) above may differ as between different applications.

26(5)   [Form and verification of information] Any information to be furnished to the Secretary of State under this section shall, if he so requires, be in such form or verified in such manner as he may specify.

Note
Concerning European investment firms, see the Investment Services Regulations 1995 (SI 1995/3275), reg. 1, 22. Concerning applications by European institutions see the Banking Coordination (Second Council Directive) Regulations 1992 (SI 1992/3218), reg. 49.

SEC. 27   Grant and refusal of authorisation

27(1)   [Power of Secretary of State] The Secretary of State may, on an application duly made in accordance with section 26 above and after being furnished with all such information as he may require under that section, grant or refuse the application.

27(2)   [Where application to be granted] The Secretary of State shall grant the application if it appears to him from the information furnished by the applicant and having regard to any other information in his possession that the applicant is a fit and proper person to carry on the investment business and provide the services described in the application.

27(3)   [Matters to be considered re other persons] In determining whether to grant or refuse an application the Secretary of State may take into account any matter relating to any person who is or will be employed by or associated with the applicant for the purposes of the business in question, to any person who is or will be acting as an appointed representative in relation to that business and—

(a)   if the applicant is a body corporate, to any director or controller of the body, to any other body corporate in the same group or to any director or controller of any such other body corporate;

(b)   if the applicant is a partnership, to any of the partners;

(c)   if the applicant is an unincorporated association, to any member of the governing body of the association or any officer or controller of the association.

27(4)   [Related business] In determining whether to grant or refuse an application the Secretary of State may also have regard to any business which the applicant proposes to carry on in connection with his investment business.

27(5)   [Business in another member State] In the case of an applicant who is authorised to carry on investment business in a member State other than the United Kingdom the Secretary of State shall have regard to that authorisation.

27(6)   [Authorisation to partnership] An authorisation granted to a partnership—

(a)   shall be granted in the partnership name; and

(b) shall authorise the carrying on of investment business in that name (or with the Secretary of State's consent in any other name) by the partnership to which the authorisation is granted, by any partnership which succeeds to that business or by any person who succeeds to that business or by any person who succeeds to that business having previously carried it on in partnership;

and, in relation to an authorisation granted to a partnership constituted under the law of England and Wales or Northern Ireland or the law of any other country or territory under which a partnership is not a legal person, references in this Act to the holder of the authorisation or the authorised person shall be construed as references to the persons or person for the time being authorised by the authorisation to carry on investment business as mentioned in paragraph (b) above.

27(7) [Authorisation to unincorporated association] An authorisation granted to an unincorporated association shall apply to the carrying on of investment business in the name of the association and in such manner as may be specified in the authorisation.

27(8) [Notice re grant] The Secretary of State shall give an applicant for authorisation written notice of the grant of authorisation specifying the date on which it takes effect.

Note

For further effect of s. 27 see the Financial Institutions (Prudential Supervision) Regulations 1996 (SI 1996/1669), reg. 9.

Concerning European investment firms, see the Investment Services Regulations 1995 (SI 1995/3275), reg. 1, 23.
Concerning European institutions and conduct by a UK institution of a listed activity, see the Banking Coordination (Second Council Directive) Regulations 1992 (SI 1992/3218), reg. 50.

SEC. 28   Withdrawal and suspension of authorisation

28(1) [Power of Secretary of State] The Secretary of State may at any time withdraw or suspend any authorisation granted by him if it appears to him—

(a) that the holder of the authorisation is not a fit and proper person to carry on the investment business which he is carrying on or proposing to carry on; or

(b) without prejudice to paragraph (a) above, that the holder of the authorisation has contravened any provision of this Act or any rules or regulations made under it or, in purported compliance with any such provision, has furnished the Secretary of State with false, inaccurate or misleading information or has contravened any prohibition or requirement imposed under this Act.

Note

Concerning European investment firms, see the Investment Services Regulations 1995 (SI 1995/3275), reg. 32 and Sch. 7, para. 5.

Concerning European institutions, see the Banking Coordination (Second Council Directive) Regulations 1992 (SI 1992/3218), reg. 55 and Sch. 9, para. 5.

28(2) [Matters in sec. 27(3), (4)] For the purposes of subsection (1)(a) above the Secretary of State may take into account any such matters as are mentioned in section 27(3) and (4) above.

28(3) [Where holder of authorisation member of SRO] Where the holder of the authorisation is a member of a recognised self-regulating organisation the rules, prohibitions and requirements referred to in paragraph (b) of subsection (1) above include the rules of that organisation and any prohibition or requirement imposed by virtue of those rules; and where he is a person certified by a recognised professional body the rules, prohibitions and requirements referred to in that paragraph include the rules of that body which regulate the carrying on by him of investment business and any prohibition or requirement imposed by virtue of those rules.

28(4) [Suspension of authorisation] The suspension of an authorisation shall be for a specified period or until the occurrence of a specified event or until specified conditions are complied with; and while an authorisation is suspended the holder shall not be an authorised person.

28(5) [Variation of matters in sec. 28(4)] Any period, event or conditions specified under subsection (4) above in the case of an authorisation may be varied by the Secretary of State on the application of the holder.

SEC. 29   Notice of proposed refusal, withdrawal or suspension

29(1) [Written notice by Secretary of State] Where the Secretary of State proposes—

(a)   to refuse an application under section 26 or 28(5) above; or
(b)   to withdraw or suspend an authorisation,

he shall give the applicant or the authorised person written notice of his intention to do so, stating the reasons for which he proposes to act.

29(2) [Contents of notice] In the case of a proposed withdrawal or suspension the notice shall state the date on which it is proposed that the withdrawal or suspension should take effect and, in the case of a proposed suspension, its proposed duration.

29(3) [Copy of notice to other persons] Where the reasons stated in a notice under this section relate specifically to matters which—

(a)   refer to a person identified in the notice other than the applicant or the holder of the authorisation; and
(b)   are in the opinion of the Secretary of State prejudicial to that person in any office or employment,

the Secretary of State shall, unless he considers it impracticable to do so, serve a copy of the notice on that person.

29(4) [Notice to include reference to Tribunal] A notice under this section shall give particulars of the right to require the case to be referred to the Tribunal under Chapter IX of this Part of this Act.

29(5) [Where no right of reference to Tribunal] Where a case is not required to be referred to the Tribunal by a person on whom a notice is served under this section the Secretary of State shall, at the expiration of the period within which such a requirement can be made—

(a)   give that person written notice of the refusal, withdrawal or suspension; or
(b)   give that person written notice of the grant of the application or, as the case may be, written notice that the authorisation is not to be withdrawn or suspended;

and the Secretary of State may give public notice of any decision notified by him under paragraph (a) or (b) above and the reasons for the decision except that he shall not do so in the case of a decision notified under paragraph (b) unless the person concerned consents to his doing so.

SEC. 30   Withdrawal of applications and authorisations by consent

30(1) [Power to withdraw application] An application under section 26 above may be withdrawn before it is granted or refused; and, subject to subsections (2) and (3) below, an authorisation granted under section 27 above may be withdrawn by the Secretary of State at the request or with the consent of the authorised person.

30(2) [Power of Secretary of State to refuse withdrawal] The Secretary of State may refuse to withdraw any such authorisation if he considers that the public interest requires any matter affecting the authorised person to be investigated as a preliminary to a decision on the question whether the Secretary of State should in respect of that person exercise his powers under section 28 above or under any other provision of this Part of this Act.

30(3) [Further power of Secretary of State] The Secretary of State may also refuse to withdraw an authorisation where in his opinion it is desirable that a prohibition or restriction should be imposed on the authorised person under Chapter VI of this Part of this Act or that a prohibition or restriction imposed on that person under that Chapter should continue in force.

30(4) [Public notice of sec. 30(1) withdrawal] The Secretary of State may give public notice of any withdrawal of authorisation under subsection (1) above.

PERSONS AUTHORISED IN OTHER MEMBER STATES

SEC. 31 Authorisation in other member State

31(1) [Authorised person] A person carrying on investment business in the United Kingdom is an authorised person if—

(a) he is established in a member State other than the United Kingdom;
(b) the law of that State recognises him as a national of that or another member State; and
(c) he is for the time being authorised under that law to carry on investment business or investment business of any particular kind.

31(2) [Establishment in another member State] For the purposes of this Act a person is established in a member State other than the United Kingdom if his head office is situated in that State and he does not transact investment business from a permanent place of business maintained by him in the United Kingdom.

31(3) [Conditions for application to persons in other member States] This section applies to a person only if the provisions of the law under which he is authorised to carry on the investment business in question—

(a) afford to investors in the United Kingdom protection, in relation to his carrying on of that business, which is at least equivalent to that provided for them by the provisions of this Chapter relating to members of recognised self-regulating organisations or to persons authorised by the Secretary of State; or
(b) satisfy the conditions laid down by a Community instrument for the co-ordination or approximation of the laws, regulations or administrative provisions of member States relating to the carrying on of investment business or investment business of the relevant kind.

31(4) [Certificate re sec. 31(3)(a)] A certificate issued by the Secretary of State and for the time being in force to the effect that the provisions of the law of a member State comply with the requirements of subsection (3)(a) above, either as respects all investment business or as respects investment business of a particular kind, shall be conclusive evidence of that matter but the absence or revocation of such a certificate shall not be regarded as indicating that those requirements are not complied with.

31(5) [Condition for sec. 31(3)(b)] This section shall not apply to a person by virtue of paragraph (b) of subsection (3) above unless the authority by which he is authorised to carry on the investment business in question certifies that he is authorised to do so under a law which complies with the requirements of that paragraph.

Note
Concerning European investment firms, see the Investment Services Regulations 1995 (SI 1995/3275), reg. 1, 24. See also note after s. 32(1).

SEC. 32   Notice of commencement of business

32(1) [Written notice to be given offence] A person who is an authorised person by virtue of section 31 above shall be guilty of an offence unless, not less than seven days before beginning to carry on investment business in the United Kingdom, he has given notice of his intention to do so to the Secretary of State either in writing or in such other manner as the Secretary of State may approve.

Note
Concerning European institutions, see the Banking Coordination (Second Council Directive) Regulations 1992 (SI 1992/3218), reg. 51, reg. 55 and Sch. 9, para. 6.

32(2) [Contents of notice] The notice shall contain—

(a)   information as to the investment business which that person proposes to carry on in the United Kingdom and the services which he will hold himself out as able to provide in the carrying on of that business;

(b)   information as to the authorisation of that person in the member State in question;

(c)   the address of a place (whether in the United Kingdom or elsewhere) for the service on that person of any notice or other document required or authorised to be served on him under this Act;

(d)   such other information as may be prescribed;

and the notice shall comply with such requirements as to the form in which any information is to be given and as to its verification as may be prescribed.

32(3) [Certificate re sec. 31] A notice by a person claiming to be authorised by virtue of subsection (3)(b) of section 31 above shall be accompanied by a copy of the certificate required by subsection (5) of that section.

32(4) [Penalty] A person guilty of an offence under subsection (1) above shall be liable—

(a)   on conviction on indictment, to a fine;

(b)   on summary conviction, to a fine not exceeding the statutory maximum.

32(5) [Defence] In proceedings brought against any person for an offence under subsection (1) above it shall be a defence for him to prove that he took all reasonable precautions and exercised all due diligence to avoid the commission of the offence.

Note
Concerning European investment firms, see the Investment Services Regulations 1995 (SI 1995/3275), reg. 32 and Sch. 7, para. 6.

SEC. 33   Termination and suspension of authorisation

33(1) [Power of Secretary of State] If it appears to the Secretary of State that a person who is an authorised person by virtue of section 31 above has contravened any provision of this Act or of any rules or regulations made under it or, in purported compliance with any such provision, has furnished the Secretary of State with false, inaccurate or misleading information or has contravened any prohibition or requirement imposed under this Act the Secretary of State may direct—

(a)   that he shall cease to be an authorised person by virtue of that section; or

(b)   that he shall not be an authorised person by virtue of that section for a specified period or until the occurrence of a specified event or until specified conditions are complied with.

33(2) [Rules in sec. 33(1) re member of SRO] In the case of a person who is a member of a recognised self-regulating organisation the rules, prohibitions and requirements referred to in subsection (1) above include the rules of that organisation and any prohibition or requirement imposed by virtue of those rules; and in the case of a person who is certified by a recognised professional body the rules, prohibitions and requirements referred to in that subsection include the rules of that body which regulate the carrying on by him of investment business and any prohibition or requirement imposed by virtue of those rules.

33(3) [Variation of matters in sec. 33(1)(b)] Any period, event or condition specified in a direction under subsection (1)(b) above may be varied by the Secretary of State on the application of the person to whom the direction relates.

33(4) [Consultation with relevant authority before direction] The Secretary of State shall consult the relevant supervisory authority before giving a direction under this section unless he considers it essential in the interests of investors that the direction should be given forthwith but in that case he shall consult the authority immediately after giving the direction and may then revoke or vary it if he considers it appropriate to do so.

33(5) [Revocation of direction] The Secretary of State shall revoke a direction under this section if he is satisfied, after consulting the relevant supervisory authority, that it will secure that the person concerned will comply with the provisions mentioned in subsection (1) above.

33(6) ["The relevant supervisory authority"] In this section "the relevant supervisory authority" means the authority of the member State where the person concerned is established which is responsible for supervising the carrying on of investment business of the kind which that person is or was carrying on.

SEC. 34   Notice of proposed termination or suspension

34(1) [Duty of Secretary of State to give written notice] Where the Secretary of State proposes—

(a)   to give a direction under section 33 above; or

(b)   to refuse an application under subsection (3) of that section,

he shall give the authorised person written notice of his intention to do so, stating the reasons for which he proposes to act.

34(2) [Where proposed direction under sec. 33] In the case of a proposed direction under section 33 above the notice shall state the date on which it is proposed that the direction should take effect and, in the case of a proposed direction under subsection (1)(b) of that section, its proposed duration.

34(3) [Copy of notice to other persons] Where the reasons stated in a notice under this section relate specifically to matters which—

s. 34(3)

(a)   refer to a person identified in the notice other than the authorised person; and
(b)   are in the opinion of the Secretary of State prejudicial to that person in any office or employment,

the Secretary of State shall, unless he considers it impracticable to do so, serve a copy of the notice on that other person.

34(4) [Notice to include reference to Tribunal] A notice under this section shall give particulars of the right to require the case to be referred to the Tribunal under Chapter IX of this Part of this Act.

34(5) [Where case not required to be referred to Tribunal] Where a case is not required to be referred to the Tribunal by a person on whom a notice is served under this section the Secretary of State shall, at the expiration of the period within which such a requirement can be made—

(a)   give that person written notice of the direction or refusal; or
(b)   give that person written notice that the direction is not to be given or, as the case may be, of the grant of the application;

and the Secretary of State may give public notice of any decision notified by him under paragraph (a) or (b) above and the reasons for the decision except that he shall not do so in the case of a decision within paragraph (b) unless the person concerned consents to his doing so.

Chapter IV — Exempted Persons

THE BANK OF ENGLAND

SEC. 35   The Bank of England

35 The Bank of England is an exempted person.

RECOGNISED INVESTMENT EXCHANGES AND CLEARING HOUSES

SEC. 36   Investment exchanges

36(1) [Recognised investment exchange] A recognised investment exchange is an exempted person as respects anything done in its capacity as such which constitutes investment business.

36(2) [References to rules of investment exchange] In this Act references to the rules of an investment exchange are references to the rules made or conditions imposed by it with respect to the matters dealt with in Schedule 4 to this Act, with respect to the admission of persons to or their exclusion from the use of its facilities or otherwise relating to its constitution.

36(3) [References to guidance issued by investment exchange] In this Act references to guidance issued by an investment exchange are references to guidance issued or any recommendation made by it to all or any class of its members or users or persons seeking to become members of the exchange or to use its facilities and which would, if it were a rule, fall within subsection (2) above.

Note
Concerning the Investment Services Directive, see the Investment Services Regulations 1995 (SI 1995/3275), reg. 1, 25.

SEC. 37   Grant and revocation of recognition

37(1) [Application to Secretary of State] Any body corporate or unincorporated association may apply to the Secretary of State for an order declaring it to be a recognised investment exchange for the purposes of this Act.

37(2) [Effect of sec. 9(2)–(5)] Subsections (2) to (5) of section 9 above shall have effect in relation to an application under subsection (1) above as they have effect in relation to an application under subsection (1) of that section; and every application under subsection (1) above shall be accompanied by—

(a)   a copy of the applicant's rules;

(b)   a copy of any guidance issued by the applicant which is intended to have continuing effect and is issued in writing or other legible form; and

(c)   particulars of any arrangements which the applicant has made or proposes to make for the provision of clearing services.

37(3) [Power of Secretary of State to make order] The Secretary of State may, on an application duly made in accordance with subsection (1) above and after being furnished with all such information as he may require in connection with the application, make or refuse to make an order ("a recognition order") declaring the applicant to be a recognised investment exchange for the purposes of this Act.

37(4) [Where Sch. 4 requirements are satisfied] Subject to Chapter XIV of this Part of this Act, the Secretary of State may make a recognition order if it appears to him from the information furnished by the exchange making the application and having regard to any other information in his possession that the requirements of Schedule 4 to this Act are satisfied as respects that exchange.

37(5) [Notice to applicant re refusal] Where the Secretary of State refuses an application for a recognition order he shall give the applicant a written notice to that effect stating the reasons for the refusal.

37(6) [Date to be stated in order] A recognition order shall state the date on which it takes effect.

37(7) [Revocation of recognition order] A recognition order may be revoked by a further order made by the Secretary of State if at any time it appears to him—

(a)   that any requirement of Schedule 4 to this Act is not satisfied in the case of the exchange to which the recognition order relates; or

(b)   that the exchange has failed to comply with any obligation to which it is subject by virtue of this Act;

and subsections (2) to (9) of section 11 above shall have effect in relation to the revocation of a recognition order under this subsection as they have effect in relation to the revocation of such an order under subsection (1) of that section.

37(8) [Effect of sec. 12] Section 12 above shall have effect in relation to a recognised investment exchange and the requirements and obligations referred to in subsection (7) above as it has effect in relation to the requirements and obligations there mentioned.

SEC. 38   Clearing houses

38(1) [Recognised clearing house] A recognised clearing house is an exempted person as respects anything done by it in its capacity as a person providing clearing services for the transaction of investment business.

s. 38(1)

38(2) [References to rules of clearing house] In this Act references to the rules of a clearing house are references to the rules made or conditions imposed by it with respect to the provision by it or its members of clearing services under clearing arrangements, that is to say, arrangements with a recognised investment exchange for the provision of clearing services in respect of transactions effected on the exchange.

38(3) [References to guidance issued by clearing house] In this Act references to guidance issued by a clearing house are references to guidance issued or any recommendation made by it to all or any class of its members or persons using or seeking to use its services and which would, if it were a rule, fall within subsection (2) above.

SEC. 39   Grant and revocation of recognition

39(1) [Application to Secretary of State] Any body corporate or unincorporated association may apply to the Secretary of State for an order declaring it to be a recognised clearing house for the purposes of this Act.

39(2) [Effect of sec. 9(2)–(5)] Subsections (2) to (5) of section 9 above shall have effect in relation to an application under subsection (1) above as they have effect in relation to an application under subsection (1) of that section; and any application under subsection (1) above shall be accompanied by—

(a)   a copy of the applicant's rules;
(b)   a copy of any guidance issued by the applicant which is intended to have continuing effect and is issued in writing or other legible form; and
(c)   particulars of any recognised investment exchange with which the applicant proposes to make clearing arrangements and of any other person (whether or not such an exchange) for whom the applicant provides clearing services.

39(3) [Power of Secretary of State to make order] The Secretary of State may, on an application duly made in accordance with subsection (1) above and after being furnished with all such information as he may require in connection with the application, make or refuse to make an order ("a recognition order") declaring the applicant to be a recognised clearing house for the purposes of this Act.

39(4) [Guidelines for making order] Subject to Chapter XIV of this Part of this Act, the Secretary of State may make a recognition order if it appears to him from the information furnished by the clearing house making the application and having regard to any other information in his possession that the clearing house—

(a)   has financial resources sufficient for the proper performance of its functions;
(b)   has adequate arrangements and resources for the effective monitoring and enforcement of compliance with its rules or, as respects monitoring, arrangements providing for that function to be performed on behalf of the clearing house (and without affecting its responsibility) by another body or person who is able and willing to perform it;
(c)   provides or is able to provide clearing services which would enable a recognised investment exchange to make arrangements with it that satisfy the requirements of Schedule 4 to this Act; and
(d)   is able and willing to comply with duties corresponding to those imposed in the case of a recognised investment exchange by paragraph 5 of that Schedule.

39(5) [Written notice to applicant re refusal] Where the Secretary of State refuses an application for a recognition order he shall give the applicant a written notice to that effect stating the reasons for the refusal.

39(6) [Order to state date] A recognition order shall state the date on which it takes effect.

39(7) [Revocation of recognition order] A recognition order may be revoked by a further order made by the Secretary of State if at any time it appears to him—

(a) that any requirement of subsection (4) above is not satisfied in the case of the clearing house; or

(b) that the clearing house has failed to comply with any obligation to which it is subject by virtue of this Act;

and subsections (2) to (9) of section 11 above shall have effect in relation to the revocation of a recognition order under this subsection as they have effect in relation to the revocation of such an order under subsection (1) of that section.

39(8) [Effect of sec. 12] Section 12 above shall have effect in relation to a recognised clearing house and the requirements and obligations referred to in subsection (7) above as it has effect in relation to the requirements and obligations there mentioned.

SEC. 40 Overseas investment exchanges and clearing houses

40(1) [Certain sec. 37(1), 39(1) applications] Any application under section 37(1) or 39(1) above by a body or association whose head office is situated in a country outside the United Kingdom shall contain the address of a place in the United Kingdom for the service on that body or association of notices or other documents required or authorised to be served on it under this Act.

40(2) [Substitutions in sec. 37(4), 39(4)] In relation to any such body or association sections 37(4) and 39(4) above shall have effect with the substitution for the requirements there mentioned of the following requirements, that is to say—

(a) that the body or association is, in the country in which its head office is situated, subject to supervision which, together with the rules and practices of that body or association, is such that investors in the United Kingdom are afforded protection in relation to that body or association at least equivalent to that provided by the provisions of this Act in relation to investment exchanges and clearing houses in respect of which recognition orders and made otherwise than by virtue of this subsection; and

(b) that the body or association is able and willing to co-operate, by the sharing of information and otherwise, with the authorities, bodies and persons responsible in the United Kingdom for the supervision and regulation of investment business or other financial services; and

(c) that adequate arrangements exist for such co-operation between those responsible for the supervision of the body or association in the country mentioned in paragraph (a) above and the authorities, bodies and persons mentioned in paragraph (b) above.

40(3) [Matter for determining whether to make sec. 40(2) order] In determining whether to make a recognition order by virtue of subsection (2) above the Secretary of State may have regard to the extent to which persons in the United Kingdom and persons in the country mentioned in that subsection have access to the financial markets in each others' countries.

40(4) [Further matters re sec. 40(2)] In relation to a body or association declared to be a

s. 40(4)

recognised investment exchange or recognised clearing house by a recognition order made by virtue of subsection (2) above—

(a)   the reference in section 36(2) above to the matters dealt with in Schedule 4 to this Act shall be construed as a reference to corresponding matters;

(b)   sections 37(7) and (8) and 39(7) and (8) above shall have effect as if the requirements mentioned in section 37(7)(a) and in section 39(7)(a) were those of subsection (2)(a) and (b) above; and

(c)   the grounds on which the order may be revoked under section 37(7) or 39(7) above shall include the ground that it appears to the Secretary of State that revocation is desirable in the interests of investors and potential investors in the United Kingdom.

40(5) ["Country"] In this section "country" includes any territory or any part of a country or territory.

40(6) ["Overseas investment exchange", "overseas clearing house"] A body or association declared to be a recognised investment exchange or recognised clearing house by a recognition order made by virtue of subsection (2) above is in this Act referred to as an "overseas investment exchange" or an "overseas clearing house".

SEC. 41   Notification requirements

41(1) [Power of Secretary of State to make regulations re notice] The Secretary of State may make regulations requiring a recognised investment exchange or recognised clearing house to give him forthwith notice of the occurrence of such events relating to the exchange or clearing house as are specified in the regulations and such information in respect of those events as is so specified.

41(2) [Regulations re furnishing information] The Secretary of State may make regulations requiring a recognised investment exchange or recognised clearing house to furnish him at such times or in respect of such periods as are specified in the regulations with such information relating to the exchange or clearing house as is so specified.

41(3) [Extent of notices and information] The notices and information required to be given or furnished under the foregoing provisions of this section shall be such as the Secretary of State may reasonably require for the exercise of his functions under this Act.

41(4) [Form, verification of information] Regulations under the foregoing provisions of this section may require information to be given in a specified form and to be verified in a specified manner.

41(5) [Notice by recognised investment exchange] Where a recognised investment exchange—

(a)   amends, revokes or adds to its rules or guidance; or
(b)   makes, terminates or varies any clearing arrangements,

it shall within seven days give written notice to the Secretary of State of the amendment, revocation or addition or, as the case may be, of the matters mentioned in paragraph (b) above.

41(6) [Notice by recognised clearing house] Where a recognised clearing house—

(a)   amends, revokes or adds to its rules or guidance; or
(b)   makes a change in the persons for whom it provides clearing services,

it shall within seven days give written notice to the Secretary of State of the amendment, revocation or addition or, as the case may be, of the change.

41(7) [Limits on notice] Notice need not be given under subsection (5) or (6) above of the revocation of guidance other than such as is mentioned in section 37(2)(b) or 39(2)(b) above or of any amendment of or addition to guidance which does not result in or consist of such guidance as is there mentioned.

Note
See the Financial Services Act 1986 (Overseas Investment Exchanges and Overseas Clearing Houses) (Notification) Regulations 1987 (SI 1987/2142).

OTHER EXEMPTIONS

SEC. 42   Lloyd's

42 The Society of Lloyd's and persons permitted by the Council of Lloyd's to act as underwriting agents at Lloyd's are exempted persons as respects investment business carried on in connection with or for the purpose of insurance business at Lloyd's.

SEC. 43   Listed money market institutions

43(1) ["Listed institution"] A person for the time being included in a list maintained by the Bank of England for the purposes of this section ("a listed institution") is an exempted person in respect of, and of anything done for the purposes of, any transaction to which Part I or Part II of Schedule 5 to this Act applies and in respect of any arrangements made by him with a view to other persons entering into a transaction to which Part III of that Schedule applies.

43(2) [Admission to list etc.] The conditions imposed by the Bank of England for admission to the list referred to in this section and the arrangements made by it for a person's admission to and removal from the list shall require the approval of the Treasury; and this section shall cease to have effect if that approval is withdrawn but without prejudice to its again having effect if approval is given for fresh conditions or arrangements.

43(3) [Publication of list] The Bank of England shall publish the list as for the time being in force and provide a certified copy of it at the request of any person wishing to refer to it in legal proceedings.

43(4) [Certified copy of list] Such a certified copy shall be evidence or, in Scotland, sufficient evidence of the contents of the list; and a copy purporting to be certified by or on behalf of the Bank shall be deemed to have been duly certified unless the contrary is shown.

Note
Concerning European investment firms, see the Investment Services Regulations 1995 (SI 1995/3275), reg. 1, 26. Concerning European institutions, see the Banking (Second Council Directive) Regulations 1992 (SI 1992/3218), reg. 52 and the Financial Services (European Institutions) Instrument 1993, para. 5.01.

SEC. 44   Appointed representatives

44(1) [Exempted person] An appointed representative is an exempted person as respects investment business carried on by him as such a representative.

44(2) [Definition] For the purposes of this Act an appointed representative is a person—

(a)   who is employed by an authorised person (his "principal") under a contract for
       services which—
       (i)   requires or permits him to carry on investment business to which this section
              applies; and
       (ii)   complies with subsections (4) and (5) below; and
(b)   for whose activities in carrying on the whole or part of that investment business his
       principal has accepted responsibility in writing;

and the investment business carried on by an appointed representative as such is the
investment business for which his principal has accepted responsibility.

44(3) [Application of section] This section applies to investment business carried on by
an appointed representative which consists of—

(a)   procuring or endeavouring to procure the persons with whom he deals to enter
       into investment agreements with his principal or (if not prohibited by his contract)
       with other persons;
(b)   giving advice to the persons with whom he deals about entering into investment
       agreements with his principal or (if not prohibited by his contract) with other
       persons; or
(c)   giving advice as to the sale of investments issued by his principal or as to the
       exercise of rights conferred by an investment whether or not issued as aforesaid.

44(4) [Contract between appointed representative and principal] If the contract
between an appointed representative and his principal does not prohibit the
representative from procuring or endeavouring to procure persons to enter into
investment agreements with persons other than his principal it must make provision for
enabling the principal either to impose such a prohibition or to restrict the kinds of
investment to which those agreements may relate or the other persons with whom they
may be entered into.

44(5) [Further matter re sec. 44(4) contract] If the contract between an appointed
representative and his principal does not prohibit the representative from giving advice
about entering into investment agreements with persons other than his principal it must
make provision for enabling the principal either to impose such a prohibition or to
restrict the kinds of advice which the representative may give by reference to the kinds
of investment in relation to which or the persons with whom the representative may
advise that investment agreements should be made.

44(6) [Responsibility of principal] The principal of an appointed representative shall
be responsible, to the same extent as if he had expressly authorised it, for anything said
or done or omitted by the representative in carrying on the investment business for
which he has accepted responsibility.

44(7) [Determining compliance of authorised person] In determining whether an
authorised person has complied with—

(a)   any provision contained in or made under this Act; or
(b)   any rules of a recognised self-regulating organisation or recognised professional
       body,

anything which a person who at the material time is or was an appointed representative
of the authorised person has said, done or omitted as respects investment business for
which the authorised person has accepted responsibility shall be treated as having been
said, done or omitted by the authorised person.

44(8) [Limit on sec. 44(7)] Nothing in subsection (7) above shall cause the knowledge
or intentions of an appointed representative to be attributed to his principal for the

purpose of determining whether the principal has committed a criminal offence unless in all the circumstances it is reasonable for them to be attributed to him.

44(9) ["Investment agreement"] In this Act "investment agreement" means any agreement the making or performance of which by either party constitutes an activity which falls within any paragraph of Part II of Schedule 1 to this Act or would do so apart from Parts III and IV of that Schedule.

Note
Concerning Investment Services Directive and European investment firms, see the Investment Services Regulations 1995 (SI 1995/3275), reg. 1, 27, 32 and Sch. 7, para. 7.
Concerning European institutions, see the Banking Coordination (Second Council Directive) Regulations 1992 (SI 1992/3218), reg. 55 and Sch. 9, para. 7.

SEC. 45   Miscellaneous exemptions

45(1) [Exempted persons] Each of the following persons is an exempted person to the extent specified in relation to that person—

(a) the President of the Family Division of the High Court when acting in the exercise of his functions under section 9 of the Administration of Estates Act 1925;
(b) the Probate Judge of the High Court of Northern Ireland when acting in the exercise of his functions under section 3 of the Administration of Estates Act (Northern Ireland) 1955;
(c) the Accountant General of the Supreme Court when acting in the exercise of his functions under Part VI of the Administration of Justice Act 1982;
(d) the Accountant of Court when acting in the exercise of his functions in connection with the consignation or deposit of sums of money;
(e) the Public Trustee when acting in the exercise of his functions under the Public Trustee Act 1906;
(f) the Master of the Court of Protection when acting in the exercise of his functions under Part VII of the Mental Health Act 1983;
(g) the Official Solicitor to the Supreme Court when acting as judicial trustee under the Judicial Trustees Act 1896;
(h) a registrar of a county court when managing funds paid into court;
(i) a sheriff clerk when acting in the exercise of his functions in connection with the consignation or deposit of sums of money;
(j) a person acting in his capacity as manager of a fund established under section 22 or 22A of the Charities Act 1960, or section 24 or 25 of the Charities Act 1993, section 25 of the Charities Act (Northern Ireland) 1964, section 11 of the Trustee Investments Act 1961 or section 42 of the Administration of Justice Act 1982;
(k) the Central Board of Finance of the Church of England or a Diocesan Authority within the meaning of the Church Funds Investment Measure 1958 when acting in the exercise of its functions under that Measure;
(l) a person acting in his capacity as an official receiver within the meaning of section 399 of the Insolvency Act 1986 or in that capacity within the meaning of any corresponding provision in force in Northern Ireland.

45(2) [Where bankruptcy order re authorised person etc.] Where a bankruptcy order is made in respect of an authorised person or of a person whose authorisation is suspended under section 28 above or who is the subject of a direction under section 33(1)(b) above or a winding-up order is made in respect of a partnership which is such a person, the trustee in bankruptcy or liquidator acting in his capacity as such is an exempted person but—

s. 45(2)

(a)   sections 48 to 71 below and, so far as relevant to any of those provisions, Chapter IX of this Part of this Act; and

(b)   sections 104, 105 and 106 below,

shall apply to him to the same extent as they applied to the bankrupt or partnership and, if the bankrupt or partnership was subject to the rules of a recognised self-regulating organisation or recognised professional body, he shall himself also be subject to those rules.

Note
Concerning European investment firms, see the Investment Services Regulations 1995 (SI 1995/3275), reg. 32 and Sch. 7, para. 8.
Concerning European institutions, see the Banking Coordination (Second Council Directive) Regulations 1992 (SI 1992/3218), reg. 55 and Sch. 9, para. 8.

45(3) [Application of sec. 45(2) to Scotland] In the application of subsection (2) above to Scotland—

(a)   for the reference to a bankruptcy order being made in respect of a person there shall be substituted a reference to the estate of that person being sequestrated;

(b)   the reference to a winding-up order in respect of a partnership is a reference to such an order made under section 72 below;

(c)   for the reference to the trustee in bankruptcy there shall be substituted a reference to the interim trustee or permanent trustee within the meaning of the Bankruptcy (Scotland) Act 1985; and

(d)   for the references to the bankrupt there shall be substituted references to the debtor.

45(4) [Application of sec. 45(2) to Northern Ireland] In the application of subsection (2) above to Northern Ireland for the reference to a bankruptcy order there shall be substituted a reference to an order of adjudication of bankruptcy and the reference to a trustee in bankruptcy shall include a reference to an assignee in bankruptcy.

SUPPLEMENTAL

SEC. 46   Power to extend or restrict exemptions

46(1) [Order by Secretary of State] The Secretary of State may by order provide—

(a)   for exemptions additional to those specified in the foregoing provisions of this Chapter; or

(b)   for removing or restricting any exemption conferred by section 42, 43 or 45 above;

and any such order may contain such transitional provisions as the Secretary of State thinks necessary or expedient.

46(2) [Approval etc. by Parliament] An order making such provision as is mentioned in paragraph (a) of subsection (1) above shall be subject to annulment in pursuance of a resolution of either House of Parliament; and no order making such provision as is mentioned in paragraph (b) of that subsection shall be made unless a draft of it has been laid before and approved by a resolution of each House of Parliament.

Notes
For Orders under s. 46 see the Financial Services Act 1986 (Miscellaneous Exemptions) Order 1988 (SI 1988/350); the Financial Services Act 1986 (Miscellaneous Exemptions) (No. 2) Order 1988 (SI 1988/723); the Financial Services Act 1986 (Miscellaneous Exemptions) Order 1989 (SI 1989/431); the Financial Services Act 1986 (Listed Money Market Institutions and Miscellaneous Exemptions) Order 1990 (SI 1990/696); the Financial Services Act 1986 (Electricity Industry Exemptions) Order 1990 (SI 1990/1492); the Financial Services Act 1986 (Electricity

Industry Exemptions) (No. 2) Order 1990 (SI 1990/2235); the Financial Services Act 1986 (Miscellaneous Exemptions) Order 1991 (SI 1991/493); the Financial Services Act 1986 (Schedule 1 (Amendment) and Miscellaneous Exemptions) Order 1991 (SI 1991/1516); the Financial Services Act 1986 (Miscellaneous Exemptions) Order 1994 (SI 1994/1517); the Financial Services Act 1986 (Miscellaneous Exemptions) Order 1995 (SI 1995/202); the Financial Services Act 1986 (EEA Regulated Markets) (Exemption) Order 1995 (SI 1995/3273); the Financial Services Act 1986 (Gas Industry Exemption) Order 1996 (SI 1996/498); the Financial Services Act 1986 (Exemption) Order 1996 (SI 1996/1587); and the Financial Services Act 1986 (Corporate Debt Exemption) Order 1997 (SI 1997/816).

CHAPTER V — CONDUCT OF INVESTMENT BUSINESS

SEC. 47   Misleading statements and practices

47(1) [Offence re statements] Any person who—

(a) makes a statement, promise or forecast which he knows to be misleading, false or deceptive or dishonestly conceals any material facts; or

(b) recklessly makes (dishonestly or otherwise) a statement, promise or forecast which is misleading, false or deceptive,

is guilty of an offence if he makes the statement, promise or forecast or conceals the facts for the purpose of inducing, or is reckless as to whether it may induce, another person (whether or not the person to whom the statement, promise or forecast is made or from whom the facts are concealed) to enter or offer to enter into, or to refrain from entering or offering to enter into, an investment agreement or to exercise, or refrain from exercising, any rights conferred by an investment.

47(2) [Offence re conduct] Any person who does any act or engages in any course of conduct which creates a false or misleading impression as to the market in or the price or value of any investments is guilty of an offence if he does so for the purpose of creating that impression and of thereby inducing another person to acquire, dispose of, subscribe for or underwrite those investments or to refrain from doing so or to exercise, or refrain from exercising, any rights conferred by those investments.

47(3) [Defence re sec. 47(2)] In proceedings brought against any person for an offence under subsection (2) above it shall be a defence for him to prove that he reasonably believed that his act or conduct would not create an impression that was false or misleading as to the matters mentioned in that subsection.

47(4) [Non-application of sec. 47(1)] Subsection (1) above does not apply unless—

(a) the statement, promise or forecast is made in or from, or the facts are concealed in or from, the United Kingdom;

(b) the person on whom the inducement is intended to or may have effect is in the United Kingdom; or

(c) the agreement is or would be entered into or the rights are or would be exercised in the United Kingdom.

47(5) [Non-application of sec. 47(2)] Subsection (2) above does not apply unless—

(a) the act is done or the course of conduct is engaged in in the United Kingdom; or

(b) the false or misleading impression is created there.

47(6) [Penalty] A person guilty of an offence under this section shall be liable—

(a) on conviction on indictment, to imprisonment for a term not exceeding seven years or to a fine or to both;

(b) on summary conviction, to imprisonment for a term not exceeding six months or to a fine not exceeding the statutory maximum or to both.

Note
See the Financial Services Act 1986 (EEA Regulated Markets) (Exemption) Order 1995 (SI 1995/3273).

SEC. 47A   Statements of principle

47A(1) [Power of Secretary of State to issue statements of principle] The Secretary of State may issue statements of principle with respect to the conduct and financial standing expected of persons authorised to carry on investment business.

47A(2) [Conduct expected] The conduct expected may include compliance with a code or standard issued by another person, as for the time being in force, and may allow for the exercise of discretion by any person pursuant to any such code or standard.

47A(3) [Consequence of failure to comply] Failure to comply with a statement of principle under this section is a ground for the taking of disciplinary action or the exercise of powers of intervention, but it does not of itself give rise to any right of action by investors or other persons affected or affect the validity of any transaction.

47A(4) [Extent of disciplinary action] The disciplinary action which may be taken by virtue of subsection (3) is—

(a)   the withdrawal or suspension of authorisation under section 28 or the termination or suspension of authorisation under section 33,
(b)   the giving of a disqualification direction under section 59,
(c)   the making of a public statement under section 60, or
(d)   the application by the Secretary of State for an injunction, interdict or other order under section 61(1);
(e)   the giving of a direction under regulation 18 of the Open-Ended Investment Companies (Investment Companies with Variable Capital) Regulations 1996 (directions) or the making of an application for an order under regulation 20 of those Regulations (application to court to remove director or depositary);

and the reference in that subsection to powers of intervention is to the powers conferred by Chapter VI of this Part.

47A(5) [Principles re compliance with code or standard] Where a statement of principle relates to compliance with a code or standard issued by another person, the statement of principle may provide—

(a)   that failure to comply with the code or standard shall be a ground for the taking of disciplinary action, or the exercise of powers of intervention, only in such cases and to such extent as may be specified; and
(b)   that no such action shall be taken, or any such power exercised, except at the request of the person by whom the code or standard in question was issued.

47A(6) [Manner of exercise of powers] The Secretary of State shall exercise his powers in such manner as appears to him appropriate to secure compliance with statements of principle under this section.

Note
For transfer of the Secretary of State's functions under s. 47A see SI 1990/354 (C. 12), art. 4(3)(a)).
Concerning European institutions, see the Banking Coordination (Second Council Directive) Regulations 1992 (SI 1992/3218), reg. 55 and Sch. 9, para. 9; and reg. 83 and Sch. 11, para. 9.
Regarding application to EC companies, see the Insurance Companies (Third Insurance Directives) Regulations 1994 (SI 1994/1696), reg. 1, 58(1).
Concerning the Investment Services Directive, see the Financial Services Act 1986 (Investment Services) (Extension of Scope of Act) Order 1995 (SI 1995/3271), reg. 1, 5.

s. 47A(1)

Concerning European investment firms, see the Investment Services Regulations 1995 (SI 1995/3275), reg. 32 and Sch. 7, para. 9, and reg. 58 and Sch. 11, para. 4.

SEC. 48   Conduct of business rules

48(1) [Power of Secretary of State to make rules] The Secretary of State may make rules regulating the conduct of investment business by authorised persons but those rules shall not apply to persons certified by a recognised professional body in respect of investment business in the carrying on of which they are subject to the rules of the body.

Note
See note after s. 48(2).

48(2) [Extent of rules] Rules under this section may in particular make provision—

(a)   prohibiting a person from carrying on, or holding himself out as carrying on—
        (i)   investment business of any kind specified in the rules; or
        (ii) investment business of a kind or on a scale other than that notified by him to the Secretary of State in connection with an application for authorisation under Chapter III of this Part of this Act, in a notice under section 32 above or in accordance with any provision of the rules or regulations in that behalf;

(b)   prohibiting a person from carrying on investment business in relation to persons other than those of a specified class or description;

(c)   regulating the manner in which a person may hold himself out as carrying on investment business;

(d)   regulating the manner in which a person makes a market in any investments;

(e)   as to the form and content of advertisements in respect of investment business;

(f)   requiring the principals of appointed representatives to impose restrictions on the investment business carried on by them;

(g)   requiring the disclosure of the amount or value, or of arrangements for the payment or provision, of commissions or other inducements in connection with investment business and restricting the matters by reference to which or the manner in which their amount or value may be determined;

(h)   enabling or requiring information obtained by an authorised person in the course of carrying on one part of his business to be withheld by him from persons with whom he deals in the course of carrying on another part and for that purpose enabling or requiring persons employed in one part of that business to withhold information from those employed in another part;

(i)   as to the circumstances and manner in which and the time when or the period during which action may be taken for the purpose of stabilising the price of investments of any specified description;

(j)   for arrangements for the settlement of disputes;

(k)   requiring the keeping of accounts and other records, as to their form and content and for their inspection;

(l)   requiring a person to whom the rules apply to make provision for the protection of investors in the event of the cessation of his investment business in consequence of his death, incapacity or otherwise.

Note
Concerning European investment firms, see the Investment Services Regulations 1995 (SI 1995/3275), reg. 32 and Sch. 7, para. 10.

48(3) [Relationship between sec. 48(1) and (2)] Subsection (2) above is without prejudice to the generality of subsection (1) above and accordingly rules under this section may make provision for matters other than those mentioned in subsection (2) or further provision as to any of the matters there mentioned except that they shall not

s. 48(3)

impose limits on the amount or value of commissions or other inducements paid or provided in connection with investment business.

48(4) [Related business] Rules under this section may also regulate or prohibit the carrying on in connection with investment business of any other business or the carrying on of any other business which is held out as being for the purposes of investment.

48(5) ["Advertisement" in sec. 48(2)(e)] In paragraph (e) of subsection (2) above "advertisement" does not include any advertisement which is subject to section 154 below or which is required or permitted to be published by listing rules under Part IV of this Act and relates to securities which have been admitted to listing under that Part.

— **48(6) [Matters done in conformity with sec. 48(2)(b)]** Nothing done in conformity with rules made under paragraph (h) of subsection (2) above shall be regarded as a contravention of section 47 above.

48(7) [Contravention of sec. 47(2)] Section 47(2) above shall not be regarded as contravened by anything done for the purpose of stabilising the price of investments if it is done in conformity with rules made under this section and—

(a)　(i)　in respect of investments which fall within any of paragraphs 1 to 5 of Schedule 1 to this Act and are specified by the rules; and

　　(ii)　during such period before or after the issue of those investments as is specified by the rules,

　　or

(b)　(i)　in respect of such investments as are mentioned in subparagraph (a)(i) above; and

　　(ii)　during a period starting with the date of the first public announcement of an offer of those investments which states the price or the minimum price at which the investments are to be sold and ending on the 30th day after the closing date specified in the announcement for acceptances of such offer.

48(7A) [Meaning of "an offer" in sec. 48(7)(b)(ii)] For the purposes of subparagraph (b)(ii) of subsection (7) above "an offer" means an offer for cash (other than in relation to the issue of the investments in question) where either—

(a)　the investments have been admitted to dealing on a recognised investment exchange or any other exchange of repute outside the United Kingdom; or

(b)　the offer is on the occasion of such admission or conditional on such admission;

and the total cost of the investments subject to the offer at the price stated in the first public announcement mentioned in subsection (7) above is at least £15,000,000 (or the equivalent in the currency or unit of account in which the price is stated on the date of the announcement).

48(8) [Power of Secretary of State to amend sec. 48(7)] The Secretary of State may by order amend subsection (7) above—

(a)　by restricting or extending the kinds of investment to which it applies;

(b)　by restricting it so as to apply only in relation to the issue of investments in specified circumstances or by extending it, in respect of investments of any kind specified in the order, so as to apply to things done during a specified period before or after events other than the issue of those investments.

Note
See the Financial Services Act 1986 (Stabilisation) Order 1988 (SI 1988/717).

48(9) [Approval by Parliament of sec. 48(4) order] No order shall be made under

s. 48(4)

subsection (8) above unless a draft of it has been laid before and approved by a resolution of each House of Parliament.

48(10) [Incidental and transitional provisions] Rules under this section may contain such incidental and transitional provisions as the Secretary of State thinks necessary or expedient.

48(11) [Effect of sec. 63A] Section 63A below (application of designated rules) has effect as regards the application of rules under this section to members of recognised self-regulating organisations in respect of investment business in the carrying on of which they are subject to the rules of the organisation.

Note
Concerning the Investment Services Directive, see the Financial Services Act 1986 (Investment Services) (Extension of Scope of Act) Order 1995 (SI 1995/3271), reg. 1, 5.
Concerning European investment firms, see the Investment Services Regulations 1995 (SI 1995/3275), reg. 58 and Sch. 11, para. 5.
Concerning European institutions, see the Banking Coordination (Second Council Directive) Regulations 1992(SI 1992/3218), reg. 55 and Sch. 9, para. 10; and reg. 83 and Sch. 11, para. 10.
Regarding application to EC companies, see the Insurance Companies (Third Insurance Directives) Regulations 1994 (SI 1994/1696), reg. 1, 58(2).

SEC. 49   Financial resources rules

49(1) [Power of Secretary of State to make rules] The Secretary of State may make rules requiring—

(a)   a person authorised to carry on investment business by virtue of section 25 or 31 above, or

(b)   a member of a recognised self-regulating organisation carrying on investment business in the carrying on of which he is subject to the rules of the organisation,

to have and maintain in respect of that business such financial resources as are required by the rules.

49(2) [Extent of rules] Without prejudice to the generality of subsection (1) above, rules under this section may—

(a)   impose requirements which are absolute or which are to vary from time to time by reference to such factors as are specified in or determined in accordance with the rules;

(b)   impose requirements which take account of any business (whether or not investment business) carried on by the person concerned in conjunction with or in addition to the business mentioned in subsection (1) above;

(c)   make provision as to the assets, liabilities and other matters to be taken into account in determining a person's financial resources for the purposes of the rules and the extent to which and the manner in which they are to be taken into account for that purpose.

49(3) [Effect of sec. 63A] Section 63A below (application of designated rules) has effect as regards the application of rules under this section to members of recognised self-regulating organisations in respect of investment business in the carrying on of which they are subject to the rules of the organisation.

Note
Concerning European investment firms, see the Investment Services Regulations 1995 (SI 1995/3275), reg. 32 and Sch. 7, para. 11, and reg. 58 and Sch. 11, para. 6.
Concerning European institutions, see the Banking Coordination (Second Council Directive) Regulations 1992(SI 1992/3218), reg. 55 and Sch. 9, para. 11; and reg. 83 and Sch. 11, para. 11.

SEC. 50   Modification of conduct of business and financial resources rules for particular cases

50(1) [Power of Secretary of State] The Secretary of State may, on the application of any person to whom any rules made under section 48 or 49 above apply, alter the requirements of the rules so as to adapt them to the circumstances of that person or to any particular kind of business carried on or to be carried on by him.

50(2) [Conditions for sec. 50(1) power] The Secretary of State shall not exercise the powers conferred by subsection (1) above in any case unless it appears to him that—

(a)   compliance with the requirements in question would be unduly burdensome for the applicant having regard to the benefit which compliance would confer on investors; and

(b)   the exercise of those powers will not result in any undue risk to investors.

50(3) [Exercise of sec. 50(1) powers] The powers conferred by subsection (1) above may be exercised unconditionally or subject to conditions.

50(4) [Effect of sec. 63B powers exercisable] The powers conferred by subsection (1) above shall not be exercised in a case where the powers conferred by section 63B below are exercisable (powers of recognised self-regulating organisation in relation to designated rules).

SEC. 51   Cancellation rules

51(1) [Power of Secretary of State] The Secretary of State may make rules for enabling a person who has entered or offered to enter into an investment agreement with an authorised person to rescind the agreement or withdraw the offer within such period and in such manner as may be prescribed.

51(2) [Extent of rules] Without prejudice to the generality of subsection (1) above, rules under this section may make provision—

(a)   for requiring the service of notices with respect to the rights exercisable under the rules;

(b)   for the restitution of property and the making or recovery of payments where those rights are exercised; and

(c)   for such other incidental matters as the Secretary of State thinks necessary or expedient.

Note
Concerning European investment firms, see the Investment Services Regulations 1995 (SI 1995/3275), reg. 32 and Sch. 7, para. 12, and reg. 58 and Sch. 11, para. 7.
Concerning European institutions, see the Banking Coordination (Second Council Directive) Regulations 1992 (SI 1992/3218), reg. 55 and Sch. 9, para. 12; and reg. 83 and Sch. 11, para. 12.

SEC. 52   Notification regulations

52(1) [Regulations re notice of certain events] The Secretary of State may make regulations requiring authorised persons to give him forthwith notice of the occurrence of such events as are specified in the regulations and such information in respect of those events as is so specified.

52(2) [Regulations re furnishing information] The Secretary of State may make regulations requiring authorised persons to furnish him at such times or in respect of such periods as are specified in the regulations with such information as is so specified.

52(3) [Exceptions to application of regulations] Regulations under this section shall not apply to a member of a recognised self-regulating organisation or a person certified by a recognised professional body unless he carries on investment business in the carrying on of which he is not subject to the rules of that organisation or body.

52(4) [Extent of regulations] Without prejudice to the generality of subsections (1) and (2) above, regulations under this section may relate to—

(a)   the nature of the investment business being carried on;

(b)   the nature of any other business carried on with or for the purposes of the investment business;

(c)   any proposal of an authorised person to alter the nature or extent of any business carried on by him;

(d)   any person becoming or ceasing to be a person of the kind to whom regard could be had by the Secretary of State under subsection (3) of section 27 above in deciding an application for authorisation under that section;

(e)   the financial position of an authorised person as respects his investment business or any other business carried on by him;

(f)   any property managed, and any property or money held, by an authorised person on behalf of other persons.

52(5) [Form, verification of information] Regulations under this section may require information to be given in a specified form and to be verified in a specified manner.

52(6) [Manner of giving notice of information] Any notice or information required to be given or furnished under this section shall be given in writing or in such other manner as the Secretary of State may approve.

Note
Concerning European institutions, see the Banking Coordination (Second Council Directive) Regulations 1992 (SI 1992/3218), reg. 55 and Sch. 9, para. 13; also reg. 83 and Sch. 11, para. 13.
Regarding application to EC companies, see the Insurance Companies (Third Insurance Directives) Regulations 1994 (SI 1994/1696), reg. 1, 58(3).
Concerning European investment firms, see the Investment Services Regulations 1995 (SI 1995/3275), reg. 32 and Sch. 7, para. 13, and reg. 58 and Sch. 11, para. 8.

SEC. 53   Indemnity rules

53(1) [Power of Secretary of State to make rules] The Secretary of State may make rules concerning indemnity against any claim in respect of any description of civil liability incurred by an authorised person in connection with his investment business.

Note
Concerning European investment firms, see the Investment Services Regulations 1995 (SI 1995/3275), reg. 32 and Sch. 7, para. 14.

53(2) [Exception to application of rules] Rules under this section shall not apply to a member of a recognised self-regulating organisation or a person certified by a recognised professional body in respect of investment business in the carrying on of which he is subject to the rules of the organisation or body unless that organisation or body has requested that rules under this section should apply to him; and any such request shall not be capable of being withdrawn after rules giving effect to it have been made but without prejudice to the power of the Secretary of State to revoke the rules if he thinks fit.

53(3) [Extent of rules providing indemnity] For the purpose of providing indemnity the rules—

(a)   may authorise the Secretary of State to establish and maintain a fund or funds;

(b)   may authorise the Secretary of State to take out and maintain insurance with insurers authorised to carry on insurance business under the law of the United Kingdom or any other member State;

(c)   may require any person to whom the rules apply to take out and maintain insurance with any such insurer.

53(4) [Further extent of rules] Without prejudice to the generality of the foregoing provisions, the rules may—

(a)   specify the terms and conditions on which, and the extent to which, indemnity is to be available and any circumstances in which the right to it is to be excluded or modified;

(b)   provide for the management, administration and protection of any fund maintained by virtue of subsection (3)(a) above and require persons to whom the rules apply to make payments to any such fund;

(c)   require persons to whom the rules apply to make payments by way of premium on any insurance policy maintained by the Secretary of State by virtue of subsection (3)(b) above;

(d)   prescribe the conditions which an insurance policy must satisfy for the purposes of subsection (3)(c) above;

(e)   authorise the Secretary of State to determine the amount which the rules require to be paid to him or an insurer, subject to such limits or in accordance with such provisions as may be prescribed by the rules;

(f)   specify circumstances in which, where sums are paid by the Secretary of State or an insurer in satisfaction of claims against a person subject to the rules, proceedings may be taken against that person by the Secretary of State or the insurer;

(g)   specify circumstances in which persons are exempt from the rules;

(h)   empower the Secretary of State to take such steps as he considers necessary or expedient to ascertain whether or not the rules are being complied with; and

(i)   contain incidental or supplementary provisions.

Note
Concerning European institutions, see the Banking Coordination (Second Council Directive) Regulations 1992 (SI 1992/3218), reg. 55 and Sch. 9, para. 14.

SEC. 54   Compensation fund

54(1) [Power of Secretary of State] The Secretary of State may by rules establish a scheme for compensating investors in cases where persons who are or have been authorised persons are unable, or likely to be unable, to satisfy claims in respect of any description of civil liability incurred by them in connection with their investment businesses.

Note
See note after s. 54(6).

54(2) [Extent of rules] Without prejudice to the generality of subsection (1) above, rules under this section may—

(a)   provide for the administration of the scheme and, subject to the rules, the determination and regulation of any matter relating to its operation by a body appearing to the Secretary of State to be representative of, or of any class of, authorised persons;

(b)   establish a fund out of which compensation is to be paid;

(c)   provide for the levying of contributions from, or from any class of, authorised persons and otherwise for financing the scheme and for the payment of contributions and other money into the fund;

(d)   specify the terms and conditions on which, and the extent to which, compensation is to be payable and any circumstances in which the right to compensation is to be excluded or modified;

(e)   provide for treating compensation payable under the scheme in respect of a claim against any person as extinguishing or reducing the liability of that person in respect of the claim and for conferring on the body administering the scheme a right of recovery against that person, being, in the event of his insolvency, a right not exceeding such right, if any, as the claimant would have had in that event; and

(f)   contain incidental and supplementary provisions.

Note
See note after s. 54(6).

54(3) [Application of scheme to SRO members etc.] A scheme under this section shall not be made so as to apply to persons who are members of a recognised self-regulating organisation except after consultation with that organisation or, except at the request of a recognised professionl body, to persons who are certified by it and subject to its rules in carrying on all the investment business carried on by them; and no scheme applying to such persons shall be made unless the Secretary of State is satisfied that the rules establishing it make sufficient provision—

(a)   for the administration of the scheme by a body on which the interests of those persons are adequately represented; and

(b)   for securing that the amounts which they are liable to contribute reflect, so far as practicable, the amount of the claims made or likely to be made or likely to be made in respect of those persons.

54(4) [Where scheme applies to persons in sec. 54(3)] Where a scheme applies to such persons as are mentioned in subsection (3) above the rules under this section may—

(a)   constitute the recognised self-regulating organisation or recognised professional body in question as the body administering the scheme in relation to those persons;

(b)   provide for the levying of contributions from that organisation or body instead of from those persons; and

(c)   establish a separate fund for the contributions and compensation payable in respect of those persons, with or without provision for payments and repayments in specified circumstances between that and any other fund established by the scheme.

54(5) [Request under sec. 54(3)] A request by a recognised professional body under subsection (3) above shall not be capable of being withdrawn after rules giving effect to it have been made but without prejudice to the power of the Secretary of State to revoke the rules if he thinks fit.

54(6) [Rules re procedure] Rules may be made—

(a)   for England and Wales, under sections 411 and 412 of the Insolvency Act 1986;

(b)   for Scotland—

   (i)   under the said section 411; and

   (ii)   in relation to the application of this section where the persons who are or have been authorised persons are persons whose estates may be sequestrated

s. 54(6)

under the Bankruptcy (Scotland) Act 1985, by the Secretary of State under this section; and

(c)   for Northern Ireland, under Article 359 of the Insolvency (Northern Ireland) Order 1989 and section 65 of the Judicature (Northern Ireland) Act 1978,

for the purpose of integrating any procedure for which provision is made by virtue of subsection (2)(e) above into the general procedure on a winding-up, bankruptcy or sequestration.

Note
Concerning European investment firms, see the Investment Services Regulations 1995 (SI 1995/3275), reg. 32 and Sch. 7, para. 15, and reg. 58 and Sch. 11, para. 9.
Concerning European institutions, see the Banking Coordination (Second Council Directive) Regulations 1992 (SI 1992/3218), reg. 55 and Sch. 9, para. 15; also reg. 83 and Sch. 11, para. 14.

SEC. 55   Clients' money

55(1) [Power of Secretary of State to make regulations] The Secretary of State may make regulations with respect to money (in this section referred to as "clients' money") which authorised persons, or authorised persons of any description, hold in such circumstances as are specified in the regulations.

55(2) [Extent of regulations] Without prejudice to the generality of subsection (1) above, regulations under this section may—

(a)   provide that clients' money held by an authorised person is held on trust;

(b)   require clients' money to be paid into an account the title of which contains the word "client" and which is with an institution of a kind specified in the regulations or, in the case of or a person certified by a recognised professional body, by the rules of that body;

(c)   make provision with respect to the opening and keeping of clients' accounts, including provision as to the circumstances in which money other than clients' money may be paid into such accounts and the circumstances in which and the persons to whom money held in such accounts may be paid out;

(d)   require the keeping of accounts and records in respect of clients' money;

(e)   require any such accounts to be examined by an accountant having such qualifications as are specified in the regulations and require the accountant to report to the Secretary of State, or in the case of a person certified by a recognised professional body, to that body, whether in his opinion the provisions of the regulations have been complied with and on such other matters as may be specified in the regulations;

(f)   authorise the retention, to such extent and in such cases as may be specified in regulations, of so much of clients' money as represents interest.

Note
See note after s. 55(6).

55(3) [Where authorised person required to have auditor] Where an authorised person is required to have an auditor, whether by virtue of any provision contained in or made under any enactment (including this Act) or of the rules of any such body as is mentioned in paragraph (b) of subsection (2) above, the regulations may require the examination and report referred to in paragraph (e) of that subsection to be carried out and made by that auditor.

Note
See note after s. 55(6).

s. 55(1)

55(4) [Liability of institution under regulations] An institution with which an account is kept in pursuance of regulations made under this section does not incur any liability as constructive trustee where money is wrongfully paid from the account unless the institution permits the payment with knowledge that it is wrongful or having deliberately failed to make enquiries in circumstances in which a reasonable and honest person would have done so.

55(5) [Application to Scotland] In the application of this section to Scotland for the reference to money being held on trust there shall be substituted a reference to its being held as agent for the person who is entitled to call for it to be paid over to him or to be paid on his direction or to have it otherwise credited to him.

55(6) [Effect of sec. 63A] Section 63A below (application of designated regulations) has effect as regards the application of regulations under this section to members of recognised self-regulating organisations in respect of investment business in the carrying on of which they are subject to the rules of the organisation.

Note
For transitional provisions in relation to amendments to s. 55 effected by CA 1989, s. 206(1), 212, Sch. 23, para. 6 and Sch. 24 see SI 1990/354 (C. 12), art. 6(4).
Concerning European institutions, see the Banking Coordination (Second Council Directive) Regulations 1992 (SI 1992/3218), reg. 55 and Sch. 9, para. 16; also reg. 83 and Sch. 11, para. 15.
Concerning European investment firms, see the Investment Services Regulations 1995 (SI 1995/3275), reg. 32 and Sch. 7, para. 16.

SEC. 56   Unsolicited calls

56(1) [Prohibition re unsolicited calls] Except so far as permitted by regulations made by the Secretary of State, no person shall in the course of or in consequence of an unsolicited call—

(a)   made on a person in the United Kingdom; or

(b)   made from the United Kingdom on a person elsewhere,

by way of business enter into an investment agreement with the person on whom the call is made or procure or endeavour to procure that person to enter into such an agreement.

56(2) [Qualification to sec. 56(1)] A person shall not be guilty of an offence by reason only of contravening subsection (1) above, but subject to subsection (4) below—

(a)   any investment agreement which is entered into in the course of or in consequence of the unsolicited call shall not be enforceable against the person on whom the call was made; and

(b)   that person shall be entitled to recover any money or other property paid or transferred by him under the agreement, together with compensation for any loss sustained by him as a result of having parted with it.

56(3) [Compensation under sec. 56(2)] The compensation recoverable under subsection (2) above shall be such as the parties may agree or as a court may, on the application of either party, determine.

56(4) [Power of court re sec. 56(2) agreements] A court may allow an agreement to which subsection (2) above applies to be enforced or money and property paid or transferred under it to be retained if it is satisfied—

(a)   that the person on whom the call was made was not influenced, or not influenced to any material extent, by anything said or done in the course of or in consequence of the call;

(b)   without prejudice to paragraph (a) above, that the person on whom the call was made entered into the agreement—

      (i)   following discussions between the parties of such a nature and over such a period that his entering into the agreement can fairly be regarded as a consequence of those discussions rather than the call; and

      (ii)   was aware of the nature of the agreement and any risks involved in entering into it; or

(c)   that the call was not made by—

      (i)   the person seeking to enforce the agreement or to retain the money or property or a person acting on his behalf or an appointed representative whose principal he was; or

      (ii)   a person who has received or is to receive, or in the case of an appointed representative whose principal has received or is to receive, any commission or other inducement in respect of the agreement from a person mentioned in sub-paragraph (i) above.

56(5) [Where agreement not performed or money recovered] Where a person elects not to perform an agreement which by virtue of this section is unenforceable against him or by virtue of this section recovers money paid or other property transferred by him under an agreement he shall repay any money and return any other property received by him under the agreement.

56(6) [Where property has passed to third party] Where any property transferred under an agreement to which this section applies has passed to a third party the references to that property in this section shall be construed as references to its value at the time of its transfer under the agreement.

56(7) [Effect of sec. 63A] Section 63A below (application of designated regulations) has effect as regards the application of regulations under this section to members of recognised self-regulating organisations in respect of investment business in the carrying on of which they are subject to the rules of the organisation.

As it applies to such persons in respect of such business the reference in subsection (1) above to conduct permitted by regulations made by the Secretary of State shall be construed—

(a)   where or to the extent that the regulations do not apply, as a reference to conduct permitted by the rules of the organisation; and

(b)   where or to the extent that the regulations do apply but are expressed to have effect subject to the rules of the organisation, as a reference to conduct permitted by the regulations together with the rules of the organisation.

56(8) ["Unsolicited call"] In this section "unsolicited call" means a personal visit or oral communication made without express invitation.

Note

Concerning European investment firms, see the Investment Services Regulations 1995 (SI 1995/3275), reg. 58 and Sch. 11, para. 10.

Concerning European institutions, see the Banking Coordination (Second Council Directive) Regulations 1992 (SI 1992/3218), reg. 83 and Sch. 11, para. 16.

SEC. 57   Restrictions on advertising

57(1) [No advertising unless approved] Subject to section 58 below, no person other than an authorised person shall issue or cause to be issued an investment advertisement in the United Kingdom unless its contents have been approved by an authorised person.

57(2) ["An investment advertisement"] In this Act "an investment advertisement" means any advertisement inviting persons to enter or offer to enter into an investment agreement or to exercise any rights conferred by an investment to acquire, dispose of, underwrite or convert an investment or containing information calculated to lead directly or indirectly to persons doing so.

57(3) [Offence, penalty] Subject to subsection (4) below, any person who contravenes this section shall be guilty of an offence and liable—

(a)   on conviction on indictment, to imprisonment for a term not exceeding two years or to a fine or to both;

(b)   on summary conviction, to imprisonment for a term not exceeding six months or to a fine not exceeding the statutory maximum or to both.

57(4) [Exception to sec. 57(3)] A person who in the ordinary course of a business other than investment business issues an advertisement to the order of another person shall not be guilty of an offence under this section if he proves that he believed on reasonable grounds that the person to whose order the advertisement was issued was an authorised person, that the contents of the advertisement were approved by an authorised person or that the advertisement was permitted by or under section 58 below.

57(5) [Effect of contravention] If in contravention of this section a person issues or causes to be issued an advertisement inviting persons to enter or offer to enter into an investment agreement or containing information calculated to lead directly or indirectly to persons doing so, then, subject to subsection (8) below—

(a)   he shall not be entitled to enforce any agreement to which the advertisement related and which was entered into after the issue of the advertisement; and

(b)   the other party shall be entitled to recover any money or other property paid or transferred by him under the agreement, together with compensation for any loss sustained by him as a result of having parted with it.

57(6) [Further effect of contravention] If in contravention of this section a person issues or causes to be issued an advertisement inviting persons to exercise any rights conferred by an investment or containing information calculated to lead directly or indirectly to persons doing so, then, subject to subsection (8) below—

(a)   he shall not be entitled to enforce any obligation to which a person is subject as a result of any exercise by him after the issue of the advertisement of any rights to which the advertisement related; and

(b)   that person shall be entitled to recover any money or other property paid or transferred by him under any such obligation, together with compensation for any loss sustained by him as a result of having parted with it.

57(7) [Compensation under sec. 57(5), (6)] The compensation recoverable under subsection (5) or (6) above shall be such as the parties may agree or as a court may, on the application of either party, determine.

57(8) [Power of court re enforcing sec. 57(5), (6) agreements] A court may allow any such agreement or obligation as is mentioned in subsection (5) or (6) above to be enforced or money or property paid or transferred under it to be retained if it is satisfied—

(a)   that the person against whom enforcement is sought or who is seeking to recover the money or property was not influenced, or not influenced to any material extent, by the advertisement in making his decision to enter into the agreement or as to the exercise of the rights in question; or

s. 57(8)

(b)   that the advertisement was not misleading as to the nature of the investment, the terms of the agreement or, as the case may be, the consequences of exercising the rights in question and fairly stated any risks involved in those matters.

57(9) [Where agreement not performed or money recovered] Where a person elects not to perform an agreement or an obligation which by virtue of subsection (5) or (6) above is unenforceable against him or by virtue of either of those subsections recovers money paid or other property transferred by him under an agreement or obligation he shall repay any money and return any other property received by him under the agreement or, as the case may be, as a result of exercising the rights in question.

57(10) [Where property has passed to third party] Where any property transferred under an agreement or obligation to which subsection (5) or (6) above applies has passed to a third party the references to that property in this section shall be construed as references to its value at the time of its transfer under the agreement or obligation.

Note
See the Financial Services Act 1986 (Investment Advertisements) (Exemptions) Order 1995 (SI 1995/1266), the Financial Services Act 1986 (Investment Advertisements) (Exemptions) (No. 2) Order 1995 (SI 1995/1536) and the Financial Services Act 1986 (Investment Advertisements) (Exemptions) Order 1996(SI 1996/1586).
Concerning European investment firms, see the Investment Services Regulations 1995 (SI 1995/3275), reg. 32 and Sch. 7, para. 17.
Concerning European institutions, see the Banking Coordination (Second Council Directive) Regulations 1992 (SI 1992/3218), reg. 55 and Sch. 9, para. 17.

SEC. 58   Exceptions from restrictions on advertising

58(1) [Non-application of sec. 57—general] Section 57 above does not apply to—

(a)   any advertisement issued or caused to be issued by, and relating only to investments issued by—
   (i)   the government of the United Kingdom, of Northern Ireland or of any country or territory outside the United Kingdom;
   (ii)   a local authority in the United Kingdom or elsewhere;
   (iii) the Bank of England or the central bank of any country or territory outside the United Kingdom; or
   (iv)   any international organisation the members of which include the United Kingdom or another member State;
(b)   any advertisement issued or caused to be issued by a person who is exempt under section 36, 38, 42, 43, 44 or 45 above, or by virtue of an order under section 46 above, if the advertisement relates to a matter in respect of which he is exempt.
(c)   any advertisement which is issued or caused to be issued by a national of a member State other than the United Kingdom in the course of investment business lawfully carried on by him in such a State and which conforms with any rules made under section 48(2)(e) above;
(d)   any advertisement which—
   (i)   is subject to section 154 below; or
   (ii)   consists of or any part of listing particulars, supplementary listing particulars, a prospectus approved in accordance with listing rules made under section 144(2) or 156A(1) below, a supplementary prospectus approved in accordance with listing rules made for the purposes of section 147(1) below as applied by section 154A or 156A(3) below or any other document required or permitted to be published by listing rules under Part IV of this Act.

58(2) (Repealed by the Public Offers of Securities Regulations 1995 (SI 1995/1537), reg. 1, 17 and Sch. 2, para. 5(c) as from 19 June 1995.)

58(3) [Non-application of sec. 57 re exempted advertisements] Section 57 above does not apply to an advertisement issued in such circumstances as may be specified in an order made by the Secretary of State for the purpose of exempting from that section—

(a)   advertisements appearing to him to have a private character, whether by reason of a connection between the person issuing them and those to whom they are issued or otherwise;

(b)   advertisements appearing to him to deal with investment only incidentally;

(c)   advertisements issued to persons appearing to him to be sufficiently expert to understand any risks involved; or

(d)   such other classes of advertisement as he thinks fit.

Note
See note after s. 58(4).

58(4) [Extent of sec. 58(3) order] An order under subsection (3) above may require any person who by virtue of the order is authorised to issue an advertisement to comply with such requirements as are specified in the order.

Note
See the Financial Services Act 1986 (Investment Advertisements) (Exemptions) Order 1996 (SI 1996/1586) and the Financial Services Act 1986 (Investment Advertisements) (Exemptions) (No. 2) Order 1995(SI 1995/1536).

58(5) [Parliament approval etc. re sec. 58(3)] An order made by virtue of paragraph (a), (b) or (c) of subsection (3) above shall be subject to annulment in pursuance of a resolution of either House of Parliament; and no order shall be made by virtue of paragraph (d) of that subsection unless a draft of it has been laid before and approved by a resolution of each House of Parliament.

58(6) [Non-application of sec. 58(1)(c), (2)] Subsection (1)(c) above does not apply to any advertisement relating to an investment falling within paragraph 5 of Schedule 1 to this Act.

SEC. 59   Employment of prohibited persons

59(1) [Power of direction by Secretary of State] If it appears to the Secretary of State that any individual is not a fit and proper person to be employed in connection with investment business or investment business of a particular kind he may direct that he shall not, without the written consent of the Secretary of State, be employed in connection with investment business or, as the case may be, investment business of that kind—

(a)   by authorised persons or exempted persons; or

(b)   by any specified person or persons, or by persons of any specified description, falling within paragraph (a) above.

59(2) ["A disqualification direction"] A direction under this section ("a disqualification direction") shall specify the date on which it is to take effect and a copy of it shall be served on the person to whom it relates.

59(3) [Consent by Secretary of State] Any consent by the Secretary of State to the employment of a person who is the subject of a disqualification direction may relate to employment generally or to employment of a particular kind, may be given subject to conditions and restrictions and may be varied by him from time to time.

59(4) [Notice by Secretary of State] Where the Secretary of State proposes—

(a)   to give a disqualification direction in respect of any person; or

(b)   to refuse an application for his consent under this section or for the variation of such consent,

s. 59(4)

he shall give that person or the applicant written notice of his intention to do so, stating the reasons for which he proposes to act and giving particulars of the right to require the case to be referred to the Tribunal under Chapter IX of this Part of this Act.

59(5) [Offence, penalty] Any person who accepts or continues in any employment in contravention of a disqualification direction shall be guilty of an offence and liable on summary conviction to a fine not exceeding the fifth level on the standard scale.

59(6) [Duty of authorised person, appointed representative] It shall be the duty of an authorised person and an appointed representative to take reasonable care not to employ or continue to employ a person in contravention of a disqualification direction.

59(7) [Revocation of disqualification direction] The Secretary of State may revoke a disqualification direction.

59(8) [Interpretation] In this section references to employment include references to employment otherwise than under a contract of service.

Note
Concerning European investment firms, see the Investment Services Regulations 1995 (SI 1995/3275), reg. 32 and Sch. 7, para. 18.
Concerning European institutions, see the Banking Coordination (Second Council Directive) Regulations 1992 (SI 1992/3218), reg. 55 and Sch. 9, para. 18.

SEC. 60   Public statement as to person's misconduct

60(1) [Power of Secretary of State to publish statement] If it appears to the Secretary of State that a person who is or was an authorised person by virtue of section 22, 24, 25 or 31 above has contravened—

(a)   any provision of rules or regulations made under this Chapter or of section 56 or 59 above; or

(b)   any condition imposed under section 50 above,

he may publish a statement to that effect.

Note
See note after s. 60(3).

60(2) [Written notice to person concerned] Before publishing a statement under subsection (1) above the Secretary of State shall give the person concerned written notice of the proposed statement and of the reasons for which he proposes to act.

60(3) [Copy of notice to other persons] Where the reasons stated in the notice relate specifically to matters which—

(a)   refer to a person identified in the notice other than the person who is or was the authorised person; and

(b)   are in the opinion of the Secretary of State prejudicial to that person in any office or employment,

the Secretary of State shall, unless he considers it impracticable to do so, serve a copy of the notice on that other person.

Note
Concerning European investment firms, see the Investment Services Regulations 1995 (SI 1995/3275), reg. 32 and Sch. 7, para. 19.

60(4) [Notice to include reference to Tribunal] A notice under this section shall give particulars of the right to have the case referred to the Tribunal under Chapter IX of this Part of this Act.

60(5) [Where case not required to be referred to Tribunal] Where a case is not required to be referred to the Tribunal by a person on whom a notice is served under this section the Secretary of State shall, at the expiration of the period within which such a requirement can be made, give that person written notice that the statement is or is not to be published; and if it is to be published the Secretary of State shall after publication send a copy of it to that person and to any person on whom a copy of the notice under subsection (2) above was served.

Note
Concerning European institutions, see the Banking Coordination (Second Council Directive) Regulations 1992 (SI 1992/3218), reg. 55 and Sch. 9, para. 19.

SEC. 61   Injunctions and restitution orders

61(1) [Power of court on application by Secretary of State] If on the application of the Secretary of State the court is satisfied—

(a)   that there is a reasonable likelihood that any person will contravene any provision of—

    (i)   rules or regulations made under this Chapter;

    (ii)   sections 47, 56, 57, or 59 above;

    (iii) any requirements imposed by an order under section 58(3) above; or

    (iv)   the rules of a recognised self-regulating organisation, recognised professional body, recognised investment exchange or recognised clearing house to which that person is subject and which regulate the carrying on by him of investment business,

or any condition imposed under section 50 above;

(b)   that any person has contravened any such provision or condition and that there is a reasonable likelihood that the contravention will continue or be repeated; or

(c)   that any person has contravened any such provision or condition and that there are steps that could be taken for remedying the contravention,

the court may grant an injunction restraining the contravention or, in Scotland, an interdict prohibiting the contravention or, as the case may be, make an order requiring that person and any other person who appears to the court to have been knowingly concerned in the contravention to take such steps as the court may direct to remedy it.

61(2) [Restriction on sec. 61(1) application] No application shall be made by the Secretary of State under subsection (1) above in respect of any such rules as are mentioned in subsection (1)(a)(iv) above unless it appears to him that the organisation, body, exchange or clearing house is unable or unwilling to take appropriate steps to restrain the contravention or to require the person concerned to take such steps as are mentioned in subsection (1) above.

61(3) [Power of court to make sec. 61(4),(5) orders] The court may, on the application of the Secretary of State, make an order under subsection (4) below or, in relation to Scotland, under subsection (5) below if satisfied—

(a)   that profits have accrued to any person as a result of his contravention of any provision or condition mentioned in subsection (1)(a) above; or

(b)   that one or more investors have suffered loss or been otherwise adversely affected as a result of that contravention.

61(4) [Order re payment into court etc.] The court may under this subsection order the person concerned to pay into court, or appoint a receiver to recover from him, such sum as appears to the court to be just having regard—

(a)   in a case within paragraph (a) of subsection (3) above, to the profits appearing to the court to have accrued;

s. 61(4)

(b)   in a case within paragraph (b) of that subsection, to the extent of the loss or other adverse effect; or

(c)   in a case within both paragraphs (a) and (b) of that subsection, to the profits and to the extent of the loss or other adverse effect.

61(5) [Order re payment of sum] The court may under this subsection order the person concerned to pay to the applicant such sum as appears to the court to be just having regard to the considerations mentioned in paragraphs (a) to (c) of subsection (4) above.

61(6) [Payment of sums in sec. 61(4),(5)] Any amount paid into court by or recovered from a person in pursuance of an order under subsection (4) or (5) above shall be paid out to such person or distributed among such persons as the court may direct, being a person or persons appearing to the court to have entered into transactions with that person as a result of which the profits mentioned in paragraph (a) of subsection (3) above have accrued to him or the loss or adverse effect mentioned in paragraph (b) of that subsection has been suffered.

61(7) [Furnishing of accounts etc. re sec. 61(3)] On an application under subsection (3) above the court may require the person concerned to furnish it with such accounts or other information as it may require for establishing whether any and, if so, what profits have accrued to him as mentioned in paragraph (a) of that subsection and for determining how any amounts are to be paid or distributed under subsection (6) above; and the court may require any such accounts or other information to be verified in such manner as it may direct.

61(8) [Exercise of jurisdiction] The jurisdiction conferred by this section shall be exercisable by the High Court and the Court of Session.

61(9) [Effect on other rights] Nothing in this section affects the right of any person other than the Secretary of State to bring proceedings in respect of the matters to which this section applies.

See 47A

SEC. 62   Actions for damages

62(1) [Certain contraventions actionable] Without prejudice to section 61 above, a contravention of—

(a)   any rules or regulations made under this Chapter;
(b)   any conditions imposed under section 50 above;
(c)   any requirements imposed by an order under section 58(3) above;
(d)   the duty imposed by section 59(6) above,

shall be actionable at the suit of a person who suffers loss as a result of the contravention subject to the defences and other incidents applying to actions for breach of statutory duty.

62(2) [Additional application of sec. 62(1)] Subsection (1) applies also to a contravention by a member of a recognised self-regulating organisation or a person certified by a recognised professional body of any rules of the organisation or body relating to a matter in respect of which rules or regulations have been or could be made under this Chapter in relation to an authorised person who is not such a member or so certified.

62(3) [Non-application of sec. 62(1)] Subsection (1) above does not apply—

(a)   to a contravention of rules made under section 49 or conditions imposed under section 50 in connection with an alteration of the requirements of those rules; or

(b)   by virtue of subsection (2) above to a contravention of rules relating to a matter in respect of which rules have been or could be made under section 49.

62(4) [No offence re contraventions] A person shall not be guilty of an offence by reason of any contravention to which subsection (1) above applies or of a contravention of rules made under section 49 above or such conditions as are mentioned in subsection (3)(a) above and no such contravention shall invalidate any transaction.

SEC. 62A   Restriction of right of action

62A(1) [When sec. 62 action not to lie] No action in respect of a contravention to which section 62 above applies shall lie at the suit of a person other than a private investor, except in such circumstances as may be specified by regulations made by the Secretary of State.

62A(2) ["Private investor"] The meaning of the expression "private investor" for the purposes of subsection (1) shall be defined by regulations made by the Secretary of State.

62A(3) [Extent of sec. 62A(1) regulations] Regulations under subsection (1) may make different provision with respect to different cases.

62A(4) [Consultation before regulations] The Secretary of State shall, before making any regulations affecting the right to bring an action in respect of a contravention of any rules or regulations made by a person other than himself, consult that person.

Note
See the Financial Services Act 1986 (Restriction of Right of Action) Regulations 1991 (SI 1991/489).

SEC. 63   Gaming contracts

63(1) [Certain contracts not void] No contract to which this section applies shall be void or unenforceable by reason of—

(a)   section 18 of the Gaming Act 1845, section 1 of the Gaming Act 1892 or any corresponding provisions in force in Northern Ireland; or
(b)   any rule of the law of Scotland whereby a contract by way of gaming or wagering is not legally enforceable.

63(2) [Application of section] This section applies to any contract entered into by either or each party by way of business and the making or performance of which by either party constitutes an activity which falls within paragraph 12 of Schedule 1 to this Act or would do so apart from Parts III and IV of that Schedule.

SEC. 63A   Application of designated rules and regulations to members of self-regulating organisations

63A(1) [Power of Secretary of State to make rules and regulations] The Secretary of State may in rules and regulations under—

(a)   section 48 (conduct of business rules),
(b)   section 49 (financial resources rules),
(c)   section 55 (clients' money regulations), or
(d)   section 56 (regulations as to unsolicited calls),

s. 63A(1)

designate provisions which apply, to such extent as may be specified, to a member of a recognised self-regulating organisation in respect of investment business in the carrying on of which he is subject to the rules of the organisation.

63A(2) [Qualification to designated rules] It may be provided that the designated rules or regulations have effect, generally or to such extent as may be specified, subject to the rules of the organisation.

63A(3) [Contravention] A member of a recognised self-regulating organisation who contravenes a rule or regulation applying to him by virtue of this section shall be treated as having contravened the rules of the organisation.

63A(4) [Modification or waiver] It may be provided that, to such extent as may be specified, the designated rules or regulations may not be modified or waived (under section 63B below or section 50) in relation to a member of a recognised self-regulating organisation.

Where such provision is made any modification or waiver previously granted shall cease to have effect, subject to any transitional provision or saving contained in the rules or regulations.

63A(5) [Extent of application of rules and regulations] Except as mentioned in subsection (1), the rules and regulations referred to in that subsection do not apply to a member of a recognised self-regulating organisation in respect of investment business in the carrying on of which he is subject to the rules of the organisation.

Note
For transfer of the Secretary of State's functions under s. 63A see SI 1990/354 (C. 12), art. 4(2)(a).

SEC. 63B   Modification or waiver of designated rules and regulations

63B(1) [Power of SRO on application of member] A recognised self-regulating organisation may on the application of a member of the organisation—

(a)   modify a rule or regulation designated under section 63A so as to adapt it to his circumstances or to any particular kind of business carried on by him, or

(b)   dispense him from compliance with any such rule or regulation, generally or in relation to any particular kind of business carried on by him.

63B(2) [When powers not exercisable] The powers conferred by this section shall not be exercised unless it appears to the organisation—

(a)   that compliance with the rule or regulation in question would be unduly burdensome for the applicant having regard to the benefit which compliance would confer on investors, and

(b)   that the exercise of those powers will not result in any undue risk to investors.

63B(3) [Extent of powers; contravention] The powers conferred by this section may be exercised unconditionally or subject to conditions; and section 63A(3) applies in the case of a contravention of a condition as in the case of contravention of a designated rule or regulation.

63B(4) [Monitoring and enforcement of compliance] The reference in paragraph 4(1) of Schedule 2 (requirements for recognition of self-regulating organisations) to monitoring and enforcement of compliance with rules and regulations includes monitoring and enforcement of compliance with conditions imposed by the organisation under this section.

SEC. 63C   Codes of practice

63C(1) [Power of Secretary of State to issue] The Secretary of State may issue codes of practice with respect to any matters dealt with by statements of principle issued under section 47A or by rules or regulations made under any provision of this Chapter.

63C(2) [Determining failure to comply with statement of principle] In determining whether a person has failed to comply with a statement of principle—

(a)   a failure by him to comply with any relevant provision of a code of practice may be relied on as tending to establish failure to comply with the statement of principle, and

(b)   compliance by him with the relevant provisions of a code of practice may be relied on as tending to negative any such failure.

63C(3) [Effect of contravention] A contravention of a code of practice with respect to a matter dealt with by rules or regulations shall not of itself give rise to any liability or invalidate any transaction; but in determining whether a person's conduct amounts to contravention of a rule or regulation—

(a)   contravention by him of any relevant provision of a code of practice may be relied on as tending to establish liability, and

(b)   compliance by him with the relevant provisions of a code of practice may be relied on as tending to negative liability.

63C(4) [Limitation of rules and regulations] Where by virtue of section 63A (application of designated rules and regulations to members of self-regulating organisations) rules or regulations—

(a)   do not apply, to any extent, to a member of a recognised self-regulating organisation, or

(b)   apply, to any extent, subject to the rules of the organisation,

a code of practice with respect to a matter dealt with by the rules or regulations may contain provision limiting its application to a corresponding extent.

Note
For transfer of the Secretary of State's functions under s. 63C see SI 1990/354 (C. 12), art. 4(3)(c).

Chapter VI — Powers of Intervention

SEC. 64   Scope of powers

64(1) [Exercise of powers] The powers conferred on the Secretary of State by this Chapter shall be exercisable in relation to any authorised person or, except in the case of the power conferred by section 65 below, any appointed representative of his if it appears to the Secretary of State—

(a)   that the exercise of the powers is desirable for the protection of investors;

(b)   that the authorised person is not fit to carry on investment business of a particular kind or to the extent to which he is carrying it on or proposing to carry it on; or

(c)   that the authorised person has contravened any provision of this Act or of any rules or regulations made under it or, in purported compliance with any such provision, has furnished the Secretary of State with false, inaccurate or misleading information or has contravened any prohibition or requirement imposed under this Act.

Note
Concerning European investment firms, see the Investment Services Regulations 1995 (SI 1995/3275), reg. 32 and Sch. 7, para. 20.

s. 64(1)

Regarding application to EC companies, see the Insurance Companies (Third Insurance Directives) Regulations 1994 (SI 1994/1696), reg. 1, 59(1).

64(2) [Matter for sec. 64(1)(b)] For the purposes of subsection (1)(b) above the Secretary of State may take into account any matters that could be taken into account in deciding whether to withdraw or suspend an authorisation under Chapter III of this Part of this Act.

64(3) [Exercise of power re sec. 28, 33(1)(b) persons] The powers conferred by this Chapter may be exercised in relation to a person whose authorisation is suspended under section 28 above or who is the subject of a direction under section 33(1)(b) above and references in this Chapter to an authorised person shall be construed accordingly.

64(4) [Powers excluded] The powers conferred by this Chapter shall not be exercisable in relation to—

(a)   an authorised person who is a member of a recognised self-regulating organisation or a person certified by a recognised professional body and is subject to the rules of such an organisation or body in carrying on all the investment business carried on by him; or

(b)   an appointed representative whose principal or, in the case of such a representative with more than one principal, each of whose principals is a member of such an organisation or body and is subject to the rules of such an organisation or body in carrying on the investment business in respect of which his principal or each of his principals has accepted responsibility for his activities;

except that the powers conferred by virtue of section 67(1)(b) below may on any of the grounds specified in subsection (1) above be exercised in relation to such a person at the request of any such organisation of which he or, in the case of an appointed representative, any of his principals is a member or any such body by which he or, as the case may be, any of his principals is certified.

Note
See notes after s. 67 and s. 70.

SEC. 65   Restriction of business

65(1) [Power of Secretary of State to prohibit] The Secretary of State may prohibit an authorised person from—

(a)   entering into transactions of any specified kind or entering into them except in specified circumstances or to a specified extent;

(b)   soliciting business from persons of a specified kind or otherwise than from such persons or in a specified country or territory outside the United Kingdom;

(c)   carrying on business in a specified manner or otherwise than in a specified manner.

65(2) [Extent of prohibition] A prohibition under this section may relate to transactions entered into in connection with or for the purposes of investment business or to other business which is carried on in connection with or for the purposes of investment business.

Note
See notes after s. 67 and s. 70.
Concerning European investment firms, see the Investment Services Regulations 1995 (SI 1995/3275), reg. 32 and Sch. 7, para. 20, 21.
Regarding application to EC companies, see the Insurance Companies (Third Insurance Directives) Regulations 1994 (SI 1994/1696), reg. 1, 59(2).

SEC. 66 Restriction on dealing with assets

66(1) [Power of Secretary of State to prohibit] The Secretary of State may prohibit an authorised person or appointed representative from disposing of or otherwise dealing with any assets, or any specified assets, of that person or, as the case may be, representative in any specified manner or otherwise than in a specified manner.

66(2) [Assets outside UK] A prohibition under this section may relate to assets outside the United Kingdom.

Note
See notes after s. 67 and s. 70.

SEC. 67 Vesting of assets in trustee

67(1) [Power of Secretary of State] The Secretary of State may impose a requirement that all assets, or all assets of any specified class or description, which at any time while the requirement is in force—

(a) belong to an authorised person or appointed representative; or
(b) belong to investors and are held by or to the order of an authorised person or appointed representative,

shall be transferred to and held by a trustee approved by the Secretary of State.

67(2) [Duty of authorised person] Where a requirement is imposed under this section it shall be the duty of the authorised person or, as the case may be, appointed representative to transfer the assets to the trustee and to give him all such other assistance as may be required to enable him to discharge his functions in accordance with the requirement.

67(3) [Release of assets etc. held by trustee] Assets held by a trustee in accordance with a requirement under this section shall not be released or dealt with except in accordance with directions given by the Secretary of State or in such circumstances as may be specified by him.

67(4) [Assets outside UK] A requirement under this section may relate to assets outside the United Kingdom.

Note
Concerning European institutions, see the Banking Coordination (Second Council Directive) Regulations 1992 (SI 1992/3218), reg. 55 and Sch. 9, para. 20–23.

SEC. 68 Maintenance of assets in United Kingdom

68(1) [Power of Secretary of State] The Secretary of State may require an authorised person or appointed representative to maintain in the United Kingdom assets of such value as appears to the Secretary of State to be desirable with a view to ensuring that the authorised person or, as the case may be, appointed representative will be able to meet his liabilities in respect of investment business carried on by him in the United Kingdom.

68(2) [Assets to be taken into account] The Secretary of State may direct that for the purposes of any requirement under this section assets of any specified class or description shall or shall not be taken into account.

Note
See note after s. 70.

s. 68(2)

SEC. 69   Rescission and variation

69 The Secretary of State may, either of his own motion or on the application of a person on whom a prohibition or requirement has been imposed under this Chapter, rescind or vary the prohibition or requirement if it appears to the Secretary of State that it is no longer necessary for the prohibition or requirement to take effect or continue in force or, as the case may be, that it should take effect or continue in force in a different form.

Note
S. 69 applies to giving of notice under the Uncertificated Securities Regulations 1992 (SI 1992/225), reg. 96(2), (5). See note after s. 70.

SEC. 70   Notices

70(1) [Power to impose prohibitions etc., by written notice] The power to impose, rescind or vary a prohibition or requirement under this Chapter shall be exercisable by written notice served by the Secretary of State on the person concerned; and any such notice shall take effect on such date as is specified in the notice.

70(2) [Written notice re refusal to rescind etc.] If the Secretary of State refuses to rescind or vary a prohibition or requirement on the application of the person to whom it applies he shall serve that person with a written notice of the refusal.

Note
S. 70(2) applies to giving of notice under the Uncertificated Securities Regulations 1992 (SI 1992/225), reg. 96(2), (5).

70(3) [Notice to state reasons] A notice imposing a prohibition or requirement, or varying a prohibition or requirement otherwise than on the application of the person to whom it applies, and a notice under subsection (2) above shall state the reasons for which the prohibition or requirement was imposed or varied or, as the case may be, why the application was refused.

70(4) [Service of copy of notice on other persons] Where the reasons stated in a notice to which subsection (3) above applies relate specifically to matters which—

(a)   refer to a person identified in the notice other than the person to whom the prohibition or requirement applies; and

(b)   are in the opinion of the Secretary of State prejudicial to that person in any office or employment,

the Secretary of State shall, unless he considers it impracticable to do so, serve a copy of the notice on that person.

70(5) [Sec. 70(3) notice to refer to Tribunal] A notice to which subsection (3) above applies shall give particulars of the right to have the case referred to the Tribunal under Chapter IX of this Part of this Act.

70(6) [Public notice by Secretary of State] The Secretary of State may give public notice of any prohibition or requirement imposed by him under this Chapter and of the rescission and variation of any such prohibition or requirement; and any such notice may, if the Secretary of State thinks fit, include a statement of the reasons for which the prohibition or requirement was imposed, rescinded or varied.

Note
For application of s. 64, 65, 66, 68, 69, 70 to a listed person see the Financial Markets and Insolvency (Money Market) Regulations 1995 (SI 1995/2049), reg. 1, 6, 8–13.

SEC. 71   Breach of prohibition or requirement

71(1) **[Effect of sec. 60, 61, 62]** Sections 60, 61, and 62 above shall have effect in relation to a contravention of a prohibition or requirement imposed under this Chapter as they have effect in relation to any such contravention as is mentioned in those sections.

71(2) **[Application of sec. 62(2)]** In its application by virtue of this section, section 62(2) shall have effect with the substitution—

(a) for the reference to the rules of a recognised self-regulating organisation of a reference to any prohibition or requirement imposed by it in the exercise of powers for purposes corresponding to those of this Chapter; and

(b) for the reference to the rules of a recognised professional body of a reference to any prohibition or requirement imposed in the exercise of powers for such purposes by that body or by any other body or person having functions in respect of the enforcement of the recognised professional body's rules relating to the carrying on of investment business.

71(3) **[Equitable remedies]** This section is without prejudice to any equitable remedy available in respect of property which by virtue of a requirement under section 67 above is subject to a trust.

Chapter VII — Winding up and Administration Orders

SEC. 72   Winding up orders

72(1) **[Power of court to wind up]** On a petition presented by the Secretary of State by virtue of this section, the court having jurisdiction under the Insolvency Act 1986 may wind up an authorised person or appointed representative to whom this subsection applies if—

(a) the person is unable to pay his debts within the meaning of section 123 or, as the case may be, section 221 of that Act; or

(b) the court is of the opinion that it is just and equitable that the person should be wound up.

72(2) **[Application of sec. 72(1)]** Subsection (1) above applies to any authorised person, any person whose authorisation is suspended under section 28 above or who is the subject of a direction under section 33(1)(b) above or any appointed representative who is—

(a) a company within the meaning of section 735 of the Companies Act 1985;

(b) an unregistered company within the meaning of section 220 of the Insolvency Act 1986;

(c) an oversea company within the meaning of section 744 of the Companies Act 1985; or

(d) a partnership.

72(3) **[Person unable to pay debts]** For the purposes of a petition under subsection (1) above a person who defaults in an obligation to pay any sum due and payable under any investment agreement shall be deemed to be unable to pay his debts.

72(4) **[Winding up of partnerships etc.]** Where a petition is presented under subsection (1) above for the winding up of a partnership on the ground mentioned in paragraph (b) of subsection (1) above or, in Scotland, on a ground mentioned in paragraph (a) or (b) of that subsection, the court shall have jurisdiction and the Insolvency Act 1986 shall have effect as if the partnership were an unregistered company within the meaning of section 220 of that Act.

72(5) [Winding up re SROs etc.] The Secretary of State shall not present a petition under subsection (1) above for the winding up of any person who is an authorised person by virtue of membership of a recognised self-regulating organisation or certification by a recognised professional body and is subject to the rules of the organisation or body in the carrying on of all investment business carried on by him, unless that organisation or body has consented to his doing so.

Note
See note after s. 74.

72(6) [Non-application of sec. 72(5)] Subsection (5) above does not apply to the presentation of a petition under subsection (1) above for the winding up of an investment company with variable capital.

SEC. 73   Winding up orders: Northern Ireland

73(1) [Power of High Court in Northern Ireland to wind up] On a petition presented by the Secretary of State by virtue of this section, the High Court in Northern Ireland may wind up an authorised person or appointed representative to whom this subsection applies if—

(a)   the person is unable to pay his debts within the meaning of Article 103 or, as the case may be, Article 185 of the Insolvency (Northern Ireland) Order 1989; or

(b)   the court is of the opinion that it is just and equitable that the person should be wound up.

73(2) [Application of sec. 73(1)] Subsection (1) above applies to any authorised person, any person whose authorisation is suspended under section 28 above or who is the subject of a direction under section 33(1)(b) above or any appointed representative who is—

(a)   a company within the meaning of Article 3 of the Companies (Northern Ireland) Order 1986;

(b)   an unregistered company within the meaning of Article 184 of the Insolvency (Northern Ireland) Order 1989; or

(c)   a Part XXIII company within the meaning of Article 2 of the Companies (Northern Ireland) Order 1986; or

(d)   a partnership.

73(3) [Person unable to pay debts] For the purposes of a petition under subsection (1) above a person who defaults in an obligation to pay any sum due and payable under any investment agreement shall be deemed to be unable to pay his debts.

73(4) [Winding up of partnerships etc.] Where a petition is presented under subsection (1) above for the winding up of a partnership on the ground mentioned in paragraph (b) of subsection (1) above, the High Court in Northern Ireland shall have jurisdiction and the Insolvency (Northern Ireland) Order 1989 shall have effect as if the partnership were an unregistered company within the meaning of Article 184 of that Order.

73(5) [Winding up re SROs etc.] The Secretary of State shall not present a petition under subsection (1) above for the winding up of any person who is an authorised person by virtue of membership of a recognised self-regulating organisation or certification by a recognised professional body and is subject to the rules of the organisation or body in the carrying on of all investment business carried on by him, unless that organisation or body has consented to his doing so.

SEC. 74   Administration orders

74   A petition may be presented under section 9 of the Insolvency Act 1986 (applications for administration orders) in relation to a company to which section 8 of that Act applies, or under Article 22 of the Insolvency (Northern Ireland) Order 1989 (applications for administration orders) in relation to a company to which Article 21 of that Order applies, which is an authorised person, a person whose authorisation is suspended under section 28 above or who is the subject of a direction under section 33(1)(b) above or an appointed representative—

(a)   in the case of an authorised person who is an authorised person by virtue of membership of a recognised self-regulating organisation or certification by a recognised professional body, by that organisation or body; and

(b)   in the case of an appointed representative or an authorised person who is not authorised as mentioned in paragraph (a) above or is so authorised but is not subject to the rules of the organisation or body in question in the carrying on of all investment business carried on by him, by the Secretary of State.

Chapter VIII — Collective Investment Schemes

PRELIMINARY

SEC. 75   Interpretation

75(1)   ["A collective investment scheme"] In this Act "a collective investment scheme" means, subject to the provisions of this section, any arrangements with respect to property of any description, including money, the purpose or effect of which is to enable persons taking part in the arrangements (whether by becoming owners of the property or any part of it or otherwise) to participate in or receive profits or income arising from the acquisition, holding, management or disposal of the property or sums paid out of such profits or income.

75(2)   [Arrangements for participants in sec. 75(1)] The arrangements must be such that the persons who are to participate as mentioned in subsection (1) above (in this Act referred to as "participants") do not have day to day control over the management of the property in question, whether or not they have the right to be consulted or to give directions; and the arrangements must also have either or both of the characteristics mentioned in subsection (3) below.

75(3)   [Characteristics in sec. 75(2)] Those characteristics are—

(a)   that the contributions of the participants and the profits or income out of which payments are to be made to them are pooled;

(b)   that the property in question is managed as a whole by or on behalf of the operator of the scheme.

75(4)   [Where pooling as in sec. 75(3)(a)] Where any arrangements provide for such pooling as is mentioned in paragraph (a) of subsection (3) above in relation to separate parts of the property in question, the arrangements shall not be regarded as constituting a single collective investment scheme unless the participants are entitled to exchange rights in one part for rights in another.

75(5) [Certain investments arrangements not a collective investment scheme]
Arrangements are not a collective investment scheme if—

(a)   the property to which the arrangements relate (other than cash awaiting investment) consists of investments falling within any of paragraphs 1 to 5, 6 (so far as relating to units in authorised unit trust schemes and recognised schemes) and 10 of Schedule 1 to this Act;

(b)   each participant is the owner of a part of that property and entitled to withdraw it at any time; and

(c)   the arrangements do not have the characteristics mentioned in paragraph (a) of subsection (3) above and have those mentioned in paragraph (b) of that subsection only because the parts of the property belonging to different participants are not bought and sold separately except where a person becomes or ceases to be a participant.

75(5A), (5B) (Repealed by Financial Services Act 1986 (Restriction of Scope of Act and Meaning of Collective Investment Scheme) Order 1990 (SI 1990/349), art. 6(a) as from 26 March 1990.)

75(6) [Further arrangements etc. not collective investment schemes] The following are not collective investment schemes—

(a)   arrangements operated by a person otherwise than by way of business;

(b)   arrangements where each of the participants carries on a business other than investment business and enters into the arrangements for commercial purposes related to that business;

(c)   arrangements where each of the participants is a body corporate in the same group as the operator;

(d)   arrangements where—

 (i)   each of the participants is a bona fide employee or former employee (or the wife, husband, widow, widower, child or step-child under the age of eighteen of such an employee or former employee) of a body corporate in the same group as the operator; and

 (ii) the property to which the arrangements relate consists of shares or debentures (as defined in paragraph 20(4) of Schedule 1 to this Act) in or of a member of that group;

(f)   franchise arrangements, that is to say, arrangements under which a person earns profits or income by exploiting a right conferred by the arrangements to use a trade name or design or other intellectual property or the good-will attached to it;

(g)   arrangements the predominant purpose of which is to enable persons participating in them to share in the use or enjoyment of a particular property or to make its use or enjoyment available gratuitously to other persons;

(h)   arrangements under which the rights or interests of the participants are investments falling within paragraph 5 of Schedule 1 to this Act;

(i)   arrangements the purpose of which is the provision of clearing services and which are operated by an authorised person, a recognised clearing house or a recognised investment exchange;

(j)   contracts of insurance;

(k)   occupational pension schemes;

(l)   arrangements which by virtue of any of paragraphs 34 to 37 of Schedule 1 to this Act are not collective investment schemes for the purposes of that Schedule.

75(7) [Certain bodies corporate not collective investment schemes] No body incorporated under the law of, or of any part of, the United Kingdom relating to building societies or industrial and provident societies or registered under any such law relating to friendly societies, and no other body corporate other than an open-ended investment company, shall be regarded as constituting a collective investment scheme.

75(8) [Definitions] In this Act—

"a unit trust scheme" means a collective investment scheme under which the property in question is held on trust for the participants;

"an open-ended investment company" means a collective investment scheme under which—

(a)   the property in question belongs beneficially to, and is managed by or on behalf of, a body corporate having as its purpose the investment of its funds with the aim of spreading investment risk and giving its members the benefit of the results of the management of those funds by or on behalf of that body; and

(b)   the rights of the participants are represented by shares in or securities of that body which—

(i)   the participants are entitled to have redeemed or repurchased, or which (otherwise than under Chapter VII of Part V of the Companies Act 1985 or the corresponding Northern Ireland provision) are redeemed or repurchased from them by, or out of funds provided by, that body; or

(ii)   the body ensures can be sold by the participants on an investment exchange at a price related to the value of the property to which they relate;

"trustee", in relation to a unit trust scheme, means the person holding the property in question on trust for the participants and, in relation to a collective investment scheme constituted under the law of a country or territory outside the United Kingdom, means any person who (whether or not under a trust) is entrusted with the custody of the property in question;

"units" means the rights or interests (however described) of the participants in a collective investment scheme;

"the operator", in relation to a unit trust scheme with a separate trustee, means the manager and, in relation to an open-ended investment company, means that company.

75(9) [Amendment of sec. 2 order etc.] If an order under section 2 above amends the references to a collective investment scheme in Schedule 1 to this Act it may also amend the provisions of this section.

Note
See the Financial Services Act 1986 (Extension of Scope of Act and Meaning of Collective Investment Scheme) Order 1988 (SI 1988/496); the Financial Services Act 1986 (Restriction of Scope of Act and Meaning of Collective Investment Scheme) Order 1988 (SI 1988/803); the Financial Services Act 1986 (Restriction of Scope of Act and Meaning of Collective Investment Scheme) Order 1990 (SI 1990/349); the Financial Services Act 1986 (Restriction of Scope of Act and Meaning of Collective Investment Scheme) (No. 2) Order 1990 (SI 1990/1493); the Financial Services Act 1986 (Schedule 1 (Amendment) and Miscellaneous Exemption) Order 1991 (SI 1991/1516) and the Financial Services Act 1986 (Restriction of Scope of Act and Meaning of Collective Investment Scheme) Order 1996 (SI 1996/2996).

PROMOTION OF SCHEMES
SEC. 76   Restrictions on promotion

76(1) [Restriction on authorised person] Subject to subsections (2), (3) and (4) below, an authorised person shall not—

s. 76(1)

(a)   issue or cause to be issued in the United Kingdom any advertisement inviting persons to become or offer to become participants in a collective investment scheme or containing information calculated to lead directly or indirectly to persons becoming or offering to become participants in such a scheme; or

(b)   advise or procure any person in the United Kingdom to become or offer to become a participant in such a scheme,

unless the scheme is an authorised unit trust scheme or an investment company with variable capital or a recognised scheme under the following provisions of this Chapter.

76(2)   [Exception re advertisement to authorised person etc.] Subsection (1) above shall not apply if the advertisement is issued to or the person mentioned in paragraph (b) of that subsection is—

(a)   an authorised person; or

(b)   a person whose ordinary business involves the acquisition and disposal of property of the same kind as the property, or a substantial part of the property, to which the scheme relates.

76(3)   [Exception re things done under regulations] Subsection (1) above shall not apply to anything done in accordance with regulations made by the Secretary of State for the purpose of exempting from that subsection the promotion otherwise than to the general public of schemes of such descriptions as are specified in the regulations.

76(4)   [Exempting single property schemes under sec. 76(1)] The Secretary of State may by regulations make provision for exempting single property schemes from subsection (1) above.

Note
See note after s. 76(6).

76(5)   [Interpretation re sec. 76(4)] For the purposes of subsection (4) above a single property scheme is a scheme which has the characteristics mentioned in subsection (6) below and satisfies such other requirements as are specified in the regulations conferring the exemption.

Note
See note after s. 76(6).

76(6)   [Characteristics in sec. 76(5)] The characteristics referred to above are—

(a)   that the property subject to the scheme (apart from cash or other assets held for management purposes) consists of—

(i)   a single building (or a single building with ancillary buildings) managed by or on behalf of the operator of the scheme; or

(ii)   a group of adjacent or contiguous buildings managed by him or on his behalf as a single enterprise,

with or without ancillary land and with or without furniture, fittings or other contents of the building or buildings in question; and

(b)   that the units of the participants in the scheme are either dealt in on a recognised investment exchange or offered on terms such that any agreement for their acquisition is conditional on their admission to dealings on such an exchange.

Note
See the Financial Services Act 1986 (Single Property Schemes) (Exemption) Regulations 1989 (SI 1989/28).

76(7)   [Extent of sec. 76(4) regulations] Regulations under subsection (4) above may contain such supplementary and transitional provisions as the Secretary of State thinks necessary and may also contain provisions imposing obligations or liabilities on the operator and trustee (if any) of an exempted scheme, including, to such extent as he

s. 76(2)

thinks appropriate, provisions for purposes corresponding to those for which provision can be made under section 85 below in relation to authorised unit trust schemes.

Note
Concerning European investment firms, see the Investment Services Regulations 1995 (SI 1995/3275), reg. 32 and Sch. 7, para. 23.
See also the Financial Services Act 1986 (Single Property Schemes) (Exemption) Regulations 1989 (SI 1989/28).
Concerning European institutions, see the Banking Coordination (Second Council Directive) Regulations 1992 (SI 1992/3218), reg. 55 and Sch. 9, para. 25.

AUTHORISED UNIT TRUST SCHEMES

SEC. 77   Applications for authorisation

77(1)   [Applicants for order] Any application for an order declaring a unit trust scheme to be an authorised unit trust scheme shall be made by the manager and trustee, or proposed manager and trustee, of the scheme and the manager and trustee shall be different persons.

77(2)   [Manner of application, other information] Any such application—

(a)   shall be made in such manner as the Secretary of State may direct; and
(b)   shall contain or be accompanied by such information as he may reasonably require for the purpose of determining the application.

77(3)   [Additional information] At any time after receiving an application and before determining it the Secretary of State may require the applicant to furnish additional information.

77(4)   [Differing directions and requirements] The directions and requirements given or imposed under subsections (2) and (3) above may differ as between different applications.

77(5)   [Form and verification of information] Any information to be furnished to the Secretary of State under this section shall, if he so requires, be in such form or verified in such manner as he may specify.

SEC. 78   Authorisation orders

78(1)   [Power of Secretary of State] The Secretary of State may, on an application duly made in accordance with section 77 above and after being furnished with all such information as he may require under that section, make an order declaring a unit trust scheme to be an authorised unit trust scheme for the purposes of this Act if—

(a)   it appears to him that the scheme complies with the requirements of the regulations made under section 81 below and that the following provisions of this section are satisfied; and
(b)   he has been furnished with a copy of the trust deed and a certificate signed by a solicitor to the effect that it complies with such of those requirements as relate to its contents.

78(2)   [Manager and trustee independent] The manager and the trustee must be persons who are independent of each other.

78(3)   [Manager and trustee member State bodies corporate] The manager and the trustee must each be a body corporate incorporated in the United Kingdom or another member State, the affairs of each must be administered in the country in which it is incorporated, each must have a place of business in the United Kingdom and, if the manager is incorporated in another member State, the scheme must not be one which satisfies the requirements prescribed for the purposes of section 86 below.

78(4) [Manager and trustee authorised persons] The manager and the trustee must each be an authorised person and neither must be prohibited from acting as manager or trustee, as the case may be, by or under rules under section 48 above, by or under the rules of any recognised self-regulating organisation of which the manager or trustee is a member or by a prohibition imposed under section 65 above.

78(5) [Name and purposes of scheme] The name of the scheme must not be undesirable or misleading; and the purposes of the scheme must be reasonably capable of being successfully carried into effect.

78(6) [Requirements re redemption of units etc.] The participants must be entitled to have their units redeemed in accordance with the scheme at a price related to the net value of the property to which the units relate and determined in accordance with the scheme; but a scheme shall be treated as complying with this subsection if it requires the manager to ensure that a participant is able to sell his units on an investment exchange at a price not significantly different from that mentioned in this subsection.

78(7) [Time for decision re application] The Secretary of State shall inform the applicants of his decision on the application not later than six months after the date on which the application was received.

78(8) [Certificate on making of order] On making an order under this section the Secretary of State may issue a certificate to the effect that the scheme complies with the conditions necessary for it to enjoy the rights conferred by any relevant Community instrument.

SEC. 79   Revocation of authorisation

79(1) [Power of Secretary of State] The Secretary of State may revoke an order declaring a unit trust scheme to be an authorised unit trust scheme if it appears to him—

(a)   that any of the requirements for the making of the order are no longer satisfied;
(b)   that it is undesirable in the interests of the participants or potential participants that the scheme should continue to be authorised; or
(c)   without prejudice to paragraph (b) above, that the manager or trustee of the scheme has contravened any provision of this Act or any rules or regulations made under it or, in purported compliance with any such provision, has furnished the Secretary of State with false, inaccurate or misleading information or has contravened any prohibition or requirement imposed under this Act.

79(2) [Matter for sec. 79(1)(b)] For the purposes of subsection (1)(b) above the Secretary of State may take into account any matter relating to the scheme, the manager or trustee, a director or controller of the manager or trustee or any person employed by or associated with the manager or trustee in connection with the scheme.

79(3) [Rules in sec. 79(1)(c)] In the case of a manager or trustee who is a member of a recognised self-regulating organisation the rules, prohibitions and requirements referred to in subsection (1)(c) above include the rules of that organisation and any prohibition or requirement imposed by virtue of those rules.

79(4) [Revocation at request of manager or trustee etc.] The Secretary of State may revoke an order declaring a unit trust scheme to be an authorised unit trust scheme at the request of the manager or trustee of the scheme; but he may refuse to do so if he considers that any matter concerning the scheme should be investigated as a preliminary to a decision on the question whether the order should be revoked or that revocation would not be in the interests of the participants or would be incompatible with a Community obligation.

SEC. 80   Representations against refusal or revocation

80(1) **[Written notice re refusal etc.]** Where the Secretary of State proposes—

(a)   to refuse an application for an order under section 78 above; or

(b)   to revoke such an order otherwise than at the request of the manager or trustee of the scheme,

he shall give the applicants or, as the case may be, the manager and trustee of the scheme written notice of his intention to do so, stating the reasons for which he proposes to act and giving particulars of the rights conferred by subsection (2) below.

80(2) **[Written representations to Secretary of State]** A person on whom a notice is served under subsection (1) above may, within twenty-one days of the date of service, make written representations to the Secretary of State and, if desired, oral representations to a person appointed for that purpose by the Secretary of State.

80(3) **[Secretary of State to have regard to representations]** The Secretary of State shall have regard to any representations made in accordance with subsection (2) above in determining whether to refuse the application or revoke the order, as the case may be.

SEC. 81   Constitution and management

81(1) **[Power of Secretary of State to make regulations]** The Secretary of State may make regulations as to the constitution and management of authorised unit trust schemes, the powers and duties of the manager and trustee of any such scheme and the rights and obligations of the participants in any such scheme.

81(2) **[Extent of regulations]** Without prejudice to the generality of subsection (1) above, regulations under this section may make provision—

(a)   as to the issue and redemption of the units under the scheme;

(b)   as to the expenses of the scheme and the means of meeting them;

(c)   for the appointment, removal, powers and duties of an auditor for the scheme;

(d)   for restricting or regulating the investment and borrowing powers exercisable in relation to the scheme;

(e)   requiring the keeping of records with respect to the transactions and financial position of the scheme and for the inspection of those records;

(f)   requiring the preparation of periodical reports with respect to the scheme and the furnishing of those reports to the participants and to the Secretary of State; and

(g)   with respect to the amendment of the scheme.

81(3) **[Contents of trust deed etc.]** Regulations under this section may make provision as to the contents of the trust deed, including provision requiring any of the matters mentioned in subsection (2) above to be dealt with in the deed; but regulations under this section shall be binding on the manager, trustee and participants independently of the contents of the deed and, in the case of the participants, shall have effect as if contained in it.

81(4) **[Remuneration to scheme manager]** Regulations under this section shall not impose limits on the remuneration payable to the manager of a scheme.

81(5) **[Incidental and transitional provisions]** Regulations under this section may

s. 81(5)

contain such incidental and transitional provisions as the Secretary of State thinks necessary or expedient.

SEC. 82   Alteration of schemes and changes of manager or trustee

82(1) [Manager to give written notice re alteration etc.] The manager of an authorised unit trust scheme shall give written notice to the Secretary of State of—

(a)   any proposed alteration to the scheme; and
(b)   any proposal to replace the trustee of the scheme;

and any notice given in respect of a proposed alteration involving a change in the trust deed shall be accompanied by a certificate signed by a solicitor to the effect that the change will not affect the compliance of the deed with the regulations made under section 81 above.

82(2) [Trustee to give written notice re replacement] The trustee of an authorised unit trust scheme shall give written notice to the Secretary of State of any proposal to replace the manager of the scheme.

82(3) [Requirements for proposal to have effect] Effect shall not be given to any such proposal unless—

(a)   the Secretary of State has given his approval to the proposal; or
(b)   one month has elapsed since the date on which the notice was given under subsection (1) or (2) above without the Secretary of State having notified the manager or trustee that the proposal is not approved.

82(4) [Limit on replacements] Neither the manager nor the trustee of an authorised unit trust scheme shall be replaced except by persons who satisfy the requirements of section 78(2) to (4) above.

SEC. 83   Restrictions on activities of manager

83(1) [Only certain activities] The manager of an authorised unit trust scheme shall not engage in any activities other than those mentioned in subsection (2) below.

83(2) [Activities in sec. 83(1)] Those activities are—

(a)   acting as manager of—
    (i)   a unit trust scheme;
    (ii)   an open-ended investment company or any other body corporate whose business consists of investing its funds with the aim of spreading investment risk and giving its members the benefit of the results of the management of its funds by or on behalf of that body; or
    (iii)   any other collective investment scheme under which the contributions of the participants and the profits or income out of which payments are to be made to them are pooled;
(aa)   acting as a director of an investment company with variable capital;
(b)   activities for the purposes of or in connection with those mentioned in paragraph (a) above.

83(3) [Sec. 65 prohibition] A prohibition under section 65 above may prohibit the manager of an authorised unit trust scheme from inviting persons in any specified country or territory outside the United Kingdom to become participants in the scheme.

SEC. 84   Avoidance of exclusion clauses

84 Any provision of the trust deed of an authorised unit trust scheme shall be void in so far as it would have the effect of exempting the manager or trustee from liability for any failure to exercise due care and diligence in the discharge of his functions in respect of the scheme.

SEC. 85   Publication of scheme particulars

85(1) **[Power of Secretary of State to make regulations]** The Secretary of State may make regulations requiring the manager of an authorised unit trust scheme to submit to him and publish or make available to the public on request a document ("scheme particulars") containing information about the scheme and complying with such requirements as are specified in the regulations.

85(2) **[Revised or further scheme particulars]** Regulations under this section may require the manager of an authorised unit trust scheme to submit and publish or make available revised or further scheme particulars if—

(a)   there is a significant change affecting any matter contained in such particulars previously published or made available whose inclusion was required by the regulations; or

(b)   a significant new matter arises the inclusion of information in respect of which would have been required in previous particulars if it had arisen when those particulars were prepared.

85(3) **[Payment of compensation]** Regulations under this section may provide for the payment, by the person or persons who in accordance with the regulations are treated as responsible for any scheme particulars, of compensation to any person who has become or agreed to become a participant in the scheme and suffered loss as a result of any untrue or misleading statement in the particulars or the omission from them of any matter required by the regulations to be included.

85(4) **[Liability apart from regulations]** Regulations under this section shall not affect any liability which any person may incur apart from the regulations.

RECOGNITION OF OVERSEAS SCHEMES

SEC. 86   Schemes constituted in other member States

86(1) **[Recognition on satisfying requirements]** Subject to subsection (2) below, a collective investment scheme constituted in a member State other than the United Kingdom is a recognised scheme if it satisfies such requirements as are prescribed for the purposes of this section.

Note
See the Financial Services (Schemes Constituted in Other Member States) Regulations 1989 (SI 1989/1585).

86(2) **[Notice re invitation by scheme operator]** Not less than two months before inviting persons in the United Kingdom to become participants in the scheme the operator of the scheme shall give written notice to the Secretary of State of his intention to do so, specifying the manner in which the invitation is to be made; and the scheme shall not be a recognised scheme by virtue of this section if within two months of receiving the notice the Secretary of State notifies—

(a)   the operator of the scheme; and

s. 86(2)

(b)　　the authorities of the State in question who are responsible for the authorisation of collective investment schemes,

that the manner in which the invitation is to be made does not comply with the law in force in the United Kingdom.

86(3)　[Requirements for sec. 86(2) notice] The notice to be given to the Secretary of State under subsection (2) above—

(a)　　shall be accompanied by a certificate from the authorities mentioned in subsection (2)(b) above to the effect that the scheme complies with the conditions necessary for it to enjoy the rights conferred by any relevant Community instrument;

(b)　　shall contain the address of a place in the United Kingdom for the service on the operator of notices or other documents required or authorised to be served on him under this Act; and

(c)　　shall contain or be accompanied by such other information and documents as may be prescribed.

86(4)　[Notice to contain reasons and sec. 86(5) rights] A notice given by the Secretary of State under subsection (2) above shall give the reasons for which he considers that the law in force in the United Kingdom will not be complied with and give particulars of the rights conferred by subsection (5) below.

86(5)　[Rights re representations] A person on whom a notice is served by the Secretary of State under subsection (2) above may, within twenty-one days of the date of service, make written representations to the Secretary of State and, if desired, oral representations to a person appointed for that purpose by the Secretary of State.

86(6)　[Withdrawal of notice after representations] The Secretary of State may in the light of any representations made in accordance with subsection (5) above withdraw his notice and in that event the scheme shall be a recognised scheme from the date on which the notice is withdrawn.

86(7)　[Application of sec. 48 rules] Rules under section 48 above shall not apply to investment business in respect of which the operator or trustee of a scheme recognised under this section is an authorised person by virtue of section 24 above except so far as they make provision as respects—

(a)　　procuring persons to become participants in the scheme and advising persons on the scheme and the exercise of the rights conferred by it;

(b)　　matters incidental to those mentioned in paragraph (a) above.

This subsection also applies to statements of principle under section 47A and codes of practice under section 63A so far as they relate to matters falling within the rule-making power in section 48.

86(8)　[Interpretation] For the purposes of this section a collective investment scheme is constituted in a member State if—

(a)　　it is constituted under the law of that State by a contract or under a trust and is managed by a body corporate incorporated under that law; or

(b)　　it takes the form of an open-ended investment company incorporated under that law.

86(9)　[Notice re cessation of recognition] If the operator of a scheme recognised under this section gives written notice to the Secretary of State stating that he desires the scheme no longer to be recognised under this section it shall cease to be so recognised when the notice is given.

s. 86(3)

SEC. 87 Schemes authorised in designated countries or territories

87(1) [Recognised scheme other than under sec. 86] Subject to subsection (3) below, a collective investment scheme which is not a recognised scheme by virtue of section 86 above but is managed in and authorised under the law of a country or territory outside the United Kingdom is a recognised scheme if—

(a) that country or territory is designated for the purposes of this section by an order made by the Secretary of State; and

(b) the scheme is of a class specified by the order.

87(2) [Requirements for Secretary of State's order] Subject to subsection (2A) below, the Secretary of State shall not make an order designating any country or territory for the purposes of this section unless he is satisfied that the law under which collective investment schemes of the class to be specified by the order are authorised and supervised in that country or territory affords to investors in the United Kingdom protection at least equivalent to that provided for them by this Chapter in the case of an authorised unit trust scheme.

87(2A) [Where requirements of s. 87(2) not needed] Nothing in subsection (2) above shall require the comparison set out in that subsection to be made where—

(a) the class of collective investment schemes to be specified in an order includes schemes having characteristics corresponding to those of an investment company with variable capital; and

(b) having regard to the characteristics of such schemes, it appears more appropriate to consider whether investors in the United Kingdom are afforded protection at least equivalent to that provided for them by the Open-Ended Investment Companies (Investment Companies with Variable Capital) Regulations 1996;

and, to the extent that the requirements of paragraph (b) above are met, the relevant comparison shall be between the protection afforded to investors in the United Kingdom by the law under which collective investment schemes of the class to be specified in the order are authorised and supervised in the country or territory concerned and the protection provided for such investors by the Open-Ended Investment Companies (Investment Companies with Variable Capital) Regulations 1996.

87(3) [Written notice by scheme operator] A scheme shall not be recognised by virtue of this section unless the operator of the scheme gives written notice to the Secretary of State that he wishes it to be recognised; and the scheme shall not be recognised if within such period from receiving the notice as may be prescribed the Secretary of State notifies the operator that the scheme is not to be recognised.

Note
See the Financial Services (Schemes Authorised in Designated Countries or Territories) (Notification) Regulations 1988 (SI 1988/1961) and the Financial Services (Schemes Authorised in Designated Countries or Territories) (Notification) Regulations 1989 (SI 1989/1584).

87(4) [Contents of sec. 87(3) notice] The notice given by the operator under subsection (3) above—

(a) shall contain the address of a place in the United Kingdom for the service on the operator of notices or other documents required or authorised to be served on him under this Act; and

(b) shall contain or be accompanied by such information and documents as may be prescribed.

s. 87(4)

87(5) [Effect of sec. 85] Section 85 above shall have effect in relation to a scheme recognised under this section as it has effect in relation to an authorised unit trust scheme, taking references to the manager as references to the operator and, in the case of an operator who is not an authorised person, references to publishing particulars as references to causing them to be published; and regulations made by virtue of this subsection may make provision whereby compliance with any requirements imposed by or under the law of a country or territory designated under this section is treated as compliance with any requirement of the regulations.

87(6) [Transitional provisions in order] An order under subsection (1) above may contain such transitional provisions as the Secretary of State thinks necessary or expedient and shall be subject to annulment in pursuance of a resolution of either House of Parliament.

Note
See the Financial Services Act 1986 (Investment Advertisements) (Exemptions) Order 1996 (SI 1996/1586); the Financial Services (Designated Countries and Territories) (Overseas Collective Investment Schemes) (Order 1988 (SI 1988/2015); the Financial Services (Designated Countries and Territories) (Overseas Collective Investment Schemes) (Guernsey) Order 1988 (SI 1988/2148); the Financial Services (Designated Countries and Territories) (Overseas Collective Investment Schemes) (Jersey) Order 1988 (SI 1988/2149); and the Financial Services (Designated Countries and Territories) (Overseas Collective Investment Schemes) Order 1988 (SI 1988/2284).

SEC. 88   Other overseas schemes

88(1) [Power of Secretary of State to make order] The Secretary of State may, on the application of the operator of a scheme which—

(a)   is managed in a country or territory outside the United Kingdom; but
(b)   does not satisfy the requirements mentioned in section 86(1) above and in relation to which there is no relevant order under section 87(1) above,

make an order declaring the scheme to be a recognised scheme if it appears to him that it affords adequate protection to the participants, makes adequate provision for the matters dealt with by regulations under section 81 above and satisfies the following provisions of this section.

88(2) [General requirements] The operator must be a body corporate or the scheme must take the form of an open-ended investment company.

88(3) [Requirements re operator] Subject to subsection (4) below, the operator and the trustee, if any, must be fit and proper persons to act as operator or, as the case may be, as trustee; and for that purpose the Secretary of State may take into account any matter relating to—

(a)   any person who is or will be employed by or associated with the operator or trustee for the purposes of the scheme;
(b)   any director or controller of the operator or trustee;
(c)   any other body corporate in the same group as the operator or trustee and any director or controller of any such other body.

88(4) [Non-application of sec. 88(3)] Subsection (3) above does not apply to an operator or trustee who is an authorised person and not prohibited from acting as operator or trustee, as the case may be, by or under rules under section 48 above, by or under the rules of any recognised self-regulating organisation of which he is a member or by any prohibition imposed under section 65 above.

88(5) [Authorised person as representative in UK] If the operator is not an authorised person he must have a representative in the United Kingdom who is an authorised person and has power to act generally for the operator and to accept service of notices and other documents on his behalf.

88(6) **[Name and purposes of scheme]** The name of the scheme must not be undesirable or misleading; and the purposes of the scheme must be reasonably capable of being successfully carried into effect.

88(7) **[Redemption of units by participants]** The participants must be entitled to have their units redeemed in accordance with the scheme at a price related to the net value of the property to which the units relate and determined in accordance with the scheme; but a scheme shall be treated as complying with this subsection if it requires the operator to ensure that a participant is able to sell his units on an investment exchange at a price not significantly different from that mentioned in this subsection.

88(8) **[Application of sec. 77(2)–(5)]** Subsections (2) to (5) of section 77 above shall apply also to an application under this section.

88(9) **[Application of sec. 82]** So much of section 82 above as applies to an alteration of the scheme shall apply also to a scheme recognised under this section, taking references to the manager as references to the operator and with the omission of the requirement relating to the solicitor's certificate; and if the operator or trustee of any such scheme is to be replaced the operator or, as the case may be, the trustee, or in either case the person who is to replace him, shall give at least one month's notice to the Secretary of State.

88(10) **[Effect of sec. 85]** Section 85 above shall have effect in relation to a scheme recognised under this section as it has effect in relation to an authorised unit trust scheme, taking references to the manager as references to the operator and, in the case of an operator who is not an authorised person, references to publishing particulars as references to causing them to be published.

Note
See the Financial Services Act 1986 (Investment Advertisements) (Exemptions) Order 1996 (SI 1996/1586).

SEC. 89   Refusal and revocation of recognition

89(1) **[Power of Secretary of State]** The Secretary of State may at any time direct that a scheme shall cease to be recognised by virtue of section 87 above or revoke an order under section 88 above if it appears to him—

(a)   that it is undesirable in the interests of the participants or potential participants in the United Kingdom that the scheme should continue to be recognised;

(b)   without prejudice to paragraph (a) above, that the operator or trustee of the scheme has contravened any provision of this Act or any rules or regulations made under it or, in purported compliance with any such provision, has furnished the Secretary of State with false, inaccurate or misleading information or has contravened any prohibition or requirement imposed under this Act; or

(c)   in the case of an order under section 88 that any of the requirements for the making of the order are no longer satisfied.

89(2) **[Matters for sec. 89(1)(a)]** For the purposes of subsection (1)(a) above the Secretary of State may take into account any matter relating to the scheme the operator or trustee, a director or controller of the operator or trustee or any person employed by or associated with the operator or trustee in connection with the scheme.

89(3) **[SRO member and sec. 89(1)(b)]** In the case of an operator or trustee who is a

s. 89(3)

member of a recognised self-regulating organisation the rules, prohibitions and requirements referred to in subsection (1)(b) above include the rules of that organisation and any prohibition or requirement imposed by virtue of those rules.

89(4) [Revocation at request of operator] The Secretary of State may give such a direction or revoke such an order as is mentioned in subsection (1) above at the request of the operator or trustee of the scheme; but he may refuse to do so if he considers that any matter concerning the scheme should be investigated as a preliminary to a decision on the question whether the direction should be given or the order revoked or that the direction or revocation would not be in the interests of the participants.

89(5) [Written notice to operator re sec. 87(3), 89(1)] Where the Secretary of State proposes—

(a)   to notify the operator of a scheme under section 87(3) above; or

·(b)   to give such a direction or to refuse to make or to revoke such an order as is mentioned in subsection (1) above,

he shall give the operator written notice of his intention to do so, stating the reasons for which he proposes to act and giving particulars of the rights conferred by subsection (6) below.

89(6) [Written representations to Secretary of State] A person on whom a notice is served under subsection (5) above may, within twenty-one days of the date of service, make written representations to the Secretary of State and, if desired, oral representations to a person appointed for that purpose by the Secretary of State.

89(7) [Secretary of State to have regard to representations] The Secretary of State shall have regard to any representations made in accordance with subsection (6) above in determining whether to notify the operator, give the direction or refuse to make or revoke the order, as the case may be.

SEC. 90   Facilities and information in the United Kingdom

90(1) [Regulations by Secretary of State] The Secretary of State may make regulations requiring operators of recognised schemes to maintain in the United Kingdom, or in such part or parts of it as may be specified in the regulations, such facilities as he thinks desirable in the interests of participants and as are specified in the regulations.

90(2) [Operator to include certain information] The Secretary of State may by notice in writing require the operator of any recognised scheme to include such explanatory information as is specified in the notice in any investment advertisement issued or caused to be issued by him in the United Kingdom in which the scheme is named.

POWERS OF INTERVENTION

SEC. 91   Directions

91(1) [Power of Secretary of State] If it appears to the Secretary of State—

(a)   that any of the requirements for the making of an order declaring a scheme to be an authorised unit trust scheme are no longer satisfied;

(b)   that the exercise of the power conferred by this subsection is desirable in the interest of participants or potential participants in the scheme; or

(c)   without prejudice to paragraph (b) above, that the manager or trustee of such a scheme has contravened any provision of this Act or any rules or regulations made under it or, in purported compliance with any such provision, has furnished the Secretary of State with false, inaccurate or misleading information or has contravened any prohibition or requirement imposed under this Act,

he may give a direction under subsection (2) below.

91(2) [Scope of directions] A direction under this subsection may—

(a)   require the manager of the scheme to cease the issue or redemption, or both the issue and redemption, of units under the scheme on a date specified in the direction until such further date as is specified in that or another direction;

(b)   require the manager and trustee of the scheme to wind it up by such date as is specified in the direction or, if no date is specified, as soon as practicable.

91(3) [Effect of revocation of order] The revocation of the order declaring an authorised unit trust scheme to be such a scheme shall not affect the operation of any direction under subsection (2) above which is then in force; and a direction may be given under that subsection in relation to a scheme in the case of which the order declaring it to be an authorised unit trust scheme has been revoked if a direction under that subsection was already in force at the time of revocation.

91(4) [Effect of sec. 60, 61, 62] Sections 60, 61 and 62 above shall have effect in relation to a contravention of a direction under subsection (2) above as they have effect in relation to any such contravention as is mentioned in those sections.

91(5) [Power to direct not to be scheme] If it appears to the Secretary of State—

(a)   that the exercise of the power conferred by this subsection is desirable in the interests of participants or potential participants in a scheme recognised under section 87 or 88 above who are in the United Kingdom;

(b)   without prejudice to paragraph (a) above, that the operator of such a scheme has contravened any provision of this Act or any rules or regulations made under it or, in purported compliance with any such provision, has furnished the Secretary of State with false, inaccurate or misleading information or has contravened any prohibition or requirement imposed under this Act; or

(c)   that any of the requirements for the recognition of a scheme under section 88 above are no longer satisfied,

he may direct that the scheme shall not be a recognised scheme for a specified period or until the occurrence of a specified event or until specified conditions are complied with.

91(6) [Matter for sec. 91(1)(b), (5)(a)] For the purposes of subsections (1)(b) and (5)(a) above the Secretary of State may take into account any matter relating to the scheme, the manager, operator or trustee, a director or controller of the manager, operator or trustee or any person employed by or associated with the manager, operator or trustee in connection with the scheme.

91(7) [Manager who is SRO member] In the case of a manager, operator or trustee who is a member of a recognised self-regulating organisation the rules, prohibitions and requirements referred to in subsections (1)(c) and (5)(b) above include the rules of that organisation and any prohibition or requirement imposed by virtue of those rules.

91(8) [Withdrawal or variation of directions] The Secretary of State may, either of his own motion or on the application of the manager, trustee or operator of the scheme concerned, withdraw or vary a direction given under this section if it appears to the Secretary of State that it is no longer necessary for the direction to take effect or continue in force or, as the case may be, that it should take effect or continue in force in a different form.

s. 91(8)

SEC. 92   Notice of directions

92(1) [Exercise of power to give direction] The power to give a direction under section 91 above in relation to a scheme shall be exercisable by written notice served by the Secretary of State on the manager and trustee or, as the case may be, on the operator of the scheme and any such notice shall take effect on such date as is specified in the notice.

92(2) [Written notice of refusal] If the Secretary of State refuses to withdraw or vary a direction on the application of the manager, trustee or operator of the scheme concerned he shall serve that person with a written notice of refusal.

92(3) [Notice to state reasons for refusal etc.] A notice giving a direction, or varying it otherwise than on the application of the manager, trustee or operator concerned, or refusing to withdraw or vary a direction on the application of such a person shall state the reasons for which the direction was given or varied or, as the case may be, why the application was refused.

92(4) [Public notice of sec. 91 direction] The Secretary of State may give public notice of a direction given by him under section 91 above and of any withdrawal or variation of such a direction; and any such notice may, if the Secretary of State thinks fit, include a statement of the reasons for which the direction was given, withdrawn or varied.

SEC. 93   Applications to the court

93(1) [Application by Secretary of State] In any case in which the Secretary of State has power to give a direction under section 91(2) above in relation to an authorised unit trust scheme or, by virtue of subsection (3) of that section, in relation to a scheme which has been such a scheme, he may apply to the court—

(a)   for an order removing the manager or trustee, or both the manager and trustee, of the scheme and replacing either or both of them with a person or persons nominated by him and appearing to him to satisfy the requirements of section 78 above; or

(b)   if it appears to the Secretary of State that no, or no suitable, person satisfying those requirements is available, for an order removing the manager or trustee, or both the manager and trustee, and appointing an authorised person to wind the scheme up.

Note
Concerning European investment firms, see the Investment Services Regulations 1995 (SI 1995/3275), reg. 32 and Sch. 7, para. 24.
Concerning European institutions, see the Banking Coordination (Second Council Directive) Regulations 1992 (SI 1992/3218), reg. 55 and Sch. 9, para. 26.

93(2) [Power of court] On an application under this section the court may make such order as it thinks fit; and the court may, on the application of the Secretary of State, rescind any such order as is mentioned in paragraph (b) of subsection (1) above and substitute such an order as is mentioned in paragraph (a) of that subsection.

93(3) [Written notice to manager of making of application] The Secretary of State shall give written notice of the making of an application under this section to the manager and trustee of the scheme concerned and take such steps as he considers appropriate for bringing the making of the application to the attention of the participants.

93(4) [Exercise of jurisdiction] The jurisdiction conferred by this section shall be exercisable by the High Court and the Court of Session.

93(5) [Non-application of sec. 83] Section 83 above shall not apply to a manager appointed by an order made on an application under subsection (1)(b) above.

SUPPLEMENTAL

SEC. 94   Investigations

94(1) [Power of Secretary of State to appoint inspectors] The Secretary of State may appoint one or more competent inspectors to investigate and report on—

(a)   the affairs of, or of the manager or trustee of, any authorised unit trust scheme;
(b)   the affairs of, or of the operator or trustee of, any recognised scheme so far as relating to activities carried on in the United Kingdom; or
(c)   the affairs of, or of the operator or trustee of, any other collective investment scheme,

if it appears to the Secretary of State that it is in the interests of the participants to do so or that the matter is of public concern.

94(2) [Powers of inspector] An inspector appointed under subsection (1) above to investigate the affairs of, or of the manager, trustee or operator of, any scheme may also, if he thinks it necessary for the purposes of that investigation, investigate the affairs of, or of the manager, trustee or operator of, any other such scheme as is mentioned in that subsection whose manager, trustee or operator is the same person as the manager, trustee or operator of the first mentioned scheme.

94(3) [Application of Companies Act 1985] Sections 434 to 436 of the Companies Act 1985 (production of documents and evidence to inspectors), shall apply in relation to an inspector appointed under this section as they apply to an inspector appointed under section 431 of that Act but with the modifications specified in subsection (4) below.

94(4) [Interpretation re sec. 94(1)–(3)] In the provisions applied by subsection (3) above for any reference to a company there shall be substituted a reference to the scheme under investigation by virtue of this section and any reference to an officer of the company shall include a reference to any director of the manager, trustee or operator of the scheme.

94(5) [Non-disclosure re legal professional privilege] A person shall not under this section be required to disclose any information or produce any document which he would be entitled to refuse to disclose or produce on grounds of legal professional privilege in proceedings in the High Court or on grounds of confidentiality as between client and professional legal adviser in proceedings in the Court of Session except that a lawyer may be required to furnish the name and address of his client.

94(6) [Where lien claimed] Where a person claims a lien on a document its production under this section shall be without prejudice to the lien.

94(7) [Disclosure re bankers] Nothing in this section requires a person (except as mentioned in subsection (7A) below) to disclose any information or produce any document in respect of which he owes an obligation of confidence by virtue of carrying on the business of banking unless—

(a)   the person to whom the obligation of confidence is owed consents to the disclosure or production, or
(b)   the making of the requirement was authorised by the Secretary of State.

94(7A) [Non-application of sec. 94(7)] Subsection (7) does not apply where the person owing the obligation of confidence or the person to whom it is owed is—

(a)   the manager, operator or trustee of the scheme under investigation, or
(b)   a manager, operator or trustee whose own affairs are under investigation.

s. 94(7A)

94(8) [Reports by inspector] An inspector appointed under this section may, and if so directed by the Secretary of State shall, make interim reports to the Secretary of State and on the conclusion of his investigation shall make a final report to him.

94(8A) [Where suggestion re criminal offence] If it appears to the Secretary of State that matters have come to light in the course of the inspectors' investigation which suggest that a criminal offence has been committed, and those matters have been referred to the appropriate prosecuting authority, he may direct the inspectors to take no further steps in the investigation or to take only such further steps as are specified in the direction.

94(8B) [Where sec. 94(8A) direction] Where an investigation is the subject of a direction under subsection (8A), the inspectors shall make a final report to the Secretary of State only where the Secretary of State directs them to do so.

94(9) [Form, publication of report] Any such report shall be written or printed as the Secretary of State may direct and the Secretary of State may, if he thinks fit—

(a)   furnish a copy, on request and on payment of the prescribed fee, to the manager, trustee or operator or any participant in a scheme under investigation or any other person whose conduct is referred to in the report; and

(b)   cause the report to be published.

94(10) [Order re expenses] A person who is convicted on a prosecution instituted as a result of an investigation under this section may in the same proceedings be ordered to pay the expenses of the investigation to such extent as may be specified in the order.

There shall be treated as expenses of the investigation, in particular, such reasonable sums as the Secretary of State may determine in respect of general staff costs and overheads.

SEC. 95   Contraventions

95(1) [Effect of contravention of Ch. VIII] A person who contravenes any provision of this Chapter, a manager or trustee of an authorised unit trust scheme who contravenes any regulations made under section 81 above and a person who contravenes any other regulations made under this Chapter shall be treated as having contravened rules made under Chapter V of this Part of this Act or, in the case of a person who is an authorised person by virtue of his membership of a recognised self-regulating organisation or certification by a recognised professional body, the rules of that organisation or body.

95(2) [Additional application of sec. 95(1)] Subsection (1) above applies also to any contravention by the operator of a recognised scheme of a requirement imposed under section 90(2) above.

95(3) [Action by virtue of sec. 47A] The disciplinary action which may be taken by virtue of section 47A(3) (failure to comply with statement of principle) includes—

(a)   the giving of a direction under section 91(2), and

(b)   the application by the Secretary of State for an order under section 93;

and subsection (6) of section 47A (duty of the Secretary of State as to exercise of powers) has effect accordingly.

Chapter IX — The Tribunal

SEC. 96   The Financial Services Tribunal

96(1) ["The Tribunal"] For the purposes of this Act shall be a Tribunal known as the Financial Services Tribunal (in this Act referred to as "the Tribunal").

96(2) [Panel of members] There shall be a panel of not less than ten persons to serve as members of the Tribunal when nominated to do so in accordance with subsection (3) below; and that panel shall consist of—

(a) persons with legal qualifications appointed by the Lord Chancellor after consultation with the Lord Advocate, including at least one person qualified in Scots law; and

(b) persons appointed by the Secretary of State who appear to him to be qualified by experience or otherwise to deal with the cases that may be referred to the Tribunal.

96(3) [Where case referred to Tribunal] Where a case is referred to the Tribunal the Secretary of State shall nominate three persons from the panel to serve as members of the Tribunal in respect of that case and nominate one of them to be chairman.

96(4) [Requirements re members] The person nominated to be chairman of the Tribunal in respect of any case shall be a person with legal qualifications and, so far as practicable, at least one of the other members shall be a person with recent practical experience in business relevant to the case.

96(5) [Where member unable to act] If while a case is being dealt with by the Tribunal one of the three persons serving as members in respect of that case becomes unable to act the case may, with the consent of the Secretary of State and of the person or persons at whose request the case was referred to the Tribunal, be dealt with by the other two members.

96(6) [Sch. 6] Schedule 6 to this Act shall have effect as respects the Tribunal and its proceedings.

SEC. 97   References to the Tribunal

97(1) [Requirement that Secretary of State make reference] Any person—

(a) on whom a notice is served under section 29, 34, 59(4), 60(2) or 70 above; or

(b) on whom a copy of a notice under section 29, 34, 60(2) or 70 above is served or on whom the Secretary of State considers that a copy of such a notice would have been served if it had been practicable to do so,

may within twenty-eight days of the date of service of the notice require the Secretary of State to refer the matter to which the notice relates to the Tribunal and, subject to the provisions of this section, the Secretary of State shall refer that matter accordingly.

97(2) [Where reference need not be made] The Secretary of State need not refer a matter to the Tribunal at the request of the person on whom a notice was served under section 29, 34, 59(4) or 60(2) above if within the period mentioned in subsection (1) above he—

(a) decides to grant the application or, as the case may be, decides not to withdraw or suspend the authorisation, give the direction or publish the statement to which the notice relates; and

(b) gives written notice of his decision to that person.

97(3) [Further non-reference situation] The Secretary of State need not refer a matter to the Tribunal at the request of the person on whom a notice is served under section 70 above if—

(a) that matter is the refusal of an application for the rescission or variation of a prohibition or requirement and within the period mentioned in subsection (1) above he—

(i)   decides to grant the application; and

(ii) gives written notice of his decision to that person; or

(b)   that matter is the imposition or variation of a prohibition or requirement, being a prohibition, requirement or variation which has not yet taken effect, and within the period mentioned in subsection (1) above and before the prohibition, requirement or variation takes effect he—

(i)   decides to rescind the prohibition or requirement or decides not to make the variation; and

(ii) gives written notice of his decision to that person.

97(4) [Where new notice after suspension or withdrawal] Where the notice served on a person under section 29 or 34 above—

(a)   proposed the withdrawal of an authorisation or the giving of a direction under section 33(1)(a) above; or

(b)   proposed the suspension of an authorisation or the giving of a direction under section 33(1)(b) above,

and at any time within the period mentioned in subsection (1) above the Secretary of State serves a new notice on that person in substitution for that previously served, then, if the substituted notice complies with subsection (5) below, subsection (1) above shall have effect in relation to the substituted notice instead of the original notice and as if the period there mentioned were twenty-eight days after the date of service of the original notice or fourteen days after the date of service of the substituted notice, whichever ends later.

97(5) [Notices under sec. 97(4)] A notice served in substitution for a notice within subsection (4)(a) above complies with this subsection if it proposes—

(a)   the suspension of an authorisation or the giving of a direction under section 33(1)(b) above; or

(b)   the exercise of the power conferred by section 60 above;

and a notice served in substitution for a notice within subsection (4)(b) above complies with this subsection if it proposes a less severe suspension or direction under section 33(1)(b) or the exercise of the power conferred by section 60 above.

97(6) [Effective date of notice] The reference of the imposition or variation of a prohibition or requirement under Chapter VI of this Part of this Act to the Tribunal shall not affect the date on which it comes into effect.

Note
See the Investment Services Regulations 1995 (SI 1995/3275), reg. 9(5) and Sch. 4, para. 2.

SEC. 98   Decisions on references by applicant or authorised person etc.

98(1) [Where case referred to Tribunal] Where a case is referred to the Tribunal at the request of a person within section 97(1)(a) above the Tribunal shall—

(a)   investigate the case; and

(b)   make a report to the Secretary of State stating what would in its opinion be the appropriate decision in the matter and the reasons for that opinion;

and it shall be the duty of the Secretary of State to decide the matter forthwith in accordance with the Tribunal's report.

98(2) [Where matter referred is refusal of application] Where the matter referred to the Tribunal is the refusal of an application the Tribunal may under this section report that the appropriate decision would be to grant or refuse the application or—

(a)   in the case of an application for the variation of a suspension, direction, consent, prohibition or requirement, to vary it in a specified manner;

(b)   in the case of an application for the rescission of a prohibition or requirement, to vary the prohibition or requirement in a specified manner.

98(3) [Where matter referred is other action of Secretary of State] Where the matter referred to the Tribunal is any action of the Secretary of State other than the refusal of an application the Tribunal may report that the appropriate decision would be—

(a)   to take or not to take the action taken or proposed to be taken by the Secretary of State or to take any other action that he could take under the provision in question; or

(b)   to take instead or in addition any action that he could take in the case of the person concerned under any one or more of the provisions mentioned in subsection (4) below other than that under which he was acting or proposing to act.

98(4) [Provisions in sec. 98(1)(b)] Those provisions are sections 28, 33 and 60 above and Chapter VI of this Part of this Act; and sections 29, 34, 60(2) and (3) and 70(2) and (4) above shall not apply to any action taken by the Secretary of State in accordance with the Tribunal's report.

98(5) [Copy of report, notice of decision] The Tribunal shall send a copy of its report under this section to the person at whose request the case was referred to it; and the Secretary of State shall serve him with a written notice of the decision made by him in accordance with the report.

Note
See the Investment Services Regulations 1995 (SI 1995/3275), reg. 9(5) and Sch. 4, para. 3.

SEC. 99   Decisions on references by third parties

99 Where a case is referred to the Tribunal at the request of a person within section 97(1)(b) above the Tribunal shall report to the Secretary of State whether the reasons stated in the notice in question which relate to that person are substantiated; and the Tribunal shall send a copy of the report to that person and to the person on whom the notice was served.

SEC. 100   Withdrawal of references

100(1) [Person may withdraw reference] A person who has required a case to be referred to the Tribunal may at any time before the conclusion of the proceedings before the Tribunal withdraw the reference.

100(2) [Secretary of State may withdraw reference] The Secretary of State may at any such time withdraw any reference made at the request of a person on whom a notice was served under any of the provisions mentioned in subsection (1)(a) of section 97 above if he—

(a)   decides as mentioned in subsection (2)(a) or (3)(a)(i) or (b)(i) of that section; and

(b)   gives such a notice as is mentioned in subsection (2)(b) or (3)(a)(ii) or (b)(ii) of that section;

but a reference shall not be withdrawn by virtue of such a decision and notice as are mentioned in paragraph (b) of subsection (3) unless the decision is made and the notice is given before the prohibition, requirement or variation has taken effect.

Note
See note after s. 100(5).

100(3) [Where case withdrawn] Where a case is withdrawn from the Tribunal under this section the Tribunal shall not further investigate the case or make a report under section 98 or 99 above; but where the reference is withdrawn otherwise than by the Secretary of State he may require the Tribunal to make a report to him on the results of its investigation up to the time when the reference was withdrawn.

100(4) [Where withdrawal by one of two or more persons] Where two or more persons have required a case to be referred to the Tribunal the withdrawal of the reference by one or more of them shall not affect the functions of the Tribunal as respects the case so far as relating to a person who has not withdrawn the reference.

100(5) [Where withdrawal by persons served with sec. 29, 34, 60 notice] Where a person on whom a notice was served under section 29, 34 or 60 above withdraws a case from the Tribunal subsection (5) of each of those sections shall apply to him as if he had not required the case to be referred.

Note
See the Investment Services Regulations 1995 (SI 1995/3275), reg. 9(5) and Sch. 4, para. 4.

SEC. 101   Reports

101(1) [Exclusion re affairs of particular person] In preparing its report on any case the Tribunal shall have regard to the need to exclude, so far as practicable, any matter which relates to the affairs of a particular person (not being a person who required or could have required the case to be referred to the Tribunal) where the publication of that matter would or might, in the opinion of the Tribunal, seriously and prejudicially affect the interests of that person.

101(2) [Publication and sale of reports] The Secretary of State may, in such cases as he thinks fit, publish the report of the Tribunal and offer copies of any such report for sale.

101(3) [Copies to interested persons] The Secretary of State may, on request and on payment of the prescribed fee, supply a copy of a report of the Tribunal to any person whose conduct is referred to in the report or whose interests as a client or creditor are affected by the conduct of a person to whom the proceedings before the Tribunal related.

101(4) [Parts of report omitted from publication] If the Secretary of State is of opinion that there is good reason for not disclosing any part of a report he may cause that part to be omitted from the report as published under subsection (2) or from the copy of it supplied under subsection (3) above.

101(5) [Admissibility as evidence] A copy of a report of the Tribunal endorsed with a certificate signed by or on behalf of the Secretary of State stating that it is a true copy shall be admissible as evidence of the opinion of the Tribunal as to any matter referred to in the report; and a certificate purporting to be signed as aforesaid shall be deemed to have been duly signed unless the contrary is shown.

Chapter X — Information

SEC. 102   Register of authorised persons and recognised organisations etc.

102(1) [Secretary of State to keep register] The Secretary of State shall keep a register containing an entry in respect of—

(a)   each person who is an authorised person by virtue of an authorisation granted by the Secretary of State;
(b)   each other person who appears to him to be an authorised person by virtue of any provision of this Part of this Act;
(c)   each recognised self-regulating organisation, recognised professional body, recognised investment exchange and recognised clearing house;
(d)   each authorised unit trust scheme and recognised scheme;
(e)   each person in respect of whom a direction under section 59 above is in force.

102(2) [Entry re each authorised person] The entry in respect of each authorised person shall consist of—

(a)   a statement of the provision by virtue of which he is an authorised person;
(b)   in the case of a person who is an authorised person by virtue of membership of a recognised self-regulating organisation or certification by a recognised professional body, the name and address of the organisation or body;
(bb)   in the case of an investment company with variable capital which is an authorised person by virtue of section 24A above, the name of the company, the address of the company's head office and the names and addresses of the directors and depositary of the company;
(c)   in the case of a person who is an authorised person by virtue of section 25 or 31 above, information as to the services which that person holds himself out as able to provide;
(d)   in the case of a person who is an authorised person by virtue of section 31 above, the address notified to the Secretary of State under section 32 above;
(e)   in the case of a person who is an authorised person by virtue of any provision other than section 31 above, the date on which he became an authorised person by virtue of that provision; and
(f)   such other information as the Secretary of State may determine.

102(3) [Entry re sec. 102(1)(c) organisations etc.] The entry in respect of each such organisation, body, exchange or clearing house as is mentioned in subsection (1)(c) above shall consist of its name and address and such other information as the Secretary of State may determine.

102(4) [Entry re sec. 102(1)(d) schemes] The entry in respect of each such scheme as is mentioned in subsection (1)(d) above shall consist of its name and, in the case of an authorised unit trust scheme, the name and address of the manager and trustee and, in the case of a recognised scheme, the name and address of the operator and of any representative of the operator in the United Kingdom and, in either case, such other information as the Secretary of State may determine.

102(5) [Entry re sec. 102(1)(e) persons] The entry in respect of each such person as is mentioned in subsection (1)(e) above shall include particulars of any consent for that person's employment given by the Secretary of State.

102(6) [Where sec. 102 (1)(a), (b) person no longer authorised] Where it appears to the Secretary of State that any person in respect of whom there is an entry in the register by virtue of subsection (1) (a), (b) or (bb) above has ceased to be an authorised person (whether by death, by withdrawal or other cessation of his authorisation, as a result of his ceasing to be a member of a recognised self-regulating organisation or otherwise) the Secretary of State shall make a note to that effect in the entry together with the reason why the person in question is no longer an authorised person.

s. 102(6)

102(7) [Note re certain events] Where—

(a)   an organisation, body, exchange or clearing house in respect of which there is an entry in the register by virtue of paragraph (c) of subsection (1) above has ceased to be recognised or ceased to exist;

(b)   an authorised unit trust scheme or recognised scheme in respect of which there is an entry in the register by virtue of paragraph (d) of that subsection has ceased to be authorised or recognised; or

(c)   the direction applying to a person in respect of whom there is an entry in the register by virtue of paragraph (e) of that subsection has ceased to have effect, the Secretary of State shall make a note to that effect in the entry.

102(8) [Removal of sec. 102(6), (7) note] An entry in respect of which a note is made under subsection (6) or (7) above may be removed from the register at the end of such period as the Secretary of State thinks appropriate.

Note
Concerning UK authorised investment firms which are authorised persons and European investment firms, see the Investment Services Regulations 1995 (SI 1995/3275), reg. 1, 28, 32 and Sch. 7, para. 25.
Concerning European institutions, see the Banking Coordination (Second Council Directive) Regulations 1992 (SI 1992/3218), reg. 55 and Sch. 9, para. 27.

SEC. 103   Inspection of register

103(1) [Inspection and publication of information] The information contained in the entries included in the register otherwise than by virtue of section 102(1)(e) above shall be open to inspection; and the Secretary of State may publish the information contained in those entries in any form he thinks appropriate and may offer copies of any such information for sale.

103(2) [Inspection re sec. 102(1)(e) entries] A person shall be entitled to ascertain whether there is an entry in the register by virtue of subsection (1)(e) of section 102 above (not being an entry in respect of which there is a note under subsection (7) of that section) in respect of a particular person specified by him and, if there is such an entry, to inspect it.

103(3) [Limit on inspection re sec. 102(1)(e) entries] Except as provided by subsection (2) above the information contained in the register by virtue of section 102(1)(e) above shall not be open to inspection by any person unless he satisfies the Secretary of State that he has a good reason for seeking the information.

103(4) [Limit on information available by sec. 103(3)] A person to whom information is made available by the Secretary of State under subsection (3) above shall not, without the consent of the Secretary of State or of the person to whom the information relates, make use of it except for the purpose for which it was made available.

103(5) [Details re inspection] Information which by virtue of this section is open to inspection shall be open to inspection free of charge but only at such times and places as the Secretary of State may appoint; and a person entitled to inspect any information may obtain a certified copy of it from the Secretary of State on payment of the prescribed fee.

103(6) [Form of register] The register may be kept by the Secretary of State in such form as he thinks appropriate with a view to facilitating inspection of the information which it contains.

SEC. 104   Power to call for information

104(1) [Information from sec. 22, 24, 25, 31 persons] The Secretary of State may by notice in writing require a person who is authorised to carry on investment business by virtue of section 22, 24, 25 or 31 above to furnish him with such information as he may reasonably require for the exercise of his functions under this Act.

Note
Concerning European investment firms, see the Investment Services Regulations 1995 (SI 1995/3275), reg. 32 and Sch. 7, para. 26.

104(2) [Information from recognised bodies etc.] The Secretary of State may by notice in writing require a recognised self-regulating organisation, recognised professional body, recognised investment exchange or recognised clearing house to furnish him with such information as he may reasonably require for the exercise of his functions under this Act.

104(3) [Time, verification re information] The Secretary of State may require any information which he requires under this section to be furnished within such reasonable time and verified in such manner as he may specify.

104(4) [Effect of sec. 60, 61, 62] Sections 60, 61 and 62 above shall have effect in relation to a contravention of a requirement imposed under subsection (1) above as they have effect in relation to a contravention of the provisions to which those sections apply.

Note
Concerning European institutions, see the Banking Coordination (Second Council Directive) Regulations 1992 (SI 1992/3218), reg. 55 and Sch. 9, para. 28.
Regarding application to EC companies, see the Insurance Companies (Third Insurance Directives) Regulations 1994 (SI 1994/1696), reg. 1, 60(1).

SEC. 105   Investigation powers

105(1) [Where Secretary of State's powers to be exercised] The powers of the Secretary of State under this section shall be exercisable in any case in which it appears to him that there is good reason to do so for the purpose of investigating the affairs, or any aspect of the affairs, of any person so far as relevant to any investment business which he is or was carrying on or appears to the Secretary of State to be or to have been carrying on.

105(2) [Limit on exercise of powers] Those powers shall not be exercisable for the purpose of investigating the affairs of any exempted person unless he is an appointed representative or the investigation is in respect of investment business in respect of which he is not an exempted person and shall not be exercisable for the purpose of investigating the affairs of a member of a recognised self-regulating organisation or a person certified by a recognised professional body in respect of investment business in the carrying on of which he is subject to its rules unless—

(a)   that organisation or body has requested the Secretary of State to investigate those affairs; or

(b)   it appears to him that the organisation or body is unable or unwilling to investigate them in a satisfactory manner.

105(3) [Power re attendance before Secretary of State] The Secretary of State may require the person whose affairs are to be investigated ("the person under investigation") or any connected person to attend before the Secretary of State at a specified time and place and answer questions or otherwise furnish information with respect to any matter relevant to the investigation.

105(4) [Power re production of documents] The Secretary of State may require the person under investigation or any other person to produce at a specified time and place any specified documents which appear to the Secretary of State to relate to any matter relevant to the investigation; and—

(a)   if any such documents are produced, the Secretary of State may take copies or extracts from them or require the person producing them or any connected person to provide an explanation of any of them;

(b)   if any such documents are not produced, the Secretary of State may require the person who was required to produce them to state, to the best of his knowledge and belief, where they are.

105(5) [Statement admissible in evidence] A statement by person in compliance with a requirement imposed by virtue of this section may be used in evidence against him.

105(6) [Legal professional privilege, confidentiality] A person shall not under this section be required to disclose any information or produce any document which he would be entitled to refuse to disclose or produce on grounds of legal professional privilege in proceedings in the High Court or on grounds of confidentiality as between client and professional legal adviser in proceedings in the Court of Session except that a lawyer may be required to furnish the name and address of his client.

105(7) (Omitted and repealed by Companies Act 1989, sec. 73(1), (2), 212 and Sch. 24 as from 21 February 1990.)

105(8) [Where lien claimed] Where a person claims a lien on a document its production under this section shall be without prejudice to the lien.

105(9) [Definitions] In this section—
"connected person", in relation to any other person means—

(a)   any person who is or was that other person's partner, employee, agent, appointed representative, banker, auditor or solicitor; and

(b)   where the other person is a body corporate, any person who is or was a director, secretary or controller of that body corporate or of another body corporate of which it is or was a subsidiary; and

(c)   where the other person is an unincorporated association, any person who is or was a member of the governing body or an officer or controller of the association; and

(d)   where the other person is an appointed representative, any person who is or was his principal; and

(e)   where the other person is the person under investigation (being a body corporate), any related company of that body corporate and any person who is a connected person in relation to that company;

"documents" includes information recorded in any form and, in relation to information recorded otherwise than in legible form, the power to require its production includes power to require the production of a copy of the information in legible form;

"related company", in relation to a person under investigation (being a body corporate), means any other body corporate which is or at any material time was—

(a)   a holding company or subsidiary of the person under investigation;

(b)   a subsidiary of a holding company of that person; or

(c)   a holding company of a subsidiary of that person,

and whose affairs it is in the Secretary of State's opinion necessary to investigate for the purpose of investigating the affairs of that person.

105(10) [Offence, penalty] Any person who without reasonable excuse fails to comply with a requirement imposed on him under this section shall be guilty of an offence and liable on summary conviction to imprisonment for a term not exceeding six months or to a fine not exceeding the fifth level on the standard scale or to both.

s. 105(5)

105(11) [Order re expenses] A person who is convicted on a prosecution instituted as a result of an investigation under this section may in the same proceedings be ordered to pay the expenses of the investigation to such extent as may be specified in the order. There shall be treated as expenses of the investigation, in particular, such reasonable sums as the Secretary of State may determine in respect of general staff costs and overheads.

Note
See notes after s. 106.

SEC. 106   Exercise of investigation powers by officer etc.

106(1) [Secretary of State may authorise officer] The Secretary of State may authorise any officer of his or any other competent person to exercise on his behalf all or any of the powers conferred by section 105 above but no such authority shall be granted except for the purpose of investigating the affairs, or any aspects of the affairs, of a person specified in the authority.

106(2) [Compliance, production of evidence re authority] No person shall be bound to comply with any requirement imposed by a person exercising powers by virtue of an authority granted under this section unless he has, if required to do so, produced evidence of his authority.

106(2A) [Disclosure by bankers] A person shall not by virtue of an authority under this section be required to disclose any information or produce any documents in respect of which he owes an obligation of confidence by virtue of carrying on the business of banking unless—

(a)   he is the person under investigation or a related company,
(b)   the person to whom the obligation of confidence is owed is the person under investigation or a related company,
(c)   the person to whom the obligation of confidence is owed consents to the disclosure or production, or
(d)   the imposing on him of a requirement with respect to such information or documents has been specifically authorised by the Secretary of State.

In this subsection "documents", "person under investigation" and "related company" have the same meaning as in section 105.

106(3) [Report by officer re exercise of powers etc.] Where the Secretary of State authorises a person other than one of his officers to exercise any powers by virtue of this section that person shall make a report to the Secretary of State in such manner as he may require on the exercise of those powers and the results of exercising them.

Note
Concerning European institutions, see the Banking Coordination (Second Council Directive) Regulations 1992(SI 1992/3218), reg. 55 and Sch. 9, para. 29.
For application of s. 105 and 106 to a listed person see the Financial Markets and Insolvency (Money Market) Regulations 1995 (SI 1995/2049), reg. 1, 6, 16, 17.
Concerning European investment firms, see the Investment Services Regulations 1995 (SI 1995/3275), reg. 32 and Sch. 7, para. 27.

Chapter XI — Auditors
SEC. 107   Appointment of auditors

107(1) [Power of Secretary of State to make rules] The Secretary of State may make rules requiring—

(a)   a person authorised to carry on investment business by virtue of section 25 or 31 above, or

(b)   a member of a recognised self-regulating organisation carrying on investment business in the carrying on of which he is subject to the rules of the organisation,

and who, apart from the rules, is not required by or under any enactment to appoint an auditor, to appoint as an auditor a person satisfying such conditions as to qualifications and otherwise as may be specified in or imposed under the rules.

Note
Regarding application to EC companies, see the Insurance Companies (Third Insurance Directives) Regulations 1994 (SI 1994/1696), reg. 1, 60(2).

107(2) [Extent of rules] Rules under this section may make provision—

(a)   specifying the manner in which and the time within which an auditor is to be appointed;

(b)   requiring the Secretary of State to be notified of any such appointment and enabling the Secretary of State to make an appointment if no appointment is made or notified as required by the rules;

(c)   with respect to the remuneration of an auditor appointed under the rules;

(d)   with respect to the term of office, removal and resignation of any such auditor;

(e)   requiring any such auditor who is removed, resigns or is not reappointed to notify the Secretary of State whether there are any circumstances connected with his ceasing to hold office which he considers should be brought to the Secretary of State's attention.

107(3) [Duty of auditor] An auditor appointed under the rules shall in accordance with the rules examine and report on the accounts of the authorised person in question and shall for that purpose have such duties and powers as are specified in the rules.

Note
Concerning European investment firms, see the Investment Services Regulations 1995 (SI 1995/3275), reg. 32 and Sch. 7, para. 28.
Concerning European institutions, see the Banking Coordination (Second Council Directive) Regulations 1992 (SI 1992/3218), reg. 55 and Sch. 9, para. 30.

107(4) [Application to SRO members] In its application to members of recognised self-regulating organisations, this section has effect subject to section 107A below.

Note
See note after s. 110.

SEC. 107A   Application of audit rules to members of self-regulating organisations

107A(1) [Power of Secretary of State to make rules] The Secretary of State may in rules under section 107 designate provisions which apply, to such extent as may be specified, to a member of a recognised self-regulating organisation in respect of investment business in the carrying on of which he is subject to the rules of the organisation.

107A(2) [Extent of rules] It may be provided that the designated rules have effect, generally or to such extent as may be specified, subject to the rules of the organisation.

107A(3) [Contravention by SRO member] A member of a recognised self-regulating organisation who contravenes a rule applying to him by virtue of that section shall be treated as having contravened the rules of the organisation.

s. 107(2)

107A(4) [Application to SRO member] Except as mentioned above, rules made under section 107 do not apply to members of recognised self-regulating organisations in respect of investment business in the carrying on of which they are subject to the rules of the organisation.

107A(5) [Power of SRO to modify or dispense from rule] A recognised self-regulating organisation may on the application of a member of the organisation—

(a)   modify a rule designated under this section so as to adapt it to his circumstances or to any particular kind of business carried on by him, or

(b)   dispense him from compliance with any such rule, generally or in relation to any particular kind of business carried on by him.

107A(6) [Condition for sec. 107A(5) power] The powers conferred by subsection (5) shall not be exercised unless it appears to the organisation—

(a)   that compliance with the rule in question would be unduly burdensome for the applicant having regard to the benefit which compliance would confer on investors, and

(b)   that the exercise of those powers will not result in any undue risk to investors.

107A(7) [Exercise of sec. 107A(5) power may be conditional] The powers conferred by subsection (5) may be exercised unconditionally or subject to conditions; and subsection (3) applies in the case of a contravention of a condition as in the case of contravention of a designated rule.

107A(8) [Monitoring and enforcement of compliance] The reference in paragraph 4(1) of Schedule 2 (requirements for recognition of self-regulating organisations) to monitoring and enforcement of compliance with rules includes monitoring and enforcement of compliance with conditions imposed by the organisation under subsection (7).

Note
For transfer of the Secretary of State's functions under s. 107A see SI 1990/354 (C.12), art. 4(5).

SEC. 108   Power to require second audit

108(1) [Power of Secretary of State] If in any case it appears to the Secretary of State that there is good reason to do so he may direct any person who is authorised to carry on investment business by virtue of section 24A, 25 or 31 above to submit for further examination by a person approved by the Secretary of State—

(a)   any accounts on which that person's auditor has reported or any information given under section 52 or 104 above which has been verified by that auditor; or

(b)   such matters contained in any such accounts or information as are specified in the direction;

and the person making the further examination shall report his conclusions to the Secretary of State.

108(2) [Expense of further examination and report] Any further examination and report required by a direction under this section shall be at the expense of the authorised person concerned and shall be carried out and made within such time as is specified in the direction or within such further time as the Secretary of State may allow.

108(3) [Power of examiner] The person carrying out an examination under this section shall have all the powers that were available to the auditor; and it shall be the duty of the auditor to afford him all such assistance as he may require.

108(4) [Report being made available] Where a report made under this section relates to accounts which under any enactment are required to be sent to or made available for inspection by any person or to be delivered for registration, the report, or any part of it (or a note that such a report has been made) may be similarly sent, made available or delivered by the Secretary of State.

Note
See note after s. 110.

SEC. 109   Communication by auditor with supervisory authorities

109(1) [Communication with Secretary of State] No duty to which an auditor of an authorised person may be subject shall be regarded as contravened by reason of his communicating in good faith to the Secretary of State, whether or not in response to a request from him, any information or opinion on a matter of which the auditor has become aware in his capacity as auditor of that person and which is relevant to any functions of the Secretary of State under this Act.

Note
Concerning European investment firms, see the Investment Services Regulations 1995 (SI 1995/3275), reg. 32 and Sch. 7, para. 29.
Concerning European institutions, see the Banking Coordination (Second Council Directive) Regulations 1992 (SI 1992/3218), reg. 55 and Sch. 9, para. 31.

109(2) [Power of Secretary of State to make rules] If it appears to the Secretary of State that any auditor or class of auditor to whom subsection (1) above applies is not subject to satisfactory rules made or guidance issued by a professional body specifying circumstances in which matters are to be communicated to the Secretary of State as mentioned in that subsection the Secretary of State may himself make rules applying to that auditor or that class of auditor and specifying such circumstances; and it shall be the duty of an auditor to whom the rules made by the Secretary of State apply to communicate a matter to the Secretary of State in the circumstances specified by the rules.

Note
See the Auditors (Financial Services Act 1986) Rules 1994 (SI 1994/526).

109(3) [Matters communicated] The matters to be communicated to the Secretary of State in accordance with any such rules or guidance may include matters relating to persons other than the authorised person.

109(4) [Approval etc. of sec. 109(2) rules] No such rules as are mentioned in subsection (2) above shall be made by the Secretary of State unless a draft of them has been laid before and approved by a resolution of each House of Parliament.

109(5) [Application of section] This section applies to—

(a) the communication by an auditor to a recognised self-regulating organisation or recognised professional body of matters relevant to its function of determining whether a person is a fit and proper person to carry on investment business; and
(b) the communication to such an organisation or body or any other authority or person of matters relevant to its or his function of determining whether a person is complying with the rules applicable to his conduct of investment business,

as it applies to the communication to the Secretary of State of matters relevant to his functions under this Act.

Note
For further effect of s. 109 see the Financial Institutions (Prudential Supervision) Regulations 1996 (SI 1996/1669), reg. 10.

SEC. 110   Overseas business

110(1) [**Auditor of overseas person**] A person incorporated or having his head office outside the United Kingdom who is authorised as mentioned in subsection (1) of section 107 above may, whether or not he is required to appoint an auditor apart from the rules made under that subsection, appoint an auditor in accordance with those rules in respect of the investment business carried on by him in the United Kingdom and in that event that person shall be treated for the purposes of this Chapter as the auditor of that person.

110(2) [**Conditions as to qualifications**] In the case of a person to be appointed as auditor of a person incorporated or having his head office outside the United Kingdom the conditions as to qualifications imposed by or under the rules made under that section may be regarded as satisfied by qualifications obtained outside the United Kingdom which appear to the Secretary of State to be equivalent.

110(3) [**Conditions to be fit and proper person under sec. 25**] A person incorporated or having his head office outside the United Kingdom shall not be regarded for the purposes of section 25 above as a fit and proper person to carry on investment business unless—

(a)   he has appointed an auditor in accordance with rules made under section 107 above in respect of the investment business carried on by him in the United Kingdom; or

(b)   he has an auditor having qualifications, powers and duties appearing to the Secretary of State to be equivalent to those applying to an auditor appointed in accordance with those rules,

and, in either case, the auditor is able and willing to communicate with the Secretary of State and other bodies and persons as mentioned in section 109 above.

Note
Concerning European investment firms, see the Investment Services Regulations 1995 (SI 1995/3275), reg. 32 and Sch. 7, para. 30.
Concerning European institutions, see the Banking Coordination (Second Council Directive) Regulations 1992 (SI 1992/3218), reg. 55 and Sch. 9, para. 32.

SEC. 111   Offences and enforcement

111(1) [**Offence, penalty**] Any authorised person and any officer, controller or manager of an authorised person, who knowingly or recklessly furnishes an auditor appointed under the rules made under section 107 or a person carrying out an examination under section 108 above with information which the auditor or that person requires or is entitled to require and which is false or misleading in a material particular shall be guilty of an offence and liable—

(a)   on conviction on indictment, to imprisonment for a term not exceeding two years or to a fine or to both;

(b)   on summary conviction, to imprisonment for a term not exceeding six months or to a fine not exceeding the statutory maximum or to both.

111(2) [**Enforcement of auditor's duty**] The duty of an auditor under section 108(3) above shall be enforceable by mandamus or, in Scotland, by an order for specific performance under section 91 of the Court of Session Act 1868.

111(3) [**Secretary of State's disqualification power**] If it appears to the Secretary of State that an auditor has failed to comply with the duty mentioned in section 109(2) above, the Secretary of State may disqualify him from being the auditor of an authorised person or any class of authorised person; but the Secretary of State may remove any disqualification imposed under this subsection if satisfied that the person in question will in future comply with that duty.

111(4) **[Appointment of disqualified person]** An authorised person shall not appoint as auditor a person disqualified under subsection (3) above; and a person who is an authorised person by virtue of membership of a recognised self-regulating organisation or certification by a recognised professional body who contravenes this subsection shall be treated as having contravened the rules of the organisation or body.

Chapter XII — Fees
SEC. 112   Application fees

112(1) **[Applicant to pay required fees]** An applicant for a recognition order under Chapter III or IV of this Part of this Act shall pay such fees in respect of his application as may be required by a scheme made and published by the Secretary of State; and no application for such an order shall be regarded as duly made unless this subsection is complied with.

112(2) **[A scheme under sec. 112(1)]** A scheme made for the purposes of subsection (1) above shall specify the time when the fees are to be paid and may—

(a) provide for the determination of the fees in accordance with a specified scale or other specified factors;

(b) provide for the return or abatement of any fees where an application is refused or withdrawn; and

(c) make different provision for different cases.

112(3) **[Date re sec. 112(1) scheme]** Any scheme made for the purposes of subsection (1) above shall come into operation on such date as is specified in the scheme (not being earlier than the day on which it is first published) and shall apply to applications made on or after the date on which it comes into operation.

112(4) **[Power in sec. 112(1) includes variation, revocation]** The power to make a scheme for the purposes of subsection (1) above includes power to vary or revoke a previous scheme made under those provisions.

112(5) **[Fee with application and notices]** Every application under section 26, 77 or 88 above shall be accompanied by the prescribed fee and every notice given to the Secretary of State under section 32, 86(2) or 87(3) above shall be accompanied by such fee as may be prescribed; and no such application or notice shall be regarded as duly made or given unless this subsection is complied with.

SEC. 113   Periodical fees

113(1) **[Recognised bodies to pay]** Every recognised self-regulating organisation, recognised professional body, recognised investment exchange and recognised clearing house shall pay such periodical fees to the Secretary of State as may be prescribed.

113(2) **[Body authorised under sec. 22]** So long as a body is authorised under section 22 above to carry on insurance business which is investment business it shall pay to the Secretary of State such periodical fees as may be prescribed.

113(3) **[Society authorised under sec. 23]** So long as a friendly society is authorised under section 23 above to carry on investment business it shall pay to the Friendly Societies Commission such periodical fees as the Commission may by regulations specify.

113(4) [Person authorised under sec. 25, 31] A person who is an authorised person by virtue of section 25 or 31 above shall pay such periodical fees to the Secretary of State as may be prescribed.

113(5) [If person fails to pay sec. 113(4) fee] If a person fails to pay any fee which is payable by him under subsection (4) above the Secretary of State may serve on him a written notice requiring him to pay the fee within twenty-eight days of service of the notice; and if the fee is not paid within that period that person's authorisation shall cease to have effect unless the Secretary of State otherwise directs.

113(6) [Sec. 113(5) direction may be retrospective] A direction under subsection (5) above may be given so as to have retrospective effect; and the Secretary of State may under that subsection direct that the person in question shall continue to be an authorised person only for such period as is specified in the direction.

113(7) [Fees as debts due to Crown] Subsection (5) above is without prejudice to the recovery of any fee as a debt due to the Crown.

113(8) [Manager, operator to pay periodical fees] The manager of each authorised unit trust scheme and the operator of each recognised scheme shall pay such periodical fees to the Secretary of State as may be prescribed.

Note

Concerning European investment firms, see the Investment Services Regulations 1995 (SI 1995/3275), reg. 32 and Sch. 7, para. 31.
See the Financial Services Act 1986 (Overseas Investment Exchanges and Overseas Clearing Houses) (Periodical Fees) Regulations 1993 (SI 1993/954).
Concerning European institutions, see the Banking Coordination (Second Council Directive) Regulations 1992 (SI 1992/3218), reg. 55 and Sch. 9, para. 33.

Chapter XIII — Transfer of Functions to Designated Agency

SEC. 114   Power to transfer functions to designated agency

114(1) [Power of Secretary of State] If it appears to the Secretary of State—

(a)   that a body corporate has been established which is able and willing to discharge all or any of the functions to which this section applies; and

(b)   that the requirements of Schedule 7 to this Act are satisfied in the case of that body,

he may, subject to the provisions of this section and Chapter XIV of this Part of this Act, make an order transferring all or any of those functions to that body.

114(2) [The Securities and Investments Board Limited] The body to which functions are transferred by the first order made under subsection (1) above shall be the body known as The Securities and Investments Board Limited if it appears to the Secretary of State that it is able and willing to discharge them, that the requirements mentioned in paragraph (b) of that subsection are satisfied in the case of that body and that he is not precluded from making the order by the subsequent provisions of this section or Chapter XIV of this Part of this Act.

114(3) ["A delegation order", "a designated agency"] An order under subsection (1) above is in this Act referred to as "a delegation order" and a body to which functions are transferred by a delegation order is in this Act referred to as "a designated agency".

114(4) [Application of section] Subject to subsections (5) and (6) below, this section applies to any functions of the Secretary of State under Chapters II to XII of this Part of this Act and to his functions under paragraphs 23 and 25(2) of Schedule 1 and paragraphs 4, 5 and 15 of Schedule 15 to this Act.

s. 114(4)

114(5) [Non-application of section] This section does not apply to any functions under—

(a)   section 31(4);
(b)   section 46;
(c)   section 48(8);
(d)   section 58(3);
(dd)   section 62A;
(e)   section 86(1) or 87(1);
(f)   section 96;
(g)   section 109(2) above.

114(6) [Overseas exchanges etc.] This section does not apply to the making or revocation of a recognition order in respect of an overseas investment exchange or overseas clearing house or the making of an application to the court under section 12 above in respect of any such exchange or clearing house.

114(7) [Transfer of functions] Any function may be transferred by a delegation order either wholly or in part.

114(8) [Functions under sec. 6, 61, 72, 94, 105, 106] In the case of a function under section 6 or 72 or a function under section 61 which is exercisable by virtue of subsection (1)(a)(ii) or (iii) of that section, the transfer may be subject to a reservation that it is to be exercisable by the Secretary of State concurrently with the designated agency and any transfer of a function under section 94, 105 or 106 shall be subject to such a reservation.

114(9) [Conditions for transfer] The Secretary of State shall not make a delegation order transferring any legislative functions unless—

(a)   the agency has furnished him with a copy of the instruments it proposes to issue or make in the exercise of those functions, and
(b)   he is satisfied that those instruments will afford investors an adequate level of protection and, in the case of such provisions as are mentioned in Schedule 8 to this Act, comply with the principles set out in that Schedule.

In this subsection "legislative functions" means the functions of issuing or making statements of principle, rules, regulations or codes of practice.

114(10) [Guidance to be furnished] The Secretary of State shall also before making a delegation order transferring any functions to a designated agency require it to furnish him with a copy of any guidance intended to have continuing effect which it proposes to issue in writing or other legible form and the Secretary of State may take any such guidance into account in determining whether he is satisfied as mentioned in subsection (9)(b) above.

114(11) [Approval of delegation order] No delegation order shall be made unless a draft of it has been laid before and approved by a resolution of each House of Parliament.

114(12) [Interpretation re guidance] In this Act references to guidance issued by a designated agency are references to guidance issued or any recommendation made by it which is issued or made to persons generally or to any class of persons, being, in either case, persons who are or may be subject to statements of principle, rules, regulations or codes of practice issued or made by it, or who are or may be recognised or authorised by it, in the exercise of its functions under a delegation order.

Note
See the Financial Services Act 1986 (Delegation) Order 1987 (SI 1987/942); the Financial Services Act 1986 (Delegation) (No. 2) Order 1988 (SI 1988/738); the Financial Services Act 1986 (Delegation) Order 1991 (SI 1991/200); and the Financial Services Act 1986 (Delegation) (No. 2) Order 1991 (SI 1991/1256).

s. 114(5)

SEC. 115   Resumption of transferred functions

115(1) [Power of Secretary of State] The Secretary of State may at the request or with the consent of a designated agency make an order resuming all or any of the functions transferred to the agency by a delegation order.

115(2) [Extent of resumption order] The Secretary of State may, in the circumstances mentioned in subsection (3), (4) or (5) below, make an order resuming—

(a)   all the functions transferred to a designated agency by a delegation order; or
(b)   all, all legislative or all administrative functions transferred to a designated agency by a delegation order so far as relating to investments or investment business of any class.

115(3) [Sec. 115(2) order if Sch. 7 not complied with] An order may be made under subsection (2) above if at any time it appears to the Secretary of State that any of the requirements of Schedule 7 to this Act are not satisfied in the case of the agency.

115(4) [Sec. 115(2) order if agency unable to discharge functions etc.] An order may be made under subsection (2) above as respects functions relating to any class of investment or investment business if at any time it appears to the Secretary of State that the agency is unable or unwilling to discharge all or any of the transferred functions in respect of all or any investments or investment business falling within that class.

115(5) [Sec. 115(2) order if agency rules do not satisfy sec. 114(9)(b)] Where the transferred functions consist of or include any legislative functions, an order may be made under subsection (2) above if at any time it appears to the Secretary of State that the instruments issued or made by the agency do not satisfy the requirements of section 114(9)(b) above.

115(6) [Approval of sec. 115(1) order by Parliament] An order under subsection (1) above shall be subject to annulment in pursuance of a resolution of either House of Parliament; and no other order shall be made under this section unless a draft of it has been laid before and approved by a resolution of each House of Parliament.

115(7) [Definitions] In this section —

(a)   "legislative functions" means functions of issuing or making statements of principle, rules, regulations or codes of practice;
(b)   "administrative functions" means functions other than legislative functions;

but the resumption of legislative functions shall not deprive a designated agency of any function of prescribing fees to be paid or information to be furnished in connection with administrative functions retained by the agency; and the resumption of administrative functions shall extend to the function of prescribing fees to be paid and information to be furnished in connection with those administrative functions.

SEC. 116   Status and exercise of transferred functions

116 Schedule 9 to this Act shall have effect as respects the status of a designated agency and the exercise of the functions transferred to it by a delegation order.

SEC. 117   Reports and accounts

117(1) [Annual report by agency] A designated agency shall at least once in each year for which the delegation order is in force make a report to the Secretary of State on the discharge of the functions transferred to it by the order and on such other matters as the order may require.

s. 117(1)

117(2) **[Copies of report before Parliament]** The Secretary of State shall lay before Parliament copies of each report received by him under this section.

117(3) **[Directions re accounts of agency]** The Secretary of State may give directions to a designated agency with respect to its accounts and the audit of its accounts; and it shall be the duty of the agency to comply with the directions.

117(4) **[Qualification to sec. 117(3)]** Subsection (3) above shall not apply to a designated agency which is a company to which section 226 of the Companies Act 1985 applies; but the Secretary of State may require any designated agency (whether or not such a company) to comply with any provisions of that Act which would not otherwise apply to it or direct that any provision of that Act shall apply to the agency with such modifications as are specified in the direction; and it shall be the duty of the agency to comply with any such requirement or direction.

117(5) **[Northern Ireland]** In subsection (4) above the references to the Companies Act 1985 and section 226 of that Act include references to the corresponding Northern Ireland provisions.

SEC. 118   Transitional and supplementary provisions

118(1) **[Things previously done]** A delegation order shall not affect anything previously done in the exercise of a function which is transferred by the order; and any order resuming a function shall not affect anything previously done by the designated agency in the exercise of a function which is resumed.

118(2) **[Transitional, supplementary provisions in delegation order]** A delegation order and an order resuming any functions transferred by a delegation order may contain, or the Secretary of State may by a separate order under this section make, such transitional and other supplementary provisions as he thinks necessary or expedient in connection with the delegation order or the order resuming the functions in question.

Note
See the Financial Services Act 1986 (Transfer of Functions Relating to Friendly Societies) (Transitional Provisions) Order 1987 (SI 1987/2069).

118(3) **[Scope of provisions under sec. 118(2)]** The provisions that may be made under subsection (2) above in connection with a delegation order include, in particular, provisions—

(a)   for modifying or excluding any provision of this Act in its application to any function transferred by the order;

(b)   for applying to a designated agency, in connection with any such function, any provision applying to the Secretary of State which is contained in or made under any other enactment;

(c)   for the transfer of any property, rights or liabilities from the Secretary of State to a designated agency;

(d)   for the carrying on and completion by a designated agency of anything in process of being done by the Secretary of State when the order takes effect; and

(e)   for the substitution of a designated agency for the Secretary of State in any instrument, contract or legal proceedings.

118(4) **[Scope of provisions under sec. 118(2) re resumption order]** The provisions that may be made under subsection (2) above in connection with an order resuming any functions include, in particular, provisions—

(a)   for the transfer of any property, rights or liabilities from the agency to the Secretary of State;

(b)   for the carrying on and completion by the Secretary of State of anything in process of being done by the agency when the order takes effect;

(c)   for the substitution of the Secretary of State for the agency in any instrument, contract or legal proceedings; and

(d)   in a case where some functions remain with the agency, for modifying or excluding any provision of this Act in its application to any such functions.

118(5) [Scope of provisions under sec. 118(2) re designated agency] In a case where any function of a designated agency is resumed and is to be immediately transferred by a delegation order to another designated agency, the provisions that may be made under subsection (2) above may include provisions for any of the matters mentioned in paragraphs (a) to (c) of subsection (4) above, taking references to the Secretary of State as references to that other agency.

118(6) [Order may be annulled by Parliament] Any order under this section shall be subject to annulment in pursuance of a resolution of either House of Parliament.

Note
See the Financial Services Act 1986 (Delegation) Order 1987 (SI 1987/942); the Financial Services Act 1986 (Delegation) (No. 2) Order 1988 (SI 1988/738); and the Financial Services Act 1986 (Delegation) Order 1991 (SI 1991/200).

Chapter XIV — Prevention of Restrictive Practices

EXAMINATION OF RULES AND PRACTICES

SEC. 119   Recognised self-regulating organisations, investment exchanges and clearing houses

119(1) [Conditions for making recognition order] The Secretary of State shall not make a recognition order in respect of a self-regulating organisation, investment exchange or clearing house unless he is satisfied that—

(a)   in the case of a self-regulating organisation, the rules and any guidance of which copies are furnished with the application for the order, together with any statements of principle, rules, regulations or codes of practice to which members of the organisation would be subject by virtue of Chapter V of this Part,

(b)   in the case of an investment exchange, the rules and any guidance of which copies are furnished with the application for the order, together with any arrangements of which particulars are furnished with the application,

(c)   in the case of a clearing house, the rules and any guidance of which copies are furnished with the application for the order,

do not have, and are not intended or likely to have, to any significant extent the effect of restricting, distorting or preventing competition or, if they have or are intended or likely to have that effect to any significant extent, that the effect is not greater than is necessary for the protection of investors.

Note
See note after s. 119(2).

119(2) [Where sec. 119(3) powers to be exercised] The powers conferred by subsection (3) below shall be exercisable by the Secretary of State if at any time it appears to him that—

(a)   in the case of a self-regulating organisation—
   (i)   any rules made or guidance issued by the organisation,
   (ii) any practices of the organisation, or

(iii) any practices of persons who are members of, or otherwise subject to the rules made by, the organisation,

together with any statements of principle, rules, regulations or codes of practice to which members of the organisation are subject by virtue of Chapter V of this Part,

(b)   in the case of a recognised investment exchange—
  (i)   any rules made or guidance issued by the exchange,
  (ii) any practices of the exchange, or
  (iii) any practices of persons who are members of, or otherwise subject to the rules made by, the exchange,
(c)   in the case of a recognised clearing house —
  (i)   any rules made or guidance issued by the clearing house,
  (ii) any practices of the clearing house, or
  (iii) any practices of persons who are members of, or otherwise subject to the rules made by, the clearing house,

or any clearing arrangements made by the clearing house,

have, or are intended or likely to have, to a significant extent the effect of restricting, distorting or preventing competition and that that effect is greater than is necessary for the protection of investors.

Note
Concerning the Investment Services Directive, see the Investment Services Regulations 1995 (SI 1995/3275), reg. 32 and Sch. 7, para. 32.
Concerning protection of investors, see the Banking Coordination (Second Council Directive) Regulations 1992 (SI 1992/3218), reg. 55 and Sch. 9, para. 34 and the Insurance Companies (Third Insurance Directives) Regulations 1994 (SI 1994/1696), reg. 1, 62(1).

119(3) [Powers re revocation etc.] The powers exercisable under this subsection are—

(a)   to revoke the recognition order of the organisation, exchange or clearing house;
(b)   to direct it to take specified steps for the purpose of securing that its rules, or the guidance, arrangements or practices in question do not have the effect mentioned in subsection (2) above;
(c)   to make alterations in its rules for that purpose;

and subsections (2) to (5), (7) and (9) of section 11 above shall have effect in relation to the revocation of a recognition order under this subsection as they have effect in relation to the revocation of such an order under subsection (1) of that section.

119(4) [Non-application of sec. 119(3)(c)] Subsection (3)(c) above does not apply to an overseas investment exchange or overseas clearing house.

119(5) [Practices in sec. 119(2)(b)] The practices referred to in paragraph (a)(ii), (b)(ii) and (c)(ii) of subsection (2) above are practices of the organisation, exchange or clearing house in its capacity as such, being, in the case of a clearing house, practices in respect of its clearing arrangements.

119(6) [Practices in sec. 119(2)] The practices referred to in paragraph (a)(iii), (b)(iii) and (c)(iii) of subsection (2) above are—

(a)   in relation to a recognised self-regulating organisation, practices in relation to business in respect of which the persons in question are subject to—
  (i)   the rules of the organisation, or
  (ii) statements of principle, rules, regulations or codes of practice to which its members are subject by virtue of Chapter V of this Part,

and which are required or contemplated by the rules of the organisation or by those statements, rules, regulations or codes, or by guidance issued by the organisation,

s. 119(3)

(b)   in relation to a recognised investment exchange or clearing house, practices in relation to business in respect of which the persons in question are subject to the rules of the exchange or clearing house, and which are required or contemplated by its rules or guidance,

or which are otherwise attributable to the conduct of the organisation, exchange or clearing house as such.

SEC. 120   Modification of sec. 119 where recognition function is transferred

120(1) [Application] This section applies instead of section 119 above where the function of making or revoking a recognition order in respect of a self-regulating organisation, investment exchange or clearing house is exercisable by a designated agency.

120(2) [Duties of designated agency] The designated agency—

(a)   shall send to the Secretary of State a copy of the rules and of any guidance or arrangements of which copies or particulars are furnished with any application made to the agency for a recognition order together with any other information supplied with or in connection with the application; and

(b)   shall not make the recognition order without the leave of the Secretary of State;

and he shall not give leave in any case in which he would (apart from the delegation order) have been precluded by section 119(1) above from making the recognition order.

120(3) [Copy of notice to Secretary of State] A designated agency shall send the Secretary of State a copy of any notice received by it under section 14(6) or 41(5) or (6) above.

120(4) [Exercise of powers by Secretary of State] If at any time it appears to the Secretary of State in the case of a recognised self-regulating organisation, recognised investment exchange or recognised clearing house that there are circumstances such that (apart from the delegation order) he would have been able to exercise any of the powers conferred by subsection (3) of section 119 above he may, notwithstanding the delegation order, himself exercise the power conferred by paragraph (a) of that subsection or direct the designated agency to exercise the power conferred by paragraph (b) or (c) of that subsection in such manner as he may specify.

SEC. 121   Designated agencies

121(1) [Conditions re transferred functions] The Secretary of State shall not make a delegation order transferring any function to a designated agency unless he is satisfied that any statements of principle, rules, regulations, codes of practice and guidance of which copies are furnished to him under section 114(9) or (10) above do not have, and are not intended or likely to have, to any significant extent the effect of restricting, distorting or preventing competition or, if they have or are intended or likely to have that effect to any significant extent, that the effect is not greater than is necessary for the protection of investors.

Note
See note after s. 121(2)

121(2) [Exercise of sec. 121(3) powers by Secretary of State] The powers conferred by subsection (3) below shall be exercisable by the Secretary of State if at any time it appears to him that—

(a)   any statements of principle, rules, regulations or codes of practice issued or made by a designated agency in the exercise of functions transferred to it by a delegation order or any guidance issued by a designated agency;

(b)   any practices of a designated agency; or

(c)   any practices of persons who are subject to statements of principle, rules, regulations or codes of practice issued or made by it in the exercise of those functions,

have, or are intended or are likely to have, to any significant extent the effect of restricting, distorting or preventing competition and that that effect is greater than is necessary for the protection of investors.

Note
Concerning the Investment Services Directive, see the Investment Services Regulations 1995 (SI 1995/3275), reg. 32 and Sch. 7, para. 33.
Concerning protection of investors, see the Banking Coordination (Second Council Directive) Regulations 1992 (SI 1992/3218), reg. 55 and Sch. 9, para. 35.

121(3) [Powers in sec. 121(2)] The powers exercisable under this subsection are—

(a)   to make an order in respect of the agency under section 115(2) above as if the circumstances were such as are there mentioned; or

(b)   to direct the agency to take specified steps for the purpose of securing that the statements of principle, rules, regulations, codes of practice, guidance or practices in question do not have the effect mentioned in subsection (2) above.

121(4) [Practices in sec. 121(2)] The practices referred to in paragraph (b) of subsection (2) above are practices of the designated agency in its capacity as such; and the practices referred to in paragraph (c) of that subsection are practices in relation to business in respect of which the persons in question are subject to any such statements of principle, rules, regulations or codes of practice as are mentioned in paragraph (a) of that subsection and which are required or contemplated by those statements of principle, rules, regulations or codes of practice or by any such guidance as is there mentioned or are otherwise attributable to the conduct of the agency in its capacity as such.

Note
Concerning investor protection, see the Insurance Companies (Third Insurance Directives) Regulations 1994 (SI 1994/1696), reg. 1, 62(2).

CONSULTATION WITH DIRECTOR GENERAL OF FAIR TRADING

SEC. 122   Reports by Director General of Fair Trading

122(1) [Secretary of State to send copies of reports etc. to Director] The Secretary of State shall before deciding—

(a)   whether to refuse to make, or to refuse leave for the making of, a recognition order in pursuance of section 119(1) or 120(2) above; or

(b)   whether he is precluded by section 121(1) above from making a delegation order,

send to the Director General of Fair Trading (in this Chapter referred to as "the Director") a copy of the rules, statements of principle, regulations and codes of practice and of any guidance or arrangements which the Secretary of State is required to consider in making that decision together with such other information as the Secretary of State considers will assist the Director in discharging his functions under subsection (2) below.

122(2) [Report to Secretary of State by Director] The Director shall report to the Secretary of State whether, in his opinion, the rules, statements of principle, regulations, codes of practice, guidance or arrangements of which copies are sent to him under subsection (1) above have, or are intended or likely to have, to any significant extent the effect of restricting, distorting, or preventing competition and, if so, what that effect is likely to be; and in making any such decision as is mentioned in that subsection the Secretary of State shall have regard to the Director's report.

122(3) [Secretary of State to send copies of notices etc. to Director] The Secretary of State shall send the Director copies of any notice received by him under section 14(6), 41(5) or (6) or 120(3) above or under paragraph 4 of Schedule 9 to this Act together with such other information as the Secretary of State considers will assist the Director in discharging his functions under subsections (4) and (5) below.

122(4) [Review and report by Director re sec. 119(2), 121(2), 122(3)] The Director shall keep under review—

(a)   the rules, statements of principle, regulations, codes of practice, guidance and arrangements mentioned in section 119(2) and 121(2) above; and

(b)   the matters specified in the notices of which copies are sent to him under subsection (3) above;

and if at any time he is of the opinion that any such rules, statements of principle, regulations, codes of practice, guidance, arrangements or matters, or any such rules, statements of principle, regulations, codes of practice, guidance or arrangements taken together with any such matters, have, or are intended or likely to have, to any significant extent the effect mentioned in subsection (2) above, he shall make a report to the Secretary of State stating his opinion and what that effect is or is likely to be.

122(5) [Report re matter in sec. 122(4)(b)] The Director may report to the Secretary of State his opinion that any such matter as is mentioned in subsection (4)(b) above does not in his opinion have, and is not intended or likely to have, to any significant extent the effect mentioned in subsection (2) above.

122(6) [Report etc. re sec. 119(2), 121(2)] The Director may from time to time consider whether any such practices as are mentioned in section 119(2) or 121(2) above have, or are intended or likely to have, to any significant extent the effect mentioned in subsection (2) above and, if so, what that effect is or is likely to be; and if he is of that opinion he shall make a report to the Secretary of State stating his opinion and what the effect is or is likely to be.

122(7) [Limit on exercise of power in sec. 119(3), 120(4), 121(3)] The Secretary of State shall not exercise his powers under section 119(3), 120(4) or 121(3) above except after receiving and considering a report from the Director under subsection (4) or (6) above.

122(8) [Publication of report by Director] The Director may, if he thinks fit, publish any report made by him under this section but shall exclude from a published report, so far as practicable, any matter which relates to the affairs of a particular person (other than the self-regulating organisation, investment exchange, clearing house or designated agency concerned) the publication of which would or might in his opinion seriously and prejudicially affect the interests of that person.

SEC. 123   Investigations by Director General of Fair Trading

123(1) [Powers of Director] For the purpose of investigating any matter with a view to its consideration under section 122 above the Director may by a notice in writing—

(a)   require any person to produce, at a time and place specified in the notice, to the Director or to any person appointed by him for the purpose, any documents which are specified or described in the notice and which are documents in his custody or under his control and relating to any matter relevant to the investigation; or

(b)   require any person carrying on any business to furnish to the Director such information as may be specified or described in the notice, and specify the time within which, and the manner and form in which, any such information is to be furnished.

123(2) [Legal professional privilege, confidentiality] A person shall not under this section be required to produce any document or disclose any information which he would be entitled to refuse to produce or disclose on grounds of legal professional privilege in proceedings in the High Court or on grounds of confidentiality as between client and professional legal adviser in proceedings in the Court of Session.

123(3) [Application of sec. 85(6)–(8) of Fair Trading Act] Subsections (6) to (8) of section 85 of the Fair Trading Act 1973 (enforcement provisions) shall apply in relation to a notice under this section as they apply in relation to a notice under subsection (1) of that section but as if, in subsection (7) of that section, for the words from "any one" to "the commission" there were substituted "the Director".

CONSEQUENTIAL EXEMPTIONS FROM COMPETITION LAW
SEC. 124   The Fair Trading Act 1973

124(1) [Consideration of whether monopoly situation] For the purpose of determining whether a monopoly situation within the meaning of the Fair Trading Act 1973 exists by reason of the circumstances mentioned in section 7(1)(c) of that Act, no account shall be taken of—

(a)   the rules made or guidance issued by a recognised self-regulating organisation, recognised investment exchange or recognised clearing house or any conduct constituting such a practice as is mentioned in section 119(2) above;

(b)   any clearing arrangements or any conduct required or contemplated by any such arrangements; or

(c)   the statements of principle, rules, regulations, codes of practice or guidance issued or made by a designated agency in the exercise of functions transferred to it by a delegation order or any conduct constituting such a practice as is mentioned in section 121(2) above.

124(2) [Qualification to sec. 124(1)] Where a recognition order is revoked there shall be disregarded for the purpose mentioned in subsection (1) above any such conduct as is mentioned in that subsection which occurred while the order was in force.

124(3) [Where monopoly situation found to exist] Where on a monopoly reference under section 50 or 51 of the said Act of 1973 falling within section 49 of that Act the Monopolies and Mergers Commission find that a monopoly situation within the meaning of that Act exists and—

(a)   that the person (or, if more than one, any of the persons) in whose favour it exists is subject to the rules of a recognised self-regulating organisation, recognised investment exchange or recognised clearing house or to the statements of principle, rules, regulations or codes of practice issued or made by a designated agency in the exercise of functions transferred to it by a delegation order; or

(b)   that any such person's conduct in carrying on any business to which those statements of principle, rules, regulations or codes of practice relate is the subject of guidance issued by such an organisation, exchange, clearing house or agency; or

(c)   that any such person is a party to any clearing arrangements; or

(d)   that the person (or, if more than one, any of the persons) in whose favour the monopoly situation exists is such an organisation, exchange or clearing house as is mentioned in paragraph (a) above or a designated agency,

the Commission, in making their report on that reference, shall exclude from their consideration the question whether the statements of principle, rules, regulations, codes of practice, guidance or clearing arrangements or any acts or omissions of such an organisation, exchange, clearing house or agency as is mentioned in paragraph (d) above in its capacity as such operate, or may be expected to operate, against the public interest; and section 54(3) of that Act shall have effect subject to the provisions of this subsection.

SEC. 125   The Restrictive Trade Practices Act 1976

125(1) [Non-application to agreement re constitution of recognised bodies] The Restrictive Trade Practices Act 1976 shall not apply to any agreement for the constitution of a recognised self-regulating organisation, recognised investment exchange or recognised clearing house, including any term deemed to be contained in it by virtue of section 8(2) or 16(3) of that Act.

125(2) [Non-application to agreement where parties include sec. 125(1) body or person subject to rules] The said Act of 1976 shall not apply to any agreement the parties to which consist of or include—

(a)   any such organisation, exchange or clearing house as is mentioned in subsection (1) above; or

(b)   a person who is subject to the rules of any such organisation, exchange or clearing house or to the rules or regulations made by a designated agency in the exercise of functions transferred to it by a delegation order,

by reason of any term the inclusion of which in the agreement is required or contemplated by the rules, regulations or guidance of that organisation, exchange, clearing house or agency.

125(3) [Non-application to clearing arrangements etc.] The said Act of 1976 shall not apply to any clearing arrangements or to any agreement between a recognised investment exchange and a recognised clearing house by reason of any term the inclusion of which in the agreement is required or contemplated by any clearing arrangements.

125(4) [Where recognition order re body revoked] Where the recognition order in respect of a self-regulating organisation, investment exchange or clearing house is revoked the foregoing provisions shall have effect as if the organisation, exchange or clearing house had continued to be recognised until the end of the period of six months beginning with the day on which the revocation takes effect.

125(5) [Where agreement no longer registered, effect] Where an agreement ceases by virtue of this section to be subject to registration—

(a)   the Director shall remove from the register maintained by him under the said Act of 1976 any particulars which are entered or filed in that register in respect of the agreement; and

s. 125(5)

(b)   any proceedings in respect of the agreement which are pending before the Restrictive Practices Court shall be discontinued.

125(6) [Where agreement no longer exempt from registration] Where an agreement which has been exempt from registration by virtue of this section ceases to be exempt in consequence of the revocation of a recognition order, the time within which particulars of the agreement are to be furnished in accordance with section 24 of and Schedule 2 to the said Act of 1976 shall be the period of one month beginning with the day on which the agreement ceased to be exempt from registration.

125(7) [Where term ceases to be within sec. 125(2), (3)] Where in the case of an agreement registered under the said Act of 1976 a term ceases to fall within subsection (2) or (3) above in consequence of the revocation of a recognition order and particulars of that term have not previously been furnished to the Director under section 24 of that Act, those particulars shall be furnished to him within the period of one month beginning with the day on which the term ceased to fall within that subsection.

125(8) [Restrictive Trade Practices (Stock Exchange) Act] The Restrictive Trade Practices (Stock Exchange) Act 1984 shall cease to have effect.

SEC. 126   The Competition Act 1980

126(1) [Sec. 119(2), 121(2) practices not anti-competitive] No course of conduct constituting any such practice as is mentioned in section 119(2) or 121(2) above shall constitute an anti-competitive practice for the purposes of the Competition Act 1980.

126(2) [Where recognition or delegation order revoked] Where a recognition order or delegation order is revoked, there shall not be treated as an anti-competitive practice for the purposes of that Act any such course of conduct as is mentioned in subsection (1) above which occurred while the order was in force.

RECOGNISED PROFESSIONAL BODIES

SEC. 127   Modification of Restrictive Trade Practices Act 1976 in relation to recognised professional bodies

127(1) [Application] This section applies to—

(a)   any agreement for the constitution of a recognised professional body, including any term deemed to be contained in it by virtue of section 16(3) of the Restrictive Trade Practices Act 1976; and

(b)   any other agreement—
    (i)   the parties to which consist of or include such a body, a person certified by such a body or a member of such a body; and
    (ii)   to which that Act applies by virtue of any term the inclusion of which in the agreement is required or contemplated by rules or guidance of that body relating to the carrying on of investment business by persons certified by it.

127(2) [Powers of Secretary of State to give direction to Directors] If it appears to the Sectretary of State that the restrictions in an agreement to which this section applies—

(a)   do not have, and are not intended or likely to have, to any significant extent the effect of restricting, distorting or preventing competition; or

(b)   if all or any of them have, or are intended or likely to have, that effect to any significant extent, that the effect is not greater than is necessary for the protection of investors, he may give a direction to the Director requiring him not to make an application to the Restrictive Practices Court under Part I of the said Act of 1976 in respect of the agreement.

127(3) [Declaration by Secretary of State] If it appears to the Secretary of State that one or more (but not all) of the restrictions in an agreement to which this section applies—

(a)   do not have, and are not intended or likely to have, to any significant extent the effect mentioned in subsection (2) above; or

(b)   if they have, or are intended or likely to have, that effect to any significant extent that the effect is not greater than is necessary for the protection of investors,

he may make a declaration to that effect and give notice of it to the Director and the Restrictive Practices Court.

127(4) [Limit re Restrictive Practices Court] The Restrictive Practices Court shall not in any proceedings begun by an application made after notice has been given to it of a declaration under this section make any finding or exercise any power under Part I of the said Act of 1976 in relation to a restriction in respect of which the declaration has effect.

127(5) [Limit on applications to Court by Director] The Director shall not make any application to the Restrictive Practices Court under Part I of the said Act of 1976 in respect of any agreement to which this section applies unless—

(a)   he has notified the Secretary of State of his intention to do so; and

(b)   the Secretary of State has either notified him that he does not intend to give a direction or make a declaration under this section or has given him notice of a declaration in respect of it;

and where the Director proposes to make any such application he shall furnish the Secretary of State with particulars of the agreement and the restrictions by virtue of which the said Act of 1976 applies to it and such other information as he considers will assist the Secretary of State in deciding whether to exercise his powers under this section or as the Secretary of State may request.

127(6) [Powers of Secretary of State re revocation, variation of declaration etc.] The Secretary of State may—

(a)   revoke a direction or declaration under this section;

(b)   vary any such declaration; or

(c)   give a direction or make a declaration notwithstanding a previous notification to the Director that he did not intend to give a direction or make a declaration;

if he is satisfied that there has been a material change of circumstances such that the grounds for the direction or declaration have ceased to exist, that there are grounds for a different declaration or that there are grounds for giving a direction or making a declaration, as the case may be.

127(7) [Notice to Director by Secretary of State] The Secretary of State shall give notice to the Director of the revocation of a direction and to the Director and the Restrictive Practices Court of the revocation or variation of a declaration; and no such variation shall have effect so as to restrict the powers of the Court in any proceedings begun by an application already made by the Director.

127(8) [Cesser of direction or declaration] A direction or declaration under this section shall cease to have effect if the agreement in question ceases to be one to which this section applies.

s. 127(8)

127(9) [Application] This section applies to information provisions as it applies to restrictions.

SUPPLEMENTAL

SEC. 128   Supplementary provisions

128(1) [Duty of Secretary of State before exercising power] Before the Secretary of State exercises a power under section 119(3)(b) or (c) above, his power to refuse leave under section 120(2) above or his power to give a direction under section 120(4) above in respect of a self-regulating organisation, investment exchange or clearing house, or his power under section 121(3)(b) above in respect of a designated agency, he shall—

(a)   give written notice of his intention to do so to the organisation, exchange, clearing house or agency and take such steps (whether by publication or otherwise) as he thinks appropriate for bringing the notice to the attention of any other person who in his opinion is likely to be affected by the exercise of the power; and

(b)   have regard to any representation made within such time as he considers reasonable by the organisation, exchange, clearing house or agency or by any such other person.

128(2) [Contents of sec. 128(1) notice] A notice under subsection (1) above shall give particulars of the manner in which the Secretary of State proposes to exercise the power in question and state the reasons for which he proposes to act; and the statement of reasons may include matters contained in any report received by him under section 122 above.

128(3) [Enforcement of directions] Any direction given under this Chapter shall, on the application of the person by whom it was given, be enforceable by mandamus or, in Scotland, by an order for specific performance under section 91 of the Court of Session Act 1868.

128(4) [Alteration of altered rules etc.] The fact that any rules or regulations made by a recognised self-regulating organisation, investment exchange or clearing house or by a designated agency have been altered by or pursuant to a direction given by the Secretary of State under this Chapter shall not preclude their subsequent alteration or revocation by that organisation, exchange, clearing house or agency.

128(5) [Assumption re acting conforming to guidance] In determining under this Chapter whether any guidance has, or is likely to have, any particular effect the Secretary of State and the Director may assume that the persons to whom it is addressed will act in conformity with it.

Chapter XV — Relations with Other Regulatory Authorities
SEC. 128A   Relevance of other controls

128A In determining—

(a)   in relation to a self-regulating organisation, whether the requirements of Schedule 2 are met, or

(b)   in relation to a professional body, whether the requirements of Schedule 3 are met,

the Secretary of State shall take into account the effect of any other controls to which members of the organisation or body are subject.

Note
For transfer of the Secretary of State's functions under s. 128A see SI 1990/354 (C. 12), art. 4(2)(b).

SEC. 128B   Relevance of information given and action taken by other regulatory authorities

128B(1) [Application] The following provisions apply in the case of—

(a)   a person whose principal place of business is in a country or territory outside the United Kingdom, or

(b)   a person whose principal business is other than investment business;

and in relation to such a person "the relevant regulatory authority" means the appropriate regulatory authority in that country or territory or, as the case may be, in relation to his principal business.

128B(2) [When Secretary of State satisfied] The Secretary of State may regard himself as satisfied with respect to any matter relevant for the purposes of this Part if—

(a)   the relevant regulatory authority informs him that it is satisfied with respect to that matter, and

(b)   he is satisfied as to the nature and scope of the supervision exercised by that authority.

128B(3) [Matters taken into account] In making any decision with respect to the exercise of his powers under this Part in relation to any such person, the Secretary of State may take into account whether the relevant regulatory authority has exercised, or proposes to exercise, its powers in relation to that person.

128B(4) [Power of Secretary of State to enter arrangements] The Secretary of State may enter into such arrangements with other regulatory authorities as he thinks fit for the purposes of this section.

128B(5) [Community and international obligations] Where any functions under this Part have been transferred to a designated agency, nothing in this section shall be construed as affecting the responsibility of the Secretary of State for the discharge of Community obligations or other international obligations of the United Kingdom.

Note
For transfer of the Secretary of State's functions under s. 128B(1)–(4) see SI 1990/354 (C. 12), art. 4(3)(c).

SEC. 128C   Enforcement in support of overseas regulatory authority

128(C)1 [Powers of Secretary of State] The Secretary of State may exercise his disciplinary powers or powers of intervention at the request of, or for the purpose of assisting, an overseas regulatory authority.

Note
See note after s. 128C(5).

128C(2) [Description of disciplinary powers] The disciplinary powers of the Secretary of State means his powers—

(a)   to withdraw or suspend authorisation under section 28 or to terminate or suspend authorisation under section 33,

(b)   to give a disqualification direction under section 59,

(c)   to make a public statement under section 60, or

(d)   to apply for an injunction, interdict or other order under section 61(1);

and the reference to his powers of intervention is to the powers conferred by Chapter VI of this Part.

Note
See note after s. 128C(5).

s. 128C(2)

128C(3) ["Overseas regulatory authority"] An "overseas regulatory authority" means an authority in a country or territory outside the United Kingdom which exercises—

(a)   any function corresponding to—
    (i)   a function of the Secretary of State under this Act, the Insurance Companies Act 1982 or the Companies Act 1985,
    (ii)   a function under this Act of a designated agency, transferee body or competent authority, or
    (iii)   a function of the Bank of England under the Banking Act 1987, or

(b)   any functions in connection with the investigation of, or the enforcement of rules (whether or not having the force of law) relating to, conduct of the kind prohibited by Part V of the Criminal Justice Act 1993 (insider dealing), or

(c)   any function prescribed for the purposes of this subsection, being a function which in the opinion of the Secretary of State relates to companies or financial services.

128C(4) [Matters to be taken into account] In deciding whether to exercise those powers the Secretary of State may take into account, in particular—

(a)   whether corresponding assistance would be given in that country or territory to an authority exercising regulatory functions in the United Kingdom;

(b)   whether the case concerns the breach of a law, or other requirement, which has no close parallel in the United Kingdom or involves the assertion of a jurisdiction not recognised by the United Kingdom;

(c)   the seriousness of the case and its importance to persons in the United Kingdom;

(d)   whether it is otherwise appropriate in the public interest to give the assistance sought.

Note
See note after s. 128C(5).

128C(5) [Undertaking from overseas regulatory authority] The Secretary of State may decline to exercise those powers unless the overseas regulatory authority undertakes to make such contribution towards the cost of their exercise as the Secretary of State considers appropriate.

Note
Concerning the Investment Services Directive, see the Investment Services Regulations 1995 (SI 1995/3275), reg. 32 and Sch. 7, para. 34.
See the Banking Coordination (Second Council Directive) Regulations 1992 (SI 1992/3218), reg. 55 and Sch. 9, para. 36.

128C(6) ["Financial Services" in sec. 128C(3)(c)] The reference in subsection (3)(c) to financial services includes, in particular, investment business, insurance and banking.

Note
For transfer of the Secretary of State's functions under s. 128C, see SI 1990/354 (C. 12), art. 4(3)(d).

PART II — INSURANCE BUSINESS

SEC. 129   Application of investment business provisions to regulated insurance companies.

129 Schedule 10 to this Act shall have effect with respect to the application of the foregoing provisions of this Act to regulated insurance companies, that is to say—

(a)   insurance companies to which Part II of the Insurance Companies Act 1982 applies; and

(b)   insurance companies which are authorised persons by virtue of section 31 above.

Note
Regarding application to EC companies, see the Insurance Companies (Third Insurance Directives) Regulations 1994 (SI 1994/1696), reg. 1, 63(1).

SEC. 130   Restriction on promotion of contracts of insurance

130(1) [Limit on advertisements] Subject to subsections (2) and (3) below, no person shall—

(a)   issue or cause to be issued in the United Kingdom an advertisement—

    (i)   inviting any person to enter or offer to enter into a contract of insurance rights under which constitute an investment for the purposes of this Act, or

    (ii)   containing information calculated to lead directly or indirectly to any person doing so; or

(b)   in the course of a business, advise or procure any person in the United Kingdom to enter into such a contract.

130(2) [Non-application of sec. 130(1)] Subsection (1) above does not apply where the contract of insurance referred to in that subsection is to be with—

(a)   a body authorised under section 3 or 4 of the Insurance Companies Act 1982 to effect and carry out such contracts of insurance;

(b)   a body registered under the enactments relating to friendly societies;

(c)   an insurance company the head office of which is in a member State other than the United Kingdom and which is entitled to carry on there insurance business of the relevant class;

(d)   an insurance company which has a branch or agency in such a member State and is entitled under the law of that State to carry on there insurance business of the relevant class;

and in this subsection "the relevant class" means the class of insurance business specified in Schedule 1 or 2 to the Insurance Companies Act 1982 into which the effecting and carrying out of the contract in question falls.

130(3) [Additional non-application of sec. 130(1)] Subsection (1) above also does not apply where—

(a)   the contract of insurance referred to in that subsection is to be with an insurance company authorised to effect or carry out such contracts of insurance in any country or territory which is for the time being designated for the purposes of this section by an order made by the Secretary of State; and

(b)   any conditions imposed by the order designating the country or territory have been satisfied.

Note
For countries and territories designated under s. 130(3) see SI 1988/439 (Guernsey and Isle of Man), SI 1989/2380 (Pennsylvania) and SI 1993/1237 (Iowa).
See note after s. 130(4).

130(4) [Limit on Secretary of State's power] The Secretary of State shall not make an order designating any country or territory for the purposes of this section unless he is satisfied that the law under which insurance companies are authorised and supervised in that country or territory affords adequate protection to policy holders and potential policy holders against the risk that the companies may be unable to meet their liabilities; and, if at any time it appears to him that the law of a country or territory which has been designated under this section does not satisfy that requirement, he may by a further order revoke the order designating that country or territory.

Note
For orders made under s. 130(3), (4) see the Financial Services (Designated Countries and Territories) (Overseas Insurance Companies) Order 1988 (SI 1988/439); the Financial Services (Designated Countries and Territories) (Overseas Insurance Companies) Order 1989 (SI 1989/2380); and the Financial Services (Designated Countries and Territories (Overseas Insurance Companies) Order 1993 (SI 1993/1237).

130(5) [Annulment of order by Parliament] An order under this section shall be subject to annulment in pursuance of a resolution of either House of Parliament.

130(6) [Offence, penalty] Subject to subsections (7) and (8) below, any person who contravenes this section shall be guilty of an offence and liable—

(a)   on conviction on indictment, to imprisonment for a term not exceeding two years or to a fine or to both;

(b)   on summary conviction, to imprisonment for a term not exceeding six months or to a fine not exceeding the statutory maximum or to both.

130(7) [Defence] A person who in the ordinary course of a business other than investment business issues an advertisement to the order of another person shall not be guilty of an offence under this section if he proves that the matters contained in the advertisement were not (wholly or in part) devised or selected by him or by any person under his direction or control and that he believed on reasonable grounds after due enquiry that the person to whose order the advertisement was issued was an authorised person.

130(8) [Further defence] A person other than the insurance company with which the contract of insurance is to be made shall not be guilty of an offence under this section if he proves that he believed on reasonable grounds after due enquiry that subsection (2) or (3) above applied in the case of the contravention in question.

SEC. 131   Contracts made after contravention of sec. 130

131(1) [Effect of contravention of sec. 130] Where there has been a contravention of section 130 above, then, subject to subsections (3) and (4) below—

(a)   the insurance company shall not be entitled to enforce any contract of insurance with which the advertisement, advice or procurement was concerned and which was entered into after the contravention occurred; and

(b)   the other party shall be entitled to recover any money or other property paid or transferred by him under the contract, together with compensation for any loss sustained by him as a result of having parted with it.

131(2) [Interest recoverable under sec. 131(1)] The compensation recoverable under subsection (1) above shall be such as the parties may agree or as a court may, on the application of either party, determine.

131(3) [Where contravention by insurance company] In a case where the contravention referred to in subsection (1) above was a contravention by the insurance company with which the contract was made, the court may allow the contract to be enforced or money or property paid or transferred under it to be retained if it is satisfied—

(a)   that the person against whom enforcement is sought or who is seeking to recover the money or property was not influenced, or not influenced to any material extent, by the advertisement or, as the case may be, the advice in making his decision to enter into the contract; or

(b)   that the advertisement or, as the case may be, the advice was not misleading as to the nature of the company with which the contract was to be made or the terms of the contract and fairly stated any risks involved in entering into it.

131(4) **[Where contravention by person other than insurance company]** In a case where the contravention of section 130 above referred to in subsection (1) above was a contravention by a person other than the insurance company with which the contract was made the court may allow the contract to be enforced or money or property paid or transferred under it to be retained if it is satisfied that at the time the contract was made the company had no reason to believe that any contravention of section 130 above had taken place in relation to the contract.

131(5) **[Where election not to perform contract unenforceable by sec. 131(1)]** Where a person elects not to perform a contract which by virtue of subsection (1) above is unenforceable against him or by virtue of that subsection recovers money paid or other property transferred by him under a contract he shall not be entitled to any benefits under the contract and shall repay any money and return any other property received by him under the contract.

131(6) **[Where property has passed to third party]** Where any property transferred under a contract to which this section applies has passed to a third party the references to that property in this section shall be construed as references to its value at the time of its transfer under the contract.

131(7) **[Contravention of sec. 130]** A contravention of section 130 above by an authorised person shall be actionable at the suit of any person who suffers loss as a result of the contravention.

131(8) **[Effect of sec. 61 on sec. 130 contravention]** Section 61 above shall have effect in relation to a contravention or proposed contravention of section 130 above as it has effect in relation to a contravention or proposed contravention of section 57 above.

SEC. 132   Insurance contracts effected in contravention of sec. 2 of Insurance Companies Act 1982

132(1) **[Contracts unenforceable against other party]** Subject to subsection (3) below, a contract of insurance (not being an agreement to which section 5(1) above applies) which is entered into by a person in the course of carrying on insurance business in contravention of section 2 of the Insurance Companies Act 1982 shall be unenforceable against the other party; and that party shall be entitled to recover any money or other property paid or transferred by him under the contract, together with compensation for any loss sustained by him as a result of having parted with it.

132(2) **[Compensation recoverable under sec. 132(1)]** The compensation recoverable under subsection (1) above shall be such as the parties may agree or as a court may, on the application of either party, determine.

132(3) **[Court may allow enforcement of sec. 132(1) contract]** A court may allow a contract to which subsection (1) above applies to be enforced or money or property paid or transferred under it to be retained if it is satisfied—

(a)   that the person carrying on insurance business reasonably believed that his entering into the contract did not constitute a contravention of section 2 of the said Act of 1982; and

(b)   that it is just and equitable for the contract to be enforced or, as the case may be, for the money or property paid or transferred under it to be retained.

132(4) [Where election not to perform unenforceable contract] Where a person elects not to perform a contract which by virtue of this section is unenforceable against him or by virtue of this section recovers money or property paid or transferred under a contract he shall not be entitled to any benefits under the contract and shall repay any money and return any other property received by him under the contract.

132(5) [Where property has passed to third party] Where any property transferred under a contract to which this section applies has passed to a third party the references to that property in this section shall be construed as references to its value at the time of its transfer under the contract.

132(6) [Effect of contravention of sec. 2 of 1982 Act] A contravention of section 2 of the said Act of 1982 shall not make a contract of insurance illegal or invalid to any greater extent than is provided in this section; and a contravention of that section in respect of a contract of insurance shall not affect the validity of any re-insurance contract entered into in respect of that contract.

Note
See the Insurance Companies (Third Insurance Directives) Regulations 1994 (SI 1994/1696), reg. 1, 64.

SEC. 133   Misleading statements as to insurance contracts

133(1) [Offence] Any person who—

(a)   makes a statement, promise or forecast which he knows to be misleading, false or deceptive or dishonestly conceals any material facts; or

(b)   recklessly makes (dishonestly or otherwise) a statement, promise or forecast which is misleading, false or deceptive,

is guilty of an offence if he makes the statement, promise or forecast or conceals the facts for the purpose of inducing, or is reckless as to whether it may induce, another person (whether or not the person to whom the statement, promise or forecast is made or from whom the facts are concealed) to enter into or offer to enter into, or to refrain from entering or offering to enter into, a contract of insurance with an insurance company (not being an investment agreement) or to exercise, or refrain from exercising, any rights conferred by such a contract.

133(2) [Conditions for sec. 133(1)] Subsection (1) above does not apply unless—

(a)   the statement, promise or forecast is made in or from, or the facts are concealed in or from, the United Kingdom;

(b)   the person on whom the inducement is intended to or may have effect is in the United Kingdom; or

(c)   the contract is or would be entered into or the rights are or would be exercisable in the United Kingdom.

133(3) [Penalty] A person guilty of an offence under this section shall be liable—

(a)   on conviction on indictment, to imprisonment for a term not exceeding seven years or to a fine or to both;

(b)   on summary conviction, to imprisonment for a term not exceeding six months or to a fine not exceeding the statutory maximum or to both.

SEC. 134   Controllers of insurance companies

134 (Ceased to have effect as a result of the Insurance Companies (Third Insurance Directives) Regulations 1994, reg. 1, 68, Sch. 8, para. 12 as from 1 July 1994.)

SEC. 135   Communication by auditor with Secretary of State

135(1) [Insertion of sec. 21A of Insurance Companies Act 1982] After section 21 of the Insurance Companies Act 1982 there shall be inserted—

"Communication by auditor with Secretary of State

21A(1) No duty to which an auditor of an insurance company to which this Part of this Act applies may be subject shall be regarded as contravened by reason of his communicating in good faith to the Secretary of State, whether or not in response to a request from him, any information or opinion on a matter of which the auditor has become aware in his capacity as auditor of that company and which is relevant to any functions of the Secretary of State under this Act.

21A(2) If it appears to the Secretary of State that any auditor or class of auditor to whom subsection (1) above applies is not subject to satisfactory rules made or guidance issued by a professional body specifying circumstances in which matters are to be communicated to the Secretary of State as mentioned in that subsection the Secretary of State may make regulations applying to that auditor or class of auditor and specifying such circumstances; and it shall be the duty of an auditor to whom the regulations made by the Secretary of State apply to communicate a matter to the Secretary of State in the circumstances specified by the regulations.

21A(3) The matters to be communicated to the Secretary of State in accordance with any such rules or guidance or regulations may include matters relating to persons other than the company.

21A(4) No regulations shall be made under subsection (2) above unless a draft of them has been laid before and approved by a resolution of each House of Parliament.

21A(5) If it appears to the Secretary of State that an auditor has failed to comply with duty mentioned in subsection (2) above, the Secretary of State may disqualify him from being the auditor of an insurance company or any class of insurance company to which Part II of this Act applies; but the Secretary of State may remove any disqualification imposed under this subsection if satisfied that the person in question will in future comply with that duty.

21A(6) An insurance company to which this Part of this Act applies shall not appoint as auditor a person disqualified under subsection (5) above."

135(2) [Insertion in sec. 71(7) of 1982 Act] In section 71(7) of that Act (which lists the provisions of that Act default in complying with which is not an offence) after the words "section 16" there shall be inserted the word "21A", and in section 97(4) of that Act (which provides that regulations under that Act are to be subject to annulment) after the word "Act" there shall be inserted the words ", except regulations under section 21A(3),".

SEC. 136   Arrangements to avoid unfairness between separate insurance funds etc.

136(1) [Insertion of sec. 31A of Insurance Companies Act 1982] After section 31 of the Insurance Companies Act 1982 there shall be inserted—

> *"Arrangements to avoid unfairness between separate insurance funds etc.*

31A(1) An insurance company to which this Part of this Act applies which carries on long term business in the United Kingdom shall secure that adequate arrangements are in force for securing that transactions affecting assets of the company (other than transactions outside its control) do not operate unfairly between the section 28 fund or funds and the other assets of the company or, in a case where the company has more than one identified fund, between those funds.

31A(2) In this section—

> 'the section 28 fund or funds' means the assets representing the fund or funds maintained by the company under section 28(1)(b) above; and
> 'identified fund', in relation to a company, means assets representing the company's receipts from a particular part of its long term business which can be identified as such by virtue of accounting or other records maintained by the company."

136(2) [Insertion in sec. 71(7) of 1982 Act] In section 71(7) of that Act (which lists the provisions of that Act default in complying with which is not an offence) before the word "or" there shall be inserted the word "31A".

SEC. 137   Regulations in respect of linked long term policies

137 In section 78(2) of the Insurance Companies Act 1982 (regulations in respect of linked long term policies) after paragraph (a) there shall be inserted—

> "(aa) restricting the proportion of those benefits which may be determined by reference to property of a specified description or a specified index;".

SEC. 138   Insurance brokers

138(1) [Rules under sec. 8 of Insurance Brokers (Registration) Act 1977] Rules made under section 8 of the Insurance Brokers (Registration) Act 1977 may require an applicant for registration or enrolment to state whether he is an authorised person or exempted person under Part I of this Act and, if so, to give particulars of the authorisation or exemption; and an individual shall be treated as satisfying the requirements of section 3(2)(a) of that Act (applicant for registration to satisfy Council as to his character and suitability) if he is an authorised person or a member of a partnership or unincorporated association which is an authorised person.

138(2) [Statement, rules under sec. 10–12 of 1977 Act] In drawing up any statement under section 10 of that Act or making any rules under section 11 or 12 of that Act after the coming into force of this section the Insurance Brokers Registration Council shall take proper account of any provisions applicable to, and powers exercisable in relation to, registered insurance brokers or enrolled bodies corporate under this Act.

138(3) [Substitution in sec. 12(1), (2) of 1977 Act] In section 12(1) and (2) of that Act (which requires the Council to make professional indemnity rules) for the words "The Council shall" there shall be substituted the words "The Council may".

138(4) [Insertion of sec. 15(2A) of 1977 Act] In section 15 of that Act (erasure from register and list for unprofessional conduct etc.) after subsection (2) there shall be inserted—

> "15(2A) The Disciplinary Committee may, if they think fit, direct that the name of a registered insurance broker or enrolled body corporate shall be erased from the register or list if it appears to the Committee that any responsible person has concluded that the broker (or a related person) or the body corporate has contravened or failed to comply with—

> (a) any provision of the Financial Services Act 1986 or any rule or regulation made under it to which he or it is or was subject at the time of the contravention or failure; or

> (b) any rule of any recognised self-regulating organisation or recognised professional body (within the meaning of that Act), to which he is or was subject at that time.

> **15(2B)** In subsection (2A) above—

> (a) 'responsible person' means a person responsible under the Financial Services Act 1986 or under the rules of any recognised self-regulating organisation or recognised professional body (within the meaning of that Act) for determining whether any contravention of any provision of that Act or rules or regulations made under it or any rules of that organisation or body has occurred; and

> (b) 'related person' means a partnership or unincorporated association of which the broker in question is (or was at the time of the failure or contravention in question) a member or a body corporate of which he is (or was at that time) a director."

138(5) [Insurance Brokers Registration Council] The Insurance Brokers Registration Council shall co-operate, by the sharing of information and otherwise, with the Secretary of State and any other authority, body or person having responsibility for the supervision or regulation of investment business or other financial services.

138(6) ["Authorised insurers"] For the purposes of the said Act of 1977 "authorised insurers" shall include—

(a) an insurance company the head office of which is in a member State other than the United Kingdom and which is entitled to carry on there insurance business corresponding to that mentioned in the definition of "authorised insurers" in that Act; and

(b) an insurance company which has a branch or agency in such a member State and is entitled under the law of that State to carry on there insurance business corresponding to that mentioned in that definition.

SEC. 139   Industrial assurance

139(1) [Interpretation of sec. 5 of Industrial Assurance Act 1923] In section 5 of the Industrial Assurance Act 1923 (prohibition on issue of illegal policies) the references to policies which are illegal or not within the legal powers of a society or company shall not be construed as applying to any policy issued—

(a)	in the course of carrying on investment business in contravention of section 3 above; or

(b)	in the course of carrying on insurance business in contravention of section 2 of the Insurance Companies Act 1982.

Note
See the Insurance Companies (Third Insurance Directives) Regulations 1994 (SI 1994/1696), reg. 1, 65.

139(2) [Interpretation of sec. 20(4), 34 of 1923 Act] In section 20(4) of the said Act of 1923 the reference to a person employed by a collecting society or industrial assurance company and in section 34 of that Act the references to a person in the regular employment of such a society or company shall include references to an appointed representative of such a society or company but as respects section 34 only if the contract in question is an investment agreement.

139(3), (4) (Repealed by Friendly Societies Act 1992, sec. 120 and Sch. 22, Pt. I as from 28 April 1993 for the purposes of incorporated friendly societies and as from 1 January 1994 for all remaining purposes.)

139(5) [Application to Northern Ireland] The foregoing provisions of this section shall apply to Northern Ireland with the substitution for the references to sections 5, 20(4), 32 and 34 of the said Act of 1923 of references to Articles 20, 27(2), 36 and 38 of the Industrial Assurance (Northern Ireland) Order 1979 and for the references to the Industrial Assurance Commissioner of references to the Industrial Asssurance Commissioner for Northern Ireland.

PART III — FRIENDLY SOCIETIES

## SEC. 140	Friendly societies

140 Schedule 11 to this Act shall have effect as respects the regulation of friendly societies.

## SEC. 141	Indemnity schemes

141(1) [Arrangement between Friendly Societies] Any two or more registered friendly societies may, notwithstanding any provision to the contrary in their rules, enter into arrangements for the purpose of making funds available to meet losses incurred by any society which is a party to the arrangements or by the members of any such society by virtue of their membership of it.

141(2) [Approval by Chief Registrar] No such arrangements shall come into force unless they have been approved by the Friendly Societies Commission.

PART IV — OFFICIAL LISTING OF SECURITIES

## SEC. 142	Official listing

142(1) [Admission to official listing] No investment to which this section applies shall be admitted to the Official List except in accordance with the provisions of this Part of this Act.

142(2) **[Application to Sch. 1 investments]** Subject to subsections (3) and (4) below, this section applies to any investment falling within paragraph 1, 2, 4 or 5 of Schedule 1 to this Act.

142(3) **[Application of paragraphs in sec. 142(2)]** In the application of those paragraphs for the purposes of subsection (2) above—

(a)   paragraphs 1, 4 and 5 shall have effect as if paragraph 1 did not contain the exclusion relating to building societies, industrial and provident societies or credit unions;

(b)   paragraph 2 shall have effect as if it included any instrument falling within paragraph 3 issued otherwise than by the government of a member State or a local authority in a member State; and

(c)   paragraphs 4 and 5 shall have effect as if they referred only to investments falling within paragraph 1.

142(4) **[Application to Sch. 1 para. 6 investments]** The Secretary of State may by order direct that this section shall apply also to investments falling within paragraph 6 of Schedule 1 to this Act or to such investments of any class or description.

Note
See the Official Listing of Securities (Units in Single Property Schemes) Order 1989 (SI 1989/29).

142(5) **[Annulment of sec. 142(4) order]** An order under subsection (4) above shall be subject to annulment in pursuance of a resolution of either House of Parliament.

142(6) **["The competent authority"]** In this Part of this Act "the competent authority" means, subject to section 157 below, The International Stock Exchange of the United Kingdom and the Republic of Ireland Limited; and that authority may make rules (in this Act referred to as "listing rules") for the purposes of any of the following provisions.

142(7) **[Other definitions]** In this Part of this Act—

"approved exchange" means, in relation to dealings in securities, a recognised investment exchange approved by the Treasury for the purposes of the Public Offers of Securities Regulations 1995 either generally or in relation to such dealings;

"issuer", in relation to any securities, means the person by whom they have been or are to be issued except that in relation to a certificate or other instrument falling within paragraph 5 of Schedule 1 to this Act it means the person who issued or is to issue the securities to which the certificate or instrument relates;

"the Official List" means the list maintained by the competent authority for the purposes of this Part of this Act;

"securities" means investments to which this section applies;

and references to listing are references to inclusion in the Official List in pursuance of this Part of this Act.

142(7A) **[What constitutes offer of securities]** For the purposes of this Act—

(a)   a person offers securities if, as principal—

(i)   he makes an offer which, if accepted, would give rise to a contract for their issue or sale (which for this purpose includes any disposal for valuable consideration) by him or by another person with whom he has made arrangements for their issue or sale; or

(ii)   he invites a person to make such an offer,

but not otherwise; and, except where the context otherwise requires, "offer" and "offeror" shall be construed accordingly; and

s. 142(7A)

(b)   whether a person offers securities to the public in the United Kingdom shall be determined in accordance with Schedule 11A to this Act.

142(8) [Exercise of functions of competent authority] Any functions of the competent authority under this Part of this Act may be exercised by its governing body or by any committee or sub-committee of that body or by any officer or servant of the authority except that listing rules—

(a)   shall be made only by the governing body of the authority or by a committee or sub-committee of that body; and

(b)   if made by a committee or sub-committee, shall cease to have effect at the end of the period of twenty-eight days beginning with the day on which they are made (but without prejudice to anything done under them) unless before the end of that period they are confirmed by the governing body of the authority.

142(9) [Effect on powers of competent authority] Nothing in this Part of this Act affects the powers of the competent authority in respect of investments to which this section does not apply and such investments may be admitted to the Official List otherwise than in accordance with this Part of this Act.

Note
See the Investment Services Regulations 1995 (SI 1995/3275), reg. 32 and Sch. 7, para. 35.

SEC. 143   Applications for listing

143(1) [Manner of making application] An application for listing shall be made to the competent authority in such manner as the listing rules may require.

143(2) [Consent of issuer of securities] No application for the listing of any securities shall be made except by or with the consent of the issuer of the securities.

143(3) [Private companies, old public companies] No application for listing shall be made in respect of securities to be issued by a private company or by an old public company within the meaning of section 1 of the Companies Consolidation (Consequential Provisions) Act 1985 or the corresponding Northern Ireland provision.

SEC. 144   Admission to list

144(1) [Requirements for listings] The competent authority shall not admit any securities to the Official List except on an application duly made in accordance with section 143 above and unless satisfied that—

(a)   the requirements of the listing rules made by the authority for the purposes of this section and in force when the application is made; and

(b)   any other requirements imposed by the authority in relation to that application, are complied with.

144(2) [Conditions re securities offered to public in UK] Listing rules shall require as a condition of the admission to the Official List of any securities for which application for admission has been made and which are to be offered to the public in the United Kingdom for the first time before admission—

(a)   the submission to, and approval by, the authority of a prospectus in such form and containing such information as may be specified in the rules; and

(b)   the publication of that prospectus.

144(2A) [Conditions re other securities] Listing rules may require as a condition of the admission to the Official List of any other securities—

(a) the submission to, and approval by, the authority of a document (in this Act referred to as "listing particulars") in such form and containing such information as may be specified in the rules; and

(b) the publication of that document;

or, in such cases as may be specified by the rules, the publication of a document other than listing particulars or a prospectus.

144(2B) [Effect of sec. 144(2) and (2A)] Subsections (2) and (2A) have effect without prejudice to the generality of the power of the competent authority to make listing rules for the purposes of this section.

144(3) [Possible grounds for refusing application] The competent authority may refuse an application—

(a) if it considers that by reason of any matter relating to the issuer the admission of the securities would be detrimental to the interests of investors; or

(b) in the case of securities already officially listed in another member State, if the issuer has failed to comply with any obligations to which he is subject by virtue of that listing.

144(4) [Notification to applicant of decision] The competent authority shall notify the applicant or its decision on the application within six months from the date on which the application is received or, if within that period the authority has required the applicant to furnish further information in connection with the application, from the date on which that information is furnished.

144(5) [If no application as in sec. 144(4)] If the competent authority does not notify the applicant of its decision within the time required by subsection (4) above it shall be taken to have refused the application.

144(6) [Once securities admitted] When any securities have been admitted to the Official List their admission shall not be called in question on the ground that any requirement or condition for their admission has not been complied with.

SEC. 145   Discontinuance and suspension of listing

145(1) [Power to discontinue listing] The competent authority may, in accordance with the listing rules, discontinue the listing of any securities if satisfied that there are special circumstances which preclude normal regular dealings in the securities.

145(2) [Power to suspend listing] The competent authority may in accordance with the listing rules suspend the listing of any securities.

145(3) [Suspended securities for sec. 153, 155] Securities the listing of which is suspended under subsection (2) above shall nevertheless be regarded as listed for the purposes of sections 153 and 155 below.

145(4) [Applications] This section applies to securities included in the Official List at the coming into force of this Part of this Act as it applies to securities included by virtue of this Part.

SEC. 146   General duty of disclosure in listing particulars

146(1) [Other information in listing particulars] In addition to the information specified by listing rules or required by the competent authority as a condition of the admission of any securities to the Official List any listing particulars submitted to the competent authority under section 144 above shall contain all such information as investors and their professional advisers would reasonably require, and reasonably expect to find there, for the purpose of making an informed assessment of—

(a)   the assets and liabilities, financial position, profits and losses, and prospects of the issuer of the securities; and

(b)   the rights attaching to those securities.

Note
See s. 156A(3)(b) re no application for listing.

146(2) [Scope of information in sec. 146(1)] The information to be included by virtue of this section shall be such information as is mentioned in subsection (1) above which is within the knowledge of any person responsible for the listing particulars or which it would be reasonable for him to obtain by making enquiries.

146(3) [Relevant matters to be considered] In determining what information is required to be included in listing particulars by virtue of this section regard shall be had—

(a)   to the nature of the securities and of the issuer of the securities;

(b)   to the nature of the persons likely to consider their acquisition;

(c)   to the fact that certain matters may reasonably be expected to be within the knowledge of professional advisers of any kind which those persons may reasonably be expected to consult; and

(d)   to any information available to investors or their professional advisers by virtue of requirements imposed under section 153 below or by or under any other enactment or by virtue of requirements imposed by a recognised investment exchange for the purpose of complying with paragraph 2(2)(b) of Schedule 4 to this Act.

SEC. 147   Supplementary listing particulars

147(1) [Notification re significant changes, new matters] If at any time after the preparation of listing particulars for submission to the competent authority under section 144 above and before the commencement of dealings in the securities following their admission to the Official List—

(a)   there is a significant change affecting any matter contained in those particulars whose inclusion was required by section 146 above or by listing rules or by the competent authority; or

(b)   a significant new matter arises the inclusion of information in respect of which would have been so required if it had arisen when the particulars were prepared,

the issuer of the securities shall, in accordance with listing rules made for the purposes of this section, submit to the competent authority for its approval and, if approved, publish supplementary listing particulars of the change or new matter.

Note
See s. 156A(3)(b) re no application for listing.

147(2) ["Significant" in sec. 147(1)] In subsection (1) above "significant" means significant for the purpose of making an informed assessment of the matters mentioned in section 146(1) above.

147(3) [Where issuer of securities not aware of change etc.] Where the issuer of the securities is not aware of the change or new matter in question he shall not be under any duty to comply with subsection (1) above unless he is notified of it by a person responsible for the listing particulars; but it shall be the duty of any person responsible for those particulars who is aware of such a matter to give notice of it to the issuer.

147(4) **[Extended application of sec. 147(1)]** Subsection (1) above applies also as respects matters contained in any supplementary listing particulars previously published under this section in respect of the securities in question.

SEC. 148   Exemptions from disclosure

148(1) **[Grounds for omission of information]** The competent authority may authorise the omission from listing particulars or supplementary listing particulars of any information the inclusion of which would otherwise be required by section 146 above—

(a)   on the ground that its disclosure would be contrary to the public interest;

(b)   subject to subsection (2) below, on the ground that its disclosure would be seriously detrimental to the issuer of the securities; or

(c)   in the case of securities which fall within paragraph 2 of Schedule 1 to this Act as modified by section 142(3)(b) above and are of any class specified by listing rules, on the ground that its disclosure is unnecessary for persons of the kind who may be expected normally to buy or deal in the securities.

148(2) **[Qualification re sec. 148(1)(b)]** No authority shall be granted under subsection (1)(b) above in respect of, and no such authority shall be regarded as extending to, information the non-disclosure of which would be likely to mislead a person considering the acquisition of the securities as to any facts the knowledge of which it is essential for him to have in order to make an informed assessment.

148(3) **[Certificate re sec. 148(1)(a)]** The Secretary of State or the Treasury may issue a certificate to the effect that the disclosure of any information (including information that would otherwise have to be included in particulars for which they are themselves responsible) would be contrary to the public interest and the competent authority shall be entitled to act on any such certificate in exercising its powers under subsection (1)(a) above.

148(4) **[Rules under sec. 156(2)]** This section is without prejudice to any powers of the competent authority under rules made by virtue of section 156(2) below.

SEC. 149   Registration of listing particulars

149(1) **[Copy of particulars to registrar]** On or before the date on which listing particulars or supplementary listing particulars are published as required by listing rules a copy of the particulars shall be delivered for registration to the registrar of companies and a statement that a copy has been delivered to him shall be included in the particulars.

149(2) **["The registrar of companies"]** In subsection (1) above "the registrar of companies" means—

(a)   if the securities in question are or are to be issued by a company incorporated in Great Britain, the registrar of companies in England and Wales or the registrar of companies in Scotland according to whether the company's registered office is in England and Wales or in Scotland;

(b)   if the securities in question are or are to be issued by a company incorporated in Northern Ireland, the registrar of companies for Northern Ireland;

(c)   in any other case, any of those registrars.

149(3) [Offence, penalty] If any particulars are published without a copy of them having been delivered as required by this section the issuer of the securities in question and any person who is knowingly a party to the publication shall be guilty of an offence and liable—

(a)   on conviction on indictment, to a fine;
(b)   on summary conviction, to a fine not exceeding the statutory maximum.

SEC. 150   Compensation for false or misleading particulars

150(1) [Liability for compensation] Subject to section 151 below, the person or persons responsible for any listing particulars or supplementary listing particulars shall be liable to pay compensation to any person who has acquired any of the securities in question and suffered loss in respect of them as a result of any untrue or misleading statement in the particulars or the omission from them of any matter required to be included by section 146 or 147 above.

150(2) [Omission of information from particulars] Where listing rules require listing particulars to include information as to any particular matter on the basis that the particulars must include a statement either as to that matter or, if such is the case, that there is no such matter, the omission from the particulars of the information shall be treated for the purposes of subsection (1) above as a statement that there is no such matter.

150(3) [Non-compliance with sec. 147] Subject to section 151 below, a person who fails to comply with section 147 above shall be liable to pay compensation to any person who has acquired any of the securities in question and suffered loss in respect of them as a result of the failure.

150(4) [Other liability] This section does not affect any liability which any person may incur apart from this section.

150(5) [Interpretation] References in this section to the acquisition by any person of securities include references to his contracting to acquire them or an interest in them.

150(6) [Exclusion of liability as promoter etc.] No person shall by reason of being a promoter of a company or otherwise incur any liability for failing to disclose any information which he would not be required to disclose in listing particulars in respect of a company's securities if he were responsible for those particulars or, if he is responsible for them, which he is entitled to omit by virtue of section 148 above.

The reference above to a person incurring liability includes reference to any other person being entitled as against that person to be granted any civil remedy or to rescind or repudiate any agreement.

SEC. 151   Exemption from liability to pay compensation

151(1) [No liability if believed statement true etc.] A person shall not incur any liability under section 150(1) above for any loss in respect of securities caused by any such statement or omission as is there mentioned if he satisfied the court that at the time when the particulars were submitted to the competent authority he reasonably believed, having made such enquiries (if any) as were reasonable, that the statement was true and not misleading or that the matter whose omission caused the loss was properly omitted and—

(a)   that he continued in that belief until the time when the securities were acquired; or
(b)   that they were acquired before it was reasonably practicable to bring a correction to the attention of persons likely to acquire the securities in question; or

(c)   that before the securities were acquired he had taken all such steps as it was reasonable for him to have taken to secure that a correction was brought to the attention of those persons; or

(d)   that he continued in that belief until after the commencement of dealings in the securities following their admission to the Official List and that the securities were acquired after such a lapse of time that he ought in the circumstances to be reasonably excused.

Note
See s. 156A(3)(b) re no application for listing.

151(2) [Where statement by expert] A person shall not incur any liability under section 150(1) above for any loss in respect of securities caused by a statement purporting to be made by or on the authority of another person as an expert which is, and is stated to be, included in the particulars with that other person's consent if he satisfies the court that at the time when the particulars were submitted to the competent authority he believed on reasonable grounds that the other person was competent to make or authorise the statement and had consented to its inclusion in the form and context in which it was included and—

(a)   that he continued in that belief until the time when the securities were acquired; or

(b)   that they were acquired before it was reasonably practicable to bring the fact that the expert was not competent or had not consented to the attention of persons likely to acquire the securities in question; or

(c)   that before the securities were acquired he had taken all such steps as it was reasonable for him to have taken to secure that that fact was brought to the attention of those persons; or

(d)   that he continued in that belief until after the commencement of dealings in the securities following their admission to the Official List and that the securities were acquired after such a lapse of time that he ought in the circumstances to be reasonably excused.

Note
See s. 156A(3)(b) re no application for listing.

151(3) [Extra matters re sec. 150(1), 151(1), (2)] Without prejudice to subsections (1) and (2) above, a person shall not incur any liability under section 150(1) above for any loss in respect of any securities caused by any such statement or omission as is there mentioned if he satisfies the court—

(a)   that before the securities were acquired a correction, or where the statement was such as is mentioned in subsection (2), the fact that the expert was not competent or had not consented had been published in a manner calculated to bring it to the attention of persons likely to acquire the securities in question; or

(b)   that he took all such steps as it was reasonable for him to take to secure such publication and reasonably believed that it had taken place before the securities were acquired.

151(4) [Where statement by official] A person shall not incur any liability under section 150(1) above for any loss resulting from a statement made by an official person or contained in a public official document which is included in the particulars if he satisfies the court that the statement is accurately and fairly reproduced.

151(5) [Statement as in sec. 150(1), (3)] A person shall not incur any liability under section 150(1) or (3) above if he satisfies the court that the person suffering the loss acquired the securities in question with knowledge that the statement was false or misleading, of the omitted matter or of the change or new matter, as the case may be.

151(6) [Change etc. as in sec. 150(3)] A person shall not incur any liability under section 150(3) above if he satisfies the court that he reasonably believed that the change or new matter in question was not such as to call for supplementary listing particulars.

151(7) ["Expert"] In this section "expert" includes any engineer, valuer, accountant or other person whose profession, qualifications or experience give authority to a statement made by him; and references to the acquisition of securities include references to contracting to acquire them or an interest in them.

SEC. 152   Persons responsible for particulars

152(1) [Persons responsible—interpretation] For the purposes of this Part of this Act the persons responsible for listing particulars or supplementary listing particulars are—

(a)   the issuer of the securities to which the particulars relate;
(b)   where the issuer is a body corporate, each person who is a director of that body at the time when the particulars are submitted to the competent authority;
(c)   where the issuer is a body corporate, each person who has authorised himself to be named, and is named, in the particulars as a director or as having agreed to become a director of that body either immediately or at a future time;
(d)   each person who accepts, and is stated in the particulars as accepting, responsibility for, or for any part of, the particulars;
(e)   each person not falling within any of the foregoing paragraphs who has authorised the contents of, or any part of, the particulars.

152(2) [Where person not responsible under sec. 152(1)(b)] A person is not responsible for any particulars by virtue of subsection (1)(b) above if they are published without his knowledge or consent and on becoming aware of their publication he forthwith gives reasonable public notice that they were published without his knowledge or consent.

152(3) [Where person only authorised part of particulars — sec. 152(1)(d), (e)] Where a person has accepted responsibility for, or authorised, only part of the contents of any particulars, he is responsible under subsection (1)(d) or (e) above for only that part and only if it is included in (or substantially in) the form and context to which he has agreed.

152(4) [Where particulars re offer by issuer etc.] Where the particulars relate to securities which are to be issued in connection with an offer by (or by a wholly-owned subsidiary of), the issuer for, or an agreement for the acquisition by (or by a wholly-owned subsidiary of) the issuer of, securities issued by another person or in connection with any arrangement whereby the whole of the undertaking of another person is to become the undertaking of the issuer (of a wholly-owned subsidiary of the issuer or of a body corporate which will become such a subsidiary by virtue of the arrangement) then if—

(a)   that other person; and
(b)   where that other person is a body corporate, each person who is a director of that body at the time when the particulars are submitted to the competent authority and each other person who has authorised himself to be named, and is named, in the particulars as a director of that body,

is responsible by virtue of paragraph (d) of subsection (1) above for any part of the particulars relating to that other person or to the securities or undertaking to which the offer, agreement or arrangement relates, no person shall be responsible for that part under paragraph (a), (b) or (c) of that subsection but without prejudice to his being responsible under paragraph (d).

152(4A) [Electricity (Northern Ireland) Order 1992] Where—

(a)   the same document contains particulars relating to the securities of two or more successor companies within the meaning of Part III of the Electricity (Northern Ireland) Order 1992; and

(b)   any person's responsibility for any information included in the document is stated in the document to be confined to its inclusion as part of the particulars relating to the securities of any one of those companies,

that person shall not be treated as responsible for that information in so far as it is stated in the document to form part of the particulars relating to the securities of any other of those companies.

152(5) [Non-application of sec. 152(1)(b), (c) re international securities] Neither paragraph (b) nor paragraph (c) of subsection (1) above applies in the case of an issuer of international securities of a class specified by listing rules for the purposes of section 148(1)(c) above; and neither of those paragraphs nor paragraph (b) of subsection (4) above applies in the case of any director certified by the competent authority as a person to whom that paragraph should not apply by reason of his having an interest, or of any other circumstances, making it inappropriate for him to be responsible by virtue of that paragraph.

152(6) ["International securities"] In subsection (5) above "international securities" means any investment falling within paragraph 2 of Schedule 1 to this Act as modified by section 142(3)(b) above which is of a kind likely to be dealt in by bodies incorporated in or persons resident in a country or territory outside the United Kingdom, is denominated in a currency other than sterling or is otherwise connected with such a country or territory.

152(7) ["Wholly-owned subsidiary"] In this section "wholly-owned subsidiary", in relation to a person other than a body corporate, means any body corporate that would be his wholly-owned subsidiary if he were a body corporate.

152(8) [Advice given in professional capacity] Nothing in this section shall be construed as making a person responsible for any particulars by reason of giving advice as to their contents in a professional capacity.

152(9) [Status of payment of compensation] Where by virtue of this section the issuer of any shares pays or is liable to pay compensation under section 150 above for loss suffered in respect of shares for which a person has subscribed no account shall be taken of that liability or payment in determining any question as to the amount paid on subscription for those shares or as to the amount paid up or deemed to be paid up on them.

Note
See s. 156A(3)(b) re no application for listing.

SEC. 153   Obligations of issuers of listed securities

153(1) [Listing rules may specify certain requirements] Listing rules may specify requirements to be complied with by issuers of listed securities and make provision with respect to the action that may be taken by the competent authority in the event of non-compliance, including provision—

(a)   authorising the authority to publish the fact that an issuer has contravened any provision of the rules; and

(b)   if the rules require an issuer to publish any information, authorising the authority to publish it in the event of his failure to do so.

153(2) [Application] This section applies to the issuer of securities included in the Official List at the coming into force of this Part of this Act as it applies to the issuer of securities included by virtue of this Part.

SEC. 154   Advertisements etc. in connection with listing applications

154(1) [Conditions re advertisement] Where listing particulars are or are to be published in connection with an application for the listing of any securities no advertisement or other information of a kind specified by listing rules shall be issued in the United Kingdom unless the contents of the advertisement or other information have been submitted to the competent authority and that authority has either—

(a)   approved those contents; or
(b)   authorised the issue of the advertisement or information without such approval.

Note
See s. 156A(3)(b) re no application for listing.

154(2) [Effect of contravention of section] An authorised person who contravenes this section shall be treated as having contravened rules made under Chapter V of Part I of this Act or, in the case of a person who is an authorised person by virtue of his membership of a recognised self-regulating organisation or certification by a recognised professional body, the rules of that organisation or body.

154(3) [Offence, penalty] Subject to subsection (4) below, a person other than an authorised person, who contravenes this section shall be guilty of an offence and liable—

(a)   on conviction on indictment, to imprisonment for a term not exceeding two years or to a fine or to both;
(b)   on summary conviction, to a fine not exceeding the statutory maximum.

154(4) [Defence] A person who in the ordinary course of a business other than investment business issues an advertisement or other information to the order of another person shall not be guilty of an offence under this section if he proves that he believed on reasonable grounds that the advertisement or information had been approved or its issue authorised by the competent authority.

154(5) [Exclusion of liability for certain persons] Where information has been approved, or its issue has been authorised, under this section neither the person issuing it nor any person responsible for, or for any part of, the listing particulars shall incur any civil liability by reason of any statement in or omission from the information if that information and the listing particulars, taken together, would not be likely to mislead persons of the kind likely to consider the acquisition of the securities in question.

The reference above to a person incurring civil liability includes a reference to any other person being entitled as against that person to be granted any civil remedy or to rescind or repudiate any agreement.

Note
Concerning European investment firms, see the Investment Services Regulations 1995 (SI 1995/3275), reg. 32 and Sch. 7, para. 36.
Concerning European institutions, see the Banking Coordination (Second Council Directive) Regulations 1992 (SI 1992/3218), reg. 55 and Sch. 9, para. 37.

SEC. 154A   Application of Part IV to prospectuses

154A Sections 146 to 152 and 154 above shall apply in relation to a prospectus required by listing rules in accordance with section 144(2) above as they apply in relation to listing particulars, but as if—

(a)   any reference to listing particulars were a reference to a prospectus and any reference to supplementary listing particulars were a reference to a supplementary prospectus; and

(b)   notwithstanding section 142(7) above, any reference in section 152 above (other than in subsection (1)(b) of that section) to the issuer of securities included a reference to the person offering or proposing to offer them.

SEC. 155   Fees

155 Listing rules may require the payment of fees to the competent authority in respect of applications for listing and the retention of securities in the Official List.

SEC. 156   Listing rules: general provisions

156(1) [Different provisions] Listing rules may make different provision for different cases.

156(2) [Dispensing with or modifying rules] Listing rules may authorise the competent authority to dispense with or modify the application of the rules in particular cases and by reference to any circumstances.

156(3) [To be made by instrument in writing] Listing rules shall be made by an instrument in writing.

156(4) [Printing, publication] Immediately after an instrument containing listing rules is made it shall be printed and made available to the public with or without payment.

156(5) [Defence re contravention of rule] A person shall not be taken to have contravened any listing rule if he shows that at the time of the alleged contravention the instrument containing the rule had not been made available as required by subsection (4) above.

156(6) [Certificate on instrument] The production of a printed copy of an instrument purporting to be made by the competent authority on which is endorsed a certificate signed by an officer of the authority authorised by it for that purpose and stating—

(a)   that the instrument was made by the authority;

(b)   that the copy is a true copy of the instrument; and

(c)   that on a specified date the instrument was made available to the public as required by subsection (4) above,

shall be prima facie evidence or, in Scotland, sufficient evidence of the facts stated in the certificate.

156(7) [Deemed signing of certificate] Any certificate purporting to be signed as mentioned in subsection (6) above shall be deemed to have been duly signed unless the contrary is shown.

156(8) [Citation of instrument in legal proceedings] Any person wishing in any legal proceedings to cite an instrument made by the competent authority may require the authority to cause a copy of it to be endorsed with such a certificate as is mentioned in subsection (6) above.

SEC. 156A   Approval of prospectus where no application for listing

156A(1) [Situations where approval required] Listing rules may also provide for a prospectus to be submitted to and approved by the competent authority where—

(a)   securities are to be offered to the public in the United Kingdom for the first time;

(b)   no application for listing of the securities has been made under this Part of this Act; and

(c)   the prospectus is submitted by or with the consent of the issuer of the securities.

156A(2) [Listing rules under sec. 156A(1)] Listing rules made under subsection (1) above may make provision—

(a)   as to the information to be contained in, and the form of, a prospectus submitted under any such rules; and

(b)   subject to the provisions of the Public Offers of Securities Regulations 1995, as to the timing and manner of publication of such a prospectus.

156A(3) [Application of sec. 146–152 and sec. 154] Sections 146 to 152 and 154 above shall apply in relation to such a prospectus as they apply in relation to listing particulars but as if—

(a)   any reference to listing particulars were a reference to a prospectus and any reference to supplementary listing particulars were a reference to a supplementary prospectus;

(b)   in section 146(1) above—

(i)   the words "as a condition of the admission of any securities to the Official List" were omitted; and

(ii)   for the words "section 144 above" there were substituted "section 156A(1) below";

(c)   in section 147(1) above, for the words "under section 144 above and before the commencement of dealings in the securities following their admission to the Official List" there were substituted "under section 156A(1) below and before the end of the period during which the offer to which the prospectus relates remains open";

(d)   in subsections (1)(d) and (2)(d) of section 151 above—

(i)   the words "that he continued in that belief until after the commencement of dealings in the securities following their admission to the Official List and" were omitted; and

(ii)   the words "and, if the securities are dealt in on an approved exchange, that he continued in that belief until after the commencement of dealings in the securities on that exchange" were added at the end;

(e)   notwithstanding section 142(7) above, any reference in section 152 above (other than in subsection (1)(b) of that section) to the issuer of securities included a reference to the person offering or proposing to offer them; and

(f)   in section 154(1) above, for the words "Where listing particulars are or are to be published in connection with an application for the listing of any securities" there were substituted "Where a prospectus is or is to be published in connection with an application for approval, then, until the end of the period during which the offer to which the prospectus relates remains open,".

s. 156A(1)

156A(4) [Payment of fees] Listing rules made under this section may require the payment of fees to the competent authority in respect of a prospectus submitted for approval under the rules.

SEC. 156B   Publication of prospectus

156B(1) [Offer without prospectus unlawful] Where listing rules made under section 144(2) above require the publication of a prospectus, it shall not be lawful, before the time of publication of the prospectus, to offer the securities in question to the public in the United Kingdom.

156B(2) [Contravention of sec. 156B(1)] An authorised person who contravenes subsection (1) above shall be treated as contravening rules made under Chapter V of Part I of this Act or, in the case of a person who is an authorised person by virtue of his membership of a recognised self-regulating organisation or certification by a recognised professional body, the rules of that organisation or body.

156B(3) [Offence, penalty] A person, other than an authorised person, who contravenes subsection (1) above shall be guilty of an offence and liable—

(a)   on conviction on indictment, to imprisonment for a term not exceeding two years or to a fine or to both;

(b)   on summary conviction, to imprisonment for a term not exceeding three months or a fine not exceeding level 5 on the standard scale.

Note
See the Public Offers of Securities Regulations 1995, reg. 1, 17 and Sch. 2, para. 3: s. 156B(3) shall not apply to a European institution carrying on home-regulated investment business in the United Kingdom which contravenes s. 156B(1), but it shall be treated for all purposes as if it is not a member of a recognised self-regulating organisation, as having contravened rules made under Pt. I, Ch. V; or if it is a member of a recognised self-regulating organisation, as having contravened the rules of that organisation.

156B(4) [Non-contravention of s. 156B(1)] Without predjudice to any liability under section 150 above, a person shall not be regarded as contravening subsection (1) above by reason only of a prospectus not having fully complied with the requirements of listing rules to its form or content.

156B(5) [Action by person suffering loss] Any contravention of subsection (1) above shall be actionable at the suit of a person who suffers loss as a result of the contravention subject to the defences and other incidents applying to actions for breach of statutory duty.

SEC. 157   Alteration of competent authority

157 (Repealed by the Official Listing of Securities (Change of Competent Authority) Regulations 1991 (SI 1991/2000), reg. 3(2) as from 2 October 1991.)

PART V — OFFERS OF UNLISTED SECURITIES

158–171 (Repealed by the Public Offers of Securities Regulations 1995 (SI 1995/1537), reg. 1, 17 and Sch. 2, para. 4 as from 19 June 1995.)

s. 156B(5)

PART VI — TAKEOVER OFFERS

SEC. 172   Takeover offers

172(1) [Substitution of sec. 428–430 of Companies Act 1985] The provisions set out in Schedule 12 of this Act shall be substituted for sections 428, 429 and 430 of the Companies Act 1985.

172(2) [Exception re sec. 172(1)] Subsection (1) above does not affect any case in which the offer in respect of the scheme or contract mentioned in section 428(1) was made before the coming into force of this section.

PART VII — INSIDER DEALING

173–176 (Repealed by Criminal Justice Act 1993, sec. 79(14) and Sch. 6, Pt. I as from 1 March 1994.)

SEC. 177   Investigations into insider dealing

177(1) [Power of Secretary of State to appoint inspectors] If it appears to the Secretary of State that there are circumstances suggesting that an offence under Part V of the Criminal Justice Act 1993 (insider dealing) may have been committed, he may appoint one or more competent inspectors to carry out such investigations as are requisite to establish whether or not any such offence has been committed and to report the results of their investigations to him.

177(2) [Scope of appointment] The appointment under this section of an inspector may limit the period during which he is to continue his investigation or confine it to particular matters.

177(2A) [Variation of appointment] At any time during the investigation the Secretary of State may vary the appointment by limiting or extending the period during which the inspector is to continue his investigation or by confining the investigation to particular matters.

177(3) [Power of inspectors re production, attendance etc.] If the inspectors consider that any person is or may be able to give information concerning any such offence they may require that person—

(a)   to produce to them any documents in his possession or under his control which appear to them to be relevant to the investigation;

(b)   to attend before them; and

(c)   otherwise to give them all assistance in connection with the investigation which he is reasonably able to give;

and it shall be the duty of that person to comply with that requirement.

177(4) [Power re examination under oath] An inspector may examine on oath any person who he considers is or may be able to give information concerning any such offence, and may administer an oath accordingly.

177(5) [Reports to Secretary of State] The inspectors shall make such interim reports to the Secretary of State as they think fit or he may direct and on the conclusion of the investigation they shall make a final report to him.

177(5A) [Direction by Secretary of State] If the Secretary of State thinks fit, he may direct the inspector to take no further steps in the investigation or to take only such further steps as are specified in the direction; and where an investigation is the subject of such a direction, the inspectors shall make a final report to the Secretary of State only where the Secretary of State directs them to do so.

177(6) [Statement may be used in evidence] A statement made by a person in compliance with a requirement imposed by virtue of this section may be used in evidence against him.

177(7) [Legal professional privilege, confidentiality] A person shall not under this section be required to disclose any information or produce any document which he would be entitled to refuse to disclose or produce on grounds of legal professional privilege in proceedings in the High Court or on grounds of confidentiality as between client and professional legal adviser in proceedings in the Court of Session.

177(8) [Disclosure by bankers] A person shall not under this section be required to disclose any information or produce any document in respect of which he owes an obligation of confidence by virtue of carrying on the business of banking unless—

(a)   the person to whom the obligation of confidence is owed consents to the disclosure or production, or

(b)   the making of the requirement was authorised by the Secretary of State.

177(9) [Where lien claimed] Where a person claims a lien on a document its production under this section shall be without prejudice to his lien.

177(10) ["Document"] In this section "document" includes information recorded in any form; and in relation to information recorded otherwise than in legible form the power to require its production includes power to require the production of a copy of the information in legible form.

177(11) [Expenses] A person who is convicted on a prosecution instituted as a result of an investigation under this section may in the same proceedings be ordered to pay the expenses of the investigation to such extent as may be specified in the order.

There shall be treated as expenses of the investigation, in particular, such reasonable sums as the Secretary of State may determine in respect of general staff costs and overheads.

SEC. 178   Penalties for failure to co-operate with sec. 177 investigations

178(1) [Certificate to court re refusal to co-operate] If any person—

(a)   refuses to comply with any request under subsection (3) of section 177 above; or

(b)   refuses to answer any question put to him by the inspectors appointed under that section with respect to any matter relevant for establishing whether or not any suspected offence has been committed,

the inspectors may certify that fact in writing to the court and the court may inquire into the case.

178(2) [Power of court] If, after hearing any witness who may be produced against or on behalf of the alleged offender and any statement which may be offered in defence, the court is satisfied that he did without reasonable excuse refuse to comply with such a request or answer any such question, the court may—

(a)   punish him in like manner as if he had been guilty of contempt of the court; or

(b)   direct that the Secretary of State may exercise his powers under this section in respect of him;

and the court may give a direction under paragraph (b) above notwithstanding that the offender is not within the jurisdiction of the court if the court is satisfied that he was notified of his right to appear before the court and of the powers available under this section.

178(3)   [Power of Secretary of State re authorised person on sec. 178(2)(b) direction] Where the court gives a direction under subsection (2)(b) above in respect of an authorised person the Secretary of State may serve a notice on him—

(a)   cancelling any authorisation of his to carry on investment business after the expiry of a specified period after the service of the notice;

(b)   disqualifying him from becoming authorised to carry on investment business after the expiry of a specified period;

(c)   restricting any authorisation of his in respect of investment business during a specified period to the performance of contracts entered into before the notice comes into force;

(d)   prohibiting him from entering into transactions of a specified kind or entering into them except in specified circumstances or to a specified extent;

(e)   prohibiting him from soliciting business from persons of a specified kind or otherwise than from such persons; or

(f)   prohibiting him from carrying on business in a specified manner or otherwise than in a specified manner.

178(4)   [Period in sec. 178(3)(a)–(c)] The period mentioned in paragraphs (a) and (c) of subsection (3) above shall be such period as appears to the Secretary of State reasonable to enable the person on whom the notice is served to complete the performance of any contracts entered into before the notice comes into force and to terminate such of them as are of a continuing nature.

178(5)   [Power of Secretary of State re unauthorised person on sec. 178(2)(b) direction] Where the court gives a direction under subsection (2)(b) above in the case of an unauthorised person the Secretary of State may direct that any authorised person who knowingly transacts investment business of a specified kind, or in specified circumstances or to a specified extent, with or on behalf of that unauthorised person shall be treated as having contravened rules made under Chapter V of Part I of this Act or, in the case of a person who is an authorised person by virtue of his membership of a recognised self-regulating organisation or certification by a recognised professional body, the rules of that organisation or body.

178(6)   [Interpretation re reasonable excuse in sec. 178(2)] A person shall not be treated for the purposes of subsection (2) above as having a reasonable excuse for refusing to comply with a request or answer a question in a case where the offence or suspected offence being investigated relates to dealing by him on the instructions or for the account of another person, by reason that at the time of the refusal—

(a)   he did not know the identity of that other person; or

(b)   he was subject to the law of a country or territory outside the United Kingdom which prohibited him from disclosing information relating to the dealing without the consent of that other person, if he might have obtained that consent or obtained exemption from that law.

178(7)   [Revocation of sec. 178(3) above] A notice served on a person under subsection (3) above may be revoked at any time by the Secretary of State by serving a revocation notice on him: and the Secretary of State shall revoke such a notice if it appears to him that he has agreed to comply with the relevant request or answer the relevant question.

178(8) [Effect of revocation of sec. 178(3)(a) above] The revocation of such a notice as is mentioned in subsection (3)(a) above shall not have the effect of reviving the authorisation cancelled by the notice except where the person would (apart from the notice) at the time of the revocation be an authorised person by virtue of his membership of a recognised self-regulating organisation or certification by a recognised professional body; but nothing in this subsection shall be construed as preventing any person who has been subject to such a notice from again becoming authorised after the revocation of the notice.

178(9) [Service of notice on designated agency, recognised body] If it appears to the Secretary of State—

(a) that a person on whom he serves a notice under subsection (3) above is an authorised person by virtue of an authorisation granted by a designated agency or by virtue of membership of a recognised self-regulating organisation or certificate by a recognised professional body; or

(b) that a person on whom he serves a revocation notice under subsection (7) above was such an authorised person at the time that the notice which is being revoked was served,

he shall serve a copy of the notice on that agency, organisation or body.

178(10) [Functions for sec. 114] The Functions to which section 114 above applies shall include the functions of the Secretary of State under this section but any transfer of those functions shall be subject to a reservation that they are to be exercisable by him concurrently with the designated agency and so as to be exercisable by the agency subject to such conditions or restrictions as the Treasury may from time to time impose.

Note
Concerning European investment firms, see the Investment Services Regulations 1995 (SI 1995/3275), reg. 32 and Sch. 7, para. 37.
See the Financial Services Act 1986 (Delegation) Order 1987 (SI 1987/942).
Concerning European institutions, see the Banking Coordination (Second Council Directive) Regulations 1992 (SI 1992/3218), reg. 55 and Sch. 9, para. 39.

PART VIII — RESTRICTIONS ON DISCLOSURE OF INFORMATION

SEC. 179   Restrictions on disclosure of information

179(1) [No disclosure without consent] Subject to section 180 below, information which is restricted information for the purposes of this section and relates to the business or other affairs of any person shall not be disclosed by a person mentioned in subsection (3) below ("the primary recipient") or any person obtaining the information directly or indirectly from him without the consent of the person from whom the primary recipient obtained the information and if different, the person to whom it relates.

179(2) [Restricted information] Subject to subsection (4) below, information is restricted information for the purposes of this section if it was obtained by the primary recipient for the purposes of, or in the discharge of his functions under, this Act or any rules or regulations made under this Act (whether or not by virtue of any requirement to supply it made under those provisions).

s. 179(2)

Note
Concerning functions, see the Banking Coordination (Second Council Directive) Regulations 1992 (SI 1992/3218), reg. 55 and Sch. 9, para. 40.

179(3) [Persons in sec. 179(1)] The persons mentioned in subsection (1) above are—

(aa) the Treasury;

(a) the Secretary of State;

(b) any designated agency, transferee body or body administering a scheme under section 54 above;

(c) the Director General of Fair Trading;

(d) the Chief Registrar of friendly societies;

(e) the Friendly Societies Commission;

(f) the Bank of England;

(g) any member of the Tribunal;

(h) any person appointed or authorised to exercise any powers under section 94, 106 or 177 above;

(i) any officer or servant of any such person as is mentioned in paragraphs (a) to (h) above;

(j) any constable or other person named in a warrant issued under this Act.

179(4) [Information not to be treated as restricted] Information shall not be treated as restricted information for the purposes of this section if it has been made available to the public by virtue of being disclosed in any circumstances in which or for any purpose for which disclosure is not precluded by this section.

179(5) [Information obtained by competent authority] Subject to section 180 below, information obtained by the competent authority in the exercise of its functions under Part IV of this Act or received by it pursuant to a Community obligation from any authority exercising corresponding functions in another member State shall not be disclosed without the consent of the person from whom the competent authority obtained the information and, if different, the person to whom it relates.

179(6) [Offence, penalty] Any person who contravenes this section shall be guilty of an offence and liable—

(a) on conviction on indictment, to imprisonment for a term not exceeding two years or to a fine or to both;

(b) on summary conviction, to imprisonment for a term not exceeding three months or to a fine not exceeding the statutory maximum or to both.

Note
See note after s. 180.

SEC. 180   Exceptions from restrictions on disclosure

180(1) [Disclosures not precluded by sec. 179] Section 179 above shall not preclude the disclosure of information—

(a) with a view to the institution of or otherwise for the purposes of criminal proceedings;

(b) with a view to the institution of or otherwise for the purposes of any civil proceedings arising under or by virtue of this Act or proceedings before the Tribunal;

(bb) for the purpose of enabling or assisting the Treasury to exercise any of their powers under this Act or under Part III or VII of the Companies Act 1989;

s. 179(3)

(c) for the purpose of enabling or assisting the Secretary of State to exercise any powers conferred on him by this Act or by the enactments relating to companies, insurance companies or insolvency or by Part II, III or VII of the Companies Act 1989 or for the purpose of enabling or assisting any inspector appointed by him under the enactments relating to companies to discharge his functions;

(d) for the purpose of enabling or assisting the Department of Economic Development for Northern Ireland to exercise any powers conferred on it by the enactments relating to companies or insolvency or for the purpose of enabling or assisting any inspector appointed by it under the enactments relating to companies to discharge his functions;

(e) for the purpose—
   (i)   of enabling or assisting a designated agency to discharge its functions under this Act or Part VII of the Companies Act 1989,
   (ii) of enabling or assisting a transferee body or the competent authority to discharge its functions under this Act, or
   (iii) of enabling or assisting the body administering a scheme under section 54 above to discharge its functions under the scheme;

(f) for the purpose of enabling or assisting the Bank of England to discharge its functions under the Banking Act 1987 or any other functions;

(g) for the purpose of enabling or assisting the Deposit Protection Board to discharge its functions under that Act;

(h) for the purpose of enabling or assisting the Friendly Societies Commission to discharge its functions under this Act, the enactments relating to friendly societies or the enactments relating to industrial assurance;

(hh) for the purpose of enabling or assisting a body established by order under section 46 of the Companies Act 1989 to discharge its functions under Part II of that Act, or of enabling or assisting a recognised supervisory or qualifying body within the meaning of that Part to discharge its functions as such;

(i) for the purpose of enabling or assisting the Industrial Assurance Commissioner or the Industrial Assurance Commissioner for Northern Ireland to discharge his functions under the enactments relating to industrial assurance;

(j) for the purpose of enabling or assisting the Insurance Brokers Registration Council to discharge its functions under the Insurance Brokers (Registration) Act 1977;

(k) for the purpose of enabling or assisting an offical receiver to discharge his functions under the enactments relating to insolvency or for the purpose of enabling or assisting a body which is for the time being a recognised professional body for the purposes of section 391 of the Insolvency Act 1986 to discharge its functions as such;

(l) for the purpose of enabling or assisting the Building Societies Commission to discharge its functions under the Building Societies Act 1986;

(m) for the purpose of enabling or assisting the Director General of Fair Trading to discharge his functions under this Act;

(n) for the purpose of enabling or assisting a recognised self-regulating organisation, recognised investment exhange, recognised professional body, or recognised clearing house to discharge its functions as such;

(nn) to an Operator approved under the Uncertificated Securities Regulations 1995 if the information is necessary to ensure the proper functioning of a relevant system within the meaning of those Regulations in relation to defaults and potential defaults by market-participants;

s. 180(1)

(o)   with a view to the institution of, or otherwise for the purposes of, any disciplinary proceedings relating to the exercise by a solicitor, auditor, accountant, valuer or actuary of his professional duties;

(oo)   with a view to the institution of, or otherwise for the purposes of, any disciplinary proceedings relating to the discharge by a public servant of his duties;

(p)   for the purpose of enabling or assisting any person appointed or authorised to exercise any powers under section 43A or 44 of the Insurance Companies Act 1982, section 447 of the Companies Act 1985, section 94, 106 or 177 above or section 84 of the Companies act 1989 to discharge his functions;

(q)   for the purpose of enabling or assisting an auditor of an authorised person or a person approved under section 108 above to discharge his functions;

(qq)   for the purpose of enabling or assisting an overseas regulatory authority to exercise its regulatory functions;

(r)   if the information is or has been available to the public from other sources;

(s)   in a summary or collection of information framed in such a way as not to enable the identity of any person to whom the information relates to be ascertained; or

(t)   in pursuance of any Community obligation.

180(1A)   [Definitions] In subsection (1)—

(a)   in paragraph (oo) "public servant" means an officer or servant of the Crown or of any public or other authority for the time being designated for the purposes of that paragraph by order of the Secretary of State; and

(b)   in paragraph (qq) "overseas regulatory authority" and "regulatory functions" have the same meaning as in section 82 of the Companies Act 1989.

180(2)   [Disclosure to Secretary of State or Treasury] Section 179 above shall not preclude the disclosure of information to the Secretary of State or to the Treasury if the disclosure is made in the interests of investors or in the public interest.

180(3)   [Disclosures assisting public authorities etc.] Subject to subsection (4) below, section 179 above shall not preclude the disclosure of information for the purpose of enabling or assisting any public or other authority for the time being designated for the purposes of this subsection by an order made by the Secretary of State to discharge any functions which are specified in the order.

Note
See note after s. 180(4).

180(4)   [Scope of sec. 180(3) order] An order under subsection (3) above designating an authority for the purposes of that subsection may—

(a)   impose conditions subject to which the disclosure of information is permitted by that subsection; and

(b)   otherwise restrict the circumstances in which that subsection permits disclosure.

Note
For orders made under s. 180(3), (4) see SI 1986/2031, SI 1987/859, SI 1987/1141, SI 1988/1058, SI 1989/940, SI 1989/2009, SI 1993/1826 and SI 1994/340.

180(5)   [Further disclosures not precluded by sec. 179] Section 179 above shall not preclude the disclosure—

(a)   of any information contained in an unpublished report of the Tribunal which has been made available to any person under this Act, by the person to whom it was made available or by any person obtaining the information directly or indirectly from him;

(b)   of any information contained in any notice or copy of a notice served under this Act, notice of the contents of which has not been given to the public, by the person on whom it was served or any person obtaining the information directly or indirectly from him;

(c) of any information contained in the register kept under section 102 above by virtue of subsection (1)(e) of that section, by a person who has inspected the register under section 103(2) or (3) above or any person obtaining the information directly or indirectly from him.

180(6) (Omitted and repealed by Companies Act 1989, sec. 75(2), (6), 212 and Sch. 24 as from 21 February 1990.)

180(7) **[Disclosures by Director General of Fair Trading]** Section 179 above shall not preclude the disclosure of information by the Director General of Fair Trading or any officer or servant of his or any person obtaining the information directly or indirectly from the Director or any such officer or servant if the information was obtained by the Director or any such officer or servant for the purposes of or in the discharge of his functions under this Act (whether or not he was the primary recipient of the information within the meaning of section 179 above) and the disclosure is made—

(a) for the purpose of enabling or assisting the Director, the Secretary of State or any other Minister, the Monopolies and Mergers Commission or any Northern Ireland department to discharge any function conferred on him or them by the Fair Trading Act 1973 (other than Part II or III of that Act), the Restrictive Trade Practices Act 1976 or the Competition Act 1980; or

(b) for the purposes of any civil proceedings under any of those provisions;

and information shall not be treated as restricted information for the purposes of section 179 above if it has been made available to the public by virtue of this subsection.

180(8) **[Modification by Secretary of State]** The Secretary of State may by order modify the application of any provision of this section so as—

(a) to prevent the disclosure by virtue of that provision; or

(b) to restrict the extent to which disclosure is permitted by virtue of that provision,

of information received by a person specified in the order pursuant to a Community obligation from a person exercising functions in relation to a collective investment scheme who is also so specified.

180(9) **[Annulment of sec. 180(1A)(a), (3), (8) order by Parliament]** An order under subsection (1A)(a), (3) or (8) above shall be subject to annulment in pursuance of a resolution of either House of Parliament.

SEC. 181 Directions restricting disclosure of information overseas

181(1) **[Power of Secretary of State]** If it appears to the Secretary of State to be in the public interest to do so, he may give a direction prohibiting the disclosure to any person in a country or territory outside the United Kingdom which is specified in the direction, or to such persons in such a country or territory as may be so specified, of such information to which this section applies as may be so specified.

181(2) **[Extent of sec. 181(1) direction]** A direction under subsection (1) above—

(a) may prohibit disclosure of the information to which it applies by all persons or only by such persons or classes of person as may be specified in it; and

(b) may prohibit such disclosure absolutely or in such cases or subject to such conditions as to consent or otherwise as may be specified in it;

and a direction prohibiting disclosure by all persons shall be published by the Secretary of State in such manner as appears to him to be appropriate.

181(3) **[Application of section]** This section applies to any information relating to the business or other affairs of any person which was obtained (whether or not by virtue of any requirement to supply it) directly or indirectly—

(a)   by a designated agency, a transferee body, the competent authority or any person appointed or authorised to exercise any powers under section 94, 106 or 177 above (or any officer or servant of any such body or person) for the purposes or in the discharge of any functions of that body or person under this Act or any rules or regulations made under this Act or of any monitoring agency functions; or

(b)   by a recognised self-regulating organisation, a recognised professional body, a recognised investment exchange or a recognised clearing house other than an overseas investment exchange or clearing house (or any officer or servant of such an organisation, body, investment exchange or clearing house) for the purposes or in the discharge of any of its functions as such or of any monitoring agency functions.

181(4) **["Monitoring agency functions" in sec. 181(3)]** In subsection (3) above "monitoring agency functions" means any functions exercisable on behalf of another body by virtue of arrangements made pursuant to paragraph 4(2) of Schedule 2, paragraph 4(6) of Schedule 3, paragraph 3(2) of Schedule 4 or paragraph 3(2) of Schedule 7 to this Act or of such arrangements as are mentioned in section 39(4)(b) above.

181(5) **[Disclosures not prohibited]** A direction under this section shall not prohibit the disclosure by any person other than a person mentioned in subsection (3) above of—

(a)   information relating only to the affairs of that person; or
(b)   information obtained by that person otherwise than directly or indirectly from a person mentioned in subsection (3) above.

181(6) **[Disclosures under Community obligations]** A direction under this section shall not prohibit the disclosure of information in pursuance of any Community obligation.

181(7) **[Offence, penalty]** A person who knowingly discloses information in contravention of a direction under this section shall be guilty of an offence and liable—

(a)   on conviction on indictment, to imprisonment for a term not exceeding two years or to a fine or to both;
(b)   on summary conviction, to imprisonment for a term not exceeding three months or to a fine not exceeding the statutory maximum or to both.

181(8) **[Exception re offence]** A person shall not be guilty of an offence under this section by virtue of anything done or omitted to be done by him outside the United Kingdom unless he is a British citizen, a British Dependent Territories citizen, a British Overseas citizen or a body corporate incorporated in the United Kingdom.

SEC. 182   Disclosure of information under enactments relating to fair trading, banking, insurance and companies

182   The enactments mentioned in Schedule 13 to this Act shall have effect with the amendments there specified (which relate to the circumstances in which information obtained under those enactments may be disclosed).

s. 181(3)

PART IX — RECIPROCITY

SEC. 183   Reciprocal facilities for financial business

183(1) **[Power of Secretary of State, Treasury to serve notice]** If it appears to the Secretary of State or the Treasury that by reason of—

(a)   the law of any country outside the United Kingdom; or

(b)   any action taken by or the practices of the government or any other authority or body in that country,

persons connected with the United Kingdom are unable to carry on investment, insurance or banking business in, or in relation to, that country on terms as favourable as those on which persons connected with that country are able to carry on any such business in, or in relation to, the United Kingdom, the Secretary of State or, as the case may be, the Treasury may serve a notice under this subsection on any person connected with that country who is carrying on or appears to them to intend to carry on any such business in, or in relation to, the United Kingdom.

183(2) **[Conditions for service of sec. 183(1) notice]** No notice shall be served under subsection (1) above unless the Secretary of State or, as the case may be, the Treasury consider it in the national interest to serve it; and before doing so the Secretary of State or, as the case may be, the Treasury shall so far as they consider expedient consult such body or bodies as appear to them to represent the interests of persons likely to be affected.

183(3) **[Contents, date of notice]** A notice under subsection (1) above shall state the grounds on which it is given (identifying the country in relation to which those grounds are considered to exist); and any such notice shall come into force on such date as may be specified in it.

183(4) **[Connection with a country—interpretation]** For the purposes of this section a person is connected with a country if it appears to the Secretary of State or, as the case may be, the Treasury—

(a)   in the case of an individual, that he is a national of or resident in that country or carries on investment, insurance or banking business from a principal place of business there;

(b)   in the case of a body corporate, that it is incorporated or has a principal place of business in that country or is controlled by a person or persons connected with that country;

(c)   in the case of a partnership, that it has a principal place of business in that country or that any partner is connected with that country;

(d)   in the case of an unincorporated association which is not a partnership, that it is formed under the law of that country, has a principal place of business there or is controlled by a person or persons connected with that country.

183(5) **["Country"]** In this section "country" includes any territory or part of a country or territory; and where it appears to the Secretary of State or, as the case may be, the Treasury that there are such grounds as are mentioned in subsection (1) above in the case of any part of a country or territory their powers under that subsection shall also be exercisable in respect of any person who is connected with that country or territory or any other part of it.

s. 183(5)

Note
For circumstances where a notice may not be served under s. 183, see the Insurance Companies (Amendment) Regulations 1993 (SI 1993/174), reg. 8 and the Banking Coordination (Second Council Directive) Regulations 1992 (SI 1992/3218), reg. 53.
See also the Investment Services Regulations 1995(SI 1995/3275). reg. 1, 29.

SEC. 184   Investment and insurance business

184(1)   [Extent of sec. 183 notice] A notice under section 183 above relating to the carrying on of investment business or insurance business shall be served by the Secretary of State and such a notice may be a disqualification notice, a restriction notice or a partial restriction notice and may relate to the carrying on of business of both kinds.

184(2)   [Effects of disqualification notice] A disqualification notice as respects investment business or insurance business shall have the effect of—

(a)   cancelling any authorisation of the person concerned to carry on that business after the expiry of such period after the service of the notice as may be specified in it;

(b)   disqualifying him from becoming authorised to carry on that business after the expiry of that period; and

(c)   restricting any authorisation of the person concerned in respect of that business during that period to the performance of contracts entered into before the notice comes into force;

and the period specified in such a notice shall be such period as appears to the Secretary of State to be reasonable to enable the person on whom it is served to complete the performance of those contracts and to terminate such of them as are of a continuing nature.

184(3)   [Effect of restriction notice] A restriction notice as respects investment business or insurance business shall have the effect of restricting any authorisation of the person concerned in respect of that business to the performance of contracts entered into before the notice comes into force.

184(4)   [Effect of partial restriction notice] A partial restriction notice as respects investment business may prohibit the person concerned from—

(a)   entering into transactions of any specified kind or entering into them except in specified circumstances or to a specified extent;

(b)   soliciting business from persons of a specified kind or otherwise than from such persons;

(c)   carrying on business in a specified manner or otherwise than in a specified manner.

184(5)   [Effect of partial restriction notice re insurance business] A partial restriction notice as respects insurance business may direct that the person concerned shall cease to be authorised under section 3 or 4 of the Insurance Companies Act 1982 to effect contracts of insurance of any description specified in the notice.

184(6)   [Copy of notice on designated agency, recognised body] If it appears to the Secretary of State that a person on whom he serves a notice under section 183 above as respects investment business is an authorised person by virtue of an authorisation granted by a designated agency or by virtue of membership of a recognised self-regulating organisation or certification by a recognised professional body he shall serve a copy of the notice on that agency, organisation or body.

s. 184(1)

184(7) **[Power of Secretary of State re certain contraventions]** If it appears to the Secretary of State—

(a) that any person on whom a partial restriction notice has been served by him has contravened any provision of that notice or, in the case of a notice under subsection (5) above, effected a contract of insurance of a description specified in the notice; and

(b) that any such grounds as are mentioned in subsection (1) of section 183 above still exist in the case of the country concerned,

he may serve a disqualification notice or a restriction notice on him under that section.

184(8) **[Effect of sec. 28, 33, 60, 61, 62 re sec. 185(4) contravention]** Sections 28, 33, 60, 61 and 62 above shall have effect in relation to a contravention of such a notice as is mentioned in subsection (4) above as they have effect in relation to any such contravention as is mentioned in those sections.

SEC. 185   Banking business

185(1) **[Service of sec. 183 notice re banks]** A notice under section 183 above relating to the carrying on of a deposit-taking business as an authorised institution within the meaning of the Banking Act 1987 shall be served by the Treasury and may be either a disqualification notice or a partial restriction notice.

185(2) **[Effect of disqualification notice]** A disqualification notice relating to such business shall have the effect of—

(a) cancelling any authorisation granted to the person concerned under the Banking Act 1987; and

(b) disqualifying him from becoming an authorised institution within the meaning of that Act.

185(3) **[Effect of partial restriction notice]** A partial restriction notice relating to such business may—

(a) prohibit the person concerned from dealing with or disposing of his assets in any manner specified in the direction;

(b) impose limitations on the acceptance by him of deposits;

(c) prohibit him from soliciting deposits either generally or from persons who are not already depositors;

(d) prohibit him from entering into any other transaction or class of transactions;

(e) require him to take certain steps, to pursue or refrain from pursuing a particular course of activities or to restrict the scope of his business in a particular way.

185(4) **[Copy of sec. 183 notice to Bank of England]** The Treasury shall serve on the bank of England a copy of any notice served by them under section 183 above.

185(5) **[Offence, penalty re partial restriction notice]** Any person who contravenes any provision of a partial restriction notice served on him by the Treasury under this section shall be guilty of an offence and liable—

(a) on conviction on indictment, to a fine;

(b) on summary conviction, to a fine not exceeding the statutory maximum.

185(6) **[Persons who may sue]** Any such contravention shall be actionable at the suit of a person who suffers loss as a result of the contravention subject to the defences and other incidents applying to actions for breach of statutory duty, but no such contravention shall invalidate any transaction.

s. 185(6)

185(7)   (Repealed by the Banking Act 1987, sec. 108(2) and Sch. 7, Pt. I as from 1 October 1987.)

SEC. 186   Variation and revocation of notices

186(1)   [Power to vary restriction notice] The Secretary of State or the Treasury may vary a partial restriction notice served under section 183 above by a notice in writing served on the person concerned; and any such notice shall come into force on such date as is specified in the notice.

186(2)   [Revocation of sec. 183 notice] A notice under section 183 above may be revoked at any time by the Secretary of State or, as the case may be, the Treasury by serving a revocation notice on the person concerned; and the Secretary of State or, as the case may be, the Treasury shall revoke a notice if it appears to them that there are no longer any such grounds as are mentioned in subsection (1) of that section in the case of the country concerned.

186(3)   [Effect of revocation of disqualification notice re investment, insurance business] The revocation of a disqualification notice as respects investment business or insurance business shall not have the effect of reviving the authorisation which was cancelled by the notice except where the notice relates to investment business and the person concerned would (apart from the disqualification notice) at the time of the revocation be an authorised person as respects the investment business in question by virtue of his membership of a recognised self-regulating organisation or certification by a recognised professional body.

186(4)   [Effect of revocation of disqualification notice re banking business] The revocation of a disqualification notice as respects banking business shall not have the effect of reviving the authorisation which was cancelled by the notice.

186(5)   [Limit on effect of sec. 186(3), (4)] Nothing in subsection (3) or (4) above shall be construed as preventing any person who has been subject to a disqualification notice as respects any business from again becoming authorised after the revocation of the notice.

186(6)   [If person served notice is authorised designated agency, recognised body] If it appears to the Secretary of State that a person on whom he serves a notice under this section as respects investment business was an authorised person by virtue of an authorisation granted by a designated agency or by virtue of membership of a recognised self-regulating organisation or certification by a recognised professional body at the time that the notice which is being varied or revoked was served, he shall serve a copy of the notice on that agency, organisation or body.

186(7)   [Copy of notice to Bank of England] The Treasury shall serve on the Bank of England a copy of any notice served by them under this section which varies or revokes a notice relating to the carrying on of a deposit-taking business as mentioned in section 185 above.

PART X — MISCELLANEOUS AND SUPPLEMENTARY

SEC. 187   Exemption from liability for damages

187(1)   [Limit on liability re SROs and members] Neither a recognised self-regulating organisation nor any of its officers or servants or members of its governing body shall be liable in damages for anything done or omitted in the discharge or purported discharge of any functions to which this subsection applies unless the act or omission is shown to have been in bad faith.

187(2) [Functions for sec. 187(1)] The functions to which subsection (1) above applies are the functions of the organisation so far as relating to, or to matters arising out of—

(a) the rules, practices, powers and arrangements of the organisation to which the requirements in paragraphs 1 to 6 of Schedule 2 to this Act apply;

(b) the obligations with which paragraph 7 of that Schedule requires the organisation to comply;

(c) any guidance issued by the organisation;

(d) the powers of the organisation under section 53(2), 64(4), 72(5), 73(5) or 105(2)(a) above; or

(e) the obligations to which the organisation is subject by virtue of this Act.

187(3) [Limit on liability of designated agency and members et al.] No designated agency or transferee body nor any member, officer or servant of a designated agency or transferee body shall be liable in damages for anything done or omitted in the discharge or purported discharge of the functions exercisable by the agency by virtue of a delegation order or, as the case may be, the functions exercisable by the body by virtue of a transfer order unless the act or omission is shown to have been in bad faith.

187(4) [Limit on liability of competent authority and members et al.] Neither the competent authority nor any member, officer, or servant of that authority shall be liable in damages for anything done or omitted in the discharge or purported discharge of any functions of the authority under Part IV of this Act unless the act or omission is shown to have been in bad faith.

Note
Re application of s. 187(4) see the Uncertificated Securities Regulations 1992 (SI 1992/225), reg. 94(6) and 117.

187(5) [Functions included in sec. 187(1), (3)] The functions to which subsections (1) and (3) above apply also include any functions exercisable by a recognised self-regulating organisation, designated agency or transferee body on behalf of another body by virtue of arrangements made pursuant to paragraph 4(2) of Schedule 2, paragraph 4(6) of Schedule 3, paragraph 3(2) of Schedule 4 or paragraph 3(2) of Schedule 7 to this Act or of such arrangements as are mentioned in section 39(4)(b) above.

187(6) [Condition in certificate by recognised professional body] A recognised professional body may make it a condition of any certificate issued by it for the purposes of Part I of this Act that neither the body nor any of its officers or servants or members of its governing body is to be liable in damages for anything done or omitted in the discharge or purported discharge of any functions to which this subsection applies unless the act or omission is shown to have been in bad faith.

187(7) [Functions for sec. 187(6)] The functions to which subsection (6) above applies are the functions of the body so far as relating to, or to matters arising out of—

(a) the rules, practices and arrangements of the body to which the requirements in paragraphs 2 to 5 of Schedule 3 to this Act apply;

(b) the obligations with which paragraph 6 of that Schedule requires the body to comply;

(c) any guidance issued by the body in respect of any matters dealt with by such rules as are mentioned in paragraph (a) above;

(d) the powers of the body under the provisions mentioned in subsection (2)(d) above or under section 54(3) above; or

(e)   the obligations to which the body is subject by virtue of this Act.

SEC. 188   Jurisdiction of High Court and Court of Session

188(1)   [Proceedings in High Court, Court of Session] Proceedings arising out of any act or omission (or proposed act or omission) of—

(a)   a recognised self-regulating organisation,
(b)   a designated agency,
(c)   a transferee body, or
(d)   the competent authority,

in the discharge or purported discharge of any of its functions under this Act may be brought in the High Court or the Court of Session.

188(2)   [Sec. 188(1) jurisdiction additional] The jurisdiction conferred by subsection (1) is in addition to any other jurisdiction exercisable by those courts.

SEC. 189   Restriction of Rehabilitation of Offenders Act 1974

189(1)   [Effect of 1974 Act] The Rehabilitation of Offenders Act 1974 shall have effect subject to the provisions of this section in cases where the spent conviction is for—

(a)   an offence involving fraud or other dishonesty; or
(b)   an offence under legislation (whether or not of the United Kingdom) relating to companies, building societies, industrial and provident societies, credit unions, friendly societies, insurance, banking or other financial services, insolvency, consumer credit or consumer protection or insider dealing.

189(2)   [Limit to sec. 4(1) of 1974 Act] Nothing in section 4(1) (restriction on evidence as to spent convictions in proceedings) shall prevent the determination in any proceedings specified in Part I of Schedule 14 to this Act of any issue, or prevent the admission or requirement in any such proceedings of any evidence, relating to a person's previous convictions for any such offence as is mentioned in subsection (1) above or to circumstances ancillary thereto.

189(3)   [Qualification re sec. 4(2) of 1974 Act] A conviction for any such offence as is mentioned in subsection (1) above shall not be regarded as spent for the purposes of section 4(2) (questions relating to an individual's previous convictions) if—

(a)   the question is put by or on behalf of a person specified in the first column of Part II of that Schedule and relates to an individual (whether or not the person questioned) specified in relation to the person putting the question in the second column of that Part; and
(b)   the person questioned is informed when the question is put that by virtue of this section convictions for any such offence are to be disclosed.

189(4)   [Limit on sec. 4(3)(b) of 1974 Act] Section 4(3)(b) (spent conviction not to be ground for excluding person from office, occupation etc.) shall not prevent a person specified in the first column of Part III of that Schedule from taking such action as is specified in relation to that person in the second column of that Part by reason, or partly by reason, of a spent conviction for any such offence as is mentioned in subsection (1) above of an individual who is—

(a)   the person in respect of whom the action is taken;
(b)   as respects action within paragraph 1 or 4 of that Part, an associate of that person; or
(c)   as respects action within paragraph 1 of that Part consisting of a decision to refuse or revoke an order declaring a collective investment scheme to be an authorised unit trust scheme or a recognised scheme, the operator or trustee of the scheme or an associate of his,

or of any circumstances ancillary to such a conviction or of a failure (whether or not by that individual) to disclose such a conviction or any such circumstances.

189(5)   [Sch. 14] Parts I, II and III of that Schedule shall have effect subject to Part IV.

189(6)   ["Associate"] In this section and that Schedule "associate" means—

(a)   in relation to a body corporate, a director, manager or controller;
(b)   in relation to a partnership, a partner or manager;
(c)   in relation to a registered friendly society, a trustee, manager or member of the committee of the society;
(d)   in relation to an unincorporated association, a member of its governing body or an officer, manager or controller;
(e)   in relation to an individual, a manager.

189(7)   [Application to Northern Ireland] This section and that Schedule shall apply to Northern Ireland with the substitution for the references to the said Act of 1974 and section 4(1), (2) and (3)(b) of that Act of references to the Rehabilitation of Offenders (Northern Ireland) Order 1978 and Articles 5(1), (2) and (3)(b) of that Order.

SEC. 190   Data protection

190   An order under section 30 of the Data Protection Act 1984 (exemption from subject access provisions of data held for the purpose of discharging designated functions conferred by or under enactments relating to the regulation of financial services etc.) may designate for the purposes of that section as if they were functions conferred by or under such an enactment as is there mentioned—

(a)   any functions of a recognised self-regulating organisation in connection with the admission or expulsion of members, the suspension of a person's membership or the supervision or regulation of persons carrying on investment business by virtue of membership of the organisation;
(b)   any functions of a recognised professional body in connection with the issue of certificates for the purposes of Part I of this Act, the withdrawal or suspension of such certificates or the supervision or regulation of persons carrying on investment business by virtue of certification by that body;
(c)   any functions of a recognised self-regulating organisation for friendly societies in connection with the supervision or regulation of its member societies.

Note
See the Data Protection (Regulation of Financial Services etc.) (Subject Access Exemption) Order 1987 (SI 1987/1905) and the Data Protection (Regulation of Financial Services etc.) (Subject Access Exemption) (Amendment) Order 1992 (SI 1992/1855).

SEC. 191   Occupational pension schemes

191(1)   [Person carrying on investment business] Subject to the provisions of this section, a person who apart from this section would not be regarded as carrying on investment business shall be treated as doing so if he engages in the activity of management falling within paragraph 14 of Schedule 1 to this Act in a case where the assets referred to in that paragraph are held for the purposes of an occupational pension scheme.

191(2) [Non-application of sec. 191(1)] Subsection (1) above does not apply where all decisions, or all day to day decisions, in the carrying on of that activity so far as relating to assets which are investments are taken on behalf of the person concerned by—

(a)   an authorised person;

(b)   an exempted person who in doing so is acting in the course of the business in respect of which he is exempt; or

(c)   a person who does not require authorisation to manage the assets by virtue of Part IV of Schedule 1 to this Act.

191(3) [Order by Secretary of State] The Secretary of State may by order direct that a person of such description as is specified in the order shall not by virtue of this section be treated as carrying on investment business where the assets are held for the purposes of an occupational pension scheme of such description as is so specified, being a scheme in the case of which it appears to the Secretary of State that management by an authorised or exempted person is unnecessary having regard to the size of the scheme and the control exercisable over its affairs by the members.

Note
See the Financial Services Act 1986 (Occupational Pension Schemes) (No. 2) Order 1988 (SI 1988/724).

191(4) [Annulment of Order by Parliament] An order under subsection (3) above shall be subject to annulment in pursuance of a resolution of either House of Parliament.

191(5) [Sch. 1, para. 14] For the purposes of subsection (1) above paragraph 14 of Schedule 1 to this Act shall be construed without reference to paragraph 22 of that Schedule.

Note
Concerning European investment firms, see the Investment Services Regulations 1995 (SI 1995/3275), reg. 32 and Sch. 7, para. 39.
Concerning European institutions, see the Banking Coordination (Second Council Directive) Regulations 1992 (SI 1992/3218), reg. 55 and Sch. 9, para. 42.

SEC. 192   International obligations

192(1) [Power of direction by Secretary of State] If it appears to the Secretary of State—

(a)   that any action proposed to be taken by an authority or body to which this section applies would be incompatible with Community obligations or any other international obligations of the United Kingdom, or

(b)   that any action which that authority or body has power to take is required for the purpose of implementing any such obligation,

he may direct the authority or body not to take or, as the case may be, to take the action in question.

192(2) [Applicable authorities and bodies] The authorities and bodies to which this section applies are the following—

(a)   a recognised self-regulating organisation,

(b)   a recognised investment exchange (other than an overseas investment exchange),

(c)   a recognised clearing house (other than an overseas clearing house),

(d)   a designated agency,

(e)   a transferee body,

(f)   a competent authority.

192(3) (Repealed by the Public Offers of Securities Regulations 1995 (SI 1995/1537), reg. 1, 17 and Sch. 2, para. 5(d) as from 19 June 1995.)

192(4) [Supplementary or incidental requirements] A direction under this section may include such supplementary or incidental requirements as the Secretary of State thinks necessary or expedient.

192(5) [Where designated agency relevant] Where the function of making or revoking a recognition order in respect of an authority or body to which this section applies is exercisable by a designated agency, any direction in respect of that authority or body shall be a direction requiring the agency to give the authority or body such a direction as is specified in the direction given by the Secretary of State.

192(6) [Enforcement of direction] A direction under this section is enforceable, on the application of the person who gave it, by injunction or, in Scotland, by an order under section 45 of the Court of Session Act 1988.

SEC. 193   Exemption from Banking Act 1979

193 (Repealed by Banking Act 1987, sec. 108(2) and Sch. 7, Pt. I as from 29 April 1988.)

SEC. 194   Transfers to or from recognised clearing houses

194(1) [Amendments in sec. 5 of Stock Exchange (Completion of Bargains) Act 1976] In section 5 of the Stock Exchange (Completion of Bargains) Act 1976 (protection of trustees etc. in case of transfer of shares etc. to or from a stock exchange nominee)—

(a)   for the words "a stock exchange nominee", in the first place where they occur, there shall be substituted the words "a recognised clearing house or a nominee of a recognised clearing house or of a recognised investment exchange";

(b)   for those words in the second place where they occur there shall be substituted the words "such a clearing house or nominee";

(c)   at the end there shall be added the words "; but no person shall be a nominee for the purposes of this section unless he is a person designated for the purposes of this section in the rules of the recognised investment exchange in question."

194(2) [Insertion of sec. 5(2) of 1976 Act] The provisions of that section as amended by subsection (1) above shall become subsection (1) of that section and after that subsection there shall be inserted—

"5(2) In this section 'a recognised clearing house' means a recognised clearing house within the meaning of the Financial Services Act 1986 acting in relation to a recognised investment exchange within the meaning of that Act and 'a recognised investment exchange' has the same meaning as in that Act."

194(3) [Amendments in art. 7 of Stock Exchange (Completion of Bargains) (Northern Ireland) Order 1977] In Article 7 of the Stock Exchange (Completion of Bargains) (Northern Ireland) Order 1977 (protection of trustees etc. in case of transfer of shares etc. to or from a stock exchange nominee)—

(a)   for the words "a stock exchange nominee", in the first place where they occur, there shall be substituted the words "a recognised clearing house or a nominee of a recognised clearing house or of a recognised investment exchange";

s. 194(3)

(b)   for those words in the second place where they occur there shall be substituted the words "such a clearing house or nominee";

(c)   at the end there shall be added the words "; but no person shall be a nominee for the purposes of this Article unless he is a person designated for the purposes of this Article in the rules of the recognised investment exchange in question".

194(4)   [Insertion of art. 7(2) of 1977 Order] The provisions of that Article as amended by subsection (3) above shall become paragraph (1) of that Article and after that paragraph there shall be inserted—

"(2) In this Article 'a recognised clearing house' means a recognised clearing house within the meaning of the Financial Services Act 1986 acting in relation to a recognised investment exchange within the meaning of that Act and 'a recognised investment exchange' has the same meaning as in that Act."

194(5)   [Amendments in sec. 185(4) of Companies Act 1985] In subsection (4) of section 185 of the Companies Act 1985 (exemption from duty to issue certificates in respect of shares etc. in cases of allotment or transfer to a stock exchange nominee)—

(a)   for the words "stock exchange nominee" in the first place where they occur there shall be substituted the words "a recognised clearing house or a nominee of a recognised clearing house or of a recognised investment exchange";

(b)   for those words in the second place where they occur there shall be substituted the words "such a clearing house or nominee";

(c)   at the end of the first paragraph in that subsection there shall be inserted the words "; but no person shall be a nominee for the purposes of this section unless he is a person designated for the purposes of this section in the rules of the recognised investment exchange in question"; and

(d)   for the second paragraph in that subsection there shall be substituted—

"'**Recognised clearing house**' means a recognised clearing house within the meaning of the Financial Services Act 1986 acting in relation to a recognised investment exchange and 'recognised investment exchange' has the same meaning as in that Act".

194(6)   [Amendments in art. 195(4) of Companies (Northern Ireland) Order 1986] In paragraph (4) of Article 195 of the Companies (Northern Ireland) Order 1986 (duty to issue certificates in respect of shares etc. in cases of allotment or transfer unless it is to a stock exchange nominee)—

(a)   for the words "a stock exchange nominee" in the first place where they occur there shall be substituted the words "a recognised clearing house or a nominee of a recognised clearing house or of a recognised investment exchange";

(b)   for those words in the second place where they occur there shall be substituted the words "such a clearing house or nominee";

(c)   at the end of the first sub-paragraph in that paragraph there shall be inserted the words "; but no person shall be a nominee for the purposes of this Article unless he is a person designated for the purposes of this Article in the rules of the recognised investment exchange in question"; and

(d)   for the second sub-paragraph in that paragraph there shall be substituted—

"'**recognised clearing house**' means a recognised clearing house within the meaning of the Financial Services Act 1986 acting in relation to a recognised investment exchange and 'recognised investment exchange' has the same meaning as in that Act.".

s. 194(4)

SEC. 195   Offers of short-dated debentures

195 As respects debentures which, under the terms of issue, must be repaid within five years of the date of issue—

(a)   section 79(2) of the Companies Act 1985 (offer of debentures of oversea company deemed not to be an offer to the public if made to professional investor) shall apply for the purposes of Chapter I of Part III of that Act as well as for those of Chapter II of that Part; and

(b)   Article 89(2) of the Companies (Northern Ireland) Order 1986 (corresponding provisions for Northern Ireland) shall apply for the purposes of Chapter I of Part IV of that Order as well as for those of Chapter II of that Part.

SEC. 196   Financial assistance for employees' share schemes

196(1)   [Amendment of sec. 153 of Companies Act 1985] Section 153 of the Companies Act 1985 (transactions not prohibited by section 151) shall be amended as follows.

196(2)   [Insertion of sec. 153(4)(bb) of 1985 Act] After subsection (4)(b) there shall be inserted—

"(bb) without prejudice to paragraph (b), the provision of financial assistance by a company or any of its subsidiaries for the purposes of or in connection with anything done by the company (or a company connected with it) for the purpose of enabling or facilitating transactions in shares in the first-mentioned company between, and involving the acquisition of beneficial ownership of those shares by, any of the following persons—

(i)   the bona fide employees or former employees of that company or of another company in the same group; or

(ii) the wives, husbands, widows, widowers, children or step-children under the age of eighteen of any such employees or former employees.".

196(3)   (Repealed by Companies Act 1989, sec. 212 and Sch. 24 as from 1 October 1991.)

196(4)   [Amendment of art. 163 of Companies (Northern Ireland) Order 1986] Article 163 of the Companies (Northern Ireland) Order 1986 (transactions not prohibited by Article 161) shall be amended as follows.

196(5)   [Insertion of art. 163 (4)(bb) of 1986 Order] After paragraph (4)(b) there shall be inserted—

"(bb) without prejudice to sub-paragraph (b), the provision of financial assistance by a company or any of its subsidiaries for the purposes of or in connection with anything done by the company (or a company connected with it) for the purpose of enabling or facilitating transactions in shares in the first-mentioned company between, and involving the acquisition of beneficial ownership of those shares by, any of the following persons—

(i)   the bona fide employees or former employees of that company or of another company in the same group; or

(ii) the wives, husbands, widows, widowers, children, step-children or adopted children under the age of eighteen of such employees of former employees."

196(6)   (Repealed by Companies (No. 2) (Northern Ireland) Order 1990 (SI 1990/1504 (NI 10)), art. 113 and Sch. 6 as from 29 March 1993.)

SEC. 197   Disclosure of interests in shares: interest held by market maker

197(1)   [Insertions in sec. 209 of Companies Act 1985] In section 209 of the Companies Act 1985 (interests to be disregarded for purposes of sections 198 to 202)—

(a)   in subsection (1)(f) after the word "jobber" there shall be inserted the words "or market maker";

(b)   after subsection (4) there shall be inserted—

"**209(4A)**   A person is a market maker for the purposes of subsection (1)(f) if—

(a)   he holds himself out at all normal times in compliance with the rules of a recognised investment exchange other than an overseas investment exchange (within the meaning of the Financial Services Act 1986) as willing to buy and sell securities at prices specified by him; and

(b)   is recognised as doing so by that investment exchange;

and an interest of such a person in shares is an exempt interest if he carries on business as a market maker in the United Kingdom, is subject to such rules in the carrying on of that business and holds the interest for the purposes of that business.".

197(2)   [Insertions in art. 217 of Companies (Northern Ireland) Order 1986] In Article 217 of the Companies (Northern Ireland) Order 1986 (interests to be disregarded for purposes of Articles 206 to 210 (disclosure of interests in shares))—

(a)   in paragraph (1)(d) after the word "jobber" there shall be inserted the words "or market maker";

(b)   after paragraph (4) there shall be inserted—

"**(4A)**   A person is a market maker for the purposes of paragraph (1)(d) if—

(a)   he holds himself out at all normal times in compliance with the rules of a recognised investment exchange other than an overseas investment exchange (within the meaning of the Financial Services Act 1986) as willing to buy and sell securities at prices specified by him; and

(b)   is recognised as doing so by that investment exchange,

and an interest of such a person in shares is an exempt interest if he carries on business as a market maker in the United Kingdom, is subject to such rules in the carrying on of that business and holds the interest for the purposes of that business.".

SEC. 198   Power to petition for winding up etc. on information obtained under Act

198(1)   (Repealed by Companies Act 1989, sec. 212 and Sch. 24 as from 21 February 1990.)

198(2)   [Amendments to sec. 8 of Company Directors Disqualification Act 1986] In section 8 of the Company Directors Disqualification Act 1986—

(a)   after the words "the Companies Act" there shall be inserted the words "or section 94 or 177 of the Financial Services Act 1986"; and

s. 196(6)

(b)   for the words "that Act" there shall be substituted the words "the Companies Act or section 105 of the Financial Services Act 1986".

198(3)   (Repealed by Companies (No. 2) (Northern Ireland) Order 1990 (SI 1990/1504 (NI 10)), art. 113 and Sch. 6 as from 1 October 1991.)

SEC. 199   Powers of entry

199(1)   **[Power of JP to issue warrant]** A justice of the peace may issue a warrant under this section if satisfied on information on oath given by or on behalf of the Secretary of State that there are reasonable grounds for believing that an offence has been committed—

(a)   under section 4, 47, 57, 130, or 133 above, or
(b)   under Part V of the Criminal Justice Act 1993 (insider dealing),

and that there are on any premises documents relevant to the question whether that offence has been committed.

199(2)   **[Further powers of JP]** A justice of the peace may also issue a warrant under this section if satisfied on information on oath given by or on behalf of the Secretary of State, or by a person appointed or authorised to exercise powers under section 94, 106 or 177 above, that there are reasonable grounds for believing that there are on any premises documents whose production has been required under section 94, 105 or 177 above and which have not been produced in compliance with the requirement.

199(3)   **[Scope of warrant]** A warrant under this section shall authorise a constable, together with any other person named in it and any other constables—

(a)   to enter the premises specified in the information, using such force as is reasonably necessary for the purpose;
(b)   to search the premises and take possession of any documents appearing to be such documents as are mentioned in subsection (1) or, as the case may be, in subsection (2) above or to take, in relation to any such documents, any other steps which may appear to be necessary for preserving them or preventing interference with them;
(c)   to take copies of any such documents; and
(d)   to require any person named in the warrant to provide an explanation of them or to state where they may be found.

199(4)   **[Duration of warrant]** A warrant under this section shall continue in force until the end of the period of one month beginning with the day on which it is issued.

199(5)   **[Period for retention of documents]** Any documents of which possession is taken under this section may be retained—

(a)   for a period of three months; or
(b)   if within that period proceedings to which the documents are relevant are commenced against any person for any criminal offence, until the conclusion of those proceedings.

199(6)   **[Offence, penalty]** Any person who intentionally obstructs the exercise of any rights conferred by a warrant issued under this section or fails without reasonable excuse to comply with any requirement imposed in accordance with subsection (3)(d) above shall be guilty of an offence and liable—

(a)   on conviction on indictment, to a fine;
(b)   on summary conviction, to a fine not exceeding the statutory maximum.

199(7)   **[Functions relevant for sec. 114]** The functions to which section 114 above applies shall include the functions of the Secretary of State under this section; but if any of those functions are transferred under that section the transfer may be subject to a reservation that they are to be exercisable by the Secretary of State concurrently with the designated agency and, in the case of functions exercisable by virtue of subsection (1) above, so as to be exercisable by the agency subject to such conditions or restrictions as the Treasury may from time to time impose.

Note
See the Financial Services Act 1986 (Delegation) Order 1987 (SI 1987/942).

199(8)   [Scotland] In the application of this section to Scotland for the references to a justice of the peace substitute references to a justice of the peace or a sheriff, and for the references to information on oath substitute references to evidence on oath.

199(8A)   [Northern Ireland] In the application of this section to Northern Ireland for the references to information on oath substitute references to complaint on oath.

199(9)   ["Documents"] In this section "documents" includes information recorded in any form.

Note
For application of s. 199 to a listed person see the Financial Markets and Insolvency (Money Market) Regulations 1995 (SI 1995/2049), reg. 1, 18.

SEC. 200   False and misleading statements

200(1)   [Furnishing false information] A person commits an offence if—

(a)   for the purposes of or in connection with any application under this Act; or
(b)   in purported compliance with any requirement imposed on him by or under this Act,

he furnishes information which he knows to be false or misleading in a material particular or recklessly furnishes information which is false or misleading in a material particular.

200(2)   [False description of person] A person commits an offence if, not being an authorised person or exempted person, he—

(a)   describes himself as such a person; or
(b)   so holds himself out as to indicate or be reasonably understood to indicate that he is such a person.

200(3)   [False description of status] A person commits an offence if, not having a status to which this subsection applies, he—

(a)   describes himself as having that status, or
(b)   so holds himself out as to indicate or be reasonably understood to indicate that he has that status.

200(4)   [Application of sec. 200(3)] Subsection (3) above applies to the status of recognised self-regulating organisation, recognised professional body, recognised investment exchange or recognised clearing house.

200(5)   [Penalty for sec. 200(1) offence] A person guilty of an offence under subsection (1) above shall be liable—

(a)   on conviction on indictment, to imprisonment for a term not exceeding two years or to a fine or to both;
(b)   on summary conviction, to imprisonment for a term not exceeding six months or to a fine not exceeding the statutory maximum or to both.

200(6)   [Penalty for sec. 200(2), (3) offences] A person guilty of an offence under subsection (2) or (3) above shall be liable on summary conviction to imprisonment for a term not exceeding six months or to a fine not exceeding the fifth level on the standard scale or to both.

200(7)   [Maximum fine in sec. 200(6) if public display] Where a contravention of subsection (2) or (3) above involves a public display of the offending description or other matter the maximum fine that may be imposed under subsection (6) above shall be an amount equal to the fifth level on the standard scale multiplied by the number of days for which the display has continued.

200(8)   [Defence re sec. 200(2), (3) offences] In proceedings brought against any person for an offence under subsection (2) or (3) above it shall be a defence for him to prove that he took all reasonable precautions and exercised all due diligence to avoid the commission of the offence.

SEC. 201   Prosecutions

201(1)   [Proceedings other than under sec. 133, 185] Proceedings in respect of an offence under any provision of this Act other than section 133 or 185 shall not be instituted—

(a)   in England and Wales, except by or with the consent of the Secretary of State or the Director of Public Prosecutions; or

(b)   in Northern Ireland, except by or with the consent of the Secretary of State or the Director of Public Prosecutions for Northern Ireland.

201(2)   [Sec. 133 proceedings] Proceedings in respect of an offence under section 133 above shall not be instituted—

(a)   in England and Wales, except by or with the consent of the Secretary of State, the Indusrial Assurance Commissioner or the Director of Public Prosecutions; or

(b)   in Northern Ireland, except by or with the consent of the Secretary of State or the Director of Public Prosecutions for Northern Ireland.

201(3)   [Sec. 185 proceedings] Proceedings in respect of an offence under section 185 above shall not be instituted—

(a)   in England and Wales, except by or with the consent of the Treasury or the Director of Public Prosecutions; or

(b)   in Northern Ireland, except by or with the consent of the Treasury or the Director of Public Prosecutions for Northern Ireland.

201(4)   [Sec. 114 functions] The functions to which section 114 above applies shall include the function of the Secretary of State under subsection (1) above to institute proceedings but any transfer of that function shall be subject to a reservation that it is to be exercisable by him concurrently with the designated agency and so as to be exercisable by the agency subject to such conditions or restrictions as the Treasury may from time to time impose.

Note
See the Financial Services Act 1986 (Delegation) Order 1987 (SI 1987/942).

SEC. 202   Offences by bodies corporate, partnerships and unincorporated associations

202(1)   [Offences by body corporate with connivance of offices] Where an offence under this Act committed by a body corporate is proved to have been committed with the consent or connivance of, or to be attributable to any neglect on the part of—

s. 202(1)

(a)   any director, manager, secretary or other similar officer of the body corporate, or any person who was purporting to act in any such capacity; or

(b)   a controller of the body corporate,

he, as well as the body corporate, shall be guilty of that offence and liable to be proceeded against and punished accordingly.

202(2) [Where affairs of body corporate managed by members] Where the affairs of a body corporate are managed by the members subsection (1) above shall apply in relation to the acts and defaults of a member in connection with his functions of management as if he were a director of the body corporate.

202(3) [Offence by partnership] Where a partnership is guilty of an offence under this Act every partner, other than a partner who is proved to have been ignorant of or to have attempted to prevent the commission of the offence, shall also be guilty of that offence and be liable to be proceeded against and punished accordingly.

202(4) [Offence by unincorporated association] Where an unincorporated association (other than a partnership) is guilty of an offence under this Act—

(a)   every officer of the association who is bound to fulfil any duty of which the breach is the offence; or

(b)   if there is no such officer, every member of the governing body other than a member who is proved to have been ignorant of or to have attempted to prevent the commission of the offence,

shall also be guilty of the offence and be liable to be proceeded against and punished accordingly.

SEC. 203   Jurisdiction and procedure in respect of offences

203(1) [Summary proceedings re place] Summary proceedings for an offence under this Act may, without prejudice to any jurisdiction exercisable apart from this section, be taken against any body corporate or unincorporated association at any place at which it has a place of business and against an individual at any place where he is for the time being.

203(2) [Proceedings against unincorporated association] Proceedings for an offence alleged to have been committed under this Act by an unincorporated association shall be brought in the name of the association (and not in that of any of its members) and for the purposes of any such proceedings any rules of court relating to the service of documents shall have effect as if the association were a corporation.

203(3) [Procedure re unincorporated associations] Section 33 of the Criminal Justice Act 1925 and Schedule 3 to the Magistrates' Courts Act 1980 (procedure on charge of offence against a corporation) shall have effect in a case in which an unincorporated association is charged in England and Wales with an offence under this Act in like manner as they have effect in the case of a corporation.

203(4) [Procedure in Scotland re unincorporated associations] In relation to any proceedings on indictment in Scotland for an offence alleged to have been committed under this Act by an unincorporated association, section 74 of the Criminal Procedure (Scotland) Act 1975 (proceedings on indictment against bodies corporate) shall have effect as if the association were a body corporate.

203(5) [Procedure in Northern Ireland re unincorporated associations] Section 18 of the Criminal Justice Act (Northern Ireland) 1945 and Schedule 4 to the Magistrates' Courts (Northern Ireland) Order 1981 (procedure on charge of offence against a corporation) shall have effect in a case in which an unincorporated association is charged in Northern Ireland with an offence under this Act in like manner as they have effect in the case of a corporation.

203(6) [Fine to be paid by unincorporated association] A fine imposed on an unincorporated association on its conviction of an offence under this Act shall be paid out of the funds of the association.

SEC. 204   Service of notices

204(1) [Effect of section] This section has effect in relation to any notice, direction or other document required or authorised by or under this Act to be given to or served on any person other than the Secretary of State or the Friendly Societies Commission.

204(2) [Service on person] Any such document may be given to or served on the person in question—

'(a)   by delivering it to him;
(b)   by leaving it at his proper address; or
(c)   by sending it by post to him at that address.

204(3) [Service on body corporate, partnership, unincorporated association, appointed representative] Any such document may—

(a)   in the case of a body corporate, be given to or served on the secretary or clerk of that body;
(b)   in the case of a partnership, be given to or served on any partner;
(c)   in the case of an unincorporated association other than a partnership, be given to or served on any member of the governing body of the association;
(d)   in the case of an appointed representative, be given to or served on his principal.

204(4) [Service by post] For the purposes of this section and section 7 of the Interpretation Act 1978 (service of documents by post) in its application to this section, the proper address of any person is his last known address (whether of his residence or of a place where he carries on business or is employed) and also any address applicable in his case under the following provisions—

(a)   in the case of a member of a recognised self-regulating organisation or a person certified by a recognised professional body who does not have a place of business in the United Kingdom, the address of that organisation or body;
(b)   in the case of a body corporate, its secretary or its clerk, the address of its registered or principal office in the United Kingdom;
(c)   in the case of an unincorporated association (other than a partnership) or a member of its governing body, its principal office in the United Kingdom.

204(5) [Where new address notified re sec. 204(4)] Where a person has notified the Secretary of State of an address or a new address at which documents may be given to or served on him under this Act that address shall also be his proper address for the purposes mentioned in subsection (4) above or, as the case may be, his proper address for those purposes in substitution for that previously notified.

SEC. 205   General power to make regulations

205 The Secretary of State or the Treasury may make regulations prescribing anything which by this Act is authorised or required to be prescribed.

Note
For transfer of the Secretary of State's functions under s. 205 see SI 1990/354 (C. 12), art. 4(5) and SI 1992/1315.

SEC. 205A   Supplementary provisions with respect to subordinate legislation

205A(1)   [Application of power of Secretary of State] Subsections (2) to (4) below apply to any power of the Secretary of State or the Treasury under this Act—

(a)   to issue statements of principle,
(b)   to make rules or regulations,
(c)   to make orders (other than such orders as are expected by subsection (4) below), or
(d)   to issue codes of practice.

205A(1A)   [Application of s. 205A(2)–(4)] Subsections (2) to (4) below also apply to any power to make regulations by virtue of regulation 6 of the Open-Ended Investment Companies (Investment Companies with Variable Capital) Regulations 1996 in the event that that power becomes exercisable by the Treasury by virtue of an order under section 115 above.

205A(2)   [Power exercisable by statutory instrument] Any such power is exercisable by statutory instrument and includes power to make different provision for different cases.

205A(3)   [Annulment of statutory instrument] Except as otherwise provided, a statutory instrument containing statements of principle, rules or regulations shall be subject to annulment in pursuance of a resolution of either House of Parliament.

205A(4)   [Non-application of sec. 205A(1)–(3)] The above provisions do not apply to a recognition order, an order declaring a collective investment scheme to be an authorised unit trust scheme or a recognised scheme or to an order revoking any such order.

Note
See the Financial Services Act 1986 (Investment Advertisements) (Exemptions) (No. 2) Order 1995 (SI 1995/1536); the Financial Services Act 1986 (Investment Services) (Extension of Scope of Act) Order 1995 (SI 1995/3271); the Financial Services Act 1986 (Gas Industry Exemption) Order 1996 (SI 1996/498); the Financial Services Act 1986 (Exemption) Order 1996 (SI 1996/1587) and the Financial Services Act 1986 (Uncertificated Securities) (Extension of Scope of Act) Order 1996 (SI 1996/1322); and the Financial Services Act 1986 (Investment Advertisements) (Exemptions) Order 1996 (SI 1996/1586).

SEC. 206   Publication of information and advice

206(1)   [Power of Secretary of State re information etc.] The Secretary of State may publish information or give advice, or arrange for the publication of information or the giving of advice, in such form and manner as he considers appropriate with respect to—

(a)   the operation of this Act and the statements of principle, rules, regulations and codes of pratice issued or made under it, including in particular the rights of investors, the duties of authorised persons and the steps to be taken for enforcing those rights or complying with those duties;
(b)   any matters relating to the functions of the Secretary of State under this Act or any such statements of principle, rules, regulations or codes of practice;
(bb)   the operation of the Open-Ended Investment Companies (Investment Companies with Variable Capital) Regulations 1996 and any regulations made by virtue of regulation 6 of those Regulations;
(bc)   any matters relating to the functions to which regulation 73 of those Regulations relates;
(c)   any other matters about which it appears to him to be desirable to publish information or give advice for the protection of investors or any class of investors.

Note
Concerning European investment firms, see the Investment Services Regulations 1995 (SI 1995/3275), reg. 32 and Sch. 7, para. 40.
Concerning European institutions, see the Banking Coordination (Second Council Directive) Regulations 1992 (SI 1992/3218), reg. 55 and Sch. 9, para. 43.

206(2) [Sale of copies of information] The Secretary of State may offer for sale copies of information published under this section and may, if he thinks fit, make a reasonable charge for advice given under this section at any person's request.

206(3) [Sec. 179] This section shall not be construed as authorising the disclosure of restricted information within the meaning of section 179 above in any case in which it could not be disclosed apart from the provisions of this section.

206(4) [Functions under sec. 114] The functions to which section 114 above applies shall include the functions of the Secretary of State under this section.

Note
See the Financial Services Act 1986 (Delegation) Order 1987 (SI 1987/942).

SEC. 207   Interpretation

207(1) [Definitions] In this Act, except where the context otherwise requires—

"**appointed representative**" has the meaning given in section 44 above;

"**authorised person**" means a person authorised under Chapter III of Part I of this Act;

"**authorised unit trust scheme**" means a unit trust scheme declared by an order of the Secretary of State for the time being in force to be an authorised unit trust scheme for the purposes of this Act;

"**body corporate**" includes a body corporate constituted under the law of a country or territory outside the United Kingdom;

"**certified**" and "**certification**" mean certified or certification by a recognised professional body for the purposes of Part I of this Act;

"**clearing arrangements**" has the meaning given in section 38(2) above;

"**competent authority**" means the competent authority for the purposes of Part IV of this Act;

"**collective investment scheme**" has the meaning given in section 75 above;

"**delegation order**" and "**designated agency**" have the meaning given in section 114(3) above;

"**director**", in relation to a body corporate, includes a person occupying in relation to it the position of a director (by whatever name called) and any person in accordance with whose directions or instructions (not being advice given in a professional capacity) the directors of that body are accustomed to act;

"**ensure**" and "**ensuring**", in relation to the performance of transactions on an investment exchange, have the meaning given in paragraph 6 of Schedule 4 to this Act;

"**exempted person**" means a person exempted under Chapter IV of Part I of this Act;

"**friendly society**", "**incorporated friendly society**" and "**registered friendly society**" have the meaning given by section 116 of the Friendly Societies Act 1992;

"**group**", in relation to a body corporate, means that body corporate, any other body corporate which is its holding company or subsidiary and any other body corporate which is a subsidiary of that holding company;

"guidance", in relation to a self-regulating organisation, professional body, investment exchange, clearing house or designated agency, has the meaning given in section 8(4), 16(4), 36(3), 38(3) or 114(12) above;

"investment advertisement" has the meaning given in section 57(2) above;

"investment agreement" has the meaning given in section 44(9) above;

"investment company with variable capital" and, in relation to such a company, **"depositary"** have the same meaning as in the Open-Ended Investment Companies (Investment Companies with Variable Capital) Regulations 1996;

"listing particulars" has the meaning given in section 144(2A) above;

"member", in relation to a self-regulating organisation or professional body, has the meaning given in section 8(2) or 16(2) above;

"occupational pension scheme" means any scheme or arrangement which is comprised in one or more instruments or agreements and which has, or is capable of having, effect in relation to one or more descriptions or categories of employment so as to provide benefits, in the form of pensions or otherwise, payable on termination of service, or on death or retirement, to or in respect of earners with qualifying service in an employment of any such description or category;

"operator", in relation to a collective investment scheme, shall be construed in accordance with section 75(8) above;

"open-ended investment company" has the meaning given in section 75(8) above;

"overseas investment exchange" and **"overseas clearing house"** mean a recognised investment exchange or recognised clearing house in the case of which the recognition order was made by virtue of section 40 above;

"participant" has the meaning given in section 75(2) above;

"partnership" includes a partnership constituted under the law of a country or territory outside the United Kingdom;

"prescribed" means prescribed by regulations made by the Secretary of State or the Treasury;

"principal", in relation to an appointed representative, has the meaning given in section 44 above;

"private company" has the meaning given in section 1(3) of the Companies Act 1985 or the corresponding Northern Ireland provision;

"recognised clearing house" means a body declared by an order of the Secretary of State for the time being in force to be a recognised clearing house for the purposes of this Act;

"recognised investment exchange" means a body declared by an order of the Secretary of State for the time being in force to be a recognised investment exchange for the purposes of this Act;

"recognised professional body" means a body declared by an order of the Secretary of State for the time being in force to be a recognised professional body for the purposes of this Act;

"recognised scheme" means a scheme recognised under section 86, 87 or 88 above;

"recognised self-regulating organisation" means a body declared by an order of the Secretary of State for the time being in force to be a recognised self-regulating organisation for the purposes of this Act;

"recognised self-regulating organisation for friendly societies" has the meaning given in paragraph 1 of Schedule 11 to this Act;

"recognition order" means an order declaring a body to be a recognised self-regulating organisation, self-regulating organisation for friendly societies, professional body, investment exchange or clearing house;

"rules", in relation to a self-regulating organisation, professional body, investment exchange or clearing house, has the meaning given in section 8(3), 16(3), 36(2) or 38(2) above;

"transfer order" and **"transferee body"** have the meaning given in paragraph 28(4) of Schedule 11 to this Act;

"the Tribunal" means the Financial Services Tribunal;

"trustee", in relation to a collective investment scheme, has the meaning given in section 75(8) above;

"unit trust scheme" and **"units"** have the meaning given in section 75(8) above.

Note
See the Financial Services (Schemes Authorised in Designated Countries or Territories) (Notification) Regulations 1989 (SI 1989/1584) and the Financial Services (Schemes Constituted in Other Member States) Regulations 1989 (SI 1989/1585).

207(2) [**"Advertisement"**] In this Act **"advertisement"** includes every form of advertising, whether in a publication, by the display of notices, signs, labels or showcards, by means of circulars, catalogues, price lists or other documents, by an exhibition of pictures or photographic or cinematographic films, by way of sound broadcasting or television or by inclusion in any programme service (within the meaning of the Broadcasting Act 1990) other than a sound or television broadcasting service, by the distribution of recordings, or in any other manner; and references to the issue of an advertisement shall be construed accordingly.

207(3) [**Issue of advertisement in UK**] For the purposes of this Act an advertisement or other information issued outside the United Kingdom shall be treated as issued in the United Kingdom if it is directed to persons in the United Kingdom or is made available to them otherwise than in a newspaper, journal, magazine or other periodical publication published and circulating principally outside the United Kingdom or in a sound or television broadcast transmitted principally for reception outside the United Kingdom.

207(4) (Repealed and omitted by Broadcasting Act 1990, sec. 203(1), (3), Sch. 20, para. 45(1)(b) and Sch. 21 as from 1 January 1991.)

207(5) [**"Controller"**] In this Act **"controller"** means—

(a)   in relation to a body corporate, a person who, either alone or with any associate or associates, is entitled to exercise, or control the exercise of, 15 per cent or more of the voting power at any general meeting of the body corporate or another body corporate of which it is a subsidiary; and

(b)   in relation to an unincorporated association—

    (i)   any person in accordance with whose directions or instructions, either alone or with those of any associate or associates, the officers or members of the governing body of the association are accustomed to act (but disregarding advice given in a professional capacity); and

    (ii)   any person who, either alone or with any associate or associates, is entitled to exercise, or control the exercise of, 15 per cent or more of the voting power at any general meeting of the association;

and for the purposes of this subsection **"associate"**, in relation to any person, means that person's wife, husband or minor child or step-child, any body corporate of which that person is a director, any person who is an employee or partner of that person and, if that person is a body corporate, any subsidiary of that body corporate and any employee of any such subsidiary.

s. 207(5)

Note
See the Investment Services Regulations 1995 (SI 1995/3275), reg. 32 and Sch. 7, para. 41.

207(6) ["Manager"] In this Act, except in relation to a unit trust scheme or a registered friendly society, **"manager"** means an employee who—

(a)   under the immediate authority of his employer is responsible, either alone or jointly with one or more other persons, for the conduct of his employer's business; or

(b)   under the immediate authority of his employer or of a person who is a manager by virtue of paragraph (a) above exercises managerial functions or is responsible for maintaining accounts or other records of his employer;

and, where the employer is not an individual, references in this subsection to the authority of the employer are references to the authority, in the case of a body corporate, of the directors, in the case of a partnership, of the partners and, in the case of an unincorporated association, of its officers or the members of its governing body.

207(7) ["Insurance business" etc.] In this Act **"insurance business"**, **"insurance company"** and **"contract of insurance"** have the same meanings as in the Insurance Companies Act 1982.

207(8) [Subsidiary, holding company] Section 736 of the Companies Act 1985 (meaning of subsidiary and holding company) shall apply for the purposes of this Act.

207(9) [Application to Scotland] In the application of this Act to Scotland, references to a matter being actionable at the suit of a person shall be construed as references to the matter being actionable at the instance of that person.

207(10) [Time limits] For the purposes of any provision of this Act authorising or requiring a person to do anything within a specified number of days no account shall be taken of any day which is a public holiday in any part of the United Kingdom.

207(11) [Investment business on behalf of Crown] Nothing in Part I of this Act shall be construed as applying to investment business carried on by any person when acting as agent or otherwise on behalf of the Crown.

Note
See the Financial Services Act 1986 (Overseas Investment Exchanges and Overseas Clearing Houses) (Periodical Fees) Regulations 1993 (SI 1993/954).

SEC. 208   Gibraltar

208(1) [Application to Gibraltar] Subject to the provisions of this section, section 31, 58(1)(c), 86 and 130(2)(c) and (d) above shall apply as if Gibraltar were a member State.

208(2) [References to national of member State] References in those provisions to a national of a member State shall, in relation to Gibraltar, be construed as references to a British Dependent Territories citizen or a body incorporated in Gibraltar.

208(3) [Reference in sec. 86(3)(a) to relevant Community instrument] In the case of a collective investment scheme constituted in Gibraltar the reference in subsection (3)(a) of section 86 above to a relevant Community instrument shall be taken as a reference to any Community instrument the object of which is the co-ordination or approximation of the laws, regulations or administrative provisions of member States relating to collective investment schemes of a kind which satisfy the requirements prescribed for the purposes of that section.

208(4) **[Power of Secretary of State to make regulations]** The Secretary of State may by regulations make such provision as appears to him to be necessary or expedient to secure—

(a) that he may give notice under subsection (2) of section 86 above on grounds relating to the law of Gibraltar; and

(b) that this Act applies as if a scheme which is constituted in a member State other than the United Kingdom and recognised in Gibraltar under provisions which appear to the Secretary of State to give effect to the provisions of a relevant Community instrument were a scheme recognised under that section.

SEC. 209   Northern Ireland

209(1) **[Extent to Northern Ireland]** This Act extends to Northern Ireland.

209(2) **[Northern Ireland Constitution Act 1973]** Subject to any Order made after the passing of this Act by virtue of subsection (1)(a) of section 3 of the Northern Ireland Constitution Act 1973 the regulation of investment business, the official listing of securities and offers off unlisted securities shall not be transferred matters for the purposes of that Act but shall for the purposes of subsection (2) of that section be treated as specified in Schedule 3 to that Act.

SEC. 210   Expenses and receipts

210(1) **[Defraying of expenses]** Any expenses incurred by the Secretary of State under this Act shall be defrayed out of moneys provided by Parliament.

210(2) **[Payment of fees etc.]** Any fees or other sums received by the Secretary of State under this Act shall be paid into the Consolidated Fund.

210(3) **[Expenses, fees re Friendly Societies Commission]** Subsections (1) and (2) above apply also to expenses incurred and fees received under this Act by the Friendly Societies Commission.

SEC. 211   Commencement and transitional provisions

211(1) **[Commencement days by Order]** This Act shall come into force on such day as the Secretary of State may by order appoint and different days may be appointed for different provisions or different purposes.

211(2) **[Commencement of sec. 195]** Subsection (1) above does not apply to section 195 which shall come into force when this Act is passed.

211(3) **[Transitional matters]** Schedule 15 to this Act shall have effect with respect to the transitional matters there mentioned.

SEC. 212   Short title, consequential amendments and repeals

212(1) **[Citation]** This Act may be cited as the Financial Services Act 1986.

212(2) **[Consequential amendments]** The enactments and instruments mentioned in Schedule 16 to this Act shall have effect with the amendments there specified, being amendments consequential on the provisions of this Act.

212(3) **[Repeals]** The enactments mentioned in Part I of Schedule 17 to this Act and the instruments mentioned in Part II of that Schedule are hereby repealed or revoked to the extent specified in the third column of those Parts.

SCHEDULES

Schedule 1 — Investments and Investment Business
Sections 1 and 2

Part I — Investments
SHARES ETC.

1 Shares and stock in the share capital of a company.

Note

> In this paragraph **"company"** includes any body corporate and also any unincorporated body constituted under the law of a country or territory outside the United Kingdom but does not, except in relation to any shares of a class defined as deferred shares for the purposes of section 119 of the Building Societies Act 1986, include a building society incorporated under the law of, or of any part of, the United Kingdom, nor does it include an open-ended investment company or any body incorporated under the law of, or of any part of, the United Kingdom relating to industrial and provident societies or credit unions.

Note

See the Financial Services Act 1986 (Investment Services) (Extension of Scope of Act) Order 1995 (SI 1995/3271), reg. 1, 3.

DEBENTURES

2 Debentures, including debenture stock, loan stock, bonds, certificates of deposit and other instruments creating or acknowledging indebtedness, not being instruments falling within paragraph 3 below.

Note

This paragraph shall not be construed as applying—

(a)   to any instrument acknowledging or creating indebtedness for, or for money borrowed to defray, the consideration payable under a contract for the supply of goods or services;

(b)   to a cheque or other bill of exchange, a banker's draft or a letter of credit; or

(c)   to a banknote, a statement showing a balance in a current, deposit or savings account or (by reason of any financial obligation contained in it) to a lease or other disposition of property, a heritable security or an insurance policy.

Note

See the Financial Services Act 1986 (Investment Services) (Extension of Scope of Act) Order 1995 (SI 1995/3271), reg. 1, 4.

GOVERNMENT AND PUBLIC SECURITIES

3 Loan stock, bonds and other instruments creating or acknowledging indebtedness issued by or on behalf of a government, local authority or public authority.

Notes

(1)   In this paragraph "government, local authority or public authority" means—

(a)   the government of the United Kingdom, of Northern Ireland, or of any country or territory outside the United Kingdom;

(b)   a local authority in the United Kingdom or elsewhere;

Sch. 1

(c) any international organisation the members of which include the United Kingdom or another member State.

(2) The Note to paragraph 2 above shall, so far as applicable, apply also to this paragraph.

(3) This paragraph does not apply to any instrument creating or acknowledging indebtedness in respect of money received by the Director of Savings as deposits or otherwise in connection with the business of the National Savings Bank or in respect of money raised under the National Loans Act 1968 under the auspices of the Director of Savings or in respect of money treated as having been so raised by virtue of section 11(3) of the National Debt Act 1972.

INSTRUMENTS ENTITLING TO SHARES OR SECURITIES

4 Warrants or other instruments entitling the holder to subscribe for investments falling within paragraph 1, 2 or 3 above.

Notes

(1) It is immaterial whether the investments are for the time being in existence or identifiable.

(2) An investment falling within this paragraph shall not be regarded as falling within paragraph 7, 8 or 9 below.

CERTIFICATES REPRESENTING SECURITIES

5 Certificates or other instruments which confer—

(a) property rights in respect of any investment falling within paragraph 1, 2, 3 or 4 above;

(b) any right to acquire, dispose of, underwrite or convert an investment, being a right to which the holder would be entitled if he held any such investment to which the certificate or instrument relates; or

(c) a contractual right (other than an option) to acquire any such investment otherwise than by subscription.

Note

This paragraph does not apply to any instrument which confers rights in respect of two or more investments issued by different persons or in respect of two or more different investments falling within paragraph 3 above and issued by the same person.

UNITS IN COLLECTIVE INVESTMENT SCHEME

6 Units in a collective investment scheme, including shares in or securities of an open-ended investment company.

OPTIONS

7 Options to acquire or dispose of—
(a) an investment falling within any other paragraph of this Part of this Schedule;
(b) currency of the United Kingdom or of any other country or territory;
(c) gold, palladium, platinum or silver; or
(d) an option to acquire or dispose of an investment falling within this paragraph by virtue of (a), (b) or (c) above.

Sch. 1

FUTURES

8 Rights under a contract for the sale of a commodity or property of any other description under which delivery is to be made at a future date and at a price agreed upon when the contract is made.

Notes

(1)   This paragraph does not apply if the contract is made for commercial and not investment purposes.

(2)   A contract shall be regarded as made for investment purposes if it is made or traded on a recognised investment exchange or made otherwise than on a recognised investment exchange but expressed to be as traded on such an exchange or on the same terms as those on which an equivalent contract would be made on such an exchange.

(3)   A contract not falling within Note (2) above shall be regarded as made for commercial purposes if under the terms of the contract delivery is to be made within seven days.

(4)   The following are indications that any other contract is made for a commercial purpose and the absence of any of them is an indication that it is made for investment purposes—

(a)   either or each of the parties is a producer of the commodity or other property or uses it in his business;

(b)   the seller delivers or intends to deliver the property or the purchaser takes or intends to take delivery of it.

(5)   It is an indication that a contract is made for commercial purposes that the price, the lot, the delivery date or the other terms are determined by the parties for the purposes of the particular contract and not by reference to regularly published prices, to standard lots or delivery dates or to standard terms.

(6)   The following are also indications that a contract is made for investment purposes—

(a)   it is expressed to be as traded on a market or on an exchange;

(b)   performance of the contract is ensured by an investment exchange or a clearing house;

(c)   there are arrangements for the payment or provision of margin.

(7)   A price shall be taken to have been agreed upon when a contract is made—

(a)   notwithstanding that it is left to be determined by reference to the price at which a contract is to be entered into on a market or exchange or could be entered into at a time and place specified in the contract; or

(b)   in a case where the contract is expressed to be by reference to a standard lot and quality, notwithstanding that provision is made for a variation in the price to take account of any variation in quantity or quality on delivery.

CONTRACTS FOR DIFFERENCES ETC.

9 Rights under a contract for differences or under any other contract the purpose or pretended purpose of which is to secure a profit or avoid a loss by reference to fluctuations in the value or price of property of any description or in an index or other factor designated for that purpose in the contract.

Notes

(1)   This paragraph does not apply where the parties intend that the profit is to be obtained or the loss avoided by taking delivery of any property to which the contract relates.

Sch. 1

(2)   This paragraph does not apply to rights under any contract under which money is received by the Director of Savings as deposits or otherwise in connection with the business of the National Savings Bank or raised under the National Loans Act 1968 under the auspices of the Director of Savings or under which money raised is treated as having been so raised by virtue of section 11(3) of the National Debt Act 1972.

LONG TERM INSURANCE CONTRACTS

10 Rights under a contract the effecting and carrying out of which constitutes long term business within the meaning of the Insurance Companies Act 1982.

Notes
(1)   This paragraph does not apply to rights under a contract of insurance if—
    (a)   the benefits under the contract are payable only on death or in respect of incapacity due to injury, sickness or infirmity;
    (b)   no benefits are payable under the contract on a death (other than a death due to accident) unless it occurs within ten years of the date on which the life of the person in question was first insured under the contract or before that person attains a specified age not exceeding seventy years;
    (c)   the contract has no surrender value or the consideration consists of a single premium and the surrender value does not exceed that premium; and
    (d)   the contract does not make provision for its conversion or extension in a manner that would result in its ceasing to comply with paragraphs (a), (b) and (c) above.
(2)   Where the provisions of a contract of insurance are such that the effecting and carrying out of the contract—
    (a)   constitutes both long term business within the meaning of the Insurance Companies Act 1982 and general business within the meaning of that Act; or
    (b)   by virtue of section 1(3) of that Act constitutes long term business notwithstanding the inclusion of subsidiary general business provisions,

references in this paragraph to rights and benefits under the contract are references only to such rights and benefits as are attributable to the provisions of the contract relating to long term business.

(3)   This paragraph does not apply to rights under a reinsurance contract.
(4)   Rights falling within this paragraph shall not be regarded as falling within paragraph 9 above.

RIGHTS AND INTERESTS IN INVESTMENTS

11 Rights to and interests in anything which is an investment falling within any other paragraph of this Part of this Schedule.

Notes
(1)   This paragraph does not apply to interests under the trusts of an occupational pension scheme.
(2)   This paragraph does not apply to rights or interests which are investments by virtue of any other paragraph of this Part of this Schedule.

Sch. 1

Part II — Activities Constituting Investment Business
DEALING IN INVESTMENTS

12 Buying, selling, subscribing for or underwriting investments or offering or agreeing to do so, either as principal or as an agent.

Notes
(1)   This paragraph does not apply to a person by reason of his accepting, or offering or agreeing to accept, whether as principal or as agent, an instrument creating or acknowledging indebtedness in respect of any loan, credit, guarantee or other similar financial accommodation or assurance which he or his principal has made, granted or provided or which he or his principal has offered or agreed to make, grant or provide.

(2)   The references in (1) above to a person accepting, or offering or agreeing to accept, an instrument include references to a person becoming, or offering or agreeing to become, a party to an instrument otherwise than as a debtor or a surety.

ARRANGING DEALS IN INVESTMENTS

13 Making, or offering or agreeing to make—

(a)   arrangements with a view to another person buying, selling, subscribing for or underwriting a particular investment; or

(b)   arrangements with a view to a person who participates in the arrangements buying, selling, subscribing for or underwriting investments.

Notes
(1)   This paragraph does not apply to a person by reason of his making, or offering or agreeing to make, arrangements with a view to a transaction to which he will himself be a party as principal or which will be entered into by him as agent for one of the parties.

(2)   The arrangements in (a) above are arrangements which bring about or would bring about the transaction in question.

(3)   This paragraph does not apply to a person ("the relevant person") who is either a money-lending company within the meaning of section 338 of the Companies Act 1985 or a body corporate incorporated under the law of, or of any part of, the United Kingdom relating to building societies or a person whose ordinary business includes the making of loans or the giving of guarantees in connection with loans by reason of the relevant person making, or offering or agreeing to make, arrangements with a view to a person ("the authorised person") who is either authorised under section 22 or 23 of this Act or who is authorised under section 31 of this Act and carries on insurance business which is investment business selling an investment which falls within paragraph 10 above or, so far as relevant to that paragraph, paragraph 11 above if the arrangements are either—

    (a)   that the authorised person or a person on his behalf will introduce persons to whom the authorised person has sold or proposes to sell an investment of the kind described above, or will advise such persons to approach, the relevant person with a view to the relevant person lending money on the security of that investment; or

    (b)   that the authorised person gives an assurance to the relevant person as to the amount which will or may be received by the relevant person, should that person lend money to a person to whom the authorised person has sold or proposes to sell an investment of the kind described above, on the surrender or maturity of that investment if it is taken as security for the loan.

(4) This paragraph does not apply to a person by reason of his making, or offering or agreeing to make, arrangements with a view to a person accepting, whether as principal or as agent, an instrument creating or acknowledging indebtedness in respect of any loan, credit, guarantee or other similar financial accommodation or assurance which he or his principal has made, granted or provided or which he or his principal has offered or agreed to make, grant or provide.

(5) Arrangements do not fall within (b) above by reason of their having as their purpose the provision of finance to enable a person to buy, sell, subscribe for or underwrite investments.

(6) This paragraph does not apply to arrangements for the introduction of persons to another person if—
  (a) the person to whom the introduction is made is an authorised or exempted person or is a person whose ordinary business involves him in engaging in activities which fall within this Part of this Schedule or would do apart from the provisions of Part III or Part IV and who is not unlawfully carrying on investment business in the United Kingdom; and
  (b) the introduction is made with a view to the provision of independent advice or the independent exercise of discretion either—
    (i)   in relation to investments generally; or
    (ii) in relation to any class of investments if the transaction or advice is or is to be with respect to an investment within that class.

(7) The references in (4) above to a person accepting an instrument include references to a person becoming a party to an instrument otherwise than as a debtor or a surety.

CUSTODY OF INVESTMENTS

13A(1) Safeguarding and administering or arranging for the safeguarding and administration of assets belonging to another where—

(a) those assets consist of or include investments; or
(b) the arrangements for their safeguarding and administration are such that those assets may consist of or include investments and the arrangements have at any time been held out as arrangements under which investments would be safeguarded and administered.

13(2) Offering or agreeing to safeguard and administer, or to arrange for the safeguarding and administration of, assets belonging to another where the circumstances fall within sub-paragraph (1)(a) or (b) above.

Notes

(1) This paragraph does not apply to a person by reason of his safeguarding and administering assets, or offering or agreeing to do so, under arrangements—
  (a) under which another person ("the primary custodian") who is permitted to provide a service falling within this paragraph, undertakes to the person to whom the assets belong a responsibility in respect of the assets which is no less onerous than the responsibility which the primary custodian would undertake to that person if the primary custodian were safeguarding and administering the assets himself, and
  (b) which are operated by the primary custodian in the course of carrying on in the United Kingdom investment business falling within this paragraph.

Sch. 1

(2)   None of the following activities constitutes the administration of assets—
    (a) providing information as to the number of units or the value of any assets safeguarded;
    (b) converting currency; and
    (c) receiving documents relating to an investment solely for the purpose of onward transmission to, from or at the direction of the person to whom the investment belongs.

(3)   For the purposes of this paragraph it is immaterial that the assets safeguarded and administered—
    (a) constitute units of a security, title to which is recorded on the relevant register of securities as being held in uncertificated form; or
    (b) may be transferred to another person, subect to a commitment by the person safeguarding and administering them, or arranging for their safeguarding and administration, that they will be replaced by equivalent assets at some future date or when so requested by the person to whom they belong.

(4)   This paragraph does not apply to arrangements for the introduction of persons to another person if—
    (a) the person to whom the introduction is made is permitted to provide a service falling within this paragraph; and
    (b) the introduction is made with a view to the provision in the United Kingdom of a service falling within this paragraph or the making of arrangements operated in the United Kingdom for the provision of a service falling within this paragraph by a person who is not connected with the person by whom the introduction is made.

For the purposes of this Note, the person making the introduction shall be regarded as connected with the other person if he is either a body corporate in the same group as that other person or remunerated by that other person.

(5)   For the purposes of Notes (1) and (4) above, a person is permitted to provide a service falling within this paragraph if—
    (a) he is an authorised person who may provide that service—
        (i)   without contravening any rules that apply to him under section 48 of this Act; or
        (ii) by virtue of his membership of a recognised self-regulating organisation or his certification by a recognised professional body; or
    (b) he is an exempted person as respects any investment business which consists of or includes that service; or
    (c) he is entitled to carry on investment business in the United Kingdom which consists of or includes that service pursuant either to regulation 5 of the Banking Coordination (Second Council Directive Regulation 1992 or to regulation 5 of the Investment Services Regulations 1995.

MANAGING INVESTMENTS

14 Managing, or offering or agreeing to manage, assets belonging to another person if—
(a)   those assets consist of or include investments; or
(b)   the arrangements for their management are such that those assets may consist of or include investments at the discretion of the person managing or offering or agreeing to manage them and either they have at any time since the date of the coming into force of section 3 of this Act done so or the arrangements have at any time (whether before or after that date) been held out as arrangements under which they would do so.

Sch. 1

INVESTMENT ADVICE

15 Giving, or offering or agreeing to give, to persons in their capacity as investors or potential investors advice on the merits of their purchasing, selling, subscribing for or underwriting an investment, or exercising any right conferred by an investment to acquire, dispose of, underwrite or convert an investment.

ESTABLISHING ETC. COLLECTIVE INVESTMENT SCHEMES

16 Establishing, operating or winding up a collective investment scheme, including acting as trustee of an authorised unit trust scheme or as depositoary or sole director of an investment company with variable capital.

SENDING DEMATERIALISED INSTRUCTIONS ETC.

16A Sending on behalf of another person dematerialised instructions relating to an investment by means of a relevant system in respect of which an Operator is approved under the Uncertificated Securities Regulations 1995, or offering or agreeing to do so, or causing on behalf of another person such instructions to be sent by such means or offering or agreeing to do so.

Notes
(1)   This paragraph does not apply to a person by reason of his sending, or causing the sending of, instructions on behalf of—
  (a)   a participating issuer or settlement bank acting in its capacity as such; or
  (b)   an offeror making a takeover offer, or by reason of his offering or agreeing to do so.
(2)   For the purposes of this paragraph a person shall be taken to cause, or to offer or agree to cause, the sending of a dematerialised instruction only if he is a system-participant.
(3)   In this paragraph—
  "dematerialised instruction", "participating issuer", "relevant system", "settlement bank", "system-participant" and "Operator" have the meanings given by regulation 3 of the Uncertificated Securities Regulations 1995; and
  "offeror" and "takeover offer" have the meanings given by section 428 of the Companies Act 1985.

Note
For exemption under Sch. 1, para. 16A, see the Financial Services Act 1986 (Exemption) Order 1996 (SI 1996/1587).

Part III — Excluded Activities
DEALINGS AS PRINCIPAL

17(1) Paragraph 12 above applies to a transaction which is or is to be entered into by a person as principal only if—
(a)   he holds himself out as willing to enter into transactions of that kind at prices determined by him generally and continuously rather than in respect of each particular transaction; or
(b)   he holds himself out as engaging in the business of buying investments with a view to selling them and those investments are or include investments of the kind to which the transaction relates; or
(c)   he regularly solicits members of the public for the purpose of inducing them to enter as principals or agents into transactions to which that paragraph applies and

Sch. 1

the transaction is or is to be entered into as a result of his having solicited members of the public in that manner.

17(2) In sub-paragraph (1) above "buying" and "selling" means buying and selling by transactions to which paragraph 12 above applies and "members of the public", in relation to the person soliciting them ("the relevant person"), means any other person except—

(a)   authorised persons, exempted persons, or persons holding a permission under paragraph 23 below;
(b)   members of the same group as the relevant person;
(c)   persons who are, or propose to become, participators with the relevant person in a joint enterprise;
(d)   any person who is solicited by the relevant person with a view to—
   (i)   the acquisition by the relevant person of 20 per cent, or more of the voting shares in a body corporate (that is to say, shares carrying not less than that percentage of the voting rights attributable to share capital which are exercisable in all circumstances at any general meeting of the body); or
   (ii)   if the relevant person (either alone or with other members of the same group as himself) holds 20 per cent, or more of the voting shares in a body corporate, the acquisition by him of further shares in the body or the disposal by him of shares in that body to the person solicited or to a member of the same group as that person; or
   (iii)   if the person solicited (either alone or with other members of the same group as himself) holds 20 per cent, or more of the voting shares in a body corporate, the disposal by the relevant person of further shares in that body to the person solicited or to a member of the same group as that person;
(e)   any person whose head office is outside the United Kingdom, who is solicited by an approach made or directed to him at a place outside the United Kingdom and whose ordinary business involves him in engaging in activities which fall within Part II of this Schedule or would do so apart from this Part or Part IV.

17(3) Sub-paragraph (1) above applies only—

(a)   if the investment to which the transaction relates or will relate falls within any of paragraphs 1 to 6 above or, so far as relevant to any of those paragraphs, paragraph 11 above; or
(b)   if the transaction is the assignment (or, in Scotland, the assignation) of an investment falling within paragraph 10 above or is the assignment (or, in Scotland, the assignation) of an investment falling within paragraph 11 above which confers rights to or interests in an investment falling within paragraph 10 above.

17(4) Paragraph 12 above does not apply to any transaction which relates or is to relate to an investment which falls within paragraph 10 above or, so far as relevant to that paragraph, paragraph 11 above nor does it apply to a transaction which relates or is to relate to an investment which falls within any of paragraphs 7 to 9 above or, so far as relevant to any of those paragraphs, paragraph 11 above being a transaction which, in either case, is or is to be entered into by a person as principal if he is not an authorised person and the transaction is or is to be entered into by him—

(a)   with or through an authorised person, an exempted person or a person holding a permission under paragraph 23 below; or
(b)   through an office outside the United Kingdom, maintained by a party to the transaction, and with or through a person whose head office is situated outside the

United Kingdom and whose ordinary business is such as is mentioned in sub-paragraph (2)(e) above.

Note
Concerning core investment services, see the Financial Services Act 1986 (Restriction of Scope of Act and Meaning of Collective Investment Scheme) Order 1996 (SI 1996/2996), art. 2 and concerning European investment firms, see the Investment Services Regulations 1995 (SI 1995/3275), reg. 32 and Sch. 7, para. 42(1). Concerning European institutions, see the Banking Coordination (Second Council Directive) Regulations 1992 (SI 1992/3218), reg. 55 and Sch. 9, para. 44(1).

GROUPS AND JOINT ENTERPRISES

18(1) Paragraph 12 above does not apply to any transaction which is or is to be entered into by a person as principal with another person if—

(a)   they are bodies corporate in the same group; or

(b)   they are, or propose to become, participators in a joint enterprise and the transaction is or is to be entered into for the purposes of, or in connection with, that enterprise.

18(2) Paragraph 12 above does not apply to any transaction which is or is to be entered into by any person as agent for another person in the circumstances mentioned in sub-paragraph (1)(a) or (b) above if—

(a)   where the investment falls within any of paragraphs 1 to 6 above or, so far as relevant to any of those paragraphs, paragraph 11 above, the agent does not—

   (i)   hold himself out (otherwise than to other bodies corporate in the same group or persons who are or propose to become participators with him in a joint enterprise) as engaging in the business of buying investments with a view to selling them and those investments are or include investments of the kind to which the transaction relates; or

   (ii)   regularly solicit members of the public for the purpose of inducing them to enter as principals or agents into transactions to which paragraph 12 above applies;

and the transaction is not or is not to be entered into as a result of his having solicited members of the public in that manner;

(b)   where the investment is not as mentioned in paragraph (a) above—

   (i)   the agent enters into the transaction with or through an authorised person, an exempted person or a person holding a permission under paragraph 23 below; or

   (ii)   the transaction is effected through an office outside the United Kingdom, maintained by a party to the transaction, and with or through a person whose head office is situated outside the United Kingdom and whose ordinary business involves him in engaging in activities which fall within Part II of this Schedule or would do so apart from this Part or Part IV.

Note
Concerning European institutions, see the Banking Coordination (Second Council Directive) Regulations 1992 (SI 1992/3218), reg. 55 and Sch. 9, para. 44(2).

18(3) Paragraph 13 above does not apply to arrangements which a person makes or offers or agrees to make if—

(a)   that person is a body corporate and the arrangements are with a view to another body corporate in the same group entering into a transaction of the kind mentioned in that paragraph; or

(b)   that person is or proposes to become a participator in a joint enterprise and the arrangements are with a view to another person who is or proposes to become a

Sch. 1

participator in the enterprise entering into such a transaction for the purposes of or in connection with that enterprise.

18(3A) Paragraph 13A above does not apply to a service which a person provides or offers or agrees to provide or to arrangements which a person makes or offers or agrees to make for the provision of a service if—

(a)   that person is a body corporate and the service is or is to be provided to a body corporate in the same group and relates or will relate to assets which belong to that other body corporate; or

(b)   that person is or proposes to become a participator in a joint enterprise and the assets to which the service relates or will relate are or are to be held on behalf of another person who is or proposes to become a participator in the enterprise and are or are to be held for the purposes of or in connection with the enterprise.

18(4) Paragraph 14 above does not apply to a person by reason of his managing or offering or agreeing to manage the investments of another person if—

(a)   they are bodies corporate in the same group; or

(b)   they are, or propose to become, participators in a joint enterprise and the investments are or are to be managed for the purposes of, or in connection with, that enterprise.

18(5) Paragraph 15 above does not apply to advice given by a person to another person if—

(a)   they are bodies corporate in the same group; or

(b)   they are, or propose to become, participators in a joint enterprise and the advice is given for the purposes of, or in connection with, that enterprise.

18(5A) Paragraph 16A does not apply to a body corporate by reason of its sending, or causing the sending of, dematerialised instructions relating to an investment or offering or agreeing to do so if—

(a)   the person on whose behalf the instructions are, or are to be, sent or caused to be sent is a body corporate in the same group; and

(b)   the investment to which the instructions relate, or will relate, is one in respect of which a body corporate in the same group is registered as the holder on the appropriate register of securities, or will be so registered as a result of the instructions.

18(5B) In sub-paragraph (5A) "register of securities" has the meaning given by regulation 3 of the Uncertificated Securities Regulations 1995.

18(6) The definitions in paragraph 17(2) above shall apply also for the purposes of sub-paragraph (2)(a) above except that the relevant person referred to in paragraph 17(2)(d) shall be the person for whom the agent is acting.

Note
Concerning core investment services, see the Financial Services Act 1986 (Restriction of Scope of Act and Meaning of Collective Investment Scheme) Order 1996 (SI 1996/2996), art. 2.
Concerning European investment firms, see the Investment Services Regulations 1995 (SI 1995/3275), reg. 32 and Sch. 7, para. 42(2).

SALE OF GOODS AND SUPPLY OF SERVICES

19(1) Subject to sub-paragraph (9) below, this paragraph has effect where a person ("the supplier") sells or offers or agrees to sell goods to another person ("the customer")

Sch. 1

or supplies or offers or agrees to supply him with services and the supplier's main business is to supply goods or services and not to engage in activities falling within Part II of this Schedule.

19(2) Paragraph 12 above does not apply to any transaction which is or is to be entered into by the supplier as principal if it is or is to be entered into by him with the customer for the purposes of or in connection with the sale or supply or a related sale or supply (that is to say, a sale or supply to the customer otherwise than by the supplier but for or in connection with the same purpose as the first-mentioned sale or supply).

19(3) Paragraph 12 above does not apply to any transaction which is or is to be entered into by the supplier as agent for the customer if it is or is to be entered into for the purposes of or in connection with the sale or supply or a related sale or supply and—

(a)   where the investment falls within any of paragraphs 1 to 5 above or, so far as relevant to any of those paragraphs, paragraph 11 above, the supplier does not—
   (i)   hold himself out (otherwise than to the customer) as engaging in the business of buying investments with a view to selling them and those investments are or include investments of the kind to which the transaction relates; or
   (ii) regularly solicit members of the public for the purpose of inducing them to enter as principals or agents into transactions to which paragraph 12 above applies; and the transaction is not or is not to be entered into as a result of his having solicited members of the public in that manner;

(b)   where the investment is not as mentioned in paragraph (a) above, the supplier enters into the transaction—
   (i)   with or through an authorised person, an exempted person or a person holding a permission under paragraph 23 below; or
   (ii) through an office outside the United Kingdom, maintained by a party to the transaction, and with or through a person whose head office is situated outside the United Kingdom and whose ordinary business involves him in engaging in activities which fall within Part II of this Schedule or would do so apart from this Part of Part IV.

19(4) Paragraph 13 above does not apply to arrangements which the supplier makes or offers or agrees to make with a view to the customer entering into a transaction for the purposes of or in connection with the sale or supply or a related sale or supply.

19(4A) Paragraph 13A above does not apply to a service which the supplier provides or offers or agrees to provide or to arrangements which the supplier makes or offers or agrees to make for the provision of a service where the assets to which the service relates or will relate are or are to be held for the purposes of or in connection with the sale or supply or a related sale or supply.

19(5) Paragraph 14 above does not apply to the supplier by reason of his managing or offering or agreeing to manage the investments of the customer if they are or are to be managed for the purposes of or in connection with the sale or supply or a related sale or supply.

19(6) Paragraph 15 above does not apply to advice given by the supplier to the customer for the purposes of or in connection with the sale or supply or a related sale or supply or to a person with whom the customer proposes to enter into a transaction for the purposes of or in connection with the sale or supply or a related sale or supply.

19(7) Where the supplier is a body corporate and a member of a group sub-paragraphs (2) to (6) above shall apply to any other member of the group as they apply to the supplier; and where the customer is a body corporate and a member of a group

Sch. 1

references in those sub-paragraphs to the customer include references to any other member of the group.

19(8) The definitions in paragraph 17(2) above shall apply also for the purposes of sub-paragraph (3)(a) above.

19(9) This paragraph does not have effect where either—

(a)   the customer is an individual; or

(b)   the transaction in question is the purchase or sale of an investment which falls within paragraph 6 or 10 above or, so far as relevant to either of those paragraphs, paragraph 11 above; or

(c)   the investments which the supplier manages or offers or agrees to manage consist of investments falling within paragraph 6 or 10 above or, so far as relevant to either of those paragraphs, paragraph 11 above; or

(d)   the advice which the supplier gives is advice on an investment falling within the paragraph 6 or 10 above or, so far as relevant to either of those paragraphs, paragraph 11 above.

Note
Concerning core investment services, see the Financial Services Act 1986 (Restriction of Scope of Act and Meaning of Collective Investment Scheme) Order 1996 (SI 1996/2996), art. 2.

EMPLOYEES' SHARE SCHEMES

20(1) Paragraphs 12, 13 and 13A above do not apply to anything done by a body corporate, a body corporate connected with it or a relevant trustee for the purpose of enabling or facilitating transactions in shares in or debentures of the first-mentioned body between or for the benefit of any of the persons mentioned in sub-paragraph (2) below or the holding of such shares or debentures by or for the benefit of any such persons.

20(2) The persons referred to in sub-paragraph (1) above are—

(a)   the bona fide employees or former employees of the body corporate or of another body corporate in the same group; or

(b)   the wives, husbands, widows, widowers, or children or step-children under the age of eighteen of such employees or former employees.

20(3) In this paragraph "a relevant trustee" means a person holding shares in or debentures of a body corporate as trustee in pursuance of arrangements made for the purpose mentioned in sub-paragraph (1) above by, or by a body corporate connected with, that body corporate.

20(4) In this paragraph "shares" and "debentures" include any investment falling within paragraph 1 or 2 above and also include any investment falling within paragraph 4 or 5 above so far as relating to those paragraphs or any investment falling within paragraph 11 above so far as relating to paragraph 1, 2, 4 or 5.

20(5) For the purposes of this paragraph a body corporate is connected with another body corporate if—

(a)   they are in the same group; or

(b)   one is entitled, either alone or with any other body corporate in the same group, to exercise or control the exercise of a majority of the voting rights attributable to the share capital which are exercisable in all circumstances at any general meeting of the other body corporate or of its holding company.

Sch. 1

SALE OF BODY CORPORATE

21(1) Paragraphs 12 and 13 above do not apply to the acquisition or disposal of, or to anything done for the purposes of the acquisition or disposal of, shares in a body corporate other than an open-ended investment company, and paragraph 15 above does not apply to advice given in connection with the acquisition or disposal of such shares, if—

(a) the shares consist of or include shares carrying 75 per cent or more of the voting rights attributable to share capital which are exercisable in all circumstances at any general meeting of the body corporate; or

(b) the shares, together with any already held by the person acquiring them, carry not less than that percentage of those voting rights; and

(c) in either case, the acquisition and disposal is, or is to be between parties each of whom is a body corporate, a partnership, a single individual or a group of connected individuals.

21(2) For the purposes of subsection (1)(c) above "a group of connected individuals", in relation to the party disposing of the shares, means persons each of whom is, or is a close relative of, a director or manager of the body corporate and, in relation to the party acquiring the shares, means persons each of whom is, or is a close relative of, a person who is to be a director or manager of the body corporate.

21(3) In this paragraph "close relative" means a person's spouse, his children and step-children, his parents and step-parents, his brothers and sisters and his step-brothers and step-sisters.

Note
Concerning core investment services, see the Financial Services Act 1986 (Restriction of Scope of Act and Meaning of Collective Investment Scheme) Order 1996 (SI 1996/2996), art. 2.

TRUSTEES AND PERSONAL REPRESENTATIVES

22(1) Paragraph 12 above does not apply to a person by reason of his buying, selling or subscribing for an investment or offering or agreeing to do so if—

(a) the investment is or, as the case may be, is to be held by him as bare trustee or, in Scotland, as nominee for another person;

(b) he is acting on that person's instructions; and

(c) he does not hold himself out as providing a service of buying and selling investments.

22(2) Paragraph 13 above does not apply to anything done by a person as trustee or personal representative with a view to—

(a) a fellow trustee or personal representative and himself engaging in their capacity as such in an activity falling within paragraph 12 above; or

(b) a beneficiary under the trust, will or intestacy engaging in any such activity,

unless that person is remunerated for what he does in addition to any remuneration he receives for discharging his duties as trustee or personal representative.

22(2A) Paragraph 13A above does not apply to anything done by a person as a trustee or personal representative unless—

(a) he holds himself out as providing a service falling within paragraph 13A above; or

(b) he is remunerated for providing such a service in addition to any remuneration he receives for discharging his duties as trustee or personal representative.

22(3) Paragraph 14 above does not apply to anything done by a person as trustee or

Sch. 1

personal representative unless he holds himself out as offering investment management services or is remunerated for providing such services in addition to any remuneration he receives for discharging his duties as trustee or personal representative.

22(4) Paragraph 15 above does not apply to advice given by a person as trustee or personal representative to—

(a)   a fellow trustee or personal representative for the purposes of the trust or estate; or

(b)   a beneficiary under the trust, will or intestacy concerning his interest in the trust fund or estate,

unless that person is remunerated for doing so in addition to any remuneration he receives for discharging his duties as trustee or personal representative.

22(4A) Paragraph 16A does not apply to a person by reason of his sending, or causing the sending of, dematerialised instructions relating to an investment held by him as trustee or as personal representative, or by reason of his offering or agreeing to do so.

22(5) Sub-paragraph (1) above has effect to the exclusion of paragraph 17 above as respects any transaction in respect of which the conditions in sub-paragraph (1)(a) and (b) are satisfied.

DEALINGS IN COURSE OF NON-INVESTMENT BUSINESS

23(1) Paragraph 12 above does not apply to anything done by a person—

(a)   as principal;

(b)   if that person is a body corporate in a group, as agent for another member of the group; or

(c)   as agent for a person who is or proposes to become a participator with him in a joint enterprise and for the purposes of or in connection with that enterprise,

if it is done in accordance with the terms and conditions of a permission granted to him by the Secretary of State under this paragraph.

23(2) Any application for permission under this paragraph shall be accompanied or supported by such information as the Secretary of State may require and shall not be regarded as duly made unless accompanied by the prescribed fee.

23(3) The Secretary of State may grant a permission under this paragraph if it appears to him—

(a)   that the applicant's main business, or if he is a member of a group the main business of the group, does not consist of activities for which a person is required to be authorised under this Act;

(b)   that the applicant's business is likely to involve such activities which fall within paragraph 12 above; and

(c)   that, having regard to the nature of the applicant's main business and, if he is a member of a group, the main business of the group taken as a whole, the manner in which, the persons with whom and the purposes for which the applicant proposes to engage in activities that would require him to be an authorised person and to any other relevant matters, it is inappropriate to require him to be subject to regulation as an authorised person.

23(4) Any permission under this paragraph shall be granted by a notice in writing; and the Secretary of State may by a further notice in writing withdraw any such permission if for any reason it appears to him that it is not appropriate for it to continue in force.

Sch. 1

23(5) The Secretary of State may make regulations requiring persons holding permissions under this paragraph to furnish him with information for the purpose of enabling him to determine whether those permissions should continue in force; and such regulations may, in particular, require such persons—

(a) to give him notice forthwith of the occurrence of such events as are specified in the regulations and such information in respect of those events as is so specified;

(b) to furnish him at such times or in respect of such periods as are specified in the regulations with such information as is so specified.

23(6) Section 61 of this Act shall have effect in relation to a contravention of any condition imposed by a permission under this paragraph as it has effect in relation to any such contravention as is mentioned in subsection (1)(a) of that section.

23(7) Section 104 of this Act shall apply to a person holding a permission under this paragraph as if he were authorised to carry on investment business as there mentioned; and sections 105 and 106 of this Act shall have effect as if anything done by him in accordance with such permission constituted the carrying on of investment business.

Note
See the Financial Services Act 1986 (Investment Services) (Extension of Scope of Act) Order 1995 (SI 1995/3271), reg. 1, 6(2).

ADVICE GIVEN OR ARRANGEMENTS MADE IN COURSE OF PROFESSION OR NON-INVESTMENT BUSINESS

24(1) Paragraph 15 above does not apply to advice—

(a) which is given in the course of the carrying on of any profession or of a business not otherwise constituting investment business; and

(b) the giving of which is a necessary part of other advice or services given in the course of carrying on that profession or business.

24(2) Paragraph 13 above does not apply to arrangements—

(a) which are made in the course of the carrying on of any profession or of a business not otherwise constituting investment business; and

(b) the making of which is a necessary part of other services provided in the course of carrying on that profession or business.

24(2A) Paragraph 13A above does not apply to the provision of a service or to arrangements made for the provision of a service where—

(a) the service is provided or the arrangements are made in the course of the carrying on of any profession or of a business not otherwise constituting investment business; and

(b) the provision of the service or the making of the arrangements is a necessary part of other services provided in the course of carrying on that profession or business.

24(3) Advice shall not be regarded as falling within sub-paragraph (1)(b) above, the making of arrangements shall not be regarded as falling within sub-paragraph (2)(b) above and the provision of a service or the arranging for the provision of a service shall not be regarded as falling within sub-paragraph (2A)(b) above if the giving of the advice, the making of the arrangements or the provision, or the arranging for the provision, of the service is remunerated separately from the other advice or services.

CUSTODY OF GROUP PENSION FUNDS BY CERTAIN INSURANCE COMPANIES

24A(1) Paragraph 13A above does not apply to anything done by a relevant insurance company in relation to the investments of any pension fund which is established solely

Sch. 1

for the benefit of the officers or employees and their dependants of that company or of any other body corporate in the same group as that company.

24A(2) In sub-paragraph (1) above "relevant insurance company" means an insurance company to which Part II of the Insurance Companies Act 1982 applies but to which section 22 of this Act does not apply.

NEWSPAPERS

25(1) Paragraph 15 above does not apply to advice given in a newspaper, journal, magazine or other periodical publication if the principal purpose of the publication, taken as a whole and including any advertisements contained in it, is not to lead persons to invest in any particular investment.

25(2) The Secretary of State may, on the application of the proprietor of any periodical publication, certify that it is of the nature described in sub-paragraph (1) above and revoke any such certificate if he considers that it is no longer justified.

25(3) A certificate given under sub-paragraph (2) above and not revoked shall be conclusive evidence of the matters certified.

ADVICE GIVEN IN TELEVISION, SOUND OR TELETEXT SERVICES

25A(1) Paragraph 15 above does not apply to any advice given in any programme included, or made for inclusion, in—

(a) any television broadcasting service or other programme service (within the meaning of Part I of the Broadcasting Act 1990); or

(b) any sound broadcasting service or licensable sound programme service (within the meaning of Part III of that Act); or

(c) any teletext service.

25A(2) For the purposes of this paragraph, "programme", in relation to a service mentioned in sub-paragraph (1) above, includes an advertisement and any other item included in the service.

INTERNATIONAL SECURITIES SELF-REGULATING ORGANISATIONS

25B(1) An activity within paragraph 13 above engaged in for the purposes of carrying out the functions of a body or association which is approved under this paragraph as an international securities self-regulating organisation, whether by the organisation or by any person acting on its behalf, shall not constitute the carrying on of investment business in the United Kingdom for the purposes of Chapter II of Part I of this Act.

25B(2) In this paragraph—

"International securities business" means the business of buying, selling, subscribing for or underwriting investments (or offering or agreeing to do so, either as principal or agent) which fall within any of the paragraphs in Part I above other than paragraph 10 and, so far as relevant to paragraph 10, paragraph 11 and which, by their nature, and the manner in which the business is conducted, may be expected normally to be bought or dealt in by persons sufficiently expert to understand any risks involved, where either the transaction is international or each of the parties may be expected to be indifferent to the location of the other, and, for the purposes of this definition, the fact that the investments may ultimately be bought otherwise than in the course of international securities business by persons not so expert shall be disregarded; and "international securities self-regulating organisation" means a body corporate or unincorporated association which

(a) does not have its head office in the United Kingdom;

(b) is not eligible for recognition under section 37 or section 39 of this Act on the ground that (whether or not it has applied, and whether or not it would be eligible on other grounds) it is unable to satisfy the requirements of section 40(2)(a) or (c) of this Act;

(c) has a membership composed of persons falling within any of the following categories, that is to say, authorised persons, exempted persons, persons holding a permission under paragraph 23 above and persons whose head offices are outside the United Kingdom and whose ordinary business is such as is mentioned in paragraph 17(2)(e) above; and

(d) which facilitates and regulates the activity of its members in the conduct of international securities business.

25B(3) The Secretary of State may approve as an international securities self-regulating organisation any body or association appearing to him to fall within sub-paragraph (2) above if, having regard to such matters affecting international trade, overseas earnings and the balance of payments or otherwise as he considers relevant, it appears to him that to do so would be desirable and not result in any undue risk to investors.

25B(4) Any approval under this paragraph shall be given by notice in writing; and the Secretary of State may by a further notice in writing withdraw any such approval if for any reason it appears to him that it is not appropriate for it to continue in force.

Part IV — Additional Exclusions for Persons Without Permanent Place of Business in United Kingdom
TRANSACTIONS WITH OR THROUGH AUTHORISED OR EXEMPTED PERSONS

26(1) Paragraph 12 above does not apply to any transaction by a person not falling within section 1(3)(a) of this Act ("an overseas person") with or through—

(a) an authorised person; or

(b) an exempted person acting in the course of business in respect of which he is exempt.

26(2) Paragraph 13 above does not apply if—

(a) the arrangements are made by an overseas person with, or the offer or agreement to make them is made by him to or with, an authorised person or an exempted person and, in the case of an exempted person, the arrangements are with a view to his entering into a transaction in respect of which he is exempt; or

(b) the transactions with a view to which the arrangements are made are, as respects transactions in the United Kingdom, confined to transactions by authorised persons and transactions by exempted persons in respect of which they are exempt.

Note
Concerning European investment firms, see the Investment Services Regulations 1995 (SI 1995/3275), reg. 32 and Sch. 7, para. 42(3).
Concerning European institutions, see the Banking Coordination (Second Council Directive) Regulations 1992 (SI 1992/3218), reg. 55 and Sch. 9, para. 44(3).

Sch. 1

UNSOLICITED OR LEGITIMATELY SOLICITED TRANSACTIONS ETC. WITH OR FOR OTHER PERSONS

27(1) Paragraph 12 above does not apply to any transaction entered into by an overseas person as principal with, or as agent for, a person in the United Kingdom, paragraphs 13, 13A, 14 and 15 above do not apply to any offer made by an overseas person to or agreement made by him with a person in the United Kingdom and paragraph 15 above does not apply to any advice given by an overseas person to a person in the United Kingdom if the transaction, offer, agreement or advice is the result of—

(a)   an approach made to the overseas person by or on behalf of the person in the United Kingdom which either has not been in any way solicited by the overseas person or has been solicited by him in a way which has not contravened section 56 or 57 of this Act; or

(b)   an approach made by the overseas person which has not contravened either of those sections.

27(2) Where the transaction is entered into by the overseas person as agent for a person in the United Kingdom, sub-paragraph (1) above applies only if—

(a)   the other party is outside the United Kingdom; or
(b)   the other party is in the United Kingdom and the transaction is the result of such an approach by the other party as is mentioned in sub-paragraph (1)(a) above or of such an approach as is mentioned in sub-paragraph (1)(b) above.

27(3) Paragraph 16A does not apply to any offer made by an overseas person to or agreement made by him with a person in the United Kingdom if the offer or agreement is the result of—

(a)   an approach made to the overseas person by or on behalf of the person in the United Kingdom which either has not been in any way solicited by the overseas person, or has been solicited by him in a way which has not contravened section 56 or 57 of this Act; or

(b)   an approach made by the overseas person which has not contravened either of those sections.

Part V — Interpretation

28(1) In this Schedule—

(a)   "property" includes currency of the United Kingdom or any other country or territory;

(b)   references to an instrument include references to any record whether or not in the form of a document;

(c)   references to an offer include references to an invitation to treat;

(d)   references to buying and selling include references to any acquisition or disposal for valuable consideration.

28(2) In sub-paragraph (1)(d) above "disposal" includes—

(a)   in the case of an investment consisting of rights under a contract or other arrangements, assuming the corresponding liabilities under the contract or arrangements;

(b)   in the case of any other investment, issuing or creating the investment or granting the rights or interests of which it consists;

(c)   in the case of an investment consisting of rights under a contract, surrendering, assigning or converting those rights.

Sch. 1

28(3) A company shall not by reason of issuing its own shares or share warrants, and a person shall not by reason of issuing his own debentures or debenture warrants, be regarded for the purpose of this Schedule as disposing of them or, by reason of anything done for the purpose of issuing them, be regarded as making arrangements with a view to a person subscribing for or otherwise acquiring them or underwriting them.

28(4) In sub-paragraph (3) above "company" has the same meaning as in paragraph 1 above, "shares" and "debentures" include any investments falling within paragraph 1 or 2 above and "share warrants" and "debenture warrants" means any investment which falls within paragraph 4 above and relates to shares in the company concerned or, as the case may be, to debentures issued by the person concerned.

29 For the purposes of this Schedule a transaction is entered into through a person if he enters into it as agent or arranges for it to be entered into by another person as principal or agent.

30(1) For the purposes of this Schedule a group shall be treated as including any body corporate in which a member of the group holds a qualifying capital interest.

30(2) A qualifying capital interest means an interest in relevant shares of the body corporate which the member holds on a long-term basis for the purpose of securing a contribution to its own activities by the exercise of control or influence arising from that interest.

30(3) Relevant shares means shares comprised in the equity share capital of the body corporate of a class carrying rights to vote in all circumstances at general meetings of the body.

30(4) A holding of 20 per cent or more of the nominal value of the relevant shares of a body corporate shall be presumed to be a qualifying capital interest unless the contrary is shown.

30(5) In this paragraph "equity share capital" has the same meaning as in the Companies Act 1985 and the Companies (Northern Ireland) Order 1986.

31 In this Schedule "a joint enterprise" means an enterprise into which two or more persons ("the participators") enter for commercial reasons related to a business or businesses (other than investment business) carried on by them; and where a participator is a body corporate and a member of a group each other member of the group shall also be regarded as a participator in the enterprise.

32 Where a person is an exempted person as respects only part of the investment business carried on by him anything done by him in carrying on that part shall be disregarded in determining whether any paragraph of Part III or IV of this Schedule applies to anything done by him in the course of business in respect of which he is not exempt.

33 In determining for the purposes of this Schedule whether anything constitutes an investment or the carrying on of investment business section 18 of the Gaming Act 1845, section 1 of the Gaming Act 1892, any corresponding provision in force in Northern Ireland and any rule of the law of Scotland whereby a contract by way of gaming or wagering is not legally enforceable shall be disregarded.

34(1) For the purposes of this Schedule arrangements are not a collective investment scheme if—

(a)   the property to which the arrangements relate (other than cash awaiting investment) consists of shares;

Sch. 1

(b)   they constitute a complying fund;

(c)   each participant is the owner of a part of the property to which the arrangements relate and, to the extent that his part of that property—

   (i)   comprises relevant shares of a class which are admitted to the Official List of any member State or to dealings on a recognised investment exchange, he is entitled to withdraw it at any time after the end of the period of five years beginning with the date on which the shares in question were issued;

   (ii)   comprises relevant shares which do not fall within sub-paragraph (i) above, he is entitled to withdraw it at any time after the end of the period of two years beginning with the date upon which the period referred to in sub-paragraph (i) above expired;

   (iii)   comprises any other shares, he is entitled to withdraw it at any time after the end of the period of six months beginning with the date upon which the shares in question ceased to be relevant shares; and

   (iv)   comprises cash which the operator has not agreed (conditionally or unconditionally) to apply in subscribing for shares, he is entitled to withdraw it at any time; and

(d)   the arrangements would meet the conditions described in section 75(5)(c) of this Act were it not for the fact that the operator is entitled to exercise all or any of the rights conferred by shares included in the property to which the arrangements relate.

34(2) For the purposes of this paragraph—

(a)   "shares" means investments falling within paragraph 1 of this Schedule;

(b)   shares shall be regarded as being relevant shares if and so long as they are shares in respect of which neither—

   (i)   a claim for relief made in accordance with section 306 of the Income and Corporation Taxes Act 1988 has been disallowed; nor

   (ii)   an assessment has been made pursuant to section 307 of that Act withdrawing or refusing relief by reason of the body corporate in which the shares are held having ceased to be a body corporate which is a qualifying company for the purposes of section 293 of that Act; and

(c)   arrangements shall be regarded as constituting a complying fund if they provide that—

   (i)   the operator will, so far as practicable, make investments each of which, subject to each participant's individual circumstances, qualify for relief by virtue of Chapter III of Part VII of the Income and Corporation Taxes Act 1988; and

   (ii)   the minimum subscription to the arrangements made by each participant must be not less than £2,000.

35 For the purposes of this Schedule the following are not collective investment schemes—

(a)   arrangements where the entire contribution of each participant is a deposit within the meaning of section 5 of the Banking Act 1987 or a sum of a kind described in subsection (3) of that section;

(b)   arrangements under which the rights or interests of the participants are represented by the following—

   (i)   investments falling within paragraph 2 of this Schedule which are issued by a single body corporate which is not an open-ended investment company or

Sch. 1

which are issued by a single issuer which is not a body corporate and are guaranteed by the government of the United Kingdom, of Northern Ireland, or of any country or territory outside the United Kingdom; or

(ii) investments falling within sub-paragraph (i) above which are convertible into or exchangeable for investments falling within paragraph 1 of this Schedule provided that those latter investments are issued by the same person as issued the investments falling within sub-paragraph (i) above or are issued by a single other issuer; or

(iii) investments falling within paragraph 3 of this Schedule issued by the same government, local authority or public authority; or

(iv) investments falling within paragraph 4 of this Schedule which are issued otherwise than by an open-ended investment company and which confer rights in respect of investments, issued by the same issuer, falling within paragraph 1 of this Schedule or within sub-paragraph (i), (ii) or (iii) above;

(c) arrangements which would fall within paragraph (b) above were it not for the fact that the rights or interests of a participant ("the counterparty") whose ordinary business involves him in engaging in activities which fall within Part II of this Schedule or would do so apart from Part III or IV are or include rights or interests under a swap arrangement, that is to say, an arrangement the purpose of which is to facilitate the making of payments to participants whether in a particular amount or currency or at a particular time or rate of interest or all or any combination of those things, being an arrangement under which—

(i) the counterparty is entitled to receive amounts (whether representing principal or interest) payable in respect of any property subject to the scheme or sums determined by reference to such amounts; and

(ii) the counterparty makes payments (whether or not of the same amount and whether or not in the same currency as those referred to in sub-paragraph (i) above) which are calculated in accordance with an agreed formula by reference to the amounts or sums referred to in sub-paragraph (i) above;

(d) arrangements under which the rights or interests of participants are rights to or interests in money held in a common account in circumstances in which the money so held is held on the understanding that an amount representing the contribution of each participant is to be applied either in making payments to him or in satisfaction of sums owed by him or in the acquisition of property or the provision of services for him;

(e) arrangements under which the rights and interests of participants are rights and interests in a fund which is a trust fund within the meaning of section 42(1) of the Landlord and Tenant Act 1987.

(f) arrangements where—

(i) each of the participants is a bona fide employee or former employee (or the wife, husband, widow, widower, or child (including, in Northern Ireland, adopted child) or step-child under the age of eighteen of such an employee or former employee) of any of the following bodies corporate, that is to say, The National Grid Company plc, Electricity Association Services Limited or any other body corporate in the same group as either of them being arrangements which are operated by any of those bodies corporate; and

(ii) the property to which the arrangements relate consists of shares or debentures (as defined in paragraph 20(4) above) in or of a body corporate which is an electricity successor company for the purposes of Part II of the Electricity Act 1989 or a body corporate which would be regarded as

Sch. 1

connected with such an electricity successor company for the purposes of paragraph 20 above,

and for the purposes of this paragraph references to former employees shall have the same meaning as in the Financial Services Act 1986 (Electricity Industry Exemptions) Order 1990.

36(1) For the purposes of this Schedule, arrangements are not a collective investment scheme if they are operated by a body corporate, a body corporate connected with it or a relevant trustee, for the purpose of enabling or facilitating transactions in shares in or debentures of the first-mentioned body between or for the benefit of any of the persons mentioned in sub-paragraph (2) below or the holding of such shares or debentures by or for the benefit of any such persons.

36(2) The persons referred to in sub-paragraph (1) above are—

(a)   the bona fide employees or former employees of the body corporate or of another body corporate in the same group; or

(b)   the wives, husbands, widows, widowers, or children or step-children under the age of eighteen of such employees or former employees.

36(3) In this paragraph, "a relevant trustee" means a person holding shares in or debentures of a body corporate as trustee in pursuance of arrangements mentioned in sub-paragraph (1) above which were made by, or by a body corporate connected with, that body corporate.

36(4) In this paragraph "shares" and "debentures" include any investment falling within paragraph 1 or 2 above and also include any investment falling within paragraph 4 or 5 above so far as relating to those paragraphs or any investment falling within paragraph 11 above so far as relating to paragraphs 1, 2, 4 or 5.

36(5) For the purposes of this paragraph a body corporate is connected with another body corporate if—

(a)   they are in the same group; or

(b)   one is entitled, either alone or with any other body corporate in the same group, to exercise or control the exercise of a majority of the voting rights attributable to the share capital which are exercisable in all circumstances at any general meeting of the other body corporate or its holding company.

37 For the purposes of this Schedule, arrangements are not a collective investment scheme if—

(a)   the purpose of the arrangements is that participants should receive, by way of reward, payments or other benefits in respect of the introduction by any person of other persons who become participants;

(b)   the arrangements are such that the payments or other benefits referred to in paragraph (a) above are to be wholly or mainly funded out of the contributions of other participants; and

(c)   the only reason why the arrangements have either or both of the characteristics mentioned in section 75(3) of this Act is because, pending their being used to fund those payments or other benefits, contributions of participants are managed as a whole by or on behalf of the operator of the scheme.

Schedule 2 — Requirements for Recognition of Self-Regulating Organisation

Section 10

MEMBERS TO BE FIT AND PROPER PERSONS

1(1) The rules and practices of the organisation must be such as to secure that its members are fit and proper persons to carry on investment business of the kind with which the organisation is concerned.

1(2) Where the organisation is concerned with investment business of different kinds its rules and practices must be such as to secure that a member carrying on investment business of any of those kinds is a fit and proper person to carry on investment business of that kind.

1(3) The matters which may be taken into account under the rules in determining whether a person is a fit and proper person must include those that the Secretary of State may take into account under section 27 above.

1(4) This paragraph does not apply to a person who is not an authorised person by virtue of being a member of the organisation.

Note
See the Investment Services Regulations 1995 (SI 1995/3275), reg. 1, 21(2)–(4).

ADMISSION, EXPULSION AND DISCIPLINE

2 The rules and practices of the organisation relating to—

(a)   the admission and expulsion of members; and

(b)   the discipline it exercises over its members,

must be fair and reasonable and include adequate provision for appeals.

Note
See the Banking Coordination (Second Council Directive) Regulations 1992 (SI 1992/3218), reg. 48(2)–(3), reg 55 and Sch. 9, para. 45.
Regarding application to EC companies, see the Insurance Companies (Third Insurance Directives) Regulations 1994(SI 1994/1696), reg. 1, 56(1).
See the Investment Services Regulations 1995 (SI 1995/3275), reg. 1, 21(5). Concerning European investment firms, see the Investment Services Regulations 1995 (SI 1995/3275), reg. 32 and Sch. 7, para. 43(1).

SAFEGUARDS FOR INVESTORS

3(1) The organisation must have rules governing the carrying on of investment business by its members which, together with the statements of principle, rules, regulations and codes of practice to which its members are subject under Chapter V of Part I of this Act, are such as to afford an adequate level of protection for investors.

3(2) In determining in any case whether an adequate level of protection is afforded for investors of any description, regard shall be had to the nature of the investment business carried on by members of the organisation, the kinds of investors involved and the effectiveness of the organisation's arrangements for enforcing compliance.

Note
For transitional provisions in relation to para. 3(1), (2) see CA 1989, s. 203(3) and SI 1990/354 (C. 2), art. 6.

3(3) The organisation must, so far as practicable, have powers for purposes corresponding to those of Chapter VI of Part I of this Act.

3(4) The rules of the organisation must enable it to prevent a member resigning from the organisation if the organisation considers that any matter affecting him should be

Sch. 2

investigated as a preliminary to a decision on the question whether he should be expelled or otherwise disciplined or if it considers that it is desirable that a prohibition or requirement should be imposed on him under the powers mentioned in sub-paragraph (3) above or that any prohibition or requirement imposed on him under those powers should continue in force.

Note
Concerning European institutions, see the Banking Coordination (Second Council Directive) Regulations 1992 (SI 1992/3218), reg. 55 and Sch. 9, para. 45(2)–(3).
Regarding application to EC companies, see the Insurance Companies (Third Insurance Directives) Regulations 1994 (SI 1994/1696), reg. 1, 56(2), (3).
Concerning European investment firms, see the Investment Services Regulations 1995 (SI 1995/3275), reg. 32 and Sch. 7, para. 43(2), (3).

TAKING ACCOUNT OF COSTS OF COMPLIANCE

3A The organisation must have satisfactory arrangements for taking account, in framing its rules, of the cost to those to whom the rules would apply of complying with those rules and any other controls to which they are subject.

Note
See CA 1989, s. 204(2), (3).

MONITORING AND ENFORCEMENT

4(1) The organisation must have adequate arrangements and resources for the effective monitoring and enforcement of compliance with its rules and with any statements of principle, rules, regulations or codes of practice to which its members are subject under Chapter V of Part I of this Act in respect of investment business of a kind regulated by the organisation.

4(2) The arrangements for monitoring may make provision for that function to be performed on behalf of the organisation (and without affecting its responsibility) by any other body or person who is able and willing to perform it.

THE GOVERNING BODY

5(1) The arrangements of the organisation with respect to the appointment, removal from office and functions of the persons responsible for making or enforcing the rules of the organisation must be such as to secure a proper balance—

(a)   between the interests of the different members of the organisation; and
(b)   between the interests of the organisation or its members and the interests of the public.

5(2) The arrangements shall not be regarded as satisfying the requirements of this paragraph unless the persons responsible for those matters include a number of persons independent of the organisation and its members sufficient to secure the balance referred to in sub-paragraph (1)(b) above.

INVESTIGATION OF COMPLAINTS

6(1) The organisation must have effective arrangements for the investigation of complaints against the organisation or its members.

6(2) The arrangements may make provision for the whole or part of that function to be performed by and to be the responsibility of a body or person independent of the organisation.

Sch. 2

PROMOTION AND MAINTENANCE OF STANDARDS

7 The organisation must be able and willing to promote and maintain high standards of integrity and fair dealing in the carrying on of investment business and to co-operate, by the sharing of information and otherwise, with the Secretary of State and any other authority, body or person having responsibility for the supervision or regulation of investment business or other financial services.

Note
Concerning the Investment Services Directive, see the Investment Services Regulations 1995 (SI 1995/3275), reg. 32, and Sch. 7, para. 43(4).
Concerning European co-operation, see the Banking Coordination (Second Council Directive) Regulations 1992 (SI 1992/3218), reg. 55 and Sch. 9, para. 45(4) and see also the Insurance Companies (Third Insurance Directives) Regulations 1994 (SI 1994/1696), reg. 1, 56(4).

Schedule 3 — Requirements for Recognition of Professional Body

Section 18

STATUTORY STATUS

1 The body must—

(a)   regulate the practice of a profession in the exercise of statutory powers; or

(b)   be recognised (otherwise than under this Act) for a statutory purpose by a Minister of the Crown or by, or by the head of, a Northern Ireland department; or

(c)   be specified in a provision contained in or made under an enactment as a body whose members are qualified to exercise functions or hold offices specified in that provision.

CERTIFICATION

2(1) The body must have rules, practices and arrangements for securing that no person can be certified by the body for the purposes of Part I of this Act unless the following conditions are satisfied.

2(2) The certified person must be either—

(a)   an individual who is a member of the body; or

(b)   a person managed and controlled by one or more individuals each of whom is a member of a recognised professional body and at least one of whom is a member of the certifying body.

2(3) Where the certified person is an individual his main business must be the practice of the profession regulated by the certifying body and he must be practising that profession otherwise than in partnership; and where the certified person is not an individual that person's main business must be the practice of the profession or professions regulated by the recognised professional body or bodies of which the individual or individuals mentioned in sub-paragraph (2)(b) above are members.

2(4) In the application of sub-paragraphs (2) and (3) above to a certificate which is to be or has been issued to a partnership constituted under the law of England and Wales or Northern Ireland or the law of any other country or territory under which a partnership is not a legal person, references to the certified person shall be construed as references to the partnership.

Sch. 3

Note
See the Investment Services Regulations 1995 (SI 1995/3275), reg. 1, 31.

SAFEGUARDS FOR INVESTORS

3(1) The body must have rules regulating the carrying on of investment business by persons certified by it which, together with the statements of principle, rules, regulations and codes of practice to which those persons are subject under Chapter V of Part I of this Act, afford an adequate level of protection for investors.

3(2) In determining in any case whether an adequate level of protection is afforded for investors of any description, regard shall be had to the nature of the investment business carried on by persons certified by the body, the kinds of investors involved and the effectiveness of the body's arrangements for enforcing compliance.

Note
For transitional provisions in relation to para. 3 see CA 1989, s. 203(3) and SI 1990/354 (C. 12), art. 6.

TAKING ACCOUNT OF COSTS OF COMPLIANCE

3A The organisation must have satisfactory arrangements for taking account, in framing its rules, of the cost to those to whom the rules would apply of complying with those rules and any other controls to which they are subject.

Note
See CA 1989, s. 204(2), (3).

MONITORING AND ENFORCEMENT

4(1) The body must have adequate arrangements and resources for the effective monitoring of the continued compliance by persons certified by it with the conditions mentioned in paragraph 2 above and rules, practices and arrangements for the withdrawal or suspension of certification (subject to appropriate transitional provisions) in the event of any of those conditions ceasing to be satisfied.

4(2) The body must have adequate arrangements and resources for the effective monitoring and enforcement of compliance by persons certified by it with the rules of the body relating to the carrying on of investment business and with any statements of principle, rules, regulations or codes of practice to which those persons are subject under Chapter V of Part I of this Act in respect of business of a kind regulated by the body.

4(3) The arrangements for enforcement must include provision for the withdrawal or suspension of certification and may include provision for disciplining members of the body who manage or control a certified person.

4(4) The arrangements for enforcement may make provision for the whole or part of that function to be performed by and to be the responsibility of a body or person independent of the professional body.

4(5) The arrangements for enforcement must be such as to secure a proper balance between the interests of persons certified by the body and the interests of the public; and the arrangements shall not be regarded as satisfying that requirement unless the persons responsible for enforcement include a sufficient number of persons who are independent of the body and its members and of persons certified by it.

4(6) The arrangements for monitoring may make provision for that function to be performed on behalf of the body (and without affecting its responsibility) by any other body or person who is able and willing to perform it.

Sch. 3

INVESTIGATION OF COMPLAINTS

5(1) The body must have effective arrangements for the investigation of complaints relating to—

(a)   the carrying on by persons certified by it of investment business in respect of which they are subject to its rules; and

(b)   its regulation of investment business.

5(2)   Paragraph 4(4) above applies also to arrangements made pursuant to this paragraph.

PROMOTION AND MAINTENANCE OF STANDARDS

6 The body must be able and willing to promote and maintain high standards of integrity and fair dealing in the carrying on of investment business and to co-operate, by the sharing of information and otherwise, with the Secretary of State and any other authority, body or person having responsibility for the supervision or regulation of investment business or other financial services.

Schedule 4 — Requirements for Recognition of Investment Exchange

Section 36 and 37

FINANCIAL RESOURCES

1 The exchange must have financial resources sufficient for the proper performance of its functions.

SAFEGUARDS FOR INVESTORS

2(1) The rules and practices of the exchange must ensure that business conducted by means of its facilities is conducted in an orderly manner and so as to afford proper protection to investors.

2(2) The exchange must—

(a)   limit dealings on the exchange to investments in which there is a proper market; and

(b)   where relevant, require issuers of investments dealt in on the exchange to comply with such obligations as will, so far as possible, afford to persons dealing in the investments proper information for determining their current value.

2(3) In the case of securities to which Part IV of this Act applies compliance by The Stock Exchange with the provisions of that Part shall be treated as compliance by it with sub-paragraph (2) above.

2(4) The exchange must either have its own arrangements for ensuring the performance of transactions effected on the exchange or ensure their performance by means of services provided under clearing arrangements made by it with a recognised clearing house.

2(5) The exchange must either itself have or secure the provision on its behalf of satisfactory arrangements for recording the transactions effected on the exchange.

Sch. 4

2(6) Sub-paragraphs (2), (4) and (5) above are without prejudice to the generality of sub-paragraph (1) above.

MONITORING AND ENFORCEMENT

3(1) The exchange must have adequate arrangements and resources for the effective monitoring and enforcement of compliance with its rules and any clearing arrangements made by it.

3(2) The arrangements for monitoring may make provision for that function to be performed on behalf of the exchange (and without affecting its responsibility) by any other body or person who is able and willing to perform it.

INVESTIGATION OF COMPLAINTS

4 The exchange must have effective arrangements for the investigation of complaints in respect of business transacted by means of its facilities.

PROMOTION AND MAINTENANCE OF STANDARDS

5 The exchange must be able and willing to promote and maintain high standards of integrity and fair dealing in the carrying on of investement business and to co-operate, by the sharing of information and otherwise, with the Secretary of State and any other authority, body or person having responsibility for the supervision or regulation of investment business or other financial services.

SUPPLEMENTARY

6(1) The provisions of this Schedule relate to an exchange only so far as it provides facilities for the carrying on of investment business; and nothing in this Schedule shall be construed as requiring an exchange to limit dealings on the exchange to dealings in investments.

6(2) The references in this Schedule, and elsewhere in this Act, to ensuring the performance of transactions on an exchange are to providing satisfactory procedures (including default procedures) for the settlement of transactions on the exchange.

Schedule 5 — Listed Money Market Institutions
Section 43

Part I — Transactions not Subject to Monetary Limit

1 This Part of this Schedule applies to any transaction entered into by the listed institution as principal (or as agent for another listed institution) with another listed institution or the Bank of England (whether acting as principal or agent) if the transaction falls within paragraph 2 or 3 below.

2(1) A transaction falls within this paragraph if it is in respect of an investment specified in sub-paragraph (2) below and—

(a)   in the case of an investment within any of paragraphs (a) to (d) of that sub-paragraph, the transaction is not regulated by the rules of a recognised investment exchange; and

Sch. 5

(b)   in the case of any other investment specified in that sub-paragraph, the transaction is not made on such an exchange or expressed to be as so made.

2(2) The investments referred to above are—

(a)   a debenture or other instrument falling within paragraph 2 of Schedule 1 to this Act which is issued on terms requiring repayment not later than five years from the date of issue;

(c)   loan stock, or any other instrument, falling within paragraph 3 of Schedule 1 to this Act which is issued on terms requiring repayment not later than one year or, if issued by a local authority in the United Kingdom, five years from the date of issue;

(d)   a warrant or other instrument falling within paragraph 4 of Schedule 1 to this Act which entitles the holder to subscribe for an investment within paragraph (a), (b) or (c) above;

(e)   any certificate or other instrument falling within paragraph 5 or 11 of Schedule 1 to this Act and relating to an investment within paragraph (a), (b) or (c) above;

(f)   an option falling within paragraph 7 of Schedule 1 to this Act and relating to—
     (i)   an investment within paragraph (a), (b) or (c) above;
     (ii)   currency of the United Kingdom or of any other country or territory; or
     (iii) gold or silver;

(g)   rights under a contract falling within paragraph 8 of Schedule 1 to this Act for the sale of—
     (i)   an investment within paragraph (a), (b) or (c) above;
     (ii)   currency of the United Kingdom or of any other country or territory; or
     (iii) gold or silver;

(h)   rights under a contract falling within paragraph 9 of Schedule 1 to this Act by reference to fluctuations in—
     (i)   the value or price of any investment falling within any of the foregoing paragraphs; or
     (ii)   currency of the United Kingdom or of any other country or territory; or
     (iii) the rate of interest on loans in any such currency or any index of such rates;

(i)   an option to aquire or dispose of an investment within paragraph (f), (g) or (h) above.

Note

Concerning European institutions, see the Banking Coordination (Second Council Directive) Regulations 1992 (SI 1992/3218), reg. 82 and Sch. 10, para. 23.

3(1) A transaction falls within this paragraph if it is a transaction by which one of the parties agrees to sell or transfer an investment falling within paragraph 2 or 3 of Schedule 1 to this Act and by the same or a collateral agreement that party agrees, or acquires an option, to buy back or re-acquire that investment or an equivalent amount of a similar investment within twelve months of the sale or transfer.

3(2) For the purposes of this paragraph investments shall be regarded as similar if they entitle their holders to the same rights against the same persons as to capital and interest and the same remedies for the enforcement of those rights.

Part II — Transactions Subject to Monetary Limit

4(1) This Part of the Schedule applies to any transaction entered into by the listed institution—

(a)   as principal (or as agent for another listed institution) with an unlisted person (whether acting as principal or agent);

Sch. 5

(b)   as agent for an unlisted person with a listed institution or the Bank of England (whether acting as principal or agent); or

(c)   as agent for an unlisted person with another unlisted person (whether acting as principal or agent),

if the transaction falls within paragraph 2 or 3 above and the conditions in paragraph 5 or, as the case may be, paragraph 7 below are satisfied.

4(2) In this Part of this Schedule and in Part III below "unlisted person" means a person who is neither a listed institution nor the Bank of England.

5(1) In the case of a transaction falling within paragraph 2 above the conditions referred to above are as follows but subject to paragraph 6 below.

5(2) The consideration for a transaction in respect of an investment falling within paragraph 2(2)(a), (b), (c) or (e) above must be not less than £100,000.

5(3) The consideration payable on subscription in the case of an investment falling within paragraph 2(2)(d) must not be less than £500,000.

5(4) The value or price of the property in respect of which an option within paragraph 2(2)(f) above is granted must not be less than £500,000.

5(5) The price payable under a contract within paragraph 2(2)(g) above must be not less than £500,000.

5(6) The value or price the fluctuation in which, or the amount the fluctuation in the interest on which, is relevant for the purposes of a contract within paragraph 2(2)(h) above must not be less than £500,000.

5(7) In the case of an option falling within paragraph 2(2)(i) above the condition in sub-paragraph (4), (5) or (6) above, as the case may be, must be satisfied in respect of the investment to which the option relates.

6 The conditions in paragraph 5 above do not apply to a transaction entered into by the listed institution as mentioned in paragraph (a), (b) or (c) of paragraph 4(1) above if—

(a)   the unlisted person mentioned in paragraph (a) or (b) or, as the case may be, each of the unlisted persons mentioned in paragraph (c) has in the previous eighteen months entered into another transaction in respect of an investment specified in paragraph 2(2) above;

(b)   those conditions were satisfied in the case of that other transaction; and

(c)   that other transaction was entered into by that person (whether acting as principal or agent) with the listed institution (whether acting as principal or agent) or was entered into by that person through the agency of that institution or was entered into by him (whether acting as principal or agent) as a result of arrangements made by that institution.

7 In the case of a transaction falling within paragraph 3 above the condition referred to in paragraph 4 above is that the consideration for the sale or transfer must be not less than £100,000.

8 The monetary limits mentioned in this Part of this Schedule refer to the time when the transaction is entered into; and where the consideration, value, price or amount referred to above is not in sterling it shall be converted at the rate of exchange prevailing at that time.

Part III — Transactions Arranged by Listed Institutions

9 Subject to paragraphs 10 and 11 below, this Part of this Schedule applies to any transaction arranged by the listed institution which—

(a)   is entered into by another listed institution as principal (or as agent for another listed institution) with another listed institution or the Bank of England (whether acting as principal or agent);

(b)   is entered into by another listed institution (whether acting as principal or agent) with an unlisted person (whether acting as principal or agent); or

(c)   is entered into between unlisted persons (whether acting as principal or agent),

if the transaction falls within paragraph 2 or 3 above.

10 In the case of a transaction falling within paragraph 2 above paragraph 9(b) and (c) above do not apply unless either the conditions in paragraph 5 above are satisfied or—

(a)   the unlisted person mentioned in paragraph (b) or, as the case may be, each of the unlisted persons mentioned in paragraph (c) has in the previous eighteen months entered into another transaction in respect of an investment specified in paragraph 2(2) above;

(b)   those conditions were satisfied in the case of that other transaction; and

(c)   that other transaction was entered into by that person (whether acting as principal or agent) with the listed institution making the arrangements (whether acting as principal or agent) or through the agency of that institution or was entered into by that person (whether acting as principal or agent) as a result of arrangments made by that institution.

11 In the case of a transaction falling within paragraph 3 above paragraph 9(b) and (c) above do not apply unless the condition in paragraph 7 above is satisfied.

Schedule 6 — The Financial Services Tribunal
Section 96(6)

TERM OF OFFICE OF MEMBERS

1(1) A person appointed to the panel mentioned in section 96(2) of this Act shall hold and vacate his office in accordance with the terms of his appointment and on ceasing to hold office shall be eligible for re-appointment.

1(2) A member of the panel appointed by the Lord Chancellor may resign his office by notice in writing to the Lord Chancellor; and a member of the panel appointed by the Secretary of State may resign his office by notice in writing to the Secretary of State.

EXPENSES

2 The Secretary of State shall pay to the persons serving as members of the Tribunal such remuneration and allowances as he may determine and shall defray such other expenses of the Tribunal as he may approve.

STAFF

3 The Secretary of State may provide the Tribunal with such officers and servants as he thinks necessary for the proper discharge of its functions.

PROCEDURE

4(1) The Secretary of State may make rules for regulating the procedure of the Tribunal, including provision for the holding of any proceedings in private, for the

Sch. 6

awarding of costs (or, in Scotland, expenses) and for the payment of expenses to persons required to attend before the Tribunal.

Note
See the Financial Services Tribunal (Conduct of Investigations) Rules 1988 (SI 1988/351).

4(2) The Tribunal may appoint counsel or a solicitor to assist it in proceedings before the Tribunal.

EVIDENCE

5(1) The Tribunal may by summons require any person to attend, at such time and place as is specified in the summons, to give evidence or to produce any document in his custody or under his control which the Tribunal considers it necessary to examine.

5(2) The Tribunal may take evidence on oath and for that purpose administer oaths or may, instead of administering an oath, require the person examined to make and subscribe a declaration of the truth of the matters in respect of which he is examined.

5(3) Any person who without reasonable excuse—

(a)   refuses or fails to attend in obedience to a summons issued by the Tribunal or to give evidence; or

(b)   alters, suppresses, conceals or destroys or refuses to produce a document which he may be required to produce for the purposes of proceedings before the Tribunal,

shall be guilty of an offence.

5(4) A person guilty of an offence under paragraph (a) of sub-paragraph (3) above shall be liable on summary conviction to a fine not exceeding the fifth level on the standard scale; and a person guilty of an offence under paragraph (b) of that sub-paragraph shall be liable—

(a)   on conviction on indictment, to imprisonment for a term not exceeding two years or to a fine or to both;

(b)   on summary conviction, to a fine not exceeding the statutory maximum.

5(5) A person shall not under this paragraph be required to disclose any information or produce any document which he would be entitled to refuse to disclose or produce on grounds of legal professional privilege in proceedings in the High Court or on grounds of confidentiality as between client and professional legal adviser in proceedings in the Court of Session except that a lawyer may be required to furnish the name and address of his client.

5(6) Any reference in this paragraph to the production of a document includes a reference to the production of a legible copy of information recorded otherwise than in legible form; and the reference to suppressing a document includes a reference to destroying the means of reproducing information recorded otherwise than in legible form.

APPEALS AND SUPERVISION BY COUNCIL ON TRIBUNALS

6 (Repealed by Tribunals and Inquiries Act 1992, sec. 18(2), 19(2) and Sch. 4, Pt. I as from 1 October 1992.)

PARLIAMENTARY DISQUALIFICATION

7(1) In Part III of Schedule 1 to the House of Commons Disqualification Act 1975 (disqualifying offices) there shall be inserted at the appropriate place "Any member of the Financial Services Tribunal in receipt of remuneration".

7(2) A corresponding amendment shall be made in Part III of Schedule 1 to the Northern Ireland Assembly Disqualification Act 1975.

Schedule 7 — Qualifications of Designated Agency

Section 114

CONSTITUTION

1(1) The constitution of the agency must provide for it to have—

(a) a chairman; and

(b) a governing body consisting of the chairman and other members;

and the provisions of the constitution relating to the chairman and the other members of the governing body must comply with the following provisions of this paragraph.

1(2) The chairman and other members of the governing body must be persons appointed and liable to removal from office by the Treasury and the Governor of the Bank of England acting jointly.

1(3) The members of the governing body must include—

(a) persons with experience of investment business of a kind relevant to the functions or proposed functions of the agency; and

(b) other persons, including regular users on their own account or on behalf of others of services provided by persons carrying on investment business of any such kind;

and the composition of that body must be such as to secure a proper balance between the interests of persons carrying on investment business and the interests of the public.

ARRANGEMENTS FOR DISCHARGE OF FUNCTIONS

2(1) The agency's arrangements for the discharge of its functions must comply with the following provisions of this paragraph.

2(2) Any statements of principle, rules, regulations and codes of practice must be issued or made by the governing body of the agency.

2(3) Any decision taken in the exercise of other functions must be taken at a level appropriate to the importance of the decision.

2(4) In the case of functions to be discharged by the governing body, the members falling respectively within paragraphs (a) and (b) of paragraph 1(3) above must, so far as practicable, have an opportunity to express their opinions.

2(5) Subject to sub-paragraphs (2) to (4) above, the arrangements may enable any functions to be discharged by a committee, sub-committee, officer or servant of the agency.

TAKING ACCOUNT OF COSTS OF COMPLIANCE

2A(1) The agency must have satisfactory arrangements for taking account, in framing any provisions which it proposes to make in the exercise of its legislative functions, of the

Sch. 7

hose to whom the provisions would apply of complying with those provisions and ... / other controls to which they are subject.

2A(2) In this paragraph "legislative functions" means the functions of issuing or making statements of principle, rules, regulations or codes of practice.

Note
See CA 1989, s. 204(5), (6).

MONITORING AND ENFORCEMENT

3(1) The agency must have a satisfactory system—

(a)   for enabling it to determine whether persons regulated by it are complying with the obligations which it is the responsibility of the agency to enforce; and

(b)   for the discharge of the agency's responsibility for the enforcement of those obligations.

3(2) The system may provide for the functions mentioned in sub-paragraph (1)(a) to be performed on its behalf (and without affecting its responsiblity) by any other body or person who is able and willing to perform them.

INVESTIGATION OF COMPLAINTS

4(1) The agency must have effective arrangements for the investigation of complaints arising out of the conduct of investment business by authorised persons or against any recognised self-regulating organisation, professional body, investment exchange or clearing house.

4(2) The arrangements must make provision for the investigation of complaints in respect of authorised persons to be carried out in appropriate cases independently of the agency and those persons.

Note
See note after para. 5.
Concerning European investment firms, see the Investment Services Regulations 1995 (SI 1995/3275), reg. 32 and Sch. 7, para. 44(1).

PROMOTION AND MAINTENANCE OF STANDARDS

5 The agency must be able and willing to promote and maintain high standards of integrity and fair dealing in the carrying on of investment business and to co-operate, by the sharing of information and otherwise, with the Secretary of State and any other authority, body or person having responsibility for the supervision or regulation of investment business or other financial services.

Note
Concerning European institutions and co-operation, see the Banking Coordination (Second Council Directive) Regulations 1992 (SI 1992/3218), reg. 55 and Sch. 9, para. 46 and see also the Insurance Companies (Third Insurance Directives) Regulations 1994 (SI 1994/1696), reg. 1, 61.
Concerning the Investment Services Directive, see the Investment Services Regulations 1995 (SI 1995/3275), reg. 32 and Sch. 7, para. 44(2).

RECORDS

6 The agency must have satisfactory arrangements for recording decisions made in the exercise of its functions and for the safe-keeping of those records which ought to be preserved.

Sch. 7

Schedule 8 — Principles Applicable to Designated Agency's Legislative Provisions

Section 114

INTRODUCTION

1(1) In this Schedule "legislative provisions" means the provisions of statements of principle, rules, regulations and codes of practice issued or made under Part I of this Act and the provisions of regulations made under regulation 6 of the Open-Ended Investment Companies with Variable Capital) Regulations 1996.

1(2) References in this Schedule to "conduct of business provisions" are to rules made under section 48 of this Act and statements of principle and codes of practice so far as they relate to matters falling within that rule-making power.

1(3) References in this Schedule to provisions made for the purposes of a specified section or Chapter are to rules or regulations made under that section or Chapter and statements of principle and codes of practice so far as they relate to matters falling within that power to make rules or regulations.

STANDARDS

1A The conduct of business provisions and the other legislative provisions must promote high standards of integrity and fair dealing in the conduct of investment business.

2 The conduct of business provisions must make proper provision for requiring an authorised person to act with due skill, care and diligence in providing any service which he provides or holds himself out as willing to provide.

3 The conduct of business provisions must make proper provision for requiring an authorised person to subordinate his own interests to those of his clients and to act fairly between his clients.

4 The conduct of business provisions must make proper provision for requiring an authorised person to ensure that, in anything done by him for the persons with whom he deals, due regard is had to their circumstances.

DISCLOSURE

5 The conduct of business provisions must make proper provision for the disclosure by an authorised person of interests in, and facts material to, transactions which are entered into by him in the course of carrying on investment business or in respect of which he gives advice in the course of carrying on such business, including information as to any commissions or other inducements received or receivable from a third party in connection with any such transaction.

6 The conduct of business provisions must make proper provision for the disclosure by an authorised person of the capacity in which and the terms on which he enters into any such transaction.

7 The conduct of business provisions, or those provisions and provisions made for the purposes of section 51 of this Act, must make proper provision for requiring an authorised person who in the course of carrying on investment business enters or offers

Sch. 8

to enter into a transaction in respect of an investment with any person, or gives any person advice about such a transaction, to give that person such information as to the nature of the investment and the financial implications of the transaction as will enable him to make an informed decision.

8 Provisions made for the purposes of section 48 of this Act regulating action for the purpose of stabilising the price of investments must make proper provision for ensuring that where action is or is to be taken in conformity with the rules adequate arrangements exist for making known that the price of the investments in respect of which the action is or is to be taken (and, where relevant, of any other investments) may be affected by that action and the period during which it may be affected; and where a transaction is or is to be entered into during a period when it is known that the price of the investment to which it relates may be affected by any such action the information referred to in paragraph 7 above includes information to that effect.

PROTECTION

9 The conduct of business provisions and any provisions made for the purposes of section 55 of this Act must make proper provision for the protection of property for which an authorised person is liable to account to another person.

10 Provisions made for the purposes of section 53 and 54 of this Act must make the best provision that can reasonably be made for the purposes of those sections.

RECORDS

11 The conduct of business provisions must require the keeping of proper records and make provision for their inspection in appropriate cases.

CLASSES OF INVESTORS

12 The conduct of business provisions and the other provisions made for the purposes of Chapter V of Part I of this Act must take proper account of the fact that provisions that are appropriate for regulating the conduct of business in relation to some classes of investors may not (by reason of their knowledge, experience or otherwise) be appropriate in relation to others.

Note
Concerning European investment firms, see the Investment Services Regulations 1995 (SI 1995/3275), reg. 32 and Sch. 7, para. 45.
Concerning European institutions, see the Banking Coordination (Second Council Directive) Regulations 1992 (SI 1992/3218), reg. 55 and Sch. 9, para. 47.

Schedule 9— Designated Agencies: Status and Exercise of Transferred Functions

Section 116

STATUS

1(1) A designated agency shall not be regarded as acting on behalf of the Crown and its members, officers and servants shall not be regarded as Crown servants.

1(2) In Part III of Schedule 1 to the House of Commons Disqualification Act 1975 (disqualifying offices) there shall be inserted at the appropriate place—

"Chairman of a designated agency within the meaning of the Financial Services Act 1986 if he is in receipt of remuneration".

1(3) An amendment corresponding to that in sub-paragraph (2) above shall be made in Part III of Schedule 1 to the Northern Ireland Assembly Disqualification Act 1975.

EXEMPTION FROM REQUIREMENT OF "LIMITED" IN NAME OF DESIGNATED AGENCY

2(1) A company is exempt from the requirements of the Companies Act 1985 relating to the use of "limited" as part of the company name if—

(a) it is a designated agency; and
(b) its memorandum or articles comply with the requirements specified in paragraph (b) of subsection (3) of section 30 of that Act.

2(2) In subsection (4) of that section (statutory declaration of compliance with requirements entitling company to exemption) the reference to the requirements of subsection (3) of that section shall include a reference to the requirements of sub-paragraph (1) above.

2(3) In section 31 of that Act (provisions applicable to exempted companies) the reference to a company which is exempt under section 30 of that Act shall include a reference to a company that is exempt under this paragraph and, in relation to such a company, the power conferred by subsection (2) of that section (direction to include "limited" in company name) shall be exercisable on the ground that the company has ceased to be a designated agency instead of the ground mentioned in paragraph (a) of that subsection.

2(4) In this paragraph references to the said Act of 1985 and sections 30 and 31 of that Act include references to the corresponding provisions in force in Northern Ireland.

THE TRIBUNAL

3(1) Where a case is referred to the Tribunal by a designated agency the Tribunal shall send the Secretary of State a copy of any report made by it to the agency in respect of that case.

3(2) Where the powers which the Tribunal could, apart from any delegation order, require the Secretary of State to exercise are by virtue of such an order or of an order resuming any function transferred by it, exercisable partly by the Secretary of State and partly by a designated agency or designated agencies the Tribunal may require any of them to exercise such of those powers as are exercisable by them respectively.

LEGISLATIVE FUNCTIONS

4(1) A designated agency shall send the Secretary of State a copy of any statements of principle, rules, regulations or codes of practice issued or made by it by virtue of functions transferred to it by a delegation order and give him written notice of any amendment or revocation of or addition to any such rules or regulations.

4(2) A designated agency shall—

(a) send the Secretary of State a copy of any guidance issued by the agency which is intended to have continuing effect and is issued in writing or other legible form; and
(b) give him written notice of any amendment, revocation of or addition to guidance issued by it;

Sch. 9

but notice need not be given of the revocation of guidance other than such as is mentioned in paragraph (a) above or of any amendment or addition which does not result in or consist of such guidance as is there mentioned.

5 Paragraphs 6 to 9 below have effect instead of section 205A of this Act in relation to statements of principle, rules, regulations and codes of practice issued or made by a designated agency in the exercise of powers transferred to it by a delegation order.

6 Any such power is exercisable by instrument in writing and includes power to make different provision for different cases.

7 The instrument shall specify the provision of this Act or, as the case may be, the provision of the Open-Ended Investment Companies (Investment Companies with Variable Capital) Regulations 1996, under which it is made.

8(1) Immediately after an instrument is issued or made it shall be printed and made available to the public with or without payment.

8(2) A person shall not be taken to have contravened any statement of principle, rule, regulation or code of practice if he shows that at the time of the alleged contravention the instrument containing the statement of principle, rule, regulation or code of practice had not been made available as required by this paragraph.

9(1) The production of a printed copy of an instrument purporting to be made or issued by the agency on which is endorsed a certificate signed by an officer of the agency authorised by it for that purpose and stating—

(a)   that the instrument was made or issued by the agency;
(b)   that the copy is a true copy of the instrument; and
(c)   that on a specified date the instrument was made available to the public as required by paragraph 8 above,

shall be prima facie evidence or, in Scotland, sufficient evidence of the facts stated in the certificate.

9(2) Any certificate purporting to be signed as mentioned in sub-paragraph (1) above shall be deemed to have been duly signed unless the contrary is shown.

9(3) Any person wishing in any legal proceedings to cite an instrument made or issued by the agency may require the agency to cause a copy of it to be endorsed with such a certificate as is mentioned in this paragraph.

FEES

10(1) A designated agency may retain any fees payable to it by virtue of the delegation order.

10(2) Any such fees shall be applicable for meeting the expenses of the agency in discharging its functions under the order and for any purposes incidental thereto.

10(3) Any fees payable to a designated agency by virtue of a delegation order made before the coming into force of section 3 of this Act may also be applied for repaying the principal of, and paying interest on, any money borrowed by the agency (or by any other person whose liabilities in respect of the money are assumed by the agency) which has been used for the purpose of defraying expenses incurred before the making of the order (whether before or after the passing of this Act) in making preparations for the agency becoming a designated agency.

11 If the function of prescribing the amount of any fee, or of making a scheme under section 112 above, is exercisable by a designated agency it may prescribe or make

Sch. 9

provision for such fees as will enable it to defray any such expenses as are paragraph 10 above.

CONSULTATION

12(1) Where a designated agency proposes, in the exercise of powers transferred to it by a delegation order, to issue or make any statements of principle, rules, regulations or codes of practice, it shall publish the proposed instrument in such manner as appears to it best calculated to bring the proposals to the attention of the public, together with a statement that representations about the proposals (and, in particular, representations as to the cost of complying with the proposed provisions) can be made to the agency within a specified time.

12(2) Before issuing or making the instrument the agency shall have regard to any representations duly made in accordance with that statement.

12(3) The above requirements do not apply—

(a)   where the agency considers that the delay involved in complying with them would be prejudicial to the interests of investors;

(b)   to the issuing or making of an instrument in the same, or substantially the same, terms as a proposed instrument which was furnished by the agency to the Secretary of State for the purposes of section 114(9) of this Act.

EXCHANGE OF INFORMATION

13(1) The Secretary of State may communicate to a designated agency any information in his possession of which he could have availed himself for the purpose of exercising any function which by virtue of a delegation order is for the time being exercisable by the agency.

13(2) A designated agency may in the exercise of any function which by virtue of a delegation order is for the time being exercisable by it communicate to any other person any information which has been communicated to the agency by the Secretary of State and which the Secretary of State could have communicated to that person in the exercise of that function.

13(3) No communication of information under sub-paragraph (1) above shall constitute publication for the purposes of the law of defamation.

Schedule 10 — Regulated Insurance Companies
Section 129

PRELIMINARY

1 In this Part of this Schedule "a regulated insurance company" means any such company as is mentioned in section 129 of this Act.

AUTHORISATIONS FOR INVESTMENT BUSINESS AND INSURANCE BUSINESS

2(1) An insurance company to which section 22 of this Act applies shall not be an authorised person except by virtue of that section.

2(2) If an insurance company to which Part II of the Insurance Companies Act 1982 applies but to which section 22 of this Act does not apply becomes an authorised person by virtue of any other provision of this Act it shall be an authorised person only as respects the management of the investments of any pension fund which is established solely for the benefit of the officers or employees and their dependants of that company or of any other body corporate in the same group as that company.

Note
See note after para. 2(3A).

2(3) An insurance company to which section 31 of this Act applies shall not, so long as it is an authorised person by virtue of that section, be an authorised person by virtue of any other provision of this Act.

2(3A) An insurance company—

(a) to which section 31 of this Act applies; and
(b) which has complied with the requirements of section 81B of the Insurance Companies Act 1982 (documents to be furnished to the Secretary of State) in relation to the provision of long term insurance in the United Kingdom,

shall be deemed to have complied with section 32 of this Act in relation to any investment business consisting in the covering of commitments for the time being mentioned in the statement given by it in accordance with subsection (1)(c) of the said section 81B.

Note
Regarding application to EC companies, see the Insurance Companies (Third Insurance Directives) Regulations 1994 (SI 1994/1696), reg. 1, 63(2).

2(3B) In sub-paragraph (3A) above "commitment" and "provision of long term insurance" have respectively the same meanings as in the Insurance Companies Act 1982.

2(4) None of the provisions of Part I of this Act shall be construed as authorising any person to carry on insurance business in any case in which he could not lawfully do so apart from those provisions.

RECOGNITION OF SELF-REGULATING ORGANISATION WITH INSURANCE COMPANY MEMBERS

3(1) In the case of a self-regulating organisation whose members include or may include regulated insurance companies the requirements of Schedule 2 to this Act shall include a requirement that the rules of the organisation must take proper account of Part II of the Insurance Companies Act 1982 or, as the case may be, of the provisions for corresponding purposes in the law of any member State in which such companies are established.

3(2) Where the function of making or revoking a recognition order in respect of such a self-regulating organisation is exercisable by a designated agency it shall not regard that requirement as satisfied unless the Secretary of State has certified that he also regards it as satisfied.

3(3) A delegation order—

(a) may reserve to the Secretary of State the function of revoking a recognition order in respect of such a self-regulating organisation as is mentioned in sub-paragraph (1) above on the ground that the requirement there mentioned is not satisfied; and
(b) shall not transfer to a designated agency the function of revoking any such recognition order on the ground that the organisation has contravened sub-

Sch. 10

paragraphs (3) or (4) of paragraph 6 below as applied by sub-paragraph (5) of that paragraph.

Note
See the Financial Services Act 1986 (Delegation) Order 1987 (SI 1987/942).

3(4) In the case of such a self-regulating organisation as is mentioned in sub-paragraph (1) above the requirements of Schedule 2 to this Act referred to in section 187(2)(a) of this Act shall include the requirement mentioned in that sub-paragraph.

MODIFICATION OF PROVISIONS AS TO CONDUCT OF INVESTMENT BUSINESS

4(1) The rules under section 48 of this Act shall not apply to a regulated insurance company except so far as they make provision as respects the matters mentioned in sub-paragraph (2) below.

4(2) The matters referred to in sub-paragraph (1) above are—

(a) procuring proposals for policies the rights under which constitute an investment for the purposes of this Act and advising persons on such policies and the exercise of the rights conferred by them;

(b) managing the investments of pension funds, procuring persons to enter into contracts for the management of such investments and advising persons on such contracts and the exercise of the rights conferred by them;

(c) matters incidental to those mentioned in paragraph (a) and (b) above.

4(2A) Sub-paragraphs (1) and (2) also apply to statements of principle under section 47A and codes of practice under section 63A so far as they relate to matters falling within the rule-making power in section 48.

4(3) The rules under section 49 of this Act shall not apply to an insurance company which is an authorised person by virtue of section 31 of this Act.

4(4) The rules under sections 53 and 54 of this Act shall not apply to loss arising as a result of a regulated insurance company being unable to meet its liabilities under a contract of insurance.

4(5) A direction under section 59 of this Act shall not prohibit the employment of a person by a regulated insurance company except in connection with—

(a) the matters mentioned in sub-paragraph (2) above; or

(b) investment business carried on in connection with or for the purposes of those matters.

4(6) The Secretary of State shall not make a delegation order transferring any functions of making rules or regulations under Chapter V of Part I of this Act in relation to a regulated insurance company unless he is satisfied that those rules and regulations will take proper account of Part II of the Insurance Companies Act 1982 or, as the case may be, of the provisions for corresponding purposes in the law of the member State in which the company is established; and in section 115(5) of this Act the reference to the requirements of section 114(9)(b) shall include a reference to the requirements of this sub-paragraph.

RESTRICTION OF PROVISIONS AS TO CONDUCT OF INSURANCE BUSINESS

5(1) Regulations under section 72 of the Insurance Companies Act 1982 (insurance advertisements) shall not apply to so much of any advertisement issued by an authorised

Sch. 10

person as relates to a contract of insurance the rights under which constitute an investment for the purposes of this Act.

5(2) No requirement imposed under section 74 of that Act (intermediaries in insurance transactions) shall apply in respect of an invitation issued by, or by an appointed representative of, an authorised person in relation to a contract of insurance the rights under which constitute an investment for the purposes of this Act.

5(3) Subject to sub-paragraph (4) below, sections 75 to 77 of that Act (right to withdraw from long-term policies) shall not apply to a regulated insurance company in respect of a contract of insurance the rights under which constitute an investment for the purposes of this Act.

5(4) Sub-paragraph (3) above does not affect the operation of the said sections 75 to 77 in a case in which the statutory notice required by those sections has been or ought to have been served before the coming into force of that sub-paragraph.

EXERCISE OF POWERS OF INTERVENTION ETC.

6(1) The powers conferred by Chapter VI of Part I of this Act shall not be exercisable in relation to a regulated insurance company on the ground specified in section 64(1)(a) of this Act for reasons relating to the ability of the company to meet its liabilities to policy holders or potential policy holders.

6(2) The powers conferred by sections 66 and 68 of this Act, and those conferred by section 67 of this Act so far as applicable to assets belonging to the authorised person, shall not be exercisable in relation to a regulated insurance company.

6(3) A designated agency shall not in the case of a regulated insurance company impose any prohibition or requirement under section 65 or 67 of this Act, or vary any such prohibition or requirement, unless it has given reasonable notice of its intention to do so to the Secretary of State and informed him—

(a)   of the manner in which and the date on or after which it intends to exercise that power; and

(b)   in the case of a proposal to impose a prohibition or requirement, on which of the grounds specified in section 64(1) of this Act it proposes to act and its reasons for considering that the ground in question exists and that it is necessary to impose the prohibition or requirement.

6(4) A designated agency shall not exercise any power to which sub-paragraph (3) above applies if the Secretary of State has before the date specified in accordance with sub-paragraph (3), above served on it a notice in writing directing it not to do so; and the Secretary of State may serve such a notice if he considers it desirable for protecting policy holders or potential policy holders of the company against the risk that it may be unable to meet its liabilities or to fulfil the reasonable expectations of its policy holders or potential policy holders.

6(5) Sub-paragraphs (3) and (4) above shall, with the necessary modifications, apply also where a recognised self-regulating organisation proposes to exercise, in the case of a member who is a regulated insurance company, any powers of the organisation for purposes corresponding to those of Chapter VI of Part I of this Act.

6(6) The powers conferred by sections 72 and 73 of this Act shall not be exercisable in relation to a regulated insurance company.

Sch. 10

WITHDRAWAL OF INSURANCE BUSINESS AUTHORISATION

7(1) At the end of section 11(2)(a) of the Insurance Companies Act 1982 (withdrawal of authorisation in respect of new business where insurance company has failed to satisfy an obligation to which it is subject by virtue of that Act) there shall be inserted the words "or the Financial Services Act 1986 or, if it is a member of a recognised self-regulating organisation within the meaning of that Act, an obligation to which it is subject by virtue of the rules of that organisation".

7(2) After subsection (2) of section 13 of that Act (final withdrawal of authorisation) there shall be inserted—

"(2A) The Secretary of State may direct that an insurance company shall cease to be authorised to carry on business which is insurance business by virtue of section 95 (c)(ii) of this Act if it appears to him that the company has failed to satisfy an obligation to which it is subject by virtue of the Financial Services Act 1986 or, if it is a member of a recognised self-regulating organisation within the meaning of that Act, an obligation to which it is subject by virtue of the rules of that organisation.

(2B) Subsections (3), (5) and (6) of section 11 and subsections (1) and (5) to (8) of section 12 above shall apply to a direction under subsection (2A) above as they apply to a direction under section 11."

7(3) The disciplinary action which may be taken by virtue of section 47A(3) of this Act (failure to comply with statement of principle) includes—

(a)   the withdrawal of authorisation under section 11(2)(a) of the Insurance Companies Act 1982, and

(b)   the giving of a direction under section 13(2A) of that Act; and subsection (6) of section 47A (duty of the Secretary of State as to exercise of powers) has effect accordingly.

TERMINATION OF INVESTMENT BUSINESS AUTHORISATION OF INSURER ESTABLISHED IN OTHER MEMBER STATE

8(1) Sections 33(1)(b) and 34 of this Act shall not apply to a regulated insurance company.

8(2) A direction under section 33(1)(a) of this Act in respect of such an insurance company may provide that the company shall cease to be an authorised person except as respects investment business of a kind specified in the direction and shall not make it unlawful for the company to effect a contract of insurance in pursuance of a subsisting contract of insurance.

8(3) Where the Secretary of State proposes to give a direction under section 33(1)(a) of this Act in respect of such an insurance company he shall give it written notice of his intention to do so, giving particulars of the grounds on which he proposes to act and of the rights exercisable under sub-paragraph (4) below.

8(4) An insurance company on which a notice is served under sub-paragraph (3) above may within fourteen days after the date of service make written representations to the Secretary of State and, if desired, oral representations to a person appointed for that purpose by the Secretary of State; and the Secretary of State shall have regard to any representations made in accordance with this sub-paragraph in determining whether to give the direction.

8(5) After giving a direction under section 33(1)(a) of this Act in respect of a regulated insurance company the Secretary of State shall inform the company in writing of the reasons for giving the direction.

8(6) A delegation order shall not transfer to a designated agency the function of giving a direction under section 33(1)(a) of this Act in respect of a regulated insurance company.

POWERS OF TRIBUNAL

9 In the case of a regulated insurance company the provisions mentioned in section 98(4) of this Act shall include sections 11 and 13(2A) of the Insurance Companies Act 1982 but where the Tribunal reports that the appropriate decision would be to take action under either of those sections or under section 33(1)(a) of this Act the Secretary of State shall take the report into consideration but shall not be bound to act upon it.

CONSULTATION WITH DESIGNATED AGENCIES

10(1) Where any functions under this Act are for the time being exercisable by a designated agency in relation to regulated insurance companies the Secretary of State shall, before issuing an authorisation under section 3 of the Insurance Companies Act 1982 to a applicant who proposes to carry on in the United Kingdom insurance business which is investment business—

(a)   seek the advice of the designated agency with respect to any matters which are relevant to those functions of the agency and relate to the applicant, his proposed business or persons who will be associated with him in, or in connection with, that business; and

(b)   take into account any advice on those matters given to him by the agency before the end of the period within which the application is required to be decided.

10(2) The Secretary of State may for the purpose of obtaining the advice of a designated agency under sub-paragraph (1) above furnish it with any information obtained by him in connection with the application.

10(3) If a designated agency by which any functions under this Act are for the time being exercisable in relation to regulated insurance companies has reasonable grounds for believing that any such insurance company has failed to comply with an obligation to which it is subject by virtue of this Act it shall forthwith give notice of that fact to the Secretary of State so that he can take it into consideration in deciding whether to give a direction in respect of the company under section 11 or 13(2A) of the said Act of 1982 or section 33 of this Act.

10(4) A notice under sub-paragraph (3) above shall contain particulars of the obligation in question and of the agency's reasons for considering that the company has failed to satisfy that obligation.

10(5) A designated agency need not give a notice under sub-paragraph (3) above in respect of any matter unless it considers that that matter (either alone or in conjunction with other matters) would justify the withdrawal of authorisation under section 28 of this Act in the case of a person to whom that section applies.

Schedule 11 — Friendly Societies

Section 140

Part I — Preliminary

1 In this Schedule—

"a regulated friendly society" means a society which is an authorised person by virtue of section 23 of this Act as respects such investment business as is mentioned in that section;

"regulated business" in relation to a regulated friendly society, means investment business as respects which the society is authorised by virtue of that section;

"a self-regulating organisation for friendly societies" means a self-regulating organisation which is permitted under its rules to admit regulated friendly societies as members and to regulate the carrying on by such societies of regulated business;

"a recognised self-regulating organisation for friendly societies" means a body declared by a recognition order for the time being in force to be a recognised self-regulating organisation for friendly societies for the purposes of this Schedule;

"a member society" means a regulated friendly society which is a member of a recognised self-regulating organisation for friendly societies and is subject to its rules in carrying on all its regulated business;

"recognition order" means —

(a) an order made by the Chief Registrar of friendly societies or the Registrar of Friendly Societies for Northern Ireland before Schedule 18 to the Friendly Societies Act 1992 came into force; or

(b) an order made by the Commission after that Schedule came into force;

"the Commission" means the Friendly Societies Commission.

Part II — Self-Regulating Organisations for Friendly Societies

RECOGNITION

2(1) A self-regulating organisation for friendly societies may apply to the Commission for an order declaring it to be a recognised self-regulating organisation for friendly societies for the purposes of this Schedule.

2(2) An application under sub-paragraph (1) above—

(a) shall be made in such manner as the Commission may direct; and

(b) shall be accompanied by such information as the Commission may reasonably require for the purpose of determining the application.

2(3) At any time after receiving an application and before determining it the Commission may require the applicant to furnish additional information.

2(4) The directions and requirements given or imposed under sub-paragraphs (2) and (3) above may differ as between different applications.

2(5) Any information to be furnished to the Commission under this paragraph shall, if the Commission so requires, be in such form or verified in such manner as the Commission may specify.

2(6) Every application shall be accompanied by a copy of the applicant's rules and of any guidance issued by the applicant which is intended to have continuing effect and is issued in writing or other legible form.

3(1) If, on an application duly made in accordance with paragraph 2 above and after being furnished with all such information as the Commission may require under that paragraph, it appears to the Commission from that information and having regard to any other information in the Commission's possession that the requirements mentioned in paragraph 4 below are satisfied as respects that organisation, the Commission may, with the consent of the Secretary of State and subject to sub-paragraph (2) below, make a recognition order in respect of the organisation declaring the applicant to be a recognised self-regulating organisation for friendly societies.

3(2) Where the Commission proposes to grant an application for a recognition order the Commission shall send to the Secretary of State a copy of the application together with a copy of the rules and any guidance accompanying the application and the Secretary of State shall not consent to the making of the recognition order unless he is satisfied that the rules and guidance of which copies have been sent to him under this sub-paragraph, together with any statements of principle, rules, regulations or codes of practice to which members of the organisation would be subject by virtue of this Schedule, do not have, and are not intended or likely to have, to any significant extent the effect of restricting, distorting or preventing competition or, if they have or are intended or likely to have that effect to any significant extent, that the effect is not greater than is necessary for the protection of investors.

3(3) Section 122 of this Act shall apply in relation to the decision whether to consent to the making of a recognition order under this paragraph as it applies to the decisions mentioned in subsection (1) of that section.

3(4) Subsections (1) and (2) of section 128 of this Act shall apply for the purposes of this paragraph as if the powers there mentioned included the power of refusing consent to the making of a recognition order under this paragraph and subsection (5) of that section shall apply for that purpose as if the reference to Chapter XIV of Part I included a reference to this paragraph.

3(5) The Commission may refuse to make a recognition order in respect of an organisation if the Commission considers that its recognition is unnecessary having regard to the existence of one or more other organisations which are concerned with such investment business as is mentioned in section 23 of this Act and which have been or are likely to be recognised under this paragraph.

3(6) Where the Commission refuses an application for a recognition order the Commission shall give the applicant a written notice to that effect specifying a requirement which in the opinion of the Commission is not satisfied, stating that the application is refused on the ground mentioned in sub-paragraph (5) above or stating that the Secretary of State has refused to consent to the making of the order.

3(7) A recognition order shall state the date on which it takes effect.

4(1) The requirements referred to in paragraph 3 above are that mentioned in sub-paragraph (2) below and those set out in paragraphs 2 to 7 of Schedule 2 to this Act as modified in sub-paragraphs (3) to (5) below.

4(2) The rules of the organisation must take proper account of Parts V and VIII of the Friendly Societies Act 1992.

4(3) References in paragraphs 2, 3, 4 and 6 of Schedule 2 to members are to members who are regulated friendly societies.

Sch. 11

4(4) In paragraph 3 of that Schedule—

(a)   in sub-paragraph (1) for the reference to Chapter V of Part I of this Act there shall be substituted a reference to paragraphs 14 to 22D below; and

(c)   in sub-paragraph (3) for the reference to Chapter VI of that Part there shall be substituted a reference to the powers exercisable by the Commission by virtue of paragraph 23 below.

4(5) In paragraph 4 of that Schedule for the reference to Chapter V of Part I of this Act there shall be substituted references to paragraphs 14 to 22D below.

REVOCATION OF RECOGNITION

5(1) A recognition order may be revoked by a further order made by the Commission if at any time it appears to the Commission—

(a)   that any requirement mentioned in paragraph 4(1) above is not satisfied in the case of the organisation to which the recognition order relates ("the recognised organisation");

(b)   that the recognised organisation has failed to comply with any obligation to which it is subject by virtue of this Act; or

(c)   that the continued recognition of the organisation is undesirable having regard to the existence of one or more other organisations which have been or are to be recognised under paragraph 3 above.

5(2) Subsections (2) to (9) of section 11 of this Act shall have effect in relation to the revocation of a recognition order under this paragraph as they have effect in relation to the revocation of a recognition order under subsection (1) of that section but with the substitution—

(a)   for references to the Secretary of State of references to the Commission;

(b)   for the reference in subsection (3) to members of a reference to members of the organisation which are member societies in relation to it; and

(c)   for the reference in subsection (6) to investors of a reference to members of the societies which are member societies in relation to the organisation.

COMPLIANCE ORDERS

6(1) If at any time it appears to the Commission—

(a)   that any requirement mentioned in paragraph 3 above is not satisfied in the case of a recognised self-regulating organisation for friendly societies; or

(b)   that such an organisation has failed to comply with any obligation to which it is subject by virtue of this Act,

the Commission may, instead of revoking the recognition order under paragraph 5 above, make an application to the court under this paragraph.

6(2) If on any such application the court decides that the requirement in question is not satisfied or, as the case may be, that the organisation has failed to comply with the obligation in question it may order the organisation concerned to take such steps as the court directs for securing that that requirement is satisfied or that that obligation is complied with.

6(3) The jurisdiction conferred by this paragraph shall be exercisable by the High Court and the Court of Session.

7 (Omitted by Companies Act 1989, sec. 206(1) and Sch. 23, para. 26, 29 as from 15 March 1990 subject to transitional provisions.)

8(1) The Commission or the Secretary of State may make regulations requiring a recognised self-regulating organisation for friendly societies to give the Commission or, as the case may be, the Secretary of State forthwith notice of the occurrence of such events relating to the organisation or its members as are specified in the regulations and such information in respect of those events as is so specified.

8(2) The Commission or the Secretary of State may make regulations requiring a recognised self-regulating organisation for friendly societies to furnish the Commission or, as the case may be, the Secretary of State at such times or in respect of such periods as are specified in the regulations with such information relating to the organisation or its members as is so specified.

8(3) The notices and information required to be given or furnished under the foregoing provisions of this paragraph shall be such as the Commission or, as the case may be, the Secretary of State may reasonably require for the exercise of his functions under this Act.

8(4) Regulations under the foregoing provisions of this paragraph may require information to be given in a specified form and to be verified in a specified manner.

8(5) A notice or information required to be given or furnished under the foregoing provisions of this paragraph shall be given in writing or such other manner as the Commission or, as the case may be, the Secretary of State may approve.

8(6) Where a recognised self-regulating organisation for friendly societies amends, revokes or adds to its rules or guidance it shall within seven days give the Commission written notice of the amendment, revocation or addition; but notice need not be given of the revocation of guidance other than such as is mentioned in paragraph 2(6) above or of any amendment of or addition to guidance which does not result in or consist of such guidance as is there mentioned.

8(7) The Commission shall send the Secretary of State a copy of any notice given to the Commission under sub-paragraph (6) above.

8(8) Contravention of or of regulations under this paragraph shall not be an offence.

9(1) A recognised self-regulating organisation for friendly societies shall not exercise any powers for purposes corresponding to those of the powers exercisable by the Commission by virtue of paragraph 23 below in relation to a regulated friendly society unless it has given reasonable notice of its intention to do so to the Commission and informed the Commission—

(a)   of the manner in which and the date on or after which it intends to exercise the power; and

(b)   in the case of a proposal to impose a prohibition or requirement, of the reason why it proposes to act and its reasons for considering that that reason exists and that it is necessary to impose the prohibition or requirement.

9(2) A recognised self-regulating organisation for friendly societies shall not exercise any power to which sub-paragraph (1)(a) above applies if before the date given in the notice in pursuance of that sub-paragraph the Commission has served on it a notice in writing directing it not to do so; and the Commission may serve such a notice if the Commission considers it is desirable for protecting members or potential members of the society against the risk that it may be unable to meet its liabilities or to fulfil the reasonable expectations of its members or potential members.

PREVENTION OF RESTRICTIVE PRACTICES

10(1) The powers conferred by sub-paragraph (2) below shall be exercisable by the Secretary of State if at any time it appears to him that—

(a) any rules made or guidance issued by a recognised self-regulating organisation for friendly societies;
(b) any practices of any such organisation; or
(c) any practices of persons who are members of, or otherwise subject to the rules made by, any such organisation,

together with any statements of principle, rules, regulations or codes of practice to which members of the organisation are subject by virtue of this Schedule, have, or are intended or likely to have, to a significant extent the effect of restricting, distorting or preventing competition and that that effect is greater than is necessary for the protection of investors.

10(2) The powers exercisable under this sub-paragraph are to direct the Commission—

(a) to revoke the recognition order of the organisation;
(b) to direct the organisation to take specified steps for the purpose of securing that its rules, or the guidance or practices in question do not have the effect mentioned in sub-paragraph (1) above;
(c) to make alterations in its rules for that purpose;

and subsections (2) to (5), (7) and (9) of section 11 of this Act, as applied by sub-paragraph (2) of paragraph 5 above, shall have effect in relation to the revocation of a recognition order by virtue of a direction under this sub-paragraph as they have effect in relation to the revocation of such an order under sub-paragraph (1) of that paragraph.

10(3) The practices referred to in paragraph (b) of sub-paragraph (1) above are practices of the organisation in its capacity as such.

10(3A) The practices referred to in paragraph (c) of sub-paragraph (1) above are practices in relation to business in respect of which the persons in question are subject to—

(a) the rules of the organisation, or
(b) statements of principle, rules, regulations or codes of practice to which its members are subject by virtue of this Schedule,

and which are required or contemplated by the rules of the organisation or by those statements, rules, regulations or codes, or by guidance issued by the organisation, or which are otherwise attributable to the conduct of the organisation as such.

10(4) Subsections (3) to (8) of section 122 of this Act shall apply for the purposes of this paragraph as if—

(a) the reference to a notice in subsection (3) included a notice received under paragraph 8(7) above or 33(4) below;
(b) the references to rules and guidance in subsection (4) included such rules and guidance as are mentioned in sub-paragraph (1) above;
(c) the reference to practices in subsection (6) included such practices as are mentioned in sub-paragraph (1) above; and

Sch. 11

(d)   the reference to the Secretary of State's powers in subsection (7) included his powers under sub-paragraph (2) above.

10(5) Section 128 of this Act shall apply for the purposes of this paragraph as if—

(a)   the powers referred to in subsection (1) of that section included the powers conferred by sub-paragraph (2)(b) and (c) above;

(b)   the references to Chapter XIV of Part I included references to this paragraph; and

(c)   the reference to a recognised self-regulating organisation included a reference to a recognised self-regulating organisation for friendly societies.

FEES

11(1) An applicant for a recognition order under paragraph 3 above shall pay such fees in respect of his application as may be required by a scheme made and published by the Commission; and no application for such an order shall be regarded as duly made unless this sub-paragraph is complied with.

11(2) Subsections (2) to (4) of section 112 of this Act apply to a scheme under sub-paragraph (1) above as they apply to a scheme under subsection (1) of that section.

11(3) Every recognised self-regulating organisation for friendly societies shall pay such periodical fees to the the Commission as the Commission may by regulations prescribe.

APPLICATION OF PROVISIONS OF THIS ACT

12(1) Subject to the following provisions of this paragraph, sections 44(7), 102(1)(c), 124, 125, 126, 180(1)(n), 181, 187, 192 and 200(4) of this Act shall apply in relation to recognised self-regulating organisations for friendly societies as they apply in relation to recognised self-regulating organisations.

12(2) In its application by virtue of sub-paragraph (1) above section 126(1) of this Act shall have effect as it the reference to section 119(2) were a reference to paragraph 10(1) above.

12(3) In its application by virtue of sub-paragraph (1) above subsection (2) of section 187 of this Act shall have effect as if—

(a)   the reference in paragraph (a) to paragraphs 1 to 6 of Schedule 2 were to paragraphs 2 to 6 of that Schedule (as they apply by virtue of paragraph 4 above) and to sub-paragraph (2) of paragraph 4 above; and

(b)   paragraph (d) referred to the powers of the organisation under paragraph 23(4) below.

12(4) A direction under subsection (1) of section 192 of this Act as it applies by virtue of sub-paragraph (1) above shall direct the Commission to direct the organisation not to take or, as the case may be, to take the action in question; and where the function of making or revoking a recognition order in respect of a self-regulating organisation for friendly societies is exercisable by a transferee body any direction under that subsection as it applies as aforesaid shall be a direction requiring the Commission to direct the transferee body to give the organisation such a direction as is specified in the direction given by the Secretary of State.

12(5) Subsection (5) of that section shall not apply to a direction given to the Commission by virtue of this paragraph.

Sch. 11

Part III — Commission's Powers in Relation to Regulated Friendly Societies

SPECIAL PROVISIONS FOR REGULATED FRIENDLY SOCIETIES

13 Paragraphs 13A to 25 below shall have effect in connection with the exercise of powers for the regulation of regulated friendly societies in relation to regulated business, but nothing in this Part of this Schedule shall affect the exercise of any power conferred by this Act in relation to a regulated friendly society which is an authorised person by virtue of section 25 of this Act to the extent that the power relates to other investment business.

CONDUCT OF INVESTMENT BUSINESS

13A(1) The Commission may issue statements of principle with respect to the conduct expected of regulated friendly societies.

13A(2) The conduct expected may include compliance with a code or standard issued by another person, as for the time being in force, and may allow for the exercise of discretion by any person pursuant to any such code or standard.

13A(3) Failure to comply with a statement of principle under this paragraph is a ground for the taking of disciplinary action or the exercise of powers of intervention, but it does not give rise to any right of action by investors or other persons affected or affect the validity of any transaction.

13A(4) The disciplinary action which may be taken by virtue of sub-paragraph (3) is—

(a)   the making of a public statement under paragraph 21, or

(b)   the application by the Commission for an injunction, interdict or other order under paragraph 22(1), or

(c)   any action under paragraph 26 or 27 of this Schedule;

and the reference in that sub-paragraph to powers of intervention is to the powers conferred by Chapter VI of Part I of this Act.

13A(5) Where a statement of principle relates to compliance with a code or standard issued by another person, the statement of principle may provide—

(a)   that failure to comply with the code or standard shall be a ground for the taking of disciplinary action, or the exercise of powers of intervention, only in such cases and to such extent as may be specified; and

(b)   that no such action shall be taken, or any such power exercised, except at the request of the person by whom the code or standard in question was issued.

13A(6) The Commission shall exercise its powers in such manner as appears to the Commission appropriate to secure compliance with statements of principle under this paragraph.

Note
For transfer of the Registrar's functions under para. 13A see SI 1990/354 (C. 12), art. 5(1).

14(1) The rules under section 48 of this Act shall not apply to a regulated friendly society but the Commission may, with the consent of the Secretary of State, make such rules as may be made under that section regulating the conduct of any such society as respects the matters mentioned in sub-paragraph (2) below.

14(2) The matters referred to in sub-paragraph (1) above are—

(a)   procuring persons to transact regulated business with it and advising persons as to the exercise of rights conferred by investments acquired from the society in the course of such business;

(b)   managing the investments of pension funds, procuring persons to enter into contracts for the management of such investments and advising persons on such contracts and the exercise of the rights conferred by them;

(c)   matters incidental to those mentioned in paragraphs (a) and (b) above.

14(2A) Paragraph 22B below has effect as regards the application of rules under this paragraph to member societies in respect of investment business in the carrying on of which they are subject to the rules of a recognised self-regulating organisation for friendly societies.

14(3) Section 50 of this Act shall apply in relation to rules under this paragraph as it applies in relation to rules under section 48 except that—

(a)   for the reference to the Secretary of State there shall be substituted a reference to the Commission;

(b)   the Commission shall not exercise the power under subsection (1) to alter the requirement of rules made under this paragraph without the consent of the Secretary of State; and

(c)   for the references in subsection (4) to section 63B and a recognised self-regulating organisation there shall be substituted references to paragraph 13B and a recognised self-regulating organisation for friendly societies.

15(1) The rules under section 51 of this Act shall not apply to any investment agreement which a person has entered or offered to enter into with a regulated friendly society if, as respects the society, entering into the agreement constitutes the carrying on of regulated business but the Commission may, with the consent of the Secretary of State, make rules for enabling a person who has entered or offered to enter into such an agreement to rescind the agreement or withdraw the offer within such period and in such manner as may be specified in the rules.

15(2) Subsection (2) of section 51 of this Act shall apply in relation to rules under this paragraph as it applies in relation to rules under that section but with the substitution for the reference to the Secretary of State of a reference to the Commission.

16(1) Regulations under section 52 of this Act shall not apply to any regulated friendly society but the Commission may, with the consent of the Secretary of State, make such regulations as may be made under that section imposing requirements on regulated friendly societies other than member societies.

16(2) Any notice or information required to be given or furnished under this paragraph shall be given in writing or in such other manner as the Commission may approve.

17(1) Rules under section 53 of this Act shall not apply to any regulated friendly society but the Commission may, with the consent of the Secretary of State make rules concerning indemnity against any claim in respect of any description of civil liability incurred by a regulated friendly society in connection with any regulated business.

17(2) Such rules shall not apply to a member society of a recognised self-regulating organisation for friendly societies unless that organisation has requested that such rules should apply to it; and any such request shall not be capable of being withdrawn after rules giving effect to it have been made but without prejudice to the power of the Commission to revoke the rules if the Commission and the Secretary of State think fit.

Sch. 11

17(3) Subsections (3) and (4) of section 53 of this Act shall apply in relation to such rules as they apply to rules under that section but with the substitution for references to the Secretary of State of references to the Commission.

18(1) No scheme established by rules under section 54 shall apply in cases where persons who are or have been regulated friendly societies are unable, or likely to be unable, to satisfy claims in respect of any description of civil liability incurred by them in connection with any regulated business but the Commission may, with the consent of the Secretary of State, by rules establish a scheme for compensating investors in such cases.

18(2) Subject to sub-paragraph (3) below, subsections (2) to (4) and (6) of that section shall apply in relation to such rules as they apply to rules under that section but with the substitution for the references to the Secretary of State, authorised persons, members and a recognised self-regulating organisation of references respectively to the Commission, regulated friendly societies, member societies and a recognised self-regulating organisation for friendly societies.

18(3) Subsection (3) of that section shall have effect with the substitution for the words "the Secretary of State is satisfied" of the words "the Commission and the Secretary of State are satisfied".

18(4) The references in section 179(3)(b) and 180(1)(e) of this Act to the body administering a scheme established under section 54 of this Act shall include the body administering a scheme established under this paragraph.

19(1) Regulations under section 55 of this Act shall not apply to money held by regulated friendly societies but the Commission may, with the consent of the Secretary of State, make regulations with respect to money held by a regulated friendly society in such circumstances as may be specified in the regulations.

19(2) Regulations under this paragraph shall not provide that money held by a regulated friendly society shall be held as mentioned in paragraph (a) of subsection (2) of that section but paragraphs (b) to (f) of that subsection and subsections (3) and (4) of that section shall apply in relation to regulations made under this paragraph as they apply in relation to regulations under that section (but with the substitution for the reference in paragraph (e) of subsection (2) to the Secretary of State of a reference to the Commission).

19(3) Paragraph 22B below has effect as regards the application of regulations under this paragraph to member societies in respect of investment business in the carrying on of which they are subject to the rules of a recognised self-regulating organisation for friendly societies.

20(1) Regulations under section 56(1) of this Act shall not permit anything to be done by a regulated friendly society but that section shall not apply to anything done by such a society in the course of or in consequence of an unsolicited call which, as respects the society, constitutes the carrying on of regulated business, if it is permitted to be done by the society by regulations made by the Commission with the consent of the Secretary of State.

20(2) Paragraph 22B below has effect as regards the application of regulations under this paragraph to member societies in respect of investment business in the carrying on of which they are subject to the rules of a recognised self-regulating organisation for friendly societies.

20(3) As it applies to such persons in respect of such business, the reference in sub-paragraph (1) above to conduct permitted by regulations made by the Commission with the consent of the Secretary of State shall be construed—

Sch. 11

(a)   where or to the extent that the regulations do not apply, as a reference to conduct permitted by the rules of the organisation; and

(b)   where or to the extent that the regulations do not apply but are expressed to have effect subject to the rules of the organisation, as a reference to conduct permitted by the regulations together with the rules of the organisation.

21(1) If it appears to the Commission that a regulated friendly society other than a member society has contravened—

(a)   any provision of rules or regulations made under this Schedule or of section 56 or 59 of this Act;

(b)   any condition imposed under section 50 of this Act as it applies by virtue of paragraph 14(3) above;

(c)   any prohibition or requirement imposed under Chapter VI of Part I of this Act as it applies by virtue of paragraph 23 below; or

(d)   any requirement imposed under paragraph 24 below;

the Commission may publish a statement to that effect.

21(2) Subsections (2) to (5) of section 60 above shall apply in relation to the power under sub-paragraph (1) above as they apply in relation to the power in subsection (1) of that section but with the substitution for the references to the Secretary of State of references to the Commission.

22(1) If on the application of the Commission the court is satisfied—

(a)   that there is a reasonable likelihood that any regulated friendly society will contravene any provision of—

(i)   any prohibition or requirement imposed under Chapter VI of Part I of this Act as it applies by virtue of paragraph 23 below;

(ii)   the rules or regulations made under this Schedule;

(iii)   any requirement imposed under paragraph 24 below;

(iv)   section 47, 56 or 59 of this Act;

(v)   the rules of a recognised self-regulating organisation for friendly societies in relation to which it is a member society,

or any condition imposed under section 50 of this Act as it applies by virtue of paragraph 14(3) above;

(b)   that any regulated friendly society has contravened any such provision or condition and that there is a reasonable likelihood that the contravention will continue or be repeated; or

(c)   that any person has contravened any such provision or condition and that there are steps that could be taken for remedying the contravention,

the court may grant an injunction restraining the contravention or, in Scotland, an interdict prohibiting the contravention or, as the case may be, make an order requiring the society and any other person who appears to the court to have been knowingly concerned in the contravention to take steps to remedy it.

22(2) No application shall be made by the Commission under sub-paragraph (1) above in respect of any such rules as are mentioned in paragraph (a)(v) of that sub-paragraph unless it appears to the Commission that the organisation is unable or unwilling to take appropriate steps to restrain the contravention or to require the society concerned to take such steps as are mentioned in sub-paragraph (1) above.

Sch. 11

22(3) Subsections (3) to (9) of section 61 of this Act apply to such a contravention as is mentioned in sub-paragraph (1)(a) above as they apply to such a contravention as is mentioned in subsection (3) of that section, but with the substitution for the references to the Secretary of State of references to the Commission.

22(4) Without prejudice to the preceding provisions of this paragraph—

(a)   a contravention of any rules or regulations made under this Schedule;

(b)   a contravention of any prohibition or requirement imposed under Chapter VI of Part I of this Act as it applies by virtue of paragraph 23 below;

(c)   a contravention of any requirement imposed under paragraph 24 below;

(d)   a contravention by a member society of any rules of the recognised self-regulating organisation for friendly societies of which it is a member relating to a matter in respect of which rules or regulations have been or could be made under this Schedule or of any requirement or prohibition imposed by the organisation in the exercise of powers for purposes corresponding to those of the said Chapter VI or paragraph 24;

shall be actionable at the suit of a person who suffers loss as a result of the contravention subject to the defences and other incidents applying to actions for breach of statutory duty, but no person shall be guilty of an offence by reason of any such contravention and no such contravention shall invalidate any transaction.

22(5) This paragraph is without prejudice to any equitable remedy available in respect of property which by virtue of a requirement under section 67 of this Act as it applies by virtue of paragraph 23 below is subject to a trust.

22A(1) No action in respect of a contravention to which paragraph 22(4) above applies shall lie at the suit of a person other than a private investor, except in such circumstances as may be specified by regulations made by the Commission.

22A(2) The meaning of the expression "private investor" for the purposes of sub-paragraph (1) shall be defined by regulations made by the Commission.

22A(3) Regulations under sub-paragraph (1) may make different provision with respect to different cases.

22A(4) The Commission shall, before making any regulations affecting the right to bring an action in respect of a contravention of any rules or regulations made by a person other than the Commission, consult that person.

Note
See the Financial Services Act 1986 (Restriction of Right of Action) (Friendly Societies) Regulations 1991 (SI 1991/538).

22B(1) The Commission may in rules and regulations under—

(a)   paragraph 14 (conduct of business rules),

(b)   paragraph 19 (clients' money regulations), or

(c)   paragraph 20 (regulations as to unsolicited calls),

designate provisions which apply, to such extent as may be specified, to a member society in respect of investment business in the carrying on of which it is subject to the rules of a recognised self-regulating organisation for friendly societies.

22B(2) It may be provided that the designated rules or regulations have effect, generally or to such extent as may be specified, subject to the rules of the organisation.

22B(3) A member society which contravenes a rule or regulation applying to it by virtue of this paragraph shall be treated as having contravened the rules of the relevant recognised self-regulating organisation for friendly societies.

Sch. 11

22B(4) It may be provided that, to such extent as may be specified, the designated rules or regulations may not be modified or waived (under paragraph 22C below or section 50) in relation to a member society.

Where such provision is made any modification or waiver previously granted shall cease to have effect, subject to any transitional provision or saving contained in the rules or regulations.

22B(5) Except as mentioned in sub-paragraph (1), the rules and regulations referred to in that sub-paragraph do not apply to a member society in respect of investment business in the carrying on of which it is subject to the rules of a recognised self-regulating organisation for friendly societies.

Note
See note after para. 22D.

22C(1) A recognised self-regulating organisation for friendly societies may on the application of a society which is a member of the organisation—

(a)   modify a rule or regulation designated under paragraph 22B so as to adapt it to the circumstances of the society or to any particular kind of business carried on by it, or

(b)   dispense the society from compliance with any such rule or regulation, generally or in relation to any particular kind of business carried on by it.

22C(2) The powers conferred by this paragraph shall not be exercised unless it appears to the organisation—

(a)   that compliance with the rule or regulation in question would be unduly burdensome for the applicant having regard to the benefit which compliance would confer on investors, and

(b)   that the exercise of those powers will not result in any undue risk to investors.

22C(3) The powers conferred by this paragraph may be exercised unconditionally or subject to conditions; and paragraph 22B(3) applies in the case of a contravention of a condition as in the case of contravention of a designated rule or regulation.

22C(4) The reference in paragraph 4(1) of Schedule 2 as applied by paragraph 4 above (requirements for recognition of self-regulating organisation for friendly societies) to monitoring and enforcement of compliance with rules and regulations includes monitoring and enforcement of compliance with conditions imposed by the organisation under this paragraph.

22D(1) The Commission may issue codes of practice with respect to any matters dealt with by statements of principle issued under paragraph 13A or by rules or regulations made under any provision of this Schedule.

22D(2) In determining whether a society has failed to comply with a statement of principle—

(a)   a failure by it to comply with any relevant provision of a code of practice may be relied on as tending to establish failure to comply with the statement of principle, and

(b)   compliance by it with the relevant provisions of a code of practice may be relied on as tending to negative any such failure.

22D(3) A contravention of a code of practice with respect to a matter dealt with by rules or regulations shall not of itself give rise to any liability or invalidate any transaction; but in determining whether a society's conduct amounts to contravention of a rule or regulation—

Sch. 11

(a) contravention by it of any relevant provision of a code of practice may be relied on as tending to establish liability, and

(b) compliance by it with the relevant provisions of a code of practice may be relied on as tending to negative liability.

22D(4) Where by virtue of paragraph 22B (application of designated rules and regulations to member societies) rules or regulations—

(a) do not apply, to any extent, to a member society of a recognised self-regulating organisation for friendly societies, or

(b) apply, to any extent, subject to the rules of the organisation,

a code of practice with respect to a matter dealt with by the rules or regulations may contain provision limiting its application to a corresponding extent.

Note
For transfer of the Registrar's functions under para. 22B, 22D see SI 1990/354 (C. 12), art. 5(1).

INTERVENTION, INFORMATION AND INVESTIGATIONS

23(1) The powers conferred by Chapter VI of Part I of this Act shall not be exercisable in relation to a regulated friendly society or the appointed representative of such a society by the Secretary of State but instead shall be exercisable by the Commission; and accordingly references in that Chapter to the Secretary of State shall as respects the exercise of powers in relation to a regulated friendly society or such a representative be taken as references to the Commission.

23(2) Section 64 of this Act shall not apply to the exercise of those powers by virtue of sub-paragraph (1) above but those powers shall only be exercisable by the Commission if it appears to the Commission—

(a) that the exercise of the powers is desirable in the interests of members or potential members of the regulated friendly society; or

(b) that the society is not a fit person to carry on regulated business of a particular kind or to the extent to which it is carrying it on or proposing to carry it on; or

(c) that the society has contravened any provision of this Act or of any rules or regulations made under it or in purported compliance with any such provision has furnished the Commission with false, inaccurate or misleading information or has contravened any prohibition or requirement imposed under this Act.

23(3) For the purposes of sub-paragraph (2)(b) above the Commission may take into account any matters that could be taken into account in deciding whether to withdraw or suspend an authorisation under Chapter III of Part I of this Act.

23(4) The powers conferred by this paragraph shall not be exercisable in relation—

(a) to a member society which is subject to the rules of a recognised self-regulating organisation for friendly societies in carrying on all the investment business carried on by it; or

(b) to an appointed representative of a member society if that member society, and each other member society which is his principal, is subject to the rules of such an organisation in carrying on the investment business in respect of which it has accepted responsibility for his activities;

except that the powers conferred by virtue of section 67(1)(b) of this Act may on any of the grounds mentioned in sub-paragraph (2) above be exercised in relation to a member society or appointed representative at the request of the organisation in relation to which the society or, as the case may be, the society which is the representative's principal is a member society.

Sch. 11

24(1) The Commission may by notice in writing require any regulated friendly society (other than a member society) or any self-regulating organisation for friendly societies to furnish the Commission with such information as the Commission may reasonably require for the exercise of the Commission's functions under this Act.

24(2) The Commission may require any information which the Commission requires under this paragraph to be furnished within such reasonable time and verified in such manner as the Commission may specify.

25(1) Where a notice or copy of a notice is served on any person under section 60 or section 70 of this Act as they apply by virtue of paragraph 21(2) or 23 above, Chapter IX of Part I of this Act (other than section 96) shall, subject to sub-paragraph (2) below, have effect—

(a)   with the substitution for the references to the Secretary of State of references to the Commission; and

(b)   as if for the references in section 98(4) to sections 28, 33 and 60 of this Act there were substituted references to paragraphs 21, 23, 24, 26 and 27 of this Schedule.

25(2) Where the friendly society in question is an authorised person by virtue of section 25 of this Act the provisions mentioned in sub-paragraph (1) above shall have effect as if the references substituted by that sub-paragraph had effect in addition to rather than in substitution for the references for which they are there substituted.

25(3) Where the Tribunal reports that the appropriate decision is to take action under paragraph 26 or 27 of this Schedule the Commission shall take the report into account but shall not be bound to act on it.

EXERCISE OF POWERS UNDER ENACTMENTS RELATING TO FRIENDLY SOCIETIES

26(1) If it appears to the Commission that a regulated friendly society which is an authorised person by virtue of section 23 of this Act—

(a)   has contravened any provision of—
    (i)   this Act or any rules or regulations made under it;
    (ii)   any requirement imposed under paragraph 24 above;
    (iii) the rules of a recognised self-regulating organisation for friendly societies in relation to which it is a member society; or

(b)   in purported compliance with any such provision has furnished false, inaccurate or misleading information,

the Commission may exercise any of the powers mentioned in sub-paragraph (2) below in relation to that society.

26(2) The powers mentioned in sub-paragraph (1) above are—

(a)   in relation to a registered friendly society, those under subsection (1) of section 87 (inspection and winding up of registered friendly societies) and subsections (1) and (2) of section 91 (cancellation and suspension of registration) of the Friendly Societies Act 1974;

(b)   in relation to an incorporated friendly society, those under section 22 (winding up by court: grounds and petitioners) of the Friendly Societies Act 1992; and

(c)   in relation to a registered friendly society or an incorporated friendly society, those under the following provisions of the Friendly Societies Act 1992, namely, section 36 (imposition of conditions on current authorisation), section 39 (power to direct application for fresh authorisation), section 40 (withdrawal of

Sch. 11

authorisation in respect of new business), section 51 (power to forbid acceptance of new members), section 52 (application to court), section 62 (power to obtain information and documents etc.), section 65 (investigations on behalf of Commission) and section 66 (inspections and special meetings: general),

and the sections referred to above shall apply in relation to the exercise of those powers by virtue of this paragraph as they apply in relation to their exercise in the circumstances mentioned in those sections.

26(3) (Repealed by Friendly Societies Act 1992, sec. 120 and Sch. 22, Pt. I as from 28 April 1993 in regard to incorporated friendly societies and as from 1 January 1994 for all remaining purposes.)

27 (Repealed by Friendly Societies Act 1992, sec. 120 and Sch. 22, Pt. I as from 28 April 1993 in regard to incorporated friendly societies and as from 1 January 1994 for all remaining purposes.)

Note
See history note at end of Sch. 11.

28(1) If it appears to the Commission—
(a)   that a body corporate has been established which is able and willing to discharge all or any of the functions to which this paragraph applies; and
(b)   that the requirements of Schedule 7 to this Act (as it has effect by virtue of sub-paragraph (3) below) are satisfied in the case of that body,

the Commission may, with the consent of the Secretary of State and subject to the following provisions of this paragraph and paragraphs 29 and 30 below, make an order transferring all or any of those functions to that body.

Note
See the Financial Services (Transfer of Functions Relating to Friendly Societies) Order (Northern Ireland) 1987 (SI 1987/228).

28(2) The body to which functions are transferred by the first order made under sub-paragraph (1) above shall be the body known as The Securities and Investments Board Limited if the Secretary of State consents to the making of the order and it appears to the Commission that that body is able and willing to discharge those functions, that the requirements mentioned in paragraph (b) of that sub-paragraph are satisfied in the case of that body and that the Commission is not precluded from making the order by the following provisions of this paragraph or paragraph 29 or 30 below.

28(3) For the purposes of sub-paragraph (1) above Schedule 7 shall have effect as if—
(a)   for references to a designated agency there were substituted references to a transferee body; and
(b)   for the reference to complaints in paragraph 4 there were substituted a reference to complaints arising out of the conduct by regulated friendly societies of regulated business.

28(4) An order under sub-paragraph (1) above is in this Act referred to as a transfer order and a body to which functions are transferred by a transfer order is in this Act referred to as a transferee body.

28(5) Subject to sub-paragraphs (6) and (8) below, this paragraph applies to the functions of the Commission under section 113(3) of this Act and paragraph 38 below and any functions conferred on the Commission by virtue of paragraphs 2 to 25 (except paragraph 22A) above other than the powers under sections 66 and 68 of this Act and, so far as applicable to assets belonging to a regulated friendly society, the power under section 67 of this Act.

28(6) If the Commission transfers its functions under Chapter VI of Part I of this Act they shall not be exercisable by the transferee body if the only reasons by virtue of which it appears to the body as mentioned in paragraph 23(2) above relate to the sufficiency of the funds of the society to meet existing claims or of the rates of contribution to cover benefits assured.

28(7) Any function may be transferred by an order under this paragraph either wholly or in part and a function may be transferred in respect of all societies or only in respect of such societies as are specified in the order.

28(8) A transfer order—

(a) may reserve to the Commission the function of revoking a recognition order in respect of a self-regulating organisation for friendly societies on the ground that the requirement mentioned in paragraph 4(2) above is not satisfied; and

(b) shall not transfer to a transferee body the function of revoking any such recognition order on the ground that the organisation has contravened the provisions of paragraph 9 above.

28(9) No transfer order shall be made unless a draft of it has been laid before and approved by a resolution of each House of Parliament.

Note
See the Financial Services (Transfer of Functions Relating to Friendly Societies) Order 1987 (SI 1987/925).

29(1) The Commission shall not make a transfer order transferring any legislative functions to a transferee body unless—

(a) the body has furnished the Commission and the Secretary of State with a copy of the instruments the body proposes to issue or make in the exercise of those functions, and

(b) the Commission and the Secretary of State are both satisfied that those instruments will—

(i) afford investors an adequate level of protection,

(ii) in the case of provisions corresponding to those mentioned in Schedule 8 to this Act, comply with the principles set out in that Schedule, and

(iii) take proper account of the supervision of friendly societies by the Commission under the enactments relating to friendly societies.

29(2) In this paragraph "legislative functions" means the functions of issuing or making statements of principle, rules, regulations or codes of practice.

30(1) The Commission shall also before making a transfer order transferring any functions to a transferee body require it to furnish the Commission and the Secretary of State with a copy of any guidance intended to have continuing effect which it proposes to issue in writing or other legible form and they may take such guidance into account in determining whether they are satisfied as mentioned in paragraph 29(b) above.

30(2) In this Act references to guidance issued by a transferee body are references to guidance issued or any recommendation made by it which is issued or made to regulated friendly societies or self-regulating organisations for friendly societies generally or to any class of regulated friendly societies or self-regulating organisations for friendly societies, being societies which are or may be subject to statements of principle, rules, regulations or codes of practice issued or made by it or organisations which are or may be recognised by it in the exercise of its functions under a transfer order.

31(1) Subject to the provisions of this paragraph, sections 115, 116, 117(3) to (5) and 118 of this Act shall apply in relation to the transfer of functions under paragraph 28 above as they apply in relation to the transfer of functions under section 114 of this Act.

Sch. 11

31(2) Subject to sub-paragraphs (5) and (6)(b) below, for references in those provisions to the Secretary of State, a designated agency and a delegation order there shall be substituted respectively references to the Commission, a transferee body and a transfer order.

31(3) The Commission may not exercise the powers conferred by subsections (1) and (2) of section 115 except with the consent of the Secretary of State.

31(4) In subsection (3) of section 115 for the reference to Schedule 7 to this Act there shall be substituted a reference to that Schedule as it has effect by virtue of paragraph 28(3) above and in subsection (5) of that section for the reference to section 114(9)(b) of this Act there shall be substituted a reference to paragraph 29(b) above.

31(5) Section 118(3)(b) shall have effect as if the reference to any provision applying to the Secretary of State were a reference to any provision applying to the Secretary of State or the Commission.

31(6) In Schedule 9 to this Act—

(a)   paragraph 1(2) and (3) shall be omitted;
(b)   paragraph 4 shall have effect as if the references to the Secretary of State were references to the Secretary of State and the Commission;
(c)   paragraph 5 shall have effect as if the reference to section 205A were a reference to paragraph 45(1) and (3) below;
(d)   paragraph 12(3) shall have effect as if the reference to section 114(9) were a reference to paragraph 29 above.

31(7) The power mentioned in paragraph 2(3) of Schedule 9 to this Act shall not be exercisable on the ground that the company has ceased to be a designated agency or, as the case may be, a transferee body if the company remains a transferee body or, as the case may be, a designated agency.

31A(1) Where any functions under this Act are for the time being exercisable by a transferee body the Commission shall, before issuing an authorisation under section 32 of the Friendly Societies Act 1992 to a friendly society which is carrying on or proposes to carry on in the United Kingdom insurance business or non-insurance business which is investment business—

(a)   seek the advice of the transferee body with respect to any matters which are relevant to those functions of the body and relate to the society, its proposed business or persons who are or will be, within the meaning of the Friendly Societies Act 1992, members of the committee of management or other officers of the society; and
(b)   take into account any advice on those matters given to the Commission by the transferee body before the application is decided.

31A(2) In sub-paragraph (1) above—

(a)   "insurance business" has the meaning given by section 117(1) of the Friendly Societies Act 1992; and
(b)   "non-insurance business" has the meaning given by section 119(1) of that Act.

31A(3) The Commission may for the purpose of obtaining the advice of a transferee body under sub-paragraph (1) above furnish it with any information obtained by the Commission in connection with the application.

32 A transferee body shall at least once in each year for which the transfer order is in force make a report to the Commission on the discharge of the functions transferred to it by the order and on such other matters as the order may require and the Commission

Sch. 11

shall send a copy of each report received by the Commission under this paragraph to the Secretary of State who shall lay copies of the report before Parliament.

33(1) This paragraph applies where the function of making or revoking a recognition order in respect of a self-regulating organisation for friendly societies is exercisable by a transferee body.

33(2) Paragraph 3(2) above shall have effect as if the first reference to the Secretary of State included a reference to the Commission.

33(3) The transferee body shall not regard the requirement mentioned in paragraph 4(2) as satisfied unless the Commission has certified that the Commission also regards it as satisfied.

33(4) A transferee body shall send the Commission and the Secretary of State a copy of any notice received by it under paragraph 8(6) above.

33(5) Where the Secretary of State exercises any of the powers conferred by paragraph 10(2) above in relation to an organisation the Commission shall direct the transferee body to take the appropriate action in relation to that organisation and such a direction shall, on the application of the Commission, be enforceable by mandamus or, in Scotland, by an order for specific performance under section 91 of the Court of Session Act 1868.

34(1) A transferee body to which the Commission has transferred any legislative functions may exercise those functions without the consent of the Secretary of State.

34(2) In this paragraph "legislative functions" means the functions of issuing or making statements of principle, rules, regulations or codes of practice.

35(1) A transferee body shall not impose any prohibition or requirement under section 65 or 67 of this Act on a regulated friendly society or vary any such prohibition or requirement unless it has given reasonable notice of its intention to do so to the Commission and informed the Commission—

(a)   of the manner in which and the date on or after which it intends to exercise the power; and

(b)   in the case of a proposal to impose a prohibition or requirement, on which of the grounds specified in paragraph 23(2) above it proposes to act and its reasons for considering that the ground in question exists and that it is necessary to impose the prohibition or requirement.

35(2) A transferee body shall not exercise any power to which sub-paragraph (1) above applies if before the date given in the notice in pursuance of sub-paragraph (1)(a) above the Commission has served on it a notice in writing directing it not to do so; and the Commission may serve such a notice if the Commission considers it is desirable for protecting members or potential members of the regulated friendly society against the risk that it may be unable to meet its liabilities or to fulfil the reasonable expectations of its members or potential members.

36(1) The Secretary of State shall not consent to the making of an order by the Commission under paragraph 28 above transferring any functions to a transferee body unless he is satisfied that any statements of principle, rules, regulations, codes of practice, guidance and recommendations of which copies are furnished to him under paragraphs 29(a) and 30(1) above do not have, and are not intended or likely to have, to any significant extent the effect of restricting, distorting or preventing competition or, if they have or are intended or likely to have that effect to any significant extent, that the effect is not greater than is necessary for the protection of investors.

36(2) Section 121(2) and (4) and sections 122 to 128 above shall have effect in relation to transferee bodies and transfer orders as they have effect in relation to designated agencies and designation orders but subject to the following modifications.

36(3) Those provisions shall have effect as if the powers exercisable under section 121(3) were—

(a) to make an order transferring back to the Commission all or any of the functions transferred to the transferee body by a transfer order; or

(b) to direct the Commission to direct the transferee body to take specified steps for the purpose of securing that the statements of principle, rules, regulations, codes of practice, guidance or practices in question do not have the effect mentioned in sub-paragraph (1) above.

36(4) No order shall be made by virtue of sub-paragraph (3) above unless a draft of it has been laid before and approved by a resolution of each House of Parliament.

36(5) For the decisions referred to in section 122(1) there shall be substituted a reference to the Secretary of State's decision whether he is precluded by sub-paragraph (1) above from giving his consent to the making of a transfer order.

36(6) Section 128 shall apply as if—

(a) the powers referred to in subsection (1) of that section included the power conferred by sub-paragraph (3)(b) above; and

(b) the references to Chapter XIV of Part I included references to this paragraph.

37(1) If a transferee body has reasonable grounds for believing that any regulated friendly society has failed to comply with an obligation to which it is subject by virtue of this Act it shall forthwith give notice of that fact to the Commission so that the Commission can take it into consideration in deciding whether to exercise in relation to the society any of the relevant powers.

37(1A) In sub-paragraph (1) above "the relevant powers" means those powers specified in paragraph 26(2).

37(2) A notice under sub-paragraph (1) above shall contain particulars of the obligation in question and of the transferee body's reasons for considering that the society has failed to satisfy that obligation.

37(3) A transferee body need not give a notice under sub-paragraph (1) above in respect of any matter unless it considers that that matter (either alone or in conjunction with other matters) would justify the withdrawal of authorisation under section 28 of this Act in the case of a person to whom that provision applies.

Part V — Miscellaneous and Supplemental

38(1) The Commission may publish information or give advice, or arrange for the publication of information or the giving of advice, in such form and manner as the Commission considers appropriate with respect to—

(a) the operation of this Schedule and the statements of principle, rules, regulations and codes of practice issued or made under it in relation to friendly societies, including in particular the rights of their members, the duties of such societies and the steps to be taken for enforcing those rights or complying with those duties;

(b) any matters relating to the functions of the Commission under this Schedule or any such statements of principle, rules, regulations or codes of practice;

Sch. 11

(c)   any other matters about which it appears to the Commission to be desirable to publish information or give advice for the protection of those members or any class of them.

38(2) The Commission may offer for sale copies of information published under this paragraph and may, if the Commission thinks fit, make reasonable charges for advice given under this paragraph at any person's request.

38(3) This paragraph shall not be construed as authorising the disclosure of restricted information within the meaning of section 179 of this Act in any case in which it could not be disclosed apart from the provisions of this paragraph.

39 In the case of an application for authorisation under section 26 of this Act made by a society which is registered under the Friendly Societies Act 1974 within the meaning of that Act or is registered or deemed to be registered under the Friendly Societies Act (Northern Ireland) 1970 ("a registered society"), section 27(3)(c) of this Act shall have effect as if it referred only to any person who is a trustee manager or member of the committee of the society.

40 Where the other person mentioned in paragraph (c) of the definition of "connected person" in section 105(9) of this Act is a registered society that paragraph shall have effect with the substitution for the words from "member" onwards of the words "trustee, manager or member of the committee of the society".

40A(1) In the case of an application for authorisation under section 26 of this Act made by an incorporated friendly society section 27(3) shall have effect as if the following paragraph were substituted for paragraph (a)—

"(a) to any member of the committee of management or any director or controller of a subsidiary of the society or of a body jointly controlled by the society".

40A(2) Where the other person mentioned in paragraph (b) of the definition of "connected person" in section 105(9) of this Act is an incorporated friendly society that paragraph shall have effect with the substitution for the words from "director" onwards of the words "member of the committee of management of the society or any director, secretary or controller of a subsidiary of the society or a body jointly controlled by the society".

41 In relation to any such document as is mentioned in subsection (1) of section 204 of this Act which is required or authorised to be given to or served on a registered society—

(a)   subsection (3)(c) of that section shall have effect with the substitution for the words from "member" onwards of the words "trustee, manager or member of the committee of the society"; and
(b)   subsection (4)(c) of that section shall have effect as if for the words from "member" onwards there were substituted the words "trustee, manager or member of the committee of the society, the office which is its registered office in accordance with its rules".

42 Rules under paragraphs 14, 15, 17 and 18 above and regulations under paragraphs 16, 19 and 20 above shall apply notwithstanding any provision to the contrary in the rules of any regulated friendly society to which they apply.

43 (Repealed by Friendly Societies Act 1992, sec. 120 and Sch. 22, Pt. I as from 28 April 1993 in regard to incorporated friendly societies and as from 1 January 1994 for all remaining purposes.)

Sch. 11

44(1) In Part III of Schedule 1 to the House of Commons Disqualification Act 1975 (disqualifying offices) there shall be inserted at the appropriate place—

"Chairman of a transferee body within the meaning of Schedule 11 to the Financial Services Act 1986 if he is in receipt of remuneration."

44(2) A corresponding amendment shall be made in Part III of Schedule 1 to the Northern Ireland Assembly Disqualification Act 1975.

45(1) Any power of the Commission to make regulations, rules or orders which is exercisable by virtue of this Act shall be exercisable by statutory instrument and the Statutory Instruments Act 1946 shall apply to any such power as if the Commission were a Minister of the Crown.

45(2) Any regulations, rules or orders made under this Schedule by the Commission may make different provision for different cases.

Schedule 11A — Offers of Securities to the Public in the United Kingdom

1 A person offers securities to the public in the United Kingdom if—

(a) to the extent that the offer is made to persons in the United Kingdom, it is made to the public; and

(b) paragraph 2 below does not apply in relation to the offer;

and, for this purpose, an offer which is made to any section of the public, whether selected as members or debenture holders of a body corpoate, or as clients of the person making the offer, or in any other manner, is to be regarded as made to the public.

2 This paragraph applies in relation to an offer of securities where, to the extent that the offer is made to persons in the United Kingdom—

(a) the condition specified in any one of the paragraphs of sub-paragraph (1) of paragraph 3 below is satisfied in relation to the offer; or

(b) paragraph 4 below applies in relation to the offer.

3(1) The following are the conditions specified in this sub-paragraph—

(a) the securities are offered to persons—

(i) whose ordinary activities involve them in acquiring, holding, managing or disposing of investments (as principal or agent) for the purposes of their businesses; or

(ii) who it is reasonable to expect will acquire, hold, manage or dispose of investments (as principal or agent) for the purposes of their businesses;

or are otherwise offered to persons in the context of their trades, professions or occupations;

(b) the securities are offered to no more than fifty persons;

(c) the securities are offered to the members of a club or association (whether or not incorporated) and the members can reasonably be regarded as having a common interest with each other and with the club or association in the affairs of the club or association and in what is to be done with the proceeds of the offer;

Sch. 11A

(d)   the securities are offered to a restricted circle of persons whom the offerer reasonably believes to be sufficiently knowledgeable to understand the risks involved in accepting the offer;

(e)   the securities are offered in connection with a bona fide invitation to enter into an underwriting agreement with respect to them;

(f)   the securities are offered to a government, local authority or public authority, as defined in paragraph 3 of Schedule 1 to this Act;

(g)   the total consideration payable for the securities cannot exceed ecu 40,000 (or an equivalent amount);

(h)   the minimum consideration which may be paid for securities acquired pursuant to the offer is at least ecu 40,000 (or an equivalent amount);

(i)   the securities are denominated in amounts of at least ecu 40,000 (or an equivalent amount);

(j)   the securities are offered in connection with a takeover offer;

(k)   the securities are offered in connection with a merger within the meaning of Council Directive No. 78855EEC;

(l)   the securities are shares and are offered free of charge to any or all of the holders of shares in the issuer;

(m)   the securities are shares, or investments falling within paragraph 4 or 5 of Schedule 1 to this Act relating to shares, in a body corporate and are offered in exchange for shares in the same body corporate, and the offer cannot result in any increase in the issed share capital of the body corporate;

(n)   the securities are issued by a body corporate and offered—

    (i)   by the issuer;

    (ii) only to qualifying persons; and

    (iii) on terms that a contract to acquire any such securities may be entered into only by the qualifying person to whom they were offered or, if the terms of the offer so permit, any qualifying person;

(o)   the securities result from the conversion of convertible securities and listing particulars or a prospectus relating to the convertible securities were or was published in the United Kingdom under or by virtue of Part IV of this Act, Part III of the Companies Act 1985 or the Public Offers of Securities Regulations 1995;

(p)   the securities are issued by—

    (i)   a charity within the meaning of section 96(1) of the Charities Act 1993;

    (ii) a housing association within the meaning of section 5(1) of the Housing Act 1985;

    (iii) an industrial or provident society registered in accordance with section 1(2)(b) of the Industrial and Provident Societies Act 1965; or

    (iv) a non-profit making association or body, recognised by the country or territory in which it is established, with objectives similar to those of a body falling within any of sub-paragraphs (i) to (iii) above;

and the proceeds of the offer will be used for the purposes of the issuer's objectives;

(q)   the securities offered are shares which are issued by, or ownership of which entitles the holder to membership of or to obtain the benefit of services provided by,—

    (i)   a building society incorporated under the law of, or of any part of, the United Kingdom;

    (ii) any body incorporated under the law of, or any part of, the United Kingdom relating to industrial and provident societies or credit unions; or

Sch. 11A

(iii) a body of a similar nature established in a Member State;
(r)   the securities offered are Euro-securities and are not the subject of advertising likely to come to the attention of persons who are not professionally experienced in matters relating to investment;
(s)   the securities are of the same class, and were issued at the same time, as securities in respect of which a prospectus has been published under or by virtue of Part IV of this Act, Part III of the Companies Act 1985 or the Public Offers of Securities Regulations 1995;
(t)   the securities are investments falling within paragraph 2 of Schedule 1 to this Act with a maturity of less than one year from their date of issue;
(u)   the securities are investments falling within paragraph 3 of Schedule 1 to this Act;
(v)   the securities are not transferable.

3(2) For the purposes of this paragraph—
"convertible securities" means—

(a)   securities falling within paragraph 2 of Schedule 1 to this Act which can be converted into, or exchanged for, or which confer rights to acquire, securities; or
(b)   securities falling within paragraph 4 or 5 of that Schedule (as applied for the purposes of section 142(2) of this Act);

and **"conversion"** in relation to convertible securities means their conversion into or exchange for, or the exercise of rights conferred by them to acquire, other securities;
"credit institution" means a credit institution as defined in Article 1 of Council Directive No. 77780EEC;
"ecu" means the European currency unit as defined in Article 1 of Council Regulation No. 3320/94/EC or any Council regulation replacing the same, in either case as amended from time to time;
"Euro-securities" means investments which—

(a)   are to be underwritten and distributed by a syndicate at least two if the members of which have their registered offices in different countries or territories;
(b)   are to be offered on a significant scale in one or more countries or territories other than the country or territory in which the issuer has its registered office; and
(c)   may be acquired pursuant to the offer only through a credit institution or other financial institution;

"financial institution" means a financial institution as defined in Article 1 of Council Directive No. 89646EEC; and
"shares", except in relation to a takeover offer, means investments which are securities by virtue of falling within paragraph 1 of Schedule 1 to this Act (as applied for the purposes of section 142(3) of this Act).

3(3) For the purposes of determining whether the condition specified in paragraph (b) or (g) of sub-paragraph (1) above is satisfied in relation to an offer, the offer shall be taken together with any other offer of the same securities which was—
(a)   made by the same person;
(b)   open at any time within the period of 12 months ending with the date on which the offer is first made; and
(c)   not an offer to the public in the United Kingdom by virtue of that condition being satisfied.

Sch. 11A

3(4) In determining for the purposes of paragraph (d) of sub-paragraph (1) above whether a person is sufficiently knowledgeable to understand the risks involved in accepting an offer of securities, any information supplied by the person making the offer shall be disregarded, apart from information about—

(a)   the issuer of the securities; or

(b)   if the securities confer the right to acquire other securities, the issuer of those other securities.

3(5) For the purposes of determining whether the condition specified in paragraph (g), (h) or (i) of sub-paragraph (1) above is satisfied in relation to an offer, an amount, in relation to an amount denominated in ecu, is an **"equivalent amount"** if it is an amount of equal value, calculated at the latest practicable date before (but in any event not more than 3 days before) the date on which the offer is first made, denominated wholly or partly in another currency or unit of account.

3(6) For the purposes of paragraph (j) of sub-paragraph (1) above, **"takeover offer"** means—

(a)   an offer which is a takeover offer within the meaning of Part XIIIA of the Companies Act 1985 (or would be such an offer if that Part of that Act applied in relation to any body corporate); or

(b)   an offer made to all the holders of shares, or of shares of a particular class, in a body corporate to acquire a specified proportion of those shares (**"holders"** and **"shares"** being construed in accordance with that Part);

but in determining for the purposes of paragraph (b) above whether an offer is made to all the holders of shares, or of shares of any class, the offeror, any associate of his (within the meaning of section 430E of that Act) and any person whose shares the offeror or any such associate has contracted to acquire shall not be regarded as holders of the shares.

3(7) For the purposes of paragraph (1) of sub-paragraph (1) above, **"holders of shares"** means the persons who, at the close of business on a date specified in the offer and falling within the period of 28 days ending with the date on which the offer is first made, were the holders of such shares.

3(8) For the purposes of paragraph (n) of sub-paragraph (1) above—

(a)   a person is a **"qualifying person"**, in relation to an issuer, if he is a bona fide employee or former employee of the issuer or of another body corporate in the same group or the wife, husband, widow, widower or child or stepchild under the age of eighteen of such an employee or former employee; and

(b)   the definition of **"issuer"** in section 142(7) applies with the omission of the words from "except that" to the end of the definition.

4(1) This paragraph applies in relation to an offer where the condition specified in one relevant paragraph is satisfied in relation to part, but not the whole, of the offer and, in relation to each other part of the offer, the condition specified in a different relevant paragraph is satisfied.

4(2) For the purposes of this paragraph, **"relevant paragraph"** means any of paragraph (a) to (f), (j) to (m), (o), (p) and (s) of paragraph 3(1) above.

Schedule 12 — Takeover Offers: Provisions Substituted for Sections 428, 429 and 430 of Companies Act 1985

Section 172

Part XIIIA — Takeover Offers

SEC. 428   "Takeover offers"

428(1) In this Part of this Act **"a takeover offer"** means an offer to acquire all the shares, or all the shares of any class or classes, in a company (other than shares which at the date of the offer are already held by the offeror), being an offer on terms which are the same in relation to all the shares to which the offer relates or, where those shares include shares of different classes, in relation to all the shares of each class.

428(2) In subsection (1) **"shares"** means shares which have been allotted on the date of the offer but a takeover offer may include among the shares to which it relates all or any shares that are subsequently allotted before a date specified in or determined in accordance with the terms of the offer.

428(3) The terms offered in relation to any shares shall for the purposes of this section be treated as being the same in relation to all the shares or, as the case may be, all the shares of a class to which the offer relates notwithstanding any variation permitted by subsection (4).

428(4) A variation is permitted by this subsection where—

(a) the law of a country or territory outside the United Kingdom precludes an offer of consideration in the form or any of the forms specified in the terms in question or precludes it except after compliance by the offeror with conditions with which he is unable to comply or which he regards as unduly onerous; and

(b) the variation is such that the persons to whom an offer of consideration in that form is precluded are able to receive consideration otherwise than in that form but of substantially equivalent value.

428(5) The reference in subsection (1) to shares already held by the offeror includes a reference to shares which he has contracted to acquire but that shall not be construed as including shares which are the subject of a contract binding the holder to accept the offer when it is made, being a contract entered into by the holder either for no consideration and under seal or for no consideration other than a promise by the offeror to make the offer.

428(6) In the application of subsection (5) to Scotland, the words "and under seal" shall be omitted.

428(7) Where the terms of an offer make provision for their revision and for acceptances on the previous terms to be treated as acceptances on the revised terms, the revision shall not be regarded for the purposes of this Part of this Act as the making of a fresh offer and references in this Part of this Act to the date of the offer shall accordingly be construed as references to the date on which the original offer was made.

428(8) In this Part of this Act **"the offeror"** means, subject to section 430D, the person making a takeover offer and **"the company"** means the company whose shares are the subject of the offer.

Sch. 12

SEC. 429   Right of offeror to buy out minority shareholders

429(1) If, in a case in which a takeover offer does not relate to shares of different classes, the offeror has by virtue of acceptances of the offer acquired or contracted to acquire not less than nine-tenths in value of the shares to which the offer relates he may give notice to the holder of any shares to which the offer relates which the offeror has not acquired or contracted to acquire that he desires to acquire those shares.

429(2) If, in a case in which a takeover offer relates to shares of different classes, the offeror has by virtue of acceptances of the offer acquired or contracted to acquire not less than nine-tenths in value of the shares of any class to which the offer relates, he may give notice to the holder of any shares of that class which the offeror has not acquired or contracted to acquire that he desires to acquire those shares.

429(3) No notice shall be given under subsection (1) or (2) unless the offeror has acquired or contracted to acquire the shares necessary to satisfy the minimum specified in that subsection before the end of the period of four months beginning with the date of the offer; and no such notice shall be given after the end of the period of two months beginning with the date on which he has acquired or contracted to acquire shares which satisfy that minimum.

429(4) Any notice under this section shall be given in the prescribed manner; and when the offeror gives the first notice in relation to an offer he shall send a copy of it to the company together with a statutory declaration by him in the prescribed form stating that the conditions for the giving of the notice are satisfied.

429(5) Where the offeror is a company (whether or not a company within the meaning of this Act) the statutory declaration shall be signed by a director.

429(6) Any person who fails to send a copy of a notice or a statutory declaration as required by subsection (4) or makes such a declaration for the purposes of that subsection knowing it to be false or without having reasonable grounds for believing it to be true shall be liable to imprisonment or a fine, or both, and for continued failure to send the copy or declaration, to a daily default fine.

429(7) If any person is charged with an offence for failing to send a copy of a notice as required by subsection (4) it is a defence for him to prove that he took reasonable steps for securing compliance with that subsection.

429(8) Where during the period within which a takeover offer can be accepted the offeror acquires or contracts to acquire any of the shares to which the offer relates but otherwise than by virtue of acceptances of the offer, then, if—

(a)   the value of the consideration for which they are acquired or contracted to be acquired ("the acquisition consideration") does not at that time exceed the value of the consideration specified in the terms of the offer; or

(b)   those terms are subsequently revised so that when the revision is announced the value of the acquisition consideration, at the time mentioned in paragraph (a) above, no longer exceeds the value of the consideration specified in those terms,

the offeror shall be treated for the purposes of this section as having acquired or contracted to acquire those shares by virtue of acceptances of the offer; but in any other case those shares shall be treated as excluded from those to which the offer relates.

SEC. 430   Effect of notice under sec. 429

430(1) The following provisions shall, subject to section 430C, have effect where a notice is given in respect of any shares under section 429.

Sch. 12

430(2) The offeror shall be entitled and bound to acquire those shares on the terms of the offer.

430(3) Where the terms of an offer are such as to give the holder of any shares a choice of consideration the notice shall give particulars of the choice and state—

(a)   that the holder of the shares may within six weeks from the date of the notice indicate his choice by a written communication sent to the offeror at an address specified in the notice; and

(b)   which consideration specified in the offer is to be taken as applying in default of his indicating a choice as aforesaid;

and the terms of the offer mentioned in subsection (2) shall be determined accordingly.

430(4) Subsection (3) applies whether or not any time-limit or other conditions applicable to the choice under the terms of the offer can still be complied with; and if the consideration chosen by the holder of the shares—

(a)   is not cash and the offeror is no longer able to provide it; or

(b)   was to have been provided by a third party who is no longer bound or able to provide it,

the consideration shall be taken to consist of an amount of cash payable by the offeror which at the date of the notice is equivalent to the chosen consideration.

430(5) At the end of six weeks from the date of the notice the offeror shall forthwith—

(a)   send a copy of the notice to the company; and

(b)   pay or transfer to the company the consideration for the shares to which the notice relates.

430(6) If the shares to which the notice relates are registered the copy of the notice sent to the company under subsection (5)(a) shall be accompanied by an instrument of transfer executed on behalf of the shareholder by a person appointed by the offeror;

and on receipt of that instrument the company shall register the offeror as the holder of those shares.

430(7) If the shares to which the notice relates are transferable by the delivery of warrants or other instruments the copy of the notice sent to the company under subsection (5)(a) shall be accompanied by a statement to that effect; and the company shall on receipt of the statement issue the offeror with warrants or other instruments in respect of the shares and those already in issue in respect of the shares shall become void.

430(8) Where the consideration referred to in paragraph (b) of subsection (5) consists of shares or securities to be allotted by the offeror the reference in that paragraph to the transfer of the consideration shall be construed as a reference to the allotment of the shares or securities to the company.

430(9) Any sum received by a company under paragraph (b) of subsection (5) and any other consideration received under that paragraph shall be held by the company on trust for the person entitled to the shares in respect of which the sum or other consideration was received.

430(10) Any sum received by a company under paragraph (b) of subsection (5), and any dividend or other sum accruing from any other consideration received by a company under that paragraph, shall be paid into a separate bank account, being an account the balance on which bears interest at an appropriate rate and can be withdrawn by such notice (if any) as is appropriate.

Sch. 12

430(11) Where after reasonable enquiry made at such intervals as are reasonable the person entitled to any consideration held on trust by virtue of subsection (9) cannot be found and twelve years have elapsed since the consideration was received or the company is wound up the consideration (together with any interest, dividend or other benefit that has accrued from it) shall be paid into court.

430(12) In relation to a company registered in Scotland, subsections (13) and (14) shall apply in place of subsection (11).

430(13) Where after reasonable enquiry made at such intervals as are reasonable the person entitled to any consideration held on trust by virtue of subsection (9) cannot be found and twelve years have elapsed since the consideration was received or the company is wound up—

(a)   the trust shall terminate;
(b)   the company or, as the case may be, the liquidator shall sell any consideration other than cash and any benefit other than cash that has accrued from the consideration; and
(c)   a sum representing—
    (i)   the consideration so far as it is cash;
    (ii)   the proceeds of any sale under paragraph (b) above; and
    (iii) any interest, dividend or other benefit that has accrued from the consideration,

shall be deposited in the name of the Accountant of Court in a bank account such as is referred to in subsection (10) and the receipt for the deposit shall be transmitted to the Accountant of Court.

430(14) Section 58 of the Bankruptcy (Scotland) Act 1985 (so far as consistent with this Act) shall apply with any necessary modifications to sums deposited under subsection (13) as that section applies to sums deposited under section 57(1)(a) of that Act.

430(15) The expenses of any such enquiry as is mentioned in subsection (11) or (13) may be defrayed out of the money or other property held on trust for the person or persons to whom the enquiry relates.

SEC. 430A   Right of minority shareholder to be bought out by offeror

430A(1) If a takeover offer relates to all the shares in a company and at any time before the end of the period within which the offer can be accepted—

(a)   the offeror has by virtue of acceptances of the offer acquired or contracted to acquire some (but not all) of the shares to which the offer relates; and
(b)   those shares, with or without any other shares in the company which he has acquired or contracted to acquire, amount to not less than nine-tenths in value of all the shares in the company,

the holder of any shares to which the offer relates who has not accepted the offer may by a written communication addressed to the offeror require him to acquire those shares.

430A(2) If a takeover offer relates to shares of any class or classes and at any time before the end of the period within which the offer can be accepted—

(a)   the offeror has by virtue of acceptances of the offer acquired or contracted to acquire some (but not all) of the shares of any class to which the offer relates; and

Sch. 12

(b)   those shares, with or without any other shares of that class which he has acquired or contracted to acquire, amount to not less than nine-tenths in value of all the shares of that class,

the holder of any shares of that class who has not accepted the offer may by a written communication addressed to the offeror require him to acquire those shares.

430A(3) Within one month of the time specified in subsection (1) or, as the case may be, subsection (2) the offeror shall give any shareholder who has not accepted the offer notice in the prescribed manner of the rights that are exercisable by him under that subsection; and if the notice is given before the end of the period mentioned in that subsection it shall state that the offer is still open for acceptance.

430A(4) A notice under subsection (3) may specify a period for the exercise of the rights conferred by this section and in that event the rights shall not be exercisable after the end of that period; but no such period shall end less than three months after the end of the period within which the offer can be accepted.

430A(5) Subsection (3) does not apply if the offeror has given the shareholder a notice in respect of the shares in question under section 429.

430A(6) If the offeror fails to comply with subsection (3) he and, if the offeror is a company, every officer of the company who is in default or to whose neglect the failure is attributable, shall be liable to a fine and, for continued contravention, to a daily default fine.

430A(7) If an offeror other than a company is charged with an offence for failing to comply with subsection (3) it is a defence for him to prove that he took all reasonable steps for securing compliance with that subsection.

SEC. 430B   Effect of requirement under sec. 430A

430B(1) The following provisions shall, subject to section 430C, have effect where a shareholder exercises his rights in respect of any shares under section 430A.

430B(2) The offeror shall be entitled and bound to acquire those shares on the terms of the offer or on such other terms as may be agreed.

430B(3) Where the terms of an offer are such as to give the holder of shares a choice of consideration the holder of the shares may indicate his choice when requiring the offeror to acquire them and the notice given to the holder under section 430A(3)—

(a)   shall give particulars of the choice and of the rights conferred by this subsection; and

(b)   may state which consideration specified in the offer is to be taken as applying in default of his indicating a choice;

and the terms of the offer mentioned in subsection (2) shall be determined accordingly.

430B(4) Subsection (3) applies whether or not any time-limit or other conditions applicable to the choice under the terms of the offer can still be complied with; and if the consideration chosen by the holder of the shares—

(a)   is not cash and the offeror is no longer able to provide it; or

(b)   was to have been provided by a third party who is no longer bound or able to provide it,

the consideration shall be taken to consist of an amount of cash payable by the offeror which at the date when the holder of the shares requires the offeror to acquire them is equivalent to the chosen consideration.

Sch. 12

SEC. 430C   Applications to the court

430C(1) Where a notice is given under section 429 to the holder of any shares the court may, on an application made by him within six weeks from the date on which the notice was given—

(a)   order that the offeror shall not be entitled and bound to acquire the shares; or
(b)   specify terms of acquisition different from those of the offer.

430C(2) If an application to the court under subsection (1) is pending at the end of the period mentioned in subsection (5) of section 430 that subsection shall not have effect until the application has been disposed of.

430C(3) Where the holder of any shares exercises his rights under section 430A the court may, on an application made by him or the offeror, order that the terms on which the offeror is entitled and bound to acquire the shares shall be such as the court thinks fit.

430C(4) No order for costs or expenses shall be made against a shareholder making an application under subsection (1) or (3) unless the court considers—

(a)   that the application was unnecessary, improper or vexatious; or
(b)   that there has been unreasonable delay in making the application or unreasonable conduct on his part in conducting the proceedings on the application.

430C(5) Where a takeover offer has not been accepted to the extent necessary for entitling the offeror to give notices under subsection (1) or (2) of section 429 the court may, on the application of the offeror, make an order authorising him to give notices under that subsection if satisfied—

(a)   that the offeror has after reasonable enquiry been unable to trace one or more of the persons holding shares to which the offer relates;
(b)   that the shares which the offeror has acquired or contracted to acquire by virtue of acceptances of the offer, together with the shares held by the person or persons mentioned in paragraph (a), amount to not less than the minimum specified in that subsection; and
(c)   that the consideration offered is fair and reasonable;

but the court shall not make an order under this subsection unless it considers that it is just and equitable to do so having regard, in particular, to the number of shareholders who have been traced but who have not accepted the offer.

SEC. 430D   Joint offers

430D(1) A takeover offer may be made by two or more persons jointly and in that event this Part of this Act has effect with the following modifications.

430D(2) The conditions for the exercise of the rights conferred by sections 429 and 430A shall be satisfied by the joint offerors acquiring or contracting to acquire the necessary shares jointly (as respects acquisitions by virtue of acceptances of the offer) and either jointly or separately (in other cases); and, subject to the following provisions, the rights and obligations of the offeror under those sections and sections 430 and 430B shall be respectively joint rights and joint and several obligations of the joint offerors.

430D(3) It shall be a sufficient compliance with any provision of those sections requiring or authorising a notice or other document to be given or sent by or to the joint offerors that it is given or sent by or to any of them; but the statutory declaration required by section 429(4) shall be made by all of them and, in the case of a joint offeror being a company, signed by a director of that company.

Sch. 12

430D(4) In sections 428, 430(8) and 430E references to the offeror shall be construed as references to the joint offerors or any of them.

430D(5) In section 430(6) and (7) references to the offeror shall be construed as references to the joint offerors or such of them as they may determine.

430D(6) In sections 430(4)(a) and 430B(4)(a) references to the offeror being no longer able to provide the relevant consideration shall be construed as references to none of the joint offerors being able to do so.

430D(7) In section 430C references to the offeror shall be construed as references to the joint offerors except that any application under subsection (3) or (5) may be made by any of them and the reference in subsection (5)(a) to the offeror having been unable to trace one or more of the persons holding shares shall be construed as a reference to none of the offerors having been able to do so.

SEC. 430E   Associates

430E(1) The requirement in section 428(1) that a takeover offer must extend to all the shares, or all the shares of any class or classes, in a company shall be regarded as satisfied notwithstanding that the offer does not extend to shares which associates of the offeror hold or have contracted to acquire; but, subject to subsection (2), shares which any such associate holds or has contracted to acquire, whether at the time when the offer is made or subsequently, shall be disregarded for the purposes of any reference in this Part of this Act to the shares to which a takeover offer relates.

430E(2) Where during the period within which a takeover offer can be accepted any associate of the offeror acquires or contracts to acquire any of the shares to which the offer relates, then, if the condition specified in subsection (8)(a) or (b) of section 429 is satisfied as respects those shares they shall be treated for the purposes of that section as shares to which the offer relates.

430E(3) In section 430A(1)(b) and (2)(b) the reference to shares which the offeror has acquired or contracted to acquire shall include a reference to shares which any associate of his has acquired or contracted to acquire.

430E(4)   In this section "associate", in relation to an offeror means—

(a)   a nominee of the offeror;
(b)   a holding company, subsidiary or fellow subsidiary of the offeror or a nominee of such a holding company, subsidiary or fellow subsidiary;
(c)   a body corporate in which the offeror is substantially interested; or
(d)   any person who is, or is a nominee of, a party to an agreement with the offeror for the acquisition of, or of an interest in, the shares which are the subject of the takeover offer, being an agreement which includes provisions imposing obligations or restrictions such as are mentioned in section 204(2)(a).

430E(5) For the purposes of subsection (4)(b) a company is a fellow subsidiary of another body corporate if both are subsidiaries of the same body corporate but neither is a subsidiary of the other.

430E(6) For the purposes of subsection (4)(c) an offeror has a substantial interest in a body corporate if—

(a)   that body or its directors are accustomed to act in accordance with his directions or instructions; or
(b)   he is entitled to exercise or control the exercise of one-third or more of the voting power at general meetings of that body.

Sch. 12

430E(7) Subsections (5) and (6) of section 204 shall apply to subsection (4)(d) above as they apply to that section and subsections (3) and (4) of section 203 shall apply for the purposes of subsection (6) above as they apply for the purposes of subsection (2)(b) of that section.

430E(8) Where the offeror is an individual his associates shall also include his spouse and any minor child or step-child of his.

SEC. 430F   Convertible securities

430F(1) For the purposes of this Part of this Act securities of a company shall be treated as shares in the company if they are convertible into or entitle the holder to subscribe for such shares; and references to the holder of shares or a shareholder shall be construed accordingly.

430F(2) Subsection (1) shall not be construed as requiring any securities to be treated—

(a)   as shares of the same class as those into which they are convertible or for which the holder is entitled to subscribe; or

(b)   as shares of the same class as other securities by reason only that the shares into which they are convertible or for which the holder is entitled to subscribe are of the same class.

Schedule 13 — Disclosure of Information

Section 182

1 In section 133(2)(a) of the Fair Trading Act 1973 after the words "the Telecommunications Act 1984" there shall be inserted the words "or Chapter XIV of Part I of the Financial Services Act 1986".

2 In section 41(1)(a) of the Restrictive Trade Practices Act 1976 after the words "the Telecommunications Act 1984" there shall be inserted the words "or Chapter XIV of Part I of the Financial Services Act 1986".

3 (Repealed by the Banking Act 1987, sec. 108(2) and Sch. 7, Pt. I as from 1 October 1987.)

4 (Repealed by the Banking Act 1987, sec. 108(2) and Sch. 7, Pt. I as from 15 July 1987.)

5 At the end of section 19(3) of the Competition Act 1980 there shall be inserted—

"(h) Chapter XIV of Part I of the Financial Services Act 1986".

6 For subsections (1) and (2) of section 47A of the Insurance Companies Act 1982 there shall be substituted—

"**(1)** Subject to the following provisions of this section, no information relating to the business or other affairs of any person which has been obtained under section 44(2) to (4) above shall be disclosed without the consent of the person from whom the information was obtained and, if different, the person to whom it relates.

(2) Subsection (1) above shall not preclude the disclosure of information to any person who is a competent authority for the purposes of section 449 of the Companies Act 1985.

(2A) Subsection (1) above shall not preclude the disclosure of information as mentioned in any of the paragraphs except (m) of subsection (1) of section 180 of the Financial Services Act 1986 or in subsection (3) or (4) of that section or as mentioned in section 449(1) of the Companies Act 1985.

(2B) Subsection (1) above shall not preclude the disclosure of any such information as is mentioned in section 180(5) of the Financial Services Act 1986 by any person who by virtue of that section is not precluded by section 179 of that Act from disclosing it."

7 After subsection (1) of section 437 of the Companies Act 1985 there shall be inserted—

"**(1A)** Any persons who have been appointed under section 431 or 432 may at any time and, if the Secretary of State directs them to do so, shall inform him of any matters coming to their knowledge as a result of their investigations.";

and subsection (2) of section 433 of that Act shall be omitted.

8 In section 446 of that Act—

(a)   in subsection (3) for the words "to 436" there shall be substituted the words "to 437"; and

(b)   subsection (5) shall be omitted.

9(1) In subsection (1) of section 449 of that Act—

(a)   for paragraphs (a) and (b) there shall be substituted—

"(a) with a view to the institution of or otherwise for the purposes of criminal proceedings;".

(b)   for paragraph (d) there shall be substituted—

"(d) for the purpose of enabling or assisting the Secretary of State to exercise any of his functions under this Act, the Insider Dealing Act, the Prevention of Fraud (Investments) Act 1958, the Insurance Companies Act 1982, the Insolvency Act 1986, the Company Directors Disqualification Act 1986 or the Financial Services Act 1986.

(dd) for the purpose of enabling or assisting the Department of Economic Development for Northern Ireland to exercise any powers conferred on it by the enactments relating to companies or insolvency or for the purpose of enabling or assisting any inspector appointed by it under the enactments relating to companies to discharge his functions";

(c)   after paragraph (e) there shall be inserted—

"(f) for the purpose of enabling or assisting the Bank of England to discharge its functions under the Banking Act 1979 or any other functions,

(g) for the purpose of enabling or assisting the Deposit Protection Board to discharge its functions under that Act,

(h) for any purpose mentioned in section 180(1)(b), (e), (h), (n) or (p) of the Financial Services Act 1986,

(i) for the purpose of enabling or assisting the Industrial Assurance Commissioner or the Industrial Assurance Commissioner for Northern Ireland to discharge his functions under the enactments relating to industrial assurance,

(j) for the purpose of enabling or assisting the Insurance Brokers Registration Council to discharge its functions under the Insurance Brokers (Registration) Act 1977,

(k) for the purpose of enabling or assisting an official receiver to discharge his functions under the enactments relating to insolvency or for the purpose of enabling or assisting a body which is for the time being a recognised

Sch. 13

professional body for the purposes of section 391 of the Insolvency Act 1986 to discharge its functions as such,

(l) with a view to the institution of, or otherwise for the purposes of, any disciplinary proceedings relating to the exercise by a solicitor, auditor, accountant, valuer or actuary of his professional duties,

(m) for the purpose of enabling or assisting an authority in a country or territory outside the United Kingdom to exercise corresponding supervisory functions.".

9(2) After subsection (1) of that section there shall be inserted—

"**(1A)** In subsection (1) above **'corresponding supervisory functions'** means functions corresponding to those of the Secretary of State or the competent authority under the Financial Services Act 1986 or to those of the Secretary of State under the Insurance Companies Act 1982 or to those of the Bank of England under the Banking Act 1979 or any other functions in connection with rules of law corresponding to the provisions of the Insider Dealing Act or Part VII of the Financial Services Act 1986.

(1B) Subject to subsection (1C), subsection (1) shall not preclude publication or disclosure for the purpose of enabling or assisting any public or other authority for the time being designated for the purposes of this section by the Secretary of State by an order in a statutory instrument to discharge any functions which are specified in the order.

(1C) An order under subsection (1B) designating an authority for the purpose of that subsection may—

(a) impose conditions subject to which the publication or disclosure of any information or document is permitted by that subsection; and

(b) otherwise restrict the circumstances in which that subsection permits publication or disclosure.

(1D) Subsection (1) shall not preclude the publication or disclosure of any such information as is mentioned in section 180(5) of the Financial Services Act 1986 by any person who by virtue of that section is not precluded by section 179 of that Act from disclosing it."

9(3) For subsection (3) of that section (competent authorities) there shall be substituted—

"**(3)** For the purposes of this section each of the following is a competent authority—

(a) the Secretary of State,

(b) the Department of Economic Development for Northern Ireland and any officer of that Department,

(c) an inspector appointed under this Part by the Secretary of State,

(d) the Treasury and any officer of the Treasury,

(e) the Bank of England and any officer or servant of the Bank,

(f) the Lord Advocate,

(g) the Director of Public Prosecutions, and the Director of Public Prosecutions for Northern Ireland,

(h) any designated agency or transferee body within the meaning of the Financial Services Act 1986 and any officer or servant of such an agency or body,

Sch. 13

(i)   any person appointed or authorised to exercise any powers under section 94, 106 or 177 of the Financial Services Act 1986 and any officer or servant of such a person,

(j)   the body administering a scheme under section 54 of or paragraph 18 of Schedule 11 to that Act and any officer or servant of such a body,

(k)   the chief Registrar of friendly societies and the Registrar of Friendly Societies for Northern Ireland and any officer or servant of either of them,

(l)   the Industrial Assurance Commissioner and the Industrial Assurance Commissioner for Northern Ireland and any officer of either of them,

(m)   any constable,

(n)   any procurator fiscal.

(4) A statutory instrument containing an order under subsection (1B) is subject to annulment in pursuance of a resolution of either House of Parliament.".

10 After section 451 of that Act there shall be inserted—

"Disclosure of information by Secretary of State

451A The Secretary of State may, if he thinks fit, disclose any information obtained under this Part of this Act—

(a)   to any person who is a competent authority for the purposes of section 449, or

(b)   in any circumstances in which or for any purpose for which that section does not preclude the disclosure of the information to which it applies."

11 After Article 430(1) of the Companies (Northern Ireland) Order 1986 there shall be inserted—

"(1A) Any persons who have been appointed under Article 424 or 425 may at any time and, if the Department directs them to do so shall, inform it of any matters coming to their knowledge as a result of their investigation.";

and Article 426(2) of that Order shall be omitted.

12 In Article 439 of that Order—

(a)   in paragraph (3) for the words "to 429" there shall be substituted the words "to 430"; and

(b)   paragraph (5) shall be omitted.

13(1) In paragraph (1) of Article 442 of that Order—

(a)   for sub-paragraphs (a) and (b) there shall be substituted—

"(a) with a view to the institution of or otherwise for the purposes of criminal proceedings;";

(b)   for sub-paragraph (d) there shall be substituted—

"(d) for the purpose of enabling or assisting the Department to exercise any of its functions under this Order, the Insider Dealing Order or the Prevention of Fraud (Investments) Act (Northern Ireland) 1940;

(dd) for the purpose of enabling or assisting the Secretary of State to exercise any functions conferred on him by the enactments relating to companies or insolvency, the Prevention of Fraud (Investments) Act 1958, the Insurance Companies Act 1982, or the Financial Services Act 1986, or for the purpose of enabling or assisting any inspector appointed by him under the enactments relating to companies to discharge his functions";

(c)   after sub-paragraph (e) there shall be inserted—

"(f) for the purposes of enabling or assisting the Bank of England to discharge its functions under the Banking Act 1979 or any other functions;

(g) for the purposes of enabling or assisting the Deposit Protection Board to discharge its functions under that Act;

(h) for any purpose mentioned in section 180(1)(b), (e), (h), (n) or (p) of the Financial Services Act 1986;

(i) for the purpose of enabling or assisting the Industrial Assurance Commissioner for Northern Ireland or the Industrial Assurance Commissioner in Great Britain to discharge his functions under the enactments relating to industrial assurance;

(j) for the purpose of enabling or assisting the Insurance Brokers Registration Council to discharge its functions under the Insurance Brokers (Registration) Act 1977;

(k) for the purpose of enabling or assisting the official assignee to discharge his functions under the enactments relating to companies or bankruptcy;

(l) with a view to the institution of, or otherwise for the purposes of, any disciplinary proceedings relating to the exercise by a solicitor, auditor, accountant, valuer or actuary of his professional duties;

(m) for the purpose of enabling or assisting an authority in a country or territory outside the United Kingdom to exercise corresponding supervisory functions.".

13(2) After paragraph (1) of that Article there shall be inserted—

"**(1A)** In paragraph (1) '**corresponding supervisory functions**' means functions corresponding to those of the Secretary of State or the competent authority under the Financial Services Act 1986 or to those of the Secretary of State under the Insurance Companies Act 1982 or to those of the Bank of England under the Banking Act 1979 or any other functions in connection with rules of law corresponding to the provisions of the Insider Dealing Order or Part VII of the Financial Services Act 1986.

(1B) Subject to paragraph (1C), paragraph (1) shall not preclude publication or disclosure for the purpose of enabling or assisting any public or other authority for the time being designated for the purposes of this Article by an order made by the Department to discharge any functions which are specified in the order.

(1C) An order under paragraph (1B) designating an authority for the purpose of that paragraph may—

(a) impose conditions subject to which the publication or disclosure of any information or document is permitted by that paragraph; and

(b) otherwise restrict the circumstances in which that paragraph permits publication or disclosure.

(1D) Paragraph (1) shall not preclude the publication or disclosure of any such information as is mentioned in section 180(5) of the Financial Services Act 1986 by any person who by virtue of that section is not precluded by section 179 of that Act from disclosing it."

13(3) For paragraph (3) of that Article (competent authorities) there shall be substituted—

"**(3)** For the purposes of this Article each of the following is a competent authority—

(a) the Department and any officer of the Department,

(b)   the Secretary of State,

(c)   an inspector appointed under this Part by the Department,

(d)   the Department of Finance and Personnel and any officer of that Department;

(e)   the Treasury and any officer of the Treasury,

(f)   the Bank of England and any officer or servant of the Bank,

(g)   the Lord Advocate,

(h)   the Director of Public Prosecutions for Northern Ireland and the Director of Public Prosecutions in England and Wales,

(i)   any designated agency or transferee body within the meaning of the Financial Services Act 1986 and any officer or servant of such an agency or body,

(j)   any person appointed or authorised to exercise any powers under section 94, 106 or 177 of the Financial Services Act 1986 and any officer or servant of such a person,

(k)   the body administering a scheme under section 54 of or paragraph 18 of Schedule 11 to that Act and any officer or servant of such a body,

(l)   the Registrar of Friendly Societies and the Chief Registrar of friendly societies in Great Britain and any officer or servant of either of them,

(m)   the Industrial Assurance Commissioner for Northern Ireland and the Industrial Assurance Commissioner in Great Britain and any officer of either of them,

(n)   any constable,

(o)   any procurator fiscal.

(4) An order under paragraph (1B) is subject to negative resolution."

14 After Article 444 of that order there shall be inserted—

"Disclosure of information by Department

444A The Department may, if it thinks fit, disclose any information obtained under this Part—

(a)   to any person who is a competent authority for the purposes of Article 442, or

(b)   in any circumstances in which or for any purpose for which that Article does not preclude the disclosure of the information to which it applies.".

Schedule 14—Restriction of Rehabilitation of Offenders Act 1974

Section 189

Part I — Exempted Proceedings

1 Any proceedings with respect to a decision or proposed decision of the Secretary of State or a designated agency—

(a)   refusing, withdrawing or suspending an authorisation;

(b)   refusing an application under section 28(5) of this Act;

(c)   giving a direction under section 59 of this Act or refusing an application for consent or for the variation of a consent under that section;

Sch. 14

(d)   exercising a power under Chapter VI of Part I of this Act or refusing an application for the rescission or variation of a prohibition or requirement imposed under that Chapter;

(e)   refusing to make or revoking an order declaring a collective investment scheme to be an authorised unit trust scheme or a recognised scheme.

2 Any proceedings with respect to a decision or proposed decision of a recognised self-regulating organisation—

(a)   refusing or suspending a person's membership of the organisation;

(b)   expelling a member of the organisation;

(c)   exercising a power of the organisation for purposes corresponding to those of Chapter VI of Part I of this Act.

3(1) Any proceedings with respect to a decision or proposed decision of a recognised professional body—

(a)   refusing or suspending a person's membership of the body;

(b)   expelling a member of the body.

3(2) Any proceedings with respect to a decision or proposed decision of a recognised professional body or of any other body or person having functions in respect of the enforcement of the recognised professional body's rules relating to the carrying on of investment business—

(a)   exercising a power for purposes corresponding to those of Chapter VI of Part I of this Act;

(b)   refusing, suspending or withdrawing a certificate issued for the purposes of Part I of this Act.

4 Any proceedings with respect to a decision or proposed decision of the competent authority under Part IV of this Act refusing an application for listing or to discontinue or suspend the listing of any securities.

5 Any proceedings with respect to a decision or proposed decision of the Friendly Societies Commission or a transferee body, exercising a power exercisable by virtue of paragraph 23 of Schedule 11 to this Act or refusing an application for the rescission or variation of a prohibition or requirement imposed in the exercise of such a power.

6 Any proceedings with respect to a decision or proposed decision of a recognised self-regulating organisation for friendly societies—

(a)   refusing or suspending a society's membership of the organisation;

(b)   expelling a member of the organisation;

(c)   exercising a power of the organisation for purposes corresponding to those for which powers are exercisable by the Friendly Societies Commission by virtue of paragraph 23 of Schedule 11 to this Act.

Part II — Exempted Questions

1 The Secretary of State or a designated agency.

    (a) An authorised person.

    (b) An applicant for authorisation under section 26 of this Act.

    (c) A person whose authorisation is suspended.

Sch. 14

(d) The operator or trustee of a recognised scheme or a collective investment scheme in respect of which a notice has been given by the operator under section 87(3) or an application made under section 88 of this Act.

(e) An individual who is an associate of a person (whether or not an individual) described in paragraph (a), (b), (c) or (d) above.

2 A recognised self-regulating organisation or recognised professional body.

(a) A member of the organisation or body.

(b) An applicant for membership of the organisation or body.

(c) A person whose membership of the organisation or body is suspended.

(d) An individual who is an associate of a person (whether or not an individual) described in paragraph (a), (b) or (c) above.

3 A recognised professional body.

(a) A person certified by the body.

(b) An applicant for certification by the body.

(c) A person whose certification by the body is suspended.

(d) An individual who is an associate of a person (whether or not an individual) described in paragraph (a), (b) or (c) above.

4 A person (whether or not an individual) described in paragraph 1(a), (b), (c) or (d), paragraph 2(a), (b) or (c) or paragraph 3(a), (b) or (c) above.

An individual who is or is seeking to become an associate of the person in column 1.

5 The competent authority or any other person.

An individual from or in respect of whom information is sought in connection with an application for listing under Part IV of this Act.

6 The competent authority.

An individual who is or is seeking to become an associate of the issuer of securities listed under Part IV of this Act and from or in respect of whom information is sought which the issuer of the securities is required to furnish under listing rules.

7 The Friendly Societies Commission or a transferee body.

An individual who is an associate of a society which is authorised under section 23 of this Act.

Sch. 14

8 A recognised self-regulating organisation for friendly societies.

An individual who is an associate of a member or an applicant for membership of the organisation or of a society whose membership of the organisation is suspended.

Part III — Exempted Actions

1 The Secretary of State, a designated agency, a recognised self-regulating organisation, a recognised professional body, any other body or person mentioned in paragraph 3(2) of Part I of this Schedule or the competent authority.

Any such decision or proposed decision as is mentioned in Part I of this Schedule.

2 A person (whether or not an individual) described in paragraph 1(a), (b), (c) or (d), paragraph 2(a), (b) or (c) or paragraph 3(a), (b) or (c) of Part II of this Schedule.

Dismissing or excluding an individual from being or becoming an associate or the person in column 1.

3 The issuer of securities listed or subject to an application for listing under Part IV of this Act.

Dismissing or excluding an individual from being or becoming an associate of the issuer.

4 The Friendly Societies Commission, a transferee body or a recognised self-regulating organisation for friendly societies.

Any such decision or proposed decision as is mentioned in Part I of this Schedule.

Part IV — Supplemental

1 In Part I of this Schedule "proceedings" includes any proceedings within the meaning of section 4 of the Rehabilitation of Offenders Act 1974.

2 In Parts II and III of this Schedule—

(a) references to an applicant for authorisation, membership or certification are references to an applicant who has not yet been informed of the decision on his application;

(b) references to an application for listing under Part IV of this Act are references to an application the decision on which has not yet been communicated to the applicant and which is not taken by virtue of section 144(5) of this Act to have been refused.

3 Paragraph 1(d) of Part II of this Schedule and so much of paragraph 1(e) as relates to it—

(a) apply only if the question is put to elicit information for the purpose of determining whether the operator or trustee is a fit and proper person to act as operator or trustee of the scheme in question;

(b) apply in the case of a scheme in respect of which a notice has been given under subsection (3) of section 87 only until the end of the period within which the operator may receive a notification from the Secretary of State under that subsection or, if earlier, the receipt by him of such a notification;

(c) apply in the case of a scheme in respect of which an application has been made under section 88 only until the applicant has been informed of the decision on the application.

Schedule 15 — Transitional Provisions

Section 211(3)

INTERIM AUTHORISATION

1(1) If before such day as is appointed for the purposes of this paragraph by an order made by the Secretary of State a person has applied—

(a) for membership of any body which on that day is a recognised self-regulating organisation; or

(b) for authorisation by the Secretary of State,

and the application has not been determined before the day on which section 3 of this Act comes into force, that person shall, subject to sub-paragraphs (2), (3) and (4) below, be treated until the determination of the application as if he had been granted an authorisation by the Secretary of State.

Note
See the Financial Services Act 1986 (Applications for Authorisation) (Appointed Day) Order 1987 (SI 1987/2157).

1(2) Sub-paragraph (1) above does not apply to a person who immediately before the day on which section 3 of this Act comes into force is prohibited by the Prevention of Fraud (Investments) Act 1958 (in this Schedule referred to as "the previous Act") from carrying on the business of dealing in securities—

(a) by reason of the refusal or revocation at any time before that day of a licence under that Act; or

(b) by reason of the revocation at any time before that day of an order declaring him to be an exempted dealer.

1(3) If a person who has made any such application as is mentioned in sub-paragraph (1) above has before the day on which section 3 of this Act comes into force been served with a notice under section 6 or 16(3) of the previous Act (proposed refusal or revocation of licence or proposed revocation of exemption order) but the refusal or revocation to which the notice relates has not taken place before that day—

(a) the provisions of that Act with respect to the refusal or revocation of a licence or the revocation of an order under section 16 of that Act shall continue to apply to him until the application mentioned in sub-paragraph (1) above is determined; and

(b) that sub-paragraph shall cease to apply to him if before the determination of the application mentioned in that sub-paragraph his application for a licence under that Act is refused, his licence under that Act is revoked or the order declaring him to be an exempted dealer under that Act is revoked.

1(4) Notwithstanding sub-paragraph (1) above section 102(1)(a) of this Act shall not apply to a person entitled to carry on investment business by virtue of that sub-paragraph but the Secretary of State may make available for public inspection the information with respect to the holders of principal's licences mentioned in section 9 of the previous Act, any information in his possession by virtue of section 15(3) or (4) of that Act and the information mentioned in section 16(4) of that Act.

1(5) Notwithstanding subsection (2) of section 3 of the previous Act a licence granted under that section before the day on which section 3 of this Act comes into force shall, unless revoked under section 6 of that Act, continue in force until that day.

Sch. 15

RETURN OF FEES ON PENDING APPLICATIONS

2 Any fee paid in respect of an application under section 3 of the previous Act which is pending on the day on which that Act is repealed shall be repaid to the applicant.

DEPOSITS AND UNDERTAKINGS

3 The repeal of section 4 of the previous Act shall not affect the operation of that section in a case where—

(a)   a sum deposited in accordance with that section has become payable as provided in subsection (2) of that section before the date on which the repeal takes effect; or

(b)   a sum has become payable before that date in pursuance of an undertaking given under subsection (4) of that section,

but, subject as aforesaid, any sum deposited under that section may be withdrawn by the depositor on application to the Accountant General of the Supreme Court and any undertaking given under that section shall be discharged.

INTERIM RECOGNITION OF PROFESSIONAL BODIES

4(1) If on an application made under section 17 of this Act it appears to the Secretary of State that any of the requirements of section 18(3) of this Act or paragraphs 2 to 6 of Schedule 3 to this Act are not satisfied he may in accordance with this paragraph make a recognition order under section 18 of this Act ("an interim recognition order") notwithstanding that all or any of those requirements are not satisfied.

4(2) The Secretary of State may, subject to sub-paragraphs (3) and (4) below, make an interim recognition order if he is satisfied—

(a)   that the applicant proposes to adopt rules and practices and to make arrangements which will satisfy such of the requirements mentioned in sub-paragraph (1) above as are not satisfied;

(b)   that it is not practicable for those rules, practices and arrangements to be brought into effect before the date on which section 3 of this Act comes into force but that they will be brought into effect within a reasonable time thereafter; and

(c)   that in the meantime the applicant will enforce its existing rules in such a way, and issue such guidance, as will in respect of investment business of any kind carried on by persons certified by it (or by virtue of paragraph 5 below treated as certified by it) afford to investors protection as nearly as may be equivalent to that provided as respects investment business of that kind by the rules and regulations under Chapter V of Part I of this Act.

4(3) Where the requirements which are not satisfied consist of or include those mentioned in paragraph 2 of Schedule 3 to this Act an application for an interim recognition order shall be accompanied by—

(a)   a list of the persons to whom the applicant proposes to issue certificates for the purposes of Part I of this Act; and

(b)   particulars of the criteria adopted for determining the persons included in the list;

and the Secretary of State shall not make the order unless it appears to him that those criteria conform as nearly as may be to the conditions mentioned in that paragraph and that the applicant will, until the requirements of that paragraph are satisfied, have arrangements for securing that no person is certified by it (or by virtue of paragraph 5 below treated as certified by it) except in accordance with those criteria and for the effective monitoring of continued compliance by those persons with those criteria.

Sch. 15

4(4) Where the requirements which are not satisfied consist of or include that mentioned in paragraph 6 of Schedule 3 to this Act, the Secretary of State shall not make an interim recognition order unless it appears to him that the applicant will, until that requirement is satisfied, take such steps for complying with it as are reasonably practicable.

4(5) An application for an interim recognition order shall be accompanied by a copy of the rules and by particulars of the practices and arrangements referred to in sub-paragraph (2)(a) above.

4(6) An interim recognition order shall not be revocable but shall cease to be in force at the end of such period as is specified in it; and that period shall be such as will in the opinion of the Secretary of State allow a reasonable time for the rules, practices and arrangements mentioned in sub-paragraph (5) above to be brought into effect.

4(7) The Secretary of State may on the application of the body to which an interim recognition order relates extend the period specified in it if that body satisfies him—

(a)   that there are sufficient reasons why the rules, practices and arrangements mentioned in sub-paragraph (5) above cannot be brought into effect by the end of that period; and

(b)   that those rules, practices and arrangements, or other rules, practices and arrangements which satisfy the requirements mentioned in sub-paragraph (2)(a) above and of which copies or particulars are furnished to the Secretary of State, will be brought into effect within a reasonable time thereafter;

but not more than one application shall be made by a body under this sub-paragraph.

4(8) A recognition order under section 18 of this Act shall cease to be an interim recognition order if before it ceases to be in force—

(a)   the rules, practices and arrangements of which copies or particulars were furnished to the Secretary of State under sub-paragraph (5) or (7)(b) above are brought into effect; or

(b)   the Secretary of State certifies that other rules, practices and arrangements which have been brought into effect comply with the requirements mentioned in sub-paragraph (1) above.

4(9) In this paragraph references to the adoption of rules or the making of arrangements include references to taking such other steps as may be necessary for bringing them into effect.

INTERIM AUTHORISATION BY RECOGNISED PROFESSIONAL BODIES

5(1) If at the time when an interim recognition order is made in respect of a professional body that body is unable to issue certificates for the purposes of this Act, any person who at that time is included in the list furnished by that body to the Secretary of State in accordance with paragraph 4(3)(a) above shall be treated for the purposes of this Act as a person certified by that body.

5(2) If at any time while an interim recognition order is in force in respect of a professional body and before the body is able to issue certificates as mentioned in sub-paragraph (1) above the body notifies the Secretary of State that a person not included in that list satisfies the criteria of which particulars were furnished by the body in accordance with paragraph 4(3)(b) above, that person shall, on receipt of the

Sch. 15

notification by the Secretary of State, be treated for the purposes of this Act as a person certified by that body.

5(3) If at any time while an interim recognition order is in force in respect of a professional body it appears to the body—

(a)   that a person treated by virtue of sub-paragraph (1) or (2) above as certified by it has ceased (after the expiration of such transitional period, if any, as appears to the body to be appropriate) to satisfy the criteria mentioned in sub-paragraph (2) above; or

(b)   that any such person should for any other reason cease to be treated as certified by it,

it shall forthwith give notice of that fact to the Secretary of State and the person in question shall, on receipt of that notification by the Secretary of State, cease to be treated as certified by that body.

5(4) Where by virtue of this paragraph a partnership is treated as certified by a recognised professional body section 15(3) of this Act shall apply as it applies where a certificate has in fact been issued to a partnership.

5(5) Where by virtue of this paragraph any persons are treated as certified by a recognised professional body the requirements of paragraph 2 of Schedule 3 to this Act so far as relating to the retention by a person of a certificate issued by that body and the requirements of paragraph 4 of that Schedule shall apply to the body as if the references to persons certified by it included references to persons treated as certified.

POWER OF RECOGNISED PROFESSIONAL BODY TO MAKE RULES REQUIRED BY THIS ACT

6(1) Where a recognised professional body regulates the practice of a profession in the exercise of statutory powers the matters in respect of which rules can be made in the exercise of those powers shall, if they would not otherwise do so, include any matter in respect of which rules are required to be made—

(a)   so that the recognition order in respect of that body can cease to be an interim recognition order; or

(b)   where the recognition order was not, or has ceased to be, an interim recognition order, so that the body can continue to be a recognised professional body.

6(2) Rules made by virtue of this paragraph may in particular make provision for the issue, withdrawal and suspension of certificates for the purposes of this Act and the making of charges in respect of their issue and may accordingly apply to persons who are, or are to be, certified or treated as certified by the body in question whether or not they are persons in relation to whom rules could be made apart from this paragraph.

6(3) Rules made by virtue of this paragraph may make different provision for different cases.

6(4) The Secretary of State may at the request of a recognised professional body by order extend, modify or exclude any statutory provision relating to the regulation of the conduct, practice, or discipline of members of that body to such extent as he thinks necessary or expedient in consequence of the provisions of this paragraph; and any order made by virtue of this sub-paragraph shall be subject to annulment in pursuance of a resolution of either House of Parliament.

Sch. 15

NOTICE OF COMMENCEMENT OF BUSINESS

7 In the case of a person who is carrying on investment business in the United Kingdom on the day on which section 31 of this Act comes into force, section 32 of this Act shall have effect as if it required him to give the notice referred to in that section forthwith.

ADVERTISEMENTS

8 (Repealed by the Public Offers of Securities Regulations 1995 (SI 1995/1537), reg. 1, 17 and Sch. 2, para. 9 as from 19 June 1995.)

AUTHORISED UNIT TRUST SCHEMES

9(1) Where an order under section 17 of the previous Act (authorisation of unit trust schemes) is in force in respect of a unit trust scheme immediately before the coming into force of Chapter VIII of Part I of this Act the scheme shall be treated as an authorised unit trust scheme under that Part and the order as an order under section 78 of this Act.

9(2) In relation to any such authorised unit trust scheme the reference in section 79(1)(a) of this Act to the requirements for the making of the order shall be construed as a reference to the requirements for the making of an order under section 78, but the scheme shall not be regarded as failing to comply with those requirements by reason of the manager or trustee not being an authorised person if he is treated as such a person by virtue of paragraph 1 above.

9(3) If before the day on which Chapter VIII of Part I comes into force a notice in respect of a scheme has been served under subsection (2) of section 17 of the previous Act (proposed revocation of authorisation of unit trust scheme) but the revocation has not taken place before that day, the provisions of that subsection shall continue to apply in relation to the scheme and sub-paragraph (1) above shall cease to apply to it if the authorisation is revoked under that subsection.

RECOGNISED COLLECTIVE INVESTMENT SCHEMES

10(1) If at any time before the coming into force of section 86 of this Act it appears to the Secretary of State that the law of a member State other than the United Kingdom confers rights on the managers and trustees of authorised unit trust schemes entitling them to carry on in that State on terms equivalent to those of that section—

(a) investment business which consists in operating or acting as trustee in relation to such schemes; and

(b) any investment business which is carried on by them in connection with or for the purposes of such schemes,

he may by order direct that schemes constituted in that State which satisfy such requirements as are specified in the order shall be recognised schemes for the purposes of this Act.

10(2) Subsections (2) to (9) of section 86 of this Act shall have effect in relation to any scheme recognised by virtue of this paragraph; and the references in section 24 and 207(1) of this Act to a scheme recognised under section 86, and in section 76(1) of this Act to a scheme recognised under Chapter VIII of Part I of this Act, shall include references to any scheme recognised by virtue of this paragraph.

10(3) In section 86(3)(a) as applied by sub-paragraph (2) above the reference to the rights conferred by any relevant Community instrument shall be construed as a reference to the rights conferred by virtue of an order made under this paragraph.

Sch. 15

Note
See the Financial Services (Recognised Collective Investment Schemes from other Member States) (Luxembourg) Order 1988 (SI 1988/2258) and the FinancialServices (Recognised Collective Investment Schemes from Other Member States) (Luxembourg) Order 1988 (Revocation) Order 1989 (SI 1989/1586).

11(1) Subsection (7) of section 88 of this Act shall not apply to a scheme which is in existence on the date on which this Act is passed if—

(a)   the units under the scheme are included in the Official List of The Stock Exchange and have been so included throughout the period of five years ending on the date on which this paragraph comes into force;

(b)   the law of the country or territory in which the scheme is established precludes the participants being entitled or the operator being required as mentioned in that subsection; and

(c)   throughout the period of five years ending on the date on which the application is made under that section, units under the scheme have in fact been regularly redeemed as mentioned in that subsection or the operator has in fact regularly ensured that participants were able to sell their units as there mentioned.

11(2) The grounds for revoking an order made under section 88 of this Act by virtue of this paragraph shall include the ground that it appears to the Secretary of State that since the making of the order units under the scheme have ceased to be regularly redeemed or the operator has ceased regularly to ensure their sale as mentioned in sub-paragraph (1)(c) above.

DELEGATION ORDERS

12(1) A delegation order may transfer a function notwithstanding that the provision conferring it has not yet come into force but no such function shall be exercisable by virtue of the order until the coming into force of that provision.

12(2) Sub-paragraph (1) above applies also to a transfer order under paragraph 28(1) of Schedule 11 to this Act.

Note
See the Financial Services (Transfer of Functions Relating to Friendly Societies) Order (Northern Ireland) 1987 (SI 1987/228); the Financial Services (Transfer of Functions Relating to Friendly Societes) Order 1987 (SI 1987/925); and the Financial Services Act 1986 (Delegation) Order 1987 (SI 1987/942).

DISCLOSURE OF INFORMATION

13 In determining for the purposes of section 180(6) of this Act and the enactments amended by paragraphs 3(2), 9(2) and 13(2) of Schedule 13 to this Act whether the functions of an authority in a country or territory outside the United Kingdom correspond to functions conferred by any of the provisions of this Act regard shall be had to those provisions whether or not they have already come into force.

TEMPORARY EXEMPTIONS FOR FRIENDLY SOCIETIES

14(1) A friendly society which transacts no investment business after the date on which section 3 of this Act comes into force except for the purpose of making or carrying out relevant existing members' contracts shall be treated for the purposes of that section as if it were an exempted person under Chapter IV of Part I of this Act.

14(2) Subject to sub-paragraph (3) below, for the purposes of this paragraph "relevant existing members' contracts", in relation to any society, means—

(a)   contracts made by the society before that date; and

(b)   in the case of a small income society—
       (i)   during the period of three years beginning with that date, tax exempt investment agreements made by it with persons who were members of the society before that date; and
      (ii)   after the expiry of that period, tax exempt investment agreements made by it with such persons before the expiry of that period.

14(3) Paragraph (b) of sub-paragraph (2) above shall not apply to a friendly society after the expiry of the period of two years beginning with that date unless before the expiry of that period it has by special resolution (within the meaning of the Friendly Societies Act 1974) determined—

(a)   to transact no further investment business except for the purpose of carrying out contracts entered into before the expiry of the said period of three years; or

(b)   to take such action as is necessary to procure the transfer of its engagements to another such society or a company or the amalgamation of the society with another such society under section 82 of the said Act of 1974,

and a copy of that resolution has been registered in accordance with section 86 of the said Act of 1974.

14(4) For the purpose of sub-paragraph (2) above a society is a small income society if its income in 1985 from members' contributions did not exceed £50,000.

14(5) For the purposes of sub-paragraph (2) above an investment agreement is a tax exempt investment agreement if the society by which it is made may obtain exemption from income and corporation tax on the profits from it under section 460(1) or 461(1) of the Income and Corporation Taxes Act 1988.

14(6) A society to which sub-paragraph (1) or (2) above applies shall not be an authorised person for the purposes of this Act nor a regulated friendly society for the purposes of the provisions of Schedule 11 to this Act.

DEALINGS IN COURSE OF NON-INVESTMENT BUSINESS

15 If before the day on which section 3 of this Act comes into force a person has applied for permission under paragraph 23 of Schedule 1 to this Act and the application has not been determined before that day, that person shall, until the determination of the application and subject to his complying with such requirements as the Secretary of State may impose, be treated as if he had been granted a permission under that paragraph.

NORTHERN IRELAND

16 The foregoing provisions shall apply to Northern Ireland with the substitution for references to the previous Act or any provision of that Act of references to the Prevention of Fraud (Investments) Act (Northern Ireland) 1940 and the corresponding provision of that Act.

Schedule 16 — Consequential Amendments

Section 212(2)

1 (Repealed by Charities Act 1993, sec. 98(2), 99(1) and Sch. 7 as from 1 August 1993.)

Sch. 16

2 In the Trustee Investments Act 1961—

(a)   in section 11(3) for the words "the Prevention of Fraud (Investments) Act 1958 or the Prevention of Fraud (Investments) Act (Northern Ireland) 1940" there shall be substituted the words "the Financial Services Act 1986";

(b)   for paragraph 3 of Part III of Schedule 1 there shall be substituted—

   "**3**   In any units of an authorised unit trust scheme within the meaning of the Financial Services Act 1986";

(c)   in paragraph 2(a) of Part IV of Schedule 1 for the words from "a recognised stock exchange" onwards there shall be substituted the words "a recognised investment exchange within the meaning of the Financial Services Act 1986";

(d)   in the definition of "securities" in paragraph 4 of Part IV of that Schedule after the word "debentures" there shall be inserted the words "units within paragraph 3 of Part III of this Schedule".

3   In section 32 of the Clergy Pensions Measure 1961 No. 3—

(a)   for paragraph (t) of subsection (1) there shall be substituted—

   "(t) in any units in any authorised unit trust scheme or a recognised scheme within the meaning of the Financial Services Act 1986"; and

(b)   in subsection (5)(a) for the words from "a recognised stock exchange" onwards there shall be substituted the words "a recognised investment exchange within the meaning of the Financial Services Act 1986.".

4 In the Stock Transfer Act 1963—

(a)   for paragraph (e) of section 1(4) there shall be substituted—

   "(e) units of an authorised unit trust scheme or a recognised scheme within the meaning of the Financial Services Act 1986"; and

(b)   in the definition of "securities" in section 4(1) for the words from "unit trust scheme" to "scheme" there shall be substituted the words "collective investment scheme within the meaning of the Financial Services Act 1986".

5 In the Stock Transfer Act (Northern Ireland) 1963—

(a)   for paragraph (e) of section 1(4) there shall be substituted—

   "(e) units of an authorised unit trust scheme or a recognised scheme within the meaning of the Financial Services Act 1986"; and

(b)   in the definition of "securities" in section 4(1) for the words from "unit trust scheme" to "scheme" there shall be substituted the words "collective investment scheme within the meaning of the Financial Services Act 1986".

6 In section 25 of the Charities Act (Northern Ireland) 1964—

(a)   subsection (16) shall be omitted; and

(b)   in subsection (17) for the words "Subsections (15) and (16)" there shall be substituted the words "Subsection (15)".

7 In the Local Authorities' Mutual Investment Trust Act 1968—

(a)   in section 1(2) for the words "recognised stock exchange within the meaning of the Prevention of Fraud (Investments) Act 1958" there shall be substituted the words "recognised investment exchange within the meaning of the Financial Services Act 1986"; and

(b)   in the definition of "unit trust scheme" in section 2 for the words "Prevention of Fraud (Investments) Act 1958" there shall be substituted the words "Financial Services Act 1986".

Sch. 16

8 In the Local Government Act 1972—

(a)   in section 98(1) for the words from "and" onwards there shall be substituted the words "means—

   (a)   investments falling within any of paragraphs 1 to 6 of Schedule 1 to the Financial Services Act 1986 or, so far as relevant to any of those paragraphs, paragraph 11 of that Schedule; or

   (b)   rights (whether actual or contingent) in respect of money lent to, or deposited with, any society registered under the Industrial and Provident Societies Act 1965 or any building society within the meaning of the Building Societies Act 1986."; and

(b)   for the definition of "securities" in section 146(2) there shall be substituted—

   "**'securities'** has the meaning given in section 98(1) above".

9   For subsection (1) of section 42 of the Local Government (Scotland) Act 1973 there shall be substituted—

   "**(1)** In sections 39 and 41 of this Act **'securities'** means—

(a)   investments falling within any of paragraphs 1 to 6 of Schedule 1 to the Financial Services Act 1986 or, so far as relevant to any of those paragraphs, paragraph 11 of that Schedule; or

(b)   rights (whether actual or contingent) in respect of money lent to, or deposited with, any society registered under the Industrial and Provident Societies Act 1965 or any building society within the meaning of the Building Societies Act 1986."

10 For paragraph 20 of Schedule 1 to the Industry Act 1975 there shall be substituted—

   "**20**   Section 57 of the Financial Services Act 1986 (restrictions on advertising) shall not apply to any investment advertisement within the meaning of that section which the Board issue or cause to be issued in the discharge of their functions."

11   (Repealed by Enterprise and New Towns (Scotland) Act 1990, sec. 38(2), 39(1), (3) and Sch. 5, Pt. I as from 1 April 1991.)

12   For paragraph 21 of Schedule 1 to the Welsh Development Agency Act 1975 there shall be substituted—

   "**21**   Section 57 of the Financial Services Act 1986 (restrictions on advertising) shall not apply to any investment advertisement within the meaning of that section which the Agency issue or cause to be issued in the discharge of their functions.".

13   In section 3(5) of the Aircraft and Shipbuilding Industries Act 1977 the words "Sections 428 to 430 of the Companies Act 1985 and" shall be omitted and for the words "those sections" there shall be substituted the words "that section".

14   In paragraph 10(1)(c) of Part II of Schedule 10 to the Finance Act 1980 for the words "sections 428 to 430" there shall be substituted the words "sections 428 to 430F".

15   For the definition of "securities" in section 3(6) of the Licensing (Alcohol Education and Research) Act 1981 there shall be substituted—

   "**'securities'** means any investments falling within any of paragraphs 1 to 6 of Schedule 1 to the Financial Services Act 1986 or, so far as relevant to any of those paragraphs, paragraph 11 of that Schedule".

Sch. 16

16 (Repealed by the Public Offers of Securities Regulations 1995 (SI 1995/1537), reg. 1, 17 and Sch. 2, para. 5(e) as from 19 June 1995.)

17 In section 163 of the Companies Act 1985—

(a)   for the words "a recognised stock exchange" in each place where they occur there shall be substituted the words "a recognised investment exchange";

(b)   for the words "that stock exchange" in subsection (1) there shall be substituted the words "that investment exchange";

(c)   in subsection (2) in paragraph (a) for the words "on that stock exchange" there shall be substituted the words "under Part IV of the Financial Services Act 1986" and in paragraph (b) for the words "that stock exchange" in both places where they occur there shall be substituted the words "that investment exchange";

(d)   after subsection (3) of that section there shall be inserted—

"**(4)**   In this section 'recognised investment exchange' means a recognised investment exchange other than an overseas investment exchange within the meaning of the Financial Services Act 1986."

18 In section 209(1)(c) of the Companies Act 1985 for the words "the Prevention of Fraud (Investments) Act 1958" there shall be substituted the words "the Financial Services Act 1986".

19 In section 265(4)(a) of the Companies Act 1985 for the words "recognised stock exchange" there shall be substituted the words "recognised investment exchange other than an overseas investment exchange within the meaning of the Financial Services Act 1986".

20 In section 329(1) of the Companies Act 1985 for the words "recognised stock exchange", "that stock exchange" and "the stock exchange" there shall be substituted respectively the words "recognised investment exchange other than an overseas investment exchange within the meaning of the Financial Services Act 1986", "that investment exchange" and "the investment exchange".

21 For paragraphs (a) to (c) of section 446(4) of the Companies Act 1985 there shall be substituted—

"(a)   to any individual who is an authorised person within the meaning of the Financial Services Act 1986;

(b)   to any individual who holds a permission granted under paragraph 23 of Schedule 1 to that Act;

(c)   to any officer (whether past or present) of a body corporate which is such an authorised person or holds such a permission;

(d)   to any partner (whether past or present) in a partnership which is such an authorised person or holds such a permission;

(e)   to any member of the governing body or officer (in either case whether past or present) of an unincorporated association which is such an authorised person or holds such a permission".

22 (Repealed by Companies Act 1989, sec. 212 and Sch. 24 as from 1 April 1990.)

23 In Schedule 4 to the Companies Act 1985—

(a)   in paragraph 45 for the words "recognised stock exchange" there shall be substituted the words "recognised investment exchange other than an overseas investment exchange within the meaning of the Financial Services Act 1986"; and

(b)   in paragraph 84 for the words from "on a recognised stock exchange" onwards there shall be substituted the words "on a recognised investment exchange other

Sch. 16

than an overseas investment exchange within the meaning of the Financial Services Act 1986 or on any stock exchange of repute outside Great Britain".

24 In Schedule 9 to the Companies Act 1985 in paragraphs 10(3) and 33 for the words "recognised stock exchange" there shall be substituted the words "recognised investment exchange other than an overseas investment exchange within the meaning of the Financial Services Act 1986".

25 In paragraph 11 of Schedule 13 to the Companies Act 1985 for paragraph (a) there shall be substituted—

"(a) any unit trust scheme which is an authorised unit trust scheme within the meaning of the Financial Services Act 1986".

26 In Schedule 22 to the Companies Act 1985, in the second column of the entry relating to section 185(4) for the words "stock exchange" there shall be substituted the words "clearing house or".

27 In Schedule 24 to the Companies Act 1985—

(a)   in the second column of the entry relating to section 329(3) for the words "stock exchange" there shall be substituted the words "investment exchange"; and

(b)   after the entry relating to section 427(5) there shall be inserted—

| "429(6) | Offeror failing to send copy of notice or making statutory declaration knowing it to be false, etc. | 1. On indictment. 2. Summary. | 2 years or a fine; or both. 6 months or the statutory maximum; or both. | One-fiftieth of the statutory maximum. |
| 430A(6) | Offeror failing to give notice of rights to minority shareholder. | 1. On indictment. 2. Summary. | A fine. The statutory maximum. | One-fiftieth of the statutory maximum." |

28 (Repealed by Criminal Justice Act 1993, sec. 79(14) and Sch. 6, Pt. I as from 1 March 1994.)

29 For paragraph (c) of section 10(1) of the Bankruptcy (Scotland) Act 1985 there shall be substituted—

"(c) a petition is before a court for the winding up of the debtor under Part IV or V of the Insolvency Act 1986 or section 72 of the Financial Services Act 1986;".

30 In section 101 of the Building Societies Act 1986—

(a)   for paragraph (1)(a) there shall be substituted—

"(a) offer for sale or invite subscription for any shares in or debentures of the company or allot or agree to allot any such shares or debentures with a view to their being offered for sale;";

(b)   in subsection (1) after the words "the effect of the offer" there shall be inserted the words "the invitation"; and

(c)   in subsection (2) for the words "the public" there shall be substituted the words ", invite subscription for,".

31 In Article 107 of the Companies (Northern Ireland) Order 1986—

(a)   in paragraph (1) after the word "conditions" there shall be inserted the words "and any conditions which apply in respect of any such payment by virtue of rules made under section 169(2) of the Financial Services Act 1986"

(b)   in sub-paragraph (2)(a) for the words from "10 per cent" onwards there shall be substituted the words—

Sch. 16

"(i) any limit imposed on it by those rules or, if none is so imposed, 10 per cent of the price at which the shares are issued; or

(ii) the amount or rate authorised by the articles, whichever is the less".

32 In Article 173 of the Companies (Northern Ireland) Order 1986—

(a) for the words "a recognised stock exchange", in each place where they occur, there shall be substituted the words "a recognised investment exchange";

(b) for the words "that stock exchange" in paragraph (1) there shall be substituted the words "that investment exchange";

(c) in paragraph (2), in sub-paragraph (a) for the words "on that stock exchange" there shall be substituted the words "under Part IV of the Financial Services Act 1986" and in sub-paragraph (b) for the words "that stock exchange" in both places where they occur there shall be substituted the words "that investment exchange";

(d) after paragraph (3) there shall be inserted—

"**(4)** In this Article **'recognised investment exchange'** means a recognised investment exchange other than an overseas investment exchange within the meaning of the Financial Services Act 1986."

33 In Article 217(1)(b) of the Companies (Northern Ireland) Order 1986 for the words "the Prevention of Fraud (Investments) Act (Northern Ireland) 1940 or of the Prevention of Fraud (Investments) Act 1958" there shall be substituted the words "the Financial Services Act 1986".

34 In Article 273(4)(a) of the Companies (Northern Ireland) Order 1986 for the words "recognised stock exchange" there shall be substituted the words "recognised investment exchange other than an overseas investment exchange within the meaning of the Financial Services Act 1986".

35 In Article 337(1) of the Companies (Northern Ireland) Order 1986 for the words "recognised stock exchange", "that stock exchange" and "the stock exchange" there shall be substituted respectively the words "recognised investment exchange", "that investment exchange" and "the investment exchange".

36 For sub-paragraphs (a) to (c) of Article 439(4) of the Companies (Northern Ireland) Order 1986 there shall be substituted—

"(a) to any individual who is an authorised person within the meaning of the Financial Services Act 1986;

(b) to any individual who holds a permission granted under paragraph 23 of Schedule 1 to that Act;

(c) to an officer (whether past or present) of a body corporate which is such an authorised person or holds such a permission;

(d) to any partner (whether past or present) in a partnership which is such an authorised person or holds such a permission;

(e) to any member of the governing body or officer (in either case whether past or present) of an unincorporated association which is such an authorised person or holds such a permission".

37 (Repealed by Companies (No. 2) (Northern Ireland) Order 1990 (SI 1990/1504 (NI 10)), art. 113 and Sch. 6 as from 11 March 1991.)

38 In Schedule 4 to the Companies (Northern Ireland) Order 1986—

(a) in paragraph 45 for the words "recognised stock exchange" there shall be substituted the words "recognised investment exchange other than an overseas investment exchange within the meaning of the Financial Services Act 1986"

Sch. 16

(b) in paragraph 83 for the words from "on a recognised stock exchange" onwards there shall be substituted the words "on a recognised investment exchange other than an overseas investment exchange within the meaning of the Financial Services Act 1986 or on any stock exchange of repute outside Northern Ireland".

39 In Schedule 9 to the Companies (Northern Ireland) Order 1986, in paragraph 10(3) and 33 for the words "recognised stock exchange" there shall be substituted the words "recognised investment exchange other than an overseas investment exchange within the meaning of the Financial Services Act 1986."

40 In paragraph 11 of Schedule 13 to the Companies (Northern Ireland) Order 1986 for paragraph (a) there shall be substituted—

"(a) any unit trust scheme which is an authorised unit trust scheme within the meaning of the Financial Services Act 1986".

41 In Schedule 21 to the Companies (Northern Ireland) Order 1986 in the second column of the entry relating to Article 195(4) for the words "stock exchange" there shall be substituted the words "clearing house or".

42 In Schedule 23 to the Companies (Northern Ireland) Order 1986 in the second column of the entry relating to Article 337(3) for the words "stock exchange" there shall be substituted the words "investment exchange".

43 (Repealed by Criminal Justice Act 1993, sec. 79(14) and Sch. 6, Pt. I as from 1 March 1994.)

Schedule 17—Repeals and Revocations

Section 212(3)

Part I — Enactments

Chapter	Short title	Extent of repeal
4 & 5 Geo. 6. c. 9 (N. I.).	The Prevention of Fraud (Investments) Act (Northern Ireland) 1940.	The whole Act.
6 & 7 Eliz. 2. c. 45.	The Prevention of Fraud (Investments) Act 1958.	The whole Act.
8 & 9 Eliz. 2. c. 58.	The Charities Act 1960.	Section 22(10).
10 & 11 Eliz. 2. c. 23.	The South Africa Act 1962.	In Schedule 4, the entry relating to the Prevention of Fraud (Investments) Act 1958.
1964 c. 33 (N. I.).	The Charities Act (Northern Ireland) 1964.	Section 25(16).
1965 c. 2.	The Administration of Justice Act 1965.	Section 14(1)(e) and 5(e). In Schedule 1, the entry relating to the Prevention of Fraud (Investments) Act 1958.

Sch. 17

Chapter	Short title	Extent of repeal
1971 c. 62.	The Tribunals and Inquiries Act 1971.	In Part I of Schedule 1, the entry relating to the tribunal constituted under section 6 of the Prevention of Fraud (Investments) Act 1958.
1972 c. 71.	The Criminal Justice Act 1972.	In Schedule 5, the entry relating to the Prevention of Fraud (Investments) Act 1958.
1975 c. 24.	The House of Commons Disqualification Act 1975.	In Part II of Schedule 1 the words "The Tribunal established under the Prevention of Fraud (Investments) Act 1958."
1975 c. 68.	The Industry Act 1975.	In Schedule 1, paragraph 19.
1975 c. 70.	The Welsh Development Agency Act 1975.	In Schedule 1, paragraph 22.
1976 c. 47.	The Stock Exchange (Completion of Bargains) Act 1976.	Section 7(2).
1977 c. 3.	The Aircraft and Shipbuilding Industries Act 1977.	In section 3(5), the words "Sections 428 to 430 of the Companies Act 1985 and".
1978 c. 23.	The Judicature (Northern Ireland) Act 1978.	Section 84(3)(c).
1979 c. 37.	The Banking Act 1979.	Section 20(1) to (3). In Schedule 1, paragraph 9. In Schedule 6, paragraphs 4 and 5.
1982 c. 50.	The Insurance Companies Act 1982.	Section 73. Section 79.
1982 c. 53.	The Administration of Justice Act 1982.	Section 42(8).
1984 c. 2.	The Restrictive Trade Practices (Stock Exchange) Act 1984.	The whole Act.
1985 c. 6.	The Companies Act 1985.	Part III. Sections 81 to 83. In section 84(1) the words from "This" onwards. In section 85(1) the words "83 or". Sections 86 and 87. In section 97, subsection (2)(b) together with the word "and" immediately preceding it and subsections (3) and (4). Section 433(2). Section 446(5) and (6). In section 449(1)(d), the words "the Prevention of Fraud (Investments) Act 1958".

Sch. 17

Chapter	Short title	Extent of repeal
		In section 693, paragraph (a) and in paragraph (d) the words "in every such prospectus as above-mentioned and". Section 709(2) and (3). In section 744, the definitions of "recognised stock exchange" and "prospectus issued generally". Schedule 3. In Schedule 22, the entries relating to Parts III and IV. In Schedule 24, the entries relating to sections 56(4), 61, 64(5), 70(1), 78(1), 81(2), 82(5), 86(6), 87(4) and 97(4).
1985 c. 8.	The Company Securities (Insider Dealing) Act 1985.	In section 3(1), the word "or" immediately preceding paragraph (c). In section 13, in subsection (1), the words from "and references" onwards and subsection (2). Section 15.
1985 c. 9.	The Companies Consolidation (Consequential Provisions) Act 1985.	Section 7. In Schedule 2, the entries relating to the Prevention of Fraud (Investments) Act 1958, paragraph 19 of Schedule 1 to the Scottish Development Agency Act 1975, paragraph 22 of Schedule 1 to the Welsh Development Agency Act 1975, the Stock Exchange (Completion of Bargains) Act 1976, section 3(5) of the Aircraft and Shipbuilding Industries Act 1977 and section 20 of the Banking Act 1979.
1986 c. 31.	The Airports Act 1986.	Section 10.
1986 c. 44.	The Gas Act 1986.	Section 58.
1986 c. 60.	The Financial Services Act 1986.	Section 195.

Sch. 17

Part II — Instruments

Number	Title	Extent of revocation
SI 1977/1254 (6 N I 21).	The Stock Exchange (Completion of Bargains) (Northern Ireland) Order 1977.	Article 2(2).
SI 1986/1032 (N I 6).	The Companies (Northern Ireland) Order 1986.	Article 2(1), the definitions of "prospectus issued generally" and "recognised stock exchange". Part IV. Articles 91 to 93. In Article 94(1) the words from "This" onwards. In Article 95(1) the words "93 or". Articles 96 and 97. In Article 107, paragraph (2)(b) together with the word "and" immediately preceding it and paragraphs (3) and (4). Article 426(2). Article 439(5) and (6). In Article 442(1)(d), the words "the Prevention of Fraud (Investments) Act (Northern Ireland) 1940". In Article 643(1), sub-paragraph (a) and in sub-paragraph (d) the words "in every such prospectus as is mentioned in sub-paragraph (a) and". Article 658(2) and (3). Schedule 3. In Schedule 21, the entries relating to Parts IV and V. In Schedule 23, the entries relating to Articles 66(4), 71, 74(5), 80(1), 88(1), 91(2), 92(5), 96(6), 97(4) and 107(4).
SI 1986/1035 (N I 9).	The Companies (Consequential Provisions) (Northern Ireland) Order 1986.	In Schedule 2, the entries relating to the Prevention of Fraud (Investments) Act (Northern Ireland) 1940 and section 20 of the Banking Act 1979.
S I 1984/716.	The Stock Exchange (Listing) Regulations 1984.	The whole Regulations.

Sch. 17

Appendix 2

CRIMINAL JUSTICE ACT 1993
(1993 Chapter 36)

[27 July 1993]

PART V — INSIDER DEALING

THE OFFENCE OF INSIDER DEALING

SEC. 521   The offence

52(1) [Primary offence] An individual who has information as an insider is guilty of insider dealing if, in the circumstances mentioned in subsection (3), he deals in securities that are price-affected securities in relation to the information.

52(2) [Additional offence] An individual who has information as an insider is also guilty of insider dealing if—

(a)   he encourages another person to deal in securities that are (whether or not that other knows it) price-affected securities in relation to the information, knowing or having reasonable cause to believe that the dealing would take place in the circumstances mentioned in subsection (3); or

(b)   he discloses the information, otherwise than in the proper performance of the functions of his employment, office or profession, to another person.

52(3) [Circumstances in sec. 52(1), (2)] The circumstances referred to above are that the acquisition or disposal in question occurs on a regulated market, or that the person dealing relies on a professional intermediary or is himself acting as a professional intermediary.

52(4) [Effect] This section has effect subject to section 53.

SEC. 53   Defences

53(1) [Defence to sec. 52(1) offence] An individual is not guilty of insider dealing by virtue of dealing in securities if he shows—

(a)   that he did not at the time expect the dealing to result in a profit attributable to the fact that the information in question was price-sensitive information in relation to the securities, or

(b)   that at the time he believed on reasonable grounds that the information had been disclosed widely enough to ensure that none of those taking part in the dealing would be prejudiced by not having the information, or

(c)   that he would have done what he did even if he had not had the information.

53(2) [Defence to sec. 52(2)(a) offence] An individual is not guilty of insider dealing by virtue of encouraging another person to deal in securities if he shows—

(a) that he did not at the time expect the dealing to result in a profit attributable to the fact that the information in question was price-sensitive information in relation to the securities, or

(b) that at the time he believed on reasonable grounds that the information had been or would be disclosed widely enough to ensure that none of those taking part in the dealing would be prejudiced by not having the information, or

(c) that he would have done what he did even if he had not had the information.

53(3) [Defence to sec. 52(2)(b) offence] An individual is not guilty of insider dealing by virtue of a disclosure of information if he shows—

(a) that he did not at the time expect any person, because of the disclosure, to deal in securities in the circumstances mentioned in subsection (3) of section 52; or

(b) that, although he had such an expectation at the time, he did not expect the dealing to result in a profit attributable to the fact that the information was price-sensitive information in relation to the securities.

53(4) [Sch. 1] Schedule 1 (special defences) shall have effect.

53(5) [Amendment of Sch. 1] The Treasury may by order amend Schedule 1.

53(6) [Interpretation] In this section references to a profit include references to the avoidance of a loss.

INTERPRETATION

SEC. 54   Securities to which Part V applies

54(1) [Application] This Part applies to any security which—

(a) falls within any paragraph of Schedule 2; and
(b) satisfies any conditions applying to it under an order made by the Treasury for the purposes of this subsection;

and in the provisions of this Part (other than that Schedule) any reference to a security is a reference to a security to which this Part applies.

54(2) [Amendment of Sch. 2] The Treasury may by order amend Schedule 2.

SEC. 55   "Dealing" in securities

55(1) [Where person deals in securities] For the purposes of this Part, a person deals in securities if—

(a) he acquires or disposes of the securities (whether as principal or agent); or
(b) he procures, directly or indirectly, an acquisition or disposal of the securities by any other person.

55(2) ["Acquire"] For the purposes of this Part, **"acquire"**, in relation to a security, includes—

(a) agreeing to acquire the security; and
(b) entering into a contract which creates the security.

55(3) ["Dispose"] For the purposes of this Part, **"dispose"**, in relation to a security, includes—

(a) agreeing to dispose of the security; and

(b)   bringing to an end a contract which created the security;

55(4) [Interpretation of sec. 55(1)] For the purposes of subsection (1), a person procures an acquisition or disposal of a security if the security is acquired or disposed of by a person who is—

(a)   his agent;
(b)   his nominee, or
(c)   a person who is acting at his direction,

in relation to the acquisiton or disposal.

55(5) [Extent of sec. 55(5)] Subsection (4) is not exhaustive as to the circumstances in which one person may be regarded as procuring an acquisition or disposal of securities by another.

SEC. 56   "Inside information", etc.

56(1) ["Inside information"] For the purposes of this section and section 57, "inside information" means information which—

(a)   relates to particular securities or to a particular issuer of securities or to particular issuers of securities and not to securities generally or to issuers of securities generally;
(b)   is specific or precise;
(c)   has not been made public; and
(d)   if it were made public would be likely to have a significant effect on the price of any securities.

56(2) ["Price-affected securities", "price-sensitive information"] For the purposes of this Part, securities are **"price-affected securities"** in relation to inside information, and inside information is **"price-sensitive information"** in relation to securities, if and only if the information would, if made public, be likely to have a significant effect on the price of the securities.

56(3) ["Price"] For the purposes of this section **"price"** includes value.

SEC. 57   "Insiders"

57(1) [Where person has information as insider] For the purposes of this Part, a person has information as an insider if and only if—

(a)   it is, and he knows that it is, insider information, and
(b)   he has it, and knows that he has it, from an insider source.

57(2) [Interpretation of sec. 57(1)] For the purposes of subsection (1), a person has information from an insider source if and only if—

(a)   he has it through—
(i)   being a director, employee or shareholder of an issuer of securities; or
(ii)   having access to the information by virtue of his employment, office or profession; or
(b)   the direct or indirect source of his information is a person within paragraph (a).

SEC. 58   Information "made public"

58(1) ["Made public"] For the purposes of section 56, "made public", in relation to information, shall be construed in accordance with the following provisions of this section; but those provisions are not exhaustive as to the meaning of that expression.

58(2) [Where information is made public] Information is made public if—

(a)   it is published in accordance with the rules of a regulated market for the purpose of informing investors and their professional advisers;

(b)   it is contained in records which by virtue of any enactment are open to inspection by the public;

(c)   it can be readily acquired by those likely to deal in any securities—
    (i)   to which the information relates, or
    (ii) of an issuer to which the information relates; or

(d)   it is derived from information which has been made public.

58(3) [Information treated as made public] Information may be treated as made public even though—

(a)   it can be acquired only by persons exercising diligence or expertise;

(b)   it is communicated to a section of the public and not to the public at large;

(c)   it can be acquired only by observation;

(d)   it is communicated only on payment of a fee; or

(e)   it is published only outside the United Kingdom.

SEC. 59   "Professional intermediary"

59(1) ["Professional intermediary"] For the purposes of this Part, a **"professional intermediary"** is a person—

(a)   who carries on a business consisting of an activity mentioned in subsection (2) and who holds himself out to the public or any section of the public (including a section of the public constituted by persons such as himself) as willing to engage in any such business; or

(b)   who is employed by a person falling within paragraph (a) to carry out any such activity.

59(2) [Activities in sec. 59(1)] The activities referred to in subsection (1) are—

(a)   acquiring or disposing of securities (whether as principal or agent); or

(b)   acting as an intermediary between persons taking part in any dealing in securities.

59(3) [Interpretation re sec. 59(2)] A person is not to be treated as carrying on a business consisting of an activity mentioned in subsection (2)—

(a)   if the activity in question is merely incidental to some other activity not falling within subsection (2); or

(b)   merely because he occasionally conducts one of those activities.

59(4) [Purposes of sec. 52] For the purposes of section 52, a person dealing in securities relies on a professional intermediary if and only if a person who is acting as a professional intermediary carries out an activity mentioned in subsection (2) in relation to that dealing.

SEC. 60   Other interpretation provisions

60(1) ["Regulated market"] For the purposes of this Part, **"regulated market"** means any market, however operated, which, by an order made by the Treasury, is identified (whether by name or by reference to criteria prescribed by the order) as a regulated market for the purposes of this Part.

s. 58(2)

60(2) **["issuer"]** For the purposes of this Part an **"issuer"**, in relation to any securities, means any company, public sector body or individual by which or by whom the securities have been or are to be issued.

60(3) **["Company", "public sector body"]** For the purposes of this Part—

(a) "company" means any body (whether or not incorporated and wherever incorporated or constituted) which is not a public sector body; and

(b) "public sector body" means—

    (i) the government of the United Kingdom, of Northern Ireland or of any country or territory outside the United Kingdom;

    (ii) a local authority in the United Kingdom or elsewhere;

    (iii) any international organisation the members of which include the United Kingdom or another member state;

    (iv) the Bank of England; or

    (v) the central bank of any sovereign State.

60(4) **[Further interpretation]** For the purposes of this Part, information shall be treated as relating to an issuer of securities which is a company not only where it is about the company but also where it may affect the company's business prospects.

SEC. 61   Penalties and prosecution

61(1) **[Penalties]** An individual guilty of insider dealing shall be liable—

(a) on summary conviction, to a fine not exceeding the statutory maximum or imprisonment for a term not exceeding six months or to both; or

(b) on conviction on indictment, to a fine or imprisonment for a term not exceeding seven years or to both.

61(2) **[Institution of proceedings]** Proceedings for offences under this Part shall not be instituted in England and Wales except by or with the consent of—

(a) the Secretary of State; or

(b) the Director of Public Prosecutions.

61(3) **[Northern Ireland]** In relation to proceedings in Northern Ireland for offences under this Part, subsection (2) shall have effect as if the reference to the Director of Public Prosecutions were a reference to the Director of Public Prosecutions for Northern Ireland.

SEC. 62   Territorial scope of offence of insider dealing

62(1) **[Condition for sec. 52(1) offence]** An individual is not guilty of an offence falling within subsection (1) of section 52 unless—

(a) he was within the United Kingdom at the time when he is alleged to have done any act constituting or forming part of the alleged dealing;

(b) the regulated market on which the dealing is alleged to have occurred is one which, by an order made by the Treasury, is identified (whether by name or by reference to criteria prescribed by the order) as being, for the purposes of this Part, regulated in the United Kingdom; or

(c) the professional intermediary was within the United Kingdom at the time when he is alleged to have done anything by means of which the offence is alleged to have been committed.

62(2) **[Conditions for sec. 52(2) offence]** An individual is not guilty of an offence falling within subsection (2) of section 52 unless—

s. 62(2)

(a)   he was within the United Kingdom at the time when he is alleged to have disclosed the information or encouraged the dealing; or

(b)   the alleged recipient of the information or encouragement was within the United Kingdom at the time when he is alleged to have received the information or encouragement.

SEC. 63   Limits on section 52

63(1) [Non-application of sec. 52] Section 52 does not apply to anything done by an individual acting on behalf of a public sector body in pursuit of monetary policies or policies with respect to exchange rates or the management of public debt or foreign exchange reserves.

63(2) [Effect on contracts] No contract shall be void or unenforceable by reason only of section 52.

SEC 64   Orders

64(1) [Orders by statutory instrument] Any power under this Part to make an order shall be exercisable by statutory instrument.

64(2) [Approval by Parliament] No order shall be made under this Part unless a draft of it has been laid before and approved by a resolution of each House of Parliament.

64(3) [Provisions in orders] An order under this Part—

(a)   may make different provision for different cases; and

(b)   may contain such incidental, supplemental and transitional provisions as the Treasury consider expedient.

Schedule 1 — Special Defences

Section 53(4)

MARKET MAKERS

1(1) An individual is not guilty of insider dealing by virtue of dealing in securities or encouraging another person to deal if he shows that he acted in good faith in the course of—

(a)   his business as a market maker, or

(b)   his employment in the business of a market maker.

1(2) A market maker is a person who—

(a)   holds himself out at all normal times in compliance with the rules of a regulated market or an approved organisation as willing to acquire or dispose of securities; and

(b)   is recognised as doing so under those rules.

1(3) In this paragraph **"approved organisation"** means an international securities self-regulating organisation approved under paragraph 25B of Schedule 1 to the Financial Services Act 1986.

MARKET INFORMATION

2(1) An individual is not guilty of insider dealing by virtue of dealing in securities or encouraging another person to deal if he shows that—

(a)   the information which he had as an insider was market information; and
(b)   it was reasonable for an individual in his position to have acted as he did despite having that information as an insider at the time.

2(2) In determining whether it is reasonable for an individual to do any act despite having market information at the time, there shall, in particular, be taken into account—

(a)   the content of the information;
(b)   the circumstances in which he first had the information and in what capacity; and
(c)   the capacity in which he now acts.

3 An individual is not guilty of insider dealing by virtue of dealing in securities or encouraging another person to deal if he shows—

(a)   that he acted—
    (i)   in connection with an acquisition or disposal which was under consideration or the subject of negotiation, or in the course of a series of such acquisitions or disposals; and
    (ii)   with a view to facilitating the accomplishment of the acquisition or disposal or the series of acquisitions or disposals; and
(b)   that the information which he had as an insider was market information arising directly out of his involvement in the acquisition or disposal or series of acquisitions or disposals.

4 For the purposes of paragraphs 2 and 3 market information is information consisting of one or more of the following facts—

(a)   that securities of a particular kind have been or are to be acquired or disposed of, or that there acquisition or disposal is under consideration or the subject of negotiation;
(b)   that securities of a particular kind have not been or are not to be acquired or disposed of;
(c)   the number of securities acquired or disposed of or to be acquired or disposed of or whose acquisition or disposal is under consideration or the subject of negotiation;
(d)   the price (or range of prices) at which securities have been or are to be acquired or disposed of or the price (or range of prices) at which securities whose acquisition or disposal is under consideration or the subject of negotiation may be acquired or disposed of;
(e)   the identity of the persons involved or likely to be involved in any capacity in an acquisition or disposal.

PRICE STABILISATION

5(1) An individual is not guilty of insider dealing by virtue of dealing in securities or encouraging another person to deal if he shows that he acted in conformity with the price stabilisation rules.

5(2) In this paragraph **"the price stabilisation rules"** means rules which—

Sch. 1

(a)   are made under section 48 of the Financial Services Act 1986 (conduct of business rules); and

(b)   make provision of a description mentioned in paragraph (i) of subsection (2) of that section (price stabilisation rules).

Schedule 2 — Securities

Section 54

SHARES

1 Shares and stock in the share capital of a company (**"shares"**).

DEBT SECURITIES

2 Any instrument creating or acknowledging indebtedness which is issued by a company or public sector body, including, in particular, debentures, debenture stock, loan stock, bonds and certificates of deposit (**"debt securities"**).

WARRANTS

3 Any right (whether conferred by warrant or otherwise) to subscribe for shares or debt securities (**"warrants"**).

DEPOSITARY RECEIPTS

4(1) The rights under any depositary receipt.

4(2) For the purposes of sub-paragraph (1) a **"depositary receipt"** means a certificate or other record (whether or not in the form of a document)—

(a)   which is issued by or on behalf of a person who holds any relevant securities of a particular issuer; and

(b)   which acknowledges that another person is entitled to rights in relation to the relevant securities or relevant securities of the same kind.

4(3) In sub-paragraph (2) **"relevant securities"** means shares, debt securities and warrants.

OPTIONS

5 Any option to acquire or dispose of any security falling within any other paragraph of this Schedule.

FUTURES

6(1) Rights under a contract for the acquisition or disposal of relevant securities under which delivery is to be made at a future date and at a price agreed when the contract is made.

6(2) In sub-paragraph (1)—

(a)   the references to a future date and to a price agreed when the contract is made include references to a date and a price determined in accordance with terms of the contract; and

Sch. 2

(b)   **"relevant securities"** means any security falling within any other paragraph of this Schedule.

CONTRACTS FOR DIFFERENCES

7(1) Rights under a contract which does not provide for the delivery of securities but whose purpose or pretended purpose is to secure a profit or avoid a loss by reference to fluctuations in—

(a)   a share index or other similar factor connected with relevant securities;
(b)   the price of particular relevant securities; or
(c)   the interest rate offered on money placed on deposit.

7(2) In sub-paragraph (1) **"relevant securities"** means any security falling within any other paragraph of this Schedule.

Schedule 5 — Consequential Amendments
Section 79(13)

THE COMPANIES ACT 1985 (c. 6)

4(1) In section 744 of the Companies Act 1985 (interpretation), for the definition of "the Insider Dealing Act", there shall be substituted—

" **"the insider dealing legislation"** means Part V of the Criminal Justice Act 1993 (insider dealing)."

4(2) In the 1985 Act for "Insider Dealing Act", wherever it occurs, there shall be substituted "insider dealing legislation".

THE FINANCIAL SERVICES ACT 1986 (c. 60)

7 The Financial Services Act 1986 shall be amended as follows.

8 In section 128C(3)(b) (enforcement in support of overseas regulatory authority) for "the Company Securities (Insider Dealing) act 1985" there shall be substituted "Part V of the Criminal Justice Act 1993 (insider dealing)".

9(1) In section 177 (investigations into insider dealing), in subsection (1)—

(a)   for the words "there may have been a contravention of section 1, 2, 4 or 5 of the Company Securities (Insider Dealing) Act 1985" there shall be substituted "an offence under Part V of the Criminal Justice Act 1993 (insider dealing) may have been committed"; and
(b)   for the words "contravention has occurred" there shall be substituted "offence has been committed".

9(2) In subsection (3) of that section—

(a)   for the word "contravention" there shall be substituted "offence"; and
(b)   in paragraph (a) for the words from "relating to" to the end there shall be substituted "which appear to them to be relevant to the investigation".

9(3) In subsection (4) of that section for the word "contravention" there shall be substituted "offence".

Sch. 5

10(1) In section 178 (penalties for failure to co-operate with sec. 177 investigations), in subsection (1) for the words "contravention has occurred" there shall be substituted "offence has been committed".

10(2) In subsection (6) of that section for the words "contravention or suspected contravention" there shall be substituted "offence or suspected offence".

11 In subsection (1) of section 189 (restriction of Rehabilitation of Offenders Act 1974), in paragraph (b) "(including insider dealing)" shall be omitted and at the end there shall be inserted "or insider dealing".

12(1) In section 199 (powers of entry), in subsection (1) for paragraph (b) there shall be substituted—

"(b) under Part V of the Criminal Justice Act 1993 (insider dealing).".

12(2) After subsection (8) of that section there shall be inserted—

"(8A) In the application of this section to Northern Ireland for the references to information on oath substitute references to complaint on oath.".

THE COMPANIES ACT 1989 (c. 40)

16 In section 82(2)(b) of the Companies Act 1989 (request for assistance by overseas regulatory authority) for "the Company Securities (Insider Dealing) Act 1985" there shall be substituted "Part V of the Criminal Justice Act 1993 (insider dealing)".

Sch. 5

Schedule 6 — Repeals and Revocations

Section 79(14)

Part I — Repeals

Chapter	Short title	Extent of repeal
1985 c. 8.	The Company Securities (Insider Dealing) Act 1985.	The whole Act.
1986 c. 60.	The Financial Services Act 1986.	Sections 173 top 176. In section 189(1)(b), the words "(including insider dealing)". In Schedule 16, paragraphs 28 and 43.
1987 c. 38.	The Criminal Justice Act 1987.	In section 3(6)(i), the words "or any corresponding enactment having effect in Northern Ireland".
1989 c. 40.	The Companies Act 1989.	Section 209.

Part II — Revocations

Number	Title	Extent of revocation
SI 1992/3218.	The Banking Coordination (Second Council Directive) Regulations 1992.	In Schedule 8, paragraphs 8(3), 9(2) and 10(3). In Schedule 10, paragraphs 17 and 25.

Sch. 6

Appendix 3
Selected statutory instruments

The Insider Dealing (Securities and Regulated Markets) Order 1994
  (SI 1994/187)

The Traded Securities (Disclosure) Regulations 1994 (SI 1994/188)

The Financial Services Act 1986 (Investment Services) (Extensions of Scope of
  Act) Order 1995 (SI 1995/3271)

The Financial Services Act 1986 (Restriction of Scope of Act and Meaning of
  Collective Investment Scheme) Order 1996 (SI 1996/2996)

THE INSIDER DEALING (SECURITIES AND REGULATED MARKETS) ORDER 1994

(SI 1994/187)

Made on 1 February 1994 by the Treasury in exercise of the powers conferred by sec. 54(1), 60(1), 62(1) and 64(3) of the Criminal Justice Act 1993. Operative from 1 March 1994.

TITLE, COMMENCEMENT AND INTERPRETATION

1 This Order may be cited as the Insider Dealing (Securities and Regulated Markets) Order 1994 and shall come into force on the twenty eighth day after the day on which it is made.

2 In this Order a "State within the European Economic Area" means a State which is a member of the European Communities and the Republics of Austria, Finland and Iceland, the Kingdoms of Norway and Sweden and the Principality of Liechtenstein.

SECURITIES

3 Articles 4 to 8 set out conditions for the purposes of section 54(1) of the Criminal Justice Act 1993 (securities to which Part V of the Act of 1993 applies).

4 The following condition applies in relation to any security which falls within any paragraph of Schedule 2 to the Act of 1993, that is, that it is officially listed in a State within the European Economic Area or that it is admitted to dealing on, or has its price quoted on or under the rules of, a regulated market.

5 The following alternative condition applies in relation to a warrant, that is, that the right under it is a right to subscribe for any share or debt security of the same class as a share or debt security which satisfies the condition in article 4.

6 The following alternative condition applies in relation to a depositary receipt, that is, that the rights under it are in respect of any share or debt security which satisfies the condition in article 4.

7 The following alternative conditions apply in relation to an option or a future, that is, that the option or rights under the future are in respect of—

(a)   any share or debt security which satisfies the condition in article 4, or
(b)   any depositary receipt which satisfies the condition in article 4 or article 6.

8 The following alternative condition applies in relation to a contract for differences, that is, that the purpose or pretended purpose of the contract is to secure a profit or avoid a loss by reference to fluctuations in—

(a)   the price of any shares or debt securities which satisfy the condition in article 4, or

(b)   an index of the price of such shares or debt securities.

REGULATED MARKETS

9 The following markets are regulated markets for the purposes of Part V of the Act of 1993—

any market which is established under the rules of an investment exchange specified in the Schedule to this Order.

UNITED KINGDOM REGULATED MARKETS

10 The regulated markets which are regulated in the United Kingdom for the purposes of Part V of the Act of 1993 are any market which is established under the rules of—

(a)   the London Stock Exchange Limited;
(b)   LIFFE Administration & Management;
(c)   OMLX, the London Securities and Derivatives Exchange Limited; and
(d)   Tradepoint Financial Networks plc.

Schedule — Regulated Markets

Article 9

Any market which is established under the rules of one of the following investment exchanges;

Amsterdam Stock Exchange.
Antwerp Stock Exchange.
Athens Stock Exchange.
Barcelona Stock Exchange.
Bavarian Stock Exchange.
Berlin Stock Exchange.
Bilbao Stock Exchange.
Bologna Stock Exchange.
Bremen Stock Exchange.
Brussels Stock Exchange.
Copenhagen Stock Exchange.
Dusseldorf Stock Exchange.
Florence Stock Exchange.
Frankfurt Stock Exchange.
Genoa Stock Exchange.
Hamburg Stock Exchange.
Hanover Stock Exchange.
Helsinki Stock Exchange.
Iceland Stock Exchange.
The Irish Stock Exchange.

Lisbon Stock Exchange.
LIFFE Administration & Management.
The London Stock Exchange Limited.
Luxembourg Stock Exchange.
Lyon Stock Exchange.
Madrid Stock Exchange.
Milan Stock Exchange.
Naples Stock Exchange.
The exchange known as NASDAQ.
The exchange known as the Nouveau Marché.
OMLX, the London Securities and Derivatives Exchange Limited.
Oporto Stock Exchange.
Oslo Stock Exchange.
Palermo Stock Exchange.
Paris Stock Exchange.
Rome Stock Exchange.
Securities Exchange of Iceland.
Stockholm Stock Exchange.
Stuttgart Stock Exchange.
Tradepoint Financial Networks plc.
Trieste Stock Exchange.
Turin Stock Exchange.
Valencia Stock Exchange.
Venice Stock Exchange.
Vienna Stock Exchange.

EXPLANATORY NOTE

(This note is not part of the Order)

Part V of the Criminal Justice Act 1993 ("the Act") establishes the offence of insider dealing. It is an offence for an individual who has information as an insider to deal on a "regulated market" or through or as a professional intermediary in "securities" whose price would be significantly affected if the inside information were made public. It is also an offence to encourage insider dealing and to disclose inside information. No offence is committed unless there is some connection with the United Kingdom which includes dealing on a regulated market which has been identified as being "regulated in the United Kingdom".

This Order specifies the securities to which the insider dealing provisions apply and identifies what is a regulated market and a market regulated in the United Kingdom. The Act defines other terms used.

Section 54(1) of the Act provides that Part V applies to any security which falls within any paragraph of Schedule 2 to the Act which satisfies any condition applying to it under an order made by the Treasury for the purposes of section 54(1). Articles 4 to 8 of this Order set out those conditions.

The first condition applies to any security falling within Schedule 2: shares, debt securities, warrants, depositary receipts, options, futures and contracts for differences.

Any security of those types which is officially listed in a State within the European Economic Area or which is admitted to dealing on, or has its price quoted on or under the rules of, a regulated market is a security for the purposes of insider dealing.

Alternative conditions apply to securities listed in Schedule 2 to the Act other than shares and debt securities. A depositary receipt is a security for the purposes of insider dealing if the rights under it are in respect of shares or debt securities which satisfy the first condition i.e. that the shares or debt securities are officially listed in a State within the European Economic Area or are admitted to dealing on or have their price quoted on or under the rules of a regulated market. A warrant is a security for the purposes of insider dealing if the right under it is a right to subscribe for any share or debt security of the same class as a share or debt security which satisfies the first condition.

An option or a future is a security for the purposes of insider dealing if the option or rights under the future are in respect of shares, debt securities or depositary receipts which satisfy the first condition or are in respect of a depositary receipt which satisfies the first condition or the rights under which are in respect of shares or debt securities which satisfy the first condition.

A contract for differences is a security for the purpose of insider dealing if the purpose or pretended purpose of the contract is to secure a profit or avoid a loss by reference to fluctuations in the price or an index of the price of shares or debt securities which meet the first condition.

Article 9 and the Schedule to the Order identify which markets are "regulated markets" for the purposes of insider dealing. They are the markets which are established under the rules of an investment exchange specified in that Schedule.

Article 10 identifies the regulated markets which are "regulated in the United Kingdom" for the purposes of the territorial scope of the offence of insider dealing. These are markets established under the rules of the International Stock Exchange of the United Kingdom and the Republic of Ireland Limited (other than the market operating in the Republic of Ireland known as the Irish Unit), of LIFFE and OMLX.

THE TRADED SECURITIES (DISCLOSURE) REGULATIONS 1994
(SI 1994/188)

Made on 1 February 1994 by the Treasury in exercise of the powers conferred on them by sec. 2(2) of the European Communities Act 1972. Operative from 1 March 1994.

CITATION AND COMMENCEMENT

1(1) These Regulations may be cited as the Traded Securities (Disclosure) Regulations 1994.

1(2) These Regulations shall come into force on 1st March 1994.

INTERPRETATION

2 In these Regulations:

"the Official List" has the meaning given by section 142(7) of the Financial Services Act 1986;

"overseas investment exchange" and **"recognised investment exchange"** have the meaning given by section 207(1) of the Financial Services Act 1986;

"regulated market" means any market in the United Kingdom on which securities are admitted to trading being a market which is regulated and supervised by a recognised investment exchange and which operates regularly and is accessible directly or indirectly to the public; and

"security" means any security which falls within any paragraph of the Schedule to these Regulations but does not include an investment which is admitted to the Official List in accordance with Part IV of the Financial Services Act 1986.

and the expressions **"admitting to trading"** and **"company"** and **"undertaking"** have the same meaning as in the Council Directive of 13th November 1989 co-ordinating regulations on insider dealing (89/592/EEC).

OBLIGATION TO DISCLOSE INFORMATION

3(1) Subject to paragraph (2) below, a company or undertaking which is an issuer of a security admitted to trading on a regulated market (an "issuer") shall inform the public as soon as possible of any major new developments in the issuer's sphere of activity which are not public knowledge and which may, by virtue of their effect on the issuer's assets and liabilities or financial position or on the general course of its business, lead to substantial movements in the price of that security.

3(2) A recognised investment exchange which regulates and supervises a regulated market on which an issuer's securities are admitted to trading may exempt the issuer from the obligation imposed by paragraph (1) above if satisfied that the disclosure of the particular information would prejudice the legitimate interests of that issuer.

3(3) The rules of a recognised investment exchange must, at least, enable the exchange, in the event of a failure by an issuer whose securities are admitted to trading on a regulated market which the exchange regulates and supervises to comply with the obligation imposed by paragraph (1) above, to do any of the following, that is to say—

(a) discontinue the admission of the securities to trading;
(b) suspend trading in the securities;
(c) publish the fact that the issuer has failed to comply with the obligation; and
(d) itself make public any information which the issuer has failed to publish.

4 The Financial Services Act 1986 shall have effect as if the requirement set out in paragraph (3) of regulation 3 above was—

(a) in the case of a recognised investment exchange which is not an overseas investment exchange, among those specified in Schedule 4 to that Act (requirements for recognition of UK investment exchange); and
(b) in the case of an overseas investment exchange, among those mentioned in section 37(7)(a) of that Act (revocation of recognition order) and specified in section

40(2) of that Act (requirements for recognition of overseas investment exchange etc.).

Schedule

Regulation 2

1 Shares and stock in the share capital of a company (**"shares"**).

2 Any instrument creating or acknowledging indebtedness which is issued by a company or undertaking, including, in particular, debentures, debenture stock, loan stock, bonds and certificates of deposit (**"debt securities"**).

3 Any right (whether conferred by warrant or otherwise) to subscribe for shares or debt securities (**"warrants"**).

4(1) The rights under any depositary receipt.

4(2) For the purposes of sub-paragraph (1) above a **"depositary receipt"** means a certificate or other record (whether or not in the form of a document)—

(a)   which is issued by or on behalf of a person who holds any relevant securities of a particular issuer, and

(b)   which acknowledges that another person is entitled to rights in relation to the relevant securities or relevant securities of the same kind.

4(3) In sub-paragraph (2) above **"relevant securities"** means shares, debt securities and warrants.

5 Any option to acquire or dispose of any security falling within any other paragraph of this Schedule.

6(1) Rights under a contract for the acquisition or disposal of relevant securities under which delivery is to be made at a future date and at a price agreed when the contract is made.

6(2) In sub-paragraph (1) above—

(a)   the references to a future date and to a price agreed when the contract is made include references to a date and a price determined in accordance with the terms of the contract; and

(b)   **"relevant securities"** means any security falling within any other paragraph of this Schedule.

7(1) Rights under a contract which does not provide for the delivery of securities but whose purpose or pretended purpose is to secure a profit or avoid a loss by reference to fluctuations in—

7(2) In sub-paragraph (1) above **"relevant securities"** means any security falling within any other paragraph of this Schedule.

(a)   a share index or other similar factor connected with relevant securities; or

(b)   the price of particular relevant securities.

EXPLANATORY NOTE

(This note is not part of the Regulations)

The Regulations give effect to the provisions of article 7 of the Council Directive of

13th November 1989 co-ordinating regulations on insider dealing (89/592/EEC OJ No. L334/30). Article 7 requires that all companies and undertakings, the transferable securities of which are, whatever their nature, admitted to trading on a market which is regulated and supervised by bodies recognised by public bodies, operates regularly and is accessible directly or indirectly to the public, should be under an obligation to inform the public as soon as possible of any major new developments in the issuer's sphere of activity which are not public knowledge and which may, by virtue of their effect on the issuer's assets and liabilities or financial position or on the general course of its business, lead to substantial movements in the price of the securities admitted to trading. The authorities responsible for the market on which securities are admitted to trading may exempt a company or undertaking from compliance with the requirement if the disclosure of the information would prejudice the legitimate interests of that company or undertaking. In the United Kingdom, the obligation extends to companies and undertakings whose securities are admitted to trading on an investment exchange recognised under the Financial Services Act 1986.

Regulation 2 of, and the Schedule to, the Regulations contain definitions which are relevant for the purposes of the Regulations.

Regulations 3(1) imposes the obligation required by article 7 except where the securities in question are admitted to listing in accordance with Part IV of the Financial Services Act. Listing rules made under that Part impose the obligation in relation to such securities.

Regulation 3(2) enables an investment exchange recognised under the Financial Services Act to dispense an issuer from compliance with the obligation in the circumstances permitted by article 7 and regulation 3(3) requires that each recognised investment exchange must have rules which enable it, at least, to discontinue or suspend trading in the relevant securities where there has been a failure to comply with the obligation.

Regulation 4 makes the obligation imposed on recognised investment exchanges by regulation 3(3) one of the requirements which an exchange must meet if it is to continue to be recognised under the Financial Services Act.

THE FINANCIAL SERVICES ACT 1986 (INVESTMENT SERVICES) (EXTENSION OF SCOPE OF ACT) ORDER 1995
(SI 1995/3271)

Made on 18 December 1995 by the Treasury under s. 2 and 205A of the Financial Services Act 1986. Operative from 1 January 1996.

CITATION AND COMMENCEMENT

1 This Order may be cited as the Financial Services Act 1986 (Investment Services) Extension of Scope of Act) Order 1995 and shall come into force on 1st January 1996.

INTERPRETATION

2(1) In this Order—

"the Act" means the Financial Services Act 1986;

"core investment service" means a service listed in Section A of the Annex to the Investment Services Directive, the text of which is set out in Part I of Schedule 1 to this Order together with the text of Section B of that Annex which is relevant to the interpretation of Section A;

"investment firm" has the meaning given in paragraph (2) below;

"the Investment Services Directive" means the Council Directive on investment services in the securities field (No. 93/22/EEC); and

"listed service" means a service listed in Section A or C of the Annex to the Investment Services Directive.

2(2) In this Order references to an investment firm are references to any person, other than one within paragraph (3) below, whose regular occupation or business is the provision of any one or more core investment services to third parties on a professional basis.

2(3) The persons within this paragraph are persons to whom the Investment Services Directive does not apply by virtue of the provisions of Article 2(2) of that Directive, the text of which is set out in Schedule 2 to this Order.

SHARES IN INDUSTRIAL AND PROVIDENT SOCIETIES

3 Paragraph 1 of Schedule 1 to the Act shall have effect as if transferable shares in a body incorporated under the law of, or of any part of, the United Kingdom relating to industrial and provident societies fell within that paragraph.

BILLS OF EXCHANGE

4 Paragraph 2 of Schedule 1 to the Act shall have effect as if bills of exchange accepted by a banker fell within that paragraph.

AMENDMENT OF PART II OF SCHEDULE 1 TO THE ACT FOR CERTAIN PURPOSES

5 For the purposes of the provisions of sections 47A and 48 of the Act, Part II of Schedule 1 to the Act shall have effect as if amongst the activities falling within that Part of that Schedule were those listed services falling within Section C of the Annex to the Investment Services Directive; and for these purposes none of the exclusions in Part III of that Schedule shall have effect.

AMENDMENT OF PART III OF SCHEDULE 1 TO THE ACT

6(1) (Revoked by Financial Services Act 1986 (Restriction of Scope of Act and Meaning of Collective Investment Scheme) Order 1996 (SI 1996/2996), art. 2(3) as from 1 January 1997).

6(2) Paragraph 23 of Schedule 1 to the Act shall have effect as if it precluded a permission being granted to any person who is an investment firm.

TRANSITIONAL PROVISIONS

7 The prohibitions in section 3 of the Act shall not, until 1 January 1997, extend to any person who is, by virtue only of any provision of this Order, carrying on, or purporting to carry on, investment business in the United Kingdom.

Schedule 1 — Annex to the Investment Services Directive
Article 2(1)

"ANNEX
SECTION A — SERVICES

1(a)   Reception and transmission, on behalf of investors, of orders in relation to one or more instruments listed in section B.

1(b)   Execution of such orders other than for own account.

2   Dealing in any of the instruments listed in Section B for own account.

3   Managing portfolios of investments in accordance with mandates given by investors on a discretionary, client-by-client basis where such portfolios include one or more of the instruments listed in section B.

4   Underwriting in respect of issues of any of the instruments listed in section B and/or the placing of such issues.

SECTION B — INSTRUMENTS

1(a)   Transferable securities.

1(b)   Units in collective investment undertakings.

2   Money-market instruments.

3   Financial-futures contracts, including equivalent cash-settled instruments.

4   Forward interest-rate agreements (FRAs).

5   Interest-rate, currency and equity swaps.

6   Options to acquire or dispose of any instruments falling within this section of the Annex, including equivalent cash-settled instruments. This category includes in particular options on currency and on interest rates.

SECTION C — NON-CORE SERVICES

1   Safekeeping and adminstration in relation to one or more of the instruments listed in Section B.

2   Safe custody services.

3   Granting credits or loans to an investor to allow him to carry out a transaction in one or more of the instruments listed in Section B, where the firm granting the credit or loan is involved in the transaction.

4   Advice to undertakings on capital structure, industrial strategy and related matters and advice and service relating to mergers and the purchase of undertakings.

5   Services related to underwriting.

6   Investment advice concerning one or more of the instruments listed in Section B.

7   Foreign-exchange service where these are connected with the provision of investment services."

Schedule 2 — Article 2.2 of the Investment Services Directive
Article 2(3)

"This Directive shall not apply to:

(a)   insurance undertakings as defined in article 1 of Directive 73/239/EEC or Article 1 or Directive 79/267/EEC or undertakings carrying on the reinsurance and retrocession activities referred to in Directive 64/225/EEC;

(b)   firms which provide investment services exclusively for their parent undertakings, for their subsidiaries or for other subsidiaries of their parent undertakings.

(c)   persons providing an investment service where that service is provided in an incidental manner in the course of a professional activity and that activity is regulated by legal or regulatory provisions or a code of ethics governing the profession which do not exclude the provision of that service;

(d)   firms that provide investment services consisting exclusively in the administration of employee-participation schemes;

(e)   firms that provide investment services that consist in providing both the services referred to in (b) and those referred to in (d);

(f)   the central banks of Member States and other national bodies performing similar functions and other public bodies charged with or intervening in the management of the public debt.

(g)   firms
—   which may not hold clients' funds or securities and which for that reason may not at any time place themselves in debit with their clients, and
—   which may not provide any investment service except the reception and transmission of orders in transferable securities and units in collective investment undertakings, and
—   which in the course of providing that service may transmit orders only to
(i)   investment firms authorised in accordance with this Directive;
(ii)   credit institutions authorised in accordance with Directives 77/780/EEC and 89/646/EEC;
(iii)   branches of investment firms or of credit institutions which are authorized in a third country and which are subject to and comply with prudential rules considered by the competent authorities as at least as stringent as those laid down in this Directive, in Directive 89/646/EEC or in Directive 93/6/EEC;

(iv) collective investment undertakings authorized under the law of a Member State to market units to the public and to the managers of such undertakings;

(v) investment companies with fixed capital, as defined in article 15(4) of Directive 79/91/EEC, the securities of which are listed or dealt in on a regulated market in a Member State;

— the activities of which are governed at national level by rules or by a code of ethics;

(h) collective investment undertakings whether coordinated at Community level or not and the depositaries and managers of such undertakings;

(i) persons whose main business is trading in commodities amongst themselves or with producers or professional users of such products and who provide investment services only for such producers and professional users to the extent necessary for their main business;

(j) firms that provide investment services consisting exclusively in dealing for their own account on financial-futures or options markets or which deal for the accounts of other members of those markets or make prices for them and which are guaranteed by clearing members of the same markets. Responsibility for ensuring the performance of contracts entered into by such firms must be assumed by clearing members of the same markets;

(k) associations set up by Danish pension funds with the sole aim of managing the assets of pension funds that are members of those associations;

(l) 'agenti di cambio' whose activities and functions are governed by Italian Royal Decree No. 222 of 7 March 1925 and subsequent provisions amending it, and who are authorized to carry on their activities under Article 19 of Italian Law No. 1 of 2 January 1991."

EXPLANATORY NOTE

(This note is not part of the Order)

The Order makes amendments to the scope of the Financial Services Act 1986 ("the Act") required to give effect to Council Directive No. 93/22/EEC on investment services in the securities field (OJ No. L141, 10.5.93, p. 27). In so far as other legislative provision is needed to implement the provisions of the directive, this is contained in the Act, in an Order to be made under section 46 of the Act and in Regulations to be made under section 2(2) of the European Communities Act 1972. The Order comes into force on 1 January 1996.

The scope of the Act is determined by section 1 of the Act. Section 2 confers power on the Treasury to make orders extending or restricting the scope of the Act for the purposes of all or any of its provisions. The exercise of this power is among the functions transferred to the Treasury by the Transfer of Functions (Financial Services) Order 1992 (SI 1992/1315).

Section 1 of the Act defines "investments" by reference to the instruments falling within Part I of Schedule 1. Articles 3 and 4 of the Order add certain instruments to the investments falling within Part I of that Schedule (certain shares in industrial and provident societies and certain bills of exchange).

Article 5 of the Order extends, for the purposes of sections 47A and 48 of the Act, the activities that are to constitute the carrying on of investment business. As required by article 11 of the directive, statements of principle and rules can now be made under those two sections in respect of all services covered by the directive.

Section 1 of the Act defines "investment business" by reference to activities which fall within Part II of Schedule 1 to the Act and which are not excluded by Part III of that Schedule. Article 6 of the Order amends the meaning of "investment business" to cover the provision of all investment services to which the directive applies.

THE FINANCIAL SERVICES ACT 1986 (RESTRICTION OF SCOPE OF ACT AND MEANING OF COLLECTIVE INVESTMENT SCHEME) ORDER 1996

(SI 1996/2996)

Made on 28 November 1996 by the Treasury under s. 2 and 75(a) of the Financial Services Act 1986. Operative from 1 January 1997.

CITATION, COMMENCEMENT AND INTERPRETATION

1(1) This Order may be cited as the Financial Services Act 1986 (Restriction of Scope of Act and Meaning of Collective Investment Scheme) Order 1996.

1(2) This Order shall come into force on 1st January 1997.

1(3) In this Order, "the Act" means the Financial Services Act 1986.

RESTRICTION OF SCOPE OF ACT
AMENDMENT OF PART III OF SCHEDULE 1 TO THE ACT

2(1) Nothing in paragraphs 17 to 19 and 21 of Schedule 1 to the Act shall have the effect that the provision of any core investment service to third parties on a professional basis is excluded from the activities which fall within the paragraphs in Part II of that Schedule in any case in which the service is provided—

(a)   by a UK investment firm; or

(b)   by an investment firm which would be a UK investment firm if it was incorporated in or formed under the law of any part of the United Kingdom or, being an individual, had his head office in the United Kingdom.

2(2) In this article "core investment service", "investment firm" and "UK investment firm" have the meanings assigned to those expressions by regulation 2 of the Investment Services Regulations 1995.

2(3) In consequence of the provisions made by this article, paragraph (1) of article 6 of the Financial Services Act 1986 (Investment Services) (Extension of Scope of Act) Order 1995 is hereby revoked.

MEANING OF COLLECTIVE INVESTMENT SCHEME

3(1) In section 75(6)(1) of the Act, for the words "paragraph 34 or 35" there shall be substituted "any of paragraphs 34 to 36".

3(2) In Schedule 1 to the Act, after paragraph 35 there shall be inserted—
[Para. 36 not reproduced here.]

EXPLANATORY NOTE

(This note is not part of the Order)

The Order restricts the scope of Part I of the Financial Services Act 1986 (the Act) and of the meaning given to the expression "collective investment scheme" in section 75 of that Act.

Article 2 of the Order amends Part III of Schedule 1 to the Act so that it does not have the effect that activities falling within the scope of Council Directive 93/22/EEC on investment services in the securities field (OJ No. L141, 11.6.93, p. 27) (the Directive) are treated as constituing investment business within the meaning of the Act for circumstances in which the Directive does not require them to be so treated. Article 2 also revokes article 6(1) of the Financial Services Act 1986 (Investment Services) (Extension of Scope of Act) Order 1995 (SI 1995/3271) which had the effect that the activities referred to above constituted investment business in circumstances not required by the Directive.

Article 3 of the Order amends the references to collective investment schemes in Schedule 1 to the Act. It excludes from those references any employees share schemes that meet the conditions set out in the inserted paragraph 36. It also amends section 75 of the Act so that such schemes are excluded from the definition contained in that section of what constitutes a collective investment scheme.

Appendix 4

Extracts from the Rules and Regulations of the Securities and Investments Board

Statements of Principle
Common Unsolicited Calls Regulations (SIB Rules Ch. IV)
Promotion of Unregulated Schemes (SIB Rules Ch. VII)

These extracts are reproduced with the kind permission of the Securities and Investments Board.

STATEMENTS OF PRINCIPLE

Statements of principle

Introduction

(1)   These principles are intended to form a universal statement of the standards expected. They apply directly to the conduct of investment business and financial standing of all authorised persons ("firms"), including members of recognised, self-regulating organisations and firms certified by recognised professional bodies.

(2)   The principles are not exhaustive of the standards expected. Conformity with the principles does not absolve a failure to observe other requirements, while the observance of other requirements does not necessarily amount to conformity with the principles.

(3)   The principles do not give rise to actions for damages, but will be available for purposes of discipline and intervention.

(4)   Where the principles refer to customers, they should be taken to refer also to clients and to potential customers, and where they refer to a firm's regulator, they mean SIB, or a self-regulating organisation or professional body which regulates the firm.

(5)   Although the principles may be taken as expressing existing standards, they come into force formally, with additional sanctions resulting, on 30th April 1990.

The Principles

(1) Integrity

A firm should observe high standards of integrity and fair dealing.

(2) Skill Care and Diligence

A firm should act with due skill, care and diligence.

(3) Market Practice

A firm should observe high standards of market conduct. It should also, to the extent endorsed for the purpose of this principle, comply with any code or standards as in force from time to time and as it applies to the firm either according to its terms or by rulings made under it.

(4) Information about Customers

A firm should seek from customers it advises or from whom it exercises discretion any information about their circumstances and investment objectives which might reasonably be expected to be relevant in enabling it to fulfil its responsibilities to them.

(5) Information for Customers

A firm should take reasonable steps to give a customer it advises, in a comprehensible and timely way, any information needed to enable him to make a balanced and informed decision. A firm should similarly be ready to provide a customer with a full and fair account of the fulfilment of its responsibilities to him.

(6) Conflicts of Interest

A firm should either avoid any conflict of interest arising or, where conflicts arise, should ensure fair treatment to all its customers by disclosure, internal rules of confidentiality, declining to act, or otherwise. A firm should not unfairly place its interests above those of its customers and, where a properly informed customer would reasonably expect that the firm would place his interests above its own, the firm should live up to that expectation.

(7) Customer Assets

Where a firm has control of or is otherwise responsible for assets belonging to a customer which it is required to safeguard, it should arrange proper protection for them, by way of segregation and identification of those assets or otherwise, in accordance with the responsibility it has accepted.

(8) Financial Resources

A firm should ensure that it maintains adequate financial resources to meet its investment business commitments and to withstand the risks to which its business is subject.

(9) Internal Organisation

A firm should organise and control its internal affairs in a responsible manner, keeping proper records, and where the firm employs staff or is responsible for the conduct of investment business by others, should have adequate arrangements to ensure that they are suitable, adequately trained and properly supervised and that it has well-defined compliance procedures.

(10) Relations with Regulators

A firm should deal with its regulator in an open and cooperative manner and keep the regulator promptly informed of anything concerning the firm which might reasonably be expected to be disclosed to it.

CHAPTER IV — UNSOLICITED CALLS REGULATIONS
COMMON UNSOLICITED CALLS REGULATIONS

Introduction

1 In principle, the effect of section 56 of the Financial Services Act 1986 is that

"no person shall in the course of or in consequence of an unsolicited call:

(a)   made on a person in the United Kingdom, or

(b)   made from the United Kingdom on a person elsewhere,

by way of business enter into an investment agreement with the person on whom the call is made or procure or endeavour to procure that person to enter into such an agreement."

2 Those restrictions may be lifted by regulations made by SIB, which is the purpose of these regulations.

3 These regulations do not apply to anything done by a person certified by a recognised professional body in carrying on investment business for which he is subject to its rules.

Part I — Non-private investors

1 Non-private investors

1(1) Unless the call is an overseas person call:

(a)   the marketing restriction is lifted to the extent that the call is made with a view to the investor entering into the investment agreement as a non-private investor; and

(b)   the dealing restriction is lifted to the extent that the investor enters into the investment agreement as a non-private investor.

1(2) Where the call is an overseas person call:

(a)   the marketing restriction is lifted to the extent that the call is made with a view to the investor entering into the investment agreement as a non-private customer; and

(b)   the dealing restriction is lifted to the extent that the investor enters into the investment agreement as a non-private customer.

Part II — Private investors

2 Sale of non-geared packaged products

2(1) In principle, the restrictions are lifted to the extent that the investment agreement concerns the provision of investment services relating to the sale to the investor of a generally marketable non-geared packaged product.

2(2) Where the call is an overseas person call, the restrictions are so lifted from the overseas person only to the extent that the call is made by an authorised or exempted person.

3 Supply of callable investment services

3 The restrictions are lifted to the extent that the investment agreement relates to the provision by an authorised or exempted person to the investor of callable investment services and either:

(a)   the agreement is otherwise subject to (or is exempted from) a cancellation or delayed entry procedure under the regulatory system; or

(b)   the services are provided under a cancellable customer agreement and it is made clear to the investor in that agreement and in any accompanying letter or promotional material that he has a seven day cooling off period.

4 Existing customers

4(1) In principle, the restrictions are lifted where:

(a)   the investor has a legitimately established existing customer relationship with the caller, the dealer, or an associate of either; and

(b)   the customer relationship is such that the investor envisages unsolicited calls of the kind concerned.

4(2) Where the investment agreement relates to a geared packaged product, the restrictions are lifted by this regulation only where the call is made by the investor's investment manager.

4(3) Where the call is an overseas person call, the restrictions are lifted by this regulation only where:

(a)   the customer relationship existed while the investor was resident outside the United Kingdom; and

(b)   the investor has been given the prescribed disclosure.

4(4) Where:

(a)   the investment agreement relates to investment services which involve contingent liability transactions or the discretionary management of the customer's assets and which the dealer may provide to the customer only under a two-way customer agreement; or

(b)   the call is an overseas person call;

the restrictions are lifted by this regulation only where the investor has indicated in writing before the call is made that he envisages receiving such calls.

5 Acquisition of investment business

5 Where one person acquires the whole or part of a business from another person, the restrictions are lifted to the extent necessary for the purposes of enabling the acquiror to invite the customers of the business acquired to establish a customer relationship with him, so long as that relationship does not envisage unsolicited calls of any kind not envisaged by the investor in his relationship with the person from whom the business was acquired.

6 Public takeovers

6 The restrictions are lifted to the extent that the call (including an overseas person call) is made by or under the supervision of an authorised person and in connection with or for the purposes of a takeover or substantial acquisition which is subject to the Takeover Code or to requirements in another member state which afford equivalent protection to investors in the United Kingdom.

7 Corporate acquisitions

7(1) The marketing restriction is lifted to the extent that:

(a) the call is made on an employee for the purposes of arranging a management buy-out relating to the whole or part of the business of his employer or of one or more other undertakings in the same group;

(b) the call is made on an employee for the purposes of arranging a management buy-in relating to a business in which he would fulfil management functions; or

(c) the call is made in connection with or for the purpose of a corporate acquisition or disposal which fulfils the requirements set out in paragraph 21 of Schedule 1 to the Act.

7(2) The dealing restriction is also lifted to that extent, so long as:

(a) the investor has been provided with a written statement containing information which is adequate to enable him to make an informed investment decision; and

(b) the investor has an adequate opportunity to seek independent advice before entering into the investment agreement.

8 Connected individuals

8(1) The restrictions are lifted for calls between business partners, fellow directors or close relatives.

8(2) The restrictions are lifted for calls between the settlor of a trust (other than a unit trust scheme), its trustees, beneficiaries and the agents of any of them, to the extent that they relate to the settlement, management or distribution of the trust fund.

8(3) The restrictions are lifted for calls between personal representatives, beneficiaries under a will or intestacy and the agents of any of them, to the extent that they relate to the management or distribution of the estate.

9 Employee shares schemes

9(1) The restrictions are lifted to the extent that the call is made:

(a) by or on behalf of a body corporate, an undertaking in the same group, or the trustee of an employee share scheme; and

(b) for the purpose of enabling or facilitating either:

   (i) transactions in shares or debentures in an undertaking in the group between or for the benefit of existing or former employees of such an undertaking and their close relatives; or

   (ii) the holding of such shares or debentures by or for the benefit of any such persons.

9(2) For this purpose, shares and debentures include share and debenture warrants, certificates representing shares or debentures, and ancillaries on any of them.

10 Occupational pension schemes

10 The restrictions are lifted to the extent that the investment agreement is a contract to manage the assets of an occupational pension scheme.

11 Calls made in non-commercial contexts

11 The restrictions are lifted to the extent that they apply because of a call made by a person:

(a)   who was not acting by way of business; and
(b)   who has been provided with no incentive to make the call.

12 Calls made in the course of a profession or non investment business

12(1) The restrictions are lifted to the extent that they apply because of a call:

(a)   made in the course of the carrying on of any profession or of a business not constituting investment business; and
(b)   giving investment advice, or making arrangements, the giving or making of which is a necessary part of other advice or services given in the course of carrying on that profession or business.

12(2) For this purpose, the giving of advice or making of arrangements is not to be regarded as a necessary part of other advice or services if it is separately remunerated.

13 Exempted persons

13 The restrictions are lifted in any case where the investment agreement is to be, or is, entered into with an exempted person (other than an appointed representative) in the course of investment business covered by the exemption.

Part III — Limits on permissions provided

14 Overseas persons

14(1) Where a regulation or any paragraph of a regulation in Part I or Part II above contains a reference to an overseas person call, that regulation lifts the restrictions for such calls only to the extent it specifies.

14(2) Where a regulation in Part I or Part II above contains no reference to an overseas person call, that regulation lifts the restrictions for such calls:

(a)   in the case of the marketing restriction, only to the extent that the marketing is done through an authorised or exempted person; and
(b)   in the case of the dealing restriction, only to the extent that the dealing is done through an authorised or exempted person.

15 Calls prohibited by telecommunications licence

15 Where the call is made with a view to the provision of investment services and is prohibited by the terms of a telecommunications licence relating to unsolicited calls, the restrictions are lifted only by the permission for calls relating to public takeovers.

16 Unlawful business

16 The only one of these regulations which lifts a restriction from anything said or done by a person in the course of carrying on investment business in contravention of section 3 of the Act is the permission for calls relating to public takeovers.

Part IV — Supplementary

17 Reasonable belief

17(1) The marketing restriction is lifted to the extent that the caller can demonstrate that he believes on reasonable grounds at the time of the call in the existence of circumstances which would mean that the restriction is lifted from him.

17(2) The dealing restriction is lifted to the extent that the dealer can demonstrate that he believes on reasonable grounds at the time of the deal in the existence of circumstances which would mean that the restriction is lifted from him.

18 Reliance on guidance

18 A person is to be taken to act in conformity with the Common Unsolicited Calls Regulations to the extent that:

(a)   the relevant regulator has issued formal guidance on compliance with them; and

(b)   in reliance on standards set in that guidance, the person concerned believes on reasonable grounds that he is acting in conformity with the regulations.

19 Calls made before commencement

19 The restrictions are lifted to the extent that:

(a)   they apply because the investment agreement is entered into in consequence of an unsolicited call made before the general commencement date of these regulations; and

(b)   the restrictions would not have applied if the investment agreement had been entered into at the time of the call.

20 General

20(1) The Financial Services Glossary 1991 (Second Edition) applies, unless the context otherwise requires, for the interpretation of these regulations.

20(2) Any other expression defined for the purposes of the Act or in the Interpretation Act 1978 has the same meanings in these regulations.

20(3) These regulations may be cited as the Common Unsolicited Calls Regulations. They are made under section 56 of, and paragraph 20 of Schedule 11 to, the Act and designated so as to apply to members of recognised self-regulating organisations under section 63A of and paragraph 22B of Schedule 11 to, the Act.

20(4) The general commencement date of these regulations is 1 September 1991. For investment agreements relating to geared packaged products, they supersede existing permissions on that date. In other cases they supersede existing permissions on 1 January 1992.

20(5) Until these regulations supersede existing permissions:

(a)   these regulations apply to the members of an SRO subject to further permissions contained in the rules of that SRO; and

(b)   the provisions of the Financial Services (Unsolicited Calls) Regulations 1987 and those of the Financial Services (Interim) Rules and Regulations 1990 relating to unsolicited calls remain in full effect.

20(6) Where these regulations supersede existing permissions either for calls relating to geared packaged products or generally, then, either for such calls or generally, these regulations no longer apply subject to further permissions contained in SRO rules and the provisions mentioned in (5)(b) of this regulation are revoked.

CHAPTER VII — PROMOTION OF UNREGULATED SCHEMES

THE FINANCIAL SERVICES (PROMOTION OF UNREGULATED SCHEMES) REGULATIONS 1991

The Securities and Investment Board, in exercise of the powers conferred by section 76(3) of the Financial Services Act 1986 and now exercisable by the Board, hereby makes the following regulations:

1.01 Citation, Commencement and Revocation

1 These Regulations, the Financial Services (Promotion of Unregulated Collective Investment Schemes) Regulations 1991, are made on 21 March 1991 and shall come into operation on that date.

2 Subject to regulation 1.03 (transitional) below, the Financial Services (Promotion of Unregulated Collective Investment Schemes) Regulations 1988 are hereby revoked with effect from 21 March 1991.

Explanation

Section 76(1) of the Act prohibits any authorised person from promoting any collective investment scheme to the public in the United Kingdom unless the scheme is a regulated collective investment scheme (that is an authorised unit trust scheme or a recognised scheme). Authorised unit trust schemes are those authorised in the United Kingdom by the Board, or under the previous legislation by the Secretary of State for Trade and Industry. Recognised schemes are those which may be promoted in the United Kingdom pursuant to recognition by the Board under section 86 (the UCITS Directive), section 87 (designated countries or territories such as certain of the Channel Islands, Bermuda and the Isle of Man) or section 88 (other individually recognised overseas schemes). Breach of the prohibition is treated as a breach of the rules binding on the authorised person, with potential civil and disciplinary consequences. Section 76(3) of the Act enables the Board to make regulations for the purpose of exempting from section 76(1) the promotion, otherwise than to the general public, of collective investment schemes, even though they are unregulated schemes. These exemptions are additional to those in section 76(2) (promotion to authorised persons and, broadly, promotion to those in the business of buying and selling property like the property in the scheme itself).

1.02 Interpretation

1.02(1) The Financial Services Glossary 1991 (Second Edition) applies to these Regulations.

1.02(2) For the purpose of these Regulations:

a person "promotes" if he

(a) issues or causes to be issued in the United Kingdom any advertisement inviting a person to become or offer to become a participant in a collective investment scheme or containing information calculated to lead directly or indirectly to a person becoming or offering to become a participant in such a scheme, or

(b) advises or procures any person in the United Kingdom to become or offer to become a participant in such a scheme;

"unregulated scheme" means a collective investment scheme which is not a regulated collective investment scheme.

1.03 Transitional

1.03 Promotion by an authorised person before 1 October 1991 in reliance on any provision in the regulations revoked by these regulations is exempted from section 76(1) of the Act.

1.04 Promotion by authorised persons

1.04 An authorised person may promote an unregulated scheme if and in so far as the promotion falls within one or more items in the Table below:

Table of promotion which is permitted

	Promotion to a person who is reasonably believed by the authorised person to be—	Promotion of a scheme which is—
1	A person who is already a participant in an unregulated scheme	Either— (a) that scheme, or (b) any other scheme whose underlying property and risk profile are both substantially similar (Note 1) to those of that scheme or

Promotion to a person who is reasonably believed by the authorised person to be—	**Promotion of a scheme which is—**
	(c) a scheme which is intended to absorb or take over the assets of that scheme, or
	(d) a scheme units in which are being offered by its operator as an alternative to cash on the liquidation of that scheme.
2 A person who has been, in the last 30 months, a participant in an unregulated scheme	A scheme within Item 1— (a) (that scheme) or (b) (a substantially similar scheme)
3 A person—	Any scheme
(a) for whom (after having sought information about his circumstances and investment objectives) the authorised person has taken reasonable steps to ensure that investment in the scheme is suitable, and	
(b) who is an established customer (Note 2) or newly accepted customer (Note 3) of the authorised person or of a person in the same group	
4 A permitted person (Note 4)	Any scheme
5 An exempted person (Note 5)	Any scheme
6 A non-private customer (Note 6)	Any scheme
7 Provided that note 6A is complied with, a person who is treated as a non-private customer	Any scheme
8 A person in circumstances where advice given to that person is or would be an excluded activity (Note 7)	Any scheme
9 Provided that Note 8 is complied with, a person who is eligible to invest in schemes falling within Note 9	A scheme falling within Note 9
10 A person who is eligible to participate in a scheme constituted under—	
(a) the Church Funds Investment Measure 1958	

Promotion to a person who is reasonably believed by the authorised person to be—	Promotion of a scheme which is—
(b) section 24 of the Charities Act 1993 or	
(c) section 25 of the Charities Act (Northern Ireland) 1964	
11 A person who is an eligible employee (Note 10)	A scheme falling within Note 11
12 A person who has asked an unauthorised person (not being an associate of the authorised person) to include that person's name in a list of persons who are willing to receive details of unregulated scheme with underlying property of a particular description from authorised persons have access to that list (provided that the authorised person has no reason to believe that the inclusion of that name was effected as a result of any contravention of section 76 of the Act or of any conduct of business ruly applying to that or any other authorised person)	A scheme of the particular description in question
13 A person who is a member of the Society of Lloyd's	A scheme in the form of a limited partnership which is established for the sole purpose of underwriting insurance business at Lloyd's

Notes

1   For example, the property of a scheme will be substantially similar to that of another scheme if in both cases the objective is to invest in the same one of the following sectors, that is

- on-exchange derivatives or warrants
- on-exchange (or quoted) securities
- the property market (whether in securities of property companies or in property itself)
- collectibles of a particular description (such as works of art, antiques, vehicles etc.)
- artistic productions (such as films, television, opera, theatre or music).

The risk profile of a scheme will be substantially similar to that of another scheme only if there is such similarity in relation to both liquidity and volatility.

2   A person is an established customer of another person where he has been and remains an actual customer in relation to investment business done with or through that other person.

3   A person is a newly accepted customer of an authorised person if—

(a) there is in existence between them a written agreement (or, in the case of a person who is normally resident outside the United Kingdom, an oral or written agreement) whenever made, relating to investment business to be done between them, and

(b) that agreement has been obtained without any contravention of section 76 of the Act, or of any conduct of business rule applying to that or (so far as the first authorised person is reasonably aware) any other authorised person.

4   That is, a person granted a subsisting permission under paragraph 23 of Schedule 1 to the Act.

5   Not including a person exempted only by section 44 of the Act (appointed representatives). Other exempted persons are included in Item 4 of the Table only if the promotion relates to their investment business covered by the exemption.

6   This includes any person who is not a private customer (and customer is defined in the glossary to include potential customer). A private customer is defined in the glossary to mean—

   (a) a customer who is an individual and who is not acting in the course of carrying on investment business; or
   (b) unless he is reasonably believed to be an ordinary business investor, a customer who is a small business investor.

   "Ordinary business investor" and "small business investor" are also defined in the glossary.

6A An authorised person may not promote in reliance on Item 7 of the Table unless it reasonably believes that the following criteria are complied with:

   (a) a firm can show that it believes on reasonable grounds that the person concerned has sufficient experience and understanding to waive the protections provided for private customers;
   (b) that firm has given a clear written warning to the customer of the protections under the regulatory system which he will lose; and
   (c) that customer has given his written consent after a proper opportunity to consider that warning (though the consent need not be in writing where the customer is ordinarily resident outside the United Kingdom and is reasonably believed not to wish to consent in writing).

7   Advice given to a person is an excluded activity where, by virtue of any provision in Part III of Schedule 1 to the Act, paragraph 15 of that Schedule does not apply. Item 8 above applies to promotion whether in the form of advice or otherwise.

8   An authorised person may not promote in reliance on Item 9 of the Table except on the basis of seeking information about the customer's circumstances and investment objectives and of taking reasonable steps to ensure that investment in the scheme is suitable for him; and he must make it plain in any promotional material and in any advice given that he will advise or procure participation on that basis only.

9   Item 9 in the Table relates to a scheme only if the instrument constituting it restricts participation in it to—

   (a) persons who are treated as wholly exempt (otherwise than by reason of residence) from capital gains tax (or corporation tax on capital gains) in the United Kingdom; and
   (b) the manager in respect of units which he holds temporarily before they are cancelled or transferred to a person falling within (a) above.

10 A person is an "eligible employee" if he is an officer or employee or former officer or former employee (or is a member of the immediate family of such a person) of an employer which is (or is in the same group as) the authorised person or which has accepted responsibility for the activities of the authorised person in carrying on the investment business in question.

11 For the purposes of Item 11 of the Table, the type of scheme which may be promoted to an eligible employee is one the instrument constituting which—

   (a) restricts the property of the scheme, apart from cash and near cash (as defined in the Financial Services (Regulated Schemes) Regulations 1991 to—
      (i)   (in a case where the employer is a body corporate), shares in and debentures of (see Note 12) that body corporate or any other connected body corporate (see Note 13), or
      (ii) (in any case), any property, provided that the scheme takes the form
         • of a limited partnership, under the terms of which the employer (or connected body corporate) will be the unlimited partner and eligible employees the limited partners, or
         • of a trust which the authorised person reasonably believes not to contain any risk that any eligible employee may be liable to make further payments (other than charges) in respect of an investment transaction earlier entered into, and
   (b) (in a case falling within (a)(i) above), restricts participation in the scheme to eligible employees, the employer and any connected body corporate.

12 "Shares" and "debentures" bear the wider meaning conferred by paragraph 20(4) of Schedule 1 to the Act, and include options purchased (or gratuitously received) on the shares or debentures in question.

13 For the purposes of Note 11 a body corporate is connected with another body corporate if

   (a) they are in the same group; or
   (b) one is entitled, either alone or with any other body corporate in the same group, to exercise or control the exercise of a majority of the voting rights attributable to the share capital which are exercisable in all circumstances at any general meeting of the other body corporate or of its holding company.

Appendix 5

Annex to the Second Banking Coordination Directive (Second Council Directive 89/646/EEC)

List of Activities Subject to Mutual Recognition

1. Acceptance of deposits and other repayable funds from the public.
2. Lending[1].
3. Financial leasing.
4. Money transmission services.
5. Issuing and administering means of payment (e.g. credit cards, travellers' cheques and bankers' drafts).
6. Guarantees and commitments.
7. Trading for own account or for account of customers in:
   (a) money market instruments (cheques, bills, CDs, etc.);
   (b) foreign exchange;
   (c) financial futures and options;
   (d) exchange and interest rate instruments;
   (e) transferable securities.
8. Participation in share issues and the provision of services related to such issues.
9. Advice to undertakings on capital structure, industrial strategy and related questions and advice and services relating to mergers and the purchase of undertakings.
10. Money broking.
11. Portfolio management and advice.
12. Safekeeping and administration of securities.
13. Credit reference services.
14. Safe custody services.

---

[1] Including *inter alia*:
— consumer credit,
— mortgage credit,
— factoring, with or without recourse,
— financing of commercial transactions (including forfaiting).

Case Table

References are to paragraph (¶) numbers

Legislation Finding List

References are to paragraph (¶) numbers

Financial Services Act 1986 – continued

SI 1996/2827 – continued

Index

References are to paragraph (¶) numbers